S0-AAD-486

LEXISNEXIS LAW SCHOOL ADVISORY BOARD

Charles P. Craver
Freda H. Alverson Professor of Law
The George Washington University Law School

Richard D. Freer
Robert Howell Hall Professor of Law
Emory University School of Law

Craig Joyce
Andrews Kurth Professor of Law &
Co-Director, Institute for Intellectual Property and Information Law
University of Houston Law Center

Ellen S. Podgor
Professor of Law &
Associate Dean of Faculty Development and Electronic Education
Stetson University College of Law

Paul F. Rothstein
Professor of Law
Georgetown University Law Center

Robin Wellford Slocum
Professor of Law & Director,
Legal Research and Writing Program
Chapman University School of Law

Charles J. Tabb
Alice Curtis Campbell Professor of Law
University of Illinois College of Law

David I. C. Thomson
LP Professor & Director, Lawyering Process Program
University of Denver, Sturm College of Law

Judith Welch Wegner
Professor of Law
University of North Carolina School of Law

CRIMINAL PROCEDURE:
THE POST-INVESTIGATIVE PROCESS
PROCESS
Third Edition

CRIMINAL PROCEDURE: THE POST-INVESTIGATIVE PROCESS

Third Edition

Neil P. Cohen
Retired W.P. Tom's Professor of Law and Distinguished Service Professor of Law,
The University of Tennessee College of Law

Donald J. Hall
Professor of Law Emeritus
Vanderbilt University

Stanley E. Adelman
Visiting Associate Professor
Albany Law School

ISBN: 9781422423998

Library of Congress Cataloging-in-Publication Data

Hall, Donald J., 1943-
Criminal procedure : the post-investigative process : cases and materials / Donald J. Hall, Neil P. Cohen,
Stanley E. Adelman. -- 3rd ed.
p. cm.
Author's names appear in different order in previous ed.; Neil P. Cohen name appears first.
Includes bibliographical references and index.
ISBN 978-1-4224-2399-8 (hardbound : alk. paper) 1. Criminal procedure--United States. I. Cohen, Neil P.
II. Adelman, Stanley E. III. Title.
KF9619.C638 2008
345.73'05--dc22
2008029330

NOTE TO USERS

To ensure that you are using the latest materials available in this area, please be sure to periodically check the LexisNexis Law School web site for downloadable updates and supplements at www.lexisnexis.com/lawschool.

Editorial Offices
744 Broad Street, Newark, NJ 07102 (973) 820-2000
201 Mission St., San Francisco, CA 94105-1831 (415) 908-3200
www.lexisnexis.com

MATTHEW◆BENDER

PREFACE TO THIRD EDITION

Historically, the course that most law schools call "Criminal Procedure" focuses on vital Fourth, Fifth, and Sixth Amendment issues, but pays scant attention to the subject matter of this book – the equally vital aspects, both practical and theoretical, of the adjudicatory process. Happily, in recent years, law schools have added a separate course on criminal adjudication and placed it on a co-equal footing with the traditional "Crim. Pro" course. It is no exaggeration (and no disrespect to the traditional Criminal Procedure course) to call this book and the course it is intended for, "the real criminal procedure."

This Third Edition continues the previous editions' focus on both the theoretical and practical aspects of the "bail to jail" aspects of American criminal procedure. Thus, it presents the major policy issues raised by the most important cases, as does any criminal procedure book, but it also discusses many practice-related issues, such as motion practice, the content and format of indictments, the impact of various parts of the system on the guilty plea process, and ethical standards and dilemmas facing lawyers (both prosecutors and defense counsel) in criminal cases. No lawyer who has handled a criminal case would contest the statement that these real-life issues are critical to an understanding of the criminal process and a capacity to serve as a competent, ethical prosecutor or defense lawyer.

This new edition also takes full advantage of the electronic age of legal scholarship, providing references where appropriate to web pages and other internet resources (even including a current "blog") that go beyond the traditional citations to case law and secondary legal authorities.

Substantively, the Third Edition is an up-to-date teaching tool that reflects the upheavals that have taken place most recently in criminal adjudication: in sentencing (particularly the Apprendi-Booker-Gall line of Supreme Court sentencing decisions); in Sixth Amendment Confrontation Clause case law; and also in death penalty and habeas corpus jurisprudence and legislation.

Our goal is simple: to provide law students with teaching materials that advance the students' understanding of the post-investigative facets of criminal procedure law and the many important hands-on issues that arise in the practice of criminal law.

Neil P. Cohen

Donald J. Hall

Stanely E. Adelman

September 2008.

ACKNOWLEDGMENTS

For assistance on previous editions, we are grateful for the assistance of Chad Riddle, Esq., a former student at the University of Tennessee College of Law, and to Morgan Gire, Esq., Patricia Judd, Esq., Eric McCord, Esq., and Michael Sherman, Esq., former students at Vanderbilt Law School. The administrative assistance of Sonya Fowler at the University of Tennessee and Nan Paden at Vanderbilt Law School, was outstanding.

For the Third Edition, we appreciate the terrific assistance of law students Stuart White, Esq., formerly a student at Santa Clara Law School; Stephanie Oliva, Joanna Sorocki, and Chow Xie of Brooklyn Law School; and Mianette Layne, Esq., formerly a student at the University of Arkansas School of Law. Fredd Brewer of Albany Law School also provided very helpful administrative assistance. Christine Frost, our editor at Lexis/Nexis, was patient with us and contributed to the quality of the final product. Deans Don Polden of Santa Clara Law School and Larry Solan of Brooklyn Law School were generous with their support of the new edition. We thank them all.

DEDICATION

First Edition

To Amy, Andy, Jack, and Nancy, and the wonderful memories of Fred.

N.P.C

To Nancy.

D.J.H.

Second Edition

To Marcella Bridges.

N.P.C

To Nancy, Kelly, and Pamela.

D.J.H.

Third Edition

To Dr. Riva Nelson

N.P.C.

To Jenny and Rob.

S.E.A.

SUMMARY TABLE OF CONTENTS

TABLE OF CONTENTS

Chapter 6   THE FIRST EVIDENTIARY HEARING: THE PRELIMINARY

EXAMINATION **123**

Chapter 1
OVERVIEW OF THE CRIMINAL JUSTICE SYSTEM

A. INTRODUCTION

This book deals with part of the criminal justice system: what happens between a suspect's arrest and the final disposition of the case via sentencing, direct appeal, or collateral (usually habeas corpus) review. In general terms, the process is complicated, varies considerably among the jurisdictions, and depends to some extent on whether the crime charged is a misdemeanor or felony. Some procedural steps are rarely or never used in misdemeanor cases. Moreover, much of the criminal justice process is informal; precise legal rules play a surprisingly minor role in the routine processing of a typical case. The cast is large, consisting of defendants, victims, witnesses, police, prosecutors, defense lawyers, judges, and probation and parole officers.

This chapter provides a general overview of common features and factors that influence the criminal justice system and of the stages of criminal process covered later in this book. Obviously a brief summary cannot be accurate for all jurisdictions. The attempt is to describe what would happen in a typical case in most American jurisdictions. Subsequent chapters of this book provide a more detailed analysis of this process.

B. GENERAL FEATURES

Despite some significant differences in the criminal justice systems of American jurisdictions, there are common features that heavily influence the way the system handles actual cases. A few of these are described below.

[1] Overworked Participants and Overcrowded Facilities

Every component of the criminal justice system purports to be overworked and underfunded. Police argue that they have too many duties, too many miles to patrol, too much paperwork, and too many lawbreakers to catch. Prosecutors, defense counsel, and judges maintain that they cannot try all the criminal cases assigned them. Many probation and parole officers have caseloads that make effective community supervision difficult, if not impossible. Jails and prisons are often so overcrowded that large numbers of additional prisoners cannot be sentenced to harsh penalties and incarcerated under conditions that would satisfy the constitutional restraints on punishment. In 2000, for example, federal prisons were operating at 134% of capacity, and state prisons were at 101% of capacity.[1] These shortages of resources have a substantial impact on the criminal justice system's capacity to prosecute and punish criminals.

In order to meet the demands placed on their various components, vast and ever increasing sums of money are spent each year on state and federal criminal justice systems. In 1982, federal, state, and local governments spent less than $36 billion on their criminal justice systems[2] By 2003, federal, state and local expenditures on police, courts, and corrections had increased to almost $186 billion.[3] Of the $186 billion spent in 2003, about $83 billion was spent on police protection, $42 billion on courts, and $61 billion on corrections.[4]

Although the amounts spent on the American criminal justice system are staggering, they are still growing at a rapid rate, particularly in the area of corrections. From 1980 to 2003, total federal, state, and local expenditures on corrections increased from about $7 billion to almost $61 billion.[5]

The dramatic rise in corrections expenditures is the product of a phenomenal and continuing increase in the number of persons under correctional supervision. Between 1980 and 2005, the number of adults under correctional supervision, including probation and parole, increased from 1.8 million to just over 7 million.[6] In 2005, over 2.18 million persons were incarcerated in federal and state prisons or local jails.[7] An additional 4 million persons were on probation, and 784,000 were on parole.[8] In 2006, local jails supervised over 60,000 persons in the community through electronic monitoring, work release, or other alternative programs.[9]

Interestingly, although the number of persons under correctional supervision continues to increase, crime has decreased significantly since 1993. Between 1992 and 2005 the estimated number of overall violent crime decreased from 1,932,274 to 1,390,695, and property crime decreased from 12,505,917 to 10,166,159 during the same time period.[10] What kinds of inferences do you think can be drawn from this at least arguable anomaly?

Even with increasing criminal justice budgets, the "system" remains hard pressed to keep up with the demands placed on it. It is simply not feasible to prosecute and defend every case to the theoretical limits, and to apprehend and punish each law violator. As a result, the system has adapted to resource limits by relying on many shortcuts through the criminal justice process.

[2] Discretion

One of the key elements in the American criminal justice system is discretion, defined for our purposes as the legal power to make decisions with little specific direction or review from higher authorities. American criminal law gives the police, victim, defendant, prosecutor, judge, and defense lawyer all considerable discretion in carrying out their functions. As discussed throughout this book and especially in Chapter 2, at many stages in the criminal justice process there is the discretion to "throw out" a case or to permit it to go to the next stage, or to not initiate a criminal case at all. The victim, for example, may or may not elect to report a crime to the police. In 2005, 47% of all violent crimes and 40% of property crimes were reported to police.[11] Once a report is made, the police may decide that there is too little evidence to justify an arrest.

After police make an arrest, the prosecutor has broad discretion in his or her decision whether to prosecute. The prosecutor may use this discretion to decide not to prosecute if there is inadequate proof to prosecute or he or she believes that somehow public policy would not be served by prosecution. The prosecutor also has broad discretion in determining which crimes to charge and which people to charge. For example, if two people commit a bank robbery, the prosecutor must decide whether to charge both of them with both robbery and conspiracy to rob the bank, or with only one of these offenses. This judgment may be based on a number of factors, such as the accused's criminal record, the severity of the crime, the role the victim played in the crime, the impact of prosecution on the accused and the victim, the need for deterrence, the likelihood of conviction, the need to obtain the defendant's cooperation in prosecuting other suspected criminals, and the availability of prosecutorial and correctional resources.

Similarly, the judge has immense discretion in criminal cases. He or she may decide to set a high or low bail, or not to require any form of bail or security at all while criminal charges are pending. Before trial, the judge may decide to have multiple defendants tried together ("joined") or separately ("severed"). At trial, the judge may cut off testimony from either side that the judge believes is redundant or irrelevant, and after conviction, the judge usually has considerable discretion in imposing the sentence.

The grand jury also has discretion in carrying out its duties. Although in theory, it must indict if it finds probable cause to believe that the defendant has committed a crime, the grand jury may decide not to indict, despite the existence of probable cause, for reasons of policy or sympathy, or based on its own notions of fairness and justice. It may also conduct its own investigation and issue an indictment for someone unsuspected by the police prior to the grand jury's investigation.

Often these exercises of discretion are poorly documented or not documented at all and are virtually unreviewable by higher judicial authority. While discretion at any stage of the process may be subject to abuse, discretion has the advantage of providing the actors in the system with a flexible process to deal with both unusual fact situations and inadequate resources. For example, a shortage of police officers or jail beds may cause some patrol officers to exercise their discretion and not charge someone with public drunkenness. The time and resources needed to arrest, process, and incarcerate the drunk offender may be needed for more important tasks. Some jurisdictions are attempting to control and structure this exercise of discretion by issuing written directives that provide police officers with guidance on how to deal with specific situations such as domestic violence and drunk driving. These directives often operate to limit or reduce an officer's discretion not to arrest if probable cause is present.

[3] Race and Gender

The role that race and gender play in the criminal justice system is beyond the scope of this book but one of the important social issues of the era. To some extent this concern is bottomed on data that show significant racial and gender differences in a number of relevant areas. An analysis of the basic statistics raises serious questions about the differential impact that the criminal justice system plays in the lives of different segments of the American community.

In most of the studies cited within this section, the demographic characteristic of "race" is divided into the following categories: "white", "black", "other race" and "two or more races." The demographic characteristic of "ethnicity" is separate from "race" and is divided into "Hispanic" or "non-Hispanic". Thus, the term "white" includes white persons of both Hispanic and non-Hispanic ethnicities, and "black" includes black persons of both ethnicities. The characteristic "other race" includes American Indians/Alaska Natives, Asians, and Native Hawaiians/other Pacific Islanders identifying a single racial background.

[a] Victimization

Race and gender appear to influence victimization. Generally, blacks are more likely than whites to be victims of violent crime, other than murder. In 2005, the rate (per 1000 persons age 12 and older) of victimization for violent crimes other than murder was about 20 for white persons and 27 for black persons.[12] Whites are slightly more likely to be victims of murder or nonnegligent manslaughter.[13] Persons of two or more races experienced overall rates of violence significantly higher than the other categories of races.[14] Generally, whites are more likely than blacks to be victims of property crime. In 2005, the estimated rate per 1,000 households of all property crimes was 155.7 when the head of household was white and 144.6 when the head of household was black.[15]

Most crime is intraracial. In a 2005 study of murders and nonnegligent manslaughters that involved one offender and one victim, of the 3,569 crimes committed by black offenders, 2,984 victims were black. Of 3,445 crimes committed by white offenders, 3,150 victims were white.[16]

As for gender, males are more likely than females to be victims of all violent crimes. In 2005, 26 males (per 1,000 persons age 12 and over), compared to 17 females, were victims of violent crime other than murder.[17] Males are also more than three times as likely as females to be the victims of homicide.[18] In 2005, 78% of murder victims were male.[19] However, females are more likely to be victims of rape/sexual assault.[20]

[b] Arrest and Conviction

Most adults arrested in the United States are white and male. In 2005, almost 70% of persons, age 18 or over, arrested were white, 27% were black, and less than 3% were other races.[21] Seventy-six percent of persons arrested were male.[22] Most adults convicted of felonies are also white males. In federal courts, in 2003, 86.8% of those convicted were men, 71.2% were white, 24.8% were black, and 4% were other races.[23] As to ethnicity, 57.4% of convicted offenders were non-Hispanic and 42.6% were Hispanic.[24] In state courts in 2004, about 82% of persons convicted of felonies were male, 59% were white, 38% were black, and 3% were another race.[25] Of federal prisoners in 2003, 93% were male, 56% were white, and 40% were black.[26]

[c] Sentencing

The median length of sentences imposed on federal offenders is longer for blacks and males than for whites and females. In 2003, of federal offenders sentenced to prison for violent offenses, blacks received an average of 77 months as compared to 60 months received by whites.[27] Female offenders convicted of violent offenses received median sentences of 46 months, and males received sentences of 63 months.[28]

Generally, the median sentences imposed in the other categories of offenses, such as property offenses, reflect the same trend. It should be noted that there are numerous factors that are considered in sentencing, for example, previous convictions that may explain the differences in the length of sentences.

In the federal system, the issue of race is especially obvious for drug sentences. In 2004, 54% of federal prisoners were incarcerated for drug offenses.[29] In 2006, 81% of persons sentenced for crack cocaine in federal court were black.[30]

Since in the federal system sentences for offenses involving crack cocaine are longer than the sentences for offenses involving powder cocaine, many critics argue that, in this and in other ways, the federal criminal justice system has singled out blacks for the harshest drug sentences. In *Kimbrough v. United States*, 128 S.Ct. 558 (2007), the Supreme Court approved the practice of departing downward from the federal sentencing guidelines (discussed more fully in Chapter 17) to lessen this disparity. Further, recent changes in those guidelines have somewhat reduced the crack/powder sentencing disparity.

[4] The Prevalence of Guilty Pleas

Despite the widespread belief that criminal cases are routinely fought out in dramatic courtroom confrontations between a zealous prosecutor and a dedicated defense lawyer, the truth is that very few criminal cases go to trial. In virtually every American jurisdiction, approximately ninety-five percent of the criminal cases are disposed of by a guilty plea.[31] This is a process in which the defendant pleads guilty, neither side presents much if any proof, and the judge typically imposes a sentence that has been negotiated by the prosecution and defense. The judge, who usually agrees with whatever "deal" has been worked out in plea bargaining, may know little about the case or the defendant and may spend no more than a few minutes on the case before accepting the plea.

Because the deal must be acceptable to both prosecution and defense, it ordinarily involves give-and-take by the prosecutor and defense lawyer. The deal may involve concessions on the charges, the sentence, or both. For example, if the defendant is charged with three burglaries, the prosecution may agree to a deal in which the defendant pleads guilty to one burglary count and the other two are dismissed. The defendant is pleased because he or she will not risk a long cumulative sentence for three offenses. The prosecution is satisfied because the defendant will serve some prison time (or be placed on probation, if the prosecution finds that agreeable) and scarce prosecutorial resources will not have to be used on trying three cases. Another model is sentence bargaining, in which the prosecution and defense agree on the sentence that the judge should impose. At the sentencing hearing, both lawyers will advise the judge that they believe that a certain sentence, for example a five year prison term, is appropriate. Usually the court will accept this recommendation and impose the agreed upon sentence.

As will be discussed in Chapter 11, views differ sharply, both among criminal justice practitioners and in society in general, as to whether plea bargaining, on the whole, is a good thing, a bad thing, or a "necessary evil." While the practice of plea bargaining has been severely questioned as both allowing the guilty to escape the full measure of justice and unduly pressuring the innocent to give up the right to trial by jury and other procedural protections, it has the advantages of allowing prosecution and defense to arrive at a shared assessment of what result is "just" in a given case, and also allows "the system" to process a large number of cases in a short period of time. A 2006 study of dispositions in federal courts found that the median time between filing charges and disposition was 7 months when there was a guilty plea and 15.7 months when there was a jury trial.[32]

[5] Differences Between Felonies and Misdemeanors

The American criminal justice system typically classifies a crime as either a felony or a misdemeanor. The obvious difference between the two is the maximum possible sentence. Ordinarily, a felony is punishable by incarceration in a state penal institution for a year or more, and a misdemeanor is punishable by a sentence of less than a year in a local or county jail or house of correction. There are other differences as well. Because a felony carries a substantial possible sentence, some procedural protections are only applicable to prosecutions for felonies. For example, in some jurisdictions a grand jury indictment is required only for felonies, but not for misdemeanors. Similarly, the federal constitutional right to trial by jury attaches to all felonies, but only to misdemeanors carrying a potential sentence of more than six months incarceration.

[6] The Cast: Lawyers and Others

The criminal justice system is comprised of many people with quite different training and responsibilities.

[a] Law Enforcement

The police constitute the "street" embodiment of the criminal justice system. They not only begin the processing of a criminal case, they also investigate it, testify (usually for the prosecution), and sometimes even staff the jails. In 2006 there were over 987,125 full-time county and local law enforcement employees.[33] About 27 % of the sworn officers are women.[34] In spite of the significant and dangerous responsibilities that police officers undertake, their salaries tend to be quite low. In 2005, the mean starting salary for entry level local police officers in cities with populations of over 10,000 people was about $37,000.[35]

[b] Prosecution

The prosecutor is the lawyer who is a government employee and represents the interests of the government and, in an indirect way, the victim. Ordinarily, the prosecutor maintains close ties with the local police, who assist the prosecutor by doing most or all of the investigation in criminal cases. Sometimes the prosecutor will also assist in training police officers, counseling them on search and arrest warrants and other legal matters, and conducting difficult investigations where legal expertise is needed. The prosecutor also plays a crucial, some would say controlling, role in the presentation of cases to the grand jury for indictment and in furnishing the grand jury with legal guidance.

In 2005 there were more than 78,000 people employed in various capacities in state and local prosecutors' offices.[36]Most prosecutors do not spend their entire professional career in this capacity. After a few years as a prosecutor, many go into private law practice, often representing criminal defendants or civil litigants, which may be far more lucrative than service as a prosecutor. New prosecutors often start out drawing up criminal complaints or handling minor cases, perhaps misdemeanors or traffic offenses. Over time, with more experience, they are given responsibility for more serious criminal matters, including felony trials and grand jury proceedings.

In the federal system, each district has a United States Attorney, appointed by the President (upon confirmation by the Senate) and who serves at the pleasure of the President. The United States Attorney recommends to the Attorney General the appointment of Assistant United States Attorneys. Unlike the United States Attorney, however, they receive civil service protection. Federal prosecutions are usually conducted by an Assistant United States Attorney, although the Justice Department or another federal agency may also participate in or even conduct the prosecution in some situations.

The head prosecutor for a state judicial district or county is almost always an elected official and is usually a full-time prosecutor. Their exact titles vary; the most common are District Attorney, County Attorney, Commonwealth Attorney, Prosecutor, and Prosecuting Attorney. Most serve a four-year term and appoint assistant prosecutors. While most prosecutors are full-time government employees, sometimes, especially in rural areas, assistant prosecutors may be hired to prosecute on a part-time basis.

[c] Defense

Right to counsel. Under the Sixth Amendment to the United States Constitution, the criminal defendant is entitled to be represented by counsel before being sentenced to incarceration of any length, *see, e.g., Scott v. Illinois*, 440 U.S. 367 (1979), or to probation if the defendant may be incarcerated for violating the conditions of probation, *see, Alabama v. Shelton*, 536 U.S. 654 (2002). In such cases, counsel must be provided free of charge to indigent defendants.

Appointed defense counsel. Defense lawyers may be either public employees or private lawyers. If a public employee, the defense counsel will usually be a public defender. Most commonly, the head public defender is elected or appointed and the assistant public defenders are appointed by the head public defender. Many public defenders are recent law school graduates with little experience who work for fairly low salaries. If the office is large, the novice public defender may handle misdemeanor or traffic cases, then move up to more difficult assignments after gaining some hands-on experience.

Retained defense counsel. Private defense counsel in criminal cases often come from small firms or are solo practitioners. Often their practice includes areas other than criminal law. In many jurisdictions, a relatively small number of criminal defense lawyers handle a large number of criminal cases. Sometimes a county will have no public defender or will need defense services beyond those provided by the public defender. In this situation the county may contract with a criminal defense lawyer or firm to provide defense services to some or all indigents in that county, often at a very modest hourly rate.

Lawyer's fee. If a private lawyer is retained or hired to represent a non-indigent defendant, very often the lawyer will require that all or a large part of the fee be paid in cash and in advance. After a client is convicted, the unsuccessful criminal defendant often will refuse or be unable to pay the defense lawyer. According to Caroline Wolf Harlow, Defense Counsel in Criminal Cases (Bureau of Justice Statistics Nov. 2000), 66% of federal felony defendants and 82% of state felony defendants (in large counties) were represented by public defenders or assigned counsel. White collar defendants were far more likely than violent offender defendants to have private defense counsel.

Interestingly, the report found that the guilty plea rate and conviction rates were almost identical irrespective of whether defense counsel was retained or appointed. A surprising statistic was that state inmates who used appointed counsel had *shorter* sentences than those with retained counsel. Why do you think this is the case?

[d] Judiciary

Judges in criminal cases range from specialists, who only handle criminal cases and may have been criminal practitioners before coming to the bench, to generalists who handle both criminal and civil cases and come to the bench from broadly diverse prior legal backgrounds. In the federal system, as of 2006 there were 678 district judgeships authorized.[37] In the same year there were 167 circuit (appellate) judgeships.[38] While virtually all state judges are lawyers, in a few jurisdictions judges may not be attorneys at the lowest court level (such as Justice of the Peace).

Criminal cases often involve more than one tier of court. For example, preliminary matters (such as bail, warrants, and preliminary hearings) may be resolved by a judge of the lowest court level. Sometimes, as in the federal system, this person is referred to as a magistrate (or magistrate judge). Subsequent proceedings may be conducted exclusively or primarily by a judge of the court of general jurisdiction. Appeals usually go to the next higher court, although in capital cases sometimes the intermediate appellate courts are bypassed.

[e] Probation and Parole

Probation and parole officers also play an important role in criminal cases. These civil servants often possess at least a bachelor's degree and must undergo regular updating and training during the work year. Frequently, probation officers will prepare a presentence report to provide the judge with information about the offense and the offender. If the defendant is placed on probation, a probation officer will supervise the offender, perhaps by meeting with him or her on a weekly or monthly basis. After incarceration and service of a specified fraction of the maximum sentence, the offender may be placed on parole or supervised release, where his or her activities will be supervised by a parole officer.

Inadequate resources have caused some probation departments to be terribly understaffed. In 2006, in the Federal Probation System, 4,695 probation officers supervised 114,002 persons.[39] Parole departments experience the same shortages of resources and understaffing as do probation departments.

[7] The Scene: Federal and State

By far, most criminal proceedings take place in state and local courts. In 2003, for example, 68,533 people were convicted in federal courts.[40] In 2004, almost one million felony convictions occurred in state courts.[41] Additional convictions occurred in various municipal courts. State courts as a general rule have jurisdiction to prosecute the vast bulk of crimes that evolved from the common law; federal criminal prosecution occurs far less frequently, usually pertaining to offenses against federal property, federal personnel, or a federal agency, or involving complex criminal enterprises or large-scale interstate drug or weapons trafficking.

In recent decades, as Congress has taken a more active interest in crime control, federal criminal jurisdiction has expanded somewhat into areas that were traditionally matters of state law enforcement, a trend that some, including the late Chief Justice William H. Rehnquist have decried as "creeping federalization" of our criminal laws. For certain offenses which Congress has brought within federal jurisdiction, there may be a choice between prosecution by either federal or state authorities, or there may even be both federal and state prosecutions for the same offenses, without violating the Double Jeopardy prohibition of the Fifth Amendment. This topic is discussed more extensively in Chapter 16.

C. STAGES OF THE CRIMINAL PROCESS

[1] Complaint

At an early stage of most criminal proceedings, a complainant (a citizen or law enforcement officer who knows or believes that a crime was committed) will sign, under oath, a *complaint*, which is a formal charge of criminal activity. The complaint will often briefly describe the basic facts of the crime, indicate what offense is being charged, and sometimes cite the relevant section of the criminal code believed to be violated. Usually a lower level judge, sometimes called a *magistrate*, must also sign the complaint. If the complaint provides a sufficient basis to show probable cause to believe a crime was committed and the defendant committed it, the magistrate may issue an arrest warrant authorizing law enforcement officers to take the accused person into custody. Chapter 3 deals with the complaint in criminal cases.

[2] Custody

When a person faces criminal prosecution, he or she may be officially notified of that fact by a summons or an arrest. The *summons* (sometimes called a *citation*) is an order to appear in court at a stated time and is used frequently in traffic and other minor cases. The accused is given a piece of paper that provides notice of the charges and the time and location of an initial hearing. Usually the accused who receives a summons is not taken to the police station. Failure to appear in court at the time scheduled on the summons may result in a court-ordered arrest and the possibility of punishment for contempt of court or a separate crime punishing the failure to appear as ordered in a summons.

In serious cases and some minor ones, the first step in a criminal prosecution is usually arrest of the accused by law enforcement officers. In 2005, there were more than fourteen million non-traffic arrests in America.[42] The arrest may occur at the crime scene immediately after the crime or may occur days or years later after a substantial investigation. Depending on the circumstances, the arrest may occur with or without a warrant. The validity of the arrest may be important in assessing the admissibility of evidence obtained during the arrest (the law of arrest, including the many complex Fourth Amendment issues, is beyond the scope of this book).

Booking process at jail. Generally, when a suspect is arrested and taken into custody, he or she will be transported to the police station and *booked*. During this administrative process, jail officials obtain and record information about the accused. The booking process may involve fingerprinting and photographing, a search of the suspect's clothing and belongings, an inventory of the possessions in the person's pocket, purse, and packages, the issuance of prison clothing to wear while incarcerated, the opportunity for the accused to make one or more telephone calls, and sometimes even a lineup and an interrogation by a police officer. During the booking process, police also run the suspect's fingerprints and other identifying information through national databases, to see if the suspect is wanted by other authorities for other criminal offenses, escape from prison, probation or parole violation, or immigration offenses.

Release from custody. If the alleged offender is taken into custody, as discussed more fully in Chapter 5, someone in the system will determine whether and under what conditions the offender will be released from custody until the case is disposed of by trial or other means. A 2002 study of state felony defendants in the 75 largest counties found that 62% were released from custody following an arrest.[43] Twenty-two percent of released felons failed to appear in court as scheduled.[44]

In the federal system, in 2004, a pretrial detention hearing was held in 56.1% of the cases. Of those, almost 79% resulted in pretrial detention.[45] In 2004, federal releasees committed no violations while on release in 80.2% of the cases.[46]Only 2.2% of those released by federal courts failed to appear.[47]

Station house bail. Frequently jail officials are authorized to use *station house bail* to release the arrestee. The jailor, or some other officer authorized to receive bail payments, will determine the financial conditions of release by consulting a written schedule that applies to all similar cases. For example, the bail schedule may authorize the sheriff to release alleged shoplifters upon payment of $250. This sum is designed to guarantee that the offender will show up for trial. If the offender is unsuccessful in obtaining station house bail, the issue of release becomes a judicial matter. The arrestee will soon be brought before a judge or magistrate who will decide the conditions of release. These may include posting an amount of money or satisfying other release conditions (such as staying within the county and surrender of the defendant's passport to the court).

Professional bond services. In some jurisdictions professional bail *bondspersons* are available to post amounts required as bail. Bondspersons earn a fee, usually approximately ten percent of the bail amount, in exchange for their promise to pay the court the total amount of bail if the offender does not appear for trial. In the shoplifting hypothetical above, the offender would pay the bondsperson twenty-five dollars as a fee. The bondsperson would then sign a promise to pay the full $250 if the offender does not appear for trial. If the offender appears for trial, he or she does not get back the $25; this sum represents the bonding company's fee for its services. In cases where the defendant does not appear for trial (usually referred to as *"defaulting"* or "bail jumping"), the judge has the discretion to order the bonding company to pay the court clerk the entire sum of the bond ($250 in the above example). But if the bonding company can produce the defaulter within a reasonable time after the court date, many courts will routinely "reward" the bonding company by not ordering it to pay the amount of the bond. This system provides bonding companies with a financial incentive to locate defaulting criminal defendants.

In some jurisdictions, the bail bondsperson is replaced by a system in which the defendant posts ten percent of the bail amount with a court clerk. If the defendant appears at trial and at all other required court proceedings, he or she gets back all or almost all of the ten percent paid to the clerk. If the defendant fails to appear as required, the court can issue an order forfeiting the ten percent already paid and decreeing that the defaulter owes the remaining ninety percent as a penalty for not appearing at the scheduled hearing. An arrest warrant will also be issued under these circumstances. Failure to appear may also be prosecuted as a separate crime.

[3] Initial Appearance

Soon after arrest, a criminal accused is brought before a judge, usually one presiding over the lowest level court in the jurisdiction. Ordinarily this hearing, frequently called an initial (or first) appearance and, as discussed in Chapter 4, is brief and relatively informal. Here the accused is formally notified of the charges and advised of basic constitutional rights, and various routine procedural matters are resolved. An attorney may be appointed if, as is often the case, the accused is indigent. The issue of bail is addressed if the accused is still in custody. At the initial appearance, or at any later time while charges are pending, the judge may also review and alter the conditions of release, and either allow the accused to be released pending trial or set more stringent release conditions or revoke bail if additional favorable or unfavorable information comes to the court's attention. Finally, the judge will set a date for the next step, usually a preliminary hearing, to be held in a week or two.

If the defendant has been arrested without an arrest warrant, a common occurrence throughout the country, the judge at the initial appearance may have an additional task (also discussed in Chapter 4): to determine whether there is probable cause to detain the accused. Since the lack of a warrant means that no judge has assessed whether there is probable cause to deprive the accused of his or her freedom, the judge must decide this question and either issue an arrest warrant or make a finding of probable cause if the accused is to remain in custody. This hearing is called a *Gerstein* hearing after the Supreme Court case mandating it.

Often the initial appearance lasts only a few minutes. A number of initial appearances may be scheduled at the same time and held one after the other. There may be no defense counsel present and the prosecutor may address only the issue of release conditions. Often the court will assign counsel to an indigent defendant at the initial appearance. No evidence is taken other than information needed to determine probable cause, the conditions of release, or eligibility for appointed counsel.

In some locales the initial appearance is conducted by videoconference. The defendant is physically located in a room at the jail and the judge is situated in the court house. A video camera and monitor at both locations allow the participants to see and speak with one another. This procedure reduces both the expense of transporting defendants from jail to court, and the risk of an escape attempt before, during, or after the initial appearance.

[4] Preliminary Hearing

Probable cause. A criminal accused is often entitled to a *preliminary hearing* (or preliminary examination), which is an adversary proceeding presided over by a judge (without a jury) and conducted by a criminal defense attorney and a prosecutor. This proceeding is discussed in Chapter 6. The usual purpose of this hearing is to determine whether there is *probable cause* to believe that (1) a crime was committed and (2) the accused committed it. This probable cause determination is designed to ensure that citizens do not have to endure the rigors and expenses of a criminal trial if there is not enough proof to show probable cause. The probable cause standard is less demanding than the burden of proving guilt beyond a reasonable doubt at trial, but still generally requires the prosecution to show that the defendant, more likely than not, committed the crime(s) charged. Jurisdictions differ as to whether the formal rules of evidence or a less restrictive set of evidence principles apply in preliminary hearings.

Entitlement to hearing. Whether a particular defendant is entitled to a preliminary hearing varies considerably among the jurisdictions and may depend on the particular procedural posture of the case. In many jurisdictions the defendant is entitled to a preliminary hearing unless a grand jury has already issued an indictment. If, as explained below, the jurisdiction permits use of an information (formal charge by the prosecutor) rather than an indictment, the defendant is usually entitled to a preliminary hearing after the prosecutor signs the information.

If probable cause is found at the preliminary hearing, in many jurisdictions the case is *bound over* or transferred to the grand jury. If probable cause is not found, the case is dismissed by the preliminary hearing judge, but ordinarily the prosecutor can still present the case to the grand jury anyway. If the grand jury then issues an indictment, the case will be scheduled for trial. It is also possible that the judge, after conducting the preliminary hearing, may find probable cause for a lesser crime (perhaps a misdemeanor instead of a felony) than the one initially charged.

Strategy at preliminary hearing. Because the probable cause standard is not as rigorous as the burden of proving guilt beyond a reasonable doubt at trial, it is relatively rare that probable cause is not found. Accordingly, often defense counsel will not make a serious effort to use the preliminary hearing to have all or some of the charges dismissed or reduced. Instead, the defense lawyer will focus on discovering information about the prosecution's case. Although the defense has the option of calling witnesses, usually the defense will call no witnesses and instead will spend its time cross-examining prosecution witnesses to discover their knowledge of the case. This enables the defense to learn about the prosecution's case without disclosing much, if anything, about the defense's strategy and proof.

[5]   Information or Grand Jury Indictment

In perhaps half the American jurisdictions, a criminal case (or at least a felony) can only be tried if the grand jury has returned an *indictment*, discussed in Chapter 7. If the jurisdiction does not utilize a grand jury or the defendant waives indictment by a grand jury, the prosecutor can proceed by *information*. An information is a formal charge by the prosecutor, stating that a named person is charged with committing a specified crime.

Organization. The grand jury is a group of 13-23 citizens usually selected from the same large group of eligible jurors (the jury pool) as the petit or trial jury. One model of the grand jury mandates that at least 12 votes (out of a larger number of grand jurors) in favor of an indictment are necessary for the indictment to be issued; the decision need not be unanimous. A survey of federal grand juries found that in 2006 the average federal grand jury session was attended by approximately twenty grand jurors, lasted almost five hours, and indicted 6.9 persons.[48]

Foreperson. The foreperson or leader of the grand jury chairs the sessions and reports to the judge on behalf of the grand jury. Sometimes, the foreperson must sign the indictment on behalf of the grand jury members.

Functions. The grand jury has several functions. Its primary function, by design, is to serve as a check on prosecutorial abuse by screening cases that do not have enough merit to justify continued processing through the criminal justice system. The test is whether there is probable cause to believe that (1) a crime was committed and (2) the defendant committed it. If the grand jury finds that probable cause is present, a *true bill* or indictment is issued. If probable cause is not found, a *no true bill* is returned and the case is dismissed, but often it can be resubmitted to the same or a different grand jury if the prosecution wants to try again for an indictment.

Ordinarily, the prosecuting attorney serves as counsel to the grand jury, facilitates the issuance of subpoenas for witnesses, documents, and other physical evidence; prepares cases for it to consider, instructs the grand jury on the applicable law, and may recommend whether to issue or not issue an indictment. This close contact between prosecutor and grand jury has led many people to argue that the grand jury does not really fulfill its intended function of shielding citizens against meritless charges, but is rather a "rubber stamp" for the prosecution. This allegation is supported by studies that show that grand juries issue an indictment in approximately 95% of the cases brought before them. A number of states have done away with the fiction of grand jury protection and either abolished it altogether or severely curtailed its use, allowing the prosecutor instead to initiate criminal charges by filing an information with the court.

The second function of the grand jury is to investigate possible violations of the criminal law. A member of the grand jury, the prosecutor, or a private citizen may suggest that the grand jury investigate a person, place, or business for possible criminal activity. If the grand jury chooses to launch this probe, it may use its power to issue *subpoenas* to compel people to testify and bring records and other things with them to the grand jury. If the grand jury finds probable cause to believe that a crime has been committed, it can issue a *presentment*, which is a formal allegation that a named person or business has committed a crime. The presentment serves exactly the same function as an indictment. Indeed, in many jurisdictions the term "presentment" is not used; the grand jury issues indictments only.

A third function of the grand jury is to oversee some public facilities or activities. In some jurisdictions, for example, the grand jury inspects certain public facilities, such as jails, and issues a report of its findings to a judicial or executive officer. The report can provide the basis for corrective action to eliminate problems identified by the grand jurors.

Secrecy. One of the unusual features of the grand jury is *secrecy.* In almost all jurisdictions the grand jury operates away from the public eye. Its sessions are closed to the public, the identity and testimony of witnesses are often secret, and grand jurors are often barred from disclosing matters they have discussed.

Subpoenas and immunity. Another important aspect of the grand jury is its legal authority to issue subpoenas, orders compelling a person to testify before or bring materials to the grand jury. A person disobeying a subpoena may be held in *contempt* of court, which can be punished by a fine or even incarceration. The grand jury in many jurisdictions may also grant or request witnesses *immunity* to encourage or require testimony from people who fear that their testimony may incriminate themselves. A grant of immunity means, in most jurisdictions, that the government cannot use the person's grand jury testimony as evidence against that person in a later criminal prosecution. Accordingly, a person granted immunity cannot refuse to testify by invoking the Fifth Amendment's privilege against self-incrimination. The immunity essentially satisfies the witness's Fifth Amendment rights by, in theory, removing the possibility of compelled self-incrimination, for the testimony cannot be used as direct evidence to incriminate the witness.

Schedule. The grand jury usually meets over a period of months or even years, but the sessions are often held many days apart. For example, a grand jury may meet one day a month for six months. The prosecutor routinely presents each case to the grand jury.

Evidence. Usually only evidence supporting the existence of probable cause is presented, but sometimes, even though not constitutionally required, countervailing evidence is also made known to the grand jury. No judge attends grand jury sessions, and usually the formal rules of evidence are not used. An indictment may be based, at least in part, on hearsay.

[6]   Arraignment and Plea

If a grand jury issues an indictment or if a case is initiated by information, the accused is brought before a judge for an arraignment, which is much like the initial appearance which follows the defendant's arrest. At this brief hearing, usually a prosecutor and defense lawyer will be present. The defendant will be informed of the charges (*i.e.* of the contents of the indictment or information) and given a chance to plead. There may be several options: guilty, not guilty, not guilty by reason of insanity (sometimes part of a "not guilty" verdict rather than a separate plea), *nolo contendere* ("I do not wish to contest the charges and I agree to be punished as if I pled guilty but I do not admit guilt"), and perhaps others.

If the defendant intends to plead guilty (either at the arraignment or at any later time), the judge will inform the defendant of the consequences of the plea, including the waiver of various rights, and then almost always will accept the plea. The defendant may then be sentenced or a decision on sentencing will be postponed until a later date. More often than not, however, the defendant offers a plea of not guilty at the arraignment.

If the defendant pleads not guilty, the court will set a date for trial. At this time, the question of bail or other conditions of release can be, but usually is not, revisited. A defendant in jail awaiting trial may request a reduction in the amount of bail or some other order that will permit him or her to be released until the trial. The prosecution may ask for additional conditions of release or even for the revocation of release on bail.

[7]   Motions

Either before or during trial, a party (usually the defense) may file one or more *motions* with the court. A motion, discussed more fully in Chapter 9, is a request for a court order. The motions may address virtually any issue. Some pretrial motions (generally referred to as *dispositive motions*) may seek to dismiss charges on grounds such as statute of limitations, double jeopardy, or a fatal flaw in the indictment, while other motions seek to gain some tactical advantage at or before trial, e.g., to order discovery, or to limit the evidence that will be used at trial.

Motions *in limine*, made just before the start of trial, may seek to limit or preclude certain lines of questioning at trial, or to affect the order or the manner in which witnesses and evidence will be presented. Motions made during trial may, for example, ask the court to dismiss some or all of the charges at the conclusion of the prosecution's case, to strike or exclude evidence or testimony or, in extreme circumstances, to declare a mistrial.

While many motions are written, others, especially ones made during the heat of trial, are oral. Sometimes the other side will file a written response to a written motion. The court may hold a hearing on the motion and will then issue an order denying or granting all or part of it.

[8]   Discovery

While discovery in civil cases is often extensive, it is usually quite limited in criminal cases, as discussed more fully in Chapter 10. The rules of criminal procedure often mandate that relatively few items be disclosed to the other side, although the Constitution requires that the prosecution disclose some information that will assist the defense. Interrogatories and depositions are rare or nonexistent in criminal cases. Accordingly, in lieu of formal discovery opportunities, both the defense and prosecution will use each hearing and motion to learn about the other side's case. In addition, in some jurisdictions there are informal discovery practices that give the two sides greater access to information than would be required by the rules of criminal procedure. Some prosecutors have an *open file* policy that gives defense lawyers full access to all or most information available to the prosecutors.

[9]   Pretrial Conference

Days or even weeks before trial, the judge may convene a pretrial conference to clarify the issues and resolve various procedural matters, such as discovery problems and scheduling. Although in many jurisdictions this practice is permissible because of the judge's inherent authority to manage the case, some jurisdictions have enacted a rule of procedure specifically addressing the pretrial conference. Federal Rule 17.1 provides, "On its own, or on a party's motion, the court may hold one or more pretrial conferences to promote a fair and expeditious trial." A few statutes even require a pretrial conference in unusual situations.

The exact content of the pretrial conference differs from judge to judge. To encourage candor, Rule 17.1 provides that admissions made by the defendant or defense counsel during pretrial conferences are not admissible against the defendant unless reduced to writing and signed by both the defendant and defense counsel. A pretrial conference is not authorized under Rule 17.1 if the defendant is not represented by counsel. Rule 43(b)(3) of the Federal Rules of Criminal Procedure suggests that the defendant need not be present at a pretrial conference.

[10]   Trial

At trial, the defendant will usually be represented by retained or appointed counsel while the government will be represented by a lawyer from the prosecutor's office. Criminal trials ordinarily do not last very long. In 2006, for example, approximately 83% of federal criminal trials took 1–2 days, while only 0.3% took 10 days or more.[49] The general format of the trial follows.

[a]   Right to Jury Trial or Trial by a Judge

If the case goes to trial, in any but the most minor cases the defendant is entitled to have a jury decide guilt or innocence. See Chapter 15. However, some defendants, for a variety of possible reasons, choose to waive their right to a trial by jury and have their guilt or innocence determined by a judge. A trial conducted by a judge sitting without a jury is often referred to as a *bench trial.*

[b]   Jury Selection

Traditionally the trial (or *petit*) jury is comprised of twelve citizens, although in a few jurisdictions juries of less than twelve (but more than five) are used in some or all criminal cases. Often one or more alternate jurors are selected to serve if one of the regular jurors must be replaced because of illness or some other reason. In almost all states the jury verdict must be unanimous either to convict or acquit; however, this is not a constitutional requirement. The jury is selected from a *jury pool* or *venire*, a large number of possible jurors selected by some random process. The actual twelve (or less)– person jury is selected from this larger group through a process called *voir dire*, during which the judge and often the lawyers for both prosecution and defense question jurors to determine possible bias and competence to serve. Although there is no single method of winnowing the total number of potential jurors down to the needed number, both the prosecutor and defense counsel are permitted to challenge and exclude some jurors.

Challenges. During the selection process, potential jurors may be excluded either for cause or by a peremptory challenge. A *challenge for cause* is determined by the judge, who may disqualify a potential juror for such reasons as a physical or mental inability to serve, a problem with devoting adequate time to jury duty, or for potential bias which may include a relationship to one of the parties or lawyers. A *peremptory challenge*, on the other hand, is made by either the defense or prosecuting attorney for any reason, other than race and gender. There are no limits on the number of challenges for cause, but there are significant numerical limits on peremptory challenges. For example, a state statute may provide each side may with eight peremptory challenges. Often trial lawyers will use their experience and instinct as guidance in using a peremptory challenge to exclude a potential juror.

Pay. Jurors are paid for their services, although the amount is hardly adequate. As of June 2003, juror fees were \$40–\$50 per day for each federal juror and from \$4 to \$50 per day for state jurors.[50]

[c]   Swearing in the Jury

A jury is usually "sworn in" after it is selected. This entails having the jurors repeat a short oath that obligates them to be fair, listen to all sides, and obey the law. It is at this juncture that *jeopardy* attaches (see Chapter 16 for full discussion of Double Jeopardy issues).

[d]   Initial Jury Instruction

Sometimes the jury is then given an introductory instruction by the judge. This brief lecture may thank the jurors for their services, inform them of their duties, and perhaps describe in general terms what is going to happen, and, in some locales, outline the law to be applied in the case.

[e]   Opening Statement

Each side ordinarily will make an opening statement, outlining the evidence and theory it will present. Traditionally the prosecution goes first, followed by the defense, although the defense may choose to defer its opening statement until the prosecution has rested its case. Many judges encourage short opening statements on the theory that the evidence, not the opening statement, is the important information for the trier of fact.

[f] Prosecution's Case

The prosecution presents its *case in chief* first. It will call witnesses and present evidence and testimony (through *direct examination*) that, the prosecution hopes, will prove each element of the crime(s) beyond a reasonable doubt. After each of these witnesses testifies for the prosecution, the defense has the opportunity to *cross examine* the witness. The prosecution may then be permitted to ask additional, but limited, questions on *redirect* exam. Sometimes the defense can then ask more questions on *recross* examination.

[g] Defense Motion to Dismiss

After the prosecution has presented its witnesses and any physical evidence and rested its case, the defense lawyer may make an oral motion to dismiss all or part of the charges. The defense may argue that the prosecution's witnesses have not proven an element of one or more of the offenses charged. While this motion is usually unsuccessful, sometimes the judge will grant the motion and dismiss or reduce some or all of the alleged offenses.

[h] Defense's Case

If the motion to dismiss does not end the trial, the next step is for the defense to present its case. The defense counsel may introduce witnesses and other evidence to counter a prosecution witness's testimony or to prove some issue, such as an affirmative defense, not addressed by the prosecution. For example, the prosecution may present proof that a homicide was an intentional killing of the defendant's enemy. The defense may offer evidence that the killing was in self defense. The prosecution has the right to cross-examine defense witnesses, including the defendant him- or herself if the defendant should choose to testify.

[i] Other Proof

After the defense has presented its case, the court may permit the prosecution to put on more evidence in *rebuttal* to counter that presented by the defense. The usual order of direct, cross, redirect, recross, etc. is used. If the defense needs to put on proof to counter the state's rebuttal proof, the court may permit *surrebuttal* evidence to be introduced. Rarely will the judge exercise his or her discretion to permit proof after surrebuttal.

[j] Closing Arguments

After both sides have presented their proof and cross-examined the other side's witnesses and rested, each side is permitted to make a closing argument. Ordinarily, each side will thank the jury for its patience, summarize the proof it has offered, and minimize the probative value of some or all the proof presented by the other side. Usually, the prosecution will make the first closing argument, the defense will make the second, and, in many jurisdictions, the prosecution will have a brief chance to make a final argument responding to the defense counsel's closing remarks.

[k] Jury Instructions

Following the closing argument, the judge gives the jury its instructions or *jury charge*. This lecture informs the jury of its responsibilities, jury procedures, and the applicable law. For example, in a case involving a homicide the jury may be told about such matters as the burden of proof, the jury's role in ascertaining the facts, the selection of a foreperson, and the definitions of the crimes with which the accused is charged.

Opportunity to support or oppose instruction. Usually counsel for both sides will have an opportunity to suggest instructions for the judge to use in the jury charge. These suggested instructions are presented to and ruled on by the judge prior to closing argument, so that counsel can find out before making the final argument how the judge will charge the jury. Sometimes the charge is also "reduced to writing" and a copy is given to each juror to use during the deliberations. The correctness (or not) of jury instructions is often a key issue for appeal, so it is of great importance that both sides make timely requests for charges that they think are appropriate, and objections and exceptions to jury charges that they believe may be in error. Failure to object to an allegedly erroneous charge will usually result in a waiver of the issue on appeal.

Early jury instruction. In a few jurisdictions, a jury reform movement has led to earlier jury instructions in order to better assist the truth-finding process. Jurors are given jury instructions about the applicable law before closing arguments. This enables counsel to address themselves to the precise language of the instructions. A brief set of instructions is also given after closing arguments to deal with administrative issues, such as the selection of the jury foreperson.

[1] Jury Deliberations

The jury will then "retire" or go to the jury room, usually a small room located near the court room. Only the jurors are permitted in this room. Often the first step is for the jury to select a *foreperson* to organize the deliberations and represent the jury in communications with the judge. In some jurisdictions, the foreperson may be chosen by lot or may be appointed by the judge.

More information. Sometimes during its deliberations the jury may feel that it needs more information. For example, after an hour of discussion about the case the jury may discover that individual jurors have different recollections about the content of a particular witness's testimony or different interpretations of several words in the jury instructions. The foreperson will communicate this in writing to the judge who ordinarily will convene a hearing to resolve the issues. Counsel for both sides and the defendant will be present. The judge will then respond to the jury's request, usually after receiving suggestions from both sides. Sometimes the court will refuse to answer an improper question, perhaps even instructing the jury not to consider the issue raised by the question. For other questions, the judge may order the stenographer to read to the jury some or all of the testimony of a witness or the court may repeat or explain the part of the jury instruction that is confusing.

Unanimity. In most jurisdictions, the jury decision must be unanimous. A conviction occurs if all twelve (sometimes less) jurors find the accused guilty beyond a reasonable doubt. In these jurisdictions, if all twelve vote that the state has not proved each element of the crime beyond a reasonable doubt, the accused is acquitted and the charges are dismissed. In some jurisdictions, however, a jury may return a verdict of guilty or not guilty on a less-than-unanimous vote.

Burden of proof. The burden of proof on defenses such as insanity or self defense is more complex, with several variations. The defendant may, in some jurisdictions, be required to both offer proof ("*burden of production*") and persuade the trier of fact ("*burden of persuasion*") as to the existence of a defense. Where the burden of proof regarding an affirmative defense is placed on the defendant, the usual standard of proof is for the defendant to establish the defense by a "preponderance of the evidence." Another model that some states use for certain defenses is that the defendant must first raise the defense by offering some evidence to support it (sometimes called the "*burden of going forward*"), and then the burden shifts to the prosecution to disprove the defense beyond a reasonable doubt.

Hung jury. If after extensive deliberation the jury cannot reach a verdict (commonly referred to as a *hung jury*), the judge then declares a *mistrial* and the prosecution is usually free to try the case again at a later date. The Double Jeopardy clause does not bar a retrial following a hung jury. Statistics show that criminal trials almost always result in a conviction.

[m] Announcement of Jury Verdict

Once the jury has made a decision, all jurors return to the courtroom where the foreperson informs the judge of the decision. The jury's written decision will be signed by the foreperson or all jurors, depending on the jurisdiction. Either the foreperson or the judge will announce the verdict to the defendant and everyone else in the court room. Usually the defendant and defense counsel will stand when the verdict is disclosed. Sometimes the jurors are polled. This means that each juror is asked in open court whether the announced guilty verdict reflects his or her own vote.

If the defendant is acquitted, in the usual case he or she is immediately released from custody and is free to return home unless the defendant is also facing other untried charges. If the jury finds the defendant guilty, the judge will again consider the issue of bail pending sentencing and appeal.

[11] Sentencing Hearing

In the typical case, there will be a delay between a jury verdict of guilty and the imposition of sentence, as discussed in Chapter 17. During this time a probation or other court officer may prepare a *presentence report* which provides data about the offense and the offender. This social history may be based in part on information supplied by the defendant and defense counsel. Ordinarily the defendant will be given access to all or most of the presentence report, and may even submit a more favorable or inclusive report for the court's consideration. The police officers involved in the case may also be asked for their version of the offense.

Hearing. If no agreement has been reached between the prosecution and defense, the judge will often conduct a full sentencing hearing. The prosecution and defense will be permitted to offer proof and arguments on the proper sentence, although the strict rules of evidence that apply at trial typically do not apply at the sentencing hearing. The accused is also permitted to speak ("*allocution*"). In some jurisdictions, the crime victim (or a family member of a deceased victim) is permitted to describe the crime's effect upon the victim or survivors through the presentation of a written *victim impact statement* or by addressing the court directly ("*victim allocution*"). The judge may also read the sentencing report and hear from the probation officer who prepared it. Finally, the judge will impose sentence on the defendant. The range of permissible sentences extends from non-custodial to custodial to capital, depending on the offense and the jurisdiction.

[12] Non-Custodial Sentences

Unless the defendant has been convicted or has pleaded guilty to a crime that carries mandatory incarceration, the judge may see fit to place the defendant on *probation* or impose a fine or some other obligation on the defendant if the judge does not believe that the facts of the case or the defendant's prior history require a sentence of incarceration. A defendant placed on probation must abide by the conditions of probation that the court has imposed, and probation may be revoked and the defendant incarcerated if the defendant commits a serious violation of probation conditions. Similarly, a defendant who willfully fails to pay a fine that he or she can afford to pay may also be incarcerated. Often fines are imposed as a condition of probation, and willful failure to pay may be grounds to revoke probation. Other non-custodial sentences may require that the defendant make restitution to the victim or perform a certain number of hours of specified community service.

[13] Custodial Sentences

Defendants sentenced to imprisonment usually serve their sentence at a penal facility determined by the state or county correctional agency. Prisoners may be assigned to a variety of possible correctional facilities, from maximum (or even recently-developed "supermax" prisons) to minimum security. For any sentence other than to death or life without parole, the convicted prisoner usually will not serve the entire sentence ordered by the court. Although jurisdictions vary considerably, most have an administrative process that shortens the sentence for good behavior or work while in prison, participation in education and other rehabilitative programs, and perhaps even because the prison is so overcrowded that bed space must be made available for new arrivals.

[14] Parole and Other Supervised Release

Most jurisdictions also use *parole*, which authorizes a parole board or commission to evaluate a prisoner's likely success on the street and to release him or her, in appropriate cases, before the end of the sentence. Statutes ordinarily determine when a prisoner becomes eligible to be considered for parole. For example, a law may provide that prisoners committing a certain class of felony are parole-eligible after serving 50% of the sentence.

A parolee usually works at a job and must satisfy a number of specific conditions, such as maintaining employment, reporting regularly to a parole officer, remaining within the state, living at a certain place, limiting (or eliminating) the use of alcohol, and avoiding violations of the law. Failure to adhere to these conditions can lead to a parole revocation hearing before the parole board or a hearing officer and a return to prison for all or part of the unexpired sentence.

Some jurisdictions, including the federal government, have eliminated parole. A prisoner must serve all or virtually all of the sentence imposed by the judge. After release from prison, however, ex-prisoners in non-parole jurisdictions usually are required to have a short period of supervised release where they are counseled and monitored by a counselor under conditions that are similar to parole supervision. Violations of the conditions of supervised release, however, are handled by the sentencing judge rather than by a parole board.

[15] Direct Appeal

If the defendant is dissatisfied with the verdict, he or she has a right to a direct appeal to the next highest court in the jurisdiction. See Chapter 18. Usually the defendant will file a notice of appeal with the trial court. The case is then transferred to the appellate court for resolution. In most states this means the state intermediate appellate court where a panel of (usually, three) judges hears the appeal. While the defendant usually has a right to file this appeal and have the case decided by the appellate court, frequently the appellate court can decide the issue summarily without hearing oral argument. The appellate briefs, documents detailing the legal arguments for each side, are deemed sufficient.

If an oral argument is held, usually there will be no decision immediately. The appellate judges will deliberate for a few days or sometimes months, and then render a written opinion. If the decision is adverse to the defendant (usually affirming the conviction and sentence), in most states the accused may seek a rehearing from the same court, perhaps this time before all the state or circuit's appellate judges (an *en banc* hearing), not just a panel of three appellate jurists.

If the defendant is dissatisfied with the intermediate appellate court's decision, usually he or she can ask the state supreme court to review the case. Often this court, however, does not have to accept the case; it may decline to review the matter, leaving intact the decision of the appellate court. If the case involves the United States Constitution, the defendant may also seek review from the United States Supreme Court.

If an appellate court decides that a serious error committed at trial or in pre-trial proceedings impaired the defendant's right to a fair trial, it will reverse the conviction and/or sentence. Certain reversals are accompanied by an order from the appellate court that the defendant receive a new trial (or a new pre-trial hearing, if that was the source of the erroneous conviction), while other reversals mandate that the indictment or information be dismissed and the defendant released from custody and spared any further criminal proceedings.

[16] Collateral Attack

After direct appeals have been exhausted, the defendant may consider bringing a *collateral attack* on the conviction. See Chapter 18. In most states this can be pursued in state court. If a constitutional violation is alleged, a state conviction may also be challenged collaterally in federal court through a petition for a *writ of habeas corpus* seeking the defendant's immediate release from allegedly unlawful confinement, but only after the habeas corpus petitioner has first exhausted all available state remedies on the issue presented. A collateral attack is a procedure used to ensure that people convicted of crimes are not punished and confined wrongfully. Because such proceedings often involve a rehash of issues already resolved at trial or on direct appeal, a number of procedural hurdles must be surmounted before a successful collateral attack may be brought. Because of these procedural requirements and because of the strong presumption of correctness given to the original conviction and subsequent direct appellate review, collateral challenges rarely succeed in reversing a conviction or sentence.

[17] Executive Clemency

Constitutions and statutes routinely permit the jurisdiction's highest executive officer or an executive department board to grant a convicted offender executive clemency. The clemency power includes the power to *pardon* an offender and to *commute* a sentence. A pardon remits any penalty resulting from conviction, possibly including not only release from imprisonment but also restoration of any other collateral penalties such as loss of a public license or civil rights. However, a pardon does not, by itself, remove or expunge a conviction completely. The pardoned offender is still technically guilty of the offense for which he or she was originally convicted — it has been said that a pardon "forgives, but does not forget, the fact of guilt." *Randall v. Florida Dep't of Law Enforcement*, 791 So. 2d 1238 (Fla. Dist. Ct. App. 2001). A pardon may be granted because a governor or the president believes that the accused was erroneously convicted, or for humanitarian reasons such as removing civil disabilities that resulted from a proper conviction.

A commutation reduces the sentence, sometimes changing a sentence of death to one of life imprisonment, or shortening a deserving prisoner's sentence to "time served." A commutation may be granted to reward extraordinary or exemplary conduct while in prison (for example, to a prisoner who risked his own life to save other prisoners' lives in a prison fire), or simply where a governor or president feels that justice requires mitigation of the court-imposed sentence.

Under one common model, the offender applies for executive clemency to a board that recommends whether it should be denied or granted. The jurisdiction's highest executive officer (the President or Governor) then decides whether to accept or reject the board's recommendation. Another model is for the offender to apply directly to the executive's office where some internal administrative structure is in place to evaluate the requests. A third model involves a petition to and decision by an executive branch board, such as a Pardon Board or the Parole Board.

Although many prisoners covet executive clemency and believe they are entitled to it, few such requests are granted. In 2006, out of the 2,764 applications pending 1,402 were denied and 39 pardons were granted.[51]

ENDNOTES

[1]   U.S. Dep't of Justice Sourcebook of Criminal Justice Statistics [online] (Ann L. Pastore and Kathleen Maguire, eds., 2006), *available at* http://www.albany.edu/sourcebook/pdf/t1102.pdf.

[2] *Id.*, at http://www.albany.edu/sourcebook/pdf/t122003.pdf.

[3] *Id.*, at http://www.albany.edu/sourcebook/pdf/t122003.pdf.

[4] *Id.*, at http://www.albany.edu/sourcebook/pdf/t122003.pdf.

[5] *Id.*, at http://www.albany.edu/sourcebook/pdf/t122003.pdf.

[6] *Id.*, at http://www.albany.edu/sourcebook/pdf/t612005.pdf.

[7] *Id.*, at http://www.albany.edu/sourcebook/pdf/t612005.pdf.

[8] *Id.*, at http://www.albany.edu/sourcebook/pdf/t612005.pdf.

[9] *Id.*, at http://www.albany.edu/sourcebook/pdf/t6152006.pdf.

[10] *Id.*, at http://www.albany.edu/sourcebook/pdf/t31062005.pdf.

[11] *Id.*, at http://www.albany.edu/sourcebook/pdf/t3332005.pdf.

[12] *Id.*, at http://www.albany.edu/sourcebook/pdf/t342005.pdf.

[13] *Id.*, at http://www.albany.edu/sourcebook/pdf/t31242005.pdf.

[14] *Id.*, at http://www.albany.edu/sourcebook/pdf/t342005.pdf.

[15] *Id.*, at http://www.albany.edu/sourcebook/pdf/t3222005.pdf.

[16] *Id.*, at http://www.albany.edu/sourcebook/pdf/t31292005.pdf.

[17] *Id.*, at http://www.albany.edu/sourcebook/pdf/t342005.pdf.

[18] *Id.*, at http://www.albany.edu/sourcebook/pdf/t31242005.pdf.

[19] *Id.*, at http://www.albany.edu/sourcebook/pdf/t31242005.pdf.

[20] *Id.*, at http://www.albany.edu/sourcebook/pdf/t3142005.pdf.

[21] *Id.*, at http://www.albany.edu/sourcebook/pdf/t4102005.pdf.

[22] *Id.*, at http://www.albany.edu/sourcebook/pdf/t482005.pdf.

[23] *Id.*, at http://www.albany.edu/sourcebook/pdf/t5182003.pdf.

[24] *Id.*, at http://www.albany.edu/sourcebook/pdf/t5182003.pdf.

[25] *Id.*, at http://www.albany.edu/sourcebook/pdf/t5452004.pdf.

[26] *Id.*, at http://www.albany.edu/sourcebook/pdf/t653.pdf.

[27] *Id.*, at http://www.albany.edu/sourcebook/pdf/t5212003.pdf.

[28] *Id.*, at http://www.albany.edu/sourcebook/pdf/t5212003.pdf.

[29] *Id.*, at http://www.albany.edu/sourcebook/pdf/t657.pdf.

[30] *Id.*, at http://www.albany.edu/sourcebook/pdf/t5392006.pdf.

[31] *Id.*, at http://www.albany.edu/sourcebook/pdf/t5462004.pdf.

[32] *Id.*, at http://www.albany.edu/sourcebook/pdf/t5432006.pdf.

[33] *Id.*, at http://www.albany.edu/sourcebook/pdf/t1682006.pdf.

[34] *Id.*, at http://www.albany.edu/sourcebook/pdf/t1682006.pdf.

[35] *Id.*, at http://www.albany.edu/sourcebook/pdf/t1692005.pdf.

[36] *Id.*, at http://www.albany.edu/sourcebook/pdf/t1852005.pdf.

[37] *Id.*, at http://www.albany.edu/sourcebook/pdf/t582006.pdf.

[38] *Id.*, at http://www.albany.edu/sourcebook/pdf/t5662006.pdf.

[39] *Id.*, at http://www.albany.edu/sourcebook/pdf/t672006.pdf.

[40] *Id.*, at http://www.albany.edu/sourcebook/pdf/t5182003.pdf.

[41] *Id.*, at http://www.albany.edu/sourcebook/pdf/t5442004.pdf.

[42] *Id.*, at http://www.albany.edu/sourcebook/pdf/t412005.pdf.

[43] *Id.*, at http://www.albany.edu/sourcebook/pdf/t5542002.pdf.

[44] *Id.*, at http://www.albany.edu/sourcebook/pdf/t5562002.pdf.

[45] *Id.*, at http://www.albany.edu/sourcebook/pdf/t5142004.pdf.

[46] *Id.*, at http://www.albany.edu/sourcebook/pdf/t5162004.pdf.

[47] *Id.*, at http://www.albany.edu/sourcebook/pdf/t5162004.pdf.

[48] *Id.*, at http://www.albany.edu/sourcebook/pdf/t1942006.pdf.

[49] *Id.*, at http://www.albany.edu/sourcebook/pdf/t5422006.pdf.

[50] *Id.*, at http://www.albany.edu/sourcebook/pdf/t196.pdf.

[51] *Id.*, at http://www.albany.edu/sourcebook/pdf/t5722006.pdf.

Chapter 2

THE DECISION TO BEGIN FORMAL CRIMINAL PROCEEDINGS

A. INTRODUCTION

Once there is reason to believe that a crime has been committed, numerous individuals may exercise discretion in ways that will have an impact upon the defendant. Initially, for example, a crime victim may elect not to report a criminal offense because he or she deems the matter too trivial to justify official intervention. Similarly, a police officer may decide to resolve what would otherwise be a criminal matter through an informal warning to the would-be defendant. Even where both the victim and police proceed with vigor, the prosecutor may likewise exercise discretion in numerous ways with respect to the accused.

The initial decision to proceed with a criminal charge against an individual is one that should not be taken lightly. The financial costs incurred in mounting a defense to a criminal charge may be quite substantial. Moreover, the accused may have been jailed even for a short period of time, causing the loss of freedom and imposing on the accused and others considerable inconvenience and humiliation. Even if charges result in an acquittal, the defendant may have lost gainful employment and experienced social and psychological damage due to the stigma of a pending criminal charge. *See, e.g., Cooper v. Dupnik*, 963 F.2d 1220 (9th Cir. 1992) (after erroneous arrest for rapes and robberies, defendant lost his job and was evicted from his apartment).

While the criminal justice system provides mechanisms to screen cases that should not proceed to trial (principally the preliminary hearing and grand jury review, discussed in Chapters 6 and 7), this chapter examines the exercise of discretion and explores both informal and formal means of influencing or restricting discretionary powers. After discussing the concept of discretion and the judiciary's acceptance of it as part of the American criminal justice system, this chapter deals with the exercise of discretion by three actors: the victim, the police, and the prosecutor.

B. DISCRETION IN GENERAL

[1] Existence of and Need for Discretion

The discretionary power of law enforcement officers is largely unrestrained in any legal sense. That power is not unique to law enforcement; indeed, it is a characteristic of many aspects of the American legal system. One of the most widely cited works addressing this issue is Kenneth Culp Davis, Discretionary Justice: A Preliminary Inquiry 162, 163, 167 (1969):[*]

> An outstanding characteristic of the American legal system, especially in contrast with European systems, is the prevalence of the discretionary power of law enforcement officers to refrain from enforcement even when enforcement is clearly appropriate. This discretionary power involves enforcement of laws of all kinds, regulatory as well as criminal law. A policeman usually assumes he has discretionary power to arrest or not to arrest a violator. A prosecutor normally assumes he has discretionary power to refrain from prosecuting even when the facts and the law clearly justify prosecution.
>
> . . . When an enforcement agency or officer has discretionary power to do nothing about a case in which enforcement would be clearly justified, the result

---

[*] Reprinted with permission. All rights reserved.

23

is a power of selective enforcement. Such power goes to selection of parties against whom the law is enforced and selection of the occasions when the law is enforced. Selective enforcement may also mean selection of the law that will be enforced and of the law that will not be enforced; an officer may enforce one statute fully, never enforce another, and pick and choose in enforcing a third.

Selective enforcement obviously may be just or unjust, depending upon how the selections are made. Theoretically possible is a system of enforcement in only a fraction of the cases in which enforcement would be appropriate, with discretionary selections made in such a way that all the cases prosecuted are more deserving of prosecution than any of the cases not prosecuted.

[2] The Problem of Unenforced Statutes

When the legislature enacts a statute that makes certain conduct a crime, it can be assumed that the legislature intends — at least in broad terms — that the statute will be enforced in appropriate cases. It sometimes is the case, however, that the legislature may approve of a law for symbolic or political reasons, thereby signifying that the legislature has little actual desire or expectation that such a law will be enforced fully. Criminal laws related to offenses involving no vocal victims, such as gambling or prostitution, may fall into this category.

Even where full enforcement of criminal statutes is desired by the legislature, however, such enforcement may be nearly impossible. Some of the more obvious reasons for this are limited numbers of police, prosecutors, courts, and jail facilities. Additionally, a police officer or prosecutor may decide that the circumstances of a specific case simply do not call for enforcement of the relevant criminal statute.

[a] General Approach

When a criminal law goes unenforced, the one person most likely to complain is the crime victim. What remedy is available to have law enforcement authorities enforce the law? Consider, in this context, the following case.

INMATES OF ATTICA CORRECTIONAL FACILITY v. ROCKEFELLER
477 F.2d 375 (2d Cir. 1973)

MANSFIELD, CIRCUIT JUDGE:

This appeal raises the question of whether the federal judiciary should, at the instance of victims, compel federal and state officials to investigate and prosecute persons who allegedly have violated certain federal and state criminal statutes. Plaintiffs in the purported class suit, which was commenced in the Southern District of New York against various state and federal officers, are present and former inmates of New York State's Attica Correctional Facility ("Attica"), the mother of an inmate who was killed when Attica was retaken after the inmate uprising in September 1971, and Arthur O. Eve, a New York State Assemblyman and member of the Subcommittee on Prisons. They appeal from an order of the district court . . . dismissing their complaint. We affirm.

The complaint alleges that before, during, and after the prisoner revolt at and subsequent recapture of Attica in September 1971, which resulted in the killing of 32 inmates and the wounding of many others, the defendants, including the Governor of New York, the State Commissioner of Correctional Services, the Executive Deputy Commissioner of the State Department of Correctional Services, the Superintendent at Attica, and certain State Police, Corrections Officers, and other officials, either committed, conspired to commit, or aided and abetted in the commission of various crimes against the complaining inmates and members of the class they seek to represent. It is charged that the inmates were intentionally subjected to cruel and inhuman treatment prior to the inmate riot, that State Police, Troopers, and Correction

Officers (one of whom is named) intentionally killed some of the inmate victims without provocation during the recovery of Attica, that state officers (several of whom are named and whom the inmates claim they can identify) assaulted and beat prisoners after the prison had been successfully retaken and the prisoners had surrendered, . . . that personal property of the inmates was thereafter stolen or destroyed, and that medical assistance was maliciously denied to over 400 inmates wounded during the recovery of the prison. [The inmates also alleged that abusive conduct would continue to occur unless the responsible state officers were prosecuted.]

The complaint further alleges that Robert E. Fischer [a special prosecutor appointed by the Governor] . . . to investigate crimes relating to the inmates' takeover of Attica and the resumption of control by the state authorities, " . . . has not investigated, nor does he intend to investigate, any crimes committed by state officers." Plaintiffs claim, moreover, that because Fischer was appointed by the Governor he cannot neutrally investigate the responsibility of the Governor and other state officers said to have conspired to commit the crimes alleged. It is also asserted that since Fischer is the sole state official currently authorized under state law to prosecute the offenses allegedly committed by the state officers, no one in the State of New York is investigating or prosecuting them.

. . . As a remedy for the asserted failure of the defendants to prosecute violations of state and federal criminal laws, plaintiffs request relief in the nature of mandamus (1) against state officials, requiring the State of New York to submit a plan for the independent and impartial investigation and prosecution of the offenses charged against the named and unknown state officers, and insuring the appointment of an impartial state prosecutor and state judge to "prosecute the defendants forthwith," and (2) against the United States Attorney, requiring him to investigate, arrest and prosecute the same state officers for having committed the federal offenses defined by 18 U.S.C. §§ 241 and 242 [involving infringing rights secured by the United States Constitution or laws]. . . .

With respect to the defendant United States Attorney, plaintiffs seek mandamus to compel him to investigate and institute prosecutions against state officers, most of whom are not identified, for alleged violations of 18 U.S.C. §§ 241 and 242. . . . Federal courts have traditionally and, to our knowledge, uniformly refrained from overturning, at the instance of a private person, discretionary decisions of federal prosecuting authorities not to prosecute persons regarding whom a complaint of criminal conduct is made. . . .

The primary ground upon which this traditional judicial aversion to compelling prosecutions has been based is the separation of powers doctrine.

> Although as a member of the bar, the attorney for the United States is an officer of the court, he is nevertheless an executive official of the Government, and it is as an officer of the executive department that he exercises a discretion as to whether or not there shall be a prosecution in a particular case. It follows, as an incident of the constitutional separation of powers, that the courts are not to interfere with the free exercise of the discretionary powers of the attorneys of the United States in their control over criminal prosecutions. *United States v. Cox*, 342 F.2d 167, 171 (5th Cir.), *cert. denied*, 381 U.S. 935 (1965).

. . . In the absence of statutorily defined standards governing reviewability, or regulatory or statutory policies of prosecution, the problems inherent in the task of supervising prosecutorial decisions do not lend themselves to resolution by the judiciary. The reviewing courts would be placed in the undesirable and injudicious posture of becoming "superprosecutors." In the normal case of review of executive acts of discretion, the administrative record is open, public and reviewable on the basis of what it contains. The decision not to prosecute, on the other hand, may be based upon the insufficiency of the available evidence, in which event the secrecy of the grand jury and of the prosecutor's file may serve to protect the accused's reputation from public damage based upon insufficient, improper, or even malicious charges. *In camera* review would not be meaningful without *access* by the complaining party to the evidence before the grand jury or United States Attorney. Such interference with the normal operations of criminal investigations, in turn, based solely upon allegations of criminal conduct, raises serious questions of potential abuse by persons seeking to have other persons prosecuted. Any person, merely by filing a complaint containing allegations in general terms (permitted by the Federal Rules) of unlawful failure to prosecute, could gain access to the prosecutor's file and the grand jury's minutes, notwithstanding the secrecy normally attaching to the latter by law.

Nor is it clear what the judiciary's role of supervision should be were it to undertake such a review. At what point would the prosecutor be entitled to call a halt to further investigation as unlikely to be productive? What evidentiary standard would be used to decide whether prosecution should be compelled? How much judgment would the United States Attorney be allowed? Would he be permitted to limit himself to a strong "test" case rather than pursue weaker cases? What collateral factors would be permissible bases for a decision not to prosecute, *e.g.*, the pendency of another criminal proceeding elsewhere against the same parties? What sort of review should be available in cases like the present one where the conduct complained of allegedly violates state as well as federal laws? With limited personnel and facilities at his disposal, what priority would the prosecutor be required to give to cases in which investigation or prosecution was directed by the court?

These difficult questions engender serious doubts as to the judiciary's capacity to review and as to the problem of arbitrariness inherent in any judicial decision to order prosecution. On balance, we believe that substitution of a court's decision to compel prosecution for the U.S. Attorney's decision not to prosecute, even upon an abuse of discretion standard of review and even if limited to directing that a prosecution be undertaken in good faith, would be unwise.

Plaintiffs urge, however, that Congress withdrew the normal prosecutorial discretion for the kind of conduct alleged here by providing in 42 U.S.C. § 1987 that the United States Attorneys are "authorized *and required* . . . to institute prosecutions against all persons violating any of the provisions of [18 U.S.C. §§ 241 and 242]" (emphasis supplied), and, therefore, that no barrier to a judicial directive to institute prosecutions remains. This contention must be rejected. The mandatory nature of the word "required" as it appears in § 1987 is insufficient to evince a broad Congressional purpose to bar the exercise of executive discretion in the prosecution of federal civil rights crimes. Similar mandatory language is contained in the general direction in 28 U.S.C. § 547(1)("each United States attorney, . . . *shall* — (1) prosecute for all offenses against the United States; . . . " (emphasis supplied)) and in other statutes in particular areas of concern, *e.g.*, 33 U.S.C. § 413 ("it shall be the duty of United States attorneys to vigorously prosecute all offenders" of certain provisions of the Rivers and Harbors Act when requested to do so by the appropriate officials). *See also* 45 U.S.C. § 152 (Tenth).

Such language has never been thought to preclude the exercise of prosecutorial discretion. . . . Nor do we find the legislative history of § 1987 persuasive of an intent by Congress to depart so significantly from the normal assumption of executive discretion. . . . [The court also rejected similar claims against state defendants.]

NOTES

1. *Judicial reluctance to interfere minimally with prosecutor's discretion.* State and federal prosecutors serve as public officials and they are charged with the responsibility of enforcing relevant criminal statutes. Why, then, would a court refuse to interfere with a prosecutor's decision not to prosecute, even by reviewing the prosecutor's decision by an abuse of discretion standard of review and even if limited to directing that a prosecution be undertaken in good faith?

2. *What could Congress have done?* If the court in *Attica* was correct in deciding that Congress did not intend to restrict the exercise of prosecutorial discretion, how could Congress construct a statute to effectuate "full" enforcement of a specific statute?

3. *Appoint special prosecutor?* Given some of the concerns expressed in this case regarding the control of prosecutorial discretion, is this case one in which a court should be authorized to appoint a special prosecutor to consider instituting criminal charges?

4. *Civil settlement in Attica case.* While "criminal remedies" were denied the victims in *Attica*, the New York Times reported January 5, 2000, that the inmates would be receiving a settlement of $12 million from the State of New York ($4 million of which was for lawyers' fees) and that the award "is believed to be the biggest ever in a prisoners' rights case."

5. *Legislative efforts to control prosecutorial discretion.* Finally, if courts are not allowed to control prosecutorial discretion what would happen if the legislature attempts to control prosecutorial discretion? In Texas, for example, the legislature passed a law requiring prosecutors (who are considered judicial officers) to first consult with the Texas Commission on Environmental Quality (an executive agency) before bringing any criminal charges against a permit holder for criminal violations. *See* 36 St. Mary's L. J. 411 (2005). This has prompted one prosecutor to say that he would not enforce an "unconstitutional law."

[b] Desuetude

The *Attica* case addressed the issue of selective nonenforcement of a viable criminal statute. Victims filed a lawsuit to require prosecution in a specific situation. In contrast, in some cases a statute will have gone unenforced (*i.e.*, no prosecutions will have occurred) for many years only to surface in a specific prosecution. In this instance, the defendant will now be the complaining party, as illustrated in the next case.

STATE v. PAUL BLAKE, PROSECUTING ATTORNEY OF FAYETTE COUNTY
213 W. Va. 656 (W. Va. 2003)

[The petitioner operated a pawnshop for ten years. Shortly after he went out of business, he was indicted for violation of W. Va. Code § 61-3-51 (1981). The statute required people in the business of buying precious metals or gems for non-personal use to (1) obtain and retain documentary proof that the seller owned the items and (2) list each such purchase, including information about the seller, in a permanent record book open to inspection by law enforcement. Violation is a felony with a maximum sentence of two years.]

[The petitioner requests that the prosecuting attorney be prohibited from proceeding against him or that the circuit court be prohibited from proceeding to trial. We issue a writ prohibiting the circuit court from proceeding to trial.]

The petitioner contends, in this original action of prohibition, that W.Va. Code § 61-3-51 (1981) has fallen into desuetude due to nonuse and lack of enforcement. Desuetude is defined as

1. Lack of use; obsolescence through disuse.

2. The doctrine holding that if a statute or treaty is left unenforced long enough, the courts will no longer regard it as having any legal effect even though it has not been repealed. Black's Law Dictionary 458 (7th ed. 1999).

> Stated more clearly, the doctrine of desuetude, the concept that a statute may be void because of its lack of use, is founded on the constitutional concept of fairness embodied in federal and state constitutional due process and equal protection clauses. In other words, "the problem [of applying, or refusing to apply, the rubric of desuetude] must be approached in terms of that fundamen-

tal fairness owed to the particular defendant that is the heart of due process." *United States v. Elliott*, 266 F. Supp. 318, 326 (S.D.N.Y. 1967).

The seminal case in West Virginia regarding desuetude is *Comm. on Legal Ethics v. Printz*, 187 W.Va. 182, 416 S.E.2d 720 (1992). In . . . *Printz*, this Court held that:

Penal statutes may become void under the doctrine of desuetude if:

(1) The statute proscribes only acts that are *malum prohibitum* and not *malum in se*;

(2) There has been open, notorious and pervasive violation of the statute for a long period; and

(3) There has been a conspicuous policy of nonenforcement of the statute.

We believe all three elements are satisfied in this case.

First, we must distinguish between crimes that are *malum prohibitum* and crimes that are *malum in se*. Crimes that are *malum in se* will not lose their criminal character through desuetude, but crimes that are *malum prohibitum* may. . . . The defense attorney . . . argued that "this kind of statute is clearly *malum prohibitum*. The whole distinction between *malum in se* and *malum prohibitum* makes it clear. This statute is not anything that came up through the common law or something that is inherently wrong." . . . . We agree [that it is *malum prohibitum*].

Second, there must be an open, notorious, and pervasive violation of the statute for a long period before desuetude will take hold. In the case before us, the defense argued that the statute had been violated "for the entire period of time the statute has been in place[.]" The assistant prosecutor did not contest this contention, but rather argued that the statute was not old enough to fall into desuetude. Finally, there is no doubt that a conspicuous policy of nonenforcement exists in Fayette County. . . . [T]he Sheriff of Fayette County . . . testified that he believes W.Va. Code § 61-3-51 has never been enforced in the county since its inception in 1981. . . . Richard Kemp, an investigator, did a survey of businesses in Fayette County which pawn or purchase gems or precious metals, to see if they have been following the provisions of 61-3-51. The State stipulated Mr. Kemp would report that no business in Fayette County was making such report.

. . . [T]he petitioner argues that W.Va. Code § 61-3-51 has fallen into desuetude and, consequently, he cannot be reindicted and tried for failure to conform to the requirements of the statute. . . . The State essentially argues that an argument based upon the ancient common law doctrine of desuetude is not indicative of a case for clear, erroneous error being established. We disagree.

. . . [Citing *Printz*, the court agreed that a law that was not prosecuted in 20 years is unfair to the one person selectively prosecuted under it.] Because W.Va. Code § 61-3-51 (1981) has fallen into desuetude, the petitioner cannot be made to stand trial for violating the statute. The . . . indictment fails and must be dismissed.

NOTES

1. *Does type of crime matter?* Why did the *Blake* court care whether the crime was *malum prohibitum* or *malum in se*? Could the answer be based, at least in part, on the concept of fair warning?

2. *Desuetude in the courts.* Desuetude is a rarely successful defense. Some jurisdictions do not recognize it as a possible defense, but focus instead on whether enforcing a long-dead statute would violate the due process guarantee of fundamental fairness. *See, e.g., United States v. Elliott*, 266 F. Supp. 318 (S.D.N.Y 1967)(refusing to apply desuetude to statute barring injury to property — here a bridge in Zambia — belonging to a foreign government; though law had not been enforced since enacted in 1917, policy underpinning still valid — to stop interference in foreign relations — and no fair notice problem because blowing up a bridge in another country has never been accepted by community mores).

3. *Minimal enforcement.* Enforcement within any remotely recent time also is fatal to a desuetude defense. *See, e.g., Leonard v. Robinson,* 477 F.3d 347 (6th Cir. 2007)(statute enforced within last ten years).

C.   VICTIM DISCRETION

Various studies have focused upon the extent to which victims play important roles in influencing the exercise of discretion by public officials. One such study found that police officers frequently rely upon the victim's complaint, whether formal or informal, in deciding whether to arrest an offender when the offense is less than a felony and not committed in the officer's presence. *See* Donald J. Hall, *The Role of the Victim in the Prosecution and Disposition of a Criminal Case,* 28 VAND. L. REV. 931 (1975).

At the arrest stage, a victim may aggressively press the police officer to arrest a suspect, may attempt to persuade the officer not to make the arrest, or may be ambivalent about the arrest decision. In responding to victim preferences, police officers may or may not show deference to the victim, depending upon one or more of the following variables:

1. Whether or not the victim was a "wrongdoer" in the alleged criminal event.

2. Whether the victim and the alleged offender are related by friendship, marriage, family, or contract.

3. The socioeconomic status of the victim.

4. The victim's underlying motive for seeking an arrest.

5. The seriousness of the underlying crime.

In addition to playing a significant role at the arrest stage, crime victims also influence the prosecutor's decision whether to prosecute. Based upon his field study, Hall reported: "[I]f the crime charged is a misdemeanor or non-serious felony, chances are good that the case will be dismissed if the victim so desires unless specific circumstances other than the victim's desires predominate. With the exception of the crime of rape, however, the reluctant victim's desires will not be heeded by the prosecutor in a serious felony case." Hall relates that prosecutors had varying opinions about the victim's influence on the choice of charge. They agreed, however, that they listen attentively to the victim who desires to "overcharge" in a serious felony case but not to the victim who desires similarly overcharging in a misdemeanor case. Victims desirous of undercharging experience more success with misdemeanors than with serious crimes.

A number of factors unique to the individual victim may account for the way discretion is exercised by prosecutorial officials. Such factors include age and stature in the community. One author concludes that perhaps the single most important variable in this context is whether the victim and defendant were strangers to one another at the time of the offense: "Prosecutors and judges view stranger crimes as more serious offenses than crimes involving a prior relationship between victim and offender; but they concentrate their resources on stranger crimes, too, because it is so much harder to get a conviction in prior relationship cases. The reason, quite simply, is that when they know the offender, victims often refuse to press charges, to testify against the offender, or to cooperate with the prosecutor in other ways." Charles E. Silberman, CRIMINAL VIOLENCE, CRIMINAL JUSTICE 359–360 (1978). Silberman also observed that police and prosecutors tend to view prior-relationship crimes as less serious than those involving strangers.

It has been argued that victims should play an even *greater* role in criminal cases. *See* Sarah N. Welling, *Victims in the Criminal Process: A Utilitarian Analysis of the Victim's Participation in the Charging Decision,* 30 ARIZ. L. REV. 85 (1988). Numerous commentators and policy-makers have championed the so-called "Victims' Rights" movement which fosters this goal. *See Victims' Rights Symposium,* 11 PEPP. L. REV. 1 (1984) and *Follow-Up Issue On Victims' Rights,* 17 PEPP. L. REV. 1 (1989).

This movement has prompted the enactment of a number of state and federal statutes, many of which ensure that crime victims have an opportunity to be active participants in some phases of the criminal case. State attorneys in Florida, for example, are under a duty to consult the victim in order to obtain the views of the victim . . . about the disposition of any criminal case . . . , including the [pre-trial] release of the accused, plea agreements, and participation in pre-trial diversion programs." Fla. Stat. § 960.001(1)(e).Similarly, the Washington state legislature has expressed its intention to "grant to victims of crime and the survivors of such victims a significant role in the criminal justice system." Wash. Rev. Code § 7.69.010. Among powers granted the victim is the right to recommend that no criminal charges be filed — but only if the case is one characterized as "relatively minor."

Should the individual crime victim be given this kind of explicit influence over the handling of the defendant's case? If, as a policy matter, you believe that the crime victims should be given such a voice, will this policy not lead to disparate treatment of similarly situated defendants? Would a prosecutor be as forceful in presenting the views of a particular victim if he or she knew that the victim was disinclined to urge harsh treatment of the defendant? For a discussion of these and other issues raised by victim participation statutes, *see* Donald J. Hall, *Victims' Voices in Criminal Court: The Need For Restraint*, 28 Am. Crim. L. Rev. 235 (1991).

D.   POLICE DISCRETION

[1]   Generally

Because police make far more discretionary determinations in individual cases than any other class of administrators, it has been said that they are "among the most important policy-makers of our entire society." Kenneth Culp Davis, Discretionary Justice 222 (1969). One of the most comprehensive studies in which the exercise of discretion by police has been described and catalogued is Wayne R. LaFave, Arrest: The Decision to Take a Suspect into Custody 9–10 (1965):

> Many persons whose conduct apparently violates the criminal law are not arrested. In some instances this may be explained by the fact that there is no legislative purpose to enforcing some statutes which are obsolete or drafted in overly general or ambiguous terms. In other instances the failure to make arrests results from the obvious fact that the resources available to law enforcement agencies make impossible the full enforcement of the existing substantive criminal law. A significant number of decisions not to arrest are unrelated to either legislative intent or resource allocation. Illustrative is the failure to arrest an informant as a reward for information.

For various reasons, as noted above, some persons who have likely violated substantive criminal laws will not be subjected to arrest. On the other hand, some individuals will be arrested for purposes other than prosecution. LaFave cites the example of arresting intoxicated persons and then releasing them when they become sober. In that instance, the underlying reason for arrest is the well-being of the individual. Similarly, certain types of offenders are arrested for the purpose of confiscation of equipment with little thought given to successful criminal prosecution (*i.e.*, suspected gamblers).

Notwithstanding the many ways in which police exercise discretion, LaFave asserts that "the police have failed to evaluate carefully such enforcement policies or even to acknowledge that such practices exist. Rather, most departments attempt to maintain the existing stereotype of the police as ministerial officers who enforce all of the laws, while they actually engage in a broad range of discretionary enforcement."

In light of concerns raised by Davis, LaFave and others, attempts have been made to address ways in which police discretion can be limited or controlled. One of the earliest detailed proposals emerged in 1973 from the *National Advisory Commission On Criminal Justice Standards and Goals, Report on Police.* The Commission urged the adoption of guidelines to limit the exercise of discretion by police in conducting investigations. With regard to alternatives to arrest, the Commission recommended guidelines that should:

1. establish the limits of discretion by specifically identifying, insofar as possible, situations calling for the use of alternatives to continued physical custody;

2. establish criteria for the selection of appropriate enforcement alternatives;

3. require enforcement action to be taken in all situations where all elements of a crime are present and all policy criteria are satisfied;

4. be jurisdictionwide in both scope and application; and

5. specifically exclude offender lack of cooperation, or disrespect toward police personnel, as a factor in arrest determination unless such conduct constitutes a separate crime.

Standard 1.3, paragraph 2.

Six years later, the American Bar Association approved *Standards for Criminal Justice, The Urban Police Function*, which recommended that police departments formulate and adopt administrative regulations to guide the exercise of their discretion. This rulemaking process should give the highest priority to the formulation of administrative rules governing the exercise of discretion, particularly in the areas of selective enforcement, investigative techniques, and enforcement methods." Standard 1-4.3.

Rulemaking by many law enforcement agencies has occurred. Professor LaFave calls this a "most encouraging development," noting that policymaking improves police performance in four major ways: (1) it enhances the quality of police decisions by promoting the decisionmaking authority in responsible and capable hands; (2) it ensures fair and equal treatment of citizens as rules reduce the influence of bias; (3) rulemaking increases visibility of police policy decisions; and (4) on the assumption that rules made by police are most likely to be obeyed by police, rulemaking offers the best hope for getting police officials to obey and enforce constitutional norms. Wayne R. LaFave, *Constitutional Rules For Police: A Matter Of Style*, 41 Syracuse L. Rev. 849, 867, 868 and 873 (1990).

A study adds a more cautionary tone, however. In street encounters between police and citizens, abuse of broad police discretion can result in unchecked discrimination against disfavored groups. For a detailed analysis of issues related to "order maintenance," as well as ways in which such discretion can be channeled and supervised, *see* Debra Livingston, *Police Discretion and the Quality of Life in Public Places: Courts, Communities and the New Policing*, 97 Colum. L. Rev. 551 (1997).

It should also be noted that police officers sometimes act as prosecutors for the government in both federal and state courts. See Andrew Horowitz, *Taking the Cop Out of Copping a Plea: Eradicating Police Prosecution of Criminal Cases*, 40 Ariz. L. Rev. 1305 (1998).

[2] Racial Profiling

A persistent issue in police discretion is *racial profiling*, in which police make discretionary decisions on the basis of profiles entirely or largely based on race. One classic study of state police searches along I-95 found that sixty-three percent of those stopped and searched were African American and only twenty-nine percent were white, though only eighteen percent of the drivers on that road were African-American. John Knowles, *et al.*, 109 J. Pol. Econ. 203 (2001). Another study in West Virginia found that black drivers were 1½ times more likely to be subjected to a traffic stop and twice as likely to have their cars searched during the stop as were white drivers. www.racialprofilinganalysis.neu.edu (Reported March 25, 2008)(extensive source for information on racial profiling). Finally, the *Boston Globe* reported that "blacks, who make up about 14 percent of the population, account for 72 percent of drivers pulled over for routine traffic stops." House OKs Study of Car Searches, The Boston Globe, Mar. 25, 1998, at A12.

Concluding that the data show that police use racial profiling in deciding whom to stop and search, many states have formally outlawed the practice and mandate that law enforcement departments keep statistics to monitor the use of this practice. Some jurisdictions require police departments to make regular reports about racial profiling practices in the jurisdiction. Many also require police officers to undergo training about race profiling,

Some economists question whether the data actually show improper racial profiling, arguing that race may be a proper factor in some discretionary police decisions. *See* Yoram Margalioth & Tomer Blumkin, 24 Yale Law & Pol'y Rev 317 (2006)("profiling is always efficient, helping the police to mitigate the screening problem when criminal activity varies across racial groups").

NOTES

1. *Racial profiling and efficiency.* If criminal activity is not equal across race lines, is racial profiling justifiable as an efficient way of assigning scarce law enforcement resources? Assuming *arguendo* that it is, is it fair in a diverse, democratic society?

2. *The special case of airport security after September 11.* Would your view change if the context were airport security rather than road or street crime? Would it make sense for airport security personnel to focus their attention on people who appear to be of Middle East descent or whose passport or background suggests they may be from that area of the world? Is there a difference in the goal of screening at airports and of stopping drivers suspected of traffic violations?

3. *State efforts to limit racial profiling.* In *Comm. v. Gonsalves,* 711 N.E.2d 108 (Mass. 1999), the Massachusetts Supreme Judicial Court held that under the state constitution's protection from unreasonable searches and seizures, police officers in routine traffic stops must have a reasonable belief that the officer or someone else's safety is in danger before ordering a driver out of a vehicle.

Judge Ireland's eloquent concurrence observed:

I write separately, however, to stress the dangers posed by unfettered police power to order individuals out of automobiles without any justification. The grant of such power is certainly, as the majority notes, "a clear invitation to discriminatory enforcement of the rule." This is precisely the type of power "that art. 14 [of the Massachusetts Constitution] was adopted to guard against," because, in the words of James Otis, it " 'places the liberty of every man in the hands of every petty officer.' " The widespread public concerns about police profiling, commonly referred to as "DWB – driving while black," has been the subject of much discussion and debate both across the country and within the Commonwealth. [United States Supreme Court decisions] which permit auto-mobile exit orders during any traffic stop "may also pose unique hardships on minorities" and could be a "clear invitation to discriminatory enforcement." Prohibiting the police from ordering people out of automobiles without any justification is a much needed step in the right direction to cure such abuses.

[3] Domestic Violence: A Case Study

As the materials above make clear, police officers have broad discretion with regard to the initial decision to arrest a suspect. In domestic violence cases, the exercise of this discretion raises some unique questions about the scope and effect of police decisionmaking. If police are summoned to a private residence in which domestic violence has recently occurred, it is not uncommon for the battered spouse (assuming that both parties do not appear to be equally culpable) to urge that the spouse "at fault" not be arrested.

It is widely believed that many police officers will not arrest a spouse unless the victim expresses clearly his or her desire for arrest of the offending spouse. Moreover, in many locales police are not authorized to arrest for a misdemeanor assault unless the officer personally witnesses the crime.

[a]   Statutory Efforts

Some state statutes have been enacted for the purpose of changing these traditional rules. One variety requires the officer to make an arrest if there is probable cause to do so (mandatory arrest); the other makes arrest the preferred option (presumptive arrest).

1. Nev. Rev. Stat. § 171.137: "[A] peace officer shall, unless mitigating circumstances exist, arrest a person when he has probable cause to believe that the person to be arrested has, within the preceding 24 hours, committed a battery upon his spouse, former spouse, a person to whom he is related by blood, a person with whom he is or was actually residing or with whom he has a child in common, his minor child or a minor child of that person. . . . A peace officer shall not base his decision whether to arrest a person pursuant to this section on his perception of the willingness of a victim or a witness to the incident to testify or otherwise participate in related judicial proceedings."

2. Tenn. Code Ann. 36-3-619: "If a law enforcement officer has probable cause to believe that a person has committed a crime involving domestic abuse, whether the crime is a misdemeanor or felony or was committed within or without the presence of the officer, the preferred response of the officer is arrest. . . . A law enforcement officer [in a domestic abuse case] shall not base the decision of whether to arrest on the consent or request of the victim or the officer's perception of the willingness of the victim or of a witness . . . to testify or participate in a judicial proceeding."

[b]   Impact of Statutory Efforts

Are these statutes likely to restrict the exercise of police discretion in any meaningful way? Do they reflect "good" public policy? With regard to the exercise of prosecutorial discretion in domestic violence cases, *see* Natalie Loder Clark, *Crime Begins At Home: Let's Stop Punishing Victims and Perpetuating Violence*, 28 WM. & MARY L. REV. 263, 268 (1987), in which the author asserts that prosecutors should seek criminal penalties in chronic and severe domestic violence cases "even if the victim does not insist upon, or even request, such action."

Professor Cheryl Hanna, expanding upon Professor Clark's argument, explores mandated victim participation in domestic violence cases from both feminist and practical perspectives and contends that while mandated participation has its costs, such participation is necessary to control domestic violence. Cheryl Hanna, *No Right to Choose: Mandated Victim Participation in Domestic Violence Prosecutions*, 109 HARV. L. REV. 1849 (1996). This article offers practical solutions to prosecuting a domestic violence case with an uncooperative victim, and Professor Hanna urges prosecutors to "take into account the circumstances of each case and not expect to rely solely on victim testimony as a matter of course."

It has been reported that the number of police departments encouraging or requiring their officers to make arrests in domestic violence cases has significantly increased. This increase follows a finding in an experimental program in Minneapolis that arrest is an effective deterrent to domestic violence. However, subsequent research has shown disturbing trends:

1. Mandatory arrest reduces domestic violence in some cities but increases it in others.

2. Mandatory arrest reduces domestic violence among employed people but increases it among unemployed people.

3. Mandatory arrest reduces violence in the short run but may increase it in the long run. **See,** Janelle D. Schmidt & Lawrence W. Sherman, *Does Arrest Deter Domestic Violence?* in Do ARRESTS AND RESTRAINING ORDERS WORK? (Buzawa & Buzawa eds. 1996).

4. Mandatory arrest has no more deterrent effect on domestic violence than does separation or counseling. R Gilles, *The Politics of Research: The Use and Misuse of Social Science Data — the Cases of Intimate Partner Violence,* 45 FAMILY CT. REV. 42 (2007).

Mandatory arrests statutes still allow police to use their discretion sometimes resulting in the arrest of both parties. To combat this, many states have enacted provisions directing police to arrest only the primary physical aggressor or the party not acting in self-defense. The issue of dual arrests is being discussed in police stations across the country especially in regards to the effects of gender stereotyping and the particularly complicated situation of same-sex abuse. *See* Elizabeth Schneider, *et al.,* DOMESTIC VIOLENCE AND THE LAW (2007).

Do you think police should be *required* to arrest a suspected spouse abuser if they have probable cause to do so? Only *encouraged* to do so? What effect would such a requirement have on the number of reported spouse abuse incidents? Should remedies such as counseling or mediation be an alternative to arrest? An alternative to prosecution? *See generally* National Institute of Justice Journal 27–28 (Oct. 1998) (5-jurisdiction study shows that arresting domestic violence suspects has a modest deterrent effect); *Developments in the Law — Legal Responses to Domestic Violence,* 106 HARV. L. REV. 1498, 1535–1541 (1993) (reporting five replication studies of the Minneapolis study; two found a decrease in domestic violence, three found an increase).

E. PROSECUTORIAL DISCRETION

[1] Generally

[a] Ethical Restrictions

Prosecutors, both state and federal, have the extraordinary power to determine whether an individual should be charged with a crime. Public prosecutors occupy a dual role of representing the government as an adversary while also seeking the objective of impartial justice. Under the American Bar Association's Model Rules of Professional Conduct, for example, a prosecutor is obligated to "refrain from prosecuting a charge that the prosecutor knows is not supported by probable cause." Model Rules of Professional Conduct Rule 3.8(a). See also Model Code of Professional Responsibility D.R. 7-103(A) (same).

While in some cases it is relatively easy to determine the charge to be placed against an individual, a number of variables are taken into account in making that decision. First and foremost, as suggested by the Rules of Professional Conduct, is the question whether there is enough evidence to support a prosecution for a particular offense.

Even if ample evidence exists, however, a prosecutor may elect to bypass prosecution because of what are believed to be legitimate reasons for not subjecting the accused to that process. Sometimes a prosecutor will forego prosecution if the defendant agrees to meet certain conditions. For example, a prosecutor may decide not to prosecute an individual found in possession of a small amount of marijuana in exchange for that person's agreement to "stay clean." On the other extreme, the maximum possible charge (or any number of charges) may be sought against an individual in order to bolster the prosecutor's position in later plea bargaining sessions, discussed more fully in Chapter 11.

[b] Legal Restrictions

Prosecutors are subject to very few legal constraints in exercising their discretion. If a prosecutor decides not to charge a criminal offense, there is little that can be done to challenge that decision, as noted in the *Attica* case. (In many jurisdictions, the political process may be the only effective means of "disciplining" a prosecutor who is thought by the public to be "soft" on crime.) Conversely, when a prosecutor elects to pursue criminal prosecution, courts generally recognize a rebuttable presumption that the prosecution has been undertaken in good faith and in compliance with constitutional mandates.

In one of the most authoritative works regarding the exercise of prosecutorial discretion, Professor Miller asserts that there are several related, but independently important issues raised in this context. First, the prosecutor must ask whether there is a sufficient probability of guilt to warrant subjecting the defendant to a trial. Next, even assuming sufficient probability of guilt, should prosecution be pursued? Finally, if the decision is made to prosecute, how should the prosecutor select the specific crime or crimes with which the person is to be charged? This decision may be influenced by such considerations as sentencing probabilities and the prosecutor's individual assessment about both the defendant's and the community's interests. Frank R. Miller, PROSECUTION: THE DECISION TO CHARGE A SUSPECT WITH A CRIME (1969).

Professor LaFave has referred to uncontrolled prosecutorial discretion as "one of the most striking features of the American system of criminal justice." Wayne R. LaFave, *The Prosecutor's Discretion in the United States*, 18 AM. J. OF COMP. LAW 532 (1970). In deciding whether or not to prosecute, he has identified "common explanations" that drive the necessity for selective enforcement. They are (1) legislative "overcriminalization," (2) limitations in available enforcement resources, and (3) a need to individualize justice.

Another commentator has observed that many times a prosecutor may reject a case that he or she feels "would not be in the public interest." For example, the prosecutor may believe that the crime is too trivial, that the defendant has already suffered enough, or that the accused will provide information in another, more important, case. Prosecutors also consider the defendant's "convictability" because they do not like to lose cases:

Several trends have intensified the power of the prosecutor in the American criminal justice system. First, by legislating numerous overlapping provisions in criminal codes, states have passed the decision of how to characterize allegedly criminal conduct to the prosecutor. Second, because of increased reporting of crime without concomitant increases in resources, the system is more dependent upon discretionary plea bargaining. Finally, the creation of sentencing guidelines has increased the importance of the initial charging decision because the sentences available to the court are almost always determined by the charging decision. Robert L. Misner, *Recasting Prosecutorial Discretion*, 86 J. CRIM. L. & CRIMINOLOGY 717 (1996).

As noted above, one reason for selective prosecution is inadequate resources. Not only does that suggest insufficient numbers of prosecutors, but it also means that there are too few jails and prisons in which to incarcerate convicted offenders. At the end of 2006, federal and state jails and prisons held 2,258,983 prisoners. *Sourcebook of Criminal Justice Statistics*, www.ojp.usdoj.gov/bjs/prisons.htm. Prosecutors sometimes take the availability of criminal justice resources into consideration in their decisions whether to prosecute and whether to accept a plea that is favorable to the defense. As penal facilities become overcrowded, the prosecutor may feel pressure to withhold prosecution or reduce charges so that the accused does not contribute to the surplus of prisoners.

By definition, a prosecutor exercises discretion only for crimes or offenders as to which he or she has knowledge. Sometimes the police know about a crime but are unable to identify the offender or gather sufficient proof of guilt. The police efforts may have been unsuccessful, or never even have begun, because many crime victims elect not to report their victimization to proper authorities. In 2005, over 23 million crimes occurred. About 57% were not reported to the police, including 51% of violent crimes, 62% of sexual assault or rape, 47% of robberies, and 60% of property crimes. *Sourcebook of Criminal Justice Statistics*, www.albany.edu/sourcebook/pdf/t3332005.pdf

[2] Challenges to Exercise of Discretion

[a] Abuse of Discretion

A defendant may challenge prosecutorial discretion in bringing criminal charges.

STATE v. BELL

69 S.W.3d 171 (Tenn. 2002)

We granted this appeal to determine the following issues: (1) whether the district attorney general abused his discretion by failing to consider and weigh evidence favorable to the defendant before denying the defendant's request for pretrial diversion; and (2) whether the trial court erred in upholding the denial of pretrial diversion despite the district attorney general's failure to consider and weigh evidence favorable to the defendant.

. . . After a thorough review of the record and relevant authority, we hold that when the district attorney general denies pretrial diversion without considering and weighing all the relevant factors, including substantial evidence favorable to the defendant, there is an abuse of prosecutorial discretion. . . . [T]he proper remedy . . . [is] for the district attorney general to consider and weigh all of the relevant factors to the pretrial diversion determination. . . .

BACKGROUND

The defendant, Johnnie Bell, Jr., was charged with vehicular homicide and aggravated assault. The charges arose from a collision between a tractor-trailer driven by Bell and a minivan driven by Mrs. Lois Bacon on July 6, 1998. Bacon was killed in the collision; and her daughter, a passenger in the minivan, was injured. Bell was not injured, and there was only minor damage to his tractor-trailer. After being charged, Bell applied for pretrial diversion.

In a statement to Kingsport Police Officer Jerry Mowell, Bell stated that he was traveling north on Interstate 81 in the right lane when the minivan in front of him entered the far right emergency lane as if to approach the exit ramp. Bell stated that he noticed cars entering the interstate northbound and two tractor-trailers and a car on the left side of his tractor-trailer. When the minivan re-entered the right lane, Bell drove as close to the center line as possible while braking, but still hit the left rear side of the minivan.

In the pretrial diversion report, Bell stated that he felt terrible about the victim's death but that the accident was unavoidable, and he was not negligent. Officer Jerry Mowell reported that Bell was truthful and cooperative during the investigation and showed extreme remorse for the accident. Officer Mowell stated that if anyone deserved pretrial diversion, Bell did; although pretrial diversion was a matter for the district attorney general's office. In a recorded telephone conversation, Officer Mowell asked Bell about the victim's entry into the emergency lane. Bell indicated that the minivan's left tires reached the solid white line that separated the right lane from the emergency lane, but he agreed that the entire minivan never completely crossed into the emergency lane.

According to the pretrial diversion report, Bell was 34 years old at the time of the accident. He had been married for thirteen years and had three children. Bell graduated from high school and served seven years in the army before receiving an honorable discharge. . . . At the time he was interviewed, Bell worked as a releasing agent for Auto Rail Services, and a representative of the company characterized him as a good employee.

The pretrial diversion report also indicated that Bell paid a fine following a conviction for defective equipment in 1994. Additionally, Bell reported incurring two speeding tickets in Ohio and having a following-too-closely offense in Louisiana. Bell reported that although he had back problems, he was in good physical health and excellent mental health. Bell also stated that he had used alcohol once, but did not like the taste. He reported no other drug use. A laboratory report revealed that Bell had not used drugs on the day of the offenses.

. . . In a letter dated March 26, 1999, the district attorney denied Bell's request for pretrial diversion, noting the following reasons:

1. The defendant takes no responsibility for his actions and blames the victim in this case. . . . The lack of acceptance of responsibility on behalf of the defendant shows that he would be a poor candidate for rehabilitation.

2. The defendant admits to having two speeding tickets and one conviction for following too closely. There is evidence that the defendant was following too closely to the victim of this fatality. The defendant has violated the motor vehicle rules in the past but chose to drive dangerously again.

3. The defendant had no hesitation in acting recklessly and did endanger several motorists other than the victims. Other motorists were in danger of serious bodily injury. Diversion would depreciate the seriousness of these crimes.

4. The defendant has an unstable work history as a truck driver. He has been terminated twice and all of his jobs have been of short duration. The defendant would be a poor candidate to complete any probationary period.

5. The driver was driving a large semi-truck. The victim was driving a Dodge Caravan. The officer states that the victim was killed in part by the fact that the defendant was following too closely. The defendant should have reasonably known of his vehicles [sic] potential for deadly force. Fatalities by large trucks are a growing problem in our community and in our nation. . . .

[The trial and appellate courts upheld the denial of diversion.]

ANALYSIS

Under the pretrial diversion program, the district attorney general is permitted to suspend a prosecution against a qualified defendant for a period of up to two years. A defendant is statutorily eligible for pretrial diversion if he or she (1) has not previously been granted diversion; (2) has no prior misdemeanor conviction for which confinement was served; (3) has no prior felony conviction within a five-year period after completing the sentence or probationary period for the conviction; and (4) is not charged with [certain specific crimes].

A person who is statutorily eligible for pretrial diversion is not presumptively entitled to diversion. Rather, the district attorney general has the sole discretion to determine whether to grant pretrial diversion to one who is statutorily eligible. In order for the district attorneys general "to properly exercise the discretion vested in them by the pretrial diversion statute," this Court has established several objective considerations:

When deciding whether to [place the defendant on pretrial diversion] . . . a prosecutor should focus on the defendant's amenability to correction. Any factors which tend to accurately reflect whether a particular defendant will or will not become a repeat offender should be considered. Such factors must, of course, be clearly articulable and stated in the record in order that meaningful appellate review may be had. Among the factors to be considered in addition to the circumstances of the offense are the defendant's criminal record, social history, the physical and mental condition of a defendant where appropriate, and the likelihood that pretrial diversion will serve the ends of justice and the best interest of both the public and the defendant.

In cases where the district attorney general denies an application for pretrial diversion, the denial must be written and must discuss all of the relevant factors considered and the weight accorded to each factor. That a defendant bears the burden of establishing suitability for diversion does not relieve the district attorney general of the obligation of examining all of the relevant factors and of setting out all of the required written findings. In addition, the denial statement must identify factual disputes between the evidence relied upon and the application filed by the defendant.

. . . With these principles in mind, we turn to the facts of this case. The district attorney general denied pretrial diversion because Bell failed to take responsibility for his actions, has a record of traffic offenses, acted recklessly, endangered persons other than the victims, and has an unstable work history. The district attorney general also cited a need to deter irresponsible driving by tractor-trailer drivers. The district attorney general, however, failed to consider evidence favorable to Bell, such as his honorable discharge from the United States Army, stable marriage of thirteen years, high school diploma, and lack of a history of drug or alcohol abuse. Moreover, the district attorney general failed to set forth this favorable evidence in writing, weigh it against the other factors, and reach a conclusion based on the relative weight of all of the factors.

This Court has stated unequivocally that the district attorney general has a duty to exercise his or her discretion by focusing on a defendant's amenability for correction and by considering all of the relevant factors, including evidence that is favorable to a defendant. . . .

Accordingly, we now reiterate the well-established rule that the district attorney general, when denying pretrial diversion, must consider all relevant factors, including evidence favorable to the defendant, must weigh each factor, and must explain in writing how the decision to deny pretrial diversion was determined. We [hold] . . . that the district attorney general abused his discretion by failing to satisfy these requirements in this case.

CONCLUSION

After a thorough review of the record and relevant authority, we hold that when the district attorney general denies pretrial diversion without considering and weighing all of the relevant factors, including substantial evidence favorable to the defendant, there is an abuse of prosecutorial discretion. We further hold that in such a case, the proper remedy under the applicable standards of review requires a remand for the district attorney general to consider and weigh all of the relevant factors to the pretrial diversion determination.

NOTES

1. *Bell as unusual case finding abuse of discretion. Bell* is an unusual case where the appellate court found the prosecutor had committed an abuse of discretion in making a discretionary decision as to the sanction to seek. The usual rule is that the prosecutor's decision is found not to be an "abuse of discretion" even when the appellate court disagrees with it.

2. *Does Bell depend on use of specific factors?* Could the *Bell* result be the product of the court's use of specific factors to be addressed by the prosecutor in deciding whether to approve a petition for diversion? Courts do not require specific facts to be assessed for most of the prosecutor's discretionary decisions.

[b] Selective Prosecution

Even though there is a widely recognized presumption that every criminal prosecution is undertaken in good faith, a defendant may challenge his or her prosecution on selective prosecution grounds. The defendant will be required to meet a relatively heavy burden of proving facts sufficient to satisfy two requirements: (1) others similarly situated have not been prosecuted; and (2) the decision to prosecute was based on impermissible considerations, such as race, religion, political affiliation, or the exercise of constitutional rights. While the most important United States Supreme Court decision was announced in 1985 (*Wayte v. United States*, below), two earlier cases are deserving of consideration.

YICK WO v. HOPKINS
118 U.S. 356 (1886)

[Yick Wo was found guilty of violating a San Francisco ordinance, which provided:

Sec. 1. It shall be unlawful, from and after the passage of this order, for any person or persons to establish, maintain, or carry on a laundry within the corporate limits of the city and county of San Francisco without having first obtained the consent of the board of supervisors, except the same be located in a building constructed either of brick or stone.

His uncontested claim was that at the time of his conviction, there were about 320 laundries in the city, of which about 240 were owned by Chinese. Pursuant to the ordinance, he and 200 of his countrymen petitioned the board of supervisors for permission to continue their laundry business. Each of their petitions was denied, yet virtually all of those who were not Chinese were granted their petitions.

The United States Supreme Court held this a violation of the fourteenth amendment equal protection guarantee.]

. . . [T]he facts shown establish an administration directed so exclusively against a particular class of persons as to warrant and require the conclusion that, whatever may have been the intent of the ordinances as adopted, they are applied by the public authorities charged with their administration, and thus representing the state itself, with a mind so unequal and oppressive as to amount to a practical denial by the state of that equal protection of the laws which is secured to the petitioners, as to all other persons, by the broad and benign provisions of the fourteenth amendment to the constitution of the United States. Though the law itself be fair on its face, and impartial in appearance, yet, if it is applied and administered by public authority with an evil eye and an unequal hand, so as practically to make unjust and illegal discriminations between persons in similar circumstances, material to their rights, the denial of equal justice is still within the prohibition of the constitution. . . .

The present cases, as shown by the facts disclosed in the record, are within this class. It appears that both petitioners have complied with every requisite deemed by the law, or by the public officers charged with its administration, necessary for the protection of neighboring property from fire, or as a precaution against injury to the public health. No reason whatever, except the will of the supervisors, is assigned why they should not be permitted to carry on, in the accustomed manner, their harmless and useful occupation, on which they depend for a livelihood; and while this consent of the supervisors is withheld from them, and from 200 others who have also petitioned, all of whom happen to be Chinese subjects, 80 others, not Chinese subjects, are permitted to carry on the same business under similar conditions. The fact of this discrimination is admitted. No reason for it is shown, and the conclusion cannot be resisted that no reason for it exists except hostility to the race and nationality to which the petitioners belong, and which in the eye of the law is not justified. The discrimination is, therefore, illegal, and the public administration which enforces it is a denial of the equal protection of the laws, and a violation of the fourteenth amendment of the constitution. . . .

OYLER v. BOLES
368 U.S. 448 (1962)

Oyler, serving a life sentence under a West Virginia habitual criminal statute [providing a mandatory life sentence upon a third conviction for a crime punishable by confinement in a penitentiary], claimed a denial of equal protection, alleging:

> Petitioner was discriminated against as an Habitual Criminal in that from January, 1940, to June, 1955, there were six men sentenced in the Taylor County Circuit Court who were subject to prosecution as Habitual offenders, Petitioner was the only man thus sentenced during this period. It is a matter of record that the five men who were not prosecuted as Habitual Criminals during this period all had three or more felony convictions and sentences as adults, and Petitioner's former convictions were a result of Juvenile Court actions.

Justice Clark, writing for a five-member majority, affirmed the denial of a writ of habeas corpus:

> . . . We note that it is not stated whether the failure to proceed against other three-time offenders was due to lack of knowledge of the prior offenses on the part of the prosecutors or was the result of a deliberate policy of proceeding only in a certain class of cases or against specific persons. The statistics merely show that according to penitentiary records a high percentage of those subject to the law have not been proceeded against. There is no indication that these records of previous convictions, which may not have been compiled until after the three-time offenders had reached the penitentiary, were available to the prosecutors. Hence the allegations set out no more than a failure to prosecute others because of a lack of knowledge of their prior offenses. This does not deny equal protection due petitioners under the Fourteenth Amendment. . . .

Moreover, the conscious exercise of some selectivity in enforcement is not in itself a federal constitutional violation. Even though the statistics in this case might imply a policy of selective enforcement, it was not stated that the selection was deliberately based upon an unjustifiable standard such as race, religion, or other arbitrary classification. Therefore grounds supporting a finding of a denial of equal protection were not alleged. . . .

[Chief Justice Warren and Justices Douglas, Black, and Brennan dissented on different grounds. They expressed no opinions relevant to the equal protection issue.]

WAYTE v. UNITED STATES
470 U.S. 598 (1985)

JUSTICE POWELL delivered the opinion of the Court.

The question presented is whether a passive enforcement policy under which the Government prosecutes only those who report themselves as having violated the law, or who are reported by others, violates the First and Fifth Amendments.

[Wayte was charged by the federal government with failure to register for the draft. He claimed that he had been singled out for criminal prosecution because of his vocal opposition to the registration system.[2]

---

[2] On August 4, 1980, for example, petitioner wrote to both the President and the Selective Service System. In his letter to the President, he stated: "I decided to obey my conscience rather than your law. I did not

Six months later, petitioner sent a second letter to Selective Service:

Last August I wrote to inform you of my intention not to register for the draft. Well, I did not register, and still plan never to do so, but thus far I have received no reply to my letter, much less any news about your much-threatened prosecutions. I must interpret your silence as meaning that you are too busy or disorganized to respond to letters or keep track of us draft-age youth. So I will keep you posted of my whereabouts.

He also stated that, although he would "be traveling the nation . . . encouraging resistance and spreading the word about peace and disarmament," he could be reached at his home address in Pasadena, California. Wayte moved to dismiss his indictment on the ground of selective prosecution, asserting that he and other vocal non-registrants were identified for prosecution because of their exercise of first amendment rights. He offered evidence that more than 650,000 persons had failed to register. Yet, only a dozen or so men had been prosecuted, all of whom were "vocal opponents of draft registration." The district court dismissed his indictment on the ground that the government had failed to rebut Wayte's prima facie case of selective prosecution. The court of appeals reversed, holding that Wayte failed to establish that the government focused its investigation on him because of his protest activities. While Wayte had shown that the government was aware that a "passive enforcement system" would result in prosecutions primarily of vocal objectors, there was no evidence of impermissible governmental motivation. The appellate court also found two legitimate explanations for the government's enforcement system: (1) identities of non-reported non-registrants were not known and (2) non-registrants who expressed refusal to register made clear their intentional violation of the law.] . . .

It is appropriate to judge selective prosecution claims according to ordinary equal protection standards. Under our prior cases, these standards require petitioner to show both that the passive enforcement system had a discriminatory effect and that it was motivated by a discriminatory purpose . . . . All petitioner has shown here is that those eventually prosecuted, along with many not prosecuted, reported themselves as having violated the law. He has not shown that the enforcement policy selected nonregistrants for prosecution on the basis of their speech. Indeed, he could not have done so given the way the "beg" policy was carried out. The Government did not prosecute those who reported themselves but later registered. Nor did it prosecute those who protested registration but did not report themselves or were not reported by others. In fact, the Government did not even investigate those who wrote letters to Selective Service criticizing registration unless their letters stated affirmatively that they had refused to comply with the law . . . . The Government, on the other hand, did prosecute people who reported themselves or were reported by others but who did not publicly protest. These facts demonstrate that the Government treated all reported nonregistrants similarly. It did not subject vocal nonregistrants to any special burden. Indeed, those prosecuted in effect selected themselves for prosecution by refusing to register after being reported and warned by the Government.

Even if the passive policy had a discriminatory effect, petitioner has not shown that the Government intended such a result . . . .

Petitioner also challenges the passive enforcement policy directly on First Amendment grounds. In particular, he claims that " "[e]ven though the [Government's passive] enforcement policy did not overtly punish protected speech as such, it inevitably created a content-based regulatory system with a concomitantly disparate, content-based impact on nonregistrants." . . . This Court has held that when, as here,

---

register for your draft. I will never register for your draft. Nor will I ever cooperate with yours or any other military system, despite the laws I might break or the consequences which may befall me." In his letter to the Selective Service System, he similarly stated: "I have not registered for the draft. I plan never to register. I realize the possible consequences of my action, and I accept them."

"speech"; and "nonspeech" elements are combined in the same course of conduct, a sufficiently important governmental interest in regulating the nonspeech element can justify incidental limitations on First Amendment freedoms." *United States v. O'Brien*, 391 U.S. 367. Government regulation is justified "if it is within the constitutional power of the Government; if it furthers an important or substantial governmental interest; if the governmental interest is unrelated to the suppression of free expression; and if the incidental restriction on alleged First Amendment freedoms is no greater than is essential to the furtherance of that interest." In the present case, neither the first nor third condition is disputed.

There can be no doubt that the passive enforcement policy meets the second condition. Few interests can be more compelling than a nation's need to ensure its own security . . . .

First, by relying on reports of nonregistration, the Government was able to identify and prosecute violators without further delay. Although it still was necessary to investigate those reported to make sure that they were required to register and had not, the Government did not have to search actively for the names of these likely violators. Such a search would have been difficult and costly at that time. Indeed, it would be a costly step in any "active" prosecution system involving thousands of nonregistrants. The passive enforcement program thus promoted prosecutorial efficiency. Second, the letters written to Selective Service provided strong, perhaps conclusive evidence of the nonregistrant's intent not to comply — one of the elements of the offense. Third, prosecuting visible nonregistrants was thought to be an effective way to promote general deterrence, especially since failing to proceed against publicly known offenders would encourage others to violate the law. . . .

We conclude that the Government's passive enforcement system together with its "beg" policy violated neither the First nor Fifth Amendment. Accordingly, we affirm the judgment of the Court of Appeals. . . .

[Justice Marshall, with whom Justice Brennan joins, dissents, arguing that the real issue is whether Wayte may discover government documents concerning selective prosecution, an issue addressed in the next case.]

NOTES

1. *Plaintiff's evidence. Wayte* states that a plaintiff in a selective prosecution case must prove both discriminatory purpose and discriminatory effect. How would a plaintiff gather the necessary information? Who would be the witnesses? What data should be gathered? Where would it come from? How much would it cost to obtain the necessary information?

2. *Discovery.* The issue of discovery addressed by the *Wayte* dissenters is frequently an important pre-trial issue in selective prosecution cases. What factual showing must be made by a complaining defendant in order to obtain information from the government regarding its charging decision? The United States Supreme Court answered that question in the following case.

UNITED STATES v. ARMSTRONG[1]
517 U.S. 456 (1996)

CHIEF JUSTICE REHNQUIST delivered the opinion of the Court.

In this case, we consider the showing necessary for a defendant to be entitled to discovery on a claim that the prosecuting attorney singled him out for prosecution on the basis of his race. We conclude that respondents failed to satisfy the threshold showing: They failed to show that the Government declined to prosecute similarly situated suspects of other races.

---

[1] This case is also discussed in Chapter 10 as it relates to discovery under Rule 16.

[In April, 1992, respondents were charged with conspiracy related to the distribution of more than 50 grams of crack cocaine and certain firearms offenses. They filed a motion for discovery, alleging that they were victims of selective prosecution based upon race. Accompanying this motion was an affidavit prepared by a paralegal stating that in every one of the twenty-four crack cocaine cases closed by that office during 1991, the defendant was black. Over government objection, the district court granted the motion and ordered the government to (1) provide a list of all cases in the last three years in which the government charged both cocaine and firearms offenses, (2) identify the race of the defendant in those cases, (3) identify levels of law enforcement involved in those cases, and (4) explain its criteria for deciding to prosecute those defendants. The government moved for reconsideration, submitting affidavits to explain why the respondents had been charged and why the respondents' "study" failed to support the inference that blacks had been singled out for prosecution. The district court denied the motion "for reconsideration and the Ninth Circuit Court of Appeals affirmed that order, holding that a defendant is not required to demonstrate that the government has failed to prosecute others who are similarly situated."]

. . . A selective-prosecution claim is not a defense on the merits to the criminal charge itself, but an independent assertion that the prosecutor has brought the charge for reasons forbidden by the Constitution. Our cases delineating the necessary elements to prove a claim of selective prosecution have taken great pains to explain that the standard is a demanding one. These cases afford a "background presumption," that the showing necessary to obtain discovery should itself be a significant barrier to the litigation of insubstantial claims.

. . . The requirements for a selective-prosecution claim draw on "ordinary equal protection standards." The claimant must demonstrate that the federal prosecutorial policy "had a discriminatory effect and that it was motivated by a discriminatory purpose." To establish a discriminatory effect in a race case, the claimant must show that similarly situated individuals of a different race were not prosecuted.

The similarly situated requirement does not make a selective-prosecution claim impossible to prove. [The court then discusses the *Yick Wo* case.]

. . . Having reviewed the requirements to prove a selective-prosecution claim, we turn to the showing necessary to obtain discovery in support of such a claim. If discovery is ordered, the Government must assemble from its own files documents which might corroborate or refute the defendant's claim. Discovery thus imposes many of the costs present when the Government must respond to a prima facie case of selective prosecution. It will divert prosecutors' resources and may disclose the Government's prosecutorial strategy. The justifications for a rigorous standard for the elements of a selective-prosecution claim thus require a correspondingly rigorous standard for discovery in aid of such a claim. The parties, and the Courts of Appeals which have considered the requisite showing to establish entitlement to discovery, describe this showing with a variety of phrases, like "colorable basis," "substantial threshold showing," "substantial and concrete basis," or "reasonable likelihood." However, the many labels for this showing conceal the degree of consensus about the evidence necessary to meet it. The Courts of Appeals "require some evidence tending to show the existence of the essential elements of the defense," discriminatory effect and discriminatory intent. *United States v. Berrios*, 501 F.2d 1207, 1211 (2d Cir. 1974).

. . . In this case we consider what evidence constitutes "some evidence tending to show the existence" of the discriminatory effect element. The Court of Appeals held that a defendant may establish a colorable basis for discriminatory effect without evidence that the Government has failed to prosecute others who were similarly situated to the defendant. We think it was mistaken in this view. The vast majority of the Courts of Appeals require the defendant to produce some evidence that similarly situated defendants of other races could have been prosecuted, but were not, and this requirement is consistent with our equal protection case law.

. . . In the present case, if the claim of selective prosecution were well founded, it should not have been an insuperable task to prove that persons of other races were being treated differently than respondents. For instance, respondents could have investigated whether similarly situated persons of other races were prosecuted by the State of California and were known to federal law enforcement officers, but were not prosecuted in federal court. We think the required threshold — a credible showing of different treatment of similarly situated persons — adequately balances the Government's interest in vigorous prosecution and the defendant's interest in avoiding selective prosecution. In the case before us, respondents' "study" did not constitute some evidence tending to show the existence of the essential elements of" a selective-prosecution claim. The study failed to identify individuals who were not black, could have been prosecuted for the offenses for which respondents were charged, but were not so prosecuted. This omission was not remedied by respondents" evidence in opposition to the Government's motion for reconsideration. The newspaper article, which discussed the discriminatory effect of federal drug sentencing laws, was not relevant to an allegation of discrimination in decisions to prosecute. Respondents' affidavits, which recounted one attorney's conversation with a drug treatment center employee and the experience of another attorney defending drug prosecutions in state court, recounted hearsay and reported personal conclusions based on anecdotal evidence. The judgment of the Court of Appeals is therefore reversed, and the case is remanded for proceedings consistent with this opinion.

JUSTICE STEVENS, dissenting.

. . . The Court correctly concludes that in this case the facts presented to the District Court in support of respondents' claim that they had been singled out for prosecution because of their race were not sufficient to prove that defense. Moreover, I agree with the Court that their showing was not strong enough to give them a right to discovery, either under Rule 16 or under the District Court's inherent power to order discovery in appropriate circumstances. Like Chief Judge Wallace of the Court of Appeals, however, I am persuaded that the District Judge did not abuse her discretion when she concluded that the factual showing was sufficiently disturbing to require some response from the United States Attorney's Office. Perhaps the discovery order was broader than necessary, but I cannot agree with the Court's apparent conclusion that no inquiry was permissible.

The District Judge's order should be evaluated in light of three circumstances that underscore the need for judicial vigilance over certain types of drug prosecutions. First, the Anti-Drug Abuse Act of 1986 and subsequent legislation established a regime of extremely high penalties for the possession and distribution of so-called "crack" cocaine. . . . These penalties result in sentences for crack offenders that average three to eight times longer than sentences for comparable powder offenders.

Second, the disparity between the treatment of crack cocaine and powder cocaine is matched by the disparity between the severity of the punishment imposed by federal law and that imposed by state law for the same conduct. For a variety of reasons, often including the absence of mandatory minimums, the existence of parole, and lower baseline penalties, terms of imprisonment for drug offenses tend to be substantially lower in state systems than in the federal system. The difference is especially marked in the case of crack offenses. The majority of States draw no distinction between types of cocaine in their penalty schemes; of those that do, none has established as stark a differential as the Federal Government. For example, if respondent Hampton is found guilty, his federal sentence might be as long as a mandatory life term. Had he been tried in state court, his sentence could have been as short as 12 years, less worktime credits of half that amount.

Finally, it is undisputed that the brunt of the elevated federal penalties falls heavily on blacks. While 65% of the persons who have used crack are white, in 1993 they represented only 4% of the federal offenders convicted of trafficking in crack. Eighty-eight percent of such defendants were black. . . .

The extraordinary severity of the imposed penalties and the troubling racial patterns of enforcement give rise to a special concern about the fairness of charging practices for crack offenses. Evidence tending to prove that black defendants charged with distribution of crack in the Central District of California are prosecuted in federal court, whereas members of other races charged with similar offenses are prosecuted in state court, warrants close scrutiny by the federal judges in that District. In my view, the District Judge, who has sat on both the federal and the state benches in Los Angeles, acted well within her discretion to call for the development of facts that would demonstrate what standards, if any, governed the choice of forum where similarly situated offenders are prosecuted.

[The separate concurring opinions by Justices Souter, Ginsburg and Breyer are omitted.]

NOTES

1. *Is a single event sufficient?* Must there be a long-standing practice of non-prosecution under the *Wayte* standard, or would it be permissible to establish such a claim based upon a single event? Consider the following case.

During a private party at a club, female nude dancers allegedly engaged in sexual conduct with male patrons in return for money. Four police officers arrested and prosecuted the four female performers, but did not seek to arrest any of the 50 to 75 men who "fondled the women performers and thrust money at them." Two officers testified that "they understood the focus of the investigation to be on the female dancers." The female defendants moved for dismissal of all charges, claiming that they could not be convicted of prostitution because of discriminatory prosecution. The government responded that the male patrons were not similarly situated with the female performers because (1) the women engaged in a larger number of criminal law violations and (2) the women received financial benefit from their actions. The government also responded that any gender-based discrimination occurred because the small number of police officers were forced to focus their resources on the smallest, most manageable group — the female performers. The Wisconsin Court of Appeals rejected the government's argument, noting that both the patrons and performers could have been convicted under the language of the Wisconsin statute:

> The plain language of that statute criminalized the behavior of both the payor and the payee. It is persuasive that the goals of both general and specific deterrence in this case would have been better served by the arrest of some of the large number of local citizens involved in illicit behavior than by the arrest of a small number of out-of-towners. Because the police intentionally focused their investigation on only the female violators, the trial court properly dismissed the criminal charges.

State v. McCollum, 15 Wis.184, 464 N.W.2d 44 (Wis. App. 1990). Was *McCollum* properly decided according to the *Wayte* standard?

2. *Outrageous intent supplanting lack of discriminatory effect?* Can outrageous discriminatory intent be sufficient to compensate for a lack of discriminatory effect on a selective prosecuted claim? The Sixth Circuit Court of Appeals held in *United States v. Jones*, 159 F.3d 969 (6th Cir. 1998), that a black defendant was entitled to discovery based upon unprofessional behavior by white police officers even though the defendant failed to establish a showing of discriminatory effect. The officers, who had arrested the defendant, had printed pictures of the defendant and his wife on the shirts worn by officers during the arrest, and one officer had sent the defendant a postcard from Mexico taunting him about his chances of acquittal at his upcoming trial.

3. *Similarly situated.* The Fourth Circuit Court of Appeals, clarifying *Armstrong's* similarly situated requirement for selective prosecution claims, held that people are

similarly situated if "their circumstances present no distinguishable legitimate prosecutorial factors that might justify making different prosecutorial decisions with respect to them." *United States v. Olvis*, 97 F.3d 739, 744 (4th Cir. 1996). The two black defendants in *Olvis* did not meet the high threshold burden for obtaining discovery where they claimed that the state had failed to indict similarly situated white conspirators in a crack cocaine conspiracy. The court found that the white conspirators presented prosecutorial profiles significantly different from those of the black defendants. For example, one white conspirator offered to go undercover and there was not sufficient evidence to prosecute the second. As for the defendants, by contrast, one was the alleged head of the organization and the other was prosecuted for committing perjury before the grand jury and for having refused to cooperate with law enforcement authorities.

4. *Impact of Armstrong in hindering selective prosecution cases.* For an insightful discussion of the way in which *Armstrong* has acted as a barrier to the establishment of selective prosecution claims, see Anne Bowen Poulin, *Prosecutorial Discretion and Selective Prosecution: Enforcing Protection After United States v. Armstrong*, 34 AM. CRIM. L. REV. 1071 (1997). Because *Armstrong* ultimately limits the ability of a defendant to obtain discovery, Professor Poulin urges the enlistment of all branches of government to eliminate selective prosecution in the judicial system. While "soft enforcement," defined as the impact of an open judicial process on the voluntary behavior of both the government and the public, serves as the most effective protector of the right against selective prosecution, the key to exercising that right is discovery:

> In most cases, *Armstrong* imposes a strict requirement that an aggrieved defendant requesting discovery prove the existence of a control group (other similarly situated violators who have not been prosecuted), making it unlikely that a defendant will win discovery. However, the decision signals that there may be an exception to the control group requirement if the defendant presents evidence of improper motive. The courts should respond to that signal and grant discovery, not only if the defendant proves direct expressions of improper motive, but also if the defendant produces other evidence that indicates improper motive, such as proof of departure from regular procedures or pretextual conduct. [*Id.* at 1124]

5. *Uncovering discriminatory charging decisions outside of formal discovery.* Assuming that *Armstrong* is a significant barrier to uncovering discriminatory charging decision, are there other ways to discover those practices? Professor Andrew Leipold suggests that race-based decisionmaking in official discretion can be reduced through the use of racial impact studies and information-gathering studies on discretionary police and prosecutor decisions. Andrew D. Leipold, *Objective Tests and Subjective Bias: Some Problems of Discriminatory Intent in the Criminal Law*, 73 CHI.-KENT. L. REV. 559, 590 (1998). Another commentator, however, argues that defendants will have a nearly impossible burden of satisfying the *Armstrong* standard where they are complaining that similarly situated whites are not prosecuted at all. He describes the following case:

> Proof problems arise when a crime is minor enough that, absent selective prosecution, it is not prosecuted at all. As one example, imagine that a federal official, motivated by racial animus, concentrates health and safety inspections on (the few) food distribution businesses owned by African Americans, Asian Americans, or Latinos. The official prosecutes a number of these minorities for criminal violations of the Food, Drug, and Cosmetic Act but prosecutes no white owners. At the time, suppose the relevant state, relying on federal efforts, brings no criminal prosecutions for these kinds of violations. Under *Armstrong* this startling racial gap would not be sufficient to permit a district court to order discovery unless the defendants can first show that similarly situated but unprosecuted whites also violated the statute. But given the difficulty of detecting such violations in private facilities — that is, after all, the whole

reason for authorizing agents to conduct surprise inspections — how can a black defendant, acting without such power, prove that his white counterparts are also violating the law? Realistically, he can't.

Richard H. McAdams, *Race and Selective Prosecution: Discovering the Pitfalls of Armstrong*, 73 CHI.-KENT L. REV. 605, 617–19 (1998).*

6. *Wealth as criterion.* Should a prosecutor pick and choose between the cases he or she pursues based upon the wealth of victims? In California, Oregon, Pennsylvania and South Carolina, prosecutors have begun soliciting and accepting private financing through voluntary contributions from the business community in order to pay costs of criminal prosecutions in certain types of cases (essentially white collar crime prosecutions). In his article, *Private Financing of Criminal Prosecutions and the Differing Protections of Liberty and Equality in the Criminal Justice System*, 23 HASTINGS CONST. L.Q. 551, 670 (1997), Joseph E. Kennedy postulates that the result of such private financing will be a "two-tiered criminal justice system" with the best efforts and resources going to the privately financed cases:

> [P]rivate financing serves economic efficiency and the interests of victims selectively, at best, and inevitably at the expense of equality interests whose importance has not been appreciated fully. Private financing in any of its likely forms threatens equality of treatment by potentially biasing the prosecutor in favor of the contributors. Such a practice sacrifices the equality of the prosecutor's choices in order to enlist the financial support of victims who have both a direct interest in the prosecution and the money to further that interest. Ultimately, the overall benefit of that support to society does not justify the damage done to the legitimacy of government prosecutions.

[c] Vindictive Prosecution

Once a prosecutor has made the basic decision to charge the defendant with a criminal offense, the next question is the precise charge or range of charges to be placed against that individual. The charging decision involves not only a consideration of "degrees" of liability within a certain crime (murder first degree versus manslaughter, aggravated robbery versus simple robbery), but also the question whether multiple counts or multiple offenses should be charged. An individual who breaks into a home at night, steals property, and threatens to assault the homeowner, may be charged with (1) burglary, (2) theft, or (3) assault, or with any combination of those three offenses. Again, the circumstances of the case and matters related to characteristics of the defendant may influence a prosecutor to charge "the maximum" or something of lesser magnitude.

A defendant may seek to have charges dismissed because of prosecutorial vindictiveness, offering to show that more serious charges were placed against the defendant in retaliation for the exercise of a constitutional or statutory right. Consider, in this context, the following decision by the United States Supreme Court.

UNITED STATES v. GOODWIN
457 U.S. 368 (1982)

[The facts of this case are best summarized in Justice Brennan's dissenting opinion: Respondent was originally charged with several petty offenses and misdemeanors — speeding, reckless driving, failing to give aid at the scene of an accident, fleeing from a police officer, and assault by striking a police officer — arising from his conduct on the Baltimore-Washington Parkway. Assuming that respondent had been convicted on every count charged in this original complaint, the maximum punishment to which he conceivably could have been exposed was fines of $3,500 and 28 months in prison.

Because all of the charges against respondent were petty offenses or misdemeanors, they were scheduled for trial before a magistrate, who was not authorized to conduct jury trials. In addition, the case was assigned to a prosecutor who, owing to inexperience, was not even authorized to try felony cases. Thus the Government recognized that respondent's alleged crimes were relatively minor, and attempted to dispose of them in an expedited manner. But respondent frustrated this attempt at summary justice by demanding a jury trial in Federal District Court. This was his right, of course, not only under the applicable statute, but also under the Constitution.

Respondent's demand required that the case be transferred from the Magistrate's Court in Hyattsville to the District Court in Baltimore, and that the prosecution be reassigned to an Assistant United States Attorney, who was authorized to prosecute cases in the District Court. The new prosecutor sought and obtained a second, four-count indictment, in which the same conduct originally charged as petty-offense and misdemeanor counts was now charged as a misdemeanor and two felonies: assaulting, resisting, or impeding a federal officer with a deadly weapon, and assault with a dangerous weapon.

[Respondent was convicted of a felony.] If we assume (as before) that respondent was convicted on all of these charges, his maximum exposure to punishment had now become fines of $11,500 and 15 years in prison. Respondent's claim below was that such an elevation of the charges against him from petty offenses to felonies, following his exercise of his statutory and constitutional right to a jury trial, reflected prosecutorial vindictiveness that denied him due process of law.]

JUSTICE STEVENS delivered the opinion of the Court.

. . . The imposition of punishment is the very purpose of virtually all criminal proceedings. The presence of a punitive motivation, therefore, does not provide an adequate basis for distinguishing governmental action that is fully justified as a legitimate response to perceived criminal conduct from governmental action that is an impermissible response to noncriminal, protected activity. Motives are complex and difficult to prove. As a result, in certain cases in which action detrimental to the defendant has been taken after the exercise of a legal right, the Court has found it necessary to "presume" an improper vindictive motive. Given the severity of such a presumption, however — which may operate in the absence of any proof of an improper motive and thus may block a legitimate response to criminal conduct — the Court has done so only in cases in which a reasonable likelihood of vindictiveness exists.

In *North Carolina v. Pearce*, 395 U.S. 711 (1969), the Court held that neither the Double Jeopardy Clause nor the Equal Protection Clause prohibits a trial judge from imposing a harsher sentence on retrial after a criminal defendant successfully attacks an initial conviction on appeal. The Court stated, however, that "[i]t can hardly be doubted that it would be a flagrant violation [of the Due Process Clause] of the Fourteenth Amendment for a state trial court to follow an announced practice of imposing a heavier sentence upon every reconvicted defendant for the explicit purpose of punishing the defendant for his having succeeded in getting his original conviction set aside." The Court continued:

> Due process of law, then, requires that vindictiveness against a defendant for having successfully attacked his first conviction must play no part in the sentence he receives after a new trial. And since the fear of such vindictiveness may unconstitutionally deter a defendant's exercise of the right to appeal or collaterally attack his first conviction, due process also requires that a defendant be freed of apprehension of such a retaliatory motivation on the part of the sentencing judge.

In order to assure the absence of such a motivation, the Court concluded:

> [W]henever a judge imposes a more severe sentence upon a defendant after a new trial, the reasons for his doing so must affirmatively appear. Those

reasons must be based upon objective information concerning identifiable conduct on the part of the defendant occurring after the time of the original sentencing proceeding. And the factual data upon which the increased sentence is based must be made part of the record, so that the constitutional legitimacy of the increased sentence may be fully reviewed on appeal.

In sum, the Court applied a presumption of vindictiveness, which may be overcome only by objective information in the record justifying the increased sentence.

In *Blackledge v. Perry*, 417 U.S. 21 (1974), the Court confronted the problem of increased punishment upon retrial after appeal in a setting different from that considered in *Pearce*. Perry was convicted of assault in an inferior court having exclusive jurisdiction for the trial of misdemeanors. The court imposed a 6-month sentence. Under North Carolina law, Perry had an absolute right to a trial *de novo* in the Superior Court, which possessed felony jurisdiction. After Perry filed his notice of appeal, the prosecutor obtained a felony indictment charging him with assault with a deadly weapon. Perry pleaded guilty to the felony and was sentenced to a term of five to seven years in prison.

. . . The Court held that the opportunities for vindictiveness in the situation before it were such "as to impel the conclusion that due process of law requires a rule analogous to that of the *Pearce* case." It explained:

> A prosecutor clearly has a considerable stake in discouraging convicted misdemeanants from appealing and thus obtaining a trial *de novo* in the Superior Court, since such an appeal will clearly require increased expenditures of prosecutorial resources before the defendant's conviction becomes final, and may even result in a formerly convicted defendant's going free. And, if the prosecutor has the means readily at hand to discourage such appeals — by "upping the ante" through a felony indictment whenever a convicted misdemeanant pursues his statutory appellate remedy — the State can insure that only the most hardy defendants will brave the hazards of a *de novo* trial.

The Court emphasized in *Blackledge* that it did not matter that no evidence was present that the prosecutor had acted in bad faith or with malice in seeking the felony indictment. As in *Pearce*, the Court held that the likelihood of vindictiveness justified a presumption that would free defendants of apprehension of such a retaliatory motivation on the part of the prosecutor. . . .

There is good reason to be cautious before adopting an inflexible presumption of prosecutorial vindictiveness in a pretrial setting. In the course of preparing a case for trial, the prosecutor may uncover additional information that suggests a basis for further prosecution or he simply may come to realize that information possessed by the State has a broader significance. At this stage of the proceedings, the prosecutor's assessment of the proper extent of prosecution may not have crystallized. In contrast, once a trial begins — and certainly by the time a conviction has been obtained — it is much more likely that the State has discovered and assessed all of the information against an accused and has made a determination, on the basis of that information, of the extent to which he should be prosecuted. Thus, a change in the charging decision made after an initial trial is completed is much more likely to be improperly motivated than is a pretrial decision. In addition, a defendant before trial is expected to invoke procedural rights that inevitably impose some "burden" on the prosecutor. Defense counsel routinely file pretrial motions to suppress evidence; to challenge the sufficiency and form of an indictment; to plead an affirmative defense; to request psychiatric services; to obtain access to government files; to be tried by jury. It is unrealistic to assume that a prosecutor's probable response to such motions is to seek to penalize and to deter. The invocation of procedural rights is an integral part of the adversary process in which our criminal justice system operates.

. . . In declining to apply a presumption of vindictiveness, we of course do not foreclose the possibility that a defendant in an appropriate case might prove objectively that the prosecutor's charging decision was motivated by a desire to punish him for doing something that the law plainly allowed him to do. In this case, however, the Court of Appeals stated: "On this record we readily conclude that the prosecutor did not act with actual vindictiveness in seeking a felony indictment." . . . Respondent does not challenge that finding. Absent a presumption of vindictiveness, no due process violation has been established.

[Justice Brennan dissented, arguing that Goodwin's claim should be analyzed as follows:]

. . . Did the elevation of the charges against respondent pose a realistic likelihood of "vindictiveness?" *See Blackledge v. Perry*, 417 U.S., at 27. Is it possible that "the fear of such vindictiveness may unconstitutionally deter" a person in respondent's position from exercising his statutory and constitutional right to a jury trial? *See North Carolina v. Pearce, supra*, 395 U.S. at 725. The answer to these questions is plainly "Yes."

The Court suggests . . . that the distinction between a bench trial and a jury trial is unimportant in this context. Such a suggestion is demonstrably fallacious. Experienced criminal practitioners, for both prosecution and defense, know that a jury trial entails far more prosecutorial work than a bench trial. . . . And there is always the specter of the " "irrational" acquittal by a jury that is unreviewable on appeal. Thus it is simply inconceivable that a criminal defendant's election to be tried by jury would be a matter of indifference to his prosecutor. On the contrary, the prosecutor would almost always prefer that the defendant waive such a "troublesome" right. And if the defendant refuses to do so, the prosecutor's subsequent elevation of the charges against the defendant manifestly poses a realistic likelihood of vindictiveness. . . .

NOTES

1. *Overcoming presumption of vindictiveness.* Assuming that a presumption of vindictiveness applies, what proof would (or should) suffice to overcome that presumption? Note that in *Texas v. McCullough*, 475 U.S. 134 (1986), the Court observed that the *Pearce* presumption could be overcome "by objective information . . . justifying the increased sentence." There, the Court approved a higher sentence imposed by a "second sentencer" because the first sentence was considered "unduly lenient in light of significant evidence not before the sentencing jury in the first trial."

2. *Vindictiveness toward people other than the defendant.* Should the *Pearce* presumption of vindictiveness apply to events that do not necessarily involve vindictiveness toward the individual defendant? Assume, for example, that a particular defense attorney has been publicly critical of policies in the local district attorney's office. Thereafter, evidence is adduced to suggest that prosecutors are being especially aggressive in charging and prosecuting defendants represented by that attorney. Should the defendant be entitled to protest that practice on the ground that the prosecutor is "punishing" the defendant because of the defense lawyer's "sins"?

3. *Appellate review.* Assume that the defendant is indicted and then obtains a change of venue to another district. A superseding indictment is obtained in the latter district in which new substantive counts are added to the original counts. The defendant moves to dismiss the new counts on prosecutorial vindictiveness grounds, but the trial judge denies the motion. Is that decision immediately appealable, or must the defendant reserve appellate review until after trial on the merits? In *United States v. Hollywood Motor Car Co., Inc.*, 458 U.S. 263 (1982), the Supreme Court held that federal appellate courts have no jurisdiction to review such an interlocutory order and, therefore, the defendant must postpone appellate review of that issue until after trial. [Note: This issue also arises in the context of speedy trial claims, which are discussed in Chapter 13.]

Although as seen above there is a clear presumption in favor of prosecutorial discretion, courts do not always find in favor of the prosecution.

UNITED STATES v. JENKINS
494 F.3d 1135 (9th Cir. 2007)

The United States appeals the district court's dismissal of an indictment of Sharon Ann Jenkins for alien smuggling. The ground of dismissal was the appearance of vindictive prosecution.

Jenkins was apprehended twice for attempting to cross the U.S.-Mexico border while driving a vehicle containing undocumented aliens. Both times, Jenkins stated that she had been paid to drive the car across the border. She was not charged with any crime. Almost three months later, Jenkins was apprehended while attempting to cross the border as a passenger in a vehicle containing marijuana. She stated that she had been paid to drive the car, which she believed contained illegal aliens, across the border. Jenkins was charged with importation of marijuana. At trial, she testified in her own defense and maintained that she believed the vehicle in which she had been a passenger contained illegal aliens because she had been paid on two previous occasions to smuggle aliens. While the jury was deliberating, the government filed alien smuggling charges against Jenkins in connection with her first two border apprehensions.

The district court found that the prosecutor's conduct created the appearance of vindictive prosecution because the alien smuggling charges were brought only after Jenkins exercised her right to testify in her own defense at her separate marijuana smuggling trial. We affirm. We conclude that, because the government could have prosecuted Jenkins for alien smuggling well before she presented her theory of defense at the marijuana smuggling trial, the timing of the charges created the appearance of vindictiveness. The government's assertion that its case against Jenkins was much stronger after her in-court admission does not suffice to dispel the appearance of vindictiveness. We therefore conclude that the indictment should be dismissed. . . .

The government violated Jenkins's right to due process of law if it filed the alien smuggling charges to penalize her for exercising a protected statutory or constitutional right. *See United States v. Goodwin*, 457 U.S. 368 (1982). Jenkins may establish prosecutorial vindictiveness by producing direct evidence of the prosecutor's punitive motivation towards her. Alternatively, she is entitled to a presumption of vindictiveness if she can show that the alien smuggling charges were filed because she exercised a statutory, procedural, or constitutional right in circumstances that give rise to an appearance of vindictiveness. This case involves the latter situation, as the record contains no direct evidence of the government's improper motivation.

A. Whether the filing of alien smuggling charges created the appearance of vindictiveness

To establish a presumption of vindictiveness, Jenkins need not show that the prosecutor acted in bad faith or that he maliciously sought the alien smuggling indictment. Rather, she must demonstrate a *reasonable likelihood* that the government would not have brought the alien smuggling charges had she not elected to testify at her marijuana smuggling trial and present her theory of the case. The mere appearance of prosecutorial vindictiveness suffices to place the burden on the government because the doctrine of vindictive prosecution "seeks[s] to reduce or eliminate apprehension on the part of an accused" that she may be punished for exercising her rights. As the district court noted, the "prophylactic" doctrine is designed, in part, to prevent chilling the exercise of legal rights by other defendants who must make their choices under similar circumstances in the future.

The case before us presents an unusual situation because the government's alien smuggling case essentially was open and shut even before Jenkins testified in court. . . . In these circumstances, the government's decision to press charges only after Jenkins asserted a reasonably credible defense to the marijuana importation charges raises, at the very least, a "reasonable or realistic likelihood" that the government's decision was motivated by a retaliatory purpose. We therefore conclude that the government's conduct created the appearance of vindictiveness.

We are sensitive to the government's concern that the dismissal of charges resulting from a defendant's in-court admission may hamstring prosecutorial efforts. This might be a different case if the government had not been equipped with Jenkins's previous admissions at the time of her in-court testimony. But the government had more than enough evidence to proceed with the alien smuggling charges prior to Jenkins's decision to testify. We therefore find it appropriate to place the burden on the government to justify its course of conduct.

Finally, we reject the government's argument that, because the alien smuggling and marijuana importation charges do not arise out of the same nucleus of operative fact, the doctrine of vindictive prosecution is inapplicable. The fact that separate charges brought against a criminal defendant are unrelated to the pending charge is not controlling in any case or dispositive on the question of vindictiveness; it is "only one of the factors bearing on the issue. . . .

B. Whether the government rebutted the presumption of vindictiveness

The presumption of vindictiveness raised by the prosecutor's decision to file alien smuggling charges against Jenkins must be overcome by objective evidence justifying the prosecutor's action. The prosecution must show that the additional charges did not stem from a vindictive motive, or were justified by independent reasons or intervening circumstances that dispel the appearance of vindictiveness.

The government argues that, even if the content of the evidence against Jenkins was available all along, the evidence was stronger once Jenkins testified in court. . . . [W]e find the government's explanation unpersuasive. As the district court noted, it was not necessary to wait to file charges until Jenkins took the witness stand and confessed under oath: cases for illegal alien smuggling in this district are proven on much less than that. . . .

We also are unconvinced by the government's argument that it brought the alien smuggling charges precisely because bringing them after trial would have seemed vindictive. From the moment she was apprehended for smuggling marijuana, Jenkins maintained that she believed she was smuggling aliens and pointed to her October apprehensions. There was no reason for the government to think that she would not continue with this defense at trial. If the government had been concerned with appearing vindictive, it could have filed the alien smuggling charges in January, when Jenkins first asserted that she did not know she was smuggling marijuana. We therefore conclude that the justifications offered by the government do not suffice to dispel the appearance of vindictiveness created by the timing of the alien smuggling charges.

NOTES

1. *Immigration issues.* An important issue that defense lawyers are beginning to notice is the immigration consequences effected by a guilty plea or specific charges. May a defendant argue that a prosecutor is vindictive in charging a specific offense knowing that it may result in severe immigration consequences such as deportation? *See United States v. Fregoso-Bonilla*, 2007 U.S. Dist. LEXIS 57273. (defendant alleged that the government filed an additional count of harboring against her in retaliation for her spurring the government's plea offer to the original charge and electing to go to trial. She further argued that under immigration law a money transmitting conviction

would not require her removal from the United States, but a harboring conviction would. The court found that her motion lacked merit.)

2. *Illegal v. legal immigrants.* Another interesting question to consider is whether there is a colorable claim for vindictiveness if prosecutorial discretion is used to target illegal rather than legal aliens.

3. *Declining to plead guilty.* What if a *federal* prosecution is begun because the defendant declined to plead guilty to *state* charges for the same conduct? In *United States v. Gray*, 382 F. Supp.2d 898 (E.D. Mich. 2005), the defendant was charged under state law with possession of a firearm by a convicted felon. When he refused to plead guilty to state charges, the state charges were dropped and he was charged with a federal offense for the same conduct. The state plea he rejected would have subjected him to 24 months of incarceration, but the federal indictment upped the possible sentence to 57-71 months. The federal court refused to dismiss the federal case or to remand the case to state court, finding that the filing of federal charges did not constitute vindictive prosecution in violation of due process. Rejecting the argument that the defendant was being penalized for rejecting the plea and waiving many constitutional rights, the District Court held that in the "give and take" of plea bargaining, there is no element of punishment as long as the defendant is free to accept or reject the prosecutor's offer. Do you agree that the defendant was not punished for asserting his right to a trial?

[d] Other Challenges

[i] Overlapping Statutorily Authorized Penalties

In some instances, a state or federal criminal defendant is subject to prosecution under more than one statute for a single criminal act. The prosecutor must choose which one to pursue. If the more severe law is used as the basis for a prosecution, the defense may challenge that decision on both due process and equal protection grounds.

UNITED STATES v. BATCHELDER
442 U.S. 114 (1979)

JUSTICE MARSHALL delivered the opinion of the Court.

[Batchelder, a convicted felon, was charged with violating 18 U.S.C. § 922(h). This statute makes it a felony for any person previously convicted of a felony "to receive any firearm . . . which has been shipped . . . in interstate . . . commerce." He received the maximum authorized sentence of 5 years' imprisonment. He was not charged under a separate statute making it a felony punishable by 2 years' imprisonment for a convicted felon to "receive, possess or transport" a firearm. 18 U.S.C. § 1202(a). The Court of Appeals affirmed the conviction but remanded for sentencing; it held that since the two statutes are identical as applied to a convicted felon who receives a firearm, the maximum allowable sentence was 2 years' incarceration under § 1202. Justice Marshall *odd* delivered the opinion for a unanimous Court, ruling that the Court of Appeals erred in reducing the 5-year sentence to 2 years. The U.S. Supreme Court found that the two statutes were unambiguous and that they were "fully capable of coexisting."]

. . . That this particular conduct may violate both Titles does not detract from the notice afforded by each. Although the statutes create uncertainty as to which crime may be charged and therefore what penalties may be imposed, they do so to no greater extent than would a single statute authorizing various alternative punishments. So long as overlapping criminal provisions clearly define the conduct prohibited and the punishment authorized, the notice requirements of the Due Process Clause are satisfied. This Court has long recognized that when an act violates more than one criminal statute, the Government may prosecute under either so long as it does not discriminate against any class of defendants. . . . Whether to prosecute and what *Rule* charge to file or bring before a grand jury are decisions that generally rest in the prosecutor's discretion. . . . Contrary to the Court of Appeals' assertions, a prosecutor's discretion to choose between §§ 922(h) and 1202(a) is not "unfettered." Selectivity in the enforcement of criminal laws is, of course, subject to constitutional constraints.[9]

And a decision to proceed under § 922(h) does not empower the Government to predetermine ultimate criminal sanctions. Rather, it merely enables the sentencing judge to impose a longer prison sentence than § 1202(a) would permit and precludes him from imposing the greater fine authorized by § 1202(a). More importantly, there is no appreciable difference between the discretion a prosecutor exercises when deciding whether to charge under one of two statutes with different elements and the discretion he exercises when choosing one of two statutes with identical elements. In the former situation, once he determines that the proof will support conviction under either statute, his decision is indistinguishable from the one he faces in the latter context. The prosecutor may be influenced by the penalties available upon conviction, but this fact, standing alone, does not give rise to a violation of the Equal Protection or Due Process Clause. . . .

NOTES

1. *Great disparity in sentences.* The sentencing disparity in the *Batchelder* case does not seem to be an extreme one. Assume that a state legislature defined the offense of burglary in two separate statutes, one of which authorized a maximum period of incarceration of five years, while the other authorized a maximum sentence of thirty years. Should a defendant prosecuted under the second statute be granted any relief, assuming that he or she cannot demonstrate impermissible selective prosecution?

2. *Ambiguity in punishment.* Overlapping statutes must be carefully examined to ascertain whether there is ambiguity regarding the choice of punishment. In *United States v. Trout*, 68 F.3d 1276 (11th Cir. 1995), a federal statute (the "Anti-Drug Abuse Amendments Act") prescribed two different punishments for the same offense. Because the government conceded that the statute was ambiguous, the appellate court upheld the district court's sentence under the "lesser punishment" section, observing, " . . . the rule of lenity directs [the court] to apply the lesser penalty when a statute presents an ambiguous choice between two punishments."

3. *Impact of charge on right to jury trial.* Defendant challenged his conviction, in the District of Columbia Superior Court, of the misdemeanor of attempted threats in violation of D.C. Code Ann. § 1803 (2001). He argued that he had been convicted of a nonexistent offense solely to deprive him of a jury trial. Two police officers overheard defendant mutter a threat to kill a police witness against him. Although he was originally charged with threatening bodily harm, he was eventually charged with and convicted of attempted threats in violation of the attempt statute rather than the threat law. The court held that since the attempt statute had always included all crimes, including those later enacted, an attempt to violate the threats statute, was also a crime. The prosecutor had discretion to charge any provable crime, and the fact that attempted threats, punishable by up to 180 days in jail, did not allow for a right to jury trial, while a charge of the misdemeanor threats offense, with a six-month possible term, did permit a defendant to have a jury, did not violate defendant's rights. *Evans v. United States*, 779 A.2d 891 (2001).

---

[9] The Equal Protection Clause prohibits selective enforcement. . . . Respondent does not allege that this prosecution was motivated by improper considerations.

[ii] Conditional Immunity Grants

As stated earlier in this chapter, prosecutors are under no legal duty to institute criminal charges in all cases in which a conviction might be obtained. Sometimes, a prosecutor will grant informal immunity to the defendant in exchange for information or testimony from that defendant considered useful by the prosecutor in other (and perhaps more serious) cases. Similarly, a prosecutor may place numerous charges against a prospective defendant so that the government will be in a superior bargaining position in the plea bargaining context. This practice will be examined further in Chapter 11.

Finally, a prosecutor might agree to dismiss criminal charges in exchange for the prospective defendant's promise not to proceed with a claim for civil damages against the government or its employees. The next case addresses whether such an agreement is enforceable.

TOWN OF NEWTON v. RUMERY
480 U.S. 386 (1987)

Justice Powell announced the judgment of the Court.

[Rumery, upon learning that a friend had been indicted, contacted the alleged sexual assault victim (an acquaintance of both the indicted friend and Rumery) to learn more about the charges. Ultimately, Rumery was accused of the felony offense of tampering with a witness. Thereafter, his attorney and the prosecutor entered into a "release-dismissal" agreement: charges against Rumery would be dismissed if he agreed to release any claims he might have against the town (and others). Ten months following the dismissal of charges pursuant to the agreement, he sued the town for false arrest, defamation, and false imprisonment.]

The defendants filed a motion to dismiss, relying on the release-dismissal agreement as an affirmative defense. Rumery argued that the agreement was unenforceable because it violated public policy. The [district] court rejected Rumery's argument and concluded that a "release of claims under section 1983 is valid . . . if it results from a decision that is voluntary, deliberate and informed." . . . The [district] court found that Rumery

> is a knowledgeable, industrious individual with vast experience in the business world. . . . [H]e intelligently and carefully, after weighing all the factors, concluded that it would be in his best interest and welfare to sign the covenant. He was also represented by a very competent attorney with more than ordinary expertise in the sometimes complex area of criminal law.

The court then dismissed Rumery's suit. On appeal, the Court of Appeals for the First Circuit reversed. It adopted a *per se* rule invalidating release-dismissal agreements. The court stated:

> It is difficult to envision how release agreements, negotiated in exchange for a decision not to prosecute, serve the public interest. Enforcement of such covenants would tempt prosecutors to trump up charges in reaction to a defendant's civil rights claim, suppress evidence of police misconduct, and leave unremedied deprivations of constitutional rights.

. . .The Court of Appeals concluded that the public interests related to release-dismissal agreements justified a *per se* rule of invalidity. We think the court overstated the perceived problems and also failed to credit the significant public interests that such agreements can further. Most importantly, the Court of Appeals did not consider the wide variety of factual situations that can result in release-dismissal agreements. Thus, although we agree that in some cases these agreements may infringe important interests of the criminal defendant and of society as a whole, we do not believe that the mere possibility of harm to these interests calls for a *per se* rule.

Rumery's first objection to release-dismissal agreements is that they are inherently coercive. He argues that it is unfair to present a criminal defendant with a choice between facing criminal charges and waiving his right to sue under § 1983. We agree that some release-dismissal agreements may not be the product of an informed and voluntary decision. The risk, publicity, and expense of a criminal trial may intimidate a defendant, even if he believes his defense is meritorious. But this possibility does not justify invalidating *all* such agreements. . . .

In many cases a defendant's choice to enter into a release-dismissal agreement will reflect a highly rational judgment that the certain benefits of escaping criminal prosecution exceed the speculative benefits of prevailing in a civil action. Rumery's voluntary decision to enter this agreement exemplifies such a judgment. Rumery is a sophisticated businessman. He was not in jail and was represented by an experienced criminal lawyer, who drafted the agreement. Rumery considered the agreement for three days before signing it. The benefits of the agreement to Rumery are obvious: he gained immunity from criminal prosecution in consideration of abandoning a civil suit that he may well have lost.

. . . We also believe the Court of Appeals misapprehended the range of public interests arguably affected by a release-dismissal agreement. The availability of such agreements may threaten important public interests. They may tempt prosecutors to bring frivolous charges, or to dismiss meritorious charges, to protect the interests of other officials. But a per se rule of invalidity fails to credit other relevant public interests and improperly assumes prosecutorial misconduct. The vindication of constitutional rights and the exposure of official misconduct are not the only concerns implicated by § 1983 suits. No one suggests that all such suits are meritorious. Many are marginal and some are frivolous. Yet even when the risk of ultimate liability is negligible, the burden of defending such lawsuits is substantial. Counsel may be retained by the official, as well as the governmental entity. Preparation for trial, and the trial itself, will require the time and attention of the defendant officials, to the detriment of their public duties. In some cases litigation will extend over a period of years. This diversion of officials from their normal duties and the inevitable expense of defending even unjust claims is distinctly not in the public interest. To the extent release-dismissal agreements protect public officials from the burdens of defending such unjust claims, they further this important public interest.

. . . Because release-dismissal agreements may further legitimate prosecutorial and public interests, we reject the Court of Appeals' holding that all such agreements are invalid *per se*.

Turning to the agreement presented by this case, we conclude that the District Court's decision to enforce the agreement was correct. As we have noted, . . . it is clear that Rumery voluntarily entered the agreement. Moreover, in this case the prosecutor had an independent, legitimate reason to make this agreement directly related to his prosecutorial responsibilities. The agreement foreclosed both the civil and criminal trials concerning Rumery, in which [the victim] would have been a key witness. She therefore was spared the public scrutiny and embarrassment she would have endured if she had had to testify in either of those cases. Both the prosecutor and the defense attorney testified in the District Court that this was a significant consideration in the prosecutor's decision.

In sum, we conclude that this agreement was voluntary, that there is no evidence of prosecutorial misconduct, and that enforcement of this agreement would not adversely affect the relevant public interests.

[Justice O'Connor did not join Justice Powell's opinion on whether the agreements were invalid *per se*, leaving only four Justices holding the Justice Powell's view. She wrote a separate concurring opinion in which she found "convincing evidence that Rumery voluntarily entered into the agreement and that it served the public interest." She noted, however, that "it would have been preferable, and made this an easier case, had the . . . agreement been concluded under some form of judicial supervision."]

JUSTICE STEVENS, with whom JUSTICE BRENNAN, JUSTICE MARSHALL and JUSTICE BLACKMUN join, dissenting.

The question whether the release-dismissal agreement signed by respondent is unenforceable is much more complex than the Court's opinion indicates. A complete analysis of the question presented by this case cannot end with the observation that respondent made a knowing and voluntary choice to sign a settlement agreement. Even an intelligent and informed, but completely innocent, person accused of crime should not be required to choose between a threatened indictment and trial, with their attendant publicity and the omnipresent possibility of wrongful conviction, and surrendering the right to a civil remedy against individuals who have violated his or her constitutional rights. Moreover, the prosecutor's representation of competing and possibly conflicting interests compounds the dangerous potential of release-dismissal agreements. . . .

Because this is the first case of this kind that the Court has reviewed, I am hesitant to adopt an absolute rule invalidating all such agreements. I am, however, persuaded that the federal policies reflected in the enactment and enforcement of § 1983 mandate a strong presumption against the enforceability of such agreements and that the presumption is not overcome in this case by the facts or by any of the policy concerns discussed by the plurality. The very existence of the statute identifies the important federal interests in providing a remedy for the violation of constitutional rights and in having the merits of such claims resolved openly by an impartial adjudicator rather than *sub silentio* by a prosecutor whose primary objective in entering release-dismissal agreements is definitely not to ensure that all meritorious § 1983 claims prevail. The interest in vindication of constitutional violations unquestionably outweighs the interest in avoiding the expense and inconvenience of defending unmeritorious claims. Paradoxically, the plurality seems more sensitive to that burden than to the cost to the public and the individual of denying relief in meritorious cases. In short, the plurality's decision seems to rest on the unstated premise that § 1983 litigation imposes a net burden on society. If that were a correct assessment of the statute, it should be repealed. Unless that is done, however, we should respect the congressional decision to attach greater importance to the benefits associated with access to a federal remedy than to the burdens of defending these cases. . . .

NOTES

1. *Impact of ban on release dismissal agreements.* If release-dismissal agreements were invalidated, a defendant still could plead guilty in exchange for a favorable deal on the charges or the sentence. How would the plea bargaining process be affected if there were no release-dismissal agreement to use as a bargaining chip? Would either side gain or lose leverage by the absence of release-dismissal agreements?

2. *Closer judicial supervision.* Would closer judicial supervision of such agreements make sense? What do you think of a rule that a release-dismissal agreement is not enforceable unless it is executed under "active judicial supervision by the criminal trial court"? Under this approach, the prosecutor presumably would have to demonstrate to the criminal trial court that the agreement is the product of a voluntary, deliberate, and informed decision by the defendant, and is in the public interest. Also, the prosecutor probably would have to file a copy of the agreement with the court. If this procedure were utilized, would *Rumery's* concerns about these agreements be alleviated? What issues would the judge address? Where would the information needed by the judge come from? Would the judge have to conduct a hearing in each case to decide whether to approve a release-dismissal agreement?

3. *Against public policy.* In *Cain v. Darby Borough*, 7 F.3d 377 (3d Cir. 1993) (en banc), Cain was arrested for several crimes of assault. At her request, she was placed in a rehabilitative program that, if successfully completed, would lead to a dismissal of charges. As a condition of participation in this program, she was required to execute a

release-dismissal agreement. When she later sued for excessive force in her arrest in the assault cases, the prosecution argued that her suit should be dismissed because she signed a release-dismissal agreement. In an *en banc* decision, the Court of Appeals held the release-dismissal agreement unenforceable as a matter of law. Such agreements are valid only if the prosecutor proves that a legitimate public policy supported the decision *in this case* to dismiss charges in exchange for a release. This could be shown if the decision to require a release-dismissal agreement somehow furthered the public's interest. It could also be shown if the prosecutor could prove that the released civil rights claim appeared marginal or frivolous at the time of the agreement. Since this agreement was not fact-specific with respect to the merits of Cain's claims, the release-dismissal agreement would not bar her action.

4. *Oral release-dismissal agreement.* Should an *oral* release-dismissal agreement be upheld? *See Livingstone v. North Belle Vernon Borough*, 91 F.3d 515 (3d Cir. 1996), holding that the burden is upon the state to prove the voluntariness of an oral release-dismissal agreement by clear and convincing evidence. The court noted that those seeking to enforce such an agreement should bear the higher proof standard and that this burden should encourage prosecutors to reduce all such agreements to writing.

5. *Wisdom of release-dismissal agreements.* Are release-dismissal agreements counterproductive to society's goal in reducing official decisions influenced by race? Recall that the court noted in *Rumery* that release-dismissal agreements "spare the local community the expense of litigation associated with some minor crimes for which there is little or no public interest in prosecution." Isn't this interest present in all cases where there is a minor offense but the defendant suspects that the motivations behind the initial stop were based on race? One commentator notes that "rules designed to streamline and simplify the justice system often work at cross-purposes with the desire to detect and correct race-based conduct. Release-dismissal agreements provide a method for masking this conduct by buying a defendant's silence, albeit at a price that may be enticing to the parties most directly involved." Andrew D. Leipold, *Objective Tests and Subjective Bias: Some Problems of Discriminatory Intent in the Criminal Law*, 73 Chi.-Kent L. Rev. 559, 578 (1998).

[iii]   Separation of Powers

Occasionally, courts use the separation of powers doctrine to restrict the exercise of a prosecutor's broad discretion. See, for example, *United States v. Hamm*, 659 F.2d 624 (5th Cir. 1981), where it was noted that because courts retain sentencing discretion, they have the power to supervise prosecutorial conduct in the sentencing process.

Under Federal Sentencing Guidelines, federal prosecutors may seek a sentence reduction based on the prosecutor's representation that a defendant has substantially cooperated with law enforcement officials. Some commentators suggest that this aspect of the federal legislation may pose a due process issue by "transferring much of the responsibility of sentencing from impartial judges to prosecutors, without providing standards to guide the prosecutors' discretion." Bennett L. Gershman, *The Most Fundamental Change in the Criminal Justice System*, Criminal Justice 3 (Fall 1990). *See also* Cynthia Lee, *Prosecutorial Discretion, Substantial Assistance, and the Federal Sentencing Guidelines*, 42 UCLA L. Rev. 105 (1994).

In *United States v. Cobbins*, 749 F. Supp. 1450 (E.D. La. 1990), defendants were tried and convicted of using and carrying firearms in relation to a drug trafficking crime. This offense carried a mandatory, consecutive five-year term under Federal Sentencing Guidelines. Defendants argued that the prosecutor's decision to include the gun count determined, at least in part, their sentences and that this violated due process by giving the prosecutor an improper role in the sentencing decision. The United States district court rejected the claim (there having been no showing that the charges were selected arbitrarily or in bad faith), observing that under Federal Sentencing Guidelines there is a "de facto transfer" of some of the responsibility for sentencing from courts to prosecutors. Nonetheless, this shift of power was found to be a legitimate policy choice by Congress that did not, in and of itself, violate due process.

[3] Control of Prosecutorial Discretion Through Internal Rules or Standards

The *National Advisory Commission on Criminal Justice Standards and Goals, Reports on Courts* (1973), adopted a series of standards calling for open recognition of the need for screening certain defendants out of the criminal justice system "when the benefits to be derived from prosecution or diversion would be outweighed by the costs of such action." Among the factors to be considered in making this determination are the following:

1. Any doubt as to the accused's guilt;

2. The impact of further proceedings upon the accused and those close to him, especially the likelihood and seriousness of financial hardship or family life disruption;

3. The value of further proceedings in preventing future offenses by other persons, considering the extent to which subjecting the accused to further proceedings could be expected to have an impact upon others who might commit such offenses, as well as the seriousness of those offenses;

4. The value of further proceedings in preventing future offenses by the offender, in light of the offender's commitment to criminal activity as a way of life; the seriousness of his past criminal activity, which he might reasonably be expected to continue; the possibility that further proceedings might have a tendency to create or reinforce commitment on the part of the accused to criminal activity as a way of life; and the likelihood that programs available as diversion or sentencing alternatives may reduce the likelihood of future criminal activity;

5. The value of further proceedings in fostering the community's sense of security and confidence in the criminal justice system;

6. The direct cost of prosecution, in terms of prosecutorial time, court time, and similar factors;

7. Any improper motives of the complainant;

8. Prolonged non-enforcement of the statute on which the charged is based;

9. The likelihood of prosecution and jurisdiction; and conviction of the offender by another;

10. Any assistance rendered by the accused in apprehension or conviction of other offenders, in the prevention of offenses by others, in the reduction of the impact of offenses committed by himself or others upon the victims, and any other socially beneficial activity engaged in by the accused that might be encouraged in others by not prosecuting the offender. *National Advisory Commission on Criminal Justice Standards and Goals*, Courts, Standard 1.1. (1973).

Other recommended standards apply to individuals who should be diverted into specific programs before trial or conviction. Included among the factors to be considered favorable to diversion are (1) youth of the offender, (2) assent by the victim, and (3) likelihood of treatment of a mental illness suffered by the defendant and which was related to the crime. Factors considered unfavorable to diversion include (1) a history of physical violence, (2) organized crime involvement, (3) need for prosecution as a means of discouraging others, and (4) "a history of anti-social conduct indicating that such conduct has become an ingrained part of the defendant's lifestyle and would be particularly resistant to change."

The proper discharge of the prosecution function is also addressed by the ABA Standards Relating to the Prosecution Function and the Defense Function. Following are the pertinent provisions from American Bar Association, Standards for Criminal Justice §§ 3-3.8, 3-3.9 (3d ed. 1993):*

Standard 3-3.8. *Discretion as to Noncriminal Disposition*

(a) The prosecutor should consider in appropriate cases the availability of noncriminal disposition, formal or informal, in deciding whether to press criminal charges which would otherwise be supported by probable cause; especially in the case of a first offender, the nature of the offense may warrant noncriminal disposition.

(b) Prosecutors should be familiar with the resources of social agencies which can assist in the evaluation of cases for diversion from the criminal process.

Standard 3-3.9. *Discretion in the Charging Decision*

(a) A prosecutor should not institute, or cause to be instituted, or permit the continued pendency of criminal charges when the prosecutor knows that the charges are not supported by probable cause. A prosecutor should not institute, cause to be instituted, or permit the continued pendency of charges in the absence of sufficient admissible evidence to support a conviction.

(b) The prosecutor is not obliged to present all charges which the evidence might support. The prosecutor may in some circumstances and for good cause consistent with the public interest decline to prosecute, notwithstanding that sufficient evidence may exist which would support a conviction. Illustrative of the factors which the prosecutor may properly consider in exercising his or her discretion are:

(i) the prosecutor's reasonable doubt that the accused is in fact guilty;

(ii) the extent of the harm caused by the offense;

(iii) the disproportion of the authorized punishment in relation to the particular offense or the offender;

(iv) possible improper motives of the complainant;

(v) reluctance of the victim to testify;

(vi) cooperation of the accused in the apprehension or conviction of others;

(vii) availability and likelihood of prosecution by another jurisdiction.

(c) A prosecutor should not be compelled by his or her supervisor to prosecute a case in which he or she has a reasonable doubt about the guilt of the accused.

(d) In making the decision to prosecute, the prosecutor should give no weight to the personal or political advantages or disadvantages which might be involved or to a desire to enhance his or her record of convictions.

(e) In cases which involve a serious threat to the community, the prosecutor should not be deterred from prosecution by the fact that in the jurisdiction juries have tended to acquit persons accused of the particular kind of criminal act in question.

(f) The prosecutor should not bring or seek charges greater in number or degree than can reasonably be supported with evidence at trial or than are necessary to fairly reflect the gravity of the offense.

(g) The prosecutor should not condition a dismissal of charges, nolle prosequi, or similar action on the accused's relinquishment of the right to seek civil

*   Reprinted with permission. All rights reserved.

redress unless the accused has agreed to the action knowingly and intelligently, freely and voluntarily, and where such waiver is approved by the court.

NOTE

How helpful are the N.A.C. and A.B.A. Standards? How should each be applied to the following cases? (The essential facts of these Problems are set forth in H. Richard Uviller, *The Virtuous Prosecutor in Quest of an Ethical Standard: Guidance from the ABA*, 71 Mich. L. Rev. 1145, 1157–1158 (1973).)

PROBLEM 2-1. I NEVER FORGET A FACE

An elderly white person is suddenly grabbed from behind in a dimly lit alley by a black youth who shows a knife and takes the victim's wallet. The entire incident lasts no more than 30 seconds. Several days later, the victim spots the defendant in the neighborhood and has him arrested by the nearest police officer. Although the prosecutor presses him hard, the victim swears that his identification of the defendant is correct. The defendant's appearance is not unusual, the victim never saw the defendant before the crime, and the victim also admits that he does not personally know many blacks. Certain about his identification, though, he insists that in those few moments of terror his attacker's face was "indelibly engraved on his memory." The defendant may have an alibi: his mother apparently will testify that the defendant was home watching television at the time of the crime (evidence which is not readily credited). Does the prosecutor have enough information to decide whether to prosecute? If not, what information is lacking?

PROBLEM 2-2. DROPSY SYNDROME

Defendant, charged with illegal possession of cocaine, has indicated to defense counsel a readiness to plead guilty. Defendant claims, however, that the police found the cocaine in an illegal search of the automobile trunk and therefore it should be suppressed. The police officer claims to have retrieved the drugs after the defendant "threw" them from the window of the vehicle at the police officer's approach. The prosecutor, based on personal experience, suspects that this officer sometimes seeks to avoid the strictures of the exclusionary rule by using the "law of abandonment" (or "dropsy" testimony) to justify what would otherwise be an illegal search and seizure.

1. If the prosecutor believes this officer may testify falsely, what steps should the prosecutor take?

2. Even if the prosecutor suspects the officer may lie, should the prosecutor accept the plea offer if the defendant had a lengthy drug record? What if this were the first offense charged against the accused?

F.   ROLE OF DEFENSE COUNSEL

Until a criminal case is formally begun, often there is relatively little that a defense attorney can do to assist his or her client. Indeed, the defendant may not even be aware of a criminal investigation until it is too late — meaning, that an information has been filed or an indictment has issued from the grand jury. In cases in which the defense attorney knows of a pending criminal investigation, however, it may be very helpful to the client to pursue a course of action designed to discourage the prosecution from moving forward. Furthermore, as discussed earlier, pre-charge bargaining with the United States Attorney may have a significant impact upon the defendant's sentence under Federal Sentencing Guidelines.

Where a criminal investigation is occurring in the corporate or commercial context, it has been reported that with increasing frequency the target defendant's first notice of a federal investigation is not by way of a grand jury subpoena, but through federal investigators in the workplace. The investigator may be representing any one of several federal agencies, including FBI, IRS, Customs Service, Postal Service, Departments of Labor, Defense, Transportation, or Health and Human Services. In this context, the following advice is given by Vaira and Backstrom:

> Counsel should attempt to determine the scope of the investigation and, specifically, determine whether the company or any of its officials are targets. Once counsel has established contact with the regional counsel of the investigating agency or the Assistant U.S. Attorney in charge of the investigation, it is imperative that a conference be scheduled with this individual. . . . A line of communication must be kept open with the government attorney, even though his or her position will become adversarial. At this point, the government attorney holds all the cards. Company counsel may want to declare war, and tell the government that the company will fight on all grounds. This may be the case, but the company cannot fight without information, and the government attorney is the best source.

They conclude with the following observation:

> If the company keeps abreast of the investigation and makes an early and informed assessment of the extent of its liability, it may be able to head off possible criminal and civil proceedings altogether.

Vaira & Backstrom, *Agents On Your Doorstep: Managing The Government Investigation*, 2 Corp. Crim. Liab. Rep. 33 (1988).

Many defense attorneys have echoed these sentiments in a broader context, encouraging involvement in a pending criminal case as soon as possible, particularly in the pre-indictment phase. Not only will the defense lawyer be in a position to influence the very decision to prosecute, but it is also possible that the prosecutor may disclose, at least in part, his or her theory of the case or an assessment of the prospective defendant's culpability. Such an "early warning" discovery process can also be helpful in preparation for representation of one's client before an investigative grand jury. Finally, it has been noted that some criminal investigations are governed by internal procedures for review of the exercise of discretion in seeking grand jury indictments. With access to such information, counsel's ability to dissuade presentation of the case to the grand jury may be enhanced.

Early and aggressive intervention by defense counsel is recommended by the American Bar Association's Standards Relating to the Defense Function. The two pertinent Standards addressing the need for such action follow.

American Bar Association, Standards for Criminal Justice (3d ed. 1993) Standard 4-4.1. *Duty to Investigate* (a) Defense counsel should conduct a prompt investigation of the circumstances of the case and explore all avenues leading to facts relevant to the merits of the case and the penalty in the event of conviction. The investigation should include efforts to secure information in the possession of the prosecution and law enforcement authorities. The duty to investigate exists regardless of the accused's admission or statements to defense counsel of facts constituting guilt or the accused's stated desire to plead guilty. (b) Defense counsel should not seek to acquire possession of physical evidence personally or through use of an investigator where defense counsel's sole purpose is to obstruct access to such evidence.

Standard 4-6.1. *Duty to Explore Disposition Without Trial* (a) Whenever the law, nature, and circumstances of the case permit, defense counsel should explore the possibility of an early diversion of the case from the criminal process through the use of other community agencies.

NOTES

1. *How aggressive?* How "aggressive" should the defense lawyer be at the pre-indictment stage? Is there not a risk that the defense attorney's vigorous advocacy will "boomerang"?

2. *Approval of victim.* Should the defense attorney attempt to contact the crime victim for the purpose of obtaining "victim approval" of "diversion of the case from the criminal process" under Standard 4-6.1? From a policy perspective, should contact with a crime victim in this fashion be discouraged? Communications between victims and defense attorneys in the pretrial setting will be explored further in Chapter 10.

Chapter 3

THE FIRST FORMAL CHARGE: THE COMPLAINT

Once a police officer, prosecutor, or private citizen has decided to "press charges," often the next step is for someone to sign a formal *complaint*, which is the initial charging document. In general terms, a criminal complaint is a written allegation that a named (or described, but not named) person committed a specified crime.

A. FUNCTIONS

The complaint serves two functions: it begins the formal criminal processes by charging the defendant with a crime, and it provides the basis for an arrest warrant. Often, both occur at the same time.

[1] Begin Formal Process

The first function can be important because the complaint both notifies the accused of the allegations and facilitates the initial appearance, discussed in the next chapter. It also may stop or "toll" the running of the statute of limitations, discussed in Chapter 13.

The exact impact of the complaint as a charging instrument varies among jurisdictions and may depend on whether the crime is a misdemeanor or felony. The complaint typically serves as the only formal charging document throughout misdemeanor cases. There may be no indictment to replace it. For felonies, on the other hand, the complaint usually will be the first formal charge, but may be replaced later in the process by a grand jury indictment or prosecutor's information, discussed in Chapter 7. Accordingly, some states require greater specificity in misdemeanor complaints than in felony complaints. *See, e.g.*, Pa. R. Crim. P. 504(6)(a) and (b) (complaint must include citation to law violated in a "summary" case, but no such requirement in "court" cases; both types of complaints must contain "a summary of the facts sufficient to advise the defendant of the nature of the offense charged.").

In a jurisdiction in which the complaint is replaced by an indictment or information, the importance of the complaint wanes considerably as the case proceeds further into the criminal justice process. Indeed, in these jurisdictions the case can be initiated by an indictment or information, thus eliminating the need for a complaint to be filed.

The American Law Institute's Model Code of Pre-Arraignment Procedure (1975), commentary on Section 340.1, recommends that all offenses — even misdemeanors — be formally prosecuted by indictment or information. Therefore, the practice of prosecuting a misdemeanor on the complaint (made with little, if any, pretrial screening) would be eliminated if such a recommendation were adopted. Some jurisdictions require that "citizen complaints" be reviewed by a prosecutor who has the authority to screen ill-founded complaints. What arguments could be advanced for allowing the prosecution of misdemeanors on the basis of the complaint, alone?

[2] Basis For Arrest Warrant

The second function of the complaint is to serve as the written basis for an arrest warrant. This function is so important that it has even been described as the principal function of the complaint. Although the law of search and seizure as governed by the Fourth Amendment is beyond the scope of this book, a few basic principles will help explain the role of the complaint in the arrest warrant process. It is clear that an arrest warrant must be based on probable cause, which may be established by a sworn affidavit presented to the judge issuing the warrant.

The sworn complaint can provide the magistrate with sufficient information to demonstrate the existence of probable cause. If the complaint (and perhaps other documents) establish probable cause to arrest, the magistrate or judge who signs the complaint may simultaneously issue an arrest warrant. These principles are embraced in Rule 4 of the Federal Rules of Criminal Procedure.

B. PROCEDURES

Despite the importance of the complaint and the fact that it is routinely described in criminal procedure rules, there are relatively few rules or decisions providing much information about the complaint process. Often a court clerk will have form copies of a complaint which a person, called a *complainant*, fills out and signs under oath. Sometimes, police departments maintain copies of the general form.

The rules of criminal procedure give little guidance about the form and content of a complaint. The Federal Rules of Criminal Procedure are typically brief, as Rule 3, below, illustrates:

FEDERAL RULES OF CRIMINAL PROCEDURE

Rule 3. *The Complaint*

The complaint is a written statement of the essential facts constituting the offense charged. It must be made under oath before a magistrate judge or, if none is reasonably available, before a state or local judicial officer.

NOTES

In general terms, both the Federal Rules of Criminal Procedure and similar state rules require that the complaint must be minimally descriptive of the accused, the alleged crime, and the victim. Federal Rule 3 embraces this principle by stating that the complaint must include the "essential facts constituting the offense charged."

UNITES STATES EX REL. SAVAGE v. ARNOLD
403 F. Supp. 172, 175 (E.D. Pa. 1975)

The foundation of relator's criminal complaint is 18 U.S.C. § 242 which deals with the willful violation of civil rights under color of law. The named defendants include 2 unknown City of Philadelphia Police Officers, 2 unknown City of Philadelphia Detectives, 1 unknown City of Philadelphia Police Official, the Police Commissioner of Philadelphia, as well as the City and County of Philadelphia, the Commissioner of Corrections of Pennsylvania, and the Commonwealth of Pennsylvania.

For present purposes, it is enough to summarize the allegations of the complaint as follows: it is charged that since October 17, 1963, the defendants, at various times and in various combinations, have conspired to falsely arrest relator without probable cause, and subsequently cause him to be brought to trial, convicted and imprisoned for nearly seven years, and thereafter conspired to deny relator's attempts to obtain postconviction relief until he was awarded a new trial, and ultimately, following a finding that his arrest was illegal and the suppression of evidence, the case against him was dismissed on October 9, 1970.

Several defects are apparent under even the most liberal reading of relator's complaint, which necessitate that it be rejected. First, and most importantly, the complaint fails to state "the essential facts constituting the offense charged." Fed.R.Crim. P. 3. Despite the long listing of abuses and deprivations which the relator alleges he suffered, the conduct of the defendants is described only in conclusory fashion without a factual basis. There are no facts to show willfulness on the part of any of the named defendants, nor to establish the alleged conspiracy. The use of a warrant where the name of the defendant is unknown can be permitted only where it "contain[s] the defendant's name or, if it is unknown, a name or description by which the defendant can be identified with reasonable certainty." Fed. R. Crim. P. 4(b)(1)(A). The use of a warrant where the name of the defendant is unknown can be permitted only where it contains "any name or description by which [the defendant] can be identified with reasonable certainty." Fed.R.Crim.P. 4(b) (1). To do otherwise would clearly violate not only the language of Rule 4(b), Federal Rules of Criminal Procedure, but would likewise fail to meet the requirements of the Fourth Amendment of the United States Constitution.

Although presumably the arrest and other police records of this case would reveal the identity of these unknown defendants, the complaint on which relator seeks to proceed is nonetheless defective. Lastly, it must be noted that relator's complaint, as presented, runs head on into the five year statute of limitations applicable to the offense he would charge. 18 U.S.C. § 3282. The operative events which relator describes occurred in 1963 and allegedly continue to the present time. Regardless of the confusion as to which of the defendants participated in the alleged conspiracy or continued to participate throughout the period of time, no "overt acts" after 1969 are alleged, even accepting the conclusory nature of all of the allegations made. Nothing is averred beyond that time except relator's own bald statement that the conspiracy to violate his constitutional rights continued and is continuing to this day. Even measuring the limitation period from the time when the last "overt act" in furtherance of the alleged conspiracy was committed, it is clear that the criminal proceeding relator seeks to commence would be barred by the statute of limitations.

NOTES

1. *Essential facts.* In order to satisfy the requirement of Rule 3 that the complaint state "the essential facts constituting the offense," what additional facts should the complainant have included in the complaint?

2. *Content differs if used for arrest warrant.* Note that the complaint in *Arnold* was attacked on several grounds, including allegations that the prosecution was barred by the statute of limitations and that the complaint was inadequate to serve as the basis for an arrest warrant. Should the contents of a complaint differ when it is used *only* to begin the prosecution and not as the basis for an arrest warrant?

3. *Contrast with notice pleading.* Contrast Rule 3 with what you learned from your Civil Procedure course about pleading in a civil action. How would you compare the Rule 3 requirement that a criminal complaint be factually specific with the predominant system of *notice pleading* that governs most modern civil litigation in the United States?

4. *State statutes on content of complaint.* In some jurisdictions, a statute or court rule describing the complaint process provides more detail about the form the complaint is to take. Occasionally, it is quite specific. Pennsylvania, for example, requires that the complaint contain ten separate items, and all complaints sought by private citizens must be submitted via affidavit to a prosecutor for approval. Pa. R. Crim. P. 504 and 506. If the prosecutor does not approve, then the affiant may seek review by a judge.

5. *Oath.* The only other typical requirement is that the complaint must be made under oath. An unsigned complaint is void. Note, however, that the rules of criminal procedure do not place limits on who can sign as the complainant. Since there is no requirement that the person signing the complaint must have personally observed the crime, virtually anyone can sign a criminal complaint and institute criminal proceedings. Presumably, the complainant can base the allegation upon hearsay. Obviously, the victim of the crime can do it. Frequently, a police officer will sign the complaint.

The oath requirement is satisfied if the complainant swears (or affirms) that he or she is telling the truth. Often the oath must be made before a specified person; a judge is ordinarily sufficient. Routinely, a United States Magistrate Judge handles the oath requirement of complaints filed in federal court.

6. *Citizen complainant.* The usual rule is that a citizen has a right to file a request for a complaint, but has no right to have the case prosecuted fully by the district attorney or even to have the judge issue the complaint. *See, e.g., Victory Distributors v. Ayer Div. Of Dist. Court,* 755 N.E.2d 273 (Mass. 2001)(citizen has right to file criminal complaint and judges must act on it, but judge need not issue the complaint and district attorney may decline to prosecute it).

7. *Prosecutor's approval.* Jurisdictions frequently add other requirements. As noted above, often a prosecuting attorney must also sign the complaint. The Federal Rules of Criminal Procedure have been interpreted as requiring that an Assistant United States Attorney must sign a criminal complaint. A citizen has no right to file a federal criminal complaint absent the prosecutor's signature. Because courts are reluctant to interfere with prosecutorial discretion, the United States Attorney's failure or refusal to sign a complaint is virtually unreviewable in federal court. *See generally United States v. Panza,* 381 F. Supp. 1133 (W.D. Pa. 1974). This recognizes the prosecutor's broad discretion by permitting the prosecutor to screen out cases that the prosecutor thinks should not be pursued.

8. *Judge as complainant.* Some jurisdictions provide a check on the prosecutor's exercise of discretion by authorizing a court to commence a formal prosecution if the district attorney refuses to do so or is unavailable to issue a complaint. *See, e.g,* Wis. Stat. Ann. § 968.02(3)(if is probable cause, judge may issue complaint if prosecutor refuses to do so).

9. *Double Jeopardy inapplicable.* Since the complaint is issued in an early stage of the criminal process, the Double Jeopardy clause does not apply. *See* Chapter 16. Accordingly, a faulty or erroneous complaint can be withdrawn and a better one issued. If the complaint is faulty and not corrected, the effect of the error depends on the circumstances. If the complaint served as the basis for an arrest warrant, the arrest could be deemed illegal, with all the attendant consequences. On the other hand, if the faulty complaint was not used as support for an arrest warrant and was used only to begin the prosecution, the harmless error rule will most likely mean that the mistake will not cause an appellate reversal. A subsequent indictment or information will be viewed as "curing" any defect in the complaint. However, a new or amended complaint may be dismissed if the court finds it was the product of an effort to harass the defendant by repeated prosecutions for the same offense.

10. *Motion practice.* Even though a complaint will most likely be "cured" by a subsequent indictment, defense counsel may still choose to attack it with a Motion to Dismiss. The motion can be based on any ground, such as the statute of limitations, insufficient description of the offense, or violation of a grant of immunity. If the motion is successful, it will have the effect of ending the prosecution, though perhaps only temporarily. A byproduct of the Motion to Dismiss, however, is that it enables defense counsel to convey the message that the prosecution is in for a major, time-consuming battle if the case is pursued. The prosecutor may choose to dismiss a borderline charge or offer a lenient plea bargain rather than face the likely time commitment necessary to take the case to trial.

PROBLEM 3-1. ALL YOU EVER DO IS COMPLAIN

Herbert Foster, age 68, and Jerold Huskey, age 51, had been quarreling neighbors ever since Huskey moved next door two years ago. One summer day, Foster was working in his yard when Huskey walked up and asked to borrow $5.00 to buy some beer. Foster showed Huskey a ten dollar bill and stated that he could not loan Huskey any money because $10 was all the money he had. When Foster replaced the $10 bill in his tee shirt pocket, Huskey roughly reached into Foster's pocket and snatched the money, stating "I'll give you the change when I get back from the store." Huskey's roughness caused Foster to fall down.

 haha

Huskey left to go buy some beer. Ten minutes later, Foster got up and called the police. The officer who came to Foster's house heard Foster's story and refused to do anything when Huskey appeared to give Foster $5 change and to thank him for the loan. The officer said it sounded like a "neighborhood matter," so Foster would have to go to the judge and "swear out a complaint" if he wanted the matter to be pursued in court.

Foster's other neighbor drove him to the court house, where Foster filled out a standard form complaint.

Assume the following laws are in effect:

Westphalia Code Ann. § 418.323 *ASSAULT*

(a) A person commits assault who:

(1) intentionally, knowingly or recklessly causes bodily injury to another;

(2) intentionally or knowingly causes another to reasonably fear imminent *unlikely* bodily injury; or

best – (3) intentionally or knowingly causes physical contact with another and knows the other will regard the contact as extremely offensive or *weak* provocative.

(b) assault is a Class A misdemeanor, punishable by a jail term of not more than six months and a fine of not more than $1000.

Westphalia Code Ann. § 418.324 *AGGRAVATED ASSAULT*

(a) A person commits aggravated assault who:

(1) commits an assault as defined in Section 418.323, and

(A) causes serious bodily injury to another; or *— no news of injury*

(B) uses a deadly weapon; . . .

(b) aggravated assault is a Class C felony, punishable by a prison term of not more than twelve years and a fine of not more than $10,000.

Review the complaint on the following page. Does this complaint satisfy Rule 3's requirement that the complaint be a "written statement of the essential facts constituting the offense charged?" If not, what should be added or deleted? Even if sufficient facts are set forth, should defense counsel move to dismiss the complaint on any other basis?

Complaint

_____   _____
Complaint Number   Warrant Number

STATE OF WESTPHALIA, COUNTY OF WASHINGTON
AFFIDAVIT
AGGRAVATED ASSAULT
(Serious Bodily Injury or Weapon)
Westphalia Code §418.323

Personally appeared before me, the undersigned, (Commissioner), (Washington County Judge),
Herb Foster and made oath in due form of law that (he) ~~(she)~~ (personally
observed) (has probable cause to believe that) _Jerry Husky_ on the _3_ day of
Aug., 20_08_ in the County aforesaid, did unlawfully,

*****STRIKE THE PORTIONS THAT DO NOT APPLY*****

~~(and intentionally, knowingly or recklessly cause bodily injury to another; to wit:~~
_____

OR

(and intentionally or knowingly cause another; to wit: ~~Herb Foster~~ to reasonably
fear imminent bodily injury;)

OR

~~(and intentionally or knowingly cause physical contact with another; to wit:~~
~~and know the other person would regard the contact as extremely~~
~~offensive or provocative;)~~

and

~~(the defendant caused serious bodily injury to the victim) or (the defendant used a deadly~~
~~weapon); and the said probable cause is as follows:~~

_took Mr. Foster's money from his
shirt pockit and pushed him—
almost causing Foster to fall
(Victim on cruches)_

Herb Foster   _1002 Meridian_   _No_
Prosecutor   Address   Phone

Sworn to and subscribed before me this _3_ day of _Aug._, 20_08_
Mary Gardner
Judge of Part _2_ of the Washington County Court/Commissioner

BOUND OVER TO THE GRAND JURY
Judge of Part _____ of the Washington County Court
THE STATE

It appearing from testimony in the case that there is probable cause to believe the Defendant guilty
of the offense of which he stands charged, it is adjudged that he be held to at the next term of
Criminal Court of Washington County, Westphalia. The offense being bailable, the amount of such
bail is fixed at $_____.

This _____ day of _____ 20_____.   _____
                                           Judge, Washington County Court

_1) add why on crutch/injury
2) if almost fell, how hurt?
3) pushed him = Stretch_

Chapter 4
THE FIRST HEARING: THE INITIAL APPEARANCE

If a criminal suspect is arrested, with or without a warrant, he or she is ordinarily brought to the police station or jail and "booked." The booking process is an administrative mechanism designed to obtain information about the accused for purposes of record keeping and checking for outstanding warrants. The accused may be fingerprinted and photographed as part of the procedure. The accused may also be interrogated about the crime for which he or she was arrested, and perhaps other unsolved offenses as well.

After (or sometimes before) this process is completed, the accused is brought before a judicial officer. In federal cases, this proceeding is called the *initial appearance before the magistrate*, but some jurisdictions describe it as the *first appearance* or even the *preliminary arraignment*.

A. PURPOSES OF INITIAL APPEARANCE

The initial appearance serves a number of purposes, ranging from a basic provision of information to decisionmaking of considerable importance to both the accused and the prosecution.

[1] Provide Information to Accused

A key function of the initial appearance is more ministerial than adversarial in nature. It involves providing the accused with important information about future proceedings and the accused's basic constitutional rights. At the initial appearance, the accused is formally notified of the charges and, in some jurisdictions, is given a copy of the complaint. Also, the accused is informed of relevant constitutional and statutory rights, such as the right to remain silent, the privilege against self-incrimination, the right to a preliminary examination, and the right either to retain counsel or, if indigent, to have counsel appointed. Pretrial release may be resolved if the defendant is still in custody. In juvenile cases, the initial appearance also ensures that the child's parents or guardians have been notified.

[2] Appoint Counsel

If the accused is indigent and wants counsel, the judge presiding over the initial appearance may appoint counsel or begin the administrative process of having a lawyer appointed. The court may first have to determine whether the accused is actually indigent and therefore qualified to receive free counsel. This procedure may require the defendant to complete a questionnaire about his or her employment, assets, liabilities, and familial responsibilities. The judge also may ask a series of questions about the accused's resources. In some jurisdictions, representatives of the public defender's office or private lawyers attend initial appearances and are appointed at that time to represent indigent defendants.

An anomaly in the Federal Rules of Criminal Procedure is contained in Rule 44(a), which specifically gives the accused a right to counsel at the initial appearance. Since counsel is ordinarily appointed at this hearing, Rule 44 is not taken literally to require appointment of counsel before the initial appearance. *See United States v. Mendoza-Cecelia*, 963 F.2d 1467, 1474 n.5 (11th Cir. 1992). In *Rothgery v. Gillespie County*, 128 S.Ct. 2578 (2008), the Supreme Court held that the initial appearance triggers attachment of the Sixth Amendment right to counsel requiring appointment of counsel at or within a reasonable time after the initial appearance.

[3] Schedule Future Proceedings

A third function of the initial appearance is to schedule future proceedings, such as the preliminary hearing. Often, a statute or court rule will prescribe the maximum delay between the initial appearance and the preliminary hearing. *See, e.g.*, Fed. R. Crim. P. 5.1(c) (preliminary examination within 10 days after initial appearance if defendant is in custody, 20 days if not in custody).

Since often the accused will not have counsel at the initial appearance, the court may delay resolving some issues for a few hours or days until counsel is retained or appointed and can attend the hearing. These issues include a decision on release conditions or a hearing to assess whether the accused is mentally competent. If a date for a later proceeding is set at the initial appearance, it is probably a "soft" date that is easily changed once counsel is appointed or retained and has a chance to check his or her calendar.

[4] Make Release Decision

If the accused is in jail at the time of the initial appearance, another important function is to determine whether the accused can be released pending trial. There are actually two facets of this process. First, if no judge has assessed whether there is probable cause to detain the accused, the judge at the initial appearance may have to resolve that issue pursuant to the Supreme Court's decision in *Gerstein v. Pugh*, discussed below. Second, if probable cause has been found by a judge or grand jury (and therefore the accused is lawfully held in custody), the judge at the initial appearance may explore various methods of release on bail or other procedures, discussed in Chapter 5. Sometimes, however, the pretrial release decision is scheduled at a different time and, in some cases, that matter is heard by a different judge.

[a] *Gerstein* Probable Cause Determination

As discussed briefly in Chapter 1 and in detail in Chapter 6, a criminal defendant actually is likely to encounter two types of pre-trial proceedings before judicial officers: the initial appearance and the preliminary examination (or, in many states, the "preliminary hearing"). In addition, since the Supreme Court decided *Gerstein v. Pugh*, 420 U.S. 103 (1975), a criminal defendant who was arrested without a warrant may also face a third pretrial proceeding: a *"Gerstein"* proceeding which tests the validity of his or her detention. Rather than have three separate hearings, judges often combine the *Gerstein* determination with either the initial appearance or the preliminary examination. On rare occasions all three are combined into one proceeding.

The issue in *Gerstein v. Pugh* was whether a person arrested without a warrant and held in jail for trial under a prosecutor's information is constitutionally entitled to a probable cause determination by a judicial officer. The two defendants in *Gerstein* were arrested pursuant to a Florida law that permitted a criminal proceeding to be initiated by an information, which is a formal, written allegation by a prosecutor that a particular person has committed one or more specified crimes. Since under Florida law the filing of an information authorized an arrest, the person accused in an information could be arrested and held in jail for a substantial period of time solely on the basis of a prosecutor's decision. Under this procedure, no judge promptly assessed whether there was probable cause to detain the accused, although this issue could be addressed a month or so later at the arraignment or preliminary hearing.

The Supreme Court in *Gerstein* noted that "the standards and procedures for arrest and detention have been derived from the Fourth Amendment and its common law antecedents." Under the Fourth Amendment, an arrest must be based on probable cause, defined as sufficient proof to cause a prudent person to believe the defendant had committed an offense. Reasoning that "the detached judgment of a neutral magistrate is essential if the Fourth Amendment is to furnish meaningful protection from unfounded interference with liberty," the United States Supreme Court held in *Gerstein* that the Fourth Amendment requires that a neutral and detached judicial officer must determine probable cause before a person can be subjected to an extended restraint of liberty after a warrantless arrest.

"Hearing" procedures. Rejecting the notion that a fully adversarial hearing is essential to this probable cause determination, the *Gerstein* Court held that the required judicial finding of probable cause may be made in an informal, non-adversary *ex parte* proceeding on the basis of oral and written hearsay testimony. Thus the judge may make the *Gerstein* determination not necessarily from a courtroom, but from home in the middle of the night or from the country club in the middle of a round of golf, on the basis of information provided over the phone. The accused is not entitled to confront or cross-examine adverse witnesses at this proceeding. For these reasons, the phrase *"Gerstein* determination" is probably a more accurate description of what takes place than the term *"Gerstein* hearing." The Court in *Gerstein* indicated that it may be desirable for the judicial officer to make the probable cause determination at the suspect's initial appearance or at a preliminary hearing held soon after arrest.

Timing of Gerstein determination: the 48 hour burden shift. *Gerstein* requires that all states provide "prompt" determinations of probable cause for detained criminal suspects arrested without a warrant, but the Court in that case set no precise time requirements for this determination. In *County of Riverside v. McLaughlin*, 500 U.S. 44 (1991), the Supreme Court held that such determinations ordinarily must occur within 48 hours of arrest. The Court explained:

> This is not to say that the probable cause determination in a particular case passes constitutional muster simply because it is provided within 48 hours. Such a hearing may nonetheless violate *Gerstein* if the arrested individual can prove that his or her probable cause determination was delayed unreasonably. Examples of unreasonable delay are delays for the purpose of gathering additional evidence to justify the arrest, a delay motivated by ill will against the arrested individual, or delay for delay's sake. In evaluating whether the delay in a particular case is unreasonable, however, courts must allow a substantial degree of flexibility. Courts cannot ignore the often unavoidable delays in transporting arrested persons from one facility to another, handling late-night bookings where no magistrate is readily available, obtaining the presence of an arresting officer who may be busy processing other suspects or securing the premises of an arrest, and other practical realities.

> Where an arrested individual does not receive a probable cause determination within 48 hours, the calculus changes. In such a case, the arrested individual does not bear the burden of proving an unreasonable delay. Rather, the burden shifts to the government to demonstrate the existence of a bona fide emergency or other extraordinary circumstance. The fact that in a particular case it may take longer than 48 hours to consolidate pretrial proceedings does not qualify as an extraordinary circumstance. Nor, for that matter, do intervening weekends. A jurisdiction that chooses to offer combined proceedings must do so as soon as is reasonably feasible, but in no event later than 48 hours after arrest.

Id. at 56–57. *See also Bryant v. City of New York*, 404 F.3d 128 (2d Cir. 2005)(detention beyond 48 hours is presumptively unreasonable).

Justice O'Connor wrote the *McLaughlin* opinion for a five-Justice majority. Justices Marshall, joined by Justices Blackmun and Stevens, wrote a short dissenting opinion, arguing that the probable cause hearing should be held immediately after completion of the administrative steps in the arrest process. Justice Scalia, also dissenting, argued forcefully for a rule that would set the limit at 24 hours in most cases. He concluded his dissent by asserting that the majority had repudiated one of the Fourth Amendment's core applications — judicial determinations of probable cause — which will result in the incarceration of presumptively innocent people.

NOTES

1. *A.L.I. Code of Pre-Arraignment Procedure.* Justice Scalia's dissent in *McLaughlin* cited the American Law Institute's Model Code of Pre-Arraignment Procedure. Under § 310.1, persons in custody must be brought before a magistrate within 24 hours of arrest. Interestingly, however, the A.L.I.'s Model Code does not require that a probable cause determination occur at the first appearance. Rather, the defendant is advised of the right to counsel. If the defendant desires to be represented by a lawyer, the hearing is adjourned for 48 hours. The second hearing (characterized as the "adjourned session of the first appearance") then takes place and the judge makes the requisite "reasonable cause" determination. In what way does the A.L.I. procedure go beyond the requirements of *Gerstein* and *McLaughlin?* In what way does it fall short of the *Gerstein/McLaughlin* guarantee?

2. *Remedy.* What is the remedy for a *Gerstein* violation? In *Gerstein*, the Supreme Court made it clear that the unlawful pretrial detention (where there has not been a prompt determination of probable cause) will not invalidate a subsequent conviction. It is possible, however, that the failure to bring the accused before a magistrate in a reasonably prompt fashion may jeopardize the admissibility of pre-appearance confessions and consensual searches. The so-called *McNabb-Mallory* rule is discussed in Part B, below.

In addition, case law has accepted the possibility that the *Gerstein* violation, combined with other factors, could require suppression of an involuntary confession made during the period of illegal detention. *Lawhorn v. Allen*, 519 Fed 3d. 1272 (11th Cir. 2008).

If no *Gerstein* determination is made after a warrantless arrest, the *Gerstein* Court held that the arrestee may obtain one by filing a declaratory judgment action against state officials.

3. *Waiver of time limits.* The defendant may make a knowing and intelligent waiver of *Gerstein's* time limits. *Commonwealth v. Jackson*, 855 N.E.2d 1097 (Mass. 2006).

[b] Conditions of Release

Assuming there is probable cause to detain a suspect, the judge at the initial appearance may have to make a decision about whether release from confinement is appropriate. This decision is discussed more fully in Chapter 5. If the defendant has been released by jail personnel on "station house" bail, the judge at the initial appearance will ordinarily confirm the release decision already made, although the prosecution may request more stringent release conditions and the defense may ask for less stringent ones. If the defendant is still in custody at the time of the initial appearance, the court may conduct a release hearing at that time or may delay the matter for a day or two until the accused has had the chance to confer with appointed or retained counsel, subject, of course, to *McLaughlin* constraints.

B. PROCEDURES

The initial appearance is likely to be the defendant's first opportunity to confront a judicial officer. The proceeding is usually of short duration (often lasting only a few minutes) and the defendant will be given little, if any, opportunity to discuss the charge with the magistrate.

Use of video. An increasing number of states now permit the "appearance" to occur "in person or by electronic audio-visual device," *e.g.*, Fla. R. Crim. P. 3.130(a), or by "two-way closed circuit television." Ill. Code Crim. P. § 109-1(a). Federal Rule 5(f) permits videoconferencing with the defendant's permission.

When video methods are used, the defendant may be taken to a room in the jail equipped with a monitor and a video camera. The judge is located in a similar room in another building, perhaps a courthouse miles away. Ordinarily the video technology allows each to see and talk with the other. The session may be videotaped to memorialize the proceeding.

[1]   Felony-Misdemeanor Distinctions

Both the content and importance of the initial appearance may turn upon the felony-misdemeanor distinction. In federal cases, and in most states, more detailed initial appearance procedures exist for misdemeanor cases. For example, some jurisdictions expressly permit the criminal accused to plead guilty at the initial appearance in a misdemeanor case. In specific federal misdemeanor cases, the magistrate judge also is empowered to take guilty pleas. *See* Fed. R. Crim. P. 58(b)(3)(A). This, in effect, turns the initial appearance into an arraignment (discussed more fully in Chapter 11).

[2]   Timing

In federal criminal cases and in approximately one-half of the states, statutes or court rules provide that the defendant must appear before the magistrate "without unnecessary delay." The federal provision is contained in Rule 5 of the Federal Rules of Criminal Procedure, discussed below. The purpose of this requirement of a rather prompt hearings is to minimize the likelihood of a coerced confession, to apprise the defendant of his or her rights, and to perform a number of routine administrative and scheduling functions.

While this standard may suggest an almost immediate appearance in court, it is possible that an accused person will be held in custody several days before making this appearance. This delay is especially likely to occur in a smaller community in which a magistrate may be available only during the five-day work week. Some states now prescribe exact time limits, ranging from twenty-four to seventy-two hours as the maximum allowable time span within which the accused must be brought before a magistrate. *See* Wendy L. Brandes, *Post-Arrest Detention and the Fourth Amendment: Refining the Standard of Gerstein v. Pugh*, 22 Colum. J. L. & Soc. Prob. 445 (1989). Of course, *McLaughlin* mandates a *Gerstein* hearing within forty-eight hours of a warrantless arrest in most cases, but remember that a *Gerstein* hearing is not necessarily an initial appearance.

[3]   Federal Rule 5

Rule 5 of the Federal Rules of Criminal Procedure provides as follows:

FEDERAL RULES OF CRIMINAL PROCEDURE

Rule 5. Initial Appearance Before the Magistrate Judge

(a) **In General.**

(1) **Appearance Upon an Arrest.**

(A) A person making an arrest within the United States must take the defendant without unnecessary delay before a magistrate judge, or before a state or local judicial officer as Rule 5(c) authorizes, unless a statute provides otherwise.

(B) A person making an arrest outside the United States must take the defendant without unnecessary delay before a magistrate judge unless a statute provides otherwise.

(2) Exceptions.

(A) An officer making an arrest under a warrant issued on a complaint charging solely a violation of 18 U.S.C. § 1073 need not comply with this rule if:

(i) the person arrested is transferred without unnecessary delay to the custody of appropriate state or local authorities in the district of arrest; and

(ii) an attorney for the government moves promptly, in the district where the warrant was issued, to dismiss the complaint.

(B) If a defendant is arrested for violating probation or supervised release, Rule 32.1 applies.

(C) If a defendant is arrested for failing to appear in another district, Rule 40 applies.

(3) Appearance Upon a Summons. When a defendant appears in response to a summons under Rule 4, a magistrate judge must proceed under Rule 5(d) or (e), as applicable.

(b) Arrest Without a Warrant. If a defendant is arrested without a warrant, a complaint meeting Rule 4(a)'s requirement of probable cause must be promptly filed in the district where the offense was allegedly committed.

(c) Place of Initial Appearance; Transfer to Another District.

(1) Arrest in the District Where the Offense Was Allegedly Committed. If the defendant is arrested in the district where the offense was allegedly committed:

(A) the initial appearance must be in that district; and

(B) if a magistrate judge is not reasonably available, the initial appearance may be before a state or local judicial officer.

(2) Arrest in a District Other Than Where the Offense Was Allegedly Committed. If the defendant was arrested in a district other than where the offense was allegedly committed, the initial appearance must be:

(A) in the district of arrest; or

(B) in an adjacent district if:

(i) the appearance can occur more promptly there; or

(ii) the offense was allegedly committed there and the initial appearance will occur on the day of arrest.

(3) Procedures in a District Other Than Where the Offense Was Allegedly Committed. If the initial appearance occurs in a district other than where the offense was allegedly committed, the following procedures apply:

(A) the magistrate judge must inform the defendant about the provisions of Rule 20;

(B) if the defendant was arrested without a warrant, the district court where the offense was allegedly committed must first issue a warrant before the magistrate judge transfers the defendant to that district;

(C) the magistrate judge must conduct a preliminary hearing if required by Rule 5.1;

(D) the magistrate judge must transfer the defendant to the district where the offense was allegedly committed if:

(i) the government produces the warrant, a certified copy of the warrant, or a reliable electronic form of either; and

(ii) the judge finds that the defendant is the same person named in the indictment, information, or warrant; and

(E) when a defendant is transferred and discharged, the clerk must promptly transmit the papers and any bail to the clerk in the district where the offense was allegedly committed.

(d) Procedure in a Felony Case.

(1) Advice. If the defendant is charged with a felony, the judge must inform the defendant of the following:

(A) the complaint against the defendant, and any affidavit filed with it;

(B) the defendant's right to retain counsel or to request that counsel be appointed if the defendant cannot obtain counsel;

(C) the circumstances, if any, under which the defendant may secure pretrial release;

(D) any right to a preliminary hearing; and

(E) the defendant's right not to make a statement, and that any statement made may be used against the defendant.

(2) Consulting with Counsel. The judge must allow the defendant reasonable opportunity to consult with counsel.

(3) Detention or Release. The judge must detain or release the defendant as provided by statute or these rules.

(4) Plea. A defendant may be asked to plead only under Rule 10.

(e) Procedure in a Misdemeanor Case. If the defendant is charged with a misdemeanor only, the judge must inform the defendant in accordance with Rule 58(b)(2).

(f) Video Teleconferencing. Video teleconferencing may be used to conduct an appearance under this rule if the defendant consents.

NOTES

1. *Impact of arrest warrant.* Note that Rule 5 mandates an initial appearance for almost every arrested person, irrespective of whether the arrest was with or without an arrest warrant. How will this hearing differ depending on whether or not there was an arrest warrant? What happens if the person was arrested by warrant charging only a violation of 18 U.S.C. § 1073, unlawful flight to avoid prosecution?

2. *Function if probable cause already found.* If the arrest was made pursuant to an arrest warrant (and therefore probable cause was found), what function(s) will the initial appearance serve?

3. *Without unnecessary delay.* Rule 5(a)(1)(A) and (B) require the defendant to be brought before a magistrate "without unnecessary delay." This standard involves a case-by-case review of a number of factors, such as the length of the delay, reasons for the delay, and whether an involuntary confession was obtained. Is this "without unnecessary delay" standard too vague? Would it be better to adopt the *McLaughlin* forty-eight hour rule for both the initial appearance and the *Gerstein* determination?

4. *Arrest in another district.* What happens if a person is arrested in a district other than that in which the offense was committed and in which the trial will be held? Rule 40(a) provides that in some such situations the person must be taken without unnecessary delay before the nearest available federal magistrate judge, in accordance with Rule 5. Rule 5 states that a person must be brought before a federal magistrate judge or a state or local officer, which could mean one in the state or district of arrest rather than the one where the charges are pending.

5. *Preliminary examination.* You will note that Rule 5 includes language regarding the defendant's right to a preliminary examination. That is the subject of the next chapter and is covered also in Rule 5.1 of the Federal Rules of Criminal Procedure.

[a] Remedy: Dismissal of Charges

What is the remedy for an unreasonably delayed initial appearance? Almost all federal courts have held that the right to timely initial appearance is procedural, not substantive, and therefore Rule 5 violations do not require dismissal of an indictment, even for extensive delays in holding the initial appearance. *See, e.g., United States v. Dyer,* 325 F. 3d 464, 470 n. 2 (3rd Cir. 2003). In *United States v. Osunde,* 638 F. Supp. 171 (N.D. Cal. 1986), however, the court characterized a 106 day delay between arrest and initial appearance as a "flagrant violation" of Rule 5 which warranted dismissal with prejudice. *Osunde* has not been followed by other federal courts.

[b] Remedy: Exclusion of Evidence

The primary remedy for violation of Rule 5 is the exclusion of evidence obtained during the period of this impermissible delay.

[i] Searches and Seizures

In some circumstances, the failure to hold a prompt initial appearance can lead to the exclusion of evidence obtained through a consensual search. The delayed hearing can cause the consent-to-search to be invalidated. *See, e.g., United States v. Iribe,* 806 F. Supp. 917 (D. Colo. 1992).

[ii] Confessions

McNabb-Mallory. The remedy for a delayed initial appearance is that confessions obtained before the hearing may be excluded as evidence at trial. According to the so-called "*McNabb-Mallory* rule," derived years before *Gerstein* from the cases of *Mallory v. United States,* 354 U.S. 449 (1957), and *McNabb v. United States,* 318 U.S. 332 (1943), statements made by suspects during a period of unnecessary delay in bringing them before a magistrate are inadmissible at a federal trial. *McNabb-Mallory* excluded the statements whether or not they were given voluntarily and irrespective of the presence or absence of *Miranda* warnings and a voluntary waiver of fifth amendment rights. As one court explained:

> [T]he protection of the right of an accused to prompt production before a judicial officer following arrest will be most effectively accomplished by a per se exclusionary rule. Not only is such a rule calculated to deter unlawful detentions and to preserve the integrity of the criminal justice system, but it is likely to assure more certain and even-handed application of the prompt presentment requirement . . .

Johnson v. Maryland, 384 A.2d 709, 717 (Md. App. 1978).

This *McNabb-Mallory* exclusionary rule was based upon the Supreme Court's supervisory authority over criminal justice in federal courts. It was not mandated by the Fourth Amendment or any other part of the United States Constitution, and applied whether the accused was arrested with or without an arrest warrant.

Since the *McNabb-Mallory* exclusionary rule is not binding upon states, the vast majority of state courts have rejected it and instead use a "totality test" to determine the admissibility of a confession under these circumstances. In these jurisdictions, a statement given by a suspect who has not been promptly presented to a judicial officer is not, per se, inadmissible; delay in presenting the suspect is simply one factor in evaluating the overall voluntariness of the confession. *See, e.g., People v. Cipriano,* 429 N.W.2d 781 (Mich. 1988) (extensive discussion).

Federal statute — the six hour "safe harbor." Congress itself reacted negatively to the *McNabb-Mallory* rule in 1968 and enacted 18 U.S.C. § 3501(c). This statute overturned one facet of McNabb-Mallory. It distinguished between delays of up to six hours and those of longer duration.

The statute established a rule that virtually insulated confessions from attack on the basis of delays of six hours or less between arrest and confession. This is the so-called "safe harbor" provision. This statute provides that a custodial confession "shall not be inadmissible [in federal court] solely because of delay in bringing [the accused] before a magistrate" if the confession was made voluntarily and within six hours (or more if reasonably necessary because of transportation requirements) of arrest. 18 U.S.C. § 3501(c).

There is a split of authority about confessions made more than six hours from arrest. One view is that a confession made in violation of the six hour rule may be excluded under the *McNabb-Mallory* rule if the delay was unreasonable and even if the confession was voluntary. *See United States v. Superville*, 40 F. Supp.2d 672 (D. V.I. 1999)(suppressing confession made 7 days after end of 6-hour safe harbor; voluntariness irrelevant); *United States v. Perez*, 733 F.2d 1026 (2d Cir. 1984).

Another view is that such confessions are inadmissible if involuntary; the length of delay alone is not sufficient reason to exclude the confession. *See, e.g., United States v. Ostrander*, 411 F.3d 684 (6th Cir. 2005); *United States v. Hornbeck*, 118 F.3d 615 (8th Cir. 1997).

Some courts have found delays beyond six hours to be reasonable under the circumstances. *See, e.g., United States v. Rivera-Ruiz*, 797 F. Supp. 78 (D. P.R. 1992) (10 hour delay between arrest and confession permissible; 6 hour rule inapplicable because extra time needed to continue boat investigation and defendant's arrest occurred at sea). In determining reasonableness, courts look at such facts as transportation and distance to the magistrate, the availability of the magistrate, the need for routine processing and lodging, and any medical or family matter that affected the delay.

Motive for delay. The government's motive is also a factor in determining reasonableness of delay. In *United States v. Wilbon*, 911 F. Supp. 1420 (D.N.M. 1995), there was a delay of thirty-eight and one-half hours between the defendant's arrest and the initial appearance. Additionally, the U.S. District Court determined that the FBI agent intentionally exploited the delay for the purpose of obtaining a "last minute" confession. Therefore, the Court held that under § 3501 the confession must be suppressed "regardless of voluntariness" as "an appropriate means to deter similar misconduct in the future."

Federal-state issues. The federal statute clearly applies to a person arrested on federal charges, but does it also apply to someone arrested on *state* charges who is in state custody but interrogated by federal agents concerning a possible federal criminal violation? In *United States v. Alvarez-Sanchez*, 511 U.S. 350 (1994), the United States Supreme Court answered that question "no." The defendant's conviction was upheld, as was the admissibility of the confession used in the federal criminal case, even though more than forty-eight hours had elapsed between his arrest and interrogation by federal officials. The Court noted that the defendant was under arrest on state charges at the time when he made inculpatory statements to Secret Service agents and that there was no evidence of a "collusive arrangement" between state and federal agents.

Rule 5, like 18 U.S.C. § 3501, also applies only to a person in federal custody. What should be the result, however, if federal and state authorities have a "working arrangement" designed to have a person arrested by state authorities so that federal authorities could conduct an interrogation unimpeded by Rule 5? *See, e.g., Anderson v. United States*, 318 U.S. 350 (1943) (strikers unlawfully arrested and held by state authorities, and interrogated by federal agents; confession held inadmissible because it was the product of an impermissible "working relationship" between state and federal officers); *United States v. Roberts*, 928 F. Supp 910 (W.D. Mo. 1996) (defendant's arrest and detention by state authorities held improper pretext for sole purpose of furthering federal criminal investigation).

The defendant has the burden of establishing collusion between state and federal officers.

Chapter 5
CUSTODY AND RELEASE PENDING TRIAL

A. INTRODUCTION

When a crime suspect is taken into custody, a number of events, both formal and informal, occur prior to final case disposition (whether by voluntary dismissal, guilty plea or trial). The lapse of time between arrest and final disposition may be from several days to many months. Occasionally, several years will elapse between arrest and trial. Perhaps one of the most extreme examples is that of Raymond Buckey, who was detained without bail for almost four years. Ultimately, he was either acquitted of child molestation charges or his trials ended in mistrials. *See* Marc Miller & Martin Guggenheim, *Pretrial Detention and Punishment*, 75 MINN. L. REV. 335, 335–338 (1990).

One study reported that defendants released pending trial waited a median time of 127 days from arrest to adjudication, while those who were detained had a median wait of only 47 days. Bureau of Justice Statistics, U.S. Dept. Of Justice, *Pretrial Release of Felony Defendants in State Courts* (Nov. 2007). This is consistent with rules or practices in many locales that give preference to trials of detained defendants. *See generally* ABA Standards for Criminal Justice, Pretrial Detention, Standard 10-5.11(3d ed. 2007)(recommending accelerated time limits for detained defendants).

The suspect may avoid being taken into custody in some circumstances. Sometimes a police official will release a defendant by means of a *citation release*. This procedure involves giving the defendant a "ticket" or written order to appear in court on a specified date. It is employed in minor cases, such as traffic violations, and it results in the immediate release of the defendant at the time of the issuance of the citation (sometimes referred to as a non-custodial arrest).

If the defendant is taken to the police station for booking, a law enforcement official may permit the immediate release of the defendant. This is done either by way of a modified citation release or by posting bail according to a bail schedule, discussed later in this chapter. Generally, persons charged with misdemeanors are routinely released. In the case of felony charges, however, the accused faces a more formidable task in obtaining freedom prior to case disposition. Generally, a judicial officer must decide whether the defendant will be released.

B. COMPETING POLICIES AND CONCERNS

[1] Society's Need for Pretrial Detention

[a] Appearance at Proceedings

The most widely accepted justification for detention of a suspect after arrest is that imprisonment guarantees presence of the defendant at his or her upcoming trial and other proceedings.

[b] Prevent Destruction or Alteration of Evidence

Similarly, to the extent that society is worried about the defendant's ability to unfairly or inappropriately "alter" evidence (through intimidation of witnesses, for example), pretrial incarceration increases the likelihood of a fair fact-finding process.

[c] Prevent Future Harm

A third, and certainly most controversial, rationale in favor of pretrial detention is that the defendant's incarceration protects society from further criminal harm that may be inflicted by the defendant prior to trial (thus the expression "preventive detention"). This rationale is troublesome on several fronts. First, since the defendant awaiting trial is presumed innocent, this justification rings of "punishment" prior to a criminal conviction. Similarly, protecting society from future criminal acts of the defendant rests upon a speculative or predictive judgment as to the defendant's likelihood to commit further criminal acts. While we may intuitively believe that a particular suspect will commit offenses prior to trial, are we capable of making that judgment in a reliable way? Many would answer "No." *See* Marc Miller & Martin Guggenheim, *Pretrial Detention and Punishment*, 75 MINN. L. REV. 335 (1990), in which these predictive judgments are characterized as unscientific and inaccurate.

[d] Terrorism: The PATRIOT Act and other Laws

The threat of terrorism has engendered a number of legal issues involving detention. One important decision held that the government may detain aliens who have been convicted of a serious crime and are awaiting deportation. *Demore v. Kim*, 538 U.S. 510 (2003).

A related issue involved the detention of foreign nationals who had been apprehended in Afghanistan after September 11, 2001, and taken to the American prison in Guantanamo Bay, Cuba. The plaintiffs in *Rasul v. Bush*, 542 U.S. 466 (2004), were nationals of countries that were not engaged in a formal war with the United States, denied any terrorist acts, and had not been charged with any crimes. The Supreme Court held that federal courts had jurisdiction in cases challenging the legality of the detainees at Guantanamo. A similar result occurred when the Court held that a United States citizen, captured in Afghanistan but held in the United States and categorized by the government as an "enemy combatant," had a due process right to challenge the factual basis for the detention by bringing the case before a neutral decision maker. *Hamdi v. Rumsfeld*, 543 U.S. 507 (2004).

Another terrorist-related detention issue is the use of the statute permitting the detention of material witnesses to be used to detain people allegedly involved in terrorist activity. This is discussed below in the context of the Federal Bail Reform Act. *See generally*, R.V. Stevens, *Keeping the U.S.A Patriot Act in Check one Material Witness at a Time*, 81 N.C.L. REV. 2157 (2003).

Since September 11, 2001, Congress has actively enacted legislation designed to fight the threat of terrorism. The primary vehicle is the 2001 PATRIOT Act, a title which stands for Providing Appropriate Tools Required to Intercept and Obstruct Terrorism. The Act embraces many topics, such as wiretapping, freezing assets, and immigration. It also covers pretrial detention. One provision authorizes the Attorney General to detain any alien whom the Attorney General certifies is engaged in any activity that endangers the national security of the United States or is involved in other anti-government pursuits and is therefore deportable. The alien must be subjected to deportation proceedings or charged with a crime no later than seven days after detention begins. 8 U.S.C. § 1226a.

Involvement in terrorist activities may also trigger pretrial detention under the Federal Bail Reform Act, discussed below. People in this category are ordinarily charged with criminal activity under federal criminal law.

[2] Defendant's Need for Freedom Pending Trial

We should never overlook the quite obvious fact that at this stage of a criminal case, guilt beyond a reasonable doubt has not been established, though there may have been an arrest warrant based on a finding that there is a reasonable probability that the defendant committed a crime. The presumptively innocent defendant, then, arguably is entitled to freedom prior to a finding of guilt beyond a reasonable doubt. Additionally, incarceration prior to trial may mean psychological harm and lost wages, at best, or a lost job or family, at worst. These financial consequences may also impair the defendant's ability to support a family and retain private defense counsel. *See generally* ABA, Standards for Criminal Justice, Pretrial Release § 10-1.1 (3d ed. 2007) (law favors pretrial release).

Even with counsel, the incarcerated defendant is at a disadvantage in assisting counsel in preparation for trial. For example, the defendant may be unable to assist in investigating the case and locating witnesses. One scholar suggests the harm is especially great when the defendant is factually innocent:

> Courts, legislatures, and commentators have acknowledged (without serious contradiction) that pretrial detention can hamper the defense by making it difficult for the suspect and his lawyer to find witnesses, gather and review evidence, and consult about strategy.
>
> The problem is that the *ex ante* decision of whether defendant will appear at trial or commit other crimes bears no necessary relationship to the degree of assistance that the accused can provide in preparing his case. . . . We might, however, hypothesize that there is a positive correlation between the falsity of the accusation and the suspect's need to assist in the defense. It might be precisely when the wrong person has been charged that factual development, alibis, and hard-to-find evidence are the most vital to the case.

Andrew D. Leipold, *How the Pretrial Process Contributes to Wrongful Convictions*, 42 Am. Crim. L. Rev. 1123, 1130 (2005).

C. HISTORY OF BAIL

The relevant language of the eighth amendment in the United States Constitution provides "excessive bail shall not be required." This clause was adopted almost verbatim from the Virginia Declaration of Rights of 1776, which, itself, was derived from the English Bill of Rights of 1689. Chief Judge Newman, writing for the District of Columbia Court of Appeals in *United States v. Edwards*, 430 A.2d 1321, 1326–1327 (1981), described the history of English bail as follows:

> The English bail system developed out of the ancient Anglo-Saxon forms of sureties into early common law bail. By the thirteenth century, . . . the sheriff exercised a broad and ill-defined discretionary power to bail the King's prisoners committed to his custody. This power was widely abused by sheriffs who extorted money from individuals entitled to release without charge and who accepted bribes from those who were not otherwise entitled to bail. The first statutory regulation of bail . . . sought to curb such abuses by carefully enumerating which offenses were bailable and which were not.
>
> Further limitations on the discretion to grant bail were enacted to cure defects in the law which the Stuarts exploited to deny release to particular prisoners. Procedural abuses by the Stuarts [eventually] led to the . . . Habeas Corpus Act of 1679, which closed the procedural loopholes by firmly establishing a means for enforcing the rights of bail and habeas corpus. When, thereafter, the protections of the Habeas Corpus Act were circumvented by the practice of setting prohibitively high bail, the excessive bail clause was drafted into the Bill of Rights of 1689, in order to correct this injustice. In sum, the excessive bail clause was developed as a specific remedy for judicial abuse of the bail procedure as otherwise established by law, and did not, in and of itself, imply any right to bail.

D. CONSTITUTIONAL CONSTRAINTS

The Eighth Amendment bans "excessive bail" but does not explicitly guarantee a right to bail. As will be seen later in this chapter, federal legislation precluding bail under some circumstances has been upheld by the United States Supreme Court. Most, if not all, states have bail provisions in their state constitutions. Some, such as Michigan and New York, have adopted the language of the federal Eighth Amendment verbatim. Others explicitly create an affirmative right to bail. The Florida Constitution, for example, provides that "unless charged with a capital offense or an offense punishable by life imprisonment and the proof of guilt is evident or the presumption is great, every person charged with a crime . . . shall be entitled to pretrial release on reasonable conditions." Fla. Const. art. I, § 14.

While all states provide that bail may be denied in capital cases, states differ with respect to which other offenses are considered non-bailable. Some states do not grant the right to bail when a defendant has been charged with an offense punishable as treason (Oregon) or cases where the defendant has been accused of a violent felony (Florida). Both California and Florida also authorize the denial of bail if the defendant poses a risk of harm to others. *See, e.g.*, Cal. Const. art. I, § 12(b) ("the court finds based on clear and convincing evidence that there is a substantial likelihood that the person's release would result in great bodily harm to others"), (c) ("the court finds based on clear and convincing evidence that the person has threatened another with great bodily harm and that there is a substantial likelihood that the person would carry out the threat if released"); Fla. Const. art. I, § 14 ("If no conditions of release can reasonably protect the community from risk of physical harm to persons, assure the presence of the accused at trial, or assure the integrity of the judicial process, the accused may be detained").

E. FORMS OF RELEASE PENDING TRIAL

If it is determined that the defendant should be released prior to trial, various forms or categories of release typically are available in each jurisdiction. Generally, the judge making the pretrial release decision has considerable discretion in selecting a particular form of release. Note, however, that the Bail Reform Act of 1984, discussed below, mandates that federal defendants be released "on personal recognizance, or upon execution of an unsecured appearance bond in an amount specified by the court" unless it is determined that either form of pretrial release will not reasonably assure appearance of the defendant at trial or will endanger the safety of the community. 18 U.S.C. § 3142(b).

The typical release categories are described below.

[1] Full Cash Bond

After a judge sets a dollar amount of bail, the defendant must post the full amount in cash with the court in order to be released from custody. If the defendant appears in court as scheduled, he or she gets back all the deposited money. If the accused fails to appear, the court can order a forfeiture of the full cash bond. For example, a person charged with aggravated robbery may be required to post bond in the amount of $25,000. Upon payment of this full amount to the court, the defendant will be released from jail. The full $25,000 will be returned to the defendant when he or she appears at trial.

A study of state pretrial release of felony defendants in the 75 largest counties found that only three percent of those released pending trial posted a full cash bond. Bureau of Justice Statistics, U.S. Dept. Of Justice, *Pretrial Release of Felony Defendants in State Courts* (Nov. 2007).

Because of concerns that the money used to post bond was obtained through illegal activities, such as drugs or gambling, the court may inquire into its source and conduct a hearing on the issue. *See United States v. Nebbia*, 357 F.2d 303 (2d Cir. 1966)(leading case). If the defendant does not account for the money or the hearing shows its source was illegal, the court may refuse to accept the money in satisfaction of the bond. The prosecution may gain considerable discovery during this hearing.

[2] Deposit Bond

The defendant is required to deposit a percentage of the full bond (usually 10 percent) with the court. Failure to appear could result in an order that the remaining amount of the bond (usually 90 percent) be paid by the defendant. Appearance at court often results in a return of the initial 10 percent deposit, but the court may retain a small percentage of that amount for administrative costs (often 10 percent of the initial 10 percent amount, or 1 percent of the total amount). Assuming the aggravated robbery defendant faces the same $25,000 bond, this procedure allows the defendant to deposit $2,500 with the court to secure immediate release. If the defendant fails to appear for trial, the court may order the defendant to pay the remaining $22,500. If the defendant appears as scheduled, however, the court will refund all of the initial $2,500 deposit, less an appropriate administrative fee (10 percent of the initial deposit, or $250).

A study of state pretrial release of felony defendants in the 75 largest counties found that only six percent of those released pending trial posted a deposit cash bond. Bureau of Justice Statistics, U.S. Dept. Of Justice, *Pretrial Release of Felony Defendants in State Courts* (Nov. 2007).

[3] Surety Bond

[a] Professional Bond Companies

This is the "traditional" form of bail in which a third party, usually a bail bonding company, signs a promissory note to the court for the full bail amount and then charges the defendant a percentage of that full amount as a fee. The "surety" ordinarily must meet statutory or court-ordered criteria to ensure its financial soundness. Nationally, there are about 14,000 commercial bail agents who secure the release of two million defendants annually. Bureau of Justice Statistics, U.S. Dept. Of Justice, *Pretrial Release of Felony Defendants in State Courts* (Nov. 2007). Four states (Illinois, Kentucky, Oregon and Wisconsin) do not allow commercial bail businesses. *Id.*

A study of state pretrial release of felony defendants in the 75 largest counties found that twenty percent of those released pending trial posted a surety bond. Bureau of Justice Statistics, U.S. Dept. Of Justice, *Pretrial Release of Felony Defendants in State Courts* (Nov. 2007).

Usually the fee is 10 percent of the total bond. If the defendant fails to appear in court as scheduled, the court can order the bonding company to pay the full bail amount to the court. Many bond companies require the defendant to post collateral to ensure that the company is protected from loss if the defendant absconds.

Often the court will give the bond company time to locate and return the defendant to court. If the company is successful in obtaining the defendant's presence at court, the judge may reward the company by refusing to require it to pay the amount of the bond. Indeed, in some locales the bond company can obtain a refund of a forfeited bond it has paid if, perhaps years after a defendant absconded, the company locates and returns him or her to court.

There is also substantial authority for the court to relieve the bond company of its contractual duty to pay the bond in the interests of "justice." *See, e.g.*, Fed. R. Crim. P. 46(f)(2)(no forfeiture ordered if "justice does not require forfeiture" of bond amount). This could occur if a defendant absconded before trial, triggering forfeiture by the bond company, but then was soon apprehended by police in another jurisdiction.

Contrary to the deposit bond, however, if the defendant makes all scheduled court appearances, he or she receives no refund of the initial 10 percent fee paid for the surety bond. The bond company retains this as its fee for the transaction. By contract, the accused is legally obligated to reimburse the bond company for any money the company has to pay to the court. Sometimes the bond company requires the offender to find a guarantor — someone who agrees to reimburse the company if it cannot locate the accused and must pay the bond amount to court.

[b]   Authority to Recapture

One of the most controversial aspects of the "traditional" bail system in the United States is the bonding company's broad authority to recapture the defendant. Using "skip tracers" (or "bounty hunters"), bond companies sometimes make substantial efforts to locate and return absconding offenders. While some states have placed statutory restrictions on the extent of the bonding company's power to arrest, the authority to arrest remains largely unrestrained. It has long been held that an American court has the power to try a defendant even though the defendant's presence was obtained by a forcible abduction. In *Frisbie v. Collins*, 342 U.S. 519 (1952), Justice Black noted that "[t]here is nothing in the Constitution that [permits] a guilty person rightfully convicted to escape justice because he was brought to trial against his will." *See also*, Andrew DeForest Patrick, Note, *Running From the Law: Should Bounty Hunters Be Considered State Actors and Thus Subject to Constitutional Restraints?*, 52 Vand. L. Rev. 171 (1998).

[c]   Policy Arguments

Many reformers have called for abolition of bail bonding companies. *See* Standards for Criminal Justice § 10-1.4 (3d ed. 2007) (compensated sureties should be abolished)(second edition commentary stated that the commercial bond business is "one of the most tawdry parts in the criminal justice system"). One argument is that law enforcement officers, not a for-profit business, should be responsible for locating and returning absconding defendants. Abusive arrests by bond company agents, sometimes constituting kidnaping, are cited in support of this argument. A second argument is that a prisoner's freedom should not be dependent on whether a for-profit business will guarantee a bond. Some critics also condemn bonding companies for excessive profits and corruption (such as bribing jailors or court personnel to recommend a particular bond company). Critics also argue that bail bonding companies actually reduce an offender's incentive to appear in court by minimizing the personal financial impact of absconding.

Defenders of bond companies argue that they save taxpayer dollars by reducing the prison population and shouldering some responsibility for ensuring that criminal defendants show up for trial or are returned to court if they abscond. This saves both correctional and police resources. Some empirical studies, however, have found that professional bonding companies are responsible for returning very few of the people who are captured after missing a scheduled court date. *See, e.g.*, Standards for Criminal Justice § 10-5.5 (2d ed. (1988)).

[4]   Unsecured Bond

This is considered to be the least restrictive financial release condition. The defendant is released from custody upon promising to pay the bond amount if he or she fails to appear in court. Initially, however, the defendant pays no money to the court, and no money changes hands if the defendant appears as scheduled. This is a preferred option in some states and in federal courts. *See* 18 U.S.C. § 3142(b). A study of state pretrial release of felony defendants in the 75 largest counties found that only four percent of those released pending trial posted an unsecured bond. Bureau of Justice Statistics, U.S. Dept. Of Justice, *Pretrial Release of Felony Defendants in State Courts* (Nov. 2007).

[5] Release on Recognizance (R.O.R.)

The court releases the defendant on the personal promise that the defendant will appear in court as required. Some jurisdictions attach conditions to the R.O.R. release, such as restricting travel or maintaining employment. In order to encourage the use of R.O.R., a number of jurisdictions have enacted laws creating a presumption of this form of release. Standards for Criminal Justice § 10-5.1(a) (3d ed. 2007) (commentary refers to 23 jurisdictions). R.O.R. is a preferred option in some states and in federal courts. This is a preferred option in some states and in federal courts. *See* 18 U.S.C. § 3142(b).

A study of state pretrial release of felony defendants in the 75 largest counties found that twenty percent of those released pending trial were released on their own recognizance. Bureau of Justice Statistics, U.S. Dept. Of Justice, *Pretrial Release of Felony Defendants in State Courts* (Nov. 2007).

[6] Citation Release

Often, a person arrested for a minor criminal offense (such as a traffic violation) is given a "citation" by the arresting officer. The citation orders the offender to appear for trial on a specific date. The defendant is not taken to a police station, is not required to make an initial court appearance, and suffers no serious deprivation of freedom. Many studies recommend the use of citation release whenever possible as a means of reducing unnecessary incarceration and saving police and correctional resources. *See, e.g.*, ABA Standards for Criminal Justice § 10-2.1 (3d ed. 2007) (citations should be used "to the maximum extent consistent with the effective enforcement of the law"). Some jurisdictions now mandate the use of citation release. *See* Cal. Penal Code § 853.6(i) (mandating citation release for misdemeanors unless one or more statutory conditions met).

If the defendant is taken to a police station for booking, the police may decide to release him or her without court involvement; this is referred to as "stationhouse release," which is another form of citation release. Another form of "at-station" release involves utilization of a bail schedule, by which a police official is permitted to receive money bail (either full cash bond or surety bond) according to a schedule calibrated to the crime allegedly committed by the defendant.

[7] Conditional Release

In addition to, or in place of, other pretrial release mechanisms, some jurisdictions provide for the release of a defendant subject to one or, usually, more conditions which are thought to assure the defendant's appearance at trial or to further safeguard the community while the defendant is free. These conditions may include restrictions on travel (including wearing a locating device), avoiding contact with identified individuals (such as witnesses or the victim), periodic reporting to law enforcement agencies, remaining in custody of a designated person, and undergoing medical treatment (including in-patient psychiatric care) or schooling. A comprehensive list of such conditions appears in § 3142(c) of the Bail Reform Act of 1984, the text of which appears in Part H. of this Chapter. Violation of a condition of release can lead to arrest and confinement pending trial or to citation for contempt of court.

A study of state pretrial release of felony defendants in the 75 largest counties found that eight percent of those released pending trial were released on conditional release. Bureau of Justice Statistics, U.S. Dept. Of Justice, *Pretrial Release of Felony Defendants in State Courts* (Nov. 2007).

Many courts have adopted the practice of conditioning pretrial release on the releasee's consent to warrantless searches and drug tests by government officials. Some authorities have held this condition, despite the defendant's "consent," violates the Fourth Amendment unless the search is based on probable cause. *See United States v. Scott*, 450 F.3d 863 (9th Cir. 2006). *See generally* Note, 119 Harv. L. Rev. 1630 (2006).

[8] Property Bond

Many states statutorily authorize a defendant who has been admitted to bail to post a property bond in lieu of the full cash bond. Some states specify that the property must have a market value of at least twice the amount of bail, *e.g.*, Cal. Penal Code § 1298, while other states require that the value of the property be at least one and one-half times the amount of bail. Tenn. Code Ann. § 40-11-122(1). States also vary with respect to deed and disclosure requirements.

A study of state pretrial release of felony defendants in the 75 largest counties found that only one percent of those released pending trial were released on a property bond. Bureau of Justice Statistics, U.S. Dept. Of Justice, *Pretrial Release of Felony Defendants in State Courts* (Nov. 2007).

F. PRETRIAL DETENTION AND RELEASE: FACTS AND FIGURES

According to a Bureau of Justice statistics study of state felony defendants in the largest counties from 1990–2004, over sixty percent of all felony defendants were released prior to case disposition. Bureau of Justice Statistics, U.S. Dept. Of Justice, *Pretrial Release of Felony Defendants in State Courts* (Nov. 2007). While various forms of pretrial release are available, generally the accused obtains release either by posting bail (a money amount designed to insure the defendant's subsequent court appearance) or by some form of non-financial release. Thirty percent of those released secured a "financial" release (surety bond, full cash bond or deposit bond), while thirty-two percent secured a "non-financial" release (release on recognizance, conditional, or unsecured bond). *Id.* Only six percent of all felony defendants were held without bail. Driving-related offenses resulted in the highest release rate (73%), while murder defendants were least likely to be released prior to trial (19%). Other release percentages for specific offenses were rape (53%), robbery (44%), burglary (49%) and drug sales (63%). *Id.*

Bail was set at a high amount or denied altogether in cases where the charges were for serious felony offenses. For example, 80% of murder defendants had either a high bail amount or were detained without bail. *Id.*

As noted above, sixty-two percent of felony defendants were released prior to disposition of their case and thirty-eight percent were detained. Of those detained, six percent were denied bail and thirty-two percent had bail set but could not find the financial resources to post the required amount. *Id.*

When bail was set, the higher the bail amount the less likely the defendant would be released on bail. Thus, the median amount of bail for detained defendants was $15,000, while it was $5,000 for those able to be released. The mean (average) numbers were more striking: $58,400 (detained) compared with $11,600 (released). When bail was set at $100,000 or more, release occurred in about 10 percent of the cases. By contrast, with bail set at under $5,000, 70% of the defendants in the study obtained pretrial release. *Id.*

The study analyzing state data from 1990–2004 found that approximately 75 percent of all felony defendants who secured release prior to trial made all scheduled court appearances. More than 10 percent of released defendants were re-arrested for a felony offense committed while on pretrial release. Defendants with one prior felony conviction had a higher rate of pretrial misconduct (rearrest or failure to appear) than defendants with a history of at least one misdemeanor conviction or no prior conviction at all. *Id.*

Looking at race, the study found that 68% of white arrestees were released, while 62% of blacks and 55% of Hispanics were released. The study noted that the low rate for Hispanics may be due to immigration "holds" causing defendants to be held pending further processing on immigration issues. *Id.*

G. THE BAIL HEARING

The bail hearing, which may occur at the defendant's initial appearance or separately, is relatively informal. Often this is the first opportunity for both the government and the accused to present arguments related to (1) whether the accused should be released pending trial, and (2) if release is deemed appropriate, the terms and conditions, which may include the specific dollar amount of bail. In cases in which a "stationhouse release" decision has been previously made, if either the government or the accused is dissatisfied with the amount or conditions of release, the court may be asked to review those matters at the initial appearance or at any other time.

Pretrial release service agency. A number of jurisdictions have established a pretrial release service agency to assist in the release process. Agency staff may interview new jail prisoners to gather data about the prisoner's history and likely conduct if released. The agency may also run programs to supervise and assist persons on pretrial release. These duties may include employment counseling, regular monitoring, and even transportation to court. *See generally* ABA Standards for Criminal Justice § 10-1.10 (3d ed. 2007) (recommending that all jurisdictions provide a pretrial services agency).

Counsel. In many cases, the defendant is not represented by counsel at the bail hearing. One commentator noted that there is "a pervasive lack of guaranteed representation at a bail hearing, despite the defense attorney's critical role at such time." Douglas L. Colbert, *Thirty-Five Years After* Gideon: *The Illusory Right to Counsel at Bail Hearings*, 1998 U. ILL. L. REV. 1, 13 (noting that only 8 states and the District of Columbia guarantee that the accused has the assistance of counsel at this hearing). A study in Baltimore reported that defendants represented by counsel at bail hearings were 2½ times more likely than unrepresented defendants to be released on their own recognizance; even if not released, they were 4 times more likely to receive a reduction in the amount of bail. *See* 13 The Crim. Practice Report 22 (Nov. 3, 1999) (discussing the "Lawyer at Bail" project). If counsel is not present when a decision is made to detail the defendant, the issue may be revisited later when counsel becomes available.

Hearing. At the bail hearing, both sides may present evidence, including live witnesses and documentary proof. The rules of evidence generally do not apply. The hearing may be somewhat informal and will rarely last longer than a few minutes.

Sometimes judges announce decisions without giving their reasons, although it is recommended that judges be required to give reasons for any decision other than release on the offender's promise to return. *See, e.g.*, Standards for Criminal Justice § 10-5.1 (3d ed. 2007). Some jurisdictions require regular reports to the judge on the status of prisoners unable to meet the conditions of release. This is designed to provide a review to ensure that efforts are being made to secure the offender's release or to expedite the proceedings and minimize pretrial detention. It is not uncommon to provide an expedited trial for offenders unable to obtain pretrial release.

Judges have considerable discretion in deciding upon the amount of bail. One commentator has noted that judges sometimes go beyond the language of bail statutes in order to achieve objectives other than guaranteeing a defendant's future appearance in court:

> First, some judges view bail as a punitive measure and set bail at a high level in the belief that the defendant has committed the crime and deserves detention or at least temporary economic hardship. Second, others view bail as a means to implement preventive detention. Bail is set at an amount which is beyond the

economic means of defendants in order to protect society from those who would, in the judge's view, commit crimes while free during the pretrial period."

Paul B. Wice, BAIL AND ITS REFORM: A NATIONAL SURVEY 5 (1973).

A judge's bail decision is subject to review by the same or an equivalent judge or one from a higher court. Either the prosecutor or the defendant may request the review.

Role of victim. The usual rule is that the victim of crimes plays no role in the decision about release from detention. However, the federal Crime Victim's Rights Act, 18 U.S.C. § 3771 changes this by giving victims the right to timely notice of any public court proceeding involving "any release" of the accused. It also states that the victim has the right to be "reasonably heard" at a public proceeding involving release and to confer with the prosecutor. Do you agree that the victim should have some say in whether a criminal accused is released from detention? How much weight should the court give the victim's preferences? If you were defense counsel, would you try to convince the victim to approve release on bail or at least not to oppose it?

PROBLEM 5-1. CLYDE'S PLIGHT

Clyde Hopkins, a 26-year old male, was charged with burglary of a home in the daytime. The offense allegedly occurred August 3. He was arrested August 10, and was in possession of a very small amount of cocaine at the time of his arrest. His record shows one prior conviction for burglary two years ago, resulting in a suspended sentence, and one conviction for possession of cocaine eighteen months ago, resulting in a jail sentence of 60 days. Hopkins lives with his mother (with whom he has lived all of his life), is presently unemployed, and is a high school graduate. He has worked as a dishwasher in several local restaurants, but has lost each job for failing to report to work on schedule. He has not had steady employment in six months. Hopkins was previously placed on parole after serving his jail term and apparently established an excellent record while on parole, which was successfully completed three months ago. He was also released on money bail in his two prior cases and appeared for trial in each case according to schedule.

Under state law the maximum sentence that could be imposed is eight years' incarceration (assuming prior convictions for burglary and possession of cocaine). In all likelihood, even if the defendant were to receive that sentence, he would be released on parole in approximately two years.

1. As prosecutor, what arguments would you make in support of a recommendation that Mr. Hopkins not be released on bail? Assuming that the court decides to release the accused, what amount would you recommend for bail? What conditions would you advocate?

2. As defense counsel, what arguments would you make in favor of releasing Hopkins on bail (or, perhaps even on personal recognizance)? Assuming that the judge has decided to release the accused, what should be the appropriate bail amount? If the judge were considering a "release on conditions" plan, what conditions would you advocate as defense counsel?

3. *Variation No. 1.* Assume that Clyde Hopkins is a first-time offender (meaning no record of prior arrests or convictions). Also assume that he has no permanent residence in the community and has described himself as "homeless." Also assume that at least three credible witnesses identified Hopkins as he left the victim's home immediately after commission of the alleged burglary. What relevance, if any, do each of these facts have with respect to the bail decision?

4. *Variation No. 2.* Assume that immediately after his arrest, Hopkins sent a letter to Ms. Adams, the burglary victim. She has turned the letter over to the prosecutor. The letter reads as follows:

Dear Ms. Adams,

I don't know why you think I am the man who stole property from your house. People have been accusing me of things all my life, and I do not know what I've done to deserve that kind of treatment. I am asking you to call the district attorney and tell her to drop these charges. Some people say I have a temper. When people don't do what I ask them to do, sometimes I get really mad.

Sincerely,

Clyde Hopkins

a. If you were the judge in a jurisdiction in which the bail statute provided that the sole issue in determining bail was "assuring the presence of the defendant at trial," would your decision with respect to the amount of bail be influenced by your knowledge of this letter?

b. Assume that your jurisdiction authorizes denial of bail (*i.e.*, preventive detention) where there is clear and convincing evidence of "future dangerousness" or "likely intimidation of witnesses." The Assistant District Attorney has recommended preventive detention based upon all the facts of this case, including the letter. As defense attorney, what arguments would you make in opposition to that motion?

NOTES

1. *Master bail schedules.* Many states continue to use *bail schedules* (sometimes known as *master bond schedules*), a system by which bail is set by the court or jail officials at a specified amount depending upon the alleged offense committed by the defendant. This system is quick and efficient because it requires virtually no exercise of discretion by the judicial officer. The use of a bail or bond schedule means that the only factor considered is the identity of the alleged offense; hence, circumstances of the individual defendant (community ties, assets, etc.) are usually irrelevant, though sometimes criminal history is considered.

The United States Supreme Court, in addressing the issue what is "excessive" under the Eighth Amendment, has said that "the fixing of bail for any individual defendant must be based upon standards relevant to the purpose of assuring the presence of that defendant." *Stack v. Boyle*, 342 U.S. 1, 5 (1951). Because the use of a bail schedule seems to run counter to the *Stack* principle, commentators have seriously questioned the constitutionality of reliance upon such schedules. *See* Steven Wisotsky, *Use of a Master Bond Schedule: Equal Justice Under Law?*, 24 U. MIAMI L. REV. 808 (1970). One unusual case holding that the practice of using a master bond list to set bail is violative of due process and equal protection is *Ackies v. Purdy*, 322 F. Supp. 38 (S.D. Fla. 1970)(hearing necessary before denial of release on bail). Another case upheld the practice of *not* including a particular crime on a master bond list. *Van Herreweghe v. Burke*, 36 P. 3d 65 (Ariz. App. 2001)(no violation of due process to omit felony DUI).

As discussed in *Ackies*, in many cases the amount of bail is set at such a high amount that it virtually ensures pretrial incarceration of the accused. A master bond list could certainly yield that result. Similarly, a judge may purposely set high bail to achieve the goal of pretrial detention. Conversely, however, the financially secure defendant is likely able to secure pretrial release if the amount of bail is arbitrarily based only on the identity of the alleged offense. As noted in *Ackies*, in both instances (virtually automatic incarceration or pretrial release), the interests of the accused and society are inadequately protected.

2. *Amount of bail.* Cases litigating the amount of bail produce few rules or patterns. In cases involving drug offenses and particularly violent crimes, appellate courts rarely hold that bail amounts are excessive. *See, e.g., Ex parte Willman*, 695 S.W.2d 752 (Tex. App. 1985) (defendant was indicted for delivery of some 2,000 grams of cocaine and faced a possible punishment of confinement for life and a fine not to exceed $250,000; bail set at $300,000; court noted that sometimes financial backers in drug cases are willing to forfeit bond money); *United States v. Auriemma*, 773 F.2d 1520 (11th Cir. 1985)($1,000,000 bail was reasonable where defendant was charged with importation of 800 pounds of cocaine and related drug offenses, even though numerous factors suggested a low risk of flight (Florida resident for 27 years, married with four children and an employment history)).

3. *Factors in bail reduction.* After a judge or bail schedule sets an amount of bail, the accused can ask the court to lower the amount. Bail reductions are ordered only when a multitude of mitigating factors are present, particularly where the defendant's indigency is clearly established. *See, e.g., Ex parte Delk*, 750 S.W.2d 816 (Tex. App. 1988) (indigent capital murder defendant received a reduction in bail from $100,000 to $35,000, even though he had made numerous attempts to escape from jail); *Short v. State*, 550 So. 2d 177 (Fla. App. 1989) (defendant, charged with attempted second degree murder, received a bail reduction from $20,000 to $5,000 because of her established indigency, family ties, and long-term residence in the community); *Vetri v. State*, 558 So. 2d 1097 (Fla. App. 1990) (defendant was charged with sexual battery upon a child and bail was set at $50,000; bail was thereafter reduced to $7,500 where he had been adjudicated indigent, had lived and worked in the community for several years, and had no prior record. *But see Lewis v. Telb*, 497 N.E.2d 1376 (Ohio App. 1985) (defendant, a 24-year old mother of two children who was unemployed and receiving welfare assistance, was charged with two counts of felonious assault and two counts of intimidation; she had previously failed to appear in court on prior charges regarding failure to confine a dog; $40,000 bail was considered neither excessive nor unreasonable; dissenting judge would have reduced her bond to $4,000).

4. *Factors in determining excessive bail.* Recall that the Eighth Amendment bans "excessive bail." Whether or not a bail schedule is used, courts tend to focus upon the nature of the offense — and likely period of incarceration, if convicted — in determining excessiveness of bail. As one court explained, "If an accused is charged with crimes the conviction for which would result in long incarceration, . . . the incentive to abscond is greater and the amount must be such as to discourage the accused from absconding." *Lewis v. Telb*, 497 N.E.2d 1376, 1380 (Ohio App. 1985).

5. *Skips.* People released on bail who abscond are often called *skips* (or *defaulters*). They are subject to arrest and prosecution for the original crime as well as for a separate offense called *bail jumping. See* 18 U.S.C. § 3146. This crime ordinarily reaches people who, released on bail or another mechanism, knowingly or wilfully fail to appear at a proceeding in violation of the terms of their release. Ordinarily the defendant may defend by proving that "uncontrollable circumstances" caused the nonappearance.

6. *Illegal immigrants.* An Arizona law barring pretrial release for felony arrestees who are illegal immigrants was upheld against an equal protection challenge as appropriate to prevent flight from the jurisdiction. *Hernandez v. Lynch*, 167 P.3d 1264 (Ariz. App. 2007). Do you agree with this approach to denial of pretrial release?

7. *Continuing problems.* Notwithstanding various reforms of bail practices in the United States, problems persist. A recent publication noted:

> Even after decades of bail reform, serious questions about the fairness and effectiveness of pretrial release in the United States have not been resolved. Continued reliance on financial bail as the currency of release decisions is a major reason. *Sub rosa* pretrial detention is the continued result, and the profiteering role of the bondsman still an unexplainable anachronism.

John Goldcamp, Michael Gottfredson, Peter Jones and Doris Weiland, Personal Liberty and Community Safety: Pretrial Release in the Criminal Court 307–308 (1995).

Professor H. Richard Uviller's thought-provoking book, The Tilted Playing Field: Is Criminal Justice Unfair? (1999), devotes one chapter (pp. 162–188) to the issue of bail.

He describes bail as "[a] nasty, miserable business that defies all pretense of reason and good judgment." Expressing wonder that judges don't "show their palms in despair every time a bail call is presented to them," he describes the bail decision as "casual, impulsive, largely idiosyncratic, totally arbitrary, wildly variable, and without any possibility of objective verification." *Id.* at 166.

H.   BAIL REFORM ACT OF 1984: INTRODUCTION

The Bail Reform Act of 1984 may be the most significant and controversial federal law ever adopted pertaining to the bail system. Not only does this statute follow the traditional view and authorize pretrial detention of defendants who will not likely appear at trial, it also permits the detention of defendants who present a risk of harm to society. Because this law has had a profound impact upon persons accused of federal crimes, coupled with the fact that it serves as a model for state legislatures, the text of the legislation appears in full below.

As you study the Bail Reform Act, keep in mind the overall significance of the legislation, perhaps best summarized as follows:

> The Bail Reform Act of 1984 attempts to solve the problem of the infliction of harm on innocent victims by defendants who have been released pending trial. Congress acknowledges that the measures it enacted to address this problem substantially depart from the principles which previously guided the bail system. The Act's new procedures are preventive in nature, authorizing detention of defendants who are determined to present an intolerable risk of committing future criminal acts before trial. In such instances, Congress has determined that the safety of the community outweighs the right of these defendants to be free until proven guilty at trial, a right which until now was generally assumed not to be subject to a balancing of interests approach. By legislatively authorizing such preventive measures, Congress has led the courts into an area which up until now they were unwilling to go, having previously limited [pretrial detention] to situations where the defendant had threatened the integrity of the judicial process.

Kenneth Frederick Berg, *The Bail Reform Act of 1984*, 34 EMORY L.J. 685, 739 (1985).

[1]   The Bail Reform Act of 1984

The following is the text of the Bail Reform Act of 1984 (as amended in 1996), 18 U.S.C. §§ 3141–3148.

§ 3141. *Release and detention authority generally*

(a) *Pending trial.* A judicial officer authorized to order the arrest of a person under section 3041 of this title before whom an arrested person is brought shall order that such person be released or detained, pending judicial proceedings, under this chapter.

(b) *Pending sentence or appeal.* A judicial officer of a court of original jurisdiction over an offense, or a judicial officer of a Federal appellate court, shall order that, pending imposition or execution of sentence, or pending appeal of conviction or sentence, a person be released or detained under this chapter.

§ 3142. *Release or detention of a defendant pending trial*

(a) *In general.* Upon the appearance before a judicial officer of a person charged with an offense, the judicial officer shall issue an order that, pending trial, the person be—

(1) released on personal recognizance or upon execution of an unsecured appearance bond, under subsection (b) of this section;

(2) released on a condition or combination of conditions under subsection (c) of this section;

(3) temporarily detained to permit revocation of conditional release, deportation, or exclusion under subsection (d) of this section; or

(4) detained under subsection (e) of this section.

(b) *Release on personal recognizance or unsecured appearance bond.* The judicial officer shall order the pretrial release of the person on personal recognizance, or upon execution of an unsecured appearance bond in an amount specified by the court, subject to the condition that the person not commit a Federal, State, or local crime during the period of release [and cooperate in providing a DNA sample], unless the judicial officer determines that such release will not reasonably assure the appearance of the person as required or will endanger the safety of any other person or the community.

(c)*Release on conditions.*

(1) If the judicial officer determines that the release described in subsection (b) of this section will not reasonably assure the appearance of the person as required or will endanger the safety of any other person or the community, such judicial officer shall order the pretrial release of the person—

(A) subject to the condition that the person not commit a Federal, State, or local crime during the period of release [and provide a DNA sample]; and

(B) subject to the least restrictive further condition, or combination or conditions, that such judicial officer determines will reasonably assure the appearance of the person as required and the safety of any other person and the community, which may include the condition that the person—

(i) remain in the custody of a designated person, who agrees to assume supervision and to report any violation of a release condition to the court, if the designated person is able reasonably to assure the judicial officer that the person will appear as required and will not pose a danger to the safety of any other person or the community;

(ii) maintain employment, or, if unemployed, actively seek employment;

(iii) maintain or commence an educational program;

(iv) abide by specified restrictions on personal associations, place of abode, or travel;

(v) avoid all contact with an alleged victim of the crime and with a potential witness who may testify concerning the offense;

(vi) report on a regular basis to a designated law enforcement agency, pretrial services agency, or other agency;

(vii) comply with a specified curfew;

(viii) refrain from possessing a firearm, destructive device, or other dangerous weapon;

(ix) refrain from excessive use of alcohol, or any use of a narcotic drug or other controlled substance, . . . [without a valid prescription];

(x) undergo available medical, psychological, or psychiatric treatment, including treatment for drug or alcohol dependency, and remain in a specified institution if required for that purpose;

(xi) execute an agreement to forfeit upon failing to appear as required, property of a sufficient unencumbered value, including money, as is reasonably necessary to assure the appearance of the person as required, and shall provide the court with proof of ownership and the value of the property along with information regarding existing encumbrances as the judicial officer may require;

(xii) execute a bail bond with solvent sureties; who will execute an agreement to forfeit in such amount as is reasonably necessary to assure appearance of the person as required and shall provide the court with information regarding the value of the assets and liabilities of the surety if other than an approved surety and the nature and extent of encumbrances against the surety's property; such surety shall have a net worth which shall have sufficient unencumbered value to pay the amount of the bail bond;

(xiii) return to custody for specified hours following release for employment, schooling, or other limited purposes; and

(xiv) satisfy any other condition that is reasonably necessary to assure the appearance of the person as required and to assure the safety of any other person and the community. [In cases involving a minor victim, a minimum condition of electronic monitoring and certain other specified conditions.]

(2) The judicial officer may not impose a financial condition that results in the pretrial detention of the person.

(3) The judicial officer may at any time amend the order to impose additional or different conditions of release.

(d) *Temporary detention to permit revocation of conditional release, deportation, or exclusion.* If the judicial officer determines that—

(1)the person—

(A)is, and was at the time the offense was committed, on—

(i) release pending trial for a felony under Federal, State, or local law;

(ii) release pending imposition or execution of sentence, appeal of sentence or conviction, or completion of sentence, for any offense under Federal, State, or local law; or

(iii) probation or parole for any offense under Federal, State, or local law; or

(B) is not a citizen of the United States or lawfully admitted for permanent residence . . . ; and

(2) such person may flee or pose a danger to any other person or the community;

such judicial officer shall order the detention of the person, for a period of not more than ten days, excluding Saturdays, Sundays, and holidays, and direct the attorney for the Government to notify the appropriate court, probation or parole official, or State or local law enforcement [or immigration] official. If the official fails or declines to take the person into custody during that period, the person shall be treated in accordance with the other provisions of this section, notwithstanding the applicability of other provisions of law governing release pending trial or deportation or exclusion proceedings. If temporary detention is sought under paragraph (1)(B) of this subsection, the person has the burden of proving to the court such person's United States citizenship or lawful admission for permanent residence.

(e) *Detention.* If, after a hearing pursuant to the provisions of subsection (f) of this section, the judicial officer finds that no condition or combination of conditions will reasonably assure the appearance of the person as required and the safety of any other person and the community, such judicial officer shall order the detention of the person before trial. In a case described in (f)(1) of this section, a rebuttable presumption arises that no condition or combination of conditions will reasonably assure the safety of any other person and the community if such judicial officer finds that—

(1) the person has been convicted of a Federal offense that is described in subsection (f)(1) of this section, or of a State or local offense that would have

been an offense described in subsection (f)(1) of this section if a circumstance giving rise to Federal jurisdiction had existed;

(2) the offense described in paragraph (1) of this subsection was committed while the person was on release pending trial for a Federal, State, or local offense; and

(3) a period of not more than five years has elapsed since the date of conviction, or the release of the person from imprisonment, for the offense described in paragraph (1) of this subsection, whichever is later.

Subject to rebuttal by the person, it shall be presumed that no condition or combination of conditions will reasonably assure the appearance of the person as required and the safety of the community if the judicial officer finds that there is probable cause to believe that the person committed an offense for which a maximum term of imprisonment of ten years or more is prescribed [for certain drug, firearms, or abuse-of-minors crimes.]

(f) *Detention hearing.* The judicial officer shall hold a hearing to determine whether any condition or combination of conditions set forth in subsection (c) of this section will reasonably assure the appearance of the person as required and the safety of any other person and the community—

(1) Upon motion of the attorney for the Government, in a case that involves—

(A) a crime of violence [or terrorism carrying a sentence of at least ten years];

(B) an offense for which the maximum sentence is life imprisonment or death;

(C) an offense for which a maximum term of imprisonment of ten years or more is prescribed in [specified drug crimes] or;

(D) any felony if such person had been convicted of two or more offenses described in subparagraphs (A) through (C) of this paragraph, or two or more State or local offenses that would have been offenses described in subparagraphs (A) through (C) of this paragraph if a circumstance giving rise to Federal jurisdiction had existed, or a combination of such offenses; or

(E) [crimes involving a minor victim or use of a firearm or destructive device or any other dangerous weapon or failure to register as a sex offender.]

(2) Upon motion of the attorney for the Government or upon the judicial officer's own motion in a case, that involves—

(A) a serious risk that such person will flee;

(B) a serious risk that the person will obstruct or attempt to obstruct justice, or threaten, injure, or intimidate, or attempt to threaten, injure, or intimidate, a prospective witness or juror.

The hearing shall be held immediately upon the person's first appearance before the judicial officer unless that person, or the attorney for the Government, seeks a continuance. Except for good cause, a continuance on motion of the person may not exceed five days (not including any intermediate Saturday, Sunday, or legal holiday), and a continuance on motion of the attorney for the Government may not exceed three days (not including any intermediate Saturday, Sunday, or legal holiday). During a continuance, the person shall be detained, and the judicial officer, on motion of the attorney for the Government or sua sponte, may order that, while in custody, a person who appears to be a narcotics addict receive a medical examination to determine whether such person is an addict. At the hearing, the person has the right to be represented by counsel, and, if financially unable to obtain adequate representation, to have counsel appointed. The person shall be afforded an opportunity to testify, to present witnesses, to cross-examine witnesses who appear at the hearing, and to present information by proffer or otherwise. The rules concerning admissibility of evidence in criminal trials do not apply to the presentation and consideration of information at the hearing. The facts the judicial officer uses to support a finding pursuant to subsection (e) that no condition or combination of conditions will reasonably assure the safety of any other person and the community shall be supported by clear and convincing evidence. The person may be detained pending completion of the hearing. The hearing may be reopened before or after a determination by the judicial officer, at any time before trial if the judicial officer finds that information exists that was not known to the movant at the time of the hearing and that has a material bearing on the issue of whether there are conditions of release that will reasonably assure the appearance of the person as required and the safety of any other person and the community.

(g) *Factors to be considered.* The judicial officer shall, in determining whether there are conditions of release that will reasonably assure the appearance of the person as required and the safety of any other person and the community, take into account the available information concerning—

(1) the nature and circumstances of the offense charged, including whether the offense is a crime of violence or [terrorism, or involves a minor victim, controlled substance, firearm, or destructive device];

(2) the weight of the evidence against the person;

(3) the history and characteristics of the person, including—

(A) the person's character, physical and mental condition, family ties, employment, financial resources, length of residence in the community, community ties, past conduct, history relating to drug or alcohol abuse, criminal history, and record concerning appearance at court proceedings; and

(B) whether, at the time of the current offense or arrest, the person was on probation, on parole, or on other release pending trial, sentencing, appeal, or completion of sentence for an offense under Federal, State, or local law; and

(4) the nature and seriousness of the danger to any person or the community that would be posed by the person's release . . . .

(h) *Contents of release order.* In a release order issued under subsection (b) or (c) of this section, the judicial officer shall—

(1) include a written statement that sets forth all the conditions to which the release is subject, in a manner sufficiently clear and specific to serve as a guide for the person's conduct; and

(2) advise the person of—

(A) the penalties for violating a condition of release, including the penalties for committing an offense while on pretrial release;

(B) the consequences of violating a condition of release, including the immediate issuance of a warrant for the person's arrest; and

(C) sections 1503 of this title (relating to intimidation of witnesses, jurors, and officers of the court), 1510 (relating to obstruction of criminal investigations), 1512 (tampering with a witness, victim, or an informant), and 1513 (retaliating against a witness, victim, or an informant).

(i) *Contents of detention order.* In a detention order issued under subsection (e) of this section, the judicial officer shall—

(1) include written findings of fact and a written statement of the reasons for the detention;

(2) direct that the person be committed to the custody of the Attorney General for confinement in a corrections facility separate, to the extent practicable, from persons awaiting or serving sentences or being held in custody pending appeal;

(3) direct that the person be afforded reasonable opportunity for private consultation with counsel; and

(4) direct that, on order of a court of the United States or on request of an attorney for the Government, the person in charge of the corrections facility in which the person is confined deliver the person to a United States marshal for the purpose of an appearance in connection with a court proceeding.

The judicial officer may, by subsequent order, permit the temporary release of the person, in the custody of a United States marshal or another appropriate person, to the extent that the judicial officer determines such release to be necessary for preparation of the person's defense or for another compelling reason.

Presumption of innocence. Nothing in this section shall be construed as modifying or limiting the presumption of innocence.

§ 3143. *Release or detention of a defendant pending sentence or appeal*

(a) Release or detention pending sentence.—

(1) Except as provided in paragraph (2), the judicial officer shall order that a person who has been found guilty of an offense and who is awaiting imposition or execution of sentence, other than a person for whom the applicable guideline promulgated pursuant to 28 U.S.C. 994 does not recommend a term of imprisonment, be detained, unless the judicial officer finds by clear and convincing evidence that the person is not likely to flee or pose a danger to the safety of any other person or the community if released under section 3142(b) or (c). If the judicial officer makes such a finding, such judicial officer shall order the release of the person in accordance with section 3142(b) or (c).

(2) The judicial officer shall order that a person who has been found guilty of an offense in a case described in subparagraph (A), (B), or (C) of subsection (f)(1) of section 3142 and is awaiting imposition or execution of sentence be detained unless—

(A)(i) the judicial officer finds there is a substantial likelihood that a motion for acquittal or new trial will be granted; or

(ii) an attorney for the Government has recommended that no sentence of imprisonment be imposed on the person; and

(B) the judicial officer finds by clear and convincing evidence that the person is not likely to flee or pose a danger to any other person or the community.

(b) Release or detention pending appeal by the defendant.—

(1) Except as provided in paragraph (2), the judicial officer shall order that a person who has been found guilty of an offense and sentenced to a term of imprisonment, and who has filed an appeal or a petition for a writ of certiorari, be detained, unless the judicial officer finds—

(A) by clear and convincing evidence that the person is not likely to flee or pose a danger to the safety of any other person or the community if released under section 3142(b) or (c) of this title; and

(B) that the appeal is not for the purpose of delay and raises a substantial question of law or fact likely to result in—

(i) reversal,

(ii) an order for a new trial,

(iii) a sentence that does not include a term of imprisonment, or

(iv) a reduced sentence to a term of imprisonment less than the total of the time already served plus the expected duration of the appeal process.

If the judicial officer makes such findings, such judicial officer shall order the release of the person in accordance with section 3142(b) or (c) of this title, except that in the circumstances described in subparagraph (B)(iv) of this paragraph, the judicial officer shall order the detention terminated at the expiration of the likely reduced sentence.

(2) The judicial officer shall order that a person who has been found guilty of an offense in a case described in subparagraph (A), (B), or (C) of subsection (f)(1) of section 3142 and sentenced to a term of imprisonment, and who has filed an appeal or a petition for a writ of certiorari, be detained.

(c) *Release or detention pending appeal by the government.* — The judicial officer shall treat a defendant in a case in which an appeal has been taken by the United States under section 3731 of this title, in accordance with section 3142 of this title, unless the defendant is otherwise subject to a release or detention order.

Except as provided in subsection (b) of this section, the judicial officer, in a case in which an appeal has been taken by the United States under section 3742, shall—

(1) if the person has been sentenced to a term of imprisonment, order that person detained; and

(2) in any other circumstance, release or detain the person under section 3142.

§ 3144. *Release or detention of a material witness*

If it appears from an affidavit filed by a party that the testimony of a person is material in a criminal proceeding, and if it is shown that it may become impracticable to secure the presence of the person by subpoena, a judicial officer may order the arrest of the person and treat the person in accordance with the provisions of section 3142 of this title. No material witness may be detained because of inability to comply with any condition of release if the testimony of such witness can adequately be secured by deposition, and if further detention is not necessary to prevent a failure of justice. Release of a material witness may be delayed for a reasonable period of time until the deposition of the witness can be taken pursuant to the Federal Rules of Criminal Procedure.

§ 3145. *Review and appeal of a release or detention order*

(a) *Review of a release order.* If a person is ordered released by a magistrate, or by a person other than a judge of a court having original jurisdiction over the offense and other than a Federal appellate court—

(1) the attorney for the Government may file, with the court having original jurisdiction over the offense, a motion for revocation of the order or amendment of the conditions of release; and

(2) the person may file, with the court having original jurisdiction over the offense, a motion for amendment of the conditions of release.

The motion shall be determined promptly.

(b) *Review of a detention order.* If a person is ordered detained by a magistrate, or by a person other than a judge of a court having original jurisdiction over the offense and other than a Federal appellate court, the person may file, with the court having original jurisdiction over the offense, a motion for revocation or amendment of the order. The motion shall be determined promptly.

(c) *Appeal from a release or detention order.* An appeal from a release or detention order, or from a decision denying revocation or amendment of such an order, is governed by the provisions of section 1291 of title 28 and section 3731 of this title. The appeal shall be determined promptly. A person subject to detention pursuant to section 3142(a)(2) or (b)(2), and who meets the conditions of release set forth in section 3142(a)(1) or (b)(1), may be ordered released, under appropriate conditions, by the judicial officer, if it is clearly shown that there are exceptional reasons why such person's detention would not be appropriate.

§ 3146. *Penalty for failure to appear*

(a)*Offense.* Whoever, having been released under this chapter knowingly—

    (1) fails to appear before a court as required by the conditions of his release; or

    (2) fails to surrender for service of sentence pursuant to a court order; shall be punished as provided in subsection (b) of this section.

(b)*Punishment.*

    (1) the punishment for an offense under this section is—

        (A) if the person was released in connection with a charge of, or while awaiting sentence, surrender for service of sentence, or appeal or certiorari after conviction, for—

            (i) an offense punishable by death, life imprisonment, or imprisonment for a term of 15 years or more, a fine under this title or imprisonment for not more than ten years, or both;

            (ii) an offense punishable by imprisonment for a term of five years or more, a fine under this title or imprisonment for not more than five years, or both;

            (iii) any other felony, a fine under this title or imprisonment for not more than two years, or both; or

            (iv) a misdemeanor, a fine under this chapter or imprisonment for not more than one year, or both; and

        (B) if the person was released for appearance as a material witness, a fine under this chapter or imprisonment for not more than one year, or both.

    (2) A term of imprisonment imposed under this section shall be consecutive to the sentence of imprisonment for any other offense.

(c) *Affirmative defense.* It is an affirmative defense to a prosecution under this section that uncontrollable circumstances prevented the person from appearing or surrendering, and that the person did not contribute to the creation of such circumstances in reckless disregard of the requirement that he appear or surrender, and that the person appeared or surrendered as soon as such circumstances ceased to exist.

(d) *Declaration of forfeiture.* If a person fails to appear before a court as required, and the person executed an appearance bond pursuant to section 3142(b) of this title or is subject to the release condition set forth in clause (xi) or (xii) of section 3142(c)(1)(B) of this title, the judicial officer may, regardless of whether the person has been charged with an offense under this section, declare any property designated pursuant to that section to be forfeited to the United States.

§ 3147. *Penalty for an offense committed while on release*

A person convicted of an offense committed while released under this chapter shall be sentenced, in addition to the sentence prescribed for the offense to—

    (1) a term of imprisonment of not more than ten years if the offense is a felony; or

(2) a term of imprisonment of not more than one year if the offense is a misdemeanor.

A term of imprisonment imposed under this section shall be consecutive to any other sentence of imprisonment.

§ 3148. *Sanctions for violation of a release condition*

(a) *Available sanctions.* A person who has been released under section 3142 of this title, and who has violated a condition of his release, is subject to a revocation of release, an order of detention, and a prosecution for contempt of court.

(b) *Revocation of release.* The attorney for the Government may initiate a proceeding for revocation of an order of release by filing a motion with the district court. A judicial officer may issue a warrant for the arrest of a person charged with violating a condition of release, and the person shall be brought before a judicial officer in the district in which such person's arrest was ordered for a proceeding in accordance with this section. To the extent practicable, a person charged with violating the condition of release that such person not commit a Federal, State, or local crime during the period of release, shall be brought before the judicial officer who ordered the release and whose order is alleged to have been violated. The judicial officer shall enter an order of revocation and detention if, after a hearing, the judicial officer—

(1) finds that there is—

(A) probable cause to believe that the person has committed a Federal, State, or local crime while on release; or

(B) clear and convincing evidence that the person has violated any other condition of his release; and

(2) finds that—

(A) based on the factors set forth in section 3142(g) of this title, there is no condition or combination of conditions of release that will assure that the person will not flee or pose a danger to the safety of any other person or the community; or

(B) the person is unlikely to abide by any condition or combination of conditions of release.

If there is probable cause to believe that, while on release, the person committed a Federal, State, or local felony, a rebuttable presumption arises that no condition or combination of conditions will assure that the person will not pose a danger to the safety of any other person or the community. If the judicial officer finds that there are conditions of release that will assure that the person will not flee or pose a danger to the safety of any other person or the community, and that the person will abide by such conditions, the judicial officer shall treat the person in accordance with the provisions of section 3142 of this title and may amend the conditions of release accordingly.

(c) *Prosecution for contempt.* The judge may commence a prosecution for contempt, under section 401 of this title, if the person has violated a condition of release.

NOTES

The federal Bail Reform Act is lengthy and complex. The following questions should help you understand some of its most important features.

1. *Appearance and safety.* The Bail Reform Act is designed to "reasonably assure" (a) "the appearance of the person as required" and that the person will not "endanger the safety of any other person or the community."

"Appearance" refers to attendance at any proceeding the defendant is ordered to attend. The "safety" concerns are quite broad, reaching particular individuals (such as potential witnesses or the victim) or the community (such as continuing drug activity or violent crimes). Which of the two concerns (appearance or safety) do you think the court is more likely to be able to predict accurately?

2. *Forms of authorized pretrial release.* What are the forms of pretrial release authorized by the Act?

3. *Preference for certain types of pretrial release.* Sections 3142 (b) and (c) of the Act create a preference for two types of pretrial release. What are they?

4. *Least restrictive form of release.* Under § 3142(c)(1)(B), conditions of release must be the least restrictive that will satisfy the appearance and safety requirements. Examine the list of fourteen conditions. Which appear to be the "least restrictive?" The "most restrictive?" Does the order of the fourteen conditions indicate a legislative judgment about the relative harshness of them? Could any condition require the accused to waive or forfeit a constitutional right? *See, e.g., United States v. Kills Enemy,* 3 F.3d 1201 (8th Cir. 1993) (submit to warrantless drug search as condition of release). *See generally* ABA Standards for Criminal Justice, Pretrial Detention, Standard 10-1.2 (3d ed. 2007)(recommending least restrictive alternative that will reasonable assure appearance and safety).

5. *Limits on financial conditions of release.* Section 3142(c)(2) bars a "financial condition that results in the pretrial detention of the accused." What does this mean? Does it bar "money bail?" If so, how do you explain § 3142(c)(1)(B)(xii), which appears to authorize a bail bond as a condition of release? How does § 3142(c)(2) limit a court's options in fashioning release conditions for an indigent or poor defendant? Could a federal court ever set bond at an amount beyond the defendant's means and then detain the defendant who cannot post the money?

6. *Temporary detention.* When and for how long is temporary detention authorized under § 3142(d)? Who has the burden of proving the necessary facts? Could temporary detention exceed ten days?

7. *Rebuttable presumption.* Section 3142(e) establishes a rebuttable presumption against conditional release in certain circumstances. What are they? What standard of proof must be satisfied before the rebuttable presumption applies? Is an indictment alone sufficient? (Yes, for certain offenses.) If the defendant rebuts the presumption, is he or she entitled to release? What must the government do to prevent release?

8. *When pretrial detention authorized.* Section 3142(e) authorizes pretrial detention if "no condition or combination of conditions will reasonably assure" the appearance and safety standards. Section 3142(c)(1)(B)(xiv) contains a catch-all provision authorizing the court to fashion "any other condition that is reasonably necessary." Does this mean that there can be no pretrial detention if safety and court-appearance would be likely if the police assigned a police officer to follow the accused everywhere? *See United States v. Tortora,* 922 F.2d 880 (1st Cir. 1990) (heroic measures not required before pretrial detention authorized).

9. *Duration of pretrial detention.* The Federal Bail Reform Act sets no time limit on pretrial detention. Several limits exist, however. The Speedy Trial Act, discussed in Chapter 13, indirectly provides limits by mandating that certain procedures be held within a certain number of days. For example, in theory at least, a trial should be started within 100 days of arrest. 18 U.S.C. § 3161.

Another limit — though lacking any definite standards — is due process. Case law suggests that at some point the government's interest in pretrial detention would give way to the defendant's interest in freedom. *See, e.g., United States v. Archambault,* 240 F.Supp.2d 1082 (D. S.D. 2002)(due process violated; 20 month delay with disposition many months away; there was release plan, and delay not caused by defendant).

10. *Public safety.* The Bail Reform Act authorizes pretrial detention if necessary to protect "the safety of any other person and the community." 18 U.S.C. § 3142(e). What threats to public safety are considered? Only crimes of violence? What if the court believes the defendant, if released, is likely to sell drugs? Commit burglaries? Obstruct justice? Take drugs?

11. *Detention hearing.* Section 3142(f) deals with the detention hearing.

a. *Motion practice.* In some situations, the hearing is initiated by a motion filed by the government. In others, either the government or the court can order a detention hearing. How do the two situations differ?

b. *Timing.* Section 3142(f) deals with the detention hearing procedures. When must the detention hearing be held? If a continuance is granted, what happens to the accused? If § 3142(f)'s time limits are violated, the accused is not necessarily entitled to be released. *See United States v. Montalvo-Murillo,* 495 U.S. 711 (1990).

c. *Defendant's rights.* What rights does the accused have at this hearing? What about the right to issue subpoenas? *See United States v. Hurtado,* 779 F.2d 1467 (11th Cir. 1985) (can deny some subpoenas; should grant one if necessary to rebut presumption). Have counsel? Testify? Present evidence? Cross examine government witnesses? (Yes to all).

d. *Evidence rules.* Considering that the accused's liberty is at stake, why do the rules of evidence not apply?

e. *Proof.* What standard of proof must be satisfied before a finding that no release condition will reasonably assure the safety of another person or the community?

f. *Crime of violence.* Note that the attorney for the government may move for a detention hearing if the case involves "a crime of violence" under § 3142(f)(1)(A). In 18 U.S.C. § 3156(a)(4) a "crime of violence" is defined to mean

(A) an offense that has as an element of the offense the use, attempted use, or threatened use of physical force against the person or property of another; or (B) any other offense that is a felony and that, by its nature, involves a substantial risk that physical force against the person or property of another may be used in the course of committing the offense.

See, e.g., United States v. Ingle, 454 F.3d 1082 (10th Cir. 2006)(felon in possession of firearm not crime of violence, but cases split); *United States v. Reiner,* 468 F.Supp.2d 393 (E.D.N.Y. 2006)(child porn possession is crime of violence). A review of cases shows that crimes of violence also include such offenses as arson, armed robbery, providing materials support to terrorist organizations, and possession of a sawed-off shotgun.

12. *Written findings.* If detention is ordered, the court must maker a written statement of its factual findings and the reasons for detention. 18 U.S.C. § 3142(I). Would a court satisfy this requirement if it orally provided the information at a hearing and the remarks were preserved in a transcript? *See United States v. Wheeler,* 795 F.2d 839 (9th Cir. 1986)(yes).

13. *Release pending appeal or sentence.* Section 3142(b) creates a preference for pretrial release. Does § 3143 create a preference for release pending sentence or appeal? Will there be many defendants released from detention pending appeal? Under the Act, who has the burden of proof? What is the standard of proof?

14. *Appeal of release decision.* The Federal Bail Reform Act authorizes both the government and the defendant to appeal a court's detention decision. 18 U.S.C. § 3145.

15. *Modification and Revocation.* The court has the authority to modify the release conditions if there is new information or changed circumstances. 18 U.S.C. § 31452(c)(3). It can also revoke the decision to release the accused, though this authority should be exercised "with circumspection." *Bitter v. United States,* 389 U.S. 15 (1967). .

16. *Preventive detention.* Many federal prosecutors have lauded the Act's preventive detention provisions. What features would please defense counsel?

17. *Academic critique.* The Bail Reform Act of 1984 has been the subject of intensive academic scrutiny. *See, e.g.*, Albert W. Alschuler, *Preventive Pretrial Detention and the Failure of Interest-Balancing Approaches to Due Process*, 85 MICH. L. REV. 510 (1986); and Marc Miller and Martin Guggenheim, *Pretrial Detention and Punishment*, 75 MINN. L. REV. 335 (1990).

18. *Constitutionality.* An obvious question is whether the federal bail act is constitutional. The next case addresses this issue.

UNITED STATES v. SALERNO
481 U.S. 739 (1987)

CHIEF JUSTICE REHNQUIST delivered the opinion of the Court.

The Bail Reform Act of 1984 (Act) allows a federal court to detain an arrestee pending trial if the Government demonstrates by clear and convincing evidence after an adversary hearing that no release conditions "will reasonably assure . . . the safety of any other person and the community." The United States Court of Appeals for the Second Circuit struck down this provision of the Act as facially unconstitutional, because, in that court's words, this type of pretrial detention violates "substantive due process." We granted certiorari because of a conflict among the Courts of Appeals regarding the validity of the Act. We hold that, as against the facial attack mounted by these respondents, the Act fully comports with constitutional requirements. We therefore reverse.

Responding to "the alarming problem of crimes committed by persons on release," Congress formulated the Bail Reform Act of 1984, as the solution to a bail crisis in the federal courts. . . . .Congress hoped to "give the courts adequate authority to make release decisions that give appropriate recognition to the danger a person may pose to others if released."

To this end, § 3141(a) of the Act requires a judicial officer to determine whether an arrestee shall be detained. Section 3142(e) provides that "[i]f, after a hearing pursuant to the provisions of subsection (f), the judicial officer finds that no condition or combination of conditions will reasonably assure the appearance of the person as required and the safety of any other person and the community, he shall order the detention of the person prior to trial." Section 3142(f) provides the arrestee with a number of procedural safeguards. He may request the presence of counsel at the detention hearing, he may testify and present witnesses in his behalf, as well as proffer evidence, and he may cross-examine other witnesses appearing at the hearing. If the judicial officer finds that no conditions of pretrial release can reasonably assure the safety of other persons and the community, he must state his findings of fact in writing, § 3142(i), and support his conclusion with "clear and convincing evidence," § 3142(f).

The judicial officer is not given unbridled discretion in making the detention determination. Congress has specified the considerations relevant to that decision. These factors include the nature and seriousness of the charges, the substantiality of the Government's evidence against the arrestee, the arrestee's background and characteristics, and the nature and seriousness of the danger posed by the suspect's release. § 3142(g). Should a judicial officer order detention, the detainee is entitled to expedited appellate review of the detention order. §§ 3145(b), (c).

Respondents Anthony Salerno and Vincent Cafaro were . . . charged in a 29-count indictment alleging various Racketeer Influenced and Corrupt Organizations Act (RICO) violations, mail and wire fraud offenses, extortion, and various criminal gambling violations. The RICO counts alleged 35 acts of racketeering activity, including fraud, extortion, gambling, and conspiracy to commit murder. At respondents' arraignment, the Government moved to have Salerno and Cafaro detained pursuant to § 3142(e), on the ground that no condition of release would assure the safety of the community or any person. The District Court held a hearing at which the Government made a detailed proffer of evidence. The Government's case showed that Salerno was the "boss" of the Genovese crime family of La Cosa Nostra and that Cafaro was a "captain" in the Genovese family. According to the Government's proffer, based in large part on conversations intercepted by a court-ordered wiretap, the two respondents had participated in wide-ranging conspiracies to aid their illegitimate enterprises through violent means. The Government also offered the testimony of two of its trial witnesses, who would assert that Salerno personally participated in two murder conspiracies. Salerno opposed the motion for detention, challenging the credibility of the Government's witnesses. He offered the testimony of several character witnesses as well as a letter from his doctor stating that he was suffering from a serious medical condition. Cafaro presented no evidence at the hearing, but instead characterized the wiretap conversations as merely "tough talk."

The District Court granted the Government's detention motion, concluding that the Government had established by clear and convincing evidence that no condition or combination of conditions of release would ensure the safety of the community or any person: "The activities of a criminal organization such as the Genovese family do not cease with the arrest of its principals and their release on even the most stringent of bail conditions."

. . . Respondents appealed, contending that to the extent that the Bail Reform Act permits pretrial detention on the ground that the arrestee is likely to commit future crimes, it is unconstitutional on its face. Over a dissent, the United States Court of Appeals for the Second Circuit agreed. Although the court agreed that pretrial detention could be imposed if the defendants were likely to intimidate witnesses or otherwise jeopardize the trial process, it found "§ 3142(e)'s authorization of pretrial detention [on the ground of future dangerousness] repugnant to the concept of substantive due process, which we believe prohibits the total deprivation of liberty simply as a means of preventing future crimes." The court concluded that the Government could not, consistent with due process, detain persons who had not been accused of any crime merely because they were thought to present a danger to the community.

. . . [A] facial challenge to a legislative Act is, of course, the most difficult challenge to mount successfully, since the challenger must establish that no set of circumstances exists under which the Act would be valid. The fact that the Bail Reform Act might operate unconstitutionally under some conceivable set of circumstances is insufficient to render it wholly invalid, since we have not recognized an "overbreadth" doctrine outside the limited context of the First Amendment. We think respondents have failed to shoulder their heavy burden to demonstrate that the Act is "facially" unconstitutional.

Respondents present two grounds for invalidating the Bail Reform Act's provisions permitting pretrial detention on the basis of future dangerousness. First, they rely upon the Court of Appeals' conclusion that the Act exceeds the limitations placed upon the Federal Government by the Due Process Clause of the Fifth Amendment. Second, they contend that the Act contravenes the Eighth Amendment's proscription against excessive bail. We treat these contentions in turn.

. . . Respondents first argue that the Act violates substantive due process [which bars government conduct that "shocks the conscience" or interferes with rights "implicit in the concept of ordered liberty"] because the pretrial detention it authorizes constitutes impermissible punishment before trial. The Government, however, has never argued that pretrial detention could be upheld if it were "punishment." The Court of Appeals assumed that pretrial detention under the Bail Reform Act is regulatory, not penal, and we agree that it is.

As an initial matter, the mere fact that a person is detained does not inexorably lead to the conclusion that the government has imposed punishment. To determine whether a restriction on liberty constitutes impermissible punishment or permissible regulation, we first look to legislative intent. Unless Congress expressly intended to impose punitive restrictions, the punitive/regulatory distinction turns on " whether an alternative purpose to which [the restriction] may rationally be connected is assignable for it, and whether it appears excessive in relation to the alternative purpose assigned [to it]."

We conclude that the detention imposed by the Act falls on the regulatory side of the dichotomy. The legislative history of the Bail Reform Act clearly indicates that Congress did not formulate the pretrial detention provisions as punishment for dangerous individuals. Congress instead perceived pretrial detention as a potential solution to a pressing societal problem. There is no doubt that preventing danger to the community is a legitimate regulatory goal.

Nor are the incidents of pretrial detention excessive in relation to the regulatory goal Congress sought to achieve. The Bail Reform Act carefully limits the circumstances under which detention may be sought to the most serious of crimes. *See* 18 U.S.C. § 3142(f) (detention hearings available if case involves crimes of violence, offenses for which the sentence is life imprisonment or death, serious drug offenses, or certain repeat offenders). The arrestee is entitled to a prompt detention hearing, and the maximum length of pretrial detention is limited by the stringent time limitations of the Speedy Trial Act.[4] Moreover . . . the conditions of confinement envisioned by the Act "appear to reflect the regulatory purposes relied upon by the" Government . . . . [T]he statute at issue here requires that detainees be housed in a "facility separate, to the extent practicable, from persons awaiting or serving sentences or being held in custody pending appeal." 18 U.S.C. § 3142(i)(2). We conclude, therefore, that the pretrial detention contemplated by the Bail Reform Act is regulatory in nature, and does not constitute punishment before trial in violation of the Due Process Clause.

The Court of Appeals nevertheless concluded that "the Due Process Clause prohibits pretrial detention on the ground of danger to the community as a regulatory measure, without regard to the duration of the detention." Respondents characterize the Due Process Clause as erecting an impenetrable "wall" in this area that "no governmental interest — rational, important, compelling or otherwise — may surmount."

We do not think the Clause lays down any such categorical imperative. We have repeatedly held that the Government's regulatory interest in community safety can, in appropriate circumstances, outweigh an individual's liberty interest. [The Court cited wartime detention of people the government considered dangerous; detention of potentially dangerous aliens pending deposition; and dangerous mentally unstable people, juveniles, and incompetent people awaiting trial.] Finally, respondents concede and the Court of Appeals noted that an arrestee may be incarcerated until trial if he presents a risk of flight or a danger to witnesses.

. . . Given the well-established authority of the government, in special circumstances, to restrain individuals' liberty prior to or even without criminal trial and conviction, we think that the present statute providing for pretrial detention on the basis of dangerousness must be evaluated in precisely the same manner that we evaluated the laws in the cases discussed above.

The government's interest in preventing crime by arrestees is both legitimate and compelling. The Bail Reform Act . . . narrowly focuses on a particularly acute problem in which the Government interests are overwhelming. The Act operates only on individuals who have been arrested for a specific category of extremely serious offenses. 18 U.S.C. § 3142(f). Congress specifically found that these individuals are far more likely to be responsible for dangerous acts in the community after arrest. Nor is the Act by any means a scattershot attempt to incapacitate those who are merely suspected of these serious crimes. The Government must first of all demonstrate

---

[4] We intimate no view as to the point at which detention in a particular case might become excessively prolonged, and therefore punitive, in relation to Congress' regulatory goal.

probable cause to believe that the charged crime has been committed by the arrestee, but that is not enough. In a full-blown adversary hearing, the Government must convince a neutral decisionmaker by clear and convincing evidence that no conditions of release can reasonably assure the safety of the community or any person. 18 U.S.C. § 3142(f). While the Government's general interest in preventing crime is compelling, even this interest is heightened when the Government musters convincing proof that the arrestee, already indicted or held to answer for a serious crime, presents a demonstrable danger to the community. Under these narrow circumstances, society's interest in crime prevention is at its greatest.

On the other side of the scale, of course, is the individual's strong interest in liberty. We do not minimize the importance and fundamental nature of this right. But, as our cases hold, this right may, in circumstances where the government's interest is sufficiently weighty, be subordinated to the greater needs of society. We think that Congress' careful delineation of the circumstances under which detention will be permitted satisfies this standard. When the Government proves by clear and convincing evidence that an arrestee presents an identified and articulable threat to an individual or the community, we believe that, consistent with the Due Process Clause, a court may disable the arrestee from executing that threat.

Under the Bail Reform Act, the procedures by which a judicial officer evaluates the likelihood of future dangerousness are specifically designed to further the accuracy of that determination. Detainees have a right to counsel at the detention hearing. 18 U.S.C. § 3142(f). They may testify in their own behalf, present information by proffer or otherwise, and cross-examine witnesses who appear at the hearing. The judicial officer charged with the responsibility of determining the appropriateness of detention is guided by statutorily enumerated factors, which include the nature and the circumstances of the charges, the weight of the evidence, the history and characteristics of the putative offender, and the danger to the community. § 3142(g). The Government must prove its case by clear and convincing evidence. § 3142(f). Finally, the judicial officer must include written findings of fact and a written statement of reasons for a decision to detain. § 3142(i). The Act's review provisions, § 3145(c), provide for immediate appellate review of the detention decision.

We think these extensive safeguards suffice to repel a facial challenge.

. . . Respondents also contend that the Bail Reform Act violates the Excessive Bail Clause of the Eighth Amendment. . . . The Eighth Amendment addresses pretrial release by providing merely that "[e]xcessive bail shall not be required." This Clause, of course, says nothing about whether bail shall be available at all. Respondents nevertheless contend that this Clause grants them a right to bail calculated solely upon considerations of flight. They rely on *Stack v. Boyle*, 342 U.S. 1 (1951), in which the Court stated that "[b]ail set at a figure higher than an amount reasonably calculated [to ensure the defendant's presence at trial] is 'excessive' under the Eighth Amendment." In respondents' view, since the Bail Reform Act allows a court essentially to set bail at an infinite amount for reasons not related to the risk of flight, it violates the Excessive Bail Clause. Respondents concede that the right to bail they have discovered in the Eighth Amendment is not absolute. A court may, for example, refuse bail in capital cases. And, as the Court of Appeals noted and respondents admit, a court may refuse bail when the defendant presents a threat to the judicial process by intimidating witnesses. Respondents characterize these exceptions as consistent with what they claim to be the sole purpose of bail — to ensure the integrity of the judicial process.

While we agree that a primary function of bail is to safeguard the courts' role in adjudicating the guilt or innocence of defendants, we reject the proposition that the Eighth Amendment categorically prohibits the government from pursuing other admittedly compelling interests through regulation of pretrial release.

. . . For even if we were to conclude that the Eighth Amendment imposes some substantive limitations on the National Legislature's powers in this area, we would still hold that the Bail Reform Act is valid. Nothing in the text of the Bail Clause limits permissible Government considerations solely to questions of flight. The only arguable substantive limitation of the Bail Clause is that the Government's proposed conditions of release or detention not be "excessive" in light of the perceived evil. Of course, to determine whether the Government's response is excessive, we must compare that response against the interest the Government seeks to protect by means of that response. Thus, when the Government has admitted that its only interest is in preventing flight, bail must be set by a court at a sum designed to ensure that goal, and no more. We believe that when Congress has mandated detention on the basis of a compelling interest other than prevention of flight, as it has here, the Eighth Amendment does not require release on bail. [Reversed.]

JUSTICE MARSHALL, with whom JUSTICE BRENNAN joins, dissenting.

This case brings before the Court for the first time a statute in which Congress declares that a person innocent of any crime may be jailed indefinitely, pending the trial of allegations which are legally presumed to be untrue, if the Government shows to the satisfaction of a judge that the accused is likely to commit crimes, unrelated to the pending charges, at any time in the future . . . . [This] decision disregards basic principles of justice established centuries ago and enshrined beyond the reach of governmental interference in the Bill of Rights.

. . . The majority approaches respondents' challenge to the Act by dividing the discussion into two sections, one concerned with the substantive guarantees implicit in the Due Process Clause, and the other concerned with the protection afforded by the Excessive Bail Clause of the Eighth Amendment. This is a sterile formalism, which divides a unitary argument into two independent parts and then professes to demonstrate that the parts are individually inadequate.

On the due process side of this false dichotomy appears an argument concerning the distinction between regulatory and punitive legislation. The majority concludes that the Act is a regulatory rather than a punitive measure.

. . . The majority proceeds as though the only substantive right protected by the Due Process Clause is a right to be free from punishment before conviction. The majority's technique for infringing this right is simple: merely redefine any measure which is claimed to be punishment as "regulation," and, magically, the Constitution no longer prohibits its imposition. Because . . . the Due Process Clause protects other substantive rights which are infringed by this legislation, the majority's argument is merely an exercise in obfuscation.

The logic of the majority's Eighth Amendment analysis is equally unsatisfactory. The Eighth Amendment, as the majority notes, states that "[e]xcessive bail shall not be required." The majority then declares, as if it were undeniable, that: "[t]his Clause, of course, says nothing about whether bail shall be available at all." If excessive bail is imposed the defendant stays in jail. The same result is achieved if bail is denied altogether. Whether the magistrate sets bail at $1 million or refuses to set bail at all, the consequences are indistinguishable. It would be mere sophistry to suggest that the Eighth Amendment protects against the former decision, and not the latter. Indeed, such a result would lead to the conclusion that there was no need for Congress to pass a preventive detention measure of any kind; every federal magistrate and district judge could simply refuse, despite the absence of any evidence of risk of flight or danger to the community, to set bail. This would be entirely constitutional, since, according to the majority, the Eighth Amendment "says nothing about whether bail shall be available at all."

The essence of this case may be found, ironically enough, in a provision of the Act to which the majority does not refer. Title 18 U.S.C. § 3142(j) provides that "[n]othing in this section shall be construed as modifying or limiting the presumption of innocence." But the very pith and purpose of this statute is an abhorrent limitation of the presumption of innocence. The majority's untenable conclusion that the present Act is constitutional arises from a specious denial of the role of the Bail Clause and the Due Process Clause in protecting the invaluable guarantee afforded by the presumption of innocence.

. . . The statute now before us declares that persons who have been indicted may be detained if a judicial officer finds clear and convincing evidence that they pose a danger to individuals or to the community. The statute does not authorize the Government to imprison anyone it has evidence is dangerous; indictment is necessary. But let us suppose that a defendant is indicted and the Government shows by clear and convincing evidence that he is dangerous and should be detained pending a trial, at which trial the defendant is acquitted. May the Government continue to hold the defendant in detention based upon its showing that he is dangerous? The answer cannot be yes, for that would allow the Government to imprison someone for uncommitted crimes based upon "proof" not beyond a reasonable doubt. The result must therefore be that once the indictment has failed, detention cannot continue. But our fundamental principles of justice declare that the defendant is as innocent on the day before his trial as he is on the morning after his acquittal.

. . . The finding of probable cause conveys power to try, and the power to try imports of necessity the power to assure that the processes of justice will not be evaded or obstructed.[7]

Pretrial detention to prevent future crimes against society at large, however, is not justified by any concern for holding a trial on the charges for which a defendant has been arrested. The detention purportedly authorized by this statute bears no relation to the Government's power to try charges supported by a finding of probable cause, and thus the interests it serves are outside the scope of interests which may be considered in weighing the excessiveness of bail under the Eighth Amendment.

[The dissent of Justice Stevens is omitted.]

NOTES

1. *Effect of Bail Reform Act's procedural protections.* Chief Justice Rehnquist's opinion in *Salerno* relies heavily on the procedural limitations in the Bail Reform Act. How important are they to the result? What if a state authorized preventive detention, but did not require "clear and convincing evidence" of the need for pretrial retention, or did not limit the categories of offenders eligible for pretrial detention? Would the statutes violate substantive due process? Procedural due process? The excessive bail clause?

2. *Regulatory or punitive.* The majority opinion makes a distinction between regulatory and punitive detention. What if the accused person were denied pretrial release and were kept in the only jail cell in a small community. Cellmates included eleven other people: five had been convicted and were serving a jail sentence; six were awaiting trial for various offenses. Assume they all have the same routine, share the same facilities, eat the same food, and are subject to the same rules. Would *Salerno* still consider this regulatory rather than punitive?

3. *Conditions of confinement.* Would *Salerno's* non-punitive logic support an argument that pretrial detainees *must* be kept separate from post-trial detainees? See § 3142(i)(2) of the Bail Reform Act. That the conditions of confinement for pretrial detainees must be reasonably comfortable and must maximize freedom consistent with

---

[7] It is also true, as the majority observes, that the Government is entitled to assurance, by incarceration if necessary, that a defendant will not obstruct justice through destruction of evidence, procuring the absence or intimidation of witnesses, or subornation of perjury. But in such cases the Government benefits from no presumption that any particular defendant is likely to engage in activities inimical to the administration of justice, and the majority offers no authority for the proposition that bail has traditionally been denied prospectively, upon speculation that witnesses would be tampered with.

security needs? *See* ABA Standards for Criminal Justice § 10-5.16 (3d ed. 2007) (recommending that pretrial detainees should be confined separately from persons already convicted, and that detainees' rights and restrictions should not be more restricted than those of convicted prisoners), and also Blackstone's Commentaries on the Laws of England, Book 4, Ch. 22: Of Commitment and Bail (1765–1769):

> Upon the whole, if the offense be not bailable, or the party cannot find bail, he is to be committed to the county gaol . . . there to abide till delivered by due course of law. But this imprisonment, as has been said, is only for safe custody, and not for punishment: therefore, in this dubious interval between the commitment and trial, a prisoner ought to be used with the utmost humanity; and neither loaded with needless fetters or subjected to other hardships than such as are absolutely requisite for the purpose of confinement only[.]

Do pretrial detainees have special needs that may merit separation from all or some other prisoners? Case law suggests the view that due process (not the cruel and unusual punishment clause of the Eighth Amendment, which applies to convicted prisoners) prohibits "deliberate indifference" or conduct "so reckless as to be tantamount to a desire to inflict harm." *Redman v. County of San Diego*, 942 F.2d 1435, 1449(9th Cir. 1991). What circumstances could meet this standard? *See, e.g., Valdez v. Rosenbaum*, 302 F.3d 1039 (9th Cir. 2002)(upholding restriction on pretrial detainees use of telephone because they could warn unarrested co-conspirators).

4. *Footnote 7.* Footnote number 7 of Justice Marshall's dissent concedes that the government is entitled to incarcerate a defendant prior to trial in the absence of an assurance "that a defendant will not obstruct justice through destruction of evidence, procuring the absence or intimidation of witnesses, or subornation of perjury." That being the case, in what way is the Bail Reform Act at odds with that power?

5. *Predictions.* The dissenters would permit detention of persons who are deemed likely to flee the jurisdiction and fail to appear at trial. Given the obvious fact that likelihood of flight involves a predictive judgment, how can that predictive judgment be distinguished from a predictive judgment of likely criminal behavior pending trial?

6. *Freedom v. crime prevention. Salerno* holds that in some circumstances the interest in preventing crime is more important than the interest in the individual's freedom. Do you agree with this weighting?

7. *Role of media and public opinion.* In rare cases, the media and public opinion call for a particular decision on pretrial release. Perhaps the case involved a public figure or a sympathetic victim. Should the public's preferences play a role in the detention decision? *See generally* ABA Standards for Criminal Justice, Pretrial Detention, Standard 10-1.8 (3d ed. 2007)(no).

8. *Material witnesses.* Examine carefully the text of § 3144, which authorizes the arrest and pretrial detention of a material witness when the witness has material testimony to offer and it may become "impracticable" to obtain the testimony by issuing a subpoena. It applies to trials, grand jury hearings, and other proceedings. In what way or ways is this provision significantly different from other provisions in the Bail Reform Act of 1984? Note the detention is not permitted if the testimony could be obtained by deposition, though temporary detention is permitted until the deposition is taken.

Most states have specific provisions permitting detention of a "material witness. *See* Stacey M. Studnicki, *Material Witness Detention: Justice Served or Denied?*, 40 WAYNE L. REV. 1533 (1994). Courts are divided on whether the material witness is entitled to appointed counsel to contest detention. Some jurisdictions compensate material witnesses during the period of detention.

Several state and federal courts have addressed various states' material witness statutes. While some states explicitly limit the reach of their material witness statutes, these statutes regularly survive constitutional challenges. *See, e.g., Iowa v. Hernandez-Lopez*, 639 N.W.2d 226 (Iowa 2002) (Iowa's material witness statute meets substantive and procedural due process requirements and is therefore constitutional); *White v. Gerbitz*, 892 F.2d 457 (6th Cir. 1989) (a police detective properly arrested a homeless man pursuant to Tennessee's material witness statute in a homicide investigation where the man was found 15 to 20 feet from homicide victim and he expressed reluctance at being a "snitch").

Following September 11, 2001, the federal government has utilized § 3144 in many instances to detain witnesses. In many cases the witnesses are Muslim men who are actually being held because of their possible link to terrorism rather than their role as a material witness. *See* Joseph G. Cook, *The Detention of Material Witnesses and the Fourth Amendment*, 76 MISS. L. J. 585 (2006)(suggesting practice raises serious Fourth Amendment concerns); *see generally* Stacey M. Studnicki and John P. Apol, *Witness Detention and Intimidation: The History and Future of Material Witness Law*, 76 ST. JOHN'S L. REV. 483 (2002). For a detailed description of the evolution of § 3144 and how that statute has been applied in cases post-9/11 see Note, *Developments in Law and Policy: The Costs of Post-9/11 National Security Strategy*, 22 YALE L. & POL'Y REV. 197 (2004).

9. *Accuracy of prediction of dangerousness.* As suggested in the dissenting opinions in *Salerno*, perhaps the most controversial aspect of the 1984 legislation is the notion of preventive detention based upon predictions of dangerousness. In this regard, it has been noted that "even the best controlled prospective prediction studies have success rates that raise serious questions about Congress's conclusions regarding the ability to predict dangerousness." Marc Miller & Martin Guggenheim, *Pretrial Detention and Punishment*, 75 MINN. L. REV. 335, 383 (1990).

A study found that, with the exception of drug arrests, there was little correlation between the crime charged and the type and frequency of pretrial violations. Thomas Bak, *Does the Offense Charged Predict the Type and Frequency of Pretrial Violations?*, 24 NEW ENG. J. ON CRIM. & CIV. CONFINEMENT 65 (1998). The study focused on closed federal court cases from the calendar year 1994. The author concluded that, "[d]espite the elevated violation rates for those accused of drug crimes, few pretrial releasees commit violations, only one in ten of these violations are felonies, and only a minority of these felony violations involve violence." Moreover, violations of special conditions of pretrial release, such as drug testing and drug counseling, constituted the largest percentage of first violations.

10 *Rebuttable presumptions.* Several "rebuttable presumptions" are explicitly identified in the Bail Reform Act in the context of determining whether the defendant will appear at trial or endanger the safety of others, or both. As one would expect, these provisions have been tested in several cases. The next case is perhaps the most widely cited in this context.

UNITED STATES v. JESSUP
757 F.2d 378 (1st Cir. 1985)

BREYER, CIRCUIT JUDGE.

This appeal challenges the constitutionality of a provision of the Bail Reform Act of 1984 that requires judicial officers making bail decisions to apply a rebuttable presumption that one charged with a serious drug offense will likely flee before trial. We find that Congress has acted within the Constitution's prescribed limits in creating this rebuttable presumption and that the magistrate and district court have acted within their lawful authority in applying it, and related statutory provisions, to the appellant Mark Jessup. We affirm the district court's decision to deny him bail and to hold him in custody pending his trial.

[Jessup was accused of arranging for the sale of two kilograms of cocaine. It was determined that the weight of evidence against the defendant was strong, that he lived in this jurisdiction (Massachusetts) for only two years and that he had been unemployed for at least six months prior to his arrest. Jessup's attorney offered the following facts to support Jessup's asserted right to pretrial release: (1) Jessup was engaged to a Massachusetts resident, (2) he had recently received a job offer and (3) he had no prior criminal record.]

The Bail Reform Act of 1984 ("the Act") makes it, in one respect, harder and, in another respect, easier for judicial officers to order pretrial detention of those accused of crimes. It makes it harder by specifying explicitly what was implicit in prior law, namely that magistrates and judges cannot impose any "financial condition" that will result in detention. High money bail cannot be used as a device to keep a defendant in custody before trial. The Act makes detention easier by broadening the category of persons whom the officer can order detained. And, the Act specifies that a judicial officer shall order detention if he finds that no condition or combination of conditions [attaching to release] will reasonably assure the appearance of the person as required and the safety of any other person and the community . . . . The Act sets forth procedures to be used in applying this standard. It provides a list of factors that the officer is to weigh when doing so, § 3142(g); and it creates several "rebuttable presumptions" that the officer is to use when applying the basic standard.

This case concerns one of the "rebuttable presumptions" that the Act creates. It states:

> Subject to rebuttal by the person, it shall be presumed that no condition or combination of conditions will reasonably assure the appearance of the person as required and the safety of the community if the judicial officer finds that there is probable cause to believe that the person committed an offense for which a maximum term of imprisonment of ten years or more is prescribed in the Controlled Substances Act . . . ."

The magistrate here used the presumption in deciding to detain appellant Jessup. The magistrate found that Jessup posed a threat to the safety of the community in that, if released, he might continue to commit crimes. The magistrate also found that, if released, there was a substantial risk that Jessup would flee. In particular, the magistrate stated:

> I am equally of the view that the defendant has not rebutted the presumption that no non-financial conditions or combination of non-financial conditions of release would reasonably assure his presence. The defendant is charged with a serious crime and the Government's evidence is strong. The defendant has been in this state for only two years; he has no family or relatives living here. In all the circumstances, I do not believe the fact that the defendant is engaged to a Massachusetts resident would deter him from fleeing the jurisdiction in view of the seriousness of the crime charged and the strength of the evidence against him.

Given this alternative basis for the magistrate's decision, we need not consider the Act's "dangerousness" provisions or the magistrate's "dangerousness" finding. It is well established that the government can keep a defendant in custody to secure his presence at trial. Thus the constitutional issue presented here is whether the government can use the Act's rebuttable presumption in doing so.

. . . We turn to Jessup's claim that use of the drug offender/flight presumption is unconstitutional because it deprives him of his "liberty . . . without due process of law." In deciding whether this presumption makes Jessup's bail procedures constitutionally unfair, we shall ask 1) whether the presumption represents a reasonable congressional response to a problem of legitimate legislative concern, and 2) whether the presumption increases the risk of an erroneous deprivation of liberty — i.e., will it likely increase the risk that magistrates will release or detain the wrong people?

The first question must be answered, on the record before us, in the government's favor. The government's interest in securing the appearance of a defendant at trial has been held important enough to warrant pretrial detention where there is a significant risk of flight.

. . . Moreover, Congress held hearings and heard considerable evidence that drug offenders posed a special risk of "flight." . . . Given Congress's constitutional authority and practical fact gathering power — a power far greater than that of courts — we are not persuaded that Congress's conclusions concerning the drug offender/flight problem are without substantial basis in fact, or that Congress's solution is unreasonable. And, we conclude that the government's interest in the presumption is a strong and legitimate one.

We also find that the presumption does not significantly increase the risk of an "erroneous deprivation" of liberty. The presumption shifts the burden of production, not the burden of persuasion. It applies only where there is probable cause to believe a person is guilty of a serious crime. The defendant can provide argument and evidence suggesting that he is not involved in the "highly lucrative" drug operations at the center of congressional concern. The Act further specifically provides a defendant with a hearing at which he:

> has the right to be represented by counsel, and, if he is financially unable to obtain adequate representation, to have counsel appointed for him. The person shall be afforded an opportunity to testify, to present witnesses on his own behalf, to cross-examine witnesses who appear at the hearing, and to present information by proffer and otherwise.

§ 3142(f)(2)(B). Although the magistrate will keep the presumption in mind in making a decision, he will do so only as a reminder of Congress's findings. Given the Act's procedural protections, the fact that the presumption does not shift the burden of persuasion, and the presumption's relation to Congress's factfinding powers, we cannot say that it promotes less, rather than more, accurate decisionmaking. Given the legitimate governmental interest in securing a defendant's appearance at trial, the presumption's restrictions on the defendant's liberty are constitutionally permissible.

. . . For reasons previously given, the presumption does not impose an excessive burden in respect to this purpose. We find no legal basis for viewing the presumption as imposing "punishment." For these reasons, we believe the presumption, as we have interpreted it, is constitutional.

NOTES

1. *Denial of dangerousness usually upheld.* A review of rulings by the federal circuit courts of appeals indicates that decisions to deny federal criminal defendants bail on grounds of predicted dangerousness are generally upheld.

2. *Absence of harm.* The most successful arguments attack bail denials based upon the absence of actual physical harm to third parties or threats to witnesses. For example, in *United States v. King*, 849 F.2d 485 (11th Cir. 1988), a United States district court in Florida had issued a pretrial detention order based upon allegations that the defendant, King, was a "leader" of a high volume and extremely profitable cocaine distribution scheme. Detention was ordered based upon both risk of flight and risk of dangerousness. The Eleventh Circuit Court of Appeals affirmed the order, notwithstanding the absence of evidence of prior physical harm or threats made by the defendant against witnesses who might testify against her at trial. With respect to detention based upon risk of flight, King presented evidence that she did not pose a likelihood of flight because she was aware of the imminence of the grand jury indictments six months prior to the time that her indictment actually was returned. Accordingly, that fact, coupled with the fact that she chose to retain counsel to contest the charges, manifested "her true intent with respect to flight." The appellate court was unpersuaded by this evidence, observing that this contention was "not sufficient to overcome the statutory presumption and other evidence adduced at the hearings." *See*

also United States v. Orena, 986 F.2d 628 (2d Cir. 1993) (gang war participant denied bail because of danger of continued participation in violent crimes); *United States v. Quartermaine*, 913 F.2d 910 (11th Cir. 1990)(willingness to commit family violence supports bail denial because it evidences violent tendency).

3. *Drug cases.* Similarly, other cases suggest that defendants accused of large-quantity drug crimes (for which the Bail Reform Act carries a presumption in favor of detention) may be detained without bail based upon a prediction of future dangerousness, even in the absence of specific evidence related either to prior physical violence or actual threats to witnesses. *See, e.g., United States v. Gebro*, 948 F.2d 1118 (9th Cir. 1991).

[2]   Implementation of Bail Reform Act of 1984

The Bail Reform Act of 1984 has resulted in the detention of a much higher percentage of people in jail awaiting trial for federal crimes. Based upon information collected in a study of pretrial incarceration in federal cases, one year before and after the Bail Reform Act went into effect, the percentage of federal defendants incarcerated until trial increased from 24% to 29%. The likelihood of being held until trial was 21% higher for violent offenses involving firearms, 20% for more serious drug offenses, 26% higher for other drug offenses, and 63% higher for defendants who caused injury. Defendants held without bail increased from 2% to 19%, while those required to post financial bail decreased from 44% to 27% (meaning pretrial detention has been substituted for money bail in some cases). The reason for incarceration pending trial changed. Before the Act, 93% of those held in jail were there for failure to meet bail conditions. After the Act, 65% were held on pretrial detention. Bureau of Justice Statistics, Pretrial Release and Detention: The Bail Reform Act of 1984 (Feb. 1988).

In 2004 about forty percent of all federal defendants were released prior to trial. Of those detained, defendants charged with violent offenses and drug crimes were detained at much higher rates than those charged with property offenses. Bureau of Justice Statistics, U.S. Dept. Of Justice, Sourcebook of Criminal Justice Statistics ("Sourcebook")[online], http://www.albany.edu/sourcebook/pdf/t5132004.pdf. Detention hearings were held for 56 percent of federal criminal defendants, and 79 percent of the hearings resulted in a detention order. Men were more likely to be detained than women, as were those with a history of prior felony convictions and those who were unemployed. *Id.*, at http://www.albany.edu/sourcebook/pdf/t5142004.pdf. *See also* Jack F. Williams, *Classifying Pre-Trial Detention Decisions Under the Bail Reform Act of 1984: A Statistical Approach*, 30 Am. Crim. L. Rev. 255 (1993) (analyzing factors affecting federal release decisions).

Of those persons arrested who were released on federal pretrial supervision in 1996, approximately 16 percent violated the terms of the release. Persons charged with drug offenses or violent crimes were most likely to commit at least one pretrial violation. A surprisingly large percentage of released federal offenders appear for their scheduled hearings. Only 2.2% of them failed to appear. Sourcebook, at http://www.albany.edu/sourcebook/pdf/t5162004.pdf

Another federal study compared release decisions in felony cases in federal and state courts in 1990. It found state offenders were more likely to be required to post a financial bond (38% of state defendants, 26% federal), less likely to be released on unsecured bond (8% state, 50% federal), and more likely to be released on their own recognizance (40% state, 21% federal) and on conditional release (12% state, 4% federal). Federal releases were faster than state (68% of federal pretrial releases occurred on the first day, 54% of state releases). State offenders were six times as likely as federal ones to be rearrested before trial (18% state, 3% federal) and eight times as likely to have a warrant issued for nonappearance (24% state, 3% federal). Bureau of Justice Statistics, Pretrial Release of Federal Felony Defendants (Feb. 1994).

I. SPECIAL CASES AND CIRCUMSTANCES

[1] Capital Cases

Almost all jurisdictions, either by constitution or statutory provision, deny a person accused of a capital offense the right to bail. As earlier noted in Part D, sometimes there is an additional requirement that bail can be denied if "proof of guilt is evident or the presumption is great." *E.g.*, Fla. Const. art. 1, § 14. In a jurisdiction with this rule, the judge in a capital case deciding a motion for release on bail must assess the strength of the government's case against the accused. While defense counsel may have little reason to expect a favorable ruling on the motion to release a capital defendant on bail, the bail hearing will afford counsel some discovery of the government's case. Considering the relatively limited right to pretrial discovery in criminal cases, discussed in Chapter 10, the bail hearing in a capital case may provide useful information not otherwise obtainable prior to trial. Irrespective of the rules applied, it is safe to say that virtually no accused capital offenders are actually released on bail.

[2] Juvenile Cases

In some jurisdictions, bail procedures are the same for children and adults. *See, e.g.*, Fla. Stat. § 903.06 ("Minors may bind themselves by a bond to secure their release on bail in the same manner as persons sui juris"). Other jurisdictions have special provisions concerning release of a juvenile to his or her parents. *See, e.g.*, Pa. C.S.A. § 6326 ("A person taking a child into custody . . . shall notify the parent, guardian or other custodian of the apprehension of the child . . . [and] shall release the child to [same] upon their promise to bring the child before the court when requested by the court.").

A number of unique issues are present in juvenile cases, which suggest that the "regular" adult bail system should not apply fully to minors. Typically, juveniles are not legally competent to enter a contract with bonding companies. Unless the juvenile's parents are willing to secure bond, no release will occur. Additionally, if the juvenile's parents will not care for the child or if a court predicts continued harm in the home situation, the child probably will not be allowed to return home pending adjudication. The only alternative at that point is a form of pretrial detention unless the law allows placement with a relative or in foster care, or the court elects to allow the child to live alone or with a friend.

What should be done in the case of a juvenile charged with having committed a serious felony and who also is deemed to be dangerous to society? In *Schall v. Martin*, 467 U.S. 253 (1984), the United States Supreme Court upheld a preventive detention statute applicable to juvenile court cases. In an opinion written by Justice Rehnquist, the Court made a number of observations that would be repeated a few years later in *Salerno*, discussed earlier in this chapter. Recognizing that the protection of the community from crime is a legitimate state objective, the Court found that interest sufficient to outweigh the juvenile's interest in freedom from restraint. And as the Court found later in *Salerno*, it concluded that the preventive detention statute was not being used or intended as punishment:

> First of all, the detention is strictly limited in time. If a juvenile is detained at his initial appearance and has denied the charges against him, he is entitled to a probable-cause hearing to be held not more than three days after the conclusion of the initial appearance or four days after the filing of the petition, whichever is sooner. If the Family Court judge finds probable cause, he must also determine whether continued detention is necessary.

> . . . Detained juveniles are also entitled to an expedited factfinding hearing.

. . . The conditions of confinement also appear to reflect the regulatory purposes relied upon by the State. When a juvenile is remanded after his initial appearance, he cannot, absent exceptional circumstances, be sent to a prison or lockup where he would be exposed to adult criminals.

Id. at 269–270.

Justices Marshall, Brennan and Stevens dissented, arguing that the harm to minors outweighed the public purpose advanced by this statute.

[3] Post-conviction Bail

As we have already seen, the federal Bail Reform Act of 1984 reverses the presumption of a right to release when the defendant is awaiting sentencing or is pursuing an appeal of his or her conviction. The following case illustrates this principle.

UNITED STATES v. MILLER
753 F.2d 19 (3d Cir. 1985)

SLOVITER, CIRCUIT JUDGE.

Before us is a motion by appellants under Fed. R. App. P. 9(b) for release upon bail pending appeal.

. . . Specifically, we focus on the meaning of the statutory language conditioning the grant of bail pending appeal upon a finding that the appeal "raises a substantial question of law or fact likely to result in reversal or an order for a new trial."

Facts

Appellants Stanton and Robert Miller are brothers who were convicted following a jury trial of one count of conspiracy to defraud the United States, two counts of filing false income tax returns, and one count of conducting an illegal gambling business. Stanton Miller was also convicted on one count of making a false oath in a bankruptcy proceeding. Briefly, the convictions arose out of defendants' operation of a large scale nightly bingo game at a Philadelphia hotel managed and partly owned by them. The bingo game was ostensibly, but not actually, church sponsored. Each defendant was sentenced to fines and terms of imprisonment concurrent with the longest sentence, 18 months imprisonment on the conspiracy count.

Defendants' motion before the district court for bail pending appeal was denied, pursuant to that court's interpretation of the Bail Reform Act of 1984 . . . . The jury's verdict of conviction was returned October 19, 1984, and defendants' sentences were imposed on November 30, 1984. Defendants have appealed from their convictions, and those appeals are presently pending in this court. Appellants' briefs on the merits are not due until next month. After denying bail, the district court ordered defendants to surrender on January 28, 1985.

. . . The relevant section of the 1984 Act governing bail pending appeal, to be codified at 18 U.S.C. § 3143, provides:

(b) RELEASE OR DETENTION PENDING APPEAL BY THE DEFENDANT

The judicial officer [of a court of original jurisdiction over an offense, or of a Federal appellate court] shall order that a person who has been found guilty of an offense and sentenced to a term of imprisonment, and who has filed an appeal or a petition for writ of certiorari, be detained, unless the judicial officer finds—

(1) by clear and convincing evidence that the person is not likely to flee or pose a danger to the safety of any person or the community if released pursuant to sections 3142(b) or (c); and (2) that the appeal is not for purpose of delay and raises a substantial question of law or fact likely to result in reversal or

an order for a new trial. If the judicial officer makes such findings, he shall order the release of the person in accordance with the provisions of sections 3142(b) or (c).

The district court found that appellants Stanton and Robert Miller satisfied subsection (1) in that they were "not likely to flee or pose a danger to the safety of another person or community if released." The district court also found that "the appeal was not for the purpose of delay." It is not clear whether the district court found that the appeal "raises substantial questions of law or fact." The court denied bail pending appeal after stating that it could not "in good faith . . . conclude that it is likely to result in a reversal or an order for a new trial."

It appears that the district court construed the statutory language to signify that it could grant bail on appeal only upon finding that its own rulings were likely to be reversed. At the hearing on the post-trial motions, the court stated that the Act "practically means that the district judge has to determine that he has probably made an error in the decision that he has rendered in the lower court . . . ." At the sentencing hearing, the district court stated that, "it would be, I think, a very rare case that the judicial officer would make such a finding, but I think that's the intent and purpose of the statute, it seems to me rather clear they do not intend persons to remain on bail where an appeal is filed." We conclude that this is not the correct interpretation of the statutory language.

The Bail Reform Act of 1984 was enacted because Congress wished to reverse the presumption in favor of bail that had been established under the prior statute, the Bail Reform Act of 1966. Under that Act, even after conviction the defendant was entitled to bail "unless the court or judge has reason to believe that no one or more conditions of release will reasonably assure that the person will not flee or pose a danger to any other person or any other community." Congressional concern with this standard was manifest. As early as 1970, Congress enacted a much more stringent rule for bail pending appeal under its authority as the legislative body for the District of Columbia, D.C. Code Ann. § 23-1325(c), the precursor of the Bail Reform Act of 1984.

The House Report on the District of Columbia Act was explicit as to the reasons for congressional dissatisfaction with the prevailing criteria for bail pending appeal. It states:

> [O]nce a person has been convicted and sentenced to jail, there is absolutely no reason for the law to favor release pending appeal or even permit it in the absence of exceptional circumstances. First and most important, the conviction, in which the defendant's guilt of a crime has been established beyond a reasonable doubt, is presumably correct in law, a presumption factually supported by the low rate of reversal of criminal convictions in the Federal system. Second, the decision to send a convicted person to jail and thereby reject all other sentencing alternatives, by its very nature includes a determination by the sentencing judge that the defendant is dangerous to the person or property of others, and dangerous when sentenced, not a year later after the appeal is decided. Third, release of a criminal defendant into the community, even after conviction, destroys whatever deterrent effect remains in the criminal law. Finally, . . . the purpose of the appellate process is not to give a convicted criminal, by means of release pending appeal, an opportunity to demonstrate a basis for reducing a sentence after the conviction has been affirmed.

The provision governing bail on appeal in the Bail Reform Act of 1984 is identical to that in the District of Columbia Code. In the three relevant Senate Reports, that body made clear that the purpose of the Act was to reverse the presumption in favor of bail, but not to deny bail entirely to persons who appeal their convictions, as the district court believed.

. . . Our task is to give a reasonable construction to the statutory language in a manner that effectuates the congressional intent. Under the new act, after first making the findings as to flight, danger, and delay, a court must determine that the question raised on appeal is a "substantial" one, *i.e.*, it must find that the significant question at issue is one which is either novel, which has not been decided by controlling precedent, or which is fairly doubtful. This represents a marked change in the inquiry into the merits in the context of a bail determination, since the 1966 act only required the court to determine whether the issue was "frivolous," *see* 18 U.S.C. § 3148 (repealed by 1984 Act).

After the court finds that the question on appeal meets the new "substantial" test, it must determine whether that issue is sufficiently important to the merits that a contrary appellate ruling is likely to require reversal or a new trial. The statutory language requiring a finding that the appeal "raises a substantial question of law or fact likely to result in reversal or an order for a new trial" cannot be read as meaning, as the district court apparently believed, that the district court must conclude that its own order is likely to be reversed.

In the first place, such a reading would render language in the statute surplusage because every question that is likely to be reversed must by definition be "substantial." In the second place, we are unwilling to attribute to Congress the cynicism that would underlie the provision were it to be read as requiring the district court to determine the likelihood of its own error. A district judge who, on reflection, concludes that s/he erred may rectify that error when ruling on post-trial motions. Judges do not knowingly leave substantial errors uncorrected, or deliberately misconstrue applicable precedent. Thus, it would have been capricious of Congress to have conditioned bail only on the willingness of a trial judge to certify his or her own error.

For a similar reason, the phrase "likely to result in reversal or an order for a new trial" cannot reasonably be construed to require the district court to predict the probability of reversal. Instead, that language must be read as going to the significance of the substantial issue to the ultimate disposition of the appeal. A question of law or fact may be substantial but may, nonetheless, in the circumstances of a particular case, be considered harmless, to have no prejudicial effect, or to have been insufficiently preserved. A court may find that reversal or a new trial is "likely" only if it concludes that the question is so integral to the merits of the conviction on which defendant is to be imprisoned that a contrary appellate holding is likely to require reversal of the conviction or a new trial.

This construction . . . effectuates congressional intent in that a defendant seeking bail on appeal must now show that his or her appeal has more merit than under the discarded "frivolous" test, but preserves the court's discretion to give bail in those cases, which will consequently be considerably reduced in number, where defendant can meet the criteria discussed above.

In summary, then, under the criteria established by the 1984 Act which the defendant now has the burden of proving if s/he seeks bail pending appeal, the court must find:

(1)   that the defendant is not likely to flee or pose a danger to the safety of any other person or the community if released;

(2)   that the appeal is not for purpose of delay;

(3)   that the appeal raises a substantial question of law or fact; and

(4)   that if that substantial question is determined favorably to defendant on appeal, that decision is likely to result in reversal or an order for a new trial of all counts on which imprisonment has been imposed.

[Remanded]

NOTES

1. *Meaning of "substantial question."* Many federal courts hold that a "substantial question" is one that is "close" or "very well could be decided the other way." *United States v. Quinn*, 416 F. Supp. 2d 133, 136 (D.D.C. 2006). A minority view is it is one that is "fairly debatable." *United States v. Montoya*, 908 F.2d 450 (9th Cir. 1990).

2. *Limits on presumption?* As a policy matter, when a defendant is pursuing an appeal, should the presumption against entitlement to release apply in all cases? For example, should the presumption apply only to "serious" offenses? Or should it apply only to cases in which the term of imprisonment exceeds five years?

3. *State variation of bail pending appeal.* A number of states are more liberal than the federal government in permitting release pending an appeal of a criminal conviction. California, for example, extends bail as a matter of right in cases where the defendant is convicted of a misdemeanor; in other cases, release on bail is discretionary and factors to be considered include whether the defendant is likely to flee or pose a danger to the safety of others. Calif. Pen. Code §§ 1272 and 1272.1. Similarly, New York permits the judge to issue an order of release on recognizance or on all bail, "unless the defendant received a Class A felony sentence." N.Y. C.P.L. § 530.50. Still other jurisdictions address the question of post-conviction bail on the basis of the specific term of years which the defendant has been ordered to serve. Pennsylvania, for example, grants the same right to bail on appeal as before verdict if the sentence is less than two years; if two years or more, bail is at the discretion of the judge. Pa. R. Crim. P. 4009(B). Texas denies the right to bail pending an appeal from any felony conviction where the punishment is 10 years confinement or greater; it is discretionary in other cases. Tex. C. Crim. P. art. 44.04(b) & (c). Another state statute reflects the same underlying policy against entitlement to bail on appeal as discussed in *Miller.* Florida prohibits a convicted felon from release on bail upon appeal "unless the defendant establishes that the appeal is taken in good faith, on grounds fairly debatable, and not frivolous." Fla. Stat. § 903.132.

PROBLEM 5-2. BLUMBERG'S APPEAL

Neal Blumberg was convicted of unlawful sexual contact with a minor, a Class B felony punishable by incarceration of 20 years. He had posted bond prior to trial and appeared as scheduled. There was no evidence of unlawful activity on his part after arrest.

He now appeals his conviction, contending that the alleged victim was coerced to testify against him by police officials. This claim was presented at trial, but rejected by both judge and jury.

1. If this case were governed by the *Miller* principles, on what bases should the attorney for the government argue that Blumberg be denied bail? How should those assertions be countered by defense counsel?

2. Assume this case were tried under Pennsylvania law, discussed in Note 3. If you were the trial judge, what facts or circumstances would be relevant to the exercise of your discretion regarding the grant of bail on appeal?

J. ETHICAL ISSUES

Pretrial release raises ethical issues for both prosecution and defense lawyers. Of course both are obligated to represent their clients competently. In the context of pretrial release, their obligations are surprisingly similar.

Both prosecutors and defense counsel have an obligation to act with reasonable diligence and promptness. *See, e.g.,* Model Rules of Professional Conduct Rule 1.3 (1995)

("A lawyer shall act with reasonable diligence and promptness in representing a client"). *See also* Model Code of Professional Responsibility Canon 7 (1980) ("A lawyer should represent a client zealously within the bounds of the law"; Model Code of Professional Responsibility DR 7-101(A)(1) (1980) ("[A lawyer shall not] intentionally fail to seek the lawful objectives of his client through reasonably available means permitted by law . . . ").

In the context of pretrial release, the American Bar Association has adopted standards requiring the prosecutor to "cooperate in good faith in arrangements for release under the prevailing system for pretrial release." Standards for Criminal Justice, Prosecution Function § 3-3.10(b) (3d ed. 1993). The commentary to this provision indicates that the prosecutor should ordinarily assist in making arrangements for pretrial release "unless unusual circumstances impose a duty to object to release." The commentary further notes:

> In most cases, there will be no basis for the prosecutor to oppose the accused's release on appropriate bond or other conditions. The prosecutor should not ask for excessive bail to prevent release or in an attempt to coerce a plea agreement or other concessions through the accused's continued incarceration.

Id. commentary at 79.

Competent defense counsel must also promptly seek pretrial release in most situations. The American Bar Association's Standards urge defense counsel to take prompt legal action, including considering such procedural matters as seeking pretrial release. Standards for Criminal Justice, Defense Function § 4-3.6 (3d ed. 1993).

Once a defendant has been released pending trial, what happens if he or she does not appear as scheduled? The ethical rules are strangely silent on the issue whether defense counsel must disclose the whereabouts of his or her client. The issue depends on the scope of the attorney's obligation of confidentiality. The American Trial Lawyer's Code of Conduct (issued in 1982 and thus far not formally adopted by any jurisdiction) reads confidentiality broadly. In an illustrative case, this Code states clearly that a lawyer, representing a client who has "jumped bail" and absconded, would commit a disciplinary violation by revealing the client's whereabouts. American Trial Lawyer's Association, The American Lawyer's Code of Conduct, Illustrative Cases 1(h).

The American Bar Association's Model Rules of Professional Conduct takes a *permissive* approach to a lawyer's actions in such situations. Model Rule 1.6 permits an attorney:[*]

> to reveal information relating to the representation of a client to the extent that the lawyer reasonably believes necessary, [*inter alia*], to prevent reasonably certain death or substantial bodily harm; to prevent the client from committing a crime or fraud that is reasonably certain to result in substantial injury to the financial interests or property of another and in furtherance of which the client has used or is using the lawyer's services; to prevent, mitigate or rectify substantial injury to the financial interests or property of another that is reasonably certain to result or has resulted from the client's commission of a crime or fraud in furtherance of which the client has used the lawyer's services; . . . to comply with other law or a court order.

Model Rules of Professional Conduct Rule 1.6 (2005). However, in all of these instances, the choice to reveal such information belongs to the attorney. Judicial opinions are split on the issues. *See generally* John M. Burkhoff, Criminal Defense Ethics § 6.5(a)(2) (rev. ed. 1999); Carolyn Crotty Guttilla, Note, *Caught Between a Rock and a Hard Place: When Can or Should an Attorney Disclose a Client's Confidence?*, 32 SUFFOLK U. L. REV. 707, 721–723 (1999) (indicating that court decisions are mixed as to whether an attorney

---

is required to disclose a fugitive client's location). Do you agree with the American Trial Lawyer's approach? Do you agree with the Model Rule's permissive standard? Would it matter whether absconding was a crime? Would it matter that the missing client is accused of a property crime or a violent crime?

Chapter 6

THE FIRST EVIDENTIARY HEARING: THE PRELIMINARY EXAMINATION

A. INTRODUCTION

In many criminal cases, the defendant has a *preliminary examination* or, as it is sometimes called, a *preliminary hearing*, a *probable cause hearing*, an *examining trial*, a *PX*, a *prelim*, or a *bindover hearing*. Although whether and when this hearing occurs varies from case to case and jurisdiction to jurisdiction, typically the defendant will first have had an initial appearance, discussed in Chapter 4, during which the presiding judge or magistrate assesses the validity of any arrest and detention, informs the defendant of various rights, and schedules the preliminary examination in a few days or weeks. Occasionally the initial appearance and preliminary examination are combined in one hearing.

[1] Overview

As discussed more fully below, the primary theoretical purpose of the preliminary examination is to determine whether there is probable cause to send the case for further proceedings. Weak cases, according to theory, should be screened out of the system so the defendant and often the defendant's family do not have to suffer the many financial and emotional harms that accompany criminal prosecution. Of course, the preliminary examination also serves many other functions, some more important than the screening function. The screening function may have little actual relevance in the typical criminal case where the government's proof is so overwhelming that probable cause is obviously present.

The preliminary examination resembles a bench trial. The defendant will be represented by counsel and the local prosecutor will present the government's case by calling one or more witnesses. The defense may or may not elect to call witnesses or offer a serious defense.

[2] Relationship to Grand Jury

If the judge in the preliminary examination finds sufficient probable cause that the crime occurred and the defendant committed it, the judge will make a formal finding that probable cause exists. Often this is referred to as a "bindover," meaning that the judge will bind (or turn) the case over to the grand jury or, in jurisdictions with a limited or nonexistent grand jury system, for an information (a formal accusation prepared by the prosecutor) or trial.

It should be noted that the crime(s) bound over for further proceedings are not necessarily the same as those included in the complaint, discussed in Chapter 3. Sometimes the judge may bind over charges that were proven by probable cause at the preliminary hearing, even though they differed from those in the complaint.

[a] Jurisdictions where Grand Jury Indictment Unnecessary

Preliminary hearing after information filed by prosecutor. In those jurisdictions that have dispensed with the grand jury, often the prosecutor will issue an *information*, which is a statement of formal charges, and the defendant is then entitled to a preliminary hearing to assess whether the charges are supported by probable cause. If probable cause is found, the case is scheduled for trial.

Information after preliminary hearing. If no information was filed before the preliminary hearing, often one must be filed after that hearing and before trial. Some locales limit the permissible scope of the information to those charges for which probable cause was found at the preliminary hearing or to charges "related to" the bound-over charges. Thus, in these jurisdictions the preliminary hearing may limit the scope of subsequent formal charges.

[b]   When Grand Jury is Used

In those jurisdictions using the grand jury, usually the next step after a preliminary hearing is for the grand jury, discussed in Chapter 7, to consider the case. As strange as it may seem, the grand jury will then make a second, seemingly redundant, probable cause determination, returning an indictment only if the proof establishes probable cause to believe a crime was committed and the defendant was the culprit.

[3]   Often the Only Adversarial Proceeding

The preliminary examination can be a very important procedural facet of the typical criminal case. Not only does it present the accused with an opportunity to learn about some of the prosecution's case and to attempt to have the case thrown out or charges reduced, it also may be the only adversary hearing that occurs in the entire case. Recall that virtually all criminal defendants eventually plead guilty. At the "change of plea" hearing, the defendant typically waives the right to trial and other related due process rights, and rarely contests the facts offered by the prosecution to support acceptance of the guilty plea by the court. Generally, a plea bargain has been made between the prosecution and defense prior to the plea hearing. The judge's acceptance of the plea and ratification of the plea agreement is most often a mere formality (except that, as discussed in Chapter 11, the judge must take pains to assure that the guilty plea is entered knowingly, intelligently, and voluntarily). Thus, the preliminary examination may actually have been the only opportunity for a judge to hear an adversarial presentation of the case and assess the strength of the prosecution's evidence.

[4]   Preliminary Hearing as "Critical Stage"

COLEMAN v. ALABAMA
399 U.S. 1 (1970

MR. JUSTICE BRENNAN announced the judgment of the Court and delivered the following opinion.

Petitioners were convicted in an Alabama Circuit Court of assault with intent to murder in the shooting of one Reynolds after he and his wife parked their car on an Alabama highway to change a flat tire.

. . . Petitioners . . . argue that the preliminary hearing prior to their indictment was a "critical stage" of the prosecution and that Alabama's failure to provide them with appointed counsel at the hearing therefore unconstitutionally denied them the assistance of counsel.

II

MR. JUSTICE DOUGLAS, MR. JUSTICE WHITE, and MR.. JUSTICE MARSHALL join Part II

. . . This Court has held that a person accused of crime "requires the guiding hand of counsel at every step in the proceedings against him," *Powell v. Alabama,* 287 U.S. 45, 69 (1932), and that that constitutional principle is not limited to the presence of counsel at trial. "It is central to that principle that in addition to counsel's presence at trial, the accused is guaranteed that he need not stand alone against the State at any stage of the prosecution, formal or informal, in court or out, where counsel's absence might derogate from the accused's right to a fair trial." *United States v. Wade,* 388 U.S. 218, 226 (1967). Accordingly, "the principle of *Powell v. Alabama* and succeeding cases requires that we scrutinize any pretrial confrontation of the accused to determine whether the presence of his counsel is necessary to preserve the defendant's basic right to a fair trial as affected by his right meaningfully to cross-examine the witnesses against him and to have effective assistance of counsel at the trial itself. It calls upon us to analyze whether potential substantial prejudice to defendant's rights inheres in the particular confrontation and the ability of counsel to help avoid that prejudice." *Id.* at 227. Applying this test, the Court has held that "critical stages" include the pretrial type of arraignment where certain rights may be sacrificed or lost, and the pretrial lineup . . . .

The preliminary hearing is not a required step in an Alabama prosecution. The prosecutor may seek an indictment directly from the grand jury without a preliminary hearing. The opinion of the Alabama Court of Appeals in this case instructs us that under Alabama law the sole purposes of a preliminary hearing are to determine whether there is sufficient evidence against the accused to warrant presenting his case to the grand jury and, if so, to fix bail if the offense is bailable. The court continued:

> . . . At the preliminary hearing . . . the accused is not required to advance any defenses, and failure to do so does not preclude him from availing himself of every defense he may have upon the trial of the case. Also *Pointer v. State,* 380 U.S. 400 (1965), bars the admission of testimony given at a pretrial proceeding where the accused did not have the benefit of cross-examination by and through counsel. Thus, nothing occurring at the preliminary hearing in absence of counsel can substantially prejudice the rights of the accused on trial.

This Court is of course bound by this construction of the governing Alabama law. However, from the fact that in cases where the accused has no lawyer at the hearing the Alabama courts prohibit the State's use at trial of anything that occurred at the hearing, it does not follow that the Alabama preliminary hearing is not a "critical stage" of the State's criminal process . . . . Plainly the guiding hand of counsel at the preliminary hearing is essential to protect the indigent accused against an erroneous or improper prosecution. First, the lawyer's skilled examination and cross-examination of witnesses may expose fatal weaknesses in the State's case that may lead the magistrate to refuse to bind the accused over. Second, in any event, the skilled interrogation of witnesses by an experienced lawyer can fashion a vital impeachment tool for use in cross-examination of the State's witnesses at the trial, or preserve testimony favorable to the accused of a witness who does not appear at the trial. Third, trained counsel can more effectively discover the case the State has against his client and make possible the preparation of a proper defense to meet that case at the trial. Fourth, counsel can also be influential at the preliminary hearing in making effective arguments for the accused on such matters as the necessity for an early psychiatric examination or bail.

The inability of the indigent accused on his own to realize these advantages of a lawyer's assistance compels the conclusion that the Alabama preliminary hearing is a "critical stage" of the State's criminal process at which the accused is "as much entitled to such aid (of counsel) . . . as at the trial itself." *Powell v. Alabama,* 287 U.S. at 57.

III

MR. JUSTICE BLACK, MR. JUSTICE DOUGLAS, MR. JUSTICE WHITE, and MR. JUSTICE MARSHALL join Part III,

There remains, then, the question of the relief to which petitioners are entitled.

. . . We accordingly vacate the petitioners' convictions and remand the case to the Alabama courts for such proceedings not inconsistent with this opinion as they may deem appropriate to determine whether such denial of counsel was harmless error and therefore whether the convictions should be reinstated or a new trial ordered.

[Omitted are the concurring opinions of JUSTICES BLACK, DOUGLAS, and WHITE; the concurring and dissenting opinion of JUSTICE HARLAN; and the dissenting opinions of

CHIEF JUSTICE BURGER and JUSTICE STEWART.]

NOTES

1. *Critical stage.* Since, according to the Supreme Court, the preliminary hearing is a "critical stage" of the criminal process that serves a number of important functions, should it be constitutionally required by the due process guarantee of a fair trial? If so, every state would have to have a preliminary hearing (or the equivalent) as part of its criminal procedures.

2. *Function of counsel.* In *Coleman*, the Supreme Court recognized that counsel at an Alabama preliminary hearing serves many important functions. Most of these are "unofficial" in that no rule of criminal procedure specifically assigns them as functions of counsel. The functions of counsel listed in *Coleman* are to: (1) expose weaknesses in the prosecution's evidence so the case can be dismissed; (2) preserve helpful testimony and fashion impeachment evidence for use at trial; (3) discover the prosecution's case to assist in trial preparation; and (4) make arguments on such matters as bail and the need for psychiatric evaluation. Has *Coleman* elevated these functions to the status of constitutional rights, so that the defendant cannot be denied the opportunity (within reasonable limits) to use the preliminary examination for discovery, evidence preservation, and gathering information for impeachment at trial?

3. *Benefits of counsel. Coleman* deals with some possible advantages accruing from a preliminary examination where the defendant is represented by counsel. Are there other advantages that the *Coleman* Court ignored? Did *Coleman* ignore some harms that could occur if the defendant has a preliminary examination without benefit of a defense lawyer?

4. *Harmless error.* You will recall that the principal purpose of the preliminary examination is to determine whether or not there is probable cause to charge the defendant with a criminal offense. There appears to be no challenge in the *Coleman* case to the fact that petitioners were found guilty beyond a reasonable doubt of assault with intent to murder. Given a conviction, in what way could it be argued that denial of counsel at the preliminary examination constituted anything other than harmless error?

B. FUNCTIONS AND STRATEGIES

The preliminary examination serves a number of functions, some obvious and others quite subtle. The strategy a lawyer adopts for the hearing depends on the functions the hearing is to serve in the case.

[1] Screening

There is general agreement that the primary function of the preliminary examination is to protect individuals from having to defend themselves against charges that are insubstantial or are brought carelessly or maliciously. The charges are dismissed if the preliminary hearing judge finds the government did not establish probable cause that the defendant committed a crime.

The preliminary examination performs a screening function — sifting out weak cases that should not be retained in an already overcrowded criminal justice system. According to an important study of the preliminary hearing, "[t]he pretrial screening decisions are designed not only to save the government and the accused from incurring unnecessary expense, but also to protect the accused from unfounded and malicious allegations, thereby avoiding the anxiety and embarrassment of trial." Deborah Day Emerson & Nancy L. Ames, THE ROLE OF THE GRAND JURY AND THE PRELIMINARY HEARING IN PRETRIAL SCREENING 3 (National Institute of Justice 1984). The preliminary examination may also spare the accused from unwarranted pretrial detention.

Logically, if the prosecution cannot offer enough proof to satisfy the probable cause standard, then there is too little justification to retain the case in the criminal justice system, since it would be unlikely that the state could later satisfy the higher trial standard of proof beyond a reasonable doubt. Certainly the state would have to offer more convincing proof at trial than it presented at the preliminary examination.

Tactical considerations. If the defense strategy at the preliminary examination is to seek a dismissal or reduction of charges, counsel should vigorously object to inadmissible evidence and aggressively cross-examine prosecution witnesses. In unusual cases, defense counsel pursuing this strategy may even elect to offer proof and consider recommending that the client testify at the preliminary examination. Often this defense proof is offered only after defense counsel has tried unsuccessfully to have the case dismissed at the end of the prosecution's proof.

However, if, as is most often the case, a finding of probable cause appears to be a foregone conclusion, then the preliminary hearing becomes more useful to the defense as a discovery vehicle than as a screening device.

[2] Discovery

Although the screening function is everywhere given as the primary (or even the sole) purpose of the preliminary examination, experienced prosecutors and criminal defense lawyers realize that another critical function is discovery by the defendant.

Limited discovery. Formal discovery is quite limited in criminal cases in virtually every jurisdiction. Usually such devices as interrogatories and depositions are either unavailable or severely limited in criminal cases. *See, e.g.,* Fed. R. Crim. P. 15 (depositions available only in extraordinary circumstances to preserve testimony). Moreover, informal discovery opportunities may also be severely limited. For example, crime victims and investigating police officers may refuse to talk with defense counsel about the crime. This means that defense counsel could first learn about their testimony when the victim or officer testifies on direct examination during the trial. The use of the preliminary examination as a discovery tool is less effective if, as discussed below, the jurisdiction permits probable cause to be established by hearsay. In such jurisdictions, one witness may summarize the testimony of many people who will not testify in person at the preliminary examination.

Tactics to obtain discovery at preliminary examination. Since this dearth of information makes it difficult to prepare for trial, defense counsel (and sometimes the prosecution) will use the preliminary examination as a vehicle to learn about the other side's case. One way is for defense counsel to listen carefully to (and sometimes cross-examine) the prosecution witnesses who testify at the preliminary examination. A related, and sometimes dangerous, way is for the preliminary hearing defense counsel to call as *defense* witnesses those people who are likely to testify for the prosecution at trial but will not be called as prosecution witnesses at the preliminary examination. This may be especially appealing if the witness has refused to talk with defense counsel during the investigation of the case. Many judges dislike this tactic and will only allow the defense to call as witnesses at a preliminary hearing those persons "whose proposed testimony would be reasonably likely to establish an affirmative defense, negate a crime element, or impeach prosecution evidence." *People v. Erwin,* 25 Cal. Rptr. 2d 348 (Cal. App. 1993).

In interrogating these prosecution witnesses, often defense counsel will probe rather than challenge, trying to get as much information as possible from each prosecution witness. For example, counsel for the defense may ask prosecution witnesses to give the names and addresses of everyone they know who has information about the event (to help locate new defense witnesses and be better prepared for unknown prosecution witnesses); to relate the witness's own history of drugs, criminal convictions, and psychological problems (to use to impeach the witness at trial); and to describe in minute detail the facts the witness knows about (to facilitate preparation for trial, perhaps by spotting a slight inconsistency or vagueness).

There are many risks when the defense lawyer calls a likely prosecution witness as a defense witness at a preliminary hearing. Unless the judge permits the witness to be declared a hostile witness, defense counsel will be limited to non-leading questions, while the prosecutor will be permitted to reshape the direct testimony by asking leading questions on cross examination. And, of course, the defense lawyer could inadvertently provide the prosecution with the name and testimony of a most helpful prosecution witness.

Jencks Act (Rule 26.2). Another opportunity for discovery by both sides is provided by the so-called Jencks Act or Rule 26.2 of the Federal Rules of Criminal Procedure. *See* Fed. R. Crim. P. 5.1(h) & 26.2(g)(1). This rule, also applicable at trial, gives either side the right to examine and use any statement of a testifying witness that relates to the subject of the testimony and is in the possession of the party calling that witness. The statement must be made available after the witness has testified at the preliminary examination, but of course can be provided earlier. Thus, if the prosecution calls an eyewitness to testify at a preliminary hearing, after that witness has testified the prosecution, under Rule 26.2, must give the defense lawyer access to any statement the eyewitness made that is relevant to the testimony. The prosecution can avoid this obligation by electing not to call the eyewitness as a witness at the preliminary examination. Rule 5.1(h) also gives the judge the discretion to not require the production of these statements "for good cause shown."

Limiting "fishing expeditions." At some point the judge or prosecutor may attempt to stop what may be characterized as a defense "fishing expedition," citing the basic rule that the preliminary examination is not designed to provide discovery. *See, e.g.,* Cal. Penal Code § 866 (preliminary examination "shall not be used for purposes of discovery"). Often this argument is made after the prosecutor believes that he or she has offered sufficient proof to satisfy the probable cause standard. If the court agrees, defense counsel then will have to curtail questions that have virtually nothing to do with the presence or absence of probable cause. A typical judicial endorsement of the anti-fishing expedition view has been stated as follows:

> The mission of the hearing is an investigation into probable cause for further proceedings against the accused. It does not include discovery for the sake of discovery. To be sure, the evidence the Government offers to establish probable cause is by nature also discovery for the accused. So also is information adduced on cross-examination of Government witnesses on the aspects of direct-examination testimony tending to build up probable cause. In those senses, some discovery becomes a by-product of the process of demonstrating probable cause. But in no sense is discovery a legitimate end unto itself.

Coleman v. Burnett, 477 F.2d 1187, 1199–1200 (D.C. Cir. 1973).

Since it is no secret that the preliminary examination can help the defense learn about the prosecution's evidence and strategy, the prosecutor will often offer only a bare bones case at the preliminary hearing so that the other defense receives only minimal discovery. Commonly, for example, the prosecution's case at the preliminary examination will consist of only a small number of the witnesses it plans to use later at trial. Sometimes only one prosecution witness will testify. Similarly, the defense usually offers few or no witnesses of its own, and may try not to disclose its theory of the case and its likely defenses.

[3] Preserve Testimony

The preliminary examination also serves to preserve testimony for use at trial. A preliminary examination will routinely satisfy the former testimony hearsay exception, permitting a record (or even memory) of the preliminary examination testimony to be used as proof in the later trial if the witness who testified at the preliminary examination becomes unavailable to testify at the later trial and the defendant had an opportunity to cross examine the witness at the hearing. *See, e.g.*, Fed. R. Evid. 804(b)(1). The confrontation clause is also satisfied by this use of the preliminary examination. *Crawford v. Washington*, 541 U.S. 36 (2004).

The prosecution in particular may utilize the preliminary examination to preserve testimony if, for example, a prosecution witness is dying or, for any number of reasons, the prosecution suspects the witness may not testify at trial despite being subpoenaed to do so. Of course, in these same cases the defense may prefer that the witness not testify at the preliminary examination so that the witness's testimony at that proceeding cannot be used later at trial if the witness is unavailable at trial. This could occur, for example, if a key government witness were terminally ill. If the witness does not testify at the preliminary examination and dies before trial, the prosecution may be barred from using the witness' statements to the police as evidence at trial. In those few jurisdictions that do not require a formal record of preliminary examinations, counsel must ensure that a proper record is made if the evidence is to be preserved for later use. A stenographic or audio record may also aid in the use of information discovered during the hearing. An indigent defendant may have to file a motion to have the government pay the costs of the transcription.

[4] Test or Prepare Witness

Sometimes the preliminary examination will serve as a testing ground for witnesses. Counsel for either side can use the hearing to assess whether a particular witness comes across well or poorly, or is even willing to testify at all. The mere experience of testifying at the preliminary examination can also help the witness become more effective at trial. The preliminary examination can serve as a dry run so that at trial the witness is not answering questions for the first time. This may be especially important for the witness who will be vigorously cross-examined at trial and can benefit from a lifelike practice session. If a witness performs poorly, counsel will have time to better prepare the witness to testify at trial.

[5] Facilitate Later Impeachment

Witnesses at the preliminary examination are usually less prepared than those at trial since lawyers (usually the prosecution) spend less time "working up" the case at the early stages. This means that adverse counsel (usually the defense) at the preliminary examination may be successful in eliciting contradictory statements or at least ambiguous or ambivalent shadings to questions on cross-examination. At the least, counsel may be able to pin down a preliminary hearing witness so that the witness may be impeached at trial if he or she deviates from the preliminary hearing testimony. Of course, this cross-examination may also cause a witness to become a better trial witness who is even more convinced of the accuracy of his or her observations.

[6] Solidify Identification

The preliminary hearing can also be used, particularly by the prosecution, to solidify a witness's identification of the accused. The process of viewing and identifying the accused during the preliminary hearing provides the witness with an additional opportunity to feel comfortable with the identification that will be sought during the subsequent criminal trial. The obvious danger that an identification made during a preliminary examination could be improperly suggestive prompted the United States Supreme Court to hold that a criminal defendant has a Sixth Amendment right to counsel at a preliminary examination where the victim will make an in-court identification of the alleged offender. In *Moore v. Illinois*, 434 U.S. 220, 229–230 (1977), the Supreme Court observed:

It is difficult to imagine a more suggestive manner in which to present a suspect to a witness for their critical first confrontation than was employed in this case. The [rape] victim, who had seen her assailant for only 10 to 15 seconds, was asked to make her identification after she was told that she was going to view a suspect, after she was told his name and heard it called as he was led before the bench [at the preliminary examination], and after she heard the prosecutor recite the evidence believed to implicate petitioner. Had petitioner been represented by counsel, some or all of this suggestiveness could have been avoided.

[7] Send Message to Witness

Some attorneys use the preliminary examination as a vehicle to communicate with a witness. During direct or cross-examination, counsel will let the witness know that certain subjects will be explored or that the cross-examination will be detailed and hostile. This may induce the witness to rethink his or her testimony. Of course it may also alert the witness or witness' counsel about weaknesses in the testimony and provide an opportunity to eliminate or at least minimize the weakness at the subsequent trial. Can an ethical lawyer use this opportunity to intimidate a witness so that the witness will change testimony or decline to testify at trial?

[8] Reality Therapy for Defendant

A criminal defendant may actually or apparently be convinced that he or she has a viable defense or that the prosecution's case is weak. Conversely, the defendant may believe that the prosecution's case is overwhelming. In either event, the defense or prosecution may use the preliminary examination to help convince the client of the strength or weakness of the prosecution or defense's case. For example, the victim may testify at the preliminary hearing and appear as a credible, convincing witness or as an unsure, weak one. This "reality therapy" may do such things as convince the defendant to be honest with defense counsel or to rethink the defendant's response to plea bargain offers.

[9] Affect Plea Bargaining

Since the overwhelming number of criminal defendants, including those who have a preliminary examination, will eventually plead guilty, the preliminary examination may have an important impact on plea negotiations. One way is that it may help either side assess its likely success if the case were to go to trial. For example, the preliminary examination may apprise the defense that the prosecution witnesses are quite strong or quite weak. In either event, the defense will have new information to use in forming its plea bargaining strategy and in deciding whether to accept or reject a plea. And, as noted above, it may provide "reality therapy" for the defendant who has steadfastly disbelieved defense counsel's assessment of the prosecution's case. Overwhelming caseloads may lead some prosecutors to offer especially lenient sentences to offenders who save the prosecution time by waiving the preliminary examination.

[10] Affect Bail Decision

The preliminary examination may also affect the bail decision. By the time of the preliminary examination, it is likely that a decision will already have been made on whether the defendant will remain in custody until the trial. The conditions of release will have been set and often satisfied. But the initial bail decision may have been made on little information and can always be reopened by either the defense or prosecution on the basis of new data. If such information is presented at the preliminary examination, the judge is authorized to alter the initial release decision. For example, if the prosecutions's preliminary examination proof turns out to be quite weak and a conviction is doubtful, the court may lower the defendant's money bond or alleviate some of the harsh release conditions. On the other hand, if a preliminary examination witness testifies that the defendant has close associates who live in another country and has secreted a good bit of money, the judge may increase the amount of the bond or forbid release entirely.

[11] Diversion

In some jurisdictions a court may use the preliminary examination to have the defendant enter a diversion program which, if successfully completed, will result in a dismissal of the charges. The defendant may be required to waive the preliminary examination in order to participate. Peggy Fulton Hora, William Schma, & John T.A. Rosenthal, *Therapeutic Jurisprudence and the Drug Treatment Court Movement*, 74 NOTRE DAME L. REV. 439, 495 (1999).

C. PROCEDURES

Although the preliminary examination is an adversary hearing, it differs in many ways from a criminal trial.

[1] Federal Rule 5.1

The preliminary examination is routinely described in general terms in a jurisdiction's rules of criminal procedure. These rules usually describe at least some of the procedures that are applicable. The Federal Rules of Criminal Procedure are typical.

FEDERAL RULES OF CRIMINAL PROCEDURE

Rule 5.1. *Preliminary Hearing*

(a) **In General.** If a defendant is charged with an offense other than a petty offense, a magistrate judge must conduct a preliminary hearing unless:

(1) the defendant waives the hearing;

(2) the defendant is indicted;

(3) the government files an information under Rule 7(b) charging the defendant with a felony;

(4) the government files an information charging the defendant with a misdemeanor; or

(5) the defendant is charged with a misdemeanor and consents to trial before a magistrate judge.

(b) **Selecting a District.** A defendant arrested in a district other than where the offense was allegedly committed may elect to have the preliminary hearing conducted in the district where the prosecution is pending.

(c) **Scheduling.** The magistrate judge must hold the preliminary hearing within a reasonable time, but no later than 10 days after the initial appearance if the defendant is in custody and no later than 20 days if not in custody.

(d) **Extending the Time.** With the defendant's consent and upon a showing of good cause — taking into account the public interest in the prompt disposition of criminal cases — a magistrate judge may extend the time limits in Rule 5.1(c) one or more times. If the defendant does not consent, the magistrate judge may extend the time limits only on a showing that extraordinary circumstances exist and justice requires the delay.

(e) **Hearing and Finding.** At the preliminary hearing, the defendant may cross-examine adverse witnesses and may introduce evidence but may not object to evidence on the ground that it was unlawfully acquired. If the magistrate judge finds probable cause to believe an offense has been committed and the defendant committed it, the magistrate judge must promptly require the defendant to appear for further proceedings.

(f) Discharging the Defendant. If the magistrate judge finds no probable cause to believe an offense has been committed or the defendant committed it, the magistrate judge must dismiss the complaint and discharge the defendant. A discharge does not preclude the government from later prosecuting the defendant for the same offense.

(g) Recording the Proceedings. The preliminary hearing must be recorded by a court reporter or by a suitable recording device. A recording of the proceeding may be made available to any party upon request. A copy of the recording and a transcript may be provided to any party upon request and upon any payment required by applicable Judicial Conference regulations.

(h) Producing a Statement.

(1) **In General**. Rule 26.2(a)–(d) and (f) applies at any hearing under this rule, unless the magistrate judge for good cause rules otherwise in a particular case.

(2) **Sanctions for Not Producing a Statement.** If a party disobeys a Rule 26.2 order to deliver a statement to the moving party, the magistrate judge must not consider the testimony of a witness whose statement is withheld.

[2]   Entitlement

Since there is no federal constitutional right to a preliminary examination, jurisdictions vary considerably in their approach to providing the defendant access to a preliminary examination. To a large extent the issue depends on whether the jurisdiction utilizes the grand jury. Approximately half the states reject the necessity of a grand jury indictment and permit a felony prosecution to be pursued by either an indictment or an information. As discussed in Chapter 7, an *indictment* is a finding by a grand jury that there is probable cause to believe a crime occurred and the defendant is the person who committed it. An information is the same, except it represents a finding by the prosecuting attorney rather than by a group of citizens who constitute the grand jury.

More than a third of American jurisdictions retain the right to a grand jury determination for all felonies or capital crimes. A few of these mandate a grand jury proceeding for all crimes, unless waived by the accused. In most other American jurisdictions, a grand jury indictment is optional. The prosecutor may use either an indictment or information.

Effect of judgment. The most typical pattern, exemplified by Federal Rule of Criminal Procedure 5.1(a), is that the defendant has a right to a preliminary examination unless there has been an indictment. Once a grand jury has issued an indictment, however, usually the defendant no longer is entitled to have a preliminary examination. *See* 18 U.S.C. § 3060(e). The grand jury's decision that there is probable cause to indict is deemed sufficient to protect the defendant's interest in having weak cases removed from the system. In jurisdictions following this model, the prosecutor can prevent the defendant from having a preliminary examination by submitting the case to the grand jury before there has been a preliminary examination. Some prosecutors have even requested a delay in the scheduled date of the preliminary examination in order to enable the grand jury to consider the case first. If the grand jury issues an indictment, the preliminary examination is then canceled.

Equal protection. Obviously the preliminary examination, which is adversarial, affords the defendant many advantages unavailable if the hearing is replaced by a grand jury indictment, which is the product of a secret, nonadversarial procedure virtually unregulated by the judiciary. In *Hawkins v. Superior Court*, 586 P.2d 916 (Cal. 1978), the California Supreme Court held that California's equal protection guarantee gives the indicted citizen a right to a post-indictment preliminary examination if there was no such hearing before the indictment. This procedure equalized the rights of all criminal defendants by providing them all with the opportunity to have a preliminary examination. *Cf. State v. Sanabria*, 474 A.2d 760 (Conn. 1984) (state constitution mandates preliminary hearing in most serious cases). *Hawkins* has been widely rejected by other state courts. In California, public outcry against *Hawkins* resulted in an amendment to the California Constitution that barred a post-indictment preliminary hearing. *See generally Bowens v. Superior Court (People)*, 820 P.2d 600, (1991). Despite the demise of *Hawkins* in California, considering the fact that the preliminary hearing actually does provide the accused with many benefits, wasn't *Hawkins* correct in recognizing that defendants deprived of the hearing because of a prior indictment are at a considerable disadvantage? Is the disadvantage so important that it creates an equal protection violation?

Use of grand jury. Studies show that prosecutors vary considerably in the percentage of cases taken directly to the grand jury. One report showed that in one large county a preliminary hearing was scheduled in a majority of cases, while in another large county of the same state the preliminary hearing was scheduled infrequently (6% of the cases) and the grand jury was relied upon as a replacement. Deborah Day Emerson & Nancy L. Ames, The Role of the Grand Jury and the Preliminary Hearing in Pretrial Screening 32, 41 (1984).

Preliminary hearing after information. As noted above, in some jurisdictions the prosecutor has the option of using the grand jury or relying on an information. Since the issuance of an information requires no real screening by anyone outside the prosecutor's office, virtually all states permitting prosecution by information give the accused the right to a preliminary examination, at least in felony cases, if an information is used in lieu of a grand jury. If probable cause is found at this preliminary hearing, the case is "bound over" for trial. Of course, if an indictment rather than information is obtained in these jurisdictions, the defendant usually loses the right to have a preliminary examination, but may still be entitled to a so-called *Gerstein* determination, discussed in Chapter 4, to assess the validity of pretrial detention. *See Gerstein v. Pugh*, 420 U.S. 103 (1975).

[3] Timing

Many jurisdictions specify that the preliminary examination must be held a certain number of days after arrest or after the initial appearance. For example, Federal Rule 5.1(c) and many similar state provisions provide that the preliminary examination must be held no later than ten days after the initial appearance if the defendant is in custody and not more than twenty days if not in custody. *See also* 18 U.S.C. § 3060(b); Cal. Penal Code § 859b (not less than 2 days or more than 10, with exceptions; complaint dismissed if preliminary hearing not held within 60 days). These deadlines can be waived with the defendant's consent. Sometimes the time limits can be extended by the judge for good cause. *See, e.g.*, 18 U.S.C. § 3060(c) (extraordinary circumstances exist and delay is indispensable to the interests of justice). Both prosecution and defense may also — and frequently do — request a continuance.

[4] Length of Preliminary Hearing

Preliminary hearings usually are fairly brief. Several studies found that they averaged from thirty to forty-five minutes. Deborah Day Emerson & Nancy L. Ames, The Role of the Grand Jury and the Preliminary Hearing in Pretrial Screening 52 (1984); Kenneth Graham & Leon Letwin, *The Preliminary Hearings in Los Angeles: Some Field Findings and Legal-Policy Observations*, 18 U.C.L.A. L. Rev. 636 (1971); Janet A. Gilboy, *Prosecutors' Discretionary Use of the Grand Jury to Initiate or to Reinitiate Prosecution*, 1984 A. Bar Found. Res. J. 1, 22 (preliminary hearing in ordinary murder case in Chicago takes 20–30 minutes).

[5] Waiver

If the defendant is entitled to a preliminary examination, ordinarily he or she may elect to waive the proceeding and proceed directly to a later stage, perhaps the grand jury, arraignment, trial, or sentencing hearing. The waiver must be knowing, intelligent, and voluntary.

Procedures. Ordinarily the waiver must be in writing and is formalized in open court. A small minority of jurisdictions mandate that defense counsel approve any such waiver. *Esparaza v. State*, 595 So.2d 418 (Miss. 1992) (defense counsel approval of waiver required by statute). There is little judicial guidance on the standards of waiver of the preliminary examination. The ordinary standard for waiver of important rights is that the waiver must be knowing, intelligent, and voluntary. But in some jurisdictions a waiver is inferred if the defendant proceeds further into the criminal justice system without requesting a preliminary hearing, *see, e.g., Flowers v. Wyrick*, 732 F.2d 659 (8th Cir.), *cert. denied*, 469 U.S. 848 (1984) (guilty plea constitutes waiver of objection to lack of preliminary hearing); *State v. Kenney*, 973 S.W.2d 536 (Mo. App. 1998) (lack of preliminary hearing waived once defendant proceeds to trial without making objection), or does not appear for the scheduled hearing. *People v. Abbott*, 638 P.2d 781 (Colo. 1981) ("implied waiver" found).

Tactical considerations. As discussed above, there are many tactical considerations in the decision whether to waive the preliminary examination. Because of the many advantages to the defense, many experienced criminal defense lawyers caution against waiver of a preliminary examination. But waiver may make sense in certain situations when the costs of the hearing exceed its benefits. Sometimes, the defendant will waive the preliminary examination as part of a deal with the prosecutor who agrees to accept a more lenient sentence in exchange for not having to spend time preparing for and conducting the preliminary examination, or who agrees to recommend release on bail if the preliminary examination is waived.

A preliminary examination could also be waived by the defense in cases where it would serve no purpose, such as where the facts are undisputed. Another ground is when the preliminary examination would actually be harmful to the defense. Perhaps it would provide too much information to the prosecution, solidify the testimony of a weak prosecution witness, preserve the testimony of an important prosecution witness who may not appear at trial, alert the prosecution to the fact the accused is charged with less serious crimes than the proof would establish, cause a witness (perhaps the victim) to get angry and become resolved to harm the defense's interests at trial, or breed too much adverse publicity that can compromise the likelihood of a fair trial or will cause an unacceptable level of embarrassment to the defendant or the defendant's family, or will induce a reconsideration of an earlier decision to release the offender on favorable bail conditions.

[6] Evidence and Witnesses

Rules of evidence. Although a preliminary examination is an adversary proceeding, American jurisdictions differ in whether the formal rules of evidence apply. Of course the rules of privilege apply in all jurisdictions. A few jurisdictions also apply the full range of evidence rules so that whatever evidence is admissible at the preliminary examination would also be admissible at trial. Most, however, apply a watered-down set of evidence rules, admitting evidence that would not necessarily be admissible at a criminal trial. For example, many jurisdictions relax or do not follow the hearsay rules at preliminary examinations. *See* Cal. Penal Code § 872(b) (at preliminary examination experienced law enforcement officer may relate hearsay statements); N.Y. Crim. Proc. L. § 180.60(8) (hearsay which court finds "sufficiently reliable" admissible at preliminary examination); Fed. R. Evid. 1101(d)(3)(rules of evidence except for privileges do not apply at preliminary hearing). Indeed, in some locales the finding of probable cause may be based entirely on hearsay.

Exclusionary rule. Many statutes or criminal procedure rules also provide that the rule excluding unconstitutionally obtained evidence does not apply at a preliminary examination. *See* Federal Rule of Criminal Procedure 5.1(e) (defendant may not object to the introduction of evidence at the preliminary hearing on the ground that it was unlawfully acquired).

Policy issues. Lax evidence rules at the preliminary examination raise several interesting questions about the role of the preliminary examination as a screening device. There are good reasons why the preliminary hearing should adhere to the same evidence rules as the trial court. If the purpose of the preliminary examination is to screen out weak cases, why admit less reliable evidence at the preliminary hearing than at trial? If at the preliminary examination the state cannot establish probable cause by producing evidence that conforms with the constitution and the rules of evidence, can it meet the higher standard of proof beyond a reasonable doubt later at trial when it must adhere to the higher evidence rules?

On the other hand, there are also reasons why the lower standard makes sense. It is well established that the grand jury may consider evidence that does not comply with some constitutional provisions or the rules of evidence. If the preliminary examination uses the rules of evidence but the grand jury does not, would prosecutors be more inclined to use the grand jury in lieu of the preliminary hearing? If so, the preliminary examination's role as a protection against unwarranted prosecution would be greatly diminished. In addition, what impact would formalizing the admissibility of evidence have on the already overwhelmed workload of some prosecutors?

Witnesses, cross-examination, and documentary evidence. Witnesses at preliminary examinations routinely testify under oath and virtually all witnesses can be excluded ("*sequestered*") from the courtroom during testimony by other witnesses. Indeed, in some jurisdictions the general public can also be excluded during some or all of the preliminary examination in narrowly circumscribed circumstances where no other reasonable alternative can protect the defendant's interests in a fair trial. *See Press-Enterprise Co. v. Superior Court*, 478 U.S. 1 (1986) (preliminary examinations in California may be closed to the public only if there are specific findings that defendant's right to a fair trial would be prejudiced by publicity and that reasonable alternatives to closure will not adequately protect defendant's rights).

Both the defense and the prosecution ordinarily have the right to subpoena and to examine and cross-examine witnesses at the preliminary examination. Because the court is only examining for probable cause, some judges will exercise their discretion to cut off the cross-examination of prosecution witnesses once the state's proof has established probable cause. This is especially likely to occur if the judge believes that defense counsel is pursuing discovery rather than honestly attempting to establish lack of probable cause. All witnesses, including the defendant, may assert their Fifth Amendment right to refuse to answer incriminating questions at the preliminary hearing. Although the defendant has the right to testify (by statute and perhaps constitution) or not testify (by statute and Fifth Amendment) at the preliminary examination, usually the defendant will not take the stand. If it is more likely that the defendant would have the case thrown out if he or she testifies at the preliminary examination, why do most criminal defendants still refuse to testify at this proceeding?

PROBLEM 6-1. TO SPEAK OR NOT TO SPEAK

Kyle French had always been a bit strange. He had few friends, and was frequently observed talking to himself. He was known to be willing to fight anyone at any time, particularly when he was drunk. A month ago, Kyle got in a fight with Seth Joiner at the Star Tavern. Joiner claims that he drew his knife to protect himself from French, and that he was then shot by French. No one witnessed the fight or the events preceding it. The defendant French maintains that he is not sure what happened, but thinks that Joiner called him names and attacked him with a knife. French has been charged with assault.

The preliminary hearing is scheduled for today. You are defense counsel.

Should your client testify if you plan to argue that:

(1)   he did not shoot Joiner? or

(2)   he was insane at the time of the assault? or

(3)   he shot Joiner in self defense?

Empirical data. Research has shown that most preliminary hearings involve relatively few witnesses. One study of two populous Arizona counties reported that the average preliminary hearing involved two witnesses. If someone other than a law enforcement official testified, that person was likely to be the victim or an eyewitness. Approximately 99% of the witnesses were called by the prosecution. Rarely did either side introduce physical or documentary evidence at the preliminary hearing. Deborah Day Emerson & Nancy L. Ames, THE ROLE OF THE GRAND JURY AND THE PRELIMINARY HEARING IN PRETRIAL SCREENING 52–53, 57 (1984).

[7]   Probable Cause

The preliminary examination determines whether at the time of the preliminary hearing there is *probable cause* to believe (1) that a crime was committed, and (2) that the defendant committed the crime. The government has the burden of proof. Although there is no precise meaning for the term "probable cause," all jurisdictions agree that it requires less convincing proof than the "beyond the reasonable doubt" standard used in criminal trials. The judicial decisions are sparse and often unhelpful in defining the standard of proof.

PEOPLE v. AYALA
770 P.2d 1265 (Colo. 1989)

ERICKSON, JUSTICE:

The prosecution appeals the dismissal of an information charging defendant Anselmo Hijinio Ayala with theft by receiving. At the conclusion of the preliminary hearing, the information was dismissed by the trial judge because of the failure of the prosecution to establish probable cause that Ayala committed the crime charged. We affirm.

. . . Ayala and Anthony Wayne Johnson saw a 1983 Chevrolet Camaro in a field near the house where Ayala and Johnson were living. A man who was removing the parts from the Camaro identified himself as "Mike Klark." The affidavit of Officer Zabukovic, the investigating officer, states that Ayala told him that "Klark" informed him and codefendant, Anthony Johnson, that the Camaro belonged to "Klark's" brother, and that his brother had had problems with the automobile and that they were "stripping the vehicle out." Officer Zabukovic testified at the preliminary hearing that Ayala and Johnson told him that the Camaro was partially dismantled when they arrived at the lot and the dashboard and other items had been removed. "Klark" told Ayala and Johnson that they could purchase the automobile for $800. Ayala and Johnson returned to their home and obtained money to purchase the car, and both defendants contributed $400 to make up the $800 purchase price. They did not receive a title to the vehicle at that time. Both defendants told the police that at the time of the purchase, "Klark" gave them a phone number and said to call him to obtain the title to the Camaro. Nothing in the record establishes the precise extent of the disassembly or the condition of the Camaro when Ayala and Johnson first saw it.

Shortly thereafter, Ayala and Johnson were using a cutting torch to take the Camaro apart when a fuel line was cut causing the Camaro to go up in flames. The defendant called the fire department and cooperated in the subsequent police investigation. The police investigation disclosed that the automobile was stolen. After the police concluded

Smooth

that the identity and telephone number provided to Ayala and Johnson by "Mike Klark" were fictitious, a theft by receiving charge was filed.

A preliminary hearing is a screening device to determine whether there is probable cause to believe that the defendant committed the crime charged . . . . Greater evidentiary and procedural latitudes are permitted at a preliminary hearing because it is not a mini-trial. The sole issue at a preliminary hearing is whether probable cause exists to bind the accused over for trial.

To meet the standard of probable cause, there must be evidence sufficient to induce a person of ordinary prudence and caution conscientiously to entertain a reasonable belief that the defendant committed the crime charged. The evidence must be viewed in the light most favorable to the prosecution, and all inferences must be resolved in favor of the prosecution. The testimony of the investigating officer and the owner of the used car lot established the time of the theft and that the price set for the sale of the Camaro was $7,995. After hearing the testimony and the arguments of counsel, the trial court found that probable cause was not established and said:

> [THE COURT]: I appreciate what the standards are for the People to have this case bound over for trial at this stage of the proceedings. . . . The only evidence I have before me is that the vehicle was stolen. There's no indication that either Mr. Johnson or Mr. Ayala had anything to do with that consistent with that time period. Again, the only evidence . . . as to how the parties came to have this car was that they contacted a person who was in a field parting the vehicle out and that the vehicle was partly dismantled at that time. And while I'm not saying that that is a perfectly plausible explanation as to what happened, that's what I have before me. It isn't a situation in which somebody came up to them and said, "Do you want to buy this car," came by peddling the car or that the car was in good driving condition or fairly good driving condition or the same kind of condition as it came off the lot. The only evidence is that the car was being parted out and I don't know to what extent that was. The offense here requires not only a knowing act but also a specific intent. And I simply don't think that there's enough evidence, regardless of what reasonable suspicions there might be, I don't believe that there's enough evidence to bind the case over.

Based upon the evidence and the testimony I've heard, the case is dismissed for lack of probable cause. Mr. Ayala is discharged from his bond and the case is dismissed.

Section 18-4-410(1), 8B C.R.S. (1986), states, in part:

> [A] person commits theft by receiving when he receives, retains, loans money by pawn or pledge on, or disposes of anything of value of another, *knowing or believing* that said thing of value has been stolen, and when he *intends* to deprive the lawful owner permanently of the use or benefit of the thing of value. (Emphasis added.)

It was incumbent [on] the prosecution to establish that Ayala, knowing and believing that the Camaro was stolen, intended to deprive the lawful owner of the Camaro. The record contains only the testimony of the owner of the used car lot and the investigating officer. The testimony establishes that the Camaro was priced at $7,995 on the used car lot at the time it was stolen. The remaining testimony describes the condition and the circumstances which led to the acquisition of the Camaro by Ayala and Johnson. The Camaro was inoperable and partially dismantled when it was purchased by Ayala and Johnson. Nothing in the record establishes whether $800 was an unreasonable price to pay for the partially dismantled and inoperable Camaro. Nothing appears in the record to show that Ayala and Johnson stole the vehicle. Therefore, as a basis for reversal we are asked to infer that a Camaro that had a price tag of $7,995 when stolen was worth more than $800 when acquired by the defendants. We must then infer that the purchase price caused Ayala to know or believe that the automobile was stolen. In *Tate v. People*, 125 Colo. 527, 247 P.2d 665 (1952), we said:

> Presumption and inferences may be drawn only from facts established, and presumption may not rest on presumption or inference on inference . . . and this rule is doubly applicable in criminal cases.

Id. at 541, 247 P.2d at 672.

In *People v. Tumbarello*, 623 P.2d 46 (Colo. 1981), a theft by receiving case, we held that a "defendant's state of mind may be inferred from his conduct or from the circumstances of the case." *Tumbarello* is factually distinguishable from this case. In *Tumbarello*, the prosecution presented evidence that an undercover officer sold defendant goods which the officer represented as "hot" and "ripped off." From that evidence it could be reasonably inferred that defendant knew the goods were stolen. Here, by contrast, any effort to infer that Ayala knew the Camaro was stolen would necessitate drawing an inference upon an inference.

As evidenced by the investigating officer's affidavit, both Ayala and Johnson gave independent and virtually identical accounts of the automobile purchase. There was no competent evidence presented at the hearing that Ayala knew or believed that the Camaro was stolen or that he intended to permanently deprive the lawful owner of the use of the automobile. The Camaro had been partially dismantled and was not operational at the time of the sale and had to be towed to a garage next to the Ayala and Johnson residence. Accordingly, the prosecution failed to establish that Ayala or Johnson knew the Camaro was stolen and had the requisite mens rea to commit theft by receiving when they took possession of the Camaro.

The prosecution claims that because the ownership of the automobile was transferred without title, it may be inferred that Ayala must have known the vehicle was stolen. Although Colorado requires the seller of a motor vehicle to transfer title to the vehicle at the time of sale, failure to deliver a certificate of title does not prevent the acquisition of ownership rights by the parties to the transaction. The mere fact that Ayala did not receive a certificate of title when he purchased the automobile does not establish probable cause that Ayala knew the vehicle was stolen.

Nothing in the record reflects an abuse of discretion by the trial court and the judgment of dismissal is accordingly affirmed.

VOLLACK, JUSTICE, dissenting:

I respectfully dissent from the majority's affirmance of the trial court's dismissal of the information filed against the defendant.

The probable cause determination which must be met at a preliminary hearing requires sufficient evidence to induce a person of ordinary prudence and caution to a reasonable belief that the accused committed the crime charged. The prosecution is not required to present evidence sufficient to support a conviction. It is not for the trial judge at a preliminary hearing to accept the defendant's version of the facts over the legitimate inferences which can be drawn from the People's evidence, and a defendant's state of mind can be inferred from his conduct, or from the circumstances of the case.

The evidence presented at a preliminary hearing must be viewed in the light most favorable to the prosecution. The issue is not the defendant's innocence or guilt; the issue at a preliminary hearing is whether the evidence is sufficient to induce a person of ordinary prudence and caution to a reasonable belief that the defendant committed the crimes charged.

Applying these principles, I do not agree with the majority's conclusion that "the prosecution failed to establish that Ayala had the mens rea required to commit theft by receiving." The owner of the used car dealership testified at the preliminary hearing that the sale price of the 1983 Camaro at his lot was $7995. Even though the vehicle was only three years old when stolen, the defendant was given the opportunity to purchase it from a stranger, with no supporting paperwork, for $800. Acquisition of recently stolen property at a ridiculously low price from an unknown person is itself sufficient to support an inference that the one acquiring the property knew the property was stolen. *United States v. Prazak*, 623 F.2d 152, 154–55 (10th Cir.), *cert. denied*, 449 U.S. 880 (1980). Reviewing the testimony in the light most favorable to the prosecution, I would conclude that the prosecution met its burden of establishing probable cause. Based on the testimony at the preliminary hearing, I would let the jury assess the witnesses' credibility and decide whether the requisite mens rea has been established beyond a reasonable doubt . . . .

NOTES

1. *Definition of probable cause. Ayala* joins many jurisdictions in holding that probable cause means that "there must be evidence sufficient to induce a person of ordinary prudence and caution conscientiously to entertain a reasonable belief that the defendant committed the crime charged." This differs markedly from the trial jury's role of finding guilt only if proof rises to the level of establishing guilt beyond a reasonable doubt. Is the *Ayala* court's test sufficiently rigorous to protect the accused from unwarranted prosecutions? What would be wrong with applying the "beyond the reasonable doubt standard" to *both* the preliminary examination and the subsequent criminal trial?

2. *Tilt toward prosecution? Ayala* follows the traditional view in indicating that the proof process at the preliminary examination is tilted in favor of the prosecution. *Ayala* states the common view that at a preliminary examination the "evidence must be viewed in the light most favorable to the prosecution, and all inferences must be resolved in favor of the prosecution." It has also been held that there is a presumption that the state will strengthen its case at trial. A related maxim was noted in *State v. Dunn*, 359 N.W.2d 151, 155 (Wis.1984):

> We stress that a preliminary hearing is not a proper forum to choose between conflicting facts or inferences, or to weigh the state's evidence against evidence favorable to the defendant. That is the role of the trier of fact at trial. If the hearing judge determines after hearing the evidence that a reasonable inference supports the probable cause determination, the judge should bind the defendant over for trial. Simply stated, probable cause at a preliminary hearing is satisfied when there exists a believable or plausible account of the defendant's commission of a felony.

Accord, People v. Northey, 591 N.W.2d 227 (Mich. App. 1998) (probable cause requires belief that evidence at preliminary examination is consistent with defendant's guilt); *State v. Hendricks*, 586 N.W.2d 413 (Minn. Ct. App. 1998) ("Probable cause exists where facts would lead a person of ordinary care and prudence to hold an honest and strong suspicion that the person under consideration is guilty of a crime"). One especially low standard is "some rational ground for assuming the possibility that he or she committed an offense." *Thompson v. Superior Court*, 110 Cal. Rptr. 2d 89 (Cal. App. 2001). Considering the relatively low standard (probable cause) used in these hearings and the fact that these hearings are designed to protect the accused from baseless criminal prosecutions, why should the tables be tilted so much in favor of the prosecution?

3. Note that three justices of the Colorado Supreme Court believed that probable cause had been established. Does the dissent or majority view best serve the primary purpose of the preliminary hearing? Which do you agree with?

In other words, do you believe that the evidence adduced at the hearing was, or was not, sufficient to justify an inference that Ayala had "the mens rea required to commit theft by receiving."? Should the ultimate facts in this case, including Ayala's mental state, be determined by the preliminary hearing judge or by a jury?

4. *Changing the Ayala facts.* Is the real problem with *Ayala* that the prosecution failed to offer adequate proof? Would the outcome have been different if the following facts had been established:

    a. A witness reported that Ayala and Johnson "dashed" home to get the money and then, with money in hand, ran back to the field where the car was being stripped by Klark.

    b. An expert on used cars testified that from Ayala's description of the car when Ayala and Johnson bought it for $800, the partially stripped car had a value of at least $2,000. Would your view change if the value were $5,000?

    c. Would it matter whether Ayala knew nothing about cars? What if he were an expert on used cars? What if Ayala knew nothing about cars but Johnson was an expert on the value of used cars?

5. *Prosecution remedies.* Note that *Ayala* involves the unusual procedural posture of an appeal by the *prosecution* to a dismissal of charges in a preliminary hearing. In many locales, the prosecution could seek the same result (a finding of probable cause) by convening another preliminary hearing before the same or a different judge (perhaps with additional proof) or by seeking an indictment.

PROBLEM 6-2. PROBABLE CAUSE OF WHAT AND AGAINST WHOM?

Berger was charged with possession with intent to deliver 1,000 tablets of pentazocine (Talwin) in violation of the drug laws. He was arrested by a police officer who came to his apartment after a neighbor complained of a noisy party. The officer knocked on the door and was invited in by one of the guests who answered the door. There were four adults and two minors obviously having a party. Everyone was in the living room. Three dozen cans of beer (some opened, some not) were on the kitchen table. In the bedroom the guest's coats were stored on the bed. On the top of the dresser was an open box containing the 1,000 pills. It was established that Berger was the only person who lived in the apartment, but his girlfriend stayed there occasionally. Berger's clothes were in the dresser and closet.

At the preliminary hearing, all six people testified that they did not know anything about the drugs.

If you were the judge, would you find that probable cause had been established as to Berger? His girlfriend? Anyone else in the apartment at the time? This issue comes up with some frequency in drug cases where multiple occupants of cars or dwellings have been arrested and the court must determine if probable cause has been established as to all, some, or none of the occupants.

[8] Empirical Studies

However the probable cause standard is phrased, it is clear that probable cause is not a difficult standard for the prosecution to meet. Studies show that almost all preliminary hearings end in a finding of probable cause, although jurisdictions do vary in this regard. *See, e.g.,* Deborah Day Emerson & Nancy L. Ames, THE ROLE OF THE GRAND JURY AND THE PRELIMINARY HEARING IN PRETRIAL SCREENING 68 (1984) (probable cause not found in 3–6% of cases in two Arizona counties); Janet A. Gilboy, *Prosecutors' Discretionary Use of the Grand Jury to Initiate or to Reinitiate Prosecution*, 1984 AM. BAR FOUND. RES. J. 1, 25 (study of murder prosecutions in Chicago; no probable cause for any crime found after preliminary hearing in 26% of cases; of remaining 74% of cases, probable cause of crime originally charged was found 92% of the time and of a lesser crime was found 8% of time); Kenneth Graham & Leon Letwin, *The Preliminary Hearings in Los Angeles: Some Field Findings and Legal-Policy Observations*, 18 U.C.L.A. L. REV. 636, 719–724 (1971) (probable cause not found in 8% of 200 California cases in study; authors estimate approximately 90% of preliminary hearings result in bindover to grand jury in California).

[9]   Motion Practice

Despite the informality of preliminary examinations in many jurisdictions, experienced lawyers often consider making various motions before, during, and after the hearing. Pre-hearing motions may seek to affect preliminary hearing procedures, such as obtaining state funds to hire a stenographer, the exclusion of witnesses from the courtroom during the hearing except when they are testifying, or to have inadmissible evidence barred from the proceeding. Pretrial motions may also ask more fundamental relief, such as dismissal of some or all charges because of the statute of limitations or double jeopardy or the court's lack of jurisdiction over the cases or some of the charges.

During or immediately after the presentation of evidence at the preliminary examination, the defense lawyer may make one or more motions, usually orally. Counsel may ask for all or some of the charges to be dismissed for any number of reasons. Most often the motion will assert that the charges are unproven (no probable cause), unconstitutionally vague, or based on constitutionally protected conduct. Another motion may ask that one or more charges be reduced to allege the commission of less severe crimes. Perhaps counsel will concede that the proof established probable cause for a lesser crime, such as public intoxication, but will argue that it was not sufficient for a more serious offense, such as driving while intoxicated. Defense counsel may also move for a reduction in the amount of bail, while the prosecution may ask that it be increased.

Failure to move to dismiss charges at or after a preliminary hearing may be viewed as a waiver of the issue. *See, e.g., State v. Mays*, 85 P.3d 1208 (Kan. 2004)(failure to file motion to dismiss charges waives issue of untimely preliminary hearing).

[10]   Effect of Decision

The preliminary examination is held at such an early stage of the criminal process that the double jeopardy guarantee does not apply. As discussed in Chapter 16, jeopardy attaches once the trial begins. This means that the judge's decision at the preliminary examination is not a final resolution. In most jurisdictions that retain the grand jury, a dismissal in a preliminary hearing does not bar a subsequent grand jury indictment. Thus, if the judge at the preliminary examination throws out the case and orders the defendant's release from custody because the state did not offer sufficient proof to meet the probable cause standard, the prosecutor can still take the case to the grand jury. If the latter issues an indictment, the case will proceed to trial. Similarly, if the judge at the preliminary examination rejects some of the charges or reduces their severity, the grand jury can restore the original charges or even indict for new ones.

One study of Chicago homicide cases found that the prosecution presented the case to the grand jury in half the cases where no probable cause was found at the preliminary examination. Surprisingly, an indictment was returned in 97% of these cases that had been first rejected in the preliminary examination. One explanation for the high success rate before the grand jury is that the prosecution may have presented stronger evidence to the grand jury than it did to the judge at the preliminary examination. Another possibility is that the grand jury's standards for probable cause were lower than that of the judge at the preliminary examination, or that the prosecution's influence over the grand jury is so great that it can get an indictment virtually any time it seeks one. Looking at the ultimate disposition of the cases that were rejected in the preliminary examination but revived with a grand jury indictment, the same study found that only 54% of the first-rejected cases produced a guilty verdict after trial. In contrast, the study found a trial conviction rate of 74% for the cases where the preliminary examination found probable cause. Janet A. Gilboy, *Prosecutors' Discretionary Use of the Grand Jury to Initiate or to Reinitiate Prosecution*, 1984 AM. BAR FOUND. RES. J. 1, 26.

After a preliminary examination judge issues a decision, an appeal is often possible, though rarely successful. Reviewing courts routinely affirm the probable cause determination unless there was an "abuse of discretion." One court stated that "every legitimate factual inference" must be drawn to uphold a magistrate's finding of probable cause at a preliminary hearing. *People v. Scott*, 90 Cal. Rptr.2d 435 (Cal. App. 1999).

In some jurisdictions where there is no grand jury, a finding of probable cause at the preliminary examination can be appealed to the court of general jurisdiction that will eventually preside over the trial of the case. But once there is a criminal conviction following an erroneous "bindover" at the preliminary hearing, courts will virtually never reverse the conviction because of the error. Usually the "harmless error" standard is used to defeat the appeal. Some courts go further, holding that a valid conviction by the trial court cures any error in the preliminary examination and bars appellate reversal for any such error.

A finding of no probable cause is rarely appealed by the prosecution to a higher court, but the prosecutor may elect to refile the complaint and request another preliminary hearing in the same or a different court with jurisdiction to hold preliminary examinations. The California Supreme Court explained in *People v. Wallace*, 93 P.3d 1037, 1043 (Cal. 2004):

> A deficiency of proof at a preliminary hearing frequently reflects a temporary state of affairs. The prosecution may discover and proffer additional proof by the time a second preliminary hearing is held or by the time the case proceeds to trial.

Refiling could be barred if the new charges are designed to harass the defendant or if the defendant is prejudiced by them. *Commonwealth v. Carbo*, 822 A.2d 60 (Pa. Super. 2003).

Ordinarily another preliminary examination hearing on exactly the same evidence is possible. In some locales the state may appeal an unsuccessful preliminary hearing and, if it loses again on appeal, convene another preliminary hearing only if there is additional evidence not presented at the first such hearing. *See State v. Huser*, 959 P.2d 908 (Kan. 1998); *State v. Zahn*, 180 P.3d 186 (Utah App. 2008)(due process bars prosecutor from refiling criminal charges dismissed at a preliminary hearing unless prosecutor can show new or previously unavailable evidence has surfaced or that other good cause justifies refiling). One study found that 10% of the dismissed cases were refiled. Kenneth Graham & Leon Letwin, *The Preliminary Hearings in Los Angeles: Some Field Findings and Legal-Policy Observations*, 18 U.C.L.A. L. REV. 636, 730 (1971).

Chapter 7
THE GRAND JURY

A. INTRODUCTION

The grand jury is a group of citizens who review cases to determine whether there is probable cause to believe that a crime was committed by the accused. In many jurisdictions, a criminal case cannot proceed to trial unless the grand jury indicts the defendant or the defendant waives an indictment. While a grand jury is an important part of federal criminal procedure, its use and procedures vary considerably among the states, and it is subject to considerable debate.

[1] Functions

The grand jury is both a "shield" and a "sword." As a shield, the grand jury acts as a buffer between the accused and society, with the grand jurors guarding against unfounded accusations. As a sword, it functions as an investigative body to gather information and determine whether a formal criminal charge should be brought.

[a] Grand Jury as Shield

The grand jury has been praised as a body that protects "the innocent against hasty, malicious, and oppressive public prosecutions." *Ex parte Bain*, 121 U.S. 1, 12 (1887). In cases in which a grand jury refuses to indict a defendant because of insufficient evidence, it protects that person "from an open and public accusation of crime, and from the trouble, expense, and anxiety of a public trial." *Id.*

[b] Grand Jury as Sword

The second function of the grand jury is to investigate possible criminal activity and initiate criminal charges when appropriate. In this capacity the grand jury serves as an inquisitorial body that has no obligation to consider both sides of a case. The individual who is the subject of grand jury investigation ordinarily has no right to appear or to present arguments with respect to the determination of probable cause. Since the grand jury typically responds to cases presented to it by the prosecuting attorney, it should come as no surprise that the grand jury is often characterized as a body serving the interests of the government.

[c] Independence or Rubber Stamp

The accusation is commonly made that grand juries are not "independent" and that they essentially act as rubber stamps for prosecutors. The California Supreme Court echoed this point of view in *Hawkins v. Superior Court*, 586 P.2d 916, 919, (1978), when it stated:

> The prosecuting attorney is typically in complete control of the total process in the grand jury room: he calls the witnesses, interprets the evidence, states and applies the law, and advises the grand jury on whether a crime has been committed. The grand jury is independent only in the sense that it is not formally attached to the prosecutor's office; though legally free to vote as they please, grand jurors virtually always assent to the recommendations of the prosecuting attorney, a fact borne out by [empirical data].

> . . . Today, the grand jury is the total captive of the prosecutor who, if he is candid, will concede that he can indict anybody, at any time, for almost anything, before any grand jury . . . .

Grand jury independence is an issue that continues to be debated. Some commentators agree with the view that grand juries are not in fact independent, with one even going so far as to consider them as "an arm of the prosecution." Gregory T. Fotus, *Reading Jurors Their Rights: The Continuing Question of Grand Jury Independence*, 79 IND. L.J. 323, 324 (2004). For an argument that the disconnect between the rhetoric and reality of the grand jury is one of the central and important features of the modern federal criminal justice system, *see* Niki Kuckes, *The Useful, Dangerous Fiction of Grand Jury Independence*, 41 AM. CRIM. L. REV. 1 (2004).

Other commentators, however, have characterized the *Hawkins* opinion as overstated, pointing out that it should come as no surprise that a group of persons hearing only one side of a case will likely agree with that side. In this sense, perhaps the grand jury's real function is to compel the government to present a defensible case before a formal charge is brought. But some even question such a notion. *See* Andrew D. Leipold, *Why Grand Juries Do Not (and Cannot) Protect the Accused*, 80 CORNELL L. REV. 260 (1995). Professor Leipold characterizes the grand jury as a shield that works poorly, attributing grand jury failings to jurors' lack of competence to perform their tasks, leading inevitably to deference to prosecutorial direction and decision. He concludes:

> [A]lthough the framers of the Bill of Rights considered grand juries an important protector of individual liberty, time and close scrutiny have shown that they are not. Despite the mechanical support voiced by courts for the institution, once the focus is placed on the jurors themselves, and their inability to perform the task assigned to them, it becomes clear that grand juries will not dissuade prosecutors from bringing unfounded charges, nor do they alter the charging decisions in any significant respect. In almost all cases, a criminal defendant would be just as well off without the grand jury as he is with it." [*Id* at 323]

[2] Use of Grand Juries

[a] Federal Use

The Fifth Amendment to the United States Constitution provides:

> [N]o person shall be held to answer for a capital, or otherwise infamous crime, unless on a presentment or indictment of a grand jury . . . .

The phrase "infamous crimes" in the Fifth Amendment has been construed to apply to all felonies. This means that a federal felony prosecution must be the product of a grand jury indictment or presentment unless waived. A federal misdemeanor offense does not require an indictment, though a federal prosecutor may choose to seek one.

A *presentment* is a formal charging document issued by a grand jury in cases that have not been initiated by the prosecutor's office. The more common charging instrument is the *indictment*, a document issued by a grand jury in cases brought to its attention by the prosecutor. The indictment and the presentment have the same legal effect since both are approved by the grand jury. This similarity occasionally produces a blurring in the distinctions between these two concepts.

The fact that the federal defendant's entitlement to grand jury review is included among the Bill of Rights underscores its role as a protective device in the federal system. In 2005, for example, federal courts impaneled 969 grand juries and convened 9,854 grand jury sessions. Each session averaged just under 5 hours and indicted an average of 7 people per session. A total of 196,197 persons (about 20 per session) served as federal grand jurors. Bureau of Justice Statistics, Sourcebook of Criminal Justice Statistics Online, Table 1.94.2005, available at www.albany.edu/sourcebook/pdf/t1942005.pdf. A total of 68,996 criminal cases were filed that year. *Id.* at Table 5.9.2005, available at www.albany.edu/sourcebook/pdf/t592005.pdf. As the result of the Fifth

Amendment, all federal felony defendants are constitutionally entitled to grand jury review.

[b] State Use

While the fifth amendment makes the grand jury an inherent part of federal criminal processes, this guarantee does not apply to state prosecutions. *See Hurtado v. California*, 110 U.S. 516 (1884) (State of California not obligated to prosecute by indictment). Accordingly, a number of states now use an information in lieu of an indictment. An *information* is the counterpart of an indictment except that it is drafted and signed by a prosecutor, not by a judge or grand jury, and it is filed in court.

Less than half of the states today *require* grand jury review for all felonies. A number of state constitutions do not make any reference to grand jury proceedings (such as Massachusetts and Michigan), while others extend the right to indictment to all felony cases, using language very similar to that of the Fifth Amendment (*see* New York, Ohio and Texas).

The "middle ground" state constitutional provisions permit the government to initiate criminal proceedings either by indictment or information (California and Illinois). In Arkansas and Oklahoma, the vast majority of felony prosecutions are formally initiated by information rather than indictment, and the grand jury has been relegated to being a back-up alternative where a judge or prosecutor is persuaded of the need in a particular case for the charging decision to come from outside the prosecutor's office.

There are also other approaches to grand jury use. In Florida, the right to grand jury proceedings is triggered only when the accused "shall be tried for a capital crime," thereby allowing other felony prosecutions to proceed either by indictment or information. Fla. Const. art. 1, § 15. Illinois has a unique constitutional provision, expressly authorizing the state legislature to "abolish the grand jury or further limit its use." Ill. Const. art. 1, § 7.

[c] Waiver

If a criminal accused is entitled to a grand jury indictment as a precondition to a criminal trial, he or she is also entitled to waive the indictment process and to proceed by information. *See, e.g.,* Fed. R. Crim. P. 7(b). The waiver must be "voluntary and intelligent" and it is routinely made in writing. Some jurisdictions also require that the waiver occur in open court.

There are several reasons why a criminal defendant might find it advantageous to waive a grand jury indictment. Perhaps the most prevalent is to speed up the trial process. An accused who wants a prompt trial or a quick resolution involving a guilty plea may save several months of pretrial delay by waiving the grand jury process. This could be important to an accused who is in jail, yet believes he or she will be acquitted at trial or simply wants the case concluded. Another reason for this is to avoid the loss of witnesses that could occur if a trial were delayed. Finally, some prosecutors will sweeten a plea offer if the accused will waive indictment, saving the prosecution the time needed to present the case to the grand jury.

[3] Legal Powers

To fulfill its roles as both a sword and a shield, a grand jury possesses considerable legal powers. First, it may use subpoenas to require witnesses to testify or produce physical evidence. Second, uncooperative grand jury witnesses face contempt sanctions by a judge. Third, the grand jury operates in almost total secrecy, thereby facilitating the investigative role in an atmosphere of non-accountability. Fourth, while grand jury witnesses are allowed to assert various constitutional rights (most notably, the Fifth

Amendment self-incrimination privilege), the grand jury may seek a grant of immunity that forces the witness to disclose what would otherwise be withheld incriminating information.

[4] Relationship to Preliminary Hearings

Recall that a significant number of states permit the prosecutor to select whether to use the grand jury or an information. When an information (formal charges prepared and filed by the prosecutor without grand jury involvement) is used, the accused usually is entitled to a preliminary hearing where a judge assesses whether there is probable cause to believe the defendant committed a certain crime. See Chapter 6 (Preliminary Hearings). If the judge at the preliminary hearing finds no probable cause, the defendant is discharged. The same result occurs if the grand jury finds no probable cause and refuses to issue an indictment. Whether discharge occurs through magistrate determination or a "no true bill" by grand jury, neither form of disposition is final because the double jeopardy clause does not attach until the criminal trial on the merits begins. Ordinarily, the government may elect to re-initiate the prosecution either by presenting the case for the first or second time to a grand jury or by filing a new information and presenting the case at a second preliminary hearing.

It is likely that the cases that are dismissed at a preliminary hearing or that are no-true-billed by a grand jury are weak. A study in Cook County, Illinois, found that one-fourth of preliminary hearings resulted in discharge of the accused after a finding of no probable cause. In approximately one-half of those discharged cases, the government reinitiated prosecution by grand jury indictment. As to those reinitiated cases, there was a significantly higher chance that they would result in acquittals or dismissals at the trial level. Additionally, it was found that those defendants were more likely to demand trial than to plead guilty, "which is another indication that reinitiated cases might be weaker, since there might be strong incentives in weak cases for defendants to seek a review of their cases." Janet A. Gilboy, *Prosecutors' Discretionary Use of the Grand Jury to Initiate or to Reinitiate Prosecution*, 1984 AM. BAR FOUND. RES. J. 1, 9 (1984).

The *Hawkins* opinion, cited earlier, also discusses many of the obvious differences between a probable cause determination by a grand jury as opposed to after a preliminary hearing:

> [At a grand jury hearing] the defendant has no right to appear or be represented by counsel, and consequently may not confront and cross-examine the witnesses against him, object to evidence introduced by the prosecutor, make legal arguments, or present evidence to explain or contradict the charge. If he is called to testify, the defendant has no right to the presence of counsel, even though, because of the absolute secrecy surrounding grand jury proceedings, he may be completely unaware of the subject of inquiry or his position as a target witness. This remarkable lack of even the most basic rights is compounded by the absence from the grand jury room of a neutral and detached magistrate, trained in the law, to rule on the admissibility of evidence and ensure that the grand jury exercises its indicting function with proper regard for the independence and objectivity so necessary if it is to fulfill its purported role of protecting innocent citizens from unfounded accusations, even as it proceeds against those who it has probable cause to believe have committed offenses. [586 P.2d at 918].

[5] Secrecy

Grand jury proceedings are conducted in secrecy. While courts and legislatures occasionally permit disclosure of some matters under very specific circumstances, the rule of secrecy promotes the following interests: (1) avoids embarrassment to persons who are investigated but not charged; (2) prevents leaks of information to prospective defendants; and (3) reduces the danger that a grand jury witness will be threatened or harassed by a prospective defendant. *See* Mark Kadish, *Behind the Locked Door of an American Grand Jury: Its History, Its Secrecy, and Its Process*, 24 Fla. St. U.L. Rev. 1 (1996) and Richard M. Calkins, *Grand Jury Secrecy*, 63 MICH. L. REV. 455 (1965).

In *United States v. Procter & Gamble*, 356 U.S. 677, 682 (1958), the United States Supreme Court affirmed the notion that secrecy encourages witnesses "to step forward and testify freely without fear or retaliation." Subsequently, however, the Court recognized that there may be circumstances in which the traditional secrecy of the grand jury may be broken:

> Parties seeking grand jury transcripts . . . must show that the material they seek is needed to avoid a possible injustice in another judicial proceeding, that the need for disclosure is greater than the need for continued secrecy, and that their request is structured to cover only material so needed. Such a showing must be made even when the grand jury whose transcripts are sought has concluded its operations. [T]he courts must consider not only the immediate effects upon a particular grand jury, but also the possible effect upon the functioning of future grand juries. Persons called upon to testify will consider the likelihood that their testimony may one day be disclosed to outside parties. Fear of future retribution or social stigma may act as powerful deterrents to those who would come forward and aid the grand jury in the performance of its duties. Thus, the interests in grand jury secrecy, although reduced, are not eliminated merely because the grand jury has ended its activities.

Douglas Oil Company of California v. Petrol Stops Northwest, 441 U.S. 211, 222 (1979).For a more detailed discussion of grand jury procedures at the state level, see Sara Sun Beale, William C. Bryson, James E. Felman and Michael J. Elston, GRAND JURY LAW AND PRACTICE § 1.5 (2d ed. updated Oct. 2007) (hereinafter cited as Grand Jury Law and Practice). For similar material applicable to federal grand juries, see James C. Cissell, FEDERAL CRIMINAL TRIALS ch. 4 (6th ed. 2003).

For a detailed discussion of changes to Rule 6(e) of the Federal Rule of Criminal Procedure in the wake of September 11, 2001 and the USA PATRIOT Act of 2001 and the resultant sharing of grand jury materials relating to intelligence matters with other federal intelligence, immigration and defense agencies, see Lori E. Shaw, *The USA PATRIOT Act of 2001, the Intelligence Reform and Terrorism Prevention Act of 2004, and the False Dichotomy Between Protecting National Security and Preserving Grand Jury Secrecy*, 35 SETON HALL L. REV. 495 (2005).

B. SELECTION OF GRAND JURORS

[1] Federal System

The selection of federal grand jurors is governed by the Jury Selection and Service Act of 1968, 28 U.S.C. §§ 1861–1869, and is discussed in greater detail in Chapter 15. In general terms, this statute requires that federal jurors be selected in a random fashion in order to guarantee that they represent a fair cross section of society. Various exemptions from jury service are recognized. Each federal judicial district must adopt a plan governing the manner in which jurors' names are to be drawn. Both the government and the defense may move for dismissal of an indictment on the ground of "substantial failure to comply with [the Act]." 28 U.S.C. § 1867.

The Supreme Court has also held that an indictment may be dismissed because of an equal violation in the selection of grand jurors. *See, e.g., Vasquez v. Hillery*, 474 U.S. 253 (1986)(race discrimination).

Rule 6 of the Federal Rules of Criminal Procedure also contains provisions pertaining to the selection of grand jurors. Notice that Rule 6(b)(2) refers to the Jury Selection and Service Act of 1968.

FEDERAL RULES OF CRIMINAL PROCEDURE

Rule 6. *The Grand Jury*

(a) Summoning a Grand Jury.

(1) In General. When the public interest so requires, the court must order that one or more grand juries be summoned. A grand jury must have 16 to 23 members, and the court must order that enough legally qualified persons be summoned to meet this requirement.

(2) Alternate Jurors. When a grand jury is selected, the court may also select alternate jurors. Alternate jurors must have the same qualifications and be selected in the same manner as any other juror. Alternate jurors replace jurors in the same sequence in which the alternates were selected. An alternate juror who replaces a juror is subject to the same challenges, takes the same oath, and has the same authority as the other jurors.

(b) Objection to the Grand Jury or to a Grand Juror.

(1) Challenges. Either the government or a defendant may challenge the grand jury on the ground that it was not lawfully drawn, summoned, or selected, and may challenge an individual juror on the ground that the juror is not legally qualified.

(2) Motion to Dismiss an Indictment. A party may move to dismiss the indictment based on an objection to the grand jury or on an individual juror's lack of legal qualification, unless the court has previously ruled on the same objection under Rule 6(b)(1). The motion to dismiss is governed by 28 U.S.C. § 1867(e). The court must not dismiss the indictment on the ground that a grand juror was not legally qualified if the record shows that at least 12 qualified jurors concurred in the indictment.

(c) Foreperson and Deputy Foreperson.
The court will appoint one juror as the foreperson and another as the deputy foreperson. In the foreperson's absence, the deputy foreperson will act as the foreperson. The foreperson may administer oaths and affirmations and will sign all indictments. The foreperson — or another juror designated by the foreperson — will record the number of jurors concurring in every indictment and will file the record with the clerk, but the record may not be made public unless the court so orders.

(d) Who May Be Present.

(1) While the Grand Jury Is in Session. The following persons may be present while the grand jury is in session: attorneys for the government, the witness being questioned, interpreters when needed, and a court reporter or an operator of a recording device.

(2) During Deliberations and Voting. No person other than the jurors, and any interpreter needed to assist a hearing impaired or speech-impaired juror, may be present while the grand jury is deliberating or voting.

(e) Recording and Disclosing the Proceedings.

(1) Recording the Proceedings. Except while the grand jury is deliberating or voting, all proceedings must be recorded by a court reporter or by a suitable recording device. But the validity of a prosecution is not affected by the unintentional failure to make a recording. Unless the court orders otherwise, an attorney for the government will retain control of the recording, the reporter's notes, and any transcript prepared from those notes.

(2) Secrecy.

(A) No obligation of secrecy may be imposed on any person except in accordance with Rule 6(e)(2)(B).

(B) Unless these rules provide otherwise, the following persons must not disclose a matter occurring before the grand jury:

(**i**) a grand juror;

(**ii**) an interpreter;

(**iii**) a court reporter;

(**iv**) an operator of a recording device;

(**v**) a person who transcribes recorded testimony;

(**vi**) an attorney for the government; or

(**vii**) a person to whom disclosure is made under Rule 6 (e)(3)(A)(ii) or (iii).

(3) Exceptions.

(A) Disclosure of a grand-jury matter — other than the grand jury's deliberations or any grand juror's vote — may be made to:

(**i**) an attorney for the government for use in performing that attorney's duty;

(**ii**) any government personnel — including those of a state, state subdivision, Indian tribe, or foreign government — that an attorney for the government considers necessary to assist in performing that attorney's duty to enforce federal criminal law; or

(**iii**) a person authorized by 18 U.S.C. § 3322.

(B) A person to whom information is disclosed under Rule 6(e)(3)(A)(ii) may use that information only to assist an attorney for the government in performing that attorney's duty to enforce federal criminal law. An attorney for the government must promptly provide the court that impaneled the grand jury with the names of all persons to whom a disclosure has been made, and must certify that the attorney has advised those persons of their obligation of secrecy under this rule.

(C) An attorney for the government may disclose any grand-jury matter to another federal grand jury.

(D) An attorney for the government may disclose any grand-jury matter involving foreign intelligence, counter-intelligence (as defined in 50 U.S.C. § 401(a)), or foreign intelligence information (as defined in Rule 6(e)(3)(D)(iii)) to any federal law enforcement, intelligence, protective, immigration, national defense, or national security official to assist the official receiving the information in the performance of that official's duties. An attorney for the government may also disclose any grand-jury matter involving, within the United States or elsewhere, a threat of attack or other grave hostile acts of a foreign power or its agent, a threat of domestic or international sabotage or terrorism, or clandestine intelligence gathering activities by an intelligence service or network of a foreign power or by its agent, to any appropriate federal, state, state subdivision, Indian tribal, or foreign government official, for the purpose of preventing or responding to such threat or activities.

(**i**) Any official who receives information under Rule 6(e)(3)(D) may use the information only as necessary in the conduct of that person's official duties subject to any limitations on the unauthorized disclosure of such information. Any state, state subdivision, Indian tribal, or foreign government official who receives information under Rule 6(e)(3)(D) may use the information only in a manner consistent with any guidelines issued by the Attorney General and the Director of National Intelligence.

(ii) Within a reasonable time after disclosure is made under Rule 6(e)(3)(D), an attorney for the government must file, under seal, a notice with the court in the district where the grand jury convened stating that such information was disclosed and the departments, agencies, or entities to which the disclosure was made.

(iii) As used in Rule 6(e)(3)(D), the term "foreign intelligence information" means:

(a) information, whether or not it concerns a United States person, that relates to the ability of the United States to protect against —

- actual or potential attack or other grave hostile acts of a foreign power or its agent;

- sabotage or international terrorism by a foreign power or its agent; or

- clandestine intelligence activities by an intelligence service or network of a foreign power or by its agent; or

(b) information, whether or not it concerns a United States person, with respect to a foreign power or foreign territory that relates to —

- the national defense or the security of the United States; or

- the conduct of the foreign affairs of the United States.

(E) The court may authorize disclosure — at a time, in a manner, and subject to any other conditions that it directs — of a grand-jury matter:

(i) preliminarily to or in connection with a judicial proceeding;

(ii) at the request of a defendant who shows that a ground may exist to dismiss the indictment because of a matter that occurred before the grand jury;

(iii) at the request of the government, when sought by a foreign court or prosecutor for use in an official criminal investigation;

(iv) at the request of the government if it shows that the matter may disclose a violation of State, Indian tribal, or foreign criminal law, as long as the disclosure is to an appropriate state, state subdivision, Indian tribal, or foreign government official for the purpose of enforcing that law; or

(v) at the request of the government if it shows that the matter may disclose a violation of military criminal law under the Uniform Code of Military Justice, as long as the disclosure is to an appropriate military official for the purpose of enforcing that law.

(F) A petition to disclose a grand-jury matter under Rule 6(e)(3)(E)(i) must be filed in the district where the grand jury convened. Unless the hearing is ex parte — as it may be when the government is the petitioner — the petitioner must serve the petition on, and the court must afford a reasonable opportunity to appear and be heard to:

(i) an attorney for the government;

(ii) the parties to the judicial proceeding; and

(iii) any other person whom the court may designate.

(G) If the petition to disclose arises out of a judicial proceeding in another district, the petitioned court must transfer the petition to the other court unless the petitioned court can reasonably determine whether disclosure is proper. If the petitioned court decides to transfer, it must send to the transferee court the material sought to be disclosed, if feasible, and a written evaluation of the need for continued grand-jury secrecy. The transferee court must afford those persons identified in Rule 6(e)(3)(F) a reasonable opportunity to appear and be heard.

(4) Sealed Indictment. The magistrate judge to whom an indictment is returned may direct that the indictment be kept secret until the defendant is in custody or has been released pending trial. The clerk must then seal the indictment, and no person may disclose the indictment's existence except as necessary to issue or execute a warrant or summons.

(5) Closed Hearing. Subject to any right to an open hearing in a contempt proceeding, the court must close any hearing to the extent necessary to prevent disclosure of a matter occurring before a grand jury.

(6) Sealed Records. Records, orders, and subpoenas relating to grand-jury proceedings must be kept under seal to the extent and as long as necessary to prevent the unauthorized disclosure of a matter occurring before a grand jury.

(7) Contempt. A knowing violation of Rule 6, or of any guidelines jointly issued by the Attorney General and the Director of National Intelligence under Rule 6, may be punished as contempt of court.

(f) Indictment and Return. A grand jury may indict only if at least 12 jurors concur. The grand jury — or its foreperson or deputy foreperson — must return the indictment to a magistrate judge in open court. If a complaint or information is pending against the defendant and 12 jurors do not concur in the indictment, the foreperson must promptly and in writing report the lack of concurrence to the magistrate judge.

(g) Discharging the Grand Jury. A grand jury must serve until the court discharges it, but it may serve more than 18 months only if the court, having determined that an extension is in the public interest, extends the grand jury's service. An extension may be granted for no more than 6 months, except as otherwise provided by statute.

(h) Excusing a Juror. At any time, for good cause, the court may excuse a juror either temporarily or permanently, and if permanently, the court may impanel an alternate juror in place of the excused juror.

(i) "Indian Tribe" Defined. "Indian tribe" means an Indian tribe recognized by the Secretary of the Interior on a list published in the Federal Register under 25 U.S.C. § 479a-1.

Federal Rule of Criminal Procedure 7, reprinted in Part E.2 of this Chapter also addresses indictments and informations.

[2] State Systems

Many states follow the federal model by requiring that grand jurors be selected according to a random process. In some states, however, a *key person* system is used. Selectors (usually either jury commissioners or judges) are given discretion to select private citizens who they believe are qualified for grand jury service.

Qualifications of those who may be selected as grand jurors vary from state to state, but it has been observed by the United States Supreme Court that the key person system is the most susceptible to abuse. This is significant because an equal protection challenge is more likely to succeed where underrepresentation of a cognizable group results from such a selection process. *See* Grand Jury Law and Practice § 3:6.

Challenges to the selection or composition of the grand jury may be brought by (1) persons eligible to serve as grand jurors, (2) the defendant whose case has been or will be heard by the grand jury, and (3) the government attorney. The usual method is a motion to dismiss the indictment. A defendant of any race, for example, may challenge the exclusion of his own or any other race from the grand jury (the United States Supreme Court held in *Campbell v. Louisiana*, 523 U.S. 392 (1998), that a white defendant has third-party standing to raise both equal protection and due process objections to discrimination against black persons in the selection of grand jurors). On the other hand, witnesses called to testify before the grand jury have not been accorded the right to challenge the selection of the grand jury. *Blair v. United States*, 250 U.S. 273 (1919).

Courts have recognized the following kinds of challenges: (1) qualifications of prospective grand jurors, (2) composition of the grand jury panel on constitutional bases (equal protection and due process), and (3) failure to comply with statutory selection requirements. For an extended analysis of challenges in each of these categories, including citations to state and federal cases, see GRAND JURY LAW AND PRACTICE, ch. 3.

C. PROCEDURES

[1] Size and Vote

Grand juries range in size from as few as 7 to as many as 23 persons (the federal rule is 16-23). Often a majority vote is required for return of a *true bill*, another expression used for an indictment. Twelve votes are needed for a federal indictment. If there is a finding of insufficient probable cause to charge a defendant, the grand jury returns what is often called a *no true bill*. An indictment may be *sealed* until the defendant is arrested or for other good reasons.

[2] Foreperson

While the empaneling court ordinarily appoints one of the jurors to serve as foreperson, in some jurisdictions the grand jurors themselves select the foreperson. The foreperson is usually charged with the responsibility of swearing witnesses, chairing the deliberations, signing indictments, and sometimes keeping records of votes and organizing the process.

[3] Duration of Term

In the federal system, a grand jury may sit for up to 18 months and may be extended for six months more. The terms of state grand juries vary widely, from as little as 10 days to a maximum of 18 months. This does not necessarily mean that the grand juror will be devoting "full time" to the jury process. He or she may be called upon to meet one particular afternoon each week, for example.

Special grand jury. Both state and federal laws authorize the court to impanel *special grand juries* to deal with specific matters, such as an antitrust or organized crime investigation. *See, e.g., Alwan v. Ashcroft*, 388 F.3d 507 (5th Cir. 2004)(special grand jury to investigate specific terrorist group, Hamas). Special grand juries are also authorized to clear up unresolved cases when a regular grand jury faces a backlog.

[4] Oath of Office

All jurisdictions require that the grand jurors be sworn. This procedure is performed by the court assigned to supervise the grand jury or by the clerk of the court. The form of the oath utilized in almost all jurisdictions, state and federal, is as follows:

> Do you . . . solemnly swear that you shall diligently inquire into and make true presentation or indictment of all such matters . . . as shall be given you in charge or otherwise come to your knowledge, touching your grand jury service; to keep secret the counsel of the [government], your fellows and yourselves; not to present or indict any person through hatred, malice or ill will; nor leave any person unrepresented or indicted through fear, favor, or affection, nor for any reward, or hope or promise thereof; but in all your presentments and indict-

ments to present the truth . . . to the best of your skill and understanding? [Grand Jury Law and Practice § 4:4]

[5] Hearings

No judicial officer is present during grand jury hearings. The proceedings are preserved by audio equipment or stenographers in most locales.

Typically, grand jurors are assisted by a prosecuting attorney who, according to many people, essentially controls the grand jury's focus and its investigative inquiries. The person who is the target or object of the grand jury probe ordinarily has no right to testify or be present in the grand jury room. Sometimes he or she does not know that the grand jury is investigating the person's possible criminal activity. Even when the person being investigated is permitted to testify before the grand jury, he or she is ordinarily not entitled to representation by counsel in the grand jury room. The obvious consequence is that the defendant cannot confront or cross-examine witnesses, object to evidence, or make any legal arguments relevant to the grand jury's decision whether or not to charge criminal behavior.

[a] Role of Judge

The judge's participatory role in the day-to-day functioning of the grand jury is quite limited. Initially, the judge administers the oath to grand jurors and is usually the person who also "charges" or informs the grand jurors about their responsibilities and duties. Once the grand jury begins its investigative processes, the judge plays no direct role in the proceedings and is not present in the grand jury room, but may intervene if problems arise.

Judges do, however, possess a broad discretionary power over the grand jury process. This control can occur in several ways:[*]

> [The judge] has the power to order the grand jury into existence; conversely, unless otherwise provided by statute, [the judge] has complete discretion to refuse to call a grand jury. [The judge] may dismiss the grand jury . . . at any time after it is called. [The judge] may deny requests to issue subpoenas . . . and, after the grand jury submits its findings, [the judge] may quash for cause any indictments returned, expunge reports or any surplusage in the indictment, and divulge the records of the secret grand jury proceedings upon a showing of "particularized need."
>
> As a practical matter, perhaps the most important of these powers is the judge's control over the issuance and enforcement of subpoenas. It allows [the judge] to maintain a degree of contact with the proceedings and to scrutinize them to a limited extent. But because of traditional restraints against interference with the scope of grand jury investigations, many trial judges have been hesitant to refuse to issue and enforce subpoenas.

Robert T. Brice, *Grand Jury Proceedings: The Prosecutor, the Trial Judge, and Undue Influence*, 39 U. Chi. L. Rev. 761, 768 (1972).

[b] Role of Prosecutor

Lawyer for the grand jury. The prosecutor initiates almost all cases handled by a grand jury. While the grand jury has the authority in many jurisdictions to investigate any matter on its own initiative, this occurs in relatively few cases. Keeping in mind that the prosecutor is the only official government "actor" and probably the only lawyer in the grand jury room, he or she also serves as the grand jury's legal adviser. The

---

prosecutor usually suggests to the grand jury the identity of the witnesses to be summoned, may actually issue the subpoenas for the grand jury, and may conduct the examination of witnesses. In the event a witness invokes the self-incrimination privilege, the prosecutor makes the initial decision whether to propose a grant of immunity to that witness in exchange for testimony. The prosecutor also interprets the evidence for the grand jurors and advises them whether there has been a sufficient showing of probable cause to believe that a crime was committed by a certain person.

Discretion not to prosecute. In many jurisdictions, including the federal system, the prosecutor has the discretion to refuse to prosecute an indictment issued by a grand jury. This is part of the prosecutor's general discretion to determine which charges to pursue. Discretion is discussed in Chapter 2.

Rubber stamp? As an advocate for the government, the prosecutor's presentation to the grand jury is designed to urge the grand jurors to agree with the prosecutor's "case." Sometimes, the prosecutor may be so overzealous that the grand jury loses its independence and becomes a "rubber stamp" for the prosecutor. This overzealousness has been condemned by the American Bar Association. *See* ABA Standards for Criminal Justice § 3-3.6(f) (3d ed. 1993) (in presenting case to a grand jury, prosecutor should not intentionally interfere with its independence, preempt a grand jury function, or abuse its processes). It has been argued that the grand jury would be more independent if it had its own lawyer. *See* Susan W. Brenner, *The Voice of the Community: A Case for Grand Jury Independence*, 3 VA. J. SOC. POL'Y & L. 67 (1995).

When a prosecutor crosses the line and becomes too partial, it does not necessarily mean, however, that the grand jury will issue an indictment inappropriately or without adequate legal and factual foundation. Moreover, since a grand jury must have confidence in the prosecuting attorney, the prosecutor will be (or should be) disinclined to ask for the issuance of an indictment in a weak case.

Exculpatory evidence. Some states require that a prosecutor inform the grand jury of exculpatory evidence, at least under some circumstances. The American Bar Association adopts this approach by recommending that "[n]o prosecutor should knowingly fail to disclose to the grand jury evidence which tends to negate guilt or mitigate the offense." ABA Standards for Criminal Justice § 3-3.6(b) (3d ed. 1993). This could mean, for example, that a prosecutor would be obligated to inform grand jurors of the possibility that a killing occurred in self-defense.

It can be argued, however, that no such duty should be placed upon a prosecutor because the grand jury's role is inquisitorial, focusing only upon the question whether there is probable cause to believe that a crime occurred. The "defendant's side" of the case is more appropriately left for consideration at trial. At least with respect to federal grand jury practice, the United States Supreme Court refused to dismiss a valid indictment upon the ground that the government attorney had failed to disclose exculpatory evidence to the grand jury.

UNITED STATES v. WILLIAMS
504 U.S. 36 (1992)

JUSTICE SCALIA delivered the opinion of the Court.

The question presented in this case is whether a district court may dismiss an otherwise valid indictment because the Government failed to disclose to the grand jury "substantial exculpatory evidence" in its possession.

[Williams was indicted for knowingly making false statements to a federally insured financial institution by overstating his assets and income so as to obtain loans. After his arraignment, he obtained portions of grand jury transcripts. He then moved to dismiss the indictment, alleging that the transcript demonstrated that the government had failed to present "substantial exculpatory evidence" to the grand jury in the form of tax returns and Williams' testimony in a bankruptcy proceeding. This evidence, according to Williams, would have shown that he accounted for certain assets truthfully, thereby negating an intent to mislead the banks.]

The District Court initially denied Williams' motion, but upon reconsideration ordered the indictment dismissed without prejudice. It found, after a hearing, that the withheld evidence was "relevant to an essential element of the crime charged," created "'a reasonable doubt about [respondent's] guilt,'" and thus "render[ed] the grand jury's decision to indict gravely suspect."

Upon the Government's appeal, the [Tenth Circuit] Court of Appeals affirmed the District Court's order.

. . . Respondent does not contend that the Fifth Amendment itself obliges the prosecutor to disclose substantial exculpatory evidence in his possession to the grand jury. Instead, building on our statement that the federal courts "may, within limits, formulate procedural rules not specifically required by the Constitution or the Congress," *United States v. Hasting*, 461 U.S. 499, 505 (1983), he argues that imposition of the Tenth Circuit's disclosure rule is supported by the courts' "supervisory power." We think not. . . . [Courts have the authority to control their own procedures and to prevent parties from benefitting or incurring harm from violations of substantive or procedural rules imposed by the Constitution or laws that govern matters apart from the trial itself. Thus, supervisory power can be used to enforce or vindicate legally compelled standards of prosecutorial conduct before the grand jury, but it cannot be used to prescribe those standards of prosecutorial conduct.] Because the grand jury is an institution separate from the courts, over whose functioning the courts do not preside, we think it clear that, as a general matter at least, no such "supervisory" judicial authority exists, and that the disclosure rule applied here exceeded the Tenth Circuit's authority.

. . . Respondent argues that the Court of Appeals' rule can be justified as a sort of Fifth Amendment "common law," a necessary means of assuring the constitutional right to the judgment "of an independent and informed grand jury," *Wood v. Georgia*, 370 U.S. 375 (1962).

Respondent makes a generalized appeal to functional notions: Judicial supervision of the quantity and quality of the evidence relied upon by the grand jury plainly facilitates, he says, the grand jury's performance of its twin historical responsibilities, i.e., bringing to trial those who may be justly accused and shielding the innocent from unfounded accusation and prosecution. We do not agree. The rule would neither preserve nor enhance the traditional functioning of the institution that the Fifth Amendment demands. To the contrary, requiring the prosecutor to present exculpatory as well as inculpatory evidence would alter the grand jury's historical role, transforming it from an accusatory to an adjudicatory body.

It is axiomatic that the grand jury sits not to determine guilt or innocence, but to assess whether there is adequate basis for bringing a criminal charge. That has always been so; and to make the assessment it has always been thought sufficient to hear only the prosecutor's side.

. . . Imposing upon the prosecutor a legal obligation to present exculpatory evidence in his possession would be incompatible with this system. If a "balanced" assessment of the entire matter is the objective, surely the first thing to be done — rather than requiring the prosecutor to say what he knows in defense of the target of the investigation — is to entitle the target to tender his own defense. To require the former while denying (as we do) the latter would be quite absurd. It would also be quite pointless, since it would merely invite the target to circumnavigate the system by delivering his exculpatory evidence to the prosecutor, whereupon it would have to be passed on to the grand jury — unless the prosecutor is willing to take the chance that a court will not deem the evidence important enough to qualify for mandatory disclosure.

Respondent acknowledges (as he must) that the "common law" of the grand jury is not violated if the grand jury itself chooses to hear no more evidence than that which suffices to convince it an indictment is proper. Thus, had the Government offered to familiarize the grand jury in this case with the five boxes of financial statements and deposition testimony alleged to contain exculpatory information, and had the grand jury rejected the offer as pointless, respondent would presumably agree that the resulting indictment would have been valid . . . . If the grand jury has no obligation to consider all "substantial exculpatory" evidence, we do not understand how the prosecutor can be said to have a binding obligation to present it.

. . . [R]espondent argues that a rule requiring the prosecutor to disclose exculpatory evidence to the grand jury would, by removing from the docket unjustified prosecutions, save valuable judicial time. That depends, we suppose, upon what the ratio would turn out to be between unjustified prosecutions eliminated and grand jury indictments challenged — for the latter as well as the former consume "valuable judicial time." We need not pursue the matter; if there is an advantage to the proposal, Congress is free to prescribe it. For the reasons set forth above, however, we conclude that courts have no authority to prescribe such a duty pursuant to their inherent supervisory authority over their own proceedings. [Reversed and remanded.]

JUSTICE STEVENS, joined by JUSTICES BLACKMUN O'CONNOR and THOMAS, dissented:

. . . In an opinion that I find difficult to comprehend, the Court today . . . seems to suggest that the court has no authority to supervise the conduct of the prosecutor in grand jury proceedings so long as he follows the dictates of the Constitution, applicable statutes, and Rule 6 of the Federal Rules of Criminal Procedure. The Court purports to support this conclusion by invoking the doctrine of separation of powers and citing a string of cases in which we have declined to impose categorical restraints on the grand jury. Needless to say, the Court's reasoning is unpersuasive.

. . . Throughout its life, from the moment it is convened until it is discharged, the grand jury is subject to the control of the court.

. . . This Court has, of course, long recognized that the grand jury has wide latitude to investigate violations of federal law as it deems appropriate and need not obtain permission from either the court or the prosecutor . . . . Correspondingly, we have acknowledged that "its operation generally is unrestrained by the technical procedural and evidentiary rules governing the conduct of criminal trials." But this is because Congress and the Court have generally thought it best not to impose procedural restraints on the grand jury; it is not because they lack all power to do so.

. . . Although the Court recognizes that it may invoke its supervisory authority to fashion and enforce privilege rules applicable in grand jury proceedings, and suggests that it may also invoke its supervisory authority to fashion other limited rules of grand jury procedure, it concludes that it has no authority to "prescrib[e] standards of prosecutorial conduct before the grand jury," because that would alter the grand jury's historic role as an independent, inquisitorial institution. I disagree.

We do not protect the integrity and independence of the grand jury by closing our eyes to the countless forms of prosecutorial misconduct that may occur inside the secrecy of the grand jury room. After all, the grand jury is not merely an investigatory body; it also serves as a [shield] . . . . It blinks reality to say that the grand jury can adequately perform this important historic role if it is intentionally misled by the prosecutor — on whose knowledge of the law and facts of the underlying criminal investigation the jurors will, of necessity, rely.

. . . Unrestrained prosecutorial misconduct in grand jury proceedings is inconsistent with the administration of justice in the federal courts and should be redressed in appropriate cases by the dismissal of indictments obtained by improper methods.

What, then, is the proper disposition of this case? I agree with the Government that the prosecutor is not required to place all exculpatory evidence before the grand jury. A grand jury proceeding is an *ex parte* investigatory proceeding to determine whether there is probable cause to believe a violation of the criminal laws has occurred, not a trial. Requiring the prosecutor to ferret out and present all evidence that could be used at trial to create a reasonable doubt as to the defendant's guilt would be inconsistent with the purpose of the grand jury proceeding and would place significant burdens on the investigation. But that does not mean that the prosecutor may mislead the grand jury into believing that there is probable cause to indict by withholding clear evidence to the contrary. I thus agree with the Department of Justice that "when a prosecutor conducting a grand jury inquiry is personally aware of substantial evidence which directly negates the guilt of a subject of the investigation, the prosecutor must present or otherwise disclose such evidence to the grand jury before seeking an indictment against such a person." . . .

NOTES

1. *Directly negating guilt.* What kind of evidence "directly negates the guilt of the subject of the investigation" (quoting Justice Stevens)? Would evidence proving the affirmative defense of insanity meet that standard?

2. *Grand jury requests exculpatory information.* Assume that the grand jury requested that the prosecutor provide it with information as to the defendant's version of the facts. Some state statutes specifically authorize the grand jury to obtain exculpatory evidence. If the prosecutor fails to provide that information and the grand jury indicts the defendant, should that be grounds for dismissal of the indictment?

3. *Denying evidence to second grand jury after first refuses to indict.* Assume that evidence presented to a previous grand jury apparently led that grand jury not to indict the defendant. The prosecutor, now presenting the case to a second grand jury, fails to present that same evidence to the grand jury, as a result of which a "true bill" issues. Have the defendant's constitutional rights been infringed? If so, in what way?

4. *Prosecuting in face of substantial evidence negating guilt.* If the prosecutor is aware of substantial evidence that would tend to negate guilt, would a reasonable prosecutor seek an indictment with the knowledge that the case will probably not result in conviction? While our intuitive answer to this question should be no, it has been suggested that prosecutors sometimes utilize the grand jury to obtain an indictment in such cases. They might do so because of (1) public pressure to prosecute, (2) a sense that this process, itself, will generate the desired sanction (*i.e.*, loss of reputation), or (3) a desire to secure a conviction through plea bargaining. *See* Janet A. Gilboy, *Prosecutors' Discretionary Use of the Grand Jury to Initiate or to Reinitiate Prosecution*, 1984 AMER. BAR. FOUND. RES. J. 1. If a prosecutor were to engage in this kind of behavior, would he or she be acting in a professionally ethical way? *See* Standards for Criminal Justice § 3-3.6(c) (3d ed. 1993) (prosecutor should recommend that grand jury not indict if evidence does not warrant an indictment under applicable law).

One commentator has suggested that a prosecutor has a responsibility to tell the grand jury about potentially exculpatory evidence because a prosecutor, as the "people's lawyer," should be more concerned with doing justice than securing an indictment. *See* H. Richard Uviller, *The Neutral Prosecutor: The Obligation of Dispassion in a Passionate Pursuit*, 68 FORDHAM L. REV. 1695, 1707 (2000).

5. *Defense counsel's options with exculpatory evidence.* Assume you are a defense attorney who has an important piece of exculpatory written evidence you would like the grand jurors to have when they consider whether to return an indictment against your client. What can you do? Should you give it to the prosecutor with a request that the evidence be submitted to the grand jury? Send it to the judge with this same request?

Mail a copy of the evidence directly to the foreperson and/or each grand juror (ordinarily, the names and addresses of the grand jurors can be obtained from the court clerk)?

6. *Dismiss without prejudice.* Recall that the District Court in *Williams* dismissed the case "without prejudice." What does that mean? This is the usual remedy for a faulty indictment. Why would defense counsel bother to file a Motion to Dismiss an indictment if the likely remedy is dismissal without prejudice?

7. *Internal policies requiring submission of exculpatory evidence.* Of course a prosecutor is free to present exculpatory evidence to a grand jury. Internal prosecution policies may require it. *See, e.g.,* U.S. Attorney's Manual 9-11.233 (Dept. of Justice policy is that prosecutor must present or otherwise describe to grand jury known evidence directly negating guilt.)

8. *State rejection of Williams.* Some state courts have rejected *Williams* and have exercised their supervisory powers to require prosecutors to present exculpatory evidence to grand juries. In *State v. Hogan,* 676 A.2d 533 (N.J. 1996), the New Jersey Supreme Court reasoned that a prosecutor has a duty to present exculpatory evidence to a grand jury in those rare case where such evidence "squarely refutes an *element* of the crime in question." The victim in *Hogan* recanted her testimony to investigators and later claimed that she did so because of death threats against her and her daughter. The court held that the prosecutor did not have a duty to disclose this evidence to the grand jury because it was not sufficiently reliable to be clearly exculpatory. *See also Trebus v. Davis,* 944 P.2d 1235, 1239 (Ariz. 1997) ("The county attorney is not obligated to present all exculpatory evidence to the grand jury absent a request by the grand jury, but must present only "clearly exculpatory" evidence. . . . Clearly exculpatory evidence is evidence of such weight that it might deter the grand jury from finding the existence of probable cause.").

[c]   Role of Target

[i]   Subpoena Target

Consistent with the grand jury's broad investigative powers, a grand jury may call any individual before it as a witness. When subpoenaed, a person has no right to refuse to testify unless certain constitutional privileges apply. The witness ordinarily must respond truthfully to questions posed by grand jurors or prosecutors. Generally, this rule also applies to an individual who may be characterized as a "target" or "subject" (or perhaps "putative defendant") of the grand jury investigation.

Most courts tend to use the terms *subject* and *target* interchangeably. Both refer to an individual who either could become an indicted defendant or, more narrowly, is the principle focus of the grand jury's attention for possible indictment. Federal prosecutors have attempted to distinguish between a subject and a target. To them, a subject is "a person whose conduct is within the scope of the grand jury's investigation." A target is "a person as to whom the prosecutor or the grand jury has substantial evidence linking him/her to the commission of a crime and who, in the judgment of the prosecutor, is a putative defendant." Grand Jury Law and Practice, § 6.23.

Whether one is or is not a target (or subject) is important because a minority of jurisdictions do not permit the prosecution to use the grand jury's subpoena authority to force either a subject or a target to appear.

[ii]   Target's Right to Appear

But what if the target (or a person who perceives that the grand jury may be investigating his or her behavior) wants to testify before the grand jury? The traditional rule is that no individual — including a putative defendant — has a right to testify before the grand jury. Similarly, no witness, including the target, has a right to cross-examine other witnesses or to present evidence, but a prosecutor may present evidence or witnesses suggested by a target or other witness. While this principle does not prohibit any individual from requesting such an appearance or to present evidence, it is within the grand jury's discretion to grant or deny the request.

If a target's request to testify voluntarily is granted, he or she may be required to waive any Fifth Amendment rights prior to testifying. *See, e.g.,* U.S. Attorney's Manual 9-11.152 (must also be represented by counsel or validly waive counsel).

A few states believe this is unfair and afford the target or subject of a grand jury proceeding the right to appear and testify. Perhaps the most protective provision is a New York statute requiring that an indictment be voided if the target is not permitted the right to testify. N.Y. Crim. Proc. Law § 190.50(5)(C).

[iii] Procedures When Target Appears

Assume that a putative defendant is subpoenaed to appear before the grand jury. Is a target witness entitled to be treated differently from any other witness? The federal government and a minority of state jurisdictions mandate that *target warnings* be given to such individuals. Such warnings may include advice that (1) the individual is the subject of the grand jury investigation, (2) the witness has no right to refuse to answer a question, except that the Fifth Amendment self incrimination guarantee may apply, (3) anything said by the witness may be used in a subsequent legal proceeding, and (4) the witness may have a reasonable opportunity to confer with retained counsel outside the grand jury room. *See generally* Standards for Criminal Justice § 3-3.6(d) (3d ed. 1993) (a prosecutor who believes a grand jury witness is a potential defendant should not compel the witness to so testify without informing the witness of possible charges and the need to seek legal advice). *See also* U.S. Attorney's Manual 9-11.150 (U.S. Attorney should first attempt to have target appear voluntarily before grand jury; targets who are subpoenaed should be notified of this status and apprised of their rights).

The general rule, however, is that a putative defendant appearing before the grand jury will be treated as any other witness and afforded no particularized warnings or special protections.

[iv] Wisdom of Target's Appearance

In the minority of jurisdictions that afford the target witness an opportunity to appear before the grand jury, would it be advisable for the target to do so? Strategically, this may pose a very difficult question for the witness and his or her counsel. The testimony before the grand jury may persuade it not to indict the witness. On the other hand, the witness has a responsibility to answer questions truthfully, except where protected by the self incrimination or another privilege. Since the witness may inadvertently answer a question under circumstances in which a self-incrimination claim could have been asserted, the target's own testimony may establish probable cause. Similarly, even seemingly insignificant responses could be used for impeachment purposes at a subsequent trial.

[d] Role of Defense Attorney

[i] Prior to Grand Jury Hearing

Sometimes, and especially in white collar crime cases, the putative defendant believes that he or she is, or soon will be, the subject of a grand jury investigation and consults an attorney before an indictment is issued. Even though the grand jury process is outside of the lawyer's control, it would be a mistake to conclude that there is nothing the lawyer can do on behalf of the client.

The defense attorney's first mission may be to persuade the prosecutor not to seek an indictment against the client. This may entail making a presentation of facts or legal theory to convince the prosecutor that a formal charge would be ill-advised. Similarly, defense counsel may succeed in urging the prosecutor to limit the indictment in various ways (*i.e.*, fewer counts or a lesser offense). In exchange, the client may agree to cooperate with the government, which may have the effect of shifting the focus to other culpable parties. Cooperation at this stage also could benefit the client at the sentencing phase of the case. Defense counsel can also request that the prosecutor submit certain exculpatory evidence to the grand jury. Finally, defense counsel should begin gathering information about the investigation in order to assist in trial preparation. One commentator recommends discussions with the prosecutor to determine the scope of the investigation and debriefing of grand jury witnesses. *See* Gerald W. Heller, *Selections for the Criminal Law Library: Effective Representation Before the Grand Jury*, 27 CRIM. L. BULL. 472, 472 473 (1991) (book review).

[ii]   During Grand Jury Hearing: Minority Rule

Many states now permit witnesses' attorneys to be present to a limited extent during grand jury proceedings. Rosalind Resnick, *Grand Jury Witnesses Get Help*, NAT'L L. J., June 1, 1992, at 3, 48. Massachusetts, for example, provides that "[t]he attorney for the witness shall make no objections or arguments or otherwise address the grand jury or the prosecuting attorney." Mass R. Crim. P. 5. Similarly, Michigan mandates that the lawyer "not participate in the proceedings other than to advise the witness." Mich. R. Crim. P. 6.005.

The right to counsel in the grand jury room is usually restricted to retained attorneys; the statutory provisions do not ordinarily provide for state-funded attorneys for indigent witnesses. A small number of states (Kansas, Michigan, Nebraska, New York and Pennsylvania) provide counsel to indigent witnesses called to testify before grand juries, while others (Colorado and Illinois) appear to limit that provision to witnesses against whom the state may be seeking an indictment.

Prosecutors generally oppose statutory provisions that permit a defense attorney to be present in the grand jury room. They argue that the lawyer will jeopardize grand jury secrecy and disrupt the grand jury process by making objections, requesting delays, and conducting lengthy legal examinations of witnesses. Do you agree that these concerns are sufficient to keep defense lawyers out of the grand jury room?

[iii]   During Grand Jury Hearing: Majority Rule

In most states and in the federal system, witnesses must enter grand jury rooms alone while their retained attorneys wait outside the grand jury room. The witness desiring to consult with counsel during the grand jury proceedings ordinarily will write down the prosecutor's question on a notepad, request permission to leave the room, consult with defense counsel in the corridor outside the grand jury room, and then return and respond to the question. The scenario is repeated with each question. One rationale for this awkward and time-consuming practice is that the grand jury is non-adversarial. Its sole task, it is argued, is to determine whether there is probable cause to indict; the presence of defense counsel would not aid in meeting that objective.

A number of issues are litigated in the context of the majority no-counsel-present rule. First, since it is well established that a grand jury witness has the right to consult with defense counsel, the witness must be afforded the right to leave the grand jury room at reasonable times to consult with the witness's lawyer. *See, e.g., Gilbert v.Conn*, 131 F.3d 793 (9th Cir. 1997). On the assumption that a non-immunized witness has more to fear in terms of self incrimination than one who has received immunity, some courts have suggested that the non-immunized witness should have broader power to interrupt the grand jury proceedings to confer with counsel. *Matter of Lowry*, 713 F.2d 616 (11th Cir. 1983).

Perhaps the most difficult issue to resolve is the question under what circumstances consultation with counsel becomes unreasonable or obstructionist. A prosecutor or the grand jury foreperson may try to restrict a witness's frequent consultations with counsel. If the witness refuses to obey such a command, the prosecutor should file a petition seeking a contempt of court order against the witness. If the judge determines that the witness is engaging in consultation either to obstruct the grand jury's investigation or for entirely frivolous reasons, the judge may cite the witness for contempt of court.

[e] Admissibility of Evidence

Given the non-adversarial nature of the grand jury investigative process, rules governing the presentation and admissibility of evidence at trial are relaxed in grand jury hearings, though privileges apply in full force. Additionally, as indicated in the counsel section above, courts are hesitant to convert grand jury proceedings into "mini-trials." They believe that extending evidentiary challenges to the grand jury could impede its investigations and sacrifice the traditional rule of grand jury secrecy.

Notwithstanding these concerns, many legislatures and courts impose some restrictions on the evidence admissible in grand jury proceedings. A few states follow relatively strict rules of evidence in grand jury proceedings. *See, e.g.*, N.Y. Crim. Pro. § 190.30 (providing that rules of evidence are generally applicable to grand jury proceedings and that the district attorney has the authority to make rulings regarding "the competency of a witness to testify or upon the admissibility of evidence").

Other states do not follow the rules of evidence, but prohibit indictments based solely on either inadmissible evidence or on no evidence at all. Most states and the federal government, however, recognize relatively few limitations (other than privileges) on the kinds of evidence admissible before the grand jury. Grand Jury Law and Practice §§ 4:19, & 4:20.

One of the earliest issues to reach the United States Supreme Court was the question of whether a federal indictment could be based entirely upon hearsay testimony.

COSTELLO v. UNITED STATES
350 U.S. 359 (1956)

MR. JUSTICE BLACK delivered the opinion of the Court.

We granted certiorari in this case to consider a single question: "May a defendant be required to stand trial and a conviction be sustained where only hearsay evidence was presented to the grand jury which indicted him?"

[Defendant was indicted for wilfully attempting to evade payment of income taxes by understating his income. The only witnesses before the grand jury were the government investigators who summarized the results of interviews with witnesses and the content of various documents.]

. . . The Fifth Amendment provides that federal prosecutions for capital or otherwise infamous crimes must be instituted by presentments or indictments of grand juries. But neither the Fifth Amendment nor any other constitutional provision prescribes the kind of evidence upon which grand juries must act. . . .

If indictments were to be held open to challenge on the ground that there was inadequate or incompetent evidence before the grand jury, the resulting delay would be great indeed. The result of such a rule would be that before trial on the merits a defendant could always insist on a kind of preliminary trial to determine the competency and adequacy of the evidence before the grand jury. This is not required by the Fifth Amendment. An indictment returned by a legally constituted and unbiased grand jury, like an information drawn by the prosecutor, if valid on its face, is enough to call for trial of the charge on the merits. The Fifth Amendment requires nothing more.

Petitioner urges that this Court should exercise its power to supervise the administration of justice in federal courts and establish a rule permitting defendants to challenge indictments on the ground that they are not supported by adequate or competent evidence. . . . It would run counter to the whole history of the grand jury institution, in which laymen conduct their inquiries unfettered by technical rules. Neither justice nor the concept of a fair trial requires such a change. In a trial on the merits, defendants are entitled to a strict observance of all the rules designed to bring about a fair verdict. Defendants are not entitled, however, to a rule which would result in interminable delay but add nothing to the assurance of a fair trial.

Mr. Justice Burton, concurring.

I agree with the denial of the motion to quash the indictment. In my view, however, this case does not justify the breadth of the declarations made by the Court. I assume that this Court would not preclude an examination of grand-jury action to ascertain the existence of bias or prejudice in an indictment. Likewise, it seems to me that if it is shown that the grand jury had before it no substantial or rationally persuasive evidence upon which to base its indictment, that indictment should be quashed. To hold a person to answer to such an empty indictment for a capital or otherwise infamous federal crime robs the Fifth Amendment of much of its protective value to the private citizen. . . .

NOTES

1. *Exclusionary rule — Inapplicable in grand jury.* A different question arises when police have obtained evidence in violation of the Fourth or Fifth Amendments and now seek to use or rely upon that evidence in presenting a case for grand jury consideration. This practice, too, has been upheld by the United States Supreme Court.

In *United States v. Calandra*, 414 U.S. 338 (1974), the issue was whether a witness testifying before a grand jury could refuse to answer questions on the ground that the specific questions were based upon evidence obtained from an unlawful search. The Court responded that the exclusionary rule does not apply to grand jury proceedings. Therefore, the witness has no right to refuse to answer the questions. Using a balancing approach, the Court noted that extending the exclusionary rule to the grand jury "would unduly interfere with the effective and expeditious discharge of the grand jury's duties." And while the purposes behind the exclusionary rule (principally deterrence of police misconduct) might be advanced by extending the rule to the grand jury proceeding, that benefit would be "uncertain at best."

The *Calandra* exception to the exclusionary rule for Fourth Amendment violations also extends to evidence obtained in violation of the Fifth Amendment's self incrimination clause. *United States v. Blue*, 384 U.S. 251 (1966). Of course evidence obtained in violation of either amendment may be excluded at trial.

2. *Exclusionary rule — Applicable in grand jury.* The exclusionary rule does apply in a few contexts in grand jury proceedings. As discussed later, an indictment may be dismissed if it was based directly or indirectly on immunized testimony of the person who was indicted. This use violates the witness' Fifth Amendment right to refuse self-incrimination. An indictment has also been dismissed for violation of the speech and debate clause. *See United States v. Swindall*, 971 F.2d 1531 (11th Cir. 1992), *cert. denied*, 114 S. Ct. 683 (1994) (former member of Congress indicted for lying to grand jury; indictment dismissed because government established his knowledge of laws by questioning him before the grand jury about his congressional committee work, in violation of speech and debate clause).

3. *Voluntary application of exclusionary rule.* The U.S. Justice Department has internal rules barring federal prosecutors from presenting to grand juries evidence "against a person whose constitutional rights clearly have been violated . . . which the prosecutor personally knows was obtained as a direct result of a violation of the constitutional violation." U.S. Attorney's Manual 9-11.231. How important is the word "clearly" in the practical impact of this rule?

4. *State variations.* A few states disagree with *Calandra* and bar indictments based solely on evidence obtained in violation of the constitution. Grand Jury Law and Practice § 4:21.

5. *Evidence rules and function of grand jury.* If a grand jury relies upon hearsay testimony, as in *Costello,* or evidence clearly inadmissible at trial, such as in *Calandra,* has it truly performed its function in serving as a buffer between the government and the accused? Can it accurately assess either the defendant's culpability or the strength of the prosecution's case? If not, does it matter?

United States Attorneys are instructed that they may use hearsay evidence in grand jury proceedings but the evidence "should be presented on its merits so that the jurors are not misled into believing that the witness is giving his or her personal account." U.S. Attorneys' Manual 9-11-232. Do you think this helps the grand jury in performing its duties?

6. *Impact of stricter evidence rules.* If stricter evidentiary rules were to apply to grand juries, to what extent would (or should) the accused be entitled to a transcript of the grand jury proceeding to determine whether the indictment was properly issued? If this were allowed, how could grand jury secrecy be preserved?

[f] Subpoena Power

The grand jury's (actually the prosecutor's) power to issue subpoenas is a potent investigative tool to obtain both tangible and testimonial evidence. A *subpoena ad testificandum* is an order compelling the named witness to appear and testify before the grand jury. A *subpoena duces tecum* is an order for the witness to appear and produce certain specified records before the grand jury.

Unlike the suspect who is interrogated in a police station, an individual who has been subpoenaed has no general right to refuse to cooperate, although the Fifth Amendment privilege against self incrimination is available to both the arrestee and the subpoenaed person.

Testimony before the grand jury will be given under oath, which means that false testimony can result in a perjury conviction. A subpoenaed witness who refuses without justification (usually based on the Fifth Amendment privilege) to give testimony may be held in contempt and jailed for the duration of the grand jury's term, or until the witness purges him- or herself of contempt by complying with the subpoena and testifying.

As discussed earlier in this chapter, many states have either abolished the grand jury or severely curtailed its use. In the federal system and in states that retain the grand jury, it is usually the prosecutor, acting on behalf or in the name of the grand jury, who issues subpoenas or moves to have a recalcitrant witness held in contempt by a judicial officer.

In non-grand jury states, the prosecutor, in the absence of a grand jury, initiates charges directly via *information* and typically has the power to summon witnesses to appear and produce documents at the prosecutor's office at a designated date and time. The Arkansas statute, conferring investigatory subpoena power directly to the prosecutor, is illustrative:

Arkansas Code, § 16-43-212

Criminal proceedings — Issuance of subpoenas pursuant to investigations

(a) The prosecuting attorneys and their deputies may issue subpoenas in all criminal matters they are investigating and may administer oaths for the purpose of taking the testimony of witnesses subpoenaed before them. Such oath when administered by the prosecuting attorney or his or her deputy shall have the same effect as if administered by the foreman of the grand jury. The subpoena shall be substantially in the following form:

"The State of Arkansas to the Sheriff of County: You are commanded to summon [name of person] to attend before the Prosecuting Attorney at [date], A.D. 20 .M., and testify in the matter of an investigation then to be conducted by the said Prosecuting Attorney growing out of a representation that [name of suspect] has committed the crime of in said County. Witness my hand this , A.D. 20.

Prosecuting Attorney
By

Deputy Prosecuting Attorney

(b) The subpoena provided for in subsection (a) of this section shall be served in the manner as provided by law and shall be returned and a record made and kept as provided by law for grand jury subpoenas.

NOTE

As explained earlier, the witness has the affirmative duty to assert the self-incrimination privilege, if applicable. The witness must be cautious to avoid making an "unwitting waiver," in which the witness who voluntarily discloses some facts to the grand jury cannot assert the privilege to refuse to answer questions about the details of those facts. *See, e.g., Rogers v. United States*, 340 U.S. 367 (1951)(federal courts have uniformly held that, where incriminating facts have been voluntarily revealed, the privilege cannot be invoked to avoid disclosure of the details). The Supreme Court later reaffirmed *Rogers*, noting that "there is no unfairness in allowing cross-examination when testimony is given without invoking the privilege." *Mitchell v. United States*, 526 U.S. 314 (1999).

[g]　Jurisdiction and Relevance

Let us assume a witness is subpoenaed to appear before the grand jury and the witness believes that the grand jury has no jurisdiction over the matter being investigated. Is the witness permitted to refuse to respond to the questioning on that basis? The United States Supreme Court answered this question in the following often-cited case.

BLAIR v. UNITED STATES
250 U.S. 273 (1919)

MR. JUSTICE PITNEY delivered the opinion of the Court.

. . . [I]t is clearly recognized that the giving of testimony and the attendance upon court or grand jury in order to testify are public duties which every person within the jurisdiction of the government is bound to perform upon being properly summoned, and for performance of which he is entitled to no further compensation than that which the statutes provide. The personal sacrifice involved is a part of the necessary contribution of the individual to the welfare of the public. The duty, so onerous at times, yet so necessary to the administration of justice according to the forms and modes established in our system of government is subject to mitigation in exceptional circumstances; there is a constitutional exemption from being compelled in any criminal case to be a witness against oneself, entitling the witness to be excused from answering anything that will tend to incriminate him; some confidential matters are shielded from considerations of policy, and perhaps in other cases for special reasons a witness may be excused from telling all that he knows.

But, aside from exceptions and qualifications — and none such is asserted in the present case — the witness is bound not only to attend but to tell what he knows in answer to questions framed for the purpose of bringing out the truth of the matter under inquiry.

He is not entitled to urge objections of incompetency or irrelevancy, such as a party might raise, for this is no concern of his.

On familiar principles, he is not entitled to challenge the authority of the court or of the grand jury, provided they have a *de facto* existence and organization.

He is not entitled to set limits to the investigation that the grand jury may conduct . . . . It is a grand inquest, a body with powers of investigation and inquisition, the scope of whose inquiries is not to be limited narrowly by questions of propriety or forecasts of the probable result of the investigation, or by doubts whether any particular individual will be found properly subject to an accusation of crime. As has been said before, the identity of the offender, and the precise nature of the offense, if there be one, normally are developed at the conclusion of the grand jury's labors, not at the beginning.

And, for the same reasons, witnesses are not entitled to take exception to the jurisdiction of the grand jury or the court over the particular subject-matter that is under investigation. In truth it is in the ordinary case no concern of one summoned as a witness whether the offense is within the jurisdiction of the court or not. At least, the court and grand jury have authority and jurisdiction to investigate the facts in order to determine the question whether the facts show a case within their jurisdiction. . . .

[h] Reasonableness

While the *Blair* opinion is very strongly worded, there are a number of limitations upon the subpoena power. The next case explores the primary limitation: reasonableness.

UNITED STATES v. R. ENTERPRISES, INC.
498 U.S. 292 (1991)

Justice O'Connor delivered the opinion of the Court.

This case requires the Court to decide what standards apply when a party seeks to avoid compliance with a *subpoena duces tecum* issued in connection with a grand jury investigation.

[A federal grand jury investigating allegations of interstate transportation of obscene materials issued subpoenas to several companies, including R. Enterprises, Inc., seeking a variety of corporate books and records. The companies moved to quash the subpoenas, arguing that the materials called for were irrelevant to the grand jury's investigation and that enforcement of the subpoenas would infringe their First Amendment rights. The District Court denied the motions to quash and later held the companies in contempt because of their continued refusal to comply. The Court of Appeals for the Fourth Circuit quashed the business records subpoenas, applying the standards set out in *United States v. Nixon*, 418 U.S. 683 (1974). It required the government to establish relevancy, admissibility and specificity in order to enforce the grand jury's subpoenas.]

. . . The grand jury occupies a unique role in our criminal justice system. It is an investigatory body charged with the responsibility of determining whether or not a crime has been committed. Unlike this Court, whose jurisdiction is predicated on a specific case or controversy, the grand jury "can investigate merely on suspicion that the law is being violated, or even just because it wants assurance that it is not." *United*

States v. Morton Salt Co., 338 U.S. 632, 642–643 (1950). The function of the grand jury is to inquire into all information that might possibly bear on its investigation until it has identified an offense or has satisfied itself that none has occurred.

A grand jury subpoena is thus much different from a subpoena issued in the context of a prospective criminal trial, where a specific offense has been identified and a particular defendant charged. "[T]he identity of the offender, and the precise nature of the offense, if there be one, normally are developed at the conclusion of the grand jury's labors, not at the beginning." *Blair v. United States*, 250 U.S. 273, 282 (1919). In short, the Government cannot be required to justify the issuance of a grand jury subpoena by presenting evidence sufficient to establish probable cause because the very purpose of requesting the information is to ascertain whether probable cause exists.

This Court has emphasized on numerous occasions that many of the rules and restrictions that apply at a trial do not apply in grand jury proceedings. This is especially true of evidentiary restrictions. The same rules that, in an adversary hearing on the merits, may increase the likelihood of accurate determinations of guilt or innocence do not necessarily advance the mission of a grand jury, whose task is to conduct an ex parte investigation to determine whether or not there is probable cause to prosecute a particular defendant. . . .

This guiding principle renders suspect the Court of Appeals' holding that the standards announced in *Nixon* as to subpoenas issued in anticipation of trial apply equally in the grand jury context. The multifactor test announced in *Nixon* would invite procedural delays and detours while courts evaluate the relevancy and admissibility of documents sought by a particular subpoena . . . . Additionally, application of the *Nixon* test in this context ignores that grand jury proceedings are subject to strict secrecy requirements.

. . . The investigatory powers of the grand jury are nevertheless not unlimited. Grand juries are not licensed to engage in arbitrary fishing expeditions, nor may they select targets of investigation out of malice or an intent to harass. In this case, the focus of our inquiry is the limit imposed on a grand jury by Federal Rule of Criminal Procedure 17(c), which governs the issuance of *subpoenas duces tecum* in federal criminal proceedings. The Rule provides that "the court on motion made promptly may quash or modify the subpoena if compliance would be unreasonable or oppressive."

This standard is not self-explanatory. As we have observed, "what is reasonable depends on the context." *New Jersey v. T.L.O.*, 469 U.S. 325, 337 (1985) . . . . In the grand jury context, the decision as to what offense will be charged is routinely not made until after the grand jury has concluded its investigation. One simply cannot know in advance whether information sought during the investigation will be relevant and admissible in a prosecution for a particular offense.

. . . Our task is to fashion an appropriate standard of reasonableness, one that gives due weight to the difficult position of subpoena recipients but does not impair the strong governmental interests in affording grand juries wide latitude, avoiding minitrials on peripheral matters, and preserving a necessary level of secrecy. We begin by reiterating that the law presumes, absent a strong showing to the contrary, that a grand jury acts within the legitimate scope of its authority . . . . Consequently, a grand jury subpoena issued through normal channels is presumed to be reasonable, and the burden of showing unreasonableness must be on the recipient who seeks to avoid compliance . . . . Drawing on the principles articulated above, we conclude that where, as here, a subpoena is challenged on relevancy grounds, the motion to quash must be denied unless the district court determines that there is no reasonable possibility that the category of materials the Government seeks will produce information relevant to the general subject of the grand jury's investigation. Respondents did not challenge the subpoenas as being too indefinite nor did they claim that compliance would be overly burdensome. The Court of Appeals accordingly did not consider these aspects of the subpoenas, nor do we.

It seems unlikely, of course, that a challenging party who does not know the general subject matter of the grand jury's investigation, no matter how valid that party's claim, will be able to make the necessary showing that compliance would be unreasonable. Consequently, a court may be justified in a case where unreasonableness is alleged in requiring the Government to reveal the general subject of the grand jury's investigation before requiring the challenging party to carry its burden of persuasion. . . . In cases where the recipient of the subpoena does not know the nature of the investigation, we are confident that district courts will be able to craft appropriate procedures that balance the interests of the subpoena recipient against the strong governmental interests in maintaining secrecy, preserving investigatory flexibility, and avoiding procedural delays. For example, to ensure that subpoenas are not routinely challenged as a form of discovery, a district court may require that the Government reveal the subject of the investigation to the trial court in camera, so that the court may determine whether the motion to quash has a reasonable prospect for success before it discloses the subject matter to the challenging party.

Applying these principles in this case demonstrates that the District Court correctly denied respondents' motions to quash. . . .

Justice Stevens, with whom Justices Marshall and Blackmun join, concurring in part and concurring in the judgment.

Federal Rule of Criminal Procedure 17(c) authorizes a Federal District Court to quash or modify a grand jury subpoena duces tecum "if compliance would be unreasonable or oppressive." This rule requires the district court to balance the burden of compliance, on the one hand, against the governmental interest in obtaining the documents on the other. A more burdensome subpoena should be justified by a somewhat higher degree of probable relevance than a subpoena that imposes a minimal or nonexistent burden. Against the procedural history of this case, the Court has attempted to define the term "reasonable" in the abstract, looking only at the relevance side of the balance. Because I believe that this truncated approach to the Rule will neither provide adequate guidance to the district court nor place any meaningful constraint on the overzealous prosecutor, I add these comments.

The burden of establishing that compliance would be unreasonable or oppressive rests, of course, on the subpoenaed witness.

. . . The moving party has the initial task of demonstrating to the Court that he has some valid objection to compliance. This showing might be made in various ways. Depending on the volume and location of the requested materials, the mere cost in terms of time, money, and effort of responding to a dragnet subpoena could satisfy the initial hurdle. Similarly, if a witness showed that compliance with the subpoena would intrude significantly on his privacy interests, or call for the disclosure of trade secrets or other confidential information, further inquiry would be required. Or, as in this case, the movant might demonstrate that compliance would have First Amendment implications.

The trial court need inquire into the relevance of subpoenaed materials only after the moving party has made this initial showing. And, as is true in the parallel context of pretrial civil discovery, a matter also committed to the sound discretion of the trial judge, the degree of need sufficient to justify denial of the motion to quash will vary to some extent with the burden of producing the requested information. For the reasons stated by the Court, in the grand jury context the law enforcement interest will almost always prevail, and the documents must be produced. I stress, however, that the Court's opinion should not be read to suggest that the deferential relevance standard the Court has formulated will govern decision in every case, no matter how intrusive or burdensome the request.

. . . I would only add that further inquiry into the possible unreasonable or oppressive character of this subpoena should also take into account the entire history of this grand jury investigation, including the series of subpoenas that have been issued to the same corporations and their affiliates during the past several years.

NOTES

1. *Rule 17(c).* As noted in *R. Enterprises*, "reasonableness" is a key limit on a subpoena. Under Rule 17(c) of the Federal Rules of Criminal Procedure, a court may quash or modify any subpoena found to be unreasonable or oppressive. According to one commentator,

> The subpoena's reasonableness comes into question only when the subpoenaed party, who bears the burden of proof, desires to quash. In order to fulfill the reasonableness requirement, the subpoena must state with particularity the materials relevant to the investigation and span a reasonable period of time. The "reasonable period of time" limitation requires that the subpoena bear "some relation" to the subject matter of the investigation. Courts have upheld subpoenas covering time spans ranging from four to twenty-seven years. Other factors bearing on reasonableness include the volume of subpoenaed records, the disruptive impact on the subpoenaed party, and the cost of compliance.

Susan L. Boccardi, et al., *Grand Jury Subpoena and Secrecy*, 28 AM. CRIM. L. REV. 749, 753–754 (1991).

2. *Identity of person subpoenaed; lawyers.* Another limit is based on the identity of the person receiving the subpoena. In *United States v. Klubock*, 832 F.2d 664 (1st Cir. 1987), it was held that prior judicial approval was necessary before serving a subpoena upon an attorney to provide evidence on the attorney's own client. *See also* U.S. Attorneys' Manual 9-11.255 (prior approval of Assistant Attorney General needed for grand jury subpoena of an attorney for information related to the representation of a client or fees paid by such client)(approval of Attorney General needed for grand jury subpoena for member of news media for information relating to news gathering function). Do you agree with this special treatment of lawyers? Should there be a similar rule for physicians? Legislators? Members of the media? (Note that the U.S. Attorneys' Manual requires permission of an *Assistant* Attorney General to subpoena a lawyer, but mandates that of the *Attorney General* for a member of the news media!)

3. *Probable cause.* The *subpoena duces tecum* requires that the subpoenaed party produce records, physical evidence, or both. While a search warrant requires probable cause for a search and seizure under the Fourth Amendment, no such probable cause requirement applies to a grand jury's subpoena duces tecum. A grand jury may decide to request documents based upon uncorroborated and unsubstantiated tips or rumors. In addition to documentary evidence, the recipient of a subpoena duces tecum may be forced to appear before a grand jury to be photographed, to have a hair sample taken, or to appear in a line-up.

Some states impose restrictions upon these activities. For example, the Illinois Supreme Court relied upon its state constitution in holding that a grand jury subpoena for "non-invasive" physical evidence (appearance in line up, fingerprint, voice or handwriting exemplars) must be predicated on some showing of individualized suspicion and relevance. A grand jury subpoena for "invasive" physical evidence (pubic hair or blood sample) must be based on the higher standard of probable cause, but the grand jury need not first obtain a search warrant. *People v. Watson*, 825 N.E.2d 257, (Ill. 2005). What, if any, practical problems are likely to surface under the Illinois rule?

4. *Voice and handwriting exemplars.* Grand jury witnesses may also be compelled to provide voice recordings or handwriting exemplars. In both instances, a witness may believe either that the Fourth Amendment or Fifth Amendment protects the witness from having to comply with such orders. The United States Supreme Court, however, has held otherwise. In *United States v. Dionisio*, 410 U.S. 1 (1973), the Court reasoned that compelled production of a voice exemplar did not violate the Fifth Amendment because self incrimination does not protect the "compelled display of identifiable physical characteristics."

Similarly, it was held that the Fourth Amendment guarantee against unreasonable searches and seizures was not infringed because "no person can have a reasonable expectation that others will not know the sound of his voice." The companion case of *United States v. Mara*, 410 U.S. 19 (1973), involving orders to produce handwriting exemplars, was resolved in like fashion under the *Dionisio* rationale. In his dissenting opinion, Justice Marshall characterized the Court's decisions as serving "only to encourage prosecutorial exploitation of the grand jury process."

5. *Procedures to challenge subpoena.* As indicated in *R. Enterprises*, any person challenging a grand jury subpoena may file a Motion to Quash, but the complainant must overcome the initial presumption of regularity in order to prevail. If the judge denies the Motion to Quash, the subpoenaed party may appeal the decision only after refusing to comply with the order and being held in contempt. The following is a list of some objections that may be raised in a Motion to Quash a subpoena:

a. The *subpoena duces tecum* is too sweeping to be regarded as reasonable. Sometimes, the argument is made that compliance with the subpoena would be "oppressive."

b. The witness may assert that materials or testimony are protected from disclosure because of a legal privilege, such as those protecting communications between attorneys and clients, spouses, physicians or psychotherapists and patients, and priests and confessors.

c. Notwithstanding *R. Enterprises*, the witness may assert that the subpoena was obtained by prosecutorial misconduct through abuse of the grand jury or interference with the independence of the grand jury's performance.

d. The witness may object that the government is using the subpoena power to elicit evidence for use in a civil proceeding, as noted in *United States v. Procter and Gamble*, 356 U.S. 677 (1958). Lower courts have differed considerably, however, over the application of the *Procter and Gamble* standard. Because white collar crime statutes often include civil penalty provisions, many defendants find themselves involved in both criminal and civil proceedings. For a review of some of the constitutional and procedural issues that arise in parallel proceedings, see *Thirteenth Survey of White Collar Crime, Procedural Issues*, 35 Am. Crim. L. Rev. 1061, 1075–1090 (1998).

e. If a grand jury continues to investigate a case after an indictment has been issued, the witness may assert that the subpoena power is being used to obtain evidence for trial. A number of courts have condemned this practice.

f. The witness may allege the subpoena was issued in bad faith for the purpose of "harassment" of a witness. One commentator has suggested that calling a witness before the grand jury solely to "trap" the witness into committing perjury is a form of unreasonable harassment. *See* Bennett L. Gershman, *The "Perjury Trap*," 129 U. Pa. L. Rev. 624 (1981).

g. The witness may assert what is now the most frequently litigated constitutional claim in the context of a *subpoena duces tecum*: the Fifth Amendment self-incrimination privilege, which is addressed in the next section.

D.   THE FIFTH AMENDMENT: SELF-INCRIMINATION

When any witness is asked to testify before a grand jury, he or she may assert that the questions require a response that may be self incriminating. If the witness wants the protection of the Fifth Amendment's self-incrimination guarantee, the witness must claim the privilege. In most jurisdictions the grand jury is not obligated to "warn" the witness in advance of the questioning that the witness has a self-incrimination privilege or that an incriminating response could be used as evidence against that person. Indeed, the United States Supreme Court has indicated that *Miranda* warnings need not be given to a witness who appears before the grand jury. *United States v. Mandujano*, 425 U.S. 564 (1976).

The Constitution also does not mandate that the witness be told he or she is the target of the grand jury probe, though in this situation the prosecution may be wise to give the witness the *Miranda* warnings. *United States v. Washington*, 431 U.S. 181 (1977). *But see United States v. Quam*, 367 F.3d 1006 (8th Cir. 2004)(target need not be given *Miranda* warnings).

In general terms, the Fifth Amendment protects against compelled testimony that incriminates the witness. Historically, subpoenaed parties have enjoyed little success in resisting mandates for production of documents. Indeed, the only reported victories at the United States Supreme Court level occurred in *Boyd v. United States*, 116 U.S. 616 (1886), holding unconstitutional a notice requiring Boyd to produce an invoice for cases of imported glass, and *United States v. Doe*, 465 U.S. 605 (1984), holding that the act of producing business records of a sole proprietorship was privileged. *Boyd* was later characterized as a unanimous holding that the Fifth Amendment protects a defendant against compelled production of books and papers. *United States v. Hubbell*, 530 U.S. 27 (2000)(Thomas, concurring).

To make a successful assertion of the Fifth Amendment privilege, a person must establish three matters. First, it must be shown that the government is "compelling" compliance with its order or demand. Second, the material or information compelled must be "testimonial" in nature. And third, since the Fifth Amendment privilege is personal, the protection extends only to incrimination of one's self by one's self.

[1]   Compelled Disclosure

A person who produces documents in response to a *subpoena duces tecum* is deemed "compelled" to do so. However, as will be seen in the cases of *Fisher* and *Doe I*, discussed later in this Chapter, where records or papers are voluntarily prepared, there is no compulsion involved with respect to the preparation, as distinguished from the production of the papers.

[2]   Testimonial

The government may compel the production of certain types of physical evidence without implicating the Fifth Amendment because such evidence is deemed non-testimonial. On the other hand, most statements, whether written or oral, are considered testimonial because they may disclose facts or information that comes "from the individual's mind." Although the distinction between physical evidence (deemed non-testimonial) and statements (testimonial) is generally accurate, it falls short of defining precisely the parameters of the testimonial requirement.

DOE v. UNITED STATES (DOE II)
487 U.S. 201 (1988)

JUSTICE BLACKMUN delivered the opinion of the Court.

This case presents the question whether a court order compelling a target of a grand jury investigation to authorize foreign banks to disclose records of his accounts, without identifying those documents or acknowledging their existence, violates the target's Fifth Amendment privilege against self-incrimination.

Petitioner, named here as John Doe, is the target of a federal grand jury investigation into possible federal offenses arising from suspected fraudulent manipulation of oil cargoes and receipt of unreported income. Doe appeared before the grand jury pursuant to a subpoena that directed him to produce records of transactions in accounts at three named banks in the Cayman Islands and Bermuda. Doe produced some bank records and testified that no additional records responsive to the subpoena were in his possession or control. When questioned about the existence or location of additional records, Doe invoked the Fifth Amendment privilege against self-incrimination.

The United States branches of the three foreign banks also were served with subpoenas commanding them to produce records of accounts over which Doe had signatory authority. Citing their governments' bank-secrecy laws, which prohibit the disclosure of account records without the customer's consent, the banks refused to comply. The Government then filed a motion with the United States District Court for the Southern District of Texas that the court order Doe to sign 12 forms consenting to disclosure of any bank records respectively relating to 12 foreign bank accounts over which the Government knew or suspected that Doe had control. The forms indicated the account numbers and described the documents that the Government wished the banks to produce.

The District Court denied the motion, reasoning that by signing the consent forms, Doe would necessarily be admitting the existence of the accounts. The District Court believed, moreover, that if the banks delivered records pursuant to the consent forms, those forms would constitute "an admission that [Doe] exercised signatory authority over such accounts." The court speculated that the Government in a subsequent proceeding then could argue that Doe must have guilty knowledge of the contents of the accounts. Thus, in the court's view, compelling Doe to sign the forms was compelling him "to perform a testimonial act that would entail admission of knowledge of the contents of potentially incriminating documents," and such compulsion was prohibited by the Fifth Amendment. The District Court also noted that Doe had not been indicted, and that his signing of the forms might provide the Government with the incriminating link necessary to obtain an indictment, the kind of "fishing expedition" that the Fifth Amendment was designed to prevent.

The Government sought reconsideration. Along with its motion, it submitted to the court a revised proposed consent directive that was substantially the same as that approved by the Eleventh Circuit in *United States v. Ghidoni*, 732 F.2d 814 (11th Cir.), *cert. denied*, 469 U.S. 932 (1984). The form purported to apply to any and all accounts over which Doe had a right of withdrawal, without acknowledging the existence of any such account.[2]

The District Court denied this motion also, reasoning that compelling execution of the consent directive might lead to the uncovering and linking of Doe to accounts that the grand jury did not know were in existence. The court concluded that execution of the proposed form would "admit signatory authority over the speculative accounts [and] would implicitly authenticate any records of the speculative accounts provided by the banks pursuant to the consent."

The Court of Appeals for the Fifth Circuit reversed in an unpublished per curiam opinion. . . . On remand, the District Court ordered petitioner to execute the consent

---

[2] The revised consent form reads: "I, , of the State of Texas in the United States of America, do hereby direct any bank or trust company at which I may have a bank account of any kind or at which a corporation has a bank account of any kind upon which I am authorized to draw, and its officers, employees and agents, to disclose all information and deliver copies of all documents of every nature in your possession or control which relate to said bank account to Grand Jury 84-2, empaneled May 7, 1984 and sitting in the Southern District of Texas, or to any attorney of the District of Texas, or to any attorney of the United States Department of Justice assisting said Grand Jury, and to give evidence relevant thereto, in the investigation conducted by Grand Jury 84-2 in the Southern District of Texas, and this shall be irrevocable authority for so doing. . . . "

directive. He refused. The District Court accordingly found petitioner in civil contempt and ordered that he be confined until he complied with the order. . . .

The Fifth Circuit affirmed the contempt order . . . . We granted certiorari to resolve a conflict among the Courts of Appeals as to whether the compelled execution of a consent form directing the disclosure of foreign bank records is inconsistent with the Fifth Amendment. We conclude that a court order compelling the execution of such a directive as is at issue here does not implicate the Amendment.

. . . The execution of the consent directive at issue in this case obviously would be compelled, and we may assume that its execution would have an incriminating effect.

The question on which this case turns is whether the act of executing the form is a "testimonial communication." . . . An examination of the [prior decisions] indicates the Court's recognition that, in order to be testimonial, an accused's communication must itself, explicitly or implicitly, relate a factual assertion or disclose information. Only then is a person compelled to be a "witness" against himself.

. . . The difficult question whether a compelled communication is testimonial for purposes of applying the Fifth Amendment often depends on the facts and circumstances of the particular case.

. . . The consent directive itself is not "testimonial." It is carefully drafted not to make reference to a specific account, but only to speak in the hypothetical. Thus, the form does not acknowledge that an account in a foreign financial institution is in existence or that it is controlled by petitioner. Nor does the form indicate whether documents or any other information relating to petitioner are present at the foreign bank, assuming that such an account does exist . . . . The form does not even identify the relevant bank. Although the executed form allows the Government access to a potential source of evidence, the directive itself does not point the Government toward hidden accounts or otherwise provide information that will assist the prosecution in uncovering evidence . . . .

Given the consent directive's phraseology, petitioner's compelled act of executing the form has no testimonial significance either. By signing the form, Doe makes no statement, explicit or implicit, regarding the existence of a foreign bank account or his control over any such account. Nor would his execution of the form admit the authenticity of any records produced by the bank. . . .

Finally, we cannot agree with petitioner's contention that his execution of the directive admits or asserts Doe's consent. The form does not state that Doe "consents" to the release of bank records. Instead, it states that the directive "shall be construed as consent" with respect to Cayman Islands and Bermuda bank-secrecy laws. Because the directive explicitly indicates that it was signed pursuant to a court order, Doe's compelled execution of the form sheds no light on his actual intent or state of mind. The form does "direct" the bank to disclose account information and release any records that "may" exist and for which Doe "may" be a relevant principal. But directing the recipient of a communication to do something is not an assertion of fact or, at least in this context, a disclosure of information. In its testimonial significance, the execution of such a directive is analogous to the production of a handwriting sample or voice exemplar: it is a nontestimonial act. In neither case is the suspect's action compelled to obtain "any knowledge he might have."

. . . Because the consent directive is not testimonial in nature, we conclude that the District Court's order compelling petitioner to sign the directive does not violate his Fifth Amendment privilege against self-incrimination. Accordingly, the judgment of the Court of Appeals is affirmed.

JUSTICE STEVENS, dissenting.

A defendant can be compelled to produce material evidence that is incriminating. Fingerprints, blood samples, voice exemplars, handwriting specimens, or other items of physical evidence may be extracted from a defendant against his will. But can he be compelled to use his mind to assist the prosecution in convicting him of a crime? I think not. He may in some cases be forced to surrender a key to a strongbox containing incriminating documents, but I do not believe he can be compelled to reveal the combination to his wall safe — by word or deed.

The document the Government seeks to extract from John Doe purports to order third parties to take action that will lead to the discovery of incriminating evidence. The directive itself may not betray any knowledge petitioner may have about the circumstances of the offenses being investigated by the grand jury, but it nevertheless purports to evidence a reasoned decision by Doe to authorize action by others. The forced execution of this document differs from the forced production of physical evidence just as human beings differ from other animals.

If John Doe can be compelled to use his mind to assist the Government in developing its case, I think he will be forced "to be a witness against himself." The fundamental purpose of the Fifth Amendment was to mark the line between the kind of inquisition conducted by the Star Chamber and what we proudly describe as our accusatorial system of justice. It reflects our respect for the inviolability of the human personality. . . . . In my opinion that protection gives John Doe the right to refuse to sign the directive authorizing access to the records of any bank account that he may control.

NOTES

1. Responding to the dissent, the majority explained in a footnote:

> We do not disagree with the dissent that "[t]he expression of the contents of an individual's mind" is testimonial communication for purposes of the Fifth Amendment. We simply disagree with the dissent's conclusion that the execution of the consent directive at issue here forced petitioner to express the contents of his mind. In our view, such compulsion is more like "be[ing] forced to surrender a key to a strongbox containing incriminating documents" than it is like "be[ing] compelled to reveal the combination to [petitioner's] wall safe."

Do you agree that the consent directive is like "being forced to surrender a key to a strongbox" rather than being "compelled to reveal the combination to one's wall safe?" Does that distinction seem meaningful for self-incrimination purposes?

2. Assume that the "combination to the safe" information is protected by the Fifth Amendment. Could a grand jury require that the owner of such a safe sign a "consent directive" to blow open the safe?

3. With respect to the dissenting opinion by Justice Stevens, should the Fifth Amendment be interpreted to protect the individual from being "compelled to use his mind to assist the government in developing its case?" If this were the proper standard, could a witness appearing in a lineup be compelled to repeat words (ostensibly being used only for identification purposes)?

4. In *Pennsylvania v. Muniz*, 496 U.S. 582 (1990), the Supreme Court held that a suspect's answer to a question regarding the date of his sixth birthday was testimonial; since it was given in custody without *Miranda* warnings, it was inadmissible. The Court distinguished *Doe*, noting that "the compelled execution of the consent directive did not force [him] to express the contents of his mind, but rather forced [him] only to make a nonfactual statement." Muniz, by contrast, was required to make a testimonial response to a question, from which the incriminating inference of impaired mental faculties stemmed.

[3] Self-Incriminatory

[a] In General

The Fifth Amendment protects the individual from information that could be used against the person in a criminal prosecution. It does not protect the witness from providing information that would be considered embarrassing to that individual or that could incriminate or otherwise harm a third person. Given the fact that there will be uncertainty in some cases as to whether a response will be legally incriminating, sometimes a grand jury witness will seek to assert the self-incrimination privilege, but the answers are ones likely not covered by the privilege.

The Fifth Amendment privilege is personal in nature, and protects only against incrimination of one's self. Therefore, Jones has no Fifth Amendment protection from production by Smith of evidence that will prove incriminating to Jones. Indeed, the Fifth Amendment "is designed to prevent the use of legal process to force from the lips of the accused individual the evidence necessary to convict him or to force him to produce and authenticate any personal documents or effects that might incriminate him." *United States v. White*, 322 U.S. 694, 698 (1944).

[b] Questions and Answers

Inquiry into whether a question asked a grand jury witness or a *subpoena duces tecum* will result in self-incrimination requires careful attention to the question "who is required to say or do what?"

HOFFMAN v. UNITED STATES
341 U.S. 479 (1951)

Mr. Justice Clark delivered the opinion of the Court.

Petitioner has been convicted of criminal contempt for refusing to obey a federal court order requiring him to answer certain questions asked in a grand jury investigation. He raises here important issues as to the application of the privilege against self-incrimination under the Fifth Amendment, claimed to justify his refusal.

A special federal grand jury was convened at Philadelphia on September 14, 1950, to investigate frauds upon the Federal Government, including violations of the customs, narcotics and internal revenue liquor laws of the United States, the White Slave Traffic Act, perjury, bribery, and other federal criminal laws, and conspiracy to commit all such offenses. In response to subpoena petitioner appeared to testify on the day the grand jury was empaneled, and was examined on October 3. The pertinent interrogation, in which he refused to answer, follows:

Q: What do you do now, Mr. Hoffman?

A: I refuse to answer.

Q: Have you been in the same undertaking since the first of the year?

A: I don't understand the question.

Q: Have you been doing the same thing you are doing now since the first of the year?

A: I refuse to answer.

Q: Do you know Mr. William Weisberg?

A: I do.

Q: How long have you known him?

A: Practically twenty years, I guess.

Q:	When did you last see him?
A:	I refuse to answer.
Q:	Have you seen him this week?
A:	I refuse to answer.
Q:	Do you know that a subpoena has been issued for Mr. Weisberg?
A:	I heard about it in Court.
Q:	Have you talked with him on the telephone this week?
A:	I refuse to answer.
Q:	Do you know where Mr. William Weisberg is now?
A:	I refuse to answer.

It was stipulated that petitioner declined to answer on the ground that his answers might tend to incriminate him of a federal offense . . . .

[Petitioner's assertion of the Fifth Amendment self incrimination privilege was challenged by the government. The district court found "no real and substantial danger of incrimination to petitioner" and therefore ordered him to answer the questions. After his refusal, he was held in contempt and sentenced to a term of imprisonment. The Court of Appeals affirmed the conviction. This was overturned by the United States Supreme Court, only Justice Reed dissenting, because, on the facts presented, "it was not perfectly clear, from a careful consideration of all the circumstances in the case, that the witness is mistaken, and that the answers cannot possibly have such tendency to incriminate."]

The privilege afforded not only extends to answers that would in themselves support a conviction under a federal criminal statute but likewise embraces those which would furnish a link in the chain of evidence needed to prosecute the claimant for a federal crime. But this protection must be confined to instances where the witness has reasonable cause to apprehend danger from a direct answer. The witness is not exonerated from answering merely because he declares that in so doing he would incriminate himself — his say-so does not of itself establish the hazard of incrimination. It is for the court to say whether his silence is justified . . . . However, if the witness, upon interposing his claim, were required to prove the hazard in the sense in which a claim is usually required to be established in court, he would be compelled to surrender the very protection which the privilege is designed to guarantee. To sustain the privilege, it need only be evident from the implications of the question, in the setting in which it is asked, that a responsive answer to the question or an explanation of why it cannot be answered might be dangerous because injurious disclosure could result. The trial judge in appraising the claim "must be governed as much by his personal perception of the peculiarities of the case as by the facts actually in evidence." . . .

[c] Business Records and Accountants

COUCH v. UNITED STATES
409 U.S. 322 (1973)

MR. JUSTICE POWELL delivered the opinion of the Court.

[Petitioner, owner of a restaurant, gave her business records to her accountant for use in preparing Petitioners' tax returns. An I.R.S. agent, investigating possible tax crimes, issued a summons to the accountant after the accountant had refused the agent's request to see Petitioners' records. After finding that the accountant had, at Petitioner's request, delivered the papers to the Petitioner's attorney, the agent sought enforcement of the summons. Petitioner intervened, claiming that her ownership of the records warranted a Fifth Amendment privilege "to bar their production."]

The question is whether the taxpayer may invoke her Fifth Amendment privilege against compulsory self-incrimination to prevent the production of her business and tax records in the possession of her accountant. Both the District Court and the Court of Appeals for the Fourth Circuit held the privilege unavailable.

. . . In the case before us the ingredient of personal compulsion against an accused is lacking. The summons and the order of the District Court enforcing it are directed against the accountant. He, not the taxpayer, is the only one compelled to do anything. And the accountant makes no claim that he may tend to be incriminated by the production.

. . . The divulgence of potentially incriminating evidence against petitioner is naturally unwelcome. But petitioner's distress would be no less if the divulgence came not from her accountant but from some other third party with whom she was connected and who possessed substantially equivalent knowledge of her business affairs. The basic complaint of petitioner stems from the fact of divulgence of the possibly incriminating information, not from the manner in which or the person from whom it was extracted. Yet such divulgence, where it does not result from coercion of the suspect herself, is a necessary part of the process of law enforcement and tax investigation.

. . . Petitioner further argues that the confidential nature of the accountant-client relationship and her resulting expectation of privacy in delivering the records protect her, under the Fourth and Fifth Amendments, from their production. Although not in itself controlling, we note that no confidential accountant-client privilege exists under federal law, and no state created privilege has been recognized in federal cases. Nor is there justification for such a privilege where records relevant to income tax returns are involved in a criminal investigation or prosecution. In *Boyd v. United States*, 116 U.S. 616 (1886), a pre-income tax case, the Court spoke of protection of privacy, but there can be little expectation of privacy where records are handed to an accountant, knowing that mandatory disclosure of much of the information therein is required in an income tax return. What information is not disclosed is largely in the accountant's discretion, not petitioner's. Indeed, the accountant himself risks criminal prosecution if he willfully assists in the preparation of a false return. His own need for self-protection would often require the right to disclose the information given him. Petitioner seeks extensions of constitutional protections against self-incrimination in the very situation where obligations of disclosure exist and under a system largely dependent upon honest self-reporting even to survive. Accordingly, petitioner here cannot reasonably claim, either for Fourth or Fifth Amendment purposes, an expectation of protected privacy or confidentiality . . . .

Mr. Justice Brennan, concurring.

I join the opinion of the Court on the understanding that it does not establish a per se rule defeating a claim of Fifth Amendment privilege whenever the documents in question are not in the possession of the person claiming the privilege. In my view, the privilege is available to one who turns records over to a third person for custodial safekeeping rather than disclosure of the information, to one who turns records over to a third person at the inducement of the Government, to one who places records in a safety deposit box or in hiding; and to similar cases where reasonable steps have been taken to safeguard the confidentiality of the contents of the records.[*]

---

[*] In some of these instances, to be sure, the person claiming the privilege would not himself have been the subject of direct Government compulsion. And there is no doubt that the Fifth Amendment is concerned solely with *compulsory* self-incrimination. But surely the availability of the Fifth Amendment privilege cannot depend on whether or not the owner of the documents is compelled personally to turn the documents over to the Government. If private, testimonial documents held in the owner's own possession are privileged under the Fifth Amendment, then the Government cannot nullify that privilege by finding a way to obtain the documents without requiring the owner to take them in hand and personally present them to the Government agents.

The privilege cannot extend, however, to the protection of a taxpayer's records conveyed to a retained accountant for use in preparation of an income tax return, where the accountant is himself obligated to prepare a complete and lawful return . . . .

Mr. Justice Douglas, dissenting.

I cannot agree with the majority that the privilege against self-incrimination was not available to the petitioner merely because she did not have possession of the documents in question and was not herself subject to compulsory process. . . . The decision today sanctions yet another tool of the ever-widening governmental invasion and oversight of our private lives. . . .

[The dissent of Justice Marshall is omitted.]

[d] Lawyers and Client's Documents

FISHER v. UNITED STATES
425 U.S. 391 (1976)

Mr. Justice White delivered the opinion of the Court.

In these two cases we are called upon to decide whether a summons directing an attorney to produce documents delivered to him by his client in connection with the attorney-client relationship is enforceable over claims that the documents were constitutionally immune from summons in the hands of the client and retained that immunity in the hands of the attorney.

[An Internal Revenue agent visited taxpayers and interviewed them in connection with possible violations of federal income tax laws. Thereafter, the taxpayers obtained from their accountants documents related to the preparation by those accountants of the taxpayers' tax returns. The documents included the accountants' work papers, retained copies of taxpayers' income tax returns for earlier years, retained copies of reports and correspondence between the accounting firm and a taxpayer and analyses by the accountant of taxpayers' income and expenses which had been copied by the accountant from taxpayers' canceled checks and deposit receipts. After obtaining the documents, the taxpayers then transferred those same documents to their lawyers (Kasmir and Fisher), each of whom was retained to assist the taxpayer in connection with the investigation. The Internal Revenue Service then served summonses on the attorneys directing them to produce those documents. In each case, the lawyer declined to comply with the summons but the District Court ordered that the summons be enforced. The Court of Appeals for the Third Circuit affirmed the enforcement order against Fisher, holding that the taxpayers had not acquired a possessory interest in the documents and that the papers were not immune in the hands of the attorney. As to Kasmir, however, the Court of Appeals for the Fifth Circuit reversed the enforcement order, reasoning that the documents would have been privileged if the summons had been directed to the taxpayer; in light of the attorney-client relationship, the taxpayer therefore retained an expectation of privacy in the materials even after transfer to his attorney and thus retained Fifth Amendment protection. The United States Supreme Court held that the documents were not privileged either in the hands of the lawyers or of their clients, and therefore affirmed the judgment in Fisher and reversed the judgment in Kasmir.]

. . . The taxpayer's privilege under this Amendment is not violated by enforcement of the summonses involved in these cases because enforcement against a taxpayer's lawyer would not "compel" the taxpayer to do anything and certainly would not compel him to be a "witness" against himself.

Where the Government takes private records from, for example, a safety deposit box against the will of the owner of the documents, the owner has been compelled, in my view, to incriminate himself within the meaning of the Fifth Amendment.

. . . In *Couch v. United States*, 409 U.S. 322 (1973), we recently ruled that the Fifth Amendment rights of a taxpayer were not violated by the enforcement of a documentary summons directed to her accountant and requiring production of the taxpayer's own records in the possession of the accountant. We did so on the ground that in such a case "the ingredient of personal compulsion against an accused is lacking."

Here, the taxpayers are compelled to do no more than was the taxpayer in *Couch.* The taxpayers' Fifth Amendment privilege is therefore not violated by enforcement of the summonses directed toward their attorneys. This is true whether or not the Amendment would have barred a subpoena directing the taxpayer to produce the documents while they were in his hands.

The fact that the attorneys are agents of the taxpayers does not change this result. . . . Nor is this one of those situations . . . where constructive possession is so clear or relinquishment of possession so temporary and insignificant as to leave the personal compulsion upon the taxpayer substantially intact. In this respect we see no difference between the delivery to the attorneys in these cases and delivery to the accountant in the *Couch* case.

[It is contended] that if the summons was enforced, the taxpayers' Fifth Amendment privilege would be, but should not be, lost solely because they gave their documents to their lawyers in order to obtain legal advice. But this misconceives the nature of the constitutional privilege. The Amendment protects a person from being compelled to be a witness against himself. Here, the taxpayers retained any privilege they ever had not to be compelled to testify against themselves and not to be compelled themselves to produce private papers in their possession.

. . . The Court of Appeals for the Fifth Circuit suggested that because legally and ethically the attorney was required to respect the confidences of his client, the latter had a reasonable expectation of privacy for the records in the hands of the attorney and therefore did not forfeit his Fifth Amendment privilege with respect to the records by transferring them in order to obtain legal advice. It is true that the Court has often stated that one of the several purposes served by the constitutional privilege against compelled testimonial self-incrimination is that of protecting personal privacy. But the Court has never suggested that every invasion of privacy violates the privilege.

. . . We cannot cut the Fifth Amendment completely loose from the moorings of its language, and make it serve as a general protector of privacy — a word not mentioned in its text and a concept directly addressed in the Fourth Amendment.

. . . Our above holding is that compelled production of documents from an attorney does not implicate whatever Fifth Amendment privilege the taxpayer might have enjoyed from being compelled to produce them himself. The taxpayers in these cases, however, have from the outset consistently urged that they should not be forced to expose otherwise protected documents to summons simply because they have sought legal advice and turned the papers over to their attorneys. The Government appears to agree unqualifiedly. The difficulty is that the taxpayers have erroneously relied on the Fifth Amendment without urging the attorney-client privilege in so many words. They have nevertheless invoked the relevant body of law and policies that govern the attorney-client privilege. In this posture of the case, we feel obliged to inquire whether the attorney-client privilege applies to documents in the hands of an attorney which would have been privileged in the hands of the client by reason of the Fifth Amendment.

. . . Since each taxpayer transferred possession of the documents in question from himself to his attorney in order to obtain legal assistance in the tax investigations in question, the papers, if unobtainable by summons from the client, are unobtainable by summons directed to the attorney by reason of the attorney-client privilege. We accordingly proceed to the question whether the documents could have been obtained by summons addressed to the taxpayer while the documents were in his possession.

The only bar to enforcement of such summons asserted by the parties or the courts below is the Fifth Amendment's privilege against self-incrimination.

. . . Accordingly, we turn to the question of what, if any, incriminating testimony within the Fifth Amendment's protection, is compelled by a documentary summons.

A subpoena served on a taxpayer requiring him to produce an accountant's work papers in his possession without doubt involves substantial compulsion. But it does not compel oral testimony; nor would it ordinarily compel the taxpayer to restate, repeat, or affirm the truth of the contents of the documents sought. Therefore, the Fifth Amendment would not be violated by the fact alone that the papers on their face might incriminate the taxpayer, for the privilege protects a person only against being incriminated by his own compelled testimonial communications. The accountant's work papers are not the taxpayer's. They were not prepared by the taxpayer, and they contain no testimonial declarations by him.

. . . The act of producing evidence in response to a subpoena nevertheless has communicative aspects of its own, wholly aside from the contents of the papers produced. Compliance with the subpoena tacitly concedes the existence of the papers demanded and their possession or control by the taxpayer. It also would indicate the taxpayer's belief that the papers are those described in the subpoena. The elements of compulsion are clearly present, but the more difficult issues are whether the tacit averments of the taxpayer are both "testimonial" and "incriminating" for purposes of applying the Fifth Amendment. These questions perhaps do not lend themselves to categorical answers; their resolution may instead depend on the facts and circumstances of particular cases or classes thereof. In light of the records now before us, we are confident that however incriminating the contents of the accountant's work papers might be, the act of producing them — the only thing which the taxpayer is compelled to do — would not itself involve testimonial self-incrimination.

It is doubtful that implicitly admitting the existence and possession of the papers rises to the level of testimony within the protection of the Fifth Amendment. The papers belong to the accountant, were prepared by him, and are the kind usually prepared by an accountant working on the tax returns of his client. Surely the Government is in no way relying on the "truth-telling" of the taxpayer to prove the existence of or his access to the documents. The existence and location of the papers are a foregone conclusion and the taxpayer adds little or nothing to the sum total of the Government's information by conceding that he in fact has the papers.

. . . Whether the Fifth Amendment would shield the taxpayer from producing his own tax records in his possession is a question not involved here; for the papers demanded here are not his "private papers." We do hold that compliance with a summons directing the taxpayer to produce the accountant's documents involved in these cases would involve no incriminating testimony within the protection of the Fifth Amendment . . . .

Mr. Justice Marshall, concurring in the judgment.

. . . The Fifth Amendment basis for resisting production of a document pursuant to subpoena, the Court tells us today, lies not in the document's contents, as we previously have suggested, but in the tacit verification inherent in the act of production itself that the document exists, is in the possession of the producer, and is the one sought by the subpoena.

This technical and somewhat esoteric focus on the testimonial elements of production rather than on the content of the evidence the investigator seeks is . . . contrary to the history and traditions of the privilege against self-incrimination both in this country and in England, where the privilege originated. A long line of precedents in this Court, whose rationales if not holdings are overturned by the Court today, support the notion that "any forcible and compulsory extortion of a man's . . . private papers to be used as evidence to convict him of crime" compels him to be a witness against himself within the meaning of the Fifth Amendment to the Constitution. [The concurring opinion of Justice Brennan is omitted]

NOTE

There has been significant litigation over the "constructive possession" or "clearly temporary relinquishment of possession" exceptions raised in both *Couch* and *Fisher*. Under these doctrines, an individual who is not in actual possession of a document that is subpoenaed from another may invoke the Fifth Amendment because the party being subpoenaed either is in constructive possession of the document or has received possession so temporarily that the subpoena's compulsion actually falls upon the non-subpoenaed party. The Tenth Circuit has interpreted this doctrine to apply to situations "in which the records sought remain within the actual physical control of the party asserting the constitutional privilege even though they may be placed with another party for custodial safekeeping." *United States v. Silvestain*, 668 F.2d 1161, 1164 (10th Cir. 1982).

After *Fisher*, three specific doctrines are pertinent to the analysis of Fifth Amendment challenges to compelled evidentiary productions. These doctrines are the Entity Rule, Required Records Doctrine, and Act of Production Doctrine.

[4] The Entity Rule

As early as 1906, in *Hale v. Henkel*, 201 U.S. 43 (1906), the United States Supreme Court recognized that the privilege against self-incrimination is unavailable to corporations which, as creatures of the state, are subject to the state's "visitatorial" powers to monitor and investigate its activities. Years later, the Court made clear that a corporation must submit its books and papers when properly ordered, and that "the visitatorial power which exists with respect to the corporation of necessity reaches the corporate books, without regard to the conduct of the custodian." *Wilson v. United States*, 221 U.S. 361, 385 (1911). In *United States v. White*, 322 U.S. 694 (1944), the Court extended the class of entities lacking the Fifth Amendment privilege from corporations to unincorporated entities (a labor union). It was also made clear that an individual acting "in a representative capacity" (that is, on behalf of the entity) cannot claim a personal Fifth Amendment privilege with respect to "entity" materials.

In the 1974 case below, the United States Supreme Court addressed the question whether the Entity Rule applies to a small law firm partnership.

BELLIS v. UNITED STATES
417 U.S. 85 (1974)

Mr. Justice Marshall delivered the opinion of the Court.

The question presented in this case is whether a partner in a small law firm may invoke his personal privilege against self-incrimination to justify his refusal to comply with a subpoena requiring production of the partnership's financial records.

[Petitioner was one of three partners in a five-lawyer firm. After leaving the firm (which was dissolved), he was served with a subpoena to produce partnership records then in his possession. He refused on self-incrimination grounds, and was held in civil contempt. The United States Supreme Court affirmed.]

It has long been established, of course, that the Fifth Amendment privilege against compulsory self-incrimination protects an individual from compelled production of his personal papers and effects as well as compelled oral testimony.

. . . On the other hand, an equally long line of cases has established that an individual cannot rely upon the privilege to avoid producing the records of a collective entity which are in his possession in a representative capacity, even if these records might incriminate him personally. This doctrine was first announced in a series of cases dealing with corporate records.

. . . To some extent, these decisions were based upon the particular incidents of the corporate form, the Court observing that a corporation has limited powers granted to it by the State in its charter, and is subject to the retained "visitorial power" of the State to investigate its activities. But any thought that the principle formulated in these decisions was limited to corporate records was put to rest in *United States v. White*, 322 U.S. 694 (1944). In *White*, we held that an officer of an unincorporated association, a labor union, could not claim his privilege against compulsory self-incrimination to justify his refusal to produce the union's records pursuant to a grand jury subpoena. *White* announced the general rule that the privilege could not be employed by an individual to avoid production of the records of an organization, which he holds in a representative capacity as custodian on behalf of the group.

. . . Since no artificial organization may utilize the personal privilege against compulsory self-incrimination, the Court found that it follows that an individual acting in his official capacity on behalf of the organization may likewise not take advantage of his personal privilege. In view of the inescapable fact that an artificial entity can only act to produce its records through its individual officers or agents, recognition of the individual's claim of privilege with respect to the financial records of the organization would substantially undermine the unchallenged rule that the organization itself is not entitled to claim any Fifth Amendment privilege, and largely frustrate legitimate governmental regulation of such organizations.

. . . [A] substantial claim of privacy or confidentiality cannot often be maintained with respect to the financial records of an organized collective entity. Control of such records is generally strictly regulated by statute or by the rules and regulations of the organization, and access to the records is generally guaranteed to others in the organization. In such circumstances, the custodian of the organization's records lacks the control over their content and location and the right to keep them from the view of others which would be characteristic of a claim of privacy and confidentiality.

. . . The analysis of the Court in *White*, of course, only makes sense in the context of what the Court described as "organized, institutional activity." This analysis presupposes the existence of an organization which is recognized as an independent entity apart from its individual members. The group must be relatively well organized and structured and not merely a loose, informal association of individuals. It must maintain a distinct set of organizational records, and recognize rights in its members of control and access to them. And the records subpoenaed must in fact be organizational records held in a representative capacity. In other words, it must be fair to say that the records demanded are the records of the organization rather than those of the individual under *White*.

. . . We think it is similarly clear that partnerships may and frequently do represent organized institutional activity so as to preclude any claim of Fifth Amendment privilege with respect to the partnership's financial records. Some of the most powerful private institutions in the Nation are conducted in the partnership form. Wall Street law firms and stock brokerage firms provide significant examples. These are often large, impersonal, highly structured enterprises of essentially perpetual duration. The personal interest of any individual partner in the financial records of a firm of this scope is obviously highly attenuated.

In this case, however, we are required to explore the outer limits of the analysis of the Court in *White*. Petitioner argues that in view of the modest size of the partnership involved here, it is unrealistic to consider the firm as an entity independent of its three partners; rather, he claims, the law firm embodies little more than the personal legal practice of the individual partners. Moreover, petitioner argues that he has a substantial and direct ownership interest in the partnership records, and does not hold them in a representative capacity.

Despite the force of these arguments, we conclude that the lower courts properly applied the *White* rule in the circumstances of this case. While small, the partnership here did have an established institutional identity independent of its individual partners. This was not an informal association or a temporary arrangement for the undertaking of a few projects of short-lived duration. Rather, the partnership represented a formal institutional arrangement organized for the continuing conduct of the firm's legal practice. The partnership was in existence for nearly 15 years prior to its voluntary dissolution.

. . . Equally important, we believe it is fair to say that petitioner is holding the subpoenaed partnership records in a representative capacity. The documents which petitioner has been ordered to produce are merely the financial books and records of the partnership.

. . . This might be a different case if it involved a small family partnership [or] if there were some other pre-existing relationship of confidentiality among the partners. But in the circumstances of this case, petitioner's possession of the partnership's financial records in what can be fairly said to be a representative capacity compels our holding that his personal privilege against compulsory self-incrimination is inapplicable.

[JUSTICE DOUGLAS dissented on the ground that the investigation was directed at Bellis personally. Therefore, he viewed Petitioner's claim to be "clearly controlled by *Boyd v. United States.*"]

NOTES

1. *What is an entity?* There has been considerable lower court litigation regarding the Entity Rule. All the usual suspects are considered entities: corporations, unincorporated associations, partnerships, and law firms.

But less formalized arrangements may be deemed not to be an "entity" for this purpose. For example, one court has held that two brothers practicing law together were not an entity for the purpose of the Fifth Amendment because they were "at most an unstructured and loose association of two individual practitioners of law." *In re Special Grand Jury No. 1*, 465 F. Supp. 800, 806 (D. Md. 1978). Another court found that individuals who conducted financial transactions involving real estate owned by them as tenants in common under an assumed name constituted an entity which was unable to assert the Fifth Amendment privilege. *In re Grand Jury Proceedings (Shiffman)*, 576 F.2d 703, 708 (6th Cir. 1978), *cert. den.*, 439 U.S. 830 (1978).

2. *Personal, business, and mixed documents.* Courts have also examined the issue of what entity documents are protected by the Fifth Amendment notwithstanding the Entity Rule. Documents can be classified as personal (or "intimate personal"), business, or mixed business and personal (such as appointment books and calendars). Personal documents, though located in the workplace, are not covered by the entity rule.

Most courts addressing this issue find that mixed documents are corporate and therefore outside the privilege. See *United States v. MacKey*, 647 F.2d 898 (9th Cir. 1981).

Another federal district court distinguished between desk calendars and pocket calendars, holding that the former had to be produced, while the latter did not. The court made clear that any purely private notations in the desk calendars could be protected. It was further held that "an officer's diary is a corporate record if it is used to record entertainment expenses and is actually submitted to the company for use as the proof required by the Internal Revenue Code " and that "the officer cannot change the nature of the document by including private and personal matters in the diaries." *In re Grand Jury Subpoena Duces Tecum dated April 23, 1981*, 522 F. Supp. 977, 982 (S.D.N.Y. 1981).

[5] The Required Records Doctrine

In *Wilson v. United States*, 221 U.S. 361 (1911), the Court held that the Fifth Amendment does not apply to "records required by law to be kept." In a later case the Court set forth three elements of this doctrine:

> First, the purposes of the United States' inquiry must be essentially regulatory; second, information is to be obtained by requiring the preservation of records of a kind which the regulated party has customarily kept; and third, the records themselves must have assumed "public aspects" which render them at least analogous to public documents.

Grosso v. United States, 390 U.S. 62, 67–68 (1968). For a careful examination of the required records doctrine, see Stephen A. Saltzburg, *The Required Records Doctrine: Its Lessons for the Privilege Against Self-Incrimination*, 53 U. Chi. L. Rev. 6 (1986).

[6] Act of Production Doctrine

In *Fisher*, the United States Supreme Court acknowledged that the act of production of evidence in responding to a subpoena may have incriminating aspects unrelated to the contents of the document, itself. Specifically, the Court has noted that the act of producing a document could incriminate an individual in one of three ways. First, production could concede the very existence of the evidence demanded. Second, producing the document acknowledges that the subpoenaed document is in the party's possession or control. Third, the act of production may be used for authentication purposes. Notice the interplay of the Act of Production Doctrine and the Entity Rule in the next two cases.

BRASWELL v. UNITED STATES

487 U.S. 99 (1988)

Chief Justice Rehnquist delivered the opinion of the Court.

This case presents the question whether the custodian of corporate records may resist a subpoena for such records on the ground that the act of production would incriminate him in violation of the Fifth Amendment. We conclude that he may not.

[A grand jury issued a subpoena to the president of two Mississippi corporations, both of which had three directors: Petitioner, his wife and his mother. The subpoena required Petitioner to produce books and records of the two corporations. It also provided, however, that Braswell was not required to testify and that he could deliver the records to the agent serving the subpoena.]

There is no question but that the contents of the subpoenaed business records are not privileged. Similarly, petitioner asserts no self-incrimination claim on behalf of the corporations; it is well established that such artificial entities are not protected by the Fifth Amendment. Petitioner instead relies solely upon the argument that his act of producing the documents has independent testimonial significance, which would incriminate him individually, and that the Fifth Amendment prohibits Government compulsion of that act.

. . . Had petitioner conducted his business as a sole proprietorship, *United States v. Doe*, 465 U.S. 605 (1984)[discussed next in this casebook], would require that he be provided the opportunity to show that his act of production would entail testimonial self-incrimination. But petitioner has operated his business through the corporate form, and we have long recognized that, for purposes of the Fifth Amendment, corporations and other collective entities are treated differently from individuals. This doctrine — known as the collective entity rule — has a lengthy and distinguished pedigree.

. . . [T]he Court has consistently recognized that the custodian of corporate or entity records holds those documents in a representative rather than a personal capacity. Artificial entities such as corporations may act only through their agents, and a custodian's assumption of his representative capacity leads to certain obligations, including the duty to produce corporate records on proper demand by the Government. Under those circumstances, the custodian's act of production is not deemed a personal act, but rather an act of the corporation. Any claim of Fifth Amendment privilege asserted by the agent would be tantamount to a claim of privilege by the corporation — which of course possesses no such privilege.

. . . Although a corporate custodian is not entitled to resist a subpoena on the ground that his act of production will be personally incriminating, we do think certain consequences flow from the fact that the custodian's act of production is one in his representative rather than personal capacity. Because the custodian acts as a representative, the act is deemed one of the corporation and not the individual. Therefore, the Government concedes, as it must, that it may make no evidentiary use of the "individual act" against the individual. For example, in a criminal prosecution against the custodian, the Government may not introduce into evidence before the jury the fact that the subpoena was served upon and the corporation's documents were delivered by one particular individual, the custodian. The Government has the right, however, to use the corporation's act of production against the custodian. The Government may offer testimony — for example, from the process server who delivered the subpoena and from the individual who received the records — establishing that the corporation produced the records subpoenaed. The jury may draw from the corporation's act of production the conclusion that the records in question are authentic corporate records, which the corporation possessed, and which it produced in response to the subpoena. And if the defendant held a prominent position within the corporation that produced the records, the jury may, just as it would had someone else produced the documents, reasonably infer that he had possession of the documents or knowledge of their contents. Because the jury is not told that the defendant produced the records, any nexus between the defendant and the documents results solely from the corporation's act of production and other evidence in the case.[11]

Consistent with our precedent, the United States Court of Appeals for the Fifth Circuit ruled that petitioner could not resist the subpoena for corporate documents on the ground that the act of production might tend to incriminate him. The judgment is affirmed.

JUSTICE KENNEDY, with whom JUSTICE BRENNAN, JUSTICE MARSHALL, AND JUSTICE SCALIA join, dissenting.

. . . The Court today denies an individual his Fifth Amendment privilege against self-incrimination in order to vindicate the rule that a collective entity which employs him has no such privilege itself. To reach this ironic conclusion, the majority must blur an analytic clarity in Fifth Amendment doctrine that has taken almost a century to emerge. After holding that corporate employment strips the individual of his privilege, the Court then attempts to restore some measure of protection by its judicial creation of a new zone of immunity in some vaguely defined circumstances. This exercise admits what the Court denied in the first place, namely, that compelled compliance with the subpoena implicates the Fifth Amendment self-incrimination privilege.

The majority's apparent reasoning is that collective entities have no privilege and so their employees must have none either. The Court holds that a corporate agent must incriminate himself even when he is named in the subpoena and is a target of the

---

[11] We reject the suggestion that the limitation on the evidentiary use of the custodian's act of production is the equivalent of constructive use immunity barred under our decision in *Doe*. Rather, the limitation is a necessary concomitant of the notion that a corporation custodian acts as an agent and not an individual when he produces corporate records in response to a subpoena addressed to him in his representative capacity. We leave open the question whether the agency rationale supports compelling a custodian to produce corporate records when the custodian is able to establish, by showing for example that he is the sole employee and officer of the corporation, that the jury would inevitably conclude that he produced the records.

investigation, and even when it is conceded that compliance requires compelled, personal, testimonial, incriminating assertions. I disagree with that conclusion; find no precedent for it; maintain that if there is a likelihood of personal self-incrimination the narrow use immunity permitted by statute can be granted without frustrating the investigation of collective entities; and submit that basic Fifth Amendment principles should not be avoided and manipulated, which is the necessary effect of this decision.

. . . Recognition of the right to assert a privilege does not mean it will exist in many cases. In many instances, the production of documents may implicate no testimonial assertions at all. . . .

Further, to the extent testimonial assertions are being compelled, use immunity can be granted without impeding the investigation. Where the privilege is applicable, immunity will be needed for only one individual, and solely with respect to evidence derived from the act of production itself. The Government would not be denied access to the records it seeks, it would be free to use the contents of the records against everyone, and it would be free to use any testimonial act implicit in production against all but the custodian it selects. In appropriate cases the Government will be able to establish authenticity, possession, and control by means other than compelling assertions about them from a suspect . . . .

UNITED STATES v. DOE (DOE I)
465 U.S. 605 (1984)

JUSTICE POWELL delivered the opinion of the Court.

This case presents the issue whether, and to what extent, the Fifth Amendment privilege against compelled self-incrimination applies to the business records of a sole proprietorship.

Respondent is the owner of several sole proprietorships. In late 1980, a grand jury, during the course of an investigation of corruption in the awarding of county and municipal contracts, served five subpoenas on respondent. [The subpoenas sought an extensive array of business records, including telephone and bank records, contracts, tax returns, sales records for stock and bond transactions, and the names and addresses of all people employed at the businesses.]

Respondent filed a motion in federal district court seeking to quash the subpoenas. The District Court for the District of New Jersey granted his motion except with respect to those documents and records required by law to be kept or disclosed to a public agency [such as tax returns and W-2 forms. The Court of Appeals affirmed.]. . . .

The Court in *Fisher* expressly declined to reach the question whether the Fifth Amendment privilege protects the contents of an individual's tax records in his possession. The rationale underlying our holding in that case is, however, persuasive here. As we noted in *Fisher*, the Fifth Amendment protects the person asserting the privilege only from compelled self-incrimination. Where the preparation of business records is voluntary, no compulsion is present. A subpoena that demands production of documents "does not compel oral testimony; nor would it ordinarily compel the taxpayer to restate, repeat, or affirm the truth of the contents of the documents sought."

. . . This reasoning applies with equal force here. Respondent does not contend that he prepared the documents involuntarily or that the subpoena would force him to restate, repeat, or affirm the truth of their contents. The fact that the records are in respondent's possession is irrelevant to the determination of whether the creation of the records was compelled. We therefore hold that the contents of those records are not privileged.

Although the contents of a document may not be privileged, the act of producing the document may be. A government subpoena compels the holder of the document to perform an act that may have testimonial aspects and an incriminating effect . . . . In *Fisher*, the Court explored the effect that the act of production would have on the taxpayer and determined that the act of production would have only minimal testimonial value and would not operate to incriminate the taxpayer. Unlike the Court in *Fisher*, we have the explicit finding of the District Court that the act of producing the documents would involve testimonial self-incrimination . . . . We therefore decline to overturn the finding of the District Court in this regard, where, as here, it has been affirmed by the Court of Appeals.[13]

The Government, as it concedes, could have compelled respondent to produce the documents listed in the subpoena [by granting immunity.]

. . . The Government did state several times before the District Court that it would not use respondent's act of production against him in any way. But counsel for the Government never made a statutory request to the District Court to grant respondent use immunity. We are urged to adopt a doctrine of constructive use immunity. Under this doctrine, the courts would impose a requirement on the Government not to use the incriminatory aspects of the act of production against the person claiming the privilege even though the statutory [immunity] procedures have not been followed.

We decline to extend the jurisdiction of courts to include prospective grants of use immunity in the absence of the formal request that the [immunity] statute requires.

. . . We conclude that the Court of Appeals erred in holding that the contents of the subpoenaed documents were privileged . . . . [Affirmed in part, reversed in part, and remanded.]

JUSTICE O'CONNOR, concurring.

I concur in both the result and reasoning of Justice Powell's opinion for the Court. I write separately, however, just to make explicit what is implicit in the analysis of that opinion: that the Fifth Amendment provides absolutely no protection for the contents of private papers of any kind. The notion that the Fifth Amendment protects the privacy of papers originated in *Boyd v. United States*, but our decision in *Fisher v. United States* sounded the death knell for *Boyd*.

JUSTICE MARSHALL, with whom JUSTICE BRENNAN joins, concurring in part and dissenting in part.

I concur in the Court's affirmance of the Court of Appeals' ruling that the act of producing the documents could not be compelled without an explicit grant of use immunity . . . .

Contrary to what Justice O'Connor contends, I do not view the Court's opinion in this case as having reconsidered whether the Fifth Amendment provides protection for the contents of "private papers of any kind." This case presented nothing remotely close to the question that Justice O'Connor eagerly poses and answers.

. . . Were it true that the Court's opinion stands for the proposition that "the Fifth Amendment provides absolutely no protection for the contents of private papers of any kind," I would assuredly dissent. I continue to believe that under the Fifth Amendment

---

[13] The Government concedes that the act of producing the subpoenaed documents might have had some testimonial aspects, but it argues that any incrimination would be so trivial that the Fifth Amendment is not implicated. The Government finds support for this argument in *Marchetti v. United States*, 390 U.S. 39 (1968). In *Marchetti*, the Court stated that a party who wishes to claim the Fifth Amendment privilege must be "confronted by substantial and 'real,' and not merely trifling or imaginary, hazards of incrimination." On the basis of the findings made in this case we think it clear that the risk of incrimination was "substantial and real" and not "trifling or imaginary." Respondent did not concede in the District Court that the records listed in the subpoena actually existed or were in his possession. Respondent argued that by producing the records, he would tacitly admit their existence and his possession. Respondent also pointed out that if the Government obtained the documents from another source, it would have to authenticate them before they would be admissible at trial.

"there are certain documents no person ought to be compelled to produce at the Government's request." . . .

UNITED STATES v. HUBBELL

530 U.S. 27 (2000)

JUSTICE STEVENS delivered the opinion of the Court.

The two questions presented concern the scope of a witness' protection against compelled self-incrimination: (1) whether the Fifth Amendment privilege protects a witness from being compelled to disclose the existence of incriminating documents that the Government is unable to describe with reasonable particularity; and (2) if the witness produces such documents pursuant to a grant of immunity, whether 18 U.S.C. § 6002 prevents the Government from using them to prepare criminal charges against him.

This proceeding arises out of the second prosecution of respondent, Webster Hubbell, commenced by the Independent Counsel appointed in August 1994 to investigate possible violations of federal law relating to the Whitewater Development Corporation. The first prosecution was terminated pursuant to a plea bargain. In December 1994, respondent pleaded guilty to charges of mail fraud and tax evasion arising out of his billing practices as a member of an Arkansas law firm from 1989 to 1992, and was sentenced to 21 months in prison. In the plea agreement, respondent promised to provide the Independent Counsel with "full, complete, accurate, and truthful information" about matters relating to the Whitewater investigation.

The second prosecution resulted from the Independent Counsel's attempt to determine whether respondent had violated that promise. In October 1996, while respondent was incarcerated, the Independent Counsel served him with a subpoena duces tecum calling for the production of 11 categories of documents before a grand jury sitting in Little Rock, Arkansas. [The appendix described the documents, and all of those requested were limited to the dates "January 1, 1993, to the present." (November 9, 1996, the required date of appearance). Examples include "any and all documents reflecting, referring, or relating to Webster Hubbell's schedule of activities, including all calendars, appointment books, diaries, records of reverse telephone toll calls, credit card calls, telephone message slips, other telephone records, minutes, databases, electronic mail messages, travel records, itineraries, tickets for transportation of any kind, payments, bills, expense backup documentation, schedules, and/or any other document or database that would disclose Webster Hubbell's activities."]

On November 19, he appeared before the grand jury and invoked his Fifth Amendment privilege against self-incrimination. In response to questioning by the prosecutor, respondent initially refused "to state whether there are documents within my possession, custody, or control responsive to the Subpoena." Thereafter, the prosecutor produced an order, which had previously been obtained from the District Court pursuant to 18 U.S.C. § 6003(a), directing him to respond to the subpoena and granting him immunity "to the extent allowed by law." Respondent then produced 13,120 pages of documents and records and responded to a series of questions that established that those were all of the documents in his custody or control that were responsive to the commands in the subpoena, with the exception of a few documents he claimed were shielded by the attorney-client and attorney work-product privileges.

The contents of the documents produced by respondent provided the Independent Counsel with the information that led to this second prosecution [for] . . . various tax-related crimes and mail and wire fraud. The District Court dismissed the indictment relying, in part, on the ground that the Independent Counsel's use of the subpoenaed documents violated [the grant of immunity through] § 6002 because all of the evidence he would offer against respondent at trial derived either directly or indirectly from the testimonial aspects of respondent's immunized act of producing those documents. Noting that the Independent Counsel had admitted that he was not investigating tax-related issues when he issued the subpoena, and that he had "learned about the unreported income and other crimes from studying the records' contents," the District Court characterized the subpoena as "the quintessential fishing expedition."

The Court of Appeals vacated the judgment and remanded for further proceedings. The majority concluded that the District Court had incorrectly relied on the fact that the Independent Counsel did not have prior knowledge of the contents of the subpoenaed documents. The question the District Court should have addressed was the extent of the Government's independent knowledge of the documents' existence and authenticity, and of respondent's possession or control of them. . . .

In the opinion of the dissenting judge, the majority failed to give full effect to the distinction between the contents of the documents and the limited testimonial significance of the act of producing them. In his view, as long as the prosecutor could make use of information contained in the documents or derived therefrom without any reference to the fact that respondent had produced them in response to a subpoena, there would be no improper use of the testimonial aspect of the immunized act of production. In other words, the constitutional privilege and the statute conferring use immunity would only shield the witness from the use of any information resulting from his subpoena response "beyond what the prosecutor would receive if the documents appeared in the grand jury room or in his office unsolicited and unmarked, like manna from heaven."

On remand, the Independent Counsel acknowledged that he could not satisfy the [independent knowledge] . . . standard prescribed by the Court of Appeals and entered into a conditional plea agreement with respondent. In essence, the agreement provides for the dismissal of the charges unless this Court's disposition of the case makes it reasonably likely that respondent's "act of production immunity" would not pose a significant bar to his prosecution. The case is not moot, however, because the agreement also provides for the entry of a guilty plea and a sentence that will not include incarceration if we should reverse and issue an opinion that is sufficiently favorable to the Government to satisfy that condition. Despite that agreement, we granted the Independent Counsel's petition for a writ of certiorari in order to determine the precise scope of a grant of immunity with respect to the production of documents in response to a subpoena. We now affirm.

. . . More relevant to this case is the settled proposition that a person may be required to produce specific documents even though they contain incriminating assertions of fact or belief because the creation of those documents was not "compelled" within the meaning of the privilege. . . . It is clear, therefore, that respondent Hubbell could not avoid compliance with the subpoena served on him merely because the demanded documents contained incriminating evidence, whether written by others or voluntarily prepared by himself.

On the other hand, we have also made it clear that the act of producing documents in response to a subpoena may have a compelled testimonial aspect. We have held that "the act of production" itself may implicitly communicate "statements of fact." By "producing documents in compliance with a subpoena, the witness would admit that the papers existed, were in his possession or control, and were authentic." Moreover, as was true in this case, when the custodian of documents responds to a subpoena, he may be compelled to take the witness stand and answer questions designed to determine whether he has produced everything demanded by the subpoena. The answers to those questions, as well as the act of production itself, may certainly communicate information about the existence, custody, and authenticity of the documents. Whether the constitutional privilege protects the answers to such questions, or protects the act of production itself, is a question that is distinct from the question whether the unprotected contents of the documents themselves are incriminating.

. . . Compelled testimony that communicates information that may "lead to incriminating evidence" is privileged even if the information itself is not inculpatory. It is the Fifth Amendment's protection against the prosecutor's use of incriminating information derived directly or indirectly from the compelled testimony of the respondent that is of primary relevance in this case.

Acting pursuant to 18 U.S.C. § 6002, the District Court entered an order compelling respondent to produce "any and all documents" described in the grand jury subpoena and granting him "immunity to the extent allowed by law."

. . . The "compelled testimony" that is relevant in this case is not to be found in the contents of the documents produced in response to the subpoena. It is, rather, the testimony inherent in the act of producing those documents.

. . . The Government correctly emphasizes that the testimonial aspect of a response to a subpoena duces tecum does nothing more than establish the existence, authenticity, and custody of items that are produced. We assume that the Government is also entirely correct in its submission that it would not have to advert to respondent's act of production in order to prove the existence, authenticity, or custody of any documents that it might offer in evidence at a criminal trial; indeed, the Government disclaims any need to introduce any of the documents produced by respondent into evidence in order to prove the charges against him. It follows, according to the Government, that it has no intention of making improper "use" of respondent's compelled testimony.

The question, however, is not whether the response to the subpoena may be introduced into evidence at his criminal trial. That would surely be a prohibited "use" of the immunized act of production. But the fact that the Government intends no such use of the act of production leaves open the separate question whether it has already made "derivative use" of the testimonial aspect of that act in obtaining the indictment against respondent and in preparing its case for trial. It clearly has.

It is apparent from the text of the subpoena itself that the prosecutor needed respondent's assistance both to identify potential sources of information and to produce those sources. Given the breadth of the description of the 11 categories of documents called for by the subpoena, the collection and production of the materials demanded was tantamount to answering a series of interrogatories asking a witness to disclose the existence and location of particular documents fitting certain broad descriptions. The assembly of literally hundreds of pages of material in response to a request for "any and all documents reflecting, referring, or relating to any direct or indirect sources of money or other things of value received by or provided to" an individual or members of his family during a 3-year period, is the functional equivalent of the preparation of an answer to either a detailed written interrogatory or a series of oral questions at a discovery deposition. Entirely apart from the contents of the 13,120 pages of materials that respondent produced in this case, it is undeniable that providing a catalog of existing documents fitting within any of the 11 broadly worded subpoena categories could provide a prosecutor with a "lead to incriminating evidence," or "a link in the chain of evidence needed to prosecute."

Indeed, the record makes it clear that that is what happened in this case. The documents were produced before a grand jury sitting in the Eastern District of Arkansas in aid of the Independent Counsel's attempt to determine whether respondent had violated a commitment in his first plea agreement. . . . It is abundantly clear that the testimonial aspect of respondent's act of producing subpoenaed documents was the first step in a chain of evidence that led to this prosecution. . . . It was only through respondent's truthful reply to the subpoena that the Government received the incriminating documents of which it made "substantial use . . . in the investigation that led to the indictment."

For these reasons, we cannot accept the Government's submission that respondent's immunity did not preclude its derivative use of the produced documents because its "possession of the documents [was] the fruit only of a simple physical act — the act of producing the documents." It was unquestionably necessary for respondent to make extensive use of "the contents of his own mind" in identifying the hundreds of documents responsive to the requests in the subpoena. . . .

In sum, we have no doubt that the constitutional privilege against self-incrimination protects the target of a grand jury investigation from being compelled to answer questions designed to elicit information about the existence of sources of potentially incriminating evidence. That constitutional privilege has the same application to the testimonial aspect of a response to a subpoena seeking discovery of those sources. . . . On appeal and again before this Court, the Government has argued that the communicative aspect of respondent's act of producing ordinary business records is insufficiently "testimonial" to support a claim of privilege because the existence and possession of such records by any businessman is a "foregone conclusion" under our decision in *Fisher v. United States*. This argument both misreads *Fisher* and ignores our subsequent decision in *United States v. Doe*.

. . . Whatever the scope of [the foregone conclusion doctrine discussed in *Fisher*], this "foregone conclusion" rationale, the facts of this case plainly fall outside of it. While in *Fisher* the Government already knew that the documents were in the attorneys' possession and could independently confirm their existence and authenticity through the accountants who created them, here the Government has not shown that it had any prior knowledge of either the existence or the whereabouts of the 13,120 pages of documents ultimately produced by respondent. The Government cannot cure this deficiency through the overbroad argument that a businessman such as respondent will always possess general business and tax records that fall within the broad categories described in this subpoena. The *Doe* subpoenas also sought several broad categories of general business records, yet we upheld the District Court's finding that the act of producing those records would involve testimonial self-incrimination.

Given our conclusion that respondent's act of production had a testimonial aspect, at least with respect to the existence and location of the documents sought by the Government's subpoena, respondent could not be compelled to produce those documents without first receiving a grant of immunity. . . . [S]uch immunity is co-extensive with the constitutional privilege. *Kastigar* requires that respondent's motion to dismiss the indictment on immunity grounds be granted unless the Government proves that the evidence it used in obtaining the indictment and proposed to use at trial was derived from legitimate sources "wholly independent" of the testimonial aspect of respondent's immunized conduct in assembling and producing the documents described in the subpoena. The Government, however, does not claim that it could make such a showing. Rather, it contends that its prosecution of respondent must be considered proper unless someone — presumably respondent — shows that "there is some substantial relation between the compelled testimonial communications implicit in the act of production (as opposed to the act of production standing alone) and some aspect of the information used in the investigation or the evidence presented at trial." We could not accept this submission without repudiating the basis for our conclusion in *Kastigar* that the statutory guarantee of use and derivative-use immunity is as broad as the constitutional privilege itself. This we are not prepared to do.

Accordingly, the indictment against respondent must be dismissed.

JUSTICE THOMAS, with whom JUSTICE SCALIA joins, concurring.

Our decision today involves the application of the act-of-production doctrine, which provides that persons compelled to turn over incriminating papers or other physical evidence pursuant to a subpoena duces tecum or a summons may invoke the Fifth Amendment privilege against self-incrimination as a bar to production only where the act of producing the evidence would contain "testimonial" features. I join the opinion of the Court because it properly applies this doctrine, but I write separately to note that this doctrine may be inconsistent with the original meaning of the Fifth Amendment's Self-Incrimination Clause. A substantial body of evidence suggests that the Fifth Amendment privilege protects against the compelled production not just of incriminating testimony, but of any incriminating evidence. In a future case, I would be willing to reconsider the scope and meaning of the Self-Incrimination Clause.

The Fifth Amendment provides that "[n]o person . . . shall be compelled in any criminal case to be a witness against himself." The key word at issue in this case is "witness." The Court's opinion, relying on prior cases, essentially defines "witness" as a person who provides testimony, and thus restricts the Fifth Amendment's ban to only those communications "that are 'testimonial' in character." None of this Court's cases, however, has undertaken an analysis of the meaning of the term at the time of the founding. A review of that period reveals substantial support for the view that the term "witness" meant a person who gives or furnishes evidence, a broader meaning than that which our case law currently ascribes to the term. If this is so, a person who responds to a subpoena duces tecum would be just as much a "witness" as a person who responds to a subpoena ad testificandum.

. . . This Court has not always taken the approach to the Fifth Amendment that we follow today. The first case interpreting the Self-Incrimination Clause — *Boyd v. United States* — was decided, though not explicitly, in accordance with the understanding that "witness" means one who gives evidence. In *Boyd*, this Court unanimously held that the Fifth Amendment protects a defendant against compelled production of books and papers. And the Court linked its interpretation of the Fifth Amendment to the common-law understanding of the self-incrimination privilege.

But this Court's decision in *Fisher v. United States*, rejected this understanding, permitting the Government to force a person to furnish incriminating physical evidence and protecting only the "testimonial" aspects of that transfer. In so doing, *Fisher* not only failed to examine the historical backdrop to the Fifth Amendment, it also required . . . a difficult parsing of the act of responding to a subpoena duces tecum.

None of the parties in this case has asked us to depart from *Fisher*, but in light of the historical evidence that the Self-Incrimination Clause may have a broader reach than *Fisher* holds, I remain open to a reconsideration of that decision and its progeny in a proper case.

[The dissent of Justice Rehnquist is omitted]

NOTE

1. *Unanswered questions.* The *Hubbell* decision leaves several questions unanswered. Professor Robert Mosteller, for example, characterizes the decision as a "major reformulation of act of production doctrine." He notes:

> How protective the courts [after *Hubbell*] will prove to be when the issue is the target's possession of an item rather than its existence and how incrimination analysis will play out as to possession are the major puzzles remaining after *Hubbell*. Resolution of these issues will likely be interconnected. The Court's conclusion either will allow the anti-inquisitorial sentiment of *Hubbell* to invalidate subpoenas demanding that targets produce evidence that could incriminate them or will permit the Court to distinguish subpoenas for documents, where production might continue in a limited fashion, from other more facially incriminating items of physical evidence, whose compelled surrender appeared to greatly trouble the courts in *Hubbell*.

See Robert P. Mosteller, *Cowboy Prosecutors and Subpoenas for Incriminating Evidence: The Consequences and Correction of Excess*, 58 WASH. & LEE L. REV. 487, 547, 548 (2001). *See also* H. Richard Uviller, *Forward:* Fisher *Goes on the Quintessential Fishing Expedition and* Hubbell *Is Off the Hook*, 91 J. CRIM. L. & CRIMINOLOGY 311, 328 (2001) (analyzing several "perplexing — and disturbing — features of this strange opinion"); Thomas K. Wedeles, Note, *Fishing for Clarity in a Post-*Hubbell *World: The Need For a Bright-Line Rule in the Self-Incrimination Clause's Act of Production Doctrine*, 56 VAND. L. REV. 613 (2003) (arguing for a reevaluation of the act of production doctrine in light of the scholarship discussed in Justice Thomas's concurrence); Ronald

J. Allen & M. Kristin Mace, *The Self-Incrimination Clause Explained and its Future Predicted*, 94 J. CRIM. L. & CRIMINOLOGY 243 (2004) (arguing that the Fifth Amendment Self-Incrimination Clause bars the government from compelling "revelation of the incriminating substantive results of cognition [defined as the product of cognition that results in holding or asserting propositions with truth-value] caused by the State" and suggesting that *Hubbell* might extend the privilege "to all cases where the substantive contents of cognition are compelled").

If the Thomas/Scalia "originalist" view should prevail in some future case (*i.e.*, that *Boyd* was right all along and *Fisher* and its progeny are wrong, and that the Fifth Amendment as intended by the Framers protects not only against testimonial use of the act of producing personal papers and documents, but also, more broadly, against compulsory production of the documents themselves), it is quite possible that the Court might substantially rework this whole area of the law. Do you agree or disagree with the views of Justices Thomas and Scalia in *Hubbell*?

2. *State deviations.* The Supreme Judicial Court of Massachusetts has declined to follow the reasoning of *Braswell*, deeming it "a fiction." *Commonwealth v. Doe*, 544 N.E.2d 860, 861–62 (Mass. 1989). In *Doe*, it was held that the custodian of corporate records could invoke his state constitutional self-incrimination claim when the act of production would be personally self-incriminating. It may be interesting to note that the Massachusetts constitutional provision in question provided that "no subject shall . . . be compelled to accuse, or furnish evidence against himself." Mass. Const. part 1, art. XII.

Is there anything fundamentally unfair, in your view, about compelling corporate officers (in the absence of any corporate privilege against self-incrimination) to produce company records where they as individuals, rather than the business entity, are the true target of the investigation?

3. *Contents of documents.* In her *Doe I* concurrence, Justice O'Connor argued that the Fifth Amendment provides no protection for the contents of any private papers. In a separate opinion, Justice Marshall maintained that certain documents should be protected. Thus, while the Fifth Amendment today generally provides no protection for private documents, there may be certain unique documents which are so personal in nature that they might qualify for some Fifth Amendment protection. For instance, the Court has never ruled on the issue of the Fifth Amendment protection as it pertains to a personal diary.

4. *Location v. production.* While a corporate custodian of records cannot assert a Fifth Amendment privilege in order to avoid production of documents, a custodian, not in possession of the documents, is protected by the privilege against self-incrimination from being compelled to testify about the documents' location. *In Re Grand Jury Subpoena Dated April 14, 1996 v. Smith*, 87 F.3d 1198 (11th Cir. 1996). The court reasoned that unlike the act of production, testimony regarding the location of records requires the witness to disclose the contents of her mind.

PROBLEMS 7-1 to 7-4. SUBPOENAS GALORE

7-1. The President of ABC, Inc., has moved to quash a subpoena duces tecum served upon the President's secretary. The subpoena directs the secretary to appear before the grand jury and produce the following materials and documents in the secretary's possession: the President's and the secretary's Rolodexes; and the secretary's appointment book, desk calendar and business expense receipts (received from the President, but left in the secretary's files.) What specific argument should be made by the President? How should the prosecuting attorney respond?

7-2. A restaurant owner has moved to quash a subpoena to produce a list of all customers who have paid by credit card in the restaurant in the previous two months. On what basis should the motion be filed? What should be the outcome?

7-3. A robbery suspect moves to quash a subpoena directing a bank manager to produce the contents of the suspect's safety deposit box in a specified branch of the bank. On what basis should the robbery suspect move to quash? How should the prosecuting attorney respond?

7-4. A homicide suspect has moved to quash a subpoena directing her suspected accomplice to produce the key to a vault in the accomplice's basement. It is believed that the vault contains weapons used by the suspect and her accomplice to commit the murder. What should be the result?

[7] Immunity

If a grand jury witness makes a legitimate claim of a Fifth Amendment privilege, the government has two choices. First, it can honor the privilege and proceed no further with the particular line of questioning. Second, it can consider granting the witness immunity, as a result of which the witness may be compelled to answer the questions.

The possibility of an immunity grant can be initiated either by the witness (with or without counsel) or by the government attorney. Sometimes the prosecuting attorney may request a "proffer" (a preview of the witness's testimony) for the purpose of judging the desirability of the immunity grant. Since this step is not technically protected by a grant of immunity or an evidentiary privilege, defense counsel should enter into a stipulation or agreement that statements made in the course of such a proffer will not constitute admissions and will not be admissible in court.

[a] Informal Immunity

Prosecutors. Immunity may be conferred in a process that is either informal or formal. *Formal immunity* is granted by a judge who issues an order pursuant to a statute. *Informal immunity* is conferred by the prosecutor without technical compliance with immunity statutes. Under the latter, a prosecutor will make an informal promise — perhaps even in the context of plea bargaining — that cooperation will result in non-prosecution of the witness. This informal agreement, sometimes known as *pocket immunity*, may have the same effect as a statutory grant of immunity: testimony is given and the witness is not prosecuted. There are some significant legal differences, however. Since the grant is informal, the witness cannot be held in contempt for refusing to testify. A witness who wants to enforce a pocket immunity agreement will rely on the due process clause or contract principles.

Police. What is the legal effect of an immunity/non-prosecution agreement between a suspect and police officials? A number of jurisdictions hold that unless there is compliance with statutory immunity procedures, such an agreement has no binding effect. *See, e.g., Tabor v. State*, 971 S.W.2d 227 (Ark. 1998).

[b] Formal Immunity

To confer statutory immunity, the prosecuting attorney must apply for a formal grant of immunity from a judge. After the court grants the immunity, the government calls (or recalls) the witness to testify.

A grant of immunity should be formalized in writing and on the record to protect the witness' interests. Courts virtually never confer "constructive immunity" on a witness who did not follow the statutory immunity procedures. *See United States v. Doe*, 465 U.S. 605 (1984).

If the immunized witness continues to assert the self-incrimination privilege, a summons will issue requiring the witness to show cause (explain) why the witness refused to testify. If the witness fails to *show cause*, the court will issue a second order compelling the witness to answer the grand jury's questions. Should the witness continue to assert the self-incrimination privilege, the witness may then be held in contempt of court.

While both civil and criminal contempt sanctions are available, most courts invoke *civil contempt*. Under the usual rules for this form of contempt, the witness is imprisoned until he or she agrees to testify or until the grand jury term is over. Some state statutes restrict civil contempt orders in various ways. *Criminal contempt* involves punishing the witness for violation of a court order. Contrary to civil contempt, punishment for criminal contempt is not necessarily rescinded when the witness complies with the subpoena or order to testify. Ordinarily, the person convicted of criminal contempt will be sentenced to a short jail term and/or a fine.

[c]   Factors in Conferring Immunity

What factors or circumstances should a prosecutor consider in determining whether or not to seek a grant of immunity? Assume that a state grand jury is investigating a conspiratorial drug case in which the leader is being sought. A witness suspected of criminal involvement in a drug enterprise appears before the grand jury. It is not known, however, whether that individual is actually involved or what role that individual may have played in the larger scheme. The grant of immunity under these circumstances may lead to the discovery of more serious criminal wrongdoing on the part of other offenders. Yet there is also a possibility that these leads may go nowhere. In either event, a criminal offender has been granted immunity and may be shielded from criminal prosecution.

Assume a grand jury issues subpoenas to a number of witnesses, each of whom may have knowledge of a drug scheme. How soon in the investigation should grants of immunity be considered? The immunity grant to an individual witness may well be helpful in building a case against other members. On the other hand, an early grant of immunity may have been inadvertently extended to the drug kingpin. Consequently, the real grand jury target has been immunized from criminal prosecution.

The Witness Immunity Act of 1970, 18 U.S.C. §§ 6001–6005, states that the grant of immunity must be based upon a determination that:

> (1) the testimony or other information from such individual may be necessary to the public interest and (2) such individual has refused or is likely to refuse to testify or provide other information on the basis of his privilege against self-incrimination.

How helpful is this language in guiding a prosecutor to seek immunity in the kinds of cases described above? Consider the advice offered by Judge Stephen S. Trott, of the U.S. Court of Appeals for the Ninth Circuit:

> Do not give up more to make a deal than you have to. This is a temptation to which too many prosecutors succumb. If you have to give up anything at all, a plea to a lesser number of counts, a reduction in the degree of a crime, or a limitation on the number of years that an accomplice will serve is frequently sufficient to induce an accomplice to testify; and it sounds better to jurors when they discover that both fish are still in the net. Total immunity from prosecution should be used only as a last resort.

Stephen S. Trott, *Words of Warning for Prosecutors Using Criminals as Witnesses*, 47 Hastings L.J. 1381, 1392 (1996).

[d]   Transactional and Use Immunity

There are two forms of immunity: *transactional immunity* and *use immunity*. A majority of states use the transactional immunity grant, which means that a witness cooperating under such an immunity order cannot be prosecuted "for or on account of any transaction, matter, or thing concerning which he may testify or produce evidence."

Once the witness has testified pursuant to the grant of transactional immunity, the witness cannot be charged with any crimes related to that testimony. Some defense lawyers characterize transactional immunity as a "total bath."

Use immunity, the immunity grant utilized in federal criminal cases and in approximately twenty states, provides less protection than transactional immunity. A typical use immunity statute provides: "No testimony or other information compelled under the immunity order (or any information directly or indirectly derived from such testimony or other information) may be used against the witness in any criminal case, except a prosecution for perjury, giving a false statement, or otherwise failing to comply with the order." 18 U.S.C. § 6002.

There continues to be considerable debate whether use immunity or transactional immunity is the appropriate form of immunity and whether use immunity is broad enough to meet the constitutional demands of the Fifth Amendment.

KASTIGAR v. UNITED STATES
406 U.S. 441 (1972)

Mr. Justice Powell delivered the opinion of the Court.

This case presents the question whether the United States Government may compel testimony from an unwilling witness, who invokes the Fifth Amendment privilege against compulsory self-incrimination, by conferring on the witness immunity from use of the compelled testimony in subsequent criminal proceedings, as well as immunity from use of evidence derived from the testimony.

[Petitioners were subpoenaed to testify before a federal grand jury. Believing that the petitioners would assert their Fifth Amendment privilege, the government applied to the District Court for a grant of immunity under 18 U.S.C. §§ 6002–6003 and an order compelling petitioners to testify. Petitioners opposed the order, arguing that the scope of any immunity would be less than that protected by the Fifth Amendment. The district court granted the government's request for immunity. When the petitioners appeared before the grand jury and refused to answer questions, they were held in contempt of court and jailed until they answered or the term of the grand jury expired. The Court of Appeals affirmed.]

. . . Petitioners contend, first, that the Fifth Amendment's privilege against compulsory self-incrimination, which is that "(n)o person . . . shall be compelled in any criminal case to be a witness against himself," deprives Congress of power to enact laws that compel self-incrimination, even if complete immunity from prosecution is granted prior to the compulsion of the incriminatory testimony. In other words, petitioners assert that no immunity statute, however drawn, can afford a lawful basis for compelling incriminatory testimony. [The Court rejected that argument on the basis that the Fifth Amendment only protects against disclosures that the witness reasonably believes could be used in a criminal prosecution or could lead to other evidence that might be so used. Immunity was found to protect this interest.]

. . . Petitioners' second contention is that the scope of immunity provided by the federal witness immunity statute, 18 U.S.C. § 6002, is not coextensive with the scope of the Fifth Amendment privilege against compulsory self-incrimination, and therefore is not sufficient to supplant the privilege and compel testimony over a claim of the privilege. The statute provides that when a witness is compelled by district court order to testify over a claim of the privilege:

> the witness may not refuse to comply with the order on the basis of his privilege against self-incrimination; but no testimony or other information compelled under the order (or any information directly or indirectly derived from such testimony or other information) may be used against the witness in any criminal case, except a prosecution for perjury, giving a false statement, or otherwise failing to comply with the order.

The constitutional inquiry, rooted in logic and history, as well as in the decisions of this Court, is whether the immunity granted under this statute is coextensive with the scope of the privilege. If so, petitioners' refusals to answer based on the privilege were unjustified, and the judgments of contempt were proper, for the grant of immunity has removed the dangers against which the privilege protects. If, on the other hand, the immunity granted is not as comprehensive as the protection afforded by the privilege, petitioners were justified in refusing to answer, and the judgments of contempt must be vacated.

Petitioners draw a distinction between statutes that provide transactional immunity and those that provide, as does the statute before us, immunity from use and derivative use. They contend that a statute must at a minimum grant full transactional immunity in order to be coextensive with the scope of the privilege.

. . . The statute's explicit proscription of the use in any criminal case of "testimony or other information compelled under the order (or any information directly or indirectly derived from such testimony or other information)" is consonant with Fifth Amendment standards. We hold that such immunity from use and derivative use is coextensive with the scope of the privilege against self-incrimination, and therefore is sufficient to compel testimony over a claim of the privilege. While a grant of immunity must afford protection commensurate with that afforded by the privilege, it need not be broader. Transactional immunity, which accords full immunity from prosecution for the offense to which the compelled testimony relates, affords the witness considerably broader protection than does the Fifth Amendment privilege. The privilege has never been construed to mean that one who invokes it cannot subsequently be prosecuted. Its sole concern is to afford protection against being "forced to give testimony leading to the infliction of 'penalties affixed to . . . criminal acts.' " Immunity from the use of compelled testimony, as well as evidence derived directly and indirectly therefrom, affords this protection. It prohibits the prosecutorial authorities from using the compelled testimony in any respect, and it therefore insures that the testimony cannot lead to the infliction of criminal penalties on the witness. [The Court then held that the witness given use immunity is protected from improper use of this testimony in a later prosecution because federal authorities have the burden of showing that their evidence in the subsequent prosecution is not tainted by the direct or indirect use of the immunized testimony. They have an affirmative duty to establish that they had an independent, legitimate source for the disputed evidence, wholly independent of the compelled testimony.]

. . . There can be no justification in reason or policy for holding that the Constitution requires an amnesty grant where, acting pursuant to statute and accompanying safeguards, testimony is compelled in exchange for immunity from use and derivative use when no such amnesty is required where the government, acting without colorable right, coerces a defendant into incriminating himself.

We conclude that the immunity provided by 18 U.S.C. § 6002 leaves the witness and the prosecutorial authorities in substantially the same position as if the witness had claimed the Fifth Amendment privilege. The immunity therefore is coextensive with the privilege and suffices to supplant it.

Mr. Justice Douglas, dissenting.

The Self-Incrimination Clause says: "No person . . . shall be compelled in any criminal case to be a witness against himself." I see no answer to the proposition that he is such a witness when only "use" immunity is granted . . . .

Mr. Justice Marshall, dissenting. Today the Court holds that the United States may compel a witness to give incriminating testimony, and subsequently prosecute him for crimes to which that testimony relates. I cannot believe the Fifth Amendment permits that result.

The Fifth Amendment gives a witness an absolute right to resist interrogation, if the testimony sought would tend to incriminate him. A grant of immunity may strip the witness of the right to refuse to testify, but only if it is broad enough to eliminate all possibility that the testimony will in fact operate to incriminate him. It must put him in precisely the same position, vis-a-vis the government that has compelled his testimony, as he would have been in had he remained silent in reliance on the privilege.

. . . The Court asserts that the witness is adequately protected by a rule imposing on the government a heavy burden of proof if it would establish the independent character of evidence to be used against the witness. But in light of the inevitable uncertainties of the fact-finding process, a greater margin of protection is required in order to provide a reliable guarantee that the witness is in exactly the same position as if he had not testified. That margin can be provided only by immunity from prosecution for the offenses to which the testimony relates, *i.e.*, transactional immunity.

I do not see how it can suffice merely to put the burden of proof on the government. First, contrary to the Court's assertion, the Court's rule does leave the witness "dependent for the preservation of his rights upon the integrity and good faith of the prosecuting authorities." For the information relevant to the question of taint is uniquely within the knowledge of the prosecuting authorities. They alone are in a position to trace the chains of information and investigation that lead to the evidence to be used in a criminal prosecution. A witness who suspects that his compelled testimony was used to develop a lead will be hard pressed indeed to ferret out the evidence necessary to prove it. And of course it is no answer to say he need not prove it, for though the Court puts the burden of proof on the government, the government will have no difficulty in meeting its burden by mere assertion if the witness produces no contrary evidence. The good faith of the prosecuting authorities is thus the safeguard. For the paths of information through the investigative bureaucracy may well be long and winding, and even a prosecutor acting in the best of faith cannot be certain that somewhere in the depths of his investigative apparatus, often including hundreds of employees, there was not some prohibited use of the compelled testimony. The Court today sets out a loose net to trap tainted evidence and prevent its use against the witness, but it accepts an intolerably great risk that tainted evidence will in fact slip through that net . . . .

NOTES

1. *Kastigar hearing.* As emphasized in *Kastigar*, a criminal prosecution brought after a grant of use immunity requires the prosecutor to shoulder a "heavy burden" of proving lack of taint once the defendant has established that the testimony was compelled. The prosecutor must demonstrate that the evidence being relied upon to convict the witness was derived from legitimate sources independent of the witness's immunized testimony. The so-called "taint" or "Kastigar" hearing requires that the government establish a separation between the immunized testimony and the evidence being relied upon to establish guilt of the defendant. Once the prosecutor establishes that a witness has not been affected by immunized testimony, the burden of going forward shifts to the defense to contest the prosecution's proof.

The general view is that the government's standard of proof is a preponderance of evidence, a surprisingly low standard considering the "heavy burden" the government bears.

2. *Government procedures to preserve options.* Prosecutors use various procedures to satisfy the heavy burden imposed by *Kastigar*. One method is to collect all evidence against the witness in written form and present this to a court prior to the receipt of the immunized testimony. This is called "canning" the evidence. Another is to have the criminal matter prosecuted by a government attorney who had no personal involvement in the immunity grant process and who has not read or otherwise been apprised of the specifics of the immunized testimony.

3. *State-federal issues.* Is it proper for a witness in a state criminal proceeding who has been granted use immunity from state prosecution to invoke the privilege against self-incrimination based upon the fear of a subsequent federal prosecution?

In *Murphy v. Waterfront Commission of New York Harbor*, 378 U.S. 52 (1964), witnesses persisted in refusing to testify based upon their fear of federal prosecution and they were held in contempt. Recognizing that if a witness could not assert the privilege in such circumstances, the witness could be "whipsawed into incriminating himself under both state and federal law," the Court held that a state witness may not be compelled to give testimony which could be incriminating under federal law "unless the compelled testimony and its fruits cannot be used in any manner by federal officials in connection with a criminal prosecution against him." The Court held that the privilege protects state witnesses against incrimination under federal as well as state law, and federal witnesses against incrimination under state as well as federal law.

If a jurisdiction grants *transactional immunity*, on the other hand, that jurisdiction may not bar another one from pursuing criminal charges. But the other jurisdiction may not use evidence or the fruit of evidence obtained through the immunity given by the first jurisdiction.

4. *Foreign country issues.* Can a witness in a federal proceeding invoke the privilege against self-incrimination based upon his fear of prosecution by a foreign nation? In *United States v. Balsys*, 524 U.S. 666 (1998), Balsys, a resident alien, was subpoenaed to testify about his wartime activities between 1940 and 1944 and his immigration to the United States. Balsys claimed the privilege against self-incrimination, based upon fear of prosecution by a foreign country, and he contended that this entitlement arose because of a real and substantial fear that his testimony could be used against him by Lithuania or Israel in a criminal prosecution for Nazi war crimes. Rejecting the claim, the United States Supreme Court held that fear and concern regarding foreign prosecution was beyond the scope of the self-incrimination clause.

5. *State variations.* A small number of states have ruled that under their state constitutional self-incrimination provisions, use immunity statutes are unconstitutional (*i.e.*, transactional immunity is constitutionally mandated). In so holding, for example, the Alaska Supreme Court in *State v. Gonzalez*, 853 P.2d 526, 530 (Alaska 1993) stated:

> We do not doubt that, in theory, strict application of [use immunity] would remove the hazard of incrimination. See *Kastigar v. United States*. In a perfect world, one could theoretically trace every piece of evidence to its source and accurately police the derivative use of compelled testimony. In our imperfect world, however, the question arises whether the judicial process can develop safeguards to prevent derivative use of compelled testimony that satisfy [the Alaska Constitution]. Because we doubt that workaday measures can, in practice, protect adequately against use and derivative use, we hold that [the use immunity statute] impermissibly dilutes the [state Constitutional self-incrimination protection].

The next case illustrates how difficult it is for the prosecution to demonstrate an absence of taint.

UNITED STATES v. NORTH
910 F.2d 843 (D.C. Cir. 1990)

[Oliver North, a member of President Ronald Reagan's National Security Staff, testified under a grant of use immunity before the United States Congress. Thereafter, North was indicted on various criminal charges, and eventually convicted on three of twelve counts. The Court of Appeals reversed the convictions because the district court erred in failing to hold a full hearing as required by *Kastigar*.]

North's primary *Kastigar* complaint is that the District Court failed to require the IC [Independent Counsel] to demonstrate an independent source for each item of evidence or testimony presented to the grand jury and the petit jury, and that the District Court erred in focusing almost wholly on the IC's leads to witnesses, rather than on the content of the witnesses' testimony. North also claims that the IC made an improper nonevidentiary use of the immunized testimony (as by employing it for purposes of trial strategy), or at least that the District Court failed to make a sufficient inquiry into the question. North also protests that his immunized testimony was improperly used to refresh the recollection of witnesses before the grand jury and at trial, that this refreshment caused them to alter their testimony, and that the District Court failed to give this question the careful examination it deserved. In our discussion here, we first consider alleged nonevidentiary use of immunized testimony by the IC. We will then proceed to consider the use of immunized testimony to refresh witnesses' recollections. Finally, we will address the distinction between use of immunized testimony as a lead to procure witnesses and use insofar as it affects the substantive content of witnesses' testimony.

Assuming without deciding that a prosecutor cannot make nonevidentiary use of immunized testimony, we conclude that the IC here did not do so and that the District Court's inquiry and findings on this issue are not clearly erroneous. Thus, we do not decide the question of the permissibility or impermissibility of nonevidentiary use. However, contrary to the District Court, we conclude that the use of immunized testimony by witnesses to refresh their memories, or otherwise to focus their thoughts, organize their testimony, or alter their prior or contemporaneous statements, constitutes evidentiary use rather than nonevidentiary use. The District Court on remand is to hold the searching type of *Kastigar* hearing described in detail below, concerning North's allegations of refreshment. Finally, because the District Court apparently interpreted *Kastigar* as prohibiting the government only from using immunized testimony as a lead rather than using it at all, we hold that the District Court's truncated *Kastigar* inquiry was insufficient to protect North's Fifth Amendment right to avoid self-incrimination.

. . . The convictions are vacated and the case is remanded to the District Court. On remand, if the prosecution is to continue, the District Court must hold a full *Kastigar* hearing that will inquire into the content as well as the sources of the grand jury and trial witnesses' testimony. That inquiry must proceed witness-by-witness; if necessary, it will proceed line-by-line and item-by-item. For each grand jury and trial witness, the prosecution must show by a preponderance of the evidence that no use whatsoever was made of any of the immunized testimony either by the witness or by the Office of Independent Counsel in questioning the witness. This burden may be met by establishing that the witness was never exposed to North's immunized testimony, or that the allegedly tainted testimony contains no evidence not "canned" by the prosecution before such exposure occurred. Unless the District Court can make express findings that the government has carried this heavy burden as to the content of all of the testimony of each witness, that testimony cannot survive the *Kastigar* test. We remind the prosecution that the *Kastigar* burden is "heavy" not because of the evidentiary standard, but because of the constitutional standard: the government has to meet its proof only by a preponderance of the evidence, but any failure to meet that standard must result in exclusion of the testimony.

If the District Court finds that the government has failed to carry its burden with respect to any item or part of the testimony of any grand jury or trial witness, it should then consider whether that failure is harmless beyond a reasonable doubt. If the District Court concludes that the government's failure to carry its burden with respect to that particular witness or item is harmless beyond a reasonable doubt, the District Court should memorialize its conclusions and rationales in writing. If the government has in fact introduced trial evidence that fails the *Kastigar* analysis, then the defendant is entitled to a new trial. If the same is true as to grand jury evidence, then the indictment must be dismissed . . . .

NOTES

1. *Prosecution's difficult position.* Can the prosecution actually satisfy the *North* decision's rigorous requirements? Imagine a case where a witness confesses to a government agent, then repeats the same confession under a grant of use immunity. Under the *North* test, could the agent satisfy *Kastigar* and be permitted to testify about the first conversation?

Because of a fear that the *North* test could not be satisfied, the charges were eventually dropped against Oliver North. For a fascinating insider's view of the Oliver North trial, see Jeffrey Toobin, OPENING ARGUMENTS: A YOUNG LAWYER'S FIRST CASE: United States v. Oliver North (1991).

2. *North modified.* The *North* decision excerpted above was later slightly modified to ease the government's *Kastigar* burden. *United States v. North*, 920 F.2d 940 (D.C. Cir. 1990), *cert. denied*, 500 U.S. 941 (1991). Nevertheless, the second *North* decision repeated the rule that *Kastigar* was violated when a prosecution witness' testimony before a grand or petit jury is shaped, directly or indirectly, by compelled testimony, irrespective of how or by whom the witness was exposed to the compelled testimony. The prosecutor's bad motives or fault were not necessary to establish a *Kastigar* violation. A vigorous dissent by Chief Judge Wald argued that the majority opinion made it so difficult to satisfy *Kastigar* that it essentially turned use immunity into transactional immunity.

3. *Variations of North.* Some courts have rejected *North* as requiring the prosecution to shoulder too great a *Kastigar* burden. In *United States v. Koon*, 34 F.3d 1416 (9th Cir. 1994), for example, the court held that the government meets its *Kastigar* burden by proving that each matter as to which the witness will testify is derived from a source independent of the immunized testimony. The government need not show that the witness has neither shaped nor altered his or her testimony in any way as a result of that exposure. The *Koon* court noted that the latter requirement would essentially bar the witness from testifying in cases where the witness was exposed to the immunized testimony because it would be virtually impossible to prove there was no indirect effect of that exposure.

E. INDICTMENT

[1] Purpose

The central purpose of the indictment is to notify the defendant of the precise crime or crimes allegedly committed by the defendant. In *Hamling v. United States*, 418 U.S. 87, 117–118 (1974), the United States Supreme Court articulated the following test for determining the legal sufficiency of an indictment:

> An indictment is sufficient if it, first, contains the elements of the offense charged and fairly informs a defendant of the charge against which he must defend, and, second, enables him to plead an acquittal or conviction in bar of future prosecutions for the same offense. It is generally sufficient that an indictment set forth the offense in the words of the statute itself, as long as "those words of themselves fully, directly, and expressly, without any uncertainty or ambiguity, set forth all the elements necessary to constitute the offense intended to be punished." [The language of the statute may be used], but it must be accompanied with such a statement of the facts and circumstances as will inform the accused of the specific offense.

[2] Contents

Examine the language found in Rule 7 of the Federal Rules of Criminal Procedure.

FEDERAL RULES OF CRIMINAL PROCEDURE

Rule 7. *The Indictment and the Information*

(a) When Used

(1) **Felony.** An offense (other than criminal contempt) must be prosecuted by an indictment if it is punishable:

(A) by death; or

(B) by imprisonment for more than one year.

(2) **Misdemeanor.** An offense punishable by imprisonment for one year or less may be prosecuted in accordance with Rule 58(b)(1).

(b) Waiving Indictment.

An offense punishable by imprisonment for more than one year may be prosecuted by information if the defendant — in open court and after being advised of the nature of the charge and of the defendant's rights — waives prosecution by indictment.

(c) Nature and Contents.

(1) **In General.** The indictment or information must be a plain, concise, and definite written statement of the essential facts constituting the offense charged and must be signed by an attorney for the government. It need not contain a formal introduction or conclusion. A count may incorporate by reference an allegation made in another count. A count may allege that the means by which the defendant committed the offense are unknown or that the defendant committed it by one or more specified means. For each count, the indictment or information must give the official or customary citation of the statute, rule, regulation, or other provision of law that the defendant is alleged to have violated. For purposes of an indictment referred to in section 3282 of title 18, United States Code, for which the identity of the defendant is unknown, it shall be sufficient for the indictment to describe the defendant as an individual whose name is unknown, but who has a particular DNA profile, as that term is defined in that section 3282.

(2) **Criminal Forfeiture.** No judgment of forfeiture may be entered in a criminal proceeding unless the indictment or the information provides notice that the defendant has an interest in property that is subject to forfeiture in accordance with the applicable statute.

(3) **Citation Error.** Unless the defendant was misled and thereby prejudiced, neither an error in a citation nor a citation's omission is a ground to dismiss the indictment or information or to reverse a conviction.

(d) Surplusage.

Upon the defendant's motion, the court may strike surplusage from the indictment or information.

(e) Amending an Information.

Unless an additional or different offense is charged or a substantial right of the defendant is prejudiced, the court may permit an information to be amended at any time before the verdict or finding.

(f) Bill of Particulars.

The court may direct the government to file a bill of particulars. The defendant may move for a bill of particulars before or within 10 days after arraignment or at a later time if the court permits. The government may amend a bill of particulars subject to such conditions as justice requires.

NOTES

1. *Contents of indictment: Rule 7.* Federal Rule 7 describes the contents of a federal indictment:

a. Statement of essential facts constituting the offense;

b. Statement should be "plain, concise, and definite";

c. Signed by attorney for government;

d. Citation to law allegedly violated; and

e. Notice if is property subject to forfeiture.

2. *Contents of indictment: Rule 6.* Rule 6(c) adds an additional element. It provides that a federal indictment must be signed by the foreperson of the grand jury.

3. *State variations; form indictments.* Many jurisdictions have similar provisions with respect to the required contents of either the indictment or the information. Additionally, a number of jurisdictions use *indictment forms.* This procedure permits a "fill-in-the-blank" approach to indictment drafting. While technically grand jurors could draft their own indictments, in many jurisdictions prosecutors routinely prepare indictments prior to the presentation of evidence, hoping (and expecting) that the grand jury will concur with the prosecutor's proposed charge. In this sense, the "rubber stamp" accusation leveled at grand juries appears literally true.

Even under Rule 7, it is unclear how much specificity must be included in the indictment or information. Each case turns upon its unique facts and circumstances. The appropriate standard for evaluating federal indictments is suggested in the next case.

RUSSELL v. UNITED STATES
369 U.S. 749 (1962)

Mr. Justice Stewart delivered the opinion of the Court.

. . . Each of the petitioners was convicted for refusing to answer certain questions when summoned before a congressional subcommittee.

. . . In each case the indictment returned by the grand jury failed to identify the subject under congressional subcommittee inquiry at the time the witness was interrogated. The indictments were practically identical in this respect, stating only that the questions to which answers were refused "were pertinent to the question then under inquiry" by the subcommittee. In each case a motion was filed to quash the indictment before trial upon the ground that the indictment failed to state the subject under investigation at the time of the subcommittee's interrogation of the defendant. In each case the motion was denied.

. . . Congress has expressly provided that no one can be prosecuted under 2 U.S.C. § 192,[1] except upon indictment by a grand jury.[2]

This Court has never decided whether the indictment must identify the subject which was under inquiry at the time of the defendant's alleged default or refusal to answer. For the reasons that follow, we hold that the indictment must contain such an averment, and we accordingly reverse the judgments before us.

---

[1] "Every person who having been summoned as a witness by the authority of either House of Congress to give testimony . . . upon any matter under inquiry before either House . . . refuses to answer any question pertinent to the question under inquiry, shall be deemed guilty of a misdemeanor . . . ."

[2] 2 U.S.C. § 194 requires grand jury review "whenever a witness summoned [under § 192] refuses to answer any question pertinent to the subject under inquiry before either House . . . ."

. . . In a number of cases the Court has emphasized two of the protections which an indictment is intended to guarantee, reflected by two of the criteria by which the sufficiency of an indictment is to be measured. These criteria are, first, whether the indictment contains the elements of the offense intended to be charged, and sufficiently apprises the defendant of what he must be prepared to meet, and, secondly, in case any other proceedings are taken against him for a similar offense whether the record shows with accuracy to what extent he may plead a former acquittal or conviction. [citations omitted.]

Without doubt the second of these preliminary criteria was sufficiently met by the indictments in these cases. Since the indictments set out not only the times and places of the hearings at which the petitioners refused to testify, but also specified the precise questions which they then and there refused to answer, it can hardly be doubted that the petitioners would be fully protected from again being put in jeopardy for the same offense, particularly when it is remembered that they could rely upon other parts of the present record in the event that future proceedings should be taken against them. The vice of these indictments, rather, is that they failed to satisfy the first essential criterion by which the sufficiency of an indictment is to be tested, i.e., that they failed to sufficiently apprise the defendant "of what he must be prepared to meet."

As has been pointed out, the very core of criminality under 2 U.S.C. § 192, is pertinency to the subject under inquiry of the questions which the defendant refused to answer. What the subject actually was, therefore, is central to every prosecution under the statute. Where guilt depends so crucially upon such a specific identification of fact, our cases have uniformly held that an indictment must do more than simply repeat the language of the criminal statute.

. . . It is argued that any deficiency in the indictments in these cases could have been cured by bills of particulars. But it is a settled rule that a bill of particulars cannot save an invalid indictment. When Congress provided that no one could be prosecuted under 2 U.S.C. § 192, except upon an indictment, Congress made the basic decision that only a grand jury could determine whether a person should be held to answer in a criminal trial for refusing to give testimony pertinent to a question under congressional committee inquiry. A grand jury, in order to make that ultimate determination, must necessarily determine what the question under inquiry was. To allow the prosecutor, or the court, to make a subsequent guess as to what was in the minds of the grand jury at the time they returned the indictment would deprive the defendant of a basic protection which the guaranty of the intervention of a grand jury was designed to secure. For a defendant could then be convicted on the basis of facts not found by, and perhaps not even presented to, the grand jury which indicted him.

This underlying principle is reflected by the settled rule in the federal courts that an indictment may not be amended except by resubmission to the grand jury, unless the change is merely a matter of form . . . .

For these reasons we conclude that an indictment under 2 U.S.C. § 192 must state the question under congressional committee inquiry as found by the grand jury. . . . Reversed.

Mr. Justice Harlan, whom Mr. Justice Clark joins, dissenting.

The ground rules for testing the sufficiency of an indictment are twofold: (1) does the indictment adequately inform the defendant of the nature of the charge he will have to meet; (2) if the defendant is convicted, and later prosecuted again, will a court, under what has been charged, be able to determine the extent to which the defense of double jeopardy is available?

. . . It is "inconceivable" to me how the indictments in the present cases can be deemed insufficient to advise these petitioners of the nature of the charge they would have to meet. The indictments gave them the name of the committee before which they had appeared; the place and the dates of their appearances; the references to the enabling legislation under which the committee acted; and the questions which the petitioners refused to answer. The subject matter of the investigations had been stated to the petitioners at the time of their appearances before the committees. And the committee transcripts of the hearings were presumably in their possession and, if not, were of course available to them . . . .

NOTES

1. In *United States v. Resendiz-Ponce*, 127 S.Ct. 782 (2007), the Supreme Court stated that while "an indictment parroting the language of a federal statute is often sufficient," *Russell* illustrates a crime "that must be charged [in the indictment] with greater specificity" in order to provide fair notice and ensure that the conviction arose out of the same theory of guilt presented to the grand jury.

2. Indictment particularity requirements vary considerably from state to state. A leading treatise summarizes some of the general rules as follows[*]:

> As courts repeatedly note, "an indictment [or information] must not only contain all the elements of the offense charged, but must also provide the accused with a sufficient description of the acts he is alleged to have committed to enable him to defend himself adequately." Precisely how much factual specificity is needed to meet that standard will necessarily vary from one case to another. Relevant factors include the nature of the offense, the likely significance of particular factual variations in determining liability, the ability of the prosecution to identify a particular circumstance without a lengthy and basically evidentiary allegation, and the availability of alternative procedures for obtaining the particular information. It generally is agreed that the issue is not whether the alleged offense could be described with more certainty, but whether there is "sufficient particularity" to enable the accused to "prepare a proper defense."

Wayne R. LaFave, Jerold H. Israel, & Nancy J. King, CRIMINAL PROCEDURE § 19.3(b), at 900 (4th ed. 2004).

PROBLEM 7-5. OVERKILL

Defendants, Vicki Lynn Kennedy and William Hargis, have been joined together in a three-count indictment. The following questions pertain to the indictment forms set out on the following pages.

1. Does the murder indictment (first count) adequately inform defendants of the alleged crime? Note that the language of the indictment specifies alternative theories upon which the State of Westphalia may rely in establishing murder. Should the government be required to "elect" its theory prior to trial?

2. What specific crime is charged in the third count? Does the language of the indictment sufficiently inform the defendants so that each can intelligently prepare her or his defense?

3. *Motion practice.* Assume that both defendants have legally sound objections to the language appearing in the third count, but fail to make appropriate motions prior to trial. What are the consequences of such inaction? Rule 12 of the Federal Rules of Criminal Procedure provides that several specified defense claims must be raised before trial and that failure to do so constitutes a waiver. Among the specific matters that must be raised are the following:

---

[*] Reprinted with permission. All rights reserved.

FEDERAL RULES OF CRIMINAL PROCEDURE

Rule 12. *Pleadings and Pretrial Motions*

. . . .

(b) Pretrial Motions.

. . . .

(3) Motions That Must Be Made Before Trial. The following must be raised before trial:

> . . . . (B) a motion alleging a defect in the indictment or information — but at anytime while the case is pending, the court may hear a claim that the indictment or information fails to invoke the court's jurisdiction or to state an offense . . . .

This rule was designed to control the defense strategy of "sandbagging." That is, the defense attorney would consciously forego making an objection regarding the language of the indictment prior to trial. After conviction, defense counsel would call the court's attention to the alleged defect in the hopes of obtaining a new trial.

4. Assume that the district attorney prosecuting this case desires to amend one or more of the indictments to correct what he or she believes to be a deficiency in the pleading language. Can the district attorney do so? How? Is additional information needed to answer this question?

State of Westphalia, Washington County

FIRST COUNT

<u>JANUARY</u> TERM OF THE CRIMINAL COURT, 2008

The Grand Jurors for the State of Westphalia, duly elected, impaneled, sworn, and charged, to inquire for the body of the County of Washington and State aforesaid, upon their oath aforesaid, present: That <u>Vicky Lynn Kennedy and William Hargis</u> of the said County, heretofore, to wit, on the <u>2d</u> day of <u>December</u>, 2007, with force and arms, in the County aforesaid, unlawfully, feloniously, willfully, deliberately, maliciously and premeditatedly or in the perpetration of a robbery did make an assault upon the body of one Cleatus Hammons and they the said Vicki Lynn Kennedy and William Hargis then and there unlawfully and feloniously did kill and murder the said Cleatus Hammons, against the peace and dignity of the State of Westphalia.

Attorney General

State of Westphalia, Washington County

SECOND COUNT

<u>JANUARY</u> TERM OF THE CRIMINAL COURT, 2008

The Grand Jurors for the State of Westphalia, duly elected, impaneled, sworn, and charged, to inquire for the body of the County of Washington and State aforesaid, upon their oath aforesaid, present: That <u>Vicky Lynn Kennedy and William Harqis</u> of the said County, heretofore, and prior to the filing of this indictment, to wit, on the <u>2d</u> day of <u>December</u>, 2007, with force and arms, in the County aforesaid, unlawfully and feloniously, did make an assault upon the body of one John Friedman, then and there unlawfully and feloniously put in fear and danger of his life, and then and there unlawfully, feloniously and violently did steal, take, and carry away from the person and against the will of the said John Friedman certain personal property, to wit: a quantity of good and lawful money of the United States of America in excess of $800, said robbery being accomplished by the use of deadly weapons, to wit: two pistols; contrary to the form of the statutes in such cases made and provided, and against the peace and dignity of the State of Westphalia.

_____

Attorney General

State of Westphalia, Washington County

THIRD COUNT

<u>JANUARY</u> TERM OF THE CRIMINAL COURT, 2008

The Grand Jurors for the State of Westphalia, duly elected, impaneled, sworn, and charged, to inquire for the body of the County of Washington and State aforesaid, upon their oath aforesaid, present: That <u>Vicky Lynn Kennedy and William Hargis</u> of the said County, heretofore, and prior to the filing of this indictment, to wit, on the <u>2d</u> day of <u>December</u>, 2007, with force and arms, in the County aforesaid, unlawfully, feloniously, willfully, deliberately, maliciously and premeditatedly or in the perpetration of a robbery did make an assault upon the body of one John Friedman, with malice aforethought, to kill, and upon him to commit the crime and felony of murder in the first degree, against the peace and dignity of the State of Westphalia.

_____
Attorney General

[3] Amending Indictment

The specific language in Federal Rule of Criminal Procedure 7(e) suggests that an amendment may be made if the charging document is an information; however, if an indictment is involved, the prosecutor does not possess that authority. This interpretation is based on the early case of *Ex parte Bain*, 121 U.S. 1 (1887), prohibiting amendment of an indictment except by resubmission to the grand jury.

The *Bain* rule does not prevent an Assistant United States Attorney from amending an indictment as to form (*i.e.*, misspellings), but it does prevent a prosecutor from amending an indictment substantively.

Surplusage. In *United States v. Miller*, 471 U.S. 130 (1985), the Court interpreted *Bain* to allow for the striking of surplusage from an indictment by the court without resubmission to the grand jury. *See also* Fed. R. Crim. P. 7(d) (on defendant's motion, court may strike surplusage from indictment). A defendant may ask that surplusage (irrelevant material that is not essential for a valid indictment) be struck so that the jury, which may be read or informed of the indictment at the start of the trial, does not learn of the irrelevant allegations. For example, an indictment may contain background information alleging new, uncharged criminal activity. Surplusage is discussed further below.

State variations. While a number of states allow a prosecutor to amend both an information and an indictment, federal courts and a significant number of states continue to adhere to the "old" rule that an indictment cannot be amended by the prosecutor.

[4] Bill of Particulars

A party who needs more information about the crime than is provided in the indictment may seek a *bill of particulars*, which is obtained through a motion requesting the court to order the government to provide additional facts about the crime. More specifically, the purpose of the bill of particulars is to give the defendant enough additional information to prepare for trial, avoid unexpected facts or legal theories at trial, and assert a double jeopardy bar for the same offense. *See* Herald Price Fahringer, *The Battle for a Bill of Particulars*, 26 Crim. L. Bull. 387, 388 (1990).

Federal Rule of Criminal Procedure 7(f) articulates no standard regarding either the granting or denial of a motion for a bill of particulars. Its only details are that the motion must be filed no later than 10 days after arraignment or later if the court permits and extension.

It is difficult to discern the proper relationship between the bill of particulars and constitutional principles governing adequacy of the content of the indictment. Additionally, it has been noted by many courts that the bill of particulars is not intended to serve as a substitute for discovery, is not designed to provide the accused with specifications of factual evidence, and does not cure an otherwise invalid indictment.

If the government provides a bill of particulars, the trial proof must conform to the bill of particulars. The defendant may rely on the facts in the bill of particulars in preparing for trial and presenting its defense. The government may amend the bill of particulars as long as it does not prejudice the defendant.

The grant or denial of a bill of particulars lies within the discretion of the trial court. Often a judge will refuse to order a bill of particulars because the indictment is deemed adequate and the defendant is simply seeking discovery, perhaps beyond that authorized in criminal cases. In addition, many judges do not want to limit the government's flexibility by forcing the government to specify some of the issues or theories it will prove at trial. In order to establish that the trial court abused its discretion by denying a motion for a bill of particulars, a defendant must show actual surprise at trial and substantial prejudice to his or her rights.

A defendant will seek a court-ordered bill of particulars by motion. The motion should request specific information, such as the date or exact location of the crime. Often defense counsel will include an affidavit describing why the information is needed. The government may respond by providing all, some, or none of the requested information and giving an explanation when it does not fully comply with the motion.

The bill of particulars is an important procedural device in complex white collar crime cases. In *United States v. Davidoff*, 845 F.2d 1151 (2d Cir. 1988), Davidoff was convicted of violating the federal RICO statute by participating in a conspiracy involving the extraction of extortionate payments from air freight companies. The indictment alleged that the offenses included, but were not limited to, extortionate demands directed against certain companies. Davidoff, a Teamsters' official, moved for a bill of particulars that would "state with particularity the unspecified violations indicated by the phrase 'but were not limited to,'" but his motion was denied. At trial, the government introduced evidence of extortionate practices directed against three companies that were not specifically identified in the indictment. Following conviction, the Second Circuit Court of Appeals ruled that the trial court exceeded its discretion by denying the motion for a bill of particulars, stating "it is unrealistic to think that a defendant preparing to meet charges of extorting funds from one company had a fair opportunity to defend against allegations of extortions against unrelated companies, allegations not made prior to trial."

In *United States v. Bortnovsky*, 820 F.2d 572 (2d Cir. 1987), defendants were charged with conspiring to defraud certain government entities by submitting false and inflated insurance claims. They requested a bill of particulars, identifying which insurance claims for burglary losses were allegedly fraudulent and which invoices were falsified. Following conviction, the Second Circuit Court of Appeals found error in the trial court's refusal to grant the motion. The Court noted that the denial of the bill of particulars forced the defendants to explain circumstances surrounding eight actual burglaries and to deal with a large amount of unnecessary documents. Therefore, the bill of particulars was "vital to [defendants'] understanding of the charges . . . and to the preparation of a defense."

PROBLEM 7-6. TELL ME MORE

Paul Lawrinson was indicted for gross sexual imposition upon a minor in violation of state law. Desiring more specificity, Lawrinson filed a bill of particulars, requesting that the government specify the date on which the alleged offense occurred. The trial judge granted the motion, whereupon the prosecution filed a bill of particulars stating that "the offense in the indictment occurred between January 1, 200X, and January 31, 200X."

1. If the indictment specifically alleges one single act of "gross sexual imposition," is the response provided by the bill of particulars sufficient? Should there also be specification with respect to the time of day and location of the alleged offense?

2. Assume that Lawrinson intends to rely upon an alibi defense. He is able to account for his whereabouts for much of the time during the period January 1 through January 31. In light of this allegation, should a more specific bill of particulars be granted?

3. Assume that the state's attorney, in response to the motion for a bill of particulars, contends that no additional information is available in the prosecutor's file. Therefore, it is asserted that a more detailed bill of particulars cannot be provided. Assume, however, that the police statement received from the victim's mother contained information that pinpointed the date of the alleged offense as either January 24 or January 25. Should the prosecutor's office be held to the level of knowledge established by information available to it in police reports?

4. Assume that a more specific bill of particulars is granted and the government states that the alleged offenses occurred on January 24th or 25th. The defendant now alleges an alibi defense for these two days. If the case proceeds to trial and the victim's mother testifies that the alleged attack may have occurred "anywhere between the 20th and 27th" of January, is the government now limited to proving that the offense occurred either on January 24 or January 25?

5. Assume that a more specific bill of particulars is not granted (meaning that the time period during which the alleged attack occurred is alleged to be January 1 through January 31). If witnesses testify that the alleged crime occurred January 18, in what way has the defendant been prejudiced in his ability to defend himself? Could prejudice be established in light of rules of criminal discovery that may require the defendant to give pretrial notice of his intention to rely on an alibi defense? If the judge grants a continuance so that the defendant can prepare his alibi defense for the specific date of January 18, does this "cure" any error in failing to grant the motion for a more specific bill of particulars?

Assume that the defendant is accused of various sexual assaults upon a minor and that the information states that the offenses occurred "on various dates between approximately June, 2006 through July, 2006." Should a trial judge's denial of the defendant's motion for a bill of particulars (for specific dates of said crimes) be upheld if the judge finds that the prosecutor had no knowledge of specific dates? In *State v. Vumback*, 819 A.2d 250 (Conn. 2003), the Connecticut Supreme Court held that the bill of particulars should have been granted because the state did not use its best efforts to provide a more narrow time frame in order to allow the defendant to defend against the crimes charged. Interestingly, the Court nonetheless concluded that the conviction must be affirmed because the defendant failed to establish that the trial judge's error prejudiced his defense. Specifically, because Vumback had access to information concerning the dates of the charged defense (via the police report and the victim's physician), he failed to show that the information "was necessary to his defense." *Id.* at 258.

[5] Variance

Assume that an indictment alleges that Defendant A committed the crime of first degree murder by means of shooting his victim in the head with a.22 caliber pistol. The government later discovers that the defendant killed his victim by shooting him in the heart with a.45 caliber pistol. If before trial the government was concerned that the indictment for Defendant A was problematic because of the misidentification of the weapon, it could replace it with a *superseding indictment* issued by a grand jury. But what if the government did not discover the error until the middle of trial when an expert witness testified about the weapon? The error in the indictment could be deemed a *fatal variance*.

[a] Limits of Variance

The defendant may assert that there is a "fatal variance" between the language of the indictment and the proof at trial. That is, the defendant was on notice that the government would prove its case according to the specifics of the charging document, but the proof at trial was at variance with the facts alleged in the indictment. How is a court to judge whether the degree of variance is permissible? According to Federal Rule of Criminal Procedure 52(a), "[a]ny error, defect, irregularity or variance that does not affect substantial rights must be disregarded." This standard was explicated in *Berger v. United States*, 295 U.S. 78, 82 (1935):

> The true inquiry . . . is not whether there has been a variance in proof, but whether there has been such a variance as to "affect the substantial rights" of the accused. The general rule that allegations and proof must correspond is based upon the obvious requirements (1) that the accused shall be definitely informed as to the charges against him, so that he may be enabled to present his defense and not be taken by surprise by the evidence offered at the trial; and (2) that he may be protected against another prosecution for the same offense.

There are times when inclusion of surplus language in the indictment is both fair and unfair to the accused. For example, if a defendant is charged with growing and producing marijuana in violation of federal law, the amount or quantity of the marijuana is not relevant to an element of that offense; reference to the quantity is not essential and may be prejudicial to the defendant. On the other hand, the quantity of marijuana grown may subject the defendant to an enhanced penalty at sentencing; inclusion of the quantity provides notice to the accused, allowing preparation for sentencing arguments.

In *United States v. Caldwell*, 176 F.3d 898 (6th Cir. 1999), the indictment charged that the defendant "did knowingly and intentionally manufacture, that is, grow and produce, more than one thousand plants of marijuana" in violation of 21 U.S.C. § 841(a)(1). The district court, in instructing the jury, noted that the indictment alleged a particular amount of marijuana. Nonetheless, the jury was told, "in order for you to find the defendant guilty of this charge, the evidence in this case need not establish that the exact amount or quantity of marijuana was as alleged in the indictment, but only that any amount or quantity of marijuana was, in fact, being manufactured, grown or produced by the defendant." After conviction, the defendant argued that the district court violated his Fifth Amendment right to an indictment by a grand jury by informing the petit jury that it need not find beyond a reasonable doubt the specific number of marijuana plants stated in the indictment (*i.e.*, the government was obligated to prove that allegation).

In affirming the defendant's conviction, the Sixth Circuit Court of Appeals held that the quantity of marijuana plants included in the indictment was not necessary to state an offense under § 841(a). Therefore, under *Miller*, that part of the indictment could be considered "a useless averment." The court observed, however, that putting the defendant on notice in the indictment that he was being charged with a specific quantity of marijuana that could subject him to an enhanced penalty "ultimately embraces the underlying notice function of the indictment." In future cases, it was suggested that district court judges should prevent specific drug-quantity language in the indictment from reaching the petit jury. "The district court could, for example, delete the specific quantity and quote the redacted indictment in the instructions to the petit jury instead of providing the petit jury with an unredacted indictment that includes the specific amount."

[b]   Procedures to Address Variance

A variance, unlike a bill of particulars, is an issue that rarely can be addressed prior to trial. While the bill of particulars is designed to afford a remedy for the individual who does not have adequate information about what the government intends to prove at trial, the variance problem only occurs at such time as proof becomes inconsistent with the language of the indictment. Sometimes, through pretrial discovery, the defense attorney may anticipate a factual variance. Moreover, a prosecutor may be in possession of information that suggests the possibility of a variance argument occurring at trial. When this occurs, the prosecutor may seek amendment of the indictment by withdrawing the indictment and presenting it to another grand jury.

[c]   Prejudice

When the proof at trial is at significant variance with the language in the indictment, an argument can be made that the crime of conviction is not the one charged by the grand jury in the indictment. Some courts refer to this kind of case as one in which the charging terms are altered such that an "unconstitutional amendment of the indictment" occurs. *See United States v. Attanasio*, 870 F.2d 809 (2d Cir. 1989)(noting that the Fifth Amendment grand jury guarantee is violated when evidence and jury instructions modify the essential elements set forth in the indictment to such an extent that the conviction offense is different from that charged in the indictment).

The central question facing state and federal appellate courts is the extent to which proof at trial varies from the language of the indictment. Simply stated, a variance occurs where the evidence at trial establishes facts different from those alleged in the indictment. Not all variances, however, are "fatal." A fatal variance is considered to be one in which the defendant suffers prejudice. This usually means that the defendant has been deprived of an adequate opportunity to prepare a defense or that he or she may be exposed to a risk of being prosecuted twice for the same crime.

[d]   Surplusage

On occasion, an indictment will contain language that is neither relevant nor material to the essential elements of the alleged crime. This excess language is considered to be *surplusage*, which the defendant may move to strike in advance of the trial. In terms of trial strategy, this is the sensible course of action because the prosecutor may be allowed to read to the jury the entire indictment, including the surplus allegations. To the extent that the excess language may prejudice the defendant, courts routinely strike the unnecessary words.

Assume, for example, that the government alleges a conspiracy to sell stolen bonds and states that the bonds in question were stolen. At trial, the government concedes that it cannot prove that the bonds actually were stolen. If the defendant claims that this constitutes a fatal variance (and therefore the conviction for conspiracy to sell bonds should be overturned), how should the court rule? In *United States v. Hughes*, 766 F.2d 875 (5th Cir. 1985), the court affirmed the conviction, holding that proof of the fact that the bonds were stolen was not essential to the conviction. Accordingly, the allegation in the indictment was mere surplusage and not material to the essential elements of the crime.

[e] Lesser Included Offenses

Another type of a variance issue arises when a defendant is indicted for one offense and yet convicted of a lesser included offense. Similarly, a defendant may be indicted as a principal but found guilty as an accessory. In both instances, it has been held that adequate notice is given the accused and therefore the variance is permissible. *See People v. Garrison*, 765 P.2d 419 (Cal. 1989). Of course, this analysis requires very close attention to the question of what constitutes a lesser included offense. For example, in *People v. Schmidt*, 533 N.E.2d 898 (Sup. Ct. Ill. 1989), the defendant was indicted for burglary but was convicted of theft. Because theft was not considered to be a lesser included offense of burglary, the conviction was overturned.

PROBLEM 7-7. FATAL VARIANCES

1. The defendant is indicted for the offense of carrying a .357 revolver during the commission of certain drug trafficking crimes. Evidence at trial suggests that the gun carried was, in fact, not a revolver but a sawed-off shotgun. The defendant's asserted defense at trial was that he was a drug user and not a drug dealer. Under these circumstances, is the variance fatal?

2. Defendant was indicted under a state statute for engaging in sexual conduct with a person under 13 years of age. The indictment alleged that the defendant engaged in this activity with his daughter on four separate occasions and that this conduct included anal intercourse and cunnilingus. At trial, the victim testified that the second incident involved fellatio (which had not been alleged in the indictment); additionally, she testified that the dates on which the second and fourth incidents occurred varied by a few days from the dates specified in the indictment. Is this fatal variance?

3. Defendant is charged with mail fraud and making a false statement to the Securities and Exchange Commission. This activity is in connection with a scheme to "defraud and obtain money and property by false and fraudulent pretenses and representations." The indictment alleges that the scheme began in February of 2000. It also identified the exact mailings in question. At trial, however, the government was able to prove that the alleged scheme actually began in August of 2000. Is this a case of fatal variance?

[6] Challenging an Indictment

[a] Introduction

A defense attorney may attempt to challenge the indictment prior to trial. This is usually accomplished through a Motion to Dismiss under Federal Rule of Criminal Procedure 12(b) or a comparable state rule or statute. While this Rule does not specifically list the grounds upon which an indictment may be dismissed, a number of state jurisdictions specify grounds in detail. For example, New York allows a motion to dismiss the indictment because of a defective indictment, defective proceeding, and (among others) because "[t]he evidence before the grand jury was not legally sufficient to establish the offense charged . . . ." N.Y. Crim. Proc. Law § 210.20(1)(a–c). Another common requirement, included in Federal Rule 52(a), is that the accused must establish that the error prejudiced the defendant in some way.

There are many reasons why courts are hesitant to afford relief when a motion to dismiss is filed. Objections to grand jury proceedings could frustrate the expeditious administration of grand jury investigations. Another consideration is the notion of grand jury secrecy, previously discussed. When a defense attorney moves for dismissal of the indictment because something allegedly occurred inside the grand jury room, in all likelihood he or she will seek more information to buttress the claim. Obviously, disclosure of such information breaches the secrecy principle.

[b] Challenges Frequently Litigated

In addition to explicit statutory bases upon which motions to dismiss indictments may be made, the most frequently litigated issues are (a) selection of grand jurors, (b) bias by grand jurors, (c) grand jury misfeasance, (d) evidentiary challenges, (e) prosecutorial misconduct, and (f) unauthorized presence. These will be treated very briefly below. For more detailed analysis, *see* Grand Jury Law and Practice Ch. 9.

Selection of grand jurors. As described above, every jurisdiction has rules regulating the selection of grand jurors. In addition, the Constitution, particularly the equal protection clause, also establishes standards for selecting grand jurors. Violation of either the statute or the constitutional rules can engender a challenge to an indictment. This matter is considered more fully in Chapter 15, where challenges to jurors are discussed in detail.

Grand juror bias. Contrary to the language found in the petit jury guarantee of the Sixth Amendment to the United States Constitution, the Fifth Amendment grand jury guarantee contains no impartiality requirement. While the United States Supreme Court has not directly ruled on the question whether a grand juror must be unbiased, in *Beck v. Washington*, 369 U.S. 541 (1962), the Court intimated that the fourteenth amendment due process clause may require "the state, having once resorted to a grand jury procedure, to furnish an unbiased grand jury." The facts presented in *Beck*, however, involved no showing of prejudice; therefore the Court's pronouncement is of questionable precedential value. Other cases also hint at the need for an unbiased grand jury.

Considerable authority exists for the proposition, however, that the defendant is *not* entitled to an unbiased grand jury. Even where a court allows a challenge based upon grand jury bias, it may require an actual showing of bias on the part of named jurors. Since it may be extremely difficult to acquire this information because of grand jury secrecy, such claims are unlikely to succeed.

Juror misfeasance. Assume that the defendant somehow learns that the federal grand jury issued an indictment after only two minutes of deliberation. Defendant now desires to challenge the indictment on the ground that the grand jurors failed to perform their duty; that is, they could not have meaningfully deliberated in that short a period of time. Hence, the defendant's right to be charged by indictment guaranteed by the Fifth Amendment has been infringed. Similar to the case in which a challenge is based upon prosecutorial misconduct, the defendant making this challenge first confronts the strong presumption of regularity of grand jury proceedings. In *United States v. Gower*, 447 F.2d 187 (5th Cir. 1971), the fact that grand jurors spent approximately 45 minutes considering the defendant's case was not deemed to be sufficient proof of failure to perform grand jurors' duty.

Evidentiary challenges. Based upon the two major United States Supreme Court cases previously discussed (*Costello* and *Calandra*), most courts will not permit an indictment to be successfully challenged on the ground of either the nature or the sufficiency of the evidence presented to and considered by the grand jury. These cases stress deference to the investigative function of the grand jury. Also, the cases reflect a disinclination to sanction any procedure that may result in significant delay prior to trial.

While a majority of states follow the *Costello* rule (either by case law or by statute), approximately one-fifth of the states permit some review of either the nature or sufficiency of evidence heard by the grand jury. In some of these states, the defendant has a broad right to inspect the grand jury transcript in order to intelligently present such an evidentiary challenge. Even where the majority *Costello/Calandra* rule is followed, are there any circumstances in which an evidentiary challenge can be brought successfully? Two cases of this sort have been recognized: the knowing presentation of perjured testimony to a grand jury and a case in which the indictment is based on no evidentiary findings whatsoever.

If a prosecutor knowingly presents perjured testimony to the grand jury, a number of courts have permitted challenges to the indictment. Sometimes, this is called the "misconduct exception" to *Costello*. The indictment may be dismissed only if the perjured testimony is "material" to the finding of probable cause. *United States v. Vallie*, 284 F.3d 917 (8th Cir. 2002). One court described the materiality standard as whether the false declaration "has a tendency to influence, impede, or hamper the grand jury from pursuing its investigation." *United States v. Percell*, 526 F.2d 189, 190 (9th Cir. 1975).

A government attorney offering perjured testimony or false evidence to a grand jury also risks disciplinary sanctions for professional misconduct. Disciplinary Rule 7-102(a)(4) of the ABA Model Code of Professional Responsibility provides that a lawyer shall not "knowingly use perjured testimony or false evidence." Similarly, Rule 3.3(a)(3) of the Model Rules of Professional Conduct provides that a lawyer shall not knowingly "offer evidence that the lawyer knows to be false."

Occasionally it is alleged that the indictment should be dismissed because the grand jury did not consider any legal evidence in making its probable cause determination. While the United States Supreme Court has not ruled directly on this question, it may be helpful to recall Justice Burton's concurring opinion in *Costello*: "It seems to me if it is shown that the grand jury had before it no substantial or rationally persuasive evidence upon which to base its indictment, that indictment should be quashed." 350 U.S. at 364. It may be very difficult for defense counsel to gather support for a motion to dismiss on this ground because of grand jury secrecy.

A federal statute bars evidence obtained through illegal electronic surveillance from being presented to a grand jury. 18 U.S.C. §§ 2510 *et seq.* An indictment based on unlawful wiretapping could be dismissed for the violation.

Prosecutorial misconduct. An indictment may be dismissed because of any of the following various types of prosecutorial misconduct in the grand jury proceedings.

1. *Inflaming grand jury.*

This form of misconduct typically refers to questions or comments by the prosecutor designed to improperly influence the grand jury. Although a grand jury must be unbiased, inflammatory remands rarely result in dismissal of an indictment because of the lack of prejudice to the accused.

2. *Stating personal views.*

Many jurisdictions consider it objectionable for a prosecutor to express a personal opinion on such matters as the sufficiency of the evidence or the credibility of a particular witness. Some jurisdictions disagree with this notion, however, apparently on the basis of the prosecutor's advisory role.

3. *Testifying before the grand jury.*

Based on the ethical norm that lawyers should not act as both advocates and witnesses in the same hearing, many jurisdictions view as improper a prosecutor acting as a witness in a grand jury session. Of course, the prosecutor is often an informal witness when he or she summarizes the available evidence.

4. *Unauthorized presence.*

It is impermissible to allow simultaneous presence and testimony of multiple witnesses. Similarly, persons other than grand jurors may not be present during deliberations and voting. But a violation of secrecy may not result in dismissal because of the harmless error rule.

5. *Rendering improper or inadequate legal advice.*

The prosecutor may be asked to render an opinion as to whether certain conduct constitutes a criminal offense. The prosecutor's inaccurate response may be grounds for dismissal of the indictment.

6. *Conflict of interest.*

Prosecutorial misconduct may occur in a case in which a prosecutor who has previously represented the accused in connection with a related matter is now presenting a matter against that individual before the grand jury.

7. *Use of grand jury for an improper purpose.*

While this category is vague, courts have indicated that it would be improper to utilize a grand jury to gather evidence for a pending civil or criminal proceeding, induce a witness to commit perjury, or harass a witness. *United States v. Apperson*, 441 F.3d 1162 (10th Cir. 2006)(grand jury process is abused when prosecutor uses it for the primary purpose of strengthening government's case on pending indictment or as substitute for discovery). On the other hand, the grand jury may be used to gather evidence for new charges.

8. *Secrecy violations.*

As previously discussed, prosecutors are generally prohibited from disclosing testimony given by grand jury witnesses. When a prosecutor discloses this information prior to issuance of an indictment, it has been suggested that the indictment should be dismissed. Nonetheless, it appears that most courts will not grant such a motion unless the secrecy violation creates a reasonable likelihood of prejudice to the defendant.

9. *Selective prosecution.* A decision to prosecute based on improper grounds such as race, gender, ethnicity, political affiliation, or as retaliation for the exercise of a constitutional right. See Chapter 2.

10. *Unreasonable delay.* The indictment may have been rendered so late that it was in violation of due process or the relevant statute of limitations. See Chapter 13.

For more detailed consideration of prosecutorial misconduct claims, *see* Wayne R. LaFave, Jerold H. Israel, & Nancy J. King, CRIMINAL PROCEDURE, §§ 15.6 & 15.7 (4th ed. 2004) and GRAND JURY LAW AND PRACTICE Ch. 9.

[c]   The Problem of Prejudice

Ordinarily, errors occurring during the grand jury process are challenged after the accused has been indicted, tried, and convicted. Thus, the appellate courts are presented with an unusual situation. A rule of grand jury procedure has been violated but the accused nevertheless received a fair trial and was found guilty beyond a reasonable doubt. The question, then, is whether the grand jury error was so egregious that it should cause the subsequent conviction to be overturned, and, if not, what remedy is appropriate?

In general, "all but most serious grand jury errors are mooted by conviction.," *United States v. Brennick*, 405 F.3d 96 (1st Cir. 2005). The Supreme Court held that an indictment should be dismissed for constitutional reasons by "a defect so fundamental that it causes the grand jury no longer to be a grand jury, or the indictment no longer to be an indictment." *Midland Asphalt Corp., v. United States*, 489 U.S. 802 (1989).

In *United States v. Mechanik*, 475 U.S. 66 (1986), two government agents testified at the same time before a federal grand jury, in violation of Rule 6(d)'s provision that only the "witness being questioned" may be present at a grand jury proceeding. The grand jury indicted and the defendants were convicted in a jury trial of drug and conspiracy offenses. Defense counsel discovered the irregularity after the trial had begun and immediately filed a motion to dismiss the indictment. The trial judge took the motion under advisement, then rejected the motion to dismiss after the jury returned a guilty verdict. The Court of Appeals reversed the conviction, irrespective of the presence or absence of prejudice, because of the Rule 6(d) violation.

The United States Supreme Court then reversed the Court of Appeals, reinstating the conviction. The Supreme Court noted that the reversal of a criminal conviction engenders substantial social costs, including the time, energy, and other resources needed to conduct the second trial, the psychological harm to the victim who must relive the event, and the difficulties caused by the passage of time and its effect on memories and the dispersion of witnesses. Because of these concerns, Rule 52(a) of the Federal Rules of Criminal Procedure provides that errors not affecting substantial rights must be disregarded. This principle also applies to "any error, defect, irregularity, or variance" occurring before a grand jury. When the petit jury found the defendants guilty beyond a reasonable doubt, according to *Mechanik*, this

> rendered harmless any conceivable error in the charging decision that might have flowed from the violation [of Rule 6(d)]. In such a case, the society costs of retrial after a jury verdict of guilty are far too substantial to justify setting aside the verdict simply because of an error in the earlier grand jury proceedings. [*Id.* at 73]

NOTES

1. After *Mechanik*, is there *any* remedy for a violation of grand jury procedures after the accused is convicted by a petit jury? Since the error is unlikely to be discovered until after the criminal trial, doesn't *Mechanik* essentially hold that any mistake is harmless error?

2. *Mechanik* involved an attack on an indictment that was resolved *after* the accused was convicted by a petit jury. The next case addresses some of the issues raised by *Mechanik*, including the proof needed to launch a pre-conviction attack on a grand jury indictment.

BANK OF NOVA SCOTIA v. UNITED STATES
487 U.S. 250 (1988)

JUSTICE KENNEDY delivered the opinion of the Court.

The issue presented is whether a district court may invoke its supervisory power to dismiss an indictment for prosecutorial misconduct in a grand jury investigation, where the misconduct does not prejudice the defendants.

[Defendants were indicted on 27 counts of conspiracy, mail fraud, and tax fraud. All counts were dismissed for various violations of Rule 6 of the Federal Rules of Criminal Procedure.]

. . . [The district court] ruled dismissal was proper under the "totality of the circumstances," including the "numerous violations of Rule 6(d) and (e), Fed. R. Crim. P., violations of 18 U.S.C. §§ 6002 and 6003, violations of the Fifth and Sixth Amendments to the United States Constitution, knowing presentation of misinformation to the grand jury and mistreatment of witnesses." We shall discuss these findings in more detail below.

The District Court determined that "[a]s a result of the conduct of the prosecutors and their entourage of agents, the indicting grand jury was not able to undertake its essential mission" to act independently of the prosecution. In an apparent alternative holding, the District Court also ruled that

> [t]he supervisory authority of the court must be used in circumstances such as those presented in this case to declare with unmistakable intention that such conduct is neither "silly" nor "frivolous" and that it will not be tolerated.

[The Court of Appeals reversed, restoring the 27 count indictment.]

. . . We hold that, as a general matter, a district court may not dismiss an indictment for errors in grand jury proceedings unless such errors prejudiced the defendants.

In the exercise of its supervisory authority, a federal court "may, within limits, formulate procedural rules not specifically required by the Constitution or the Congress." . . . Our previous cases have not addressed explicitly whether this rationale bars exercise of a supervisory authority where, as here, dismissal of the indictment would conflict with the harmless-error inquiry mandated by the Federal Rules of Criminal Procedure.

We now hold that a federal court may not invoke supervisory power to circumvent the harmless-error inquiry prescribed by Federal Rule of Criminal Procedure 52(a). Rule 52(a) provides that "[a]ny error, defect, irregularity or variance which does not affect substantial rights shall be disregarded."

. . . Our conclusion that a district court exceeds its powers in dismissing an indictment for prosecutorial misconduct not prejudicial to the defendant is supported by other decisions of this Court. In *United States v. Mechanik*, 475 U.S. 66 (1986), we held that there is "no reason not to apply [Rule 52(a)] to 'errors, defects, irregularities, or variances' occurring before a grand jury just as we have applied it to such error occurring in the criminal trial itself."

. . . Having concluded that our customary harmless-error inquiry is applicable where, as in the cases before us, a court is asked to dismiss an indictment prior to the conclusion of the trial, we turn to the standard of prejudice that courts should apply in assessing such claims. We adopt for this purpose, at least where dismissal is sought for nonconstitutional error, the standard articulated by Justice O'Connor in her concurring opinion in *United States v. Mechanik*. Under this standard, dismissal of the indictment is appropriate only "if it is established that the violation substantially influenced the grand jury's decision to indict," or if there is "grave doubt" that the decision to indict was free from the substantial influence of such violations.

. . . To be distinguished from the cases before us are a class of cases in which indictments are dismissed, without a particular assessment of the prejudicial impact of the errors in each case, because the errors are deemed fundamental. These cases may be explained as isolated exceptions to the harmless-error rule. We think, however, that an alternative and more clear explanation is that these cases are ones in which the structural protections of the grand jury have been so compromised as to render the proceedings fundamentally unfair, allowing the presumption of prejudice. These cases are exemplified by *Vasquez v. Hillery*, 474 U.S. 254 (1986), where we held that racial discrimination in selection of grand jurors compelled dismissal of the indictment. In addition to involving an error of constitutional magnitude, other remedies were impractical and it could be presumed that a discriminatorily selected grand jury would treat defendants unfairly. We reached a like conclusion in *Ballard v. United States*, 329 U.S. 187 (1946), where women had been excluded from the grand jury. The nature of the violation allowed a presumption that the defendant was prejudiced, and any inquiry into harmless error would have required unguided speculation. Such considerations are not presented here, and we review the alleged errors to assess their influence, if any, on the grand jury's decision to indict in the factual context of the cases before us.

. . . The District Court found that the Government had violated Federal Rule of

Criminal Procedure 6(e) by: (1) disclosing grand jury materials to Internal Revenue Service employees having civil tax enforcement responsibilities; (2) failing to give the court prompt notice of such disclosures; (3) disclosing to potential witnesses the names of targets of the investigation; and (4) instructing two grand jury witnesses, who had represented some of the defendants in a separate investigation of the same tax shelters, that they were not to reveal the substance of their testimony or that they had testified before the grand jury. The court also found that the Government had violated Federal Rule of Criminal Procedure 6(d) in allowing joint appearances by IRS agents before the grand jury for the purpose of reading transcripts to the jurors.

The District Court further concluded that one of the prosecutors improperly argued with an expert witness during a recess of the grand jury after the witness gave testimony adverse to the Government. It also held that the Government had violated the witness immunity statute, 18 U.S.C. §§ 6002, 6003, by the use of "pocket immunity" (immunity granted on representation of the prosecutor rather than by order of a judge), and that the Government caused IRS agents to mischaracterize testimony given in prior proceedings. Furthermore, the District Court found that the Government violated the Fifth Amendment by calling a number of witnesses for the sole purpose of having them assert their privilege against self-incrimination and that it had violated the Sixth Amendment by conducting postindictment interviews of several high-level employees of The Bank of Nova Scotia. Finally, the court concluded that the Government had caused IRS agents to be sworn as agents of the grand jury, thereby elevating their credibility.

As we have noted, no constitutional error occurred during the grand jury proceedings. The Court of Appeals concluded that the District Court's findings of Sixth Amendment postindictment violations were unrelated to the grand jury's independence and decisionmaking process because the alleged violations occurred after the indictment. We agree that it was improper for the District Court to cite such matters in dismissing the indictment. The Court of Appeals also found that no Fifth Amendment violation occurred as a result of the Government's calling seven witnesses to testify despite an avowed intention to invoke their Fifth Amendment privilege. We agree that, in the circumstances of these cases, calling the witnesses was not error. The Government was not required to take at face value the unsworn assertions made by these witnesses outside the grand jury room. Once a witness invoked the privilege on the record, the prosecutors immediately ceased all questioning. Throughout the proceedings, moreover, the prosecution repeated the caution to the grand jury that it was not to draw any adverse inference from a witness' invocation of the Fifth Amendment.

In the cases before us we do not inquire whether the grand jury's independence was infringed. Such an infringement may result in grave doubt as to a violation's effect on the grand jury's decision to indict, but we did not grant certiorari to review this conclusion. We note that the Court of Appeals found that the prosecution's conduct was not "a significant infringement on the grand jury's ability to exercise independent judgment," and we accept that conclusion here. Finally, we note that we are not faced with a history of prosecutorial misconduct, spanning several cases, that is so systematic and pervasive as to raise a substantial and serious question about the fundamental fairness of the process which resulted in the indictment.

We must address, however, whether, despite the grand jury's independence, there was any misconduct by the prosecution that otherwise may have influenced substantially the grand jury's decision to indict, or whether there is grave doubt as to whether the decision to indict was so influenced. Several instances of misconduct found by the District Court — that the prosecutors manipulated the grand jury investigation to gather evidence for use in civil audits; violated the secrecy provisions of Rule 6(e) by publicly identifying the targets and the subject matter of the grand jury investigation; and imposed secrecy obligations in violation of Rule 6(e) upon grand jury witnesses — might be relevant to an allegation of a purpose or intent to abuse the grand jury process. Here, however, it is plain that these alleged breaches could not have affected the charging decision. We have no occasion to consider them further.

We are left to consider only the District Court's findings that the prosecutors: (1) fashioned and administered unauthorized "oaths" to IRS agents in violation of Rule 6(c); (2) caused the same IRS agents to "summarize" evidence falsely and to assert incorrectly that all the evidence summarized by them had been presented previously to the grand jury; (3) deliberately berated and mistreated an expert witness for the defense in the presence of some grand jurors; (4) abused its authority by providing "pocket immunity" to 23 grand jury witnesses; and (5) permitted IRS agents to appear in tandem to present evidence to the grand jury in violation of Rule 6(d). We consider each in turn.

The Government administered oaths to IRS agents, swearing them in as "agents" of the grand jury. Although the administration of such oaths to IRS agents by the Government was unauthorized, there is ample evidence that the jurors understood that the agents were aligned with the prosecutors. At various times a prosecutor referred to the agents as "my agent(s)," and, in discussions with the prosecutors, grand jurors referred to the agents as "your guys" or "your agents." There is nothing in the record to indicate that the oaths administered to the IRS agents caused their reliability or credibility to be elevated, and the effect, if any, on the grand jury's decision to indict was negligible.

The District Court found that, to the prejudice of petitioners, IRS agents gave misleading and inaccurate summaries to the grand jury just prior to the indictment. Because the record does not reveal any prosecutorial misconduct with respect to these summaries, they provide no ground for dismissing the indictment. The District Court's finding that the summaries offered by IRS agents contained evidence that had not been presented to the grand jury in prior testimony boils down to a challenge to the reliability or competence of the evidence presented to the grand jury. We have held that an indictment valid on its face is not subject to such a challenge. To the extent that a challenge is made to the accuracy of the summaries, the mere fact that evidence itself is unreliable is not sufficient to require a dismissal of the indictment. In light of the record, the finding that the prosecutors knew the evidence to be false or misleading, or that the Government caused the agents to testify falsely, is clearly erroneous. Although the Government may have had doubts about the accuracy of certain aspects of the summaries, this is quite different from having knowledge of falsity.

The District Court found that a prosecutor was abusive to an expert defense witness during a recess and in the hearing of some grand jurors. Although the Government concedes that the treatment of the expert tax witness was improper, the witness himself testified that his testimony was unaffected by this misconduct. The prosecutors instructed the grand jury to disregard anything they may have heard in conversations between a prosecutor and a witness, and explained to the grand jury that such conversations should have no influence on its deliberations. In light of these ameliorative measures, there is nothing to indicate that the prosecutor's conduct toward this witness substantially affected the grand jury's evaluation of the testimony or its decision to indict.

The District Court found that the Government granted "pocket immunity" to 23 witnesses during the course of the grand jury proceedings. Without deciding the propriety of granting such immunity to grand jury witnesses, we conclude the conduct did not have a substantial effect on the grand jury's decision to indict, and it does not create grave doubt as to whether it affected the grand jury's decision. Some prosecutors told the grand jury that immunized witnesses retained their Fifth Amendment privilege and could refuse to testify, while other prosecutors stated that the witnesses had no Fifth Amendment privilege, but we fail to see how this could have had a substantial effect on the jury's assessment of the testimony or its decision to indict. The significant point is that the jurors were made aware that these witnesses had made a deal with the Government.

Assuming the Government had threatened to withdraw immunity from a witness in order to manipulate that witness' testimony, this might have given rise to a finding of prejudice. There is no evidence in the record, however, that would support such a finding. The Government told a witness' attorney that if the witness "testified for Mr. Kilpatrick, all bets were off." The attorney, however, ultimately concluded that the prosecution did not mean to imply that immunity would be withdrawn if his client testified for Kilpatrick, but rather that his client would be validly subject to prosecution for perjury. Although the District Court found that the Government's statement was interpreted by the witness to mean that if he testified favorably for Kilpatrick his immunity would be withdrawn, neither Judge Winner nor Judge Kane made a definitive finding that the Government improperly threatened the witness. The witness may have felt threatened by the prosecutor's statement, but his subjective fear cannot be ascribed to governmental misconduct and was, at most, a consideration bearing on the reliability of his testimony.

Finally, the Government permitted two IRS agents to appear before the grand jury at the same time for the purpose of reading transcripts. Although allowing the agents to read to the grand jury in tandem was a violation of Rule 6(d), it was not prejudicial. The agents gave no testimony of their own during the reading of the transcripts. The grand jury was instructed not to ask any questions and the agents were instructed not to answer any questions during the readings. There is no evidence that the agents' reading in tandem enhanced the credibility of the testimony or otherwise allowed the agents to exercise undue influence.

In considering the prejudicial effect of the foregoing instances of alleged misconduct, we note that these incidents occurred as isolated episodes in the course of a 20-month investigation, an investigation involving dozens of witnesses and thousands of documents. In view of this context, those violations that did occur do not, even when considered cumulatively, raise a substantial question, much less a grave doubt, as to whether they had a substantial effect on the grand jury's decision to charge.

Errors of the kind alleged in these cases can be remedied adequately by means other than dismissal. For example, a knowing violation of Rule 6 may be punished as a contempt of court. In addition, the court may direct a prosecutor to show cause why he should not be disciplined and request the bar or the Department of Justice to initiate disciplinary proceedings against him. The court may also chastise the prosecutor in a published opinion. Such remedies allow the court to focus on the culpable individual rather than granting a windfall to the unprejudiced defendant.

We conclude that the District Court had no authority to dismiss the indictment on the basis of prosecutorial misconduct absent a finding that petitioners were prejudiced by such misconduct. The prejudicial inquiry must focus on whether any violations had an effect on the grand jury's decision to indict. If violations did substantially influence this decision, or if there is grave doubt that the decision to indict was free from such substantial influence, the violations cannot be deemed harmless. The record will not support the conclusion that petitioners can meet this standard. The judgment of the Court of Appeals is affirmed.

[The concurring opinion of Justice Scalia is omitted]

Justice Marshall, dissenting.

I cannot concur in the Court's decision to apply harmless-error analysis to violations of Rule 6 of the Federal Rules of Criminal Procedure. I already have outlined my objections to the Court's approach, which converts "Congress' command regarding the proper conduct of grand jury proceedings to a mere form of words, without practical effect." *United States* v. *Mechanik*, 475 U.S. 66, 84 (1986) (MARSHALL, J., dissenting). . . . Given the nature of grand jury proceedings, Rule 6 violations can be deterred and redressed effectively only by a per se rule of dismissal. Today's decision reduces Rule 6 to little more than a code of honor that prosecutors can violate with virtual impunity. I respectfully dissent.

NOTES

1. *Burden of proof.* The Court in *Bank of Nova Scotia* held that the harmless error rule applies to most errors in grand jury proceedings. Who has the burden of proof? Must the defendant prove that there was harm or does the prosecution have to prove there was no harm?

2. *Proof of harm limited by grand jury secrecy.* Recall that grand jury proceedings are usually secret. This means that the defendant will not know who testified or what evidence the grand jury considered. If the burden of proving harm is on the defendant, how will he or she satisfy this?

3. *Substantial effect?* The Court holds that the many errors did not raise a substantial question or even a grave doubt about whether they had a substantial effect on the grand jury's decision. Do you agree? Did the Court have enough information to decide this? Would you have preferred more data?

For an unusual case finding that the *Bank of Nova Scotia* standard was met, see *United States v. Breslin*, 916 F. Supp. 438 (E.D. Pa. 1996) (holding that prosecutorial misconduct warranted dismissal of the indictment without prejudice, thereby allowing the government to present the case "to another grand jury and start with a clean slate").

4. *Remedies other than dismissal.* The Court suggests that there are remedies other than dismissal that are adequate to remedy the errors. These include contempt of court, professional discipline, and public chastisement. Do you agree that these are adequate under the circumstances? Would dismissal be appropriate *in addition*? Would it matter if it were dismissal with or without prejudice?

5. *Presumed prejudice. Bank of Nova Scotia* also indicated that there are some situations where no prejudice need be proven because the error was "fundamental." In such cases prejudice is presumed. Note that the two examples involve errors in the selection of grand jurors. Can you think of other situations where the "fundamental error" approach is appropriate?

F. TIME FOR REFORM?

While commentators continue to question whether the modern grand jury should be retained, the fact remains that it is constitutionally required in felony cases in federal prosecutions and in a significant number of states. Short of abolition efforts through the time-consuming process of amending constitutions, should statutory measures be adopted to revise the grand jury process?

Hyde Amendment. In 1997, Representative Henry Hyde, Chairman of the House Judiciary Committee, sponsored legislation allowing individual and small businesses that were grand jury targets and subject to "bad faith, vexatious or frivolous" federal prosecutions to file motions to recoup their costs in defending against those prosecutions. This law became known as the Hyde Amendment. For background on this law, *see* National Association of Criminal Defense Lawyers, *Federal Grand Jury Reform, Report and Bill of Rights* (May 2000), available at www.nacdl.org.

Grand Jury Bill of Rights. The National Association of Criminal Defense Lawyers, echoing an American Bar Association proposal, has proffered a "Grand Jury Bill of Rights" which argues that the following rules and procedures should be followed by federal prosecutors when seeking indictments:

(1) A grand jury witness that has not received immunity should have the right to be accompanied by counsel during his or her appearance.

(2) Prosecutors should not intentionally withhold clearly exculpatory information from a grand jury.

(3) Prosecutors should not present evidence to the grand jury that they know to be inadmissible at trial because a trial court ruled on its admissibility.

(4) A grand jury target or subject should have the right to testify before the grand jury. A grand jury target should also be permitted to provide written information to the grand jury foreperson for consideration by the grand jury.

(5) Grand jury witnesses should be allowed to receive a transcript of their own testimony.

(6) The grand jury should not name a person in an indictment as an unindicted co-conspirator.

(7) All non-immunized subjects or targets called before a grand jury should receive *Miranda* warnings.

(8) Grand jury subpoenas ordinarily should be issued at least 72 hours before the scheduled appearance.

(9) Grand jurors should receive meaningful instructions concerning the charges they are to consider.

(10) Prosecutors should not call before a grand jury any subject or target who has stated that he or she intends to invoke the constitutional privilege against self-incrimination.

With which recommendations do you agree? Disagree? Assuming that it would be constitutional to do so, should prosecutors have the option to charge either by indictment or by information?

Grand jury's own counsel. Another suggestion is that the prosecutor should be replaced as the grand jury's lawyer by counsel that represents the grand jury rather than the prosecution. This lawyer would be a buffer between the grand jury and the prosecution, advise the grand jury on the law, and provide them with information, such as evidence presented by the prosecutor was seized illegally and could not be used at trial. Susan W. Brenner, *The Voice of the Community: A Case for Grand Jury Independence*, 3 Va. J. Soc. Pol'y & L. 67 (1995).

Chapter 8
JOINDER AND SEVERANCE

A. INTRODUCTION

Questions of joinder and severance may arise when a person commits more than one crime or when two or more people join together to engage in criminal activity. For example, assume that A and B conspire together and rob the Superior Convenient Mart. Assume further that A, acting alone and without the knowledge of B, also robbed the Minit Save Convenient Market the following week. B was not involved in any way in the second heist.

The prosecutor will have to decide several questions. The first is whether A and B can be indicted or tried together or separately. The second is whether A can be indicted or tried at the same time for the Superior robbery and the Minit Save robbery, or whether the two robberies will have to be handled separately. Finally, can both defendants and both robberies be joined in one indictment or trial, or will there have to be two or even three proceedings?

American criminal procedure analyzes these issues in terms of the closely related concepts of *joinder* and *severance*. *Joinder* is the process of joining two people or crimes together into one indictment or trial. *Severance* is the process of undoing a joinder. After a severance, the crimes or people would be tried separately.

Returning to the crimes of A and B, there are a number of possibilities. If there were total trial joinder (which is unlikely) in the above hypothetical, there would be one trial: A and B would be tried for the robbery of the Superior Mart and, during that same trial, A would also be tried for the robbery of the Minit Save Market. Another possibility is that A and B would be tried together for the robbery of the Superior Mart and A would be tried at another proceeding for the crime at the Minit Save. Still another possible arrangement is that A would face two trials: one for the robbery of each convenience store; B would be tried alone at a third proceeding for the theft at the Superior Mart.

B. POLICIES

Joinder and severance questions initially involve two often conflicting policies: efficiency and fairness. In an effort to conserve scarce human and physical resources, judges and prosecutors (and sometimes defense counsel) often prefer to join crimes and defendants together and have one trial. For example, in the above hypothetical, in order to resolve the Superior Mart case, it would be more efficient to have a trial in which A and B were co-defendants, as opposed to having two trials, one for each defendant. At the joint trial, everyone would save time.

The judge would have to preside over only one proceeding. The prosecutor would have to appear at only one trial. If one lawyer represents both A and B (which is unlikely because of a substantial possibility of a conflict of interest), it would save professional time if the lawyer had to participate in only one trial. Since the prosecution's witnesses are probably the same in the cases against both A and B, these witnesses and some defense witnesses who would testify for both defendants would welcome the opportunity to testify only once. Other savings also could be realized. The courtroom, court clerks, bailiffs, and the like could be used for other proceedings if only one trial were held for A and B. The obvious efficiencies inherent in virtually all joint trials have led courts to favor joinder. Some courts have even stated that there is a preference in having joint trials for persons who were jointly indicted. *See, e.g., United States v. Davis*, 397 F.3d 173 (3d Cir. 2005).

Even though joinder may be efficient in many cases, it does not necessarily ensure a fair trial. Sometimes joinder may actually promote unfairness. In *Drew v. United States*, 331 F.2d 85, 88 (D.C. Cir. 1964), the court observed:

> The justification for a liberal rule on joinder of offenses appears to be the economy of a single trial. The argument against joinder is that the defendant may be prejudiced for one or more of the following reasons: (1) he may become embarrassed or confounded in presenting separate defenses; (2) the jury may use the evidence of one of the crimes charged to infer a criminal disposition on the part of the defendant from which is found his guilt of the other crime or crimes charged; or (3) the jury may cumulate the evidence of the various crimes charged and find guilt when, if considered separately, it would not so find. A less tangible, but perhaps equally persuasive, element of prejudice may reside in a latent feeling of hostility engendered by the charging of several crimes as distinct from only one. Thus, in any given case the court must weigh prejudice to the defendant caused by the joinder against the obviously important considerations of economy and expedition in judicial administration.

C. EFFECTS OF JOINDER

Social scientists have studied the issue of joinder and severance. The results of a recent study are summarized in Andrew D. Leipold, *How the Pretrial Process Contributes to Wrongful Convictions*, 42 AM. CRIM. L. REV. 1123 (2005). This study looked at various aspects of the pre-trial process and analyzed their impact on convictions and how these processes can hamper a defense. The study analyzed the trials of over 20,000 federal defendants from 1997 through 2001. The conviction rates from these trials show a trend toward a higher rate of conviction when multiple counts or defendants are joined. Defendants who were tried alone on a single count had a 66% conviction rate, but when they were tried on more than one count, "the defendant was more likely to be convicted of something . . . [and] also more likely to be convicted of the most serious charge against them."

Defendants tried on two charges were convicted of all counts in 72% of the cases, and the most serious count in 82%. When the trial was of three or more charges, defendants were convicted of all counts in 78% of the trials, and of the most serious count in 88%. The same trend was found when multiple defendants were tried together.

Defendants who stood trial alone and went to judgment on the most serious charge had a conviction rate of 73%, which increased to 83% when the defendant was joined with at least one other defendant. When both defendants and offenses were joined, a defendant charged with multiple counts has a higher conviction rate than one charged with a single count (85% to 77%), though the numbers are similar for defendants charged with multiple counts regardless of whether they are were joined with other defendants. The study points out, however, that these numbers do not prove that joinder of counts or defendants causes unjust treatment of defendants, even though the numbers suggest a "prejudicial overlay."

This study was further analyzed and expanded in Andrew D. Leipold and Hossein A. Abbasi, *The Impact of Joinder and Severance on Federal Criminal Cases: An Empirical Study*, 59 VAND. L. REV. 349 (2006).

The results of a prior study are summarized in James Farrin, Note, *Rethinking Criminal Joinder: An Analysis of the Empirical Research and Its Implications for Justice*, 52 LAW & CONTEMP. PROBS. 325 (1989). The note reports that virtually all of the studies concerning joinder (at least to the date of the note) focus on joinder of offenses rather than joinder of offenders. One common research method is to have mock jurors see a videotape or read a transcript of evidence in a criminal case. The jurors then decide whether the defendant(s) is (are) guilty or not guilty, and answer questions about their views of the case and the defendant(s). According to this article, when offenses are joined in one trial, many (though not all) studies show that jurors get confused about the facts of each offense, but, surprisingly, most studies also show that the confusion did not produce biased verdicts. There is, however, substantial indication that multiple charges lead a jury to believe that the defendant has a criminal personality. In general, according to this report, "the studies are unanimous in finding that defendants do face a greater likelihood of conviction if offenses are tried jointly rather than separately. Furthermore, the effect of joinder increases with the number of offenses charged." Looking at the scant data available on joinder of defendants, the report noted that social psychological research has found "a strong tendency for people to attribute similarity to all group members when people are presented as a group." Combining these data with those available on joinder of offenses, the author suggests that it is likely that "jurors are biased against joined defendants in a trial under Rule 8(b), and that the existing curative conditions are insufficient to cure the prejudice."

D. STRATEGIC CONSIDERATIONS

Counsel faced with the possibility of joint trials must carefully weigh the wisdom of requesting a severance. As the above studies show, defense counsel may opt to move for a severance because a joinder could increase the chance of a conviction. Sometimes evidence admissible against X in a joint trial of X and Y would be inadmissible in a separate trial against Y. Defense counsel for Y may move for a severance in order to keep the jury in Y's case from hearing this damaging proof. For example, assume that Mary and Bill extort money from a politician in exchange for a promise to keep certain information confidential. Bill is arrested and confesses, implicating himself and Mary. At the joint trial of Mary and Bill, assume that Bill's confession was made in conformity with constitutional guarantees and is admissible against Bill. It is possible, however, that Bill's confession may be inadmissible against Mary. Since the jury will hear Bill's confession and may use it against Bill but should not consider it as evidence against Mary, Mary's defense counsel may request a severance in order to ensure that the jury is not polluted by hearing the confession implicating Mary. Counsel may believe that jury instructions — requiring the jury to consider the confession only against Bill — will be inadequate to protect Mary from being harmed by the damaging statement. The prosecution may also seek a severance so that Bill's confession may be used against only Bill. (The trial court may have ruled that the confession is inadmissible in a joint trial and could only be used if Bill were tried alone.)

A severance motion may have other beneficial effects as well. A severance may permit the defendant to testify in one case and remain silent in the other. It may also avoid presenting seemingly inconsistent defenses to the same jury. Assume a defendant is charged with two robberies. She maintains she had an alibi for the first and was too drunk to formulate the intent for the second. While a jury presented with only one of these defenses may be persuaded to accept the defense, a jury presented with both may find neither persuasive or even plausible.

In addition, since a severance motion requires the prosecution to devote time to answer the motion and, if the motion is granted, additional resources commanded by two or more trials, it is possible that a severance motion could induce a prosecutor to offer the defendant a better deal during plea bargaining negotiations. Conversely, the government's initial decision to join offenses or offenders may have been prompted by a prosecutor's desire to obtain an advantage during plea bargaining negotiations.

Another possible defense advantage in seeking a severance is that the motion process may provide discovery. The judge at the pretrial hearing on the severance motion may require the state to disclose some of its trial proof in order to establish the prerequisites for joinder. For example, the prosecutor may have to inform the court of the government's proof of a "common scheme or plan," as required by Rule 8(a) for the joinder of offenses. This helpful defense information may have been unavailable through normal discovery processes.

On the other hand, defense counsel may prefer that two crimes or defendants be tried at the same time. If two defendants are tried together and represented by different counsel (or, rarely, even the same counsel), the combined resources of the clients may permit additional investigators and experts to be hired to assist both defendants. If two lawyers are involved, they can split up legal research and drafting tasks where the clients are pursuing compatible theories.

Joinder of two or more offenses may also be advantageous to the defense, especially if a guilty plea is likely. A single judge will handle the consolidated cases and may be more likely to give concurrent sentences on all charges.

PROBLEM 8-1. TACTICAL CHOICES

Can you think of any other tactical reasons why defense counsel would want a severance? Are there cases where the prosecutor would want a severance, despite the additional time and resources that separate proceedings will cost?

NOTES

1. *Partial waiver of jury trial.* An unusual situation occurs when the defendant wants a jury trial for some charges and a bench trial for others. Is consolidation appropriate? There are several possibilities. A court might permit a consolidation in this scenario. The judge would resolve the bench-tried issues and the jury handles the others, or the judge would order a jury trial on all the issues. Another approach is for the court to disapprove of this procedure and grant a severance of the jury and bench cases. To prevent defense counsel from manipulating the severance rules by waiving a jury trial on some issues, a number of locales permit this severance only with the prosecutor's approval.

2. *Dual juries.* Another option, used in a small number of cases, is for the trial court to seat *two* juries, one for each defendant. The jury for defendant A is excluded from the courtroom during testimony not admissible against this defendant, but admissible against defendant B. Appellate courts have tolerated this device. *See, e.g., United States v. Sidman*, 470 F.2d 1158 (9th Cir. 1972); *State v. Avery*, 571 N.W.2d 907 (Wis. App. 1997).

The many practical problems with this procedure were noted in the Oklahoma City bombing case, *United States v. McVeigh*, 169 F.R.D. 362, 371 (D. Colo. 1996), where the trial court ordered severance of the defendants' trials because the government intended to use several statements of one of the defendants against him but not anyone else. The court rejected all possible mechanisms for remedying the problem, finding that the difficulty of administering the solutions would counteract any efficiency achieved by a joint trial. With respect to the possibility of seating two juries, Judge Matsch observed:

> The possibility of a joint trial with separate juries has been considered. Conceptually, that is a convenient solution. Logistically, it is impracticable. If 6 alternate jurors were seated with each jury, the courtroom would have to accommodate 36 jurors for most of the trial. Moreover, the use of two juries would . . . not relieve the prejudice to each of the defendants from their antagonistic defenses requiring different tactics and strategies during the trial proceedings. It is reasonable to anticipate a need for extensive hearings outside the presence of the jury to consider conflicting defense objections and requests for cautionary instructions during the presentation of the evidence, including arguments about whether both juries can hear particular testimony or see certain exhibits. The resulting delays would interrupt the rhythm and flow of the proceedings and risk unforeseeable adverse consequences.

E. JOINDER AND SEVERANCE RULES

Both state and federal rules of criminal procedure deal with joinder and severance.

[1] Federal

The federal rules are as follows:

FEDERAL RULES OF CRIMINAL PROCEDURE

Rule 8. Joinder of Offenses or Defendants

(a) Joinder of Offenses. The indictment or information may charge a defendant in separate counts with 2 or more offenses if the offenses charged — whether felonies or misdemeanors or both — are of the same or similar character, or are based on the same act or transaction, or are connected with or constitute parts of a common scheme or plan.

(b) Joinder of Defendants. The indictment or information may charge 2 or more defendants if they are alleged to have participated in the same act or transaction, or in the same series of acts or transactions, constituting an offense or offenses. The defendants may be charged in one or more counts together or separately. All defendants need not be charged in each count.

Rule 13. *Joint Trial of Separate Cases*

The court may order that separate cases be tried together as though brought in a single indictment or information if all offenses and all defendants could have been joined in a single indictment or information.

Rule 14. *Relief from Prejudicial Joinder*

(a) Relief. If the joinder of offenses or defendants in an indictment, an information, or a consolidation for trial appears to prejudice a defendant or the government, the court may order separate trials of counts, sever the defendants' trials, or provide any other relief that justice requires.

(b) Defendant's Statements. Before ruling on a defendant's motion to sever, the court may order an attorney for the government to deliver to the court for in camera inspection any defendant's statement that the government intends to use as evidence.

[a] In General

The above three rules should be read and applied together. In general terms, Rule 8 details when offenses (Rule 8(a)) and offenders (Rule 8(b)) may be joined in an indictment or information. Although Rule 13 describes when offenses and offenders may be tried at the same time, it contains no separate standard for either. Rather, Rule 13 indicates that crimes or defendants may be *tried* together if, under Rule 8, they could have been *indicted* together. If offenses or offenders are properly joined under Rules 8 or 13, the trial court has the discretion under Rule 14 to grant a severance if joinder would cause prejudice to either the defendant or the government.

Note that in some situations *both* 8(a)(joinder of crimes) and 8(b)(joinder of defendants) could apply. This could occur when A and B work together to carry out a series of bank robberies or drug transactions. Which rule is to assess joinder? The answer is 8(b), not 8(a). The two are deemed mutually exclusive. If more than one defendant is to be indicted or tried, Rule 8(b) provides the standards for joinder.

[b] Joinder of Offenses

Rule 8(a) covers joinder of offenses and does not limit the number of crimes that may be joined. Looking more carefully at Rule 8, it is clear that the standard for joinder of offenses differs from that for joinder of defendants. Joinder of offenses is possible if any of three criteria is satisfied. First, Rule 8(a) permits joinder if the crimes are of the *same or similar character*. This means that a defendant could be indicted in a single indictment for two robberies or several drug sales. Second, joinder of offenses is possible if the crimes were based on the *same act or transaction*. Third, joinder is permissible if the crimes were *connected with or constitute parts of a common scheme or plan.* The third approach would permit joinder of an auto theft, robbery, and homicide that were part of a grand scheme to steal a car to use in robbing a bank, during which robbery a homicide occurred. In most situations, joinder requires the crimes to have been committed in the same jurisdiction.

UNITED STATES v. JAWARA
462 F.3d 1173 (9th Cir. 2006)

[In December 2000, Haji Jawara executed an INS application for asylum in which he claimed to be a native of Sierra Leone. Three years later . . . it was discovered that Haji Jawara was a second name used by Mohamed Jawara, and that in 1999 Mohamed Jawara had submitted applications for a visa and a social security number in which he claimed Gambia as his birthplace. The following year, Jawara approached a friend for help in finding a citizen to marry an acquaintance for immigration purposes, not knowing that his friend was a paid informant working with federal law enforcement authorities. In June 2004, the informant met Jawara and they discussed the mechanics of a potential sham marriage. Some months later, the informant had another meeting with Jawara at which Jawara sought his help in finding a wife for himself. Both meetings were recorded.

A grand jury indicted Jawara on one count of fraud related to immigration documents and one count of conspiracy to commit marriage fraud. . . . A forensic document examiner testified [at trial] that Jawara's Sierra Leone documents were counterfeit. The informant testified that . . . he and Jawara had spoken about document fraud for immigration purposes. The meeting recordings were played for the jury.

At trial, Jawara testified that his real name was Haji, he was born in Sierra Leone, and Mohamed Jawara was the name of his Gambian cousin whose passport he borrowed to enter the United States. He admitted using Mohamed Jawara's passport and name to obtain various identity cards in the United States. Jawara acknowledged several falsehoods in his asylum application, but maintained that he was unaware of the falsehoods at the time the application was filed because aside from providing copies of his Sierra Leone documents, he had no role in preparing the application and did not read it before signing. Jawara maintained that the informant initiated the fraudulent marriage idea.]

McKeown, Circuit Judge:

Mohamed Jawara . . . appeals from his convictions for document fraud related to his personal asylum application and conspiracy to commit marriage fraud to avoid the immigration laws. . . . Jawara argues the two counts were improperly joined under Rule 8(a). Alternatively, he argues that even if the initial joinder was proper, the district court should have severed the counts under Rule 14 because the joinder was prejudicial.

Rule 8(a) provides for joinder of offenses against a single defendant in the indictment if one of three conditions is satisfied. The offenses charged must be: (1) "of the same or similar character;" (2) "based on the same act or transaction;" or (3) "connected with or constitut[ing] parts of a common scheme or plan." . . .

Rule 14 permits the district court to "order separate trials of counts" at its discretion "[i]f the joinder of offenses . . . in an indictment . . . appears to prejudice a defendant." . . . Thus, even if joinder is permissible under Rule 8, a party who feels prejudiced by joinder may move to sever pursuant to [Rule] 14.

We take the view that "[b]ecause Rule 8 is concerned with the propriety of joining offenses in the indictment, the validity of the joinder is determined solely by the allegations in the indictment." *United States v. Terry*, 911 F.2d 272, 276 (9th Cir. 1990) . . . .

Because Rule 14 is available as a remedy for prejudice that may develop during the trial, Rule 8 has been broadly construed in favor of initial joinder . . . . Nonetheless, the joinder decision warrants scrutiny, and Rule 14 should not be viewed as a backstop or substitute for the initial analysis required under Rule 8(a). At least one of Rule 8(a)'s three conditions must be satisfied for proper joinder, and those conditions, although phrased in general terms, are not infinitely elastic. . . . In Jawara's case, the government invokes two of the three bases for joinder: that the counts formed part of a "common scheme or plan" to engage in immigration fraud, and that the counts were of a "similar character."

We have not specifically defined the requisite nexus for a "common scheme or plan" . . . Courts generally permit joinder under this test where the counts grow out of related transactions. Stated another way, we ask whether "[c]ommission of one of the offenses either depended upon or necessarily led to the commission of the other; proof of the one act either constituted or depended upon proof of the other." *United States v. Halper*, 590 F.2d 422, 429 (2d Cir. 1978) . . . .

Restricting our inquiry to the allegations in the . . . indictment, nothing suggests such a nexus between the two counts. The document fraud count describes acts — knowingly making false statements on an asylum application — that were completed as of December 23, 2000. The marriage fraud conspiracy count describes very different acts — the two meetings between Jawara and a "cooperating witness . . . " — that occurred several years later, on June 24, 2004 and November 13, 2004. The document fraud charge makes no reference to the "cooperating witness" that is central to the marriage fraud charge, and the marriage fraud charge makes no reference to the asylum application that is central to the document fraud charge. Aside from the subject matter of immigration, the . . . indictment does not offer a discernible link between the two offenses or suggest any overlapping evidence. No plan or common scheme links the charges nor can any commonality be inferred from the indictment.

. . . Here, there is no direct connection between the acts other than Jawara's participation in both events. For example, the false statements were not made to bolster or help conceal the marriage fraud conspiracy, nor can it be said that the marriage fraud conspiracy flowed from the document fraud crime. . . . [T]he alleged acts underlying the two offenses had no temporal connection and were separated by several years.

The more difficult question is the government's alternate basis for joinder — that the offenses are of a "similar character" because they relate to immigration fraud. . . .

[We consider the] immediate question: does the fact that the two offenses relate to immigration fraud make them of a "similar character" for joinder purposes? . . .

We consider it appropriate to consider factors such as the elements of the statutory offenses, the temporal proximity of the acts, the likelihood and extent of evidentiary overlap, the physical location of the acts, the modus operandi of the crimes, and the identity of the victims in assessing whether an indictment meets the "same or similar character" prong of Rule 8(a). The weight given to a particular factor will depend on the specific context of the case and the allegations in the indictment. But the bottom line is that the similar character of the joined offenses should be ascertainable — either readily apparent or reasonably inferred — from the face of the indictment. Courts should not have to engage in inferential gymnastics or resort to implausible levels of abstraction to divine similarity. Thus, where the government seeks joinder of counts on the basis of "same or similar character," it crafts a barebones indictment at its own risk.

Applying this inquiry to the indictment here, it is apparent that the two counts are not of the "same or similar character." The indictment alleges two different statutory violations requiring proof of different elements. The underlying acts alleged in the indictment are separated by three-and-a-half years . . . . The lack of any temporal connection is all the more significant because the counts do not stem from common events. As for potential evidentiary overlap . . . the cooperating witness whose centrality to the marriage fraud charge is obvious from the indictment, is notably absent from the document fraud charge; nor is any other evidentiary link ascertainable from the indictment. The indictment evinces no similar mode of operation with respect to the two crimes — lying about being from Sierra Leone on an asylum application is vastly different from facilitating or procuring meetings with prospective marriage candidates. The counts do not involve related geographic locations or related victims of the fraud. Ultimately, the only similarity discernible from the indictment is that both counts involve immigration. Such a vague thematic connection cannot, in and of itself, justify joinder.

The immigration document fraud charge is, in essence, a perjury claim related to Jawara's national origin. The other charge stems from an arrangement to facilitate sham marriages. The proof is in the framing. We interpret "similar" to mean something beyond facial similarity of subject matter. Looking at the allegations in the indictment, including any reasonable inferences of the connections and similarities that maybe drawn about these two counts, we hold that the counts do not qualify as "same or similar" under Rule 8.

According to the Supreme Court, our inquiry does not end here. "A violation of Rule 8 'requires reversal only if the misjoinder results in actual prejudice because it had a substantial and injurious effect or influence in determining the jury's verdict.'" *Terry*, 911 F.2d at 277 (quoting *United States v. Lane*, 474 U.S. 438, 449 (1986)). This standard . . . is less exacting than Rule 14's "manifest prejudice" standard.

In *Lane*, the Supreme Court considered a variety of factors in resolving that misjoinder under Rule 8 did not have a "substantial and injurious" effect on the jury's verdict, including the "overwhelming evidence of guilt shown," the provision of a "proper limiting instruction . . . admonish[ing] the jury to consider each count and defendant separately," and the likelihood that evidence admitted on the misjoined count would have been admissible in a separate trial as evidence of intent . . . . The Court also refused to "necessarily assume that the jury misunderstood or disobeyed" the district court's limiting instruction, and noted that the evidence as to one count "was distinct and easily segregated from evidence" relating to the other counts.

After carefully reviewing the trial record as a whole, we are comfortable in our analysis that misjoinder did not have a "substantial and injurious" effect on the verdict. A number of factors support this conclusion. We begin with the fact that the district court instructed the jury to treat the charges separately . . . . In addition, the evidence of guilt was overwhelming as to both counts. . . . Given the strength of the individual cases, we do not confront a situation where prejudice might stem from a disparity of evidence — i.e., a weak case joined with a strong case.

Finally, for many of the same reasons that we determined the charges are not similar — the differences in applicable statute, modes of operation, evidence, and time frame — the jury likewise would have had no difficulty distinguishing between the charges and the evidence. . . . The issues in this four-day trial were relatively simple, and the evidence central to the document fraud count — the asylum application, the Sierra Leonean identity documents . . . — was distinct and easily segregated from evidence central to the marriage fraud count — the recordings and [witness] testimony.

In claiming prejudice as a result of the joinder, Jawara offers the general assertion that "evidence of alleged material misstatements in an asylum application would not have been admissible against [him] in a separate trial on the charge of conspiracy to commit marriage fraud, and vice versa." We have observed that one of the ways that joinder of offenses may prejudice a defendant is that the jury may use the evidence of one of the crimes charged to infer a criminal disposition on the part of the defendant from which is found his guilt of the other crime or crimes charged. Jawara does not point to any specific "inadmissible" evidence in support of this assertion. Even if some of the evidence would not have been cross-admissible in separate trials, it is likely that the jury was able to "compartmentalize the evidence" in light of the other factors we have described.

In the absence of prejudice, reversal is not required. Since Jawara has not established that he was prejudiced by the violation of Rule 8, he cannot satisfy the burden of demonstrating "manifest prejudice" under Rule 14. . . .

REINHARDT, CIRCUIT JUDGE, dissenting from the judgment:

[Judge Reinhardt dissented from the majority on the issue of harmless error in the misjoinder. He found that the evidence with respect to falsifying immigration documents was not overwhelming and that the critical issue with respect to this charge was Jawara's credibility — if the jury believed Jawara's testimony, it would have acquitted him of that charge.]

In the vast majority of cases, and especially in cases in which a defendant's credibility is the crucial issue, the most prejudicial evidence the prosecution can present — perhaps aside from a confession — is testimony establishing that the defendant has committed other serious crimes and is a bad person generally. Evidence of other crimes is particularly damning when the other crimes, as in this case, are of the same general type (here, immigration offenses) as the offense with which the defendant is charged. . . .

Prejudice can arise even more readily than in the average case when there is misjoinder of a crime that would be particularly disturbing to the average juror. Conspiring to violate the immigration laws by aiding a number of aliens to remain in the country unlawfully and obtain permanent resident status would be highly offensive to many jurors these days. . . . [T]he jury likely was influenced, in determining whether Jawara was guilty of submitting his own fraudulent immigration document, by its conclusion that he had in fact conspired to commit immigration fraud to aid others over an extended period of time. . . .

[Furthermore, by] hearing far stronger evidence on the conspiracy charge than the document fraud charge, the jury may have experienced the human tendency to draw a conclusion which is impermissible in the law: because he did it before, he must have done it again.

Although the majority relies heavily on its technical arguments that the district court's error was mitigated by the instruction that the jury consider the counts separately . . . and that the jury could compartmentalize the evidence as to each charge, these factors, while not irrelevant, are hardly sufficient to overcome the overwhelming actual prejudice created in this case by joinder with the conspiracy charge.

For these reasons, I would find the improper joinder prejudicial, at least with respect to the document fraud charge.

NOTES

1. *Applying Rule 8(a).* An application of Rule 8(a) often requires a detailed look at the facts of a case, meaning that appellate precedents are of limited value.

2. *Same or similar character.* Rule 8(a) permits joinder of crimes that are of the same or similar character. Many relevant factors were listed in *Jawara*. Because of the possibility that crimes of the same or similar character may actually be unrelated to one another and proof of them will involve totally different witnesses, severance is more readily ordered under Rule 14's generic authority to sever crimes because of the potential prejudice of joinder and the reduced administrative efficiencies in a joint trial.

3. *Same act or transaction.* Rule 8(a) also permits joinder of crimes that "are based on the same act or transaction." A fact-specific inquiry is necessary. Some courts ask whether the offenses come from the same sequence of events. Ordinarily this means that the crimes will have some common relationship that is described in the indictment.

4. *Connected with or constitute parts of a common scheme or plan.* The last joinder alternative under Rule 8(a) is for crimes connected with or part of a common scheme or plan. Often the commonality is established by proof of a common purpose of that the offenses shared parties, time, and location. *See, e.g., United States v. Dominguez,* 226 F.3d 1235 (11th Cir. 2000)(filing fraudulent mortgage application, designed to hide drug proceeds, properly joined with drug trafficking charges); *United States v. Nettles,* 476 F.3d 508 (7th Cir. 2007)(upholding joinder of counterfeiting and plan to blow up a federal building since former done to obtain money for latter). Examples include a joinder of a bank robbery and firearms charge involving a robbery committed with a pistol. On the other hand, joinder should not have been permitted in a case involving harboring aliens and a firearms offense since the firearm was not used in connection with the harboring aliens offense.

5. The court in *Jawara* found that the document fraud crime was unrelated to the marriage conspiracy count. Yet in both instances Jawara was attempting to procure legal status to stay in the U.S. (applying for first a visa, then asylum, then meeting with the informant to acquire a wife for himself for immigration purposes). Could these instances of conduct be considered a "common scheme or plan" of immigration fraud to obtain legal status for himself in the U.S.? What about these acts being of a "similar character" for the same reason?

6. The majority and dissent disagree on whether Jawara was prejudiced by the joinder. Was the majority or the dissent correct in its analysis? Was it probable that the jury was able to keep the two charges and evidence separate during deliberations? Would a jury find Jawara's attempted marriage fraud "particularly disturbing" or "highly offensive" as the dissent claims? Would Jawara have been convicted of both counts if there had been separate trials?

7. In *United States v. Terry,* 911 F.2d 272 (9th Cir. 1990), the court indicated that persons seeking a severance under Rules 8 and 14 must engage in different motion practices. The Motion for Relief under Rule 8 need not be renewed at the end of the trial, but a Motion for Severance under Rule 14 must be renewed or it is waived. The court reasoned:

> The rationale behind the renewal requirement in the Rule 14 context is inapplicable to Rule 8. A Rule 14 motion must be renewed in order to allow the trial court to assess whether the joinder was prejudicial and to prevent a defendant from deliberately failing to make a meritorious motion and waiting to see what verdict the jury returns.

> A Rule 8 motion, in contrast to Rule 14, disputes the propriety of joining charges in the indictment. Rather than being decided at the discretion of the lower court judge it permits joinder only under certain specific circumstances- . . . . Because the propriety of a Rule 8 joinder is determined solely by the initial allegations of the indictment, there is no need to assess what actually happened in the trial. . . . [I]t is unnecessary to renew a Rule 8 misjoinder objection to preserve it for appeal . . . .

Do you agree with the court's reasoning for this distinction?

8. *Focus on indictment.* The *Jawara* opinion, following a common approach, holds that the trial court is to assess the propriety of a misjoinder by looking "solely" to the allegations in the indictment. This means that a knowledgeable prosecutor, who drafts an indictment, should be able to include the necessary facts to make joinder of crimes or defendants very likely. If you were the prosecutor drafting the indictment in the *Jawara* case, what would you include to maximize the chances that a joinder would be permitted?

9. *Effect of acquittal.* If a jury acquits a defendant of one of several crimes joined under Rule 8(a), it does not mean that joinder was improper or that the convictions on the remaining joined offenses should be reversed for prejudice. Rather than assume the convictions were the product of prejudice, appellate courts often reason the acquittal proves the opposite — the jury was able to consider each crime on its own merits.

PROBLEM 8-2. A THIEF IS A THIEF IS A THIEF

Kerry was arrested for two crimes: robbery (defined as theft by use of force) of a convenience food market and shoplifting from a department store. Because of a heavy trial docket caused by inadequate numbers of lawyers in the district attorney's office, the prosecutor would like to join the two offenses in a single indictment and trial. Under Rule 8(a), are the two crimes of the same or similar character? What facts should the prosecutor seek to discover in order to prove that they satisfied the "connected together" and "common scheme or plan" requirement of Rule 8(a)?

[c]   Joinder of Defendants

Joinder of defendants, governed by Rule 8(b), is similar to but more restrictive than the provisions in Rule 8(a) for joinder of offenses. Joinder of defendants is permissible only if they participated in the *same act or transaction or series of acts or transactions constituting the crime(s)*. Thus, X and Y could not be joined together in the same indictment simply because they both robbed the Safelock Bank. There must be some connection between the offenders. Under Rule 8(b), X and Y could be included in the same indictment only if they both participated in the same robbery. In other words, if A and B *together* carried out the Safelock Bank job, they could be indicted together. If X and Y conspired to rob the Safelock Bank, a joint indictment and trial under Rule 8(b) would be likely for both the conspiracy and substantive offenses stemming from the conspiracy. But if each did an independent crime without the participation of the other, then a joint indictment would not be permissible under Rule 8(b). Each would have to be indicted in a separate indictment and tried in a separate trial.

Note that the necessary connection virtually always involves a conspiracy, though a conspiracy count is not needed for joinder of defendants. The key is that the indictment allege that all the defendants participated together in the criminal enterprise.

UNITED STATES v. SATTERFIELD
548 F.2d 1341 (9th Cir. 1977)

Anthony M. Kennedy, Circuit Judge:

In this case we reverse a robbery conviction, for the appellant was improperly joined with a codefendant for trial.

On October 9, 1974 a ten-count indictment was returned against appellant Satterfield and one Harvey Willard Merriweather. The charges pertained to five Oregon bank robberies committed in the greater Portland area during the summer of 1974. Merriweather and Satterfield were joined in a single indictment charging that Merriweather alone had perpetrated the first, second, and fifth robberies, and that Merriweather and appellant Satterfield together had committed the third and the fourth.

It was never alleged that Satterfield was involved in the first, second, and fifth robberies, whether as a participant in a common plan or in any other manner. . . . A jury found both defendants guilty as charged.

. . . At various stages of the proceedings below, Satterfield timely moved for a separate trial on the ground that under Fed. R. Crim. P. 8(b), he had been improperly joined in the indictment. He contends that the trial court erred in refusing to grant his motions. We agree.

. . . Rule 8(a) applies only to joinder of offenses against a single defendant. Where more than one defendant is named in an indictment, the provisions of rule 8(b) control. Nevertheless, in evaluating an allegation of misjoinder of persons under rule 8(b), the controlling standards for such joinder are best understood by contrasting them with the standards for joinder of offenses in a single defendant trial under rule 8(a). While rule 8(a) permits joinder against one defendant of offenses "of the same or similar character," even where those offenses arise out of wholly separate, unconnected transactions, rule 8(b) treats joinder of multiple defendants differently. In *United States v. Roselli*, 432 F.2d 879, 898 (9th Cir. 1970), we described the operation of the rule as follows:

> Under Rule 8(b), the sole basis for joinder of charges against multiple defendants is that the defendants "are alleged to have participated in the same act or transaction or in the same series of acts or transactions constituting an offense or offenses." It is irrelevant that Rule 8(a) permits charges "of the same or similar character" to be joined against a single defendant, even though they do not arise out of the same or connected transactions. Charges against multiple defendants may not be joined merely because they are similar in character, and even dissimilar charges may be joined against multiple defendants if they arise out of the same series of transactions constituting an offense or offenses.

From the foregoing, it follows that Satterfield [charged only with involvement in two of the five robberies] was properly joined in the indictment and for trial only if all of the offenses charged in the indictment arose out of the same series of transactions. Joinder under rule 8(b) cannot be based on a finding that the offenses charged were merely of the same or a similar character. In considering what constitutes a "series of transactions" we have stated that the term "transaction" is a word of flexible meaning. Whether or not multiple offenses joined in an indictment constitute a "series of acts or transactions" turns on the degree to which they are related. In the cases under rule 8(b), that relation is most often established by showing that substantially the same facts must be adduced to prove each of the joined offenses. We have thus stated that rule 8(b)'s goal of maximum trial convenience consistent with minimum prejudice is best served by permitting initial joinder of charges against multiple defendants whenever the common activity constitutes a substantial portion of the proof of the joint charges. Other logical relationships might also be sufficient to establish that a group of offenses constitutes a "series of acts or transactions," but a mere showing that the events occurred at about the same time, or that the acts violated the same statutes, is not enough.

Notwithstanding our express policy that rule 8(b) should be construed broadly in favor of initial joinder, we are convinced that in the instant case Satterfield was improperly joined with the codefendant, Merriweather.

Most of the testimony at the trial related to the first, second, and fifth robberies, which were committed by Merriweather alone. The evidence against Merriweather was strong.

. . . The evidence adduced at trial relative to the first, second, and fifth robberies pertained solely to acts undertaken by Merriweather alone. Furthermore, in a separate trial of Satterfield for the third and fourth robberies, evidence pertaining to the first, second, and fifth robberies would have been irrelevant. Thus, this is not a situation where substantially the same facts would have been adduced at separate trials. Since a nexus between each offense charged in the indictment was absent, we cannot say, on these facts, that the five robberies each arose out of the same series of acts or transactions. Joinder of Satterfield cannot be justified merely because the robberies which Merriweather perpetrated alone were somewhat similar in character to the robberies in which both defendants participated.

Relying on our holding in *United States v. Patterson*, 455 F.2d 264 (9th Cir. 1972), the Government nevertheless argues that joinder was proper in this case because one of the defendants named in the indictment was mentioned in every count and because the modus operandi in each bank robbery was similar. It contends that this similarity provides the needed nexus between the joined offenses and establishes that the offenses charged constituted "a series of transactions." In *Patterson*, the indictment charged that the appellant and one Mortillaro had engaged in multiple counts of mail fraud; it was also alleged that Mortillaro and a third defendant, one Aquino, had engaged in offenses with substantially the same modus operandi. In holding that joinder under rule 8(b) was proper, we noted that Mortillaro was a common participant in each count and that the modus operandi in each count was "basically the same." We concluded that appellant and the others were charged with the same basic fraudulent scheme which they jointly and individually executed within a six month period.

Patterson is distinguishable from this case on various grounds. First, a mere similarity in the manner in which several offenses are carried out — a similar "modus operandi" — is insufficient by itself to justify joinder under rule 8(b), absent some factual or logical relation among those offenses. In *Patterson*, the indictment charged that each incident of mail fraud had been carried out in an intricate and highly sophisticated manner that suggested a close connection among the offenses charged against the three defendants. Indeed, we found the existence of a "scheme" that had been jointly and individually executed. In this case, as noted above, the Government conceded at trial that the first, second, and fifth robberies were not part of any common scheme or plan in which Satterfield had participated.

As a practical matter, moreover, the five robberies in this case did not reflect a distinct pattern. They were certainly not virtually identical. Although the robbers were disguised during the robberies, the disguises were not the same every time. In any event, use of disguises is so common in bank robberies that resorting to the device on different occasions does not by itself constitute a common pattern. Any similarity between the disguises worn at the several robberies fails to reach the level of similarity present in *Patterson*, where each count charged that the defendants had engaged in complex criminal ventures that had been carried out in virtually the same manner. Given these factors, we reject the Government's claim that a similar modus operandi justified joining Satterfield in an indictment that charged Merriweather with the five robberies.

The Government makes a second argument, related to the "modus operandi" justification discussed above. It claims that evidence as to all the robberies would have been admissible to establish Merriweather's motive, intent, etc., even if he and Satterfield had been tried jointly in a prosecution limited to the third and fourth robberies . . . . [T]he Government concludes that because the evidence as to all robberies would have been admissible in a trial limited to the crimes in which both defendants allegedly participated, joinder was proper.

Although superficially appealing, the argument, on closer scrutiny, is unpersuasive. Even assuming that at a joint trial limited to the third and fourth robberies evidence of Merriweather's involvement in the other three offenses would have been admissible against him to show motive, etc., it does not follow that joinder under rule 8(b) was proper. The evidence put forth to prove an offense for which a defendant is tried will generally be more extensive, and thus more damaging, than that which would be adduced to establish a prior crime as proof of such matters as motive or intent. At a joint trial, where one defendant is charged with offenses in which the other defendants did not participate, the detailed evidence introduced to establish guilt of the separate offenses may shift the focus of the trial to the crimes of the single defendant. In such cases, codefendants run a high risk of being found guilty merely by association. That risk was present here, where highly probative evidence was introduced to show that Merriweather had committed the first, second, and fifth robberies.

It is also significant that where evidence of prior criminal acts is proffered, the trial court has discretion to limit, or even to exclude, such evidence if its probative value is substantially outweighed by the danger of unfair prejudice, confusion of the issues, or misleading the jury, or by considerations of undue delay, waste of time, or needless presentation of cumulative evidence. Where multiple offenses are charged in an indictment, however, a trial judge must permit the prosecution to establish each of those offenses beyond a reasonable doubt.

. . . Finally, the Government argues that if joinder under rule 8(b) was improper the error was harmless and reversal is not required. The foregoing discussion, however, shows that Satterfield was substantially prejudiced by joinder with Merriweather. To reiterate: The jury first heard evidence on the fifth robbery, proof of which was exceptionally strong against Merriweather. Subsequently, the jury heard evidence pertaining to the first and second robberies. This evidence, relating to Merriweather alone, could have had no other effect than to prejudice Satterfield in the precise manner against which rule 8(b) seeks to protect. Furthermore, the case against Merriweather for the three robberies committed by him alone was stronger than the case against Satterfield for the third and fourth robberies. Although the trial court instructed the jury that the evidence relating to the first, second, and fifth robberies concerned Merriweather alone, in our view the substantial proof of Merriweather's involvement in these robberies prejudiced Satterfield.

We recognize that even permissible joinder will often result in some prejudice to a defendant. The purpose of rule 8(b) is to limit joinder to those cases where considerations of trial efficiency clearly outweigh a defendant's interest in a separate trial. In this case, serious prejudice to Satterfield has been demonstrated. Misjoinder under rule 8(b) therefore requires that his conviction be set aside.

NOTES

1. Recall that the jury found both Satterfield and Merriweather guilty as charged. Thus, Merriweather was convicted of offenses involving all five robberies, but three of them he did alone, without any assistance from Satterfield. Satterfield was convicted of the two robberies he committed with Merriweather. The court found that Satterfield's case had been improperly joined with Merriweather's, but upheld (in an unpublished opinion) Merriweather's convictions. If Satterfield was improperly joined with Merriweather, was Merriweather improperly joined with Satterfield?

2. *Efficiency.* One of the reasons for joinder is efficiency. What efficiencies occurred when the five robberies were joined in a single trial?

3. *Conspiracy.* Note that Merriweather and Satterfield were not charged with conspiracy. For purposes of joinder, would it have mattered whether the indictment alleged a conspiracy to commit the two robberies that Satterfield and Merriweather allegedly committed together?

4. *Prejudice.* The *Satterfield* court found that Satterfield had suffered "serious prejudice" from the misjoinder. Based on the reasons given in the opinion, are you convinced that this actually occurred?

5. *Inconsistent theories.* Assume that defendants A and B are charged with murder committed in the course of a felony. While clear proof exists that they both committed the predicate felony, there is no definitive evidence as to who fired the fatal shot. A motion to sever is granted, and at A's trial the prosecutor argues that A was the triggerman. Following A's conviction, the same prosecutor argues at B's subsequent trial that B (and not A) pulled the trigger. Is such an inconsistent argument permitted? *See* Anne Bowen Poulin, *Prosecutorial Inconsistency, Estoppel, and Due Process: Making the Prosecution Get Its Story Straight,* 89 CAL. L. REV. 1423 (2001) (describing such cases, noting that courts thus far have often refused to give the defendant relief, and proposing that this practice be controlled either through estoppel or due process theories).

In *Bradshaw v. Stumpf*, 545 U.S. 175 (2005), the U.S. Supreme Court held that prosecutorial inconsistencies regarding the identity of the triggerman did not invalidate the defendant's plea of guilty. With regard to the death penalty imposed on Stumpf, however, the case was remanded for a determination whether the allegedly inconsistent theories may have affected the sentence to such an extent that it violated due process.

6. *Not all counts.* Though under Rule 8(b) defendants joined in an indictment must have shared a common activity, each need not have been charged in every count. For example, assume that A, B, and C formed a conspiracy three years ago and last year D joined it. All four may be joined for conspiracy and substantive drug crimes, but D may not be mentioned in the substantive drug counts that were completed before D joined the plot.

7. *Retroactive correction of misjoinder.* Since the validity of a joinder of defendants is essentially determined by the allegations in the indictment, what happens if the proof at trial does not support the linkage described in the indictment? For example, assume that A and B are indicted for conspiracy to commit fraud and four counts of fraud. The jury acquits on the conspiracy charge. Is joinder of the substantive fraud charges still permissible? Most courts uphold the joinder's propriety as assessed by the indictment, not trial, unless the defendants can establish the prosecutor's bad faith in preparing the indictment.

PROBLEM 8-3. BY THE TIME WE GET TO BOSTON

Sam and Oliver each owned a small business in Boston. Sam ran a barber shop and Oliver owned a dry cleaning store. They were arrested after an anonymous informant telephoned the police and reported that they had committed insurance fraud. Within a week before the informant's tip, both of their businesses had burned down. Each was insured by the All Safe Insurance Company. Both Sam and Oliver filed claims for damages caused by the fires.

The local prosecutor believes that Sam and Oliver worked together to defraud the All Safe Insurance Company and would like to indict and try them together under Rule 8(b). What facts should the prosecutor seek to establish?

[d] Discretionary Relief from Prejudicial Joinder

Rule 14 is an important rule. Federal Rules 8(a) and (b) are quite liberal and permit a joinder in many situations. When an indictment (under Rule 8) or trial (under Rule 13) permits a joinder of defendants or crimes or both, either the government or defense counsel can request a severance pursuant to Rule 14.

The criteria are vague. Rule 14 authorizes a severance if either side is "prejudiced" by the joinder, but does not define prejudice or provide guidance in the logic the court is to follow. Often Rule 14 is read as authorizing a court to balance the likelihood of prejudice against the interests of judicial economy. Prejudice is frequently said to require more than an increased likelihood that the defendant would have been acquitted if there had been no joinder. One court, for example, said that the defendant can obtain a severance if he or she can show an inability to obtain a fair trial. *United States v. Serpico*, 320 F.3d 691 (7th Cir. 2003). Another court, *United States v. Foutz*, 540 F.2d 733, 736 (4th Cir. 1976), summarized the kind of proof of prejudice in joinder of offense cases as follows:

> When two or more offenses are joined for trial . . . , three sources of prejudice are possible which may justify the granting of a severance under Rule 14: (1) the jury may confuse and cumulate the evidence, and convict the defendant of one or both crimes when it would not convict him of either if it could keep the evidence properly segregated; (2) the defendant may be confounded in presenting defenses, as where he desires to assert his privilege against self-incrimination with respect to one crime but not the other; or (3) the jury may conclude that the defendant is guilty of one crime and then find him guilty of the other because of his criminal disposition.

The considerations are slightly different when defendants are joined together.

Prejudice from joinder of defendants may arise in a wide variety of circumstances as, for example, where one defendant makes an inculpatory statement inadmissible against his codefendant, where the defendants present conflicting and irreconcilable defenses and there is a danger that the jury will unjustifiably infer that this conflict alone demonstrates that both are guilty, and where only one defendant testifies and urges the jury to draw an adverse inference from his codefendant's silence.

Rhone v. United States, 365 F.2d 980, 981 (D.C. Cir. 1966) (citations omitted).

NOTES

1. *Discretion and burden of proof.* The trial judge is given wide discretion in ruling on severance issues. On appeal the trial judge's decision is reviewed under the forgiving standard of whether there was an "abuse of discretion." A person requesting severance under Rule 14 has the burden of proof. Often this burden is characterized as being quite substantial. *See, e.g., United States v. Mitchell*, 484 F.3d 762 (5th Cir. 2007) (defendant seeking severance from codefendants bears burden of showing specific and compelling prejudice that resulted in unfair trial).

2. *Jury instructions to limit use of evidence.* Obviously, prejudice will be difficult to prove if the jury could easily compartmentalize the evidence. Sometimes prejudice may be present or possible, but severance is denied because the court can minimize or eliminate the harm by giving curative jury instructions that are usually viewed as effective in ensuring that the jury can perform in a fair, unbiased way. *See, e.g., United States v. Mitchell*, 484 F.3d 762 (5th Cir. 2007).

3. *Options if prejudice appears.* In some cases, before the trial, counsel cannot tell whether joinder will be prejudicial. During the trial, however, the theories of the case and the testimony of witnesses may strongly suggest that joinder is prejudicial or inappropriate. In such cases the trial judge has several options. One is to grant a mistrial and schedule separate proceedings at a later date. Another option is to require the prosecution to elect which charge(s) or defendant(s) to try at this time. A severance would then be granted for the remaining defendant(s) or charge(s).

4. *Illustrations of severance under Rule 14.* Although the vast variety of facts in these cases makes it difficult to generalize about the situations meriting a severance under Rule 14, examples of successful reasons supporting a severance include: mutually antagonistic defenses by two defendants such that acceptance of one defendant's defense would preclude acquittal of the other defendant; two robberies joined in one trial when the proof of one of the crimes was very weak; use of one codefendant's confession implicating another codefendant; and exceptionally complex, lengthy evidence involving multiple defendants where a jury could not reasonably be expected to separate the evidence.

ZAFIRO v. UNITED STATES
506 U.S. 534 (1993)

Justice O'Connor delivered the opinion of the Court.

Rule 8(b) of the Federal Rules of Criminal Procedure provides that defendants may be charged together "if they are alleged to have participated in the same act or transaction or in the same series of acts or transactions constituting an offense or offenses." Rule 14 of the Rules, in turn, permits a district court to grant a severance of defendants if "it appears that a defendant or the government is prejudiced by a joinder." In this case, we consider whether Rule 14 requires severance as a matter of law when codefendants present "mutually antagonistic defenses." Gloria Zafiro, Jose Martinez, Salvador Garcia, and Alfonso Soto were accused of distributing illegal drugs in the Chicago area, operating primarily out of Soto's bungalow in Chicago and Zafiro's apartment in Cicero, a nearby suburb. One day, government agents observed Garcia and Soto place a large box in Soto's car and drive from Soto's bungalow to Zafiro's apartment. The agents followed the two as they carried the box up the stairs. When the agents identified themselves, Garcia and Soto dropped the box and ran into [Zafiro's] apartment. The agents entered the apartment in pursuit and found the four petitioners in the living room. The dropped box contained 55 pounds of cocaine. [Agents also found cocaine, heroin, marijuana and cash in the apartment.]

The four petitioners were indicted and brought to trial together. At various points during the proceeding, Garcia and Soto moved for severance, arguing that their defenses were mutually antagonistic. Soto testified that he knew nothing about the drug conspiracy. He claimed that Garcia had asked him for a box, which he gave Garcia, and that he (Soto) did not know its contents until they were arrested. Garcia did not testify, but his lawyer argued that Garcia was innocent: The box belonged to Soto and Garcia was ignorant of its contents.

Zafiro and Martinez also repeatedly moved for severance on the ground that their defenses were mutually antagonistic. Zafiro testified that she was merely Martinez's girlfriend and knew nothing of the conspiracy. She claimed that Martinez stayed in her apartment occasionally, kept some clothes there, and gave her small amounts of money. Although she allowed Martinez to store a suitcase in her closet, she testified, she had no idea that the suitcase contained illegal drugs. Like Garcia, Martinez did not testify. But his lawyer argued that Martinez was only visiting his girlfriend and had no idea that she was involved in distributing drugs.

The District Court denied the motions for severance. The jury convicted all four petitioners of conspiring to possess cocaine, heroin, and marijuana with the intent to distribute. In addition, Garcia and Soto were convicted of possessing cocaine with the intent to distribute, and Martinez was convicted of possessing cocaine, heroin, and marijuana with the intent to distribute. Petitioners appealed their convictions. Garcia, Soto, and Martinez claimed that the District Court abused its discretion in denying their motions to sever. (Zafiro did not appeal the denial of her severance motion, and thus, her claim is not properly before this Court.) [The Court of Appeals affirmed the convictions because the defendants had not suffered prejudice from the denial of a severance.] . . . We granted the petition for certiorari and now affirm the judgment of the Court of Appeals.

Rule 8(b) states that "[t]wo or more defendants may be charged in the same indictment or information if they are alleged to have participated in the same act or transaction or in the same series of acts or transactions constituting an offense or offenses." There is a preference in the federal system for joint trials of defendants who are indicted together. Joint trials play a vital role in the criminal justice system. They promote efficiency and serve the interests of justice by avoiding the scandal and inequity of inconsistent verdicts. For these reasons, we repeatedly have approved of joint trials. But Rule 14 recognizes that joinder, even when proper under Rule 8(b), may prejudice either a defendant or the Government. Thus, the Rule provides,

> [i]f it appears that a defendant or the government is prejudiced by a joinder of . . . defendants . . . for trial together, the court may order an election or separate trials of counts, grant a severance of defendants or provide whatever other relief justice requires.

In interpreting Rule 14, the Courts of Appeals frequently have expressed the view that "mutually antagonistic" or "irreconcilable" defenses may be so prejudicial in some circumstances as to mandate severance. Notwithstanding such assertions, the courts have reversed relatively few convictions for failure to grant a severance on grounds of mutually antagonistic or irreconcilable defenses. The low rate of reversal may reflect the inability of defendants to prove a risk of prejudice in most cases involving conflicting defenses.

Nevertheless, petitioners urge us to adopt a bright-line rule, mandating severance whenever codefendants have conflicting defenses. We decline to do so. Mutually antagonistic defenses are not prejudicial per se. Moreover, Rule 14 does not require severance even if prejudice is shown; rather, it leaves the tailoring of the relief to be granted, if any, to the district court's sound discretion.

We believe that, when defendants properly have been joined under Rule 8(b), a district court should grant a severance under Rule 14 only if there is a serious risk that a joint trial would compromise a specific trial right of one of the defendants, or prevent the jury from making a reliable judgment about guilt or innocence. Such a risk might occur when evidence that the jury should not consider against a defendant and that would not be admissible if a defendant were tried alone is admitted against a codefendant. . . . Conversely, a defendant might suffer prejudice if essential exculpatory evidence that would be available to a defendant tried alone were unavailable in a joint trial. The risk of prejudice will vary with the facts in each case, and district courts may find prejudice in situations not discussed here. When the risk of prejudice is high, a district court is more likely to determine that separate trials are necessary, but . . . less drastic measures, such as limiting instructions, often will suffice to cure any risk of prejudice.

Turning to the facts of this case, we note that petitioners do not articulate any specific instances of prejudice. Instead they contend that the very nature of their defenses, without more, prejudiced them. Their theory is that when two defendants both claim they are innocent and each accuses the other of the crime, a jury will conclude (1) that both defendants are lying and convict them both on that basis, or (2) that at least one of the two must be guilty without regard to whether the Government has proved its case beyond a reasonable doubt.

As to the first contention, it is well settled that defendants are not entitled to severance merely because they may have a better chance of acquittal in separate trials. Rules 8(b) and 14 are designed to promote economy and efficiency and to avoid a multiplicity of trials, so long as these objectives can be achieved without substantial prejudice to the right of the defendants to a fair trial. While an important element of a fair trial is that a jury consider *only* relevant and competent evidence bearing on the issue of guilt or innocence, a fair trial does not include the right to exclude relevant and competent evidence. A defendant normally would not be entitled to exclude the testimony of a former codefendant if the district court did sever their trials, and we see no reason why relevant and competent testimony would be prejudicial merely because the witness is also a codefendant.

As to the second contention, the short answer is that petitioners' scenario simply did not occur here. The Government argued that all four petitioners were guilty and offered sufficient evidence as to all four petitioners; the jury in turn found all four petitioners guilty of various offenses. Moreover, even if there were some risk of prejudice, here it is of the type that can be cured with proper instructions, and "juries are presumed to follow their instructions." The District Court properly instructed the jury that the Government had "the burden of proving beyond a reasonable doubt" that each defendant committed the crimes with which he or she was charged. The court then instructed the jury that it must "give separate consideration to each individual defendant and to each separate charge against him. Each defendant is entitled to have his or her case determined from his or her own conduct and from the evidence [that] may be applicable to him or to her." In addition, the District Court admonished the jury that opening and closing arguments are not evidence and that it should draw no inferences from a defendant's exercise of the right to silence. These instructions sufficed to cure any possibility of prejudice.

Rule 14 leaves the determination of risk of prejudice and any remedy that may be necessary to the sound discretion of the district courts. Because petitioners have not shown that their joint trial subjected them to any legally cognizable prejudice, we conclude that the District Court did not abuse its discretion in denying petitioners' motions to sever. [Affirmed]

JUSTICE STEVENS, concurring in the judgment.

. . . The burden of overcoming any individual defendant's presumption of innocence, by proving guilt beyond a reasonable doubt, rests solely on the shoulders of the prosecutor. Joinder is problematic in cases involving mutually antagonistic defenses because it may operate to reduce the burden on the prosecutor, in two general ways. First, joinder may introduce what is in effect a second prosecutor into a case, by turning each codefendant into the other's most forceful adversary. Second, joinder may invite a jury confronted with two defendants, at least one of whom is almost certainly guilty, to convict the defendant who appears the more guilty of the two regardless of whether the prosecutor has proven guilt beyond a reasonable doubt as to that particular defendant. Though the Court is surely correct that this second risk may be minimized by careful instructions insisting on separate consideration of the evidence as to each codefendant, the danger will remain relevant to the prejudice inquiry in some cases.

. . . I agree with the Court that a "bright-line rule, mandating severance whenever codefendants have conflicting defenses" is unwarranted. For the reasons discussed above, however, I think district courts must retain their traditional discretion to consider severance whenever mutually antagonistic defenses are presented. . . .

NOTES

1. *Deference to trial judge.* Since decisions under Rule 14 involve a heavy dose of the trial judge's discretion, appellate courts are quite deferential to the lower court's ruling. Does this make sense? What information will the trial court need to assess whether there was prejudice? Is this any different than a trial court's decision about the meaning of words in a statute, where little or no deference is given the trial court's ruling?

2. *Standard of prejudice.* What is the standard of "prejudice" in *Zafiro*? Must the defendants prove actual prejudice? Must they prove that the result *would* have been different had a severance been granted? That it *might* have been different? How would they prove this?

3. *Spillover evidence.* A common ground for a Rule 14 motion is "spillover" — evidence admissible against one or more defendants, but not against others, will be improperly used against the latter offenders. Was this risk adequately considered in *Zafiro*?

4. *Mutually antagonistic defenses.* *Zafiro* follows the traditional view that mutually antagonistic defenses are grounds for a discretionary severance under Rule 14 if the necessary prejudice is shown. In these cases, ordinarily the jury will be forced to believe one defendant and disbelieve another. The typical pattern is that each defendant offers a defense to his or her charge but supports the guilt of the other defendant. Why should this typical factfinding process be grounds for a severance under Rule 14?

5. *Jury instructions.* *Zafiro* also suggests that jury instructions can often cure problems arising from mutually antagonistic defenses and other joinder problems. Do you agree? Can a jury really obey such instructions? Note that the *Zafiro* Court found that the curative instructions "sufficed to cure any possibility of prejudice." Do you agree?

[2]   State Provisions

State statutes and rules on joinder and severance often resemble the federal rules described above. Joinder and severance are both discretionary when the stated criteria are met. The criteria are often the same as the federal approach: whether the offenses are of the same or similar character or the offenses or offenders were part of the same act, transaction, or common plan. Some states also permit joinder of defendants if it would be difficult to separate the proof against the accused, if all the defendants are charged as accomplices in the offenses, or if the defendants are involved in the same conspiracy.

[a] Right to Sever

Some state provisions, however, are quite different. One view greatly facilitates separate proceedings by permitting joined defendants to obtain a severance simply by a timely motion. *See, e.g.*, Ala. Code § 15-14-20 (joined defendants "may be tried either jointly or separately, as either may elect"); Ga. Code Ann. § 17-8-4 (capital defendants have right to severance; severance discretionary for other defendants). This view makes it easier for the defendants to avoid the prejudicial facets of joinder and may provide them with some clout during plea bargaining sessions.

A related approach gives a defendant, whose offenses have been joined for trial, a right to a severance of joinder in specified circumstances. *See, e.g., Markee v. State*, 494 S.E.2d 551 (Ga. App. 1997) (right to severance of crimes joined solely because were of same or similar character); Tex. Penal Code § 3.04 (right to severance of offenses joined because arose from same criminal episode).

[b] Mandatory Joinder

Just as some state statutes make severance easier, others make joinder more likely than the federal approach. A handful of jurisdictions have adopted so-called mandatory joinder provisions. Sometimes mandatory joinder of offenses is provided:

> *(a)(1) Mandatory Joinder [of Offenses].* If several offenses are actually known to the prosecuting attorney at the time of commencing the prosecution and were committed within his judicial district, all such offenses upon which the prosecuting attorney elects to proceed must be prosecuted by separate counts in a single prosecution if they are based on the same act or series of acts arising from the same criminal episode. Any such offense not thus joined by separate count cannot thereafter be the basis of a subsequent prosecution . . . .

Colo. R. Crim. P. 8. Other provisions, following Model Penal Code § 1.07(2) (Proposed Official Draft 1962), require mandatory joinder of defendants.

> Cal. Penal Code § 1098. *Trial of defendants jointly charged with offense; Separate trials.*
>
> When two or more defendants are jointly charged with any public offense, whether felony or misdemeanor, they must be tried jointly, unless the court orders separate trials. . . .

Mandatory joinder is an interesting and complex approach. Clearly, mandatory joinder rules conserve the resources of both prosecution and defense (as well as the psychological health of the accused) by forcing both sides to resolve the defendant's criminal liability at one time. In addition, they clearly interfere with traditional notions of prosecutorial freedom by requiring the prosecution to proceed with charges when, for any number of reasons, the district attorney would prefer to wait, perhaps to have time to build a stronger case. Mandatory joinder issues also could raise double jeopardy concerns, discussed in Chapter 16.

[c] Joinder of Several Cases or Counts

Some state provisions also deal specifically with those cases where someone wants a joinder of cases or counts that are scheduled to be handled separately. An unusual state rule gives either party the right to a joinder. *See, e.g.*, Ariz. R. Crim. P. 13.3 (either party may file a motion requesting a joinder of offenses or defendants). Another rule specifically recognizes the hardship that can result from separate trials and authorizes joinder of offenses that would not otherwise be dealt with in the same proceeding:

> Mass. R. Crim. P. 9(a)(4). *Joinder of Unrelated Offenses.* Upon the written motion of a defendant, or with his written consent, the trial judge may join for trial two or more charges of unrelated offenses upon a showing that failure to try the charges together would constitute harassment or unduly consume the

time or resources of the parties. The trial judge shall join the charges for trial unless he determines that joinder is not in the best interests of justice.

American Bar Association. The American Bar Association, Standards for Criminal Justice, Standard 13-2.3(a) (2d ed. Supp. 1986) favors joint proceedings by providing that a defendant's motion to join "related offenses"

> should be granted unless the court determines that, because the prosecuting attorney does not have sufficient evidence to warrant trying some of the offenses at that time, or for some other reason, the ends of justice would be defeated if the motion were granted in whole or in part.

F. PROCEDURES

[1] Motion to Sever or Join

Ordinarily the prosecutor decides whether to join defendants and/or offenders in a single indictment or information or trial. The defendant is virtually always the party who seeks a severance, but on rare occasions he or she may ask that additional counts or people be joined in an indictment, information, or trial. If a change, whether joinder or severance, is sought, the person seeking the change would usually file a written motion requesting the relief, although the court can order a severance *sua sponte* without a request by either party.

Failure to make a timely severance motion may constitute a waiver of the issue. In a typical case where two defendants are charged in one indictment and want their cases tried separately, they should file a Motion to Sever. Several theories are possible.

One argument, usually unsuccessful, is that joinder was improper under Rules 8(a) or (b). On appeal, parties rarely obtain a reversal if the trial court erred in joining defendants or offenses. According to the United States Supreme Court, improper joinder is subject to a harmless error analysis. It will lead to a reversal "only if the misjoinder results in actual prejudice because it had substantial and injurious effect or influence in determining the jury's verdict." *United States v. Lane,* 474 U.S. 438, 449 (1986).

A second, more frequent argument is that severance should be ordered under Rule 14 because joinder is prejudicial. Since a Rule 14 motion addresses itself to the discretion of the trial court, appellate courts give the trial courts wide latitude in resolving such motions. The trial court is free to balance prejudice against trial efficiency on a case by case basis. The person requesting severance has the burden of demonstrating that prejudice is present and cannot be alleviated by remedies short of a severance.

[2] Timing of Motion

In order to permit the trial court to rule on a severance motion before the trial begins, the motion should be filed well before that date. A severance motion filed after trial has begun can be denied because of the tardy filing. Of course, the motion can be filed during trial if the reasons for it first surface during proof. Statutes, court rules, or local practice in some jurisdictions mandate that severance petitions be filed by a specific time in the proceedings. For example, a jurisdiction may require filing five days before trial. Rule 12(b)(3)(D) of the Federal Rules of Criminal Procedure requires severance motions under Rule 14 to be filed "prior to trial."

[3] Proof

A common issue is whether the standards for joinder are assessed on the basis of the allegations in the charging instrument (complaint, indictment, or information) or by the proof presented at trial. What if the indictment alleges facts constituting a "common scheme," in compliance with the joinder standard of Rule 8(a), but the proof at the joint trial fails to establish this element? In this situation some courts hold the defendants were improperly joined for trial and are therefore entitled to a mistrial. Other courts apply a harmless error analysis, granting a mistrial only if the misjoinder caused prejudice.

When a severance motion is filed before trial, the court may delay ruling on the motion until some time during the trial when sufficient proof has been tendered to determine whether the defendant will be prejudiced by the joinder. If a Motion to Sever is denied, the defendant would be wise to renew the motion during the trial when the proof that necessitates the motion has been presented. Of course, courts may be especially reluctant to grant this mid-trial motion since both time and resources have already been devoted to the case and will be wasted if the motion is successful.

[4] Inconsistent Positions

Assume that two defendants in a single homicide are tried separately. At the trial of defendant A, the prosecutor argues that A was the trigger person. A is convicted and sentenced to death. At the subsequent trial of defendant B, the prosecutor now argues that B was the actual killer and that A was a minor participant. Is this permissible? If A and B had been tried together, the prosecutor could not assert such inconsistent positions. One author argues that this practice is unethical since it casts a doubt on the accuracy of the verdict in each case. Moreover, the prosecutor is barred from perpetrating a fraud on the court. J. Vincent Aprile, II, *Criminal Justice Matters*, 14 CRIMINAL JUSTICE 59 (1999). The author suggests that this possibility requires defense counsel to monitor the prosecution's activities in both prior and subsequent trials of the same incident. Counsel at the second trial may be able to use the prosecutor's arguments and evidence at the first trial to impeach testimony and arguments at the later one. *See also* Anne Bowen Poulin, *Prosecutorial Inconsistency, Estoppel, and Due Process: Making the Prosecution Get Its Story Straight*, 89 CAL. L. REV. 1423 (2001) (describing specific cases, noting that courts thus far have often refused to give the defendant relief, and proposing that this practice be controlled either through estoppel or due process theories).

PROBLEM 8-4. LAWYER'S ADVICE

Smith and Phillips were sports agents who represented football players. They secured some of their player-clients by paying cash bonuses, no-interest loans and sports cars, then signing the athletes to secret postdated contracts while the players were still members of their college football teams. Since college rules bar such contracts, the understanding was that each player would lie about the contracts until the end of the player's college eligibility. Before beginning their business adventure, Smith and Phillips consulted Ms. Lowell, a lawyer specializing in sports law. Each provided her with a significant amount of confidential information.

Smith and Phillips are scheduled to be tried for mail fraud, stemming from the players' lies on routine forms the players mailed to the NCAA in which they denied signing any contracts with sports agents. At the trial, Smith plans to argue that he is not guilty of mail fraud because he had no intent to defraud, one of the elements of mail fraud. He maintains that he was told by Ms. Lowell, his attorney, that the scheme was legal. To prove this, Smith plans to call Ms. Lowell as a crucial defense witness.

Phillips' attorney has decided that it would be unwise for Phillips to rely on the advice-of-counsel defense. It is feared that Ms. Lowell's testimony will likely include confidential information that Mr. Phillips provided Ms. Lowell. Accordingly, the lawyer has filed, pursuant to Rule 14, a Motion to Sever, arguing that Smith's defense will force Phillips to assert the same advice-of-counsel defense and that this will have negative consequences for Phillips because privileged communications will probably be revealed by Ms. Lowell. What result?

PROBLEM 8-5. BOOZE BROTHERS

Four people were indicted for conspiracy to violate the revenue laws in that they were involved in making and transporting illegal whiskey. The one count indictment alleged the following facts. On January 6th Defendants A and B were arrested for transporting 90 gallons of untaxed spirits. After the arrest, they went to Defendant C's house to sleep. On July 19th Defendant C drove a heavily loaded truck near Defendant D's house. The truck, no longer loaded, was seen an hour later traveling away from D's house, where an illegal still was located the same day. Twenty thousand pounds of sugar, used to make moonshine whiskey, were found at the still.

Was joinder correct under Rule 8(b)? If so, should there be a severance under Rule 14?

Assume also that the indictment contained other counts: In Count Two, Defendants A and B were charged with the substantive offense of transporting untaxed whiskey. In Count Three, Defendants C and D were charged with the crime of illegal manufacture of intoxicating liquors. Was joinder correct under Rule 8(a)? Under Rule 8(b)? Should there be a severance under Rule 14? If a severance is appropriate, which defendant(s) and crime(s) should be severed?

Chapter 9
MOTION PRACTICE IN CRIMINAL CASES

A. INTRODUCTION

Motion practice is a very important facet of criminal representation. Although many cases are won or lost on the basis of motion practice, it is often ignored in law school and is described in only the most general terms in the rules of criminal procedure. This chapter provides an overview of motion practice and the strategic and ethical questions it raises. For additional information regarding the myriad of motions that may be filed in a criminal case, including grounds for motions and an examination of governing legal principles, see James A. Adams and Daniel D. Blinka, PRETRIAL MOTIONS IN CRIMINAL PROSECUTIONS (3d ed. 2004).

A motion is a formal request for a judge to issue an order. The requested order may direct a clerk or someone else to do or not do something (such as give counsel access to a sealed file) or, may regulate some future aspect of the case (perhaps excluding certain proof at trial), or may even end the case. More than one motion can be filed at the same time. Sometimes, counsel will file motions in the alternative. If Motion A is not granted, then counsel asks for relief under Motion B. The danger of alternative motions, of course, is that the dual approach may undercut the strength of the argument for each motion. The court may get the feeling that counsel is not serious about either motion.

Once made, a motion triggers a series of events. The opposing counsel is given an opportunity to respond (perhaps arguing that the motion should be denied for certain specific reasons), and often the judge will rule on the motion (perhaps granting or denying all or part of it, or postponing a decision).

Motions can be filed by the prosecutor or defense counsel, and sometimes by other people as well. For example, a witness may file a motion to quash a subpoena issued to compel the witness to testify at trial.

B. FUNCTIONS OF MOTIONS — DISPOSITIVE AND TACTICAL

[1] Types of Motions

Some defense motions (generally referred to as *dispositive motions*) may seek to dismiss charges, ending the case against the defendant. Examples of dispositive motions include motions to dismiss for insufficient evidence usually brought at the close of the prosecution's case in chief (sometimes called a *motion for directed verdict of acquittal*), or on grounds such as *statute of limitations, double jeopardy*, or a fatal flaw in the indictment. Some motions, while not technically dispositive (not automatically requiring dismissal by themselves), nonetheless turn out to be dispositive in effect — for example, a *motion to suppress* evidence which if granted will leave the prosecution without sufficient evidence to sustain the charge(s).

Other motions, in contrast, seek to gain some tactical advantage at or before trial, e.g., to permit discovery, or to limit the evidence that will be used at trial. For obvious reasons, the prosecution may only bring tactical motions, but not dispositive motions, in criminal cases.

[2] Functions of Motions

Motions serve a number of important functions. Some are the product of legal rules requiring that certain motions be made and eliminating some options if the motions are not made. Others stem from strategic considerations aside from legal requirements.

[a] Obtain Specific Result

The most obvious reason for making a motion is to obtain a court ruling on the matter raised in the motion. For example, if counsel wants to sever defendants so that two defendants are tried in separate trials rather than one trial, a Motion to Sever Defendants should be filed in order to obtain a court ruling on severance.

[b] Prerequisite to Raising Certain Legal Issues

Some important issues in criminal cases can only be raised by written motion. The failure to file the appropriate motion may preclude the party from obtaining a court order that would have been given if correct motion practice had been followed.

[c] Preserve Issue for Appeal

If a party does not formally request a court ruling on an issue, ordinarily the party cannot later appeal the fact that the court made no such ruling. Often the issue is considered to have been waived. Thus, a motion, even though denied, may keep an issue alive for presentation to an appellate court. *See, e.g., United States v. Yousef*, 327 F.3d 56 (2d Cir. 2003)(failure to file pretrial suppression motion bars later consideration of issue of involuntary confession).

Two closely related, tragic cases illustrate the importance of preserving an issue for appellate review. In August 1974, John Eldon Smith and his wife Rebecca Smith Machetti were involved in a double murder of Rebecca's former husband and the former husband's new wife. The homicides were committed to obtain life insurance proceeds. John and Rebecca were tried in state court for the murders in separate trials in the same Georgia county a few weeks apart in early 1975. Both were convicted and sentenced to death. The juries for both trials were selected in a way that underrepresented women, in violation of decisions by the United States Supreme Court. Rebecca's attorney raised the issue of the invalid jury selection process at an early stage of the proceedings and a federal appellate court eventually overturned her conviction. *Machetti v. Linahan*, 679 F.2d 236 (11th Cir. 1982), *cert. denied*, 459 U.S. 1127 (1983).

John's attorney, on the other hand, was unaware of the United States Supreme Court's decisions, the most important of which was decided five days before John's trial, indicating that the Georgia jury selection procedure was unconstitutional. Consequently, he did not raise the issue of the invalid jury selection process until eight years later, after Rebecca's convictions had been set aside by a federal appellate court. She was retried and received a life sentence. Her husband was not as fortunate. Under Georgia law, a defendant's challenge to jury composition had to be made at or before the jury is "put upon him." Because John's lawyer failed to make a timely objection to the unconstitutionally selected jury, he waived the issue under Georgia law and both Georgia and federal courts refused to intervene because of this waiver. *Smith v. Kemp*, 715 F.2d 1459 (11th Cir. 1983), *cert. denied*, 464 U.S. 1003 (1983). John Smith was executed by Georgia authorities on December 15, 1983. *See generally* Stephen B. Bright, *Death by Lottery — Procedural Bar of Constitutional Claims in Capital Cases Due to Inadequate Representation of Indigent Defendants*, 92 W. Va. L. Rev. 679 (1990).

[d] Counter Prosecutor's Claim of Inadvertent Mistake

Defendants sometimes appeal their convictions (rarely successfully) alleging that they were harmed ("prejudiced") by prosecutorial misconduct. Sometimes a prosecutor's motivation for making a comment or taking an action, later held to be inappropriate or legally unfounded, is a factor that will be considered by an appellate court in determining whether to reverse a conviction because of the prosecutor's error.

Whether motives for trial counsel's mistakes were proper or improper are also considered by trial courts in deciding whether to grant a dismissal or a mistrial for trial error by counsel.

A motion may set the stage for a later argument that adversary counsel's motivations were unacceptable or at least suspect. For example, defense counsel may file a motion requesting a court order that the prosecution not do certain things. Even though the motion may be denied as premature, it will set the stage for a trial or appellate court reversal if the subject of the motion actually happens. To illustrate, assume that defense counsel fears that a prosecutor or prosecution witness will refer to evidence (perhaps a baggie of drugs) that has been ruled inadmissible as the result of a successful Motion to Suppress. Counsel may file a Motion to Prevent the Prosecution from Referring Directly or Indirectly to Suppressed Evidence. Some judges will deny the motion as too speculative (no one knows whether the prosecution will actually engage in this unethical behavior or whether a witness will venture into forbidden topics). But if during the trial the prosecutor or a prosecution witness actually does make a reference to the suppressed evidence, even an "unsuccessful" motion will make it unlikely that either the trial or appellate court will view such behavior as inadvertent.

[e] Provide Discovery

As described elsewhere in this book, in most jurisdictions, discovery is quite limited in criminal cases. Depositions are rare and interrogatories nonexistent. Some witnesses may refuse to speak with lawyers for the other side until the witness testifies in court. Sometimes motion practice may provide a little discovery for both sides. If, for example, the defense files a motion, the prosecution's response may provide an indication of the prosecution's view of the case. The judge's ruling on the motion may also provide insight into the judge's attitude toward the case. If there is a hearing on the motion, counsel may learn something about the other side's evidence and view of the case and may get to hear and cross-examine witnesses or, if hearsay evidence is presented, at least to find something out about the information that some likely witnesses have. On rare occasions, the motion hearing will be used by counsel to give friendly witnesses experience testifying and to assess the person's credibility as a witness.

[f] Assist in Planning Trial Strategy

Some motions are used to assist in planning trial strategy. For example, assume that defense counsel files a pretrial motion to exclude certain evidence that could be used in cross-examining one of the defense's key witnesses, perhaps even the criminal accused. If the motion is granted and the evidence barred, counsel may decide to call the person as a witness since the harmful impeaching proof cannot be used. But if the motion is denied and the harmful evidence is admissible to impeach, counsel may elect to proceed without benefit of this witness's testimony. This sophisticated motion practice should increase counsel's capacity to plan an effective presentation of the client's case.

[g] Affect Plea Bargaining

Since it is statistically likely that a criminal defendant will plead guilty, serious attention to motion practice could contribute to the defendant's ability to get a better deal from the prosecutor. It demonstrates to the prosecutor that defense counsel is willing to "go to the mat" on this case. The prosecutor may dread the realization that a time-consuming, protracted series of procedural hurdles and hearings is ahead. In too many American jurisdictions, prosecutors are overworked. They have far more cases scheduled than they can handle except in a most perfunctory way. When an overworked prosecutor is deluged with defense motions and faces the prospect of a fight over matters considered by the prosecutor to be trivial or not worth the time to deal with them, a natural response may be to offer an attractive deal so that the accused will plead guilty and the motions will not have to be answered, and a motion hearing can be avoided, conserving limited prosecutorial resources.

Motion practice may also encourage negotiations by creating or exposing weaknesses in the prosecution's case. For example, a Motion to Suppress Defendant's Confession may, if granted, severely reduce the likelihood of a conviction and therefore encourage the prosecutor to make an attractive offer in order to avoid the risk of an acquittal or hung jury. Similarly, if the court erroneously denies a defense motion and thereby creates a viable appellate issue, the prosecution may be willing to agree to a minimal sentence so that it does not have to risk a time-consuming appellate process followed by another trial.

[h] Educate Participants in the Case

Motions not only seek a result, they also educate those persons involved in the motion practice. As noted above, motion practice can let the prosecutor know that the defense is taking the case seriously and will be fighting every step of the way. This can affect plea bargaining. Motion practice also educates the judge about counsel and counsel's case. It alerts the judge to issues that will arise in the case. For example, if a judge is not familiar with a technical facet of the case, a motion dealing with that issue will force the judge to learn about the issue before it arises in court. This may make it easier to present the case at trial. Finally, motion practice may help educate the client. It tells the client that counsel is aggressively pursuing the case and may make the client feel better about the quality of legal work and the fairness of the proceeding.

[i] Protect Attorney from Malpractice Action

Today lawyers, like physicians, always face the possibility of a malpractice action. Good motion practice may help prevent or defeat malpractice claims. An attorney who files a motion has created a documented record of efforts to represent the accused competently. The motions are available to prove that the lawyer aggressively protected the client's rights.

On the other hand, poor motion practice can provide strong evidence of incompetent representation. Counsel may be forced to explain why certain motions were not filed or were drafted in a particular way.

[j] Gain Time to Further Prepare Case

As discussed below, an ethical attorney should not file motions as a pretext to delay a pending criminal trial (unless, of course, the motion specifically addresses that issue; an example would be a Motion for a Continuance). Nevertheless, sometimes a motion will have the effect of delaying criminal proceedings by requiring time to permit the other lawyers and the judge an opportunity to respond and rule on the motion. This delay can be beneficial and is a by-product of motion practice in some jurisdictions.

C. FORM OF MOTIONS

There is surprisingly little law that describes the form of motions. Often the best way to find out what a motion is supposed to look like is to study motions that have been successfully used in the court where the motion will be filed. Local rules of court should also be carefully consulted, for they may establish time limits for filing and serving motions, and rules for such important matters as the length and propriety of supporting documents, the need for a pre-filing conference with opposing counsel, the need for a written response to a motion, and the procedures used in hearings on motions.

[1]   Written or Oral

Although many motions can be made either in writing or orally, some must be in writing. Rule 47 of the Federal Rules of Criminal Procedure, for example, states:

FEDERAL RULES OF CRIMINAL PROCEDURE

Rule 47. *Motions and Supporting Affidavits*

(a) **In general.** A party applying to the court for an order must do so by motion.

(b) **Form and Content of a Motion.** A motion — except when made during a trial or hearing — must be in writing, unless the court permits the party to make the motion by other means. A motion must state the grounds on which it is based and the relief or order sought. A motion may be supported by affidavit.

(c) **Timing of a Motion.** A party must serve a written motion — other than one that the court may hear ex parte — and any hearing notice at least 5 days before the hearing date, unless a rule or court order sets a different period. For good cause, the court may set a different period upon ex parte application.

(d) **Affidavit Supporting a Motion.** The moving party must serve any supporting affidavit with the motion. A responding party must serve any opposing affidavit at least one day before the hearing, unless the court permits later service.

NOTES

1. Rule 47 requires that motions be in writing unless (a) made during a trial or hearing, or (2) the court excuses the requirement for a written motion. Rule 12 reinforces this by providing that pretrial motions "may be written or oral at the discretion of the judge."

2. *Advantages of written motions.* A written motion has many advantages. It provides a formal record that the motion was made and it provides accurate notice to all parties of the content of the motion. It also allows counsel to draft the motion carefully so that it includes the proper requests. This ensures that the right issue is raised and therefore preserved for appellate review. An oral motion, on the other hand, does permit counsel to respond quickly to a fast-moving situation during the course of a hearing or trial and calls for the other side to respond with little time for reflection. Since appellate courts may refuse to review an issue not properly raised at trial, a lawyer making an oral motion should make sure the court reporter accurately preserves the motion and the court's ruling.

[2]   Content of Motions

Criminal procedure rules are surprisingly silent on the content of motions. Many questions are simply not addressed. Local rules and custom determine the acceptable content of a motion, but generalizations are possible because motions are usually quite similar irrespective of the jurisdiction.

In general terms, a motion should contain a clear statement of what is requested and why it is requested. More particularly, the motion will ordinarily contain the following ten parts:

1. *Court where filed.* At the top of most motions is a statement of the court in which the motion is filed. For example, the motion may indicate that it is filed in the United States District Court for the Southern District of New York. This helps counsel and court clerks keep track of motions filed in different courts.

2. *Style or Caption of case (names of parties).* Near the top of the motion, counsel should include the names of the parties. Ordinarily in a criminal case, one of the parties will be a government entity (State of X or United States of America) and the other will be one or more defendants. For example, a motion may be styled:

UNITED STATES OF AMERICA

vs.

JONATHAN BLAIR DOE

Obviously this is crucial in ensuring that the motion is considered in the correct case and filed in the correct folder.

3. *Case number.* The court clerk's office assigns each criminal case a unique number. This facilitates record keeping in a potentially confusing situation where thousands of cases may be active at the same time and many defendants have the same or similar names or face multiple charges. Counsel filing a motion should insert the case number near the top of the motion.

4. *Title that summarizes content of motion.* In most jurisdictions, somewhere near the top of each motion is a sparsely worded title indicating the substance of the motion. This helps distinguish one document from another in cases where many items are filed. While this statement should be brief, it must be sufficiently inclusive to be helpful. For example, a motion titled simply "Motion" does not provide adequate guidance. A better title would be "Motion to Sever Offenses" or "Motion to Suppress Product of Unconstitutional Search" or "Motion to Reduce Bail."

5. *Statement of relief requested and the party requesting it.* The heart of a motion is contained in the first paragraph of the body of the document. This indicates which party is making the request and includes a conclusory statement of the relief sought. In some locales this paragraph begins with a stilted (and unnecessary) opening line such as, "Comes now the Defendant Jonathan Blair Doe by and through counsel Elizabeth Adams. . . . " A more modern plain-English rendition is, "Defendant Jonathan Blair Doe moves the court for an order. . . . "

After the party making the request is identified, the motion may contain a recitation of the authority permitting the motion to be made. For example, the motion may indicate that the motion is made "pursuant to Rule 47 of the Rules of Criminal Procedure."

The next item is a conclusory statement of the relief requested. This should be sufficiently precise to indicate exactly what order is sought. For example, the motion may indicate that the defendant is moving to have the defendant's case severed from that of a co-defendant. Obviously the relief requested must be described with great care to avoid waiving matters not mentioned in the motion. *See, e.g, United States v. Mathison,* 157 F.3d 541 (8th Cir. 1998)(motion to severe offenses does not constitute motion to severe one codefendant).

6. *Statement of underlying facts.* Sometimes the motion will include a brief statement of facts underlying the motion. One or more affidavits or other documents may also be attached to the motion. Rules of criminal procedure are usually silent on whether the motion must adhere to the usual civil standard of being stated "with particularity." This factual description will provide background for the judge to use in ruling on the motion. Some lawyers prefer to disclose as few facts and theories as possible in order to avoid providing adversary counsel with discovery.

Obviously these facts must be stated accurately, for counsel may have to prove them if a hearing is held to determine whether the motion should be granted. For example, in a Motion to Dismiss Because of the Statute of Limitations, the motion may include a brief recitation of such facts as the alleged date of the crime and the date of the indictment. A copy of the indictment may be attached to the motion.

7. *Statement of reasons why entitled to relief.* The motion must also include a brief statement about why the relief requested should be granted. If there are many reasons for granting the request, the motion should include them all. For example, if a motion is designed to exclude the defendant's confession to the police, the Motion to Exclude the Defendant's Confession may argue that the confession should be barred because it was obtained in violation of the Fifth Amendment's self-incrimination guarantee, the

Fourteenth Amendment's due process clause, and the Sixth Amendment's right to counsel. Many experienced criminal trial lawyers will list the reasons in separately numbered paragraphs. Often counsel will include a citation to statutes, rules, or cases supporting the request, but in most courts this citation to authority should be quite brief. An extensive memorandum of law, described below, can be attached to the motion to provide a full justification for the requested court order.

8. *Concluding paragraph.* Many lawyers include a final paragraph summarizing once again the relief sought. For example, the motion may state, "For the reasons given, the defendant Jonathan Blair Doe moves for an order that his case be severed from that of co-defendant."

9. *Signed by lawyer offering the motion.* Usually motions must be signed by the attorney filing them. Some courts even refuse to accept unsigned motions. Beneath the lawyer's signature, virtually every motion includes the name (and often address and telephone number) of the attorney filing it. This *signature block* provides a quick way for the court and adversary counsel to identify the source of the motion and to contact the lawyer if necessary. This may be especially helpful in cases involving many defendants and numerous lawyers.

10. *Indication of service on opposing party.* In most jurisdictions, a lawyer who files a motion with a court has the responsibility of providing a copy to the other lawyers in the case. To prove that service on all lawyers was made, frequently a *certificate of service* will be included at the end of a motion, indicating that a copy of the motion was mailed or hand delivered to one or more lawyers whose names and addresses are listed in this part of the motion.

D.   SUPPORTING DOCUMENTS

Since a motion is usually quite conclusory and contains few facts and citations to relevant cases, rules, statutes, and constitutional provisions, often counsel will want to submit an affidavit and/or a brief or memorandum in support of the motion. These documents provide the court with more detailed information and authorities and may be instrumental in obtaining a favorable ruling on the motion.

Although these supporting affidavits, memoranda and briefs are common in many jurisdictions, they may be virtually unregulated by formal court rules. Sometimes local rules will prescribe some of the process (perhaps by establishing standards for the size of the paper used for the memorandum or brief, or limits on the number of pages that can be submitted in support of a motion). Usually, however, informal local practice establishes the parameters of this facet of motion practice.

[1]   Affidavit

An *affidavit* is a sworn statement. It provides facts or expert opinions helpful or necessary in resolving the motion. An affidavit may be made by a party or anyone else, including an expert or even a lawyer. The only limit is that the affiant (the person whose statement is in the affidavit) must be competent to testify as a witness. The affidavit is signed by the person providing the information and usually is also signed by a notary. Although hearsay, an affidavit may be admissible to support a motion because the formal rules of evidence usually do not apply to motion hearings. Rule 47(b) of the Federal Rules of Criminal Procedure specifically provides that a motion "may be supported by affidavit." Rule 47(d) states that an affidavit should be served on all parties at the same time as the motion it supports.

An affidavit has several advantages. First, it provides the court with important factual information that has been carefully scrutinized by counsel submitting it. Second, it does so in a way that cannot be cross-examined by opposing counsel. Thus, a criminal defendant can submit an affidavit without having to take the stand at a hearing on a motion. On occasion, a judge may permit the motion to be resolved on the basis of facts submitted in affidavits by both sides. This procedure avoids the discovery and delay that may occur if the judge holds a full evidentiary hearing on the motion.

Another consideration arises in jurisdictions where one judge resolves motions based solely on affidavits and another judge decides those requiring an evidentiary hearing. Counsel may use one or the other procedures in order to affect the assignment of judges.

Because of the lack of rules regulating this facet of motion practice, there is significant confusion about what is appropriate to include in an affidavit. For the reasons stated above, counsel may prefer to rely on an affidavit rather than a live witness. But there are authorities for the view that so-called "speaking motions" are impermissible since they are a substitute for live testimony at a hearing.

Although far from clear, the proper use of affidavits probably depends on the issue raised in the motion. Except in unusual cases, affidavits should not be permitted to counter the allegations in an indictment. The government is entitled to prove its case through direct and cross examination and other evidence. On the other hand, if the issue can be resolved by undisputed facts, affidavits may be an appropriate and sufficient source of factual data. This is especially true for legal (as opposed to factual) issues.

In *United States v. Jones*, 542 F.2d 661 (6th Cir. 1976), for example, the court upheld the use of affidavits to provide a factual basis for a motion to dismiss an indictment on the basis of a statutory exemption from prosecution. The facts needed to resolve the legal issue could be established by affidavits. Similarly, in *United States v. J.R. Watkins Co.*, 16 F.R.D. 229 (D. Minn. 1954), the court held that a motion to dismiss because of a violation of the statute of limitations can be resolved on the basis of affidavits and exhibits. However, the court held further that the defendant's motion opposing the government's characterization of facts alleged in the indictment (that use of a code number constituted a "representation" and therefore violated federal requirements mandating the provision of certain information) must be resolved at trial rather than through affidavits because it is the factual heart of the prosecution.

Sealed affidavit. On rare occasions, counsel may be placed in the difficult position of needing to file an affidavit, yet fearing that doing so will adversely affect the case. For example, defense counsel may believe that a defense motion should be supported by an affidavit from a key defense witness. But if the affidavit is filed and read by the prosecutor, important defense strategy will be revealed and the prosecutor may get significant discovery about a defense witness's likely testimony at trial. In this situation, the defense counsel can file a *sealed affidavit* and a motion that requests the court to consider the affidavit *ex parte*, without disclosure to the prosecution. Since some judges are reluctant to permit *ex parte* affidavits, counsel seeking to offer one may elect first to file a Motion to File a Sealed Affidavit. This motion may trigger a hearing on the issue and result in a ruling that, itself, could be a ground for appeal.

[2] Supporting Memoranda and Briefs

A *memorandum* or *brief* contains legal argument and authorities in support of a motion. They may also include details about the procedural history of the case. These are especially appropriate for motions that raise questions of law and need supporting legal arguments and citations to relevant authorities. Memoranda and briefs are written by an advocate for a particular position and are rarely neutral in their approach.

Form varies markedly. The form of memoranda and briefs varies considerably among lawyers and jurisdictions. Some are quite lengthy, while others consist of a short summary of arguments and authorities. State or local rules of court may place page or size limits on these documents, and may require them in certain situations. Sometimes counsel will attach copies of relevant rules, cases, and statutes to the memorandum.

Sometimes these items will be combined. A motion may be filed, accompanied by a memorandum which includes an appendix containing an affidavit. In some courts, the memorandum and affidavit may be filed after the motion is filed. The needs of each case and the rules and preferences of the court will determine when and what items, if any, are submitted with a motion.

[3] Proposed Order

In some jurisdictions, counsel will submit a *proposed order* with the motion. This is a draft of a court order that implements the motion. The trial judge may sign the draft order (or one based on the draft order) if the motion is granted. Many courts prefer that the draft order be signed by all lawyers in the case, indicating it has been approved by all parties. This ensures that the order is accurate, acceptable, and virtually immune from appellate reversal. Obviously, the procedure of submitting a draft order saves the court time. It also gives counsel a chance to affect the exact wording of the judge's decree.

E. SAMPLE MOTION

The following sample motion illustrates what a typical motion looks like. The parts of the motion are bracketed in bold. In this case, Jonathan Blair Doe is a police officer charged with multiple cocaine sales. Because of Doe's job, the local and national media have covered the crime in great detail, decrying corruption by public officials. Investigative reporters have combed the crime scene, interviewed every possible person in the case, and heavily covered every legal proceeding. For the past five months, the local papers have published daily stories on some facet of the case.

UNITED STATES DISTRICT COURT FOR THE EASTERN DISTRICT OF STATALINA [Court]

UNITED STATES
OF AMERICA,

vs.

JONATHAN BLAIR DOE
[Title of motion] [Case number]
Case No. Cr. 00-1382

s.s.:

MOTION FOR EXCLUSION OF PUBLIC FROM PRELIMINARY HEARING

[Relief requested]

The Defendant Jonathan Blair Doe moves the court for an order excluding the general public from a Preliminary Hearing in the instant case set for August 3, 200X, at 1:30 P.M.

[Underlying facts and reasons motion should be granted]

In support of this motion, the defendant states:

1. That there will be extensive press coverage of this hearing, and

2. Evidence that will not be admitted at trial will be introduced and reported, and

3. That this press coverage will make it substantially probable that the defendant will be unable to have a fair trial because the extensive publicity will make it impossible to select an unbiased jury, and

4. That no reasonable alternatives exist to protect the defendant's rights to a fair trial. *Press-Enterprise Co. v. Superior Court*, 478 U.S. 1 (1986).

[Concluding paragraph]

THEREFORE, defendant respectfully moves this Court to order that the above-described preliminary hearing be closed to the general public and that attendance be limited to the defendant, legal counsel for all parties, the judge, necessary court officers, and witnesses permitted to remain in the courtroom pursuant to the Statalina Rules of Evidence.

Date
[Signature block]

Pat Ferguson
Attorney for Defendant,
Jonathan Blair Doe
Ferguson & Mancuso
2317 Main Street
Center, Statalina 37924
Tel. (234)567-8910

[Proof of service]

Certificate

I hereby certify that on July 18, 200X, I mailed a copy of the foregoing Motion to the United States Attorney for the Eastern District of Statalina, Federal Court House, 239 Court Street, Center, Statalina 37924.

Pat Ferguson

NOTES

1. *Additional information.* Although this Motion for Exclusion of Public from Preliminary Hearing does contain both facts and a citation to a leading case, more information may be helpful to the court. Accordingly, many lawyers would at least file a memorandum. Since this particular motion has constitutional overtones, a legal brief, titled "Memorandum of Law in Support of Defendant's Motion for Exclusion of Public from Preliminary Hearing," would be essential to educate the judge and persuade him or her to rule in the defendant's favor. This document would present the legal arguments and authorities supporting the defendant's motion.

One or more affidavits may also be furnished so that the court has more detailed information about such matters as the quantity and quality of publicity to date, the precise evidence that is likely to be introduced at the preliminary hearing but unavailable at the trial, and the practical pitfalls of other methods of controlling the dissemination of information about the preliminary hearing. The prosecution, of course, would have an opportunity to file its memorandum in opposition, containing its counterarguments, before the judge rules on the motion.

2. *Ruling on motion.* If you were the judge, would you grant the defendant's motion? If not, what additional information would change your mind? How should the information be furnished? In an affidavit? Memorandum? Hearing?

3. *Role of third parties.* Should the press be able to intervene in opposition to the defendant's motion? If so, what limits should there be on interventions by third parties? Should the victim be permitted to express an opinion as to the presence of the press? If so, how should the victim's opinion be presented to the court?

F. PROCEDURE

[1] Timing and Waiver

Motions can be made before, during, and after a criminal trial. Sometimes court rules mandate that certain motions be filed at or before a specified time in the proceedings. These time limits must be explored carefully and taken seriously. Failure to adhere to them can constitute a waiver of the issue the motion addresses. Fed. R. Crim. P. 12(e).

However, the waiver rule is not absolute; the court has the discretion to refuse to find that an issue has been waived because of an untimely motion. *See* Rule 12(e): "For good cause, the court may grant relief from the waiver." Typical reasons for a late motion include that counsel was too busy to complete and file the motion (a reason that is unlikely to be viewed with favor by the trial judge), counsel rendered ineffective assistance, or, despite due diligence, counsel was unaware of the defect addressed in the motion.

The Federal Rules of Criminal Procedure provide an example of time requirements for filing motions:

FEDERAL RULES OF CRIMINAL PROCEDURE

Rule 12. *Pleadings and Pretrial Motions*

. . . .

(b) Pretrial Motions.

(1) In General. Rule 47 applies to a pretrial motion.

(2) Motions That May Be Made Before Trial. A party may raise by pretrial motion any defense, objection, or request that the court can determine without a trial of the general issue.

(3) Motions That Must Be Made Before Trial. The following must be raised before trial:

(A) a motion alleging a defect in instituting the prosecution;

(B) a motion alleging a defect in the indictment or information — but at any time while the case is pending, the court may hear a claim that the indictment or information fails to invoke the court's jurisdiction or to state an offense;

(C) a motion to suppress evidence;

(D) a Rule 14 motion to sever charges or defendants; and

(E) a Rule 16 motion for discovery.

(4) Notice of the Government's Intent to Use Evidence.

(A) *At the Government's Discretion.* At the arraignment or as soon afterward as practicable, the government may notify the defendant of its intent to use specified evidence at trial in order to afford the defendant an opportunity to object before trial under Rule 12(b)(3)(C).

(B) *At the Defendant's Request.* At the arraignment or as soon afterward as practicable, the defendant may, in order to have an opportunity to move to suppress evidence under Rule 12(b)(3)(C), request notice of the government's intent to use (in its evidence-in-chief at trial) any evidence that the defendant may be entitled to discover under Rule 16.

(c) Motion Deadline. The court may, at the arraignment or as soon afterward as practicable, set a deadline for the parties to make pretrial motions and may also schedule a motion hearing.

(d) Ruling on a Motion. The court must decide every pretrial motion before trial unless it finds good cause to defer a ruling. The court must not defer ruling on a pretrial motion if the deferral will adversely affect a party's right to appeal. When factual issues are involved in deciding a motion, the court must state its essential findings on the record. . . .

NOTES

1. *Pretrial motions.* It is obvious from Rule 12 that time limits for filing certain motions must be researched carefully. Commonly, criminal procedure rules mandate that certain motions must be filed pretrial. The requirement of an early filing is designed to facilitate the use of a single hearing on all motions in the case and to permit the court and the parties time to implement any court decision. Typical motions that must be filed before trial include motions alleging defects in the institution of the prosecution, indictment, or information; motions to suppress evidence; discovery motions; selective prosecution; speedy trial; statute of limitations; double jeopardy; and motions seeking a severance of offenses or charges.

Even when a rule does not require a pretrial motion, many judges prefer or require that motions affecting a trial be filed sufficiently in advance of the trial to permit the parties to prepare for it if the motion is granted or denied. Thus, when possible, certain motions should be filed before a trial even though no court rule so states. Examples include a motion for a continuance, for support services during trial, for special trial arrangements (such as letting two counsel do closing argument, permitting the client to serve as co-counsel, permitting the defense to argue last), or narrowing the scope of the trial by eliminating certain issues or evidence.

2. *Post-trial motions.* Just as some motions must be filed before trial, other motions must be filed after the trial has ended. These vary among the jurisdictions but include such motions as a motion for judgment of acquittal, motion in arrest of judgment, and motion for a new trial.

3. *In-trial motions.* Still other motions are filed during the trial. For example, often after the prosecution has put on its case, the defense will make a motion for judgment of acquittal, alleging that the prosecution has not met its burden of proving guilt beyond a reasonable doubt. *See* Fed. R. Crim. P. 29(a).

4. *Any time motions.* Other motions can be filed at any time. Rule 12(b)(3) specifies that a motion alleging a defect in the indictment or information on the ground that "it fails to invoke the court's jurisdiction in the court or to state an offense" may be brought and ruled on at any time while the case is pending.

5. *Tactical considerations in timing of motions.* If counsel has a choice of when to file a particular motion, there are many tactical considerations to take into account. An early filing may engender an early resolution, which may or may not be desired. For example, an unresolved issue may be more of a plea bargaining advantage than one that was rejected in an early motion process. Conversely, an early pretrial motion may prompt an early decision and the greater possibility of an interlocutory appeal to the losing side. It may also avoid lengthy jury-out hearings that will bore and perhaps even anger some jurors.

[2]   Timing and Waiver

A motion and its supporting documents must be *filed* with the court. This means that they must be presented to the court clerk who usually will make an official record that the item was submitted and will write or stamp on the item the date and time it was filed. Usually the clerk then routinely sends the motion to the file, the judge, or other appropriate location.

[3]   Service

Motions must be filed with the court clerk as well as served on all other parties. Since in criminal cases where motions are used, all parties will probably be represented by counsel, service on a party's lawyer is sufficient. Although the legal system sometimes provides that the court clerk performs service on all parties, in most jurisdictions service on other parties is the responsibility of the party submitting the motion. Ordinarily the motion itself will indicate the people who were served with copies. Service is usually accomplished by delivering or mailing a copy of the motion to opposing counsel's office.

As seen below, the Federal Rules of Criminal Procedure deal briefly with service:

FEDERAL RULES OF CRIMINAL PROCEDURE

Rule 47. *Motions and Supporting Affidavits*

. . . .

(c) Timing of a Motion. A party must serve a written motion — other than one that the court may hear ex parte — and any hearing notice at least 5 days before the hearing date, unless a rule or court order sets a different period. For good cause, the court may set a different period upon ex parte application.

(d) Affidavit Supporting a Motion. The moving party must serve any supporting affidavit with the motion. A responding party must serve any opposing affidavit at least one day before the hearing, unless the court permits later service.

Rule 49. *Serving and Filing Papers*

(a) When Required. A party must serve on every other party any written motion (other than one to be heard ex parte), written notice, designation of the record on appeal, or similar paper.

(b) How Made. Service must be made in the manner provided for a civil action. When these rules or a court order requires or permits service on a party represented by an attorney, service must be made on the attorney instead of the party, unless the court orders otherwise.

. . . .

(d) Filing. A party must file with the court a copy of any paper the party is required to serve. A paper must be filed in a manner provided for in a civil action.

[4] Response by other Parties

The rules of criminal procedure are quite sketchy on the issue of what happens after a motion is filed and served on all parties. The general rule is that a party does not have to file a written response to a motion, but some courts have adopted local rules that require a written response to some or all motions. If no written reply is necessary, the party can wait until the hearing and respond orally. Even if no written response is required, all parties have the option of providing one. They can file a responsive pleading entitled, for example, "Government's Response to Defendant's Motion to Dismiss Indictment." Memoranda and affidavits can also be included in these responsive pleadings. Of course, all such documents must be served on all parties and filed with the court. Rule 47(d) states that opposing affidavits must be served at least one day before a hearing on the motion unless the court grants an extension.

Because of their crowded dockets, some prosecutors do not respond in writing to some or all motions. Their practice is to wait until the motion hearing to respond orally. Since many criminal defendants will plead guilty before the motion hearing is held, many defense motions are never answered by the prosecution. The issues they present become moot when the defendant pleads guilty.

[5] Amendment and Withdrawal of Motions

As counsel gets further into case preparation, new information and ideas may suggest that a motion that has been filed is no longer adequate. Counsel may want to amend the original motion or withdraw it altogether. Rules regulating motion practice rarely deal with the propriety of amending or withdrawing motions. Because of this lack of direction, in most jurisdictions motions can be freely amended or withdrawn, at least before a motion hearing.

The amended motion may markedly or only slightly change the original motion. For example, counsel may file an Amended Motion to Dismiss that adds an additional ground for relief. This document may be quite brief, simply indicating that a sentence should be added to the original motion. The amended motion should be filed and served in the same way as the original. Similarly, counsel may have a change of strategy or enter a deal with the prosecution that makes it necessary to withdraw a motion. The notice of withdrawal must also be filed and served on all parties. Sometimes courts will refuse to permit withdrawal of a motion after a hearing on the motion has commenced.

[6] Burden of Proof

Irrespective of the type of motion, the general rule, subject to few exceptions, is that the movant has the burden of establishing the merits of the motion. *See, e.g., United States v. Briscoe*, 896 F.2d 1476 (7th Cir.1990) (defendants' motions for severance were properly denied because they did not sustain their burden of proving joinder caused actual prejudice); *United States v. Olafson*, 203 F.3d 560 (9th Cir. 2000)(party moving for a deposition has burden of proving witness will be unavailable at trial).

The matter becomes more complex when the motion addresses constitutional issues. To some extent, the difficulty is caused by the lack of an authoritative resolution of many burden of proof issues in criminal constitutional law. Although a detailed analysis of this area of constitutional law is beyond the scope of this book, a few examples illustrate this murky area. For example, when the defendant files a motion to suppress evidence allegedly seized in violation of the Fourth Amendment, the general rule is that the defendant has the burden of proof of challenging a search based on a warrant, but the prosecution has the burden on a search conducted without a warrant. *See, e.g., United States v. Jones*, 374 F.Supp.2d 143 (D.D.C. 2005). In other areas, the defendant has been given the burden of proof. *See, e.g., Wayte v. United States*, 470 U.S. 598 (1985), discussed in Chapter 2, (on motion to dismiss for selective prosecution, defendant has burden of proving discriminatory enforcement of criminal laws).

Surprisingly, there is little law describing exactly what standard of proof must be met. For many motions raising non-constitutional matters, the issue is especially difficult because state jurisdictions are generally free to resolve them using their own policies. Some motions raise questions of law, as to which there may be a clear answer governed by the Constitution or a federal or state statute. Appellate courts reviewing rulings on motions that raise questions of law usually apply a *de novo* standard of review — the appellate court is free to review the motion judge's ruling "anew," and determine for itself whether the ruling was correct or erroneous.

Many other motions, however, address themselves not to clearly governing rules of law, but rather to the *discretion* of the court. Most "housekeeping" rulings on motions regarding the timing and manner of presentation of evidence at the trial fall into this category. Appellate courts are extremely reluctant to reverse discretionary rulings, and typically will only (and rarely) do so if they find that the trial court's decision on the motion was an "abuse of discretion." *See, e.g., United States v. Nettles*, 476 F.3d 508 (7th Cir. 2007)(abuse of discretion standard used to review decision on transfer of case for trial under Rule 21); *United States v. Lore*, 430 F.3d 190 (3d Cir. 2005)(motion to sever offenses or defendants under Rule 14).

The few cases on point often indicate that many motions can be sustained if the party who has the burden of proof provides sufficient evidence to satisfy the preponderance of evidence test. *See, e.g., Lego v. Twomey*, 404 U.S. 477 (1972) (in response to motion to exclude a confession, the voluntariness of the confession can be established by preponderance of evidence); *Medina v. California*, 505 U.S. 437 (1992) (not unconstitutional for state to allocate to the defense the burden of persuasion on issue of defendant's competency to stand trial).

[7] Hearing

Law and practice are quite murky with regard to the procedures following the filing of a motion. The typical procedure is that a hearing on the motion is available, although many jurisdictions' criminal procedure rules do not mandate a hearing. Local court rules, however, will often provide for a hearing on some or all motions. Sometimes counsel must request a hearing. Such requests should be in writing to facilitate appellate review. By custom or local rule, in some courts a lawyer notifies adversary counsel of an intent to argue a particular motion at a specific future motion hearing. This practice allows counsel to determine the sequence of consideration of motions. Of course the court must consent to the hearing time and date.

Scheduling hearing. Some judges have a "motion day" on which they conduct hearings on motions. Many judges in criminal cases automatically schedule motion hearings a set time before trial. Perhaps the most sophisticated approach is the *omnibus hearing*, a wide-ranging hearing used in some jurisdictions. Scheduled automatically a number of days before each criminal trial, the omnibus hearing tries to resolve all outstanding motions and to deal with many other administrative matters that will speed up the criminal process.

Often informal. Motion hearings are usually quite informal, although their exact contours differ markedly among jurisdictions and judges. Usually oral argument by counsel is permitted but not required. Counsel submitting the motion may argue why it should be granted. Opposing counsel may then argue why it should be denied. The court may permit the parties to take turns until no one has anything else to say. The court can ask for the parties to provide a brief on certain legal issues.

At some motion hearings, especially where the outcome of the motion may depend on the court's determination of certain facts (*e.g.*, a motion to suppress, where the actions and knowledge of the officer who seized the contested evidence are in dispute), the court will hold an *evidentiary hearing*, where both parties can present witnesses and physical evidence. Where determination of facts is not crucial to the outcome of the motion, counsel may simply summarize the relevant facts or rely on affidavits submitted with the motion or response. One benefit of an evidentiary hearing on a motion is that it may provide an opportunity for both sides to preview the likely trial testimony of witnesses who testify at the motion hearing. Where facts are not in dispute and there is no need for an evidentiary hearing, the hearing on the motion is simply an opportunity for the lawyers to offer oral and written arguments in support of their positions.

[8] Ruling by Court

As strange as it may seem, on occasion a motion is filed, perhaps a hearing is held, and no decision on it is ever reached. The court may "take the matter under advisement" or simply refuse or forget to render a decision. When this occurs, appellate review of the issue is virtually foreclosed. Counsel submitting a motion must ensure that a decision is made on the motion if counsel wants to preserve the issue for appellate review. Whenever possible, counsel should urge the judge to indicate why the judge denied or granted a motion. Any such ruling on a motion should be on the record so the appellate court has a clear understanding of what happened and why. Rule 12(d) provides that "[w]hen factual issues are involved in deciding a motion, the court must state its essential findings on the record."

Counsel will usually prefer that the court make a prompt ruling on a motion so counsel can plan for other motions or proceedings that will be affected by the ruling. Rule 12(d) of the Federal Rules of Criminal Procedure clearly indicates that a pretrial motion should be determined before trial unless a later determination is needed "for good cause." Some judges delay such decisions in order to obtain more information. For example, they may postpone until trial the decision on a pretrial motion asking that evidence be excluded as too prejudicial. The judge may feel that the motion cannot be assessed without an understanding of how this evidence will complement other evidence and affect the outcome of the trial. No such delay is permissible, however, "if a party's right to appeal is adversely affected." Fed. R. Crim. P. 12(d).

The difficulty of rendering a pretrial decision on a motion was highlighted in *Luce v. United States*, 469 U.S. 38 (1984). The defendant had filed a pretrial motion to exclude evidence of his prior criminal conviction. Presumably, the defendant would testify if the impeaching conviction were barred, but would not testify if it were admissible. The district court denied the motion and the defendant did not testify at trial, where he was convicted of various drug offenses. The United States Supreme Court held that the defendant was not entitled to appellate review of the trial court's denial of the motion to exclude the conviction. The Court stated,

> . . . [H]ad petitioner testified and been impeached by evidence of a prior conviction . . . [t]he Court of Appeals would then have had a complete record detailing the nature of petitioner's testimony, the scope of the cross-examination, and the possible impact of the impeachment on the jury's verdict.

> A reviewing court is handicapped in any effort to rule on subtle evidentiary questions outside a factual context. . . . Any possible harm flowing from a district court's *in limine* ruling permitting impeachment by a prior conviction is wholly speculative. The ruling is subject to change when the case unfolds, particularly if the actual testimony differs from what was contained in the defendant's proffer. . . . When the defendant does not testify, the reviewing court also has no way of knowing whether the government would have sought

to impeach with the prior conviction. . . . Even if these difficulties could be surmounted, the reviewing court would still face the question of harmless error. . . . Were *in limine* rulings under [Federal Rules of Evidence] Rule 609(a) reviewable on appeal, almost any error would result in the windfall of automatic reversal; the appellate court could not logically term "harmless" an error that presumptively kept the defendant from testifying. Requiring that a defendant testify in order to preserve Rule 609(a) claims [dealing with the admissibility of prior criminal convictions to impeach] will enable the reviewing court to determine the impact any erroneous impeachment may have had in light of the record as a whole; it will also tend to discourage making such motions solely to "plant" reversible error in the event of conviction. [469 U.S. at 41–42]

NOTES

1. *Impact of Luce on planning.* What effect will *Luce* have on defense planning for trial? For prosecution planning?

2. *Motion in limine.* The *Luce* opinion makes reference to the district court's ruling *in limine*. A motion *in limine*, meaning literally, in Latin, a motion brought "at the threshold" of trial, asks the judge to make a ruling about the conduct of the trial. Common motions *in limine* include a motion to sequester witnesses, to allow a defendant in custody to appear in trial in civilian clothing instead of a jail uniform, or to preclude or limit the other side from questioning witnesses about certain subjects. These motions are often heard at the pretrial conference (see Rule 17.1 of the Federal Rules of Criminal Procedure) rather than during the trial itself, so as to anticipate and resolve contested procedural issues in advance of the trial and thereby minimize interruptions in the presentation of evidence during the trial, and to let the parties know in advance what kinds of questioning of witnesses will or will not be permitted.

3. *Luce and other types of motions.* *Luce* dealt with one kind of motion: suppressing evidence of a prior criminal conviction. Does the Court's logic in *Luce* apply to other motions as well? Could a trial court use *Luce* to delay ruling on a Motion to Dismiss Because of the Statute of Limitations? What about a Motion to Dismiss Because of Extensive, Harmful Pretrial Publicity That Makes a Fair Trial Impossible?

[9] Appeal from Adverse Ruling

The law regulating appeals of unsuccessful motions is quite complex and beyond the scope of this book. Nevertheless, a few general principles should be kept in mind. Often appeals of motions are governed by the rules of appellate procedure rather than the rules of criminal procedure. The appellate rules ordinarily permit appeals of final orders and, in the discretion of the appellate court, interlocutory appeals. These principles are interpreted to place severe limits on the appeal of unsuccessful motions in criminal cases.

The general approach is that unsuccessful motions may not be appealed until after the defendant is convicted. The alleged erroneous rulings on motions are considered as part of the normal appellate review process. For example, if the court erroneously denies a defense motion to exclude certain evidence, ordinarily the appellate courts will not hear the appeal of the decision on the motion until the defendant is convicted and appeals. On appeal, the allegedly wrongful admission of evidence against the accused will be one ground used to challenge the conviction.

A few motions are reviewable by an *interlocutory appeal* to an appellate court before the defendant is convicted. Often the motions for which interlocutory review is allowed are specified in a statute or appellate rule. For example, federal law provides that a criminal defendant denied release pending trial can appeal the detention decision to the Court of Appeals. *See* 18 U.S.C. § 3145(c). Similarly, another federal statute lists ral situations where the government can appeal successful defense motions. *See* 18 .C. § 3731 (government can appeal granting of defense motion to dismiss indictment nformation, suppressing or excluding evidence or requiring the return of seized property, and granting release of a person pending trial; all subject to double jeopardy limitations).

G. VARIETIES OF MOTIONS

The list of motions that can be filed in criminal cases is limited only by the imagination of counsel. Virtually any topic can be addressed. To give you a sense of the variety and scope of motions in criminal cases, the descriptive titles of some that have been filed in actual criminal cases are listed below.

Motions seeking dismissal. A Motion to Dismiss a criminal prosecution can be based on a number of grounds. Examples include Motions to Dismiss for Failure to State a Criminal Offense, because Statute is Unconstitutional, for Lack of Jurisdiction, for Improper Venue, for Denial of Speedy Trial, for Delay in Returning Indictment, for Failure to Prosecute, for Prejudicial Pretrial Delay, because Barred by Statute of Limitations, because of Immunity From Prosecution, because Barred by Double Jeopardy Clause, for Violation of Ex Post Facto Clause, for Prosecutorial Misconduct, for Insufficient Indictment, for Grand Jury Abuse, for Illegally Constituted Grand Jury, for Loss or Destruction of Indispensable Evidence, for Failure to Honor Grant of Immunity, for Prejudicial Pretrial Publicity, for Failure to Grant a Preliminary Hearing, and for Judgment of Acquittal.

Motions affecting evidence. Counsel may file a written motion in order to obtain a ruling on an evidentiary issue. Often these evidentiary motions are filed as motions *in limine*, which, in most jurisdictions, are made and ruled on before the start of the trial. These can include motions *in limine* to exclude or to admit evidence. Examples are: Motions to Suppress Unconstitutionally Seized Evidence, to Bar Reference to Past Convictions, to Produce an Incarcerated Witness, to Exclude a Coconspirator's Statement, to Disclose the Existence of Electronic Surveillance, to Permit Defendant to Testify in Narrative Style, and to Permit Introduction of Results of a Polygraph Test.

Motions affecting pretrial proceedings. Pretrial proceedings may also be addressed by motions. For example, a lawyer may file a Motion for a Prompt Preliminary Hearing, or a Speedy Grand Jury Hearing, to Intervene in a Grand Jury Proceeding, to Exclude Evidence from the Grand Jury or the Preliminary Hearing, and to Testify Before the Grand Jury.

Motions affecting trial procedure. Virtually any aspect of the trial can be altered by court order responding to a motion. These requests can include such motions as a Motion to Withdraw Guilty Plea, to Sever Counts, to Sever Defendants, to Withdraw a Plea, to Change Venue, to Disqualify the Judge, to Disqualify the Prosecutor, to Disqualify Defense Counsel, to Disqualify an Improperly Selected Jury, to Grant a Continuance, to Permit the Defendant to Appear Without Shackles, to Have the Defendant's Mother Sit at Counsel's Table, to Exclude the Media from the Trial (or certain proceedings, such as a suppression hearing), to Interrogate Potential Jurors Individually Rather than as a Group, to Preclude Discriminatory Use of Peremptory Challenges, for Additional Peremptory Challenges, for Daily Transcripts, and for a Written Jury Charge.

Motions involving defendant's activities. If the defendant wants a court to modify a previous order to facilitate new activities or alter conditions of release or confinement, various motions can be filed. These include motions to Grant Bail, to Change the Conditions of Release, to Lower the Amount of Bail, to Quash Arrest Warrant, to Travel Out of State to Interview a Witness, to Transfer Cells, to Receive Medicine While Incarcerated, to Increase Opportunities to Meet with Defense Counsel, and to be Present at All Hearings.

Motions to assist in gathering evidence. Many aspects of the process of gathering information for use in preparing for trial or another proceeding merit a motion in order to obtain a court order. Examples of these motions are a Motion to Produce a Witness in Government Control for Purposes of Interview, to Compel a Witness to Be Interviewed by Defense Counsel, to Grant Immunity to Defense or Prosecution Witness, to Inspect Jencks Act Material (discussed in Chapter 10), to Grant a Protective Order, to Order a Mental Examination of the Defendant (or a named witness or the victim), to Have a List of Prosecution (or Defense) Witnesses, for State Paid Investigator (or forensic expert, handwriting expert, etc.), for a Bill of Particulars (to get more information about the allegations; discussed in Chapter 7), for Discovery and Inspection (Rule 16 motion), for Disclosure of Evidence Favorable to Accused, to Reveal the Deal (disclosure of any government promises to prosecution witnesses), for Demographic Information about Potential Jurors, and to Inspect the Grand Jury Minutes.

Motions incorporating other motions. Sometimes a motion will seek an order to have other motions deemed applicable to the movant. This may occur in a case involving two defendants represented by different lawyers. Lawyer X may file a Motion to Suppress Evidence. If Lawyer Y wants that motion to apply to her case as well, she may file a Motion to Adopt Codefendant's Motion to Suppress. Sometimes a lawyer will even offer a Motion to Adopt All of Codefendant's Motions. This type of motion may be adequate to raise an issue and, if necessary, preserve it for appeal without the need to replicate it verbatim.

H.   ETHICAL FACETS OF MOTION PRACTICE

There is no doubt that counsel must conduct motion practice in many criminal cases if the client is to be represented competently. The American Bar Association, for example, recommends that defense counsel routinely consider all procedural steps that can be taken in good faith. These include a host of motions, including those for pretrial release, psychiatric examination, change of venue, continuance, suppression of evidence, severance, and dismissal. Standards for Criminal Justice § 4-3.6 (3d ed. 1993). As noted above, issues and opportunities can be lost if proper motions are not made in a timely manner.

The failure to file appropriate motions can constitute ineffective assistance of counsel in violation of the Sixth Amendment. However, if a motion is not pursued because of a trial tactic, usually the failure will not constitute ineffective assistance. The United States Supreme Court recognized that "[o]ften the interests of the accused are not advanced by challenges that would only delay the inevitable date of prosecution . . . or by contesting all guilt." *Tollett v. Henderson*, 411 U.S. 258, 268 (1973). More specifically, "The decision whether or not to make various pretrial motions is a matter of trial tactics generally not reviewable under a claim of ineffective assistance. Moreover, counsel is not required to make futile or frivolous motions." *United States v. Ritch*, 583 F.2d 1179, 1182 (1st Cir.), *cert. denied*, 439 U.S. 970 (1978) (citations omitted). In *Strickland v. Washington*, 466 U.S. 668 (1984), discussed below, the Supreme Court established general standards for assessing whether defense counsel's representation satisfied the Sixth Amendment's guarantee of "the effective assistance of counsel."

Because of the virtually unlimited array of possible motions, counsel must decide which ones to pursue. To some lawyers, the issue is made easier by the fact that engaging in motion practice may, by itself, give defense counsel some clout in plea negotiations and additional time to prepare the case. These benefits may create a significant ethical dilemma as counsel has to resolve difficult questions about the extent of motion practice that should be pursued in this case. Should counsel file discovery motions to obtain information not required to be disclosed by existing law in the jurisdiction? Should counsel seek release on bail in a capital case where such motion stands no chance of success but where the hearing on it may provide some needed discovery into the prosecution's case?

The ethical precepts of the legal profession are not very helpful on these issues. The two widely recognized sets of rules detailing professional standards, although vague, focus on two issues: good faith and frivolousness. A lawyer must file motions in good faith and cannot file frivolous motions.

Model Code of Professional Responsibility. The American Bar Association approved the Model Code of Professional Responsibility in 1969, which was widely adopted by American jurisdictions. Canon 6 states that "A lawyer should represent a client competently." Canon 7 makes it more emphatic: "A lawyer should *represent a client zealously within the bounds of the law*" (emphasis added). More particularly, a client is entitled "to seek any lawful objective through legally permissible means, and to present for adjudication any lawful claim, issue, or defense." (EC 7-1) If there is any doubt about what the law allows, "a lawyer should resolve in favor of his client doubts as to the bounds of the law." (EC 7-3) Thus, the attorney is to be an aggressive advocate for the client. But how far can counsel go in arguing what is permissible? The Model Code is helpful in a general way. The lawyer's conduct is permissible "if the position taken is supported by the law or is supportable by a good faith argument for an extension, modification, or reversal of the law." (EC 7-4).

The key concept is *good faith*. The contrasting principle is frivolousness. Counsel may not, consistent with the Model Code, assert "a position in litigation that is frivolous." (EC 7-4) More specifically, DR 7-102 states that a lawyer cannot "assert a position, conduct a defense, delay a trial, or take other action on behalf of his client when he knows or when it is obvious that such action would serve merely to harass or maliciously injury another." The lawyer also may not "[k]nowingly advance a claim or defense that is unwarranted under existing law, except that he may advance such claim or defense if it can be supported by good faith argument for an extension, modification, or reversal of existing law." *Id.*

Model Rules of Professional Conduct. In response to significant criticisms of the Model Code, the American Bar Association adopted the Model Rules of Professional Conduct in 1983, then substantially updated in 2002. A majority of American jurisdictions have now adopted all or part of the Model Rules in lieu of the Model Code. The new Rules, however, are no more helpful than the Model Code on the issue of the ethics of motion practice. The same themes of requiring good faith and barring frivolous motions are present. Rule 3.1 states that a lawyer cannot "bring or defend a proceeding, or assert or controvert an issue therein, unless there is a basis for doing so that is not frivolous, which includes a good faith argument for an extension, modification or reversal of existing law." The Comment to this section explains that an action is frivolous "if the lawyer is unable either to make a good faith argument on the merits of the action taken or to support the action taken by a good faith argument for an extension, modification or reversal of existing law." A more specific reference to frivolous motion practice is in Rule 3.4: "A lawyer shall not . . . (d) in pretrial procedure, make a frivolous discovery request or fail to make reasonably diligent effort to comply with a legally proper discovery request by an opposing party."

The Model Rules also address the issue of delay. Rule 3.2 states that "[a] lawyer shall make reasonable efforts to expedite litigation consistent with the interests of the client." The Comment to Rule 3.2 explains that an action done solely for the purpose of delay is improper:

> The question is whether a competent lawyer acting in good faith would regard the course of action as having some substantial purpose other than delay. Realizing financial or other benefit from otherwise improper delay in litigation is not a legitimate interest of the client.

See also Standards for Criminal Justice § 4-1.3(d) (3d ed. 1993) (defense counsel should not intentionally use procedural devices for delay for which there is no legitimate basis).

PERRON v. PERRIN

742 F.2d 669 (1st Cir. 1984)

GIERBOLINI, DISTRICT JUDGE.

Petitioner appeals from an order of the U.S. District Court for the District of New Hampshire dismissing his petition for a writ of habeas corpus for failure to show that he had been denied effective assistance of counsel and that he had been deprived of his right to a speedy trial. We affirm.

At approximately 8:30 p.m. on November 6, 1979, Robert D. O'Neal, a Dartmouth undergraduate, was beaten and robbed near the center of the Dartmouth College campus. [A jury convicted the defendant of robbery and assault. After his convictions were upheld by the New Hampshire Supreme Court, the defendant filed a habeas corpus petition alleging that his Sixth Amendment rights were violated when his trial counsel rendered ineffective assistance.]

. . . Over the years, the Supreme Court has repeatedly recognized the Sixth Amendment right to counsel, and its necessity to protect the fundamental right to a fair trial. . . .

In *Strickland v. Washington*, 466 U.S. 668 (1984), the Court clearly set forth the standard for determining effective assistance of counsel. "The benchmark for judging any claim of ineffectiveness must be whether counsel's conduct so undermined the proper functioning of the adversarial process that the trial cannot be relied on as having produced a just result." The Court reasoned that the well established right to counsel played a crucial role in the adversarial system embodied in the Sixth Amendment. Indeed, without access to counsel's skill and knowledge defendants would effectively be denied "the 'ample opportunity to meet the case of the prosecution' to which they are entitled."

To determine whether assistance of counsel was in actuality so defective as to warrant reversal, the Court formulated a two-pronged test. The criminal defendant must prove first, that counsel's performance was deficient, and second, that the deficient performance prejudiced the defense thus depriving him of a fair trial.

The proper standard for judging attorney's performance is that of reasonably effective assistance, taking into consideration all the circumstances. A convicted defendant must show that counsel made errors so serious that counsel's representation fell below an objective standard of reasonableness. In cases where it does, criminal defendants would not have received a fair trial.

The Court emphasized that judicial scrutiny of counsel's performance must be highly deferential. It confirmed the rule in this circuit that reviewing courts shall not use the benefit of hindsight to second-guess tactical decisions made by an attorney unless they are unreasonable. Instead, after the defendant has identified the acts or omissions of counsel alleged to be ineffective, the reviewing court must reconstruct the circumstances of counsel's conduct and evaluate it from counsel's perspective at the time. Because of the difficulties inherent in making such evaluation, a court must indulge a strong presumption that counsel's conduct falls within the wide range of reasonable professional assistance.

With regard to the second prong, "[i]t is not enough for the defendant to show that [counsel's] errors had some conceivable effect on the outcome of the proceeding." Defendant bears the heavier burden of affirmatively showing that "there is a reasonable probability that, but for counsel's unprofessional errors, the result of the proceeding would have been different." In making the above determination a court hearing an ineffective assistance claim must consider the totality of the evidence before it.

In short, the appropriate inquiry in ineffective assistance claims focuses on the adversarial process. If counsel is a reasonably effective advocate, and has not substantially prejudiced his client, he has met the constitutional standards.

. . . Petitioner's main allegation of ineffective assistance was that defense counsel failed to secure a decision on a motion in limine to prohibit the state from using details of a prior conviction if petitioner took the stand to testify on his own behalf. Petitioner argues that counsel improperly advised him that if he took the stand, he would be subject to cross-examination with respect to those details, and consequently, he gave up his right to testify on his own behalf.

Petitioner filed a motion in limine two days prior to trial wherein he sought to prohibit the state from raising on cross-examination the details of his prior conviction of aggravated assault upon an eighteen-month old child. No objection was made to the mere fact of the felony conviction and subsequent confinement being presented to the jury.

At the commencement of petitioner's case, his counsel requested a ruling on the motion in limine and the court responded that a hearing outside the presence of the jury would be held in the afternoon, provided his client would be testifying. After discussions with his client, defense counsel stated: "I have . . . advised my client fully as to his right to testify and his right not to testify and we discussed the scope of cross-examination which would be allowed if he did testify, and he has chosen not to testify."

In the affidavit in support of this motion petitioner stated: "My attorney informed me that the court would not rule on the motion in limine unless I first appeared on the witness stand. That I further understood from my attorney that the motion in limine would probably be denied and that if I took the witness stand and it was denied the court would allow full cross-examination of me including the details of my prior conviction."

The district court acknowledged that defense counsel should have demanded a ruling on petitioner's motion in limine but, in so doing, suggested that failure to do so was of little significance since the court would have denied it anyway.

Petitioner argues that while the fact of his aggravated assault conviction would have been admissible for impeachment purposes, further details of the offense would not have been admissible, either substantively or to test his credibility, since in either event their prejudicial effect would outweigh their probative value. Petitioner, however, has done little to explain precisely what "details" he wished to have excluded and whether any of these were revealed in his record of conviction. Even had all "details" been excluded, the admission of a prior conviction for aggravated assault in a case of this nature would obviously have been extremely detrimental.

According to New Hampshire law, "[n]o person shall be incompetent to testify on account of his having been convicted of an infamous crime, but the record of such conviction may be used to affect his credit as a witness." N.H. Rev. Stat. § 516.33.

. . . As defense counsel acknowledged, defendant's prior conviction would undoubtedly have been admissible for the purpose of impeaching his credibility during cross-examination. Under these circumstances, the withdrawal of the motion in limine based on his client's decision not to testify on his own behalf can only be characterized as a sound tactical choice which falls within the wide range of reasonable professional assistance.

In briefly addressing counsel's failure to secure a ruling on the motion in limine, we note that it is counsel's responsibility to assure that the record is complete. This entails obtaining the trial judge's ruling on the admissibility of a prior conviction on the record in order to remove any uncertainty as to the actual reasons for the trial judge's decision and to preserve the arguments made to him by counsel. However, counsel's failure to do so here constitutes at most harmless error when viewed against the totality of the circumstances and facts surrounding the trial.

Even assuming that counsel's performance was deficient and that his errors caused petitioner not to testify, petitioner's Sixth Amendment claim must still be rejected for he has failed to show that "there is a reasonable probability that, but for counsel's unprofessional errors, the result of the proceeding would have been different."

Petitioner avers that his failure to testify due to the allegedly erroneous advice given by his counsel, could have made a critical difference at trial. In an affidavit submitted he states that he would have testified (1) that he did not commit the alleged crime, (2) that at all times he was clean-shaven and thus, did not meet the description provided by the victim, and (3) that he never permitted other persons to drive his vehicle and therefore, could not have been the person who stepped out of the passenger seat to assault the victim.

Notwithstanding this argument, the record indicates that defense witnesses testified that petitioner was clean-shaven on the night of the assault. There was also testimony to the effect that Perron did not allow others to drive his vehicle. When viewed against the totality of the evidence presented at trial, we do not believe that petitioner has shown a reasonable probability that his testimony would have made a difference. . . .

NOTES

1. *Tactics or carelessness.* Was defense counsel's failure to obtain a ruling on the motion *in limine* a tactical decision or a careless oversight? Would the difference affect the outcome in *Perron?*

2. *Strickland tests.* In *Strickland v. Washington,* 466 U.S. 668 (1984), cited in *Perron,* the United States Supreme Court established a two-fold test to use in determining whether criminal defense counsel was ineffective in violation of the Sixth Amendment. The test, described in greater detail below, focuses on the quality of the lawyer's work and the effects of alleged deficiencies in the representation. *Strickland* involved a convicted murderer who received three death sentences. The defendant challenged the effectiveness of defense counsel's decisions to withhold certain proof during the sentencing hearing.

The first prong of the *Strickland* test states that the client-defendant must prove that counsel's performance was deficient. This requires showing that counsel made errors so serious that counsel was not functioning as the "counsel" guaranteed by the Sixth Amendment. . . . When a convicted defendant complains of the ineffectiveness of counsel's assistance, the defendant must show that counsel's representation fell below an objective standard of reasonableness. 466 U.S. at 687–688. What kinds of errors in motion practice would satisfy this test? Would your answer be affected by the *Strickland* Court's view that "the court could recognize that counsel is strongly presumed to have rendered adequate assistance and made all significant decisions in the exercise of reasonable professional judgment.[?]" 466 U.S. at 690.

The second prong of *Strickland* looks at the consequences of the ineffective counsel. The key is the defendant's burden of proving prejudice.

> Second, the defendant must show that the deficient performance prejudiced the defense. This requires showing that counsel's errors were so serious as to deprive the defendant of a fair trial, a trial whose result is reliable. [466 U.S. at 687]

More particularly,

> The defendant must show that there is a reasonable probability that, but for counsel's unprofessional errors, the result of the proceeding would have been different. A reasonable probability is a probability sufficient to undermine confidence in the outcome. [466 U.S. at 694]

What kinds of errors in motion practice are likely to rise to the level of "prejudice" as defined in *Strickland?* Counsel's defective representation that results in an increase in a prison term is prejudicial under *Strickland. Glover v. United States,* 531 U.S. 198 (2001).

I. THE MOTION FOR A CONTINUANCE: CASE STUDY AND PROBLEM

A detailed discussion of all criminal motions is far beyond the scope of this book. Nevertheless, to provide a better understanding of motion practice, this section will describe one motion, the Motion for a Continuance, as an illustration of motion practice.

A Motion for a Continuance is a request for a postponement of a scheduled hearing or other proceeding. If counsel for one party wants a continuance, in many jurisdictions that matter is worked out informally between the lawyers. The lawyer seeking the postponement will contact the other lawyers who, as a matter of professional courtesy, will agree to the postponement and may even try to agree on an alternate day that is convenient for both sides and the court. The court's calendar clerk is then notified of the lawyers' agreement and will routinely reschedule the matter at a time acceptable to everyone.

When a formal Motion for a Continuance is used, courts prefer that the motion be filed well before the scheduled hearing, although often the delay is sought because of an unexpected last-minute matter and advance filing of the motion is impossible. Advance filing lets the court efficiently handle its calendar by scheduling another matter in place of the postponed one.

There are virtually no limits on the grounds that can support a Motion for a Continuance. Typical grounds include counsel's conflict with another case scheduled at the same time; illness of counsel, the defendant, or a witness; newly discovered evidence; incomplete expert evaluation of the defendant or evidence; incomplete investigation; inadequate time to complete legal research; and active, intense media coverage that makes a fair trial unlikely at that time.

Judges are given the discretion to control their dockets. Accordingly, continuance motions are held to be within the discretion of the trial judge and will be overturned on appeal only for an abuse of discretion. Speedy trial statutes, however, may put some limits on the judge's discretion to grant a continuance. *See* Chapter 13. These statutes often establish time limits for various proceedings. *See, e.g.*, 18 U.S.C. § 3161 *et seq.* Unless these time limits are waived by the accused, the court cannot grant a continuance in violation of the speedy trial statute. The continuance is discussed more fully in Chapter 12.

PROBLEM 9-1. JUSTICE DELAYED IS . . . JUSTICE

Bennett Foster is charged with several federal drug charges. An undercover federal agent allegedly bought drugs from Bennett in an area of town known to be the center of local drug activity. Bennett Foster has an identical twin brother, Barry, who is heavily involved in the drug trade. For several months, Bennett told defense counsel that he (Bennett) was innocent and did not know anything about the crime. Yesterday, Bennett told defense counsel that Barry sold the drugs alleged in the indictment. He believes that Barry will confess if confronted with the allegations. The problem is that Bennett has not seen Barry for two months and does not know where he is, but Bennett does believe that Barry is still in the area. An even bigger problem is that the trial is scheduled to begin in five days.

Defense counsel has filed the following motion:

UNITED STATES DISTRICT COURT FOR EASTERN WESTPHALIA

UNITED STATES OF AMERICA,

vs.

BENNETT FOSTER,
Defendant

Case No. 00-C24792

MOTION FOR TIME

The Defendant Bennett Foster moves the court for more time to prepare for trial.

Robert Wenterbright
Wenterbright Building
Suite 500
Marion, Westphalia 35678

1. Assess the adequacy of the Motion for Time. If you were the judge, would you grant it? Why or why not?

2. Review the suggested contents of a motion. What, if anything, is missing in the Motion for Time?

3. Recall that sometimes counsel attaches affidavit(s) and/or a memorandum to a motion. Would either of these be appropriate here? Would either one increase the likelihood that the motion will be granted? If you believe that something should be attached to this motion, what would that be? From whom? What should it say?

J.　COMMUNICATING WITH THE OTHER SIDE

The preceding motion for continuance is but one of many possible examples where it may be of significant benefit (and in some cases, a matter of practical necessity) for either prosecution or defense to use informal channels of communication with the other side (the conversation can be designated beforehand, if necessary, as "off the record") before filing a formal motion. A lot can be worked out through discussion and stipulation between the parties or, even if a formal motion and court order are required, via an *assented to* (sometimes called *agreed motion*), or at least *unopposed* motion. Sometimes the cooperation is reflected in a motion signed by both counsel who jointly ask for the relief requested in the motion.

Establishing credibility in the value of a lawyer's word and a reputation for veracity, reasonableness, and reciprocity can serve both the attorney and the client very well in achieving desired results on motions, especially those which might not be particularly controversial. Being reasonable when your opponent seeks a time extension makes it all the more likely that your opponent will be reasonable in return when and if you find yourself in a similar position.

Judges usually prefer not to decide any more than they have to. An assented to motion relieves the judge of having to decide who wins and who loses the motion. Also, oftentimes when presented with a motion for decision, the judge will ask the moving party, "Have you discussed this with the other side?" Counsel can look foolish taking up the court's time with a formal a motion where a phone call might have sufficed, or where the other side might have assented if asked. Unless doing so might somehow compromise the defense (and the same goes for prosecution motions too), it is usually better, at least with relatively routine, housekeeping-type motions (*e.g.*, for continuance), to talk to the other side first.

Chapter 10
DISCOVERY, DISCLOSURE, AND PRESERVATION

A. INTRODUCTION

This chapter deals with three critically important and related issues: the defense or prosecution's right to gather factual information from the other side, each side's duty to disclose information to the other side, and to preserve evidence it obtains on its own. These matters are important because they affect trial preparation and conduct as well as decisions in guilty plea negotiations. Assume that the defendant is charged with vehicular homicide after a hit-and-run incident. The prosecution has photographed, measured, and preserved (using a plaster cast) tireprints from the car that struck the victim. If the defense can get access to the photographs, measurements, and casts of the prints, it can have its own expert examine them to assess whether they match the tires on the defendant's car. Moreover, if the prosecution has had an expert conduct these tests, the defense would benefit considerably if permitted to read the prosecution expert's written report and to depose the expert to determine the expert's assessment of the similarity between the tireprints at the scene and those from the defendant's vehicle. The prosecution would also like to get access to any tireprint information the defense counsel has gathered. If the prosecution were satisfied that the tireprints at the scene matched those on the defendant's car, perhaps the prosecution would insist on a stiff sentence during plea negotiations. Conversely, if the prosecution believed that the tireprints did not match those of the defendant, perhaps the case would be dropped.

B. DISCOVERY AND DISCLOSURE: IN GENERAL

[1] Civil and Criminal Discovery

The law of discovery in criminal cases differs markedly from that in civil cases. In general terms, criminal discovery is far more limited than civil discovery. Much less information must be disclosed to the other side. For example, most jurisdictions severely limit depositions in criminal cases while routinely permitting them in civil cases. Similarly, interrogatories are often unknown in criminal cases but are quite prevalent in civil cases. The usual explanation, to be explored at the end of this chapter, is that the criminal defendant cannot be trusted to know much about the prosecution's case because the accused will tamper with the evidence or witnesses, or will commit or suborn perjury. Another explanation for some differences is that the Fifth Amendment bars some discovery by the prosecution, but does not limit discovery by the defense.

The substantial differences between civil and criminal discovery have led both prosecutors and defense lawyers to attempt to use the more liberal civil discovery procedures in order to obtain information for use in a criminal case. This practice is theoretically not difficult since many crimes are also torts or other civil actions. It is clear, however, that courts will not permit civil discovery to be used as a subterfuge for criminal discovery. *See, e.g., Application of Eisenberg,* 654 F.2d 1107 (5th Cir. 1981) (defendant cannot use civil discovery as disguised "back door" attempt at criminal discovery; preindictment deposition not permitted); *United States v. Tison,* 780 F. 2d 1569 (11th Cir. 1986) (government similarly barred from bringing a civil action to generate discovery for a criminal case). The possibility or existence of criminal charges does not *per se* bar legitimate civil discovery in a civil case, but sometimes courts stay discovery in civil cases until completion of all related criminal proceedings.

In some situations where both civil and criminal actions are possible, special procedural rules have been formulated to resolve questions about the proper scope of discovery. *See, e.g.,* 15 U.S.C. § 1312 (extensive discovery, called civil investigative demands, available in antitrust cases before filing of either civil or criminal antitrust proceedings); 18 U.S.C. § 1345(b) (civil injunctions authorized in certain fraud and banking violations; discovery governed by civil procedure rules until indictment returned, then criminal procedure discovery rules applicable).

The issue of discovery is also addressed in legal areas that could be characterized as either criminal or civil. For example, discovery in habeas corpus proceedings by state prisoners attacking convictions on federal constitutional grounds is governed by the federal rules of civil procedure (with some judicial discretion), while discovery for federal prisoners attacking federal convictions is governed by either civil or criminal discovery rules. *Compare* Rules Governing § 2254 Cases, Rule 6 *with* Rules Governing § 2255 Cases, Rule 6.

[2] Formal vs. Informal Discovery

One trend in criminal procedure, discussed below, is for rules of discovery to be codified in a jurisdiction's statutes or rules of criminal procedure. In addition, some important judicial decisions mandate discovery in certain situations. These rules, statutes and judicial decisions provide a mechanism of *formal discovery*, often involving written motions and responses, and sometimes closely supervised by a judge.

While these methods of discovery are quite important, there is also another method of discovery that may have an even greater actual impact. In many jurisdictions, discovery occurs routinely through an *informal discovery* system that has developed. Often the product of continuing relationships between prosecutors and defense counsel, the informal processes facilitate the sharing of information without resort to the formal discovery processes authorized by rules and statutes. One example of this is the so-called *open file* practice. A prosecutor may routinely give defense counsel access to most or all of the information available to the prosecution. Another model is for the prosecutor and defense counsel to exchange information about the case, perhaps in an informal telephone call or chat in the courthouse corridor.

[3] Trend Toward Mutuality

Discovery in criminal cases is ordinarily reciprocal. In most situations, if one side must turn over something to the other side, the other side must reciprocate. The primary limits on this approach are constitutional, particularly the Fifth Amendment privilege against self-incrimination which limits the materials the defense must furnish the prosecution.

[4] Overview of Discovery and Disclosure Law

In general terms, discovery and disclosure are governed by three sources of rules, each discussed in greater detail below. First, the United States Constitution itself mandates certain disclosure. Second, formal discovery in criminal cases is governed, in perhaps every jurisdiction, by statutes or court rules that are designed to avoid surprise. As discussed below, these rules usually give the prosecution and defense counsel the right to obtain certain information from the other side. Typically, the two sides will exchange information about physical evidence, expert testimony, and prior statements of witnesses. Often the prosecution or defense must also provide the other side with advance notice of certain proof or theories to be used at trial. The rules may also require disclosure of the names of witnesses to be used at trial, and may embrace a limited right to depose friendly and hostile witnesses. The third source of discovery and disclosure rules is the trial court's inherent authority to regulate many facets of the practice of criminal proceedings. Some judges use this authority to issue orders requiring the disclosure of certain information, such as the names and addresses of witnesses who will be called to testify at trial.

C.   DISCOVERY AND DISCLOSURE: CONSTITUTIONAL ISSUES

It has often been held that there is no constitutional right to discovery. While this is true in the most general sense, in several situations the Constitution does create a right to discovery or at least raises questions about a right to discovery.

[1]   Discovery by the Defendant

The due process guarantee in the Fifth and Fourteenth Amendments gives the criminal accused the right to a fair trial. In some situations, a fair trial is possible only if the accused is accorded some discovery from the prosecution. The leading case, *Brady v. Maryland*, engendered the so-called "Brady Rule."

BRADY v. MARYLAND
373 U.S. 83 (1963)

Opinion of the Court By Mr. Justice Douglas, Announced By Mr. Justice Brennan.

Petitioner and a companion, Boblit, were found guilty of murder in the first degree and were sentenced to death, their convictions being affirmed by the Court of Appeals of Maryland . . . .

. . . Their trials were separate, petitioner being tried first. At his trial Brady took the stand and admitted his participation in the crime, but he claimed that Boblit did the actual killing. And, in his summation to the jury, Brady's counsel conceded that Brady was guilty of murder in the first degree, asking only that the jury return that verdict "without capital punishment." Prior to the trial petitioner's counsel had requested the prosecution to allow him to examine Boblit's extrajudicial statements. Several of those statements were shown to him; but one dated July 9, 1958, in which Boblit admitted the actual homicide, was withheld by the prosecution and did not come to petitioner's notice until after he had been tried, convicted, and sentenced, and after his conviction had been affirmed.

Petitioner moved the trial court for a new trial based on the newly discovered evidence that had been suppressed by the prosecution. Petitioner's appeal from a denial of that motion was dismissed by the Court of Appeals without prejudice to relief under the Maryland Post Conviction Procedure Act . . . .

We agree with the Court of Appeals that suppression of this confession was a violation of the Due Process Clause of the Fourteenth Amendment . . . .

This ruling is an extension of *Mooney v. Holohan*, 294 U.S. 103 (1935), where the Court ruled on what nondisclosure by a prosecutor violates due process:

> It is a requirement that cannot be deemed to be satisfied by mere notice and hearing if a state has contrived a conviction through the pretense of a trial which in truth is but used as a means of depriving a defendant of liberty through a deliberate deception of court and jury by the presentation of testimony known to be perjured. Such a contrivance by a state to procure the conviction and imprisonment of a defendant is as inconsistent with the rudimentary demands of justice as is the obtaining of a like result by intimidation.

. . . We now hold that the suppression by the prosecution of evidence favorable to an accused upon request violates due process where the evidence is material either to guilt or to punishment, irrespective of the good faith or bad faith of the prosecution.

The principle of *Mooney v. Holohan* is not punishment of society for misdeeds of a prosecutor but avoidance of an unfair trial to the accused. Society wins not only when the guilty are convicted but when criminal trials are fair; our system of the administration of justice suffers when any accused is treated unfairly. An inscription on the walls of the

Department of Justice states the proposition candidly for the federal domain: "The United States wins its point whenever justice is done its citizens in the courts." A prosecution that withholds evidence on demand of an accused which, if made available, would tend to exculpate him or reduce the penalty helps shape a trial that bears heavily on the defendant. That casts the prosecutor in the role of an architect of a proceeding that does not comport with standards of justice, even though, as in the present case, his action is not "the result of guile," to use the words of the Court of Appeals. Affirmed.

NOTES

1. *Open file not required.* Brady confirmed a number of decisions that held that in some circumstances the prosecution had to provide the defense with information that could help the criminal defendant be acquitted or receive a more favorable punishment. But it must be stressed that *Brady* did not require an "open file" policy in which the prosecution had to disclose *everything* to the defense, even though this policy would provide the defense with the maximum assistance in its case.

2. *Many unanswered questions.* Because of the general language and the particular facts presented in *Brady,* the decision left many questions unanswered. These include the precise extent of the prosecution's obligations to search its files and those of other government agencies for proof that could assist the defendant. A related issue is to what extent the prosecution's obligations depend on whether the defense asked for information. Finally, how should an appellate court review allegations that information was withheld?

3. *Appellate review: Agurs.* In *United States v. Agurs,* 427 U.S. 97 (1976), discussed in *Bagley, infra,* the Supreme Court resolved some of these issues. *Agurs* involved a homicide in a hotel room. The defendant argued that she killed in self-defense after a violent struggle when the victim attacked her with a knife. After being convicted of second degree murder, the defendant sought a new trial because the prosecution did not disclose that the homicide victim had a prior criminal record involving violence. Defense counsel had not requested this information from the prosecution, but argued that it should have been disclosed anyway because it would have helped prove the victim had a violent character and therefore was the aggressor.

The *Agurs* Court held that *Brady* applied in three situations that raised different questions about the standard of appellate review. First, when the prosecution knew or should have known that it used perjured testimony, the conviction should be reversed if there is any reasonable likelihood that the false testimony could have affected the jury's judgment. Second, if the defense made a specific request for information, perhaps in a discovery motion, the Court observed that the prosecution's failure to make an appropriate response is rarely excusable, but the Court did not articulate a standard of review for the prosecution's failure to comply with the request. The third situation involved either a general request ("give me all the *Brady* materials") or no request (perhaps no discovery motion was filed) for helpful information. In such cases, according to *Agurs,* the appellate court should reverse the conviction if the undisclosed evidence created a reasonable doubt that did not otherwise exist. As applied to the facts of *Agurs,* the Court found no violation of the due process guarantee.

Nine years later, a divided Court in *United States v. Bagley* reconsidered the *Agurs* tests and formulated a "unified" rule for the appellate review of cases where the prosecution failed to disclose information that might have been helpful to the defense.

UNITED STATES v. BAGLEY
473 U.S. 667 (1985)

JUSTICE BLACKMUN announced the judgment of the Court and delivered an opinion of the Court except as to Part III.

In *Brady v. Maryland,* 373 U.S. 83, 87 (1963), this Court held that "the suppression by the prosecution of evidence favorable to an accused upon request violates due process where the evidence is material either to guilt or punishment." The issue in the present case concerns the standard of materiality to be applied in determining whether a conviction should be reversed because the prosecutor failed to disclose requested evidence that could have been used to impeach Government witnesses.

[Several weeks before trial on numerous narcotics and firearms charges, the defendant filed a discovery motion. The motion requested the names and addresses of witnesses who the government intended to call at trial, as well as the prior criminal records of witnesses, "and any deals, promises or inducements made to witnesses in exchange for their testimony." The Government's two principal witnesses at the trial were James F. O'Connor and Donald E. Mitchell, who were state law enforcement officers working as federal undercover agents.]

. . . The Government's response to the discovery motion did not disclose that any "deals, promises or inducements" had been made to O'Connor or Mitchell. In apparent reply to a request in the motion's ninth paragraph for "[c]opies of all Jencks Act [covering a witness's prior statement] material," the Government produced a series of affidavits that O'Connor and Mitchell had signed between April 12 and May 4, 1977, while the undercover investigation was in progress. These affidavits recounted in detail the undercover dealings that O'Connor and Mitchell were having at the time with respondent. Each affidavit concluded with the statement, "I made this statement freely and voluntarily without any threats or rewards, or promises of reward having been made to me in return for it."

[At trial, O'Connor and Mitchell testified about both the firearms and the narcotics charges, and the respondent was found guilty on the narcotics charges, but not guilty on the firearms charges. In mid-1980, respondent used the Freedom of Information Act and the Privacy Act of 1974, 5 U.S.C. §§ 552 & 552(a), to obtain copies of contracts that O'Connor and Mitchell signed in May 1977. The contracts stated that the two would provide information to the government and] . . . "upon the accomplishment of the objective sought to be obtained by the use of such information to the satisfaction of said Regional Director, the United States will pay to said vendor a sum commensurate with services and information rendered." Each form contained the following typewritten description of services:

> That he will provide information regarding T-I and other violations commit-
> ted by Hughes A. Bagley, Jr.; that he will purchase evidence for ATF [Bureau
> of Alcohol, Tobacco and Firearms]; that he will cut [sic] in an undercover
> capacity for ATF; that he will assist ATF in gathering of evidence and testify
> against the violator in federal court.

*> contract
w/ undercove*

The figure "$300.00" was handwritten in each form on a line entitled "Sum to Be Paid to Vendor."

Because these contracts had not been disclosed to respondent in response to his pretrial discovery motion, respondent moved . . . to vacate his sentence. He alleged that the Government's failure to disclose the contracts, which he could have used to impeach O'Connor and Mitchell, violated his right to due process under *Brady v. Maryland*.

ΔΛ

[At an evidentiary hearing it was established that the printed form contracts were blank when O'Connor and Mitchell signed them, that the contracts were not signed by an ATF representative until after the trial, and that on January 4, 1978, following the trial and decision in respondent's case, ATF made payments of $300.00 to both O'Connor and Mitchell pursuant to the contracts.

Based on these facts, the District Court held that it was "probable" that O'Connor and Mitchell expected to receive compensation, in addition to their expenses, for their assistance, "though perhaps not for their testimony."]

TC hold

. . . The District Court found beyond a reasonable doubt, however, that had the existence of the agreements been disclosed to it during trial, the disclosure would have had no effect upon its finding that the Government had proved beyond a reasonable doubt that respondent was guilty of the offenses for which he had been convicted. The District Court reasoned: Almost all of the testimony of both witnesses was devoted to the firearms charges in the indictment. Respondent, however, was acquitted on those charges. The testimony of O'Connor and Mitchell concerning the narcotics charges was relatively very brief. On cross-examination, respondent's counsel did not seek to discredit their testimony as to the facts of distribution but rather sought to show that the controlled substances in question came from supplies that had been prescribed for respondent's personal use. The answers of O'Connor and Mitchell to this line of cross-examination tended to be favorable to respondent. Thus, the claimed impeachment evidence would not have been helpful to respondent and would not have affected the outcome of the trial. Accordingly, the District Court denied respondent's motion to vacate his sentence.

[The Court of Appeals granted an "automatic" reversal, apparently finding that the defendant's right to confront adverse witnesses was impaired by the government's failure to disclose the requested *Brady* information.]

. . . We granted certiorari, and we now reverse.

The holding in *Brady v. Maryland* requires disclosure only of evidence that is both favorable to the accused and "material either to guilt or to punishment." The Court explained in *United States v. Agurs*, 427 U.S. 97 (1976): "A fair analysis of the holding in *Brady* indicates that implicit in the requirement of materiality is a concern that the suppressed evidence might have affected the outcome of the trial."

. . . The *Brady* rule is based on the requirement of due process. Its purpose is not to displace the adversary system as the primary means by which truth is uncovered, but to ensure that a miscarriage of justice does not occur. Thus, the prosecutor is not required to deliver his entire file to defense counsel, but only to disclose evidence favorable to the accused that, if suppressed, would deprive the defendant of a fair trial . . . .

In *Brady* and *Agurs*, the prosecutor failed to disclose exculpatory evidence. In the present case, the prosecutor failed to disclose evidence that the defense might have used to impeach the Government's witnesses by showing bias or interest. Impeachment evidence, however, as well as exculpatory evidence, falls within the *Brady* rule . . . .

[The Court then rejected the Court of Appeals "automatic reversal" approach. That court's] reliance on *Davis v. Alaska* for its "automatic reversal" rule is misplaced. In *Davis*, the defense sought to cross-examine a crucial prosecution witness concerning his probationary status as a juvenile delinquent. The defense intended by this cross-examination to show that the witness might have made a faulty identification of the defendant in order to shift suspicion away from himself or because he feared that his probationary status would be jeopardized if he did not satisfactorily assist the police and prosecutor in obtaining a conviction. Pursuant to a state rule of procedure and a state statute making juvenile adjudications inadmissible, the trial judge prohibited the defense from conducting the cross-examination. This Court reversed the defendant's conviction, ruling that the direct restriction on the scope of cross-examination denied the defendant "the right of effective cross-examination which [merited automatic reversal irrespective of prejudice] . . . ."

The present case, in contrast, does not involve any direct restriction on the scope of cross-examination. The defense was free to cross-examine the witnesses on any relevant subject, including possible bias or interest resulting from inducements made by the Government. The constitutional error, if any, in this case was the Government's failure to assist the defense by disclosing information that might have been helpful in conducting the cross-examination . . . . [S]uch suppression of evidence amounts to a constitutional violation only if it deprives the defendant of a fair trial. Consistent with "our overriding concern with the justice of the finding of guilt," a constitutional error occurs, and the conviction must be reversed, only if the evidence is material in the sense that its suppression undermines confidence in the outcome of the trial.

III

It remains to determine the standard of materiality applicable to the nondisclosed evidence at issue in this case. Our starting point is the framework for evaluating the materiality of *Brady* evidence established in *United States v. Agurs.* The Court in *Agurs* distinguished three situations involving the discovery, after trial, of information favorable to the accused that had been known to the prosecution but unknown to the defense. The first situation was the prosecutor's knowing use of perjured testimony or, equivalently, the prosecutor's knowing failure to disclose that testimony used to convict the defendant was false. The Court noted the well-established rule that "a conviction obtained by the knowing use of perjured testimony is fundamentally unfair, and must be set aside if there is any reasonable likelihood that the false testimony could have affected the judgment of the jury." Although this rule is stated in terms that treat the knowing use of perjured testimony as error subject to harmless-error review, it may as easily be stated as a materiality standard under which the fact that testimony is perjured is considered material unless failure to disclose it would be harmless beyond a reasonable doubt. The Court in *Agurs* justified this standard of materiality on the ground that the knowing use of perjured testimony involves prosecutorial misconduct and, more importantly, involves "a corruption of the truth-seeking function of the trial process."

At the other extreme is the situation in *Agurs* itself, where the defendant does not make a *Brady* request and the prosecutor fails to disclose certain evidence favorable to the accused. . . .

The third situation identified by the Court in *Agurs* is where the defense makes a specific request and the prosecutor fails to disclose responsive evidence. . . .

[Noting that subsequent cases reformulated the *Agurs* tests, the *Bagley* Court adopted the test articulated in *Strickland v. Washington*, 466 U.S. 668 (1984), to cover the "no request," "general request," and "specific request" cases of prosecutorial failure to disclose evidence favorable to the accused: evidence is "material only if there is a reasonable probability that, had the evidence been disclosed to the defense, the result of the proceeding would have been different." A "reasonable probability" was defined as "a probability sufficient to undermine confidence in the outcome."]

The Government suggests that a materiality standard more favorable to the defendant reasonably might be adopted in specific request cases. The Government notes that an incomplete response to a specific request not only deprives the defense of certain evidence, but also has the effect of representing to the defense that the evidence does not exist. In reliance on this misleading representation, the defense might abandon lines of independent investigation, defenses, or trial strategies that it otherwise would have pursued.

We agree that the prosecutor's failure to respond fully to a *Brady* request may impair the adversary process in this manner. And the more specifically the defense requests certain evidence, thus putting the prosecutor on notice of its value, the more reasonable it is for the defense to assume from the nondisclosure that the evidence does not exist, and to make pretrial and trial decisions on the basis of this assumption. This possibility of impairment does not necessitate a different standard of materiality, however, for under the *Strickland* formulation the reviewing court may consider directly any adverse effect that the prosecutor's failure to respond might have had on the preparation or presentation of the defendant's case. The reviewing court should assess the possibility that such effect might have occurred in light of the totality of the circumstances and with an awareness of the difficulty of reconstructing in a post-trial proceeding the course that the defense and the trial would have taken had the defense not been misled by the prosecutor's incomplete response.

In the present case, we think that there is a significant likelihood that the prosecutor's response to respondent's discovery motion misleadingly induced defense counsel to believe that O'Connor and Mitchell could not be impeached on the basis of bias or interest arising from inducements offered by the Government . . . . While the Government is technically correct that the blank contracts did not constitute a "promise of reward," the natural effect of these affidavits would be misleadingly to induce defense counsel to believe that O'Connor and Mitchell provided the information in the affidavits, and ultimately their testimony at trial recounting the same information, without any "inducements."

. . . Accordingly, we reverse the judgment of the Court of Appeals and remand the case to that court for a determination whether there is a reasonable probability that, had the inducement offered by the Government to O'Connor and Mitchell been disclosed to the defense, the result of the trial would have been different.

JUSTICE POWELL took no part in the decision of this case.

JUSTICE WHITE, with whom THE CHIEF JUSTICE and JUSTICE REHNQUIST join, concurring in part and concurring in the judgment.

I agree with the Court that respondent is not entitled to have his conviction overturned unless he can show that the evidence withheld by the Government was "material," and I therefore join Parts I and II of the Court's opinion. I also agree with Justice BLACKMUN that for purposes of this inquiry, "evidence is material only if there is a reasonable probability that, had the evidence been disclosed to the defense, the result of the proceeding would have been different." . . . Given the flexibility of the standard and the inherently factbound nature of the cases to which it will be applied, however, I see no reason to attempt to elaborate on the relevance to the inquiry of the specificity of the defense's request for disclosure, either generally or with respect to this case. I would hold simply that the proper standard is one of reasonable probability and that the Court of Appeals' failure to apply this standard necessitates reversal. I therefore concur in the judgment.

JUSTICE MARSHALL, with whom JUSTICE BRENNAN joins, dissenting.

When the Government withholds from a defendant evidence that might impeach the prosecution's *only witness*, that failure to disclose cannot be deemed harmless error. Because that is precisely the nature of the undisclosed evidence in this case, I would affirm the judgment of the Court of Appeals and would not remand for further proceedings.

. . . Instead of affirming, the Court today chooses to reverse and remand the case for application of its newly stated standard to the facts of this case. While I believe that the evidence at issue here, which remained undisclosed despite a particular request, undoubtedly was material under the Court's standard, I also have serious doubts whether the Court's definition of the constitutional right at issue adequately takes account of the interests this Court sought to protect in its decision in *Brady v. Maryland*.

. . . When the state does not disclose information in its possession that might reasonably be considered favorable to the defense, it precludes the trier of fact from gaining access to such information and thereby undermines the reliability of the verdict . . . .

. . . *Brady v. Maryland*, of course, established this requirement of disclosure as a fundamental element of a fair trial by holding that a defendant was denied due process if he was not given access to favorable evidence that is material either to guilt or punishment . . . . To my mind, the *Brady* decision, the reasoning that underlay it, and the fundamental interest in a fair trial, combine to give the criminal defendant the right to receive from the prosecutor, and the prosecutor the affirmative duty to turn over to the defendant, all information known to the government that might reasonably be considered favorable to the defendant's case.

. . . The Court, however, offers a complex alternative. It defines the right not by reference to the possible usefulness of the particular evidence in preparing and presenting the case, but retrospectively, by reference to the likely effect the evidence will have on the outcome of the trial . . . . By adhering to the view articulated in *United States v. Agurs* — that there is no constitutional duty to disclose evidence unless nondisclosure would have a certain impact on the trial — the Court permits prosecutors to withhold with impunity large amounts of undeniably favorable evidence, and it imposes on prosecutors the burden to identify and disclose evidence pursuant to a pretrial standard that virtually defies definition.

. . . I would return to the original theory and promise of *Brady* and reassert the duty of the prosecutor to disclose all evidence in his files that might reasonably be considered favorable to the defendant's case. No prosecutor can know prior to trial whether such evidence will be of consequence at trial; the mere fact that it might be, however, suffices to mandate disclosure.

In so saying, I recognize that a failure to divulge favorable information should not result in reversal in all cases. It may be that a conviction should be affirmed on appeal despite the prosecutor's failure to disclose evidence that reasonably might have been deemed potentially favorable prior to trial. The state's interest in nondisclosure at trial is minimal, and should therefore yield to the readily apparent benefit that full disclosure would convey to the search for truth. After trial, however, the benefits of disclosure may at times be tempered by the state's legitimate desire to avoid retrial when error has been harmless. However, in making the determination of harmlessness, I would apply our normal constitutional error test and reverse unless it is clear beyond a reasonable doubt that the withheld evidence would not have affected the outcome of the trial . . . .

[JUSTICE STEVENS dissented, arguing that *Brady* applied to the facts since a specific request for the information was made. He would apply the *Brady* test of materiality and reverse if there was "any reasonable likelihood" that the information "could have affected the judgment of the trier of fact."]

Brady test

NOTES

1. *Uniform standard.* In combination, the Blackmun and White opinions in *Bagley* establish a uniform standard for reviewing the no request, general request, and specific request cases. How does that standard differ from the one used for the knowing use of perjured testimony? How does it differ from *Agurs*? *Bagley* held that exculpatory and impeachment evidence are the same for *Brady* purposes. Do you agree?

2. *Standard based on request.* *Bagley* provides that the "reasonable probability" test applies to appeals in cases where the defense made a specific request for materials. Yet, recall that Justice Blackmun observed that nondisclosure after a specific disclosure request may be more misleading than that after no request or a general request. Moreover, nondisclosure after a specific request involves greater prosecutorial carelessness or even intentional misrepresentation. Was *Bagley* right in lumping together the appellate review standards for specific request, no request, and general request cases?

Under *Bagley*, favorable evidence is material if there is a "reasonable probability" that, had the evidence been disclosed to the defense, the result of the proceeding would have been different. Many courts, despite *Bagley*, still distinguish between the specific, general, and no request situations. One court observed:

> As the specificity of the defendant's request increases, a lesser showing of materiality will suffice to establish a [*Brady*] violation.

United States v. Anderson, 31 F. Supp. 2d 933, 940 (D. Kan. 1998). Is this interpretation of "materiality" consistent with *Bagley*?

3. *Kyles.* In *Kyles v. Whitley*, 514 U.S. 419 (1995), the United States Supreme Court held that this materiality standard is defined in terms of the cumulative effect of all suppressed evidence favorable to the defense, not the evidence considered item-by-item. Justice Souter, writing for the majority, emphasized four aspects of materiality under *Bagley*:

1. A showing of materiality does not require demonstration by a preponderance of evidence that disclosure of the suppressed evidence would have resulted ultimately in the defendant's acquittal; the question is whether the defendant received a fair trial resulting in a verdict worthy of confidence.

2. *Bagley* is not a sufficiency of evidence test in that the accused must demonstrate that after discounting the inculpatory evidence in light of the undisclosed evidence, there was not enough evidence left to convict. Rather, the accused must show that the favorable evidence could reasonably be taken to put the case in such a different light as to undermine confidence in the verdict.

3. Once a reviewing court has found constitutional error under *Bagley*, there is no need for further harmless-error review; no such error could be deemed harmless since the accused did not receive a fair trial worthy of confidence.

4. As stated above, materiality is defined in terms of suppressed evidence considered collectively, not item-by-item. Thus, the prosecution must gauge the likely net effect of all *Brady* evidence and make disclosure when the point of "reasonable probability" is reached. As a subsequent decision noted, until that point, there is no *Brady* violation. *Strickler v. Greene*, 527 U.S. 263 (1999) (there is never a *Brady* violation unless nondisclosure was so serious that there is a reasonable probability the suppressed evidence would have produced a different result).

4. *Duty to correct concealment of Brady materials.* The U.S. Supreme Court's most recent *Brady* decision analyzes and applies the major decisions (*Brady, Bagley, Kyles and Strickler*) to a Texas death penalty case. In *Banks v. Dretke*, 540 U.S. 668 (2004), Justice Ginsburg, writing for the Court, provides this succinct overview:

Petitioner Delma Banks, Jr., was convicted of capital murder and sentenced to death. Prior to trial, the State advised Banks's attorney there would be no need to litigate discovery issues, representing: "[W]e will, without the necessity of motions[,] provide you with all discovery to which you are entitled." Despite that undertaking, the State withheld evidence that would have allowed Banks to discredit two essential prosecution witnesses. The State did not disclose that one of those witnesses was a paid police informant, nor did it disclose a pretrial transcript revealing that the other witness' trial testimony had been intensively coached by prosecutors and law enforcement officers.

Furthermore, the prosecution raised no red flag when the informant testified, untruthfully, that he never gave the police any statement and, indeed, had not talked to any police officer about the case until a few days before the trial. Instead of correcting the informant's false statements, the prosecutor told the jury that the witness "ha[d] been open and honest with you in every way," and that his testimony was of the "utmost significance." Similarly, the prosecution allowed the other key witness to convey, untruthfully, that his testimony was entirely unrehearsed. Through direct appeal and state collateral review proceedings, the State continued to hold secret the key witnesses' links to the police and allowed their false statements to stand uncorrected.

Ultimately, through discovery and an evidentiary hearing authorized in a federal habeas corpus proceeding, the long-suppressed evidence came to light. The District Court granted Banks relief from the death penalty, but the Court of Appeals reversed. In the latter court's judgment, Banks had documented his claims of prosecutorial misconduct too late and in the wrong forum; therefore he did not qualify for federal-court relief. We reverse that judgment. When the police or prosecutors conceal significant exculpatory or impeaching material in the State's possession, it is ordinarily incumbent on the State to set the record straight.

5. *Cumulative evidence.* In light of the Court's decisions in *Bagley* and *Kyles*, lower courts have attempted to delineate what cumulative amount of evidence constitutes materiality under the *Brady* standard. In *United States v. Sipe*, 388 F.3d 471 (5th Cir. 2004), the Fifth Circuit Court of Appeals struggled with this question in a case involving the conviction of a Border Patrol Agent on charges that the agent used excessive force while arresting a Mexican national who entered the United States illegally. The *Sipe* court, in a 2-1 decision, upheld the trial court's decision to grant defendant's motion for a new trial, stating, in part, "[e]ven if none of the nondisclosures [by the government] standing alone could have affected the outcome, when viewed cumulatively in the context of the full array of facts, we cannot disagree with the conclusion of the district judge that the government's nondisclosures undermined confidence in the jury's verdict." While the court noted that " [u]nquestionably, there is sufficient evidence to support a finding of guilt in this case," it concluded that "[g]iven the closeness of this case based solely on those facts presented at trial, the government's failure to disclose copious amounts of evidence casting doubt upon the credibility of almost all of the key witnesses severely undermines our confidence in the outcome of this case."

6. *Special case of perjury.* Justice Blackmun's opinion in *Bagley* characterized the perjury cases as following the traditional harmless error standard of review (any reasonable likelihood that the false testimony could have affected the jury's decision). He then said this "may as easily be stated as a materiality standard under which the fact that testimony is perjured is considered material unless failure to disclose it would be harmless beyond a reasonable doubt." Are these two standards the same? Why should perjured testimony be reviewed by a higher standard than the other three classes of materials (specific request, no request, general request)?

7. *Promise of leniency and impeachment: Giglio.* In *Giglio v. United States*, 405 U.S. 150 (1972), a key government witness in a forged money order case falsely testified that he had not been promised leniency in exchange for his testimony. The prosecutor repeated this statement during closing argument. Later it was discovered that, unknown to the prosecuting attorney, another prosecutor had promised the witness leniency. The Supreme Court reversed because the prosecution's nondisclosure of important impeachment proof violated due process. Many lawyers now use the expression "*Giglio* materials" in referring to proof that would help impeach a government witness by establishing a deal for leniency in exchange for testimony. Isn't *Giglio* just an application of *Brady, Agurs, Bagley,* and *Kyles*?

8. *Inadmissible Brady evidence.* Assume that the prosecution searches its files and finds information that would be helpful to the defense but which would be inadmissible at trial. If the government does not disclose this information, what result under *Bagley* and *Brady*?

If the information in the government's files would likely be inadmissible, but could lead to admissible evidence if defense investigators used it well, *Brady* and *Bagley* may require disclosure. *See East v. Johnson*, 123 F.3d 235 (5th Cir. 1997). What if the evidence were inadmissible but could somehow help the defense formulate its trial strategy?

The United States Supreme Court addressed some of these questions in *Wood v. Bartholomew*, 516 U.S. 1 (1995). The defendant sought habeas relief based upon the prosecutor's failure to turn over results of a polygraph examination of a key witness. Though the polygraph information was inadmissible even for impeachment under state law, the Ninth Circuit Court of Appeals reversed, reasoning that the withholding of such information might have had an adverse effect on pretrial preparation by the defense. In a *per curiam* reversal, the Supreme Court characterized the lower court's decision as a misapplication of *Brady* jurisprudence. The Court explained that evidence is "material" under *Brady* only where there exists a "reasonable probability" that had the evidence been disclosed the result at trial would have been different. Concluding that any adverse impact on the defendant in the present case was little more than speculative, the Court declined to grant habeas relief.

9. *Information defense could have obtained or did know about.* What if the prosecution withholds material *Brady* information that the defense could obtain on its own? *See United States v. Rodriguez,* 162 F.3d 135 (1st Cir. 1998) (prosecutor must disclose *Brady* information if defense could not obtain the information through reasonable diligence, but defense "knew full well" of witness' long prior criminal record, therefore no *Brady* violation for government's nondisclosure of its notice of intention to seek enhanced recidivist penalties for that witness).

A similar result occurs if defendant knew of the *Brady* materials. *See, e.g., United States v. Runyan,* 290 F.3d 223 (5th Cir. 2002)(no *Brady* violation when defendant already had possession of defendant's computer).

10. *Prosecutor's dilemma.* How does a prosecutor know whether evidence is subject to disclosure under *Brady*? While some *Brady* proof is obvious, other such evidence is not. To know what to disclose, must the prosecutor anticipate the defenses that might be raised?

If you were a prosecutor, would you adopt an open file rule to satisfy *Brady*? An open file policy may satisfy *Brady* if the *Brady* materials are actually disclosed. *See, e.g., United States v. Mmahat,* 106 F.3d 89 (5th Cir. 1997) (*Brady* satisfied if necessary materials are in file or papers that are given to defense; prosecution has no duty to point out *Brady* materials); *Smith v. Secretary, DOC,* 50 F.3d 801 (10th Cir. 1995) (open file practice is inadequate if *Brady* materials are not included because they were given orally or were in a police file).

11. *Types of Brady information.* What type of information is covered by *Brady*? Clearly evidence that is favorable to the defense on issues of guilt or punishment or that would assist in cross-examining prosecution witnesses. There are countless illustrations. *See, e.g., Paradis v. Arave,* 130 F.3d 385 (9th Cir. 1997) (location of crime to establish lack of jurisdiction); *Banks v. Reynolds,* 54 F.3d 1508 (10th Cir. 1995) (identity of person suspected of committing the offense); *United States v. Wilson,* 135 F.3d 291 (4th Cir. 1998) (information contradicting government's theory of case).

12. *False information.* What if the prosecutor believes the possibly exculpatory evidence is false? *See United States v. Alvarez,* 86 F.3d 901 (9th Cir. 1996) (prosecutor should turn over evidence believed false; criminal trial will resolve truthfulness).

13. *Timing of Brady decision.* When must the prosecution turn over *Brady* material? What if it waits until the eve of trial, so that the defense cannot have full use of it in planning and investigating the defense? In *United States v. Coppa,* 267 F.3d 132 (2d Cir. 2001), a lower court's ruling that *immediate* disclosure of *Brady* material is required upon the defendant's request was overturned. Rather, such material must be disclosed in time for its effective use at trial or at a plea proceeding. Additionally, however, the Second Circuit Court of Appeals added that the time required "for effective use" will depend on the likely materiality of that evidence (characterized as a predictive "result-affecting test") and the particular circumstances of the case. The same court in another recent case also discussed the question of timing of disclosures. *See Leka v. Portuondo,* 257 F.3d 89 (2d Cir. 2001), holding that *Brady* material (a former police officer's observation of the crime that cast doubt upon the prosecutor's theory) disclosed three days before trial was "too little [the disclosure consisted only of the officer's name and address] too late" and therefore merited "suppression" for *Brady* purposes.

The conflict between the timeliness of disclosure of *Brady* and Rule 26.2 materials is discussed later in this chapter.

14. *Effect of guilty plea.* Should *Brady* material be disclosed if the accused pleads guilty? Will such disclosure increase the accuracy of fact-finding during plea proceedings in court? The Supreme Court rejected these claims in *U.S. v. Ruiz*, 536 U.S. 622 (2002) (discussed in Chapter 11), holding that the prosecution may constitutionally require the defendant to waive the right under *Brady* to receive exculpatory materials prior to pleading guilty.

15. *Who is the "government?"* The prosecution represents the "government," which includes many different agencies and departments. Obviously *Brady* applies to information physically in the files in the prosecution's office. *Kyles v. Whitley*, 514 U.S. 419, 437 (1995), held that the prosecutor under *Brady* also has a duty to seek out evidence known to the police or any other persons acting on the government's behalf in the case. This means that disclosure is required even if no prosecutor has actual knowledge of the *Brady* materials. *See, e.g., United States v. Kearns*, 5 F.3d 1251 (9th Cir. 1993) (destruction by police of written agreement for witness to cooperate, without disclosing it to prosecution, arguably violated *Brady*, but dismissal of charges not justified where less drastic sanctions would have sufficed).

Similarly, *Brady* also applies to promises made by individual prosecutors, whether or not the promise was known by other prosecutors. *See Giglio v. United States*, 405 U.S. 150 (1972) (one prosecutor, apparently without informing other prosecutors, promised a witness immunity in exchange for testimony; a promise by one prosecutor is attributed to the government and must be disclosed to the defense).

Do *Bagley* and *Brady* also apply to data in files of all other government agencies involved somehow in the case or only to those agencies directly investigating the case? Recall that *Kyles v. Whitley*, discussed above, imposes on the prosecutor a duty "to learn of any favorable evidence known to the others acting on the government's behalf in the case, including the police." *Kyles*, 514 U.S. at 437. Does it extend to data in files of government agencies having no obvious connection with the investigation? In a court's possession? Does it extend across the borders between state and federal agencies or between agencies of different states or localities or countries? *See* Peter J. Henning, *Defense Discovery in White Collar Criminal Prosecutions*, 15 Ga. St. U. L. Rev. 601, 616 (1999) (arguing that the definition of "government" under *Brady* is not as broad as that for discovery under Rule 16, discussed later in this chapter; *Brady* only reaches the prosecutor's office and other government offices "closely allied with the investigation" because a broader definition "would be disruptive to the [offices'] operations without much benefit to ensuring the fairness of the trial"). Do you agree with professor Henning?

16. *Independent* source. *Brady* requires the prosecution to turn over exculpatory and impeachment proof. Does it also require the government to seek such proof from independent sources? *See Commonwealth v. Beal*, 709 N.E.2d 413 (Mass. 1999) (*Brady* only requires disclosure of information in possession of prosecutor and those subject to prosecutor's control; prosecutor need not interrogate rape victim to assist defendant in obtaining new exculpatory information).

17. *Brady codified.* Some jurisdictions have attempted to codify *Brady*. *See, e.g.,* Ariz. R. Crim. P. 15.1(a)(8) (by 10 days after arraignment, state must provide defendant with "all material or information which tends to mitigate or negate the defendant's guilt" or punishment); Md. R. Crim. P. 4-262(a)(1) (same); Mont. Code Ann. § 46-15-322(1)(e) (same).

18. *State variations.* States are ordinarily free to interpret their state constitutions to allow greater constitutional protections than analogous provisions of the federal constitution. In *People v. Vilardi*, 76 N.Y.2d 67, 556 N.Y.S.2d 518, 555 N.E.2d 915 (1990), the New York Court of Appeals interpreted the New York due process clause as rejecting the "lesser protections of *Bagley*" and following the analysis outlined in *Agurs*. The *Vilardi* case involved the government's failure to disclose an expert's report that had been specifically requested by the defense. The New York Court of Appeals held that under state law the correct standard of materiality was whether there was a "reasonable possibility" that nondisclosure "contributed to the verdict." How does this test differ from *Bagley*? Do you think the New York Court of Appeals was correct when it said that this test would better encourage the prosecution to comply with its discovery obligations?

The New Hampshire Supreme Court, relying upon its state constitution, concluded that *Bagley* places too severe a burden on defendants, and therefore held that where a defendant is able to show that favorable exculpatory evidence has been knowingly withheld by the prosecution, the burden shifts to the state to prove beyond a reasonable doubt that the undisclosed evidence would not have affected the verdict. *New Hampshire v. Laurie*, 653 A.2d 549 (N.H. 1995). The case was remanded for a new trial because the conviction depended upon the testimony of a particular detective and the prosecutor failed to turn over the detective's employment records (which may have affected the verdict because they reflected negatively upon the detective's character and credibility).

19. *Additional sanctions for deliberate misconduct.* If a prosecutor were to deliberately withhold *Brady* material, are additional sanctions or remedies needed? In *United States v. Ranger Electronic Communications, Inc.*, 22 F.Supp.2d 667 (W.D. Mich. 1998), a U.S. district court ordered the federal government to pay a corporate criminal defendant's attorney's fees as a sanction for the prosecution's failure to disclose exculpatory evidence. Following dismissal of the criminal case, the defendant moved for attorney's fees of $404,737 under the Hyde Amendment. This statute (Pub. L. No. 105–119, 111 Stat. 2440, 2519 (Nov. 26, 1997), noted in comments after 18 U.S.C. § 3006A), permits an award of reasonable attorney's fees to a prevailing criminal defendant "where the court finds that the position of the United States was vexatious, frivolous, or in bad faith." Because the prosecution's failure to disclose information constituted "bad faith" under the Hyde provision, attorneys' fees were appropriate. The District Court construed the Amendment as one designed "specifically to curb abuses associated with . . . the failure to disclose exculpatory evidence." It also should be noted that the District Court ordered the responsible federal prosecutor to show cause why he should not be disciplined for violating a state rule of professional conduct provision. *See also* Edward L. Wilkinson, *Brady and Ethics: A Prosecutor's Evidentiary Duties to the Defense Under the Due Process Rules and Their Relation to the State Bar Rules*, 61 TEX. BAR J. 435 (1998) (noting the dramatically different duties required by *Brady* and lawyer's ethical rules).

[2] Discovery by the Government

As the cases above suggest, the United States Constitution provides the criminal defendant with a right to discovery in a narrow category of situations. Perhaps in an effort to counteract the impact of defense discovery, in recent years many jurisdictions have created rules of criminal procedure that provide the *government* with a right to discover certain items possessed by or known to the defense. Such efforts raise serious constitutional issues because the accused, unlike the government, is protected by the Fifth Amendment's right of silence and the Sixth Amendment's guarantee of the assistance of counsel.

[a] Defenses

WILLIAMS v. FLORIDA
399 U.S. 78 (1970)

MR. JUSTICE WHITE delivered the opinion of the Court.

Prior to his trial for robbery in the State of Florida, petitioner filed a "Motion for a Protective Order," seeking to be excused from the requirements of Rule 1.200 of the Florida Rules of Criminal Procedure. That rule requires a defendant, on written demand of the prosecuting attorney, to give notice in advance of trial if the defendant intends to claim an alibi, and to furnish the prosecuting attorney with information as to the place where he claims to have been and with the names and addresses of the alibi witnesses he intends to use. In his motion petitioner openly declared his intent to claim an alibi, but objected to the further disclosure requirements on the ground that the rule "compels the Defendant in a criminal case to be a witness against himself" in violation of his Fifth and Fourteenth Amendment rights. The motion was denied . . . . Petitioner was convicted as charged and was sentenced to life imprisonment. . . . We granted certiorari.

Florida's notice-of-alibi rule is in essence a requirement that a defendant submit to a limited form of pretrial discovery by the State whenever he intends to rely at trial on the defense of alibi. In exchange for the defendant's disclosure of the witnesses he proposes to use to establish that defense, the State in turn is required to notify the defendant of any witnesses it proposes to offer in rebuttal to that defense. Both sides are under a continuing duty promptly to disclose the names and addresses of additional witnesses bearing on the alibi as they become available. The threatened sanction for failure to comply is the exclusion at trial of the defendant's alibi evidence — except for his own testimony — or, in the case of the State, the exclusion of the State's evidence offered in rebuttal of the alibi.

In this case, following the denial of his Motion for a Protective Order, petitioner complied with the alibi rule and gave the State the name and address of one Mary Scotty. Mrs. Scotty was summoned to the office of the State Attorney on the morning of the trial, where she gave pretrial testimony. At the trial itself, Mrs. Scotty, petitioner, and petitioner's wife all testified that the three of them had been in Mrs. Scotty's apartment during the time of the robbery. On two occasions during cross-examination of Mrs. Scotty, the prosecuting attorney confronted her with her earlier deposition in which she had given dates and times that in some respects did not correspond with the dates and times given at trial. Mrs. Scotty adhered to her trial story, insisting that she had been mistaken in her earlier testimony. The State also offered in rebuttal the testimony of one of the officers investigating the robbery who claimed that Mrs. Scotty had asked him for directions on the afternoon in question during the time when she claimed to have been in her apartment with petitioner and his wife.

We need not linger over the suggestion that the discovery permitted the State against petitioner in this case deprived him of "due process" or a "fair trial." Florida law provides for liberal discovery by the defendant against the State, and the notice-of-alibi rule is itself carefully hedged with reciprocal duties requiring state disclosure to the defendant. Given the ease with which an alibi can be fabricated, the State's interest in protecting itself against an eleventh-hour defense is both obvious and legitimate. Reflecting this interest, notice-of-alibi provisions, dating at least from 1927, are now in existence in a substantial number of States. The adversary system of trial is hardly an end in itself; it is not yet a poker game in which players enjoy an absolute right always to conceal their cards until played. We find ample room in that system, at least as far as "due process" is concerned, for the instant Florida rule, which is designed to enhance the search for truth in the criminal trial by insuring both the defendant and the State ample opportunity to investigate certain facts crucial to the determination of guilt or innocence.

Petitioner's major contention is that he was "compelled . . . to be a witness against himself" contrary to the commands of the Fifth and Fourteenth Amendments because the notice-of-alibi rule required him to give the State the name and address of Mrs. Scotty in advance of trial and thus to furnish the State with information useful in convicting him. No pretrial statement of petitioner was introduced at trial; but armed with Mrs. Scotty's name and address and the knowledge that she was to be petitioner's alibi witness, the State was able to take her deposition in advance of trial and to find rebuttal testimony. Also, requiring him to reveal the elements of his defense is claimed to have interfered with his right to wait until after the State had presented its case to decide how to defend against it. We conclude, however, as has apparently every other court that has considered the issue, that the privilege against self-incrimination is not violated by a requirement that the defendant give notice of an alibi defense and disclose his alibi witnesses.[14]

The defendant in a criminal trial is frequently forced to testify himself and to call other witnesses in an effort to reduce the risk of conviction. When he presents his witnesses, he must reveal their identity and submit them to cross-examination which in itself may prove incriminating or which may furnish the State with leads to incriminating rebuttal evidence. That the defendant faces such a dilemma demanding a choice between complete silence and presenting a defense has never been thought an invasion of the privilege against compelled self-incrimination. The pressures generated by the State's evidence may be severe but they do not vitiate the defendant's choice to present an alibi defense and witnesses to prove it, even though the attempted defense ends in catastrophe for the defendant. However "testimonial" or "incriminating" the alibi defense proves to be, it cannot be considered "compelled" within the meaning of the Fifth and Fourteenth Amendments.

Very similar constraints operate on the defendant when the State requires pretrial notice of alibi and the naming of alibi witnesses. Nothing in such a rule requires the defendant to rely on an alibi or prevents him from abandoning the defense; these matters are left to his unfettered choice. . . . Response to that kind of pressure by offering evidence or testimony is not compelled self-incrimination transgressing the Fifth and Fourteenth Amendments.

In the case before us, the notice-of-alibi rule by itself in no way affected petitioner's crucial decision to call alibi witnesses or added to the legitimate pressures leading to that course of action. At most, the rule only compelled petitioner to accelerate the timing of his disclosure, forcing him to divulge at an earlier date information that the petitioner from the beginning planned to divulge at trial. Nothing in the Fifth Amendment privilege entitles a defendant as a matter of constitutional right to await the end of the State's case before announcing the nature of his defense, any more than it entitles him to await the jury's verdict on the State's case-in-chief before deciding whether or not to take the stand himself.

Petitioner concedes that absent the notice-of-alibi rule the Constitution would raise no bar to the court's granting the State a continuance at trial on the ground of surprise as soon as the alibi witness is called. Nor would there be self-incrimination problems if, during that continuance, the State was permitted to do precisely what it did here prior to trial: take the deposition of the witness and find rebuttal evidence. But if so utilizing a continuance is permissible under the Fifth and Fourteenth Amendments, then surely the same result may be accomplished through pretrial discovery, as it was here, avoiding the necessity of a disrupted trial. We decline to hold that the privilege against compulsory self-incrimination guarantees the defendant the right to surprise the State with an alibi defense . . . .

. . . Mr. Chief Justice Burger, concurring.

I join fully in Mr. Justice White's opinion for the Court. I see an added benefit to the notice-of-alibi rule in that it will serve important functions by way of disposing of cases without trial in appropriate circumstances — a matter of considerable importance when courts, prosecution offices, and legal aid and defender agencies are vastly overworked. The prosecutor upon receiving notice will, of course, investigate prospective alibi witnesses. If he finds them reliable and unimpeachable he will doubtless re-examine his

---

[14] We emphasize that this case does not involve the question of the validity of the threatened sanction, had petitioner chosen not to comply with the notice-of-alibi rule. Whether and to what extent a State can enforce discovery rules against a defendant who fails to comply, by excluding relevant, probative evidence is a question raising Sixth Amendment issues which we have no occasion to explore. It is enough that no such penalty was exacted here.

entire case and this process would very likely lead to dismissal of the charges. In turn he might be obliged to determine why false charges were instituted and where the breakdown occurred in the examination of evidence that led to a charge . . . .

MR. JUSTICE BLACK, with whom MR. JUSTICE DOUGLAS joins, concurring in part and dissenting in part.

. . . The Court also holds that a State can require a defendant in a criminal case to disclose in advance of trial the nature of his alibi defense and give the names and addresses of witnesses he will call to support that defense. This requirement, the majority says, does not violate the Fifth Amendment prohibition against compelling a criminal defendant to be a witness against himself. Although this case itself involves only a notice-of-alibi provision, it is clear that the decision means that a State can require a defendant to disclose in advance of trial any and all information he might possibly use to defend himself at trial. This decision, in my view, is a radical and dangerous departure from the historical and constitutionally guaranteed right of a defendant in a criminal case to remain completely silent, requiring the State to prove its case without any assistance of any kind from the defendant himself.

. . . When a defendant is required to indicate whether he might plead alibi in advance of trial, he faces a vastly different decision from that faced by one who can wait until the State has presented the case against him before making up his mind. Before trial the defendant knows only what the State's case might be. Before trial there is no such thing as the "strength of the State's case"; there is only a range of possible cases. At that time there is no certainty as to what kind of case the State will ultimately be able to prove at trial.

. . . The Florida system, as interpreted by the majority, plays upon this inherent uncertainty in predicting the possible strength of the State's case in order effectively to coerce defendants into disclosing an alibi defense that may never be actually used.

. . . The Court apparently also assumes that a defendant who has given the required notice can abandon his alibi without hurting himself. Such an assumption is implicit in and necessary for the majority's argument that the pretrial decision is no different from that at the trial itself. I, however, cannot so lightly assume that pretrial notice will have no adverse effects on a defendant who later decides to forgo such a defense. Necessarily the defendant will have given the prosecutor the names of persons who may have some knowledge about the defendant himself or his activities. Necessarily the prosecutor will have every incentive to question these persons fully, and in doing so he may discover new leads or evidence. Undoubtedly there will be situations in which the State will seek to use such information — information it would probably never have obtained but for the defendant's coerced cooperation.

It is unnecessary for me, however, to engage in any such intellectual gymnastics concerning the practical effects of the notice-of-alibi procedure, because the Fifth Amendment itself clearly provides that "[n]o person . . . shall be compelled in any criminal case to be a witness against himself." If words are to be given their plain and obvious meaning, that provision, in my opinion, states that a criminal defendant cannot be required to give evidence, testimony, or any other assistance to the State to aid it in convicting him of crime. The Florida notice-of-alibi rule in my opinion is a patent violation of that constitutional provision because it requires a defendant to disclose information to the State so that the State can use that information to destroy him.

. . . On the surface this case involves only a notice-of-alibi provision, but in effect the decision opens the way for a profound change in one of the most important traditional safeguards of a criminal defendant. The rationale of today's decision is in no way limited to alibi defenses, or any other type or classification of evidence. The theory advanced goes at least so far as to permit the State to obtain under threat of sanction complete disclosure by the defendant in advance of trial of all evidence, testimony, and tactics he plans to use at that trial. In each case the justification will be that the rule affects only the "timing" of the disclosure, and not the substantive decision itself . . . .

[The dissent of JUSTICE MARSHALL is omitted.]

NOTES

1. *Unanswered questions.* In clearly stating that the Fifth Amendment's self-incrimination provision and the due process clause do not bar at least some pretrial disclosure to the prosecution, *Williams* resolved a number of doubts about the validity of the trend toward requiring the defense to disclose information to the prosecution before trial. But *Williams* did not answer all questions.

For example, the Florida provision requires the defense to disclose the names and addresses of defense alibi witnesses. Would the Fifth Amendment or due process clause be violated if the rule also required disclosure of the expected *content* of the defense witness's alibi testimony?

What if the defense had to notify the prosecution of an intent to use self-defense and to list the witnesses on this issue? What if a rule required each side to provide an "open file" to the other side? Would this be constitutional?

2. *Justice Black's literal view.* Justice Black's literal reading of the Fifth Amendment was clearly rejected in *Williams.* If it had been accepted, would any pretrial discovery by the prosecution be permissible?

3. Justice Black argues that defense counsel has to guess whether to provide pretrial notice of an alibi defense since counsel does not know what the State will prove and therefore does not know whether he or she should invoke an alibi defense. Is this an accurate perception of the defense lawyer's dilemma? Recall that the prosecution must prove beyond a reasonable doubt that the defendant committed the crime. Usually this means the prosecution must prove that the defendant was at the scene of the crime. Since the alibi defense essentially says, "I was not there, I was elsewhere," is there any reason the defense would hinge the decision to use it on the proof offered by the prosecution?

4. *Non-reciprocal alibi rule.* Note that *Williams* considered a Florida provision involving the reciprocal exchange of information about alibi witnesses. Would *Williams* also uphold a state rule mandating that the defense disclose data about its alibi witnesses to the prosecution, but not requiring that the prosecution provide the same information to the defense? In *Wardius v. Oregon,* 412 U.S. 470 (1973), the defendant refused to comply with Oregon's notice-of-alibi defense that required the defense to disclose alibi witnesses, but did not obligate the state to disclose its rebuttal witnesses. The Supreme Court in *Wardius* held that alibi-disclosure rules violate due process unless the defendant also is given information about the prosecution's case. The Court observed:

> In the absence of a strong showing of state interests to the contrary, discovery must be a two-way street. The State may not insist that trials be run as a "search for truth" so far as defense witnesses are concerned, while maintaining "poker game" secrecy for its own witnesses. It is fundamentally unfair to require a defendant to divulge the details of his own case while at the same time subjecting him to the hazard of surprise concerning refutation of the very pieces of evidence which he disclosed to the State.

Id. at 475. Does *Wardius* also support an argument in favor of reciprocal discovery for the *prosecution*?

5. *State variations.* Since *Williams,* many states have enacted statutes or court rules requiring the defense to notify the prosecution of an intent to use a particular defense, such as alibi, insanity, duress, intoxication, and the like. These rules are discussed in greater detail later in this chapter.

[b] Work Product

UNITED STATES v. NOBLES
422 U.S. 225 (1975)

Mr. Justice Powell delivered the opinion of the Court.

In a criminal trial, defense counsel sought to impeach the credibility of key prosecution witnesses by testimony of a defense investigator regarding statements previously obtained from the witnesses by the investigator. The question presented here is whether in these circumstances a federal trial court may compel the defense to reveal the relevant portions of the investigator's report for the prosecution's use in cross-examining him . . . . *Issue*

Respondent was tried and convicted on charges arising from an armed robbery of a federally insured bank. The only significant evidence linking him to the crime was the identification testimony of two witnesses, a bank teller and a salesman who was in the bank during the robbery . . . .

In the course of preparing respondent's defense, an investigator for the defense interviewed both witnesses and preserved the essence of those conversations in a written report. When the witnesses testified for the prosecution, respondent's counsel relied on the [investigator's] report in conducting their cross-examination. Counsel asked the bank teller whether he recalled having told the investigator that he had seen only the back of the man he identified as respondent. The witness replied that he did not remember making such a statement. He was allowed, despite defense counsel's initial objection, to refresh his recollection by referring to a portion of the investigator's report. The prosecutor also was allowed to see briefly the relevant portion of the report. The witness thereafter testified that although the report indicated that he told the investigator he had seen only respondent's back, he in fact had seen more than that and continued to insist that respondent was the bank robber.

The other witness acknowledged on cross-examination that he too had spoken to the defense investigator. Respondent's counsel twice inquired whether he told the investigator that "all blacks looked alike" to him, and in each instance the witness denied having made such a statement. The prosecution again sought inspection of the relevant portion of the investigator's report, and respondent's counsel again objected. The court declined to order disclosure at that time, but ruled that it would be required if the investigator testified as to the witnesses' alleged statements from the witness stand. The court further advised that it would examine the investigator's report in camera and would excise all reference to matters not relevant to the precise statements at issue.

After the prosecution completed its case, respondent called the investigator as a defense witness. The court reiterated that a copy of the report, inspected and edited in camera, would have to be submitted to Government counsel at the completion of the investigator's impeachment testimony. When respondent's counsel stated that he did not intend to produce the report, the court ruled that the investigator would not be allowed to testify about his interviews with the witnesses.

The Court of Appeals for the Ninth Circuit . . . found that the Fifth Amendment prohibited the disclosure condition imposed in this case. . . . Decisions of this Court *AC* repeatedly have recognized the federal judiciary's inherent power to require the prosecution to produce the previously recorded statements of its witnesses so that the defense may get the full benefit of cross-examination and the truth-finding process may be enhanced. At issue here is whether, in a proper case, the prosecution can call upon that same power for production of witness statements that facilitate "full disclosure of all the [relevant] facts."

In this case, the defense proposed to call its investigator to impeach the identification testimony of the prosecution's eyewitnesses. It was evident from cross-examination that the investigator would testify that each witness' recollection of the appearance of the individual identified as respondent was considerably less clear at an earlier time than it was at trial. It also appeared that the investigator and one witness differed even as to what the witness told him during the interview. The investigator's contemporaneous report might provide critical insight into the issues of credibility that the investigator's testimony would raise. It could assist the jury in determining the extent to which the investigator's testimony actually discredited the prosecution's witnesses. If, for example, the report failed to mention the purported statement of one witness that "all blacks looked alike," the jury might disregard the investigator's version altogether. On the other hand, if this statement appeared in the contemporaneously recorded report, it would tend strongly to corroborate the investigator's version of the interview and to diminish substantially the reliability of that witness' identification.

It was therefore apparent to the trial judge that the investigator's report was highly relevant to the critical issue of credibility. In this context, production of the report might substantially enhance "the search for truth. We must determine whether compelling its production was precluded by some privilege available to the defense in the circumstances of this case.

. . . In this instance disclosure of the relevant portions of the defense investigator's report would not impinge on the fundamental values protected by the Fifth Amendment. The court's order was limited to statements allegedly made by third parties who were available as witnesses to both the prosecution and the defense. Respondent did not prepare the report, and there is no suggestion that the portions subject to the disclosure order reflected any information that he conveyed to the investigator. The fact that these statements of third parties were elicited by a defense investigator on respondent's behalf does not convert them into respondent's personal communications. Requiring their production from the investigator therefore would not in any sense compel respondent to be a witness against himself or extort communications from him.

We thus conclude that the Fifth Amendment privilege against compulsory self-incrimination, being personal to the defendant, does not extend to the testimony or statements of third parties called as witnesses at trial. The Court of Appeals' reliance on this constitutional guarantee as a bar to the disclosure here ordered was misplaced.

. . . Respondent contends further that the work-product doctrine exempts the investigator's report from disclosure at trial. While we agree that this doctrine applies to criminal litigation as well as civil, we find its protection unavailable in this case.

[The Court reaffirmed the validity of the work-product doctrine, announced in *Hickman v. Taylor*, 329 U.S. 495 (1947), as providing a privileged area within which lawyers in both civil and criminal cases can analyze and prepare their clients' cases without disclosing the lawyers' mental processes. The Court also observed that the work-product doctrine provides protection both before and during the trial, and reaches materials prepared by the attorney and agents for the attorney.]

. . . We need not, however, undertake here to delineate the scope of the doctrine at trial, for in this instance it is clear that the defense waived such right as may have existed to invoke its protection.

The privilege derived from the work-product doctrine is not absolute. Like other qualified privileges, it may be waived. Here respondent sought to adduce the testimony of the investigator and contrast his recollection of the contested statements with that of the prosecution's witnesses. Respondent, by electing to present the investigator as a witness, waived the privilege with respect to matters covered in his testimony. . . .

Finally, our examination of the record persuades us that the District Court properly exercised its discretion in this instance. The court authorized no general "fishing expedition" into the defense files or indeed even into the defense investigator's report. Rather, its considered ruling was quite limited in scope, opening to prosecution scrutiny only the portion of the report that related to the testimony the investigator would offer to discredit the witnesses' identification testimony. The court further afforded respondent the maximum opportunity to assist in avoiding unwarranted disclosure or to exercise an informed choice to call for the investigator's testimony and thereby open his report to examination.

The court's preclusion sanction was an entirely proper method of assuring compliance with its order. Respondent's argument that this ruling deprived him of the Sixth Amendment rights to compulsory process and cross-examination misconceives the issue. The District Court did not bar the investigator's testimony. It merely prevented respondent from presenting to the jury a partial view of the credibility issue by adducing the investigator's testimony and thereafter refusing to disclose the contemporaneous report that might offer further critical insights. The Sixth Amendment does not confer the right to present testimony free from the legitimate demands of the adversarial system . . . .

[The *Nobles* Court also held that Rule 16 of the Federal Rules of Criminal Procedure did not bar the trial court from requiring disclosure of the defense's investigatory report.]

NOTES

1. *Mutual work product waiver.* Consistent with *Williams v. Florida*, the Court in *Nobles* stressed that pretrial discovery serves the important interest of finding the truth. Accordingly, *Nobles* held that in extreme situations the Fifth Amendment does not limit pretrial disclosure of defense investigators' reports of interviews with potential witnesses. In order to facilitate the finding of the "truth," would the Court also have approved a rule requiring disclosure of the defendant's statements to a defense investigator?

2. *Good cause for work product waiver. Nobles* also found a waiver of the work-product rule. That rule has always been flexible, permitting disclosure of most work-product when there is good cause. Was there good cause here? Could the government have obtained the same information by carefully interviewing these witnesses or by questioning them during the trial? *See generally* Rand L. Koler, Note, 16 Santa Clara L. Rev. 391 (1976).

3. *Waiver required in plea bargain.* Although *Nobles* held that neither the Fifth Amendment nor the work-product rule prevents mandatory disclosure of the defense investigator's report, other data in the defense's file may be protected by these or other provisions. Accordingly, prosecutors frequently require a corporation, negotiating a guilty plea to corporate offenses, to waive its attorney-client and work-product privileges as a condition of the plea bargain. The records and other information obtained from the corporation are then used as evidence against employees of the corporation who are prosecuted personally for their involvement in the corporation's crimes.

D. PRESERVATION OF EVIDENCE

In many criminal cases the police and other investigatory agencies and the defense will gather evidence that could be used for or against the accused at trial. Because of *Brady v. Maryland, supra,* and the rules of criminal procedure, discussed *infra,* sometimes this evidence must be turned over to the other side before trial. The other side may want to conduct its own scientific tests to ascertain whether the evidence could help its case. The most common example may be drugs found at the defendant's home. Both the defense and prosecution may want to have the drugs chemically analyzed by their own independent experts to determine the precise content of the substance. While the rules of criminal procedure and constitutional law will generally permit this, the analysis is only possible if the items have been preserved. The matter is made more complicated by the fact that the first analysis of the substance may destroy or alter it so that subsequent analyses are impossible. In such cases, the first analysis may reveal a chemical composition that is devastating to the other side, which cannot conduct its own independent tests of the now-destroyed or altered substance. Must efforts be made to preserve such evidence?

ARIZONA v. YOUNGBLOOD
488 U.S. 51 (1988)

CHIEF JUSTICE REHNQUIST delivered the opinion of the Court.

[A jury convicted defendant Youngblood of child molestation, sexual assault, and kidnapping. The 10 year old victim was abducted from a carnival and sexually assaulted numerous times. After being released, the victim was taken to a hospital where a "sexual assault kit" was used routinely to obtain evidence for police use. Saliva, hair, blood, and microscopic samples were taken from the victim. His underwear and tee shirt were also obtained by the police but were not refrigerated.

The defendant was later identified from a photograph and arrested. The police criminologist who processed the data in the sexual assault kit testified that he determined that a sexual assault occurred, but he and other police experts testified that other tests were unsuccessful in detecting blood group substances. A police criminologist also was unable to obtain useful information from semen stains on the victim's underwear and tee shirt.]

. . . Respondent's principal defense at trial was that the boy had erred in identifying him as the perpetrator of the crime. In this connection, both a criminologist for the State and an expert witness for respondent testified as to what might have been shown by tests performed on the samples shortly after they were gathered, or by later tests performed on the samples from the boy's clothing had the clothing been properly refrigerated. The court instructed the jury that if they found the State had destroyed or lost evidence, they might "infer that the true fact is against the State's interest."

The jury found respondent guilty as charged, but the Arizona Court of Appeals reversed the judgment of conviction. It stated that "when identity is an issue at trial and the police permit the destruction of evidence that could eliminate the defendant as the perpetrator, such loss is material to the defense and is a denial of due process." The Court of Appeals concluded on the basis of the expert testimony at trial that timely performance of tests with properly preserved semen samples could have produced results that might have completely exonerated respondent. The Court of Appeals reached this conclusion even though it did "not imply any bad faith on the part of the State." The Supreme Court of Arizona denied the State's petition for review, and we granted certiorari. We now reverse.

Decision of this case requires us to again consider what might loosely be called the area of constitutionally-guaranteed access to evidence. In *Brady v. Maryland* we held "that the suppression by the prosecution of evidence favorable to the accused upon request violates due process where the evidence is material either to guilt or to punishment, irrespective of the good faith or bad faith of the prosecution." In *United States v. Agurs*, we held that the prosecution had a duty to disclose some evidence of this description even though no requests were made for it, but at the same time we rejected the notion that a "prosecutor has a constitutional duty routinely to deliver his entire file to defense counsel."

. . . There is no question but that the State complied with *Brady* and *Agurs* here . . . .

If respondent is to prevail on federal constitutional grounds, then, it must be because of some constitutional duty over and above that imposed by cases such as *Brady* and *Agurs*. Our most recent decision in this area of the law, *California v. Trombetta*, 467 U.S. 479 (1984), arose out of a drunk driving prosecution in which the State had introduced test results indicating the concentration of alcohol in the blood of two motorists. The defendants sought to suppress the test results on the ground that the State had failed to preserve the breath samples used in the test. We rejected this argument for several reasons: first, the officers here were acting in good faith and in accord with their normal practice; second, in the light of the procedures actually used the chances that preserved samples would have exculpated the defendants were slim; and, third, even if the samples might have shown inaccuracy in the tests, the defendants had alternative means of demonstrating their innocence. In the present case, the likelihood that the preserved materials would have enabled the defendant to exonerate himself appears to be greater than it was in *Trombetta*, but here, unlike in *Trombetta*, the State did not attempt to make any use of the materials in its own case in chief.

Our decisions in related areas have stressed the importance for constitutional purposes of good or bad faith on the part of the Government when the claim is based on loss of evidence attributable to the Government. . . . [I]n *United States v. Valenzuela-Bernal*, 458 U.S. 858 (1982), we considered whether the Government's deportation of two witnesses who were illegal aliens violated due process. We held that the prompt deportation of the witnesses was justified "upon the Executive's good-faith determination that they possess no evidence favorable to the defendant in a criminal prosecution."

The Due Process Clause of the Fourteenth Amendment, as interpreted in *Brady*, makes the good or bad faith of the State irrelevant when the State fails to disclose to the defendant material exculpatory evidence. But we think the Due Process Clause requires a different result when we deal with the failure of the State to preserve evidentiary material of which no more can be said than that it could have been subjected to tests, the results of which might have exonerated the defendant. Part of the reason for the difference in treatment is found in the observation made by the Court in *Trombetta* that "[w]henever potentially exculpatory evidence is permanently lost, courts face the treacherous task of divining the import of materials whose contents are unknown and, very often, disputed." Part of it stems from our unwillingness to read the "fundamental fairness" requirement of the Due Process Clause as imposing on the police an undifferentiated and absolute duty to retain and to preserve all material that might be of conceivable evidentiary significance in a particular prosecution. We think that requiring a defendant to show bad faith on the part of the police both limits the extent of the police's obligation to preserve evidence to reasonable bounds and confines it to that class of cases where the interests of justice most clearly require it, i.e., those cases in which the police themselves by their conduct indicate that the evidence could form a basis for exonerating the defendant. We therefore hold that unless a criminal defendant can show bad faith on the part of the police, failure to preserve potentially useful evidence does not constitute a denial of due process of law.

In this case, the police collected the rectal swab and clothing on the night of the crime; respondent was not taken into custody until six weeks later. The failure of the police to refrigerate the clothing and to perform tests on the semen samples can at worst be described as negligent. None of this information was concealed from respondent at trial, and the evidence — such as it was — was made available to respondent's expert who declined to perform any tests on the samples. The Arizona Court of Appeals noted in its opinion — and we agree — that there was no suggestion of bad faith on the part of the police. It follows, therefore, from what we have said, that there was no violation of the Due Process Clause.

The Arizona Court of Appeals also referred somewhat obliquely to the State's "inability to quantitatively test" certain semen samples with the newer P-30 test. If the court meant by this statement that the Due Process Clause is violated when the police fail to use a particular investigatory tool, we strongly disagree. The situation here is no different than a prosecution for drunk driving that rests on police observation alone; the defendant is free to argue to the finder of fact that a breathalyzer test might have been exculpatory, but the police do not have a constitutional duty to perform any particular tests. The judgment of the Arizona Court of Appeals is reversed and the case remanded for further proceedings not inconsistent with this opinion.

JUSTICE STEVENS, concurring in the judgment.

Three factors are of critical importance to my evaluation of this case. First, at the time the police failed to refrigerate the victim's clothing, and thus negligently lost potentially valuable evidence, they had at least as great an interest in preserving the evidence as did the person later accused of the crime. Indeed, at that time it was more likely that the evidence would have been useful to the police — who were still conducting an investigation — and to the prosecutor — who would later bear the burden of establishing guilt beyond a reasonable doubt — than to the defendant.

. . . Second, although it is not possible to know whether the lost evidence would have revealed any relevant information, it is unlikely that the defendant was prejudiced by the State's omission. In examining witnesses and in her summation, defense counsel impressed upon the jury the fact that the State failed to preserve the evidence and that the State could have conducted tests that might well have exonerated the defendant. More significantly, the trial judge instructed the jury: "If you find that the State has . . . allowed to be destroyed or lost any evidence whose content or quality are in issue, you may infer that the true fact is against the State's interest." As a result, the uncertainty as to what the evidence might have proved was turned to the defendant's advantage.

Third, the fact that no juror chose to draw the permissive inference that proper preservation of the evidence would have demonstrated that the defendant was not the assailant suggests that the lost evidence was "immaterial." Our cases make clear that "[t]he proper standard of materiality must reflect our overriding concern with the justice of the finding of guilt," and that a State's failure to turn over (or preserve) potentially exculpatory evidence therefore "must be evaluated in the context of the entire record." In declining defense counsel's and the court's invitations to draw the permissive inference, the jurors in effect indicated that, in their view, the other evidence at trial was so overwhelming that it was highly improbable that the lost evidence was exculpatory . . . . Presumably, in a case involving a closer question as to guilt or innocence, the jurors would have been more ready to infer that the lost evidence was exculpatory.

With these factors in mind, I concur in the Court's judgment. I do not, however, join the Court's opinion because it announces a proposition of law that is much broader than necessary to decide this case. It states "that unless a criminal defendant can show bad faith on the part of the police, failure to preserve potentially useful evidence does not constitute a denial of due process of law." In my opinion, there may well be cases in which the defendant is unable to prove that the State acted in bad faith but in which the loss or destruction of evidence is nonetheless so critical to the defense as to make a criminal trial fundamentally unfair. This, however, is not such a case. Accordingly, I concur in the judgment.

JUSTICE BLACKMUN, with whom JUSTICE BRENNAN AND JUSTICE MARSHALL join, dissenting.

The Constitution requires that criminal defendants be provided with a fair trial, not merely a "good faith" try at a fair trial. Respondent here, by what may have been nothing more than police ineptitude, was denied the opportunity to present a full defense. That ineptitude, however, deprived respondent of his guaranteed right to due process of law. In reversing the judgment of the Arizona Court of Appeals, this Court, in my view, misreads the import of its prior cases and unduly restricts the protection of the Due Process Clause. An understanding of due process demonstrates that the evidence which was allowed to deteriorate was "constitutionally material," and that its absence significantly prejudiced respondent. Accordingly, I dissent.

The Court, with minimal reference to our past cases and with what seems to me to be less than complete analysis, announces "that unless a criminal defendant can show bad faith on the part of police, failure to preserve potentially useful evidence does not constitute a denial of due process of law." This conclusion is claimed to be justified because it limits the extent of police responsibility "to that class of cases where the interests of justice most clearly require it, i.e., those cases in which the police themselves by their conduct indicate that the evidence could form a basis for exonerating the defendant." The majority has identified clearly one type of violation, for police action affirmatively aimed at cheating the process undoubtedly violates the Constitution. But to suggest that this is the only way in which the Due Process Clause can be violated cannot be correct. Regardless of intent or lack thereof, police action that results in a defendant's receiving an unfair trial constitutes a deprivation of due process . . . .

NOTES

1. *Youngblood and Brady.* Recall that *Brady v. Maryland,* discussed *supra* and cited by the Court in *Youngblood,* holds that the due process clause requires the state to disclose certain evidence that the defense requests and that is helpful to the accused, irrespective of the prosecution's good or bad faith. Is *Youngblood* inconsistent with this when it held that the state, though obligated to disclose information, is not obligated to preserve such information?

2. *Importance of unpreserved evidence.* In *Youngblood,* what is the relationship between the government's good faith and the importance (materiality) to the defendant of the lost evidence? If the government acted in good faith but the evidence could have definitely exonerated the accused, would *Youngblood* excuse the loss of the evidence? What if the government in bad faith destroyed the evidence but the evidence would have been of virtually no use to the defense?

3. *Inculpatory evidence.* Assume that evidence is subjected to scientific analysis and the results provide strong proof that the defendant is guilty. Must the evidence be preserved under *Youngblood* so that the defendant can have an independent analysis conducted that could prove the defendant innocent? *See, e.g., United States v. Gibson,* 963 F.2d 708 (5th Cir. 1992) (80 pounds of marijuana destroyed; lab samples and photographs preserved; no error absent proof of bad faith by government).

The trial court's inherent authority to control the proceedings is probably broad enough to permit it to order preservation for this purpose in appropriate cases. Moreover, some prosecutors routinely provide the defense with a sample of the evidence, whenever possible, to facilitate scientific analysis. *See also* Standards for Criminal Justice § 11-3.2 (3d ed. 1996) (either party intending to destroy or transfer from its possession any discoverable objects or information must so notify the other party; either party should be permitted to evaluate or test discoverable physical evidence in the other party's possession, subject to appropriate court orders).

4. *Apparent exculpatory value.* A footnote in *Youngblood* suggests that the state's responsibility to preserve evidence is triggered if the evidence has "apparent" exculpatory value. If the evidence has not been tested or retested, what would satisfy this standard?

5. *Practical problems.* What practical problems would result had *Youngblood* required the preservation of any evidence that could exonerate the defendant?

6. *Proof of bad faith.* How could defense counsel ever prove bad faith when a police officer disposed of evidence that may have helped the accused if it had been analyzed? *See, e.g., United States v. Cooper,* 983 F.2d 928 (9th Cir. 1993) (indictment dismissed because government, in bad faith, failed to preserve laboratory equipment that could have exonerated defendants in drug manufacturing case; before equipment destroyed, defense counsel had alerted government to its importance, had demanded its return, and had been assured it would be preserved).

An obvious example of bad faith would be if a police officer destroyed evidence for the purpose of preventing defense counsel from having it analyzed by an independent laboratory. Fortunately, bad faith is rare. Moreover, since proof of bad faith may involve proof of what was in an officer's mind months or years ago, it is virtually impossible to prove. For an example of possible bad faith, see *Miller v. Vasquez*, 868 F.2d 1116 (9th Cir. 1989) (in remanding for resolution of the bad faith claim, the Court of Appeals noted that the police officer, who failed to obtain evidence that could have exonerated the accused, had referred to the accused using an "extremely derogative expletive," was not credible in claiming to have forgotten the evidence, and had tried to dissuade witnesses from testifying for the accused).

7. *Pending discovery request.* Assume that a defendant charged with possession of cocaine files a motion for discovery of physical evidence the government intends to use at his trial. Prior to the time for response, the defendant (who has been released on bond) fails to appear and remains a fugitive for over ten years. Upon his renewed request, the government responds by establishing that the evidence (cocaine) had been destroyed in good faith pursuant to established police procedures. Would a court violate *Youngblood* by dismissing criminal charges? Yes, answered the U.S. Supreme Court in *Illinois v. Fisher*, 540 U. S. 544 (2004). In a *per curiam* decision, the Court stated, "[w]e have never held or suggested that the existence of a pending discovery request eliminates the necessity of showing bad faith on the part of police." The Court also responded to a related argument by clarifying that the bad-faith requirement does not depend on the "centrality of the contested evidence;" it depends only upon the "distinction between 'material exculpatory' evidence and 'potentially useful' evidence."

8. *Negligent conduct.* Does "bad faith" also embrace acts that do not rise to the level of intentional misconduct? Recall that the *Youngblood* opinion indicated that the police misconduct "at worst can be described as negligent." This suggests that simple negligence is insufficient to require a reversal under *Youngblood*. But what if the government were *grossly negligent* in destroying evidence? In *Doggett v. United States*, 505 U.S. 647, 657 (1992), a case discussed in Chapter 13 and dealing with whether the speedy trial guarantee was violated, the Court cited *Youngblood* for the proposition that "our toleration of such [governmental] negligence varies inversely with its protractedness."

9. *Remedy for bad faith.* If it is established that the government destroyed evidence in bad faith, should the conviction be reversed automatically or should a "harmless error" analysis be performed?

10. *State variations.* A number of states do not follow *Youngblood*'s bad faith approach. Relying on state law, they impose a higher standard on the prosecution's duty to preserve evidence. Most use a balancing test. *See, e.g., State v. Morales*, 657 A.2d 585 (Conn. 1995) (police returned sexual assault victim's jacket to her though it contained semen stains from rapist; *Youngblood* interprets federal due process clause, but Connecticut constitution's due process clause uses balancing test that assesses materiality of missing evidence, likelihood of mistaken interpretation of it by jury, reason evidence is unavailable to defense, and prejudice caused by unavailability of the evidence); *Hammond v. State*, 569 A.2d 81 (Del. 1989) (when potentially exculpatory evidence is lost or destroyed by state, Delaware due process clause requires analysis of 3 factors: degree of negligence or bad faith, importance of missing evidence, and degree of prejudice to defendant). *See, contra, Collins v. Commonwealth*, 951 S.W. 2d 569 (Ky. 1997) (following *Youngblood*'s bad faith requirement as a matter of state constitutional law).

Other jurisdictions require government culpability that is not as egregious as *Youngblood*'s bad faith. *See State v. Smagula*, 578 A.2d 1215 (N.H. 1990) (state must act without "culpable negligence," which is less than gross negligence but more than ordinary negligence).

11. *Duty to gather evidence.* If *Trombetta* and *Youngblood* require the prosecution to preserve obviously exculpatory evidence in some cases, do they impose a duty on the police to *gather* exculpatory proof? Courts have not gone so far as to require that the government obtain exculpatory evidence. In *Miller v. Vasquez*, 868 F.2d 1116 (9th Cir. 1989), the defendant was charged with assault and false imprisonment after allegedly accosting a female acquaintance and forcing her into his car. He argued that due process was violated when the police did not gather two items of evidence that would have exonerated him. First, the investigating officer did not collect the victim's jacket which contained blood from the culprit who was bitten on the arm during the attack. Second, after the defendant was arrested, the police did not photograph his arm (presumably the photos would show no bite marks). The Court of Appeals rejected the claim, noting that due process does not impose a duty to obtain evidence. The *Vasquez* court cited *Youngblood* for the proposition that "even failure to preserve evidence that is only *potentially* useful does not violate due process in the absence of bad faith on the part of the police." But *Vasquez* also noted that a "bad faith failure to collect potentially exculpatory evidence would violate the due process clause."

The American Bar Association has gone further than the cases demand. "A prosecutor should not intentionally avoid pursuit of evidence because he or she believes it will damage the prosecution's case or aid the accused." Standards for Criminal Justice § 3-3.11(c) (3d ed. 1993). Although this passage could be read as not mandating a *search* for pro-defense evidence, the commentary to this section makes it clear that the "duty of the prosecutor is to acquire all the relevant evidence without regard to its impact on the success of the prosecution." *Id.* commentary. Does this mean that the prosecution must continue looking for evidence after it has gathered enough to convict the accused?

12. *Youngblood's subsequent history.* The subsequent history of Larry Youngblood and the crime victim is interesting and sobering. Though the sexual assault occurred in 1983 and the trial in 1985, the jury took only 95 minutes to convict Youngblood of kidnaping, sexual assault and child molestation, and the United States Supreme Court upheld the conviction in 1988, Youngblood did not report to prison until 1993 because of subsequent appeals to Arizona courts.

Recall that Justice Stevens' concurring opinion in *Youngblood* noted that "the jurors, in effect indicated that, in their view, the other evidence at trial was so overwhelming that it was highly improbable that the lost evidence was exculpatory."

Youngblood was released from prison in 1998, then rearrested in 1999 for failure to report a change in his address, in violation of a requirement under Arizona law (all other states have recently enacted similar legislation, commonly known as "Megan's Laws") that convicted sex offenders register into a central data base and report any new address to law enforcement authorities. In August 2000, DNA testing of a cotton swab retained from the sexual assault kit proved that Youngblood, now 47 years old, was innocent of the 1983 crime and he was released from jail where he was awaiting trial for the Megan's Law violation. In order to obtain a state-paid DNA test, Youngblood was required by police authorities to sign a waiver barring a suit against several state agencies for wrongful conviction. His later civil action to have the waiver declared invalid was unsuccessful.

The ten year-old victim of the sexual assault, wrongly attributed to Youngblood, also went to prison in 1993 when, as a twenty year-old adult, he assaulted his girlfriend. He was released, then convicted again for a serious assault on another woman.

E.   ACCESS TO WITNESSES AND OTHER EVIDENCE

Both prosecution (and the police and other law enforcement officials) and defense counsel will often attempt to interview potential witnesses to find out what happened, to locate other witnesses and evidence, and to prepare for guilty plea negotiations and trial. The usual format is for a police investigator or the lawyer prosecuting or defending the case to contact possible witnesses. Sometimes the task is as simple as placing a telephone call to a crime witness and asking what the witness saw. Often, particularly for key witnesses, a personal interview will be held. The session may be held at such locations as the witness's home or job, or at the police station or defense lawyer's office. Often it will be tape recorded.

Absent a court order (which is rare), a crime witness (or anyone else, for that matter) does not have to speak with either the prosecution or defense representatives. When a witness will not voluntarily talk with the prosecution or defense, either lawyer may use a subpoena to require the witness to appear and provide information at a preliminary hearing or trial. In addition, the prosecution can also subpoena a witness to testify before a grand jury. The use of a subpoena in such cases may be dangerous, however, if the witness, whose testimony is not known, testifies in a way harmful to the side that issued the subpoena. Accordingly, it is better to interview the witness informally before deciding whether to subpoena the witness to testify at a formal hearing.

Another way to compel a potential witness to provide pretrial information is the deposition, discussed later in this chapter. While some jurisdictions allow a potential witness in a criminal case to be deposed, usually it is permissible only in extraordinary circumstances by court order. *See* Fed. R. Crim. P. 15.

[1]   Ethical and Professional Restrictions

In an adversary system, sometimes one side would prefer that the other side not have contact with the first side's witnesses before trial. For example, the prosecutor may prefer that defense counsel not conduct pretrial interviews of police officers who may be prosecution witnesses at trial. Since gathering pretrial information may be critical to adequate trial preparation, the ethical standards of the legal profession severely limit a lawyer's efforts to prevent adversary counsel from conducting a full pretrial investigation of the case. Rule 3.4 of The Model Rules of Professional Conduct provides:

A Lawyer shall not:

(a) unlawfully obstruct another party's access to evidence or unlawfully alter, destroy or conceal a document or other material having potential evidentiary value. A lawyer shall not counsel or assist another person to do any such act;

. . . .

(f) request a person other than a client to refrain from voluntarily giving relevant information to another party unless:

(1) the person is a relative or an employee or other agent of a client; and

(2) the lawyer reasonably believes that the person's interests will not be adversely affected by refraining from giving such information.

Moreover, the American Bar Association's Standards for Criminal Justice provide specific guidance for both prosecutors and defense counsel. The Standards bar lawyers both from discouraging or obstructing communication between prospective witnesses and counsel for the other side. More specifically, a prosecutor "should not" and "it is unprofessional conduct" for defense counsel to advise any person or cause any person (other than a defense lawyer's client) to be advised to decline to give to counsel for the other side "information which such person has the right to give." STANDARDS FOR CRIMINAL JUSTICE §§ 3-3.1(d) (prosecutor), 4-4.3(d) (defense counsel) (3d ed. 1993). The

Code of Professional Responsibility focuses on a slightly different issue: "A lawyer shall not advise or cause a person to secrete himself or to leave the jurisdiction of a tribunal for the purpose of making him unavailable as a witness therein." American Bar Association, Model Code of Professional Responsibility, DR 7-109(B) (1969, as amended).

[2]   Constitutional Restrictions

Just as the ethical standards of the legal profession bar a lawyer from preventing a non-client from talking with counsel for the other side, the United States Constitution also has been read as barring such conduct by the *prosecution.* In general terms, the criminal defense lawyer has a right to attempt to interview potential witnesses without unreasonable interference by either the police or the prosecuting attorneys. This right has been attributed to a number of constitutional provisions: the due process clause, the Sixth Amendment right to the effective assistance of counsel, and the Sixth Amendment right to compulsory process. In order to establish a due process or Sixth Amendment violation, however, a defendant who has been denied access to potential witnesses by the government must show that the denial has been prejudicial — i.e., that the missing witnesses would have provided material testimony favorable to the defense. *See, e.g., United States v. Valenzuela-Bernal,* 458 U.S. 858 (1982) (no constitutional violation where defendant could not show prejudice from deportation of potential witnesses).

[3]   Other Restrictions

In addition, some courts use their inherent authority to supervise the practice of criminal law in their courts to restrict interference with access to potential witnesses. *See generally Gregory v. United States,* 369 F.2d 185 (D.C. Cir. 1966).

Statutes in a few jurisdictions also forbid interference with investigation. *See, e.g.,* Ark. R. Crim. P. 19.1 (neither prosecutor nor defense counsel shall advise persons other than the defendant to refrain from discussing the case with opposing counsel or from showing opposing counsel any relevant information).

[4]   Duty to Ensure Access

A few cases have required the prosecution to take positive steps to ensure defense access to exculpatory witnesses. In a rare case reaching this result, the court in *Government of Virgin Islands v. Smith,* 615 F.2d 964 (3d Cir. 1980), held that if the government's refusal to grant immunity to a potential defense witness intentionally distorts the factfinding process, then due process may require the government to give use immunity so that the witness will testify. *But see Commonwealth v. Beal,* 709 N.E.2d 413 (Mass. 1999) (refusing defendant's motion to require prosecutor to interrogate rape victim about exculpatory information; prosecutor has no duty to help defendant generate information from independent witness); *State v. Gorrio,* 726 So. 2d 832 (Fla. Dist. Ct. App. 1999) (state has no duty to procure witnesses for defense discovery).

[5]   Remedy

What happens when one side improperly impedes access to information? If the government's impropriety affected the fairness of the proceeding, perhaps dismissal would be appropriate in extreme cases. Of course, contempt of court and professional ethical sanctions are also possible. Another possibility is to adjust the discovery rules to offset the harm. *See, e.g., United States v. Carrigan,* 804 F.2d 599 (10th Cir. 1986) (court invoked its inherent authority to supervise its own proceedings in order to assure fair administration of justice and permitted defense to depose government witness, beyond the normal scope of criminal discovery rules, where government had attempted to discourage its witnesses from talking to defense counsel).

PROBLEM 10-1. DO WHAT YOU WANT TO DO

Margaret was the victim of a street robbery. A young man held a knife to her throat and threatened to kill her unless she gave him her purse. She readily complied and he ran away. Margaret gave the police a detailed description of the robber, and Seth Brownlow was arrested a month later and charged with the robbery.

Defense counsel has begun the investigation. Obviously, she would like to interview Margaret, the victim and primary government witness. Margaret has called the prosecutor to ask for advice. She wants to know to what extent she must cooperate with the defense lawyer's investigator who has just called her to schedule an interview.

Assess the validity of the following advice the prosecutor gave Margaret.

1. "You do not have to talk to anyone."

2. "You do not have to talk to anyone. If you want to talk to someone and would like for me to be present, let me know and I'll be there to help you."

3. "You do not have to talk to anyone. If you do, I would like to be present."

4. "You do not have to talk to anyone, but you are free to do so. If you do talk to the defense, they will try to use what you say against you at trial."

5. "The defense will try to trick you with their questions, but you don't have to cooperate with them."

F. SPECIFIC MODES OF DISCOVERY

As noted at the first of this chapter, discovery in criminal cases is quite restricted in most jurisdictions. Consequently, both sides may avail themselves of the few avenues of discovery permitted by the rules of criminal procedure. Some discovery occurs as the byproduct of various pretrial proceedings where information about the case is disclosed as an essential part of the process. Examples include hearings on bail, suppression of evidence under Rule 41(h), venue, and jury selection, as well as preliminary hearings and grand jury proceedings. There are also a number of provisions that specifically authorize discovery.

Although each of these modes provides only a limited amount of information, sometimes in the aggregate they do afford counsel considerable information about the other side's case. One commentator has characterized some criminal defense lawyers as engaged in the "pasta theory of discovery" in which they throw "out to the court as many potential grounds for discovery as possible to see what will stick." Peter J. Henning, *Defense Discovery in White Collar Criminal Prosecutions*, 15 GA. ST U. L. REV. 601, 619 (1999).

[1] Bill of Particulars

As described more fully in Chapter 7, an indictment or information should provide the accused with sufficient information about the charges so that counsel can prepare for trial and assert the double jeopardy guarantee if the same case is charged again. If an indictment contains too few facts to satisfy these goals, the rules of criminal procedure ordinarily permit the accused to file a Bill of Particulars, which is a formal request for more information about the charges. *See* Fed. R. Crim. P. 7(f).

If the court orders the prosecution to comply with the request, the prosecution will submit a written document providing more information about the crime. For example, if an indictment for armed robbery does not indicate where and when the robbery occurred, defense counsel may file a Motion for a Bill of Particulars to force the prosecution to disclose this information. The prosecution's response could provide defense counsel with some discovery about the case. Absent some detailed information about the offense, the defendant may find it difficult or impossible to defend. Returning to the armed robbery hypothetical, the defendant cannot investigate a possible alibi until he or she knows where and when the alleged robbery occurred.

Note that the Bill of Particulars is not mutual. The defense requests it from the government, but the government is not authorized to demand one from the defense. Should the rules of criminal procedure require the defense to inform the prosecution of details of the defense's likely proof? For example, should the defense have to tell the prosecution what its approach will be (for example, arguing criminal insanity, alibi, prosecution witnesses are lying, self-defense)?

Some discovery rules are reciprocal. If the defense requests and receives certain items, it is then obligated to turn over similar items to the prosecution. The Bill of Particulars could follow this model. If the defense sought a Bill of Particulars, it would have to inform the prosecution of its likely defenses. Would this make sense?

[2]   Notice to the Other Side

A significant trend in American criminal law is to minimize trial surprises by requiring the parties to provide one another with some information about their case. Obviously the indictment serves this purpose since it informs the defendant of the charges and some of the facts to be addressed at trial.

[a]   Evidence Rules

The rules of evidence occasionally provide some discovery in criminal cases. Perhaps the best examples are rape shield laws, which limit the proof that is admissible about the sexual assault victim's sexual history. Typically, these rules bar the defendant in sexual assault cases from introducing some data about the victim's sexual past unless the accused first notifies the prosecution (and sometimes the victim as well) of the intent to use such evidence. *See, e.g.,* Fed. R. Evid. 412 (c)(1). Usually the notice also includes an "offer of proof" that summarizes the evidence to be introduced. It may also include the names and addresses of witnesses on the issue. According to the United States Supreme Court, the rape shield notice provisions serve a number of purposes, including protecting the government against a surprise at trial. Once notified that certain evidence will be introduced, the prosecutor now has some understanding of the defense theory and can investigate the alleged facts to determine their veracity. *See Michigan v. Lucas,* 500 U.S. 145 (1991).

Other evidence rules also mandate notice to the other side. *See, e.g.,* Fed. R. Evid. 807 ("residual" hearsay exception available only if adverse party given advance notice of intent to offer the evidence and name and address of declarant); 609(b) (convictions more than 10 years old may be used to impeach if proponent gives adverse party advance written notice of intent to use such evidence); 404(b) (upon request of defendant, prosecution intending to use evidence of other crimes, wrongs, or acts to prove such issues as intent or motive must ordinarily give defense advance notice of nature of such evidence).

[b]   Alibi

Just as the rules of evidence require notice to the other side if certain proof is to be used, the rules of criminal procedure mandate notice to the other side if certain defenses are used.

Many jurisdictions require the defense to notify the prosecution if the defense intends to use an alibi defense. This prevents surprise at trial and permits both sides to investigate the alibi defense and gather proof to counter the other side's witnesses. It also facilitates more predictable court scheduling as it may remove a ground for a government request for a continuance shortly before trial to permit the government to prepare for unexpected alibi testimony.

Without advance notice of an intent to use an alibi defense, the prosecution will find it difficult to cross-examine defense alibi witnesses and provide proof that the alibi witnesses are mistaken or lying. Assume, for example, that the accused is charged with committing a one-person bank robbery in San Francisco. Of course the prosecution must prove beyond a reasonable doubt that the accused was the person who robbed that particular bank. Assume further that the defendant will assert at trial that she was in Los Angeles at a rock concert at the moment of the robbery in San Francisco. Unless the prosecution knows in advance of this alibi defense, it will be limited to proving presence in San Francisco. It will not have a real opportunity to prove that the defendant was not in Los Angeles by producing witnesses to testify that there was no record that defendant purchased a ticket to the concert, stayed at a hotel in Los Angeles, charged gas or anything else in Los Angeles on her credit card, visited her best friend who lives in Los Angeles, and the like.

The Federal Rules of Criminal Procedure mandate notice in such cases.

FEDERAL RULES OF CRIMINAL PROCEDURE

Rule 12.1 *Notice of an Alibi Defense*

(a) Government's Request for Notice and Defendant's Response.

(1) **Government's Request.** An attorney for the government may request in writing that the defendant notify an attorney for the government of any intended alibi defense. The request must state the time, date, and place of the alleged offense.

(2) **Defendant's Response.** Within 10 days after the request, or at some other time the court sets, the defendant must serve written notice on an attorney for the government of any intended alibi defense. The defendant's notice must state:

(A) each specific place where the defendant claims to have been at the time of the alleged offense; and

(B) the name, address, and telephone number of each alibi witness on whom the defendant intends to rely.

(b) Disclosing Government Witnesses.

(1) **Disclosure.** If the defendant serves a Rule 12.1(a)(2) notice, an attorney for the government must disclose in writing to the defendant or the defendant's attorney:

(A) the name, address, and telephone number of each witness the government intends to rely on to establish the defendant's presence at the scene of the alleged offense; and

(B) each government rebuttal witness to the defendant's alibi defense.

(2) **Time to Disclose.** Unless the court directs otherwise, an attorney for the government must give its Rule 12.1(b)(1) disclosure within 10 days after the defendant serves notice of an intended alibi defense under Rule 12.1(a)(2), but no later than 10 days before trial.

(c) Continuing Duty to Disclose. Both an attorney for the government and the defendant must promptly disclose in writing to the other party the name, address, and telephone number of each additional witness if:

(1) the disclosing party learns of the witness before or during trial; and

(2) the witness should have been disclosed under Rule 12.1(a) or (b) if the disclosing party had known of the witness earlier.

(d) Exceptions. For good cause, the court may grant an exception to any requirement of Rule 12.1(a)-(c).

(e) Failure to Comply. If a party fails to comply with this rule, the court may exclude the testimony of any undisclosed witness regarding the defendant's alibi. This rule does not limit the defendant's right to testify.

(f) Inadmissibility of Withdrawn Intention. Evidence of an intention to rely on an alibi defense, later withdrawn, or of a statement made in connection with that intention, is not, in any civil or criminal proceeding, admissible against the person who gave notice of the intention.

NOTES.

1. *Triggered by government notice.* Rule 12.1 contains an unusual feature. Note that it is triggered by a written "demand" by the government. The defendant cannot initiate the reciprocal discovery process of Rule 12.1. If the government does not initiate the notice process, Rule 12.1 is inapplicable and neither side is obligated to follow its procedures. In such cases, the defense may offer a full alibi defense without providing any alibi notice to the government.

Why would the government initiate the Rule 12.1 process? What does it have to gain? To lose? When would it choose to not do so in a case where an alibi defense is possible? If you were the United States Attorney, would you routinely provide a Rule 12.1 demand notice in every case? Note that some courts have held that the government cannot request a continuance because of a surprise alibi defense if it does not provide the "demand" required by Rule 12.1.

On rare occasions the defense may voluntarily provide information about its alibi witnesses without a prior formal request by the government. This could occur if the defense were using the possibility of an alibi defense to have charges not filed or dropped, or to gain an advantage in plea bargaining. The defense will disclose the possible alibi defense so the prosecutor will possibly be moved to make the decision the defense wants. In this situation, Rule 12.1 does not apply and the prosecution need not file either a request (including the time, date, and location of the crime) or a list of its own witnesses to rebut the alibi.

2. *Sequence of events.* Rule 12.1 prescribes a series of three actions by the government and the defense. First, the prosecution begins the process by providing a written "demand" which indicates details about the time and location of the offense. Second, within ten days the defense must then notify the prosecution of any intent to offer an alibi defense, the location where the defendant claims to have been, and the witness who will support the alibi. Third, ten days later (but at least ten days before trial) the government must then disclose the names and addresses of the witnesses who will place the defendant at the scene of the crime and those who will rebut the defense's alibi claim. The court has the discretion to dispense with the time requirements in appropriate cases. If the required demand is made, both sides have a continuing duty to continue to supply the names of witnesses identified later.

3. *What must be disclosed.* Note that Rule 12.1 requires the two sides to exchange information about alibi witnesses but not other witnesses. Thus, Rule 12.1 is an exception to the general, though not universal, rule that parties in a criminal case need not exchange a list of witnesses to be called at trial. If the accused relies on an alibi, often the alibi witnesses are the only defense witnesses since the defendant claims to know nothing about the event and does not dispute that it happened. On the other hand, the prosecution will have witnesses both to prove the crime and disprove the alibi. This means that the defense must disclose its main and perhaps only witnesses, but the prosecution need disclose only some of its witnesses. Is this fair?

Rule 12.1 requires each side to disclose its witnesses' name, address, and telephone number. If any of this information is not known, the party must do its best to comply and is under a continuing duty to provide the missing information when it becomes available.

The witnesses to be disclosed include government witnesses both placing the defendant at the crime scene as well as those rebutting defense alibi witnesses, perhaps establishing that the defendant was not where the alibi witnesses claimed.

Another issue is whether it is fair to require the defense to disclose its primary defense, but not to require the government to disclose its theory of the case. Should the government be required to inform the defendant of such matters as its theory of intent or motive? Would it make sense to require the government to disclose its theory of the case in exchange for learning the defense's theory?

4. *Penalty for failure to comply.* If the government provides the necessary "demand," both sides must comply with Rule 12.1's disclosure rules unless the court, in its discretion, grants an exception to the provisions of Rule 12.1. Under Rule 12.1(e), the court has the discretion to exclude the testimony of a "location" witness who was not disclosed to the other side. Of course, this penalty does not apply to the defendant, who need not be mentioned in the exchange of witnesses under Rule 12.1.

In *Taylor v. Illinois*, 484 U.S. 400 (1988), the Supreme Court held there are some limits on barring a defense witness from testifying as a sanction for violation of a discovery order. In *Taylor*, when the defense did not list a particular person on its court-ordered witness list, the trial judge refused to allow the witness to testify. While this order was upheld by the Supreme Court, it noted that the compulsory process guarantee of the Sixth Amendment gives the criminal accused the right to present favorable witnesses to the jury. This right severely limits a trial judge's authority to bar such witnesses as a sanction for discovery violations. The trial court should find out the reason for noncompliance. If the noncompliance was willful and motivated by a desire to obtain a tactical advantage, it may be appropriate to bar the witness from testifying. On the other hand, if the harm of noncompliance could be cured by a continuance, the court should consider this alternative. The Supreme Court in *Taylor* noted that sanctions for noncompliance with discovery should be resolved on a case-by-case basis, giving appropriate weight to the defendant's right to present witnesses.

In deciding whether exclusion of a witness is proper for noncompliance with Rule 12.1, the court looks at a number of factors, including the prejudice caused by the failure to disclose, any evidence of actions mitigating the prejudice, the reason for nondisclosure, and the weight of evidence of guilt. *See United States v. Burkhalter*, 735 F.2d 1327 (11th Cir. 1984). *See also United States v. Levy-Cordero*, 67 F.3d 1002 (1st Cir. 1995) (several weeks into trial, defense counsel filed emergency motion to present alibi evidence; court of appeals remanded for hearing on whether, under *Taylor*, alibi notice could have been filed in timely fashion or whether delay was wilful and done to obtain tactical advantage and therefore alibi proof should be excluded).

Prejudice would be difficult to prove if the unidentified witness were known to the other side, such as when the witness was already named on a list of trial witnesses (as some judges require) or had identified the defendant in a line up where defense counsel was present. Intentional withholding, on the other hand, will be viewed with extreme disfavor and may well lead to the exclusion of the unidentified witness, even without a showing of prejudice.

[c] Mental Condition Defense

Just as many rules of criminal procedure mandate notice of alibi, a large number establish a somewhat complex procedure when the defendant intends to use a defense, such as insanity, that is based on a mental disease or defect. The overall purpose of these rules is to provide the prosecution with an opportunity to have the defendant examined before trial by a neutral expert. If there were no such rules, the defense could surprise the prosecution at trial by raising, without prior indication, the insanity defense and producing defense experts who testify that the accused was insane. The prosecution would not have had a chance to have its own experts examine the accused and may find it difficult to counter the defense proof, especially in jurisdictions where the defendant must raise the insanity defense and then the prosecution has the burden of proving that the accused was sane.

FEDERAL RULES OF CRIMINAL PROCEDURE

Rule 12.2 *Notice of an Insanity Defense; Mental Examination*

(a) Notice of an Insanity Defense. A defendant who intends to assert a defense of insanity at the time of the alleged offense must so notify an attorney for the government in writing within the time provided for filing a pretrial motion, or at any later time the court sets. A defendant who fails to do so cannot rely on an insanity defense. The court may, for good cause, allow the defendant to file the notice late, grant additional trial-preparation time, or make other appropriate orders.

(b) Notice of Expert Evidence of a Mental Condition. If a defendant intends to introduce expert evidence relating to a mental disease or defect or any other mental condition of the defendant bearing on the issue of guilt, the defendant must — within the time provided for filing a pretrial motion or at any later time the court sets — notify an attorney for the government in writing of this intention and file a copy of the notice with the clerk. The court may, for good cause, allow the defendant to file the notice late, grant the parties additional trial-preparation time, or make other appropriate orders.

(c) Mental Examination.

    (1) Authority to Order an Examination; Procedures.

        (A) The court may order the defendant to submit to a competency examination under 18 U.S.C. § 4241.

        (B) If the defendant provides notice under Rule 12.2(a), the court must, upon the government's motion, order the defendant to be examined under 18 U.S.C. § 4242. If the defendant provides notice under Rule 12.2(b) the court may, upon the government's motion, order the defendant to be examined under procedures ordered by the court.

    (2) Disclosing Results and Reports of Capital Sentencing Examination. The results and reports of any examination conducted solely under Rule 12.2(c)(1) after notice under Rule 12.2(b)(2) must be sealed and must not be disclosed to any attorney for the government or the defendant unless the defendant is found guilty of one or more capital crimes and the defendant confirms an intent to offer during sentencing proceedings expert evidence on mental condition.

    (3) Disclosing Results and Reports of the Defendant's Expert Examination. After disclosure under Rule 12.2(c)(2) of the results and reports of the government's examination, the defendant must disclose to the government the results and reports of any examination on mental condition conducted by the defendant's expert about which the defendant intends to introduce expert evidence.

    (4) Inadmissibility of a Defendant's Statements. No statement made by a defendant in the course of any examination conducted under this rule (whether conducted with or without the defendant's consent), no testimony by the expert based on the statement, and no other fruits of the statement may be admitted into evidence against the defendant in any criminal proceeding except on an issue regarding mental condition on which the defendant:

        (A) has introduced evidence of incompetency or evidence requiring notice under Rule 12.2(a) or (b)(1), or

(B) has introduced expert evidence in a capital sentencing proceeding requiring notice under Rule 12.2(b)(2).

(d) Failure to Comply.

(1) Failure to Give Notice or to Submit to Examination. The court may exclude any expert evidence from the defendant on the issue of the defendant's mental disease, mental defect, or any other mental condition bearing on the defendant's guilt or the issue of punishment in a capital case if the defendant fails to:

(A) give notice under Rule 12.2(b); or

(B) submit to an examination when ordered under Rule 12.2(c).

(2) Failure to Disclose. The court may exclude any expert evidence for which the defendant has failed to comply with the disclosure requirement of Rule 12.2(c)(3).

(e) Inadmissibility of Withdrawn Intention. Evidence of an intention as to which notice was given under Rule 12.2(a) or (b) later withdrawn, is not, in any civil or criminal proceeding, admissible against the person who gave notice of the intention.

NOTES

1. *Mental conditions covered.* Rule 12.2 applies whenever the defense intends to raise a defense based on insanity (Rule 12.2(a)) or to use an expert on a "mental disease or defect or any other mental condition . . . bearing upon the issue of . . . guilt" (Rule 12.2(b)).

In order to reduce the impact of expert testimony in criminal cases, evidence rules may limit an expert's testimony on whether a criminal accused did or did not have a particular mental state or condition constituting an element of the crime charged or a defense to the charge. *See, e.g.,* Fed. R. Evid. 704(b).

2. *Triggered by defense notice.* The reciprocal notice provisions of Rule 12.2 are triggered by the defense's written notice of an intent to rely upon an insanity defense or to use expert testimony to the effect that the defendant's mental condition affected guilt. Why would Rule 12.2 be written so that defense counsel does not have to notify the prosecution of an intent to use an expert for a defense based on insanity (notice only must be given of the intent to use the insanity defense, irrespective of the use of expert testimony), but must provide such notice if it wants to use expert testimony on other mental condition defenses?

3. *Timing of notice.* Rule 12.2(a) & (b) provides that the defense notice shall be filed within the time provided for filing pretrial motions or later with the court's permission. After the deadline, late notice is still permissible "for cause shown." Counsel seeking to give late notice may file a Motion to Provide Late Notice under Rule 12.1 and should be prepared to justify the tardy notice. Some courts are quite flexible in enforcing the notice deadline. *See, e.g., United States v. Vega-Penarete,* 137 F.R.D. 233 (E.D.N.C. 1991) (even though defense's Rule 12.2 notice was filed late, the district court refused to exclude defendant's expert witnesses on battered wife syndrome because the government had actual knowledge of defendant's intent to use this defense, the case was serious, and no continuance would be necessary).

4. *Compelled mental examination.* The key to Rule 12.2 is that it authorizes the court to order the defendant to undergo a mental examination. Note that the rule does not say anything about the qualifications of the person who will conduct the exam, the location of the exam, the type of exam, whether there will be a written report by the examining expert, who has access to any such report, and who will pay for the expert's services. Some of the answers to these questions are provided by 18 U.S.C. §§ 4241 (determination of mental competency to stand trial), 4242 (determination of insanity at time of offense), and 4247 (various procedures).

In general terms, these provisions indicate that the exam is to be conducted by a psychiatrist or clinical psychologist. The defendant can be committed to a mental institution for a short period of time to facilitate the examination. The examining expert must prepare a written report which is given to all parties and the court. Rule 16(a)(1)(F), discussed below, also requires disclosure of reports of scientific tests. Moreover, Rules 16(a)(1)(G) and 16(b)(1)(C) often mandate disclosure of a summary of expert testimony to be presented on the defendant's mental condition.

Since the government pays for these compelled mental examinations, sometimes the defense files a notice under Rule 12.2 in order to obtain a free evaluation. This is especially likely if the defendant has too few assets to hire independent mental health professionals for a private evaluation.

On the other hand, some defendants have challenged the propriety of a compelled mental examination. In *United States v. Bell*, 855 F. Supp. 239 (N.D. Ill. 1994), for example, the court held that the defendant's duress defense, unlike an insanity defense, was not based on defendant's "mental capacity" and therefore denied the government's motion to compel to the defendant to submit to a compulsory mental examination under Rule 12.2. Do you agree? *Cf. United States v. Vega-Penarete*, 137 F.R.D. 233 (E.D.N.C. 1991) (battered wife syndrome defense is covered by Rule 12.2 and mental examination ordered).

5. *Information obtained in examination.* During the mental examination ordered pursuant to Rule 12.2, the defendant may well discuss the crime at issue, other crimes that have not been discovered, and other issues that may be relevant to either guilt or the sentence. If disclosed in court, this information could lead the defendant to be convicted of the case at hand as well as others not yet filed. Despite these significant self-incrimination concerns, courts have consistently held that this mandated examination does not violate the defendant's Fifth Amendment rights. Rule 12.2(c) eliminates most of the Fifth Amendment concerns by providing that any statement the defendant gives during the exam, any testimony of the examining expert based on that statement, and any fruit of the defendant's statement are inadmissible on any matter other than the mental condition at issue.

For example, assume that Foster is being evaluated under Rule 12.2 for a possible insanity defense in a homicide trial. During the psychologist's interview, Foster admitted that he killed the victim. Foster's admission to the psychologist is admissible at trial to support the expert's opinion on Foster's insanity, but is not admissible on the issue whether Foster killed the victim. The problem, of course, is that insanity is ordinarily decided by the same jury that decides whether Foster killed the victim. Can the jury hear this evidence and apply it only to the former issue but not the latter?

In order to protect against this dilemma, some defense counsel will encourage their clients undergoing a Rule 12.2 evaluation to avoid discussions of criminal activity. A few defense lawyers have even asked the court's permission to attend the evaluation sessions to protect their client's interests. *See, e.g., United States v. Cohen*, 530 F.2d 43 (5th Cir.), *cert. denied*, 429 U.S. 855 (1976)(defense counsel not entitled to attend evaluation).

6. *Sanctions for noncompliance.* Failure to comply with Rule 12.2 can cause drastic consequences for the defense. If notice is not given under Rule 12.2(a) and (b), the defendant may be barred from offering an insanity defense or an expert witness on the defendant's mental condition. A similar result may occur if the defendant refuses to participate in a court-ordered evaluation.

PROBLEM 10-2. MENTAL ISSUES

1. Assume that defendant X is charged with the "knowing and wilful attempt to evade federal income taxes." Defense counsel would like to call a psychiatrist to testify that the defendant was "too stupid to understand the intricacies of the reporting requirements under the federal tax laws." Must defense counsel provide notice under Rule 12.2? *See United States v. Edwards*, 90 F.R.D. 391 (E.D. Va. 1981) (notice requirements of Rule 12.2 apply to "stupidity" defense); *United States v. Beers*, 91 F.3d 1201 (8th Cir. 1996) (trial court did not abuse discretion in disallowing defendant from presenting expert testimony on issue of insanity where defense had not complied with Rule 12.2 notice requirement).

2. Defendant Y is charged with selling drugs to a police undercover agent. Y's defense is entrapment. Y maintains that she had no predisposition to sell drugs and was entrapped by a government agent who overcame her resistance by repeatedly offering her large sums of money to obtain a small quantity of drugs for the agent. Y plans to call a clinical psychologist to testify that the defendant's psychological characteristics and subnormal intelligence combined to make Y particularly susceptible to persuasion and psychological pressure. Must defense counsel provide notice under Rule 12.2? *See United States v. Lewis*, 53 F.3d 29 (4th Cir. 1995); *United States v. Hill*, 655 F.2d 512 (3d Cir. 1981)(holding the rule's notice requirement inapplicable to expert testimony relative to defense of entrapment). *But see, contra, United States v. Sullivan*, 919 F. 2d 1403 (10th Cir. 1990)(notice requirement held applicable to mental condition evidence in entrapment defenses).

3. Defendant Z was charged with perjury and obstructing justice for lying to a grand jury about a bid-rigging in which she denied involvement. As a defense, Z would like to call a physician to testify that at the time of the grand jury hearing she was taking medicine for a benign tumor. The medicine caused a short-term memory loss and therefore she had no criminal intent when she falsely denied involvement in the bid-rigging. Assume that no notice was provided by the defense attorney under Rule 12.2. As Assistant United States Attorney, what arguments would you make in support of your claim that the physician's testimony should not be allowed? *See United States v. Cervone*, 907 F.2d 332 (2d Cir. 1990); *United States v. Kim*, 303 F. Supp. 2d 150 (D. Conn. 2004)(good cause not shown for late disclosure of proffered expert witness; proffered expert testimony relative to defendant's history of family abuse and mental illness as explanation for defendant's criminal activity disallowed).

[d]   Other Notice Rules

Following the well recognized lead of Rules 12.1 and 12.2, some jurisdictions have recognized a need to prevent trial surprise for other defenses. For Example, Rule 12.3 of the Federal Rules of Criminal Procedure requires the defense to notify the prosecution of an intent to "assert a defense of actual or believed exercise of public authority on behalf of a law enforcement agency or federal intelligence agency at the time of the alleged offense." The notice must identify the agency and personnel involved and when the authority existed. The government then becomes obligated to admit or deny the existence of the public authority identified in the defendant's notice. Both sides must then exchange the names and addresses of witnesses on this issue.

Other jurisdictions have gone much further than the federal government. Arizona represents one of the most expansive approaches to the disclosure of defenses:

> Within the time specified in Rule 15.2(d), the defendant shall provide a written notice to the prosecutor specifying all defense as to which the defendant intends to introduce evidence at trial, including, but not limited to, alibi, insanity, self-defense, defense of others, entrapment, impotency, marriage, insufficiency of a prior conviction, mistaken identity, and good character. The notice shall specify for each defense the persons, including the defendant, whom the defendant intends to call as witnesses in support of each defense.

Ariz. R. Crim. P. 15.2(b). *See also* Ark. R. Crim. P. 18.3 (disclose nature of any defense to be used at trial and witnesses on that issue); Ill. Sup. Ct. R. 413(d) (any defenses); Mass. R. Crim. P. 14(b)(3) (disclosure of defense based upon license, claim of authority or ownership, or exemption). Do you agree with the Arizona approach? Should it be reciprocal, requiring the prosecution to disclose its theories and witnesses? Would it make sense to limit this disclosure to surprise witnesses or theories? Do you think it will speed up, slow down, or not affect the trial process?

[3] Depositions

While depositions are a common and important feature of discovery in civil cases, they are rare or nonexistent in criminal cases in most jurisdictions. When permitted in criminal cases by court rule or statute, often they are limited to unusual situations. The federal approach, embraced in Rule 15, is typical.

FEDERAL RULES OF CRIMINAL PROCEDURE

Rule 15. *Depositions*

(a) When Taken.

(1) In General. A party may move that a prospective witness be deposed in order to preserve testimony for trial. The court may grant the motion because of exceptional circumstances and in the interest of justice. If the court orders the deposition to be taken, it may also require the deponent to produce at the deposition any designated material that is not privileged, including any book, paper, document, record, recording, or data.

(2) Detained Material Witness. A witness who is detained under 18 U.S.C. § 3144 may request to be deposed by filing a written motion and giving notice to the parties. The court may then order that the deposition be taken and may discharge the witness after the witness has signed under oath the deposition transcript.

(b) Notice.

(1) In General. A party seeking to take a deposition must give every other party reasonable written notice of the deposition's date and location. The notice must state the name and address of each deponent. If requested by a party receiving the notice, the court may, for good cause, change the deposition's date or location.

(2) To the Custodial Officer. A party seeking to take the deposition must also notify the officer who has custody of the defendant of the scheduled date and location.

(c) Defendant's Presence.

(1) Defendant in Custody. The officer who has custody of the defendant must produce the defendant at the deposition and keep the defendant in the witness's presence during the examination, unless the defendant:

(A) waives in writing the right to be present; or

(B) persists in disruptive conduct justifying exclusion after being warned by the court that disruptive conduct will result in the defendant's exclusion.

(2) Defendant Not in Custody. A defendant who is not in custody has the right upon request to be present at the deposition, subject to any conditions imposed by the court. If the government tenders the defendant's expenses as provided in Rule 15(d) but the defendant still fails to appear, the defendant — absent good cause — waives both the right to appear and any objection to the taking and use of the deposition based on that right.

(d) Expenses. If the deposition was requested by the government, the court may — or if the defendant is unable to bear the deposition expenses, the court must — order the government to pay:

(1) any reasonable travel and subsistence expenses of the defendant and the defendant's attorney to attend the deposition; and

(2) the costs of the deposition transcript.

(e) Manner of Taking. Unless these rules or a court order provides otherwise, a deposition must be taken and filed in the same manner as a deposition in a civil action, except that:

(1) A defendant may not be deposed without that defendant's consent.

(2) The scope and manner of the deposition examination and cross-examination must be the same as would be allowed during trial.

(3) The government must provide to the defendant or the defendant's attorney, for use at the deposition, any statement of the deponent in the government's possession to which the defendant would be entitled at trial.

(f) Use as Evidence. A party may use all or part of a deposition as provided by the Federal Rules of Evidence.

(g) Objections. A party objecting to deposition testimony or evidence must state the grounds for the objection during the deposition.

(h) Depositions by Agreement Permitted. The parties may by agreement take and use a deposition with the court's consent.

NOTES

1. *Limited use.* Rule 15 makes it clear why depositions are so rare in federal criminal cases. They are available only by court order "to preserve testimony for trial" and the trial court is given significant discretion in deciding whether to issue the order. One court's analysis is typical:

> . . . [T]he language of . . . [Rule 15] suggests that the trial court's discretion is not broad and should be exercised carefully. Allowing depositions too freely would create the risks that parties would seek to use depositions as a discovery device in criminal cases, or would try to use depositions in lieu of live testimony at trial in contravention of the spirit of the Sixth Amendment.

United States v. Mann, 590 F.2d 361, 365 (1st Cir. 1978). *See also, United States v. Kim,* 303 F.Supp.2d 150 (D. Conn. 2004).

2. *Preserve testimony for trial.* Rule 15(a) makes it clear that depositions are only authorized to "preserve testimony for trial." This limitation is widely interpreted as barring a deposition simply for discovery. Ordinarily the person deposed will likely be unavailable for trial.

3. *Exceptional circumstances or interests of justice.* Consistent with the preference against the use of depositions in criminal cases, Rule 15 places two significant limits on depositions. Rule 15(a) states that a deposition is authorized only in "exceptional circumstances" in the "interests of justice." The party requesting the deposition has the burden of establishing that this test is satisfied. The trial judge is given great discretion in deciding whether to order the deposition.

Although there is no generally recognized definition of these terms, courts consider the facts of each case and look at four factors: the importance of the testimony, the likelihood that the witness will be able to testify personally at trial, the financial and other costs that would be saved by the deposition, and the fact the witness is that of the party taking the deposition.

Courts have found this standard was met when an important government witness was too ill to attend court, when witnesses were out of the country and could not be subpoenaed, and when the costs of taking depositions would be far less than that necessary to bring the witnesses to the site of a suppression hearing. With regard to taking a deposition of a fugitive who refuses to return to the United States for fear of prosecution, *see, United States v. Hernandez-Escarsega,* 886 F.2d 1560 (9th Cir. 1989) (fugitive status not an absolute bar to taking out-of-country deposition, but "exceptional circumstances" not shown under the facts presented).

4. *State expansions of depositions.* Some states are less restrictive in their allowance of depositions in criminal cases. But there are routinely more restrictions than are present in civil cases. *See*, e.g, Ariz. R. Crim. P. 15.3 (depositions permissible if party shows that deponent's testimony is material to case, to prepare a defense, or investigate the offense and deponent was not witness at preliminary hearing and will not grant personal interview); Colo. R. Crim. P. 15(a) (deposition permissible if deponent may be unable to attend hearing and deposition necessary to prevent injustice); Tex. Crim. Proc. Code Ann. § 39.02 (deposition for "good reason").

A few jurisdictions have rejected the traditional reservations about depositions in criminal cases. *See, e.g.,* Fla. R. Crim. P. 3.220(h)(1) ("At any time after the filing of the charging document any party may take the deposition upon oral examination of any [authorized] person) (*see generally* John F. Yetter, *Discovery Depositions in Florida Criminal Proceedings: Should They Survive?*, 16 FLA. ST. U. L. REV. 675 (1988)); Vt. R. Crim. P. 15 (either side may take deposition of witness, subject to appropriate protective orders). New Mexico rules allow both sides to obtain discovery in criminal cases similarly to the ways in which discovery is undertaken in civil cases (limited only by claims of privilege and irrelevance), and permit either prosecution or defense to subpoena "any person, other than the defendant" to give a "statement" and to produce "materials to be examined during the statement." *See*, N.M. R. Crim. P. 5-503. Missouri's rules authorize the prosecutor to "obtain the deposition of any person on oral examination" in the same manner as "governed by the rules relating to the taking of depositions in civil cases." Mo. R. Crim. P. 25.15.

5. *Policy rationales.* Why are depositions ordinarily more limited in criminal than civil cases? One argument is that victims and other witnesses will be harassed. *See* Vt. R. Crim. P. 15 (extensive provisions to protect deponents, including victim's right to have lawyer and victim-advocate present at deposition; judge or special master may be present if necessary; judge may limit deposition to written questions; judge may limit people present at deposition; and judge may deny taking of deposition); Fla. R. Crim. P. 3.220(h)(7) (defendant has no right to be physically present at deposition unless good cause shown; court may consider "intimidating effect of the defendant's presence on the witness"). What can be done to minimize this possibility?

Another issue is expense. While this is especially a concern for indigent or poor defendants, prosecutors likewise object that they cannot afford to allocate scarce resources, including personnel, to the deposition process. Is the cure for this to deny depositions to rich and poor alike? A third problem is that depositions could result in inequality between the two sides since the defendant can assert the Fifth Amendment to prevent being deposed by the government. Could the defendant be required to waive the Fifth Amendment in exchange for the right to depose police officers who investigated the case?

An argument in favor of increased use of depositions is that it will promote dispositions (guilty plea or dropped charges) short of trial. Do you agree?

6. *Includes testimony and non-privileged materials.* Although Federal Rule 15(a) is titled "depositions," it reaches further than that. It not only can compel a party's witness to appear for deposition, it also can require the witness to bring "any designated book, paper, document, record, recording, or other material not privileged."

7. *Form of deposition.* Federal Rule 15(e) provides little specific guidance on the method of taking the deposition. It does indicate that the deposition is to be taken and filed "in the manner provided in civil actions" with a few exceptions. Thus, one must consult the Federal Rules of Civil Procedure to determine the precise form of depositions in criminal cases. Courts have permitted such depositions by videotape, telephone, and, for foreign deponents, "letters rogatory" (pursuant to Federal Rule of Civil Procedure 28(b)(2)).

Rule 15(e) does contain two exceptions. First, in order to satisfy the Fifth Amendment's self-incrimination guarantee, a party defendant cannot be deposed without his or her permission. Second, the scope and manner of direct and cross examination at the deposition are the same as that of the trial. To facilitate cross-examination, Rule 15(e) also requires the government at the deposition to provide defense counsel with any statement of the deponent that the defense would be entitled to at trial.

8. *Procedures.* Federal Rule 15 outlines the procedures to be followed in those rare cases where a deposition is taken in a criminal case. According to Rule 15(b), the party seeking the deposition must notify the other parties of the time and place of the deposition. The defendant has a right to attend the deposition in person.

Rule 15(c) provides that the government may be ordered to pay the expenses of a deposition requested by either the government or an indigent defendant. But the government does not pay lawyer's fees of retained defense counsel for depositions requested by the government.

9. *Use of Deposition.* Recall that many judicial decisions hold that a deposition under Rule 15 is designed to preserve testimony rather than to discover evidence. Federal Rule 15(f) provides that these depositions are admissible "as provided by the Federal Rules of Evidence." Thus a deposition can be admissible for several purposes. First, if the deponent is unavailable at trial, as defined by the rules of evidence, the deposition may be admissible as substantive evidence through the former testimony hearsay exception in Rule 804(b)(1). Second, if the declarant testifies at trial, the deposition can be used as substantive evidence as a prior inconsistent statement. Third, the deposition is admissible to impeach or contradict the deponent's trial testimony.

UNITED STATES v. ESQUIVEL
755 F. Supp. 434 (D.D.C. 1990)

ROBINSON, CHIEF JUDGE

[Defendants Novo and Diaz are charged with the homicide of Letelier.]

. . . Defendant seeks leave to depose three individuals in Chile, Manuel Contreras, Pedro Espinoza and Lilliana Walker. Contreras and Espinoza are co-defendants who have been fugitives since the indictment was handed up. Walker is an unindicted co-conspirator. Defendant proffers that "[t]he testimony of these three witnesses will show that DINA [Chilean Intelligence] and the Chilean government planned and directed the murder of Letelier and that DINA had the resources and its own agents in the United States to carry out the killing of Letelier." Defendant also believes that the deposition testimony will contradict the probable testimony of Townley [prosecution's primary witness].

. . . The burden rests with the movant [under Rule 15] to show the necessity of preserving a prospective witnesses' testimony by a deposition. Materiality of the testimony and the unavailability of the witness are the critical factors. In the criminal context, a defendant typically demonstrates the "exceptional circumstances" necessary for success on a Rule 15(a) motion by some preliminary showing that the testimony will exculpate him.

Defendant here has not carried his burden of showing materiality as to any of the three proposed deponents, and failed to show the unavailability of Walker. Defendant has provided no specific information about the probable testimony these witnesses could offer, other than unsubstantiated speculation that it will exculpate him. In fact, the government proffers that Contreras and Espinoza have consistently denied their participation in the Letelier bombing. With regard to Walker, she has not been indicted in this case and apparently faces no other criminal charges in the United States. There is no evidence whatsoever that Walker is unable or unwilling to attend trial in the United States.

In any event, Contreras and Espinoza are co-defendants, and defendant has not shown that they consent to the giving of testimony. Clearly they maintain a Fifth Amendment privilege in the United States. The Rule requires consent, and defendant has not provided it. On this ground alone, defendant's motion must be denied.

NOTES

1. Is it fair to say that the *Esquivel* court says that a deposition requested by a defendant will be granted *only* when it will exculpate the accused? If not, in what other situations?

2. *Preindictment deposition.* Can a defendant, who fears that he or she will be indicted, obtain a court order under Rule 15 for a preindictment deposition? If not, can the person use Rule 27 of the Federal Rules of Civil Procedure to obtain a preindictment deposition if a civil case is likely? *See Application of Eisenberg,* 654 F.2d 1107 (5th Cir. 1981) (cannot use civil discovery as disguised attempt at criminal discovery).

3. *Proof of materiality.* If the witnesses whose deposition is sought will not talk to the defendant, how can the defendant establish the materiality of the testimony since the content of that testimony is unknown?

4. *Absent defense witness.* Assume that an important defense alibi witness has fled the jurisdiction and is unavailable to testify at trial. Should the defendant be heard to complain of any disadvantage resulting from the failure of that witness to appear at trial? *See Ray v. United States,* 367 F.2d 258 (8th Cir. 1966), *cert. denied,* 386 U.S. 913 (1967).

5. *Detention of material witness.* If it appears that a material witness will be unreachable by subpoena, a federal statute authorizes a federal judge or magistrate judge to order the person arrested. But no material witness may be detained "if the testimony of such witness can adequately be secured by deposition." 18 U.S.C. § 3144. Release can be delayed until the deposition is taken.

6. *Witness-initiated deposition.* Recall that a deposition, when allowed under Rule 15, is routinely taken by either the government or the defendant. Can a potential *witness* at a criminal trial initiate the deposition process under Rule 15(a)? Why would a witness want to do this? *See United States v. Allie,* 978 F.2d 1401 (5th Cir. 1992)(deposition to avoid pretrial detention).

7. *Closed circuit television as alternative.* In an unusual case where both the defendant and the deponent were too ill to travel and the former was in a secret location for his own protection, the court held that a deposition was appropriate. In lieu of a deposition, however, the court upheld the use at trial of two-way closed-circuit television testimony. The confrontation clause was not violated. *United States v. Gigante,* 166 F.3d 75 (2d Cir. 1999).

[4]   Pretrial Discovery: Statements, Tests, Objects, etc.

The primary focus of pretrial discovery in criminal cases is on providing access to some statements, tests, and objects in the possession of the other side. Usually these rules are reciprocal: if one side must give X proof (perhaps a copy of a scientific test of the weapons used in the crime) to the other side, the requesting party must give Y proof (a copy of its own tests of the weapon) to the party who provided X proof.

Under federal law, Rule 16 gives each side rights to some such information before trial. This rule does not, however, give defense counsel total access to the prosecution's files. In reading Rule 16, note both what is and what is not included.

FEDERAL RULES OF CRIMINAL PROCEDURE

Rule 16. *Discovery and Inspection*

(a) Government's Disclosure.

(1) Information Subject to Disclosure.

(A) Defendant's Oral Statement. Upon a defendant's request, the government must disclose to the defendant the substance of any relevant oral statement made by the defendant, before or after arrest, in response to interrogation by a person the defendant knew was a government agent if the government intends to use the statement at trial.

(B) Defendant's Written or Recorded Statement. Upon a defendant's request, the government must disclose to the defendant, and make available for inspection, copying, or photographing, all of the following:

(i)   any relevant written or recorded statement by the defendant if:

- the statement is within the government's possession, custody, or control; and

- the attorney for the government knows — or through due diligence could know — that the statement exists;

(ii)   the portion of any written record containing the substance of any relevant oral statement made before or after arrest if the defendant made the statement in response to interrogation by a person the defendant knew was a government agent; and

(iii) the defendant's recorded testimony before a grand jury relating to the charged offense.

(C) Organizational Defendant. Upon a defendant's request, if the defendant is an organization, the government must disclose to the defendant any statement described in Rule 16(a)(1)(A) and (B) if the government contends that the person making the statement:

(i)   was legally able to bind the defendant regarding the subject of the statement because of that person's position as the defendant's director, officer, employee, or agent; or

(ii)   was personally involved in the alleged conduct constituting the offense and was legally able to bind the defendant regarding that conduct because of that person's position as the defendant's director, officer, employee, or agent.

(D) Defendant's Prior Record. Upon a defendant's request, the government must furnish the defendant with a copy of the defendant's prior criminal record that is within the government's possession, custody, or control if the attorney for the government knows — or through due diligence could know — that the record exists.

(E) Documents and Objects. Upon a defendant's request, the government must permit the defendant to inspect and to copy or photograph books, papers, documents, data, photographs, tangible objects, buildings or places, or copies or portions of any of these items, if the item is within the government's possession, custody, or control and:

(i)   the item is material to preparing the defense;

(ii)   the government intends to use the item in its case-in-chief at trial; or

(iii) the item was obtained from or belongs to the defendant.

(F) Reports of Examinations and Tests. Upon a defendant's request, the government must permit a defendant to inspect and to copy or photograph the results or reports of any physical or mental examination and of any scientific test or experiment if:

(i)   the item is within the government's possession, custody, or control;

(ii)   the attorney for the government knows — or through due diligence could know — that the item exists; and

    (iii) the item is material to preparing the defense or the government intends to use the item in its case-in-chief at trial.

(G) Expert witnesses. — At the defendant's request, the government must give to the defendant a written summary of any testimony that the government intends to use under Rules 702, 703, or 705 of the Federal Rules of Evidence during its case-in-chief at trial. If the government requests discovery under subdivision (b)(1)(C)(ii) and the defendant complies, the government must, at the defendant's request, give to the defendant a written summary of testimony that the government intends to use under Rules 702, 703, or 705 of the Federal Rules of Evidence as evidence at trial on the issue of the defendant's mental condition. The summary provided under this subparagraph must describe the witness's opinions, the bases and reasons for those opinions, and the witness's qualifications.

(2) Information Not Subject to Disclosure. Except as Rule 16(a)(1) provides otherwise, this rule does not authorize the discovery or inspection of reports, memoranda, or other internal government documents made by an attorney for the government or other government agent in connection with investigating or prosecuting the case. Nor does this rule authorize the discovery or inspection of statements made by prospective government witnesses except as provided in 18 U.S.C. § 3500.

(3) Grand Jury Transcripts. This rule does not apply to the discovery or inspection of a grand jury's recorded proceedings, except as provided in Rules 6, 12(h), 16(a)(1), and 26.2.

(b) Defendant's Disclosure.

    (1) *Information Subject to Disclosure.*

    (A) Documents and Objects. If a defendant requests disclosure under Rule 16(a)(1)(E) and the government complies, then the defendant must permit the government, upon request, to inspect and to copy or photograph books, papers, documents, data, photographs, tangible objects, buildings or places, or copies or portions of any of these items if:

    (i) the item is within the defendant's possession, custody, or control; and

    (ii) the defendant intends to use the item in the defendant's case-in-chief at trial.

    (B) Reports of Examinations and Tests. If a defendant requests disclosure under Rule 16(a)(1)(F) and the government complies, the defendant must permit the government, upon request, to inspect and to copy or photograph the results or reports of any physical or mental examination and of any scientific test or experiment if:

    (i) the item is within the defendant's possession, custody, or control; and

    (ii) the defendant intends to use the item in the defendant'case-in-chief at trial, or intends to call the witness who prepared the report and the report relates to the witness's testimony.

    (C) Expert witnesses. — The defendant must, at the government's request, give to the government a written summary of any testimony that the defendant intends to use under Rules 702, 703, or 705 of the Federal Rules of Evidence as evidence at trial, if —

    (i) the defendant requests disclosure under subdivision (a)(1)(G) and the government complies; or

    (ii) the defendant has given notice under Rule 12.2(b) of an intent to present expert testimony on the defendant's mental condition. The summary must describe the witness's opinions, the bases and reasons for those opinions, and the witness's qualifications.

(2) Information Not Subject to Disclosure. Except for scientific or medical reports, Rule 16(b)(1) does not authorize discovery or inspection of:

(A) reports, memoranda, or other documents made by the defendant, or the defendant's attorney or agent, during the case's investigation or defense; or

(B) a statement made to the defendant, or the defendant's attorney or agent, by:

(i)   the defendant;

(ii)   a government or defense witness; or

(iii)   a prospective government or defense witness.

(c) Continuing Duty to Disclose. A party who discovers additional evidence or material before or during trial must promptly disclose its existence to the other party or the court if:

(1) the evidence or material is subject to discovery or inspection under this rule; and

(2) the other party previously requested, or the court ordered, its production.

(d) Regulating Discovery.

(1) Protective and Modifying Orders. At any time the court may, for good cause, deny, restrict, or defer discovery or inspection, or grant other appropriate relief. The court may permit a party to show good cause by a written statement that the court will inspect ex parte. If relief is granted, the court must preserve the entire text of the party's statement under seal.

(2) Failure to Comply. If a party fails to comply with this rule, the court may:

(A) order that party to permit the discovery or inspection; specify its time, place, and manner; and prescribe other just terms and conditions;

(B) grant a continuance;

(C) prohibit that party from introducing the undisclosed evidence; or

(D) enter any other order that is just under the circumstances.

[a]   Overview

Rule 16 is the primary criminal procedure rule regulating pretrial discovery. The general features are outlined below and discussed in greater detail in subsequent subsections.

[i]   Mutual Discovery

In general terms, Rule 16 establishes a regime of *mutual discovery*. This obligates each side to provide the other with information after certain procedures are followed.

[ii]   Begun by Defendant's Request

The defendant begins the Rule 16 discovery process by making a *request* for the prosecution to turn over specified categories of information. These categories are the defendant's own statements and criminal record, relevant documents and objects, requests of examinations and tests, and information about expert witnesses to be used at trial.

[iii]   Prosecution Responds

Once the prosecution complies with the defendant's requests, the defendant must turn over the same type of information to the prosecution. The defendant, however, need not disclose his or her own statements or criminal record.

[iv]   Continuing Duty

Each side is under a continuing duty to disclose information acquired after the initial compliance with discovery.

[v]   Information Not Subject to Disclosure

Certain information is not subject to disclosure under Rule 16. This includes work product of either side, defendant's statements in the possession of the defense, and the identity of confidential informants.

[vi]   Protective Order

Rule 16 gives the court the authority to issue a protective order to avoid discovery abuses.

[vii]   Great Discretion in Remedy for Violation

Federal Rule of Criminal Procedure 16 gives the trial judge great discretion in ordering sanctions for discovery violations.

[b]   Statements

[i]   Defendant's Statements in Prosecution's Possession

The rules of criminal procedure routinely authorize pretrial disclosure of the defendant's own statements and sometimes also mandate disclosure of those of other defendants or even of all witnesses. This disclosure should facilitate trial preparation as it alerts the defense to key evidence available to the prosecution. It may also assist in locating new witnesses or evidence.

Federal Rule16(a)(1), typical of most discovery rules, gives the defense a right to inspect and copy four types of prior statements of the defendant that are relevant to the case:

> (1) relevant written or recorded statements of the defendant which the government has in its possession, custody or control and knows or should know about (through "due diligence");

> (2) the substance of any oral statement by the defendant, made to a known government agent during interrogation, which the government intends to offer in evidence;

> (3) the portion of any written record containing the substance of any relevant oral statement made by the defendant during interrogation to a known government agent; and

> (4) recorded statements the defendant made to a grand jury relating to the instant offense.

It must be noted that this discovery is triggered by "request" of the defendant, usually in a discovery "motion" or "request" filed before trial. One article claims that the discovery of the defendant's statement is "the most significant discovery" under the federal rules. Jeffrey E. Stone & Corey B. Rubenstein, *Criminal Discovery: Leveling the Playing Field*, 23 Litigation 45 (Winter 1997). Why is this information so critical to defense counsel?

Virtually all states also require disclosure of the defendant's statements in government possession. *See, e.g.,* N.Y. Crim. Proc. Law § 240.20(1)(a) (defendant's statement to public servant engaged in law enforcement activity or person under that person's direction or in cooperation with that person). Some even require disclosure of the names of witnesses to the defendant's statements. *See, e.g.,* Ill. Sup. Ct. R. 412(a)(i).

Note the severe limitations of Federal Rule 16. While it does give the accused access to many of his or her own statements, it does not provide discovery of all of them. For example, it does not reach statements which the government has in its possession but could not, through due diligence, find. This may occur because many federal agencies may be involved in an investigation and the communication between them may be poor.

Rule 16(a)(1) also does not require disclosure of the substance of oral statements the defendant made outside of interrogation or to people who conducted an interrogation but the accused did not know were government agents. This result is not changed if the government agent made a written memorandum of the oral statements. For example, if the defendant confessed to a neighbor who told an FBI agent who wrote a memorandum describing the neighbor's information, Rule 16 does not mandate disclosure of the agent's memorandum. But if the government has obtained a written version or a recording of such statements, they must be disclosed under Rule 16(a)(1)(B). *See State v. Vanderford*, 980 S.W.2d 390 (Tenn. Crim. App. 1997) (state court's interpretation of provision identical to Rule 16 that audio recording of conversation between defendant and "wired" undercover agent is discoverable if the defendant's statements to agent are "relevant" to the crime charged; statements on audio tape here found not relevant).

The American Bar Association recommends broader discovery of a criminal defendant's statements. The prosecution must give the defendant all written and oral statements of the defendant that are within the possession or control of the prosecution and that relate to the subject matter of the offense charged. Standards for Criminal Justice § 11-2.1(a) (3d ed. 1996). Is this model superior to the federal one?

[ii] Defendant's Statements in Defense Counsel's Possession

While Rule 16(a) requires the government to give the defendant copies of virtually all of defendant's statements the prosecution has, the discovery is not mutual. Because of concerns about the lawyer-client privilege, the self incrimination guarantee in the Fifth Amendment, and the guarantee of counsel in the Sixth Amendment, Rule 16 does not obligate the defense to provide the prosecution with copies of statements made by the defendant or actual or potential witnesses. Disclosure may be required under Rule 26.2, however, if the defendant or witness testifies.

[iii] Third Parties' Statements

Finally, Rule 16 does not cover statements of persons (except for experts, as described below) other than the accused. Thus, the defendant may not discover statements of witnesses or codefendants unless exculpatory and disclosure is required by *Brady v. Maryland*, supra. Of course if the statements are recordings of the defendant speaking to a third person, the recording is covered by Rule 16(a)(1). But note that Rule 16(a)(1)(C) does include statements by various representatives of a defendant which is an organization, such as a corporation or labor union.

A number of states expand their discovery rules to include statements of third persons. *See, e.g.,* Ala. R. Crim. P. 16.1(b) (defense entitled to discover statements of codefendants and accomplices); Ariz. R. Crim. P. 15.1(b) (statements of state's witnesses and of all people to be tried with defendant); N.Y. Crim. Proc. Law § 240.20(a) (statements of defendant and jointly tried codefendant). *See also State v. Rodriguez*, 985 S.W.2d 863 (Mo.App. 1998) (defense entitled to disclosure of statement of defense witness (given to prosecution without knowledge of defense lawyer) that related earlier inculpatory statement of defendant).

[iv]   Recommendations

The American Bar Association recommends broader discovery of witnesses' statements. The prosecution must give the defense the names, addresses, and relevant written statements of all persons known to the prosecution to have information concerning the offense charged. It must also identify the persons it intends to call as witnesses. Standards for Criminal Justice § 11-2.1(a)(ii) (3d ed. 1996). The defense, according to the ABA, need only disclose the names, addresses, and statements of witnesses it intends to call as witnesses for its case-in-chief; statements of defense witnesses used solely to impeach a prosecution witness need not be disclosed until after the witness has testified at trial. *Id.* § 11-2.2(a)(i). Rule 26.2, discussed below, mandates disclosure of a witness' statement after the witness has testified on direct examination.

[c]   Tests

Rule 16 establishes reciprocal discovery for the reports of physical or mental examinations and other scientific tests or experiments. Note that Rule 16(a)(1)(F) focuses on "results or reports" of tests. It does not appear to reach log notes and other internal lab documents from which the report was written, yet these documents may be critical if the report is to be re-evaluated by other experts. *See United States v. Iglesias*, 881 F.2d 1519 (9th Cir. 1989), *cert. denied*, 493 U.S. 1088 (1990). Rule 16(a)(1)(E) may reach these items, however, if they form the basis for expert testimony. *United States v. W.R. Grace*, 233 F.R.D. 586 (D. Mont. 2005) (disclosure ordered prior to trial of documents underlying government's test results).

Test results. Upon request by the defendant, the government must provide the "results or reports" to the defense if available (including through "due diligence") to the government and which the government intends to use at trial or which are material to the defense's trial preparation. Once the government complies with this request, it is entitled to ask the defendant for the same access to results or reports in the control or possession of the defendant if the defense intends to introduce them as evidence or which were prepared by an expert the defense intends to call as a defense witness. Note that the standards for prosecution and defense differ slightly. The defense receives various reports that are "material" to "trial preparation," but the prosecution receives only those related to proof to be used at trial. What is the practical effect of these differing approaches? Why are the standards different? Should they be the same?

Rule 16 does not appear to limit the type of tests subject to discovery. Moreover, it does not embrace purely oral reports, nor does it obligate the government to conduct tests.

Work product. Since some of the data covered by this provision are also included in the work-product rule, Rule 16 creates an exception to the work-product rule. If the defense asks for the government test results, the defense is viewed as waiving the work-product protection for its own test results. The defense does not have to disclose such data, however. Since the entire process is started by the "request" of the defense, the defense can opt to forego this facet of discovery under Rule 16. This means that the defense does not get access to test and related results in the government's file, but it also does not have to disclose such items in its own file.

Conduct tests. A related issue is whether the defense has a right to conduct tests or retests of items relating to the offense. Some state discovery rules specifically authorize this. *E.g.*, Fla. R. Crim. P. 3.220(b)(1); Wis. Stat. Ann. § 971.23(5) (testing subject to conditions court may specify in order). Other jurisdictions find a right to conduct "reasonable" tests on evidence from general discovery rules that permit "inspection" or from due process concerns. *See, e.g., United States v. Sullivan*, 578 F. 2d 121 (5th Cir. 1978); *State v. Cloutier*, 302 A.2d 84 (Me. 1973) (court may order that independent analysis be done at State laboratory under State supervision). *But see Frias v. State,*

547 N.E.2d 809 (Ind. 1989), *cert. denied,* 495 U.S. 921 (1990). Should the defendant have a right to test evidence found at a crime scene?

Should court approval be required? *See generally* Paul C. Giannelli, *Criminal Discovery, Scientific Evidence, and DNA,* 44 Vand. L. Rev. 791 (1991). Should an indigent defendant have the right to a *potentially exonerating* court-ordered DNA test at the government's expense? Should the government have the right to compel the defendant to submit to a *potentially incriminating* DNA test? See discussion, below, of discovery of persons' physical characteristics.

[d]   Summary of Expert Witnesses' Testimony

Rule 16(a)(1)(G) partially rejects the view that one side's expert witnesses can surprise the other side. The rule requires disclosure of (1) an intent to rely on expert opinion testimony; the (2) content and (3) bases of that testimony; and (4) the qualifications of the expert witness. This rule is designed to reduce the need for continuances and to permit expert opinion testimony to be evaluated by both effective cross-examination and the use of counter testimony by other experts.

This rule follows the pattern of other portions of Rule 16. It is triggered by a defense request. Once the prosecution complies, the defense must give reciprocal disclosure of defense expert witnesses. This means that the defense can avoid disclosing information about its own experts by refusing to request data about prosecution expert witnesses.

The government's responsibility is to give information that is either material to the preparation of the defense or intended for use in the government's case in chief (but not rebuttal).

This provision must be read in conjunction with Rule 16(a)(1)(F), which requires disclosure of various test reports. Sometimes, an expert will testify without having prepared a report covered by Rule 16(a)(1)(F). Rule 16 now mandates pretrial disclosure of both the expert's reports and a summary of the expert's testimony. If the expert changes his or her view, the new opinion ordinarily must be provided under Rule 16 and, sometimes, *Brady.*

[e]   Documents and Objects

Rule 16 also creates a reciprocal discovery process for various documents and tangible objects, such as books, papers, photographs, buildings, and places. These items must be in the government's possession, custody, or control. They may have been obtained by a search warrant. Since many documents important to the defense may not be in the *prosecutor's* files, how far does the definition of "government" reach to require disclosure of items in various agency files? *See* Peter J. Henning, *Defense Discovery in White Collar Criminal Prosecutions,* 15 Ga. State U. L. Rev. 601, 618 (1999) (arguing for a broad reading of "government" because Rule 16 is designed to provide discovery).

Material to defense preparation or used as government proof at trial. To be discoverable by the defense, they must be material to the preparation of the defense, intended for use as evidence by the government, or belong to or be obtained from the defendant.

Does the phrase "material to the preparation of the defendant's defense" include allegations of selective prosecution? The United States Supreme Court answered that question in *United States v. Armstrong,* 517 U.S. 456 (1996), discussed in Chapter 2. According to Chief Justice Rehnquist, writing for the Court:

> Respondents argue that documents "within the possession . . . of the government" that discuss the government's prosecution strategy for cocaine cases are "material" to respondents' selective-prosecution claim. Respondents argue that the Rule applies because any claim that "results in nonconviction" if

successful is a "defense" for the Rule's purposes, and a successful selective-prosecution claim has that effect.

We reject this argument, because we conclude that in the context of Rule 16 "the defendant's defense" means the defendant's response to the Government's case-in-chief. . . . If "defense" means an argument in response to the prosecution's case-in-chief, there is a perceptible symmetry between documents "material to the preparation of the defendant's defense," and, in the very next phrase, documents "intended for use by the government as evidence in chief at the trial."

If this symmetry were not persuasive enough, paragraph (a)(2) of Rule 16 establishes beyond peradventure that "defense" in section (a)(1)[E] can refer only to defenses in response to the Government's case-in-chief. Rule 16(a)(2), as relevant here, exempts from defense inspection "reports, memoranda, or other internal government documents made by the attorney for the government or other government agents in connection with the investigation or prosecution of the case."

Under Rule 16(a)(1)[E], a defendant may examine documents material to his defense, but, under Rule 16(a)(2), he may not examine Government work product in connection with his case. If a selective-prosecution claim is a "defense," Rule 16(a)(1)(C) gives the defendant the right to examine Government work product in every prosecution except his own. Because respondents' construction of "defense" creates the anomaly of a defendant's being able to examine all Government work product except the most pertinent, we find their construction implausible. We hold that Rule 16(a)(1)[E] authorizes defendants to examine Government documents material to the preparation of their defense against the Government's case-in-chief, but not to the preparation of selective-prosecution claims.

Justice Breyer, who concurred in the final judgment, nonetheless disagreed with Chief Justice Rehnquist's analysis:

I write separately because, in my view, Federal Rule of Criminal Procedure 16 does not limit a defendant's discovery rights to documents related to the Government's case-in-chief. The Rule says that "the government shall permit the defendant to inspect and copy" certain physical items (I shall summarily call them "documents") "which are material to the preparation of the defendant's defense." A "defendant's defense" can take many forms, including (1) a simple response to the Government's case-in-chief, (2) an affirmative defense unrelated to the merits (such as a Speedy Trial Act claim), (3) an unrelated claim of constitutional right, (4) a foreseeable surrebuttal to a likely Government rebuttal, and others. The Rule's language does not limit its scope to the first item on this list. To interpret the Rule in this limited way creates a legal distinction that, from a discovery perspective, is arbitrary. It threatens to create two full parallel sets of criminal discovery principles. And, as far as I can tell, the interpretation lacks legal support . . . .

[Justice Breyer concluded, nonetheless, that the defendants had failed to satisfy the Rule's requirement that the discovery be "material to the preparation of the defendant's defense" because they failed to establish that there had been some instances in which the government had failed to prosecute similarly situated Caucasian defendants.]

Documents not covered. This required disclosure of "documents" does not include statements of other witnesses (covered by Rule 26.2) or government work product.

Defendant's items. Rule 16(a)(1)(E) requires the government to disclose items belonging to or obtained from the defendant. Note compliance is not based on either use at trial by the government or material to the defense.

Reciprocity. Under Rule 16(b)(1)(A), after the government complies with the defense's request for this tangible proof, the defense must provide the government with access to the same items in the defendant's possession, custody, or control and which the defendant intends to use as evidence in chief. Again, note that the defense gets items "material" to "preparation of the defense," but the government receives only items which the defense intends to use as evidence in its case in chief.

The reciprocal discovery process is begun by the "request" of the defense. If the defendant does not want to be compelled to turn over this kind of information to the prosecution, the defendant can opt not to request it from the prosecution under Rule 16.

Mechanics of discovery. For documents and tangible objects covered by Rule 16, the other side is entitled "to inspect and copy or photograph" the items. Ordinarily the two sides, without court involvement, work out the details of this process using common sense and professional courtesy. For example, the prosecution may copy the documents for the defense.

Sometimes the mechanics of this discovery become complicated. Since one side may be concerned about chain of custody, loss, or spoliation of evidence, inspection and copying may have to be done under supervision in a restricted environment. Other restrictions may also be appropriate depending on the particular circumstances. *See, e.g., United States v. Horn,* 187 F.3d 781 (8th Cir. 1999) (trial court correctly denied defendant's request to copy pornographic video tapes, which were contraband; defendant limited to having expert view the tapes); *United States v. Hsu,* 185 F.R.D. 192 (E.D. Pa. 1999) (defendant entitled to limited disclosure of documents protected as trade secrets).

[f] Prior Criminal Record

Record of defendant. Under Rule 16, upon request by the defense, the prosecution must provide the defense with a copy of the defendant's criminal record if that record is in the possession, custody, or control of the government and its existence is known or could be known through due diligence. It does not require disclosure of pending or likely criminal charges.

Note that this rule is not reciprocal. The defendant need not supply the government with a copy of the defendant's record. This means that Rule 16 does not require the defendant to inform the prosecution about criminal convictions, such as those from other states, that are not in the prosecutor's files.

Record of witnesses. Federal Rule 16 does not require disclosure of the criminal record of witnesses, though *Brady v. Maryland,* discussed earlier in this chapter, does compel such disclosure to assist in impeaching government witnesses.

Some state provisions, however, require the prosecution to disclose the prior criminal record of prosecution witnesses. *See, e.g.,* Ariz. R. Crim. P. 15.1(d)(1) and (2) (state must "make available to the defendant of the prior felony convictions of witnesses whom the prosecutor expects to call at trial" in both felony and misdemeanor cases); Minn. R. Crim. P. 9.01 subd. 1(1)(a) (prosecution must inform defendant of prior conviction record of witnesses prosecution intends to call at trial). Does *Brady* require this as a matter of constitutional law? *Cf. State v. Thomas,* 514 S.E.2d 486 (N.C. 1999) (to establish due process violation for prosecution's refusal to disclose criminal records of prosecution witnesses, defendant must establish witness had a significant record and that disclosure would have created reasonable doubt of guilt that did not otherwise exist).

Record of jurors. What about the criminal records of prospective jurors? *See State v. Thompson,* 985 S.W.2d 779 (Mo. 1999) (state need not disclose arrest records of venire persons absent showing of pending charges against one or that there could have been a leniency deal or threat to one).

ABA Recommendations. The American Bar Association recommends substantial defense discovery of criminal records. The prosecution should disclose any record of prior convictions, pending charges, or probationary status of the defendant and any codefendant. The same is true for the information about any witness (of any party) if the information is known to the prosecution and may be used to impeach the witness. Standards for Criminal Justice § 11-2.1(a)(vi) (3d ed. 1996).

[g] Witness List

Rule 16 does not require either side in advance of trial to provide the other with a list of witnesses, other than those who have provided expert assistance with tests and the like. Some federal courts, however, utilize their inherent authority to regulate criminal discovery and require each side to inform the other side of its likely witnesses. Some federal courts even have a "standing order" requiring the exchange of witness lists. *See, e.g., United States v. Combs,* 267 F.3d 1167 (10th Cir. 2001). Others refuse to order such disclosure in typical cases but occasionally will mandate disclosure when there is a "compelling need" for it.

Many states now require or permit pretrial disclosure of the names and addresses of witnesses to be called at trial. *See, e.g.,* Ariz. R. Crim. P. 15.1(b)(1) (pretrial disclosure of names, addresses, and statements of witnesses to be called in case-in-chief; defense need not list defendant or provide defendant's statements); Ill. Sup. Ct. Rules 412, 413 (pretrial disclosure of names, addresses, and statements of prosecution and defense witnesses); Mass. R. Crim. P. 14(a)(1)(A) (automatic discovery of names and addresses of prosecution's prospective witnesses). Some rules specifically embrace rebuttal witnesses. *See, e.g., Williams v. State,* 992 S.W.2d 89 (Ark. 1999) (defense must provide names of rebuttal witnesses after state has presented its case; recess allowable if necessary to permit state to prepare). A slightly different approach requires disclosure of names and addresses of witnesses "on whose evidence the charge is based." Neb. Rev. Stat. § 29-1912(1)(d).

Capital cases. A separate federal statute requires disclosure of the names and addresses of government witnesses who will testify in a federal trial for treason or other capital offenses. 18 U.S.C. § 3432. This law is not reciprocal; it does not obligate the defense to provide the government with a list of defense witnesses. Since both treason and capital cases are rare in federal courts, this provision is infrequently used.

Policy issue. Should witness lists be exchanged in all criminal trials? Why or why not? Recall that federal law already requires disclosure of *some* witnesses (*e.g.* experts). Would pretrial disclosure of all witnesses provide a trial more likely to reach the truth? What about also requiring disclosure of the *content* of a witness's likely testimony?

[h] Person's Physical Characteristics

Sometimes a person's physical characteristics may be an important part of proof. For example, a criminal defendant may have left blood stains at a crime scene. The prosecution will seek a court order compelling the accused to provide a blood sample.

Inherent authority. Rule 16 does not mention discovery of the defendant's physical characteristics. But federal and state courts often use their inherent authority to require a witness or other person to submit to various tests. *See, e.g., United States v. Benn,* 476 F.2d 1127 (D.C. Cir. 1973) (using its inherent authority, court may order mentally retarded witness to submit to psychiatric examination for assessing her competency or credibility), *but see, contra, Nobrega v. Commonwealth,* 628 S.E. 2d 922 (Va. 2006) (noting that compelled psychiatric examination can be especially traumatic to sex offense victim); *Clark v. Commonwealth,* 521 S.E.2d 313 (Va. App. 1999) (trial court has inherent authority to require sex offense victim to undergo independent medical examination, but only if defendant demonstrates compelling reason). *See generally* Troy Andrew Eid, Note, 57 U. Chi. L. Rev. 873 (1990).

State variations. Some state provisions specifically authorize discovery of the defendant's physical characteristics. *See, e.g.,* N.Y. Crim. Proc. Law 240.40(2) (prosecutor may obtain court order requiring defendant to appear in line-up, speak for identification, be fingerprinted, pose for photograph (but not reenact the event), provide handwriting sample, submit to a bodily physical inspection or medical examination, or permit the taking of an array of physical samples, such as hair, blood, saliva, or urine). *See also* Ala. R. Crim. P. 16.2(b) (same, plus try on clothing); Utah R. Crim. P. 16(h) (same, plus allow hair to grow to approximate appearance at time of offense). *See also* Standards for Criminal Justice § 11-2.3 (3d ed. 1996) (prosecution given access to extensive physical and related information about defendant). Query: what showing, if any (e.g., probable cause, reasonable suspicion, or no evidentiary showing at all), should be required for the prosecution to obtain a court order or warrant requiring the defendant to submit to a DNA test to determine identity?

The defendant may be able to affect the fairness of some identification procedures. In *Moore v. Illinois,* 434 U.S. 220, 230 n.5 (1977), the Supreme Court noted that the trial court has the discretion to grant a criminal accused's request that a lineup be conducted in a way that is not unduly suggestive of guilt. This issue is also discussed in Chapter 6.

[i]   Other Information

State discovery provisions mandate discovery of various information not covered by Rule 16. Some of these are designed to alert the defendant to possible issues to address or to possible sources of information. Examples of the data required to be disclosed to the defense are: the use of electronic surveillance, Ariz. R. Crim. P. 15.1(b)(9); the use of an informant, Ariz. R. Crim. P. 15.1(b)(11); whether the state has any material or information provided by a confidential informant, Fla. R. Crim. P. 3.220(1)(G); the existence of a search warrant, Ariz. R. Crim. P. 15.1(b)(10); the relationship a state witness has to the prosecution (for example, whether the witness is on probation, a paid informant, or a government employee), Ark. R. Crim. P. 17.1(b)(iii); names and addresses of all persons known to prosecutor to have information relevant to the crime or a defense, Fla. R. Crim. P. 3.220(b)(1)(A); a prosecution witness's pretrial identification of the defendant, Md. R. Crim. P. 4-263(a)(2); and information indicating entrapment, Wash. Super. Ct. Crim. R. 4.7(a)(2)(iii).

Arizona's rules authorize a prosecutor, upon a showing of "substantial need . . . for material or information not otherwise covered" by the rules of criminal discovery and an inability "without undue hardship to obtain the substantial equivalent by other means," to obtain a court order requiring "any person to make such material or information available to the prosecutor." Ariz. R. Crim. P. 15.2(g).

See also Standards for Criminal Justice § 11-2.1 (3d ed. 1996) (prosecution must disclose the relationship between the prosecution and any of its witnesses; information about lineups and other identifications; materials relating to searches in which prosecution evidence was obtained; and if there was electronic surveillance of the defendant's conversations or premises).

[j]   Information Not Subject to Disclosure

Work product. Rule 16 and most state rules of criminal procedure routinely list information that is not subject to disclosure under the general discovery provision. The most common example is work-product information. *See, e.g.,* Fed. R. Crim. P. 16(a)(2). Note that this provision extends to documents made by the prosecuting attorney "or any other government agent investigating or prosecuting the case." *See United States v. Wilkerson,* 189 F.R.D. 14 (D. Mass. 1999) (Rule 16 does not require disclosure of "working papers" of examiner who tested substance for cocaine; papers were not "reports" or "results of tests" and examiner was an "investigating" government agent).

The concept of government agent investigating the case could even extend to local police investigating a case when their reports were later shared with federal law enforcement authorities. *United States v. Fort*, 472 F.3d 1106 (9th Cir. 2007).

The ban also extends to work product of the defendant's attorney or agent. Rule 16(b)(2). Of course the ban on work-product disclosure is not absolute, since Rule 16 itself mandates some such disclosure by both sides.

Informant's identity. In some cases courts are permitted to protect the identity of law enforcement informants. The Supreme Court, recognizing the need to encourage people to provide information about criminal activity, has held the government possesses a *qualified privilege* to withhold such information. The privilege does not apply if the information would be helpful to the defense or essential to a fair trial. *Rovario v. United States*, 33 U.S. 53 (1957). The defense has the burden of establishing that the informant's identity is helpful or essential. *See, e.g., United States v. Hollis*, 245 F.3d 671 (8th Cir. 2001). Disclosure is more likely to be required if the informant actually participated in the crime rather than simply provided a tip to the police. Some state provisions also ban disclosure of the names of government informants if disclosure would risk either the informant's health or operational effectiveness. *See, e.g.,* Ariz. R. Crim. P. 15.4(b)(2); Mont. Code Ann. § 46-15-324(3).

Of course, disclosure of an informant's identity may be required by the due process clause if necessary to assure that the trial is fundamentally fair. *See, e.g., Roviaro v. United States*, 353 U.S. 53 (1957); *Gaines v. Hess*, 662 F.2d 1364 (10th Cir. 1981) (disclosure may be made *in camera*).

Grand jury testimony. Another category of nondiscoverable evidence relates to grand jury testimony not otherwise authorized to be disclosed. *See, e.g.,* Ore. Rev. Stat. § 135.855(1)(c).

PROBLEM 10-3. YOU SHOW ME YOURS, I'LL SHOW YOU MINE

Barret was killed when a bomb planted in his car exploded while the car was parked in Barret's garage. Defendant D, a tall (6' 2") man with long black hair, was arrested and charged with the homicide. Defense counsel is now assessing what proof is discoverable under Rule 16.

1. After the explosion, a team of government investigators carefully sifted through the rubble and took thirty-two bags of materials to the F.B.I. laboratory for analysis.

    a. Are the thirty-two bags discoverable under Rule 16? Do you need any additional facts to answer this question? If so, what are they? *See United States v. Esquivel*, 755 F. Supp. 434 (D.D.C. 1990).

    b. If the thirty-two bags are discoverable under Rule 16, how would this be accomplished? Should the prosecution simply deliver the bags to defense counsel? Obviously, taking a photograph of the outside of the thirty-two bags would be of little help. What should defense counsel do?

    c. Assume that defense counsel utilized Rule 16 to obtain the contents of the thirty-two bags. Assume further that both defense and prosecution had them analyzed by their own experts, who have submitted written reports detailing their findings.

        i. The prosecution's expert submitted a report to the prosecutor indicating that the explosion was caused by dynamite triggered by a wind-up alarm clock. Is the defense entitled to a copy of this report under Rule 16? Reread Rule 16(a)(1)(E) and (F). Do you need additional facts to answer this question?

        ii. Assume that the report by the prosecution expert has been turned over to the defense under Rule 16. Assume also that the defense expert has submitted a report to defense counsel indicating that a new photographic process revealed that the clock used to trigger the explosion contained fingerprints. An Appendix to the report included a photograph of the fingerprints. Defense counsel fears that the fingerprints belong to Defendant D. Must defense counsel give a copy of the expert's report, including the Appendix, to the prosecution pursuant to Rule 16(b)(1)(B)?

iii. Assume that the prosecution's expert witness told the prosecutor about what the witness will say at trial. Is the defense entitled to know about the substance of this conversation? Would it matter whether the prosecution intended to use the witness only if necessary as a rebuttal witness? *See* Rule 16(a)(1)(G).

2. Defendant D was questioned about the incident. Assume that the interrogation was conducted in strict conformity with all constitutional requirements.

a. Officer Lynch interviewed Defendant D at the police station. He is prepared to testify from memory that Defendant D told him that shortly before the explosion D saw a short, blond man wearing yellow pants run from the area near Barret's garage. Is the defense team entitled to interview Officer Lynch before trial to determine what he recalls about D's statement, pursuant to Rule 16?

b. Shortly after the interview with Defendant D, Officer Lynch returned to his desk and wrote out a short summary of the interview, including D's description of the man with the yellow pants. The memorandum is in the police department's "Barret Homicide" file. Is the defense entitled to discover this memorandum under Rule 16?

c. Officer Lynch tape recorded the entire interview with Defendant D. Is the tape recording discoverable under Rule 16? If so, in what form? Is the government obligated to provide defense counsel with a copy of the tape?

d. A police secretary made a transcript of the tape recording of D's statement. Is the defense entitled to discover the transcript under Rule 16? If so, what role would the government and defense play in the mechanics of obtaining the information for the defense?

3. An anonymous telephone call alerted the police to D's possible involvement in the homicide. The police questioned D's neighbors, one of whom (Neville) gave the police a photocopied booklet entitled, "How To Build A Car Bomb." Neville said that the booklet belonged to D who loaned it to Neville to use in writing a college term paper on violence in our society. Is the photocopied booklet discoverable under Rule 16?

4. The police received an anonymous letter stating that D planted the bomb in Barret's car. The police have no idea who authored the letter and do not plan to use it at trial. Is the letter discoverable under Rule 16? *See United States v. Parikh*, 858 F.2d 688 (11th Cir. 1988).

5. D suspects that the prosecution will call Neville as a witness.

a. Does Rule 16 entitle D to discover Neville's prior criminal record to use to impeach Neville at trial?

b. Officer Lynch also interviewed Neville and made a post-interview memorandum of the interview. Is the defense entitled to discover this memorandum pursuant to Rule 16? Review Rule 16(a)(2). Does it matter whether the government plans to introduce this memorandum into evidence at trial?

6. The prosecutor has learned that D was under investigation for another car bombing in another state. The prosecutor telephoned the police chief in that other state and was informed of the evidence against D on the other bombing. D fears that evidence of the out-of-state bombing will be used at D's trial for Barret's murder. Does Rule 16 permit D to discover the records of the out-of-state bombing? If the Barret prosecutor dictated a memorandum of the conversation with the out-of-state police chief, is D entitled to discover the memorandum under Rule 16?

7. The government has compiled an extensive list of Defendant D's past criminal convictions.

a. Is the defendant entitled to this list under Rule 16?

b. Assume that defense counsel successfully uses Rule 16 to obtain a copy of D's prior record. Assume further that the Defendant D has carefully reviewed this list and has discovered that it does not include two out-of-state felony convictions and eight misdemeanor convictions. At defense counsel's suggestion, Defendant D has prepared a complete list of his prior crimes. Must defense counsel turn over this complete list to the prosecution pursuant to Rule 16?

[k]   Procedural Issues of Rule 16

[i]   Initiated By Motion (or Request)

Request. Rule 16 is not self executing. All five categories of prosecution information covered by Rule 16 are only available "upon request" of the defendant. Often the defense will make this request in a lengthy discovery motion that covers materials embraced by Rule 16 as well as those covered by other rules and constitutional provisions. A common illustration is a general discovery motion covering Rule 16, *Brady*, and, as discussed next, notice of intent to use Rule 16 evidence (Rule 12(b)(4)).

Timing of request. Rule 16 is silent as to when the request for discovery or a response to this request must be made. The request cannot be made before the defendant is formally charged. Often the issue is resolved by an agreement between the prosecutor and defense lawyer. Some courts announce a deadline for filing this and other motions and schedule a motion hearing (sometimes called an "omnibus hearing") to resolve issues raised by motion practice.

Role of judge. Once the defendant makes the request, the government should comply without a court order. The court may become involved in the Rule 16 process only if there is a problem. For example, if the defendant requests materials arguably not covered by Rule 16, the government may refuse to comply and the defense or prosecution will request a judicial hearing on the matter. The court must then decide whether the materials are discoverable and issue an appropriate order.

[ii]   Continuing Duty

Rule 16 specifically imposes a continuing duty to comply. For example, if a party turns over test results then gets new ones, the new ones also must be disclosed in a timely fashion.

[iii]   Mechanics of Compliance

Often the government will comply with a discovery request by notifying the defense of the discoverable materials and making arrangements for access. The court gets involved only if there is a problem.

[iv]   Notice of Intent to Use Rule 16 Evidence

In order to facilitate the pretrial determination of the admissibility of discoverable evidence, Rule 12(b)(4)(B) authorizes the defendant to request the government to provide notice of its intent to use, as evidence in chief at trial, evidence the defendant may be entitled to discover under Rule 16.

FEDERAL RULES OF CRIMINAL PROCEDURE

Rule 12. *Pleadings and Motions Before Trial;*

Defenses and Objections

. . . .

(b) Pretrial Motions.

. . . .

(4) Notice of the Government's Intent to Use Evidence.

(A) *At the Government's Discretion.* At the arraignment or as soon afterward as practicable, the government may notify the defendant of its intent to use specified evidence at trial in order to afford the defendant an opportunity to object before trial under Rule 12(b)(3)(C).

(B) *At the Defendant's Request.* At the arraignment or as soon afterward as practicable, the defendant may, in order to have an opportunity to move to suppress evidence under Rule 12(b)(3)(C), request notice of the government's intent to use (in its evidence-in-chief at trial) any evidence that the defendant may be entitled to discover under Rule 16.

NOTES

1. This mechanism assists both the defense and prosecution in planning for trial and will help reduce the number of mid-trial suppression hearings that disrupt the orderly process of the trial. Note that subdivision (b)(4)(B) does not deal with evidence to be used in rebuttal or on cross-examination.

2. *Compliance.* Because Rule 12(b)(4)(B) is written in general terms, it is not clear what constitutes compliance. What if the government responds that the defense should assume all items disclosed under Rule 16 would be used during the prosecution's case-in-chief? In *United States v. Gullo*, 672 F. Supp. 99 (W.D. N.Y. 1987), the court upheld this response. Do you agree that it comports with the purpose of Rule 12(b)(4)? What if the government responds that it has provided the defense with "open file" discovery? Does this satisfy Rule 12(b)(4)(B)? *See United States v. Anderson*, 416 F.Supp.2d 110 (D.D.C. 2006) (open file policy does not satisfy Rule 12(b)(4) because it does not specify what evidence the prosecution intends to use).

What if the evidence is clearly admissible? Must the prosecution still provide it under 12(b)(4)(B) upon the defendant's timely request?

3. *Sanction for noncompliance.* What is the sanction if the government does not comply with a Rule 12(b)(4) request? *See United States v. de la Cruz-Paulino*, 61 F.3d 986 (1st Cir. 1995) (reversal of conviction for Rule 12(b)(4) violation ordered only if defendant can prove prejudice by the noncompliance). If prejudice must be demonstrated, can the defendant ever succeed if the prosecution had provided Rule 16 discovery so the accused was actually aware of the items that could be the object of a motion to suppress evidence because of a Rule 12(b)(4) violation?

4. *Government's discretionary notice.* A similar provision, Rule 12(b)(4)(A), authorizes the government to give notice to the defendant of the government's intention to use specified evidence (whether or not discoverable under Rule 16) at trial. Although there is no similar rule permitting the defense to provide the government with pretrial notice of defense proof, surely the typical "unwritten" court procedures permit the defense to do so in order to obtain a pretrial ruling on the matter.

[v] Protective Order

Although Rule 16 makes it likely that some important evidence will be shared with the other side before trial, it also contains a procedure to protect against the possible misuse of the disclosures. Rule 16(d)(1) provides that the court may, "for good cause, deny, restrict, or defer discovery or inspection, or grant other appropriate relief." The court is given no guidance in determining when this protective order should be given or how it should be structured. In those unusual cases where confidential information justifies the protective order, Rule 16(d)(1) permits the court to issue the protective order after an *ex parte* process. The record of the *ex parte* process should be preserved for possible appellate review.

Rule 16(d) is vague on the contents of the protective order. Apparently it can do two things. First, it can limit the information otherwise available under Rule 16. Thus, it could be used to protect trade secrets or the identity of government witnesses whose safety could be jeopardized by discovery, or to prevent the abusive use of criminal discovery to aid a civil case.

Second, it can order the defendant or others to refrain from contacting witnesses or otherwise tampering with witnesses. Do you think the latter would be effective in protecting witnesses from abuse by the defendant personally or through the defendant's "friends"?

Both civil and criminal remedies may also be available to protect witnesses. *E.g.*, 18 U.S.C. § 1512 (crime to tamper with witness); 42 U.S.C. § 1985 (civil rights action for conspiracy to interfere with witness). State provisions also routinely authorize the court to place limits on discovery on a case-by-case basis. *See, e.g.*, N.Y. Crim. P. Law § 240.50.

[5] Pretrial and Trial Discovery: Subpoena

Federal Rule 17(c) deals with the processes for obtaining and serving subpoenas for evidence and documents. While ordinarily this rule has primary application in obtaining an item's presence at trial or another proceeding, it also has a limited role in pretrial discovery.

FEDERAL RULES OF CRIMINAL PROCEDURE

Rule 17. *Subpoena*

. . . .

(c) Producing Documents and Objects.

(1) **In General.** A subpoena may order the witness to produce any books, papers, documents, data, or other objects the subpoena designates. The court may direct the witness to produce the designated items in court before trial or before they are to be offered in evidence. When the items arrive, the court may permit the parties and their attorneys to inspect all or part of them.

(2) **Quashing or Modifying the Subpoena.** On motion made promptly, the court may quash or modify the subpoena if compliance would be unreasonable or oppressive.

. . . .

(h) Information Not Subject to a Subpoena. No party may subpoena a statement of a witness or of a prospective witness under this rule. Rule 26.2 governs the production of the statement.

NOTES

1. *Relation to Sixth Amendment.* Rule 17 provides a formal method for both sides to issue subpoenas in criminal cases. Its application to the criminal accused satisfies the Sixth Amendment's right to compulsory process.

2. *Issued by court clerk.* Rule 17 follows the traditional view that parties obtain a subpoena from the court clerk. To preserve the parties' right to conduct their own case, Rule 17 specifically authorizes the clerk to provide subpoenas in blank, to be filled in and served by the party issuing the subpoenas. Service under Rule 17(d) may be made by a Marshall or any adult who is not a party.

3. *For any proceeding.* The subpoena under Rule 17 may compel attendance at any criminal proceeding, including trial, deposition, and various hearings (such as suppression, preliminary, and grand jury). But Rule 17 does not authorize a subpoena for a witness to attend a private interview with a government agent. *See, e.g., United States v. Villa-Chaparro,* 115 F.3d 797 (10th Cir. 1997).

4. *Production before trial.* Note that Rule 17(c) directs production of various items "before the court at any time prior to the trial when they are to be offered into evidence" and authorizes the court to permit the parties and their attorney to inspect the items when produced. Does Rule 17(c) provide both sides with a discovery tool? Can a defense lawyer issue a subpoena for documents not discoverable through Rule 16 or other rules? For example, while Rule 16 mandates discovery of some items in the *government's* possession, custody, or control, it does not apply to items in the hands of private parties. Can the defense lawyer subpoena such items for delivery to the court and inspection, say, five months before the trial date?

The Supreme Court has answered "sometimes." In *United States v. Nixon,* 418 U.S. 683 (1974), a prosecutor issued a Rule 17(c) subpoena to President Nixon to produce certain tape recordings and documents involving the President's conversations with various aides. The items could be evidence in a trial scheduled of other people in five months. Rejecting the President's motion to quash the subpoena, the Supreme Court held that Rule 17(c) permitted such subpoenas in limited circumstances. The *Nixon* Court first noted that precedent had established that Rule 17(c) was designed to expedite a trial by providing a time and place before trial for the parties to inspect the subpoenaed items; it was "not intended to provide a means of discovery for criminal cases." *Id.* at 698. The Court also cited favorably prior case law limiting Rule 17(c) to cases where the items are not procurable in advance of trial by due diligence, the party needs the pretrial inspection to prepare for trial and avoid a trial delay, and the subpoena is issued in good faith, not as a fishing expedition. Accordingly, the person seeking the subpoena must establish that the items subpoenaed are described with specificity, are relevant to the trial, and contain admissible evidence.

Noting that *Nixon* severely restricts Rule 17(c) as a discovery device, Professor Peter Henning argues that Rule 17(c) should be construed to provide defendants (though not prosecutors) with a means to supplement discovery under Rule 16. He asserts that *Nixon* imposes an unrealistic standard on the defense because it is nearly impossible to establish that the items are relevant and admissible without first examining the documents to ascertain their content. Peter J. Henning, *Defense Discovery in White Collar Prosecution,* 15 GA. STATE U. L. REV. 601, 642 (1999). Do you agree?

5. *Witness' statements excluded.* Rule 17(h) specifies that a subpoena may not be issued for a statement of a witness or prospective witness. Witness statements are generally covered by Rule 26.2, discussed below.

6. *Sanction for noncompliance.* A subpoena is a court order. Rule 17(g) makes failure to abide by the subpoena punishable as contempt of court under Rule 42.

[6] In-trial Discovery: Statements of Witnesses (jencks)

In order to prepare for trial, both the defense counsel and prosecutor would like to see or hear about any statements made by their own or the other side's witnesses. For example, assume that M is a key prosecution witness who saw the crime occur. The defense would be most interested in any prior statements M made about the event. Perhaps M's earlier remarks will differ from M's court testimony. The earlier statement could be used to impeach M at trial and perhaps even as substantive evidence for the defense, and could also provide a lead to new witnesses who could help the defense. The obvious problem is that the defense lawyer may never learn that witness M made an earlier statement, for the rules of criminal procedure often do not require disclosure of such statements. In extreme cases where the defendant can prove prejudice, the due process clause may require disclosure of such statements. *See, e.g., Clewis v. Texas,* 386 U.S. 707, 712 n.8 (1967) (in some circumstances due process mandates disclosure of defendant's own statements to the police).

A limited amount of such disclosure is mandated by several rules of criminal procedure. Recall that Rule 16(a)(1) of the Federal Rules of Criminal Procedure gives the defendant a right to pretrial discovery of some information about the defendant's prior statements. This information will make it easier for defense counsel to prepare for trial and to decide whether to encourage the defendant to testify. Moreover, Rule 16(a)(1)(F) requires disclosure of certain statements by experts who conducted various tests or examinations. And Rule 15 permits the limited use of depositions to obtain statements of possible witnesses.

Nothing in the Federal Rules of Criminal Procedure or those of most states provides generally for the pretrial discovery of statements by all witnesses. In 1957 the United States Supreme Court exercised its supervisory power over federal courts and required disclosure of prior statements of government witnesses to facilitate impeachment by the criminal accused. *Jencks v. United States,* 353 U.S. 657 (1957). Congress responded by enacting 18 U.S.C. § 3500, known as the Jencks Act, which requires the government to disclose to defense counsel statements made by government witnesses who testify at trial. But this disclosure does not occur until after the witness has testified on direct examination. This last-minute disclosure is justified on the theory that if disclosure were earlier, the criminal accused may try to harm the witness or otherwise affect the witness's testimony or tailor defense proof to counter the prosecution witness's testimony.

Rule 26.2 of the Federal Rules of Criminal Procedure, added in 1979, repeats most of the Jencks Act. It was included in the rules of criminal procedure because of a belief that procedural rules should be readily available in a complete package of provisions rather than scattered throughout both the rules of criminal procedure and various separate statutes. *See generally* Ellen S. Podgor, *Criminal Discovery of Jencks Witness Statements: Timing Makes a Difference,* 15 GA. STATE U. L. REV. 651 (1999).

Rule 26.2 provides a minimal level of discovery of witnesses' statements by requiring disclosure of such statements after a witness has testified on direct examination. Thus, it is a departure from the traditional view that such statements are not discoverable, perhaps because part of counsel's work-product.

FEDERAL RULES OF CRIMINAL PROCEDURE

Rule 26.2. *Producing a Witness' Statement*

(a) Motion to Produce. After a witness other than the defendant has testified on direct examination, the court, on motion of a party who did not call the witness, must order an attorney for the government or the defendant and the defendant's attorney to produce, for the examination and use of the moving party, any statement of the witness that is in their possession and that relates to the subject matter of the witness's testimony.

(b) Producing the Entire Statement. If the entire statement relates to the subject matter of the witness's testimony, the court must order that the statement be delivered to the moving party.

(c) Producing a Redacted Statement. If the party who called the witness claims that the statement contains information that is privileged or does not relate to the subject matter of the witness's testimony, the court must inspect the statement in camera. After excising any privileged or unrelated portions, the court must order delivery of the redacted statement to the moving party. If the defendant objects to an excision, the court must preserve the entire statement with the excised portion indicated, under seal, as part of the record.

(d) Recess to Examine a Statement. The court may recess the proceedings to allow time for a party to examine the statement and prepare for its use.

(e) Sanction for Failure to Produce or Deliver a Statement. If the party who called the witness disobeys an order to produce or deliver a statement, the court must strike the witness's testimony from the record. If an attorney for the government disobeys the order, the court must declare a mistrial if justice so requires.

(f) "Statement" Defined. As used in this rule, a witness's "statement" means:

(1) a written statement that the witness makes and signs, or otherwise adopts or approves;

(2) a substantially verbatim, contemporaneously recorded recital of the witness's oral statement that is contained in any recording or any transcription of a recording; or

(3) the witness's statement to a grand jury, however taken or recorded, or a transcription of such a statement.

(g) Scope. This rule applies at trial, at a suppression hearing under Rule 12, and to the extent specified in the following rules:

(1) Rule 5.1(h) (preliminary hearing);

(2) Rule 32(i)(2) (sentencing);

(3) Rule 32.1(e) (hearing to revoke or modify probation or supervised release);

(4) Rule 46(j) (detention hearing); and

(5) Rule 8 of the Rules Governing Proceedings under 28 U.S.C. § 2255.

NOTES

1. *Mutuality.* Several features of Rule 26.2 are important. Unlike the Jencks Act, Rule 26.2 requires disclosure by both the defense and the prosecution of any statement, whether inculpatory, exculpatory, or neither, but it does not mandate that any statements be memorialized at all or in any specific way. Either side may request and receive relevant statements made by the other side's witnesses after the witness has completed direct examination. But Rule 26.2 is not identical for the two sides. The rule does not mandate disclosure to the prosecution of prior statements by the defendant.

Note that Rule 26.2(g) applies at sentencing, suppression hearings, detention hearings, and, important for discovery purposes, preliminary examinations. Of course, the prosecutor (and defense lawyer on rare occasions when defense witnesses are called at a preliminary examination) can avoid compliance with Rule 26.2's disclosure requirement at preliminary examinations for Witness X's statement by not calling Witness X at the preliminary examination.

2. *Sanctions for noncompliance.* Another difference in the treatment of prosecution and defense is in the sanctions for noncompliance. If Rule 26.2 is violated by either side's failure to produce a witness's statement, the authorized sanction differs for the two sides. The court is required by Rule 26.2(e) to order the testimony of that witness stricken from the record. In addition, if the government was at fault, the court must declare a mistrial "if required by the interest of justice." Rule 26.2 does not specifically permit the court to declare a mistrial for the defendant's failure to comply with Rule 26.2, but it may have the inherent authority to do so anyway in extraordinary situations.

3. *Deleting some information.* Rule 26.2 answers several practical problems that arise regularly. Sometimes a witness will provide a written statement dealing with many facts and issues, some of which the witness mentions on direct examination. Rule 26.2(c) permits the court, in camera, to review the statement and excise the irrelevant parts before the statement is turned over to the other side.

Since Rule 26.2 deals with statements by the witness, if the statement also contains remarks by other people, the latter's comments need not be produced under Rule 26.2. In addition, Rule 26.2 does not authorize one side to peruse the other side's records to determine whether the records contain a witness's statement. Each side is obligated to review its own records to assess whether it has a statement covered by Rule 26.2.

4. *Statements.* Rule 26.2(f) defines "statement" as including a written statement made by the witness that was signed or adopted or approved by the witness, a "substantially verbatim" recital of a witness' oral statement that was recorded contemporaneously, and a grand jury statement. This definition does not include an investigator's rough notes or brief summary of a witness' statement. *See United States v. Norris*, 56 F. Supp. 2d 1043 (N.D. Ind. 1998). It was viewed as unfair to permit a brief summary of a statement to be used for impeachment since the person preparing the summary may have selectively included portions of the statement and may have added his or her interpretations or extrapolations of what the witness actually said. Do you agree that this rationale is an adequate justification to exclude summaries from disclosure under Rule 26.2?

5. *Possession of party.* Rule 26.2 covers statements in the "possession" of a party. For the prosecution, this may include various government agencies. *See, e.g., United States v. Moore*, 452 F.3d 382 (5th Cir. 2006) (Bureau of Prisons, irrespective of whether statement's existence was known to anyone in entire Justice Department); *Cole v. State*, 835 A.2d 600 (Md. 2003)(police department internal affairs division).

6. *Timing of disclosure.* Another practical problem is caused by the timing of disclosure under Rule 26.2. What if a prosecution witness provides the prosecution with a one hundred page statement and then testifies for four days on direct examination at trial? As soon as the direct exam is completed, the prosecution gives the defense a copy of the lengthy statement. Obviously, it will take defense counsel hours to read and digest this statement and think about how to use it in cross-examining the witness. *See United States v. Holmes*, 722 F.2d 37 (4th Cir. 1983) (one day before trial, prosecution gave defense Jencks materials consisting of an 8-inch stack of papers including 1,000 pages of testimony from 10 witnesses, a 45-minute tape recording, and other documents; *Jencks* violation to not give defense lawyers adequate time to examine and prepare to use these materials).

Some courts follow the *Holmes* early disclosure requirement while others either reject it as unauthorized by the Rules (*see United States v. Mariani*, 7 F. Supp. 2d 556, 564 (M.D. Pa. 1998)), or limit it to "rare" situations where, as in *Holmes*, the *Jencks* materials are complex and overwhelming in volume (*see United States v. Riggs*, 739 F.Supp. 414 (N.D. Ill. 1990)).

Rule 26(d) specifically authorizes the trial court to grant a recess in the trial to facilitate the defense's need for time to review the witness's statement. But many defense counsel report that courts apply subtle and sometimes blatant pressure to "get on with it" to avoid delays in the proceedings. This judicial encouragement may cause some defense counsel to rush their reading of the statement and their preparation for its use on cross-examination. A defense counsel's failure to ask for an adequate continuance or recess so he or she has time to read the Rule 26.2 statement may cause an appellate court to reject an appeal on the basis of the inadequate time.

Although some courts reject the notion that they have the authority, either under the rule or under their inherent authority, to order early release of *Jencks* materials, some lawyers (with not-so-subtle judicial encouragement) may voluntarily provide early access to Rule 26.2 statements. In *Mariani, supra*, for example, the prosecutor agreed to provide these statements one week before trial. Professor Podgor recommends that Rule 26.2 should be amended to permit the judge to utilize non-mandatory guidelines and require pretrial release of Rule 26.2 statements unless the government obtains a protective order delaying this release. Ellen S. Podgor, *Criminal Discovery of Jencks Witness Statements: Timing Makes a Difference*, 15 GA. STATE U. L. REV. 651 (1999).

7. *Electronic statements.* Paperless trials, where documents are presented via computer monitors, raise new problems with respect to the disclosure of witness statements. In *United States v. Labovitz,* 1996 WL 417113 (D. Mass. 1996), the court granted the government's motion for a paperless trial provided that the government agree to make its witness statements available thirty days before the trial's commencement. Acknowledging that the court lacks power in the ordinary case to require the government to produce witness statements before the witness has completed direct examination, the court commented:

> A "paperless trial," however, presents special problems, which require the court to be alert to possible unfairness to the defendant. The defendant must be given sufficient time to prepare his case, and particularly the documents to be used in cross-examining witnesses, through the special procedures and techniques to be used in this "paperless" case. For example, documents the defense intends to use on cross-examination must be "imaged" and indexed in some manner to make them accessible to defense counsel before the trial commences. Without some opportunity to review witness statements before trial, select the documents for cross-examination and prepare them for use in the system, the "paperless" approach will place defense counsel at an unfair disadvantage. For this reason, the court has conditioned the use of the "paperless" procedure upon the disclosure by the Government of *Jencks* material thirty days in advance of trial.

8. *State adoptions.* States routinely adopt a version of Federal Rule 26.2. Sometimes it is more expansive. *See, e.g.,* N.Y. Crim. P. Law § 240.45 (defendant entitled to government witnesses' prior statements before prosecutor's opening argument at trial; prosecution entitled to defendant's witnesses' statements before defense counsel presents defense evidence in chief).

9. *Jencks and Brady.* In some cases, *Jencks* material and *Brady* material overlap. For example, a *Jencks* statement may constitute exculpatory or impeachment evidence; if so, it constitutes *Brady* material as well. *Brady* materials are ordinarily disclosed before trial to permit adequate trial preparation. When this dual coverage occurs, courts differ as to the timing of disclosure. Some hold that *Brady*'s pretrial disclosure rule must be followed in the event of *Brady/Jencks* overlap, *see, e.g., United States v. Starusko,* 729 F.2d 256 (3rd Cir. 1984); others find that the Rule 26.2 *Jencks* procedures prevail, *see, e.g., United States v. Causey* [and Jeffrey Skilling and Kenneth Lay — the much publicized Enron securities fraud prosecution], 356 F.Supp.2d 681 (S.D. Tex. 2005). Still other courts adopt a middle ground. *See e.g., United States v. Beckford,* 962 F. Supp. 780 (E.D. Va. 1997) (adopting a balancing approach and holding that except in limited circumstances, disclosure of evidence constituting both *Brady* and *Jencks* material need not occur earlier than as provided by the Jencks Act). *See generally* Ellen S. Podgor, *Criminal Discovery of Jencks Witness Statements: Timing Makes a Difference,* 15 GA. STATE U. L. REV. 651, 673 (1999).

PROBLEM 10-4. TO GIVE OR NOT TO GIVE, THAT IS THE QUESTION

You are the prosecutor in a bank fraud case involving misrepresentation of the value of assets listed on the defendant's loan application. Your first witness, Sally Lightner, is President of the First State Bank that was the victim of the scam. President Lightner has just completed her direct examination, during which she described the loan procedures used by the bank and the falsehoods in the defendant's loan application. The defense has filed a Motion for Production of Witness Statements Under Rule 26.2. You have carefully reviewed your files and have found several items that could possibly be covered by the defense's motion. Assuming that each related to Lightner's direct testimony at the trial, which of the following must you disclose to the defense under Rule 26.2?

1. President Lightner was interviewed two times by investigators from your office.

a. Agent A visited Lightner at her office at the bank after Lightner called your office to report the scam. The session lasted 45 minutes. Agent A made handwritten notes of Lightner's description of the offense. The notes cover two handwritten pages in Agent A's notebook and generally summarize Lightner's information. Are Agent A's handwritten notes covered by Rule 26.2?

Would your answer be different if the notes were twenty pages in length?

What if Agent A concluded the interview by saying, "Let me see if I have everything." He then spent five minutes summarizing the data in his notes. He then asked Lightner, "Is this basically it?" She responded, "Yes, that's about it." Are his notes now discoverable under Rule 26.2?

b. Agent A returned to his office where he dictated a ten page memorandum describing the interview with Ms. Lightner. He used his handwritten notes to supplement his memory of the interview. Is the ten page memorandum covered by Rule 26.2? Is the tape recording he dictated?

c. Four days after the interview, Agent A received a letter from President Lightner. The letter said that after the interview she remembered several facts that she had forgotten to mention. The letter then detailed the information omitted during the interview. Is the letter discoverable under Rule 26.2?

d. Agent B conducted the second interview with Lightner a month before trial. Agent B tape recorded the entire interview. Must the entire tape recording be turned over to the defense under Rule 26.2?

Assume that during Agent B's interview with Lightner, the bank's Vice President was called and asked to participate in the last half of the interview. The Vice President agreed to do so and participated in the interview. Assume that Lightner and the Vice President spoke for about the same length of time while jointly interviewed and that this portion of the interview lasted about 30 minutes. Is this part of the tape discoverable under Rule 26.2?

2. You have carefully prepared for trial. Your trial notebook includes a section for each witness. In the section labeled "Lightner," you summarize her likely testimony in two typed pages. Should you disclose these two pages to the defense pursuant to Rule 26.2?

[7] Grand Jury Evidence

An important principle of American law, discussed more fully in Chapter 7, is that the grand jury's processes are generally regarded as secret. Accordingly, transcripts of grand jury hearings are usually deemed secret. Of course, defense counsel would love to have access to these transcripts, for key government witnesses will testify both before the grand jury and later at trial. A witness's grand jury testimony would likely provide important information about the witness's trial testimony and could also be used to impeach the witness at trial and to gather other information that might benefit the defense. This information is particularly desirable when the grand jury witness refuses to talk about the case with defense counsel or a defense investigator.

The rules of criminal procedure often provide some flexibility in the dissemination of transcripts of testimony before the grand jury. Federal law, for example, specifically authorizes their disclosure to the prosecution to assist in preparing for trial. Moreover, there is some flexibility that permits the court to order disclosure to defense counsel.

FEDERAL RULES OF CRIMINAL PROCEDURE

Rule 6. *The Grand Jury*

. . . .

(e) Recording and Disclosing the Proceedings.

(1) Recording the Proceedings. Except while the grand jury is deliberating or voting, all proceedings must be recorded by a court reporter or by a suitable recording device. But the validity of a prosecution is not affected by the unintentional failure to make a recording. Unless the court orders otherwise, an attorney for the government will retain control of the recording, the reporter's notes, and any transcript prepared from those notes.

(2) Secrecy.

(A) No obligation of secrecy may be imposed on any person except in accordance with Rule 6(e)(2)(B).

(B) Unless these rules provide otherwise, the following persons must not disclose a matter occurring before the grand jury:

(i) a grand juror;

(ii) an interpreter;

(iii) a court reporter;

(iv) an operator of a recording device;

(v) a person who transcribes recorded testimony;

(vi) an attorney for the government; or

(vii) a person to whom disclosure is made under Rule 6(e)(3)(A)(ii) or (iii).

(3) Exceptions.

(A) Disclosure of a grand-jury matter — other than the grand jury's deliberations or any grand juror's vote — may be made to:

(i) an attorney for the government for use in performing that attorney's duty;

(ii) any government personnel — including those of a state or state subdivision or of an Indian tribe — that an attorney for the government considers necessary to assist in performing that attorney's duty to enforce federal criminal law; or

(iii) a person authorized by 18 U.S.C. § 3322.

(B) A person to whom information is disclosed under Rule 6(e)(3)(A)(ii) may use that information only to assist an attorney for the government in performing that attorney's duty to enforce federal criminal law. An attorney for the government must promptly provide the court that impaneled the grand jury with the names of all persons to whom a disclosure has been made, and must certify that the attorney has advised those persons of their obligation of secrecy under this rule.

(C) An attorney for the government may disclose any grand-jury matter to another federal grand jury.

(D) An attorney for the government may disclose any grand-jury matter involving foreign intelligence, counterintelligence (as defined in 50 U.S.C. § 401a), or foreign intelligence information (as defined in Rule 6(e)(3)(D)(iii)) to any federal law enforcement, intelligence, protective, immigration, national defense, or national security official to assist the official receiving the information in the performance of that official's duties. An attorney for the government may also disclose any grand-jury matter involving, within the United States or elsewhere, a threat of attack or other grave hostile acts of a foreign power or its agent, a threat of domestic or international sabotage or terrorism, or clandestine intelligence gathering activities by an intelligence service or network of a foreign power or by its agent, to any appropriate federal, state, state subdivision, Indian tribal, or foreign government official, for the purpose of preventing or responding to such threat or activities.

(i) Any official who receives information under Rule 6(e)(3)(D) may use the information only as necessary in the conduct of that person's official duties subject to any limitations on the unauthorized disclosure of such information. Any state, state subdivision, Indian tribal, or foreign government official who receives information under Rule 6(e)(3)(D) may use the information only in a manner consistent with any guidelines issued by the Attorney General and the Director of National Intelligence.

(ii) Within a reasonable time after disclosure is made under Rule 6(e)(3)(D), an attorney for the government must file, under seal, a notice with the court in the district where the grand jury convened stating that such information was disclosed and the departments, agencies, or entities to which the disclosure was made.

(iii) As used in Rule 6(e)(3)(D), the term "foreign intelligence information" means:

(a) information, whether or not it concerns a United States person, that relates to the ability of the United States to protect against —

- actual or potential attack or other grave hostile acts of a foreign power or its agent;
- sabotage or international terrorism by a foreign power or its agent; or
- clandestine intelligence activities by an intelligence service or network of a foreign power or by its agent; or

(b) information, whether or not it concerns a United States person, with respect to a foreign power or foreign territory that relates to —

- the national defense or the security of the United States; or
- the conduct of the foreign affairs of the United States.

(E) The court may authorize disclosure — at a time, in a manner, and subject to any other conditions that it directs — of a grand-jury matter:

(i) preliminarily to or in connection with a judicial proceeding;

(ii) at the request of a defendant who shows that a ground may exist to dismiss the indictment because of a matter that occurred before the grand jury;

(iii) at the request of the government if it shows that the matter may disclose a violation of state or Indian tribal criminal law, as long as the disclosure is to an appropriate state, state subdivision, or Indian tribal official for the purpose of enforcing that law; or

(iv) at the request of the government if it shows that the matter may disclose a violation of military criminal law under the Uniform Code of Military Justice, as long as the disclosure is to an appropriate military official for the purpose of enforcing that law.

(F) A petition to disclose a grand-jury matter under Rule 6(e)(3)(D)(i) must be filed in the district where the grand jury convened. Unless the hearing is ex parte — as it may be when the government is the petitioner — the petitioner must serve the petition on, and the court must afford a reasonable opportunity to appear and be heard to:

(i) an attorney for the government;

(ii) the parties to the judicial proceeding; and

(iii) any other person whom the court may designate.

NOTES

1. *Particularized need.* Although Rule 6 authorizes the trial judge to order disclosure of grand jury transcripts, most federal courts do so only upon a showing of a "particularized need" which outweighs the policy of grand jury secrecy. *Pittsburgh Plate Glass Co. v. United States,* 360 U.S. 395 (1959).

2. *Application of Jencks Act (Rule 26.2).* Rule 26.2(f) of the Federal Rules of Criminal Procedure also authorizes disclosure of grand jury testimony. After a witness testifies on direct, the other side is entitled to a copy of the witness's prior statements, including those made before a grand jury.

3. *Defendant's own grand jury testimony.* Rule 16(a)(1)(B)(iii) authorizes a defendant to discover his or her own grand jury testimony. This provision will rarely be invoked, however, because defendants rarely testify before a grand jury.

Some state rules are more liberal, authorizing pretrial disclosure of grand jury statements, *see, e.g.,* Mass R. Crim. P. 14(a)(1)(ii) (defendant to receive relevant written or recorded statements of grand jury witnesses), and the identities of grand jury witnesses, *see, e.g.,* Minn. R. Crim. P. 9.01, subd. 1(1)(c) (names and addresses of grand jury witnesses).

[8]   Court's Inherent Authority to Order Disclosure

Although the rules of criminal procedure do not accord full discovery in criminal cases, the courts have some inherent authority to extend discovery beyond that specifically authorized in the rules. This inherent authority is used routinely by some judges and sparingly by others. One area in which it has been used is to correct interference by one side with the other side's access to potential witnesses.

UNITED STATES v. CARRIGAN
804 F.2d 599 (10th Cir. 1986)

Logan, Circuit Judge.

[In a mail fraud case, several government witnesses indicated a willingness to be interviewed by defense counsel, then changed their minds and refused to do so. There was some proof that the refusal came after a government agent met with the witnesses and expressed a preference that the witnesses not discuss the case with defense counsel. The defendants then filed a motion to depose the witnesses. The trial court granted the order and the government sought a writ of mandamus to vacate the district court's order.]

. . . Does a district court have authority in a criminal case, in any circumstances, to order pretrial depositions of the prosecution's witnesses by a defendant? In searching for this power we must consider these sources: Federal Rules of Criminal Procedure 15(a) and 16(d), and the court's inherent power to control the conduct of its trials and to impose sanctions in connection with that supervisory power.

Fed. R. Crim. P. 15 explicitly treats depositions. Under subsection (a) depositions of "a prospective witness of a party" may be taken when in the exceptional circumstances of the case such taking is in the interest of justice. The advisory and legislative committee notes make clear that Rule 15 does not authorize a party to take discovery depositions of the adversary party's witnesses. The case law has confirmed this construction of Rule 15, holding that it does not contemplate use of depositions of adverse witnesses as discovery tools in criminal cases.

Rule 16 treats discovery and inspection in criminal cases. Rule 16(d) places the regulation of discovery in the hands of the trial judge. The subsection appears to give the district court significant discretionary power to make such orders as are appropriate. In context, however, Rule 16 appears to limit discovery to items other than depositions. The rule states that the court may permit a defendant to have access to tangible items, to copy written papers, and to receive statements under certain circumstances. Moreover, in 1974, amendments to Rule 16 were proposed to permit parties' access, in normal circumstances, to the names and addresses of the other side's witnesses. Those proposed amendments were rejected . . . . In view of Congress' explicit rejection of discovery of the identity of witnesses, we cannot read Rule 16 as providing a basis for the trial court to order the depositions of adverse witnesses in criminal prosecutions.

In our view, the only possible source for the district court's authority to make the order it did in the present case is in its inherent power to control and supervise its own proceedings. As a sanction for government misbehavior, can the trial court order the depositions of specific government witnesses by defendants?

Against finding that the court had the inherent authority to make this order is the scheme of the Federal Rules of Criminal Procedure, which provide detailed rules for essentially all aspects of criminal trials and contain no explicit statement that the trial court has such power. Those rules authorize certain explicit sanctions for particular infractions: Rule 26.2(e) permits the court to strike the testimony of a witness or to declare a mistrial for failure to comply with an order to deliver a statement; Rule 48(b) permits the court to dismiss a case if there is unnecessary delay in presenting charges to a grand jury or to a court, or there is unnecessary delay in bringing a defendant to trial; Rule 16(d)(2) permits the court to prohibit a party from introducing evidence it has not disclosed as the court required. What the district court did here is nowhere specifically authorized as a sanction.

On the other hand, the courts have long recognized that trial judges must be able to control their own proceedings to ensure the fair administration of justice within the confines of the law. We have recognized the principle that witnesses in a criminal prosecution belong to no one, and that, subject to the witness' right to refuse to be interviewed, both sides have the right to interview witnesses before trial . . . . This view is bolstered by the American Bar Association's Standards for Criminal Justice § 3–3.01(c), providing that the prosecutor will not discourage or obstruct communications between prospective witnesses and defense counsel and that it is unprofessional conduct for the prosecutor to advise a prospective witness to decline to give the defense information that person has a right to give. *See also* Model Rules of Professional Conduct Rule 3.4(f).

Additionally, a number of cases, including at least one from this circuit, while denying relief on various grounds, assume that the district court has the power, at least in unusual circumstances, to order the taking of adverse witnesses' depositions in criminal cases.

. . . Although the question is a close one, we cannot find the order entered here as a sanction for the government's interference with a defendant's access to potential prosecution witnesses to be wholly beyond the district court's jurisdiction. An order merely to cease such interference, after the fact, might be insufficient because the witnesses' free choice might have been already perverted and the witnesses likely to refuse voluntary interviews. Accordingly, we are unwilling to issue a writ of mandamus on this ground . . . .

NOTES

1. *Inherent authority.* A court's inherent authority to grant discovery has also been accorded in "special circumstances" where an unusual factual situation makes it appropriate to grant discovery beyond that traditionally available.

An excellent example is *United States v. Stubblefield*, 325 F. Supp. 485 (E.D. Tenn. 1971). The defendant was found competent to stand trial, although a psychiatrist testified that the defendant suffered an "alcoholic blackout" rendering it impossible for him to recall the events at issue in the case. The trial court found that this condition would impair the defendant's ability to consult with his lawyer, to testify in his behalf, and to have a fair trial. Accordingly, the court stated:

> These considerations render it imperative that the prosecution assist the defendant and his counsel in reconstructing, extrinsic to the defendant's recollection, the evidence in suit relating to the crime charged as well as any reasonably possible alibi or other defense. Under these special circumstances- . . . the Court hereby orders the prosecution attorneys herein to open their files forthwith to defense counsel as to all matters relating to the evidence of the crime charged and any reasonable defense and to keep those files open continually to defense counsel until, during and after the trial herein.

Id. at 486. *Contra, United States v. Hearst*, 412 F. Supp. 863, 866 (N.D. Cal. 1975) (*Stubblefield* not followed because of inadequate proof that Patty Hearst suffered such severe amnesia that she could not assist in the reconstruction of the events at issue).

2. *Codification of expansive judicial discretion.* Some states have essentially codified the court's inherent authority to order discovery by authorizing the court to order discovery beyond that mandated by the discovery rules. *See, e.g.,* Ark. R. Crim. P. 17.4(a) (court may require disclosure to defense counsel of other information material to preparation of the defense); Ill. Sup. Ct. Rules 412(h), 413(e) (reasonable disclosure to either side of relevant material not covered by discovery rules).

3. *Examination of victim.* Sometimes the inherent authority extends to require a physical or mental examination of a witness or victim. *See, e.g., Clark v. Commonwealth,* 521 S.E.2d 313 (Va. App. 1999) (independent physical examination of sexual assault victim, upon showing of compelling need).

[9] Other Sources and Limits of Discovery

[a] Electronic Surveillance

Sometimes discovery in criminal cases is authorized by laws other than the usual rules of evidence or criminal procedure. While these rules are beyond the scope of this book, one merits mention. It provides an important discovery device for criminal defendants who fear that inadmissible evidence obtained through illegal electronic surveillance of them will be used against them. A federal statute provides that in any trial, hearing, or other proceeding, including grand jury hearings, a party claiming that evidence is inadmissible because it was procured through illegal electronic surveillance of that party is entitled to have the opponent of the claim affirm or deny the occurrence of the alleged wrongful act. 18 U.S.C. § 3504. The party alleging the illegality must make a prima facie showing of electronic surveillance (usually through an affidavit), and then the government must affirm or deny that the illegal surveillance occurred.

This statute can be illustrated by assuming that Defendant D believes that her phone was illegally tapped by the police and that some of her conversations were used to obtain evidence against her. She cannot prove it because she cannot locate the wiretap, perhaps because it had been removed by government technicians. Under § 3504, Defendant D can assert that there was an illegal wiretap of her house telephone. The government must then affirm or deny the wiretap. Ordinarily, the government's response is in the form of a written document entitled something like "Answer to Defendant's Motion Pursuant to 18 U.S.C. § 3504." The government will most likely attach affidavits from appropriate government officials detailing the presence or absence of the illegal wiretap.

Courts disagree on how specific the complainant must be in alleging government illegality. Some decisions have held that the complaint should allege details about the illegal surveillance, including such items as which phones were tapped, which government agency did the tapping, which conversations were overheard, and how the government took advantage of the illegally obtained information. Most courts reject as too general an allegation that the government "may have obtained information from an illegal wiretap."

[b] Freedom of Information Act

Another source of discovery is the Freedom of Information Act (F.O.I.A.), 5 U.S.C. § 552. Some states have similar "open records laws." The federal F.O.I.A. law provides the public with a right of access to various federal government materials. It also mandates procedures for obtaining this information. In order to avoid interference with law enforcement activities, some data are excluded from discovery under the F.O.I.A. Statutes also exempt materials from release under the Act. *See, e.g., Fund for Constitutional Government v. National Archives and Records Service,* 656 F.2d 856 (D.C. Cir. 1981) (Rule 6 of Federal Rules of Criminal Procedure exempts federal grand jury matters from release under the Freedom of Information Act).

Case law has shown a judicial reluctance to allow the F.O.I.A. as a substitute for the more rigorous requirements of discovery under the Federal Rules of Criminal Procedure. *See, e.g., United States v. United States District Court,* 717 F.2d 478 (9th Cir. 1983).

[c] National Security

On rare occasions the government will argue it cannot comply with a pretrial discovery request because of national security concerns. In such cases courts routinely try to accommodate those concerns by reviewing the discovery request in an *ex parte* setting and making feasible adjustments in the discovery compliance. *See* classified Information Protection Act, 18 U.S.C. App. § 4. Courts seek to balance the defendant's need for the information against the government's need to keep the data from being revealed.

Often the court will accommodate both sides by permitting the government to summarize or redact the information. In *United States v. O'Hara,* 301 F.3d 563 (7th Cir. 2002), for example, the court redacted sensitive documents in a manner that still disclosed *Brady* materials.

If disclosure is needed because redaction or other remedies are inadequate, the court will order it. To avoid a dismissal for refusing to obey the court-ordered discovery, the government may be forced to drop charges.

[10] Remedies for Violation of Discovery Order

Rules requiring disclosure of information also authorize the trial judge to take various steps when disclosure is improperly withheld. Because these violations of the discovery rules may be based on unique facts or have consequences unique to the case, both the discovery rules and appellate courts usually give the trial judge discretion in fashioning an appropriate remedy. Federal Rule 16(d)(2) is typical.

FEDERAL RULES OF CRIMINAL PROCEDURE

Rule 16. *Discovery and Inspection*

. . .

(d)(2) Failure to Comply. If a party fails to comply with this rule, the court may:

(A) order that party to permit the discovery or inspection; specify its time, place, and manner; and prescribe other just terms and conditions;

(B) grant a continuance;

(C) prohibit that party from introducing the undisclosed evidence; or

(D) enter any other order that is just under the circumstances.

NOTES

1. *General pattern of noncompliance sanctions.* Other discovery rules also deal with sanctions for their violation. The general pattern is to authorize, but not require, the court to exclude evidence. For example, if either side fails to comply with the notice of alibi requirements in Federal Rule of Criminal Procedure 12.1, the court may exclude the testimony of an undisclosed witness, other than the defendant. Fed. R. Crim. P. 12.1(e). *See also* Fed. R. Crim. P. 12.2(d)(1) (if defendant fails to give required notice of mental condition defense or to submit to mental exam, defense expert witnesses may be barred); 26.2(e) (if either side does not disclose a witness's prior statement as required by "*Jencks*" rule, court must order witness's direct testimony stricken or, if the refusal was by the government, must order a mistrial).

2. *Case-by-case approach.* Even though a court may be authorized to exclude otherwise admissible evidence as a sanction for violation of a disclosure rule, the Sixth Amendment's right to present witnesses and evidence may place limits on the court's options to exclude defense evidence. Courts routinely look at the particular facts of the case in deciding what sanction to apply. One court expressed the test as follows:

> In addition to preventing surprise, other factors considered before a witness preclusion sanction is employed to enforce discovery rules are: the effectiveness of less severe sanctions, the materiality of the testimony to the outcome of the case, prejudice to the other party caused by the testimony, and the evidence of bad faith in the violation of the discovery rules.

United States ex rel. Enoch v. Hartigan, 768 F.2d 161, 163 (7th Cir. 1985).

Often courts prefer the least harsh sanction. *See, e.g., United States v. Golyansky,* 291 F.3d 1245 (10th Cir. 2002)(excluding witness was not the least restrictive sanction to avoid prejudice); United *States v. DeCoteau,* 186 F.3d 1008 (8th Cir. 1999) (for prosecution's violation of Rule 16, court should impose least severe sanction that will adequately punish the government and secure future compliance, in absence of a finding of prejudice to the defendant or bad faith by the prosecution).

3. *Intentional nondisclosure.* Intentional nondisclosure is treated more harshly than negligent nondisclosure. *See, e.g., United States v. Charley,* 189 F.3d 1251 (10th Cir. 1999) (in assessing sanction for government's failure to disclose written summary of expert testimony, court should consider as factor whether government acted in bad faith); *United States v. Katz,* 178 F.3d 368 (5th Cir. 1999) (trial court properly excluded pornographic color photos when defense, during discovery, had been given only poor quality black-and-white photos; government either tried to sandbag defense or engaged in highly unprofessional conduct).

4. *Minimizing harm.* Courts also look at the options available to minimize the harm caused by nondisclosure. For example, a continuance may be ordered if it would cure any harm caused by nondisclosure. *See, e.g., Berry v. State,* 715 N.E.2d 864 (Ind. 1999) (generally, continuance is proper remedy for discovery violation absent prejudice or deliberate misconduct).

Similarly, courts often ask whether the "harmed" party could have alleviated any prejudice. For example, in one case the judge refused to impose sanctions for a violation of Rule 26.2 because the defense could have minimized any harm by trying to interview the source of undisclosed information in the report. *United States v. Gotchis,* 803 F.2d 74 (2d Cir. 1986).

5. *Harmless error.* The harmless error rule is also used in deciding the proper sanction for a violation of a discovery rule. If the government's failure to disclose was of little consequence, the error will usually not cause a reversal of a conviction. *See, e.g., United States v. Riley,* 189 F.3d 802 (9th Cir. 1999) (violation of Jencks Act will cause striking of witness' testimony only after consideration of government's culpability and prejudice to the defendant); *Rose v. State*, 563 S.E.2d 865 (Ga. 2002) (state's failure to list witness on formal witness list will not bar that witness' testimony when identity and involvement of that witness were disclosed in discovery).

On the other hand, if the nondisclosure actually made it impossible for the other side to investigate an issue or obtain proof, the court may bar evidence or even declare a mistrial. *See, e.g., United States v. Buchbinder*, 796 F.2d 910 (7th Cir. 1986) (defendant failed to provide notice of intent to use an expert in violation of Rule 12; trial court properly excluded defense expert witness on issue of mental condition because defense's failure to give notice deprived government of opportunity to have defendant examined by government psychiatrist; nonexpert proof on mental condition permitted).

In extreme situations, involving flagrant conduct or substantial prejudice, the court may even dismiss the case. *See, e.g., United States v. Jacobs*, 855 F.2d 652 (9th Cir. 1988).

6. *Constitutional limits on barring defendant's testimony and witnesses.* Similarly, it is arguably unconstitutional to bar the defendant from testifying because defense counsel did not provide adequate disclosure of a witness list or a particular defense. The defendant may have a right to testify that cannot be abridged through counsel's error. *See, e.g., Alicea v. Gagnon*, 675 F.2d 913 (7th Cir. 1982) (defense counsel failed to give notice of alibi defense as required by state rules of criminal procedure, and state trial judge barred defendant from testifying about his whereabouts; criminal defendant has constitutional right to testify under Fifth, Sixth, and Fourteenth Amendments). *But see, contra, Burroughs v. State*, 344 N.W. 149 (Wis. 1984).

Some decisions have also held that it is unconstitutional to bar defense witnesses from testifying as a sanction for the defense's failure to comply with a discovery rule. *See, e.g., Fendler v. Goldsmith*, 728 F.2d 1181 (9th Cir. 1983) (Sixth Amendment prevents exclusion of defense witnesses who were barred when defense counsel failed to list the addresses of 131 potential defense witnesses as required by state discovery rules); *Taylor v. Illinois*, 484 U.S. 400 (1988)(while upholding the exclusion of a defense witness, the Court discussed limits on barring defense witnesses because of a violation of a discovery rule) (discussed *supra*); *State v. Harris*, 979 P.2d 1201 (Idaho 1999) (Sixth Amendment violated when trial court barred important defense witness who defense counsel inadvertently omitted from witness list; exclusion permissible if omission was wilful). *See generally* Note, *The Preclusion Sanction — A Violation of the Constitutional Right to Present a Defense*, 81 Yale L.J. 1342 (1972); *see also* Charles A. Pulaski, Jr., *Extending the Disclosure Requirements of the Jencks Act to Defendants: Constitutional and Nonconstitutional Considerations*, 64 Iowa L. Rev. 1 (1978).

If important defense evidence is barred because of defense counsel's discovery errors, could this constitute ineffective assistance of counsel in violation of the Sixth Amendment? *See Commonwealth v. Sena*, 709 N.E.2d 1111 (Mass. 1999) (yes).

7. *Appellate review.* In general, a trial judge's decision on discovery is deemed *interlocutory* and not subject to pretrial appellate review. Appellate courts use the abuse of discretion standard in reviewing the trial judge's decision. Some cases do allow the government to appeal if the court excludes evidence because of the government's failure to provide discovery. *See, e.g., United States v. Golyansky*, 291 F.3d 1245 (10th Cir. 2005).

[11] Ethical Issues in Discovery

While some ethical issues have already been discussed in this chapter, several others bear mention. Lawyers are held to high ethical standards in the area of discovery. As noted earlier in this chapter, the Model Rules of Professional Conduct deal in considerable detail with discovery. They not only ban obstructing adversary counsel's access to evidence, they also prohibit falsifying evidence, disobeying an obligation imposed by court rules (unless the court rules are openly challenged), making a frivolous discovery request, and failing to make a reasonably diligent effort to comply with a proper discovery request by adversary counsel. Model Rules of Professional Conduct Rule 3.4 (1983). See also Standards for Criminal Justice §§ 3–3.11(b) (3d ed. 1993) (prosecutor must make reasonably diligent effort to comply with proper discovery request), 4-4.5 (same for defense counsel).

G. A BETTER SYSTEM

[1] Arguments Against Extensive Discovery in Criminal Cases

Now that you are familiar with discovery in criminal cases, you have seen how less extensive it is than that allowed in civil cases. For example, while depositions and interrogatories are common in civil cases, they are virtually nonexistent in criminal cases. These differences may be surprising because in other areas, such as the right to free counsel for indigents, criminal procedure offers more protection for the defendant than does civil procedure. To a large extent, the greater protections given the criminal accused in many areas of criminal procedure are based on the theory that these protections are appropriate since the defendant's liberty (as opposed to the civil defendant's money) is at stake.

What are the reasons for the limited scope of discovery in criminal cases? Several rationales are repeated commonly.

[a] Harm or Intimidate Witnesses

Perhaps the most prevalent argument is that extensive discovery would allow the criminal accused to learn the identity and likely testimony of prosecution witnesses. To avoid conviction, the accused would intimidate or harm these witnesses to prevent or alter their trial testimony. This risk may also deter some potential witnesses from agreeing to testify or even providing the prosecution with information.

There is some evidence that this fear is real, although we do not know its extent or whether it is confined to certain types of cases. A federal prosecutor reported that a survey of United States Attorneys found over 700 instances of witness intimidation, assault, or assassination. Edward S.G. Dennis, Jr., *The Discovery Process in Criminal Prosecutions: Toward Fair Trials and Just Verdicts*, 68 WASH. U. L.Q. 63, 65 (1990).

[b] Commit or Suborn Perjury

A related argument is that the accused would learn the likely prosecution evidence and then tailor his or her own testimony or that of other defense witnesses to meet the likely government evidence. While this possibility is also present in civil cases, for some reason it is rarely discussed.

[c] Violate Adversary Process

A third argument is that full discovery would undermine the adversary process, particularly if disclosure were not identical for both sides. Some adherents of this view note that the burden of proof in criminal cases weighs heavily against the government, yet the defendant can withhold critical information, helpful to the prosecution, because of the protection of the Fifth Amendment. If the defendants had full discovery of the government's file plus the advantages of a "tilted" burden of proof, the resulting adversary process would not be a fair one for both sides. Judge Learned Hand observed in an often-quoted passage:

> Under our criminal procedure the accused has every advantage. While the prosecution is held rigidly to the charge, he need not disclose the barest outline of his defense. He is immune from question or comment on his silence; he cannot be convicted when there is the least fair doubt in the minds of any of the twelve.

Why in addition he should in advance have the whole evidence against him to pick over at his leisure, and to make his defense, fairly or foully, I have never been able to see . . . . Our dangers do not lie in too little tenderness to the accused. Our procedure has been always haunted by the ghost of the innocent man convicted. It is an unreal dream. What we need to fear is the archaic formalism and the watery sentiment that obstructs, delays, and defeats the prosecution of crime.

United States v. Garsson, 291 F. 646, 649 (S.D.N.Y. 1923).

NOTES

1. *Defendant as threat to witnesses.* Obviously the first two of these rationales are based on a view of the criminal accused as a dangerous person who will do (virtually) anything to escape conviction. How does this view accord with reality? Does this describe some/most/all criminal defendants? Could discovery rules be written to protect witnesses in those cases where such protection is necessary, but to permit broad discovery in other cases? What procedures would have to be provided if this individualized model were adopted? Who would have the burden of proof and what would have to be proven?

One suggestion to improve the existing system is to create a presumption *in favor of* early and full discovery by the defendant. Under this model, the government must provide full disclosure unless it could demonstrate to the court that there really is a danger that the defendant will tamper with evidence, intimidate witnesses, or commit perjury. When the government satisfies this standard, the trial court would restrict discovery only to the extent necessary to avoid the dangers established by the government's proof. *See* H. Lee Sarokin & William E. Zuckerman, *Presumed Innocent? Restrictions on Criminal Discovery in Federal Court Belie This Presumption*, 43 RUT. L. REV. 1089, 1090 (1991). Do you agree with this approach? Are there any problems with it?

2. *Eventually the defendant will know.* Does the witness intimidation argument make sense since the defendant will eventually learn both the prosecution witness's identity and testimony when the witness testifies at trial? Is there less fear of post-testimony retribution than of pre-testimony harm?

3. *Presumption of innocence.* Discovery rules obviously apply to criminal defendants who are actually guilty as well as to those who are innocent. Does the limit on discovery assume that the defendant is guilty? Does it square with the presumption of innocence?

4. *Role of defense counsel.* The intimidation and perjury theories assume the worst type of defendant while ignoring the role of counsel. According to a distinguished jurist, Judge Frankel, the perjury theory overlooks

that it is a lawyer who ordinarily moves for discovery, representing that he has a proper purpose for what is on its face a responsible professional request . . . . [We should not abandon the presumption] that members of our bar behave regularly and refrain from suborning perjury.

United States v. Projansky, 44 F.R.D. 550 (S.D.N.Y. 1968). Do you agree with Judge Frankel?

5. *Impact on government-defendant balance.* How will increased discovery affect the current prosecution-defense balance in the adversary process of American criminal procedure?

An Assistant Attorney General for the United States Department of Justice's Criminal Division observed:

Fairness in criminal cases is due not only the defendant but also the general public, whose interest is represented by the government. Defendants should not be protected against tripping themselves up when they testify falsely or fabricate defenses. The "surprise" that results when the government puts on a witness who thwarts such efforts to distort justice is of the very essence of fairness in our system and promotes the reaching of just verdicts.

Edward S.G. Dennis, Jr., *The Discovery Process in Criminal Prosecutions: Toward Fair Trials and Just Verdicts,* 68 WASH. U. L.Q. 63, 65 (1990). Do you agree?

6. *Speeding up process.* One argument in favor of more discovery in criminal cases is that it would speed up the proceedings. Is this argument valid?

7. *Facilitate plea bargaining.* Another argument is that more discovery in criminal cases would facilitate plea bargaining (and therefore help alleviate crowded dockets) by giving the defendant a good sense of the strength of the government's case that will be presented if there is a trial. Will an increase in discovery in criminal cases lead to more guilty pleas? If so, is this progress for the American criminal justice system? *See* H. Lee Sarokin & William E. Zuckerman, *Presumed Innocent? Restrictions on Criminal Discovery in Federal Court Belie This Presumption,* 43 RUT. L. REV. 1089 (1991) (arguing in favor of more criminal discovery).

[2] More Disclosure: The California Model

Since little of the law of discovery in criminal cases is mandated by the Constitution, jurisdictions have considerable leeway in fashioning their discovery rules. While most jurisdictions have laws that resemble the federal approach, a few jurisdictions have considerably broadened the scope of discovery in criminal cases.

A popular example is the California discovery process, added by the Crime Victim's Justice Reform Act through a citizen's initiative in 1990. *See generally* Deborah Glynn, *Proposition 115: The Crime Victims Justice Reform Act,* 22 PAC. L. J. 1010 (1991). To a large extent, these rules were a reaction to California judicial decisions severely limiting discovery by the prosecution in criminal cases.

California Penal Code

§ 1054.1. *Prosecuting attorney; disclosure of materials to defendant*

The prosecuting attorney shall disclose to the defendant or his or her attorney all of the following materials and information, if it is in the possession of the prosecuting attorney or if the prosecuting attorney knows it to be in the possession of the investigating agencies:

(a) The names and addresses of persons the prosecutor intends to call as witnesses at trial.

(b) Statements of all defendants.

(c) All relevant real evidence seized or obtained as a part of the investigation of the offenses charged.

(d) The existence of a felony conviction of any material witness whose credibility is likely to be critical to the outcome of the trial.

(e) Any exculpatory evidence.

(f) Relevant written or recorded statements of witnesses or reports of the statements of witnesses whom the prosecutor intends to call at the trial, including any reports or statements of experts made in conjunction with the case, including the results of physical or mental examinations, scientific tests, experiments, or comparisons which the prosecutor intends to offer in evidence at the trial.

§ 1054.2. *Disclosure of address or telephone number of victim or witness; prohibition; exception*

(a)(1) Except as provided in paragraph (2), no attorney may disclose or permit to be disclosed to a defendant, members of the defendant's family, or anyone else, the address or telephone number of a victim or witness whose name is disclosed to the attorney pursuant to subdivision (a) of Section 1054.1, unless specifically permitted to do so by the court after a hearing and a showing of good cause.

(2) Notwithstanding paragraph (1), an attorney may disclose or permit to be disclosed the address or telephone number of a victim or witness to persons employed by the attorney or to persons appointed by the court to assist in the preparation of a defendant's case if that disclosure is required for that preparation. Persons provided this information by an attorney shall be informed by the attorney that further dissemination of the information, except as provided by this section, is prohibited.

(3) Willful violation of this subdivision by an attorney, persons employed by the attorney, or persons appointed by the court is a misdemeanor.

(b) If the defendant is acting as his or her own attorney, the court shall endeavor to protect the address and telephone number of a victim or witness by providing for contact only through a private investigator licensed by the Department of Consumer Affairs and appointed by the court or by imposing other reasonable restrictions, absent a showing of good cause as determined by the court.

§ 1054.3. *Defense counsel; disclosure of information to prosecution*

The defendant and his or her attorney shall disclose to the prosecuting attorney:

(a) The names and addresses of persons, other than the defendant, he or she intends to call as witnesses at trial, together with any relevant written or recorded statements of those persons, or reports of the statements of those persons, including any reports or statements of experts made in connection with the case, and including the results of physical or mental examinations, scientific tests, experiments, or comparisons which the defendant intends to offer in evidence at the trial.

(b) Any real evidence which the defendant intends to offer in evidence at the trial.

§ 1054.5. *Criminal cases; discovery orders; informal request; testimony of witnesses; prohibition*

. . . .

(b) Before a party may seek court enforcement of any of the disclosures required by this chapter, the party shall make an informal request of opposing counsel for the desired materials and information. If within 15 days the opposing counsel fails to provide the materials and information requested, the party may seek a court order. Upon a showing that a party has not complied with Section 1054.1 or 1054.3 and upon a showing that the moving party complied with the informal discovery procedure provided in this subdivision, a court may make any order necessary to enforce the provisions of this chapter, including, but not limited to, immediate disclosure, contempt proceedings, delaying or prohibiting the testimony of a witness or the presentation of real evidence, continuance of the matter, or any other lawful order. Further, the court may advise the jury of any failure or refusal to disclose and of any untimely disclosure.

(c) The court may prohibit the testimony of a witness pursuant to subdivision (b) only if all other sanctions have been exhausted. The court shall not dismiss a charge pursuant to subdivision (b) unless required to do so by the Constitution of the United States.

§ 1054.6. *Work product privilege*

Neither the defendant nor the prosecuting attorney is required to disclose any materials or information which are work product . . . or which are privileged pursuant to an express statutory provision, or are privileged as provided by the Constitution of the United States.

§ 1054.7. *Disclosure of information; time limitations*

The disclosures required under this chapter shall be made at least 30 days prior to the trial, unless good cause is shown why a disclosure should be denied, restricted, or deferred. If the material and information becomes known to, or comes into the possession of, a party within 30 days of trial, disclosure shall be made immediately, unless good cause is shown why a disclosure should be denied, restricted, or deferred. "Good cause" is limited to threats or possible danger to the safety of a victim or witness, possible loss or destruction of evidence, or possible compromise of other investigations by law enforcement.

Upon the request of any party, the court may permit a showing of good cause for the denial or regulation of disclosures, or any portion of that showing, to be made in camera. A verbatim record shall be made of any such proceeding. If the court enters an order granting relief following a showing in camera, the entire record of the showing shall be sealed and preserved in the records of the court, and shall be made available to an appellate court in the event of an appeal or writ. In its discretion, the trial court may after trial and conviction, unseal any previously sealed matter.

NOTES

1. While California mandates extensive pretrial discovery, it has not adopted an open-file rule that requires each side to turn over its entire file to the other. What would be wrong with an open-file rule? Wouldn't it speed up the trial process and promote the ascertainment of truth by eliminating surprise at trial and providing each side with its best opportunity to present its case?

2. Examine the California discovery rules. Do they mandate that California law enforcement authorities *gather* exculpatory evidence? Should they?

3. The California provisions have different standards for defense and prosecution discovery. Does this make sense?

4. What if both sides conduct extensive investigation and find witnesses helpful to the other side. Must the prosecution give the defense this information? Does the defense have to do so for the prosecution? Do you agree with this result?

5. Must the identities and statements of rebuttal witnesses be disclosed? *See People v. Hammond*, 28 Cal. Rptr. 2d 180 (Cal. App. 1994) (due process requires that prosecution disclose rebuttal witnesses it intends to call if defense must disclose witnesses it intends to use).

6. Should this discovery process apply even to misdemeanors?

7. Is the California discovery process better than the federal one?

Chapter 11
PLEAS AND PLEA BARGAINING

A. INTRODUCTION

Criminal cases, like civil cases, rarely go to trial. Where civil litigation typically is resolved by settlement, criminal cases are resolved in overwhelming proportion, in both state and federal courts, by the process of *plea bargaining*, which results in a negotiated *guilty plea*. This chapter is devoted to the process, the constitutional constraints, and the policy concerns surrounding plea bargaining in our nation's courts.

The criminal defendant who pleads guilty admits responsibility for one or more of the crimes charged (perhaps in the form of a lesser included offense), agrees to be punished in accordance with the criminal laws, and waives the right to trial and other procedural rights under the Fifth and Sixth Amendments. Although statistics vary somewhat from jurisdiction to jurisdiction, approximately 90% of criminal convictions are the product of guilty pleas. A study of state felony convictions found that 95% of convictions resulted from guilty pleas, 2% from jury trials, and 3% from bench trials. U.S. Dep't of Justice Sourcebook of Criminal Justice Statistics [online] (Ann L. Pastore and Kathleen Maguire, eds., 2006), *available at* http://www.albany.edu/sourcebook/pdf/t5462004.pdf. Similar numbers are reported in U.S. District Courts. *Id.*, at http://www.albany.edu/sourcebook/pdf/t5242006.pdf. Therefore, an understanding of the plea bargaining process is critically important if one is to understand the American criminal justice system.

B. PLEA OPTIONS AVAILABLE TO THE DEFENDANT

In federal cases and in almost all of the states, a defendant may enter one of three pleas to a criminal charge: not guilty, *nolo contendere*, or guilty. *E.g.*, Fed. Rule Crim. P. 11(a)(1). In addition, some jurisdictions also allow the separate plea of "not guilty by reason of insanity" or "guilty but mentally ill." *See, e.g.*, Ohio R. Crim. P. 11(A); Mich. R. Crim. P. 6.303, 6.304. In contrast with the federal rule, New York does not allow the plea of *nolo contendere* "as a matter of right," while Illinois only allows the *nolo* plea for those defendants charged with a violation of the state income tax law. *See* N.Y. Crim. Proc. Law § 220.10; Ill. Cons. Stat. ch. 725, art. 113-4.1.

[1] Plea of Not Guilty

By pleading not guilty, the defendant requires the government to prove its case, thereby placing in issue each material element specified in the indictment. This plea also preserves many constitutional rights, including the right to jury trial, the privilege against self-incrimination, and the right to confront one's accusers.

A plea of not guilty is a *legal assertion of rights*, rather than a sworn *statement of fact*. Therefore, a defendant who is guilty of the crime(s) charged but pleads not guilty in order to exercise his or her right to trial by jury, does *not* thereby commit an act of perjury.

[2] Plea of *Nolo Contendere* (No Contest)

A plea of *nolo contendere*, like a plea of guilty, involves a waiver of the right to a trial and other related procedural rights. Fed. R. Crim. P. 11(b)(1)(F). A *nolo* plea is a formal declaration that the defendant will not contest the charge and it has the same legal effect as a guilty plea in terms of its finality. Therefore, judgment following entry of a *nolo contendere* plea is a criminal conviction which sometimes may be admitted as evidence in other proceedings where the fact of conviction has legal significance. *But see* Fed. R. Evid. 803(22)(conviction on *nolo* plea inadmissible in later proceedings).

In contrast to the plea of guilty, however, the legal consequences of a *nolo* plea are different in one critical respect. In most jurisdictions, the *nolo* plea may not be used in a later civil case as proof of the fact that the defendant committed the offense. That is, the plea of *nolo* may not be used as direct evidence of liability in a civil suit. In fact, some jurisdictions even provide that the plea of no contest may not be used against the defendant in any subsequent civil *or* criminal proceeding. *See, e.g.*, Ohio R. Crim. P. 11(B)(2). This feature explains why a person facing both civil and criminal proceedings might prefer to plead *nolo contendere* to resolve the criminal matter without compromising the subsequent civil proceedings.

The defendant does not have an absolute right to plead *nolo contendere*. In federal cases, the *nolo* plea requires the consent of the court and "such a plea shall be accepted by the court only after due consideration of the views of the parties and the interest of the public in the effective administration of justice." Fed. R. Crim. P. 11(a)(3). In practice, this rule has been construed to vest the trial judge with broad discretion to refuse to accept a *nolo* plea. *See United States v. David E. Thompson, Inc.*, 621 F.2d 1147 (1st Cir. 1980) (district court did not abuse its discretion in rejecting a *nolo* plea in a criminal antitrust action where entry of the plea would have deprived the victims of the antitrust conspiracy of a significant opportunity in subsequent civil actions to benefit from the government's efforts). Most states follow the same rule. Many judges are reluctant to permit *nolo* pleas since this plea leaves unresolved the issue of actual responsibility for the crime.

A minority of jurisdictions do not permit a *nolo* plea. *See, e.g., Corbin v. State*, 713 N.E.2d 906 (Ind. App. 1999) (*nolo* pleas not permitted because guilty plea in Indiana requires admission of crime charged).

[3] Plea of Guilty

By pleading guilty, the defendant consents to entry of a judgment of conviction without trial and jury verdict. Although a plea of guilty is usually entered before trial, it may also be entered at any point during trial before the jury returns its verdict.

The guilty plea waives the right to be tried by a jury and also the defendant's other constitutional trial-related rights, including the right to the assistance of trial counsel, the right to confront and cross-examine adverse witnesses, and the right against compelled self-incrimination. Fed. R. Crim. P. 11(b)(1)(F). Consequently, before accepting a plea of guilty and a waiver of these rights, the court must determine that the accused is acting voluntarily and understands the charges. The plea itself is an admission of guilt and the accepted plea is essentially a criminal conviction. The judge's only remaining tasks are to enter judgment and impose sentence.

C. THE PLEA BARGAINING PROCESS

Virtually all attorneys involved in the criminal justice system — whether a prosecutor or defense attorney, whether federal or state — participate in plea bargaining. Simply put, plea bargaining is a form of plea negotiation in which the prosecutor agrees to make certain concessions in exchange for the defendant's guilty or *nolo contendere* plea. Both the government and the defendant may benefit from a negotiated resolution of the case. First, a trial on the merits is time consuming and, for the defendant who has hired a private attorney, quite expensive. Second, there is a certain amount of unpredictability with respect to the outcome of a criminal trial. Both prosecution and defense may prefer the certainty of the guilty plea, which establishes guilt as well as the level of criminal culpability. Third, even if the defendant is convicted at trial, the sentence imposed by the court may exceed what the defendant expected or may be less than the prosecution thinks is appropriate. Hence, a bargained-for sentence may be seen as beneficial to both sides by virtue of the certainty and finality it provides to all concerned, including not only the prosecution and defense attorneys but also the crime victim, the police, the public, and the defendant himself.

In federal criminal cases, there are essentially four types of plea agreements available: (1) charge agreements; (2) recommendation agreements; (3) specific sentence agreements; and (4) fact stipulation agreements.

[1] Charge Agreements

A charge agreement is one in which the government agrees that the defendant will plead guilty to one or more specific charges in exchange for the government's assent to dismiss other pending charges. If this kind of agreement is reached prior to the issuance of an indictment, the government agrees not to pursue one or more particular charges (sometimes referred to as placing the other charges *on file*). If the agreement is reached following indictment, the government agrees to dismiss one or more existing charges. This agreement also may be used in a single-count charge to reduce the charge to a lesser offense (*i.e.*, a defendant charged with second degree murder may agree to plead guilty to involuntary manslaughter).

For example, assume that Luther has been indicted for robbery, burglary, and two counts of receiving and concealing stolen property. He could enter a plea agreement in which he agrees to plead guilty to robbery (the most serious of his charges) in exchange for the government's agreement to dismiss the burglary and the receiving and concealing charges.

[2] Recommendation Agreements

A recommendation agreement is one in which the defendant agrees to plead guilty in exchange for the prosecutor's willingness either to recommend a particular sentence or not to resist or oppose a sentence recommendation made by the defense. In federal cases, the agreement may entail precise commitments — perhaps from both prosecution and defense — regarding departures from the sentence prescribed by the federal sentencing guidelines.

Return to the example involving Luther who was indicted for robbery, burglary, and two counts of receiving and concealing stolen property. Perhaps he would agree to plead guilty to all four crimes if the prosecution would recommend to the judge that he be given a sentence of ten years in prison for the robbery and three year prison sentences each for the other three offenses, all to be served concurrently with the ten-year robbery sentence. If (as is likely) the recommendation is accepted by the judge, Luther will have served all four sentences by the time he completes the ten-year term for robbery.

[3] Specific Sentence Agreements

Similar to a recommendation agreement, a specific sentence agreement entails a guilty plea in exchange for an agreement from the government that the court will impose a specific sentence or use a certain sentencing range or use (or not use) a particular sentencing guideline or factor.

While the judge may (and usually does) choose to abide by such an agreement, the court has the authority to reject the specific agreed-upon sentence. In that event, the defendant is allowed to withdraw the guilty plea. Withdrawals of guilty pleas are discussed in further detail later in this chapter.

Returning again to the hypothetical involving Luther, assume that the plea agreement involved a specific (as opposed to a recommended) ten-year sentence for robbery (with the other three sentences to be served concurrently). If the judge accepts the deal, Luther must be sentenced to the ten-year term in accordance with the agreement. If the judge refuses to accept the agreement, perhaps believing it to be too lenient, Luther has the option of withdrawing his plea and going to trial on all four charges (of course, this entails a substantial risk that if he is convicted, the sentence will be more than what could be negotiated in a plea agreement the court would accept).

[4] Fact Stipulation Agreements

A fact stipulation agreement, while not a traditional form of plea negotiation, is a separate agreement in which pertinent facts and circumstances surrounding the offense are agreed upon. These agreements are contemplated by federal sentencing guidelines and their purpose is to explicate specific facts which the federal judge relies upon to support the particular sentence within statutory ranges. For a more detailed discussion of plea bargaining under federal sentencing guidelines, see Tony Garoppolo, *Fact Bargaining: What the Sentencing Commission Hath Wrought*, 10 BNA Criminal Practice Manual 405 (1996) and William L. Gardner & Davis S. Rifkind, *A Basic Guide to Plea Bargaining Under the Federal Sentencing Guidelines*, 7 Crim. Just. 14 (Summer, 1992). For a critical view, arguing that some fact stipulations between prosecution and defense (such as an agreement to treat a repeat offender as a first offender for sentencing purposes) may inappropriately, even fraudulently, shield certain relevant facts from the sentencing judge's view, see the *cri de coeur* of one federal district judge:

> The most repugnant of the [Justice] Department's tactics is to lie to the Court in order to induce a guilty plea. This is the process known as "fact bargaining." It occurs when a departmental attorney "swallows the drugs" or "the gun" as the case may be, i.e., fails to report to the probation officer in rendering its descriptions of offense conduct (and then later fails to bring to the attention of the Court) relevant evidence that may affect the [Federal Sentencing G]uidelines calculation in order to reduce that calculation to secure a disposition to which it and defense counsel have agreed. This, of course, is flat-out illegal.

U.S. v. Green, 346 F. Supp. 2d 259, 278 (D. Mass. 2004, Young, C.J.), vacated *sub nom. U.S. v. Yeje-Cabrera*, 430 F. 3d 1 (1st Cir. 2005).

[5] Plea Bargaining Variations

[a] Conditional Pleas

A *conditional plea* is designed to make it possible for the defendant to enter a guilty plea yet preserve the pretrial motion ruling for appellate review. It is specifically authorized by federal law, as shown below.

FEDERAL RULES OF CRIMINAL PROCEDURE

Rule 11. *Pleas*

(a) **Entering a Plea.**

. . . .

(2) **Conditional Plea.** With the consent of the court and the government, a defendant may enter a conditional plea of guilty or nolo contendere, reserving in writing the right to have an appellate court review an adverse determination of a specified pretrial motion. A defendant who prevails on appeal may then withdraw the plea.

Essentially, when a conditional guilty plea is accepted by the court, the defendant reserves the right to appeal the adverse pretrial motion. If the appellate court affirms the pretrial ruling, the guilty plea stands. If the appellate court upholds the defendant's claim, however, the guilty plea may then be withdrawn.

1. *Hypothetical.* Assume a case in which the defendant's apartment is searched by a police officer without a search warrant. As a result of this search, cocaine is found and the defendant is charged with possession of cocaine. The defense attorney files a pretrial suppression motion arguing that the search was unlawful and the drugs should be excluded from evidence. Without this evidence, the prosecution's case is so weak that the charges would likely be dismissed. Assume also that defense counsel's suppression motion is denied by the trial judge, but the defense attorney believes that the appellate court will probably exclude the evidence. The general rule is that a guilty plea waives all non-jurisdictional defects in the case. Therefore, if the defendant wishes to preserve the evidentiary issue for review by an appellate court, he or she cannot plead guilty; the case must go to trial.

In the above hypothetical, however, assume that the defendant enters a conditional guilty plea, reserving the right to appeal the issue of the admissibility of the cocaine. If the appeal is unsuccessful, the defendant's plea is valid and will subject him or her to the criminal sanctions agreed to in the plea bargain. On the other hand, if the appeal is successful and the evidence is ruled inadmissible, the defendant's plea can be withdrawn and, if it is, the prosecution has the option of dropping the charges, setting the case for trial, or engaging in further plea bargaining.

2. *Mutual benefit.* Both defense and prosecution may benefit from a conditional plea. The defendant benefits by not having to go to trial in order to appeal an important issue, such as the admissibility of a confession. The government gains by avoiding the waste of time that would occur if the defendant went through a trial, then successfully appealed and had the conviction overturned. The government would then have to launch a second trial if it could not work out a deal or did not want to drop charges.

[b] Agreements for Cooperation

A somewhat different form of plea bargaining has emerged in recent years: the "agreement for cooperation." Unlike the traditional plea bargaining, this form of agreement contemplates a favorable disposition for the accused in exchange for cooperation with the government, usually in the form of testimony against other defendants. Professor Graham Hughes describes this compact as one involving "contested issues that must be negotiated, sometimes for months, and that eventually are embodied in letter agreements that range from the fairly straightforward to the extremely complicated."

As Professor Hughes also explains, cooperation agreements entail a very precise description of the cooperation promised by the accused as well as a clear delineation of the scope of immunity or nature of the plea bargain benefit extended by the government. Subsequent litigation between the contracting parties necessarily hinges upon the very terms of the contract. Graham Hughes, *Agreements for Cooperation in Criminal Cases*, 45 Vand. L. Rev. 1 (1992). This issue will be explored later in *Ricketts v. Adamson*, 483 U.S. 1 (1987).

Sometimes a cooperation agreement may be accompanied by a *consistency agreement*, which obligates the offender to testify against others in a way that is consistent with the offender's prior statements. Since these provisions discourage the offender from recanting or altering the earlier statement that may have been incomplete or untruthful, consistency agreements are disfavored in many courts. *See, e.g., State v. Kayer*, 984 P.2d 31 (Ariz. 1999)(agreements that oblige the defendant to testify truthfully and completely are valid, but those that oblige the defendant to testify to certain stipulated facts are not).

[c]   Bargaining for Unusual Sentencing Provisions

Sometimes, judges, prosecutors and defense attorneys use the plea bargaining process to reach results in individual cases that allow for unusual punishments or sentencing results that are not specifically provided for under the sentencing laws. For example, an agreed upon guilty plea may require the defendant to stay out of certain cities or geographical areas, engage in unpaid charitable contributions or labors, enter the armed services (if the military is willing to induct the defendant), or to undergo certain "scarlet letter" punishments (such as wearing a confessional sandwich-board in a public place or write a public letter of apology for the crime).

Views differ on the appropriateness of bargaining for particular sentencing outcomes that fall outside the express provisions of the sentencing laws. On the one hand, Professor Joseph A. Colquitt, *Ad Hoc Plea Bargaining*, 75 TULANE L. REV. 695, 699 (2001), argues that such ad hoc settlements are outside the law and must be controlled:

> Prosecutors and defense attorneys should not be allowed to assume the legislative functions of defining crimes and establishing the types and ranges of punishments. Giving them the option to settle criminal cases through the use of ad hoc alternatives to legal punishments does precisely that. They establish the law of the locale rather than apply the laws of the state. Moreover, the "punishments" they negotiate most often fail to address penological goals. Ad hoc justice commonly leaves much to be desired.

On the other hand, as discussed in Chapter 17, courts have broad discretionary powers to fashion specific conditions of probation appropriate to the facts and circumstances of each particular case, and often impose these kinds of individualized alternative sanctions as conditions of probation.

D.   PLEA BARGAINING POLICY CONSIDERATIONS PRO AND CON: NECESSARY EVIL, NECESSARY GOOD, OR JUST PLAIN EVIL?

Opinions about the value and fairness of plea bargaining differ sharply. To oversimplify somewhat, views on plea bargaining tend to fall into three schools of thought. Some view plea bargaining itself as inherently unfair, compromising of justice, and even unconstitutional. Others regard it as a kind of necessary evil without which the criminal justice system would grind to a halt, but which should be subject to close legislative and judicial oversight. Still others regard the plea bargaining process as not only necessary, but also one which tends to yield fair and just results when the adversary system works properly. This section of the chapter explores these contrasting viewpoints, and although somewhat more space is given to the "cons" than the "pros" of plea bargaining, students are encouraged to think for themselves and come to their own conclusions after reading these materials. Students should consider also whether the potential evils of plea bargaining can adequately be addressed by procedurally "policing" the process, or whether plea bargaining should be severely limited or abolished altogether.

[1]   Administrative Convenience/Necessity

Many persons — judges and advocates included — maintain that plea bargaining in our society is a necessary part of the criminal justice system. This argument rests upon two assumptions. First, without plea bargaining, it is argued, many criminal defendants will have little incentive to plead guilty and will insist on a trial. Second, we have inadequate resources (prosecutors, defense attorneys, judges, courtrooms, *etc.*) to conduct a full trial in every criminal case. We would have to devote massive additional funding to the criminal justice system if many more defendants demanded all the rights guaranteed by the Constitution. This would be a waste of resources, it is argued, since most defendants really are guilty and the proof against them is overwhelming. These arguments are buttressed by the fact that currently there is roughly one trial for every ten guilty pleas. What would happen to our already overburdened system if a much larger percentage of criminal defendants elected to face trial rather than plead guilty?

In recent years, some jurisdictions have tested this argument by attempting to ban plea bargaining altogether (isolated jurisdictions within the states of Texas, Michigan, and New York, and state-wide in Alaska, among others). The few empirical studies that have examined those efforts suggest that bargaining prohibitions have not caused courts and criminal justice officials to be overwhelmed. In Alaska, where the State Attorney General banned plea negotiations in 1975 (but recognized possible exceptions to the ban where suspects exchange helpful information), a study found that (1) defendants continued to plead guilty at about the same rate as before the ban, (2) the rate of trials increased, but the number of trials remained low, and (3) conviction rates changed very little. Other studies have found that such bans produced increases in sentencing severity, especially for minor offenses. As to the hypothesis that banning plea bargaining would substantially disrupt the criminal justice system (through increased trial rates, case backlogs, and lengthened case processing times), none of these adverse effects occurred (except in New York, according to one study). *See* Sandra Shane-Dubow, Alice P. Brown & Erik Olsen, SENTENCING REFORM IN THE UNITED STATES: HISTORY, CONTENT, AND EFFECT (1985); Michael H. Tonry, SENTENCING REFORM IMPACTS (1987).

Where plea bargaining has been "eliminated," two important points must be kept in mind. First, banning the practice of plea bargaining does not preclude a defendant from pleading guilty to the charge or charges and asking for "the mercy of the court." Second, some commentators believe that prohibiting explicit plea bargaining will never eliminate "implicit plea bargaining," defined as an informal understanding among prosecutors, defense attorneys, and judges that the guilty defendant who enters a plea of guilty should and will receive a reduced sentence. Similarly, banning plea bargaining could have the effect of shifting the exercise of discretion to a less visible stage of the criminal case. For example, California's attempt to ban plea bargaining through a constitutional amendment ("Proposition 8") did not produce that result. Rather, it had the effect of encouraging guilty pleas at earlier stages of the process than before. This result led one commentator to observe: "Paradoxically, . . . Proposition 8 strengthened plea bargaining rather than eliminating it." Candace McCoy, Politics and Plea Bargaining: VICTIMS' RIGHTS IN CALIFORNIA 179 (1993).

[2]   Fair and Accurate Results

Many people believe that our current plea bargaining system produces results that are both unfair and inaccurate. The charge of unfairness is premised upon the assertion that the offender who negotiates a "sweet deal" may receive an inappropriately lenient sentence. The "accuracy" concern rests upon the contention that the enticement to plead guilty may be so attractive that an innocent defendant will plead guilty rather than face the possibility of a false conviction at trial. While the latter hypothesis is difficult to test, some commentators assert that a significant number of legally innocent defendants are persuaded to enter pleas of guilty. On the assumption that a prosecutor's reputation may be based upon the conviction rate, sometimes a very favorable plea bargain may be offered to avoid the possibility of an acquittal. *See* Albert W. Alschuler, *The Prosecutor's Role in Plea Bargaining*, 36 U. CHI. L. REV. 50, 59 (1968) (one prosecutor interviewed by Professor Alschuler admitted, "when we have a weak case for any reason, we'll reduce to almost anything rather than lose."). Professor H. Richard Uviller, while defending plea bargaining as a necessary aspect of the criminal justice system, offers a proposal for insuring fair and accurate results from the plea bargaining process. Specifically, he recommends that for each defendant, a conference should be held among opposing counsel and the presiding judge "during which the individual case is fully evaluated on its special merits and an appropriate sentence settled upon." H. Richard Uviller, VIRTUAL JUSTICE: THE FLAWED PROSECUTION OF CRIME IN AMERICA 177, 198 (1996).

[3] Disparity

Another concern about plea bargaining is that it may contribute to sentencing disparity as similar defendants receive different sentences. Evidence suggests that sentencing disparities result from differential plea bargaining rather than from real distinctions in offenders or offenses. It is well established that defendants who bargain for a plea receive lower sentences than those who are convicted at trial. For example, in 1986, among state felony defendants convicted after a trial, the average sentence was 145 months; the comparable figure for defendants who pled guilty was 72 months. Robert E. Scott & William J. Stuntz, *Plea Bargaining as Contract*, 101 YALE L.J. 1909 (1992). Similarly, defendants who plead guilty in federal court receive sentences from 25 to 75 percent lower than the sentences imposed on comparable defendants convicted at trial. Stephen J. Schulhofer, *Plea Bargaining as Disaster*, 101 YALE L.J. 1979, 1993 (1992).

As noted later in this chapter, the United States Supreme Court has held that the Constitution does not bar sentencing defendants who plead guilty to a lesser sentence than those who go to trial. *Brady v. United States*, 397 U.S. 742 (1970). Those who plead are rewarded for accepting their responsibility, saving government resources, and sparing victims and witnesses the burdens and anxieties of testifying at trial. Conversely, it is widely held that the trial court cannot penalize defendants who go to trial by giving them a longer sentence. Of course, it is difficult for some to understand how the longer sentence following a trial is not, in essence, a penalty for exercising an important constitutional right.

Consider the following recommendations of the American Bar Association:

> (a) The fact that a defendant has entered a plea of guilty . . . should not, by itself alone, be considered by the court as a mitigating factor in imposing sentence. It is proper for the court to approve or grant charge and sentence concessions to a defendant who enters a plea of guilty . . . when consistent with governing law . . . .

> (b) The court shall not impose upon a defendant any sentence in excess of that which would be justified by any of the protective, deterrent, or other purposes of the criminal law because the defendant has chosen to require the prosecution to prove guilt at trial rather than to enter a plea of guilty . . . .

STANDARDS FOR CRIMINAL JUSTICE § 14-1.8 (3d ed. 1999).

The potential for both disparity and dishonesty is inherent in a wide-open system of plea bargaining. With respect to the crime of conviction, similarly situated offenders who have committed identical crimes may not be treated identically. They may bargain for different crimes or sentences, or one may demand a trial and receive a harsher sentence than the co-defendant who pleads guilty. One commentator has characterized this aspect of plea bargaining as "willful mislabeling" which has "turned our criminal statistics into a pack of lies." John H. Langbein, *On the Myth of Written Constitutions: The Disappearance of Criminal Jury Trial*, 15 HARV. J.L. & PUB. POL. 119, 125 (1992) (examples cited by Professor Langbein include the person who commits murder but who is "pretended to have committed manslaughter" and the person whose "real crime" was child molesting but is convicted of loitering around a schoolyard).

On the other hand, it would be naive to believe that simply eliminating plea bargaining would cure the long-standing and well-documented sentencing disparities that have existed in state and federal courts. See Ch. 17 for fuller discussion of the issues surrounding disparity in sentencing practices and of various efforts to reduce unwarranted disparities.

[4]   Invisibility

Because plea negotiation is essentially a process that occurs in private and replaces the public trial, it is an invisible procedure that may keep information away from the public. Many commentators believe that there is a strong public interest in full, open and public inquiry and adjudication. An example frequently cited in this context is the murder plea accepted from James Earl Ray, who was charged with killing Rev. Martin Luther King, Jr. Society's interest in discovering the facts about the assassination of a public figure is frustrated by private plea discussions and the absence of a public trial. Professor Abraham Goldstein argues that the public interest in a public trial is so strong in some cases that judges should not be allowed to "deny the public [the] educative and deterrent role that attaches to a contested and visible public trial." Abraham S. Goldstein, *Converging Criminal Justice Systems: Guilty Pleas and the Public Interest*, 49 S.M.U.L. Rev. 567 (1996). In these cases, if:

> the trial judge determines that the public interest requires a public airing of the facts culminating in a criminal charge, he should do one of two things: (1) he should reject the plea and insist on the prosecution putting its witnesses on record, with the defendant either challenging those witnesses or acquiescing in what they have said; or (2) if he decides to accept a guilty plea, he should follow the English practice and require a presentation, in open court, of the testimony of the principal witnesses and such stipulations of fact as make a contested trial inappropriate.

[5]   Effect Upon Counsel

With the realization that relatively few criminal cases go to trial, routine plea bargaining may encourage lackadaisical preparation by both prosecution and defense lawyers. Since the case will likely be settled by a plea bargain, too many lawyers wait until the eve of trial to "work up" the case. If there is no trial, they save the time they would have devoted to a full investigation of all the factual and legal issues in the case. This means that they will engage in plea negotiations without having fully explored these matters. Yet, they cannot know the strengths and weaknesses of their case without a full investigation prior to plea negotiations. To the extent that either prosecution or defense attorneys engage in this less-than-zealous representation, the possibility of an inappropriate guilty plea is heightened. In addition, defense counsel's sloppy pre-plea preparation may violate the defendant's Sixth Amendment right to effective counsel as well as the lawyer's professional obligation to provide competent legal assistance.

[6]   Overcharging

The plea negotiation process can be a complicated, time consuming, give-and-take procedure. Given the high probability that a criminal charge will be bargained "down," the initial "asking price" in plea negotiations is the prosecutor's determination of the initial charges. Most defense attorneys believe that many prosecutors inflate those charges, a practice called "overcharging." Albert W. Alschuler, *The Prosecutor's Role in Plea Bargaining*, 36 U. Chi. L. Rev. 50, 85 (1968).

One way for the prosecutor to raise the ante in plea bargaining is to multiply the number of accusations against a single defendant. Professor Alschuler refers to this practice as "horizontal overcharging." *Id.* at 85. For example, the defendant alleged to have committed an armed robbery may be charged with robbery, assault, and possessing unlawful weapons; the maximum possible sentence may be in excess of fifty years in prison. The objective is to use the lengthy possible sentence to convince the defendant to plead guilty to a few of the charges in exchange for a dismissal of the others. Somewhat ironically, even where the defendant succeeds in persuading the prosecutor to dismiss some of the additional counts, very little actual benefit may be realized. This is because consecutive sentences are rare and also because the sentencing judge may take into account the dismissed charge in determining the sentence.

Another prosecutorial strategy is "vertical overcharging," the practice of charging a single offense at a high level and then bargaining for a plea to a lesser included or lower offense. *Id.* at 86. Many defense attorneys believe that vertical overcharging occurs as a matter of course in homicide cases. Prosecutors defend the practice of vertical overcharging because facts and circumstances may emerge between the initial charge and trial that would warrant a finding of guilt as to the crime charged. If the initial charge is set at a level that does not adequately gauge the defendant's culpability, a guilty plea may be entered to the lower offense, with the result that an "inaccurate" judgment will have been entered. Whatever their motivations, prosecutors usually charge the "highest and most" that the evidence permits. *Id.* at 88–89. *See also*, Donald G. Gifford, *Meaningful Reform of Plea Bargaining: The Control of Prosecutorial Discretion*, 1983 U. ILL. L. REV. 37, 47–49.

One may well ask the question, exactly what is overcharging? Is charging the "highest and most" really overcharging? Is it "overcharging" to bring charges at the highest level that the prosecutor in good faith believes are potentially sustainable given the facts and the law, and then let a jury sort it out if the plea bargaining process is unsuccessful? Or does overcharging consist in bringing more, or more serious charges, than the prosecutor in good faith believes can be sustained at trial? Definitions and views of overcharging may vary, but ethically, the existence of *probable cause* and a good faith assessment of "tryability" are what set the limit on the number and severity of charges a prosecutor may responsibly bring.

[7]   The Views of Police and Crime Victims

Depending on the policies and practices of prosecutors' offices, the plea bargaining process may either include or exclude the possibility of the views of police and crime victims being taken into consideration in the negotiation of an agreed upon guilty plea. Views among police and crime victims also differ. Some police may see their front-line law enforcement efforts being undermined by prosecutors who they think are too eager and willing to bargain out a "good" case and accept lenient punishment. Others, especially at the administrative level, may appreciate that plea bargaining, by eliminating unnecessary trials, enables police agencies to keep their personnel "on the street" more and tied up in court less.

Similarly, some crime victims see trials as part of their own healing process and their opportunity to affect the outcome of the case and may feel excluded by the plea bargaining process, while others may appreciate being spared by a guilty plea from having to undergo the rigors and sometimes the re-inflicted trauma of the crime occasioned by having to testify and undergo cross examination at trial. Many prosecutors' offices now have victims' assistance units, which not only provide victims with access to therapeutic services, but also operate to ensure that victims' views are heard and taken appropriately into consideration in the plea bargaining process.

[8]   Plea Bargaining Seen As Furthering Justice

In addition to the utilitarian justifications for plea bargaining mentioned in the preceding discussion (conserving limited police, judicial, prosecution, and defense resources, and sparing victims the potential trauma of having to testify at trial and pretrial proceedings and being confronted again by those who injured them), plea bargaining is also sometimes seen as a means to achieve justice while protecting the rights and interests of all concerned. *See, Bordenkircher v. Hayes*, 434 U.S. 357, 361–362 (1978)(discussed later in this chapter), "the guilty plea and the often concomitant plea bargain are important components of this country's criminal justice system. Properly administered, they can benefit all concerned." (majority opinion of

Justice Stewart); *see also*, Justice Powell's dissenting opinion in *Bordenkircher*: "The plea-bargaining process. . . . normally affords genuine benefits to defendants as well as to society." *Id.*, at 672.

Implicit in the assumption of Justice Stewart and the *Bordenkircher* majority that the plea bargaining process is being "properly administered," is the notion that the adversary system is functioning properly — with fair and competent judges, prosecutors, and defenders. Experienced and conscientious practitioners have a good sense of the "market value" range of reasonable outcomes for a given offense considered in light of the defendant's personal background and prior criminal history. According to this "market value" view, the plea negotiation process in a properly functioning adversary system appropriately takes into account the relative strengths and weaknesses of the prosecution and defense cases, and results in outcomes that, on the whole, do justice to defendants, victims, and society.

Of course, this idealized notion of the adversary system can (and sometimes does) tend to break down in the real world, as observed by some of the skeptics of plea bargaining cited above. Therefore, federal and state rules have been developed (*see, especially*, Fed. R. Crim. P. 11's detailed procedural requirements, emulated by many states) which are aimed at "policing" the system to provide the greatest possible degree of procedural fairness and transparency to the processes and the outcomes of plea bargaining.

E. PLEA BARGAINING: CONSTITUTIONAL ISSUES

[1] Introduction

It may be surprising to know that plea bargaining was not officially "discovered" until about 1921. Before that time there were no records in existence to document the extent to which plea bargaining was occurring in either state or federal cases. Indeed, some of the early nineteenth century cases suggest that any inducement to secure a guilty plea from the accused was prohibited. One author has concluded that "early American decisions exhibited judicial disdain for plea bargaining." Jay Wishingrad, *The Plea Bargain in Historical Perspective*, 23 BUFF. L. REV. 499, 525 (1974). Professor George Fisher, on the other hand, describes plea bargaining in the nineteenth century, observing that "individual prosecutors [at that time] found a personal and political advantage in securing the easy victories that plea bargaining afforded. [P]rosecutors may have believed that the more clandestinely they could secure those victories, the better." George Fisher, *Plea Bargaining's Triumph*, 109 YALE L.J. 857, 935–36 (2000).

Nonetheless, it is widely believed that various forms of plea bargaining were practiced long before the adoption of statutes and rules explicitly sanctioning the plea negotiation process. We can speculate, however, that, due to the fear that judges would not accept guilty pleas resulting from the negotiation process, prosecutors, defense attorneys, and defendants routinely may have withheld information about their deals from the judges (or perhaps, in some cases, flatly misrepresented the truth) in order to secure judicial acceptance of negotiated pleas.

In recent years, however, plea bargaining has "come out of the closet" as a recognized facet of the American criminal justice system. To some extent, this recognition is the product of judicial decisions that have "constitutionalized" some of the procedures involved in guilty pleas. Once guilty pleas became subject to judicial scrutiny, it was no longer possible to pretend that they did not exist or to downplay their prevalence and importance.

[2]　Does Plea Bargaining Impermissibly Burden the Exercise of the Constitutional Right to Trial by Jury?

In *United States v. Jackson*, 390 U.S. 570 (1968), three defendants were indicted by a federal grand jury and charged with kidnapping under the Federal Kidnapping Act, which provided:

> whoever knowingly transports in interstate . . . commerce, any person who has unlawfully . . . kidnapped . . . and held for ransom . . . shall be punished (1) by death if the kidnapped person has not been liberated unharmed, and if the verdict of the jury shall so recommend, or (2) by imprisonment for any term of years or for life, if the death penalty is not imposed.

Because the statute authorized the death penalty only if a *jury* so recommended, this allowed a defendant to avoid the death penalty by waiving a jury trial and facing the possibility of a conviction after a bench trial or a guilty plea. The United States Supreme Court held that this death penalty provision imposed an impermissible burden on the exercise of the defendant's constitutional right to trial by jury. Therefore, the Court invalidated the death penalty provision in the kidnapping statute, but also held it severable from the rest of the statute. Therefore, the Court ruled, Jackson could be retried under the kidnapping statute but not put to death if convicted on retrial. Justice Stewart explained:

> Under the Federal Kidnapping Act . . . the defendant who abandons the right to contest his guilt before a jury is assured that he cannot be executed; the defendant ingenious enough to seek a jury acquittal stands forewarned that, if the jury finds him guilty and does not wish to spare his life, he will die . . . . The inevitable effect of any such provision, is of course, to discourage assertion of the Fifth Amendment right not to plead guilty and to deter exercise of the Sixth Amendment right to demand a jury trial. If the provision had no other purpose or effect than to chill the assertion of constitutional rights by penalizing those who choose to exercise them, then it would be patently unconstitutional. [*Id.* at 581]

Jackson raised the question as to whether plea bargaining may unconstitutionally chill or penalize a defendant's exercise of the right to trial by jury, insofar as a prosecutor's plea offer may discourage the accused from asserting that right (because of the real or perceived likelihood of a more severe sentence if the defendant rejects the plea offer and goes to trial). Such a claim was presented squarely to the Supreme Court two years later.

BRADY v. UNITED STATES
397 U.S. 742 (1970)

Mr. Justice White delivered the opinion of the Court.

In 1959, petitioner was charged with kidnaping in violation of 18 U.S.C. § 1201(a) [the statute quoted above]. Since the indictment charged that the victim of the kidnaping was not liberated unharmed, petitioner faced a maximum penalty of death if the verdict of the jury should so recommend. Petitioner, represented by competent counsel throughout, first elected to plead not guilty. Apparently because the trial judge was unwilling to try the case without a jury, petitioner made no serious attempt to reduce the possibility of a death penalty by waiving a jury trial. Upon learning that his codefendant, who had confessed to the authorities, would plead guilty and be available to testify against him, petitioner changed his plea to guilty. His plea was accepted after the trial judge twice questioned him as to the voluntariness of his plea. Petitioner was sentenced to 50 years' imprisonment, later reduced to 30.

In 1967, petitioner sought relief . . . claiming that his plea of guilty was not voluntarily given because § 1201(a) operated to coerce his plea, because his counsel exerted impermissible pressure upon him, and because his plea was induced by representations with respect to reduction of sentence and clemency . . . . [The District Court and Court of Appeals denied relief.] . . .

The Court of Appeals for the Tenth Circuit affirmed. We granted certiorari to consider the claim that the Court of Appeals was in error in not reaching a contrary result on the authority of this Court's decision in *United States v. Jackson*, 390 U.S. 570 (1968). We affirm.

. . . Brady contends that *Jackson* requires the invalidation of every plea of guilty entered under that section, at least when the fear of death is shown to have been a factor in the plea. Petitioner, however, has read far too much into the *Jackson* opinion.

The Court made it clear in *Jackson* that it was not holding § 1201(a) inherently coercive of guilty pleas: "the fact that the Federal Kidnaping Act tends to discourage defendants from insisting upon their innocence and demanding trial by jury hardly implies that every defendant who enters a guilty plea to a charge under the Act does so involuntarily."

. . . Plainly, it seems to us, *Jackson* ruled neither that all pleas of guilty encouraged by the fear of a possible death sentence are involuntary pleas nor that such encouraged pleas are invalid whether involuntary or not. *Jackson* prohibits the imposition of the death penalty under § 1201(a), but that decision neither fashioned a new standard for judging the validity of guilty pleas nor mandated a new application of the test theretofore fashioned by courts and since reiterated that guilty pleas are valid if both "voluntary" and "intelligent."

. . . Central to the plea and the foundation for entering judgment against the defendant is the defendant's admission in open court that he committed the acts charged in the indictment. He thus stands as a witness against himself and he is shielded by the Fifth Amendment from being compelled to do so — hence the minimum requirement that his plea be the voluntary expression of his own choice. But the plea is more than an admission of past conduct; it is the defendant's consent that judgment of conviction may be entered without a trial — a waiver of his right to trial before a jury or a judge. Waivers of constitutional rights not only must be voluntary but must be knowing, intelligent acts done with sufficient awareness of the relevant circumstances and likely consequences. On neither score was Brady's plea of guilty invalid.

. . . Petitioner, advised by competent counsel, tendered his plea after his codefendant, who had already given a confession, determined to plead guilty and became available to testify against petitioner. It was this development that the District Court found to have triggered Brady's guilty plea.

. . . The record before us also supports the conclusion that Brady's plea was intelligently made. He was advised by competent counsel, he was made aware of the nature of the charge against him, and there was nothing to indicate that he was incompetent or otherwise not in control of his mental faculties; once his confederate had pleaded guilty and became available to testify, he chose to plead guilty, perhaps to ensure that he would face no more than life imprisonment or a term of years. Brady was aware of precisely what he was doing when he admitted that he had kidnaped the victim and had not released her unharmed.

It is true that Brady's counsel advised him that § 1201(a) empowered the jury to impose the death penalty and that nine years later in *United States v. Jackson*, the Court held that the jury had no such power as long as the judge could impose only a lesser penalty if trial was to the court or there was a plea of guilty. But these facts do not require us to set aside Brady's conviction.

Often the decision to plead guilty is heavily influenced by the defendant's appraisal of the prosecution's case against him and by the apparent likelihood of securing leniency should a guilty plea be offered and accepted. Considerations like these frequently present imponderable questions for which there are no certain answers; judgments may be made that in the light of later events seem improvident, although they were perfectly sensible at the time. The rule that a plea must be intelligently made to be valid does not require that a plea be vulnerable to later attack if the defendant did not correctly assess every relevant factor entering into his decision. A defendant is not entitled to withdraw his plea merely because he discovers long after the plea has been accepted that his calculus misapprehended the quality of the State's case or the likely penalties attached to alternative courses of action . . . . A plea of guilty triggered by the expectations of a competently counseled defendant that the State will have a strong case against him is not subject to later attack because the defendant's lawyer correctly advised him with respect to the then existing law as to possible penalties but later pronouncements of the courts, as in this case, hold that the maximum penalty for the crime in question was less than was reasonably assumed at the time the plea was entered.

. . . Although Brady's plea of guilty may well have been motivated in part by a desire to avoid a possible death penalty, we are convinced that his plea was voluntarily and intelligently made and we have no reason to doubt that his solemn admission of guilt was truthful. Affirmed.

NOTES

1. *Brady's contemporary: Parker.* In *Parker v. North Carolina*, 397 U.S. 790 (1970), decided the same day as *Brady*, the United States Supreme Court followed the *Brady* analysis. Parker pled guilty to burglary in the first degree. Under the then-applicable North Carolina statute, the maximum penalty available in the event of a plea of guilty was life imprisonment, whereas the death penalty could have been imposed had he elected to contest the criminal charge. Parker also claimed that his guilty plea was invalid because it was the product of a coerced confession he had given to the police shortly after his arrest. This claim was rejected because "even if Parker's counsel was wrong in his assessment of Parker's confession, it does not follow that his error was sufficient to render the plea unintelligent and entitle Parker to disavow his admission in open court that he committed the offense with which he was charged." After assessing the facts related to Parker's confession and guilty plea, the Court concluded that the lawyer's advice to Parker "was well within the range of competence required of attorneys representing defendants in criminal cases."

Justice Brennan, joined by Justices Douglas and Marshall, dissented in *Parker*. In their opinion, Parker would be entitled to relief "if he can demonstrate that the unconstitutional capital punishment scheme was a significant factor in his decision to plead guilty." The same Justices concurred in *Brady*, however, because of the findings made below that his decision to plead guilty rested upon bases other than the Kidnapping Act.

2. *Unconstitutional conditions.* The concept of "unconstitutional conditions" has been described as a ban on the government's power to condition the grant of a benefit upon the recipient's willingness to forego the exercise of a constitutional right. Do the *Jackson* and *Brady* decisions address the unconstitutional conditions doctrine? It has been suggested that the plea bargaining process violates the unconstitutional conditions doctrine, but this argument has not found judicial acceptance. For a thoughtful analysis of this issue, see Thomas R. McCoy & Michael J. Mirra, *Plea Bargaining as Due Process in Determining Guilt*, 32 STAN. L. REV. 887 (1980).

[3] Plea Bargaining and Competent Counsel

In *Brady*, the United States Supreme Court emphasized that the defense attorney in that case had met the standard of competent counsel. The question of an attorney's effective representation in the context of plea bargaining also was addressed in *McMann v. Richardson*, 397 U.S. 759 (1970). There, the defendant challenged his guilty plea in a collateral proceeding by asserting that the plea had been motivated by a prior coerced confession. Finding that the plea of guilty was not open to such attack, the

United States Supreme Court emphasized that the plea had been tendered after an assessment of the case by the defendant's attorney. Therefore, the question whether the plea was subject to attack depends upon " . . . whether that advice was within the range of competence demanded of attorneys in criminal cases." Whether the petitioner's attorney met that standard, however, was left "to the good sense and discretion of the trial courts with the admonition . . . that judges should strive to maintain proper standards of performance by attorneys."

Not until 1984, in *Strickland v. Washington*, 466 U.S. 668 (1984), did the United States Supreme Court delineate a constitutional standard for judging claims of attorney incompetency. The following year, in the excerpted case below, the Court evaluated the application of *Strickland* to the guilty plea process.

HILL v. LOCKHART
474 U.S. 52 (1985)

Justice Rehnquist delivered the opinion of the Court.

Petitioner William Lloyd Hill pleaded guilty in the Arkansas trial court to charges of first-degree murder and theft of property. More than two years later he sought federal habeas relief on the ground that his court-appointed attorney had failed to advise him that, as a second offender, he was required to serve one-half of his sentence before becoming eligible for parole. [The District Court and Court of Appeals denied relief.]

. . . . We affirm the judgment of the Court of Appeals for the Eighth Circuit because we conclude that petitioner failed to allege the kind of prejudice from the allegedly incompetent advice of counsel that would have entitled him to a hearing.

. . . Our concern in *McMann v. Richardson*, 397 U.S. 759 (1970), with the quality of counsel's performance in advising a defendant whether to plead guilty stemmed from the more general principle that all "defendants facing felony charges are entitled to the effective assistance of competent counsel." Two Terms ago, in *Strickland v. Washington*, 466 U.S. 668 (1984), we adopted a two-part standard for evaluating claims of ineffective assistance of counsel. There, citing *McMann*, we reiterated that "[w]hen a convicted defendant complains of the ineffectiveness of counsel's assistance, the defendant must show that counsel's representation fell below an objective standard of reasonableness." We also held, however, that "[t]he defendant must show that there is a reasonable probability that, but for counsel's unprofessional errors, the result of the proceeding would have been different." This additional "prejudice" requirement was based on our conclusion that "[a]n error by counsel, even if professionally unreasonable, does not warrant setting aside the judgment of a criminal proceeding if the error had no effect on the judgment."

Although our decision in *Strickland v. Washington* dealt with a claim of ineffective assistance of counsel in a capital sentencing proceeding, and was premised in part on the similarity between such a proceeding and the usual criminal trial, the same two-part standard seems to us applicable to ineffective-assistance claims arising out of the plea process. Certainly our justifications for imposing the "prejudice" requirement in *Strickland v. Washington* are also relevant in the context of guilty pleas:

> The government is not responsible for, and hence not able to prevent, attorney errors that will result in reversal of a conviction or sentence. Attorney errors come in an infinite variety and are as likely to be utterly harmless in a particular case as they are to be prejudicial. They cannot be classified according to likelihood of causing prejudice. Nor can they be defined with sufficient precision to inform defense attorneys correctly just what conduct to avoid. Representation is an art, and an act or omission that is unprofessional in one case may be sound or even brilliant in another. Even if a defendant shows that particular errors of counsel were unreasonable, therefore, the defendant must show that they actually had an adverse effect on the defense.

In addition, we believe that requiring a showing of "prejudice" from defendants who seek to challenge the validity of their guilty pleas on the ground of ineffective assistance of counsel will serve the fundamental interest in the finality of guilty pleas we identified in *United States v. Timmreck*, 441 U.S. 780 (1979):

> Every inroad on the concept of finality undermines confidence in the integrity of our procedures; and, by increasing the volume of judicial work, inevitably delays and impairs the orderly administration of justice. The impact is greatest when new grounds for setting aside guilty pleas are approved because the vast majority of criminal convictions result from such pleas. Moreover, the concern that unfair procedures may have resulted in the conviction of an innocent defendant is only rarely raised by a petition to set aside a guilty plea.

We hold, therefore, that the two-part *Strickland v. Washington* test applies to challenges to guilty pleas based on ineffective assistance of counsel. In the context of guilty pleas, the first half of the *Strickland v. Washington* test is nothing more than a restatement of the standard of attorney competence already set forth in *Tollett v. Henderson* 411 U.S. 258 (1973), and *McMann v. Richardson*. The second, or "prejudice," requirement, on the other hand, focuses on whether counsel's constitutionally ineffective performance affected the outcome of the plea process. In other words, in order to satisfy the "prejudice" requirement, the defendant must show that there is a reasonable probability that, but for counsel's errors, he would not have pleaded guilty and would have insisted on going to trial.

In many guilty plea cases, the "prejudice" inquiry will closely resemble the inquiry engaged in by courts reviewing ineffective-assistance challenges to convictions obtained through a trial. For example, where the alleged error of counsel is a failure to investigate or discover potentially exculpatory evidence, the determination whether the error "prejudiced" the defendant by causing him to plead guilty rather than go to trial will depend on the likelihood that discovery of the evidence would have led counsel to change his recommendation as to the plea. This assessment, in turn, will depend in large part on a prediction whether the evidence likely would have changed the outcome of a trial.

. . . In the present case the claimed error of counsel is erroneous advice as to eligibility for parole under the sentence agreed to in the plea bargain. We find it unnecessary to determine whether there may be circumstances under which erroneous advice by counsel as to parole eligibility may be deemed constitutionally ineffective assistance of counsel, because in the present case we conclude that petitioner's allegations are insufficient to satisfy the *Strickland v. Washington* requirement of "prejudice." Petitioner did not allege in his habeas petition that, had counsel correctly informed him about his parole eligibility date, he would have pleaded not guilty and insisted on going to trial. He alleged no special circumstances that might support the conclusion that he placed particular emphasis on his parole eligibility in deciding whether or not to plead guilty. Indeed, petitioner's mistaken belief that he would become eligible for parole after serving one-third of his sentence would seem to have affected not only his calculation of the time he likely would serve if sentenced pursuant to the proposed plea agreement, but also his calculation of the time he likely would serve if he went to trial and were convicted.

Because petitioner in this case failed to allege the kind of "prejudice" necessary to satisfy the second half of the *Strickland v. Washington* test, the District Court did not err in declining to hold a hearing on petitioner's ineffective assistance of counsel claim. The judgment of the Court of Appeals is therefore affirmed.

[The concurring opinion of JUSTICE WHITE, joined by JUSTICE STEVENS, is omitted.]

NOTES

1. *Counsel's questionable recommendations.* Most cases involving competency of counsel in the plea bargaining context concern attorneys who recommended acceptance of a plea bargain in the face of facts indicating either (1) the bargain was not especially favorable to the accused or (2) the case should have proceeded to trial on the merits. How would (or should) a reviewing court ascertain whether defense counsel has rendered competent assistance under the *Lockhart* standard?

2. *Post-trial plea issues.* In some cases, the question of effectiveness of counsel arises after the defendant has been convicted at trial. Defendants may argue that the defense attorney incompetently (1) refused to enter into plea negotiations with the prosecutor or (2) incompetently recommended rejection of a tendered plea agreement.

Assume, for example, that the defendant is charged with the crime of forcible rape, carrying with it a maximum penalty of 30 years incarceration. The prosecution offers to accept a plea of guilty to the crime of sexual battery, coupled with the prosecutor's agreement to recommend a sentence of no more than five years imprisonment. The defense attorney urges the defendant to reject the agreement, boasting that "you'll be acquitted at trial." What factors should be considered in determining whether the attorney has rendered reasonably effective assistance? Assume that it is determined that the lawyer in this hypothetical violated the *Lockhart* standard. What would be the appropriate remedy?

3. *Types of ineffective assistance claims.* One commentator has noted that ineffective assistance of counsel claims in the plea bargaining context can be categorized as follows: (1) the attorney failed to inform the defendant of the plea offer altogether; (2) the attorney offered no advice regarding the wisdom of accepting or rejecting the plea; (3) inaccurate information was provided by the lawyer; or (4) the attorney coerced the defendant into either accepting or rejecting a plea offer. This commentator urges attorneys to adopt a client-centered counseling strategy, whereby they are obligated to listen to their clients and insure that the clients assume an active and primary role in making decisions about their cases. See Steven Zeidman, *To Plead or Not to Plead: Effective Assistance and Client-Centered Counseling*, 39 B.C.L. REV. 841 (1998). Courts tend, however, to look very skeptically at well worn after-the-fact ineffective assistance claims by remorseful defendants that "my lawyer made me do it."

4. *Lawyer's obligation to advise on plea.* In *Purdy v. United States*, 208 F.3d 41 (2d Cir. 2000), the court held that there is no *per se* rule that a lawyer *must* advise the client whether or not to plead guilty. In so holding, the court recognized that defense counsel sometimes faces a difficult choice as to how to best advise a client in order to avoid, on the one hand, failing to give advice, and on the other, coercing the client's plea. When counsel is rendering advice in this critical area, he or she may take into account "the defendant's chances of prevailing at trial, the likely disparity in sentencing after a full trial as compared to a guilty plea, whether the defendant has maintained his innocence, and the defendant's comprehension of the various factors that will inform his plea decision." *Id.* at 45.

5. *Incomplete advice.* Assume that the defense attorney informs the defendant of the direct consequences of the guilty plea (i.e., period of incarceration and monetary fine), but fails to explain collateral consequences of the plea, such as suspension of a driver's license, ineligibility for educational aid or loss of the right to vote. Could this constitute ineffective assistance of counsel? Notwithstanding American Bar Association Standards requiring defense counsel to advise the accused of such matters prior to the entry of a plea, virtually all jurisdictions hold that the lawyer has not rendered ineffective assistance. *See* Gabriel J. Chin and Richard W. Holmes, Jr., *Effective Assistance of Counsel and the Consequences of Guilty Pleas*, 87 CORNELL L. REV. 697, 742 (2002)

(asserting that because such a result is inconsistent with the *Strickland v. Washington* framework, the "collateral consequences rule" should be abandoned).

6. *Advice concerning appeal.* As discussed in Chapter 18, defense attorneys are strongly advised to consult with the defendant after conviction regarding the possibility of pursuing an appeal. If counsel fails to follow the defendant's instructions with respect to an appeal by failing to file a notice of appeal, then counsel performs in a professionally unreasonable manner, as the Supreme Court held in *Roe v. Flores-Ortega*, 528 U.S. 470 (2000) (applying *Strickland v. Washington* to such a claim). Must a defense attorney consult with his or her client about an appeal, as a constitutional matter, in *every* case? Not according to the Court in *Flores-Ortega*. That duty exists only when counsel has reason to think that his or her client has reasonably demonstrated an interest in appealing or that a rational defendant would want to appeal. The court noted, however, that it would be "highly relevant" to that inquiry as to whether the conviction followed trial or a guilty plea:

> [This is important, although not determinative,] both because a guilty plea reduces the scope of potentially appealable issues and because such a plea may indicate that the defendant seeks an end to judicial proceedings. Even in cases when the defendant pleads guilty, the court must consider such factors as whether the defendant received the sentence bargained for as a part of the plea and whether the plea expressly reserved or waived some or all appeal rights. [*Id.* at 1036]

Justice Ginsburg, who concurred in part and dissented in part, noted that after a defendant pleads guilty or is convicted, the Sixth Amendment "hardly ever" permits defense counsel to walk away, leaving the defendant uncounseled about his or her appeal rights.

[4]   Plea Bargaining and Vindictiveness

Plea bargaining involves a give-and-take process among participants who often have unequal bargaining power. One of the advantages the prosecution has is its ability to control the charges against the defendant. Ordinarily, the defendant knows the charges before the plea bargaining process begins. But sometimes the prosecution has not sought an indictment for all *possible* charges. In order to secure an advantage during plea negotiations, can the prosecution threaten to bring new charges against the defendant or others if the defendant does not accept a certain deal? If the defendant yields to pressure and accepts the deal rather than face additional charges, can he or she later invalidate the plea because it was coerced and therefore involuntary?

BORDENKIRCHER v. HAYES
434 U.S. 357 (1978)

Mr. Justice Stewart delivered the opinion of the Court.

The question in this case is whether the Due Process Clause of the Fourteenth Amendment is violated when a state prosecutor carries out a threat made during plea negotiations to reindict the accused on more serious charges if he does not plead guilty to the offense with which he was originally charged.

The respondent was indicted by a grand jury on a charge of uttering a forged instrument in the amount of $88.30, an offense then punishable by a term of 2 to 10 years in prison. After arraignment, Hayes, his retained counsel, and the Commonwealth's Attorney met in the presence of the Clerk of the Court to discuss a possible plea agreement. During these conferences the prosecutor offered to recommend a sentence of five years in prison if Hayes would plead guilty to the indictment. He also said that if Hayes did not plead guilty and "save the court the inconvenience and necessity of a trial," he would return to the grand jury to seek an indictment under the Kentucky Habitual Criminal Act, which would subject Hayes to a mandatory sentence of life imprisonment by reason of his two prior felony convictions.

Hayes chose not to plead guilty, and the prosecutor did obtain an indictment charging him under the Habitual Criminal Act. It is not disputed that the recidivist charge was fully justified by the evidence, that the prosecutor was in possession of this evidence at the time of the original indictment, and that Hayes' refusal to plead guilty to the original charge was what led to his indictment under the habitual criminal statute.

[A jury found Hayes guilty of uttering a forged instrument and of having two prior felonies, resulting in a life sentence as an habitual criminal. After an unsuccessful appeal, Hayes filed for federal habeas corpus. The District Court denied his petition, but the Sixth Circuit Court of Appeals reversed the conviction, holding that the prosecutor violated *Blackledge v. Perry*, 417 U.S. 21 (1974), by engaging in the vindictive exercise of prosecutorial discretion.]

It may be helpful to clarify at the outset the nature of the issue in this case. While the prosecutor did not actually obtain the recidivist indictment until after the plea conferences had ended, his intention to do so was clearly expressed at the outset of the plea negotiations. Hayes was thus fully informed of the true terms of the offer when he made his decision to plead not guilty. This is not a situation, therefore, where the prosecutor without notice brought an additional and more serious charge after plea negotiations relating only to the original indictment had ended with the defendant's insistence on pleading not guilty. As a practical matter, in short, this case would be no different if the grand jury had indicted Hayes as a recidivist from the outset, and the prosecutor had offered to drop that charge as part of the plea bargain.

The Court of Appeals nonetheless drew a distinction between "concessions relating to prosecution under an existing indictment," and threats to bring more severe charges not contained in the original indictment — a line it thought necessary in order to establish a prophylactic rule to guard against the evil of prosecutorial vindictiveness. Quite apart from this chronological distinction, however, the Court of Appeals found that the prosecutor had acted vindictively in the present case since he had conceded that the indictment was influenced by his desire to induce a guilty plea. The ultimate conclusion of the Court of Appeals thus seems to have been that a prosecutor acts vindictively and in violation of due process of law whenever his charging decision is influenced by what he hopes to gain in the course of plea bargaining negotiations.

We have recently had occasion to observe: "[W]hatever might be the situation in an ideal world, the fact is that the guilty plea and the often concomitant plea bargain are important components of this country's criminal justice system. Properly administered, they can benefit all concerned." *Blackledge v. Allison*, 431 U.S. 63 (1977).

. . . [In *North Carolina v. Pearce*, 395 U.S. 711 (1969)[limiting sentence that could be imposed in a second trial after defendant successfully appealed a conviction in the first trial] and *Blackledge v. Perry* [limiting charges that can be filed after a defendant exercises the right to seek a trial *de novo* in a higher court] the Court was dealing with the State's unilateral imposition of a penalty upon a defendant who had chosen to exercise a legal right to attack his original conviction — a situation "very different from the give-and-take negotiation common in plea bargaining between the prosecution and defense, which arguably possess relatively equal bargaining power." The Court has emphasized that the due process violation in cases such as *Pearce* and *Perry* lay not in the possibility that a defendant might be deterred from the exercise of a legal right but rather in the danger that the State might be retaliating against the accused for lawfully attacking his conviction.

To punish a person because he has done what the law plainly allows him to do is a due process violation of the most basic sort, and for an agent of the State to pursue a course of action whose objective is to penalize a person's reliance on his legal rights is "patently unconstitutional." But in the "give-and-take" of plea bargaining, there is no such element of punishment or retaliation so long as the accused is free to accept or reject the prosecution's offer.

Plea bargaining flows from "the mutuality of advantage" to defendants and prosecutors, each with his own reasons for wanting to avoid trial. Defendants advised by competent counsel and protected by other procedural safeguards are presumptively capable of intelligent choice in response to prosecutorial persuasion, and unlikely to be driven to false self-condemnation. Indeed, acceptance of the basic legitimacy of plea bargaining necessarily implies rejection of any notion that a guilty plea is involuntary in a constitutional sense simply because it is the end result of the bargaining process. By hypothesis, the plea may have been induced by promises of a recommendation of a lenient sentence or a reduction of charges, and thus by fear of the possibility of a greater penalty upon conviction after a trial.

. . . It is not disputed here that Hayes was properly chargeable under the recidivist statute, since he had in fact been convicted of two previous felonies. In our system, so long as the prosecutor has probable cause to believe that the accused committed an offense defined by statute, the decision whether or not to prosecute, and what charge to file or bring before a grand jury, generally rests entirely in his discretion. Within the limits set by the legislature's constitutionally valid definition of chargeable offenses, "the conscious exercise of some selectivity in enforcement is not in itself a federal constitutional violation" so long as "the selection was [not] deliberately based upon an unjustifiable standard such as race, religion, or other arbitrary classification."

. . . There is no doubt that the breadth of discretion that our country's legal system vests in prosecuting attorneys carries with it the potential for both individual and institutional abuse. And broad though that discretion may be, there are undoubtedly constitutional limits upon its exercise. We hold only that the course of conduct engaged in by the prosecutor in this case, which no more than openly presented the defendant with the unpleasant alternatives of forgoing trial or facing charges on which he was plainly subject to prosecution, did not violate the Due Process Clause of the Fourteenth Amendment. [Reversed]

MR. JUSTICE BLACKMUN, with whom MR. JUSTICE BRENNAN and MR. JUSTICE MARSHALL join, dissenting.

I feel that the Court, although purporting to rule narrowly . . . is departing from, or at least restricting, the principles established in [*Pearce* and *Perry*]. If those decisions are sound and if those principles are salutary, as I must assume they are, they require, in my view, an affirmance, not a reversal, of the judgment of the Court of Appeals in the present case.

. . . The Court now says . . . that this concern with vindictiveness is of no import in the present case, despite the difference between five years in prison and a life sentence, because we are here concerned with plea bargaining where there is give-and-take negotiation, and where, it is said, "there is no such element of punishment or retaliation so long as the accused is free to accept or reject the prosecution's offer." Yet in this case vindictiveness is present to the same extent as it was thought to be in *Pearce* and in *Perry*; the prosecutor here admitted that the sole reason for the new indictment was to discourage the respondent from exercising his right to a trial. Even had such an admission not been made, when plea negotiations, conducted in the face of the less serious charge under the first indictment, fail, charging by a second indictment a more serious crime for the same conduct creates "a strong inference" of vindictiveness . . . . I therefore do not understand why, as in *Pearce*, due process does not require that the prosecution justify its action on some basis other than discouraging respondent from the exercise of his right to a trial.

It might be argued that it really makes little difference how this case, now that it is here, is decided. The Court's holding gives plea bargaining full sway despite vindictiveness. A contrary result, however, merely would prompt the aggressive prosecutor to bring the greater charge initially in every case, and only thereafter to bargain. The consequences to the accused would still be adverse, for then he would bargain against a greater charge, face the likelihood of increased bail, and run the risk that the court would be less inclined to accept a bargained plea. Nonetheless, it is far preferable to hold the prosecution to the charge it was originally content to bring and to justify in the eyes of its public.

Even if overcharging is to be sanctioned, there are strong reasons of fairness why the charges should be presented at the beginning of the bargaining process, rather than as a filliped threat at the end. First, it means that a prosecutor is required to reach a charging decision without any knowledge of the particular defendant's willingness to plead guilty; hence the defendant who truly believes himself to be innocent, and wishes for that reason to go to trial, is not likely to be subject to quite such a devastating gamble since the prosecutor has fixed the incentives for the average case.

Second, it is healthful to keep charging practices visible to the general public, so that political bodies can judge whether the policy being followed is a fair one. Visibility is enhanced if the prosecutor is required to lay his cards on the table with an indictment of public record at the beginning of the bargaining process, rather than making use of unrecorded verbal warnings of more serious indictments yet to come.

Finally, I would question whether it is fair to pressure defendants to plead guilty by threat of reindictment on an enhanced charge for the same conduct when the defendant has no way of knowing whether the prosecutor would indeed be entitled to bring him to trial on the enhanced charge. Here, though there is no dispute that respondent met the then-current definition of a habitual offender under Kentucky law, it is conceivable that a properly instructed Kentucky grand jury . . . in response to the same considerations that ultimately moved the Kentucky Legislature to amend the habitual offender statute, would have refused to subject respondent to such an onerous penalty for his forgery charge. There is no indication in the record that, once the new indictment was obtained, respondent was given another chance to plead guilty to the forged check charge in exchange for a five-year sentence.

Mr. Justice Powell, dissenting.

Although I agree with much of the Court's opinion, I am not satisfied that the result in this case is just or that the conduct of the plea bargaining met the requirements of due process.

. . . There may be situations in which a prosecutor would be fully justified in seeking a fresh indictment for a more serious offense. The most plausible justification might be that it would have been reasonable and in the public interest initially to have charged the defendant with the greater offense. In most cases a court could not know why the harsher indictment was sought, and an inquiry into the prosecutor's motive would neither be indicated nor likely to be fruitful. In those cases, I would agree with the majority that the situation would not differ materially from one in which the higher charge was brought at the outset.

But this is not such a case. Here, any inquiry into the prosecutor's purpose is made unnecessary by his candid acknowledgment that he threatened to procure and in fact procured the habitual criminal indictment because of respondent's insistence on exercising his constitutional rights . . . .

The plea-bargaining process, as recognized by this Court, is essential to the functioning of the criminal-justice system. It normally affords genuine benefits to defendants as well as to society. And if the system is to work effectively, prosecutors must be accorded the widest discretion, within constitutional limits, in conducting bargaining. This is especially true when a defendant is represented by counsel and presumably is fully advised of his rights. Only in the most exceptional case should a court conclude that the scales of the bargaining are so unevenly balanced as to arouse suspicion. In this case, the prosecutor's actions denied respondent due process because their admitted purpose was to discourage and then to penalize with unique severity his exercise of constitutional rights. Implementation of a strategy calculated solely to deter the exercise of constitutional rights is not a constitutionally permissible exercise of discretion. I would affirm the opinion of the Court of Appeals on the facts of this case.

NOTES

1. *Impact of Bordenkircher.* The United States Supreme Court in *Bordenkircher* found no due process violation even though there was clear evidence that the prosecutor sought the new indictment for the purpose of dissuading the defendant from exercising his right to a trial. Are you satisfied with the treatment of this issue by the majority? If you are persuaded by the dissenters that relief should have been provided, would such a holding exacerbate the "overcharging" phenomenon discussed earlier? Would such a holding also have the effect of influencing prosecutors to falsely state reasons for plea agreement concessions?

2. *Package deal.* In a separate footnote, the *Bordenkircher* majority noted that tying an individual defendant's guilty plea together with other individuals' pleas "might pose a greater danger of inducing a false guilty plea by skewing the assessment of the risks a defendant must consider." 434 U.S. at 364 n. 8. This concern arises in a "package deal" plea agreement. Under these agreements, as one court explained:

> [S]everal confederates plead together and the government gives them a volume discount — a better deal than each could have gotten separately. Consistent with the package nature of the agreement, defendants' fates are often bound together: If one defendant backs out, the deal's off for everybody. This may well place additional pressure on each of the participants to go along with the deal despite misgivings they might have.

United States v. Caro, 997 F.2d 657, 658–59 (9th Cir. 1993).

Does this mean that a package deal plea agreement is *per se* impermissible? In *Caro*, the Court found one such agreement invalid because the trial judge failed to conduct a "careful examination" into whether the confederates had pressured Caro into accepting the plea agreement. Furthermore, the court held that since the real issue was one of voluntariness, the error could not be found harmless.

The Minnesota Supreme Court announced special rules for acceptance and withdrawal of package deal (or, in its words, "wired") plea agreements. The state must inform the trial judge of the details of such agreements, and the court must conduct a further inquiry (focusing upon such factors as (1) the degree to which the defendant was influenced to plead by the state's offer of leniency to a third party, and (2) the strength of the factual basis for the plea) to determine the plea's voluntariness. *Minnesota v. Danh*, 516 N.W. 2d 539 (Minn. 1994). *See also People v. Fiumefreddo*, 626 N.Y.2d 536, 626 N.E.2d 646 (Ct. App. 1993) (third party's benefit from plea bargain is one factor in assessing whether plea was voluntary; special procedures unnecessary).

3. *Impermissible discrimination.* Toward the end of the majority opinion, the *Bordenkircher* Court alludes to the fact that selectivity in enforcement of the criminal law is constitutionally permissible so long as the selection is not "based upon an unjustifiable standard such as race, religion, or other arbitrary classification." It is widely recognized that prosecutors possess broad discretion regarding whether or not to negotiate with an individual defendant with respect to a plea agreement. Additionally, the terms of such agreements lie within that same discretion. This means that in some instances, similarly situated defendants who have committed very similar crimes are dealt with in dissimilar ways by prosecutors. In such a situation, it is possible that the defendant will raise the claim that the disparity in treatment was based upon race, sex, national origin, religion, or some other impermissible classification.

Rarely are discrimination claims presented in the context of plea bargaining, and it is extremely difficult for such a claim to succeed. For example, in *United States v. Moody*, 778 F.2d 1380 (9th Cir. 1985), several defendants were charged with conspiracy to import a controlled substance. While one defendant was permitted to plead, two others were not allowed to do so. They asserted that this was impermissibly discriminatory, offering to show that the other defendant, who was given a favorable plea bargain, was actually more culpable than the two who were not. Recognizing that a defendant has no constitutional right to a plea bargain, the appellate court held that there was no connection between the defendants' race or any other impermissible factor and the prosecutor's refusal to plea bargain. In order to prevail, a defendant must show that he or she was singled out because of race or some other arbitrary classification, and that such treatment was intentional. The defendants' assertions in *Moody* were too vague to establish a prima facie case of discrimination.

By contrast, impermissible discrimination in plea bargaining was found in *United States v. Redondo-Lemos*, 955 F.2d 1296 (9th Cir. 1992). Defendant, charged with possession with intent to distribute marijuana, was offered a plea agreement in which the prosecutor would recommend the minimum statutory imprisonment of five years. The United States District Court judge, finding that the United States Attorney's Office was treating this male defendant differently from other similarly situated female defendants (who were receiving sentences of approximately eighteen months), held that the equal protection guarantee required that the defendant's sentence be reduced to eighteen months. The Ninth Circuit Court of Appeals reversed and remanded, requiring that further hearings be held to allow the prosecutor to present non-gender based reasons for the perceived discriminatory treatment. After such a hearing, the district court found that a prima facie case of discrimination had been established and that the prosecution had been unable to rebut this showing. *United States v. Redondo-Lemos*, 817 F. Supp. 812 (D. Ariz. 1993). Ultimately, however, the district court's decision was reversed because of the appellate court's determination that the government had "amply demonstrated that it acted on the basis of . . . non-discriminatory criteria." *United States v. Redondo-Lemos*, 27 F.3d 439 (9th Cir. 1994).

Procedurally, the defendant should raise the claim of discrimination prior to trial. Also, evidence in support of the challenge must be as precise and specific as possible. *See e.g., United States v. Bernal-Rojas*, 933 F.2d 97 (1st Cir. 1991) (the claim of impermissible discrimination was vague and failed to establish a prima facie case; also, challenge was not raised until the sentencing phase of the trial).

4. *Statutory benefits for entering plea.* In *Corbitt v. New Jersey*, 439 U.S. 212 (1978), the defendant was tried and convicted of murder in the first degree and received a mandatory life prison sentence. If he had entered a nolo plea to the same charge, however, his sentence could have been either life imprisonment or a term of not more than thirty years. The defendant claimed that this sentencing scheme constituted an unconstitutional burden upon his right to trial by jury. The United States Supreme Court rejected that contention, holding that it was permissible for New Jersey to encourage a guilty plea by offering a benefit in return for the plea. The Court also found "no difference of constitutional significance between *Bordenkircher* and this case":

> There, as here, the defendant went to trial on an indictment that included a count carrying a mandatory life term under the applicable state statutes. There, as here, the defendant could have sought to counter the mandatory penalty by tendering a plea. In *Bordenkircher*, as permitted by state law, the prosecutor was willing to forgo the habitual criminal count if there was a plea, in which event the mandatory sentence would have been avoided. Here, the state law empowered the judge to impose a lesser term either in connection with a plea bargain or otherwise. In both cases, the defendant gave up the possibility of leniency if he went to trial and was convicted on the count carrying the mandatory penalty. In *Bordenkircher*, the probability or certainty of leniency in return for a plea did not invalidate the mandatory penalty imposed after a jury trial. It should not do so here, where there was no assurance that a plea would be accepted if tendered, and, if it had been, no assurance that a sentence less

than life would be imposed. Those matters rested ultimately in the discretion of the judge, perhaps substantially influenced by the prosecutor and the plea-bargaining process permitted by New Jersey law. [*Id.* at 221–222]

5. *Capital cases.* Does *Bordenkircher* apply in death penalty cases? In *State v. Mann,* 959 S.W.2d 503 (Tenn. 1997), the Tennessee Supreme Court answered this question in the affirmative. There, the Court found that the defendant's constitutional rights had not been violated by the government's decision to seek the death penalty after the defendant had rejected a plea offer of life imprisonment. Following the rejection of that offer, the defendant was convicted of premeditated first degree murder, aggravated rape and aggravated burglary, and was sentenced to death. Noting that *Bordenkircher* applies even to situations in which the death penalty ultimately is imposed, the Court reasoned:

> A defendant who pleads guilty extends a substantial benefit to the criminal justice system, and in exchange, the State is entitled to extend a less harsh sentence than might otherwise be given. Likewise, if a plea offer is rejected, the State may prosecute the defendant to the fullest extent possible and seek whatever punishment is appropriate under the law.

[5] Waiver Limitations?

May the prosecutor, as a part of the plea bargain, demand that the defendant waive the right to appeal? If so, what protections remain for the defendant if the court fails to apply the proper sentence? Does the waiver bar a claim of ineffective assistance of counsel? Consider the following case.

JONES v. UNITED STATES
167 F.3d 1142 (7th Cir. 1998)

On March 3, 1995 a jury convicted Shawn Jones of conspiring to distribute cocaine and marijuana . . . . After trial and prior to sentencing, Jones entered into a cooperation agreement with the government, which contained a waiver of his rights to appeal and to file a habeas motion under 18 U.S.C. § 2255. The district court subsequently sentenced Jones to 144 months imprisonment, five years of supervised release and a mandatory special assessment of $100. Notwithstanding the waiver, Jones . . . moved under § 2255 [habeas corpus] to vacate, set aside or correct his sentence. The issue here is whether a cooperation agreement that waives the right to file a [habeas] petition under § 2255 bars a defendant from arguing that he received ineffective assistance of counsel when negotiating the agreement or that the agreement was involuntary . . . . [T]he district court denied the motion.

We have routinely held that a defendant may waive the right to a direct appeal as part of a written plea agreement. See *United States v. Wooley,* 123 F.3d 627 (7th Cir. 1997) ("the right to appeal is a statutory right, and like other rights — even constitutional rights — which a defendant may waive, it can be waived in a plea agreement"). The validity of an appeal waiver rests on whether it is "express and unambiguous" and whether . . . it was made "knowingly and voluntarily." [In accepting a plea agreement] the court is not required to conduct a specific dialogue with the defendant concerning the appeal waiver, so long as the record contains sufficient evidence to determine whether the defendant's acceptance of the waiver was knowing and voluntary.

We have recognized that the right to appeal survives where the agreement is involuntary, or the trial court relied on some constitutionally impermissible factor (such as race), or . . . the sentence exceeded the statutory maximum. [Other] circuits have held that a plea agreement waiver cannot bar an appeal based on the Sixth Amendment right to effective counsel.

. . . Justice dictates that a claim of ineffective assistance of counsel in connection with the negotiation of a cooperation agreement cannot be barred by the agreement itself . . . . To hold otherwise would deprive a defendant of an opportunity to assert his Sixth Amendment right to counsel where he had accepted the waiver in reliance on delinquent representation. Similarly, where a waiver is not the product of the defendant's free will — for example, where it has been procured by government coercion or intimidation — the defendant cannot be said to have knowingly and voluntarily relinquished his rights. It is intuitive that in those circumstances the waiver is ineffective against a challenge based on involuntariness.

. . . [W]e cannot approve the district court's determination that the waiver was effective and we hold that Jones was entitled to file a [habeas] petition under § 2255 challenging the cooperation agreement on the grounds of involuntariness and ineffective assistance of counsel.

[The court did, however, affirm the district court's decision to deny the petitioner's motion to vacate the sentence. The Court of Appeals found that the petitioner failed to adequately specify his claims of ineffective assistance of counsel and involuntariness.]

NOTES

1. *Appeal sentence severity.* Where the appeal relates to the severity of the sentence, rather than the integrity of the bargain, and the sentence falls within statutory guidelines, most courts hold that such a waiver is valid and enforceable. *See Watson v. United States*, 165 F.3d 486 (6th Cir. 1999) (the right to collaterally attack a sentence is statutory and may be waived as part of a plea bargaining agreement); *Davila v. United States*, 258 F.3d 448 (6th Cir. 2001) (an informed and voluntary waiver of post-conviction relief upheld); *In re Acosta*, 480 F.3d 421 (6th Cir. 2007)(appeal of the determination of degree of culpability may be waived).

2. *Public policy concerns.* The Second Circuit Court of Appeals as well as district courts in both Massachusetts and the District of Columbia have refused to enforce such waivers on the ground that they are contrary to public policy. *See, United States v. Goodman*, 165 F.3d 169 (2d Cir. 1999) (refusing to enforce a broad waiver of appeal including the right to appeal from an upward departure from the applicable United States Sentencing Guidelines, which would subject the defendant to risk of sentencing error or abuse), (*but see, contra, United States v. Montano*, 472 F. 3d 1202 (10th Cir. 2007)); *United States v. Raynor*, 989 F.Supp. 43 (D.D.C. 1997)(disallowing waiver of appeal on the ground that it cannot be considered to be "informed and intelligent" because the sentence has not been imposed at the time of the waiver), (*but see, contra, United States v. Hahn*, 359 F. 3d 1315 (10th Cir. 2004)). Consider Judge Gertner's opinion in *United States v. Perez*, 46 F.Supp.2d 59 (D. Mass. 1999):

> In a guideline regime that presumes that the correct guideline sentence is a fair sentence, a sentence based on mistake is plainly unfair. Moreover, in a guideline regime that emphasizes rational pre-sentence investigations and sentencing hearings, that seeks to stem unwarranted disparities in sentence through a reasonable analysis at the trial court level and through appellate review of sentencing, the suppression of the right to appeal judicial errors is anathema.

> Despite the attraction of the idea of maximizing a defendant's power by allowing him to sell whatever he has, the market for plea bargains, like every other market, should not be so deregulated that the conditions essential to assuring basic fairness are undermined.

> . . . In finding the "syllogism" that runs from the premise that defendants can waive various constitutional rights to the conclusion that defendants can waive the statutory right to appeal a sentence overlooks both the significance of sentence appeals in the criminal justice system, and the limits on the waivability of rights. Second, I find that there is a due process problem with pressuring defendants, in a plea bargain setting, to waive their appeal rights. Third, I find

that appeal waiver clauses are inconsistent with and would systematically undermine, the Congressional intent in drafting the Sentencing Reform Act of 1984. Fourth, I find that there are contractual problems with appeal waivers in plea bargains. Fifth, I find that the government's interest in enforcing appeal waivers is not very substantial.

. . . It is [not] acceptable, I hold, for the United States Attorney's Office to make a deal with a defendant only on the condition that he waive his right to appeal errors the court may make in determining his ultimate sentence.

. . . In a regime in which almost all defendants plea guilty, rather than go to trial, it is crucial for carrying out the intent of Congress . . . that misapplications of the sentencing guidelines be appealable after a plea as well as after trial . . . . The result of a general pattern of appeals waivers would be a return to a regime in which the disparities Congress sought to eliminate would go generally unchecked.

. . . In addition, allowing appeals waivers would have a cost in terms of the development of appellate law necessary to clarify how the guidelines should be applied.

. . . There is also a more insidious systemic effect. If appeals waivers are generally accepted, then the baseline for cooperation will shift so that only a defendant who has something exceptionally valuable for the government will be able to maintain his right to appeal. Rather than seeing waiver of appeal rights as a bargaining chip, defendants will have to bargain for the ability to keep it.

. . . There is an additional problem of systemic distortion which arises from the fact that many appeal waivers . . . are asymmetrical; the defendant waives appeal rights which the government does not waive.

. . . To understand why a plea bargain with an appeal waiver clause is an unenforceable contract, one has to appreciate that defendants frequently get rewarded for making deals early on, before they know much about the government's case against them. It is not unusual for probation to come in with a pre-sentence report that brings to light facts that the parties did not consider in their plea negotiations.

3. *Rule 11's appeal waiver rule.* Rule 11 of the Federal Rules of Criminal Procedure, as recently amended, contains the following provision relating to plea waivers:

Rule 11. *Pleas*

(b)(1) *Advising and Questioning the Defendant.* Before the court accepts a plea of guilty or nolo contendere, . . . the court must address the defendant personally in open court [and] . . . inform the defendant of, and determine that the defendant understands, the following:

. . . .

(N) the terms of any plea-agreement provision waiving the right to appeal or to collaterally attack the sentence.

4. *Other waivers. Jones* and *United States v. Hahn*, 359 F. 3d 1315 (10th Cir. 2004), hold that a claim of ineffective assistance of counsel in connection with the negotiation of a cooperation agreement cannot be barred by the agreement itself. Are there other rights that can never be waived? In *United States v. Ruiz*, 536 U.S. 622 (2002), the United States Supreme Court unanimously held that it was constitutionally permissible for the government to insist as a part of a plea bargain that the defendant waive the right to receive "impeachment information relating to any informants or other witnesses [and] information supporting any affirmative defense the defendant raises if the case goes to trial." Noting that this particular agreement obligated the government to provide information establishing the defendant's factual innocence, the Court found it "difficult to distinguish, in terms of importance, (1) a defendant's ignorance of grounds for impeachment of potential witnesses . . . from (2) the varying forms of ignorance in [such cases as *Brady* (quality of state's case), *McMann* (admissibility of a confession), *Broce* (a potential defense), or *Tollett* (a potential constitutional infirmity in the grand jury proceeding)]." The Court also observed that a contrary rule could "significantly" interfere with the plea bargaining process itself.

F. PROCEDURES

Now that plea bargaining is a visible part of the criminal justice system, statutes and rules exist in virtually all jurisdictions pertaining to the way in which guilty pleas — whether the result of bargaining or not — are to be accepted. The first procedural step in the guilty plea process is the arraignment, governed by Rule 10.

[1] Arraignment

The exact nature of an arraignment varies among the jurisdictions, but in general terms it presents the defendant with the formal charges (indictment or information for felonies), allows the defendant to plead (guilty, not guilty, or *nolo contendere* in most locales), and schedules trial (if the defendant pleads not guilty) or sentencing (if the plea is guilty or *nolo contendere*).

FEDERAL RULES OF CRIMINAL PROCEDURE

Rule 10. *Arraignment*

(a) In General. An arraignment must be conducted in open court and must consist of:

(1) ensuring that the defendant has a copy of the indictment or information;

(2) reading the indictment or information to the defendant or stating to the defendant the substance of the charge; and then

(3) asking the defendant to plead to the indictment or information.

(b) Waiving Appearance. A defendant need not be present for the arraignment if:

(1) the defendant has been charged by indictment or misdemeanor information;

(2) the defendant, in a written waiver signed by both the defendant and defense counsel, has waived appearance and has affirmed that the defendant received a copy of the indictment or information and that the plea is not guilty; and

(3) the court accepts the waiver.

(c) Video Teleconferencing. Video teleconferencing may be used to arraign a defendant if the defendant consents.

NOTES

1. *Enters no plea.* If the defendant refuses to enter a plea at the arraignment, the court will treat it as if the defendant pled "not guilty" and will schedule trial.

2. *Right to counsel.* The Sixth Amendment guarantee of counsel extends to an arraignment. *Fellows v. United States*, 540 U.S. 519 (2004). Thus, a judge who sees a defendant who is not represented by counsel at an arraignment should inquire whether the defendant wants a lawyer or is willing to waive counsel.

3. *Informing defendant of charges.* A primary function of the arraignment is to inform defendant of the charges, usually by providing the defendant or defense counsel with a copy of the indictment or information. While Rule 10 technically requires the court to *read* the indictment to the defendant or at least to summarize the "substance of the charge," ordinarily this process is waived or simply not offered if the defendant in fact has received a copy of the indictment or information.

4. *Waiver of defendant's presence.* Rule 10 specifically authorizes an indicted defendant (or one facing misdemeanor charges by a filed information) to waive personal appearance at an arraignment. The waiver must be signed by both the defendant and defense counsel. It must state that the defendant received a copy of the indictment or information and pleads not guilty. The court is not obligated to accept the waiver and can require the defendant to be physically present for the arraignment.

5. *Waiver of arraignment.* While Rule 10 specifically allows defendant to waive presence at an arraignment, it does not permit waiver of the arraignment itself.

6. *Videoconferencing.* Any arraignment may be held by videoconferencing if the defendant consents. Rule 10(c).

7. *Rule 11 applies if sentence imposed at arraignment.* If the defendant pleads not guilty, or simply refuses to enter any plea (in which case the court automatically enters a plea of not guilty on behalf of the defendant), the court will ordinarily set the case for trial. On the other hand, if the defendant pleads guilty or *nolo contendere* at the arraignment, the court may accept the plea and then either schedule a sentencing hearing in the future or impose sentence at that time. If a sentence is to be imposed, the court must follow the detailed requirements of Rule 11, printed below, which governs all federal cases and has been the model for most state provisions.

[2] Rule 11

By far the most important rule of criminal procedure is Rule 11, which governs — sometimes in great detail — the conduct of proceedings where defendant pleads guilty or *nolo* contendere. It should be studied carefully since it impacts over ninety percent of criminal defendants.

FEDERAL RULES OF CRIMINAL PROCEDURE

Rule 11. *Pleas*

(a) Entering a Plea.

    (1) *In General.* A defendant may plead not guilty, guilty, or (with the court's consent) nolo contendere.

    (2) *Conditional Plea.* With the consent of the court and the government, a defendant may enter a conditional plea of guilty or nolo contendere, reserving in writing the right to have an appellate court review an adverse determination of a specified pretrial motion. A defendant who prevails on appeal may then withdraw the plea.

    (3) *Nolo Contendere Plea.* Before accepting a plea of nolo contendere, the court must consider the parties' views and the public interest in the effective administration of justice.

    (4) *Failure to Enter a Plea.* If a defendant refuses to enter a plea or if a defendant organization fails to appear, the court must enter a plea of not guilty.

(b) Considering and Accepting a Guilty or Nolo Contendere Plea.

    (1) *Advising and Questioning the Defendant.* Before the court accepts a plea of guilty or nolo contendere, the defendant may be placed under oath, and the court must address the defendant personally in open court. During this address, the court must inform the defendant of, and determine that the defendant understands, the following:

        (A) the government's right, in a prosecution for perjury or false statement, to use against the defendant any statement that the defendant gives under oath;

(B) the right to plead not guilty, or having already so pleaded, to persist in that plea;

(C) the right to a jury trial;

(D) the right to be represented by counsel — and if necessary have the court appoint counsel — at trial and at every other stage of the proceeding;

(E) the right at trial to confront and cross-examine adverse witnesses, to be protected from compelled self-incrimination, to testify and present evidence, and to compel the attendance of witnesses;

(F) the defendant's waiver of these trial rights if the court accepts a plea of guilty or nolo contendere;

(G) the nature of each charge to which the defendant is pleading;

(H) any maximum possible penalty, including imprisonment, fine, and term of supervised release;

(I) any mandatory minimum penalty;

(J) any applicable forfeiture;

(K) the court's authority to order restitution;

(L) the court's obligation to impose a special assessment;

(M) [the court's obligation to calculate the sentencing guideline range and to consider possible departures and other sentencing factors]; and

(N) the terms of any plea-agreement provision waiving the right to appeal or to collaterally attack the sentence.

(2) *Ensuring That a Plea Is Voluntary.* Before accepting a plea of guilty or nolo contendere, the court must address the defendant personally in open court and determine that the plea is voluntary and did not result from force, threats, or promises (other than promises in a plea agreement).

(3) *Determining the Factual Basis for a Plea.* Before entering judgment on a guilty plea, the court must determine that there is a factual basis for the plea.

(c) Plea Agreement Procedure.

(1) *In General.* An attorney for the government and the defendant's attorney, or the defendant when proceeding pro se, may discuss and reach a plea agreement. The court must not participate in these discussions. If the defendant pleads guilty or nolo contendere to either a charged offense or a lesser or related offense, the plea agreement may specify that an attorney for the government will:

(A) not bring, or will move to dismiss, other charges;

(B) recommend, or agree not to oppose the defendant's request, that a particular sentence or sentencing range is appropriate or that a particular provision of the Sentencing Guidelines, or policy statement, or sentencing factor does or does not apply (such a recommendation or request does not bind the court); or

(C) agree that a specific sentence or sentencing range is the appropriate disposition of the case, or that a particular provision of the Sentencing Guidelines, or policy statement, or sentencing factor does or does not apply (such a recommendation or request binds the court once the court accepts the plea agreement).

(2) *Disclosing a Plea Agreement.* The parties must disclose the plea agreement in open court when the plea is offered, unless the court for good cause allows the parties to disclose the plea agreement in camera.

(3) *Judicial Consideration of a Plea Agreement.*

(A) To the extent the plea agreement is of the type specified in Rule 11(c)(1)(A) or (C), the court may accept the agreement, reject it, or defer a decision until the court has reviewed the pre-sentence report.

(B) To the extent the plea agreement is of the type specified in Rule 11(c)(1)(B), the court must advise the defendant that the defendant has no right to withdraw the plea if the court does not follow the recommendation or request.

(4) *Accepting a Plea Agreement.* If the court accepts the plea agreement, it must inform the defendant that to the extent the plea agreement is of the type specified in Rule 11(c)(1)(A) or (C), the agreed disposition will be included in the judgment.

(5) *Rejecting a Plea Agreement.* If the court rejects a plea agreement containing provisions of the type specified in Rule 11(c)(1)(A) or (C), the court must do the following on the record and in open court (or, for good cause, in camera):

(A) inform the parties that the court rejects the plea agreement;

(B) advise the defendant personally that the court is not required to follow the plea agreement and give the defendant an opportunity to withdraw the plea; and

(C) advise the defendant personally that if the plea is not withdrawn, the court may dispose of the case less favorably toward the defendant than the plea agreement contemplated.

(d) Withdrawing a Guilty or Nolo Contendere Plea. A defendant may withdraw a plea of guilty or nolo contendere:

(1) before the court accepts the plea, for any reason or no reason; or

(2) after the court accepts the plea, but before it imposes sentence if:

(A) the court rejects a plea agreement under Rule 11(c)(5); or

(B) the defendant can show a fair and just reason for requesting the withdrawal.

(e) Finality of a Guilty or Nolo Contendere Plea. After the court imposes sentence, the defendant may not withdraw a plea of guilty or nolo contendere, and the plea may be set aside only on direct appeal or collateral attack.

(f) Admissibility or Inadmissibility of a Plea, Plea Discussions, and Related Statements. The admissibility or inadmissibility of a plea, a plea discussion, and any related statement is governed by Federal Rule of Evidence 410.

(g) Recording the Proceedings. The proceedings during which the defendant enters a plea must be recorded by a court reporter or by a suitable recording device. If there is a guilty plea or a nolo contendere plea, the record must include the inquiries and advice to the defendant required under Rule 11(b) and (c).

(h) Harmless Error. A variance from the requirements of this rule is harmless error if it does not affect substantial rights.

[3] Requirement of a Record

In order to facilitate appellate review, Rule 11(g) requires a verbatim record of the plea proceeding. Assuming acceptance of the plea, the court must inform the defendant that disposition provided for in the plea agreement, per Rule 11(c)(4), "will be included in the judgment."

Constitutional basis for requiring a record. There is also a constitutional dimension to the requirement of a guilty plea acceptance record. Since a guilty plea serves to relinquish several fundamental constitutional rights, the guilty plea proceeding must ensure that the defendant's abandonment of those rights is voluntary and knowing. *See*

Boykin v. Alabama, 395 U.S. 238 (1969) (a plea of guilty must be voluntary and knowing). Additionally, *Boykin* held that a waiver of constitutional rights cannot be presumed "from a silent record."

Absence of record. While the *Boykin* case may be interpreted to require that all guilty pleas be invalidated in the absence of an explicit record, this is not the uniform rule. For example, in *United States v. Ferguson*, 935 F.2d 862 (7th Cir. 1991), the defendant argued that his sentence could not be enhanced because of prior convictions since at least one of those convictions was based upon a guilty plea which was not entered voluntarily and knowingly. In support of his claim, he alleged that there was no transcript of the guilty plea proceeding in the Illinois state court. Noting that the defendant had not previously challenged his plea of guilty and also interpreting *Boykin* to permit the federal court to examine "custom, practice and law applicable to Illinois guilty pleas," the federal circuit court rejected his claim. It held that, despite the lack of a record of the guilty plea proceedings, the defendant had not satisfied his burden of proving that his prior conviction was unconstitutional. Illinois law, which is presumed to have been followed, mandated that the trial court explain fully the defendant's rights before accepting a plea. Moreover, the judgment of conviction entered after each guilty plea clearly stated that the defendant had been apprised of his rights. His prior conviction based upon a recordless guilty plea therefore was valid for the purpose of federal sentence enhancement.

Burden of proof. States may place the burden of proving a defective guilty plea on the person challenging the validity of a prior conviction based on the allegedly defective guilty plea. *Parke v. Raley*, 506 U.S. 20 (1992). In the absence of a record of the guilty plea, this burden will be difficult to satisfy.

[4] Disclosing Agreement in Open Court

Rule 11(c)(2) mandates that the plea agreement must be disclosed "in open court" when the plea is offered. For "good cause," the agreement may be disclosed *in camera*. This requirement ensures that all parties and the judge understand the deal and allows the judge to decide whether to honor it.

[5] Role of Victim

Participate in plea process. In recent years, the victim's role in the plea bargaining process has expanded dramatically. Many states have statutory provisions that guarantee the victim certain rights in the plea bargaining context. Idaho's statute is a good example of the trend to enable victims to become much more active participants in the adjudication process. Idaho Code § 19-5306(1)(e) and (f) provides victims the right to "be advised of any proposed plea agreement by the prosecuting attorney prior to entering into a plea agreement in criminal or juvenile cases involving crimes of violence, sex crimes or crimes against children," and to be heard upon request at all guilty plea and sentencing hearings. Many states now allow victims to address the court through direct testimony at the time of plea or sentencing (*"victim allocution"*) or via a "victim impact statement" in a presentence report. *See* Ariz. Rev. Stat. § 13-4423(A) (1991): "On request of the victim, the victim has the right to be present and be heard at any proceeding in which a negotiated plea . . . will be presented to the court."

Recommendations. These kinds of provisions mirror the recommendations made by a number of organizations. For example, the American Bar Association recommends: "The prosecuting attorney should make every effort to remain advised of the attitudes and sentiments of the victims . . . before reaching a plea agreement." STANDARDS FOR CRIMINAL JUSTICE § 14-3.1(e) (3d ed. 1999). The 1992 Uniform Victims of Crime Act, promulgated by the National Conference of Commissioners on Uniform State Laws, recommends that all states enact legislation providing that: "To the extent practicable, the [prosecutor] shall confer with the victim before amending or dismissing a charge or agreeing to a [negotiated plea] . . . ." Commentary to this recommendation offers the following supporting rationale:

> Expanding the victim's role will . . . increase cooperation in the reporting of crimes and the prosecution of criminal offenders. Affording victims information concerning the crimes and any negotiated plea will lead to greater victim satisfaction with the criminal justice system which translates into greater cooperation of victims in the prosecution of criminal offenders.

For consideration of competing views regarding the expansion of the victim's role in the plea bargaining process, see Josephine Gittler, *Expanding the Role of the Victim in a Criminal Action: An Overview of Issues and Problems*, 11 PEPP. L. REV. 117 (1984); Sarah N. Welling, *Victim Participation in Plea Bargains*, 65 WASH. U.L.Q. 301 (1987); and Donald J. Hall, *Victims' Voices in Criminal Court: The Need for Restraint*, 28 AM. CRIM. L. REV. 233 (1991).

PROBLEM 11-1. VICTIM'S REVENGE

Alvin Wilson was indicted by a state grand jury in connection with an attack upon Sheila Claycomb. Wilson entered into a plea agreement with the prosecuting attorney. He agreed to plead guilty to assault in the second degree and the government promised to recommend the minimum sentence of five years, "while taking no stand on probation." The plea of guilty was accepted and the government recommended the minimum sentence of five years, as promised.

At the time of sentencing, Wilson moved for release on probation. Ms. Claycomb appeared at the hearing and argued against probation. She also submitted a victim's impact statement (VIS) pursuant to a statute granting the victim the right to provide a written "description of the nature and extent of harm suffered by the victim and the victim's recommendation for an appropriate sentence." Another portion of the statute mandates that the victim impact statement "shall be considered by the court prior to any decision on the sentencing or release, including probation, of the defendant." After considering the victim's statement and all other evidence, the judge sentenced Wilson to five years in prison and denied release on probation.

1. Assume that the defendant appealed the denial of the grant of probation, arguing that the "victim was bound by the government's plea bargain." As prosecutor, how would you respond to such a contention?

2. Assume that Wilson's plea agreement contained a pre-printed signature line for the "prosecuting witness" and that Ms. Claycomb signed on that line. As prosecutor, could you make a good faith assertion that "signing off on the plea bargaining" did not constitute a waiver of her right to make a victim impact statement under the state statute?

3. Assume that Wilson sought to withdraw his plea on grounds that it was not freely, voluntarily and knowingly entered. Should the victim's sentiments be considered in ruling upon such a motion? Similarly, should a trial judge consider the likely outcome of the case when determining the validity of Wilson's plea agreement? Both of those questions were addressed in *State v. Van Camp*, 569 N.W.2d 577 (Wis. 1997). The Wisconsin Supreme Court held that the trial judge's refusal to allow withdrawal of the plea because to do so "would further punish the victim" was improper. Second, the Court also held it improper for the trial judge to focus upon the eventual outcome of a trial when considering whether a defendant should be allowed to withdraw a plea.

[6] Ensuring Voluntariness of Plea

Rule 11(b)(2) requires that the court determine that a plea of guilty or nolo contendere is voluntary. The United States Supreme Court has held on numerous occasions that a guilty plea must be voluntary. *See, e.g., Brady v. United States*, 397

U.S. 742, 750 (1970) (a plea may not be produced "by actual or threatened physical harm or by mental coercion overbearing the will of the defendant"); *Godinez v. Moran*, 509 U.S. 389 (1993) (guilty plea decision must be "uncoerced"). Notice how closely Rule 11(b)(2) makes it clear that the court must also determine whether the defendant's desire to plead guilty is the result of the plea negotiation process.

Case-by-case determination. In determining the voluntariness of a plea, the trial judge must evaluate all of the surrounding circumstances on a case-by-case basis. For example, in *Manley v. United States*, 396 F.2d 699 (5th Cir. 1968), the appellate court interpreted Rule 11 to require that the trial judge determine the effect of narcotics administered to a defendant upon the voluntariness of his proffered plea. There, the trial court's finding of voluntariness was overturned. Interestingly, the appellate court noted that "generally the burden of proof is on a defendant to show that he was under the influence of a narcotic, but in the instant case that burden was shifted to the government because the Assistant United States Attorney had made an innocent misrepresentation that the defendant was not under the influence of narcotics at the time the guilty plea was proffered."

Judge's duty to probe. If there is any credible evidence that the defendant's proffered plea was not the product of free will, a more searching inquiry must be undertaken by the trial judge. For instance, in *Mack v. United States*, 635 F.2d 20 (1st Cir. 1980), the defendant was asked the standard series of questions surrounding the guilty plea, one of which was, "Is your plea entirely free and voluntary?" Mack answered, "Yes, it is." However, some time prior to that, in the context of an inquiry concerning competency to stand trial, Mack stated, "I would like to state that I am being pressured into making the plea. I am not doing it of my own free will." The First Circuit Court of Appeals concluded: "In view of Mack's earlier statement that he was pressured into making a plea, his subsequent answer should have triggered a deeper probe for the purpose of reconciling the clearly contradictory comments." *Id.* at 25.

Kinds of pressures argued to create involuntary plea. There is no shortage of reasons defendants give for seeking to overturn their plea as involuntary. The obvious ones, threats to harm the defendant physically, are rare. More common ones are threats of increased charges unless a plea is entered (not successful); threats to prosecute third parties, such as loved ones (relatives, friends, lovers) unless the defendant pleads (cases divided; sometimes unsuccessful if there is a good faith basis for believing the third party has committed a crime); and threats by the judge (successful if can be proven).

Standard of mental competence to plead. In *Godinez v. Moran*, 509 U.S. 389 (1993), the United States Supreme Court held that if the defendant is adjudged competent to stand trial, the accused is also competent to plead guilty. In so holding, the Court rejected the argument that the competency standard for pleading guilty or waiving the right to counsel should be a more demanding one than competency for standing trial. The test for both is whether the defendant has sufficient present ability to consult with defense counsel and has an understanding of the nature of the proceedings at hand.

If the judge, prosecutor, or defense counsel has a reason to question the defendant's competency, the judge should convene a hearing on the issue. The court has the authority to order the defendant to be examined by a mental health professional and both sides would be permitted to offer evidence at the competence hearing.

[7] Advice to Defendant: In General

Rule 11(b)(1) explicitly requires the judge to address the defendant personally and to inform the defendant of specific rights listed. These rights include full awareness of the nature of the charge and possible penalties, right to be represented by counsel, right to plead not guilty, right to jury trial, right to confront and cross-examine witnesses, right not to incriminate himself or herself, and consequences of statements made under oath.

By requiring that the court must personally address the defendant, Rule 11 aims to assure that the trial judge will be better able to ascertain that the plea is voluntary. Subdivisions (b)(1)(B)–(N) also assure that the defendant's waiver of rights when pleading guilty is both knowing and voluntary, in compliance with the standard articulated in *Boykin v. Alabama*, 395 U.S. 238 (1969).

Rule 11(b) requires the judge to do two things: (1) convey information specified in the Rule and (2) "determine that the defendant understands" all of the information communicated by the court. A finding that the defendant knows and understands the rights being waived provides the groundwork for one of the critically important constitutional aspects of the plea hearing: the determination that the defendant's plea of guilty is a knowing and intelligent one.

[8]   Knowing and Intelligent Plea

Because a guilty plea involves a waiver of many constitutional rights, the plea is constitutionally valid only if it is "knowing and intelligent." This means that the accused must understand both the charges and the penalties.

[a]   Understanding the Charge

[i]   Judge's Duty to Inform

Before accepting a guilty plea, the judge must determine whether the defendant understands the charges. This standard is mandated by both Rule 11(b)(1) and the United States Supreme Court:

> [A plea of guilty] cannot support a judgment of guilt unless it was voluntary in a constitutional sense. And clearly the plea could not be voluntary in the sense that it constituted an intelligent admission that [the defendant] committed the offense unless the defendant received "real notice of the true nature of the charge against him, the first and most universally recognized requirement of due process." *[Henderson v. Morgan*, 426 U.S. 637 (1976).]

In *Henderson*, the defendant pled guilty to second degree murder. At the sentencing hearing, the trial judge did not discuss the elements of that offense or the requirement of actual intent to cause death. Concluding that the defendant did not receive adequate notice of the offense to which he pled guilty, the United States Supreme Court held that "it is impossible to conclude that his plea to the unexplained charge of second degree murder was voluntary." The Court observed:

> Normally the record contains either an explanation of the charge by the trial judge, or at least a representation by defense counsel that the nature of the offense has been explained to the accused. Moreover, even without such an express representation, it may be appropriate to presume that in most cases defense counsel routinely explained the nature of the offense in sufficient detail to give the accused notice of what he is being asked to admit. This case is unique because the trial judge found as a fact that the element of intent was not explained to respondent. [*Id.* at 647]

Judge's actual performance: empirical evidence. Despite the clear language of Rule 11 (and similar state provisions) and the constitutional underpinning for it, a 1987 survey of felony-level judicial practices in six jurisdictions found that many judges simply fail to inform the defendant of the necessary matters. The average court time per felony plea was 9.9 minutes and per misdemeanor plea was 5.2 minutes. About three-quarters of the defendants were addressed individually by the judge. They were informed of their rights to the following degree: right to a jury trial (70% of defendants were informed); to confront witnesses (44%); to remain silent (38%). In more than half the cases it was noted that defense counsel had explained the rights to the defendant. The charges were explained to the defendant in almost seventy percent of the cases. In less than half the cases (48%) they were told the maximum possible sentence. The plea agreement's terms were entered in the record in 71% of the cases. The pleas were rejected in less than two percent of the cases. Interviews with defendants who had pled guilty showed that 80% said they understood what had been said about the charges and the rights they would waive. William F. McDonald, *Judicial Supervision of the Guilty Plea Process: a Study of Six Jurisdictions*, 70 JUDICATURE 203 (1987).

[ii]   How Informed Must Defendant Be?

While *Henderson* holds that a defendant must know certain information about the offense to which the guilty plea is addressed, the decision is unclear about how fully informed the defendant must be. It has been held, for example, that the mere reading of the indictment may be insufficient to inform the defendant of the charge. Similarly, simply asking the defendant if he or she understands the charge may not be enough. At least one court has suggested that the exchange between defendant and judge will vary from case to case depending upon the complexity of the charges and the relative sophistication of the defendant.

[iii]   Role of Defense Counsel

Note that *Henderson* presumes that normally defense counsel informs the defendant of specific elements of the charges. Does this mean that the defense attorney may serve as a "substitute" for the judge with respect to compliance with Rule 11(b)? Courts have split on this question. In *Horsely v. United States*, 583 F.2d 670 (3d Cir. 1978), the trial judge asked the defendant, "Have you had an opportunity to go over [the indictment] with your attorney?" The defendant responded in the affirmative. There was nothing in the record to show that the elements of the offense had been explained by the judge. Therefore, notwithstanding the defendant's response, this was held to be error under Rule 11. The defendant's sentence was vacated and the plea withdrawn so that he could be permitted to plead anew.

By contrast, in *United States v. Butcher*, 926 F.2d 811 (9th Cir. 1991), the defendant's trial attorney testified that it was his "standard procedure . . . to advise his clients of the nature and elements of the offenses with which the defendant is charged and the possible defenses." The Ninth Circuit, citing *Henderson* for the proposition that "notice of the true nature of a charge does not require a description of every element of the offense," held that it was appropriate to rely upon the attorney's representations and therefore the plea was properly accepted.

[b]   Understanding the Penalty

Rules 11(b)(1)(H)–(M) require that the defendant understand the penalties associated with the charge to which the plea is offered. The defendant must understand the mandatory minimum penalty, if any, and the maximum possible penalty, including the effect of any supervised release term. Advisory Committee Notes observe that "giving this advice tells a defendant the shortest mandatory sentence and also the longest possible sentence for the offense to which he is pleading guilty."

Rules 11(b)(1)(H)–(M) also mandate that the defendant be apprised in general that the court must consider any applicable federal sentencing guidelines, including the fact that the court may depart from them under some circumstances. This rule does not prohibit the trial judge from providing additional information about sentencing guidelines; rather, it sets forth only the minimum information that must be conveyed to the defendant by the court. The Advisory Committee Notes to Rule 11 explain:

> This requirement assures that the existence of guidelines will be known to a defendant before a plea of guilty . . . is accepted. Since it will be impracticable, if not impossible, to know which guidelines will be relevant prior to the formulation of a presentence report and resolution of disputed facts, the

amendment does not require the court to specify which guidelines will be important or which grounds for departure might prove to be significant . . . . By giving the advice, the court places the defendant and defense counsel on notice of the importance that guidelines may play in sentencing and of the possibility of a departure from those guidelines. A defendant represented by competent counsel will be in a position to enter an intelligent plea.

Collateral consequences. Although a number of indirect or collateral consequences may flow from a judgment of guilty, Rule 11(b) does not require that such information be conveyed to the defendant. It has been held, for example, that the defendant need not be told of the loss of the right to vote or the possibility of deportation upon entry of the guilty plea.

[c]   Understanding the Defendant's Rights and the Fact of Waiver

Rule 11 provides an extensive laundry list of rights that the judge is to tell the defendant are available if he or she wants a trial and that those rights are waived by a plea. These include such fundamental rights as the right to plead not guilty, to have a jury trial, to be represented by counsel, and to confront and cross-examine witnesses at that trial.

[d]   Inadmissibility of Statements Made in the Course of Plea Discussions

Statements during negotiations inadmissible. In order to encourage plea bargaining, Rule 11(f) and Federal Rule of Evidence 410 provide that statements made in the course of plea discussions between a criminal defendant and a prosecutor are inadmissible against the defendant if the defendant does not actually plead guilty or pleads guilty but then withdraws the guilty plea. Note, however, that these rules do not exclude such statements if the defendant *does plead guilty.* This means that the exclusionary rule in Rule 11(f) does not apply in most cases since the usual practice is for the defendant to enter a guilty plea after the plea negotiations.

Waiver of rule making plea discussion statements inadmissible. What if a prosecutor indicates to the defendant, represented by counsel, that plea negotiations can occur only if the defendant agrees that any statements made during the meeting could be used to impeach any contradictory testimony he or she might give at trial if the case proceeds that far? In response, the defendant and his or her attorney agree to proceed according to those terms. At the later trial, the prosecutor cross-examines the defendant about inconsistent statements made during the unsuccessful plea negotiations. In *United States v. Mezzanatto*, 513 U.S. 196 (1995), the United States Supreme Court held, under those facts, that absent some affirmative indication that the agreement was entered into unknowingly or involuntarily, "an agreement to waive the exclusionary provisions of the plea-statement Rules is valid and enforceable."

[e]   Plea and Waiver of Fifth Amendment

A defendant who pleads guilty waives the Fifth Amendment with regard to the plea proceedings. He or she will "confess" in open court as part of the plea process. But does a guilty plea waive the privilege against self-incrimination in the sentencing phase of the case? In *Mitchell v. United States*, 526 U.S. 314 (1999), the Court held, by a 5 to 4 vote, that the plea does not operate as a waiver of the privilege at sentencing. In *Mitchell* the defendant pled guilty to three counts of distributing cocaine near a school ground and to conspiracy to distribute five or more kilograms of cocaine. At the plea colloquy, the U.S. District Court judge, while assessing whether there was a factual basis for the plea, asked her whether she had done the things to which she was pleading guilty. She admitted to doing "some of it," but reserved the right to contest the drug quantity under the conspiracy charge at sentencing. The Court accepted the guilty plea. At sentencing, she did not testify regarding the quantity of drugs. The sentencing judge concluded that her guilty plea waived her Fifth Amendment self-incrimination privilege and therefore the judge could draw an adverse inference from her silence at the sentencing hearing. In reversing, the U.S. Supreme Court explained:

> The Fifth Amendment by its terms prevents a person from being "compelled in any criminal case to be a witness against himself." To maintain that sentencing proceedings are not part of "any criminal case" is contrary to the law and to common sense. [In this case] the defendant was less concerned with the proof of her guilt or innocence than with the severity of her punishment. Petitioner faced imprisonment from one year upwards to life, depending on the circumstances of the crime. To say that she had no right to remain silent but instead could be compelled to cooperate in the deprivation of her liberty would ignore the Fifth Amendment privilege at the precise stage where, from her point of view, it was most important.

The Court also concluded that by drawing an adverse inference from Mitchell's silence, the sentencing judge imposed an impermissible burden on her attempt to exercise her privilege against self-incrimination.

The issue of a defendant's right not to testify under *Griffin v. Illinois*, 380 U.S. 609 (1965), and later cases is explored more fully in Chapter 15. It is worth noting here, however, that the dissenters in *Mitchell* argue vigorously that *Griffin* was erroneously decided. Justice Scaila, joined by the three other dissenters, would refuse to extend *Griffin* in any way; Justice Thomas would take the further step of considering overruling *Griffin* and its progeny in an appropriate future case. 326 U.S. at 331 (dissent of Scalia, J.), 341 (dissent of Thomas, J.). The holdings of both *Griffin* and *Mitchell*, therefore, may be vulnerable in the future.

[9]   Factual Basis

Purpose. Rule 11(b)(3) requires that the judge not accept a guilty plea without first determining that there is a *factual basis* for it. The court should ascertain that the conduct the defendant admits to having done constitutes the crime for which the defendant will plead. The purpose of the factual basis rule is to provide at least some assurance that the defendant actually is guilty of the charges. This procedure also is used to deny later motions seeking a reversal on the basis of innocence.

How determined. The Rule does not specify the particular kind of inquiry required, however. According to the Advisory Committee Notes, "[a]n inquiry might be made of the defendant, of the attorneys for the government and the defense, of the presentence report when one is available, or by whatever means is appropriate in a specific case." Sometimes a law enforcement officer or the victim will testify about the defendant's involvement in the crime.

A study of felony practices in six jurisdictions showed that the factual basis was determined most frequently (in 40% of the cases) by asking the defendant if he or she committed the offense. The factual basis was also established by having the prosecutor provide additional information about the crime (48% of the cases) and/or questioning the defendant about the offense (36%). William F. McDonald, *Judicial Supervision of the Guilty Plea Process: a Study of Six Jurisdictions*, 70 JUDICATURE 203 (1987).

Standard of certainty. Note that under Rule 11(b)(3) the court must make an inquiry "as shall satisfy it that there is a factual basis for the plea." In an unusual case, *United States v. Ventura-Cruel*, 35 F.3d55 (1st Cir. 2003), the trial court accepted a guilty plea, then later rejected it when information at the subsequent sentencing hearing cast doubt on the defendant's guilt. The First Circuit upheld the court's decision based on concerns that there was inadequate factual basis for the plea.

Does the "satisfy" standard require proof beyond a reasonable doubt? By a preponderance of the evidence? By clear and convincing evidence? If the test is less rigorous than the usual criminal case standard of beyond a reasonable doubt, does this mean that the court would accept a guilty plea (and enter a judgment of conviction) on less convincing evidence than would be required for a criminal trial? Keep this question in mind as you read the next case, which deals with the question of whether a judge may accept a guilty plea in the face of the defendant's assertion of innocence.

G.   GUILTY BUT NOT GUILTY?

NORTH CAROLINA v. ALFORD
400 U.S. 25 (1970)

MR. JUSTICE WHITE delivered the opinion of the Court.

On December 2, 1963, Alford was indicted for first-degree murder, a capital offense under North Carolina law. The court appointed an attorney to represent him, and this attorney questioned all but one of the various witnesses who appellee said would substantiate his claim of innocence. The witnesses, however, did not support Alford's story but gave statements that strongly indicated his guilt. Faced with strong evidence of guilt and no substantial evidentiary support for the claim of innocence, Alford's attorney recommended that he plead guilty, but left the ultimate decision to Alford himself. The prosecutor agreed to accept a plea of guilty to a charge of second-degree murder, and on December 10, 1963, Alford pleaded guilty to the reduced charge.

Before the plea was finally accepted by the trial court, the court heard the sworn testimony of a police officer who summarized the State's case. Two other witnesses besides Alford were also heard. Although there was no eyewitness to the crime, the testimony indicated that shortly before the killing Alford took his gun from his house, stated his intention to kill the victim, and returned home with the declaration that he had carried out the killing. After the summary presentation of the State's case, Alford took the stand and testified that he had not committed the murder but that he was pleading guilty because he faced the threat of the death penalty if he did not do so.[3]

In response to the questions of his counsel, he acknowledged that his counsel had informed him of the difference between second-and first-degree murder and of his rights in case he chose to go to trial. The trial court then asked appellee if, in light of his denial of guilt, he still desired to plead guilty to second-degree murder and appellee answered, "Yes, sir. I plead guilty on — from the circumstances that he (Alford's attorney) told me." After eliciting information about Alford's prior criminal record, which was a long one, the trial court sentenced him to 30 years' imprisonment, the maximum penalty for second-degree murder.

Alford sought post-conviction relief in the state court. Among the claims raised was the claim that his plea of guilty was invalid because it was the product of fear and coercion. After a hearing, the state court in 1965 found that the plea was "willingly,

---

[3] After giving his version of the events of the night of the murder, Alford stated: "I pleaded guilty on second degree murder because they said there is too much evidence, but I ain't shot no man, but I take the fault for the other man. We never had an argument in our life and I just pleaded guilty because they said if I didn't they would gas me for it, and that is all." In response to questions from his attorney, Alford affirmed that he had consulted several times with his attorney and with members of his family and had been informed of his rights if he chose to plead not guilty. Alford then reaffirmed his decision to plead guilty to second-degree murder: Q. (by Alford's attorney). "And you authorized me to tender a plea of guilty to second degree murder before the court?" A. "Yes, sir." Q. "And in doing that, that you have again affirmed your decision on that point?" A. "Well, I'm still pleading that you all got me to plead guilty. I plead the other way, circumstantial evidence; that the jury will prosecute me on — on the second. You told me to plead guilty, right. I don't — I'm not guilty but I plead guilty."

knowingly, and understandingly" made on the advice of competent counsel and in the face of a strong prosecution case.

. . . State and lower federal courts are divided upon whether a guilty plea can be accepted when it is accompanied by protestations of innocence and hence contains only a waiver of trial but no admission of guilt. . . . [W]hile most pleas of guilty consist of both a waiver of trial and an express admission of guilt, the latter element is not a constitutional requisite to the imposition of criminal penalty. An individual accused of crime may voluntarily, knowingly, and understandingly consent to the imposition of a prison sentence even if he is unwilling or unable to admit his participation in the acts constituting the crime.

Nor can we perceive any material difference between a plea that refuses to admit commission of the criminal act and a plea containing a protestation of innocence when, as in the instant case, a defendant intelligently concludes that his interests require entry of a guilty plea and the record before the judge contains strong evidence of actual guilt. Here the State had a strong case of first-degree murder against Alford. Whether he realized or disbelieved his guilt, he insisted on his plea because in his view he had absolutely nothing to gain by a trial and much to gain by pleading. Because of the overwhelming evidence against him, a trial was precisely what neither Alford nor his attorney desired. Confronted with the choice between a trial for first-degree murder, on the one hand, and a plea of guilty to second-degree murder, on the other, Alford quite reasonably chose the latter and thereby limited the maximum penalty to a 30-year term. When his plea is viewed in light of the evidence against him, which substantially negated his claim of innocence and which further provided a means by which the judge could test whether the plea was being intelligently entered, its validity cannot be seriously questioned. In view of the strong factual basis for the plea demonstrated by the State and Alford's clearly expressed desire to enter it despite his professed belief in his innocence, we hold that the trial judge did not commit constitutional error in accepting it.[11]

MR. JUSTICE BRENNAN, with whom MR. JUSTICE DOUGLAS and MR. JUSTICE MARSHALL join, dissenting.

. . . Today the Court makes clear that its previous holding [in *Brady*] was intended to apply even when the record demonstrates that the actual effect of the unconstitutional threat was to induce a guilty plea from a defendant who was unwilling to admit his guilt.

I adhere to the view that, in any given case, the influence of such an unconstitutional threat "must necessarily be given weight in determining the voluntariness of a plea." And, without reaching the question whether due process permits the entry of judgment upon a plea of guilty accompanied by a contemporaneous denial of acts constituting the crime, I believe that at the very least such a denial of guilt is also a relevant factor in determining whether the plea was voluntarily and intelligently made. With these factors in mind, it is sufficient in my view to state that the facts set out in the majority opinion demonstrate that Alford was "so gripped by fear of the death penalty" that his decision to plead guilty was not voluntary but was "the product of duress as much so as

---

[11] Our holding does not mean that a trial judge must accept every constitutionally valid guilty plea merely because a defendant wishes so to plead. A criminal defendant does not have an absolute right under the Constitution to have his guilty plea accepted by the court, although the States may by statute or otherwise confer such a right. Likewise, the States may bar their courts from accepting guilty pleas from any defendants who assert their innocence. Cf. Fed. Rule Crim. Proc. 11, which gives a trial judge discretion to "refuse to accept a plea of guilty . . . ." We need not now delineate the scope of that discretion.

choice reflecting physical constraint." . . .

NOTES

1. *Discretion in accepting Alford plea.* As suggested in footnote 11 of *Alford*, trial judges have considerable discretion whether or not to accept a guilty plea from a defendant who asserts factual innocence. One commentator has observed that there are no standards for the acceptance and use of the *Alford* plea, which has led to excessive judge shopping. *See* Curtis J. Shipley, Note, *The Alford Plea: A Necessary But Unpredictable Tool for the Criminal Defendant*, 72 Iowa L. Rev. 1063 (1987). A few jurisdictions reject *Alford* and require an admission of guilt to the crime charged as a precondition to a valid guilty plea. *See, e.g. Sims v. State*, 873 N.E.2d 204 (Ind. App. 2007)(reversible error to accept guilty plea when defendant maintains his innocence).

2. *Encouraging lies?* Some have suggested that a defendant who asserts innocence while pleading guilty may not be amenable to correctional measures. If true, this notion argues in favor of having guilt or innocence established at the trial stage rather than by a guilty plea. If this practice were followed, however, would it encourage defendants to be less than candid at the plea hearing?

3. *Factual basis matching crime elements.* Under Rule 11(b) the court must find a "factual basis" before accepting a guilty plea. When an *Alford* plea is offered and the defendant essentially denies guilt, the factual basis still is necessary but will not be based on the defendant's own statements. Other sources, such as law enforcement or even the victim, may have to provide the necessary link between the defendant and the crime for which the plea will be entered.

Another issue sometimes confronted by courts in *Alford* plea cases is how close the evidence establishing a factual basis must match the elements of the offense to which the plea is entered. For example, assume that the defendant is charged with aggravated robbery under a statute defining the offense as the "(1) intentional taking from the person of another property of any value by violence or putting the person in fear and (2) the robbery is accomplished with a deadly weapon or by display of any article used or fashioned to lead the victim to reasonably believe it to be a deadly weapon." As a result of plea negotiations, the defendant is permitted to plead guilty to the crime of simple robbery, which requires only the intentional taking of property by violence or putting the person in fear. At the plea hearing, the trial judge ascertains that the defendant actually accomplished the robbery by using a loaded pistol, satisfying the elements of aggravated robbery. A very strict interpretation of the factual basis requirement might lead the trial judge to reject the guilty plea because the facts established do not comport with the statutory definition of simple robbery. It appears, however, that most courts have little difficulty finding the guilty plea valid under these circumstances. The Supreme Court of California has suggested that the appropriate test in this context is whether the defendant's guilty plea (to an uncharged offense) is "reasonably related to the defendant's conduct." *People v. Jackson*, 694 P.2d 736, 742 (Cal. 1985).

4. *Should judge accept an Alford plea?* The decision whether to accept a proffered *Alford* plea, or not to, may place some judges in a moral/ethical quandary. If you were the judge, would you have any qualms about accepting a plea of guilty from a defendant who still protested his or her innocence? On the other hand, would you have qualms about rejecting a proffered *Alford* plea and as a result, subjecting the defendant to enhanced punishment (possibly even including exposure to the death penalty, as was the circumstance in the *Alford* case itself)?

H. BREACH OF PLEA AGREEMENT

Given the contractual nature of plea agreements, at times either the prosecutor or defendant may refuse or fail to comply with certain terms of the bargain. The American Bar Association states plainly that "[a] prosecutor should not fail to comply with a plea agreement unless a defendant fails to comply with a plea agreement or other extenuating circumstances are present." Standards for Criminal Justice § 3-4.2(c) (3d ed. 1993). More particularly, the prosecutor should "comply scrupulously with the letter and spirit of plea agreements." *Id.* commentary. When compliance is questioned, a determination must be made whether a breach occurred and, if it did, what remedy is appropriate.

SANTOBELLO v. NEW YORK
404 U.S. 257 (1971)

Mr. Chief Justice Burger delivered the opinion of the Court.

We granted certiorari in this case to determine whether the State's failure to keep a commitment concerning the sentence recommendation on a guilty plea required a new trial.

[The defendant agreed to plead guilty to a gambling crime which carried a maximum sentence of one year imprisonment, and the prosecutor agreed to make no recommendation as to the sentence. Following a series of delays, defendant appeared for sentencing. At that time, a different prosecutor than the one who had negotiated the plea appeared for the state and recommended the maximum one-year sentence. Defense counsel immediately objected, but the prosecutor asserted that there was no record to support the defendant's claim of a no-sentence-recommendation promise by the state. In subsequent proceedings, however, the state no longer contested the fact that the earlier promise had been made.]

. . . This record represents another example of an unfortunate lapse in orderly prosecutorial procedures, in part, no doubt, because of the enormous increase in the workload of the often understaffed prosecutor's offices. The heavy workload may well explain these episodes, but it does not excuse them. The disposition of criminal charges by agreement between the prosecutor and the accused, sometimes loosely called "plea bargaining," is an essential component of the administration of justice. Properly administered, it is to be encouraged. If every criminal charge were subjected to a full-scale trial, the States and the Federal Government would need to multiply by many times the number of judges and court facilities.

Disposition of charges after plea discussions is not only an essential part of the process but a highly desirable part for many reasons. It leads to prompt and largely final disposition of most criminal cases; it avoids much of the corrosive impact of enforced idleness during pre-trial confinement for those who are denied release pending trial; it protects the public from those accused persons who are prone to continue criminal conduct even while on pretrial release; and, by shortening the time between charge and disposition, it enhances whatever may be the rehabilitative prospects of the guilty when they are ultimately imprisoned.

. . . This phase of the process of criminal justice, and the adjudicative element inherent in accepting a plea of guilty, must be attended by safeguards to insure the defendant what is reasonably due in the circumstances. Those circumstances will vary, but a constant factor is that when a plea rests in any significant degree on a promise or agreement of the prosecutor, so that it can be said to be part of the inducement or consideration, such promise must be fulfilled.

On this record, petitioner "bargained" and negotiated for a particular plea in order to secure dismissal of more serious charges, but also on condition that no sentence recommendation would be made by the prosecutor. It is now conceded that the promise to abstain from a recommendation was made, and at this stage the prosecution is not in a good position to argue that its inadvertent breach of agreement is immaterial. The staff lawyers in a prosecutor's office have the burden of "letting the left hand know what the right hand is doing" or has done. That the breach of agreement was inadvertent does not lessen its impact.

We need not reach the question whether the sentencing judge would or would not have been influenced had he known all the details of the negotiations for the plea. He stated that the prosecutor's recommendation did not influence him and we have no reason to doubt that. Nevertheless, we conclude that the interests of justice and appropriate recognition of the duties of the prosecution in relation to promises made in the negotiation of pleas of guilty will be best served by remanding the case to the state courts for further consideration. The ultimate relief to which petitioner is entitled we leave to the discretion of the state court, which is in a better position to decide whether the circumstances of this case require only that there be specific performance of the agreement on the plea, in which case petitioner should be resentenced by a different judge, or whether, in the view of the state court, the circumstances require granting the relief sought by petitioner, i.e., the opportunity to withdraw his plea of guilty. We emphasize that this is in no sense to question the fairness of the sentencing judge; the fault here rests on the prosecutor, not on the sentencing judge.

The judgment is vacated and the case is remanded for reconsideration not inconsistent with this opinion.

[JUSTICE DOUGLAS concurred, arguing that the trial court should decide the remedy for the government's error, but the defendant's preference should be given great weight since the prosecutor violated the defendant's right in breaching the plea bargain. JUSTICE MARSHALL, joined by JUSTICES BRENNAN and STEWART, concurred in part and dissented in part. He believed that the defendant should be permitted to withdraw the plea, which was the relief requested. The government had taken no action in reliance on the plea and would suffer no harm from having to go to trial.]

In the *Santobello* case, there was little doubt that the plea agreement had been breached by the prosecution. Sometimes it is not clear whether a breach — either by the government or by the defendant — took place.

RICKETTS v. ADAMSON
483 U.S. 1 (1987)

JUSTICE WHITE delivered the opinion of the Court.

The question for decision is whether the Double Jeopardy Clause bars the prosecution of respondent for first-degree murder following his breach of a plea agreement under which he had pleaded guilty to a lesser offense, had been sentenced, and had begun serving a term of imprisonment. The Court of Appeals for the Ninth Circuit held that the prosecution of respondent violated double jeopardy principles and directed the issuance of a writ of habeas corpus. We reverse.

In 1976, Donald Bolles, a reporter for the Arizona Republic, was fatally injured when a dynamite bomb exploded underneath his car. Respondent was arrested and charged with first-degree murder in connection with Bolles' death. Shortly after his trial had commenced, while jury selection was underway, respondent and the state prosecutor reached an agreement whereby respondent agreed to plead guilty to a charge of second-degree murder and to testify against two other individuals — Max Dunlap and James Robison — who were allegedly involved in Bolles' murder. Specifically, respondent agreed to "testify fully and completely in any Court, State or Federal, when requested by proper authorities against any and all parties involved in the murder of Don Bolles . . . ." The agreement provided that "[s]hould the defendant refuse to testify or should he at any time testify untruthfully . . . then this entire agreement is null and void and the original charge will be automatically reinstated."[1]

---

[1] The agreement further provided that, in the event respondent refused to testify, he "will be subject to the charge of Open Murder, and if found guilty of First Degree Murder, to the penalty of death or life imprisonment requiring mandatory twenty-five years actual incarceration, and the State shall be free to file any charges, not yet filed as of the date of this agreement."

The parties agreed that respondent would receive a prison sentence of 48–49 years, with a total incarceration time of 20 years and 2 months. In January 1977, the state trial court accepted the plea agreement and the proposed sentence, but withheld imposition of the sentence. Thereafter, respondent testified as obligated under the agreement, and both Dunlap and Robison were convicted of the first-degree murder of Bolles. While their convictions and sentences were on appeal, the trial court, upon motion of the State, sentenced respondent. In February 1980, the Arizona Supreme Court reversed the convictions of Dunlap and Robison and remanded their cases for retrial. This event sparked the dispute now before us.

The State sought respondent's cooperation and testimony in preparation for the retrial of Dunlap and Robison. On April 3, 1980, however, respondent's counsel informed the prosecutor that respondent believed his obligation to provide testimony under the agreement had terminated when he was sentenced. Respondent would again testify against Dunlap and Robison only if certain conditions were met, including, among others, that the State release him from custody following the retrial. [2]

The State then informed respondent's attorney on April 9, 1980, that it deemed respondent to be in breach of the plea agreement. On April 18, 1980, the State called respondent to testify in pretrial proceedings. In response to questions, and upon advice of counsel, respondent invoked his Fifth Amendment privilege against self-incrimination.

[After the State filed a new information charging respondent with first-degree murder, respondent filed a motion to quash the information on grounds of a double jeopardy violation. The Arizona Supreme Court rejected the challenge, holding that the plea agreement "by its very terms waives the defense of double jeopardy if the agreement is violated."]

. . . Respondent was then convicted of first-degree murder and sentenced to death.

. . . We may assume that jeopardy attached at least when respondent was sentenced in December 1978, on his plea of guilty to second-degree murder. Assuming also that under Arizona law second-degree murder is a lesser included offense of first-degree murder, the Double Jeopardy Clause, absent special circumstances, would have precluded prosecution of respondent for the greater charge on which he now stands convicted. The State submits, however, that respondent's breach of the plea arrangement to which the parties had agreed removed the double jeopardy bar to prosecution of respondent on the first-degree murder charge. We agree with the State.

. . . The agreement specifies in two separate paragraphs the consequences that would flow from respondent's breach of his promises. Paragraph 5 provides that if respondent refused to testify, "this entire agreement is null and void and the original charge will be automatically reinstated." (emphasis added). Similarly, Paragraph 15 of the agreement states that "[i]n the event this agreement becomes null and void, then the parties shall be returned to the positions they were in before this agreement." Respondent unquestionably understood the meaning of these provisions.

. . . The terms of the agreement could not be clearer: in the event of respondent's breach occasioned by a refusal to testify, the parties would be returned to the status quo ante, in which case respondent would have no double jeopardy defense to waive. And, an agreement specifying that charges may be reinstated given certain circumstances is, at least under the provisions of this plea agreement, precisely equivalent to an agreement waiving a double jeopardy defense.

---

[2] Respondent's other conditions — which he characterized as "demands" — included that he be held in a nonjail facility with protection during the retrials, that he be provided with new clothing, that protection be afforded his ex-wife and son, that a fund be provided for his son's education, that he be given adequate resources to establish a new identity outside Arizona following his release from custody, and that he be granted "full and complete immunity for any and all crimes in which he may have been involved."

. . . We are also unimpressed by the Court of Appeals' holding that there was a good-faith dispute about whether respondent was bound to testify a second time and that until the extent of his obligation was decided, there could be no knowing and intelligent waiver of his double jeopardy defense. But respondent knew that if he breached the agreement he could be retried, and it is incredible to believe that he did not anticipate that the extent of his obligation would be decided by a court. Here he sought a construction of the agreement in the Arizona Supreme Court, and that court found that he had failed to live up to his promise. The result was that respondent was returned to the position he occupied prior to execution of the plea bargain: he stood charged with first-degree murder. Trial on that charge did not violate the Double Jeopardy Clause.

. . . Finally, it is of no moment that following the Arizona Supreme Court's decision respondent offered to comply with the terms of the agreement. At this point, respondent's second-degree murder conviction had already been ordered vacated and the original charge reinstated. The parties did not agree that respondent would be relieved from the consequences of his refusal to testify if he were able to advance a colorable argument that a testimonial obligation was not owing. The parties could have struck a different bargain, but permitting the State to enforce the agreement the parties actually made does not violate the Double Jeopardy Clause. [Reversed]

JUSTICE BRENNAN, with whom JUSTICE MARSHALL, JUSTICE BLACKMUN, and JUSTICE STEVENS join, dissenting.

The critical question in this case is whether Adamson ever breached his plea agreement. Only by demonstrating that such a breach occurred can it plausibly be argued that Adamson waived his rights under the Double Jeopardy Clause.

. . . Without disturbing the conclusions of the Arizona Supreme Court as to the proper construction of the plea agreement, one may make two observations central to the resolution of this case. First, the agreement does not contain an explicit waiver of all double jeopardy protection.

. . . Second, Adamson's interpretation of the agreement — that he was not required to testify at the retrials of Max Dunlap and James Robison — was reasonable. Nothing in the plea agreement explicitly stated that Adamson was required to provide testimony should retrials prove necessary . . . .

. . . This Court has yet to address in any comprehensive way the rules of construction appropriate for disputes involving plea agreements. Nevertheless, it seems clear that the law of commercial contract may in some cases prove useful as an analogy or point of departure in construing a plea agreement, or in framing the terms of the debate. It is also clear, however, that commercial contract law can do no more than this, because plea agreements are constitutional contracts. The values that underlie commercial contract law, and that govern the relations between economic actors, are not coextensive with those that underlie the Due Process Clause, and that govern relations between criminal defendants and the State. Unlike some commercial contracts, plea agreements must be construed in light of the rights and obligations created by the Constitution.

. . . Of course, far from being a commercial actor, Adamson is an individual whose "contractual" relation with the State is governed by the Constitution. The determination of Adamson's rights and responsibilities under the plea agreement is controlled by the principles of fundamental fairness imposed by the Due Process Clause. To grant to one party — here, the State — the unilateral and exclusive right to define the meaning of a plea agreement is patently unfair. Moreover, such a grant is at odds with the basic premises that underlie the constitutionality of the plea-bargaining system. Guilty pleas are enforceable only if taken voluntarily and intelligently. It would be flatly inconsistent with these requirements to uphold as intelligently made a plea agreement which provided that, in the future, the agreement would mean whatever the State interpreted it to mean. Yet the Court upholds today the equivalent of such an agreement. The logic of the plea-bargaining system requires acknowledgment and protection of the defendant's right to advance against the State a reasonable interpretation of the plea agreement.

This right requires no exotic apparatus for enforcement. Indeed, it requires nothing more than common civility. If the defendant offers an interpretation of a plea agreement at odds with that of the State, the State should notify the defendant of this fact, particularly if the State is of the view that continued adherence to defendant's view would result in breach of the agreement. If the State and the defendant are then unable to resolve their dispute through further discussion, a ready solution exists — either party may seek to have the agreement construed by the court in which the plea was entered. By following these steps the State would have placed far fewer demands on the judicial process than were in fact imposed here, and would have fulfilled its constitutional obligation to treat all persons with due respect.

The unfairness of the Court's decision does not end here. Even if one assumes, arguendo, that Adamson breached his plea agreement by offering an erroneous interpretation of that agreement, it still does not follow that the State was entitled to retry Adamson on charges of first degree murder. As the Court acknowledges, immediately following the decision of the Arizona Supreme Court adopting the State's construction of the plea agreement, Adamson sent a letter to the State stating that he was ready and willing to testify. At this point, there was no obstacle to proceeding with the retrials of Dunlap and Robison; each case had been dismissed without prejudice to refiling, and only about one month's delay had resulted from the dispute over the scope of the plea agreement. Thus, what the State sought from Adamson — testimony in the Dunlap and Robison trials — was available to it.

. . . The Court's decision flouts the law of contract, due process, and double jeopardy. It reflects a world where individuals enter agreements with the State only at their peril, where the Constitution does not demand of the State the minimal good faith and responsibility that the common law imposes on commercial enterprises, and where, in blind deference to state courts and prosecutors, this Court abdicates its duty to uphold the Constitution. I dissent.

NOTES

1. *Need for careful drafting.* The *Ricketts* case underscores the significance of drafting precise plea agreements. Note, for example, that the plea agreement did not explicitly state that the defendant was required to testify in any future proceedings that might take place after appellate review. A number of commentators have asserted that Adamson's interpretation of the agreement was a reasonable one. *See* Graham Hughes, *Agreements for Cooperation in Criminal Cases*, 45 VAND. L. REV. 1 (1992); *Mark V. Tushnet, The Politics of Executing the Innocent: The Death Penalty in the Next Century?*, 53 U. PITT. L. REV. 261, 263 (1991) (noting, sarcastically, that the United States Supreme Court apparently believes that "the death penalty is an appropriate sanction for breach of contract."). Professor Tushnet points out, however, that Adamson ultimately was spared the death penalty through some "bizarre" developments that occurred after the case was remanded to the Ninth Circuit Court of Appeals. *Id.* at 264, n.8.

2. *Interpretation of plea agreements and the role of contract law.* Is the commercial contract analogy the appropriate one in deciding whether or not a breach of a plea agreement has occurred? In many breach-of-plea-bargain cases, courts address a variety of contract concepts, such as inducements to bargain, expectations of the parties, and receipt of benefit of the bargain. *See In re Alfro*, 180 F.3d 372 (2d Cir. 1999) (plea agreements are interpreted under contract law but there are unique due process concerns for fairness and procedural safeguards).

In *United States v. Wood*, 378 F.3d 342, (4th Cir. 2004), the court observed:

The law governing the interpretation of plea agreements is an "amalgam of constitutional, supervisory, and private [contract] law concerns. In most cases, contract principles will be wholly dispositive because neither side should be able, any more than would be private contracting parties, unilaterally to renege or seek modification simply because of uninduced mistake or change of mind. A plea agreement, however, is not simply a contract between two parties. It necessarily implicates the integrity of the criminal justice system and requires the courts to exercise judicial authority in considering the plea agreement and in accepting or rejecting the plea. Consequently, we hold the Government to a greater degree of responsibility than the defendant (or possibly than would be either of the parties to commercial contracts) for imprecisions or ambiguities in plea agreements."

3. *Construe against government.* A number of courts have observed that ambiguities in the plea agreement should be construed against the government due to the unequal bargaining power between the government and the defendant. *See, e.g., United States v. Vaval,* 404 F.3d 144 (2d Cir. 2005)(plea agreements construed against government; government's conduct must comport with highest standards of fairness).

4. *Too vague to enforce.* A plea agreement may involve such vague terms that all or part of it is unenforceable. *See, e.g., State v. Nason,* 981 P.2d 866 (Wash. App. 1999) (defendant pled guilty on agreement that "no other charges will be filed"; applying contract principle of lack of mutual assent, court found this language ambiguous and refused to bar new charges for conduct unknown to prosecutor at time of plea).

5. *Sentence recommendations.* A large number of plea bargain breach cases involve situations related to promises from the government concerning sentencing recommendations. In *United States v. Brummett,* 786 F.2d 720 (6th Cir. 1986), the plea agreement provided that the government would make no recommendation as to the sentence. At the sentencing hearing, however, the prosecutor stated that while no specific recommendation would be made, "a lengthy incarceration" was necessary because of the defendant's criminal behavior. Because the prosecutor did not make a "specific" recommendation, the court held that there was no breach of the plea agreement.

By contrast, in *United States v. Crusco,* 536 F.2d 21 (3d Cir. 1976), the government agreed to take no position at the sentencing hearing. When the hearing was held, however, the prosecutor attacked the defendant's character and reputation and also provided details as to the defendant's criminal record. On these facts, the court ruled that the government had breached the agreement: "We see the government's characterization [of the defendant] as a transparent effort to influence the severity of [the defendant's] sentence." 536 F.2d at 26. *See also United States v. Johnson,* 187 F.3d 1129 (9th Cir. 1999) (plea agreement said government would recommend a 4-level enhancement for possession of firearm but would not recommend any other enhancement or departure; condition violated when prosecutor introduced victim impact statement in attempt to increase sentence); *United States v. Camarillo-Tello,* 236 F.3d 1024 (9th Cir. 2001)(prosecutor who had agreed to recommend a 4-level downward guideline departure could not change that recommendation at sentencing hearing by joining probation officer's recommendation that court grant only a 2-level downward departure).

6. *Require prosecutor to be "enthusiastic?"* In *United States v. Benchimol,* 471 U.S. 453 (1985), a per curiam decision, the United States Supreme Court reviewed a case in which the government had agreed to recommend probation with restitution in exchange for the defendant's guilty plea. At the sentencing hearing, the defense attorney informed the judge that the presentence report erroneously stated that the government would "stand silent." The Assistant United States Attorney remarked that the defense attorney had made an "accurate representation" in so correcting the presentence report. A lower court found that the government had breached the agreement because the government attorney "made no effort to explain [the recommendation] but rather left an impression with the court of less-than-enthusiastic support for leniency." Reversing that decision, the United States Supreme Court found no breach:

> It may well be that the Government in a particular case might commit itself to "enthusiastically" make a particular recommendation to the court, and it may be that the Government in a particular case might agree to explain to the court the reasons for the Government's making a particular recommendation. But respondent does not contend, nor did the Court of Appeals find, that the Government had in fact undertaken to do either of these things here. The Court of Appeals simply held that as a matter of law such an undertaking was to be implied from the Government's agreement to recommend a particular sentence. But our view of Rule 11 is that it speaks in terms of what the parties in fact agree to, and does not suggest that such implied-in-law terms as were read into this agreement by the Court of Appeals have any place under the Rule. [*Id.* At 455]

[1]   Remedies for Breach of Plea Agreement

[a]   Breach by Defendant

Recall *Santobello's* discussion of the question of remedy. Where the defendant breaches the plea agreement, the prosecution no longer is required to uphold its end of the bargain. Thus, the government may re-charge the defendant and proceed to trial. And, as noted in *Ricketts*, the defendant's breach also removes a double jeopardy bar to prosecution of the defendant on a higher charge than the one to which the defendant initially pled guilty.

[b]   Breach by Government

When the prosecutor breaks the plea agreement, however, there are three options available to the court. First, the court may view the breach as not meriting any remedy. Second, specific performance of the agreement can be demanded, meaning that the defendant insists upon full compliance with the plea agreement. Third, the defendant may be allowed to withdraw the plea.

[i]   No Remedy Necessary for Breach

Many cases holds that the defendant is entitled to relief whenever the government breaches the plea agreement after the plea is entered, irrespective of whether the defendant suffers prejudice. The government is held to a high standard of integrity. In two situations, however, some courts have held no remedy is needed despite the government's breach.

De minimis harm. In some situations the government or court commits a technical violation of the plea agreement but the defendant suffers no real harm and gets essentially what was expected in the bargain. No remedy is ordered. In *Paradiso v. United States*, 689 F.2d 28 (2dCir. 1982), for example, the defendant entered a plea bargain that sentences would run concurrently rather than consecutively and would not total more than ten years. Although the trial judge sentenced him to serve the two sentences consecutively, the Court of Appeals imposed no remedy for the breach of the agreement because the total number of years did not exceed ten, which was characterized as the real essence of the plea agreement.

Government later remedies the breach. In a few unusual cases, the government breaches a plea agreement then later "cures" it by subsequent action that satisfies the defendant's expectations in making the deal. For example, in *United States v. Brody*, 808 F.2d (2d Cir. 1986), the plea agreement obligated the government to tell the court of the defendant's cooperation with law enforcement, but at sentencing the prosecution did not do so. Nevertheless, at a subsequent hearing on a motion to reduce sentence, the prosecution complied with the agreement. No remedy was ordered because the defendant received the benefit he had bargained for in the plea agreement.

[ii]   Specific Performance

When specific performance is deemed the proper remedy for the government's breach of a plea agreement, the case is routinely remanded to the trial court to implement the agreement. As suggested in *Santobello*, the new sentencing should occur before a different judge and the prosecutor would then be compelled to adhere to the plea agreement in full. It should be noted, however, that some courts have questioned whether reassignment to a different judge is required in all cases. *See, e.g., State v. Bracht*, 573 N.W.2d 176 (S.D. 1997).

In federal cases, it appears that specific performance is the remedy usually ordered by trial judges. Appellate courts routinely defer to the trial judge's decision. *See United States v. Moscahlaidis*, 868 F.2d 1357 (3d Cir. 1989).

What factors should a trial judge use in deciding upon the appropriate remedy? Some states, influenced by Justice Douglas's concurring opinion in *Santobello*, hold that the defendant's preference should be given considerable weight. *Brooks v. Narick*, 243 S.E.2d 841 (W. Va. 1978). For more on remedies for broken plea agreements, see Peter Westen & David Westin, *A Constitutional Law of Remedies for Broken Plea Bargains*, 66 Cal. L. Rev. 471 (1978).

[iii]   Withdrawal of Guilty Plea

The other remedy available to the defendant is to withdraw the guilty plea, returning both the government and the defendant to their original positions.

[2]   Specifying Remedy in Plea Agreement

As discussed earlier, plea agreements must be as thorough and precise as possible. The agreement should also include the issue of remedy in the event of breach. For a good example of such a written agreement, see *United States v. Jefferies*, 908 F.2d 1520 (11th Cir. 1990) (the plea agreement contained a provision that any breach of the agreement by defendants for failure to forfeit identified property would (1) not relieve the defendants of their obligation to continue in their original plea of guilty, (2) permit the government to reinstate and proceed with other identified criminal charge, and (3) permit the government to "instigate and proceed with any prosecution of any other offenses now known to the government."). *See also Jones v. Commonwealth*, 995 S.W.2d 363 (Ky. 1999) (defendant violated valid plea agreement that required him to appear for sentencing hearing or prosecutor would recommend sentence of 20 years instead of 6).

I.   EFFECT OF RULE 11 VIOLATIONS

Rule 11 obligates the court to perform a litany of specific tasks. Common experience teaches that any such comprehensive rule will be violated on occasion, whether accidentally or purposefully. What is the legal effect of a trial judge's failure to comply with every detail of Rule 11? One approach would be to hold that any violation, however slight or unintentional, invalidates the guilty plea. While this result could be rationalized as technically appropriate, it could be seen as unjust because guilty pleas would be invalidated for technical reasons when the defendant was not actually misled about anything. For example, assume that the trial judge did not apprise the defendant of the mandatory minimum penalty in a case in which the defendant had agreed to plead guilty and receive a sentence that far exceeded the minimum penalty. Should the defendant's plea be invalidated because of that minor and seemingly irrelevant oversight?

[1]   Harmless Error: Defense Objection

Rule 11(h) establishes the harmless error standard, specifying that a variance from Rule 11 procedures which "does not affect substantial rights" shall be considered harmless error. In other words, such minor errors are not grounds for invalidating or undoing the plea. The rule does not define the meaning of "substantial rights"; that is left to the courts. This short provision is very important because it means that literal word-for-word compliance with all Rule 11 provisions is not necessarily required.

The difficult judicial task is to ascertain circumstances in which noncompliance with Rule 11 affected substantial rights and will result in vacating the defendant's conviction and remanding for new proceedings. The Tenth Circuit Court of Appeals has held that the appropriate standard is whether the failure to comply with Rule 11 "had a significant influence on [the defendant's] decision to plead guilty." *United States v. Barry*, 895 F.2d 702, 704 (10th Cir. 1990).

If the defendant objected to the court's Rule 11 violation, the burden is on the government to prove the error was harmless. Some Rule 11 errors have been deemed of sufficient magnitude that they were not harmless. *See, e.g., United States v. Harrington*, 354 F.3d 178 (2d Cir. 2004)(failure to apprise defendant of restitution possibility not harmless if restitution ordered).

With respect to Rule 11 violations raised on direct appeal, the Advisory Committee Notes (1983 amendment) provide:

> . . . [I]t is fair to say that the kinds of Rule 11 violations which might be found to constitute harmless error upon direct appeal are fairly limited. Illustrative are: where the judge's compliance with subdivision (c)(1) was not absolutely complete, in that some essential element of the crime was not mentioned, but the defendant's responses clearly indicate his awareness of that element; where the judge's compliance with subdivision (c)(2) was erroneous in part in that the judge understated the maximum penalty somewhat, but the penalty actually imposed did not exceed that indicated in the warnings; and where the judge completely failed to comply with subdivision (c)(5), which of course has no bearing on the validity of the plea itself.

As the Advisory Committee Notes to Rule 11 also make clear, however, the harmless error rule is not to be construed by trial judges as an invitation to be sloppy in conducting Rule 11 proceedings: "[Rule 11(h)] makes no change in the responsibilities of the judge at Rule 11 proceedings, but instead merely rejects the extreme sanction of automatic reversal." The Advisory Committee concludes with a reiteration of the importance of compliance with Rule 11:

> . . . [t]houghtful and careful compliance with Rule 11 best serves the cause of fair and efficient administration of criminal justice, as it will help reduce the great waste of judicial resources required to process the frivolous attacks on guilty plea convictions that are encouraged, and are more difficult to dispose of, when the original record is inadequate. It is, therefore, not too much to require that, before sentencing defendants to years of imprisonment, district judges take the few minutes necessary to inform them of their rights and to determine whether they understand the action they are taking.

[2]   Plain Error: No Objection by Defense

Assume that a Rule 11 violation is committed by the U.S. District Court judge during the plea colloquy. Assume, further, that the defendant fails to lodge a contemporaneous objection thereto. After the guilty plea is accepted and the defendant is sentenced, an appeal is filed. By what standard is the appellate court to ascertain whether the defendant is entitled to relief?

In *United States v. Dominguez Benitez*, 542 U.S. 74 (2004), the Supreme Court held that because no objection was made at the time of the error, appellate courts may correct a plain error only under Rule 52(b). This provision allows for a correction of a "plain error that affects substantial rights." (See fuller discussion of the plain error doctrine in Chapter 18.) This, in turn, means that the defendant "is obliged to show a reasonable probability that, but for the error, he would not have entered the plea." The Court noted that because of the error, "probability of a different result is sufficient to undermine confidence in the outcome of the proceeding.

Under this standard, plain error has been found in a fairly small number of cases. Courts look at the "totality of circumstances" in the entire record to determine whether the defendant has satisfied his or her burden of proof. For example, in *United States v. Martinez*, 289 F.3d 1023 (7th Cir. 2002), the trial judge violated Rule 11 by not informing defendant of the maximum possible sentence or the elements of two drug offenses. Nevertheless, the Seventh Circuit found no plain error since the prosecutor had informed the defendant of the maximum sentence, the court told defendant of the nature (thought not the elements) of the charge, the defendant, represented by two lawyers, agreed that the government could prove their case, and defendant told the judge that he understood the charges and consequences of pleading guilty.

[3] Collateral Attack

Whether relief will be granted for failure to comply fully with Rule 11 procedures may hinge upon the way in which relief is sought. For example, the defendant may pursue a collateral attack upon the plea pursuant to 28 U.S.C. § 2255. Such an action was brought in *United States v. Timmreck*, 441 U.S. 780 (1979), where the trial judge had failed to inform the defendant of a mandatory special parole term following imprisonment. Since the error did not result in a "complete miscarriage of justice" or in a proceeding "inconsistent with the rudimentary demands of fair procedure," relief was denied. The United States Supreme Court also noted that Timmreck's claim was one of a "technical violation" of Rule 11 and that the claim could have been raised on direct appeal.

J. FINALITY

[1] Withdrawal of Plea

[a] Withdrawal by defendant

[i] Type of Plea

Sometimes a defendant who has entered into a plea agreement will desire to withdraw the guilty plea either for the purpose of proceeding to trial or for the purpose of trying to negotiate a more favorable agreement. Consideration of this issue requires careful attention to Rules 11(c) and 32(d) and to the exact nature of the plea. Under Rule 11(c)(1), the government, in exchange for the defendant's guilty plea, may agree to do any one or more of the following three options: move for dismissal of other charges, make a non-binding recommendation for a particular sentence, or agree that a specific sentence is appropriate. Rule 11(c) requires close attention to the type of agreement specified because if the agreement is of the type specified in subdivision (c)(3)(B) [a non-binding recommendation for a particular sentence], "the court must advise the defendant that the defendant has no right to withdraw the plea if the court does not follow the recommendation or request."

As to the other types of agreements, however, the court must either accept or reject the agreement "so that it may be determined whether the defendant shall receive the bargained-for concessions or shall instead be afforded an opportunity to withdraw his plea." Notes of Advisory Committee on Rules (1979 Amendment).

[ii] Before or After Imposition of Sentence

A defendant may seek to get out of a guilty plea at any of three times.

Before entering plea. If the defendant works out a deal with the prosecution but has a change of mind before actually entering the plea in court, he or she may back out of the deal for any reason.

After plea entered but before judge accepts it and imposes sentence. After the defendant enters a plea in court but before the court accepts it and imposes sentence, Rule 11(d)(2)(B) provides that the court may permit withdrawal if the defendant shows any "fair and just reason," discussed below.

After judge accepts plea and imposes sentence. In contrast, the rules change once the judge has accepted the plea and imposed sentence. Federal Rule of Criminal Procedure 11(e) provides, "After the court imposes sentence, the defendant may not withdraw a plea of guilty or nolo contendere, and the plea may be set aside only on direct appeal or collateral attack."

This rule recognizes the clear dichotomy between pre-sentence and post-sentence motions to withdraw the guilty plea. In the former instance, the defendant's motion to withdraw the plea is governed by the "fair and just reason" standard, as opposed to the more restrictive standard applicable to relief sought under § 2255 [federal post conviction relief]: "a fundamental defect which inherently results in a complete miscarriage of justice or an omission inconsistent with the rudimentary demands of fair procedure."

[iii] Fair and Just Reason to Withdraw

If defendant seeks to withdraw a plea after it is made and accepted but before the judge imposes sentence, the defendant has the burden of showing a "fair and just" reason for withdrawal of the plea. Recognizing that this standard is inexact, Notes of the Advisory Committee (1983 amendment) observed:

> Whether the [defendant] has asserted his legal innocence is an important factor to be weighed, as is the reason why the defenses were not put forward at the time of the original pleading. The amount of time which as passed between the plea and the motion must also be taken into account.

> If the defendant establishes such a reason, it is then appropriate to consider whether the government would be prejudiced by withdrawal of the plea. Substantial prejudice may be present for a variety of reasons [citing cases in which physical evidence had been discarded, the chief government witness had died, other defendants with whom defendant had been joined for trial had already been tried in a lengthy trial, and the fact that prosecution had dismissed more than fifty witness who had traveled long distances for the trial.]

[iv] State Variations

Among state jurisdictions, there is little consistency with respect to rules governing the withdrawal of guilty pleas. Typically, a state statute or rule of criminal procedure addresses two basic issues: (1) at what point during the proceeding withdrawal is allowed, and (2) the standard to be employed. Consistent with the federal model, most states insist upon a more demanding withdrawal standard after sentencing than when the motion to withdraw is filed before sentence is imposed. *See* Wayne R. LaFave, Jerold H. Israel, and Nancy J. King, CRIMINAL PROCEDURE § 21.5(a) (4th ed. 2004).

[v] Deferral of Decision on Permitting Withdrawal

On occasion, a district court judge will accept a guilty plea (finding, of course, that the defendant was acting knowingly, voluntarily, and intelligently, and that there was a factual basis for the plea) but defer a decision on whether to accept the plea *agreement* until after completion of a presentence report. Assume that a defendant moves to withdraw the guilty plea *before* the trial judge has ruled whether to accept the plea agreement. Does the defendant have an absolute right to do so, or must he or she provide a "fair and just reason" for the withdrawal as required by Rule 11(d)(2)(B)? The Supreme Court ruled unanimously in *United States v. Hyde*, 520 U.S. 670 (1997) that Rule 11(d)(2)(B) (formerly Rule 32 (e)) governs and thus the defendant cannot withdraw the plea "simply on a lark."

[b] Withdrawal by Government

[i] Before Plea Entered

A different question — not addressed in the Federal Rules of Criminal Procedure — is whether the government is allowed to withdraw a plea offer before the plea is entered in court. In *Mabry v. Johnson*, 467 U.S. 504 (1984), the defendant was tried and convicted on charges of burglary, assault and murder. After the murder conviction was set aside by the state supreme court, plea negotiations ensued. The prosecutor proposed that in exchange for a plea of guilty to the charge of accessory after felony murder, the prosecutor would recommend a sentence of 21 years to be served *concurrently* with the burglary and assault sentences. The next day, defendant's lawyer called the prosecutor to convey his acceptance of the offer but "was told that a mistake had been made" and the prosecutor therefore withdrew the offer. Instead, the prosecutor now proposed to recommend the sentence of 21 years to be served *consecutively* to the other sentences. Ultimately, the defendant accepted the prosecutor's second offer.

Following the district court's dismissal of his habeas corpus petition, defendant appealed to the Eighth Circuit Court of Appeals, which reversed. The Circuit Court concluded that " 'fairness' precluded the prosecution's withdrawal of a plea proposal once accepted by respondent." A unanimous United States Supreme Court reversed. Citing *Santobello v. New York*, the Court acknowledged that when the prosecution breaches its promise with respect to an *executed* plea agreement, the defendant pleads guilty on a false premise and therefore the conviction cannot stand. This case, however, is fundamentally different:

> *Santobello* demonstrates why respondent may not successfully attack his plea of guilty. Respondent's plea was in no sense induced by the prosecutor's withdrawn offer; unlike Santobello, who pleaded guilty thinking he had bargained for a specific prosecutorial sentencing recommendation which was not ultimately made, at the time respondent pleaded guilty he knew the prosecution would recommend a 21-year consecutive sentence. Respondent does not challenge the District Court's finding that he pleaded guilty with the advice of competent counsel and with full awareness of the consequences — he knew that the prosecutor would recommend and that the judge could impose the sentence now under attack. Respondent's plea was thus in no sense the product of governmental deception; it rested on no "unfulfilled promise" and fully satisfied the test for voluntariness and intelligence.

Thus, because it did not impair the voluntariness or intelligence of his guilty plea, respondent's inability to enforce the prosecutor's offer is without constitutional significance. Neither is the question whether the prosecutor was negligent or otherwise culpable in first making and then withdrawing his offer relevant. The Due Process Clause is not a code of ethics for prosecutors; its concern is with the manner in which persons are deprived of their liberty. Here respondent was not deprived of his liberty in any fundamentally unfair way. Respondent was fully aware of the likely consequences when he pleaded guilty; it is not unfair to expect him to live with those consequences now. [467 U.S. at 510]

[ii]   Exception for Detrimental Reliance

Although the government may withdraw from a plea deal any time until the plea is entered, a few cases hold the government may not do so if the defendant detrimentally relied on the deal.

[2]   Conditional Pleas

The conditional plea, discussed earlier in this chapter, is governed by Rule 11(a)(2). It allows a defendant to plead guilty while reserving an issue for appeal. If the appeal is successful, the defendant may withdraw the plea. The Rule states that the conditional plea can be made only with the consent of the court and the government. The defendant is required to file a written document reserving the right to appeal an adverse ruling on a specific pretrial motion. This document should describe the precise issue that will be appealed.

The unusual requirement of a *written* conditional plea is designed to serve several functions. It assures that the government considered the issue and acquiesced in the precise plea. Second, it prevents the defendant from claiming that a plea should be deemed conditional when the oral record is ambiguous and the defendant was unsuccessful on important motions. Finally, it allows both the trial and appellate court to know precisely which issues are reserved for appeal and to ascertain that those issues are material to the case. If the defendant succeeds on appeal, the defendant is allowed to withdraw the guilty plea. Many states have identical rules. *See, e.g.*, Mich. Court Rule 6.301(C)(2).

Notwithstanding the criticism that the conditional plea strikes at the notion of finality in the criminal process, many courts and commentators applaud this procedure. Indeed, in *Lefkowitz v. Newsome*, 420 U.S. 283 (1975), the United States Supreme Court indicated its approval of a New York conditional plea statute as a procedure "which permits a defendant to obtain appellate review of certain pretrial constitutional claims without imposing on the state the burden of going to trial." Even in jurisdictions that have not provided for the conditional plea explicitly, courts have recognized that the parties may negotiate a "plea-with-reservation" arrangement whereby the defendant's guilty plea is offered while expressly reserving to the defendant the right to appeal a specified pretrial ruling. *See* Wayne R. LaFave, Jerold H. Israel, and Nancy J. King, CRIMINAL PROCEDURE § 21.6(b) (4th ed. 2004).

NOTES

1. *Appellate court's limited information.* When the defendant enters a conditional plea and then pursues appellate review of a pretrial motion, the trial record will be limited to those matters considered at the pretrial stage along with the record of the conditional guilty plea. Thus, the appellate court will not have the full trial record normally available to it when reviewing a lower court's ruling. For this reason, it has been suggested that the conditional plea is inappropriate. Do you agree?

2. *Wisdom of allowing conditional plea.* The conditional plea actually gives the defendant the best of both worlds: the defendant is permitted to seek review of an adverse pretrial ruling yet is not required to undergo the time, expense, and risk involved in a full trial on the merits. Since the plea negotiation process entails the waiver or forfeiture of many significant constitutional rights, why shouldn't appellate review also be one of those rights waived by guilty plea? Stated differently, is it not fair to require the defendant who desires appellate review to "jump through the hoop" of trial on the merits?

[3] Post-Conviction Review

Sometimes a criminal defendant pleads guilty to a crime but believes that he or she could challenge some legal infirmity in the case. One way to ensure that this is possible is through a conditional plea, discussed above, that preserves the issue for appeal.

In the absence of a conditional plea, a subsequent challenge following a guilty plea may be difficult and limited to a few issues. Recall that one of the critical consequences of a guilty plea is that the accused forgoes a number of rights, such as the rights to confront accusers and, in more serious cases, to have a jury trial. Rule 11 is designed to ensure — and provide a written record — that the waiver of these various rights is knowing, intelligent, and voluntary. If the plea is knowing, intelligent, and voluntary, the accused is thereafter barred from raising most issues on appeal or through various collateral remedies such as habeas corpus or post-conviction relief procedures. The obvious rationale is that the accused has the option of waiving these rights and has done so in order to obtain an advantage during plea negotiations. Although post-conviction procedures are discussed in more detail in Chapter 18, this section provides a few general principles that are uniquely applicable to legal challenges launched by criminal defendants who pled guilty.

Ordinarily, a person convicted of a crime has a right to appeal the case to an appellate court in that jurisdiction. These appeals must be taken within a relatively short time from the conviction. After that time, the only remedy is some sort of post-conviction "collateral" proceeding, such as habeas corpus or a state post-conviction relief procedure. Often the latter are limited to constitutional or jurisdictional issues.

Appeal. Under both state and federal procedure, the defendant may file a direct appeal from the judgment of guilt based upon the guilty plea. Usually this must be done relatively promptly after the conviction. The applicable statute normally specifies the grounds upon which the appeal can be based. In many respects, the direct appeal from a plea conviction in a federal case is the most desirable form of post-conviction review:

> Direct appeal is . . . the most advantageous route for challenging a federal conviction [because of] the potential for reversal on a showing of error of less than constitutional, jurisdictional, or fundamental magnitude [and because the defendant] is entitled to both court-appointed counsel and necessary transcripts.

Paul D. Borman, *The Hidden Right to Direct Appeal from a Federal Plea Conviction,* 64 Cornell L. Rev. 319, 371 (1979).

General waiver rule. As the result of a long series of judicial decisions, it has been held that the person who pleads guilty waives appeal or collateral relief on most issues, including many not covered specifically in the waiver provisions of Rule 11. *See, e.g., United States v. Tolson,* 988 F.2d 1494 (7th Cir. 1993)(defendant who voluntarily and intelligently pled guilty to marijuana conspiracy cannot appeal the facts of the indictment for that crime), *but see, United States v. Morales-Martinez,* 496 F. 3d 356 (5th Cir. 2007)(recognizing authority in some jurisdictions for a narrower waiver which treats guilty pleas as an admission of only those facts necessary to support conviction); *Mills v. State,* 999 S.W.2d 674 (Ark. 1999) (guilty plea waives right to post-conviction challenge to voluntariness of custodial confessions). As discussed earlier, the plea agreement itself may contain a specific provision in which the accused agrees to waive an appeal. Generally such waivers are upheld.

Knowing and voluntary exception. In the context of a habeas corpus case, the United States Supreme Court expressed the general waiver rule and discussed an exception in *Tollett v. Henderson,* 411 U.S. 258, 267 (1973):

When a criminal defendant has solemnly admitted in open court that he is in fact guilty of the offense with which he is charged, he may not thereafter raise independent claims relating to the deprivation of constitutional rights that occurred prior to the entry of the guilty plea. He may only attack the voluntary and intelligent character of the guilty plea by showing that the advice he received from counsel was not within the standards [of competency for a criminal defense attorney].

Although *Tollett* specifically dealt with federal habeas corpus relief, the principles in it are often cited as providing limits on direct appeals. *See, e.g., United States v. Cortez*, 973 F.2d 764 (9th Cir. 1992) (guilty plea may constitute waiver of right to appeal ruling on selective prosecution, citing *Tollett*). Thus, *Tollett* and other decisions permit the defendant to attack the guilty plea if the "voluntary and intelligent" standards are not met. The reason is that the plea itself is invalid if the defendant was coerced into pleading or did so with inadequate knowledge or legal assistance. *See, e.g., United States v. Brady*, 397 U.S. 742 (1970) (plea upheld because facts show it was knowing and intelligent); *McMann v. Richardson*, 397 U.S. 759 (1970) (upholding plea of guilty based on reasonably competent advice of counsel that confession was admissible; plea was intelligent and habeas corpus hearing denied); *Wilson v. United States*, 962 F.2d 996 (11th Cir. 1992) (guilty plea involves waiver of all nonjurisdictional challenges to constitutionality of conviction and only attack left is on the voluntary and knowing nature of the plea).

Jurisdiction exception. Other decisions have added another exception: the defendant who pled guilty may also attack certain jurisdictional defects in the proceeding. *See United States v. Broce*, 488 U.S. 563 (1989)(person entering guilty plea may still appeal that the trial court had no power to enter the conviction or impose the sentence).

Statute of limitations. Although it is not clear exactly what jurisdictional defects are preserved after a guilty plea, the statute of limitations is often listed as one that is. However, a waiver of the statute of limitations is permissible if specific. *See, e.g., United States v. Del Percio*, 870 F.2d 1090 (6th Cir. 1989) (specific waiver of statute of limitations upheld). When, one might ask, would it be in the defendant's interest to waive a statute of limitations provision? Given the general rule that misdemeanor offenses carry shorter statutes of limitations periods than felonies, a defendant charged with a felony may seek a charge reduction to a lesser-included — but time-barred — misdemeanor. A plea of guilty under such circumstances could necessitate a specific statute of limitations waiver.

Failure to recuse. Another defect that may be preserved after a guilty plea is a denial of a recusal motion where the trial judge's impartiality is questioned (discussed more fully in Chapter 15, Part B). The federal circuit courts are divided on this issue. *Contrast, United States v. Chantal*, 902 F.2d 1018 (1st Cir. 1990) (holding that the guilty plea was not a waiver of the right to appeal a denied recusal motion) with *United States v. Patti*, 337 F.3d 1317 (11th Cir. 2003) (holding that this issue is not preserved where the recusal motion is based upon 28 U.S.C. § 455(a)). One commentator argues that federal courts should recognize that an unconditional guilty plea is not *a per se* waiver of the defendant's right to disqualify the judge when the judge's impartiality is reasonably in question. *See* Nancy B. Pridgen, Note, *Avoiding the Appearance of Bias: Allowing a Federal Criminal Defendant to Appeal a Denial of a Recusal Motion Even After Entering an Unconditional Guilty Plea*, 53 Vand. L. Rev. 983 (2000).

K. ETHICAL ISSUES

Plea bargaining generates a number of important — and often unrecognized — issues for the judge, prosecutor, and defense lawyer. As one would expect, often there are no clear answers to the important questions about what is ethical and what is not.

[1] Judge

[a] Majority Rule: Judge Barred from Participating in Plea Discussions

In most jurisdictions, the role of the judge in plea bargaining is clear: the judge is barred from participating in the process. Rule 11(c)(1) of the Federal Rules of Criminal Procedure states unequivocally that "[t]he court must not participate in [plea negotiation] discussions." A presidential commission summarized the judge's role:

> The judge's function is to insure the appropriateness of the correctional disposition reached by the parties and to guard against any tendency of the prosecution to overcharge or to be excessively lenient . . . . The judge's role is not that of one of the parties to the negotiation, but that of an independent examiner to verify that the defendant's plea is the result of an intelligent and knowing choice and not based on misapprehension or the product of coercion.

President's Commission on Law Enforcement and Administration of Justice, The Challenge of Crime in a Free Society 167 (1967).

Rationale. Several reasons are given for this ban. A defendant who refuses to plead guilty despite the judge's involvement in the negotiations may believe that a fair trial or a fair sentence is impossible by that same judge whose desire for a negotiated sentence was thwarted. Similarly, the judge's position of power by itself may give him or her sufficient clout to convince the defendant to plead guilty, irrespective of actual guilt or innocence. Judicial involvement in plea bargaining may also make it impossible for the judge to determine objectively whether a plea was voluntary, since the judge may have participated in the alleged coercive process. Finally, the judge who actively participates in plea bargaining may shift from neutral decisionmaker to advocate for a side or disposition. This would alter the traditional role of neutrality that is a hallmark of the American judiciary. It would leave the defendant with the impression that the judge is simply another arm of the prosecution trying to convince the defendant to accept a lengthy prison term. *See generally* Albert W. Alschuler, *The Judge's Role in Plea Bargaining*, Part I, 76 Colum. L. Rev. 1059 (1976).

[b] Minority View: Permit Judicial Involvement in Plea Discussions

While Rule 11 appears to bar judges from involvement in any plea discussions, the Notes of the Advisory Committees on Rules indicate that Rule 11 bars only judicial involvement in plea discussions that *lead to a plea agreement.* After the agreement is announced in court, the judge is not prohibited from discussing it with the parties. It is not clear, however, to what extent the court should become involved in resolving ambiguities or suggesting specific changes in the deal that the parties worked out.

While Rule 11's ban on judicial participation represents the prevailing view, there are several other approaches that permit much greater involvement by the judge. North Carolina, for example, specifically authorizes the judge to participate in plea discussions. N.C. Gen. Stat. § 15a-1021 (a). This provision was adopted to facilitate the expeditious resolution of criminal cases. North Carolina judges use this authority frequently, sometimes forcefully encouraging plea negotiations the day before trial or even during the trial. *See generally* Norman Lefstein, *Plea Bargaining and the Trial Judge: the New ABA Standards, and the Need to Control Judicial Discretion*, 59 N.C. L. Rev. 477, 486 (1981). *See also* Ill. Sup. Ct. R. 402(d) (trial judge may not initiate plea discussions, but may participate in them). A few jurisdictions also authorize the parties to submit a proposed deal to the judge for an advisory opinion as to whether the bargain will be accepted. Ill. Sup. Ct. R. 402; N.C. Gen. Stat. § 15A-1021(c).

The American Bar Association has recommended greater judicial participation in plea bargaining than is permitted by Rule 11. Under the Bar Association's proposals, the judge is specifically authorized to play a limited, non-directive role in discussions between the prosecutor and defense counsel if the two are unable to reach agreement on a plea and both request the judge's participation. Upon request of the parties, the judge is allowed to evaluate a proposed plea agreement and "may indicate whether the court would accept the terms as proposed and if relevant, indicate what sentence would be imposed." Nonetheless, this standard holds to the view that a judge "should not ordinarily participate in plea negotiation discussions among the parties" and "should not . . . communicate to the defendant . . . that a plea agreement should be accepted or that a guilty plea should be entered." STANDARDS FOR CRIMINAL JUSTICE § 14-3.3 (3d ed. 1999).

[2] Lawyers

Plea negotiations create a number of ethical issues for both the prosecution and the defense lawyer.

[a] Duty to Explore Possibility of Plea

Both the prosecutor and defense attorney will ordinarily benefit from exploring the possibility of a guilty plea, although "there is no constitutional right to plea bargain; the prosecutor need not do so if he prefers to go to trial." *Weatherford v. Bursey*, 429 U.S. 545, 561 (1977). The American Bar Association specifically recommends that the prosecutor should have a general policy of discussing the possibility of disposing of a case without trial. Standards for Criminal Justice § 3-4.1(a) (3d ed. 1993). The ABA also indicates that defense counsel should normally seek discussions about a plea negotiation unless there is a good reason for not doing so. *Id.* § 4-6.1 commentary. Neither side, however, should enter plea negotiations without first becoming familiar with the case, including the available evidence. This may mean deferring plea discussions until after formal and informal discovery has occurred.

[b] Negotiations

[i] Zealous Advocate

During negotiations, each advocate has an important duty to represent the client zealously. The Model Rules of Professional Conduct provide that "[a] lawyer should act with commitment and dedication to the interests of the client and with zeal in advocacy upon the client's behalf." Model Rules of Professional Conduct Rule 1.3 cmt. (1983). Similarly, the Model Code of Professional Responsibility states that "[a] lawyer shall not intentionally . . . fail to seek the lawful objectives of his clients through reasonably available means permitted by law and the Disciplinary rules." Model Code of Professional Responsibility DR 7-101A (1969).

These guidelines mean that both prosecutors and defense lawyers should try to advance their clients' interests in plea discussions, although these interests will differ for the two sides. The prosecutor has a unique role in the criminal justice adversary system. According to the American Bar Association, "[t]he prosecutor is an administrator of justice, an advocate, and an officer of the court; the prosecutor must exercise sound discretion in the performance of his or her functions." Standards for Criminal Justice § 3-1.2(b) (3d ed. 1993). Defense counsel, on the other hand, is ordinarily not described as an "administrator for justice." Defense counsel's role is to further "the defendant's interest to the fullest extent that the law and the applicable standards of professional conduct permit." *Id.* § 4-1.2 commentary. "Once a case has been undertaken, a lawyer is obliged not to omit any essential lawful and ethical step in the defense . . . ." *Id.* For a thorough treatment of general negotiation principles as they apply to the plea bargaining of criminal cases, see Rodney J. Uphoff, *The Criminal Defense Lawyer as Effective Negotiator: A Systemic Approach*, 2 CLIN. L. REV. 73 (1995).

[ii] Candor

Although an attorney must be a zealous advocate, there are serious limitations on the actions that can be taken. In the context of plea negotiations, a key restriction is the obligation for both the prosecutor and defense lawyer to be truthful. Both the Model Rules and the Model Code prohibit a lawyer from knowingly making a false statement of law or material fact to anyone during the course of representation. Model Rules of Professional Conduct Rule 4.1(a) (1983); Model Code of Professional Responsibility DR 7-102(A)(5) (1969).

The American Bar Association appears to apply this standard differently to the two sides. The prosecutor's duties are stated exactly as described above. Standards for Criminal Justice § 3-4.1(c) (3d ed. 1993). The defense lawyer, on the other hand, is only barred from "knowingly mak[ing] false statements concerning the evidence in the course of plea discussions with the prosecutor." *Id.* § 4-6.2(c). The Commentary to the ABA standards is consistent with the differences in the standards themselves. Prosecutors are under no obligation to reveal evidence during plea negotiations, but they must be truthful when presenting the facts of the case and must "avoid the use of deception in dealing with the evidence and must refrain from misrepresenting the law or sentencing practices of the court." *Id.* § 3-4.1 commentary. Defense counsel appear to have a more limited responsibility. They need not reveal evidence to the prosecution, but must be truthful when they present to the prosecutor "facts relating to the case or any mitigating facts." *Id.* § 4-6.2 commentary.

The duty of candor can be difficult in negotiations when each side may try to ignore or "favorably shade" its own weaknesses and to emphasize its strong points while denigrating those of the adversary. Puffery in negotiations has long been tolerated, while outright lying is impermissible. See, for example, *People v. Jones*, 375 N.E. 2d 41 (Ct. App. N.Y. 1978), in which no due process violation was found where the state failed to disclose during plea negotiations that it had received information that the complaining witness had died. The court noted that there was no claim of affirmative misrepresentation, and that the undisclosed information did not involve exculpatory evidence. Do these ordinary negotiation tactics offend the lawyer's ethical duty of candor? The Model Rules of Professional Conduct try to address this concern by providing a flexible definition of "facts."

> Under generally accepted conventions in negotiation, certain types of statements ordinarily are not taken as statements of material facts. Estimates of price or value placed on the subject of a transaction and a party's intentions as to an acceptable settlement of a claim are in this category . . . .

Model Rules of Professional Conduct Rule 4.1 comment (1983).

A shorthand way of analyzing this issue is to view some such statements as *fact* and others as *opinion*. Even this dichotomy, however, may be imprecise in particular instances.

An increasing number of commentators are addressing matters relating to instances in which an innocent person is wrongfully convicted. Some suggest that prosecuting attorneys should be more mindful of these injustices and should temper their adversarial tendencies. *See* Abbe Smith, *Can You Be A Good Person and A Good Prosecutor?* 14 GEO. J. LEGAL ETHICS 355, 390 (2001) (describing several instances in which the prosecutor's desire for victory "wins out over matters of procedural fairness, such as disclosure"); Bennett L. Gershman, *The Prosecutor's Duty to Truth*, 14 GEO. J. LEGAL ETHICS 309, 316 (2001) (noting numerous instances of wrongful convictions and asserting that a prosecutor has an obligation not to proceed with a prosecution "without being personally convinced of the defendant's guilt").

PROBLEM 11-2. DO I HAVE A DEAL FOR YOU

John Hobart and Francine Pickens are charged with burglary and theft of a painting from the Seaside Art Gallery. The indictment alleges the two entered the gallery during normal business hours, then hid in a storeroom until midnight when they took an original McClintock watercolor worth $5500 from a gallery wall and exited through a fire door.

1. You represent Hobart. Do the following statements violate ethical norms?

    a. "You have no case against my client."

        i. Assume that defense counsel does not know the strength of the government's case.

        ii. What if you are convinced the government has an airtight case against your client and that the chances of a conviction approach 100% if there is a trial?

    b. "My client did not take the painting from the wall; Pickens did."

        i. Assume that your client told you in confidence that he did take the painting from the wall.

        ii. What if you do not know who took the painting? Your client refuses to tell you despite your persistent questioning. Would it matter if you did not ask?

    c. "My client will agree to nothing more than a one year prison term. We go to trial for anything more."

        i. Assume that your client told you that he would accept the best deal you can get for him.

        ii. What if your client told you that he would accept no more than a three year prison sentence, but would prefer a maximum of one year in prison?

2. You are now the Assistant District Attorney prosecuting the case. Do the following statements violate ethical norms?

    a. "We have an eyewitness who saw your client [Hobart] take the painting."

        i. Assume that there is no such eyewitness.

        ii. What if you, the prosecutor, are confident that you will eventually induce Pickens to testify against Hobart (and state that she saw Hobart take the painting), but so far Pickens has refused to discuss the case with you?

    b. "My boss said I have to get five years from your client."

        i. Assume that you and your boss (the District Attorney) have never discussed this case.

        ii. Although you and the District Attorney have never discussed this case, you honestly believe that the D.A. would insist upon a minimum of five years' incarceration.

[c]   Defense Counsel's Obligation to Client

Plea negotiations present the defense attorney with special ethical obligations with regard to relations with the client. The client should be kept informed about the status of plea negotiations and any significant proposals made by the prosecution. STANDARDS FOR CRIMINAL JUSTICE § 4-6.2 (3d ed. 1993). A failure to apprise the defendant of an offer has been held to deny the defendant the right to effective counsel guaranteed by the sixth amendment. *See, e.g., People v. Todd*, 465 N.W.2d 380 (Mich. App. 1990) (defendant convicted of first degree murder; defense counsel failed to inform defendant of prosecution's offer to accept plea to second degree murder).

The client should also be told the lawyer's professional opinion of the likely outcome of the case and the ramifications of possible plea deals. The defense attorney must be sensitive to the fact that the ultimate decision whether to plead guilty or to proceed to trial rests with the client. Yet the way in which the attorney conveys information to the client (*i.e.*, "I'm positive that a jury will return a guilty verdict") can (and most certainly does on occasion) dictate the client's "choice." Additionally, defense counsel may be called upon by the client to make the decision (*i.e.*, "I'm not the lawyer . . . you are. You tell me what to do.").

Significant issues arise where the attorney faces possible conflicts of interest. An obvious one is when defense counsel represents two or more defendants during plea negotiations. Sometimes the deal may require one to testify against the other or to accept a greater punishment than the other. While separate defense counsel for both defendants is best, if the defendants want to be represented by the same lawyer, there must be complete candor so that each defendant is fully apprised of the situation. Sometimes the conflict of interest will cause a reversal for ineffective assistance of counsel. *See Burden v. Zant*, 498 U.S. 433 (1991) (counsel representing two alleged murderers negotiated immunity for one to testify against the other; reversal ordered).

Another source of conflict is between the interests of the present client and that of future clients. For example, a busy criminal defense lawyer may engage in routine plea negotiations with a prosecutor several times a week on various unrelated cases. The defense lawyer may be tempted not to "upset the apple cart" by having heated negotiations on a particular case. If the prosecutor were angered, future discussions on other cases may be compromised. Of course, this may violate the defense lawyer's ethical duty to represent each client with undivided loyalty.

[d] Prosecution's Contact with Defendant

If the defendant is represented by counsel, the prosecutor must not engage in plea negotiations directly with the client unless defense counsel specifically consents. *See* Model Rules of Professional Conduct Rule 4.2; Model Code of Professional Responsibility DR 7-104(A)(1). Such discussions should ordinarily take place only with defense counsel. The defendant need not be personally present for the negotiation.

If the defendant has waived counsel, the prosecution may negotiate directly with the defendant. To protect against claims of undue influence or overreaching by the prosecutor, the American Bar Association recommends that the prosecutor make and preserve a record of negotiations with uncounseled defendants. STANDARDS FOR CRIMINAL JUSTICE § 3-4.1(b) (3d ed. 1993).

Chapter 12
CONTINUANCE

A. INTRODUCTION

In order to facilitate efficient use of both human and physical resources and to permit adequate preparation in criminal cases, hearings are often scheduled days or weeks in advance. Not uncommonly, the judge or one or more lawyers finds that the scheduled hearing date is inconvenient or impossible to meet. A *continuance* or postponement may be sought. A few jurisdictions distinguish a continuance from a *recess*. The latter involves a temporary adjournment of an ongoing proceeding; the former is the postponement of a scheduled hearing. The word *adjournment* has also been used for one or both concepts. For purposes of this chapter, both concepts will be discussed as a continuance.

There is no limit to the reasons why a continuance may be sought. Sometimes a judge will grant a continuance because an earlier trial ran longer than anticipated and the courtroom and judge are simply unavailable on the scheduled date. Obviously the illness of the judge, prosecutor, or defense counsel may prompt a continuance. Other typical reasons for a continuance include a lawyer's inability to attend because he or she is also scheduled to appear at that time in another courtroom in another case; one or both of the lawyers has not had time to adequately prepare for the hearing; a key witness or the defendant is ill or absent; the defendant wants to fire the defense lawyer and hire another lawyer who needs time to prepare; or either side needs time to have an expert witness conduct a scientific test or to locate or analyze evidence that has just been discovered.

If the continuance is needed because the judge cannot or will not be available, he or she simply reschedules the hearing as part of the court's inherent authority to control its docket. Unless a rule of criminal procedure or a statute, such as a speedy trial law, would be violated by the judge's postponement, no hearing is necessary, although a brief meeting or telephone conference may be held to reschedule at a time convenient to the lawyers and parties. If the continuance is sought by either the prosecutor or defense attorney, the judge may or may not hold a hearing on whether to order the continuance, depending on the reasons given for the requested delay. For example, if the prosecutor becomes quite ill and is hospitalized the day before the trial, the judge may grant a continuance without first having a hearing on whether the delay should be ordered.

Though continuances are granted frequently, many judicial decisions reflect a preference to deny a continuance motion to permit courts to schedule and handle cases efficiently. Some cases, for example, state that a continuance should be given only when really necessary.

There are important ethical issues raised by a request for a continuance. As discussed more fully in Chapter 9 in the context of motion practice, the ethical precepts of the legal profession, in general terms, require that lawyers file motions in good faith and avoid ones that are frivolous. *See* MODEL CODE OF PROFESSIONAL RESPONSIBILITY EC 7-4 (1980) (good faith standard); MODEL RULES OF PROFESSIONAL CONDUCT Rules 3.1 (good faith, non-frivolous standard) & 3.2 cmt. (1983) (action done solely for purposes of delay is improper); STANDARDS FOR CRIMINAL JUSTICE § 4-1.3(b) (3d ed. 1993) (defense counsel should avoid unnecessary delay in the disposition of cases).

B. STANDARDS FOR CONTINUANCE

There is little helpful law on the issue of when and whether a continuance should be granted or denied. The appellate decisions virtually always involve appeals by criminal defendants who were convicted after their requests for continuance were denied. Rarely, a defendant appeals the granting of a continuance for the government. There are few, if any, cases where the prosecution appeals the granting or denial of a continuance motion.

The decision to grant or deny a continuance motion is ordinarily left to the discretion of the judge, who controls the court calendar. The exercise of this discretion is rarely overturned on appeal. Appellate courts routinely ask whether the denial of a continuance was an "abuse of discretion." They also inquire whether the defendant can prove that the denial caused him or her "actual prejudice," a showing that is quite difficult to make. *See, e.g., United States v. Allmon*, 500 F.3d 800 (8th Cir. 2007)(trial courts have "broad discretion" in ruling on continuance; reversal only for abuse of discretion and prejudice caused by denial).

This is well illustrated by *McFadden v. Cabana*, 851 F.2d 784 (5th Cir. 1988), in which a Mississippi prisoner tried to overturn a robbery conviction via a federal habeas corpus petition. He and three others were indicted on September 16th. Over the next three days, his public defender attorney filed a motion for a continuance, contending that there would be an alibi defense and that the public defender, who had three trials scheduled on the three days immediately before McFadden's trial, did not have adequate time to prepare. The continuance motion was denied and the one-day trial was held on September 26th, only ten days after the indictment. Four eyewitnesses testified for the prosecution. The three defense witnesses testified about a lineup that was overly suggestive. Defense counsel offered no alibi witness. The defendant was convicted and given a life sentence. The Court of Appeals, despite what it regarded as the "unseemly haste" with which the defendant was forced to trial, upheld the denial of habeas relief because McFadden could not prove that the denial of the continuance was prejudicial.

Do you agree with the result in *McFadden v. Cabana*? Did the "unseemly haste" with which the defendant was tried render his trial so fundamentally unfair as to amount to a denial of due process, even without a showing of actual prejudice?

Some jurisdictions have statutes, court rules, or local practices that deal with the request for a continuance. Often these provisions are quite general, giving the court discretion to grant or deny a continuance. The American Bar Association's Standards Relating to Criminal Justice express the prevailing approach:

> The Court should grant a continuance only upon a showing of good cause and only for so long as is necessary, taking into account not only the request or consent of the prosecution or defense, but also the public interest in prompt disposition of the case.

STANDARDS FOR CRIMINAL JUSTICE § 12-1.3 (2d ed. 1986). *See, e.g.*, Cal. Penal Code § 1050 (e) (continuances granted only for "good cause;" convenience or stipulation of parties alone insufficient); Fla. Stat. Ann. § 907.055 (continuance can be granted for "good cause"); Ga. Code Ann. §§ 17-8-20 (party applying for continuance must have used "due diligence"), 17-8-22 (continuance granted or refused as the ends of justice may require); La. Code Crim. Proc. Ann. art 712 (continuance granted, in the discretion of the court, for "good ground"); Tex. Code Crim. Proc. art. 29.03 (continuance for "sufficient cause shown").

A few jurisdictions list the factors to be considered. *See, e.g.*, Ga. Code Ann. § 17-8-23 *et seq.* (continuance authorized for absence of party, counsel, witness, or Attorney General, for attendance at General Assembly or state Board of Human Resources, or active duty with National Guard). In rare situations, a statute places time limits on various procedures and may dictate when the limits may be exceeded, thus placing limits on the grant of a continuance.

Moreover, several constitutional issues may be involved in a request to alter the date of a hearing. A number of other issues are also routinely involved in continuance issues, leading most courts to adopt a "factor approach" in assessing requests for a continuance.

UNITED STATES v. POPE

841 F.2d 954 (9th Cir. 1988)

FLETCHER, CIRCUIT JUDGE:

Appellant Pope appeals his conviction for escape and interstate transportation of a stolen vehicle. We reverse.

Edward Pope was convicted in April 1983, in Idaho, of interstate transportation of a stolen car. He was sentenced to prison and sent to the federal correctional facility in Springfield, Missouri. In January 1985, Pope was transferred to the Community Treatment Center at Channel Enterprises in Boise, Idaho — a halfway house that houses inmates near the ends of their sentences.

On February 26, 1985, Pope left Channel for a few hours to look for a job. He did not return. The next day, he took a pickup truck from a car dealer for a test drive. He called the dealer half an hour later to say he was going to the bank to get money to buy the truck. He never returned the truck. He was arrested a week later, on March 4, while driving the truck in Illinois.

On March 14, 1985, he was indicted in federal court in Idaho for escape and interstate transportation of a stolen vehicle, in violation of 18 U.S.C. §§ 751(a) and 2312. He was arraigned on March 20, and a jury trial was set for May 8. On April 12, Pope's attorney, John Lynn, gave notice his client would rely on an insanity defense. The prosecution moved for a pretrial psychiatric examination on April 19. On April 24, the defense made an *ex parte* request for the appointment of a psychiatrist, and on May 3 filed a Motion for Excludable Time, requesting a continuance of the trial to have psychiatric tests conducted. The trial court granted the motions. On May 23, it ordered psychologist Craig Beaver and psychiatrist Dr. Thomas Kruzich to examine the defendant. The court continued the trial to July 25, 1985.

On May 28, Lynn sent Dr. Kruzich, whom he hoped to use as a witness, a letter with a copy of the court's order appointing Kruzich to examine his client. On June 19, a psychologist evaluated Pope in the county jail and found him suicidal and homicidal. On the basis of that finding, the court ordered Pope transported back to the federal prison in Missouri for a mental evaluation.

In late July, Lynn again wrote Kruzich to tell him Pope had been sent to Missouri. He included with the letter a packet of medical records from a hospital where Pope had been previously hospitalized, and a copy of the psychologist's report. Pope returned from Missouri on August 6. For the next five weeks, Lynn tried several times to reach Kruzich by phone to schedule the evaluation of Pope, but succeeded only in leaving messages. Because of "scheduling conflicts," the two were unable to speak directly.

On August 21, trial was again continued to September 23. On September 10, two weeks before trial was to start, Lynn wrote Kruzich a third time, reminding him of the needed evaluation and including a copy of the evaluation done in Missouri. On September 19, the court held a sanity hearing to determine whether Pope was competent to stand trial. At the hearing, Pope asked the court to appoint him a different attorney, because Lynn had yet to contact Kruzich. The court denied the request for change of counsel and found Pope competent to stand trial.

On September 23, 1985, before trial began, Lynn asked for a continuance in order that Kruzich could examine Pope. The motion was denied, and trial commenced.

Pope testified that he had left Channel to go to a job interview. He said he had taken several drugs that day, had spoken to the devil and to his grandparents in a suburb of Heaven. He testified that he could remember nothing else until waking up in the Salt Lake City jail. The psychologist who had interviewed Pope testified for the government that at the time of his interview with Pope, June 19, he concluded Pope was suffering from schizophrenia and should be hospitalized. Another psychologist told the jury that Pope had possibly abused drugs, was depressed and had a psychosocial personality difficulty. He did not think Pope was schizophrenic, however, and concluded he had the capacity to appreciate the nature of the charge against him and assist in his defense.

The jury found Pope guilty on both counts. The court denied his motions for a new trial and sentenced him to a total of seven years. [After several procedural steps, this appeal was filed.]

A. The Denial of a Continuance

. . . Pope claims that the district court abused its discretion in denying his motion for a continuance that would have enabled him to have a psychiatric evaluation by a doctor appointed for the defense. The district court has considerable latitude in granting or denying continuances. *United States v. Flynt*, 756 F.2d 1358 (9th Cir. 1985). To establish abuse, a party must show that the denial was "arbitrary or unreasonable." *Id.*

Flynt sets forth the four factors that are relevant in reviewing a denial of a continuance for abuse of discretion: (1) the requester's diligence in preparing for trial; (2) the likely utility of the continuance, if granted; (3) the inconvenience to the court and the other side; and (4) prejudice from the denial.

1. Diligence

It is plain that defense counsel did not exercise adequate diligence in his pursuit of Dr. Kruzich to examine his client. After acquiring Dr. Kruzich's agreement to examine his client, Lynn allowed the four months before trial to pass without again talking directly with Dr. Kruzich. Two weeks before the continued trial date, Lynn wrote Dr. Kruzich, reminding him of the need to examine Pope, but neither talked with Kruzich directly nor sought another doctor. He asked for another continuance on the morning of trial but offered no adequate explanation for his request.

Appellant concedes that his counsel was not diligent, but the same cannot be said of appellant. Before trial he did the best he could to help himself. At his sanity hearing four days before trial, Pope asked the court to appoint him a new attorney. He stated that "Mr. Lynn hasn't got a hold of none of the witnesses for me that I asked him to get a hold of. This Mr. Kruzich, the doctor that was supposed to come and examine me for Mr. Lynn, he hasn't came and seen me yet. I'm supposed to go to the trial Monday and he hasn't got a hold of none of my witnesses." The court denied Pope's request.

On the morning of trial after Lynn had requested the continuance, the court questioned Pope as to his wishes. Pope said he wanted to "get it over with" so he could be returned to regular prison, "instead of over there in that isolation cell." He then told the court: Saturday night I'm sitting there reading the Bible and one of them comes over the speaker talking about, "This is God. Don't do that, and don't do this, and don't do that," you know. I can't deal with that. You know, if you call them good conditions, I don't think they're too humane, you know. After making sure that the witnesses who had examined appellant for the government would be available for cross-examination, the court, "in view of the defendant's feeling in this matter," denied the continuance.

We have no difficulty concluding that the diligence of Pope was adequate. The questions, however, are whether the court should have (1) allowed the failures of his counsel to deprive him of the only defense he had; and (2) paid heed to Pope's preference to proceed to trial without further delays. The first answers itself. Pope, when he realized that his counsel had not succeeded in getting Dr. Kruzich to examine him, asked for new counsel who would pursue the preparation of the defense. He should not be deprived of a defense. The answer to the latter is less clear. However, the court's colloquy with Pope should have alerted the court to the defendant's flawed perception of reality and should have underscored the importance of a continuance to enable the defense to secure a psychiatric evaluation.

The government contends that to establish the utility of a continuance Pope must show, inter alia, not only who the witnesses are, but also what they would say in testimony, and that they could be obtained if the continuance were granted. *United States v. Hoyos*, 573 F.2d 1111, 1114 (9th Cir. 1978). In *Flynt*, however, we distinguished *Hoyos*, noting the inability to state what the testimony would be where the continuance was sought to provide time for a psychiatric evaluation. Since the requested continuance was to permit time for evaluation, Flynt "obviously could not present to the court the substance of [the witnesses'] testimony." We held it should have been apparent from Flynt's behavior that such testimony would be relevant. Nothing more should be required.

This case is similar. Appellant cannot tell us what Dr. Kruzich's evaluation would be. But since insanity was Pope's only defense, testimony from Dr. Kruzich would have been relevant. The fact that Dr. Kruzich was available and had expressed a willingness to conduct the examination, indicates his testimony could have been obtained had the court granted the continuance. The continuance, therefore, would have been useful.

2. Inconvenience

We must examine the extent to which the court and the opposing party, including its witnesses, would have been inconvenienced by a continuance.

Unlike *Flynt*, where only a hearing on a show cause order was involved, here the court was faced with a requested continuance on the day of a trial with jurors present, and seven government witnesses waiting, two of whom had come from out-of-state. We held in *Armant v. Marquez*, 772 F.2d 552, 557 (9th Cir. 1985), that recalendaring a one-day trial would not have created grave scheduling difficulties, but that was a case where the government's three witnesses all were local. Undeniably, this district court faced greater potential inconvenience.

Nonetheless, the district court could have held the continuance Pope sought to one or two days. Indeed, the district court could have taken an active role in making sure the evaluation took place and quickly. Balanced against the importance to Pope's defense of a psychiatric evaluation, the inconvenience did not justify the denial.

3. Prejudice

To warrant reversal the defendant must show prejudice from the denial of the continuance.

In the context of this case, . . . the prejudice is the inability, without the continuance, to obtain the only testimony potentially supportive of his insanity defense . . . . Facing an irrefutable factual case by the government that he committed the acts charged, Pope's only defense was insanity. He had identified his expert, made arrangements to be examined as to his sanity, and identified the defense he hoped to establish. And there was substantial evidence to suggest that Pope was insane. He had been diagnosed as schizophrenic. The reason he found jail conditions intolerable was the constant intrusion of messages from God coming over the loudspeaker. During his jail stay, a psychologist was called because of his observed mental state that was concerning to his jailers. He recommended hospitalization.

The court's denial of even a brief continuance thus deprived Pope of the only testimony that could plausibly have helped him. He was clearly prejudiced.

We review the denial of a continuance on a case-by-case basis. There are no mechanical or exact measures to determine when reversal is warranted. We conclude: Pope was diligent in pursuing his defense, the continuance could have been brief enough to cause only minimal inconvenience, and would have been useful; by denying Pope's motion, the district court prejudiced his defense. On these facts, we find that the district court abused its discretion.

. . . On the facts of this case, the court abused its discretion in denying a continuance. Pope is entitled to a new trial.

Reversed and Remanded.

NOTES

1. *Factors.* Every court considering whether to approve a motion for a continuance uses a laundry list of factors. The court in *Pope* uses four factors in assessing whether the denial of a continuance was an abuse of discretion. Should these factors be given equal weight? Are there additional factors that should be taken into account?

2. *Diligence.* One factor, used throughout the country, is the "requester's diligence in preparing for trial." The *Pope* court finds that Pope "did the best he could to help himself." Do you agree? Does his obvious mental problem affect your response? Why is this even a factor? Should the court expect the client to do anything to prepare for trial? Isn't that the job of trial counsel?

3. *Inconvenience to other parties.* Another factor is inconvenience to the opposing parties and all witnesses. The court minimizes this inconvenience, noting that "the district court could have held the continuance Pope sought to one or two days." What proof supports this conclusion? Would the result have been different had Dr. Kruzich informed the court that he could not examine the defendant for a week? A month? Note how important it is for a party seeking a continuance to get the approval (or at least acquiescence) of the other side?

4. *Special procedures to reduce need for continuance.* In some jurisdictions, the courts have developed a special procedure designed to reduce the need for continuances in cases where one is sought so that an absent witness can be produced. When a continuance motion is filed for this reason, the adverse party can admit that the witness, if produced, would testify as described in the continuance motion. The court may then deny the continuance and inform the jury that both sides agree what the witness would have said. Sometimes the court may also condition the denial of the motion on the adverse party's admission that the absent witness's evidence was true. *See, e.g.*, La. Code Crim. Proc. Ann. art. 710 (following ALI Code of Crim. Proc. § 303); Ind. Stat. Ann. § 35–36-7-1. Would either rule have been helpful in *Pope*?

5. *Actual prejudice.* The key factor is whether the defendant would suffer actual prejudice unless a continuance were ordered. General allegations are routinely rejected. The party seeking a continuance must articulate specifically how the case would be prejudiced without a continuance. This may be very difficult in some cases, especially since often a continuance actually benefits the accused.

[1] Expert Witness

As discussed in *Pope*, sometimes a continuance is sought so that expert testimony can be produced. If given for this reason, the continuance may have to be for a substantial time period so that the expert can be located, scheduled, and given time to perform scientific or other evaluations. Courts often look with suspicion when such motions are filed shortly before trial. Key factors are diligence in obtaining the expert, the length of the continuance, and prejudice if a continuance is denied.

Cases are resolved based on their unique facts. When a continuance should have been given to obtain expert testimony, the evidence is virtually always of critical importance. *See, e.g., United States v. Ellis*, 2008 WL341711 (4th Cir.)(abuse of discretion to deny continuance in telephone bomb threat case; defendant's voice identification expert would be in Russia on trial date; defense counsel provided a report about the anticipated expert testimony exonerating the defendant; stated no substitute expert was available; government did not object to continuance; and continuance was only for two weeks); *State v. Hunter*, 177 P.3d 1001 (Kan. App. 2008)(reversal for failure to grant continuance so defense counsel could obtain expert testimony on proper interview techniques of child victim witness in child rape cases; testimony "of utmost importance").

Most often the denial of a continuance is upheld. *See, e.g., Johnson v. Puckett*, 176 F.3d 809 (5th Cir. 1999) (upholding denial of continuance motion to permit defendant to obtain testimony of two forensic scientists who would support defense theory that cuts on defendant's hands were consistent with defendant's assisting in rescue of homicide victim; motion filed only 10 days before trial, no affidavits submitted establishing materiality or necessity of testimony, and no statement of when experts would be available); *United States v. Wagner*, 834 F.2d 1474 (9th Cir. 1987) (trial court properly denied defense motion for continuance, requested on the first day of trial, to permit the defendant to be examined by a government psychiatrist in accordance with a pretrial order issued six weeks before trial; defendant had refused to make reasonable efforts to schedule this examination and no prejudice shown).

[2] Lay Witness and Other Evidence

A related reason for a continuance sought by either the prosecution or defense is the need to locate or produce helpful lay witnesses. The continuance motion is more compelling if the party seeking it can establish the likely content and importance of the testimony, efforts made to secure the testimony (especially whether a subpoena was served), the likelihood of locating the witness if a continuance is granted, the length of the requested continuance, and the likely prejudice if the continuance motion is denied. *See, e.g., State v. Wilcox*, 487 F.3d 1163 (8th Cir. 2007)(upholding continuance denial to allow ambulance driver to testify about victim's mother's behavior on way to hospital; testimony marginally relevant on credibility and partially cumulative); *United States v. Kidwell*, 217 Fed. Appx. 441 (6th Cir. 2007)(upholding continuance denial to locate 20 witnesses who would support an invalid defense of drug legalization); *State v. Iniquez*, 2008 WL 962634 (Wash. App.)(upholding continuance for absent prosecution witness).

A continuance may be requested to permit a party or witness to observe a religious holy day. *See, e.g.*, Tex. Code Crim. Proc. art. 29.011 (continuance to permit party to observe religious holy day). A failure to grant this continuance may raise equal protection and First Amendment issues.

Counsel also may ask for continuances to secure other kinds of evidence. *See, e.g., State v. Carr*, 610 S.W.2d 296 (Mo. App. 1980) (x-rays); *King v. State*, 656 S.W.2d 544 (Tex. App. 1983) (latent fingerprints taken from vehicle); *Ex parte Hays*, 518 So.2d 768 (Ala. 1986) (state given one day continuance to obtain physical evidence being tested by out-of-state laboratory). Presumably, a continuance to allow time for DNA identification testing requested by either prosecution or defense, or both jointly, would also be in order.

[3] Secure Counsel and Adequate Preparation Time

Another basis for requesting a continuance is that time is needed to secure counsel, to replace existing counsel with a more acceptable lawyer, or to permit counsel to prepare for the hearing. A continuance on this basis is often sought pursuant to the due process guarantee of a fair trial and the Sixth Amendment's guarantee of the effective assistance of counsel. Sometimes a statute or court rule specifically authorizes a continuance for this reason. *See, e.g.*, Ga. Code Ann. § 17-8-24 (authorizing continuance for illness or absence of sole or leading counsel).

The ground for a continuance also applies to the government when, for example, the prosecutor handling the case is occupied in another trial. *State v. Chichester*, 170 P.2d 583 (Wash. App. 2007).

It can also be an issue when the defendant waives counsel and represents himself. A last-minute continuance request to allow the defendant more time to prepare may be rejected. *See, e.g., State v. Moore*, 920 So.2d 334 (La. App. 2006)(no need for continuance when defendant was already familiar with defense witnesses).

[a] Judicial Discretion

In a case in which a defendant was given five days notice of a hearing and on the day of the hearing requested a continuance in order to permit retained counsel to become familiar with the record, the United States Supreme Court noted:

> The matter of continuance is traditionally within the discretion of the trial judge, and it is not every denial of a request for more time that violates due process even if the party [seeking the continuance] fails to offer evidence or is compelled to defend without counsel. Contrariwise, a myopic insistence upon expeditiousness in the face of a justifiable request for delay can render the right to defend with counsel an empty formality. There are no mechanical tests for deciding when a denial of a continuance is so arbitrary as to violate due process. The answer must be found in the circumstances present in every case, particularly in the reasons presented to the trial judge at the time the request is denied.

Ungar v. Sarafite, 376 U.S. 575, 589 (1964) (citations omitted). In another case, the Supreme Court observed:

> Trial judges necessarily require a great deal of latitude in scheduling trials. Not the least of their problems is that of assembling the witnesses, lawyers, and jurors at the same place at the same time, and this burden counsels against continuances except for compelling reasons. Consequently, broad discretion must be granted trial courts on matters of continuances; only an unreasoning and arbitrary "insistence upon expeditiousness in the face of a justifiable request for delay" violates the right to the assistance of counsel.

Morris v. Slappy, 461 U.S. 1, 11–12 (1983) (upholding denial of continuance to permit representation by defendant's preferred counsel). *Cf. United States v. Cronic*, 466 U.S. 648 (1984) (no Sixth Amendment violation for ineffective assistance of counsel even though inexperienced counsel given only 25 days to prepare for trial involving complex issues and almost inaccessible witnesses).

One case, *United States v. Flanders*, 491 F.3d 1197 (10th Cir. 2007), described the factors in deciding whether there should be a continuance for the defendant to obtain new counsel:

> We review the district court's decision for abuse of discretion, balancing the defendant's constitutional right to retain counsel of . . . choice against the need to maintain the highest standards of professional responsibility, the public's confidence in the integrity of the judicial process and the orderly administration of justice, In striking that balance, we consider whether: 1) the continuance would inconvenience witnesses, the court, counsel, or the parties; 2) other continuances have been granted; 3) legitimate reasons warrant a delay; 4) the defendant's actions contributed to the delay; 5) other competent counsel is prepared to try the case; 6) rejecting the request would materially prejudice or substantially harm the defendant's case; 7) the case is complex; and 8) any other case-specific factors necessitate or weigh against further delay. [citations omitted]

[b] Efforts to Avoid Continuance

In resolving requests for a continuance to secure the services of well prepared counsel of choice, courts routinely ask whether the delay could have been avoided. If the need for new counsel arose because the original lawyer suddenly became ill or otherwise had to withdraw on short notice from representation, continuances are routinely given in those cases where the prosecution or the defendant made reasonable efforts to find substitute counsel on a timely basis.

On the other hand, if the accused had adequate time to secure the services of acceptable counsel, in some cases the continuance will be denied, resulting in a trial with defense counsel who had been fired by the defendant, with no defense lawyer at all, or with counsel who had inadequate time to prepare for the proceeding. *See, e.g., United States v. Kikumura*, 947 F.2d 72 (3d Cir. 1991) (denial of continuance upheld because accused had 4 months notice of resentencing hearing and appointed counsel adequately represented him; constitution only requires defendant be given fair and reasonable opportunity to have counsel of choice); *United States v. Poulack*, 556 F.2d 83 (1st Cir. 1977) (right to retained counsel of choice "cannot be insisted upon in a manner that will obstruct reasonable and orderly court procedure;" court gave 3 month continuance to permit defendant to be represented by particular lawyer; additional 3 month continuance properly denied and representation by appointed counsel permissible); *State v. Divine*, 738 So. 2d 614 (La. App. 1999) (defendant "cannot, by last minute change of counsel, force a postponement;" trial scheduled two months in advance; on day of trial original defense counsel asked for continuance so new retained counsel could prepare; continuance denied because defendant had adequate time to hire counsel of choice).

[c] Factor Approach

As with other grounds for continuance, a "factor approach" is also used in assessing whether a continuance should have been given to allow counsel to prepare for trial. *See, e.g., United States v. Tingle*, 183 F.3d 719 (7th Cir. 1999) (upholding trial court's refusal to give new defense counsel more than 2 week continuance to prepare for trial; factors include amount of time available to prepare, likelihood of prejudice from denial of additional time, complexity of case, adequacy of defense actually provided, counsel's skill and experience, and work of other lawyers assisting in the case).

Occasionally the denial of a continuance causes reversible error. *See, e.g., Grant v. Dortch*, 993 S.W.2d 506 (Ky. App. 1999) (due process violated when trial court denied continuance motion to permit defense counsel, appointed minutes before contempt trial, to confer with defendant and prepare case).

[4] Harmful Publicity

In cases that have generated significant pretrial publicity, defendants (and occasionally prosecutors) will ask for a continuance to permit the harmful effects of the press coverage to diminish. As discussed more fully in Chapter 15, the due process right to a fair trial and the Sixth Amendment right to an impartial jury guarantee a jury that has not been too tainted by exposure to media reports of the case. To effectuate those rights, sometimes a continuance is granted until the publicity has abated. According to the Supreme Court, "That time soothes and erases is a perfectly natural phenomenon, familiar to all." *Patton v. Yount*, 467 U.S. 1025, 1034 (1984).

Change of venue. Another alternative, often used in lieu of or in addition to a continuance, is for the trial court to grant a change of venue, discussed in Chapter 14, or to rely on extensive voir dire of potential jurors to alleviate the harmful impact of substantial pretrial publicity. *See, e.g., United States v. Moreno Morales*, 815 F.2d 725 (1st Cir. 1987) (where media gave extensive coverage to case involving alleged police murders of Puerto Rican independence workers, trial court correctly granted only one continuance to permit media impact to subside; change of venue is preferred method of countering substantial pretrial publicity; jury voir dire was extensive, taking 17 days and involving 195 potential jurors).

[5]   Death Penalty Cases

Continuances are often sought in death penalty cases after the defendant has been convicted and before the sentencing phase of the trial has begun. Defense counsel may request a continuance in order to have time to prepare for the death penalty phase of the proceeding. *See generally* Robin E. Abrams, Note, *A Capital Defendant's Right to a Continuance Between the Two Phases of a Death Penalty Trial*, 64 N.Y.U. L. Rev. 579 (1989) (arguing a continuance of at least 72 hours should be granted automatically after the death penalty phase of a capital case so that defense counsel can adequately prepare for the sentencing hearing; such continuances should actually be given for an average of 30 days). As a general rule, because the stakes are so high, courts are often sympathetic to continuance requests in death penalty cases.

[6]   Appeal

On appeal, in cases where a continuance was denied, the issue usually is whether the due process right to a fair trial was violated when the trial court denied the request for a continuance. Courts take a factor approach in resolving the issue, looking at the source, content, and relevance of the evidence; whether the witness or other evidence will actually be produced if the continuance is granted; the diligence used to obtain the proof by the original trial date; the inconvenience to the court and all parties; the length of the requested continuance; and the prejudice caused to the accused if the continuance is not granted.

C.   PROCEDURAL ISSUES

Request and motion practice. A party seeking a continuance must request one. Failure to ask for a continuance will bar appellate review of a claim that the trial court should have delayed a proceeding.

In some courts, a request for a continuance must be made by written motion which must give the reasons why the continuance is sought. *See, e.g.*, Cal. Penal Code § 1050(b) (written notice of request for continuance); La. Code Crim. Proc. Ann. art. 707 (grounds for continuance must be in writing and must state grounds upon which based).

In response to a concern that a delay will be sought to obtain a tactical advantage, some state rules mandate that the continuance motion must indicate that it is made in "good faith." *See, e.g.*, Fla. R. Crim. Proc. 3.190(g)(4); Tex. Code Crim. Proc. art. 29.06 (continuance motion based on absence of witness must state that motion not made for delay).

Affidavit. Often the motion for a continuance will be accompanied by an affidavit that provides specific facts in support of the motion. For example, if a continuance is sought because trial counsel has two trials scheduled on the same date, he or she may file a Motion for a Continuance accompanied by an Affidavit in which the lawyer details such matters as the location, date, judge, and time of the two conflicting proceedings. If the affidavit will reveal strategy or provide unnecessary discovery (such as the name or likely testimony of a witness) to adversary counsel, the lawyer submitting it may file it, in some jurisdictions, as a sealed document to be read only by the judge.

Timing. Because requests for a continuance may cause a judge and other parties in this and later cases considerable inconvenience, requests for a continuance should be made as soon as possible. A request made a month before trial may be viewed more favorably than one made the day before trial. Obviously, any such request should include a detailed statement of why the continuance is needed and how long a delay is sought.

Sometimes a statute or court rule will mandate that a request for a continuance should ordinarily be made a specified time in advance of the proceeding. *See, e.g.*, Ind. Stat. Ann. § 35–36–7-1 (continuance motion ordinarily must be filed at least 5 days before trial); La. Code Crim. Proc. Ann. art. 707 (continuance motion must be filed at least 7 days before trial).

As discussed in Chapter 9, informal communication between prosecution and defense, and reasonable give-and-take over scheduling issues can sometimes be more efficient and effective than going through the formalities of motion practice to obtain a continuance. An assented to or unopposed motion by either side is unlikely to be denied, unless the court is facing external pressures to have the case tried quickly, or subject to local rules that limit its ability to grant a continuance. Sometimes a continuance can even be obtained by a phone call to the court clerk, who will reschedule the proceeding.

A formal motion for continuance is always an option for either side if informal channels of communication between parties are unsuccessful.

Notice to other side. Because a continuance may cause witnesses and others considerable inconvenience, the better practice is for counsel seeking a continuance to notify the other side as soon as possible that a continuance will be requested. This courteous practice will permit witnesses, lawyers, and others to be informed that the hearing will not be held as originally scheduled. It will also make it more likely that the judge will look favorably on the request, since efforts were made to minimize the ill effects of the delay.

Hearing. Trial judges are given broad discretion in deciding when to schedule a hearing on a Motion for a Continuance. If the continuance is sought because of an illness or other physical or mental disability, the court may hold the evidentiary hearing shortly before the scheduled trial date. This will enable the court to base its decision on the most current medical and other information. It may also give the court sufficient information to deny the continuance but structure the trial so that it minimizes possible harm to parties or witnesses who are ill or disabled.

Record. In order to facilitate appellate review if a continuance motion is denied, counsel who seek a continuance should ensure that the record reflects the formal request, the reasons why the request was made, the pertinent dates (for example, the date counsel was retained), the reasons why the continuance was denied, and the harm caused by the denial. For instance, if a judge denies a continuance motion that requests time to prepare for trial, the lawyer who lost the motion should make efforts to include in the record specific reasons why the lawyer's trial performance was impeded by inadequate preparation time.

Speedy trial. Sometimes a request for a continuance may conflict with an accused's constitutional or statutory rights to a speedy trial, discussed more fully in Chapter 13. If the continuance request is made by the accused, often the Sixth Amendment's speedy trial rights are not violated since one factor in assessing such rights is whether the accused sought a trial or asked for a continuance. *See Barker v. Wingo*, 407 U.S. 514 (1972). On the other hand, if the prosecution seeks the continuance, the court may deny the motion because the continuance would cause the accused's Sixth Amendment speedy trial rights to be violated.

Similarly, if the speedy trial rights originate in a statute, often the defendant's request for a continuance tolls the right to a trial within the mandated time frame. For example, the Federal Speedy Trial Act, which sets specific time limits for various criminal proceedings in each case, does not count:

> any period of delay resulting from a continuance granted by any judge on his own motion or at the request of the defendant or his counsel or at the request of the attorney for the Government, if the judge granted such continuance on the basis of his findings that the ends of justice served by taking such action outweigh the best interest of the public and the defendant in a speedy trial.

18 U.S.C. § 3161(h)(8)(A). The federal judge must include in the record the reasons for finding that the ends of justice outweigh the interests of the public and the defendant in a speedy trial. The statute also provides the judge with a list of some of the factors to

consider in this decision. They include whether the grant of a continuance would make it possible to conduct the proceeding eventually or would result in a miscarriage of justice, whether the case is so unusual or complex the usual time limits are unreasonable, and whether the failure to grant the delay would unreasonably deny the defendant time to obtain counsel or either side time to prepare adequately. 18 U.S.C. § 3161(h)(8)(B). A continuance may not toll the speedy trial time limits if based on either the court's congested calendar or the government's lack of diligence in preparing its case. 18 U.S.C. § 3161(h)(8)(C).

The matter is especially complex if there are multiple defendants, only one of whom requests a continuance. Since the speedy trial rights of the remaining defendants may have to be respected, the trial court may have to sever the trial of the one defendant if the continuance is granted for that defendant but not the other offenders.

Other justifications for a delay. Although this chapter has focused on the issue of a continuance, delays in proceedings may also occur for other procedural reasons. In many jurisdictions, for example, the prosecutor may withdraw the charges or enter a *nolle prosequi* at any time before the trial begins. Both of these procedures terminate the prosecution, but not necessarily permanently. In some localities, the prosecution can then renew the prosecution, without court approval, by seeking a new indictment or issuing a new information. The net result of this process is that the prosecution gets a delay in the proceeding without having to obtain a court-ordered continuance. There may be both statutory and constitutional limits on this practice. For example, the delay cannot violate the accused's Sixth Amendment or statutory speedy trial rights. In addition, some jurisdictions permit the prosecution to withdraw or *nolle prosequi* cases only with the approval of the trial judge.

PROBLEM 12-1. THE TIME HAS COME, THE WALLRUSS SAID

On January 3rd, Byron Abbot was arrested and charged with bank robbery. Abbot's mother immediately hired Tasheka Cogdon, a local criminal defense lawyer, to represent him. Cogdon thoroughly investigated the case over the next three months. Trial was to begin on June 15th. When Abbot and Cogdon could not agree on a defense strategy, Abbot fired her on May 3rd. On May 29th, he retained attorney William Bell, who studied the case file and discussed the case with prosecutors for almost two weeks. Bell was the senior partner in a five-lawyer office. The case has been assigned to Judge Jane Wallruss.

On June 10th, Bell filed a Motion for a Continuance, based on two grounds: he needed time to locate witnesses who may be able to testify that Abbot was not the robber; and, as the result of a jail fight, Abbot had sustained a bad concussion and a broken jaw that needed surgery in the next few weeks.

1. With regard to the request for a continuance based on the need to investigate further, what facts should defense attorney Bell allege in an Affidavit filed with the continuance motion? How long a delay should he seek? Would your answer depend on whether Bell was (1) a recent law school graduate or (2) had been a prosecutor for ten years and then a leading defense lawyer for eight more years?

2. With respect to defendant Abbot's physical injuries, what facts should the defense counsel allege in an Affidavit filed with the continuance motion? Whose affidavit(s) should be included? How long a continuance should the defense counsel seek? What if Abbot started the fight and was clearly at fault in getting injured?

3. If you were Judge Wallruss, would you grant the continuance on either ground? If so, for how long? How would your answer change if you believed the trial would take only two days? Three weeks?

4. In lieu of a continuance, sometimes a judge will structure the trial (duration of hearings each day, number and length of recesses each trial day, physical arrangement of the courtroom, in-court presence of medical personnel to assist, etc.) to accommodate the unusual medical or other needs of parties or witnesses. Would this approach be helpful in this case?

5. Note that defense counsel Bell filed the Motion for a Continuance on June 10th. Should he have done this earlier? Why? What additional information, if any, would be relevant to your assessment whether Bell was tardy in filing the motion?

6. If you were Judge Wallruss, would you conduct a hearing on the Motion for a Continuance? When would you schedule the hearing? Would you have to delay the start of trial in order to have a full hearing on the continuance motion?

Chapter 13

TIME LIMITATIONS

A. INTRODUCTION AND OVERVIEW

After the police have identified a particular person as having committed a crime, there may be considerable delay between the date of the crime (or identification of the alleged criminal) and the date of various proceedings. For example, assume that a crime was committed in January, 2003. The accused could be identified shortly afterward or years after the offense. After being identified, he or she may be arrested anywhere from days to years later. Other proceedings may also be held promptly or after considerable delay. The prosecution could obtain an indictment shortly after the culprit was identified or years afterwards. Similarly, the trial and sentencing could occur shortly after the crime or indictment, or years after one or both.

One could easily imagine a robbery occurring in 2006, an arrest (following an extensive investigation) made in 2007, an indictment in 2008, and a trial in 2009. Although there may be valid reasons why each of these events occurred when it did, the significant time between the crime, formal charges, and the trial may cause considerable problems for both the defense and the prosecution. The defendant may have spent months or years in jail awaiting trial. Moreover, evidence for both sides may have disappeared or become less reliable as memories fade and witnesses become difficult to trace. The public itself may lose confidence in a judicial system that takes so long to discharge its important responsibilities.

Because of these important concerns, American law has long placed some limits on these delays. In general terms, some proceedings cannot be delayed too long without offending statutes, procedural rules, or state and federal constitutional guarantees. Delays between the commission of the crime and the institution of formal charges are often referred to as *pre-accusation delays* and are addressed principally through state and federal statutes of limitations. These requirements place pressure on the police to expedite investigations and to institute formal processes in a timely fashion.

Delays in convening a trial are addressed explicitly by the Sixth Amendment's speedy trial provision that "[i]n all criminal prosecutions, the accused shall enjoy the right to a speedy and public trial." Virtually all state constitutions have similar speedy trial guarantees. Additionally, a variety of state and federal statutes and rules of procedure establish precise time limitations upon formal charges and trials. These rules bar the prosecution from indefinitely postponing trials and other criminal proceedings. Finally, the due process clause places general limits on delays in every portion of the criminal justice process, but its most significant impact is restricted to pre-accusation and post-conviction phases of the criminal case.

Because the United States Supreme Court decisions address principally post-accusation delays, this chapter begins with an examination of those issues. It concludes with consideration of pre-charge and post-conviction matters.

B. POST-ACCUSATION DELAYS

One possible delay is the period between the institution of formal charges (either an arrest or an indictment) and the beginning of a trial. For example, an accused could be indicted in 2006 but not tried until 2008 or 2009, the time lag being caused by an infinite variety of circumstances. At one end of the spectrum, the accused may have escaped shortly after being indicted, causing delay of the trial until the escapee is apprehended. On the other hand, trial could have been delayed because judicial or prosecutorial resources were committed to other trials involving other defendants, because the prosecution needed more time to investigate this offense, because the prosecution was waiting for an important witness to recover from a serious illness, because the defense lawyer was ill or had requested the delays, or because the case got forgotten in an overloaded system with far too few prosecutors and inadequate records.

There are several important limitations on this delay. The speedy trial guarantee, contained in the Sixth Amendment to the federal constitution, places some restrictions upon tardy trials. Statutory "speedy trial" laws do so as well.

[1]   Constitutional Speedy Trial Guarantee

In *Klopfer v. North Carolina*, 386 U.S. 213 (1967), the United States Supreme Court held that the Sixth Amendment right to speedy trial applies to the states through the due process clause of the Fourteenth Amendment. It was not until 1972, however, that the Court, in the next case, addressed the two most significant questions related to that guarantee: (1) by what standard is a court to determine whether the right to a speedy trial has been violated and (2) what remedy is required for such a violation?

BARKER v. WINGO
407 U.S. 514 (1972)

Mr. Justice Powell delivered the opinion of the Court.

[Barker was indicted September 15, 1958, in connection with a double homicide. Because the state wanted to obtain the testimony of his co-defendant, Manning, the decision was made to proceed first against Manning. Assuming Manning's conviction, he would then be available to testify against Barker. This strategy resulted in a series of some sixteen continuances of Barker's trial, to which Barker did not object. Because of various difficulties (mistrials and reversals of convictions), Manning's convictions did not occur until late 1962.]

In February 1963, the first term of court following Manning's final conviction, the Commonwealth moved to set Barker's trial for March 19. But on the day scheduled for trial, it again moved for a continuance until the June term. It gave as its reason the illness of the ex-sheriff who was the chief investigating officer in the case. To this continuance, Barker objected unsuccessfully.

The witness was still unable to testify in June, and the trial, which had been set for June 19, was continued again until the September term over Barker's objection. This time the court announced that the case would be dismissed for lack of prosecution if it were not tried during the next term. The final trial date was set for October 9, 1963. On that date, Barker again moved to dismiss the indictment, and this time specified that his right to a speedy trial had been violated. The motion was denied; the trial commenced with Manning as the chief prosecution witness; Barker was convicted and given a life sentence.

. . . The right to a speedy trial is generically different from any of the other rights enshrined in the Constitution for the protection of the accused. In addition to the general concern that all accused persons be treated according to decent and fair procedures, there is a societal interest in providing a speedy trial which exists separate from, and at times in opposition to, the interests of the accused. The inability of courts to provide a prompt trial has contributed to a large backlog of cases in urban courts which, among other things, enables defendants to negotiate more effectively for pleas of guilty to lesser offenses and otherwise manipulate the system. In addition, persons released on bond for lengthy periods awaiting trial have an opportunity to commit other crimes. It must be of little comfort to the residents of Christian County, Kentucky, to know that Barker was at large on bail for over four years while accused of a vicious and brutal murder of which he was ultimately convicted. Moreover, the longer an accused is free awaiting trial, the more tempting becomes his opportunity to jump bail and escape. Finally, delay between arrest and punishment may have a detrimental effect on rehabilitation.

. . . A second difference between the right to speedy trial and the accused's other constitutional rights is that deprivation of the right may work to the accused's advantage. Delay is not an uncommon defense tactic. As the time between the commission of the crime and trial lengthens, witnesses may become unavailable or their memories may fade. If the witnesses support the prosecution, its case will be weakened, sometimes seriously so. And it is the prosecution which carries the burden of proof. Thus, unlike the right to counsel or the right to be free from compelled self-incrimination, deprivation of the right to speedy trial does not per se prejudice the accused's ability to defend himself.

Finally, and perhaps most importantly, the right to speedy trial is a more vague concept than other procedural rights. It is, for example, impossible to determine with precision when the right has been denied. We cannot definitely say how long is too long in a system where justice is supposed to be swift but deliberate. As a consequence, there is no fixed point in the criminal process when the State can put the defendant to the choice of either exercising or waiving the right to a speedy trial.

. . . The amorphous quality of the right also leads to the unsatisfactorily severe remedy of dismissal of the indictment when the right has been deprived. This is indeed a serious consequence because it means that a defendant who may be guilty of a serious crime will go free, without having been tried. Such a remedy is more serious than an exclusionary rule or a reversal for a new trial, but it is the only possible remedy.

Perhaps because the speedy trial right is so slippery, two rigid approaches are urged upon us as ways of eliminating some of the uncertainty which courts experience in protecting the right. The first suggestion is that we hold that the Constitution requires a criminal defendant to be offered a trial within a specified time period. The result of such a ruling would have the virtue of clarifying when the right is infringed and of simplifying courts' application of it. Recognizing this, some legislatures have enacted laws, and some courts have adopted procedural rules which more narrowly define the right.

. . . But such a result would require this Court to engage in legislative or rulemaking activity, rather than in the adjudicative process to which we should confine our efforts. We do not establish procedural rules for the States, except when mandated by the Constitution. We find no constitutional basis for holding that the speedy trial right can be quantified into a specified number of days or months. The States, of course, are free to prescribe a reasonable period consistent with constitutional standards, but our approach must be less precise.

The second suggested alternative would restrict consideration of the right to those cases in which the accused has demanded a speedy trial. Most States have recognized what is loosely referred to as the "demand rule," although eight States reject it. It is not clear, however, precisely what is meant by that term. Although every federal court of appeals that has considered the question has endorsed some kind of demand rule, some have regarded the rule within the concept of waiver, whereas others have viewed it as a factor to be weighed in assessing whether there has been a deprivation of the speedy trial right. We shall refer to the former approach as the demand-waiver doctrine. The demand-waiver doctrine provides that a defendant waives any consideration of his right to speedy trial for any period prior to which he has not demanded a trial. Under this rigid approach, a prior demand is a necessary condition to the consideration of the speedy trial right.

Such an approach, by presuming waiver of a fundamental right from inaction, is inconsistent with this Court's pronouncements on waiver of constitutional rights. The Court has defined waiver as "an intentional relinquishment or abandonment of a known right or privilege."

. . . In excepting the right to speedy trial from the rule of waiver we have applied to other fundamental rights, courts that have applied the demand-waiver rule have relied on the assumption that delay usually works for the benefit of the accused and on the absence of any readily ascertainable time in the criminal process for a defendant to be given the choice of exercising or waiving his right. But it is not necessarily true that delay benefits the defendant. There are cases in which delay appreciably harms the defendant's ability to defend himself. Moreover, a defendant confined to jail prior to trial is obviously disadvantaged by delay as is a defendant released on bail but unable to lead a normal life because of community suspicion and his own anxiety.

The nature of the speedy trial right does make it impossible to pinpoint a precise time in the process when the right must be asserted or waived, but that fact does not argue for placing the burden of protecting the right solely on defendants. A defendant has no duty to bring himself to trial; the State has that duty as well as the duty of insuring that the trial is consistent with due process. Moreover, for the reasons earlier expressed, society has a particular interest in bringing swift prosecutions, and society's representatives are the ones who should protect that interest.

. . . We reject, therefore, the rule that a defendant who fails to demand a speedy trial forever waives his right. This does not mean, however, that the defendant has no responsibility to assert his right. We think the better rule is that the defendant's assertion of or failure to assert his right to a speedy trial is one of the factors to be considered in an inquiry into the deprivation of the right. Such a formulation avoids the rigidities of the demand-waiver rule and the resulting possible unfairness in its application. It allows the trial court to exercise a judicial discretion based on the circumstances, including due consideration of any applicable formal procedural rule. It would permit, for example, a court to attach a different weight to a situation in which the defendant knowingly fails to object from a situation in which his attorney acquiesces in long delay without adequately informing his client, or from a situation in which no counsel is appointed. It would also allow a court to weigh the frequency and force of the objections as opposed to attaching significant weight to a purely pro forma objection.

In ruling that a defendant has some responsibility to assert a speedy trial claim, we do not depart from our holdings in other cases concerning the waiver of fundamental rights, in which we have placed the entire responsibility on the prosecution to show that the claimed waiver was knowingly and voluntarily made. Such cases have involved rights which must be exercised or waived at a specific time or under clearly identifiable circumstances, such as the rights to plead not guilty, to demand a jury trial, to exercise the privilege against self-incrimination, and to have the assistance of counsel. We have shown above that the right to a speedy trial is unique in its uncertainty as to when and under what circumstances it must be asserted or may be deemed waived. But the rule we announce today, which comports with constitutional principles, places the primary burden on the courts and the prosecutors to assure that cases are brought to trial. We hardly need add that if delay is attributable to the defendant, then his waiver may be given effect under standard waiver doctrine, the demand rule aside.

We, therefore, reject both of the inflexible approaches — the fixed-time period because it goes further than the Constitution requires; the demand-waiver rule because it is insensitive to a right which we have deemed fundamental. The approach we accept is a balancing test, in which the conduct of both the prosecution and the defendant are weighed.

A balancing test necessarily compels courts to approach speedy trial cases on an ad hoc basis. We can do little more than identify some of the factors which courts should assess in determining whether a particular defendant has been deprived of his right. Though some might express them in different ways, we identify four such factors: length of delay, the reason for the delay, the defendant's assertion of his right, and prejudice to the defendant.

The length of the delay is to some extent a triggering mechanism. Until there is some delay which is presumptively prejudicial, there is no necessity for inquiry into the other factors that go into the balance. Nevertheless, because of the imprecision of the right to speedy trial, the length of delay that will provoke such an inquiry is necessarily dependent upon the peculiar circumstances of the case. To take but one example, the delay that can be tolerated for an ordinary street crime is considerably less than for a serious, complex conspiracy charge.

Closely related to length of delay is the reason the government assigns to justify the delay. Here, too, different weights should be assigned to different reasons. A deliberate attempt to delay the trial in order to hamper the defense should be weighted heavily against the government. A more neutral reason such as negligence or overcrowded courts should be weighted less heavily but nevertheless should be considered since the ultimate responsibility for such circumstances must rest with the government rather than with the defendant. Finally, a valid reason, such as a missing witness, should serve to justify appropriate delay.

We have already discussed the third factor, the defendant's responsibility to assert his right. Whether and how a defendant asserts his right is closely related to the other factors we have mentioned. The strength of his efforts will be affected by the length of the delay, to some extent by the reason for the delay, and most particularly by the personal prejudice, which is not always readily identifiable, that he experiences. The more serious the deprivation, the more likely a defendant is to complain. The defendant's assertion of his speedy trial right, then, is entitled to strong evidentiary weight in determining whether the defendant is being deprived of the right. We emphasize that failure to assert the right will make it difficult for a defendant to prove that he was denied a speedy trial.

A fourth factor is prejudice to the defendant. Prejudice, of course, should be assessed in the light of the interests of defendants which the speedy trial right was designed to protect. This Court has identified three such interests: (i) to prevent oppressive pretrial incarceration; (ii) to minimize anxiety and concern of the accused; and (iii) to limit the possibility that the defense will be impaired. Of these, the most serious is the last, because the inability of a defendant adequately to prepare his case skews the fairness of the entire system. If witnesses die or disappear during a delay, the prejudice is obvious. There is also prejudice if defense witnesses are unable to recall accurately events of the distant past. Loss of memory, however, is not always reflected in the record because what has been forgotten can rarely be shown.

We have discussed previously the societal disadvantages of lengthy pretrial incarceration, but obviously the disadvantages for the accused who cannot obtain his release are even more serious. The time spent in jail awaiting trial has a detrimental impact on the individual. It often means loss of a job; it disrupts family life; and it enforces idleness. Most jails offer little or no recreational or rehabilitative programs. The time spent in jail is simply dead time. Moreover, if a defendant is locked up, he is hindered in his ability to gather evidence, contact witnesses, or otherwise prepare his defense. Imposing those consequences on anyone who has not yet been convicted is serious. It is especially unfortunate to impose them on those persons who are ultimately found to be innocent. Finally, even if an accused is not incarcerated prior to trial, he is still disadvantaged by restraints on his liberty and by living under a cloud of anxiety, suspicion, and often hostility.

We regard none of the four factors identified above as either a necessary or sufficient condition to the finding of a deprivation of the right of speedy trial. Rather, they are related factors and must be considered together with such other circumstances as may be relevant. In sum, these factors have no talismanic qualities; courts must still engage in a difficult and sensitive balancing process. But, because we are dealing with a fundamental right of the accused, this process must be carried out with full recognition that the accused's interest in a speedy trial is specifically affirmed in the Constitution.

The difficulty of the task of balancing these factors is illustrated by this case, which we consider to be close. It is clear that the length of delay between arrest and trial — well over five years — was extraordinary. Only seven months of that period can be attributed to a strong excuse, the illness of the ex-sheriff who was in charge of the investigation. Perhaps some delay would have been permissible under ordinary circumstances, so that Manning could be utilized as a witness in Barker's trial, but more than four years was too long a period, particularly since a good part of that period was attributable to the Commonwealth's failure or inability to try Manning under circumstances that comported with due process.

Two counterbalancing factors, however, outweigh these deficiencies. The first is that prejudice was minimal. Of course, Barker was prejudiced to some extent by living for over four years under a cloud of suspicion and anxiety. Moreover, although he was released on bond for most of the period, he did spend 10 months in jail before trial. But there is no claim that any of Barker's witnesses died or otherwise became unavailable owing to the delay. The trial transcript indicates only two very minor lapses of memory — one on the part of a prosecution witness — which were in no way significant to the outcome.

More important than the absence of serious prejudice, is the fact that Barker did not want a speedy trial. Counsel was appointed for Barker immediately after his indictment and represented him throughout the period. No question is raised as to the competency of such counsel. Despite the fact that counsel had notice of the motions for continuances, the record shows no action whatever taken between October 21, 1958, and February 12, 1962, that could be construed as the assertion of the speedy trial right. On the latter date, in response to another motion for continuance, Barker moved to dismiss the indictment. The record does not show on what ground this motion was based, although it is clear that no alternative motion was made for an immediate trial. Instead the record strongly suggests that while he hoped to take advantage of the delay in which he had acquiesced, and thereby obtain a dismissal of the charges, he definitely did not want to be tried.

. . . We do not hold that there may never be a situation in which an indictment may be dismissed on speedy trial grounds where the defendant has failed to object to continuances. There may be a situation in which the defendant was represented by incompetent counsel, was severely prejudiced, or even cases in which the continuances were granted *ex parte*. But barring extraordinary circumstances, we would be reluctant indeed to rule that a defendant was denied this constitutional right on a record that strongly indicates, as does this one, that the defendant did not want a speedy trial. We hold, therefore, that Barker was not deprived of his due process right to a speedy trial. Affirmed.

[The concurring opinion of JUSTICE WHITE is omitted.]

NOTES

1. *Demand by defendant.* One of the important factors to be weighed in the balance is, according to *Barker*, "the defendant's assertion of his right [to a speedy trial]." While *Barker* makes clear that it is not absolutely essential that the defendant "demand" a speedy trial, the Court observed that finding a violation in the absence of such a demand will be "difficult for a defendant to prove."

Should this factor be weighted differently if a defendant is proceeding *pro se*? When the defendant is represented by counsel, should this not be a threshold requirement for a finding of a speedy trial violation in *all* cases? One commentator, sympathetic to this notion, criticized the Court's analysis, comparing it "to repealing the law requiring motorists to drive on the right-hand side of the road and decreeing instead that, in tort suits following motor vehicle accidents, it shall be a 'factor' relevant to the defendant's liability whether he was driving on the right or the left." Anthony Amsterdam, *Speedy Criminal Trial: Rights and Remedies*, 27 STAN. L. REV. 525, 540 (1975). By contrast, another commentator has asserted that the defendant's true desire for a speedy trial should not govern the grant of the protection. Professor Richard Uviller would replace the Court's "distorted formula" with the following test:

> Absent an explicit and competent waiver for the period in question, the accused is denied his right to a speedy trial by the passage of an unreasonable period of time without a demonstration by the state of good and sufficient reason or necessity therefor; and further, prejudice presumptively increases with the length of elapsed time, imposing upon the state the increasing burden of proving the delay harmless by reasons more particular and persuasive than convenience, negligence, or the hope of tactical advantage.

H. Richard Uviller, *Barker v. Wingo: Speedy Trial Gets a Fast Shuffle*, 72 COLUM. L. R. 1376, 1400 (1972).

2. *Length of delay.* Regarding the length of delay question, the *Barker* Court alluded to the assumed fact that "delay . . . can be tolerated [more so] for a serious, complex conspiracy charge [than] an ordinary street crime." Did the Court act with haste in selecting these examples? Is it not probable that many conspiracy cases are far *less* complex in terms of case preparation than street crimes?

One commentator has observed that courts tend to treat delays of eight months or more as presumptively prejudicial to the accused, while delays of less than five months generally are not deemed to be prejudicial. *See* Gregory P.N. Joseph, *Speedy Trial Rights in Application*, 48 FORDHAM L. REV. 611 (1980). Yet this rule of thumb is not without exceptions. *Contrast, State v. Goss*, 777 P.2d 781, 785 (Kan. 1989) (finding that a delay of more than one year was not presumptively prejudicial) with *State v. Weaver*, 78 P. 3d 397 (Kan. 2003)(fourteen month delay held presumptively prejudicial, but presumption held to be rebutted applying the *Barker* factors to the circumstances of the case).

3. *Reasons For delay.* Another factor identified by the *Barker* Court in assessing a speedy trial claim is the reason offered by the government to justify a delay between the formal charge and trial. Sometimes a trial is delayed for a considerable period of time because of interlocutory appeals from pre-trial decisions. And a lengthy appellate process may postpone a trial for years. How should that kind of delay be factored into the balance?

In *United States v. Loud Hawk*, 474 U.S. 302 (1986), the United States Supreme Court explicitly adopted the *Barker* test to determine the extent to which appellate time consumed in the review of pretrial motions should weigh towards a speedy trial claim. While recognizing that a 90-month delay was presumptively prejudicial, the Court in *Loud Hawk* found no speedy trial violation because an interlocutory appeal was deemed to be "ordinarily . . . a valid reason that justifies the delay." Factors to be considered in this context include the strength of the government's position on the issue appealed, the importance of the issue and the seriousness of the underlying offense. Justice Marshall, joined by Justices Brennan, Blackmun and Stevens, dissented. He maintained that it was the government, rather than the defendant, who should suffer the consequences attributable to the slow appellate process, which he characterized in the case as being "patently unreasonable."

The *Barker* Court explicitly recognized that if the prosecution delayed a defendant's trial because of a missing witness, this would normally be justified. Other situations falling within this category include incompetency of the defendant and unavailability of a codefendant where the two are being tried jointly. *See* Wayne R. LaFave, Jerold H. Israel & Nancy J. King, CRIMINAL PROCEDURE § 18.2(c) (4th ed. 2004). On the other hand, delaying a trial because of the fear that evidence would not support a guilty verdict has been characterized as an "extremely unsatisfactory" justification for delay. *Arrant v. Wainwright*, 468 F.2d 677, 681 (5th Cir. 1972).

In *State v. Spivey*, 579 S.E.2d 251 (N.C. 2003), defendant's murder trial was delayed four and one-half years because, according to the prosecutor, of court congestion. While acknowledging that the delay was "presumptively prejudicial," the North Carolina Supreme Court found no Sixth Amendment speedy trial violation because the defendant failed to establish prejudice. Two dissenting justices noted that almost forty homicide cases arose after Spivey's arrest, but were disposed of before his, demonstrating indifference by the prosecutor and "precisely the type of neglect [constituting] a violation of [the] right to a speedy trial." *Id.* at 260.

4. *Prejudice.* In explaining the balancing test, the Supreme Court declared that no one factor is "either a necessary or sufficient condition to the finding of a deprivation of the right of speedy trial." However, it noted that the most significant harm is the possibility the defense will be impaired. On the facts presented in *Barker*, two factors were considered to be detrimental to Barker's claim of a violation: (1) prejudice was deemed to be "minimal," and (2) Barker apparently did not desire a speedy trial. The second factor (absence of demand) was considered to be the "more important" of the two. Assume that a defendant is able to demonstrate serious prejudice due to post-accusation delays attributable to the government (for example, the government delayed the defendant's trial until after a key defense witness was deported from the country and the government had knowledge that a prompt trial would have allowed the witness to testify). In that kind of case, should not the presence of demonstrable prejudice be sufficient, alone, for a finding of a speedy trial violation?

5. *Interests analysis.* Given the fact that the speedy trial guarantee protects against the three harms identified in *Barker*, does it follow that the right either is or is not categorically violated? That is, is it not possible that a specific kind of delay may infringe upon one of the defendant's interests (for example, prolonged pretrial detention), but not upon others? Professor Anthony Amsterdam maintains that this aspect of the *Barker* analysis is "plainly unsound." Amsterdam, *supra*, at 537.

6. *Interlocutory appeal.* Assume that you represent a person whose trial has been delayed repeatedly, notwithstanding your persistent insistence upon speedy trial. After six continuances, you file a motion for dismissal of the indictment under *Barker*, but the trial judge denies the motion. It is your position at that time that the judge erroneously weighed the *Barker* factors and that appellate review of that decision should be pursued immediately, thereby avoiding the time and cost associated with trial on the merits. Do you (or should you) have a right to an interlocutory appeal?

The United States Supreme Court answered "no" in *United States v. MacDonald*, 435 U.S. 850 (1978), holding that federal circuit courts have no jurisdiction to hear such claims prior to trial. Accordingly, the defendant was required to proceed to trial, reserving appellate review of the speedy trial issue until after verdict. The Court emphasized that "resolution of a speedy trial claim necessitates a careful assessment of the particular facts of the case [and therefore such claims] are best considered only after the relevant facts have been developed at trial." Additionally, the Court rejected the notion that the speedy trial guarantee encompasses a right not to be tried. In the Court's words, "it is the delay before trial, not the trial itself, that offends against the [right to] a speedy trial."

DOGGETT v. UNITED STATES
505 U.S. 647 (1992)

JUSTICE SOUTER delivered the opinion of the Court.

In this case we consider whether the delay of 8 1 / 2 years between petitioner's indictment and arrest violated his Sixth Amendment right to a speedy trial. We hold that it did.

On February 22, 1980, petitioner Marc Doggett was indicted for conspiring with several others to import and distribute cocaine. Douglas Driver, the Drug Enforcement Administration's principal agent investigating the conspiracy, told the United States Marshal's Service that the DEA would oversee the apprehension of Doggett and his confederates. On March 18, 1980, two police officers set out under Driver's orders to arrest Doggett at his parents' house in Raleigh, North Carolina, only to find that he was not there. His mother told the officers that he had left for Colombia four days earlier.

To catch Doggett on his return to the United States, Driver sent word of his outstanding arrest warrant to all United States Customs stations and to a number of law enforcement organizations. He also placed Doggett's name in the Treasury Enforcement Communication System (TECS), a computer network that helps Customs agents screen people entering the country, and in the National Crime Information Center computer system, which serves similar ends. The TECS entry expired that September, however, and Doggett's name vanished from the system.

In September 1981, Driver found out that Doggett was under arrest on drug charges in Panama and, thinking that a formal extradition request would be futile, simply asked Panama to "expel" Doggett to the United States. Although the Panamanian authorities promised to comply when their own proceedings had run their course, they freed Doggett the following July and let him go to Colombia, where he stayed with an aunt for several months. On September 25, 1982, he passed unhindered through Customs in New York City and settled down in Virginia. Since his return to the United States, he has married, earned a college degree, found a steady job as a computer operations manager, lived openly under his own name, and stayed within the law.

Doggett's travels abroad had not wholly escaped the Government's notice, however. In 1982, the American Embassy in Panama told the State Department of his departure to Colombia, but that information, for whatever reason, eluded the DEA, and Agent Driver assumed for several years that his quarry was still serving time in a Panamanian prison. Driver never asked DEA officials in Panama to check into Doggett's status, and only after his own fortuitous assignment to that country in 1985 did he discover Doggett's departure for Colombia. Driver then simply assumed Doggett had settled there, and he made no effort to find out for sure or to track Doggett down, either abroad or in the United States. Thus Doggett remained lost to the American criminal justice system until September 1988, when the Marshal's Service ran a simple credit check on several thousand people subject to outstanding arrest warrants and, within minutes, found out where Doggett lived and worked. On September 5, 1988, nearly 6 years after his return to the United States and 8 1 / 2 years after his indictment, Doggett was arrested.

He naturally moved to dismiss the indictment, arguing that the Government's failure to prosecute him earlier violated his Sixth Amendment right to a speedy trial. . . . The Magistrate found that the delay between Doggett's indictment [Feb. 1980] and arrest [Sept. 1988] was long enough to be "presumptively prejudicial," that the delay "clearly [was] attributable to the negligence of the government," and that Doggett could not be faulted for any delay in asserting his right to a speedy trial, there being no evidence that he had known of the charges against him until his arrest. The Magistrate also found, however, that Doggett had made no affirmative showing that the delay had impaired his ability to mount a successful defense or had otherwise prejudiced him. In his recommendation to the District Court, the Magistrate contended that this failure to demonstrate particular prejudice sufficed to defeat Doggett's speedy trial claim.

[The District Court and Court of Appeals denied relief. Doggett then entered a conditional guilty plea under Federal Rule of Criminal Procedure 11(a)(2), expressly reserving the right to appeal his ensuing conviction on the speedy trial claim.]

. . . The Sixth Amendment guarantees that, "[i]n all criminal prosecutions, the accused shall enjoy the right to a speedy . . . trial. . . . " On its face, the Speedy Trial Clause is written with such breadth that, taken literally, it would forbid the government to delay the trial of an "accused" for any reason at all. Our cases, however, have qualified the literal sweep of the provision by specifically recognizing the relevance of four separate enquiries: whether delay before trial was uncommonly long, whether the government or the criminal defendant is more to blame for that delay, whether, in due course, the defendant asserted his right to a speedy trial, and whether he suffered prejudice as the delay's result.

The first of these is actually a double enquiry. Simply to trigger a speedy trial analysis, an accused must allege that the interval between accusation and trial has crossed the threshold dividing ordinary from "presumptively prejudicial" delay, since, by definition, he cannot complain that the government has denied him a "speedy" trial if it has, in fact, prosecuted his case with customary promptness. If the accused makes this showing, the court must then consider, as one factor among several, the extent to which the delay stretches beyond the bare minimum needed to trigger judicial examination of the claim. This latter enquiry is significant to the speedy trial analysis because, as we discuss below, the presumption that pretrial delay has prejudiced the accused intensifies over time. In this case, the extraordinary 8 1 / 2 year lag between Doggett's indictment and arrest clearly suffices to trigger the speedy trial enquiry. . . .[1]

As for *Barker*'s second criterion, the Government claims to have sought Doggett with diligence. The findings of the courts below are to the contrary, however, and we review trial court determinations of negligence with considerable deference. . . . While the Government's lethargy may have reflected no more than Doggett's relative unimportance in the world of drug trafficking, it was still findable negligence, and the finding stands.

The Government goes against the record again in suggesting that Doggett knew of his indictment years before he was arrested. Were this true, *Barker*'s third factor, concerning invocation of the right to a speedy trial, would be weighed heavily against him. But here again, the Government is trying to revisit the facts. At the hearing on Doggett's speedy trial motion, it introduced no evidence challenging the testimony of Doggett's wife, who said that she did not know of the charges until his arrest, and of his mother, who claimed not to have told him or anyone else that the police had come looking for him.

. . . The Government is left, then, with its principal contention: that Doggett fails to make out a successful speedy trial claim because he has not shown precisely how he was prejudiced by the delay between his indictment and trial.

We have observed in prior cases that unreasonable delay between formal accusation and trial threatens to produce more than one sort of harm, including "oppressive pretrial incarceration," "anxiety and concern of the accused," and "the possibility that the [accused's] defense will be impaired" by dimming memories and loss of exculpatory evidence. Of these forms of prejudice, "the most serious is the last, because the inability of a defendant adequately to prepare his case skews the fairness of the entire system." Doggett claims this kind of prejudice, and there is probably no other kind that he can claim, since he was subjected neither to pretrial detention nor, he has successfully contended, to awareness of unresolved charges against him.

The Government answers Doggett's claim by citing language in three cases, *United States v. Marion*, 404 U.S. 307 (1971), *United States v. MacDonald*, 456 U.S. 1 (1982), and *United States v. Loud Hawk*, 474 U.S. 302 (1986), for the proposition that the Speedy Trial Clause does not significantly protect a criminal defendant's interest in fair adjudication. In so arguing, the Government asks us, in effect, to read part of *Barker* right out of the law, and that we will not do.

. . . As an alternative to limiting *Barker*, the Government claims Doggett has failed to make any affirmative showing that the delay weakened his ability to raise specific defenses, elicit specific testimony, or produce specific items of evidence. Though Doggett did indeed come up short in this respect, the Government's argument takes it only so far: Consideration of prejudice is not limited to the specifically demonstrable, and, as it concedes, affirmative proof of particularized prejudice is not essential to every

---

[1] Depending on the nature of the charges, the lower courts have generally found postaccusation delay "presumptively prejudicial" at least as it approaches one year. We note that, as the term is used in this threshold context, "presumptive prejudice" does not necessarily indicate a statistical probability of prejudice; it simply marks the point at which courts deem the delay unreasonable enough to trigger the *Barker* enquiry.

speedy trial claim. *Barker* explicitly recognized that impairment of one's defense is the most difficult form of speedy trial prejudice to prove because time's erosion of exculpatory evidence and testimony "can rarely be shown." . . . Thus, we generally have to recognize that excessive delay presumptively compromises the reliability of a trial in ways that neither party can prove or, for that matter, identify. While such presumptive prejudice cannot alone carry a Sixth Amendment claim without regard to the other *Barker* criteria, it is part of the mix of relevant facts, and its importance increases with the length of delay.

This brings us to an enquiry into the role that presumptive prejudice should play in the disposition of Doggett's speedy trial claim. We begin with hypothetical and somewhat easier cases and work our way to this one.

Our speedy trial standards recognize that pretrial delay is often both inevitable and wholly justifiable. The government may need time to collect witnesses against the accused, oppose his pretrial motions, or, if he goes into hiding, track him down. We attach great weight to such considerations when balancing them against the costs of going forward with a trial whose probative accuracy the passage of time has begun by degrees to throw into question. Thus, in this case, if the Government had pursued Doggett with reasonable diligence from his indictment to his arrest, his speedy trial claim would fail. Indeed, that conclusion would generally follow as a matter of course however great the delay, so long as Doggett could not show specific prejudice to his defense.

The Government concedes, on the other hand, that Doggett would prevail if he could show that the Government had intentionally held back in its prosecution of him to gain some impermissible advantage at trial. That we cannot doubt. *Barker* stressed that official bad faith in causing delay will be weighed heavily against the government and a bad-faith delay the length of this negligent one would present an overwhelming case for dismissal.

Between diligent prosecution and bad-faith delay, official negligence in bringing an accused to trial occupies the middle ground. While not compelling relief in every case where bad-faith delay would make relief virtually automatic, neither is negligence automatically tolerable simply because the accused cannot demonstrate exactly how it has prejudiced him.

. . . Although negligence is obviously to be weighed more lightly than a deliberate intent to harm the accused's defense, it still falls on the wrong side of the divide between acceptable and unacceptable reasons for delaying a criminal prosecution once it has begun. And such is the nature of the prejudice presumed that the weight we assign to official negligence compounds over time as the presumption of evidentiary prejudice grows. Thus, our toleration of such negligence varies inversely with its protractedness, and its consequent threat to the fairness of the accused's trial. Condoning prolonged and unjustifiable delays in prosecution would both penalize many defendants for the state's fault and simply encourage the government to gamble with the interests of criminal suspects assigned a low prosecutorial priority. . . .

To be sure, to warrant granting relief, negligence unaccompanied by particularized trial prejudice must have lasted longer than negligence demonstrably causing such prejudice. But even so, the Government's egregious persistence in failing to prosecute Doggett is clearly sufficient. The lag between Doggett's indictment and arrest was 8 1 / 2 years, and he would have faced trial 6 years earlier than he did but for the Government's inexcusable oversights. . . . When the Government's negligence thus causes delay six times as long as that generally sufficient to trigger judicial review, and when the presumption of prejudice, albeit unspecified, is neither extenuated, as by the defendant's acquiescence, nor persuasively rebutted,[4] the defendant is entitled to relief.

---

[4] While the Government ably counters Doggett's efforts to demonstrate particularized trial prejudice, it has

[Reversed and remanded.]

JUSTICE O'CONNOR, dissenting.

. . . The only harm to petitioner from the lapse of time was potential prejudice to his ability to defend his case. We have not allowed such speculative harm to tip the scales. Instead, we have required a showing of actual prejudice to the defense before weighing it in the balance. . . .

JUSTICE THOMAS, with whom THE CHIEF JUSTICE and JUSTICE SCALIA join, dissenting.

. . . [T]he Speedy Trial Clause's core concern is impairment of liberty. Whenever a criminal trial takes place long after the events at issue, the defendant may be prejudiced in any number of ways. But "[t]he Speedy Trial Clause does not purport to protect a defendant from all effects flowing from a delay before trial."

. . . A lengthy pretrial delay, of course, may prejudice an accused's ability to defend himself. But . . . prejudice to the defense is not the sort of impairment of liberty against which the Clause is directed. "Passage of time, whether before or after arrest, may impair memories, cause evidence to be lost, deprive the defendant of witnesses, and otherwise interfere with his ability to defend himself. But this possibility of prejudice at trial is not itself sufficient reason to wrench the Sixth Amendment from its proper context." Even though a defendant may be prejudiced by a pretrial delay, and even though the government may be unable to provide a valid justification for that delay, the Clause does not come into play unless the delay impairs the defendant's liberty.

. . . [P]rejudice to the defense stems from the interval between crime and trial, which is quite distinct from the interval between accusation and trial. If the Clause were indeed aimed at safeguarding against prejudice to the defense, then it would presumably limit all prosecutions that occur long after the criminal events at issue. A defendant prosecuted 10 years after a crime is just as hampered in his ability to defend himself whether he was indicted the week after the crime or the week before the trial — but no one would suggest that the Clause protects him in the latter situation, where the delay did not substantially impair his liberty, either through oppressive incarceration or the anxiety of known criminal charges. . . . The initiation of a formal criminal prosecution is simply irrelevant to whether the defense has been prejudiced by delay.

. . . So engrossed is the Court in applying the multifactor balancing test set forth in *Barker* that it loses sight of the nature and purpose of the speedy trial guarantee set forth in the Sixth Amendment. The Court's error [is] . . . in its failure to recognize that the speedy trial guarantee cannot be violated — and thus *Barker* does not apply at all — when an accused is entirely unaware of a pending indictment against him.

. . . Today's opinion, I fear, will transform the courts of the land into boards of law-enforcement supervision. For the Court compels dismissal of the charges against Doggett not because he was harmed in any way by the delay between his indictment and arrest,[6] but simply because the Government's efforts to catch him are found wanting. . . . By divorcing the Speedy Trial Clause from all considerations of prejudice to an accused, the Court positively invites the Nation's judges to indulge in ad hoc and result-driven second-guessing of the government's investigatory efforts. Our

---

not, and probably could not have, affirmatively proved that the delay left his ability to defend himself unimpaired.

[6] It is quite likely, in fact, that the delay benefitted Doggett. At the time of his arrest, he had been living an apparently normal, law-abiding life for some five years — a point not lost on the District Court Judge, who, instead of imposing a prison term, sentenced him to three years' probation and a $1000 fine. Thus, the delay gave Doggett the opportunity to prove what most defendants can only promise: that he no longer posed a threat to society. There can be little doubt that, had he been tried immediately after his cocaine-importation activities, he would have received a harsher sentence.

Constitution neither contemplates nor tolerates such a role. I respectfully dissent.

NOTES

1. *Meanings of prejudice.* Take note of how Justice Souter has characterized the issue of "prejudice" in two different ways. First, prejudice is a component of the finding that the interval between accusation and trial was not prompt enough. Second, it is a separate factor for consideration as the delay lengthens. Does it seem logical to you that prejudice is necessarily a part of the "initial delay" analysis? Could the defendant satisfy the first "prejudice" test without any proof of prejudice to his or her case?

2. *Negligence v. bad faith.* Did the Court provide any helpful guidance with respect to the distinction between "bad-faith government delay" and "negligent government delay"? The importance of such a distinction is clearly underscored in that portion of the opinion noting that "where bad-faith delay [occurs], relief [is] virtually automatic."

The line between negligence and bad faith is not always clear. What if the police force were so shorthanded it could not investigate cases in a timely fashion? Is this negligence or bad faith? If this police force refused to prod politicians for more resources, would "bad faith" be present? To avoid a bad faith finding, would the police have to reassign officers from traffic and other responsibilities to ensure timely investigations? If the lack of resources persists, at some point is there "bad faith"? Would it be bad faith or negligence to assign a case to an incompetent detective who failed to investigate the case despite knowledge of the offender's identity?

3. *Time frame of prejudice.* Do you agree with Justice Thomas' statement in the dissent that "the initiation of a formal criminal prosecution is simply irrelevant to whether the defendant has been prejudiced by delay"? If you disagree, how would you respond to his observation that "prejudice to the defense stems from the interval between crime and trial, which is quite distinct from the interval between accusation and trial"?

4. *Rebutting presumption of prejudice.* Justice Souter acknowledged that the government may be able to defeat a speedy trial claim if it could "persuasively rebut" the presumption of prejudice. Footnote 4, however, appears to make it next to impossible for the government to carry this burden. In *United States v. Shell*, 974 F.2d 1035 (9th Cir. 1992), the Court of Appeals found that a five-year delay between indictment and arrest was attributable to the government's negligence (the defendant's file had been misplaced and the government thereafter made no attempt to locate him), creating a strong presumption of prejudice. The government attempted to "persuasively rebut" the presumption of prejudice by pointing to the fact that the defendant actually conceded that "most of the essential witnesses and documentary evidence [were] still available." While the court acknowledged that *Doggett* "did not define precisely what type of evidence must be shown to rebut the presumption," it concluded that the government failed to meet that burden.

5. *Remedy for speedy trial violation.* In *Barker*, the Supreme Court held that the remedy for a speedy trial violation is dismissal of the indictment. Justice Powell characterized the remedy as an "unsatisfactorily severe remedy . . . because it means that a defendant who may be guilty of a serious crime will go free, without having been tried." Nonetheless, he declared this to be "the only possible remedy." One year later, in *Strunk v. United States*, excerpted below, the Court was presented the opportunity to reconsider the question of remedy.

STRUNK v. UNITED STATES
412 U.S. 434 (1973)

Opinion of the Court by Mr. Chief Justice Burger, announced by Mr. Justice Douglas.

Petitioner was found guilty in United States District Court of transporting a stolen automobile from Wisconsin to Illinois in violation of 18 U.S.C. § 2312 and was sentenced to a term of five years. The five-year sentence was to run concurrently with a sentence of one to three years that petitioner was then serving in the Nebraska State Penitentiary pursuant to a conviction in the courts of that State.

Prior to trial, the District Court denied a motion to dismiss the federal charge, in which petitioner argued that he had been denied his right to a speedy trial. At trial petitioner called no witnesses and did not take the stand; the jury returned a verdict of guilty. The Court of Appeals reversed the District Court, holding that petitioner had in fact been denied a speedy trial. However, the court went on to hold that the "extreme" remedy of dismissal of the charges was not warranted; the case was remanded to the District Court to reduce petitioner's sentence to the extent of 259 days in order to compensate for the unnecessary delay which had occurred between return of the indictment and petitioner's arraignment.

. . . It is correct, as the Court of Appeals noted, that *Barker* prescribes "flexible" standards based on practical considerations. However, that aspect of the holding in *Barker* was directed at the process of determining whether a denial of speedy trial had occurred; it did not deal with the remedy for denial of this right. By definition, such denial is unlike some of the other guarantees of the Sixth Amendment. For example, failure to afford a public trial, an impartial jury, notice of charges, or compulsory service can ordinarily be cured by providing those guaranteed rights in a new trial. The speedy trial guarantee recognizes that a prolonged delay may subject the accused to an emotional stress that can be presumed to result in the ordinary person from uncertainties in the prospect of facing public trial or of receiving a sentence longer than, or consecutive to, the one he is presently serving — uncertainties that a prompt trial removes. We recognize that the stress from a delayed trial may be less on a prisoner already confined, whose family ties and employment have been interrupted, but other factors such as the prospect of rehabilitation may also be affected adversely. The remedy chosen by the Court of Appeals does not deal with these difficulties.

The Government's reliance on *Barker* to support the remedy fashioned by the Court of Appeals is further undermined when we examine the Court's opinion in that case as a whole. It is true that *Barker* described dismissal of an indictment for denial of a speedy trial as an "unsatisfactorily severe remedy." Indeed, in practice, "it means that a defendant who may be guilty of a serious crime will go free, without having been tried." But such severe remedies are not unique in the application of constitutional standards. In light of the policies which underlie the right to a speedy trial, dismissal must remain, as *Barker* noted, "the only possible remedy."

Given the unchallenged determination that petitioner was denied a speedy trial, the District Court judgment of conviction must be set aside; the judgment is therefore reversed and the case remanded to the Court of Appeals to direct the District Court to set aside its judgment, vacate the sentence, and dismiss the indictment. Reversed and remanded.

[2] Statutes And Rules Of Procedure

Although the Sixth Amendment's speedy trial guarantee has been effective in some cases to compel prompt criminal proceedings, the *Barker* factors may be difficult for the accused to establish. Often, for example, the defendant will not have demanded a speedy trial and cannot prove prejudice by the delay. The result is a system of delayed criminal proceedings that, as *Barker* noted, deprives the public of its interest in the timely resolution of criminal cases.

Because the constitutional speedy trial guarantee has not eliminated delays in criminal proceedings, both federal and state legislative bodies have passed statutory speedy trial laws establishing maximum time limits for various proceedings in criminal cases. The next few sections describe three such efforts: the federal speedy trial statute, state speedy trial provisions, and a uniform act that facilitates prompt resolution of criminal charges against people imprisoned in other jurisdictions.

[a] The Federal Speedy Trial Act

The Speedy Trial Act, which governs only federal criminal prosecutions, establishes precise time limits for processing a federal criminal case. First, the information or indictment must be filed within 30 days of arrest or service of summons. Second, the trial must take place within 70 days of the filing of the formal charge (information or indictment) or 70 days from the date on which the defendant appears before a judicial officer, whichever is later. Various "tolling" provisions apply to dismissals of the indictment, mistrials, etc. A variety of matters that occur prior to trial also are excluded from the stated time limits. In the event of a violation of the statute, the case against the defendant is dismissed either with or without prejudice. Additionally, certain actions by an attorney for either the defendant or the government are subject to sanctions.

SPEEDY TRIAL ACT OF 1974
18 U.S.C. §§ 3161, 3162, 3164 & 3173

§ 3161. *Time limits and exclusions*

(a) *[Expedited Trial Date]* In any case involving a defendant charged with an offense, the appropriate judicial officer, at the earliest practicable time, shall, after consultation with the counsel for the defendant and the attorney for the Government, set the case for trial on a day certain, or list it for trial on a weekly or other short-term trial calendar at a place within the judicial district, so as to assure a speedy trial.

(b) *[Thirty Day Filing Date for Information or Indictment]* Any information or indictment charging an individual with the commission of an offense shall be filed within thirty days from the date on which such individual was arrested or served with a summons in connection with such charges. If an individual has been charged with a felony in a district in which no grand jury has been in session during such thirty-day period, the period of time for filing of the indictment shall be extended an additional thirty days.

(c)(1) *[Seventy Day Trial Date Deadline]* In any case in which a plea of not guilty is entered, the trial of a defendant charged in an information or indictment with the commission of an offense shall commence within seventy days from the filing date (and making public) of the information or indictment, or from the date the defendant has appeared before a judicial officer of the court in which such charge is pending, whichever date last occurs. If a defendant consents in writing to be tried before a magistrate on a complaint, the trial shall commence within seventy days from the date of such consent.

(2) *[Not Less Than Thirty Days]* Unless the defendant consents in writing to the contrary, the trial shall not commence less than thirty days from the date on which the defendant first appears through counsel or expressly waives counsel and elects to proceed pro se.

(d)(1) If any indictment or information is dismissed upon motion of the defendant, or any charge contained in a complaint filed against an individual is dismissed or otherwise dropped, and thereafter a complaint is filed against such defendant or individual charging him with the same offense or an offense based on the same conduct or arising from the same criminal episode, or an information or indictment is filed charging such defendant with the same offense or an offense based on the same conduct or arising from the same criminal episode, the provisions of subsections (b) and (c) of this section shall be applicable with respect to such subsequent complaint, indictment, or information, as the case may be.

(2) If the defendant is to be tried upon an indictment or information dismissed by a trial court and reinstated following an appeal, the trial shall commence within seventy days from the date the action occasioning the trial becomes final, except that the court retrying the case may extend the period for trial not to exceed one hundred and eighty days from the date the action occasioning the trial becomes final if the unavailability of witnesses or other factors resulting from the passage of time shall make trial within seventy days impractical. The periods of delay enumerated in section 3161(h) are excluded in computing the time limitations specified in this section. The sanctions of section 3162 apply to this subsection.

(e) *[Retrial After Mistrial or New Trial]* If the defendant is to be tried again following a declaration by the trial judge of a mistrial or following an order of such judge for a new trial, the trial shall commence within seventy days from the date the action occasioning the retrial becomes final. If the defendant is to be tried again following an appeal or a collateral attack, the trial shall commence within seventy days from the date the action occasioning the retrial becomes final, except that the court retrying the case may extend the period for retrial not to exceed one hundred and eighty days from the date the action occasioning the retrial becomes final if unavailability of witnesses or other factors resulting from passage of time shall make trial within seventy days impractical. The periods of delay enumerated in section 3161(h) are excluded in computing the time limitations specified in this section. The sanctions of section 3162 apply to this subsection.

[Subsections (f) and (g) are omitted. They provided for a graduated phasing in of the Act. In the first year after passage of the Act, for example, the time limit between arrest and indictment was 60 days; between arraignment and trial, it was 180 days.]

(h) *[Periods Excluded from Deadlines]* The following periods of delay shall be excluded in computing the time within which an information or an indictment must be filed, or in computing the time within which the trial of any such offense must commence:

(1) Any period of delay resulting from other proceedings concerning the defendant, including but not limited to —

(A) *[Mental Examinations]* delay resulting from any proceeding, including any examinations, to determine the mental competency or physical capacity of the defendant;

(B) delay resulting from any proceeding, including any examination of the defendant, pursuant to section 2902 of title 28, United States Code;

(C) *[Deferred Prosecution]* delay resulting from deferral of prosecution pursuant to section 2902 of title 28, United States Code;

(D) *[Trial on Other Charges]* delay resulting from trial with respect to other charges against the defendant;

(E) *[Interlocutory Appeal]* delay resulting from any interlocutory appeal;

(F) *[Motions]]* delay resulting from any pretrial motion, from the filing of the motion through the conclusion of the hearing on, or other prompt disposition of, such motion;

(G) *[Transfer of Case]* delay resulting from any proceeding relating to the transfer of a case or the removal of any defendant from another district under the Federal Rules of Criminal Procedure;

(H) *[Transportation to Another District]* delay resulting from transportation of any defendant from another district, or to and from places of examination or hospitalization, except that any time consumed in excess of ten days from the date an order of removal or an order directing such transportation, and the defendant's arrival at the destination shall be presumed to be unreasonable;

(I) *[Consideration of Plea Agreement]* delay resulting from consideration by the court of a proposed plea agreement to be entered into by the defendant and the attorney for the Government; and

(J) *[While Under Advisement by Court]* delay reasonably attributable to any period, not to exceed thirty days, during which any proceeding concerning the defendant is actually under advisement by the court.

(2) *[Deferred Prosecution]* Any period of delay during which prosecution is deferred by the attorney for the Government pursuant to written agreement with the defendant, with the approval of the court, for the purpose of allowing the defendant to demonstrate his good conduct.

(3)(A) *[Absence or Unavailability of Witness]* Any period of delay resulting from the absence or unavailability of the defendant or an essential witness.

(B) For purposes of subparagraph (A) of this paragraph, a defendant or an essential witness shall be considered absent when his whereabouts are unknown and, in addition, he is attempting to avoid apprehension or prosecution or his whereabouts cannot be determined by due diligence. For purposes of such subparagraph, a defendant or an essential witness shall be considered unavailable whenever his whereabouts are known but his presence for trial cannot be obtained by due diligence or he resists appearing at or being returned for trial.

(4) *[Mental or Physical Incompetency]* Any period of delay resulting from the fact that the defendant is mentally incompetent or physically unable to stand trial.

(5) *[Drug Treatment]* Any period of delay resulting from the treatment of the defendant pursuant to section 2902 of title 28, United States Code.

(6) *[Government Dismisses and Then Refiles Charges]* If the information or indictment is dismissed upon motion of the attorney for the Government and thereafter a charge is filed against the defendant for the same offense, or any offense required to be joined with that offense, any period of delay from the date the charge was dismissed to the date the time limitation would commence to run as to the subsequent charge had there been no previous charge.

(7) *[Joint Trial]* A reasonable period of delay when the defendant is joined for trial with a codefendant as to whom the time for trial has not run and no motion for severance has been granted.

(8)(A) *[Continuance]* Any period of delay resulting from a continuance granted by any judge on his own motion or at the request of the defendant or his counsel or at the request of the attorney for the Government, if the judge granted such continuance on the basis of his findings that the ends of justice served by taking such action outweigh the best interest of the public and the defendant in a speedy trial. No such period of delay resulting from a continuance granted by the court in accordance with this paragraph shall be excludable under this subsection unless the court sets forth, in the record of the case, either orally or in writing, its reasons for finding that the ends of justice served by the granting of such continuance outweigh the best interests of the public and the defendant in a speedy trial.

(B) *[Factors in Considering Continuance]* The factors, among others, which a judge shall consider in determining whether to grant a continuance under subparagraph (A) of this paragraph in any case are as follows:

(i) Whether the failure to grant such a continuance in the proceeding would be likely to make a continuation of such proceeding impossible, or result in a miscarriage of justice.

(ii) Whether the case is so unusual or so complex, due to the number of defendants, the nature of the prosecution, or the existence of novel questions of fact or law, that it is unreasonable to expect adequate preparation for pretrial proceedings or for the trial itself within the time limits established by this section.

(iii) Whether, in a case in which arrest precedes indictment, delay in the filing of the indictment is caused because the arrest occurs at a time such that it is unreasonable to expect return and filing of the indictment within the period specified in section 3161(b), or because the facts upon which the grand jury must base its determination are unusual or complex.

(iv) Whether the failure to grant such a continuance in a case which, taken as a whole, is not so unusual or so complex as to fall within clause (ii), would deny the defendant reasonable time to obtain counsel, would unreasonably deny the defendant or the Government continuity of counsel, or would deny counsel for the defendant or the attorney for the Government the reasonable time necessary for effective preparation, taking into account the exercise of due diligence.

(C) *[Congested Court Calendar]* No continuance under subparagraph (A) of this paragraph shall be granted because of general congestion of the court's calendar, or lack of diligent preparation or failure to obtain available witnesses on the part of the attorney for the Government.

(9) *[Evidence in Foreign Country]* Any period of delay, not to exceed one year, ordered by a district court upon an application of a party and a finding by a preponderance of the evidence that an official request, as defined in section 3292 of this title, has been made for evidence of any such offense and that it reasonably appears, or reasonably appeared at the time the request was made, that such evidence is, or was, in such foreign country.

(i) *[Withdrawn Plea]* If trial did not commence within the time limitation specified in section 3161 because the defendant had entered a plea of guilty or nolo contendere subsequently withdrawn to any or all charges in an indictment or information, the defendant shall be deemed indicted with respect to all charges therein contained within the meaning of section 3161, on the day the order permitting withdrawal of the plea becomes final.

(j)(1) *[Incarcerated Defendant]* If the attorney for the Government knows that a person charged with an offense is serving a term of imprisonment in any penal institution, he shall promptly —

(A) undertake to obtain the presence of the prisoner for trial; or

(B) cause a detainer to be filed with the person having custody of the prisoner and request him to so advise the prisoner and to advise the prisoner of his right to demand trial.

(2) If the person having custody of such prisoner receives a detainer, he shall promptly advise the prisoner of the charge and of the prisoner's right to demand trial. If at any time thereafter the prisoner informs the person having custody that he does demand trial, such person shall cause notice to that effect to be sent promptly to the attorney for the Government who caused the detainer to be filed.

(3) Upon receipt of such notice, the attorney for the Government shall promptly seek to obtain the presence of the prisoner for trial.

(4) When the person having custody of the prisoner receives from the attorney for the Government a properly supported request for temporary custody of such prisoner for trial, the prisoner shall be made available to that attorney for the Government (subject, in cases of interjurisdictional transfer, to any right of the prisoner to contest the legality of his delivery).

(k)(1) *[Absent Defendant]* If the defendant is absent (as defined by subsection (h)(3)) on the day set for trial, and the defendant's subsequent appearance before the court on a bench warrant or other process or surrender to the court occurs more than 21 days after the day set for trial, the defendant shall be deemed to have first appeared before a judicial officer of the court in which the information or indictment is pending within the meaning of subsection (c) on the date of the defendant's subsequent appearance before the court.

(2) If the defendant is absent (as defined by subsection (h)(3)) on the day set for trial, and the defendant's subsequent appearance before the court on a bench warrant or other process or surrender to the court occurs not more than 21 days after the day set for trial, the time limit required by subsection (c), as extended by subsection (h), shall be further extended by 21 days.

§ 3162. *Sanctions*

(a)(1) *[Untimely Indictment or Information]* If, in the case of any individual against whom a complaint is filed charging such individual with an offense, no indictment or information is filed within the time limit required by section 3161(b) as extended by section 3161(h) of this chapter, such charge against that individual contained in such complaint shall be dismissed or otherwise dropped. In determining whether to dismiss the case with or without prejudice, the court shall consider, among others, each of the following factors: the seriousness of the offense; the facts and circumstances of the case which led to the dismissal; and the impact of a reprosecution on the administration of this chapter and on the administration of justice.

(2) *[Untimely Trial]* If a defendant is not brought to trial within the time limit required by section 3161(c) as extended by section 3161(h), the information or indictment shall be dismissed on motion of the defendant. The defendant shall have the burden of proof of supporting such motion but the Government shall have the burden of going forward with the evidence in connection with any exclusion of time under subparagraph 3161(h)(3). In determining whether to dismiss the case with or without prejudice, the court shall consider, among others, each of the following factors: the seriousness of the offense; the facts and circumstances of the case which led to the dismissal; and the impact of a reprosecution on the administration of this chapter and on the administration of justice. Failure of the defendant to move for dismissal prior to trial or entry of a plea of guilty or nolo contendere shall constitute a waiver of the right to dismissal under this section.

(b) *[Sanctions for Lawyer Misconduct]* In any case in which counsel for the defendant or the attorney for the Government

(1) knowingly allows the case to be set for trial without disclosing the fact that a necessary witness would be unavailable for trial; (2) files a motion solely for the purpose of delay which he knows is totally frivolous and without merit; (3) makes a statement for the purpose of obtaining a continuance which he knows to be false and which is material to the granting of a continuance; or (4) otherwise willfully fails to proceed to trial without justification consistent with section 3161 of this chapter, the court may punish any such counsel or attorney, as follows:

(A) in the case of an appointed defense counsel, by reducing the amount of compensation that otherwise would have been paid to such counsel pursuant to section 3006A of this title in an amount not to exceed 25 per centum thereof;

(B) in the case of a counsel retained in connection with the defense of a defendant, by imposing on such counsel a fine of not to exceed 25 per centum of the compensation to which he is entitled in connection with his defense of such defendant;

(C) by imposing on any attorney for the Government a fine of not to exceed $250;

(D) by denying any such counsel or attorney for the Government the right to practice before the court considering such case for a period of not to exceed ninety days; or

(E) by filing a report with an appropriate disciplinary committee.

The authority to punish provided for by this subsection shall be in addition to any other authority or power available to such court.

(c) The court shall follow procedures established in the Federal Rules of Criminal Procedure in punishing any counsel or attorney for the Government pursuant to this section.

§ 3164. *Persons detained or designated as being of high risk*

(a) The trial or other disposition of cases involving —

(1) a detained person who is being held in detention solely because he is awaiting trial, and

(2) a released person who is awaiting trial and has been designated by the attorney for the Government as being of high risk,

shall be accorded priority.

(b) The trial of any person described in subsection (a) (1) or (a) (2) of this section shall commence not later than ninety days following the beginning of such continuous detention or designation of high risk by the attorney for the Government. The periods of delay enumerated in section 3161(h) are excluded in computing the time limitation specified in this section.

(c) Failure to commence trial of a detainee as specified in subsection (b), through no fault of the accused or his counsel, or failure to commence trial of a designated releasee as specified in subsection (b), through no fault of the attorney for the Government, shall result in the automatic review by the court of the conditions of release. No detainee, as defined in subsection (a), shall be held in custody pending trial after the expiration of such ninety-day period required for the commencement of his trial. A designated releasee, as defined in subsection (a), who is found by the court to have intentionally delayed the trial of his case shall be subject to an order of the court modifying his nonfinancial conditions of release under this title to insure that he shall appear at trial as required.

§ 3173. *Sixth Amendment rights*

No provision of this chapter shall be interpreted as a bar to any claim of denial of speedy trial as required by amendment VI of the Constitution.

NOTES

1. *No Trial Before Thirty Days.* Examine § 3161(c)(2), which is designed to protect against the defendant's trial commencing in a "too speedy" fashion (see discussion of *McFadden v. Cabana* in Chapter 12, where a robbery defendant was forced to go to trial only ten days after his indictment). Congress has declared, in effect, that forcing a person to trial in less than 30 days after first appearance would be fundamentally unfair due to the presumed inability of the accused and counsel to adequately prepare for trial.

2. *Indictment or information within thirty days of arrest or summons.* Note that the general rule is that an information of indictment must be filed within thirty days of the date the defendant was arrested or summoned *in connection with such charges.* 18 U.S.C. § 3161(b). Arrest for another charge may not trigger the speedy trial clock. *See, e.g, United States v. Congdon,* 54 Fed. App. 638 (9th Cir. 2002)(arrest for state parole violation does not begin 30 day deadline under Speedy Trial Act).

3. *Trial within seventy days of filing information or indictment or of appearance before judicial officer where charge is pending.* The second significant deadline is that the trial must be commenced within seventy days of the filing of the information or indictment or the date the defendant first appeared before a judicial officer in the court where the information or indictment is pending, *whichever is last.* Thus, if the government begins the process by obtaining an indictment (a frequent sequence in federal cases) and the defendant is then arraigned on that indictment (see Rule 10), the seventy-day period begins to run at the arraignment.

4. *Exclusions from time periods.* Note how § 3161(h) contains an extensive list of exclusions from the calculation of the thirty-and seventy-day deadlines. This list is so comprehensive that it results in routine violations of the two deadlines. For example, the filing of a pretrial motion, so common in federal criminal trials, stops the running of the deadline until the motion is disposed of by the court.

a. *Continuance.* It is routine in a criminal case for one or even both sides to request a continuance that will postpone a Speedy Trial Act deadline. For example, the accused may assert that there has been insufficient time to prepare for trial. This is especially true when there has been a change of attorneys between the initial charge and trial. Normally, the newly appointed or retained lawyer will file a motion for a continuance, arguing that it would be unfair to try the defendant because of inadequate time to prepare the case. See Chapter 12.

Trial judges have considerable discretion in determining whether to grant a motion for a continuance. The factors include inconvenience to parties, whether the requested delay is for a legitimate reason (or deemed to be dilatory or contrived), whether other counsel is prepared to try the case, and whether the denial of the continuance will result in prejudice to the defendant. *United States v. Burton*, 584 F.2d 485 (D.C. Cir. 1978). *Burton* has been frequently cited and applied in numerous jurisdictions.

In *United States v. Poston*, 902 F.2d 90 (D.C. Cir. 1990), the defendant filed a motion for a continuance the day before the trial was to begin. The trial judge announced that a continuance would be granted only on the condition that the defendant agree to pay all expenses incurred by the court, but the insolvent defendant was unable to meet that requirement. On appeal, Circuit Judge Clarence Thomas, writing for the majority, ruled that the continuance motion was properly denied. Judge Thomas, examining the factors outlined in *Burton*, emphasized that the defendant had replaced his court appointed attorney the day before trial and therefore contributed to the circumstances leading to the motion for a continuance. Additionally, the new attorney stated that he was ready for trial. Finding no violation of due process, the court affirmed the conviction.

Do you agree with the *Poston* analysis? If it is true that the new attorney entered the case one day before trial, was denial of the continuance tantamount to condoning less than effective representation to the accused? By conditioning the grant of a continuance upon the defendant's willingness to "pay all expenses incurred by the Court," did the trial judge violate the equal protection guarantee?

Ends of justice. Rule 3161(h)(8)(A) authorizes the trial court to grant a continuance on is own motion or that of either the government or defense if the court makes a finding that the "ends of justice" outweigh the "best interest of the public and the defendant in a speedy trial." The time of the continuance is not counted in assessing whether the trial, indictment, or indictment was timely.

Note that this rule only applies when the judge makes a finding on the record that the ends-of-justice reasons for the continuance outweigh the interests of the defendant and public in a speedy trial. The harmless error rule is inapplicable when the judge fails to make these findings, meaning that the time of the continuance is not excluded from the time limits of the Speedy Trial Act. *Zedner v. United States*, 547 U.S. 489 (2006).

Court congestion. With regard to the granting of a continuance under the Speedy Trial Act, § 3161(h)(8)(C) bars the granting of a continuance "because of general congestion of the court's calendar, or lack of diligent preparation or failure to obtain available witnesses on the part of the attorney for the government." What are the possible ramifications of this provision? With the expanding federal criminal law jurisdiction, is it not inevitable that federal civil cases will be delayed even longer than before?

b. *Mental competency.* Periods of time needed to determine the defendant's mental competency (including period needed for examination and for related judicial proceedings) are not counted under the Speedy Trial Act. 18 U.S.C. § 3161(h)(1)(a). There is no time limit for this delay. Likewise, periods during which the defendant was mentally incompetent or physically unable to attend trial are not counted. 18 U.S.C. § 3161(h)(4).

c. *Interlocutory appeal.* The Speedy Trial Act also excludes delays caused by pursuit of an interlocutory appeal by either side. 18 U.S.C. § 3161(h)(1)(E).

d. *Motions.* Motion practice may stop the Speedy Trial Act clock. Periods between the filing of a motion and its disposition by the court are not counted. 18 U.S.C. § 3161(h)(F). A review of recent cases shows this exclusion was given for such motions as a motion for acquittal (filed after a first trial ended in a hung jury), discovery motions, motion *in limine* to exclude evidence, motion to delay bail decision, motion to seal indictment, motion to modify conditions of pretrial release, motion for a severance, and a motion for a continuance. This is a common way that Speedy Trial Act timetables are extended.

e. *Plea agreements.* To encourage guilty pleas, the Speedy Trial Act excludes delays resulting from the court's consideration of a proposed plea agreement.

8. *Dismissal with or without prejudice.* Under § 3162, the trial judge is to consider specific factors in determining whether a violation of the Act should result in a dismissal of charges "with or without prejudice." If dismissed "with prejudice," the government is barred from refiling the case. If 'without prejudice,' on the other hand, the government may refile the case as long as the statute of limitations has not elapsed.

In *United States v. Taylor*, 487 U.S. 326 (1988), the district court ordered that the indictment against the defendant be dismissed with prejudice due to a violation of the Speedy Trial Act. In a 6-to-3 decision (Justices Stevens, Brennan, and Marshall in dissent), the United States Supreme Court held that the trial judge committed error by failing to consider all of the factors listed in the Act. Additionally, the majority found that the factors relied upon were not adequately supported by factual findings or evidence in the record. Therefore, even though the Court recognized that "ordinarily, a trial judge is endowed with great discretion to make decisions concerning trial schedules and to respond to abuse and delay where appropriate," the decision was reversed.

In *Taylor*, apparently the district court judge dismissed the indictment with prejudice because dismissal without prejudice "would tacitly condone the government's behavior." As to the effectiveness (or ineffectiveness) of dismissal without prejudice, Justice Blackmun stated for the Court:

> Dismissal without prejudice is not a toothless sanction: It forces the Government to obtain a new indictment if it decides to reprosecute, and it exposes the prosecution to dismissal on statute of limitations grounds. Given the burdens borne by the prosecution and the effect of delay on the Government's ability to meet those burdens, substantial delay well may make reprosecution, even if permitted, unlikely.

487 U.S. at 342.

9. *Waiver of deadlines.* The Speedy Trial Act provides specific deadlines but by many actions the defendant may essentially "waive" those deadlines, such as by filing a motion that is taken under advisement. The Supreme Court has held that the Speedy Trial Act contains no provision authorizing the defendant to waive the deadlines. Rather, the issue is handled by a continuance motion, as described above. *United States v. Zedner*, 547 U.S. 489 (2006).

Timely motion to dismiss to avoid waiver. Rule 3162(a)(2) provides that a defendant who seeks to dismiss charges because of a Speedy Trial violation must file an appropriate motion before trial or entry of a guilty or *nolo contendere* plea. Failure to file this motion in a timely fashion constitutes a waiver of the right to dismiss charges for the violation. The Supreme Court in *United States v. Zedner*, 547 U.S. 489, 502–503 (2006). explained the purpose of this time limit:

> First, § 3162(a)(2) assigns the role of spotting violations of the Act to defendants-for the obvious reason that they have the greatest incentive to perform this task. Second, by requiring that a defendant move before the trial starts or a guilty plea is entered, § 3162(a)(2) both limits the effects of a dismissal without prejudice (by ensuring that an expensive and time-consuming trial will not be mooted by a late-filed motion under the Act) and prevents undue defense gamesmanship.

Waiver for all time. If the speedy trial statute is designed to foster the defendant's interest in having charges resolved, may the defendant waive the Act for all time? In *Zedner*, the Supreme Court held that the defendant could not waive the application of the Act "for all time" since the Speedy Trial Act was also designed to protect the public's interest in an efficient disposition of criminal charges.

10. *Role of Victim.* The traditional rule is that the victim plays no role in decisions concerning speedy trial. Modern victim's rights laws, however, change this in some locales. The federal Crime Victim's Rights Act, 18 U.S.C. § 3771, gives federal crime victims many rights, including the right to "timely notice of any public court proceeding," the right not to be excluded from any such proceeding, and the right to "proceedings free from unreasonable delay." The statute gives victims standing to assert these right in federal court. Though the statute is vague about the victim's participation in matters involving trial or other delays, it has been held that the Act gives victims the right to be notified of, and to attend and be heard in court proceedings about trial delays. *See, e.g, United States v. Turner*, 367 F. Supp.2d 319 (E.D.N.Y. 2005)(victim has right to be heard at hearing on continuance but not with regard to a written waiver of the Speedy Trial Act in a written request, signed by both the U.S. Attorney and defense counsel, for a continuance that will not involve a public hearing to resolve).

PROBLEM 13-1. JUSTICE DELAYED

1. P. Stamp, a postal service employee, was arrested and charged on June 10th with felony mail theft and the misdemeanor of opening mail without authority. Allegedly, Stamp had taken a ring from a package he was to deliver. He was promptly arraigned and then released after he entered a plea of not guilty. Nothing further occurred until July 31st, the same year, when the government made an ex parte motion for dismissal of the charges. The United States magistrate granted the motion. The government admitted that the delay was caused by simple oversight; no other excuse was proffered. Thereafter, an information was filed, charging Stamp with the misdemeanor offense.

    a. With respect to the 51-day delay, was the Speedy Trial Act of 1974 violated?

    b. If you conclude that there was a violation, should the dismissal (July 31) have been with or without prejudice?

2. Harry Woods, indicted by a federal grand jury on the charge of distributing eight ounces of cocaine, was brought to trial 90 days after indictment. He moves for dismissal of the charge with prejudice, though he is unable to identify specific ways in which his defense would be prejudiced by the 90-day delay. The Assistant U.S. Attorney, while acknowledging a violation of the Speedy Trial Act, asserts that (1) the government did not purposely delay matters, but was "merely lax" in pursuing Woods' case, (2) Woods suffered no prejudice, and (3) the action should not be dismissed with prejudice because of the seriousness of the offense and the "impact of reprosecution on administration of the Act and justice in general."

> **a.** If you were the trial judge, how would you rule? Would your answer change if it were proven that the United States Attorney's Office in that district frequently violated the Speedy Trial Act?

> **b.** How should the trial judge evaluate the "impact of reprosecution on the Act and justice in general" factor? Is this nothing more than another way to weigh the seriousness of the underlying crime?

3. James "Peewee" May was arrested January 5th, following a search of his residence in which contraband was discovered. On February 22, the same year, a federal grand jury returned a six-count indictment, charging May with federal narcotics and firearms offenses. This indictment was dismissed without prejudice four weeks later at the government's request during an *ex parte* hearing before a magistrate. The next day, March 20th, May was reindicted. Following reindictment, May filed a motion asserting that the initial indictment should have been dismissed with prejudice because of the 47-day delay between arrest and indictment.

> **a.** The trial judge inquires of the Assistant U.S. Attorney why the indictment was not obtained within 30 days of May's arrest. The attorney offered no explanation whatsoever. As defense counsel, what is the significance of the government's failure to explain the delay?

> **b.** Should the length of delay be factored into the court's analysis? If so, how?

[b]   State Speedy Trial Provisions

With the exception of New York, all state constitutions guarantee to the accused the right to a speedy trial. Slightly less than one-half of the states also have statutory provisions establishing precise time limitations and remedies for speedy trial violations. These laws vary markedly and it appears that very few states have modeled their statutes after the Speedy Trial Act of 1974.

In Florida, for example, the defendant is entitled, absent "exceptional circumstances" to be tried within 90 days if the charge is a misdemeanor or 175 days if the charge is a felony. Additionally, special provisions are applicable if the defendant serves a "Demand for Speedy Trial" upon the prosecution. Fla. R. Crim. Pro. 3.191. Other states, such as North Carolina, use less precise time limits more for effectuating the defendant's right to a speedy trial. N.C. Crim. Pro. § 15-10 (upon the defendant's demand, if the accused is not "indicted and tried at the second term of the court, he shall be discharged from his imprisonment").

[c]   The Imprisoned Defendant

On occasion, the defendant formally charged with commission of a criminal offense is in prison for another crime at the time of the charge. If the defendant is incarcerated in an institution within that geographic jurisdiction, obviously it is relatively easy to proceed against that defendant on those pending charges. Every jurisdiction has adopted procedures enabling a prisoner to be transported to another location in the same jurisdiction to participate in various proceedings involving unresolved criminal charges. It is more complicated, however, in a case in which the defendant is incarcerated in another jurisdiction, as in the next case.

SMITH v. HOOEY
393 U.S. 374 (1969)

Mr. Justice Stewart delivered the opinion of the Court.

In *Klopfer v. North Carolina*, 386 U.S. 213 (1967), this Court held that, by virtue of the Fourteenth Amendment, the Sixth Amendment right to a speedy trial is enforceable against the States as "one of the most basic rights preserved by our Constitution." The case before us involves the nature and extent of the obligation imposed upon a State by that constitutional guarantee, when the person under the state criminal charge is serving a prison sentence imposed by another jurisdiction.

In 1960 the petitioner was indicted in Harris County, Texas, upon a charge of theft. He was then, and still is, a prisoner in the federal penitentiary at Leavenworth, Kansas. Shortly after the state charge was filed against him, the petitioner mailed a letter to the Texas trial court requesting a speedy trial. In reply, he was notified that "he would be afforded a trial within two weeks of any date (he) might specify at which he could be present." Thereafter, for the next six years, the petitioner, "by various letters, and more formal so-called 'motions,'" continued periodically to ask that he be brought to trial. Beyond the response already alluded to, the State took no steps to obtain the petitioner's appearance in the Harris County trial court. Finally, in 1967, the petitioner filed in that court a verified motion to dismiss the charge against him for want of prosecution. No action was taken on the motion.

. . . There can be no doubt that if the petitioner in the present case had been at large for a six-year period following his indictment, and had repeatedly demanded that he be brought to trial, the State would have been under a constitutional duty to try him. And Texas concedes that if during that period he had been confined in a Texas prison for some other state offense, its obligation would have been no less. But the Texas Supreme Court has held that because petitioner is, in fact, confined in a federal prison, the State is totally absolved from any duty at all under the constitutional guarantee. We cannot agree.

. . . At first blush it might appear that a man already in prison under a lawful sentence is hardly in a position to suffer from "undue and oppressive incarceration prior to trial." But the fact is that delay in bringing such a person to trial on a pending charge may ultimately result in as much oppression as is suffered by one who is jailed without bail upon an untried charge. First, the possibility that the defendant already in prison might receive a sentence at least partially concurrent with the one he is serving may be forever lost if trial of the pending charge is postponed. Secondly, under procedures now widely practiced, the duration of his present imprisonment may be increased, and the conditions under which he must serve his sentence greatly worsened, by the pendency of another criminal charge outstanding against him.

And while it might be argued that a person already in prison would be less likely than others to be affected by "anxiety and concern accompanying public accusation," there is reason to believe that an outstanding untried charge (of which even a convict may, of course, be innocent) can have fully as depressive an effect upon a prisoner as upon a person who is at large. In the opinion of the former Director of the Federal Bureau of Prisons,

> [I]t is in their effect upon the prisoner and our attempts to rehabilitate him that detainers are most corrosive. The strain of having to serve a sentence with the uncertain prospect of being taken into the custody of another state at the conclusion interferes with the prisoner's ability to take maximum advantage of his institutional opportunities. His anxiety and depression may leave him with little inclination toward self-improvement.

Finally, it is self-evident that "the possibilities that long delay will impair the ability of an accused to defend himself" are markedly increased when the accused is incarcerated in another jurisdiction. Confined in a prison, perhaps far from the place where the offense covered by the outstanding charge allegedly took place, his ability to confer with potential defense witnesses, or even to keep track of their whereabouts, is obviously impaired. And, while "evidence and witnesses disappear, memories fade, and events lose their perspective," a man isolated in prison is powerless to exert his own investigative efforts to mitigate these erosive effects of the passage of time.

Despite all these considerations, the Texas Supreme Court has said that the State is under no duty even to attempt to bring a man in the petitioner's position to trial, because "(t)he question is one of power and authority and is in no way dependent upon how or in what manner the federal sovereignty may proceed in a discretionary way under the doctrine of comity." Yet Texas concedes that if it did make an effort to secure a federal prisoner's appearance, he would, in fact, "be produced for trial in the state court."

. . . [W]e think the Texas court was mistaken in allowing doctrinaire concepts of "power" and "authority" to submerge the practical demands of the constitutional right to a speedy trial. Indeed, the rationale upon which the Texas Supreme Court based its denial of relief in this case was wholly undercut [in an earlier case in which the U.S. Supreme Court had held that a state could not excuse its failure to obtain a state's witness where that witness was in an out-of-state federal prison and the state had failed to make a good faith effort to obtain his presence].

. . . By a parity of reasoning we hold today that the Sixth Amendment right to a speedy trial may not be dispensed with so lightly either. Upon the petitioner's demand, Texas had a constitutional duty to make a diligent, good-faith effort to bring him before the Harris County court for trial.

[The concurring opinions of Justices Black, Harlan and White are omitted.]

NOTES

1. *Federal defendant in state prison: Speedy Trial Act.* Where a defendant in a pending federal criminal case is also serving a state prison sentence on other charges, the Speedy Trial Act of 1974 has a specific provision for having the prisoner tried in a timely manner in federal court. Under § 3161(j), the federal prosecutor may either attempt to have the defendant temporarily transferred from state to federal custody for purposes of trial, or may lodge a "detainer" with the appropriate prison official requesting that official to advise the defendant of the defendant's right to demand trial. If the defendant then informs the prison official that he or she does, in fact, desire a trial, notice is to be forwarded promptly to the federal prosecutor who must then seek to obtain the defendant's presence for trial.

2. *State defendant incarcerated in another state: pretrial problems.* While the federal Speedy Trial Act provides guidance for federal prosecutors involved in cases where there are outstanding criminal charges against a prisoner, it has no bearing on state prosecutions of out-of-state prisoners. Assume, for example, that Karen goes on an interstate crime spree. She commits a murder in State A and a kidnaping in State B, where she is apprehended. Assume also that Karen is tried, convicted, and sentenced to a twenty-year prison term in State B for the kidnaping. While the law enforcement officials in State B may be satisfied because Karen is punished for violating State B's criminal laws, officials in State A will want to prosecute Karen for the homicide committed in that state. The problem is that Karen may be incarcerated in State B for the next twenty years. If the prosecutors in State A wait for twenty years to begin the trial against Karen, key government witnesses may be unavailable and a conviction impossible. Karen, too, may prefer that the charges in State A be resolved. She may fear losing a defense during the twenty-year period or may prefer to get the State A charges resolved and, if convicted, seek to get concurrent sentences on the two charges (letting her earn credit for State A and State B sentences at the same time). How should a prosecutor in State A proceed with the outstanding murder charges against Karen?

3. *Extradition.* One statutory solution is that the law enforcement officials in State A can obtain Karen's presence in State A by utilizing cumbersome extradition proceedings involving the governors of both states. *See* Uniform Criminal Extradition Act. But the extradition process sometimes is slow and cumbersome.

In general terms, the process is begun when the governor of a state from which the defendant fled makes a written demand on the governor of the state where the fugitive is found. The initial application is ordinarily made by a local prosecutor who asks the governor to make a formal demand for extradition. The demand states that the person is a fugitive who is charged with a crime in the demanding state. This suffices to establish probable cause of the crime in the demanding state. A judge in the "asylum" state may then order the defendant arrested and held until further proceedings authorize the defendant to be taken to the demanding state.

4. *Interstate Agreement on Detainers (IAD).* In order to simplify the process of getting a prisoner in one jurisdiction to a trial in another, forty-eight states, the District of Columbia, and the federal government have adopted the Interstate Agreement on Detainers (IAD), sometimes referred to as the Interstate Compact on Detainers or the Uniform Detainer Act.

A *detainer*, used frequently throughout the country, is a request by one criminal justice agency addressed to another such agency that is incarcerating a particular individual. The detainer asks the latter agency to notify the former agency before the prisoner is released or to hold the prisoner until the requesting agency can obtain the legal right to take the prisoner into its custody. This latter procedure is referred to as a *hold* in some jurisdictions.

The IAD provides that when an individual is indicted for a crime in one jurisdiction, yet is imprisoned in another, the prisoner can be transported to the demanding state (the "requesting jurisdiction") as long as both jurisdictions are parties to the agreement. Extradition procedures are not used.

Under the IAD's procedures, the requesting jurisdiction sends the appropriate detainer to the prospective defendant. The IAD's provisions are then activated to deal with an "untried indictment, information, or complaint." (but not an arrest warrant, sentencing proceeding, or parole or probation violation). Upon receipt of the detainer, the prisoner has the option of demanding speedy trial. If this option is exercised, the prisoner must communicate a written demand to the prison warden, who sends it to both the prosecuting attorney and the appropriate court in the jurisdiction filing the detainer. Trial must be held within 180 days of the date the demand is delivered to the court and the prosecutor. Trial must also be within 120 days of the prisoner's arrival in the requesting state.

If the prisoner is returned to the sending state before trial is held, under the IAD the indictment, information, or complaint in the requesting state must be dismissed with prejudice in the requesting state. *Alabama v. Bozeman*, 533 U.S. 146 (2001) (under IAD prisoner brought from federal prison to Alabama where he had an initial appearance and counsel was appointed, then he was returned to the federal prison; Alabama was barred from returning prisoner to Alabama for trial because once prisoner was in Alabama under the IAD's "anti-shuttling" provision, he had to be kept there until the trial was completed).

C. PRE-CHARGE DELAYS

The prior section dealt with post-accusation delays: those between the arrest or filing of formal charges and the trial. As we have seen, both constitutional and statutory speedy trial provisions place limits on the extent of these delays. We now turn to the question of limits on the time between the commission of the crime and the defendant's arrest or the filing of criminal charges. For example, assume that Harry commits arson on February 1, 2007, is arrested on January 1, 2008, and is indicted on February 1, 2008.

There has been an eleven-month delay between the crime and the arrest, and a twelve-month delay between the crime and the indictment. Has this delay violated any constitutional or statutory provisions?

In general terms, there are two legal limits on such delays. As described in *Marion*, the statute of limitations bars some prosecutions because of pre-charge delays. Both *Marion* and *Lovasco* also describe the second such limitation: the due process clause.

[1]   General Approaches: Speedy Trial, Statutes of Limitation, and Due Process

UNITED STATES v. MARION

404 U.S. 307 (1971)

MR. JUSTICE WHITE delivered the opinion of the Court.

This appeal requires us to decide whether dismissal of a federal indictment was constitutionally required by reason of a period of three years between the occurrence of the alleged criminal acts and the filing of the indictment.

On April 21, 1970, the two appellees were indicted and charged in 19 counts with operating a business known as Allied Enterprises, Inc., which was engaged in the business of selling and installing home improvements such as intercom sets, fire control devices, and burglary detection systems. Allegedly, the business was fraudulently conducted and involved misrepresentations, alterations of documents, and deliberate nonperformance of contracts. The period covered by the indictment was March 15, 1965, to February 6, 1967; the earliest specific act alleged occurred on September 3, 1965, the latest on January 19, 1966.

On May 5, 1970, appellees filed a motion to dismiss the indictment "for failure to commence prosecution of the alleged offenses charged therein within such time as to afford (them their) rights to due process of law and to a speedy trial under the Fifth and Sixth Amendments to the Constitution of the United States."

. . . Appellees moved to dismiss because the indictment was returned "an unreasonably oppressive and unjustifiable time after the alleged offenses." They argued that the indictment required memory of many specific acts and conversations occurring several years before, and they contended that the delay was due to the negligence or indifference of the United States Attorney in investigating the case and presenting it to a grand jury. No specific prejudice was claimed or demonstrated. The District Court judge dismissed the indictment for "lack of speedy prosecution" at the conclusion of the hearing and remarked that since the Government must have become aware of the relevant facts in 1967, the defense of the case "is bound to have been seriously prejudiced by the delay of at least some three years in bringing the prosecution that should have been brought in 1967, or at the very latest early 1968."

. . . Appellees do not claim that the Sixth Amendment [right to a speedy trial] was violated by the two-month delay between the return of the indictment and its dismissal. Instead, they claim that their rights to a speedy trial were violated by the period of approximately three years between the end of the criminal scheme charged and the return of the indictment; it is argued that this delay is so substantial and inherently prejudicial that the Sixth Amendment required the dismissal of the indictment. In our view, however, the Sixth Amendment speedy trial provision has no application until the putative defendant in some way becomes an "accused," an event that occurred in this case only when the appellees were indicted on April 21, 1970.

The Sixth Amendment provides that "[i]n all criminal prosecutions, the accused shall enjoy the right to a speedy and public trial. . . . " On its face, the protection of the Amendment is activated only when a criminal prosecution has begun and extends only to those persons who have been "accused" in the course of that prosecution. These provisions would seem to afford no protection to those not yet accused, nor would they seem to require the Government to discover, investigate, and accuse any person within any particular period of time.

. . . It is apparent also that very little support for appellees' position emerges from a consideration of the purposes of the Sixth Amendment's speedy trial provision, a guarantee that this Court has termed "an important safeguard to prevent undue and oppressive incarceration prior to trial, to minimize anxiety and concern accompanying public accusation and to limit the possibilities that long delay will impair the ability of an accused to defend himself." Inordinate delay between arrest, indictment, and trial may impair a defendant's ability to present an effective defense. But the major evils protected against by the speedy trial guarantee exist quite apart from actual or possible prejudice to an accused's defense. To legally arrest and detain, the Government must assert probable cause to believe the arrestee has committed a crime. Arrest is a public act that may seriously interfere with the defendant's liberty, whether he is free on bail or not, and that may disrupt his employment, drain his financial resources, curtail his associations, subject him to public obloquy, and create anxiety in him, his family and his friends. . . . So viewed, it is readily understandable that it is either a formal indictment or information or else the actual restraints imposed by arrest and holding to answer a criminal charge that engage the particular protections of the speedy trial provision of the Sixth Amendment.

Invocation of the speedy trial provision thus need not await indictment, information, or other formal charge. But we decline to extend that reach of the amendment to the period prior to arrest. Until this event occurs, a citizen suffers no restraints on his liberty and is not the subject of public accusation: his situation does not compare with that of a defendant who has been arrested and held to answer. Passage of time, whether before or after arrest, may impair memories, cause evidence to be lost, deprive the defendant of witnesses, and otherwise interfere with his ability to defend himself.[13] But this possibility of prejudice at trial is not itself sufficient reason to wrench the Sixth Amendment from its proper context. Possible prejudice is inherent in any delay, however short; it may also weaken the Government's case.

The law has provided other mechanisms to guard against possible as distinguished from actual prejudice resulting from the passage of time between crime and arrest or charge. . . . [Statutes of limitations] represent legislative assessments of relative interests of the State and the defendant in administering and receiving justice; they "are made for the repose of society and the protection of those who may (during the limitation) . . . have lost their means of defence." These statutes provide predictability by specifying a limit beyond which there is an irrebuttable presumption that a defendant's right to a fair trial would be prejudiced.

. . . [I]t is appropriate to note here that the statute of limitations does not fully define the appellees' rights with respect to the events occurring prior to indictment. Thus, the Government concedes that the Due Process Clause of the Fifth Amendment would require dismissal of the indictment if it were shown at trial that the pre-indictment delay in this case caused substantial prejudice to appellees' rights to a fair trial and that the delay was an intentional device to gain tactical advantage over the accused. However, we need not, and could not now, determine when and in what circumstances actual prejudice resulting from pre-accusation delays requires the dismissal of the prosecution. Actual prejudice to the defense of a criminal case may

---

[13] Extending a Sixth Amendment right to a period prior to indictment or holding to answer would also create procedural problems: "[W]hile other rights may be violated by delay in arrest or charge, it does not follow that the time for trial should be counted from any date of inaction preceding filing of the charge or holding the defendant to answer. To recognize a general speedy trial right commencing as of the time arrest or charging was possible would have unfortunate consequences for the operation of the criminal justice system. Allowing inquiry into when the police could have arrested or when the prosecutor could have charged would raise difficult problems of proof. . . . " [citation omitted]

result from the shortest and most necessary delay; and no one suggests that every delay-caused detriment to a defendant's case should abort a criminal prosecution. To accommodate the sound administration of justice to the rights of the defendant to a fair trial will necessarily involve a delicate judgment based on the circumstances of each case. It would be unwise at this juncture to attempt to forecast our decision in such cases.

. . . The 38-month delay between the end of the scheme charged in the indictment and the date the defendants were indicted did not extend beyond the period of the applicable statute of limitations here. Appellees have not, of course, been able to claim undue delay pending trial, since the indictment was brought on April 21, 1970, and dismissed on June 8, 1970. Nor have appellees adequately demonstrated that the pre-indictment delay by the Government violated the Due Process Clause. No actual prejudice to the conduct of the defense is alleged or proved, and there is no showing that the Government intentionally delayed to gain some tactical advantage over appellees or to harass them. Appellees rely solely on the real possibility of prejudice inherent in any extended delay: that memories will dim, witnesses become inaccessible, and evidence be lost. In light of the applicable statute of limitations, however, these possibilities are not in themselves enough to demonstrate that appellees cannot receive a fair trial and to therefore justify the dismissal of the indictment. Events of the trial may demonstrate actual prejudice, but at the present time appellees' due process claims are speculative and premature. Reversed.

MR. JUSTICE DOUGLAS, with whom MR. JUSTICE BRENNAN and MR. JUSTICE MARSHALL join, concurring in the result.

I assume that if the three-year delay in this case had occurred after the indictment had been returned, the right to a speedy trial would have been impaired and the indictment would have to be dismissed. I disagree with the Court that the guarantee does not apply if the delay was at the pre-indictment stage of a case.

. . . The Sixth Amendment, to be sure, states that "the accused shall enjoy the right to a speedy and public trial." But the words "the accused," as I understand them in their Sixth Amendment setting, mean only the person who has standing to complain of prosecutorial delay in seeking an indictment or filing an information. The right to a speedy trial is the right to be brought to trial speedily which would seem to be as relevant to pre-indictment delays as it is to post-indictment delays.

. . . Undue delay may be as offensive to the right to a speedy trial before as after an indictment or information. The anxiety and concern attendant on public accusation may weigh more heavily upon an individual who has not yet been formally indicted or arrested for, to him, exoneration by a jury of his peers may be only a vague possibility lurking in the distant future. Indeed, the protection underlying the right to a speedy trial may be denied when a citizen is damned by clandestine innuendo and never given the chance promptly to defend himself in a court of law. Those who are accused of crime but never tried may lose their jobs or their positions of responsibility, or become outcasts in their communities.

The impairment of the ability to defend oneself may become acute because of delays in the pre-indictment stage. Those delays may result in the loss of alibi witnesses, the destruction of material evidence, and the blurring of memories. At least when a person has been accused of a specific crime, he can devote his powers of recall to the events surrounding the alleged occurrences. When there is no formal accusation, however, the State may proceed methodically to build its case while the prospective defendant proceeds to lose his.

. . . In the present case, two to three years elapsed between the time the District Court found that the charges could and should have been brought and the actual return of the indictment. The justifications offered were that the United States Attorney's office was "not sufficiently staffed to proceed as expeditiously" as desirable and that priority had been given to other cases. . . . But on the bare bones of this record I hesitate to say that the guarantee of a speedy trial has been violated. Unless appellees on remand demonstrate actual prejudice, I would agree that the prosecution might go forward. Hence I concur in the result.

[2] Statutes of Limitation

[a] Purpose

While *Marion* recognized that there may be due process protections with respect to pre-charge delay, it stressed the importance of statutes of limitations insofar as they operate "to guard against possible . . . prejudice resulting from the passage of time between crime and arrest or charge." Quoting from *Toussie v. United States*, 397 U.S. 112, 114–115 (1970), the Court noted:

> The purpose of a statute of limitations is to limit exposure to criminal prosecution to a certain fixed period of time following the occurrence of those acts the legislature has decided to punish by criminal sanctions. Such a limitation is designed to protect individuals from having to defend themselves against charges when the basic facts may have become obscured by the passage of time and to minimize the danger of official punishment because of acts in the far-distant past. Such a time limit may also have the salutary effect of encouraging law enforcement officials promptly to investigate suspected criminal activity. [404 U.S. at 323]

[b] Illustrative Statutes of Limitation

Almost all states have precise statutes of limitations specifying the time periods within which a criminal prosecution must be brought. Generally, the length of the limitation period increases with the seriousness of the crime. *See, e.g.*, Cal. Pen. Code Ann. §§ 799–802 (offenses punishable by death — no limit; offenses punishable by 8 years' imprisonment or more — 6 year limit; most other felonies — 3 year limit; most misdemeanors — 1 year limit); Tex. Code Crim. Pro. art. 12.01 (murder or manslaughter — no limit; certain sexual assaults — 10 year limit; theft and burglary — 5 year limit; all other felonies — 3 year limit). Many jurisdictions have no statutes of limitations applicable to capital crimes. Often there are generic statutes setting time limitations based upon the classification of offenses. *See, e.g.*, Model Penal Code § 1.06 (1) and (2) (no limitation as to the offense of murder, limitation of six years for a felony of the first degree, limitation of three years for any other felony, limitation of two years for a misdemeanor and limitation of six months for a petty misdemeanor or violation).

[c] Procedural issues

If the statute of limitations has run, the crime can no longer be prosecuted, irrespective of the strength of the prosecution's case against the accused. Thus, the statute of limitations is a defense to criminal prosecution, and is usually raised formally in a Motion to Dismiss. The burden of persuasion, however, generally is on the government, which must prove beyond a reasonable doubt that the statute of limitations was not violated.

[d] Periods Calculated; Tolling

Usually the statute of limitations begins to run when the crime is committed, and ends when either an arrest is made or an indictment or information is issued. According to statute or case law, the running of the statute of limitations is *tolled* or stopped during various periods, such as when the existence of the crime is hidden or when the accused is out of state.

[e]   Waiver

Some states will permit a waiver of a statute of limitations defense when the defendant agrees to plead guilty to a crime that is time-barred. For example, in *Cowan v. Superior Court*, 926 P.2d 438 (Cal. 1996), the defendant, charged with having committed three murders, entered into a plea agreement whereby he would plea no contest to one count of voluntary manslaughter. Because the statute of limitations had run on the crime of voluntary manslaughter, the trial court set aside the guilty plea prior to sentencing. Reasoning that a trial court has jurisdiction over a time-barred lesser charge by virtue of the valid greater charge, the California Supreme Court held that the guilty plea was valid so long as the defendant's waiver of the statute of limitations was knowing, intelligent, voluntary, and made for the defendant's benefit after consultation with counsel.

[3]   Due Process

UNITED STATES v. LOVASCO
431 U.S. 783 (1977)

Mr. Justice Marshall delivered the opinion of the Court.

We granted certiorari in this case to consider the circumstances in which the Constitution requires that an indictment be dismissed because of delay between the commission of an offense and the initiation of prosecution.

On March 6, 1975, respondent was indicted for possessing eight firearms stolen from the United States mails, and for dealing in firearms without a license. The offenses were alleged to have occurred between July 25 and August 31, 1973, more than 18 months before the indictment was filed. Respondent moved to dismiss the indictment due to the delay.

The District Court conducted a hearing on respondent's motion at which the respondent sought to prove that the delay was unnecessary and that it had prejudiced his defense. In an effort to establish the former proposition, respondent presented a Postal Inspector's report on his investigation that was prepared one month after the crimes were committed, and a stipulation concerning the post-report progress of the probe. The report stated, in brief, that within the first month of the investigation respondent had admitted to Government agents that he had possessed and then sold five of the stolen guns, and that the agents had developed strong evidence linking respondent to the remaining three weapons. The report also stated, however, that the agents had been unable to confirm or refute respondent's claim that he had found the guns in his car when he returned to it after visiting his son, a mail handler, at work. The stipulation into which the Assistant United States Attorney entered indicated that little additional information concerning the crimes was uncovered in the 17 months following the preparation of the Inspector's report.

To establish prejudice to the defense, respondent testified that he had lost the testimony of two material witnesses due to the delay. The first witness, Tom Stewart, died more than a year after the alleged crimes occurred. At the hearing respondent claimed that Stewart had been his source for two or three of the guns. The second witness, respondent's brother, died in April 1974, eight months after the crimes were completed. Respondent testified that his brother was present when respondent called Stewart to secure the guns, and witnessed all of respondent's sales. Respondent did not state how the witnesses would have aided the defense had they been willing to testify.[4]

The Government made no systematic effort in the District Court to explain its long

---

[4] Respondent admitted that he had not mentioned Stewart to the Postal Inspector when he was questioned about his source of the guns. He explained that this was because Stewart "was a bad tomato" and "was liable to take a shot at me if I told (on) him." Respondent also conceded that he did not mention either his brother's

delay. The Assistant United States Attorney did expressly disagree, however, with defense counsel's suggestion that the investigation had ended after the Postal Inspector's report was prepared.

. . . Following the hearing, the District Court filed a brief opinion and order. The court found that by October 2, 1973, the date of the Postal Inspector's report, "the Government had all the information relating to defendant's alleged commission of the offenses charged against him," and that the 17-month delay before the case was presented to the grand jury "had not been explained or justified" and was "unnecessary and unreasonable." The court also found that "(a)s a result of the delay defendant has been prejudiced by reason of the death of Tom Stewart, a material witness on his behalf." Accordingly, the court dismissed the indictment [and the Eighth Circuit Court of Appeals affirmed].

. . . Respondent seems to argue that due process bars prosecution whenever a defendant suffers prejudice as a result of preindictment delay. To support that proposition respondent relies on the concluding sentence of the Court's opinion in *Marion* where, in remanding the case, we stated that "(e)vents of the trial may demonstrate actual prejudice, but at the present time appellees' due process claims are speculative and premature." But the quoted sentence establishes only that proof of actual prejudice makes a due process claim concrete and ripe for adjudication, not that it makes the claim automatically valid. Indeed, two pages earlier in the opinion we expressly rejected the argument respondent advances here: "(W)e need not . . . determine when and in what circumstances actual prejudice resulting from preaccusation delays requires the dismissal of the prosecution. Actual prejudice to the defense of a criminal case may result from the shortest and most necessary delay; and no one suggests that every delay-caused detriment to a defendant's case should abort a criminal prosecution." Thus *Marion* makes clear that proof of prejudice is generally a necessary but not sufficient element of a due process claim, and that the due process inquiry must consider the reasons for the delay as well as the prejudice to the accused.

. . . It requires no extended argument to establish that prosecutors do not deviate from "fundamental conceptions of justice" when they defer seeking indictments until they have probable cause to believe an accused is guilty; indeed it is unprofessional conduct for a prosecutor to recommend an indictment on less than probable cause. It should be equally obvious that prosecutors are under no duty to file charges as soon as probable cause exists but before they are satisfied they will be able to establish the suspect's guilt beyond a reasonable doubt.

It might be argued that once the Government has assembled sufficient evidence to prove guilt beyond a reasonable doubt, it should be constitutionally required to file charges promptly, even if its investigation of the entire criminal transaction is not complete. Adopting such a rule, however, would have many of the same consequences as adopting a rule requiring immediate prosecution upon probable cause.

First, compelling a prosecutor to file public charges as soon as the requisite proof has been developed against one participant on one charge would cause numerous problems in those cases in which a criminal transaction involves more than one person or more than one illegal act. In some instances, an immediate arrest or indictment would impair the prosecutor's ability to continue his investigation, thereby preventing society from bringing lawbreakers to justice. In other cases, the prosecutor would be able to obtain additional indictments despite an early prosecution, but the necessary result would be multiple trials involving a single set of facts. Such trials place needless burdens on defendants, law enforcement officials, and courts.

Second, insisting on immediate prosecution once sufficient evidence is developed to obtain a conviction would pressure prosecutors into resolving doubtful cases in favor of

---

or Stewart's illness or death to the Postal Inspector on the several occasions in which respondent called the Inspector to inquire about the status of the probe.

early and possibly unwarranted prosecutions. The determination of when the evidence available to the prosecution is sufficient to obtain a conviction is seldom clear-cut, and reasonable persons often will reach conflicting conclusions. . . .

Finally, requiring the Government to make charging decisions immediately upon assembling evidence sufficient to establish guilt would preclude the Government from giving full consideration to the desirability of not prosecuting in particular cases.

. . . We therefore hold that to prosecute a defendant following investigative delay does not deprive him of due process, even if his defense might have been somewhat prejudiced by the lapse of time.

In the present case, the Court of Appeals stated that the only reason the Government postponed action was to await the results of additional investigation. Although there is, unfortunately, no evidence concerning the reasons for the delay in the record, the court's "finding" is supported by the prosecutor's implicit representation to the District Court, and explicit representation to the Court of Appeals, that the investigation continued during the time that the Government deferred taking action against respondent. The finding is, moreover, buttressed by the Government's repeated assertions in its petition for certiorari, its brief, and its oral argument in this Court, "that the delay was caused by the government's efforts to identify persons in addition to respondent who may have participated in the offenses." We must assume that these statements by counsel have been made in good faith. In light of this explanation, it follows that compelling respondent to stand trial would not be fundamentally unfair. The Court of Appeals therefore erred in affirming the District Court's decision dismissing the indictment.

In *Marion* we conceded that we could not determine in the abstract the circumstances in which preaccusation delay would require dismissing prosecutions. More than five years later, that statement remains true. Indeed, in the intervening years so few defendants have established that they were prejudiced by delay that neither this Court nor any lower court has had a sustained opportunity to consider the constitutional significance of various reasons for delay. We therefore leave to the lower courts, in the first instance, the task of applying the settled principles of due process that we have discussed to the particular circumstances of individual cases. We simply hold that in this case the lower courts erred in dismissing the indictment. Reversed.

[The dissent of JUSTICE STEVENS is omitted]

NOTES

1. *Charge dismissed, then reinstituted.* How should *Marion* and *Lovasco* apply to a situation in which there is a formal charge brought, then dismissed, and later the defendant is formally charged again? In *United States v. Loud Hawk*, 474 U.S. 302 (1986), an indictment was issued in late 1975, but was dismissed in March of 1976. The government appealed the dismissal order, making it clear that it desired to prosecute the defendant. Due to various interlocutory appeals, the defendant was not reindicted until more than seven years had elapsed. In a five-to-four decision, the United States Supreme Court held that the time during which the indictment was dismissed was to be excluded from the length of delay considered under the speedy trial guarantee. This ruling was based upon the earlier case of *United States v. MacDonald*, 456 U.S. 1 (1982), holding that the time between the dismissal of military charges and the subsequent indictment on civilian charges is not to be considered in determining whether a speedy trial violation occurred.

2. *Defendant's proof of pre-charge delay.* In applying the *Marion* due process standard to pre-charge delays, most courts require the defendant to prove (1) actual prejudice and (2) malicious prosecutorial intent (based upon that portion of the opinion suggesting that there must be a "showing that the Government intentionally delayed to gain some tactical advantage over [the defendant] or to harass [the defendant]"). *See*

United States v. Crouch, 84 F.3d 1497 (5th Cir. 1996) (expressly adopting that standard and noting that "[a] significant majority of our sister circuits appear to now follow the same rule"); *but see Howell v. Barker*, 904 F.2d 889 (4th Cir. 1990) (minority view, holding that where the defendant establishes prejudice, there is no absolute requirement that the defendant also must prove improper prosecutorial motive).

Under the demanding *Marion* standard, it is exceedingly difficult for defendants to prove improper prosecutorial motive. For example, in *State v. Wilson*, 440 N.W.2d 534 (Wis. 1989), there was a sixteen-year delay between the offense and the indictment. While the defendant was able to show actual prejudice, there was no evidence that the delay was used by the prosecution deliberately to gain a tactical advantage. Therefore, no due process violation was found. Similarly, in *Commonwealth v. Patten*, 513 N.E.2d 689 (Mass. 1987), ten years elapsed between the offense and the indictment. While some evidence was misplaced during this period of time, the defendant could not prove actual prejudice because he could not demonstrate that this missing evidence would have helped his case. Furthermore, there appeared to be no evidence of improper prosecutorial intent. Therefore, the Court found no due process violation.

3. *Some state standards less exacting.* Contrary to the *Marion* standard, recognized by a majority of states, some courts have adopted a less exacting standard. Under this approach, once the defendant has demonstrated actual prejudice, a balancing test is used, weighing prejudice to the defendant against the prosecutor's reasons for delay.

In *State v. Cyr*, 588 A.2d 753 (Me. 1991), the defendant was indicted for arson five years after the crime had been committed (within the six-year statute of limitation for arson). This was more than five years after the investigation had been completed and during which time no new evidence was found, no new studies were conducted, and no new witnesses or statements regarding the fire were available to authorities. Cyr moved to dismiss the indictment, but the trial judge reserved judgment until after trial. Following his conviction, the court determined that the defendant had established actual and unjustifiable prejudice as a result of the pre-indictment delay and granted the motion to dismiss the indictment. The Supreme Court of Maine affirmed, noting that during this period of delay, the state had misplaced several pieces of evidence that possessed exculpatory value. Because the state had offered no reason for the delay in seeking the indictment, dismissal on due process grounds was affirmed.

D. POST-CONVICTION DELAYS

[1] Delay Between Conviction and Beginning of Service of Sentence

Once the defendant is convicted and the sentence is imposed, it can be expected in most cases that the defendant will begin serving the sentence within a relatively short period of time. Due to jail and prison overcrowding, however, there may be a significant delay between the sentencing decision and its actual execution. When this occurs, are there legal constraints upon such delays?

There appears to be no uniform constitutional standard applied in such cases. Nonetheless, some courts have granted relief to the defendant upon due process grounds. *See People v. Levandoski*, 603 N.W.2d 831 (Mich. App. 1999) (based upon a totality of circumstances approach, including fact that defendant requested that he be allowed to serve his ninety-day sentence, five-year delay "is inconsistent with fundamental principles of liberty and justice").

Other courts have fashioned remedies based upon statutory provisions. *See State v. Walker*, 905 S.W.2d 554 (Tenn. 1995)(defendants, facing twenty-day jail sentences who experienced more than one-year delays, granted "dismissals" of sentences based upon statutes requiring that sentences "begin to run when the judgment of conviction becomes final or the prisoner is actually incarcerated, whichever is earlier").

[2] Delay Between Conviction and Appellate Review

Perhaps the most visible post-conviction delay is the delay in obtaining appellate review of the verdict of conviction, sentence, or both. Indeed, delays in the appellate process are sometimes so extreme that prisoners serve their full sentences before their appeals are even considered. The Second Circuit Court of Appeals observed that appellate delays of even six years were not "unusual." *Mathis v. Hood*, 851 F.2d 612, 614 (2d Cir. 1988). Reasons for significant delays range from overcrowded appellate court dockets to the failure of court reporters to prepare transcripts of trials, without which appellate review is impossible.

The very language of the Sixth Amendment (the phrase "criminal prosecutions") suggests that there is no constitutional right to a speedy appellate process. Nonetheless, a number of courts have found a right to a speedy criminal appeal. This right has been gleaned from both due process and equal protection principles. In *United States v. DeLeon*, 444 F. 3d 41 (1st Cir. 2006), the First Circuit held:

> Extreme delay in the processing of an appeal may amount to a due process violation, and delays caused by court reporters are attributable to the government for purposes of determining whether a defendant has been deprived of due process. . . . " However, "mere delay, in and of itself will not give rise to a due process infraction. The defendant must show prejudice. Furthermore, as the Supreme Court has said in the context of pre-indictment delay, even proof of actual prejudice does not make a due process claim "automatically valid." *United States v. Lovasco*, 431 U.S. 783. The court "must consider the reasons for the delay as well as the prejudice to the [defendant]." The showing of prejudice is therefore a threshold requirement. The prejudice must be such as to render the proceedings fundamentally unfair. [citing *Lovasco*.]

In *United States v. Johnson*, 732 F.2d 379, 382 (4th Cir. 1984), the court, applying the *Barker* test, concluded that a two-year delay in preparation of the transcript "may have violated due process" but ruled that the defendant was not entitled to release because his appeal had been heard and found lacking in merit.

Is the *Barker v. Wingo* test (discussed at the beginning of this chapter) appropriate in the context of appellate delay cases? Even if the test applies, is the *Barker* dismissal remedy appropriate? Professor Mark Arkin argues for a "sliding scale of remedies," including such alternatives as ordering release of the defendant if the appeal is not heard within a relatively short period, ordering release of the defendant on bail pending resolution of the appeal, or reducing the defendant's sentence in proportion to the length of the appellate delay. Marc Arkin, *Speedy Criminal Appeal: A Right Without a Remedy*, 74 MINN. L. REV. 437 (1990).

Chapter 14
JURISDICTION AND VENUE

A. INTRODUCTION

The location of criminal proceedings is important, though not a contested issue in the typical criminal case. Assume that a bank robbery occurs in Washington County, State X. For most people involved in the crime and its investigation and prosecution, the most convenient location for the trial is the courthouse in Washington County. Many, if not most, witnesses probably live in or near that county. The investigating police officers and the prosecuting lawyers from that area will find it convenient to do their work there since the crime scene and witnesses will be close to their offices and staff. The defendant may also live in that county and therefore have family, character witnesses, and a lawyer who also reside nearby. Routinely, the trial would be scheduled and held in Washington County and no one would think about the issue.

But sometimes the facts are more complex. What if the defendant lived in a different county or state than Washington County, State X? It could be more convenient for the defendant if the trial were held in his or her home county rather than in Washington County where the crime occurred. The defendant's character witnesses and family attorney would be closer to the courthouse. Moreover, what if the crime had generated a lot of media attention in Washington County? The defendant may fear that the Washington County jurors would have heard or read this publicity and perhaps formed an opinion about guilt before they heard any evidence in the case. To reduce the risk of a trial before a guilt-prone jury, the defendant may prefer to have the case tried in a county other than Washington County.

In unusual situations, the prosecution may also prefer that the case be tried in another county. Perhaps the accused is from a highly respected Washington County family. The prosecution may suspect that the jury will be prone to believe the accused because of his or her family's stature in the community. This concern could be alleviated if the trial were held in another area. Similarly, a prosecutor may prefer trial outside Washington County in order to make the defense's work more difficult. If defense character witnesses find it difficult to attend trial held many miles from where they live, the prosecution may believe it has achieved an advantage.

The question becomes more muddled as the facts become more intricate. For example, perhaps there were two bank robbers in the above Washington County bank robbery. One of them lived in Lincoln County, the other in Jefferson County. The two talked about the crime on the phone while at home each night. The bank robbery was planned in detail in Kent County where they both worked. They stole the "getaway" car in Hamilton County, obtained the gun in Cobb County, and hid the money in an abandoned shack in Florence County. After hiding the money, they fled to Belton County, State Y, where they were arrested. Where did the crime occur? Although the bank was located in Washington County, State X, other facets of the crime were carried out in six other counties and one other state. Could the joint trial of the two defendants be held in Lincoln County where one of them lived and used the telephone to discuss the crime with the other defendant? In Cobb County where they obtained the gun used in the robbery? In Belton County, State Y, where they fled and were apprehended?

These questions address the issues of venue and jurisdiction in criminal cases. *Venue* refers to the physical location where a trial or other proceeding may be held. *Jurisdiction* refers to the power of a court to resolve an issue or case.

Venue and jurisdiction are closely related and the lines between them are often blurred. Sometimes it is held that venue is jurisdictional. This means that the procedural rules of venue establish certain court(s) in a specific geographical area as the only court(s) authorized to hear a particular case. For example, if, as is discussed below, state law provides that a criminal trial must be held in the same county where the crime occurred, the venue for the case is that county. Criminal courts in that county must determine where the crime occurred. If it occurred in their county, they have jurisdiction to handle the case, while courts in other counties do not, unless, as is often the case, state law permits the defendant to waive jurisdiction and request a trial in another county.

This chapter deals with both venue and jurisdiction as applied in criminal cases. It also explores many policy, procedural, and strategic issues that may arise when more than one court may be empowered to handle all or part of a case.

B. JURISDICTION

Terminology. As noted above, jurisdiction refers to a court's power or authority to resolve a case or issue. There are two types of jurisdiction. If a court has *exclusive* jurisdiction, it is the only court authorized to handle a case. On the other hand, two courts may have *concurrent* jurisdiction, giving each of them the power to resolve a case. Sometimes if there is concurrent jurisdiction, a case begun in one court can be *removed* or transferred to the other court with concurrent jurisdiction. Depending on the statutory scheme, the removal may occur because one or both parties request it, or because of administrative concerns.

[1] Limited Jurisdiction

In criminal cases, there are actually two situations raising jurisdiction issues. First, by statute, court rule, or constitution, some courts have jurisdiction over only certain types of criminal cases. For example, in many states some courts have jurisdiction to try misdemeanors and/or city ordinance violations but not felonies. Often impeachment trials can only be held in one or both houses of the state legislature. *E.g.*, Ark. Stat. Ann. § 16-88-101(a) (impeachment trial in Arkansas Senate).

There is a similar pattern in the federal system. The United States Magistrate Judge is authorized to conduct trials of persons charged with federal misdemeanors occurring in the judicial district. The magistrate judge can also resolve many pretrial issues in felony cases. Appeal is to the United States District Judge for that judicial district. 28 U.S.C. § 636; 18 U.S.C. § 3401 *et seq.* The United States district judge conducts trials for felonies and decides certain procedural matters in criminal cases.

Specialized courts. A related model, used rarely and then in response to a particular need for specialized expertise or prompt action in certain cases, creates quite specialized courts that handle only a narrow category of criminal cases, such as drunk driving or drug cases. These courts do not have (or choose to exercise) jurisdiction over other types of cases.

[2] Geographical Jurisdiction

The second type of jurisdiction can be described as geographical jurisdiction and is the subject of this chapter. As discussed more fully below, usually courts in criminal cases have jurisdiction only for crimes somehow related to the geographical area the court covers. Ordinarily, this means that the court in a judicial district has jurisdiction only over crimes where at least some action or result occurred in that judicial district. To clarify the precise borders of an area, sometimes a jurisdiction will enact a detailed law describing precisely the boundaries of the jurisdiction. *See, e.g.*, Ark. Stat. Ann. § 16-88-106 (detailed description of boundaries of Arkansas at bank of Mississippi River).

C. VENUE

[1] Where the Crime is Committed

The rules of venue in criminal cases are the product of a set of statutes, rules, and constitutional provisions. Absent a waiver of the issue, improper venue may be challenged in a motion to acquit or a motion to dismiss an indictment. *Cf. United States v. Trie*, 21 F. Supp. 2d 7 (D.D.C. 1998) (government's failure to allege basis for venue should be addressed first in bill of particulars, not in motion to dismiss).

Judicial district or county. Ordinarily, venue in federal court is based on the federal *judicial district*, while venue in state court is based on a county or judicial district. This means that usually a federal court will deal with crimes that occur in its own judicial district. A state court will usually be authorized to handle those that occur in the county or the judicial district where the state court holds sessions. *But see* Fla. Stat. Ann. § 910.06 (West) (if person in one county commits an offense in another county, the offender may be tried in either county).

[a] Origins of Venue Rules

Often, venue principles are actually established by laws that limit the location of jury trials (an issue sometimes referred to as *vicinage*, the geographical area from which jurors are selected). In the early history of the United States, the colonists were outraged when the English Parliament enacted a number of laws permitting the colonists to be tried in England for certain crimes committed in an American colony. *See* William Wirt Blume, *The Place of Trial of Criminal Cases*, 43 Mich. L. Rev. 59 (1944). The colonists objected to the inconvenience and unfairness of being tried so far from home and the location of their misdeeds and to the likelihood that English jurors would be biased against the American colonists. These complaints surfaced in the Declaration of Independence. In its list of the "repeated injuries and usurpations" of the English King, the Declaration of Independence noted:

> He has combined with others to subject us to a jurisdiction foreign to our constitution, and unacknowledged by our laws . . . . [He has transported] us beyond Seas to be tried for pretended offences . . . .

[b] Constitutional Venue Limitations

The colonists' strong sentiments resulted in two constitutional provisions on point.

[i] Article III, § 2

Article III, § 2 of the United States Constitution provides:

> The trial of all Crimes, except in Cases of Impeachment, shall be by Jury; and such Trial shall be held in the State where the said Crimes shall have been committed; but when not committed within any State, the trial shall be at such Place or Places as the Congress may by Law have directed.

Note that this provision recognizes a right to (1) trial by jury in a federal case, and (2) venue in a federal case in the state where the crime was committed. It does not combine these guarantees and place limits on where jurors must be selected from. Theoretically, it would permit jurors from Alaska to be used in a federal trial in Texas involving a crime committed in Texas.

[ii] Sixth Amendment

The Sixth Amendment, on the other hand, deals specifically with the question of *vicinage*:

> In all criminal prosecutions, the accused shall enjoy the right to a . . . trial . . . by an impartial jury of the State and District wherein the crime shall have been committed, which district shall have been previously ascertained by law . . . .

U.S. Const. amend. VI. Since this provision indicates that the accused in a federal case has a right to a trial by a jury from both the state and district of the crime, it places a potentially significant limit on the location of a federal trial.

[iii] Modern Rules

Early in America's history, this restriction was not severe. It meant that the trial had to be somewhere in the state, for most federal judicial districts covered a whole state. Now, on the other hand, a small state, such as Utah, may contain one federal judicial district, while large states may contain more. For example, Michigan has two federal judicial districts, Illinois contains three, while California and New York each have four districts. Thus, ordinarily a bank robbery in Chicago must be tried in the United States District Court for the Northern District of Illinois. This rule is also embodied in the Federal Rules of Criminal Procedure.

FEDERAL RULES OF CRIMINAL PROCEDURE

Rule 18. *Place of Prosecution and Trial*

> Unless a statute or these rules permit otherwise, the government must prosecute an offense in a district where the offense was committed. The court must set the place of trial within the district with due regard for the convenience of the defendant and the witnesses, and the prompt administration of justice.

NOTES

1. *Federal venue.* Note that although Rule 18 specifies that the federal criminal trial must be conducted somewhere in the federal district where the offense was committed, it does not indicate precisely where in the district the trial must be held. This is an important question because a federal district may cover hundreds of miles and utilize federal courthouses in several towns. A United States District Judge may travel to the various federal courthouses around the district or one or more district judges may work full time in each of the federal courthouses. Each of these courthouses is located in the federal judicial district and therefore would satisfy both Article III, § 2 and the Sixth Amendment as the proper venue for a crime committed in that district.

In deciding which of the courthouses in the district to use for a particular trial, Rule 18 requires the judge to take into consideration two factors. The first is convenience to the defendant and the witnesses. Note that convenience to the prosecuting lawyers is not mentioned, but the convenience of prosecution witnesses may be considered. The second factor is the "prompt administration of justice," a vague term that permits the court to use a number of factors in making its decision.

2. *State venue.* The Article III and Rule 18 provisions concerning venue are obviously limits on the *federal* government, not state prosecutions. Moreover, a clear majority of state courts hold that the Sixth Amendment vicinage requirement also does not apply to the states through the Due Process Clause, though the Supreme Court has not spoken on the issue. *See, e.g., Price v. Superior Court*, 25 Cal. 4th 1046 (2001)(upholding California rule that in certain child sex abuse cases committed against the same child in more than one California jurisdiction, venue is permitted in any jurisdiction where one of the offenses occurred; Sixth Amendment's vicinage rule does not apply to the states; extensive discussion). Nevertheless, most states follow the federal lead and authorize a trial in the county or district where the crime occurred.

[2]   Criminal Acts or Results in Multiple Counties, Districts, or States

A common pattern is that a crime involves acts or consequences occurring in more than one district. For example, a person may be poisoned in District A and die in District B. Where is venue? Many jurisdictions have passed statutes resolving these issues. The usual pattern is to provide for flexibility in venue. Some of these laws are generic, establishing venue in any jurisdiction where the crime was begun, or where criminal acts or the forbidden result occurred. *See, e.g.*, 18 U.S.C. § 3237 (federal crime begun in one district and completed in another or committed in more than one district may be prosecuted in any district in which the offense was begun, continued, or completed). Thus, the poisoning case could be prosecuted in either District A (where the poison was administered) or District B (where death occurred). The prosecutor decides which district will be used. If the defendant is dissatisfied with this decision, he or she can file a Motion for a Change of Venue, described below.

State laws on this issue are quite similar throughout the country. By statute or court rule, states have established several general principles about venue when acts occur in more than one county or judicial district. Often two states or counties have venue. Because of the "separate sovereign" rule in double jeopardy cases, discussed more fully in Chapter 16, two states can convict an offender for a crime committed in both states. *But see* Cal. Penal Code § 793 (conviction or acquittal in another state is bar to prosecution in California).

[a]   Commenced in One Location, Consummated in Another

According to the usual state rules, when the offense is begun or "commenced" in State A and finished or "consummated" in State B, venue lies both in the county or district in State A where the crime was commenced and the county or district in State B where it was consummated. If both states have adopted these rules, the result is that both states have venue, since the crime was commenced in one state and consummated in another. For example, if a robbery were planned in State A and carried out in State B where the bank was located, both states could have venue if their legislatures had enacted the typical venue rules giving jurisdiction whenever a crime was commenced or consummated within the state. The robbers could be convicted of robbery in two states, even though the bank was located in State B.

[b]   Acts in More Than One Location

Similar rules exist for actions occurring in more than one county. The usual rule is that if a crime is committed partly in one county and partly in another or the acts or effects constituting the crime occur in two or more counties, venue is appropriate in any of the counties where an act or effect occurred. For example, if a robbery were planned in County M and carried out in County N, venue would lie in either county, under the most prevalent venue laws.

[c]   Acts Near Border

In order to alleviate concern in those unusual cases where criminal acts occur on or quite near a county border, state rules often provide that in such cases venue is appropriate in either county. For example, assume that a homicide occurs on the border between Counties C and D. A state statute may well indicate that the homicide can be prosecuted in either county. *See, e.g.*, Cal. Penal Code § 782 (for offense committed on boundary of 2 or more judicial territories or within 500 yards thereof, jurisdiction is in either jurisdictional territory).

[d] Crime in Moving Vehicle

A related statute deals with the problem of establishing the location of a crime committed on a moving vehicle. If a crime is committed on a railroad car, vehicle, watercraft or aircraft and it cannot be ascertained precisely where the offense occurred, a statute may provide that jurisdiction lies in any county through which the vehicle traveled. Sometimes the accused is permitted to elect which of these counties will conduct the trial. *See* Fla. Stat. Ann. § 910.02 (West).

[e] When Impossible to Determine Where Crime Occurred

Perhaps the most flexible of all statutes gives the prosecutor plenary authority to select a venue in those unusual cases where it is impossible to determine where the crime occurred. *See* Mich. Comp. Laws Ann. § 762.3 (West) (if it appears to the attorney general that a felony was committed within the state and it is impossible to determine the county, the crime may be prosecuted in any county designated by the attorney general).

[f] Venue for Specific Crimes

States have also enacted a host of venue provisions relating to specific offenses. Examples include: property stolen in one judicial district and carried into another can be tried in either judicial district, Conn. Stat. Ann. § 51-352; an accessory after the fact to a felony may be tried in the county where he or she became an accessory or in any county in which the principal may be tried, Fla. Stat. Ann. § 910.13 (West); bigamy can be tried in the county where the invalid marriage ceremony was performed or in any county in which the bigamous cohabitation occurred, Kan. Stat. Ann. § 22-2613; the crime of failure to file a mandatory report can be tried in the county of the residence of the person failing to file, Mo. Ann. Stat. § 541.035 (Vernon).

[3] Continuing Crimes

Some crimes are classified as *continuing crimes*, meaning that they are ongoing until something happens to end them. The most common example is conspiracy, which may involve many conspirators performing acts helpful to the conspiracy in many jurisdictions. In a large scale drug conspiracy, for example, there may be dealers in many states or judicial districts, suppliers in other locations, and a fleet of people transporting the drugs to and from the suppliers and dealers. The general rule is that conspiracy may be prosecuted in any district where the conspiracy was formulated or where any conspirator did an overt act in furtherance of the conspiracy.

Statutes in many jurisdictions provide that venue in a continuing crime case is in any district or county where an act occurred that was part of the crime. *See* 18 U.S.C. § 3237(a). Typical is Delaware, which provides that venue in a conspiracy case is in any county where the defendant entered the conspiracy or where someone in the conspiracy committed an overt act. Del. Code Ann. tit. 11 § 522. *See also* Cal. Penal Code § 784.5 (in child abduction case, venue lies where the victim resided at time of abduction, or where the minor child was taken, detained, concealed or found).

[4] Outside any County, District, or State

Sometimes a crime occurs in an area other than a clearly defined district or county. For example, a crime may occur in the middle of a lake that separates two counties or states. Or it may occur on the high seas. Where is venue? Both constitutional and statutory provisions address these issues.

For federal crimes, recall that Article III, § 2 of the United States Constitution provides that a federal crime committed in no state shall be tried "at such Place or

Places as the Congress may by Law have directed." U.S. Const., Art. III, § 2. Congress has exercised its authority and enacted a statute providing that:

> The trial of all offenses begun or committed upon the high seas, or elsewhere out of the jurisdiction of any particular State or district, shall be in the district in which the offender, or any one or two or more joint offenders is arrested or is first brought; but if such offender or offenders are not so arrested or brought into any district, an indictment or information may be filed in the district of the last known residence of the offender or of any one of two or more joint offenders, or if no such residence is known the indictment or information may be filed in the District of Columbia. [18 U.S.C. § 3238]

Sometimes this provision causes some confusion. *See, e.g., United States v. Biao*, 51 F. Supp. 2d 1042 (S.D. Cal. 1999) (smuggling aliens case where defendant was arrested on high seas, then indictment was issued in Southern District of California where defendants were first brought by ship after the indictment; indictment permissible in Southern District, not in Central District of California where defendant last lived ten years earlier, because that is where defendants were "first brought"); *United States v Liang*, 224 F.3d 1057 (9th Cir. 2000) (venue was proper only in the district in whose territorial waters defendant committed the offense of attempted alien smuggling, and no alternative venue was provided by the statute concerning offenses committed on the high seas since defendant was not first brought into or arrested in the second district).

The "first brought" provision was also applied in the prosecution of the notorious would-be "shoe bomber," Richard Reid, who attempted to blow up a plane over the Atlantic Ocean. The flight, originally destined from Paris to Miami, was diverted to Boston, the nearest major international airport, and Reid was subsequently tried and convicted in the United States District Court for the District of Massachusetts.

States have also enacted statutes establishing the venue in such cases. *See, e.g.*, 720 Ill. Comp. Stat. Ann. 5/1-6(e) (Smith-Hurd) (venue of offense committed on navigable waters bordering Illinois is in any county adjacent to the body of navigable water).

[5]   Removal to Federal Court

On rare occasions, state criminal proceedings may be removed to federal court. Because of federalism concerns, such removals are rare and federal courts are hesitant to order them.

[a]   Federal Officials

Concerned with the possibility that a state could interfere with the federal government's activities by prosecuting federal officials who are performing their duties, Congress enacted 28 U.S.C. § 1442, which authorizes removal to federal courts of a state criminal prosecution against federal officers acting under color of their office. The United States Supreme Court has narrowed the reach of this provision by adding a requirement that removal is permissible only if the federal official raises a federal defense, such as official immunity. *Mesa v. California*, 489 U.S. 121 (1989). *See generally* Andrew J. Field, *Removing State Criminal Charges Against a Federal Officer to Federal Court*, 14 Crim. Justice 20 (Winter 2000). In *Mesa* the federal defense requirement barred removal for postal workers charged with traffic offenses while delivering mail. Defense counsel seeking removal must file a notice of removal in the federal district court that has jurisdiction in the locale of the state criminal charges. 28 U.S.C. § 1446(c).

[b]   State Defendant Claiming Denial of Equal Rights

Just as a federal official may remove certain state criminal cases to federal court, any state criminal defendant may do so if unable to enforce equal civil rights in the state court. 28 U.S.C. § 1443. This provision has been limited to civil rights based on racial equality. *Georgia v. Rachel*, 384 U.S. 780 (1966) (permitting removal to federal court of state criminal trespass cases stemming from civil rights demonstrations in racially segregated restaurants in Atlanta). The accused must establish that some formal expression of state law prevents the enforcement of the race-related federal civil right. *See People v. Bailey*, 885 F. Supp. 167 (W.D. Mich. 1995) (removal denied for state criminal prosecution by state inmate charged with assaulting staff; no evidence offered that enforcement of race-related rights would not occur in Michigan courts); *Michigan v. Garner*, 2006 WL 696518 (W.D. Mich.)(refusing to remove state child non-support prosecution to federal court).

D. LOCATION OF THE CRIME

Since the general rule is that the venue of a criminal proceeding is where the crime occurred, it is essential to know precisely where it was committed. As the above bank robbery hypothetical illustrates, sometimes this is easy to determine and sometimes quite difficult. In a simple crime where one person does all acts necessary for the crime in a single county or judicial district, venue will lie in that district. In more complex cases, however, the answers are not always clear. They may depend on the resolution of questions about where various facets of the crime occurred or on a precise interpretation of the criminal law allegedly violated. Ordinarily the statute's key verbs are critical.

TRAVIS v. UNITED STATES
364 U.S. 631 (1961)

Mr. Justice Douglas delivered the opinion of the Court.

In this case petitioner was charged on four counts of an indictment with the making and filing of false non-Communist affidavits required by § 9(h) of the National Labor Relations Act . . . . The indictment charged that the affidavits were false writings or documents made and executed in Colorado and filed in Washington, D.C., with the National Labor Relations Board.

. . . Before the first trial, petitioner moved to dismiss the indictment on the ground that venue was improperly laid in Colorado. [The District Court and Court of Appeals approved venue in Colorado and we address this issue.]

. . . It is agreed that the affidavits were executed by petitioner as a union officer in Colorado and mailed there to the Board in Washington, D.C., where they were received and filed [regulations required that the affidavits be kept on file with the NLRB in Washington, D.C]. The prosecution contends . . . that the offense was begun in Colorado and completed in the District of Columbia. In that view venue was properly laid in Colorado by virtue of 18 U.S.C. § 3237(a), which provides:

> Except as otherwise expressly provided by enactment of Congress, any offense against the United States begun in one district and completed in another . . . may be inquired of and prosecuted in any district in which such offense was begun . . . or completed.

We start with the provision of Art. III, § 2 of the Constitution that criminal trials "shall be held in the State where the said crimes shall have been committed," a safeguard reinforced by the command of the Sixth Amendment that the criminal trial shall be before an impartial jury of "the State and district wherein the crime shall have been committed." We start also with the assumption that Colorado, the residence of petitioner, might offer conveniences and advantages to him which a trial in the District of Columbia might lack. We are also aware that venue provisions in Acts of Congress should not be so freely construed as to give the Government the choice of "a tribunal favorable" to it. We therefore begin our inquiry from the premise that questions of venue are more than matters of mere procedure. They raise deep issues of public policy in the light of which legislation must be construed.

Where various duties are imposed, some to be performed at a distant place, others at home, the Court has allowed the prosecution to fix the former as the venue of trial. The use of agencies of interstate commerce enables Congress to place venue in any district where the particular agency was used. "The constitutional requirement is as to the locality of the offense, and not the personal presence of the offender." *Armour Packing Co. v. U.S.*, 209 U.S. 56, 76 (1908). Where the language of the Act defining venue has been construed to mean that Congress created a continuing offense, it is held, for venue purposes, to have been committed wherever the wrongdoer roamed. The decisions are discrete, each looking to the nature of the crime charged. Thus, while the use of the mails might be thought to allow venue to be laid either at the sending or receiving end, the trial was recently restricted to the district of the sender, in light of the constitutional provisions already mentioned and the phrasing of a particular criminal statute. Where Congress is not explicit, "the *locus delicti* must be determined from the nature of the crime alleged and the location of the act or acts constituting it." *United States v. Anderson*, 328 U.S. 699, 703 (1946).

Section 9(h) of the National Labor Relations Act, with which we are concerned, did not require union officers to file non-Communist affidavits. If it had, the whole process of filing, including the use of the mails, might logically be construed to constitute the offense. But this statutory design is different. It requires that the Board shall make no investigation nor issue any complaint in the matters described in § 9(h) "unless there is on file with the Board" a non-Communist affidavit of each union officer. The filings are conditions precedent to a union's use of the Board's procedures. The false statement statute, under which the prosecution is brought, penalizes him who knowingly makes any "false" statement "in any matter within the jurisdiction of any department or agency of the United States." There would seem to be no offense, unless petitioner completed the filing in the District of Columbia. The statute demanded that the affidavits be on file with the Board before it could extend help to the union; the forms prescribed by the Board required the filing in the District of Columbia; the indictment charged that petitioner filed the affidavits there. The words of the Act — "unless there is on file with the Board" — suggest to us that the filing must be completed before there is a "matter within the jurisdiction" of the Board within the meaning of the false statement statute. When § 9(h) provides the criminal penalty, it makes the penal provisions applicable "to such affidavits," viz., to those "on file with the Board."

The Government admits that the filing is necessary to the "occurrence" of the offense, but it argues that the offense has its "beginning" in Colorado, because it was there that "the defendant had irrevocably set in motion and placed beyond his control the train of events which would normally result (and here did result) in the consummation of the offense." We do not agree with this analysis. Venue should not be made to depend on the chance use of the mails, when Congress has so carefully indicated the locus of the crime. After mailing, the affidavit might have been lost; petitioner himself might have recalled it. Multiple venue in general requires crimes consisting of "distinct parts" or involving "a continuously moving act." *United States v. Lombardo*, 241 U.S. 73, 77 (1916). When a place is explicitly designated where a paper must be filed, a prosecution for failure to file lies only at that place, [the District of Columbia. Reversed.]

Mr. Justice Harlan, whom Mr. Justice Frankfurter and Mr. Justice Clark join, dissenting.

Title 18 U.S.C. § 3237(a) provides in pertinent part:

> Except as otherwise expressly provided by enactment of Congress, any offense against the United States *begun* in one district and *completed* in another . . . may be inquired of and prosecuted in any district in which such offense was begun . . . or completed. (Emphasis added.)

In my view of the offense with which Travis is charged, I think that under [§ 3237(a)] the Government was entitled to proceed either in Colorado, where this affidavit was made, or in the District of Columbia, where the affidavit was filed, and therefore dissent from the Court's holding that venue was improperly laid in Colorado.

. . . If this crime may properly be viewed as having been begun in the district of Colorado and completed in the district of the District of Columbia, then venue may be laid in either district under 18 U.S.C. § 3237(a). Whether that is the proper view of this offense is an issue on which the authorities in this Court are at best inconclusive . . . . *United States v. Lombardo*, 241 U.S. 73 (1916), which the Court considers particularly significant, is not controlling, since in that case the offense charged was the failure to file with the Commissioner General of Immigration certain information concerning an alien woman whom the defendant was harboring for purposes of prostitution. In such a charge it is difficult to see how the defendant does anything at all except at the place where he fails to file. In contrast, the false affidavit in the present case first came into existence in Colorado, having been made and sworn to there.

. . . In these circumstances, the proper course to follow appears to me to be to determine the appropriate venue "from the nature of the crime alleged and the location of the act or acts constituting it," *United States v. Anderson*, 328 U.S. 699, 703 (1946), and that determination should take into account that:

. . . The provision for trial in the vicinity of the crime is a safeguard against the unfairness and hardship involved when an accused is prosecuted in a remote place. Provided its language permits, the Act in question should be given that construction which will respect such considerations. *United States v. Cores*, 356 U.S. 405, 407 (1958).

In this kind of case, prosecution in the district in which the affidavit was executed, most often I would suppose the place where the union offices are located, is more likely to respect the basic policy of the Sixth Amendment than would a prosecution in the district where the affidavit was filed. The witnesses and relevant circumstances surrounding the contested issues in such cases more probably will be found in the district of the execution of the affidavit than at the place of filing which, as in this instance will often be for the defendant "a remote place," — that is the District of Columbia where the headquarters of the National Labor Relations Board are located in the case of officers of international unions, or elsewhere throughout the country where the Board has branch offices in the case of local union officers.

This is not to say that venue must be limited to the place of execution of the affidavit, but only that there is no lack of consonance with the underlying policy of the Sixth Amendment in permitting venue to be laid there if the elements of the crime allow. In holding that the crime for which this petitioner was prosecuted does not allow venue to be laid in the district of the making of the affidavit, the Court considers the essence of the crime to be the filing of the affidavit, and until that is accomplished it holds that the crime is not even begun. . . .

It is of course true that the offense is not completed until the affidavit is filed with the Board, but I do not think it adds anything to say, as the Court does, that until such time as the affidavit is filed with the Board there is no matter "within the jurisdiction of any department or agency of the United States." The fact that the filing completes the offense by giving the Board jurisdiction over the matter does not, in my view, detract from the conclusion that the offense was begun when and where the affidavit was executed. Indeed this would seem to be the very type of situation contemplated by 18 U.S.C. § 3237(a) . . . .

NOTES

1. *Travis reverses usual preferences of the parties.* In cases where venue is challenged, a common pattern is that the defendant seeks to have the case tried where he or she lives or works. The government prefers some other location. Is that pattern present in *Travis*? Why or why not?

2. Note that 18 U.S.C. § 3237(a), discussed in *Travis*, provides that a crime that is begun in one district and completed in another may be prosecuted in both. Did the *Travis* Court hold that the crime was not begun in Colorado, where the false statements were made and mailed? Did the crime occur in Washington, D.C. even though no defendant was physically present in that locale?

3. *Venue policies.* Which location, Colorado or Washington, D.C., better serves the policies underlying Article III, § 2 and the Sixth Amendment of the Constitution?

4. *Ways of approaching meaning of statutes.* Note that the Supreme Court in *Travis* strictly construed criminal statutes in ascertaining the proper venue for their enforcement. The Court looked carefully at the wording of the criminal statute to determine exactly where the offense occurred. The Justices gave little attention to the question of where a fair trial was most likely to occur. This literal approach is reflected in a number of cases. *See, e.g., Wurster v. State*, 715 N.E.2d 341 (Ind. 1999) (crime of filing perjurious affidavit with Bureau of Motor Vehicles was committed in county where defendant submitted affidavit, not in county where affidavit was forwarded for processing).

Other Supreme Court decisions are more flexible. For example, in *United States v. Cores*, 356 U.S. 405 (1958), the defendant was a non-American crew member of a ship that landed in Philadelphia. When the defendant failed to leave the country within twenty-nine days, as required by his conditional immigration permit, he was prosecuted for violation of a federal statute making it a crime to "willfully remain" in the United States after the expiration of the conditional entry permit. Apparently the defendant arrived in Philadelphia, then went to New York for a year. He was apprehended and prosecuted in Connecticut after leaving New York. The District Court dismissed the federal charges because there was no venue in Connecticut since the entry permit had long expired before the defendant entered that state.

The defendant had argued that the offense was completed the moment his permit expired. The government, on the other hand, maintained that the crime was a continuing crime that could be prosecuted in any state where the accused is found. The Supreme Court agreed with the government, holding that the essence of the crime is "remaining" after the permit has expired. Accordingly, venue was permissible in any district where the crewman willfully went more than twenty-nine days after his entry into the United States. The Supreme Court noted that the legislative history of the federal offense was not "inconsistent" with this result. Moreover, the *Cores* Court reasoned that the result was consistent with the policy of sparing the criminal accused the hardships associated with having to endure a criminal prosecution far from home.

Although *Cores* makes it more likely that some offenders will face a federal trial in a location close to home rather than many miles away, the decision may cause the opposite result in other cases. If *Cores* can be prosecuted in Connecticut where he was found, can he also be prosecuted in Philadelphia or New York where he lived after the expiration of his entry permit? After all, he "remained" in those jurisdictions with no valid immigration permit. If so, then the *Cores* interpretation could be used by the government to try him in a forum that is very inconvenient to the accused. The only protection for defendants in cases where there are numerous permissible trial locations is the possibility of obtaining a change of venue to a more convenient location. This topic is discussed in the next section.

5. *Expanded scope of federal crimes.* Increased federalization of criminal law requires close attention to venue questions. Each statute and act must be carefully scrutinized. For example, assume that a person deposits $40,000 in a Florida bank and shortly thereafter withdraws $9,500 on four separate occasions. The money that was withdrawn is traced to earlier drug transactions in the state of Missouri, but the person who deposited the $40,000 in Florida is not charged with involvement in the Missouri drug deals. The defendant is charged with (1) conspiracy to violate a federal statute pertaining to money laundering and (2) violation of a statute pertaining to monetary transactions in criminally-derived property of a value greater than $10,000. Does venue lie in the state of Missouri? In *United States v. Cabrales*, 524 U.S. 1 (1998), the Supreme Court held that because the laundering alleged in the indictment occurred in Florida and because the defendant was not alleged to have transported any of the funds from Missouri to Florida, Missouri was not a proper venue for trial.

The money laundering statute has since been amended to provide that venue is proper in any district in which the financial transaction was conducted or any district where a prosecution for the underlying criminal conduct "could be brought" as long as the defendant participated in the transfers of the proceeds of the underlying offense from the district where that offense occurred to the district where the money-laundering occurred. *See* 18 U.S.C. § 1956 (i).

Compare *Cabrales* with *United States v. Rodrigues-Moreno*, 526 U.S. 275 (1999), involving the following facts: The defendant, Jacinto, kidnaped his victim, Ephraim, in Texas after a drug deal gone bad. Jacinto and others drove Ephraim from Texas to New York to New Jersey to Maryland. A handgun was used in Maryland during and in relation to the kidnapping, but there was no evidence of the gun having been used in any of the other states. A federal statute makes it a crime to use a firearm during and in relation to any crime of violence. Defendant was charged with this offense in New Jersey and he moved to dismiss, arguing that venue was proper only in Maryland. The United States Supreme Court held that venue was proper in any district where the crime of violence was committed, even if the firearm was used or carried only in a single district. The Court read the statute as containing two conduct elements: "using and carrying" a gun and the "commission of a kidnaping." The crime was characterized as a "continuing crime of violence" and venue was permissible in any district where part of the kidnaping was committed. Justices Scalia and Stevens dissented, arguing that *Cabrales* requires a careful examination of "the nature of the crime alleged and the location of the act or acts constituting it." Based upon their examination of the text of this federal statute, the dissenters concluded that venue is proper only where the defendant engages in both the predicate offense and uses or carries the gun. For a brief analysis of the implications of increased federalization of criminal law upon venue, see Geoffrey Mearns and Stanley Okula Jr., *Venue and Federalizing Crime: Will the Supreme Court Tell Prosecutors Where to Go?*, 13 CRIM. JUST. 20 (Winter 1999).

6. *Different approach: contacts test.* When faced with a crime involving more than one jurisdiction and a criminal statute where venue is unclear, some jurisdictions have rejected the formalistic approach in *Travis* and have adopted the "substantial contacts test."

UNITED STATES v. WILLIAMS
788 F.2d 1213 (6th Cir. 1986)

MILBURN, CIRCUIT JUDGE.

[Defendant was convicted under 18 U.S.C. § 3150 (now § 3146) for willfully failing to appear after having been released on bond. He was indicted on a firearms charge in the Eastern District of Kentucky and arrested in the Southern District of Indiana. After being released on bond in Indiana on the condition that he report for arraignment in Kentucky, he absconded and did not appear in Kentucky. A Kentucky federal grand jury indicted him for failure to appear and he was arrested in Kentucky. The federal appellate courts were split on whether the proper venue was in the district where the defendant was released on bail (Indiana) or where he failed to appear (Kentucky). An earlier Sixth Circuit case had held that venue was proper in the district where the defendant was released. In this case the court asked whether venue is also appropriate in the district where the defendant was to appear. The court first noted that the accused has a constitutional right to be tried in the state and district where the crime was committed.]

In *United States v. Reed*, 773 F.2d 477 (2d Cir. 1985), the court addressed this problem in the context of statutes, such as bail jumping, which contain no venue provision. The court began by pointing out that "where the acts constituting the crime and the nature of the crime charged implicate more than one location, the constitution does not command a single venue." After discussing Supreme Court venue cases, the *Reed* court concluded:

> a review of relevant authorities demonstrates that there is no single defined policy or mechanical test to determine constitutional venue. Rather, the test is best described as a substantial contacts rule that takes into account a number of factors — the site of the defendant's acts, the elements and nature of the crime, the locus of the effect of the criminal conduct, and the suitability of each district for accurate fact finding . . . .

We now adopt the substantial contacts test as well as the rationale and framework of analysis articulated by the *Reed* court.[3] Applying the substantial contacts test to prosecutions under 18 U.S.C. § 3150, we hold that there are substantial contacts both in the district releasing a defendant and in the district in which he is ordered to appear.

The first factor — the site of the defendant's acts — is applicable when certain affirmative acts trigger criminal liability. Thus, for example, the act of assaulting a witness could trigger criminal liability for obstruction of justice under 18 U.S.C. § 1503. In such a case, the affirmative acts could, under the substantial contacts test, establish venue in the district where the acts were committed. However, since § 3150 proscribes the failure to act, "the site of defendant's acts" does little to establish the requisite substantial contacts in either district.

The second factor has two considerations. First, we look to the elements of the crime. In interpreting the elements of a crime in order to determine where the crime was committed and thus where venue lies, courts have often examined the key verbs of statutes defining criminal offenses . . . . Based on this analysis, courts and commentators have concluded that where "the statute makes it a crime to fail to do some act required by law, the failure takes place in, and the proper venue is, the district in which the act should have been done." 2 Charles Alan Wright, Federal Practice and Procedure § 302, at 198 (1982).

Although consideration of the elements of 18 U.S.C. § 3150 establishes venue in the district where a defendant is ordered to appear, as *United States v. Roche*, 611 F.2d 1180 (6th Cir. 1980), demonstrates, substantial contacts, and thus venue, can be found in the district releasing a defendant by considering the remaining factors. In this connection, we turn to the next consideration of the second factor: the nature of the crime. In *Roche* we relied heavily on the nature of the crime in holding venue was proper in the court releasing the defendant. For example, we noted that: In our view when a bailed defendant willfully disobeys a court order requiring him to report for commencement of his prison term, the nature of that failure constitutes an affront to the power and dignity of the court which admitted him to bail and a most flagrant breach of the conditions of his lawful release. Under the substantial contacts test, this suggests, as we held in *Roche*, that venue lies in the district releasing a defendant.

The third factor — the locus of the effect of the criminal conduct — also demonstrates that substantial contacts are likely in both districts. As we noted in *Roche*, the "primary effect [of bail jumping] is upon the proper administration of justice in the court which admits one to bail and is akin to a 'constructive contempt of court.' " *Roche*, 611 F.2d at 1183 (quoting *O'Donnell*, 510 F.2d at 1195). Although the primary effect may be in the district which admits one to bail, the effect in the district where a defendant is ordered to appear cannot be underestimated. By failing to appear a delay in trial is necessitated,

---

[3] The substantial contacts test is adopted to aid in the determination of where venue lies when Congress has not prescribed venue for the offense. We, of course, do not alter the principle that "Congress may provide that venue for the crimes it creates will lie in any district having minimal contacts with the offense." Note, Criminal Venue in the Federal Courts: The Obstruction of Justice Puzzle, 82 Mich. L. Rev. 90, 95 (1983).

and society's legitimate interest in bringing a suspected criminal to trial is frustrated.

. . . The final factor in the substantial contacts test is the suitability of each district for accurate fact-finding. It is important to point out that determining the proper venue under particular statutes is done, not by examining the evidence in each individual case, but by scrutinizing the definition of the crime and the likely location of evidence of such crimes generally." Similarly, we think it is important to consider potential defenses to a given crime and the location of evidence necessary to establish or support such a defense.

. . . A defendant, for example, might raise his failure to receive the order to appear as a defense. This would suggest that the district in which the order was issued (here the Southern District of Indiana) would be best suited for accurate fact-finding. On the other hand, a trial in the district where a defendant was ordered to appear (here the Eastern District of Kentucky) would be best suited for determining whether the order was complied with and, if not, the willfulness of the failure. In this connection we note that, as revised, the failure to appear statute expressly provides [an affirmative defense if "uncontrollable circumstances prevented the person from appearing"] . . . Although these "uncontrollable circumstances" can arise in any district, it seems most likely that they will arise in the district where performance was required.

. . . In summary, we hold that venue under 18 U.S.C. § 3150 is proper both in the district issuing the order to appear and in the district where a defendant is ordered to appear. Affirmed.

NOTES

1. *Travis or Williams?* Compare the approach in *Travis* with that in *Williams.* Which do you prefer?

2. *Switching tests.* Would the result in *Travis* have been different if the Supreme Court had used the "substantial contacts" test? Would the result in *Williams* have been different had the court used the approach of the *Travis* case?

3. *Policy analysis.* Which test is more consistent with Article III, § 2 and the Sixth Amendment? With the policies behind those provisions?

4. *Information to make contacts assessment.* Note that under the substantial contacts approach the trial judge must have some information about the case in order to resolve the first (site of defendant's acts) and fourth (suitability of the district for accurate fact-finding) factors. But how much information is needed? And who will furnish it? For example, how will the court know about the site of the defendant's acts without hearing proof from both defense and prosecution witnesses at the trial? Similarly, how will the court know what the defendant's defenses will be without getting this information from defense counsel, who may be reluctant or unable to disclose this information early in the criminal process? Should the court hold a hearing to determine the proper venue and call witnesses to resolve the above questions? Or should the court base its venue decision on speculation about where the acts could have occurred or what defenses could be offered?

5. *Minimal contacts needed.* There is some indication that Congress has some "contacts" limits on where it can place venue. *See United States v. Trie*, 21 F. Supp. 2d 7 (D.D.C. 1998) (Congress may define where crime was committed; can be in district other than location of defendant's acts as long as the offense has some minimal contacts with that district).

E.   PROCEDURAL ISSUES

[1]   Grounds for Transfer of Venue

Although the Sixth Amendment and other court rules establish the general rule that venue lies in the district (or county) where the crime occurred, sometimes the accused or the prosecution would like the venue changed. The person seeking this will file a Motion for a Change of Venue.

Court rules often authorize a change of venue for a trial. A venue change may also be permitted when the defendant foregoes a trial and pleads guilty or *nolo contendere* and is sentenced. The Federal Rules of Criminal Procedure specifically provide for these possibilities.

[a]   Transfer for Plea and Sentence

Sometimes a criminal defendant will live or work in one area and commit a crime in another. Ordinarily, of course, the venue for the proceeding would be in the district where the crime was committed. But sometimes the accused is going to plead guilty and would like the matter to be handled in the district where he or she lives rather than where the crime occurred. This will facilitate testimony by the accused's character witnesses and will make it easier for the defendant to live at home and continue working while the sentencing matter is being studied and resolved. If the offender is likely to receive probation, the early transfer will facilitate the offender's efforts to cooperate with the probation officer in the offender's home area.

Rule 20 of the Federal Rules of Criminal Procedure specifically authorizes a criminal defendant to request that the case be transferred from the district of the crime to that where the accused was arrested, held, or is present. *See also* Fla. Stat. Ann. § 910.035 (West) (transfer to county where defendant was arrested or is held). The request for a change of venue is viewed as a waiver of the ordinary venue rule. The government's interests are safeguarded in the transfer process since the United States Attorneys for both districts must agree to the transfer.

FEDERAL RULE OF CRIMINAL PROCEDURE

Rule 20. *Transfer for Plea and Sentence*

(a) **Consent to Transfer.** A prosecution may be transferred from the district where the indictment or information is pending, or from which a warrant on a complaint has been issued, to the district where the defendant is arrested, held, or present if:

(1) the defendant states in writing a wish to plead guilty or nolo contendere and to waive trial in the district where the indictment, information, or complaint is pending, consents in writing to the court's disposing of the case in the transferee district, and files the statement in the transferee district; and

(2) the United States attorneys in both districts approve the transfer in writing.

(b) **Clerk's Duties.** After receiving the defendant's statement and the required approvals, the clerk where the indictment, information, or complaint is pending must send the file, or a certified copy, to the clerk in the transferee district.

(c) **Effect of a Not Guilty Plea.** If the defendant pleads not guilty after the case has been transferred under Rule 20(a), the clerk must return the papers to the court where the prosecution began, and that court must restore the proceeding to its docket. The defendant's statement that the defendant wished to plead guilty or nolo contendere is not, in any civil or criminal proceeding, admissible against the defendant.

(d) **Juveniles.**

(1) Consent to Transfer. A juvenile, as defined in 18 U.S.C. § 5031, may be proceeded against as a juvenile delinquent in the district where the juvenile is arrested, held, or present if:

> **(A)** the alleged offense that occurred in the other district is not punishable by death or life imprisonment;

> **(B)** an attorney has advised the juvenile;

> **(C)** the court has informed the juvenile of the juvenile's rights — including the right to be returned to the district where the offense allegedly occurred — and the consequences of waiving those rights;

> **(D)** the juvenile, after receiving the court's information about rights, consents in writing to be proceeded against in the transferee district, and files the consent in the transferee district;

> **(E)** the United States attorneys for both districts approve the transfer in writing; and

> **(F)** the transferee court approves the transfer.

(2) Clerk's Duties. After receiving the juvenile's written consent and the required approvals, the clerk where the indictment, information, or complaint is pending or where the alleged offense occurred must send the file, or a certified copy, to the clerk in the transferee district.

[b] Transfer of Trial

Just as a criminal defendant may prefer to plead and be sentenced in a district other than that where the crime occurred, he or she may also want a trial in another district. Both state and federal statutes authorize the defendant to request a change of venue. Sometimes the rules are quite specific in authorizing a change of venue for a specific reason. *See, e.g.*, Ala. Code § 15-2-21 (danger of mob violence and need for military guard).

As a general principle, courts are reluctant to grant a venue change. If the request is made because of concerns about an inability to obtain a fair trial in the original venue, the judge in that venue may be unwilling to admit that he or she cannot provide a fair trial. And some courts may believe that the local populace has a right to have the case tried where the crime occurred.

Rule 21 of the Federal Rules of Criminal Procedure permits the accused to file a Motion for Transfer to accomplish this. Note that the transfer request may be based on three grounds: prejudice against the defendant (Rule 21(a)), convenience of the parties or witnesses (Rule 21(b)), or the interest of justice (Rule 21(b)). Because venue is a right conferred on the defendant, the government cannot obtain a change of venue to another district without the defendant's consent. The defendant's consent to a change is viewed as a waiver of venue rights. The government's consent is not necessary.

FEDERAL RULE OF CRIMINAL PROCEDURE

Rule 21. *Transfer for Trial*

(a) For Prejudice. Upon the defendant's motion, the court must transfer the proceeding against that defendant to another district if the court is satisfied that so great a prejudice against the defendant exists in the transferring district that the defendant cannot obtain a fair and impartial trial there.

(b) For Convenience. Upon the defendant's motion, the court may transfer the proceeding, or one or more counts, against that defendant to another district for the convenience of the parties and witnesses and in the interest of justice.

(c) Proceedings on Transfer. When the court orders a transfer, the clerk must send to the transferee district the file, or a certified copy, and any bail taken. The prosecution will then continue in the transferee district.

(d) Time to File a Motion to Transfer. A motion to transfer may be made at or before arraignment or at any other time the court or these rules prescribe.

[i]   Transfer Because of Prejudice (Usually Hostile Publicity)

Transfer under Rule 21(a) requires a transfer if there is so much prejudice in the locale that the defendant cannot obtain a fair trial. Ordinarily, the prejudice is caused by hostile pretrial medial coverage. When pretrial publicity is the culprit, it raises serious issues about the defendant's right to a fair trial by an impartial jury and to have the case tried pursuant to the usual venue rules, and the media's rights to press freedom as well as the citizens' right to have a trial in their area.

When the court finds that the defendant cannot obtain a fair and impartial trial because of prejudice, it *must* transfer the proceeding under Rule 21(a). This could occur in cases that have attracted a lot of media attention. The accused may believe that a fair trial is impossible in the district where there is venue. Perhaps the media has depicted the defendant as guilty, disclosed inadmissible evidence, or caused outrage about the crime.

The next case illustrates that prejudice could be caused by sources other than pretrial publicity.

UNITED STATES v. NETTLES
476 F.3d 508 (6th Cir. 2007)

Boyce F. Martin, Jr., Circuit Judge.

Gale Nettles was charged with attempting to destroy the federal courthouse in Chicago, attempting to provide material support to terrorism, manufacturing counterfeit money, and distributing counterfeit money. After a jury trial, he was convicted on all charges except for attempting to provide material support to terrorism, and sentenced to 160 years. On appeal, Nettles alleges that the district court erred by refusing to transfer the proceedings to a different venue . . . . [Convictions affirmed.]

[While in prison for counterfeiting, Nettles met Cecil Brown and the two discussed bombing the federal courthouse, the Dirksen Building, in Chicago. Nettles explained his plan to put a bomb in a tractor trailer at the building's loading dock. Brown informed federal officials. These officials put Brown in touch with the FBI. Under the FBI's direction, Brown gave Nettles the phone number of Brown's alleged nephew, Beasley, who was actually an undercover F.B.I. agent claiming to be a Louisiana farmer with access to ammonium nitrate fertilizer. Agent Beasley, in turn, put Nettles in contact with other F.B.I. undercover agents who agreed to buy counterfeit money from Nettles and who posed as Al-Qaeda and Hamas operatives willing to buy explosive fertilizer from Nettles. On July 31, 2004, Nettles met with several informants, described to them how to create a time bomb using diesel fuel and ammonium nitrate, and again mentioned that he had the Dirksen Federal Building in mind as a target. Nettles noted the "impact" it would make on the country if this happened while judges were inside.]

. . . On January 14, 2004, Beasley came to Chicago and met with Nettles. Nettles told agent Beasley that he wanted to build a bomb that would bring down the entire Dirksen Federal Building because he was upset with the federal judicial system and further, because the building blocked the view of the lake.

On August 2, 2004, undercover agent Beasley told Nettles that he had packed a ton of ammonium nitrate on his truck. [Two days later Nettles was arrested during the process of transferring "fertilizer" (actually a harmless substance) from agent Beasley's truck to a locker and to the truck of the supposed Al-Qaeda contact.]

On September 1, 2004, a grand jury returned a nine-count indictment charging Nettles with attempting to destroy a federal building by fire and explosive, attempting to destroy a building used in interstate commerce by fire and explosive, attempting to provide material support to terrorism, manufacturing counterfeit currency, and five counts of transferring counterfeit currency.

Before trial, Nettles moved [to] . . . transfer to another district. Both motions were denied. [The Court of Appeals ordered the district judge to recuse himself but did not rule on the transfer motion.] . . . .

. . . The district court denied Nettles's motion to transfer, finding that there was no showing that Nettles could not receive a fair and impartial trial in the Northern District of Illinois. . . . Nettles was convicted by a jury on September 15, 2005, on all counts but the count for attempting to provide material support to terrorism. He was sentenced on January 12, 2006, to eight consecutive terms of 20 years each, for a total of 160 years.

Nettles sought a transfer of venue under Fed.R.Crim.P. 21(a), which requires a change of venue "if the court is satisfied that so great a prejudice against the defendant exists in the transferring district that the defendant cannot obtain a fair and impartial trial there." The district court denied the request, noting that the jurors in Nettles's case would not have been jurors at the time Nettles intended to destroy the courthouse, that the pretrial publicity had been less pervasive in Nettles's case than in other cases from the Northern District of Illinois that were not transferred, and that "[n]othing has been presented to the Court to demonstrate that defendant cannot receive a fair and impartial trial in the Northern District of Illinois with a jury from the district. Nettles challenges this ruling on appeal, asserting that jurors sitting in the very building he was accused of attempting to destroy could not realistically be asked to put out of mind the potential death and destruction his acts would have caused.

We review a denial of a request for change of venue under Rule 21(a) for abuse of discretion. Abuse of discretion will not be found unless the facts compel — and not merely support — a finding that a change in venue is necessary.

Courts have typically analyzed whether there is prejudice under Rule 21 by looking to pretrial publicity. Prejudice can be established by either a showing of actual prejudice, for example, when jurors can be shown to have exposure to pretrial publicity that prevents them from judging the case impartially, or by presumed prejudice, which occurs in cases surrounded by a carnival atmosphere, where pervasive and inflammatory pretrial publicity makes juror bias inevitable. In reviewing denials of requests to change venue, we have stated that the ultimate question is whether it is possible to select a fair and impartial jury, and in most situations the voir dire examination adequately supplies the facts upon which to base that determination.

In his brief, Nettles does not point to any actual prejudice, as he does not identify anything in the record that would indicate any given juror had been exposed to pretrial publicity. Further, he acknowledges that the pretrial publicity in this case was not nearly as pervasive as in other cases in which motions for transfer were denied. Instead, he seems to rely on the idea of presumed prejudice, stating that "juror[s] sitting for a week or more in a building which the government argued was intended to be destroyed by a huge explosion and fire, killing most or all of the persons who worked therein, including jurors, would inevitably have their judgment clouded by that fact."

The district court conducted a careful voir dire process to prevent the presence of juror bias. As we have noted, this approach usually satisfies the "ultimate question" of whether particular jurors can be fair and impartial.[1] However, Nettles argues that the effectiveness of voir dire is irrelevant, because it can only eliminate the taint of pretrial publicity, and here, "the prejudice of the jurors is based on a state of mind which is not nearly as easy to quantify and articulate as a submission of a volume of press clippings would be." In other words, unlike in the case of pretrial publicity, here, the "anxiety" of

---

[1] Only one venire member indicated that he had heard of the case. He was eventually dismissed.

the jurors concerning a potential threat to their own safety made them unable to assess their ability to fairly deliberate and assess the evidence. Nettles argues that it was impossible for these jurors "to put out of their mind the inevitable and natural human thought, 'that could have been me working in this building on that day.'" He makes the bold assertion that as a matter of law, it would be impossible for him to be tried by an impartial jury in the Dirksen Federal Building.

Although Nettles effectively distinguishes this type of case from those involving pretrial publicity, it does not necessarily follow that voir dire is a less valuable tool to screen for juror prejudice in this context. The questioning of jurors regarding their ability to be impartial need not be limited to their prior knowledge of the case. Nettles also could have requested that the jurors be asked about their ability to fairly assess evidence pertaining to a threat to the courthouse within which they were sitting, and yet he failed to do so. We find Nettles's full scale attack on our reliance on the voir dire process, based simply on the possibility of "juror anxiety," to be unconvincing.

Nettles relies on the case of *United States v. McVeigh*, 918 F.Supp. 1467 (W.D.Okla.1996), in support of his claim for a transfer. There are some key distinctions between this case and *McVeigh* that make it inapposite here. First and foremost, McVeigh actually executed his plan to destroy the federal building in Oklahoma City, which, as the district court noted, caused the deaths of 168 identified men, women and children, injuries to hundreds of other people, the complete destruction of the Alfred P. Murrah Federal Office Building and collateral damage to other buildings, including the United States Courthouse . . . [as well as] immeasurable effects on the hearts and minds of the people of Oklahoma from the blast and its consequences. In addition to the fact that Nettles was unsuccessful in carrying out his plan, we note that it was entirely impossible for Nettles to destroy the Dirksen Federal Building because (1) every person involved in his plot was an FBI informant, and (2) he was actually given urea, which does not have the explosive attributes of ammonium nitrate. Perhaps more significantly, *McVeigh* is a district court case, and only represents an example of a district court judge exercising his discretion to grant a change of venue. It offers no support for a reviewing court to reverse a denial of a motion to transfer. Therefore, we do not believe the *McVeigh* case is of much relevance here.

To be sure, the argument that jurors' impartiality would be affected by the fact they sit in the very building that was targeted would indeed be compelling in some instances. However, in this particular case, the alleged facts simply do not compel a finding that, as a matter of law, jurors were prejudiced. As noted above, Nettles's attempted crime was a failure and had a zero percent chance of success given the FBI's involvement. Further, given the improbability of this crime ever coming to fruition, we find that the potential of a juror thinking "it could have been me," would have been just as likely for any juror in any federal courthouse. Admittedly, the facts of this case were enough to convince the prior panel that neither a judge from the Northern District of Illinois, nor a judge from the Seventh Circuit, should hear this case. However, as recorded statements by Nettles reveal, Nettles admitted his desire to kill judges, but not jurors, inside the courthouse. Had Nettles stated that he wished to kill jurors, perhaps our decision would be different.

We reject Nettles's argument that the jury was prejudiced and hold that the district court did not abuse its discretion.[2]

NOTES

1. *Are judges less neutral?* The Court of Appeals in *Nettles* recused judges in the Northern District of Illinois as well as from the Seventh Circuit (who had offices in the Dirksen Building) from presiding over the trial, yet allowed jurors in that same building

---

[2] Additionally, although this does not affect our determination, we note that Nettles merely moved to

to be seated in the case. If the judges could not be impartial, how could the jurors be expected to be impartial?

2. *Nettles: unusual Rule 21(a) issue. Nettles* involved a motion to transfer under Rule 21(a) because of prejudice, but not for the usual reason of widespread pretrial publicity. Is the "prejudice" *Nettles* discussed significantly different than that generated by hostile pretrial publicity?

3. *A more typical pretrial publicity case.* In *Rideau v. Louisiana,* 373 U.S. 723 (1963), the defendant was sentenced to death for armed robbery, kidnaping, and murder. Shortly after his arrest, he gave a twenty minute interview to the Sheriff, during which he confessed to the crimes. This interview was filmed and later broadcast three times over local television. Convinced that the pretrial publicity made a fair trial impossible, the defense lawyer moved for a change of venue. The trial court denied the motion. The United States Supreme Court reversed.

> [W]e hold that it was a denial of due process of law to refuse the request for a change of venue, after the people of Calcasieu Parish had been exposed repeatedly and in depth to the spectacle of Rideau personally confessing in detail to the crimes with which he was later to be charged. For anyone who has ever watched television the conclusion cannot be avoided that this spectacle, to the tens of thousands of people who saw and heard it, in a real sense *was* Rideau's trial — at which he pleaded guilty to murder. Any subsequent court proceedings in a community so pervasively exposed to such a spectacle could be but a hollow formality. [*Id.*, at 726].

4. *Actual v. presumed prejudice. Nettles,* like many courts, categorize prejudice as *actual* and *presumed.* Which is really at issue here? Considering that the trial would occur in the very building that Nettles planned to bomb, do you agree with the court's refusal to find at least presumed prejudice?

5. *Presumed prejudice.* Courts rarely find presumed prejudice sufficient to trigger a venue change. *United States v. Campa,* 459 F.3d 1121 (11th Cir. 2006), explained:

> A district court must presume that so great a prejudice exists against the defendant as to require a change of venue under Rule 21 if the defendant shows: (1) that widespread, pervasive prejudice against him and prejudicial pretrial publicity saturates the community where he is to be tried and (2) that there is a reasonable certainty that such prejudice will prevent him from obtaining a fair trial by an impartial jury. The presumed prejudice principle is rarely applicable and is reserved for an "extreme situation. The burden placed upon the defendant to show that pretrial publicity deprived him of his right to a fair trial before an impartial jury is an extremely heavy one." Once the defendant puts forth evidence of the pervasive prejudice against him, the government can rebut any presumption of juror prejudice by demonstrating that the district court's careful and thorough voir dire, as well as its use of prophylactic measures to insulate the jury from outside influences, ensured that the defendant received a fair trial by an impartial jury.

6. *How likely must prejudice be under Rule 21(a).* Rule 21(a) requires a transfer of venue when the court is "satisfied" that the defendant cannot obtain a fair and impartial

---

transfer to a different district, without suggesting the logical solution of simply transferring his case to the Western Division of the Northern District of Illinois. This would have allowed Nettles to be tried in the courthouse in Rockford, Illinois, rather than the Dirksen Federal Building, without having to transfer to another district. At oral argument, Nettles's counsel conceded that this would have been a viable alternative which would have eliminated the need to appeal on this issue. Despite his failure to craft a more particularized motion to transfer, because we find that Nettles was in no way prejudiced by having his trial held in the Dirksen Federal Building, we need not address whether an intradistrict transfer would have been a more appropriate solution.

trial in the venue. Often the standard of "satisfied" is interpreted as meaning that the court must find a *reasonable likelihood* or *reasonable certainty* that there cannot be a fair trial.

7. *Empirical findings about pretrial publicity.* Social scientists have studied the impact of pretrial publicity on jurors' perceptions. The overwhelming result is that jurors are affected by exposure to pretrial publicity. One author noted that research has shown that jurors views are shaped by the jurors' knowledge of inadmissible evidence, a prior arrest record, a confession, performance on a lie detector, negative facets of a defendant's character, and "emotional" publicity (arousing an emotional reaction, as provided by a graphic description of a homicide victim's injuries). Vineet R. Shahani, Note, 42 Am. Crim. L. Rev. 93, 101 (2005).

8. *Possible remedies other than venue change for hostile pretrial publicity.* As discussed more fully in Chapter 15, when pretrial publicity interferes with an accused's rights to a fair trial by an impartial jury, there are a number of possible remedies. One is for the court to grant a continuance to permit the media attention to extinguish. *See* Chapter 12. Another remedy is to use the jury selection process to winnow out persons who were too affected by the publicity or to sequester the jurors to protect them from the media coverage. When pretrial publicity is an issue, trial judges routinely allow potential jurors to be questioned about their exposure to the publicity and the impact of the publicity on the jurors' impartiality. Many judges also instruct jurors to ignore pretrial publicity in their deliberations on the case.

9. *Procedures to obtain venue change for hostile publicity.* A third remedy is for the trial court to grant a change of venue. Sometimes the trial court will consider the venue motion only after an unsuccessful attempt to seat an untainted jury.

10. *Additional items filed with transfer motion.* Rule 21(a) authorizes the defendant to waive venue and file a motion for a change of venue to a location where pretrial media coverage will not compromise a fair trial. The motion may be accompanied by an appendix containing copies of relevant newspaper articles and transcripts or audio or videotapes of radio or television coverage. Affidavits from people familiar with local public opinion and from experts who conducted public opinion polls may also be helpful.

If the judge holds a hearing on the motion, the above information may be presented through exhibits and live witnesses. In addition, there have even been cases where the lawyers called as witnesses a number of passersby who happened to be near the courthouse. These witnesses are asked to share their knowledge of the case and the extent of their prejudice. Though far less expensive than formal public opinion polls, this practice is dangerous because the witnesses' testimony may be unfavorable.

11. *Burden of proof.* Ordinarily the defendant has the burden of establishing that hostile publicity makes a venue change necessary. Sometimes there is a presumption that the jury in the locale of the crime can provide a fair trial. *See, e.g., Swisher v. Commonwealth*, 506 S.E.2d 763 (Va. 1998).

12. *Source of pretrial publicity.* Often neither the prosecution nor defense is responsible for the damaging pretrial publicity. However, if the victim or prosecution were at fault in generating the publicity, courts are more inclined to transfer venue. *See, e.g., State v. Lee*, 976 So.2d 109 (La. 2008).

13. *Public's Right to Local Venue.* In Steven A. Engel, *The Public's Vicinage Right: A Constitutional Argument*, 75 N.Y.U L. Rev. 1658, 1664 (2000), the author argues that the public at large has a *vicinage* right in criminal trials; that is, the public has a right to see that a defendant from their community is tried in that community:

> The vicinage right, like the right of public access, serves interests beyond those of the criminal defendant. Like the right of public access, it has longstanding roots in our legal tradition that testify to the favorable judgement of historical experience in that period. . . . Recognizing the right not only would ensure that courts consider the community's interests, but also would

allow representatives of the affected community itself to bring claims before the court that might be ignored by the prosecution and the defense.

14. *Fair trial impossible but no venue change.* Note that while *Rideau* indicates that the criminal defendant may have a right to a change of venue in situations where the media has created an overwhelmingly hostile environment, the case does not hold that the accused *must* request a venue change in this situation. What if the hostile publicity has risen to the level that *Rideau* finds sufficient for a constitutional violation, but the accused does not want a change of venue and yet demands a fair trial by an impartial jury as guaranteed by the Sixth Amendment and the due process clause? Should the accused have to waive the right to venue in order to assert the crucial right to a fair trial? Can a change of venue be forced on the accused in order to protect the accused's right to a fair trial?

The usual judicial response to this unusual dilemma is to avoid it by finding that a fair trial is possible in the original place of venue (by granting a continuance and liberal jury voir dire to ensure impartiality). In rare circumstances, on the other hand, a court may dismiss the charges because there is no place in the proper venue where a fair trial is possible. But of course this extreme remedy is a last resort. As was said in *United States v. Abbott Laboratories*, 505 F.2d 565, 572 (4th Cir. 1974), *cert. denied*, 420 U.S. 990 (1975):

> Although a change of venue under Rule 21 cannot be imposed on a defendant against his will, the availability of a change of venue as a corrective device undergirds the requirement that a defendant, who declines to request a change of venue but who seeks dismissal of an indictment against him because of allegedly prejudicial pretrial publicity, demonstrates the existence of actual prejudice far more convincingly than was done in the case at bar. A defendant who has unused means [i.e. a motion for a change of venue] to protect his rights [to a trial by an impartial jury] should not lightly be granted the extreme remedy of dismissal of the charges against him on less than a conclusive showing that the unused means would be ineffective.

See generally Scott Kafker, Comment, *The Right to Venue and the Right to an Impartial Jury: Resolving the Conflict in the Federal Constitution*, 52 U. CHI. L. REV. 729 (1985) (arguing that the history of the Sixth Amendment demonstrates that the venue rule was designed to protect both the defendant's *and* the government's rights in a fair trial; therefore, the court should be permitted to order a change of venue to another district rather than dismiss charges if an impartial jury cannot be found in the correct venue).

15. *Impartial jury unavailable.* A related issue arises when massive publicity makes it impossible to obtain an impartial jury anywhere in the country (for federal crimes) or state (for state offenses). Even if the accused is willing to request a change of venue for the purpose of securing an impartial jury, the efforts may be fruitless. Imagine a trial if Adolf Hitler had somehow been arrested in the United States and somehow was charged in an American court with a violation of American homicide law for his part in the Holocaust, or if Osama Bin Laden were to be captured and tried in connection with the thousands of deaths that took place on 911. In such high visibility, emotionally charged cases, it is arguable that the case would have to be dismissed because a fair trial before an impartial jury is simply impossible. *See State v. Banks*, 387 N.W.2d 19 (S.D. 1986) (defendant has right under South Dakota law to be tried by impartial jury in county where crime occurred; if an impartial jury cannot be secured in that county, there can be no lawful conviction). Can you imagine the public outcry if a dismissal of charges against a genocidal mass murderer were to be ordered because it was impossible to find an impartial jury anywhere?

Such an argument was raised, unsuccessfully, in the case of Timothy McVeigh, tried for the 1995 bombing of the Murrah Building in Oklahoma City, a case discussed in *Nettles*. Because of the intense emotional impact of the bombing on the community, the

District Court judge transferred the case from Oklahoma to Denver, Colorado. Thereafter, McVeigh argued that because of massive national coverage by the media, the case should be dismissed or, in the alternative, a lengthy continuance should be granted to permit the media attention to diminish. In denying the motion, the trial judge took a number of measures to ensure that jurors would remain impartial, including lengthy questionnaires in the selection process and detailed instructions admonishing the jurors to set aside any preconceived impressions they might have. The appellate court concluded that the trial court ruled correctly, noting that the defendant failed to make "the strong showing that would be necessary for the court to presume prejudice as a result of the publicity." *United States v. McVeigh*, 153 F.3d 1166 (10th Cir. 1998).

One possible solution is to authorize transfer to an adjoining county if an impartial jury cannot be seated. *See* Cal. Penal Code § 1033(b). Do you think this will solve the problem in a case involving massive pretrial publicity? Would it matter if the new venue had a much larger population than the original one?

[ii] Transfer for Convenience or in the Interests of Justice

A criminal accused may seek a transfer for reasons other than adverse publicity. Rule 21(b) recognizes that a transfer may be appropriate, upon the motion of the defendant, for either the convenience of the parties or witnesses or in the interests of justice. Courts faced with a motion under Rule 21(b) use a factor approach.

PLATT v. MINNESOTA MINING & MANUFACTURING CO.
376 U.S. 240 (1964)

MR. JUSTICE CLARK delivered the opinion of the Court.

[The defendant, Minnesota Mining and Manufacturing Company, was indicted for several antitrust violations for efforts to monopolize commerce in pressure-sensitive tape and other products. The indictment was issued by a federal grand jury in the Eastern District of Illinois. It was agreed that the indictment could have also been returned in the District of Minnesota and several other districts.

The defendant filed a motion under Rule 21(b), based on the "interests of justice," to transfer the case from the Eastern District of Illinois to the District of Minnesota where it had its headquarters. The District Court denied the motion on the grounds that the factors of convenience, expense, and early trial, together with the probability that it "would be more difficult (for the Government) to get a fair and impartial jury in the Minnesota District," convinced him that "the interests of justice" would not be promoted by a transfer.

The Court of Appeals found that the trial judge had treated the factor of a fair and impartial trial as the "most important item" in his decision and that this was not an appropriate criterion. It concluded that in addition to "the essential elements of convenience, expense and early trial, constituting 'interest of justice' in a civil case," a criminal case was "impressed with the fundamental historical right of a defendant to be prosecuted in its own environment or district . . . ." Upon reviewing the record, the Court of Appeals substituted its own findings for those of the trial judge and ordered the case transferred from Illinois to Minnesota.]

. . . We believe that the Court of Appeals erred in ordering the transfer . . .

. . . The Court of Appeals found, in contradiction to the finding of the District Court, that a trial in the Eastern District of Illinois would result in unjustifiable increased expenses to the respondent of "at least $100,000, great inconvenience of witnesses, serious disruption of business and interference of contact between the (respondent's) executives and its trial attorneys . . . ." It also found that respondent had no office, plant, or other facility in the Eastern District and that there was less congestion in the docket of the Minnesota District than in the Eastern District of Illinois. The court concluded that this was a "demonstration by proof or admission of the essential elements of convenience, expense and early trial, constituting 'interest of justice' in a civil case," which, augmented by the additional consideration that this was a criminal action, compelled the granting of the motion to transfer.

. . . [T]he Court of Appeals placed particular weight on the trial judge's finding that it "would be more difficult to get a fair and impartial jury in the Minnesota District than in the Eastern District of Illinois." The Court of Appeals stated that this finding, if true (which it doubted), "would not justify a refusal to make a transfer otherwise proper under rule 21(b) . . . ." and concluded that "it would be an unsound and dangerous innovation in our federal court system for a judge in any district to appraise or even speculate as to the efficacy of the operations of a federal court of concurrent jurisdiction in another district. It follows that no order in any way based upon such reasoning can stand, even under the guise of an exercise of discretion."

. . . The trial judge in his memorandum decision listed a number of items as pertinent in the determination of whether the case should be transferred to Minnesota "in the interest of justice" as required by Rule 21(b). As Chief Judge Hastings pointed out in his dissent, these "factors were (1) location of corporate defendant; (2) location of possible witnesses; (3) location of events likely to be in issue; (4) location of documents and records likely to be involved; (5) disruption of defendant's business unless the case is transferred; (6) expense to the parties; (7) location of counsel; (8) relative accessibility of place of trial; (9) docket condition of each district or division involved; and (10) any other special elements which might affect the transfer."

It appears that both parties and the Court of Appeals agree that the first nine factors enumerated were appropriate. As we have noted, the Court of Appeals struck the fair and impartial jury finding as not being a proper factor and the Government does not challenge that action here . . . . This leaves before us the question of whether the Court of Appeals erred in considering the motion to transfer de novo on the record made in the District Court and ordering transfer to the District of Minnesota.

. . . The District Court's use of an inappropriate factor did not empower the Court of Appeals to order the transfer. The function of the Court of Appeals in this case was to determine the appropriate criteria and then leave their application to the trial judge on remand . . . . Here, however, the Court of Appeals undertook a de novo examination of the record and itself exercised the discretionary function which the rule commits to the trial judge . . . .

Since the trial court must reconsider the motion, effective judicial administration requires that we comment upon the erroneous holding of the Court of Appeals that criminal defendants have a constitutionally based right to a trial in their home districts . . . . As we said in *United States v. Cores*, 356 U.S. 405, 407 (1958): "The Constitution makes it clear that determination of proper venue in a criminal case requires determination of where the crime was committed . . . . The provision for trial in the vicinity of the crime is a safeguard against the unfairness and hardship involved when an accused is prosecuted in a remote place." The fact that Minnesota is the main office or "home" of the respondent has no independent significance in determining whether transfer to that district would be "in the interest of justice," although it may be considered with reference to such factors as the convenience of records, officers, personnel and counsel.

The judgment of the Court of Appeals is therefore reversed and the cause is remanded to that court with instructions to vacate the judgment of the District Court and to remand the case for reconsideration of the motion for transfer, without reference to the ability of the United States to receive a fair and impartial trial in Minnesota.

[The concurring opinion of JUSTICE HARLAN is omitted.]

NOTES

1. *Government's interest.* Recall that Rule 21(b) authorizes a transfer "[f]or the convenience of parties and witnesses, and in the interest of justice." Note also that in *Platt* venue was appropriate in either the Eastern District of Illinois or the District of Minnesota (as well as several other districts). Apparently the prosecution decided to seek the indictment in Illinois rather than Minnesota. The defendant corporation wanted to move the case to Minnesota, its home base. The *Platt* Court seems to suggest that the trial court could not consider the *government's* interest in an impartial jury. Why not? Isn't the government entitled to a fair trial? Don't the "interests of justice" by definition include the likelihood of a fair trial?

In a few states the defendant's venue rights are not absolute; the government may obtain a change of venue when necessary to empanel a fair and impartial jury. *See Sailor v. State*, 733 So. 2d 1057 (Fla. App. 1999); *State v. House*, 978 P.2d 967 (N.M. 1999) (state given change of venue to county with fewer Native Americans).

2. Can the government invoke Rule 21(a) or (b) to obtain a change of venue to a location where it believes a fairer trial is likely? Why or why not? Would your answer change if the government's request were based on convenience to its witnesses? The government's lawyers?

3. *Pretrial publicity and Rule 21(b).* While Rule 21(a) specifically addresses pretrial publicity and mandates a venue change if the court finds the defendant is unlikely to get a fair and impartial trial, the court may also order a venue change for hostile publicity under Rule 21(b), involving the convenience of the parties and the "interests of justice." One author summarized the cases as suggesting that courts apply the "interests of justice" standard by looking at five factors: the nature and extent of pretrial publicity, the size and demographic composition of current and potential trial venues, the nature and gravity of the offense, the interests of the defendant and the victim, and the existence of any government-sponsored publicity. Vineet R. Shahani, Note, 42 AM. CRIM. L. REV. 93, 108 (2005).

4. *Choice of new location.* Note that Rule 21 does not indicate to which district the case should be transferred. Nowhere does Rule 21 indicate that it must be one suggested by the defendant. Fed. R. Crim. P. 21(a). Many states provide similar flexibility.

Some state statutes are more specific. *E.g.*, Ala. Stat. Ann. § 15-2-24 (new venue must be nearest county free from the reasons mandating the change). Do you favor a rule restricting the new location of the trial? How will the likely locale of the proceeding, if the change-of-venue motion is successful, affect counsel's decision whether to seek a venue change?

A recent trend is for a state to authorize the court to consider the racial composition of the venues to which the trial could be transferred. If the defendant is not guaranteed a trial of any particular racial composition, does it make sense to allow the judge to consider the racial composition of potential trial sites?

5. *Victim's preferences.* Courts deciding whether to order a venue change often take into consideration the victim's interests. Some states require it as part of their victim's rights laws. *See, e.g.*, N.J.S.A. § 52:4B-36 (victims entitled to have inconvenience to their participation in court proceedings minimized to fullest extent possible).

6. *Limit on number of venue changes.* Rule 21 contains no limit on the number of times venue can be changed. Some state laws do. *E.g.*, Ala. Stat. Ann. § 15-2-24 (only 1 venue change permitted). Should such limits be placed on a change of venue?

[c] Transfer of Jury

One solution to the problem of a jury tainted by local publicity is to select a *foreign jury* from another area and then transport the jurors to the original venue of the offense. Under this model, the jury should have less exposure to the local media coverage and the accused will have a trial in the locality of the crime. In federal cases, the district court judge has discretion to select jurors from areas other than the one in which the crime occurred so long as the jurors reside within the federal district where the crime occurred. *See, e.g., United States v. Ford*, 958 F.2d 372 (6th Cir. 1992) (jury selected from Jackson, Tennessee, then transported to Memphis for trial; publicity concerns justify intra-district transfers). Many states also permit the use of foreign jurors if the accused waives venue. *See, e.g., State v. Harris*, 716 A.2d 458 (N.J. 1998).

In deciding whether to change venue or use a foreign venue, courts often use a factor approach. One often-ignored factor is convenience to the victim who desires to attend. *See State v. Timmendequas*, 737 A.2d 55 (N.J. 1999) (New Jersey Victims Rights Amendment requires trial court to consider convenience to victim as factor in deciding whether to change venue or use a foreign jury).

[d] Return to Original Venue

On rare occasions the reasons for a venue change are no longer valid. Some state statutes specifically authorize the court in the new venue to return the case to the original venue after holding a hearing on the issue. *E.g.*, Cal. Penal Code § 1033.1.

[2] Timing of Transfer Motion

Because a successful motion for a change of venue has a significant impact on the court calendar as well as that of the other participants in the trial, the motion should be made as early in the proceedings as feasible. Some such motions have been denied because, in part, they were filed shortly before the trial was to begin. *See, e.g, United States v. Keuylian*, 602 F.2d 1033, 1038 (2d Cir. 1979). On the other hand, some courts are more forgiving. *See, e.g., United States v. Carreon-Palacio*, 267 F.3d 381 (5th Cir. 2001)(no waiver of venue if testimony puts venue in issue and defendant requests a jury instruction on venue; pretrial motion unnecessary in this situation).

Some statutes or court rules establish timetables for these motions. Rule 21 of the Federal Rules of Criminal Procedure is quite broad, authorizing a venue motion to be filed at or before arraignment or at any other time the court or rules prescribe.

FEDERAL RULES OF CRIMINAL PROCEDURE

Rule 21. *Transfer for Trial*

. . . .

(d) Time to File a Motion to Transfer. A motion to transfer may be made at or before arraignment or at any other time the court or these rules prescribe.

NOTE

1. *Before or after voir dire.* Since a venue change motion may be made before or after jury selection, defense counsel may struggle with the decision whether to seek the change before the *voir dire* process has explored jurors' exposure to the publicity. It is possible that the jury selection process itself could provide counsel with potent ammunition for the venue change as the potential jurors reveal how pervasive the pretrial publicity has been. For example, if the court excused for cause a large percentage of potential jurors, the defense may argue that a venue change is needed because of the proven harm of the hostile publicity.

2. *Local practice rules concerning venue motion.* Pursuant to a court's broad authority in scheduling cases, some federal judges have adopted local practice rules setting a specific date for most motions, including a motion to change venue. For example, a court rule could mandate that motions be filed fifteen days before trial. A motion filed after the deadline can be denied for this reason alone, absent some significant excuse for the tardy motion.

State rules are often similar to the federal Rule 21. Some indicate a preference for a motion filed early in the proceedings. *See, e.g.*, Ala. Stat. Ann. § 15-2-20(a) (application for change of venue should be made "as early as practicable before the trial").

3. *Motion to acquit for improper venue.* By way of contrast, a motion to acquit because of improper venue has fewer time limits than one to transfer venue. Since the court may not be able to assess whether the state met its burden of proving venue until after the proof, a motion to acquit for failure to prove venue often may be filed as late as before the jury verdict is returned. *See, e.g.*, *United States v. Robinson*, 167 F.3d 824 (3d Cir. 1999); *see also United States v. Biao*, 51 F. Supp. 2d 1042 (S.D. Cal. 1999) (motion to dismiss for lack of venue may be brought before close of government's case, but must be raised before trial if claim is that the indictment is defective on its face).

[3] Content of Transfer Motion

Statutes or court rules detailing the requirements for a change of venue must be consulted carefully. Often they indicate what facts must be alleged. An affidavit, establishing the necessary facts, may be necessary.

The exact facts that must be proved vary according to the theory of the motion to change venue. For example, if the change of venue is sought because of adverse publicity that has polluted the jury pool so that it will be impossible to select an impartial jury, the venue motion must include sufficient facts to raise a serious question on this issue. One way to do this is to include an Appendix that reproduces the newspaper and other articles about the defendant and the trial. If funds permit, defense counsel may also want to commission a trial consultant to conduct a study of community attitudes. The results of this could also be included in the Appendix to the venue motion. *See generally* Edward R. Shohat & Pamela I. Perry, *International Drug Cartels: Miami Vice or Government Spice*, 40 Am. U. L. Rev. 849 (1991).

Besides proving that there is negative publicity, many courts have begun to rely on public opinion surveys. *See*, 42 Am. Crim. L. Rev. 93 (2005). In fact, one court actually denied a change of venue primarily due to a defendant's failure to submit a public opinion survey despite his producing a quantity of media coverage. *See, State v Erickstad*, 620 N.W.2d 136 (N.D. 2000).

[4] Multiple Parties and Multiple Counts

Questions of venue become difficult if there are multiple parties with different views of the proper or best venue for a joint trial or if there is one defendant facing several counts who believes that the venue should not be the same for all counts. In such cases the trial court may grant a severance of defendants or counts pursuant to Rules 8, 13, and 14 of the Federal Rules of Criminal Procedure, discussed in Chapter 8.

Because a joint trial of multiple offenders or counts will probably save judicial and prosecutorial resources, most judges are disinclined to grant a severance and change of venue on some defendants or some counts. One court noted the practical problems associated with such requests:

> We have already discussed the government's interest in judicial economy and how the "convenience" of the government is fostered by the policy favoring joint trials for persons who are properly joined together in a single indictment. If Williams was entitled to a separate trial in Jacksonville, then surely co-defendant Elizah Jackson was entitled to a separate trial in Savannah and

co-defendant Isom Clemon was entitled to a separate trial in Mobile. Such an approach, however, would deprive the valid interest in judicial economy of all force.

United States v. Kopituk, 690 F.2d 1289, 1322 (11th Cir. 1982). *See also United States v. United States District Court*, 693 F.2d 68 (9th Cir. 1982) (district court permitted to transfer venue of tax evasion counts while retaining that for conspiracy to commit tax evasion pursuant to statute permitting transfer of former cases; appellate court noted that the government would have to conduct two lengthy trials and the only connection one trial location had was that the defendants lived there).

[5] Proof of Venue and Waiver

Although venue is not specifically part of the legal definition of a crime, the venue of the crime is usually stated in the indictment or information. Generally venue is established through the facts of the case, and is considered in some sense to be an "element" of the crime charged inasmuch as the prosecution has the burden to prove that venue is proper if the defendant contests it. However, venue is not a "substantive element" of a crime which must necessarily be proved to the jury beyond a reasonable doubt. In order to properly raise and preserve a challenge to venue, the defendant may place the question of venue "in issue," which may sometimes be decided by the judge, and sometimes by the jury (see below). *See, United States v. Perez*, 280 F. 3d 318 (3d Cir. 2002); *see also*, Comment, 76 TEMP. L REV. 883 (2003).

Standard of proof. When the government does prove venue, the general rule is that the government need only satisfy the preponderance of evidence standard. Some courts also view proof of venue in the light most favorable to the government. *See, e.g., United States v. Tingle*, 183 F.3d 719, 726 (7th Cir. 1999). Proof beyond a reasonable doubt is not required. Sometimes venue is established by judicial notice. For example, the trial judge in King County may take judicial notice that the Safety Bank on West Broadway in Central City is located in King County.

Putting venue in issue. When a defendant chooses to challenge venue, he or she must put it "in issue." In *United States v. Miller*, 111 F.3d 747 (10th Cir. 1997), for example, venue was based on acts of a coconspirator in Wyoming who had pled guilty, and no evidence was offered that defendant had ever traveled to or committed overt acts in Wyoming in furtherance of the conspiracy. Despite defendant's objections, the trial court refused to instruct the jury on the element of venue, and defendant appealed. The court reversed, holding that the failure to instruct on venue was not harmless error because it was not beyond a reasonable doubt that the jury's guilty verdict on the charged offense necessarily incorporated a finding of proper venue.

Unlike the Tenth circuit, most federal circuits take a more narrow approach. Some require three things a defendant must do in order to obtain a jury charge on venue.

> 1. The defendant must preserve the issue by raising it in a motion for acquittal at or before the close of the government's case-in-chief;

> 2. The defendant must present some evidence that the issue of venue is in genuine dispute; and

> 3. The defendant must have made a proper request to charge the jury with this issue.

See, United States v. Perez, 280 F.3d 318 (3d Cir. 2002); *United States v. Bala*, 236 F.3d 87 (2d Cir. 2000).

Waiver. Since venue provisions are designed to assist the accused, he or she can waive them. Sometimes a waiver has been inferred when the defendant did not object to the lack of venue. This may mean the jury is not charged with making a finding on venue. Note that this is a more relaxed standard than usual for waiver of a constitutional right, which usually requires an affirmative showing of a knowing and voluntary waiver. *See, e.g., United States v. Carreon-Palacio*, 267 F.3d 381 (5th Cir. 2001)(extensive discussion of venue procedures). Venue, as stated by the Second Circuit in *Perez*, "occup[ies] a lesser station in the hierarchy of constitutionally derived rights." 280 F. 3d at 328.

More frequently, a formal waiver of venue occurs when the defendant requests a change of venue pursuant to Rules 20 and 21 of the Federal Rules of Criminal Procedure, or their equivalent.

PROBLEM 14-1. BYRDS OF A FEATHER

Karen Byrd-Forrester and Kyle Byrd were twenty-nine year old twins. Although born in Miami, Karen moved to Chicago six years ago where she lived with her husband and two children. Kyle remained in Miami with the rest of the family. Karen and Kyle were engaged in a scam involving fraudulent mortgages. They talked on the phone almost daily about their "deals" and traveled as necessary to carry them out. Since Karen was an accountant, she kept the records of their deals in her professional office in Chicago.

Federal law authorized the United States Department of Housing and Urban Development (HUD) to insure mortgages for certain condominiums. A person who lived in the condominium could get a mortgage that covered 97% of the cost, while a non-occupant person could get only an 85% mortgage. Karen and Kyle paid Oliver Stohn $1500 to buy a condo with money from a 97% HUD-insured loan, then immediately to sell the condo to Karen and Kyle for the original purchase price. In order to qualify for the federal mortgage insurance, Stohn signed an application (drafted by Karen) in which Stohn stated that he would personally live in the condominium, located in Virginia just outside Washington, D.C., although in truth he never had any intent to do so. The mortgage documents were actually signed in a motel room in Maryland, then taken to Virginia where they were submitted to the lending bank, First Virginia Bank and Trust. After the bank processed and approved the loan, the papers were mailed to the HUD office in Washington, D.C. for approval.

Since the mortgages were assumable, Stohn immediately sold the condominium and the government-insured mortgage to Karen and Kyle. This scheme gave Karen and Kyle a 97% government insured mortgage (minus the $1500 fee), although they were non-occupant owners and entitled to no more than an 85% mortgage.

Karen and Kyle were indicted for (1) conspiracy to commit offenses against the United States, and (2) making a false statement in violation of 18 U.S.C. § 1001:

> [W]hoever, in any matter within the jurisdiction of any department or agency of the United States knowingly and willfully falsifies, conceals or covers up by trick, scheme, or device a material fact, or makes any false, fictitious or fraudulent statements or representations, or makes or uses any false writing or document knowing the same to contain any false, fictitious or fraudulent statement or entry, shall be fined not more than $10,000 or imprisoned not more than five years, or both.

1. Note that Karen and Kyle were charged with two offenses. List all possible locations where there is venue for the conspiracy charge. Which would the government prefer? Karen? Kyle?

2. Where is venue for the false statement charge? Which would the government prefer? Karen? Kyle?

3. Assume that the government chose the federal district in Virginia as the locale for the trial. Assume further that the media in the Washington-Virginia area had launched a blistering campaign against mortgage fraud. There are daily articles in the local papers and regular features about the case on local television stations. You represent Karen. Would you seek a change of venue under Federal Rules of Criminal Procedure, Rule 21? To where? Could you get the case tried in Chicago? What would you include in your Motion to Change Venue? Would you file an Affidavit? What would you expect the judge to do with your Motion?

4. Assume that Kyle's lawyer does not agree with the concept of a venue change and does not request one for Kyle. If the district judge agrees that there should be a venue change for Karen because of hostile publicity, can the judge order one for Kyle as well?

5. Although the government chose Virginia for the case, it now prefers Washington, D.C., where the HUD records and officials are located. Can the government obtain a venue change under Rule 21?

Chapter 15
TRIAL

A. PUBLIC TRIAL

[1]   Constitutional Right

The Sixth Amendment to the Constitution provides that "the accused shall enjoy the right to a . . . public trial." This right, extended to the states, establishes a strong presumption in favor of openness of criminal trials. Since the defendant's Sixth Amendment right to a public trial is personal to the accused, it confers no general right of access to the press or members of the community. The First Amendment, however, protects press coverage and will be discussed below.

The Supreme Court has recognized that the public trial guarantee serves many important functions. It ensures that judges, lawyers, witnesses and jurors will perform their various functions more responsibly when those tasks are carried out in public view rather than in secret proceedings. Additionally, a public trial is thought to encourage witnesses to come forward and also to discourage perjury. Finally, the public trial guarantee has an educative effect upon the public and is thought to be an effective restraint upon the possible abuse of judicial power.

[2]   Extended Meaning of "Trial"

While the Sixth Amendment public trial guarantee does not apply to juvenile proceedings, it extends to all criminal proceedings and goes beyond the actual trial. For example, the Court in *Waller v. Georgia*, 467 U.S. 39 (1984), held that the right applies to a pretrial hearing to suppress wrongfully seized evidence. It also applies to documents filed in a case. With respect to the trial, the right to a public trial extends to impaneling the jury, opening statements, all facets of presentation of evidence, closing arguments, jury instructions, and final verdict.

[3]   *Waller's* Four Requirements for Permitting Total or Partial Closure

The defendant's right to a public and open trial is not absolute. There is a *presumption of openness*. While this presumption is characterized as *strong*, it can be overcome. According to the leading case, *Waller v. Georgia*, 467 U.S. 39 (1984), the presumption is overcome only by establishing four items:

> [1] an overriding interest that is likely to be prejudiced [by a public trial], [2] the closure must be no broader than necessary to protect that interest, [3] the trial court must consider reasonable alternatives to closing the proceeding, and [4] it must make findings adequate to support the closure.

NOTES

1. *Judicial findings.* Before a trial court excludes some or all of the public from a hearing, *Waller* requires that it make findings identifying the interest served by the closure and the alternatives considered in lieu of closure. This ensures the court addresses the issues and facilitates appellate review.

2. *Closely circumscribed closure rules.* If all or part of the proceeding is closed to some or all of the public, the court must fashion the closure as narrowly as possible to achieve the objectives that merit closure.

3. *Illustration of application of Waller elements.* In *Smith v. Hollins*, 448 F.3d 533 (2d Cir. 2006), the trial court ordered the drug defendant's brother and sister either to sit behind a screen or leave the courtroom during the testimony of an undercover agent. The court was concerned that the agent's safety and future usefulness would be compromised if the mother and sister could see the agent. While recognizing that the safety of the agent is a legitimate government concern, the appellate court held that the trial court's ruling violated the defendant's right to a public trial. The trial court should have made the necessary findings that the screen-or-exclusion rule was necessary. The appellate court noted that other relatives were permitted to remain in the courtroom in full view of the undercover agent-witness, so the agent's identity was easily ascertainable by the brother and sister. Also, the court held that a defendant's relatives deserve special consideration in allowing them to attend the trial.

[4]   Illustrations of Permissible Trial Closures

Among reasons accepted by courts ordering total or partial closure of trials are the following:

(1) *Welfare of crime victim.* Courts consider the victim's age, psychological makeup, nature of the offense, etc. (discussed more specifically in the next section).

(2) *Protection of witness from threatened harm.*

(3) *Protection of an undercover agent's identity.* Courts may take administrative steps to protect the identity of an undercover agent. This is deemed important to protect the agent's well being and to permit continued employment in subsequent criminal investigations.

Another approach is to permit particular persons to attend a trial only if they submit to an obscured view. *See, e.g., People v. Hargett,* 742 N.Y.S.2d 638, 2002 N.Y. App. Div. LEXIS 4089 (App. Div. 2002) (closure of courtroom to general public and use of blackboard to block view of defendant's family did not violate defendant's right to a public trial; undercover officer-witness testified that he feared for his safety and that of his team which was still working in the area where the defendant's relatives lived).

But absolute exclusion is impermissible for this purpose unless the closure is necessary to protect the safety of the officers and the integrity of their ongoing investigations. *People v. Akaydin,* 685 N.Y.S.2d 737, 1999 N.Y. App. Div. LEXIS 785 (App. Div. 1999).

(4) *National security concerns.*

(5) *Court security concerns. See, e.g, People v. Perez,* 665 N.Y.S.2d 647, 1997 N.Y. App. Div. LEXIS 12839 (App. Div. 1997)(screening of spectators permitted as security precaution).

(6) *Practical reasons related to space.* For obvious practical reasons, some persons desiring to attend a public trial may be excluded due to the lack of available seating. *See, e.g., United States v. Kobli,* 172 F.2d 919, 923 (3d Cir. 1949) (Sixth Amendment precludes the indiscriminate exclusion of the public from a criminal trial, but recognizes that some persons may be barred when exclusion is justified by lack of space or for reasons particularly applicable to those persons).

(7) *Practical reasons related to orderly proceedings.* Courts routinely uphold short-term closures, such as to prevent interruptions during opening and closing statements or jury instructions.

(8) *Exclusion because of particular attributes of person excluded.* Courts routinely uphold the exclusion of people for misbehavior or other reasons that may compromise a fair trial. *See, e.g., Andrade v. State,* 246 S.W.3d 217 (Tex. App. 2007)(exclusion of one lawyer for arguing with judge; court has authority to control behavior of people in courtroom); *State v. Momah,* 171 P.3d 1064 (Wash. App. 2007)(exclusion of disruptive spectator).

[5]   Remedy for Violation of Right

[a]   Prejudice not Required

Waller v. Georgia, supra, held that if the public trial right is infringed, the defendant is not required to prove actual prejudice to obtain relief. The Court reasoned that it may well be impossible for the defendant to establish actual prejudice because of the nature of the right to a public trial. By contrast, it is interesting to note that if a defendant alleges ineffective assistance of counsel, a showing of prejudice is required. Does the "no-prejudice" public trial rule, however, require that the defendant receive a new trial whenever his or her right to a public trial is violated?

[b]   Trivial Error Exception

Not every minor error in according a defendant a public trial is recognized as violating the Sixth Amendment. Courts have held that errors characterized as *trivial* do not merit any remedy. Thus, in *Peterson v. Williams*, 85 F.3d 39 (2d Cir. 1996), the appellate court found that the trial court had made a trivial error in inadvertently keeping the courtroom closed to the public beyond the time needed to protect the identity of an undercover agent. The failure to reopen the court was not noticed until after the next witness, the defendant, had testified briefly.

[c]   Flexible Remedy Appropriate to Violation

In *Waller*, the Court refused to adopt the rule that a new trial was necessary when the right to a public trial was violated. Rather, the Court held that the remedy "should be appropriate to the violation." *Waller* involved evidence from wiretaps and searches that was used in a gambling trial. Before trial, the court held a suppression hearing in accordance with the defendant's motion to exclude this evidence. At the prosecutor's request, the trial court restricted the people attending the suppression hearing, permitting only the parties, lawyers, court personnel, and witnesses. The exclusion was authorized because of a Georgia statute that rendered inadmissible at trial evidence obtained from a wiretap if the wiretap proof was unnecessarily published. Some evidence was suppressed at this hearing, but the defendant was still convicted. The Supreme Court in *Waller* held that the public trial guarantee was violated when the public was excluded from the suppression hearing. Turning to the remedy for this error, the Court held that since the closure order related to the suppression hearing, a new trial would be required only if the new public suppression hearing resulted in a material change in the position of the parties, such as the suppression of material evidence not suppressed at the defendant's first trial. Does this remedy make sense? Why should a different ruling on *suppression* issues determine whether there will be a new *trial*?

[d]   Illustrations of Remedy for Denial of Public Trial

Federal and state lower court decisions strongly support the *Waller* proposition that the remedy for a public trial violation "should be appropriate to the violation." *See People v. Guevara*, 521 N.Y.S.2d 785, 1987 N.Y. App. Div. LEXIS 52510 (App. Div. 1987) ("The appropriate remedy for a violation of the defendant's right to a public trial at the pretrial stage is not a new trial but a new public suppression hearing"); *In re Orange*, 100 P.3d 291 (Wash. 2004) (defendant's public trial right was violated when trial judge closed the courtroom to spectators during voir dire; remedy is a new trial); *P.M.M. v. State*, 762 So. 2d 384 (Ala. Crim. App. 1999) (court's closure of courtroom to the public for the duration of the entire trial is a violation of public trial right; remedy in this case, explicitly citing *Waller*, is a new trial); *United States v. Canady*, 126 F.3d 352 (2d Cir. 1997) (public trial violation where court *mailed* its decision of defendant's guilt to defendant and never made announcement in open court with both defendant and the public present; remedy was for court to vacate defendant's conviction and for the court "to announce its decision in open court").

[6] Press Controls

The Sixth Amendment's public trial guarantee appears to be a right given only to the defendant. If that were the case, then logically the defendant could choose to waive that right and thereby deny public access to the trial. Stated differently, if the defendant possessed unlimited control (via waiver) of the public trial right, in some cases both the public and the press would be denied access to one of the most important functions of our government.

It was not until *Richmond Newspapers, Inc. v. Virginia*, 448 U.S. 555 (1980), that the United States Supreme Court explicitly recognized a right of the public under both the First and Fourteenth Amendments to attend criminal trials. While acknowledging that the First Amendment rights of the public and representatives of the press are not absolute, the plurality opinion held that "absent an overriding interest articulated in findings, the trial of a criminal case must be open to the public." In condemning the trial judge's action of clearing the courtroom (upon motion of the defendant and without objection from the prosecution), the opinion explained:

> The First Amendment, in conjunction with the Fourteenth, prohibits governments from "abridging the freedom of speech, or of the press; or the right of the people peaceably to assemble, and to petition the Government for a redress of grievances." These expressly guaranteed freedoms share a common core purpose of assuring freedom of communication on matters relating to the functioning of government. Plainly it would be difficult to single out any aspect of government of higher concern and importance to the people than the manner in which criminal trials are conducted. . . .
>
> . . . [T]he conduct of trials "before as many of the people as chose to attend" was regarded as one of "the inestimable advantages of a free English constitution of government." In guaranteeing freedoms such as those of speech and press, the First Amendment can be read as protecting the right of everyone to attend trials so as to give meaning to those explicit guarantees . . . . Free speech carries with it some freedom to listen . . . . What this means in the context of trials is that the First Amendment guarantees of speech and press, standing alone, prohibit government from summarily closing courtroom doors which had long been open to the public at the time that Amendment was adopted.
>
> . . . We hold that the right to attend criminal trials is implicit in the guarantees of the First Amendment; without the freedom to attend such trials, which people have exercised for centuries, important aspects of freedom of speech and "of the press could be eviscerated."
>
> Having concluded there was a guaranteed right of the public under the First and Fourteenth Amendments to attend the trial of Stevenson's case, we return to the closure order challenged by appellants . . . . Despite the fact that this was the fourth trial of the accused, the trial judge made no findings to support closure; no inquiry was made as to whether alternative solutions would have met the need to ensure fairness; there was no recognition of any right under the Constitution for the public or press to attend the trial . . . . There was no suggestion that any problems with witnesses could not have been dealt with by their exclusion from the courtroom or their sequestration during the trial. Nor is there anything to indicate that sequestration of the jurors would not have guarded against their being subjected to any improper information. All of the alternatives admittedly present difficulties for trial courts, but none of the factors relied on here was beyond the realm of the manageable. Absent an

overriding interest articulated in findings, the trial of a criminal case must be open to the public. [448 U.S. at 575, 576, 580–581]

NOTES

Note that *Richmond Newspapers* recognized a First Amendment right of the *public* to attend criminal trials, yet it was the *press* that sought access to the proceeding. In one case, the judge barred the media from the voir dire examinations of prospective jurors held in the robing room but provided for the release of these transcripts with the juror's names redacted. The appellate court vacated that decision, finding that the district court did not have enough evidence to warrant a closed-court voir dire. *ABC, Inc. v. Stewart*, 360 F.3d 90 (2nd Cir. 2004).

Does the Court in *Richmond Newspapers* suggest the right of the press *is the same as* that of the public? If not, could a judge exclude the press but not the general public from all or part of a criminal trial? What about the reverse? Could it exclude the public but not the press? *See Stephens v. State*, 405 S.E. 2d 483 (Ga. 1991) (holding it was reversible error to exclude the public because of insufficient findings therefor; error not ameliorated by allowing media representatives to attend).

Under what circumstances might it be permissible to bar both members of the press and public from the defendant's trial?

GLOBE NEWSPAPER CO. v. SUPERIOR COURT
457 U.S. 596 (1982)

JUSTICE BRENNAN delivered the opinion of the Court.[1]

[A Massachusetts statute required that trial judges exclude the press and the public from the courtroom during testimony given by victims of specified sexual offenses when victims are under the age of eighteen. The trial judge, over objections both by Globe Newspaper and the defendant, ordered that the courtroom be closed. The prosecution attempted to distance itself from the trial court's order, stating that the closure decision was made on the court's own motion and not at the request of the prosecution. The United States Supreme Court held that the trial judge's decision was a violation of *Richmond Newspapers* right of access to criminal trials].

The state interests asserted to support Massachusetts statute § 16A, though articulated in various ways, are reducible to two: the protection of minor victims of sex crimes from further trauma and embarrassment; and the encouragement of such victims to come forward and testify in a truthful and credible manner.

. . . We agree with appellee that the first interest — safeguarding the physical and psychological well-being of a minor — is a compelling one. But as compelling as that interest is, it does not justify a *mandatory* closure rule, for it is clear that the circumstances of the particular case may affect the significance of the interest. A trial court can determine on a case-by-case basis whether closure is necessary to protect the welfare of a minor victim. Among the factors to be weighed are the minor victim's age, psychological maturity and understanding, the nature of the crime, the desires of the victim, and the interests of parents and relatives. Section 16A, in contrast, requires closure even if the victim does not seek the exclusion of the press and general public, and would not suffer injury by their presence. In the case before us, for example, the names of the minor victims were already in the public record, and the record indicates that the victims may have been willing to testify despite the presence of the press. If

---

[1] Massachusetts General Laws Annotated, ch. 278, § 16A (West 1981): "At the trial of a complaint or indictment for rape, incest, carnal abuse or other crime involving sex, where a minor under eighteen years of age is the person upon, with or against whom the crime is alleged to have been committed, . . . the presiding judge shall exclude the general public from the courtroom, admitting only such persons as may have a direct interest in the case."

the trial court had been permitted to exercise its discretion, closure might well have been deemed unnecessary. In short, § 16A cannot be viewed as a narrowly tailored means of accommodating the State's asserted interest: That interest could be served just as well by requiring the trial court to determine on a case-by-case basis whether the State's legitimate concern for the well-being of the minor victim necessitates closure. Such an approach ensures that the constitutional right of the press and public to gain access to criminal trials will not be restricted except where necessary to protect the State's interest.

Nor can § 16A be justified on the basis of the Commonwealth's second asserted interest — the encouragement of minor victims of sex crimes to come forward and provide accurate testimony. The Commonwealth has offered no empirical support for the claim that the rule of automatic closure contained in § 16A will lead to an increase in the number of minor sex victims coming forward and cooperating with state authorities. Not only is the claim speculative in empirical terms, but it is also open to serious question as a matter of logic and common sense. Although § 16A bars the press and general public from the courtroom during the testimony of minor sex victims, the press is not denied access to the transcript, court personnel, or any other possible source that could provide an account of the minor victim's testimony. Thus § 16A cannot prevent the press from publicizing the substance of a minor victim's testimony, as well as his or her identity. If the Commonwealth's interest in encouraging minor victims to come forward depends on keeping such matters secret, § 16A hardly advances that interest in an effective manner. And even if § 16A effectively advanced the State's interest, it is doubtful that the interest would be sufficient to overcome the constitutional attack, for that same interest could be relied on to support an array of mandatory closure rules designed to encourage victims to come forward: Surely it cannot be suggested that minor victims of sex crimes are the only crime victims who, because of publicity attendant to criminal trials, are reluctant to come forward and testify.

. . . For the foregoing reasons, we hold that § 16A, as construed by the Massachusetts Supreme Judicial Court, violates the First Amendment to the Constitution.[27]

[The concurring and dissenting opinions are omitted.]

NOTES

1. *Particular proceedings. Richmond* and *Globe* established that the public and the press have a right of access to criminal trials. Subsequent decisions dealt with access to other parts of the judicial process. In *Press-Enterprise Co. v. Superior Court* (Press-Enterprise I), 464 U.S. 501 (1984), the Supreme Court indicated that a newspaper reporter had a right of access, guaranteed by the First Amendment, to the voir dire examination of trial jurors. Two years later, in *Press-Enterprise Co. v. Superior Court* (Press-Enterprise II), 478 U.S. 1 (1986), the right of access guarantee was extended to preliminary hearings (at least as then conducted in California), with the admonition that such proceedings could not be closed to the press unless specific findings were made on the record demonstrating that closure was essential to preserve higher values and that such closure was narrowly tailored to serve those interests.

2. *ABA Recommendations.* The American Bar Association has adopted a comprehensive policy that recognizes the right of public and press access to "criminal proceedings" (defined as "all legal events that involve the exercise of judicial authority

---

[27] We emphasize that our holding is a narrow one: that a rule of mandatory closure respecting the testimony of minor sex victims is constitutionally infirm. In individual cases, and under appropriate circumstances, the First Amendment does not necessarily stand as a bar to the exclusion from the courtroom of the press and general public during the testimony of minor sex-offense victims. But a mandatory rule, requiring no particularized determinations in individual cases, is unconstitutional.

and materially affect the . . . interests of the parties, including courtroom proceedings, applications, motions, plea-acceptances, correspondence, arguments, hearings, trials and similar matters, but shall not include bench conferences or conferences on matters customarily conducted in chambers"). Nonetheless, a closure order may be issued, after notice and opportunity to be heard, if the court finds that (1) access would pose more harm "to the fairness of the trial or other overriding interest" than the defendant's right to a public trial, (2) the closure order will effectively prevent such harm, and (3) there is no less restrictive alternative available to prevent that harm. STANDARDS FOR CRIMINAL JUSTICE § 8-3.2 (3d ed. 1992). *See also* American Bar Association, Principles for Juries and Jury Trials, Prin. 7(A)(1) (voir dire should be open to public view unless court finds a threat to the safety of jurors or evidence of attempt to intimidate or influence the jury).

[7] Electronic Access

A separate issue frequently arising in the context of the First Amendment right of access to criminal trials is the extent to which electronic access (by means of cameras, recording devices, etc.) is allowed. Federal courts have consistently denied requests for televising criminal trials. *See Westmoreland v. CBS*, 596 F. Supp. 1166 (S.D.N.Y.), *aff'd* 752 F.2d 16 (2d Cir. 1984). In addition, Rule 53 of the Federal Rules of Criminal Procedure specifically bans taking photographs during judicial proceedings and broadcasting of such proceedings from the courtroom. Fed. R. Crim. P. 53. Courts have held that this rule violates no right of the defendant. *United States v. Hastings*, 695 F.2d 1278 (11th Cir.), *cert. denied*, 461 U.S. 931 (1983).

State courts. In contrast to the federal trend, one study found that 47 states permitted some form of live television coverage of trials as of 1996. *See* Christo Lassiter, *TV or Not TV That is the Question*, 86 J. CRIM. L. & CRIMINOLOGY 928, 929 (1996). Professor Lassiter points out, however, that television coverage of trials is not as overwhelming as is sometimes reported, observing that in only about 26 states are cameras allowed on a regular basis in the courtroom. He also provides a comprehensive survey of state restrictions on television coverage of trials.

ABA recommendations. The American Bar Association condemns unregulated camera coverage of criminal cases, but endorses judicially supervised coverage so long as the coverage is done "in a manner that will be unobtrusive, will not distract or otherwise adversely affect witnesses or other trial participants, and will not otherwise interfere with the administration of justice." STANDARDS FOR CRIMINAL JUSTICE § 8-3.8 (3d ed. 1992). *See also* American Bar Association, PRINCIPLES FOR JURIES AND JURY TRIALS, Prin. 7(C)(if cameras are allowed in court, should not be allowed to show jurors' faces).

NOTES

1. *Impact of television coverage.* What is the effect of increased television coverage on jurors' impartiality? Is sequestration an option that can or should be used more frequently? What are the problems, if any, with that solution?

2. *Fees for media access.* In cases in which electronic access has been allowed, should the government be able to charge the media for such access? Some have suggested this solution as a means to redirect the profit stemming from the entertainment value of the proceedings. For arguments on both sides, *see* Honorable William L. Howard, *Televised Trials: Can the Government Market Electronic Access?*, 49 S.C. L. REV. 55 (1997); Stephen D. Easton, *No Pay, No Play: Trial Broadcast Fees are Constitutional*, 49 S.C. L. REV. 73 (1997).

B. JUDGE: DISQUALIFICATION/RECUSAL

[1] Right to Impartial Judge

A bedrock principle of the American judicial system is that the judge presiding at trial must be neutral and unbiased. Only if the judge is impartial can a person accused of crime be afforded the requisite fairness guaranteed by the due process clause of the United States Constitution. Almost seventy years ago, the United States Supreme Court recognized this very important principle: "It . . . deprives a defendant in a criminal case of due process of law to subject his liberty or property to the judgment of a court, the judge of which has a direct, personal, substantial pecuniary interest in reaching a conclusion against him in his case." *Tumey v. Ohio*, 273 U.S. 510 (1927).

While bias based upon a pecuniary interest is relatively obvious, the Supreme Court has also recognized that the requirement of judicial impartiality can be infringed where the judge has a personal, though not pecuniary, interest in the proceedings. In *Taylor v. Hayes*, 418 US. 488 (1974), for example, the Court held that contempt charges against a defense attorney should have been heard by a judge other than the one who had observed the "attorney's behavior that gave rise to the charges." The defense attorney in *Taylor*, while defending a person charged with double murder, was held in contempt nine times and given prison sentences that totaled more than four years. Although the Supreme Court found that the defendant's conduct did not constitute a personal attack on the judge, the circumstances created a likelihood of judicial bias or at least the appearance of bias.

[2] Statutes Related to Judge Disqualification

[a] Federal

Two statutes directly address the disqualification of a district court judge in a federal criminal trial. One, 28 U.S.C. § 144, allows for a peremptory challenge of judges; the other, 28 U.S.C. § 455, involves self-disqualification. Because grounds for judicial disqualification in 28 U.S.C. § 455 and 28 U.S.C. § 144 are so similar, they may be considered together. *Jacobson v Everson*, 2005 WL 2781951 (W.D. Wis. 2005).

Peremptory challenge. The peremptory challenge procedure in 28 U.S.C. § 144 allows a party to a proceeding who believes that the trial judge is in any way personally prejudiced to file an affidavit, setting out in detail the facts and reasons supporting the belief that bias exists. Only one such affidavit may be filed for each case, and it must be accompanied by a certificate from counsel that the challenge is made in good faith. Once the affidavit is filed, disqualification is *mandatory* — hence the notion that this is a "peremptory" challenge statute. Indeed, the statute explicitly leaves nothing to the discretion of the challenged judge; he or she is immediately disqualified and another judge must be appointed.

The seminal case under this statute is *Berger v. United States*, 255 U.S. 22 (1920). Defendants, charged with violations of the Espionage Act, asserted by affidavit that the trial judge held strong anti-German beliefs and therefore would be biased against them because of their German origin. The challenged judge denied the motion for disqualification. The United States Supreme Court recognized that the district court judge may determine whether the affidavit, on its face, is sufficient under the statute. Having once done so, however, the judge is not permitted to rule on the truth of the matters alleged; they must be assumed as true. The *Berger* decision means that the party seeking to disqualify a judge is entitled to the disqualification if the statutory requirements are met with respect to the appropriate affidavit.

Because the statute is weighed heavily in favor of recusal, the filing requirements are strictly construed. *See, e.g., United States v. Sykes*, 7 F.3d 1331 (7th Cir. 1993) (holding recusal not required because the affidavit had "procedural and substantive shortcomings"); *Levine v Gerson*, 334 F. Supp. 2d 376 (S.D.N.Y. 2003) (unlike 28 U.S.C., § 455 self-disqualification, which may be invoked by motion of party or by judge *sua sponte*, 28 U.S.C. § 144 self-disqualification is triggered by an affidavit of a party. This affidavit must be accompanied by certificate of counsel of record, and pursuant to § 144, the district judge must recuse himself if the affidavit states that the judge has personal bias or prejudice either for or against one of parties and it provides facts and reasons supporting the statement that prejudice or bias exists. The affidavit must show an objectionable inclination or disposition of judge; it must give fair support to a charge of a bent of mind that may prevent or impede impartiality of judgment.)

Self-disqualification. Self-disqualification under 28 U.S.C. § 455 directs the federal trial judge to excuse himself or herself in any case in which the judge's "impartiality might reasonably be questioned." The remainder of the statute catalogs specific reasons for disqualification, including personal bias towards one of the parties or instances in which the trial judge may have served as an attorney for one of the parties at an earlier date. This statute permits the judge either to disqualify without motion from either party or disqualify after a party has moved for recusal.

By focusing on circumstances in which the trial judge should recuse when his or her impartiality might *reasonably* be questioned, the statute creates an objective rather than a subjective standard. For example, in *Liljeberg v. Health Services Acquisition Company*, 486 U.S. 847 (1988), the United States Supreme Court held that the district court judge, who had a financial interest in the matter but was unaware of this interest, should have been disqualified because an objective observer would have questioned the judge's ability to judge impartially.

At one time, the appellate courts construed this self-disqualification statute to require that the judge's bias or prejudice *must* be directed *against the defendant*, personally, and also must be extra-judicial in nature. *See, e.g., Rivera Perez v. United States*, 508 F. Supp.2d 150 (D. P.R. 2007)(source of alleged bias was judge's handling of previous case against defendant; was not extra-judicial source); *United States v. Carignan*, 600 F.2d 762 (9th Cir. 1979) (judge was prejudiced, if at all, against the defendant's attorney rather than the defendant herself; the prejudice, if any, was not extra-judicial in nature and therefore did not fulfill the requirements of the statute); *United States v. Cepeda Penes*, 577 F.2d 754 (1st Cir. 1978) (no "personal bias or prejudice" had been established even though the trial judge presiding over the defendant's drug-related case was the same one who had denied the defendant's attempt to plead nolo contendere to the charge).

The United States Supreme Court has articulated a somewhat different interpretation of the federal recusal statutes. In *Liteky v. United States*, 510 U.S. 540, 554 (1994), the Court held that while an extra-judicial source of prejudice is *a* factor in determining whether the trial judge should be disqualified, extra-judicial prejudice is neither mandatory nor sufficient on its own:

> The fact that an opinion held by a judge derives from a source outside judicial proceedings is not a *necessary* condition for "bias or prejudice" recusal, since predispositions developed during the course of a trial will sometimes (albeit rarely) suffice. Nor is it a *sufficient* condition for "bias or prejudice" recusal, since *some* opinions acquired outside the context of judicial proceedings. . .will *not* suffice.

Accordingly, the Supreme Court held that the district court judge acted properly in denying the disqualification motion (which relied on events that had occurred during an earlier trial and which involved one of the defendants before the same judge). In sum, courts have held recusal to be appropriate when the judge expresses personal bias concerning the outcome of the case at issue and when the judge has a direct personal or fiduciary interest in the outcome of case. However, when the alleged interest of the judge is not direct, but is remote, contingent, or speculative, it is not the kind of interest that reasonably brings into question judge's impartiality. *Gerson* 334 F. Supp. 2d 376 (S.D.N.Y. 2003).

[b] States

Many states, including California and New York, have adopted statutes modeled after the federal statute, 28 U.S.C., § 455. The main difference between the state and federal systems with respect to judicial recusal is treatment of the peremptory challenge issue. According to *United States v. Escobar*, 803 F. Supp. 611 (E.D.N.Y. 1992), only 19 states allowed peremptory challenges.

C. DEFENDANT'S PRESENCE AT TRIAL

[1] Right to Attend

Defendants in all criminal cases have the right to attend their criminal trials. They should be situated in the courtroom so that they can consult with their counsel and see and hear the proceedings. Sources of this right include common law, constitutional guarantees (such as due process and the Sixth Amendment right of confrontation), and statutory rules of procedure. Many states have based their right of presence provisions upon Federal Rule of Criminal Procedure 43, reproduced below.

FEDERAL RULES OF CRIMINAL PROCEDURE

Rule 43. *Defendant's Presence*

(a) When Required. Unless this rule, Rule 5, or Rule 10 provides otherwise, the defendant must be present at:

(1) the initial appearance, the initial arraignment, and the plea;

(2) every trial stage, including jury impanelment and the return of the verdict; and

(3) sentencing.

(b) When Not Required. A defendant need not be present under any of the following circumstances:

(1) **Organizational Defendant.** The defendant is an organization represented by counsel who is present.

(2) **Misdemeanor Offense.** The offense is punishable by fine or by imprisonment for not more than one year, or both, and with the defendant's written consent, the court permits arraignment, plea, trial, and sentencing to occur in the defendant's absence.

(3) **Conference or Hearing on a Legal Question.** The proceeding involves only a conference or hearing on a question of law.

(4) **Sentence Correction.** The proceeding involves the correction or reduction of sentence under Rule 35 or 18 U.S.C. § 3582(c).

(c) Waiving Continued Presence.

(1) **In General.** A defendant who was initially present at trial, or who had pleaded guilty or nolo contendere, waives the right to be present under the following circumstances:

(A) when the defendant is voluntarily absent after the trial has begun, regardless of whether the court informed the defendant of an obligation to remain during trial;

(B) in a noncapital case, when the defendant is voluntarily absent during sentencing; or

(C) when the court warns the defendant that it will remove the defendant from the courtroom for disruptive behavior, but the defendant persists in conduct that justifies removal from the courtroom.

(2) Waiver's Effect. If the defendant waives the right to be present, the trial may proceed to completion, including the verdict's return and sentencing, during the defendant's absence.

[2]   Scope of Right to Attend

[a]   General Rule: Broad Right to Attend

Rule 43 requires the presence of the defendant at the initial appearance, arraignment, time of plea, and every stage of the trial including the impaneling of the jury and the return of the verdict, and at the imposition of sentence. Notwithstanding this relatively clear language, a number of cases, state and federal, have addressed the question whether particular aspects of the criminal trial require presence of the defendant.

[b]   Proceedings Where There is Right to Attend

The United States Supreme Court has declared that the defendant's right of presence applies to any proceeding or portion thereof that "has a relation, reasonably substantial, to the fullness of his opportunity to defend against the charge . . . ." *Snyder v. Massachusetts*, 291 U.S. 97, 105 (1934) (holding no constitutional violation occurred where the defendant was not permitted to be present at jury view of murder scene). This includes jury selection, jury instructions, rereading testimony to the jury, return of the verdict, and sentencing.

[c]   Proceedings Where There is No Right to Attend

Courts have found that a defendant does not have a right to be present during purely legal aspect of trial. Thus, case law holds that the defendant has no right to be present at various in-chamber conferences, bench conferences conducted outside the jury's hearing, conferences and rulings on jury instructions, and other matters relating principally to questions of law rather than questions of fact. *See, e.g., State v. Swoopes,* 166 P.3d 945 (Ariz. App. 2007)(defendant did not have a right to be present when trial judge answered question from jury during deliberations; judge did not read testimony back to the jury or provide it with any factual information in the case, but rather, he merely provided a legal answer to jurors' question).

In *United States v. Gagnon,* 470 U.S. 522 (1985), for example, the district court judge, in the presence of the defendant's attorney, conferred in chambers with a juror over the possibility that the juror may have been prejudiced against the defendant. Emphasizing that this encounter "was a short interlude in a complex trial," and that the defendant could not have gained anything by attending the encounter, the Court held that his Fifth Amendment due process rights were not violated.

[d]   Waiver

It is well accepted that in most situations a defendant may waive presence at trial. Rule 43(b) a authorizes an organization (such as a corporation) or a misdemeanor defendant to waive presence. As discussed later in this chapter, the defendant may sometimes waive presence by fleeing or disruptive behavior.

Waivers also may occur by acquiescence or specific acts and may waive presence for only part of a trial. For example, in *State v. Newman,* 738 N.W.2d 887 (N.D. 2007), the defense counsel specifically approved the procedure by which the judge alone met with an errant juror (because of an unauthorized cell phone use) and then with the rest of the jurors. The court found the defendant had knowingly and voluntarily waived his presence when defendant was present when the procedure was discussed and acquiesced in it. *See also, Com. v. Hill, 737 A.2d 255* (Pa. Super. 1999) (repeated absence from trial without cause constituted a voluntary waiver of right to be present at trial even though defendant was absent prior to trial and was never informed that trial could proceed in his absence.)

[e] Harmless Error

When a defendant's right to be present is violated, courts ordinarily assess whether the error was harmless. One theme is that defense counsel's participation, despite defendant's absence, sometimes renders the violation harmless and without remedy. The outcome depends on the type of proceeding and the length of the defendant's absence.

The United States Supreme Court has noted that the defendant's right to be present at the criminal trial is based, in large measure, upon the defendant's right to confront and cross-examine the accuser. In *Kentucky v. Stincer*, 482 U.S. 730 (1987), the defendant was not present during a competency hearing to determine whether two children, who were the victims of the alleged crime, were competent to testify. The hearing was held in the judge's chambers. Finding no confrontation clause violation, the Supreme Court approached the issue by asking whether the exclusion of the defendant from the hearing interfered with his opportunity for effective cross-examination. No such interference was found because both of the witnesses appeared and testified in open court, subject to full and complete cross-examination. The Court also observed that any questions that might have been asked during the competency hearing, attended by defendant's attorney, could have been repeated during direct examination and cross-examination at trial in the defendant's presence. For similar reasons, the Court also ruled that the defendant's rights under the due process clause were not violated by his exclusion from the competency hearing.

Justice Marshall, joined by Justices Brennan and Stevens, dissented in *Stincer*. He asserted that the physical presence of the defendant enhances reliability of the fact finding process. He noted that "it is both functionally inefficient and fundamentally unfair to attribute to the defendant's attorney complete knowledge of the facts which the trial judge, in the defendant's involuntary absence, deems relevant to the competency determination." Justice Marshall also pointed out that a defendant who appears *pro se* would be entitled to attend such a competency hearing. Therefore, this case may create for the accused a difficult dilemma. "A choice between continuing to exercise his right to assistance of counsel, thereby being excluded from the competency hearing, and appearing *pro se* so that he may be in attendance at this critical stage of his trial."

NOTES

1. *Medicated defendant.* Could a defendant be both present and not present at the same time? What if the defendant were physically present but heavily medicated so that the defendant's mind was fuzzy and he or she was unable to remember the trial or consult with counsel? *Riggins v. Nevada*, 504 U.S. 127 (1992), is the seminal case on the subject. The defendant in *Riggins* was being treated for a psychiatric disorder by means of an extremely high dose of antipsychotic medication that caused drowsiness, confusion, and possibly severe interference with mental processes. Citing the Sixth and Fourteenth Amendments, the defendant requested that he be allowed to refrain from taking the medication for the duration of his trial. First, he said that the calm, sedate appearance caused by the medication interfered with his ability to present an insanity defense. Second, he claimed that the medicine interfered with his thought processes and his ability to mentally follow the trial and consult with his counsel.

The Supreme Court held that, once a defendant raises a claim that forced administration of medication affects his constitutional rights to a fair trial, the state must prove that the "treatment with antipsychotic medication [is] medically appropriate and, considering less intrusive alternatives, essential for the sake of [the defendant's] own safety or the safety of others." 504 U.S. at 135. The defendant's conviction was reversed because the trial court had not made the necessary findings to support the forced administration of medication.

Competence to stand trial. Questions were raised in *Riggins* about the defendant's competence to stand trial without the medicine. Can a court order administration of medication against a defendant's will in order to *make* him or her competent to stand trial? The majority in *Riggins* seemed to say yes: "[T]he State might have been able to justify medically appropriate, involuntary treatment with the drug by establishing that it could not obtain an adjudication of Riggins' guilt or innocence by using less intrusive means."

The United States Supreme Court sharpened the *Riggins* analysis in *Sell v. United States,* 539 U.S. 166 (2003), by holding that "the Constitution permits the government involuntarily to administer antipsychotic drugs to a mentally ill defendant facing serious criminal charges in order to render that defendant competent to stand trial, but only if the treatment is medically appropriate and substantially likely to render the defendant competent to stand trial, is substantially unlikely to have side effects that may undermine the fairness of the trial, and, taking account of less intrusive alternatives, is necessary significantly to further important governmental trial-related interests. *See also, United States v. Gomes,* 305 F. Supp. 2d 158 (D. Conn. 2004).

2. *Right to be absent.* While Rule 43 confers a right of presence, is it inconsistent with a right to be absent? Many statutes mandate the defendant's presence in capital cases. But what if the defendant wants to be absent, perhaps for political or tactical reasons? While the defendant can be forced to appear for purposes of identification, some courts have held the state cannot force a defendant to attend some proceedings if there is a knowing and voluntary waiver of presence. *See, e.g., Nixon v. State,* 572 So. 2d 1336 (Fla. 1990)(defendant will not be forced to attend his capital trial if his actions or the means to ensure his presence would prejudice him in the eyes of the jury). Does this approach adequately consider the interests of the court and the public?

3. *Video technology.* Is the right of presence satisfied when the defendant views the proceedings and communicates with those in the courtroom from a remote location, using videoconferencing? Recent advances in technology have allowed for the increased use of videoconferencing in trials, enabling the defendant to participate in the trial proceedings without being physically present. Many states authorize a wide range of court proceedings by videoconferencing when the defendant is incarcerated.

In federal criminal cases, teleconferencing is permitted at the initial appearance and the arraignment if the defendant consents (Fed. R. Crim P. 5(f) and 10(c)). Rule 43 specifically approves of presence-by-video in these proceedings. Benefits of the videoconferencing technique include reduced consumption of time and resources in moving an incarcerated defendant to the courthouse from distant facilities, increased security in proceedings that are open to the public, and efficient handling of cases. However, the use of videoconferencing may place constraints on the judicial process that detrimentally affect criminal defendants, outweighing any perceived benefits of the technology. *See* Anne Bowen Poulin, *Criminal Justice and Videoconferencing Technology: The Remote Defendant,* 78 Tul. L. Rev. 1089 (2004) (asserting that videoconferencing techniques distort normal communication between the defendant and counsel, and that viewing the defendant on remote television may cause the judge and jury to develop unwarranted negative impressions of the defendant).

[3] The Escaping Defendant

While Rule 43 literally mandates the presence of defendant at certain critical states of the criminal case, under some circumstances, discussed below, it also permits a trial to proceed in the defendant's absence. Does this rule also mean that a trial may not be held in the case of a defendant who escapes prior to trial? The Supreme Court read Rule 43 literally and answered this question in the affirmative.

CROSBY v. UNITED STATES
506 U.S. 255 (1993)

Justice Blackmun delivered the opinion of the Court.

This case requires us to decide whether Federal Rule of Criminal Procedure 43 permits the trial in absentia of a defendant who absconds prior to trial and is absent at its beginning. We hold that it does not.

[The defendant and others were indicted in April, 1988, on a number of counts of mail fraud. He appeared before a federal magistrate and entered a not guilty plea. Following his conditional release (one of the conditions being that he would remain in Minnesota), he attended "pretrial conferences and hearings" with counsel and was informed that his trial was to begin on October 12. When he failed to appear for his trial, it was delayed five days. The District Court commenced the trial, finding that (1) Crosby had notice of the trial date, (2) his absence was "knowing and deliberate," resulting in a voluntary waiver of his right to be present, and (3) the trial would proceed in his absence because not doing so would mean severing him from the trial of his co-defendants, causing "extreme difficulty for the Government, witnesses, counsel, and the court." Defendant and two co-defendants were convicted; Crosby's attorney participated actively at trial. Crosby was later arrested in Florida and returned to Minnesota where he was sentenced on the mail fraud convictions. The Eighth Circuit Court of Appeals upheld the convictions, concluding that the District Court's decision to try the defendant in absentia was not prohibited by Rule 43.]

In *Diaz v. United States*, 223 U.S. 442 (1912), a case that concerned a defendant who had absented himself voluntarily on two occasions from his ongoing trial in the Philippines, this Court authorized a limited exception to the general rule, an exception that was codified eventually in Rule 43(b). Because it did "not seem to us to be consonant with the dictates of common sense that an accused person, being at large upon bail, should be at liberty, whenever he pleased, to withdraw himself from the courts of his country and to break up a trial already commenced," the Court held:

> [W]here the offense is not capital and the accused is not in custody, . . . if, *after the trial has begun in his presence*, he voluntarily absents himself, this does not nullify what has been done or prevent the completion of the trial, but, on the contrary, operates as a waiver of his right to be present and leaves the court free to proceed with the trial in like manner and with like effect as if he were present. 223 U.S. at 455 (emphasis added).

Diaz was cited by the Advisory Committee that drafted Rule 43. The Committee explained: "The second sentence of the rule is a restatement of existing law that, except in capital cases, the defendant may not defeat the proceedings by voluntarily absenting himself after the trial has been commenced in his presence." There is no reason to believe that the drafters intended the Rule to go further.

. . . The Court of Appeals in the present case recognized that this Court in *Diaz* had not addressed the situation of the defendant who fails to appear for the commencement of trial. Nevertheless, the court concluded: "It would be anomalous to attach more significance to a defendant's absence at commencement than to absence during more important substantive portions of the trial." While it may be true that there are no "talismanic properties which differentiate the commencement of a trial from later stages," we do not find the distinction between pre- and midtrial flight so farfetched as to convince us that Rule 43 cannot mean what it says. As a general matter, the costs of suspending a proceeding already under way will be greater than the cost of postponing a trial not yet begun. If a clear line is to be drawn marking the point at which the costs of delay are likely to outweigh the interests of the defendant and society in having the defendant present, the commencement of trial is at least a plausible place at which to draw that line.

There are additional practical reasons for distinguishing between flight before and flight during a trial. As did *Diaz*, the Rule treats midtrial flight as a knowing and voluntary waiver of the right to be present. Whether or not the right constitutionally may be waived in other circumstances — and we express no opinion here on that subject — the defendant's initial presence serves to assure that any waiver is indeed knowing. "Since the notion that trial may be commenced in absentia still seems to shock most lawyers, it would hardly seem appropriate to impute knowledge that this will occur to their clients." It is unlikely, on the other hand, "that a defendant who flees from a courtroom in the midst of a trial — where judge, jury, witnesses and lawyers are present and ready to continue — would not know that as a consequence the trial could continue in his absence." *Taylor v. United States*, 414 U.S. 17 (1973).

The language, history, and logic of Rule 43 support a straightforward interpretation that prohibits the trial in absentia of a defendant who is not present at the beginning of trial. Because we find Rule 43 dispositive, we do not reach Crosby's claim that his trial in absentia was also prohibited by the Constitution.

The judgment of the Court of Appeals is reversed and the case is remanded for further proceedings consistent with this opinion.

NOTES

1. *Capital case exception.* Note that the *Diaz* decision suggests that capital cases may not proceed in the absence of the accused even where the accused was present for the beginning of the trial. Why should that be?

2. *Constitutional limits. Crosby* dealt with a defendant's rights under Criminal Procedure Rule 43. In the absence of Rule 43, should there be any *constitutional* bar to a trial in absentia of a defendant who flees the jurisdiction before trial commences? *See* Neil P. Cohen, *Can They Kill Me If I'm Gone: Trial In Absentia in Capital Cases*, 36 U. FLA. L. REV. 273 (1984), in which Professor Cohen describes a death penalty case in which such a trial was held under these circumstances (but noting that the jury returned verdicts of guilty to less serious homicide charges).

Case law recognizes that the Due Process and Confrontation Clauses confer a right of the defendant to attend various proceedings, but also approve of a knowing and voluntary waiver of that right by a voluntary absence. *See, e.g., Pinkney v. State*, 711 A.2d 205 (Md. 1998) (state and federal constitution permit trial court to conduct a trial in defendant's absence where defendant was aware of time and place of trial and judge determines that absence was voluntary); *United States v. Sharp*, 38 M.J. 33 (C.M.A. 1993) (defendant who voluntarily absented himself after arraignment could be tried *in absentia* even without being notified of exact trial date).

3. *Allowing defendant to explain absence.* When a defendant is absent, he or she should be allowed to give a reason to ensure that the absence was knowing and voluntary. *See, e.,g., Tweedy v. State*, 845 A.2d 1215 (Md. 2004)(error not to have at least allowed defendant an opportunity to show good reason for his absence during sentencing); *Robinson v. Commonwealth*, 837 N.E.2d 241 (Mass. 2005)(if a defendant does not appear at a scheduled hearing on a motion to suppress, the judge should determine whether the defendant's absence was voluntary by making a reasonable inquiry into the circumstances surrounding the defendant's failure to appear).

4. *Court's options when defendant absent.* While Rule 43 permits a court to proceed with the trial if the defendant waives presence, the court has the option of declaring a mistrial or granting a continuance (perhaps to await the defendant's capture or return).

5. *No need to warn of consequences of absence. Taylor v. United States*, 414 U.S. 17 (1973), cited in *Crosby*, involved a claim by the defendant, who had voluntarily absented himself during trial, that such voluntary absence, alone, cannot be construed as an effective waiver of his right to be present. In a *per curiam* ruling in which that claim was rejected, the Court found that his absence was the product of his voluntary choice and that it was not necessary in establishing waiver that the defendant be expressly warned by the trial court of the consequences of his absence. The Court, however, did not abandon the requirement that a waiver of presence must be "knowing and voluntary." Rather it held that it "seemed incredible" that the defendant would not have known the trial would continue in his absence. Moreover, the Court noted the defendant did not contend he was unaware that the trial would go on despite his escape.

What should be the result if the court believes the defendant really did not know the consequences of flight? Could *Taylor* be viewed as creating a rebuttable presumption of this knowledge? Rule 43(c)(1) provides the defendant may waive presence by voluntary absence "regardless of whether the court informed the defendant of an obligation to remain during trial." Does this deal with the issue whether defendant knew the trial would proceed in his or her absence?

6. *Service by publication.* Civil actions sometimes commence against parties who are notified of proceedings through publication (*i.e.*, a formal notice published in a newspaper). Why should that procedure not be utilized in criminal cases?

[4] The Disruptive Defendant

ILLINOIS v. ALLEN
397 U.S. 337 (1970)

MR. JUSTICE BLACK delivered the opinion of the Court.

. . . The question presented in this case is whether an accused can claim the benefit of his constitutional right to remain in the courtroom while at the same time he engages in speech and conduct which is so noisy, disorderly, and disruptive that it is exceedingly difficult or wholly impossible to carry on the trial.

[The defendant, charged with armed robbery, refused court-appointed counsel and was allowed by the trial judge to proceed *pro se* — but only if the appointed lawyer remained at trial "to protect the record." During voir dire, the defendant was admonished to confine the examination to pertinent matters.]

. . . At that point, the petitioner started to argue with the judge in a most abusive and disrespectful manner. At last, and seemingly in desperation, the judge asked appointed counsel to proceed with the examination of the jurors. The petitioner continued to talk, proclaiming that the appointed attorney was not going to act as his lawyer. He terminated his remarks by saying, "When I go out for lunchtime, you're (the judge) going to be a corpse here." At that point he tore the file which his attorney had and threw the papers on the floor. The trial judge thereupon stated to the petitioner, "One more outbreak of that sort and I'll remove you from the courtroom." This warning had no effect on the petitioner. He continued to talk back to the judge, saying, "There's not going to be no trial, either. I'm going to sit here and you're going to talk and you can bring your shackles out and straight jacket and put them on me and tape my mouth, but it will do no good because there's not going to be no trial." After more abusive remarks by the petitioner, the trial judge ordered the trial to proceed in the petitioner's absence. The petitioner was removed from the courtroom. The voir dire examination then continued and the jury was selected in the absence of the petitioner.

After a noon recess and before the jury was brought into the courtroom, the petitioner, appearing before the judge, complained about the fairness of the trial and his appointed attorney. He also said he wanted to be present in the court during his trial. In reply, the judge said that the petitioner would be permitted to remain in the courtroom if he "behaved (himself) and (did) not interfere with the introduction of the case." The jury was brought in and seated. Counsel for the petitioner then moved to exclude the witnesses from the courtroom. The (petitioner) protested this effort on the part of his attorney, saying: "There is going to be no proceeding. I'm going to start talking and I'm going to keep on talking all through the trial. There's not going to be no trial like this. I want my sister and my friends here in court to testify for me." The trial judge thereupon ordered the petitioner removed from the courtroom.

After this second removal, Allen remained out of the courtroom during the presentation of the State's case-in-chief, except that he was brought in on several occasions for purposes of identification. During one of these latter appearances, Allen responded to one of the judge's questions with vile and abusive language. After the prosecution's case had been presented, the trial judge reiterated his promise to Allen that he could return to the courtroom whenever he agreed to conduct himself properly. Allen gave some assurances of proper conduct and was permitted to be present through the remainder of the trial, principally his defense, which was conducted by his appointed counsel.

. . . The Court of Appeals [holding that Allen should not have been removed from the courtroom] felt that the defendant's Sixth Amendment right to be present at his own trial was so "absolute" that, no matter how unruly or disruptive the defendant's conduct might be, he could never be held to have lost that right so long as he continued to insist upon it, as Allen clearly did. Therefore the Court of Appeals concluded that a trial judge could never expel a defendant from his own trial and that the judge's ultimate remedy when faced with an obstreperous defendant like Allen who determines to make his trial impossible is to bind and gag him. We cannot agree that the Sixth Amendment, the cases upon which the Court of Appeals relied, or any other cases of this Court so handicap a trial judge in conducting a criminal trial . . . . Although mindful that courts must indulge every reasonable presumption against the loss of constitutional rights, we explicitly hold today that a defendant can lose his right to be present at trial if, after he has been warned by the judge that he will be removed if he continues his disruptive behavior, he nevertheless insists on conducting himself in a manner so disorderly, disruptive, and disrespectful of the court that his trial cannot be carried on with him in the courtroom. Once lost, the right to be present can, of course, be reclaimed as soon as the defendant is willing to conduct himself consistently with the decorum and respect inherent in the concept of courts and judicial proceedings.

It is essential to the proper administration of criminal justice that dignity, order, and decorum be the hallmarks of all court proceedings in our country. The flagrant disregard in the courtroom of elementary standards of proper conduct should not and cannot be tolerated. We believe trial judges confronted with disruptive, contumacious, stubbornly defiant defendants must be given sufficient discretion to meet the circumstances of each case. No one formula for maintaining the appropriate courtroom atmosphere will be best in all situations. We think there are at least three constitutionally permissible ways for a trial judge to handle an obstreperous defendant like Allen: (1) bind and gag him, thereby keeping him present; (2) cite him for contempt; (3) take him out of the courtroom until he promises to conduct himself properly.

Trying a defendant for a crime while he sits bound and gagged before the judge and jury would to an extent comply with that part of the Sixth Amendment's purposes that accords the defendant an opportunity to confront the witnesses at the trial. But even to contemplate such a technique, much less see it, arouses a feeling that no person should be tried while shackled and gagged except as a last resort. Not only is it possible that the sight of shackles and gags might have a significant effect on the jury's feelings about the defendant, but the use of this technique is itself something of an affront to the very dignity and decorum of judicial proceedings that the judge is seeking to uphold. Moreover, one of the defendant's primary advantages of being present at the trial, his ability to communicate with his counsel, is greatly reduced when the defendant is in a condition of total physical restraint. It is in part because of these inherent disadvantages and limitations in this method of dealing with disorderly defendants that we decline to hold with the Court of Appeals that a defendant cannot under any possible circumstances be deprived of his right to be present at trial. However, in some situations which we need not attempt to foresee, binding and gagging might possibly be the fairest and most reasonable way to handle a defendant who acts as Allen did here.

In a footnote the Court of Appeals suggested the possible availability of contempt of court as a remedy to make Allen behave in his robbery trial, and it is true that citing or threatening to cite a contumacious defendant for criminal contempt might in itself be sufficient to make a defendant stop interrupting a trial. If so, the problem would be solved easily, and the defendant could remain in the courtroom. Of course, if the defendant is determined to prevent any trial, then a court in attempting to try the defendant for contempt is still confronted with the identical dilemma that the Illinois court faced in this case. And criminal contempt has obvious limitations as a sanction when the defendant is charged with a crime so serious that a very severe sentence such as death or life imprisonment is likely to be imposed. In such a case the defendant might not be affected by a mere contempt sentence when he ultimately faces a far more serious sanction. Nevertheless, the contempt remedy should be borne in mind by a judge in the circumstances of this case.

Another aspect of the contempt remedy is the judge's power, when exercised consistently with state and federal law, to imprison an unruly defendant such as Allen for civil contempt and discontinue the trial until such time as the defendant promises to behave himself. This procedure is consistent with the defendant's right to be present at trial, and yet it avoids the serious shortcomings of the use of shackles and gags. It must be recognized, however, that a defendant might conceivably, as a matter of calculated strategy, elect to spend a prolonged period in confinement for contempt in the hope that adverse witnesses might be unavailable after a lapse of time. A court must guard against allowing a defendant to profit from his own wrong in this way.

The trial court in this case decided under the circumstances to remove the defendant from the courtroom and to continue his trial in his absence until and unless he promised to conduct himself in a manner befitting an American courtroom. As we said earlier, we find nothing unconstitutional about this procedure. Allen's behavior was clearly of such an extreme and aggravated nature as to justify either his removal from the courtroom or his total physical restraint. Prior to his removal he was repeatedly warned by the trial judge that he would be removed from the courtroom if he persisted in his unruly conduct, and . . . the record demonstrates that Allen would not have been at all dissuaded by the trial judge's use of his criminal contempt powers. Allen was constantly informed that he could return to the trial when he would agree to conduct himself in an orderly manner. Under these circumstances we hold that Allen lost his right guaranteed by the Sixth and Fourteenth Amendments to be present throughout his trial.

. . . We do not hold that removing this defendant from his own trial was the only way the Illinois judge could have constitutionally solved the problem he had. We do hold, however, that there is nothing whatever in this record to show that the judge did not act completely within his discretion. Deplorable as it is to remove a man from his own trial, even for a short time, we hold that the judge did not commit legal error in doing what he did. [Reversed]

Mr. Justice Brennan, concurring.

. . . I would add only that when a defendant is excluded from his trial, the court should make reasonable efforts to enable him to communicate with his attorney and, if possible, to keep apprised of the progress of his trial. Once the court has removed the contumacious defendant, it is not weakness to mitigate the disadvantages of his expulsion as far as technologically possible in the circumstances.

[The separate opinion by JUSTICE DOUGLAS is omitted.]

NOTES

1. *Technological presence.* Given today's technological capabilities, could you envision a case in which a defendant, removed under the *Allen* standard, would not be able to follow the trial as it occurs? Even if you believe that technology should provide a disruptive defendant with the capacity to see courtroom proceedings (through live telecast, for example), in what way could such a procedure not ensure "fairness" to the defendant?

2. *Pro se disruptive defendant.* What will a court do with a disruptive defendant who chooses to proceed *pro se*? The fact of self-representation must be considered in selecting the appropriate sanction. In *Biglari v. State*, 847 A.2d 1239 (Md. App. 2004), defendant fired his counsel during trial and represented himself. When defendant was taken from the courtroom due to his disruptive behavior, the trial judge erred in not giving him the chance to return upon a promise to behave properly. After instructing the jury, the trial court should have (1) sent the jury to the jury room, (2) brought defendant into the courtroom, (3) told defendant he could object to the instructions, and (4) told defendant, if he promised to behave properly, he could give a closing argument and stay in the courtroom for closing argument.

In another illustrative case, the *pro se* defendant was removed from the courtroom for inappropriate conduct and was denied the opportunity to exercise peremptory challenges. Finding this gave the prosecution an unfair advantage, the court reversed the conviction and held that the defendant's Sixth Amendment rights were violated. *People v. Cohn*, 160 P.3d 336 (Colo. App. 2007). The court suggested that a trial judge facing a contumacious *pro se* defendant could appoint standby counsel to take over if necessary or could allow the defendant to participate by remote video technology.

If standby counsel is available to handle the case when a disruptive *pro se* defendant is removed from the courtroom, courts usually uphold the proceedings and find harmless error. *See, e.g., United States v. Williams*, 431 F.3d 1115 (8th Cir. 2005)(disruptive *pro se* defendant removed from courtroom, partly to protect him from prejudicing his own case; standby counsel took over; harmless error and waiver of right to be present found).

3. *Shackles.* As noted in *Allen*, shackling (defined by one court as all forms of hand-cuffs, leg irons, restraining belts and the like) a defendant in the courtroom may be highly prejudicial to the accused. As one court stated, "the presumption of innocence requires the garb of innocence, and regardless of the ultimate outcome, or the evidence awaiting presentation, every defendant is entitled to be brought before the court with the appearance, dignity, and self-respect of a free and innocent man." *Eaddy v. People*, 174 P.2d 717, 718–719 (Colo. 1946). While there may be circumstances in which the decision to shackle a defendant is fully warranted, the Sixth Circuit Court of Appeals has held that "a defendant should never be shackled during his trial before a jury except in extraordinary circumstances. [Noting the inherent prejudice to the accused], only upon a clear showing of necessity should shackles ever be employed." *Kennedy v. Cardwell*, 487 F.2d 101, 111 (6th Cir. 1973).

In *Deck v. Missouri*, 544 U.. 622 (2005), the Supreme Court, by a 7 to 2 vote, held that it is not permissible to shackle a convicted offender during the penalty phase of a capital case unless such use is justified by "an essential state interest." The court reasoned as follows:

> The considerations that militate against the routine use of visible shackles during the guilt phase of a criminal trial apply with like force to penalty proceedings in capital cases. This is obviously so in respect to the latter two

considerations mentioned, securing a meaningful defense and maintaining dignified proceedings. It is less obviously so in respect to the first consideration mentioned, for the defendant's conviction means that the presumption of innocence no longer applies. Hence shackles do not undermine the jury's effort to apply that presumption.

Nonetheless, shackles at the penalty phase threaten related concerns. Although the jury is no longer deciding between guilt and innocence, it is deciding between life and death.

Neither is accuracy in making that decision any less critical. The Court has stressed the "acute need" for reliable decisionmaking when the death penalty is at issue. The appearance of the offender during the penalty phase in shackles, however, almost inevitably implies to a jury, as a matter of common sense, that court authorities consider the offender a danger to the community — often a statutory aggravator and nearly always a relevant factor in jury decisionmaking, even where the State does not specifically argue the point. It also almost inevitably affects adversely the jury's perception of the character of the defendant. And it thereby inevitably undermines the jury's ability to weigh accurately all relevant considerations — considerations that are often unquantifiable and elusive — when it determines whether a defendant deserves death. In these ways, the use of shackles can be a "thumb [on] death's side of the scale."

Given the presence of similarly weighty considerations, we must conclude that courts cannot routinely place defendants in shackles or other physical restraints visible to the jury during the penalty phase of a capital proceeding. The constitutional requirement, however, is not absolute. It permits a judge, in the exercise of his or her discretion, to take account of special circumstances, including security concerns, that may call for shackling. In so doing, it accommodates the important need to protect the courtroom and its occupants. But any such determination must be case specific; that is to say, it should reflect particular concerns, say special security needs or escape risks, related to the defendant on trial.

Hidden shackles. Another consideration is whether the jury actually sees the shackles and is prejudiced by their presence. For example, in *United States v. Orris*, 86 Fed. Appx. 82 (6th Cir. 2004), the defendant argued that the district court committed reversible error when it required that his legs be shackled under the defense table, which was draped with a shroud so that the shackles could not be seen. The table occupied by the prosecutors was draped in the same way. The court held that . . . a defendant may permissibly be shackled only upon a *clear showing* of necessity . . . and only as a "last resort." The burden "to show the necessity of any extreme physical security measures" is on the prosecution." The standard of review is abuse of discretion. The Sixth Circuit held that the district court should have more clearly stated on the record, based upon facts in the record, the reasons he believed that shackling was necessary. However, the appellate court also noted that there was no indication whatsoever in the record that the shackling prevented Orris from consulting with his attorney, was ever seen by the jury, or otherwise prejudiced.

Electronic shackles. Besides hidden shackles, are other methods, such as electronic shackling, which is undetectable, allowed? In *People v. Garcia*, 56 Cal. App. 4th 1349 (Cal. Ct. App. 1997), the California Court of Appeals upheld the use of an electronic "React" belt worn under the defendant's clothes despite the fact that the defendant did not engage in disruptive behavior while in the courtroom. The court described the "React" belt as the modern, electronic version of the "ball and chain" which accomplishes the same goals as physical shackling while remaining functionally invisible. The court noted that the "React" belt will deliver 50,000 volts of electricity if activated by a remote transmitter that is controlled by the attending officer, and that this shock will immobilize the wearer. Additionally, the belt could be activated upon any outburst or quick movement, tampering with the belt, or any attempt to escape custody. Because the electronic belt is unlike a traditional physical restraint, the California court held its use is permitted under a good cause standard, which requires that the trial court consider the totality of facts and circumstances.

By contrast, the Supreme Court of Indiana held in *Wrinkles v. State*, 749 N.E.2d 1179 (Ind. 2001), that stunbelts may not be used on Indiana defendants, observing:

> . . . we believe that [handcuffs, shackles, security chairs, and gagging a defendant] can do the job without inflicting the mental anguish that results from simply wearing the stunbelt and the physical pain that results if the belt is activated. [*Id.* at 1195]

Courts will analyze this need carefully because of the ramifications of a stun belt. In one case, the court remanded after it determined it was prejudicial error to require the defendant to wear a stunbelt absent a "manifest need" and there was a reasonable probability that the error affected the trial's outcome by affecting the defendant's demeanor during his crucial testimony. *People v Mar*, 28 Cal. 4th 1201 (Cal. 2002).

4. *Jury instructions concerning restraints.* If a criminal accused is physically restrained in the jurors' presence, should the judge instruct the jurors that the restraint should not be considered in assessing credibility or determining guilt? *See* STANDARDS FOR CRIMINAL JUSTICE § 15-3.2(d) (3d ed. 1996) (yes). Could this make matters worse?

5. *Police visibly present.* If shackles are prejudicial, what about large numbers of police officers standing near the defendant during trial? *See Middlebrooks v. State*, 363 S.E. 2d 39 (Ga. App.1987) (not ground for automatic mistrial).

6. *Prison or jail clothing.* The Supreme Court has held that the government cannot, consistently with due process, "compel an accused to stand trial before a jury while dressed in identifiable prison clothes." *Estelle v. Williams*, 425 U.S. 501, 512 (1976). Because of defense counsel's failure to object to this practice, however, relief was denied.

D. BURDEN OF PROOF

[1] Crime Elements: Beyond a Reasonable Doubt

It was not until 1970 that the United States Supreme Court explicitly held that the due process clause "protects the accused against conviction except upon proof beyond a reasonable doubt of every fact necessary to constitute the crime with which he is charged." *In re Winship*, 397 U.S. 358, 364 (1970). Noting that the reasonable doubt standard plays a "vital role" in the criminal case, the Court in *Winship* characterized the standard as a "prime instrument for reducing the risk of convictions resting on factual error." The Court further explained:

> The accused during a criminal prosecution has at stake interests of immense importance, both because of the possibility that he may lose his liberty upon conviction and because of the certainty that he would be stigmatized by the conviction. Accordingly, a society that values the good name and freedom of every individual should not condemn a man for commission of a crime when there is reasonable doubt about his guilt.
>
> . . . Moreover, use of the reasonable-doubt standard is indispensable to command the respect and confidence of the community in applications of the criminal law. It is critical that the moral force of the criminal law not be diluted by a standard of proof that leaves people in doubt whether innocent men are being condemned. It is also important in our free society that every individual going about his ordinary affairs have confidence that his government cannot adjudge him guilty of a criminal offense without convincing a proper factfinder of his guilt with utmost certainty. [397 U.S. at 363–364]

While *Winship* establishes an important burden-of-proof principle, it does not answer the question whether proof of some evidentiary matters can be placed upon the *defendant*. For example, could a state require the defense to prove by a preponderance of the evidence that the defendant was "acting in the heat of passion on sudden provocation" so as to reduce a murder charge to manslaughter? The United States Supreme Court held in *Mullaney v. Wilbur*, 421 U.S. 684 (1975), that it could not do so. This result meant the government had to prove *absence* of provocation beyond a reasonable doubt. The *Mullaney* decision was based on an interpretation of Maine homicide law:

> Absent justification or excuse, all intentional or criminally reckless killings are felonious homicides. Felonious homicide is punished as murder . . . unless the defendant proves by a fair preponderance of the evidence that it was committed in the heat of passion on sudden provocation, in which case it is punished as manslaughter . . . . [421 U.S. at 691–92].

In an opinion that can be charitably characterized as unclear, the Court in *Mullaney* held that murder and manslaughter are punishment categories of the "single offense of felonious homicide." Therefore, the state, in order to prove guilt of murder, must disprove manslaughter. This requires the state to prove the lack of heat of passion.

Two years later, however, the Supreme Court upheld a state statute that required the defendant to prove extreme emotional disturbance by the civil "preponderance" standard in order to reduce a murder charge to manslaughter. *Patterson v. New York*, 432 U.S. 197 (1977). The *Patterson* Court reasoned that under New York homicide law, second degree murder required the government to prove beyond a reasonable doubt that the defendant intended to and did cause death. As an affirmative defense, the defendant could reduce a murder to the lesser crime of manslaughter by proving that he or she acted "under the influence of extreme emotional disturbance." Finding that the government's proof of intent and causation for second degree murder did not negate extreme emotional disturbance, the Court held that allocating proof of the latter to the accused did not violate *Mullaney v. Wilbur*. Some, including the *Patterson* dissenters, find it difficult to reconcile the two cases. *See* Ronald J. Allen, *The Restoration of In re Winship: A Comment on Burdens of Persuasion in Criminal Cases After Patterson v. New York*, 76 Mich. L. Rev. 30 (1977); Barbara D. Underwood, *The Thumb of the Scales of Justice: Burdens of Persuasion in Criminal Cases*, 86 Yale L.J. 1299 (1977).

[2] Defenses: Wide Variation

After *Patterson*, it is clear that the government must prove each element of the crime beyond a reasonable doubt, but can require the defendant to prove various defenses. Generally, the defendant may be responsible for proving insanity, self-defense, or duress; the standard of proof in such cases usually is a preponderance of the evidence. In some jurisdictions there is a "burden-shifting." After the defendant offers some proof of the existence of a defense, such as insanity, the burden shifts to the government to prove beyond a reasonable doubt or a lesser standard that the defense did not exist.

[3] Presumptions and Inferences

In some cases, the prosecution has attempted to lighten its burden of proof through the utilization of jury instructions related to specific factual findings. For example, in a homicide case, the prosecutor may seek to have the jury instructed that the defendant's state of mind can be proven through the use of a presumption based upon the proven physical acts of the defendant. Such a proposed instruction might be phrased as follows:

> A person is presumed to intend the natural and probable consequences of his or her acts.

In *Francis v. Franklin*, 471 U.S. 307 (1985), however, the United States Supreme Court held that such an instruction creates a presumption, thereby relieving the government of its burden of proving the defendant's mental state beyond a reasonable doubt. The quoted language was characterized by the Court as having "undeniably created an unconstitutional burden-shifting presumption with respect to the element of intent," and therefore violated the due process clause.

As a result of *Francis*, the government relies on "permissive inferences" rather than burden-shifting presumptions. For example, the jury is instructed, "You may infer that the defendant intended to kill from the fact (if so found beyond a reasonable doubt) that he aimed his weapon at the victim, and fired the shots that caused the victim's death."

E.   ORDER OF PROOF

After the judge and lawyers select a jury and the judge informs the jury of the formal charges (often by reading the indictment), the prosecution begins presentation of its case.

[1]   Opening Statements

Unless the prosecution waives its option (which rarely occurs), the first step is for the prosecution to give an opening statement, which is designed simply as an overview of the alleged offense, the government's theory of the case, and the evidence it will offer to establish guilt beyond a reasonable doubt. The defense ordinarily will respond with its own opening statement, sketching its theory of the case and the proof it intends to offer. In some courts the defense is permitted to delay its opening statement until after the prosecution has presented its proof.

[2]   Prosecution's Proof

The prosecution then presents its case "in chief" to satisfy its responsibility of proving guilt beyond a reasonable doubt. This may consist of testimonial evidence, such as that of the victim, other witnesses to the crime, and expert testimony, and may also include physical evidence, such as drugs, clothing found at the scene of the offense, the weapon used to commit the crime, and various documents. If the defendant has confessed to the offense yet is denying guilt at trial, the confession is generally offered by presenting testimony from the police officer who obtained the defendant's statement. Sometimes, a written or videotaped version of the admission will accompany the officer's testimony. The defendant is entitled under the Sixth Amendment to the United States Constitution to confront and cross-examine the government's witnesses, as discussed in the next section. Upon presentation of all of its evidence, the prosecution "rests its case."

[3]   Defense Motion for Acquittal

The defense attorney may then move for an acquittal, asserting that the government has failed to offer sufficient proof of the defendant's guilt to satisfy the beyond-a-reasonable-doubt standard. Rule 29 provides procedures for acquittal motions.

FEDERAL RULES OF CRIMINAL PROCEDURE

Rule 29. *Motion for a Judgment of Acquittal*

(a) **Before Submission to the Jury.** After the government closes its evidence or after the close of all the evidence, the court on the defendant's motion must enter a judgment of acquittal of any offense for which the evidence is insufficient to sustain a conviction. The court may on its own consider whether the evidence is insufficient to sustain a conviction. If the court denies a motion for a judgment of acquittal at the close of the government's evidence, the defendant may offer evidence without having reserved the right to do so.

(b) Reserving Decision. The court may reserve decision on the motion, proceed with the trial (where the motion is made before the close of all the evidence), submit the case to the jury, and decide the motion either before the jury returns a verdict or after it returns a verdict of guilty or is discharged without having returned a verdict. If the court reserves decision, it must decide the motion on the basis of the evidence at the time the ruling was reserved.

(c) After Jury Verdict or Discharge.

(1) Time for a Motion. A defendant may move for a judgment of acquittal, or renew such a motion, within 7 days after a guilty verdict or after the court discharges the jury, whichever is later, or within any other time the court sets during the 7-day period.

(2) Ruling on the Motion. If the jury has returned a guilty verdict, the court may set aside the verdict and enter an acquittal. If the jury has failed to return a verdict, the court may enter a judgment of acquittal.

(3) No Prior Motion Required. A defendant is not required to move for a judgment of acquittal before the court submits the case to the jury as a prerequisite for making such a motion after jury discharge.

(d) Conditional Ruling on a Motion for a New Trial.

(1) Motion for a New Trial. If the court enters a judgment of acquittal after a guilty verdict, the court must also conditionally determine whether any motion for a new trial should be granted if the judgment of acquittal is later vacated or reversed. The court must specify the reasons for that determination.

(2) Finality. The court's order conditionally granting a motion for a new trial does not affect the finality of the judgment of acquittal.

(3) Appeal.

(A) **Grant of a Motion for a New Trial.** If the court conditionally grants a motion for a new trial and an appellate court later reverses the judgment of acquittal, the trial court must proceed with the new trial unless the appellate court orders otherwise.

(B) **Denial of a Motion for a New Trial.** If the court conditionally denies a motion for a new trial, an appellee may assert that the denial was erroneous. If the appellate court later reverses the judgment of acquittal, the trial court must proceed as the appellate court directs.

NOTES

When considered at the close of the government's case under Rule 29(a), a motion for judgment of acquittal asks the trial judge to ascertain whether a jury could, based upon the evidence presented, find guilt beyond a reasonable doubt. If at that point, that particular evidentiary standard has been met, the motion will be denied and the defendant will have the opportunity to present evidence. As provided in Rule 29(b), the judge may decide to delay a decision on the motion until after the return of a verdict (discussed in further detail at the end of this chapter).

[4] Defendant's Proof

The defense has the right to "rest" and present no contradictory evidence whatsoever in response to the government's proof. This option, while risky, is chosen in cases in which the defense attorney believes that the government's evidence fails to satisfy the beyond-a-reasonable-doubt standard. The defendant is entitled to remain completely silent under the Fifth Amendment self-incrimination privilege. Ordinarily, however, the defense will present the same kind of evidence offered by the prosecution (witnesses, physical evidence, etc.).

[5] Rebuttal Proof

Most judges permit the government to offer rebuttal evidence to respond to new evidence or theories presented by defendant's proof. The defense may also be permitted to introduce rebuttal proof if the prosecutor's rebuttal raises new issues.

[6] Closing Arguments

Upon completion of prosecution and defense evidence, both prosecution and defense are allowed to present summations or closing arguments to the trier of fact. Indeed, the Supreme Court held in *Herring v. New York*, 422 U.S. 853 (1975), that denying defense counsel the opportunity to present a closing argument in a non-jury criminal trial is a violation of the Sixth Amendment assistance of counsel guarantee. During closing argument, each side will summarize its own evidence, question the reliability or meaning of the other side's proof, and try to convince the trier of fact that the necessary burden of proof has or has not been satisfied.

Prosecution may have two. In many American jurisdictions, as exemplified by Rule 29.1 of the Federal Rules of Criminal Procedure, the prosecution actually gets to make *two closing arguments.* The prosecutor makes the first closing argument. The defense lawyer makes the second closing argument. Then the prosecutor is permitted to reply to the defendant's argument. This order means that the prosecution gets the last chance to influence the trier of fact.

Legal limits. There is relatively little law on the closing argument. The trial court is given broad discretion in controlling the content, duration, and form of closing argument. For example, appellate courts have upheld a trial court's discretion on whether to permit counsel in closing argument to read from a trial transcript, to give a jury instruction correcting defense counsel's legal analysis in closing argument, to limit inflammatory remarks, and to set time limits for each side.

Many appellate courts have addressed the propriety of prosecutors' closing arguments (inflammatory, expressing personal opinions of guilt, etc.), but reversal is rare even when error is found. The harmless error doctrine is relied upon to uphold convictions in such instances. *See Darden v. Wainwright*, 477 U.S. 168 (1986)(prosecutor's closing argument deserved "condemnation" but reversal not ordered because trial not fundamentally unfair).

On the other hand, in a review of selected 1999 state and federal cases in which reversals were ordered because of improper closing arguments by prosecutors ("arguing facts not in evidence, calling the defendant a liar, and appealing to the passion of the jury"), the author concluded that convictions will be lost if " . . . the case was close, the comment went to a central issue, and the curative instructions were insufficient." *Prosecutors Checked by Round of Recent Decisions*, 13 CRIM. PRACTICE RPT. 176 (1999).

[7] Jury Instruction and Verdict

After both sides have completed their closing arguments, the judge instructs the jury (as discussed later in this chapter) and, after deliberation, the jury returns with its verdict.

F. DEFENDANT'S RIGHT TO TESTIFY

The United States Constitution contains no explicit guarantee of the right to testify on one's own behalf. While the notion of the right to "take the stand" appears to be unquestioned, this principle was not definitively established by the United States Supreme Court until *Rock v. Arkansas*, 483 U.S. 44 (1987). There, the defendant was charged with manslaughter in the death of her husband. When she could not remember the details of the shooting incident, her attorney suggested that she submit to hypnosis to refresh her memory. After hypnosis, she could remember some of the details concerning the incident. Upon learning of the hypnosis sessions, the prosecutor filed a motion to exclude the defendant's testimony. The motion was granted by the state court on the ground that under Arkansas law hypnotically-refreshed testimony is always unreliable.

The United States Supreme Court held that the state's "per se rule" of inadmissibility infringed impermissibly on the defendant's right to testify on her own behalf. The Court stated that a defendant has "the right to take the witness stand and to testify in his or her own defense." Sources of this right include (1) the Fifth Amendment's due process of law, (2) the Sixth Amendment's compulsory process clause, (3) the Sixth Amendment's right to self-representation, and (4) the Fifth Amendment's self-incrimination privilege (as a "corollary" thereto). Justices Rehnquist, White, O'Connor and Scalia dissented, arguing that the state court's decision was an "entirely permissible response to a novel and difficult question."

Polygraph evidence. In contrast to *Rock*, the United States Supreme Court has ruled that a defendant is not denied the right to present a defense where, by reason of an evidentiary rule, results of polygraph examinations (favorable to the accused) are ruled inadmissible, *United States v. Scheffer*, 523 U.S. 303 (1998). While acknowledging that individual jurisdictions may reach differing conclusions as to whether polygraph results should be admitted, the *per se* rule of exclusion (Military Rule of Evidence 707) was found to serve legitimate interests in the criminal trial process. Because Rule 707 did not preclude the defendant from introducing any factual evidence (other than the unreliable polygraph proof) pertaining to guilt or innocence, this case was distinguished from *Rock* because there, the defendant was barred from testifying in her own behalf. Justice Stevens dissented, asserting that a categorical rule that prohibits the admission of polygraph evidence in all cases, no matter how reliable or probative, is unconstitutional.

Risks of cross examination. A defendant facing the strategic issue whether or not to testify must carefully assess the risks associated with the cross-examination process. Many persons accused of crime elect not to testify on their own behalf because cross-examination by the prosecutor may disclose past criminal activity of the accused. *See* Fed. R. Evid. 609. In this sense, then, a defendant does not have an absolutely "unfettered" right to testify. Some states depart from the federal model and place tighter limits upon the prosecutor's ability to cross-examine defendants with prior crimes evidence.

Procedural hurdles. The defendant's right to testify may also be impeded by various procedural rules. For example, in *Brooks v. Tennessee*, 406 U.S. 605 (1972), a Tennessee statute required that a defendant "desiring to testify shall do so before any other testimony for the defense is heard." The United States Supreme Court found this statute to be an infringement of due process:

> Whether the defendant is to testify is an important tactical decision as well as a matter of constitutional right. By requiring the accused and his lawyer to make that choice without an opportunity to evaluate the actual worth of their evidence, the statute restricts the defense — particularly counsel — in the planning of its case. Furthermore, the penalty for not testifying first is to keep the defendant off the stand entirely, even though as a matter of professional judgment his lawyer might want to call him later in the trial. The accused is

thereby deprived of the "guiding hand of counsel" in the timing of this critical element of his defense. While nothing we say here otherwise curtails in any way the ordinary power of a trial judge to set the order of proof, the accused and his counsel may not be restricted in deciding whether, and when in the course of presenting his defense, the accused should take the stand. [406 U.S. at 612–613]

G.   DEFENDANT'S RIGHT TO NOT TESTIFY

Under the Fifth Amendment the criminal accused has a right to refuse to testify. But does this mean he or she cannot suffer any adverse legal consequences of from the decision to remain silent? The Supreme Court addresses one form of harm in the next case.

GRIFFIN v. CALIFORNIA
380 U.S. 609 (1965)

Mr. Justice Douglas delivered the opinion of the Court.

Petitioner was convicted of murder in the first degree after a jury trial in a California court. He did not testify at the trial on the issue of guilt, though he did testify at the separate trial on the issue of penalty. The trial court instructed the jury on the issue of guilt, stating that a defendant has a constitutional right not to testify. But it told the jury:

> As to any evidence or facts against him which the defendant can reasonably be expected to deny or explain because of facts within his knowledge, if he does not testify or if, though he does testify, he fails to deny or explain such evidence, the jury may take that failure into consideration as tending to indicate the truth of such evidence and as indicating that among the inferences that may be reasonably drawn therefrom those unfavorable to the defendant are the more probable.

It added, however, that no such inference could be drawn as to evidence respecting which he had no knowledge. It stated that failure of a defendant to deny or explain the evidence of which he had knowledge does not create a presumption of guilt nor by itself warrant an inference of guilt nor relieve the prosecution of any of its burden of proof.

. . . If this were a federal trial, reversible error would have been committed . . . . But that is the beginning, not the end, of our inquiry. The question remains whether- . . . the comment rule, approved by California, violates the Fifth Amendment.

We think it does. It is in substance a rule of evidence that allows the State the privilege of tendering to the jury for its consideration the failure of the accused to testify. No formal offer of proof is made as in other situations; but the prosecutor's comment and the court's acquiescence are the equivalent of an offer of evidence and its acceptance.

. . . [C]omment on the refusal to testify is a remnant of the "inquisitorial system of criminal justice," which the Fifth Amendment outlaws. It is a penalty imposed by courts for exercising a constitutional privilege. It cuts down on the privilege by making its assertion costly. It is said, however, that the inference of guilt for failure to testify as to facts peculiarly within the accused's knowledge is in any event natural and irresistible, and that comment on the failure does not magnify that inference into a penalty for asserting a constitutional privilege. What the jury may infer, given no help from the court, is one thing. What it may infer when the court solemnizes the silence of the accused into evidence against him is quite another.

. . . We . . . hold that the Fifth Amendment, in its direct application to the Federal Government and in its bearing on the States by reason of the Fourteenth Amendment, forbids either comment by the prosecution on the accused's silence or instructions by the court that such silence is evidence of guilt. Reversed.

THE CHIEF JUSTICE took no part in the decision of this case.

[JUSTICE HARLAN concurred and JUSTICES STEWART and WHITE dissented.]

NOTES

1. *Invocation of Miranda's right to remain silent.* It is well established that no negative inference can be drawn against a defendant for exercising his or her Fifth Amendment right at trial or sentencing. *Fuller v. State*, 860 A.2d 324 (Del. 2004). This extends to the prosecutor's trying to discredit the defendant's trial testimony by bringing out the defendant's assertion of *Miranda* rights after arrest. *United States v. Hill*, 222 Fed. Appx. 635 (9th Cir. 2007).

2. *Jury instructions on silence.* If the defendant chooses not to testify, no reference can be drawn from the silence. But can the judge instruct the jury to give the defendant's decision no significance? In *Lakeside v. Oregon*, 435 U.S. 333 (1978), over the defendant's objection, the trial judge instructed the jury as follows:

> Under the laws of this state a defendant has the option to take the witness stand to testify in his or her own behalf. If a defendant chooses not to testify, such a circumstance gives rise to no inference or presumption against the defendant, and this must not be considered by you in determining the question of guilt or innocence.

The defense counsel argued that the effect of such a jury instruction was like "waving a red flag in front of the jury." The United States Supreme Court rejected the claim, holding that the giving of such an instruction over the defendant's objection does not violate *Griffin*; nor does it violate the Fifth Amendment self-incrimination guarantee. The Court explained:

> The petitioner's argument would require indulgence in two very doubtful assumptions: First, that the jurors have not noticed that the defendant did not testify and will not, therefore, draw adverse inferences on their own; second, that the jurors will totally disregard the instruction, and affirmatively give weight to what they have been told not to consider at all. Federal constitutional law cannot rest on speculative assumptions so dubious as these. [435 U.S. at 340]

Entitlement to no-inference instruction. While *Lakeside* addresses the question of the propriety of giving a "no adverse inference instruction," it does not address the question whether a defendant is *entitled* to such an instruction. In *Carter v. Kentucky*, 450 U.S. 288 (1981), the United States Supreme Court held that state trial judges have a constitutional obligation, upon proper request, to give such an instruction. In that case, the defendant had requested that the jury be told that "the defendant is not compelled to testify and the fact that he does not cannot be used as an inference of guilt and should not prejudice him in any way."

3. *Sentencing.* The Court also held in *Mitchell v. United States*, 526 U.S. 314 (1999), that Griffin's no adverse inference rule also applies to defendants who do not testify at a sentencing hearing:

> The concerns which mandate the rule against negative inferences at a criminal trial apply with equal force at sentencing. Without question, the stakes are high: Here, the inference drawn by the District Court from petitioner's silence may have resulted in decades of added imprisonment. The Government often has a motive to demand a severe sentence, so the central purpose of the privilege — to protect a defendant from being the unwilling instrument of his or her own condemnation — remains of vital importance.

Note, however, that *Mitchell* was decided on a bare 5-4 majority, and that several of the dissenting Justices called the correctness of *Griffin* into question and indicated a willingness to reconsider it in the future.

4. *Comment on fact defendant testified after hearing government witnesses.* Assume that the defendant testifies after having heard the government's witnesses testify. During closing argument, the government's attorney calls the jury's attention to this fact, suggesting that the defendant's credibility should be questioned because of the opportunity afforded him to tailor his testimony to that of the witnesses. Is the prosecutor's argument prohibited by *Griffin*? The Supreme Court held in *Portuondo v. Agard*, 529 U.S. 61 (2000), that it would not "extend" *Griffin* to this practice. It reasoned that (1) *Griffin* prohibits a prosecutor from urging the jury to do something that it is not permitted to do, whereas here the jury is "perfectly entitled' to do what it was invited to do; and (2) *Griffin* prohibits comments that suggest that the defendant's silence is evidence of guilt, whereas here the comments concerned the defendant's credibility as a witness.

H.   DEFENDANT'S ACCESS TO EVIDENCE AND COMPULSORY PROCESS

[1]   Constitutional Right to Offer Witnesses

The Sixth Amendment to the United States Constitution provides, in part, that "in all criminal prosecutions, the accused shall enjoy the right . . . to have compulsory process for obtaining witnesses in his favor." In *Washington v. Texas*, 388 U.S. 14, 19 (1967), the United States Supreme Court held that this guarantee was a fundamental element of due process of law:

> The right to offer the testimony of witnesses, and to compel their attendance, if necessary, is in plain terms the right to present a defense, the right to present the defendant's version of the facts as well as the prosecution's to the jury so that it may decide where the truth lies. Just as an accused has the right to confront the prosecution's witnesses for the purpose of challenging their testimony, he has the right to present his own witnesses to establish a defense.

Under a Texas statute, the petitioner, Washington, was denied the opportunity to present the testimony of an alleged accomplice, Fuller, who "would have testified that [Washington] pulled at him and tried to persuade him to leave, and that [Washington] ran before Fuller fired the fatal shot [in the murder case]." The statute provided that persons charged or convicted as co-participants in the same crime could not testify for one another, although there was no bar to their testifying for the state. Under these circumstances, the Supreme Court held that the defendant's compulsory process rights had been denied: We hold that the petitioner . . . was denied his right to have compulsory process for obtaining witnesses in his favor because the State arbitrarily denied him the right to put on the stand a witness who was physically and mentally capable of testifying to events that he had personally observed, and whose testimony would have been relevant and material to the defense. [388 U.S. at 23]

By way of a footnote, however, the Court observed that the decision would have no bearing upon privileges such as the privilege against self-incrimination, or the lawyer-client or husband-wife privileges. This could deny a defendant the testimony of a helpful witness. Similarly, the opinion did not address what the Court called "nonarbitrary state rules that disqualify as witnesses persons who, because of mental infirmity or infancy, are incapable of observing events or testifying about them."

Chambers v. Mississippi. Six years later, the Court again evaluated rules of procedure and evidence that limited defense proof and, again, found their application constitutionally impermissible. Defendant Chambers, charged with murdering a police officer, attempted to present evidence that a third person (McDonald) actually committed the offense. Under Mississippi's "voucher rule" and its hearsay rule, however, the defense was unable to cross-examine McDonald or to present witnesses who would have testified that McDonald was responsible for the murder. While reaffirming that states possess the power to establish "their own criminal trial rules," the Court held that the exclusion of this "critical evidence . . . denied [Chambers] a trial in accord with traditional and fundamental standards of due process." *Chambers v. Mississippi*, 410 U.S. 284, 302 (1973).

In another illustrative case the United States Supreme Court reversed a death sentence because the defendant was denied the right to introduce evidence that a third party had committed the crime. *Holmes v. South Carolina*, 547 U.S. 319 (2006) (defendant's constitutional right to present a complete defense cannot be denied by evidence rules that are arbitrary or disproportionate to the interests they are to serve; state evidence law barred weak defense evidence of third person's guilt in face of strong forensic evidence of guilt).

Hypnotic refreshment again. Recall that the United States Supreme Court held in *Rock v. Arkansas*, 483 U.S. 44 (1987), that a *per se* rule of inadmissibility regarding hynotically-refreshed testimony infringed upon the *defendant*'s right to testify in her own behalf. What if such a *per se* rule barred a defense *witness* from testifying to hynotically-enhanced memories? In *Burral v. State*, 724 A.2d 65 (Md. App. 1999), the state appellate court held that the *Rock* rule does not apply to hypnosis testimony of other defense witnesses. The court explained that the rights upon which *Rock* relied were unique to defendants. Is this decision consistent with *Washington v. Texas*? With *Chambers v. Mississippi*?

[2] Subpoena Process

An important right of the criminal accused, guaranteed by the Sixth Amendment, is the right "to have compulsory process for obtaining witnesses in his favor." Rule 17 and similar rules in all jurisdictions implement this critical procedure by providing a mechanism for both sides to subpoena witnesses.

FEDERAL RULES OF CRIMINAL PROCEDURE

Rule 17. *Subpoena*

(a) Content. A subpoena must state the court's name and the title of the proceeding, include the seal of the court, and command the witness to attend and testify at the time and place the subpoena specifies. The clerk must issue a blank subpoena — signed and sealed — to the party requesting it, and that party must fill in the blanks before the subpoena is served.

(b) Defendant Unable to Pay. Upon a defendant's ex parte application, the court must order that a subpoena be issued for a named witness if the defendant shows an inability to pay the witness's fees and the necessity of the witness's presence for an adequate defense. If the court orders a subpoena to be issued, the process costs and witness fees will be paid in the same manner as those paid for witnesses the government subpoenas.

(c) Producing Documents and Objects.

(1) In General. A subpoena may order the witness to produce any books, papers, documents, data, or other objects the subpoena designates. The court may direct the witness to produce the designated items in court before trial or before they are to be offered in evidence. When the items arrive, the court may permit the parties and their attorneys to inspect all or part of them.

(2) Quashing or Modifying the Subpoena. On motion made promptly, the court may quash or modify the subpoena if compliance would be unreasonable or oppressive.

(d) Service. A marshal, a deputy marshal, or any nonparty who is at least 18 years old may serve a subpoena. The server must deliver a copy of the subpoena to the witness and must tender to the witness one day's witness-attendance fee and the legal mileage allowance. The server need not tender the attendance fee or mileage allowance when the United States, a federal officer, or a federal agency has requested the subpoena.

(e) Place of Service.

(1) In the United States. A subpoena requiring a witness to attend a hearing or trial may be served at any place within the United States.

(2) In a Foreign Country. If the witness is in a foreign country, 28 U.S.C. § 1783 governs the subpoena's service.

(f) Issuing a Deposition Subpoena.

(1) Issuance. A court order to take a deposition authorizes the clerk in the district where the deposition is to be taken to issue a subpoena for any witness named or described in the order.

(2) Place. After considering the convenience of the witness and the parties, the court may order — and the subpoena may require — the witness to appear anywhere the court designates.

(g) Contempt. The court (other than a magistrate judge) may hold in contempt a witness who, without adequate excuse, disobeys a subpoena issued by a federal court in that district. A magistrate judge may hold in contempt a witness who, without adequate excuse, disobeys a subpoena issued by that magistrate judge as provided in 28 U.S.C. § 636(e).

(h) Information Not Subject to a Subpoena. No party may subpoena a statement of a witness or of a prospective witness under this rule. Rule 26.2 governs the production of the statement.

NOTES

1. *Issued in blank.* Note that Rule 17 requires the court clerk to issue a subpoena *in blank.* This allows the prosecutor or defense counsel to fill in the blank subpoena and serve it without letting the other side know about the subpoena. This is consistent with the limited discovery of potential adverse witnesses in criminal cases.

2. *Includes items.* Rule 17(c)(1) authorizes a subpoena to order the witness to bring various items, but not statements of witnesses covered by Rules 16 (expert) and 26.2 (after witness testifies, witness's statement must be released to adverse party).

3. *Many proceedings.* Rule 17 permits subpoenas for virtually any proceeding, including grand jury, trials, preliminary hearings, and depositions.

4. *Service of subpoena.* Rule 17 follows the typical pattern of permitting service to be made by a law enforcement person or any adult who is not a party. This procedure allows each side to serve its subpoenas without informing the other side.

5. *Compliance and motion to quash.* A person receiving a subpoena must comply or face possible contempt of court under Rule 17(g). But Rule 17(c) authorizes a person to file a *motion to quash* the subpoena as being *unreasonable or oppressive.* This could occur if the subpoena requests a large number of documents, costs too much to comply, or were too broad.

The person who is subpoenaed may also assert a privilege, such as the Fifth Amendment's self incrimination ban.

6. *Indigent's special procedures.* Examine the language of paragraph (b), pertaining to cases in which the defendant is unable to pay the fees of the witness. By requiring that the indigent defendant establish that "the presence of the witness is necessary to an adequate defense," is not the accused required, in effect, to disclose the theory of his or her defense? The problem is solved by having the indigent seek the subpoena in an *ex parte* proceeding where the prosecutor is not present. *See United States v. Abreu,* 202 F.3d 386 (1st Cir. 2000) (for sentencing purposes because defendant was indigent, his counsel applied for government funding of expert services and sought an evaluation by a licensed psychologist. Although 18 U.S.C. § 3006A made such applications an *ex parte* hearing, the trial court held an adversary proceeding because it said only sentencing was involved. The appellate court vacated the sentence, holding an *ex parte* hearing had to be conducted to protect appellant from revealing his defense prior to sentencing and to prevent him from being punished for being indigent).

Actual prejudice. The defendant has the burden of showing actual prejudice if an error occurs in an indigent's efforts to obtain the free subpoena. *See United States v. Meriwether*, 486 F.2d 498 (5th Cir. 1973)(prosecutor's presence during defendant's *ex parte* application for subpoenas was error, but that defendant did not meet burden of showing actual prejudice because the error occurred before the second trial of the case and prosecutor had been informed of defendant's witness list during first trial); *United States v. Brinkman*, 739 F.2d 977 (4th Cir. 1984) (defendant failed to meet the burden of showing prejudice where the government did not contact any of the defense's witnesses and the only action taken by the government as a result was to quash a subpoena of its own for a witness it already knew about).

7. *Subpoena of expert.* While the defendant may be disadvantaged by the procedures in Rule 17, it can also be argued that the indigent defendant has an advantage over the non-indigent accused in some respects. For example, the language of Rule 17(b) may enable the indigent defendant to obtain expert testimony (in an insanity defense case, for example), while the non-indigent would be financially unable to obtain the same kind of expert testimony. Note that if an indigent defendant wants to subpoena an expert, he or she has the burden of proving that the expert's services are "necessary to an adequate defense" under Rule 17(b). Trial courts are given wide discretion in determining when the defendant has met this burden, and the standard of review is abuse of discretion. These determinations are extremely fact-specific.

For instance, in *United States v. Julian*, 469 F.2d 371 (10th Cir. 1972), the court found that a trial court's denial of defendant's request to have a psychiatrist subpoenaed was an abuse of discretion where the defendant was raising the insanity defense and the only other available witness had committed himself to the notion that the defendant was sane at the time of the offense. By contrast, the Fifth Circuit, in *United States v. Joyner*, 494 F.2d 501 (5th Cir. 1974), found no abuse of discretion where defendant wanted to subpoena a witness at government expense to impeach the key government witness, defendant's co-conspirator, by saying that the government witness had a reputation for lying and untrustworthiness. Defendant presented no evidence that this character witness knew anything about the origin of these accusations or the community in which they allegedly existed. Thus, the appellate court concluded that the trial court's denial of the request was well within that court's discretion.

8. *Due process mandated payment of expert's fees.* Due process may require the appointment of a state-paid expert to assist the defense in unusual cases. *See, e.g., Ake v. Oklahoma*, 470 U.S. 68 (1985) (state must pay for psychiatric examination of indigent criminal defendant whose sanity was seriously in question). *See generally* Gordon B. Burns, *The Right to the Effective Assistance of a Psychiatrist Under Ake v. Oklahoma*, 30 Crim. L. Bull., 429 (1994). Statutes may also provide government funds to pay defense experts. *See, e.g.*, 18 U.S.C. § 3006A(e)(1) (federal funding available to federal defendants unable to afford necessary "investigative, expert, or other services").

9. *Government's special responsibilities for defense witnesses.* Does the compulsory process guarantee place any significant restrictions on the way in which the government deals with individuals who might be witnesses for the accused? In *United States v. Valenzuela-Bernal*, 458 U.S. 858 (1982), the defendant was indicted for transporting an illegal alien in violation of federal law. Two of the three passengers who admitted that they were illegally in the country were immediately deported to Mexico after an Assistant United States Attorney concluded that they possessed no evidence material to the prosecution or defense. A third passenger was detained to provide a nonhearsay basis for establishing that the defendant had violated the federal statute. The accused moved to dismiss the indictment, claiming that the deportation of the two passengers violated his Fifth Amendment right to due process and his Sixth Amendment right to compulsory process for obtaining favorable witnesses. The motion was denied and the defendant was convicted.

The United States Supreme Court concluded that the government's action was proper. First, it held that prompt deportation of such witnesses who were determined by the government to possess no material evidence was justified by practical considerations (pointing out overcrowded detention facilities and related budgetary limitations). Second, the Court emphasized that the defendant had failed to make at least a plausible showing of how the deported aliens' testimony would have been both material and favorable to his defense. The Court concluded:

> [T]he responsibility of the Executive Branch faithfully to execute the immigration policy adopted by Congress justifies the prompt deportation of illegal-alien witnesses upon the Executive's good faith determination that they possess no evidence favorable to the defendant in a criminal prosecution. The mere fact that the Government deports such witnesses is not sufficient to establish a violation of the Compulsory Process Clause of the Sixth Amendment or the Due Process Clause of the Fifth Amendment. A violation of these provisions requires some showing that the evidence lost would be both material and favorable to the defense. [458 U.S. at 872–873]

Justices Brennan and Marshall dissented, pointing out that in this case the government had deported these witnesses before the defendant or his attorney had an opportunity to interview them, thereby "depriving [the defendant] of the surest and most obvious means by which he could establish the materiality and relevance of such witnesses' testimony."

Do you agree with the majority in *Valenzuela-Bernal*? Would your view change if the government had deported the two passengers after learning that they could provide testimony helpful to the defense?

If you believe the government should not have been permitted to deport these potential defense witnesses, what should it have done? Kept the two in jail until trial (recall they were in the country illegally)? Released them but monitored their whereabouts? If the witnesses had been released, would the government have to allow them to work (recall they were in the country illegally)? If not, how would they have supported themselves?

10. *Disclosure of informant's identity.* What if the defendant desires to learn of the identity of a prosecution witness so that the witness can be interviewed by the defense? In *Roviaro v. United States*, 353 U.S. 53 (1957), cited and discussed in the *Valenzuela-Bernal* opinion, the United States Supreme Court held on the specific facts of the case that the government was obligated to disclose to the defense the name of an informer-eyewitness. While the government maintained that the refusal to disclose was justified based upon the traditional informant privilege, the Court held that disclosure was required because, on the facts of the case, the informer's testimony would be highly relevant:

> This is a case where the Government's informer was the sole participant, other than the accused, in the transaction charged. The informer was the only witness in a position to amplify or contradict the testimony of government witnesses. Moreover, a government witness testified that [the informer] denied knowing petitioner or ever having seen him before. We conclude that, under these circumstances, the trial court committed prejudicial error in permitting the Government to withhold the identity of its undercover employee in the face of repeated demands by the accused for his disclosure. [353 U.S. at 64–65]

As explained by the Court in *Valenzuela-Bernal*, *Roviaro* imposes upon the defendant who has not had the opportunity to interview a witness "a difficult task in making a showing of materiality [but] the task is not an impossible one." Finally, it was pointed out that the *Roviaro* ruling was not decided on the basis of constitutional claims. It should be noted, however, that the majority opinion in *Roviaro* characterized its analysis in the following terms:

> The problem is one that calls for balancing the public interest in protecting the flow of information against the individual's right to prepare his defense. Whether a proper balance renders nondisclosure erroneous must depend on the particular circumstances of each case, taking into consideration the crime charged, the possible defenses, the possible significance of the informer's testimony, and other relevant factors. [353 U.S. at 62]

See also Banks v. Dretke, 540 U.S. 668 (2004)(prosecution failed to disclose the informant's status and did not correct the informant's false testimony that he did not talk to police until shortly before trial; inmate's failure to investigate the witness's status as an informant resulted from the prosecution's believable persistent misrepresentations and omissions concerning such status; defendant was prejudiced since the prosecution relied heavily on the informant's penalty phase testimony about the inmate's propensity to commit further crimes).

11. *Immunity for defense witnesses.* If it is appropriate, according to *Roviaro*, to request the government to relinquish the informer's privilege to remain anonymous so as to assist the defendant's right to gain access to an important witness, could (or should) the same principle apply in the case of a witness for the *defense* who refuses to testify by asserting his or her self-incrimination privilege? The issue is raised when the defense asks the trial judge to confer use immunity on such witnesses so the witnesses will be able to testify and can no longer invoke the Fifth Amendment. In *United States v. Wilson*, 715 F.2d 1164 (7th Cir. 1983), this argument was summarily rejected:

> That power [to request immunity] belongs exclusively to the executive branch. And, we will not review a prosecutor's immunization decisions in the absence of substantial evidence showing that the prosecutor's actions amounted to a clear abuse of discretion violating the due process clause. Defendants have made no such showing here. Thus, we hold that the district court properly denied defendants' request to order use immunity for certain witnesses, and that there was no abuse of discretion in government's decision not to confer immunity. [715 F.2d at 1172]

In a later case, the Seventh Circuit Court of Appeals expressed the view that such an abuse of discretion occurs "when a prosecutor intends to use his authority under the immunity statute to distort the judicial fact-finding process." *United States v. Taylor*, 728 F.2d 930, 935 (7th Cir. 1984).

One court studied the few cases on point and recognized two theories supporting the conclusion that due process and compulsory process require the state to immunize defense witnesses. The two are the *effective defense* theory (the defense is significantly hampered without immunity) and the *prosecutorial misconduct* theory (prosecutor forces defense witnesses to assert Fifth Amendment or engages in a discriminatory grant of immunity to obtain an advantage). *State v. Ayuso*, 937 A.2d 1211 (Conn. App. 2008).

12. *Court's obligation to assist defense.* Besides the government, the court also has a burden to assure that a defendant has a chance to present witnesses. In one case, the defendant contended that the trial court erred by precluding him from calling the alleged victim of the assault as a witness. The court of appeals held that although the victim had refused to cooperate at appellant's first trial, which ended in a mistrial, the appellant still had a right under the Sixth Amendment to call the victim as a witness at the second trial. Therefore, they held the trial court had abused its discretion by denying the request without first determining whether the victim would, indeed, refuse to cooperate in the second trial. *State v. Carlos*, 17 P.3d 118 (Ariz. App. 2001).

13. *Ex post facto considerations.* Sometimes a rule of evidence or similar statutory provision is amended in such a way as to ease the government's burden of proof. When this occurs, the *ex post facto* guarantee may be implicated. In *Carmell v. Texas*, 529 U.S. 513 (2000), a Texas statute authorized conviction of certain offenses on the victim's testimony alone. The previous statute, however, required both the victim's testimony and other corroborating evidence to convict. Carmell's trial occurred *after* the effective date of the "new" statute, but the offense occurred before that effective date. Quoting from *Calder v. Bull*, 3 Dall. 386, 390 (1798), the Supreme Court recognized that the *ex post facto* prohibition applies to "every law that alters the legal rules of evidence, and receives less, or different, testimony, than the law required at the time of the commission of the offense, in order to convict the offender." Finding that this provision plainly applies to Carmell and that "fundamental justice" requires the government to abide by its own rules, the court held that Carmell's convictions using the new rules could not be sustained under the *ex post facto* clause. The four dissenters argued that it is permissible to retroactively apply changes in rules concerning admissibility of evidence and competency of witnesses.

I. THE RIGHT TO CROSS-EXAMINE AND CONFRONT WITNESSES

[1] Cross-Examination

In *Pointer v. Texas*, 380 U.S. 400 (1965), the United States Supreme Court held that the accused in a criminal case has both the right to confront witnesses and, as a necessary corollary, the right of cross-examination. While this principle is considered essential to a fundamentally fair trial, numerous issues arise with respect to limitations upon the cross-examination right.

Scope of cross examination: limited and wide-open approaches. Under the Federal Rules of Evidence and in a majority of states, for example, cross-examination is restricted to matters testified to by the witness on direct examination and to issues of credibility. See Fed. R. Evid. 611(b). This is often called the *limited* or *federal* approach.

Approximately fifteen states, on the other hand, adopt the so-called *wide open* approach in which the witness may be cross-examined about any subject relevant to any of the issues in the entire case, including facts related solely to the cross-examiner's own case or to an affirmative defense. In some of those jurisdictions, the trial judge may, in the interest of justice, limit the scope of cross-examination with respect to matters not testified to on direct. *See, e.g.,* Ky. R. Evid. 611(b); N.H. R. Evid. 611(b); Wisc. Stat. § 906.11(2).

Constitutionality of limits on cross examination. Are statutes or court rulings that impose limits on cross-examination constitutionally permissible? In *Delaware v. Van Arsdall*, 475 U.S. 673, 679 (1986), the United States Supreme Court ruled that appropriate limitations may be imposed:

> [T]rial judges retain wide latitude insofar as the Confrontation Clause is concerned to impose reasonable limits on such cross-examination based on concerns about, among other things, harassment, prejudice, confusion of the issues, the witness' safety, or interrogation that is repetitive or only marginally relevant. [The Confrontation Clause] guarantees an opportunity for effective cross-examination, not cross-examination that is effective in whatever way, and to whatever extent, the defense might wish.

Time limits. Similarly, time constraints upon cross-examination have been upheld. *See United States v. Vest*, 116 F.3d 1179 (7th Cir. 1997) (holding that trial judge properly exercised discretion in placing time limits on defense counsel's cross-examination of government's experts).

Name and address of witness. The Supreme Court has held that the accused is entitled under the Sixth Amendment to cross-examine an informer who was the principal prosecution witness as to his actual name and address:

> [The defendant] was denied the right to ask the principal prosecution witness either his name or where he lived, although the witness admitted that the name he had first given was false. Yet when the credibility of a witness is in issue, the very starting point in "exposing falsehood and bringing out the truth" through cross-examination must necessarily be to ask the witness who he is and where he lives. The witness' name and address open countless avenues of in-court examination and out-of-court investigation. To forbid this most rudimentary inquiry at the threshold is effectively to emasculate the right of cross-examination itself. [*Smith v. Illinois*, 390 U.S. 129, 131 (1968)]

Status as probationer. Similarly, in *Davis v. Alaska*, 415 U.S. 308 (1974), the Court held that the trial court erred in refusing to allow the defendant to cross-examine a key prosecution witness to show that the witness had been placed on probation following an adjudication of juvenile delinquency. The state claimed that cross-examination had been properly restricted because of its interest in protecting the anonymity of juvenile offenders. The defense desired to pursue this line of questioning, however, in the hopes that it would show that the government had control over the witness's post-testimony freedom. While the Court acknowledged that states may implement policies to protect juvenile offenders, such an interest was outweighed, on the facts of this case, by the defendant's Sixth Amendment right to cross-examine the witness to determine whether the witness was biased.

NOTES

1. *Remedy for violation of right to impeach witnesses.* Assume that a defendant is denied the right to impeach a witness through appropriate cross-examination questioning. Following conviction, must the appellate court automatically reverse or is such an error subject to harmless error analysis? In *Delaware v. Van Arsdall, supra,* the Court rejected the *per se* reversal rule, holding that harmless-error analysis applies:

> The correct inquiry is whether, assuming that the damaging potential of the cross-examination were fully realized, a reviewing court might nonetheless say that the error was harmless beyond a reasonable doubt. Whether such an error is harmless in a particular case depends upon a host of factors, all readily accessible to reviewing courts. These factors include the importance of the witness' testimony in the prosecution's case, whether the testimony was cumulative, the presence or absence of evidence corroborating or contradicting the testimony of the witness on material points, the extent of cross-examination otherwise permitted, and, of course, the overall strength of the prosecution's case. [475 U.S. at 684]

Justice Marshall dissented, expressing the view that "a complete denial of otherwise proper cross-examination concerning the potential bias of a prosecution witness should lead to no less than a reversal of the conviction." He explained:

> [A]n appellate court attempting to apply harmless-error analysis is faced with a formidable burden. The court cannot merely satisfy itself that the jury would have reached the same result had the witness in question not appeared at all; it must be convinced beyond a reasonable doubt that the jury would have reached the same result even if cross-examination had led the jury affirmatively to believe that the witness was lying. Moreover, the court must conclude, beyond a reasonable doubt, that no evidence exculpatory to the defendant could

have emerged from a genuinely adversarial testing of the witness. I think that a court can make such a determination only in the rarest of circumstances, and a rule of *per se* reversal is therefore justified. [475 U.S. at 688]

2. *Limits on cross examination of victims of sexual assault.* Almost all jurisdictions, including the federal government, have *rape shield* laws restricting the defendant's ability to cross-examine rape victims with regard to evidence of past sexual history. Rule 412 of the Federal Rules of Evidence, following the pattern established by state statutes, disallows such evidence but recognizes situations in which such inquiry will be allowed, such as where the past sexual behavior was with a person other than the accused and is offered by the defendant to explain the source of semen or injury to the victim. *See,* Shawn J. Wallach, Note, *Rape Shield Laws: Protecting the Victim at the Expense of the Defendant's Constitutional Rights*, 13 N.Y.L. Sch. J. Hum. Rts. 485 (1997) (identifying and evaluating four approaches to rape shield legislation taken by different jurisdictions).

Some commentators have argued that these statutes, by prohibiting access to potentially relevant evidence, may run afoul of the cross-examination guarantee. *See* J. Alexander Tanford & Anthony J. Bocchino, *Rape Victim Laws and the Sixth Amendment*, 128 U. Pa. L. Rev. 544 (1980).

[2]   Confrontation

The preceding section related to cross-examination assumes that a witness has testified for the prosecution and is physically available for cross-examination. In most instances, testimony from a witness deemed favorable to the prosecution will be presented in "live" form. On occasion, however, testimony is offered in a way that effectively deprives the defendant of the right to confront the witness physically.

A literal interpretation of the confrontation clause of the Sixth Amendment would require the physical presence of all adverse witnesses. As this section of the chapter demonstrates, the Sixth Amendment does not require actual presence of witnesses in all cases.

Both confrontation and cross-examination issues may arise in those instances in which the government seeks to offer testimonial evidence from a person not physically testifying in open court. Sometimes a witness is not brought to open court in order to protect him or her from real or perceived harm (for example, child witnesses). More commonly, the government may seek to offer hearsay testimony under circumstances in which a witness is not physically available to testify at trial.

[a]   "In-Court" Testimony and the Confrontation Clause

[i]   Face to Face Confrontation and Use of Videoconferencing

In order to protect child witnesses from the trauma that may be associated with testifying in open court about the abuse they experienced, a number of jurisdictions have adopted various procedures that shelter such witnesses from having to testify in an open courtroom atmosphere.

In *Coy v. Iowa*, 487 U.S. 1012 (1988), two thirteen-year-old sexual assault victims were permitted to testify by being seated behind a large screen placed between the accused and the witness stand. The witnesses would not be able to see the defendant, but with lighting adjustments the defendant would be "dimly [able] to perceive the witnesses." The United States Supreme Court, holding that the defendant's Sixth Amendment rights were violated, concluded that the confrontation clause guarantees the defendant a face-to-face meeting with witnesses:

It is always more difficult to tell a lie about a person "to his face" than "behind his back." . . . The Confrontation Clause does not, of course, compel the witness to fix his eyes upon the defendant; he may studiously look elsewhere, but the trier of fact will draw its own conclusions . . . . The State can hardly gainsay the profound effect upon a witness of standing in the presence of the person the witness accuses, since that is the very phenomenon it relies upon to establish the potential "trauma" that allegedly justified the extraordinary procedure in the present case. That face-to-face presence may, unfortunately, upset the truthful rape victim or abused child; but by the same token it may confound and undo the false accuser, or reveal the child coached by a malevolent adult. It is a truism that constitutional protections have costs. [487 U.S. at 1019–1020]

The state asserted that the defendant's confrontation rights were outweighed by the necessity of protecting the minor witnesses. While the Court in *Coy* acknowledged that confrontation rights may, in some circumstances, give way to other important interests, such a determination could not be made in this case because there had been "no individualized findings that these particular witnesses needed special protection."

[ii] Videoconferencing

Two years later, the Supreme Court addressed the constitutionality of another procedure designed to protect the child witness: one-way closed circuit television.

MARYLAND v. CRAIG
497 U.S. 836 (1990)

JUSTICE O'CONNOR delivered the opinion of the Court.

This case requires us to decide whether the Confrontation Clause of the Sixth Amendment categorically prohibits a child witness in a child abuse case from testifying against a defendant at trial, outside the defendant's physical presence, by one-way closed circuit television. . . .

[Defendant Craig was indicted for various sex offenses against a six-year-old girl who attended a kindergarten and prekindergarten center owned and operated by the defendant.]

In March 1987, before the case went to trial, the State sought to invoke a Maryland statutory procedure that permits a judge to receive, by one-way closed circuit television, the testimony of a child witness who is alleged to be a victim of child abuse. To invoke the procedure, the trial judge must first "determin[e] that testimony by the child victim in the courtroom will result in the child suffering serious emotional distress such that the child cannot reasonably communicate." Md. Cts. & Jud. Proc. Code Ann. § 9-102(a)(1)(ii) (1989). Once the procedure is invoked, the child witness, prosecutor, and defense counsel withdraw to a separate room; the judge, jury, and defendant remain in the courtroom. The child witness is then examined and cross-examined in the separate room, while a video monitor records and displays the witness's testimony to those in the courtroom. During this time the witness cannot see the defendant. The defendant remains in electronic communication with defense counsel, and objections may be made and ruled on as if the witness were testifying in the courtroom.

In support of its motion invoking the one-way closed circuit television procedure, the State presented expert testimony that the named victim as well as a number of other children who were alleged to have been sexually abused by Craig, would suffer "serious emotional distress such that [they could not] reasonably communicate," § 9-102(a)(1)(ii), if required to testify in the courtroom. The Maryland Court of Appeals characterized the evidence as follows:

The expert testimony in each case suggested that each child would have some or considerable difficulty in testifying in Craig's presence. For example, as to one child, the expert said that what "would cause him the most anxiety would be to testify in front of Mrs. Craig . . . ." The child "wouldn't be able to communicate effectively." As to another, an expert said she "would probably stop talking and she would withdraw and curl up." With respect to two others, the testimony was that one would "become highly agitated, that he may refuse to talk or if he did talk, that he would choose his subject regardless of the questions" while the other would "become extremely timid and unwilling to talk."

Craig objected to the use of the procedure on Confrontation Clause grounds, but the trial court rejected that contention, concluding that although the statute "take[s] away the right of the defendant to be face to face with his or her accuser," the defendant retains the "essence of the right of confrontation," including the right to observe, cross-examine, and have the jury view the demeanor of the witness. The trial court further found that, "based upon the evidence presented . . . the testimony of each of these children in a courtroom will result in each child suffering serious emotional distress . . . such that each of these children cannot reasonably communicate." The trial court then found the named victim and three other children competent to testify and accordingly permitted them to testify against Craig via the one-way closed circuit television procedure.

[Craig was convicted by a jury on all counts, but the Maryland appellate court reversed, holding that the showing made by the state was insufficient to reach the threshold required by *Coy* for invocation of the statute. The U.S. Supreme Court granted certiorari.]

. . . [I]n *Coy v. Iowa*, we expressly "le[ft] for another day . . . the question whether any exceptions exist" to the "irreducible literal meaning of the Clause: 'a right to meet face to face all those who appear and give evidence at trial.' " The procedure challenged in *Coy* involved the placement of a screen that prevented two child witnesses in a child abuse case from seeing the defendant as they testified against him at trial. In holding that the use of this procedure violated the defendant's right to confront witnesses against him, we suggested that any exception to the right "would surely be allowed only when necessary to further an important public policy" — *i.e.*, only upon a showing of something more than the generalized, "legislatively imposed presumption of trauma" underlying the statute at issue in that case. We concluded that "[s]ince there ha[d] been no individualized findings that these particular witnesses needed special protection, the judgment [in the case before us] could not be sustained by any conceivable exception." Because the trial court in this case made individualized findings that each of the child witnesses needed special protection, this case requires us to decide the question reserved in *Coy*.

The central concern of the Confrontation Clause is to ensure the reliability of the evidence against a criminal defendant by subjecting it to rigorous testing in the context of an adversary proceeding before the trier of fact. The word "confront," after all, also means a clashing of forces or ideas, thus carrying with it the notion of adversariness. As we noted in our earliest case interpreting the Clause:

> The primary object of the constitutional provision in question was to prevent depositions or *ex parte* affidavits, such as were sometimes admitted in civil cases, being used against the prisoner in lieu of a personal examination and cross-examination of the witness in which the accused has an opportunity, not only of testing the recollection and sifting the conscience of the witness, but of compelling him to stand face to face with the jury in order that they may look at him, and judge by his demeanor upon the stand and the manner in which he gives his testimony whether he is worthy of belief. *Mattox v. United States*, 156 U.S. 237, 242–243 (1895).

As this description indicates, the right guaranteed by the Confrontation Clause includes not only a "personal examination," but also "(1) insures that the witness will give his statements under oath — thus impressing him with the seriousness of the matter and guarding against the lie by the possibility of a penalty for perjury; (2) forces the witness to submit to cross-examination, the 'greatest legal engine ever invented for the discovery of truth'; [and] (3) permits the jury that is to decide the defendant's fate to observe the demeanor of the witness in making his statement, thus aiding the jury in assessing his credibility."

. . . [W]e have never insisted on an actual face-to-face encounter at trial in every instance in which testimony is admitted against a defendant. Instead, we have repeatedly held that the Clause permits, where necessary, the admission of certain hearsay statements against a defendant despite the defendant's inability to confront the declarant at trial . . . . Thus, in certain narrow circumstances, "competing interests, if 'closely examined,' may warrant dispensing with confrontation at trial."

. . . Maryland's statutory procedure, when invoked, prevents a child witness from seeing the defendant as he or she testifies against the defendant at trial. We find it significant, however, that Maryland's procedure preserves all of the other elements of the confrontation right: The child witness must be competent to testify and must testify under oath; the defendant retains full opportunity for contemporaneous cross-examination; and the judge, jury, and defendant are able to view (albeit by video monitor) the demeanor (and body) of the witness as he or she testifies. Although we are mindful of the many subtle effects face-to-face confrontation may have on an adversary criminal proceeding, the presence of these other elements of confrontation — oath, cross-examination, and observation of the witness' demeanor — adequately ensures that the testimony is both reliable and subject to rigorous adversarial testing in a manner functionally equivalent to that accorded live, in-person testimony. These safeguards of reliability and adversariness render the use of such a procedure a far cry from the undisputed prohibition of the Confrontation Clause: trial by *ex parte* affidavit or inquisition.

. . . We likewise conclude today that a State's interest in the physical and psychological well-being of child abuse victims may be sufficiently important to outweigh, at least in some cases, a defendant's right to face his or her accusers in court. That a significant majority of States have enacted statutes to protect child witnesses from the trauma of giving testimony in child abuse cases attests to the widespread belief in the importance of such a public policy.

. . . In sum, we conclude that where necessary to protect a child witness from trauma that would be caused by testifying in the physical presence of the defendant, at least where such trauma would impair the child's ability to communicate, the Confrontation Clause does not prohibit use of a procedure that, despite the absence of face-to-face confrontation, ensures the reliability of the evidence by subjecting it to rigorous adversarial testing and thereby preserves the essence of effective confrontation. Because there is no dispute that the child witnesses in this case testified under oath, were subject to full cross-examination, and were able to be observed by the judge, jury, and defendant as they testified, we conclude that, to the extent that a proper finding of necessity has been made, the admission of such testimony would be consonant with the Confrontation Clause.

[The Maryland Court of Appeals appeared to have rested its conclusion on the trial court's failure to observe the child witness' behavior in the defendant's presence and also its failure to explore less restrictive alternatives to the use of the closed circuit television procedure. The Supreme Court declined to establish, as a matter of federal constitutional law, that any such categorical evidentiary prerequisite was necessary for the use of the closed circuit television procedure. But because the Maryland appellate court held that the trial judge had not made the requisite finding of necessity, the case was vacated and remanded for further proceedings.]

JUSTICE SCALIA, with whom JUSTICE BRENNAN, JUSTICE MARSHALL, and JUSTICE STEVENS join, dissenting.

Seldom has this Court failed so conspicuously to sustain a categorical guarantee of the Constitution against the tide of prevailing current opinion. The Sixth Amendment provides, with unmistakable clarity, that "[i]n all criminal prosecutions, the accused shall enjoy the right . . . to be confronted with the witnesses against him." The purpose of enshrining this protection in the Constitution was to assure that none of the many policy interests from time to time pursued by statutory law could overcome a defendant's right to face his or her accusers in court. The Court, [in the majority opinion] however, says:

> We . . . conclude today that a State's interest in the physical and psycho-logical well-being of child abuse victims may be sufficiently important to outweigh, at least in some cases, a defendant's right to face his or her accusers in court. That a significant majority of States have enacted statutes to protect child witnesses from the trauma of giving testimony in child abuse cases attests to the widespread belief in the importance of such a public policy.

Because of this subordination of explicit constitutional text to currently favored public policy, the following scene can be played out in an American courtroom for the first time in two centuries: A father whose young daughter has been given over to the exclusive custody of his estranged wife, or a mother whose young son has been taken into custody by the State's child welfare department, is sentenced to prison for sexual abuse on the basis of testimony by a child the parent has not seen or spoken to for many months; and the guilty verdict is rendered without giving the parent so much as the opportunity to sit in the presence of the child, and to ask, personally or through counsel, "it is really not true, is it, that I — your father (or mother) whom you see before you — did these terrible things?" Perhaps that is a procedure today's society desires; perhaps (though I doubt it) it is even a fair procedure; but it is assuredly not a procedure permitted by the Constitution.

Because the text of the Sixth Amendment is clear, and because the Constitution is meant to protect against, rather than conform to, current "widespread belief," I respectfully dissent.

According to the Court, "we cannot say that [face-to-face] confrontation [with witnesses appearing at trial] is an indispensable element of the Sixth Amendment's guarantee of the right to confront one's accusers." That is rather like saying "we cannot say that being tried before a jury is an indispensable element of the Sixth Amendment's guarantee of the right to jury trial." The Court makes the impossible plausible by recharacterizing the Confrontation Clause, so that confrontation (redesignated "face-to-face confrontation") becomes only one of many "elements of confrontation." The reasoning is as follows: The Confrontation Clause guarantees not only what it explicitly provides for — "face-to-face" confrontation — but also implied and collateral rights such as cross-examination, oath, and observation of demeanor (TRUE); the purpose of this entire cluster of rights is to ensure the reliability of evidence (TRUE); the Maryland procedure preserves the implied and collateral rights (TRUE), which adequately ensure the reliability of evidence (perhaps TRUE); therefore the Confrontation Clause is not violated by denying what it explicitly provides for — "face-to-face" confrontation (unquestionably FALSE). This reasoning abstracts from the right to its purposes, and then eliminates the right. It is wrong because the Confrontation Clause does not guarantee reliable evidence; it guarantees specific trial procedures that were thought to assure reliable evidence, undeniably among which was "face-to-face" confrontation. Whatever else it may mean in addition, the defendant's constitutional right "to be confronted with the witnesses against him" means, always and everywhere, at least what it explicitly says: the "right to meet face to face all those who appear and give evidence at trial." . . .

NOTES

1. *Craig v. Coy.* Note the adamant dissent in *Craig* by Justice Scalia, the author of the *Coy* opinion. Are the *Coy* and *Craig* cases reconcilable? Is Justice Scalia correct in his assertion that the *Craig* majority eviscerates the central holding in *Coy* that the constitution guarantees a face-to-face meeting between defendant and accuser?

2. *Shield between defendant and witness.* Assume that a state statute allows a child victim to testify by way of closed-circuit television if it is determined by the judge that in-court testimony "will result in the child's suffering serious emotional distress." If the judge decides that the child would not suffer such distress if testifying in the presence of the *jury* so long as she could not observe the *defendant*, would it be constitutionally permissible to erect a shield between the defendant and the witness as a "modified courtroom setup" to avoid use of the closed-circuit television procedure? In *People v. Lofton*, 740 N.E.2d 782 (Ill. 2000), the Illinois Supreme Court held that this procedure violated the defendant's right to confrontation under both the United States and Illinois Constitutions:

> Here the defendant's ability to observe the manner of the witness while testifying could have prejudiced him by limiting his ability to suggest lines of examination to his attorney that might have been indispensable to effective cross-examination. Unlike the use of one-way closed-circuit television provided for by the legislature . . . and found permissible in *Craig*, the barricade . . . erected [between the witness and the accused] precluded the defendant from seeing her while she testified. [*Id.* at 794]

Does it seem sensible that trial judges should be limited to either "full" in-court testimony, consistent with *Coy*, or the closed-circuit television "out of court" procedure authorized by *Craig*?

3. *Effect on jurors' perceptions.* What are the effects of closed-circuit technology on jurors' perceptions of witnesses and defendants? In one study, it was found that when children testified by means of closed-circuit television, the defendant was no more likely to be convicted; additionally, the trial was not viewed as more unfair to the defendant. By contrast, the use of closed-circuit technology was associated with a negative juror bias against child witnesses. Children who testified via closed-circuit television were viewed as less believable than children who testified in open court. Gail S. Goodman, et al., *Face-to-Face Confrontation: Effects of Closed-Circuit Technology on Children's Eyewitness Testimony and Jurors' Decisions*, 22 LAW & HUM. BEHAV., 165 (1998).

4. *Effect on defendant's communications with defense counsel.* If the witness is to testify outside the physical presence of the defendant and defense counsel, the process must ensure that the defendant can communicate effectively with defense counsel during the testimony. *See, e.g., United States v. Miguel*, 111 F.3d 666 (9th Cir. 1997)(rejecting procedure by which child sex abuse victim gave deposition in presence of judge and lawyer with defendant watching on television but unable to communicate with defense lawyer; violates defendant's right to contemporaneous communication with his lawyer).

5. *Impact in pro se cases.* In the cases above, the Supreme Court stressed that, while the defendant has been separated from the witness by a physical barrier, the defense attorney retains full access to the witness. What are the implications of such procedural mechanisms on defendants wishing to represent themselves? *See* William F. Lane, Note, *Explicit Limitations on the Implicit Right to Self-Representation in Child Sexual Abuse Trials: Fields v. Murray*, 74 N.C. L. REV. 863 (1996).

6. *State permutations.* Some state courts have refused to go as far as the United States Supreme Court in upholding the use of these special procedures for child witnesses. In *Commonwealth v. Bergstrom*, 524 N.E.2d 366 (Mass. 1988), the Massachusetts Supreme Judicial Court held that a closed-circuit testimony procedure violated the defendant's state constitutional confrontation guarantees. Similarly, in *Myles v. State*, 602 So. 2d 1278 (Fla. 1992), the Florida Supreme Court held that a closed-circuit procedure which included an oral relay system whereby the defendant was required to communicate with counsel by oral messages delivered by the bailiff to the room in which the child was testifying, violated the defendant's right to the assistance of counsel under the state constitution and infringed on the privacy of attorney-client communications.

7. *Federal legislative response to Craig.* Shortly after *Craig*, Congress enacted 18 U.S.C. § 3509 under which a court may order that a child witness testify "in a room outside the courtroom . . . televised by a 2-way closed circuit television." This procedure requires the trial court to determine that "the child is unable to testify in open court in the presence of the defendant" because "of fear" or "a substantial likelihood, established by expert testimony, that the child would suffer emotional trauma from testifying." In *United States v. Etimani*, 382 F.3d 493 (9th Cir. 2003), the statute was held constitutional and properly applied; the court also rejected the defendant's argument that the statute required that the television monitor be located directly in the child's field of vision while the child testified.

8. *Suggested alternate means of taking child testimony.* Although many states have enacted legislation to comply with the strict constitutional standards set forth in *Maryland v. Craig*, no formal structure is given to attorneys and courts as to when and under what circumstances alternative means of taking child testimony should take place. To remedy this, the National Conference of Commissioners on Uniforms State Laws proposed the Uniform Act on Taking Testimony of Children by Alternative Methods. The act applies to all children under the age of thirteen who may be called as witnesses in either criminal or noncriminal proceedings. It gives direction and structure across state jurisdictions for handling particularly vulnerable child witnesses, while aiming to strike a balance between protecting the interests of child witnesses and the rights of parties. The Uniform Act has now been adopted by a few states and is being considered in others.

[b]   "Out-of-Court" Testimony and the Confrontation Clause

As noted earlier, if the confrontation clause were interpreted to guarantee an absolute right to confront and cross-examine the declarant, then many exceptions to the rule against hearsay, such as dying declarations, would be inadmissible as evidence.

[i]   *Ohio v. Roberts*

The current approach to the problem of confrontation and the unavailable witness begins with *Ohio v. Roberts*, 448 U.S. 56 (1980), in which the United States Supreme Court upheld a state trial court's admission of an absent witness' preliminary hearing testimony. In reaching this conclusion, the Court held that the confrontation clause seeks to ensure that government-offered hearsay is reliable and establishes a preference for face-to-face confrontation which requires the prosecution either to produce the declarant or demonstrate the declarant's unavailability. Upon a satisfactory showing of unavailability, the hearsay statement must be shown to be trustworthy. The Court explained:

> [The] statement is admissible only if it bears adequate "indicia of reliability." Reliability can be inferred without more in a case where the evidence falls within a firmly rooted hearsay exception. In other cases, the evidence must be excluded, at least absent a showing of particularized guarantees of trustworthiness. [448 U.S. at 66]

A number of subsequent Supreme Court decisions dealt with whether particular hearsay exceptions were firmly rooted, thus satisfying the confrontation clause without an additional showing of trustworthiness.

Six years after the Supreme Court set forth the *Roberts* two-prong test, it severely limited its application. In *United States v. Inadi*, 475 U.S. 387 (1986), the prosecution sought to introduce taped statements of co-conspirators at the defendant's trial under the co-conspirator exception to the hearsay rule, Rule 801. Even though there was no showing of unavailability, the Supreme Court upheld the admission of the testimony, choosing to confine *Roberts'* unavailability analysis to situations involving *prior testimony* by a witness. Thus, the *Inadi* Court held that statements made by co-conspirators are inherently reliable because of the context in which they are made, rendering further in-court investigation of the declarant unhelpful.

In *Idaho v. Wright*, 497 U.S. 805 (1990), the Supreme Court shifted its focus to the second prong of the original *Roberts* test — the reliability requirement. In a trial for sexual abuse of a minor, the trial court had admitted statements made by a three-year-old girl to her doctor under a state "residual hearsay" exception. The Idaho Supreme Court reversed the resulting conviction, holding that the admission of this hearsay testimony violated the confrontation clause, and the United States Supreme Court affirmed. There was no dispute over unavailability, so the opinion focused on the reliability prong of the *Roberts* test. Since the residual hearsay exception was not found to be "firmly rooted," the prosecution had to show that the child's statements carried "particularized guarantees of trustworthiness."

In its holding, the Court elaborated on the appropriate means of establishing these "particularized guarantees of trustworthiness." The Court held that these "particularized guarantees" could be based on circumstances surrounding the making of the statement (*i.e.*, ways of showing that the statement was particularly worthy of belief), but that a showing of trustworthiness could not be based on physical corroborating evidence. The Court reasoned that using corroborating evidence in this fashion would permit admission of a presumptively unreliable statement by allowing it to be boot-strapped onto other evidence admitted at trial.

[ii]   *Crawford v. Washington*: The Revolution in Confrontation Analysis

The next case represents the current approach to Confrontation, which overruled *Ohio v. Roberts* and substituted a "testimonial" approach.

CRAWFORD v. WASHINGTON
541 U.S. 36 (2004)

JUSTICE SCALIA delivered the opinion of the Court.

Petitioner Michael Crawford stabbed a man who allegedly tried to rape his wife, Sylvia. At his trial, the State played for the jury Sylvia's tape-recorded statement to the police describing the stabbing, even though he had no opportunity for cross-examination [because Sylvia did not testify at trial. Sylvia's statement to some extent contradicted the defendant's testimony that the stabbing was in self defense; she testified she did not see a weapon in the victim's hand.] The Washington Supreme Court upheld petitioner's conviction [under *Roberts*] after determining that Sylvia's statement was reliable. The question presented is whether this procedure complied with the Sixth Amendment's guarantee that, "[i]n all criminal prosecutions, the accused shall enjoy the right . . . to be confronted with the witnesses against him."

. . . The State charged petitioner with assault and attempted murder. At trial, he claimed self-defense. Sylvia did not testify because of the state marital privilege, which generally bars a spouse from testifying without the other spouse's consent. In Washington, this privilege does not extend to a spouse's out-of-court statements admissible under a hearsay exception, so the State sought to introduce Sylvia's tape-recorded statements to the police as evidence that the stabbing was not in self-defense. Noting that Sylvia had admitted she led petitioner to Lee's apartment and thus had facilitated the assault, the State invoked the hearsay exception for statements against penal interest.

Petitioner countered that, state law notwithstanding, admitting the evidence would violate his federal constitutional right to be "confronted with the witnesses against him." According to our description of that right in *Ohio v. Roberts*, 448 U.S. 56 (1980), it does not bar admission of an unavailable witness's statement against a criminal defendant if the statement bears "adequate 'indicia of reliability.' " To meet that test, evidence must either fall within a "firmly rooted hearsay exception" or bear "particularized guarantees of trustworthiness." The trial court here admitted the statement on the latter ground, offering several reasons why it was trustworthy: Sylvia was not shifting blame but rather corroborating her husband's story that he acted in self-defense or "justified reprisal"; she had direct knowledge as an eyewitness; she was describing recent events; and she was being questioned by a "neutral" law enforcement officer. The prosecution played the tape for the jury and relied on it in closing, arguing that it was "damning evidence" that "completely refutes [petitioner's] claim of self-defense." The jury convicted petitioner of assault.

The Washington Court of Appeals reversed [because Sylvia's statement did not bear sufficient particularized guarantees of trustworthiness]. . . . The Washington Supreme Court reinstated the conviction, unanimously concluding under *Roberts* that, although Sylvia's statement did not fall under a firmly rooted hearsay exception, it bore guarantees of trustworthiness: "[W]hen a codefendant's confession is virtually identical [to, *i.e.*, interlocks with,] that of a defendant, it may be deemed reliable."

We granted certiorari to determine whether the State's use of Sylvia's statement violated the Confrontation Clause. The Sixth Amendment's Confrontation Clause provides that, "[i]n all criminal prosecutions, the accused shall enjoy the right . . . to be confronted with the witnesses against him." We have held that this bedrock procedural guarantee applies to both federal and state prosecutions. *Pointer v. Texas*, 380 U.S. 400, 406 (1965). As noted above, *Roberts* says that an unavailable witness's out-of-court statement may be admitted so long as it has adequate indicia of reliability — *i.e.*, falls within a "firmly rooted hearsay exception" or bears "particularized guarantees of trustworthiness." Petitioner argues that this test strays from the original meaning of the Confrontation Clause and urges us to reconsider it.

The Constitution's text does not alone resolve this case. One could plausibly read "witnesses against" a defendant to mean those who actually testify at trial. We must therefore turn to the historical background of the Clause to understand its meaning.

The right to confront one's accusers is a concept that dates back to Roman times. The founding generation's immediate source of the concept, however, was the common law. English common law has long differed from continental civil law in regard to the manner in which witnesses give testimony in criminal trials. The common-law tradition is one of live testimony in court subject to adversarial testing, while the civil law condones examination in private by judicial officers.

Nonetheless, England at times adopted elements of the civil-law practice. Justices of the peace or other officials examined suspects and witnesses before trial. These examinations were sometimes read in court in lieu of live testimony. . . .

. . . The most notorious instances of civil-law examination occurred in the great political trials of the 16th and 17th centuries. One such was the 1603 trial of Sir Walter Raleigh for treason. Lord Cobham, Raleigh's alleged accomplice, had implicated him in an examination before the Privy Council and in a letter. At Raleigh's trial, these were read to the jury. Raleigh argued that Cobham had lied to save himself. . . . Suspecting that Cobham would recant, Raleigh demanded that the judges call him to appear, arguing that "[t]he Proof of the Common Law is by witness and jury: let Cobham be here, let him speak it. Call my accuser before my face . . . ." The judges refused, and, despite Raleigh's protestations that he was being tried "by the Spanish Inquisition," the jury convicted, and Raleigh was sentenced to death.

. . . Through a series of statutory and judicial reforms, English law developed a right of confrontation that limited these abuses. . . . Courts, meanwhile, developed relatively strict rules of unavailability, admitting examinations only if the witness was demonstrably unable to testify in person. . . .

Controversial examination practices were also used in the Colonies. . . . Many declarations of rights adopted around the time of the Revolution guaranteed a right of confrontation . . . . The proposed Federal Constitution, however, did not. At the Massachusetts ratifying convention, Abraham Holmes objected to this omission precisely on the ground that it would lead to civil-law practices . . . . The First Congress responded by including the Confrontation Clause in the proposal that became the Sixth Amendment. . . .

This history supports two inferences about the meaning of the Sixth Amendment. First, the principal evil at which the Confrontation Clause was directed was the civil-law mode of criminal procedure, and particularly its use of *ex parte* examinations as evidence against the accused. . . . The Sixth Amendment must be interpreted with this focus in mind. . . .

This focus also suggests that not all hearsay implicates the Sixth Amendment's core concerns. An off-hand, overheard remark might be unreliable evidence and thus a good candidate for exclusion under hearsay rules, but it bears little resemblance to the civil-law abuses the Confrontation Clause targeted. On the other hand, *ex parte* examinations might sometimes be admissible under modern hearsay rules, but the Framers certainly would not have condoned them.

The text of the Confrontation Clause reflects this focus. It applies to "witnesses" against the accused — in other words, those who "bear testimony." 1 N. Webster, An American Dictionary of the English Language (1828). "Testimony," in turn, is typically "[a] solemn declaration or affirmation made for the purpose of establishing or proving some fact." *Ibid.* An accuser who makes a formal statement to government officers bears testimony in a sense that a person who makes a casual remark to an acquaintance does not. The constitutional text, like the history underlying the common-law right of confrontation, thus reflects an especially acute concern with a specific type of out-of-court statement.

Various formulations of this core class of "testimonial" statements exist: "*ex parte* in-court testimony or its functional equivalent — that is, material such as affidavits, custodial examinations, prior testimony that the defendant was unable to cross-examine, or similar pretrial statements that declarants would reasonably expect to be used prosecutorially," Brief for Petitioner 23; "extrajudicial statements . . . contained in formalized testimonial materials, such as affidavits, depositions, prior testimony, or confessions," *White v. Illinois*, 502 U.S. 346, 365 (1992) (THOMAS, J., joined by SCALIA, J., concurring in part and concurring in judgment); "statements that were made under circumstances which would lead an objective witness reasonably to believe that the statement would be available for use at a later trial," Brief for National Association of Criminal Defense Lawyers et al. as *Amici Curiae* 3. These formulations all share a common nucleus and then define the Clause's coverage at various levels of abstraction around it. Regardless of the precise articulation, some statements qualify under any definition — for example, *ex parte* testimony at a preliminary hearing.

Statements taken by police officers in the course of interrogations are also testimonial under even a narrow standard. Police interrogations bear a striking resemblance to examinations by justices of the peace in England. The statements are not sworn testimony, but the absence of oath was not dispositive.

. . . That interrogators are police officers rather than magistrates does not change the picture either. . . . . The involvement of government officers in the production of testimonial evidence presents the same risk, whether the officers are police or justices of the peace. . . . In sum, even if the Sixth Amendment is not solely concerned with testimonial hearsay, that is its primary object, and interrogations by law enforcement officers fall squarely within that class.

The historical record also supports a second proposition: that the Framers would not have allowed admission of testimonial statements of a witness who did not appear at trial unless he was unavailable to testify, and the defendant had had a prior opportunity for cross-examination. . . . As the English authorities above reveal, the common law in 1791 conditioned admissibility of an absent witness's examination on unavailability and a prior opportunity to cross-examine. The Sixth Amendment therefore incorporates those limitations.

. . . We do not read the historical sources to say that a prior opportunity to cross-examine was merely a sufficient, rather than a necessary, condition for admissibility of testimonial statements. They suggest that this requirement was dispositive, and not merely one of several ways to establish reliability. This is not to deny, as THE CHIEF JUSTICE notes, that "[t]here were always exceptions to the general rule of exclusion" of hearsay evidence. Several had become well established by 1791. But there is scant evidence that exceptions were invoked to admit testimonial statements against the accused in a criminal case. . . .

Our case law has been largely consistent with these two principles. . . . [The Court analyzes a series of confrontation clause cases where a prior opportunity to cross-examine was mentioned as a component of the right of confrontation.]

. . . Our cases have thus remained faithful to the Framers' understanding: Testimonial statements of witnesses absent from trial have been admitted only where the declarant is unavailable, and only where the defendant has had a prior opportunity to cross-examine.

Although the results of our decisions have generally been faithful to the original meaning of the Confrontation Clause, the same cannot be said of our rationales. *Roberts* conditions the admissibility of all hearsay evidence on whether it falls under a "firmly rooted hearsay exception" or bears "particularized guarantees of trustworthiness." This test departs from the historical principles identified above in two respects. First, it is too broad: It applies the same mode of analysis whether or not the hearsay consists of ex parte testimony. This often results in close constitutional scrutiny in cases that are far removed from the core concerns of the Clause. At the same time, however, the test is too narrow: It admits statements that do consist of ex parte testimony upon a mere finding of reliability. This malleable standard often fails to protect against paradigmatic confrontation violations.

Members of this Court and academics have suggested that we revise our doctrine to reflect more accurately the original understanding of the Clause. They offer two proposals: First, that we apply the Confrontation Clause only to testimonial statements, leaving the remainder to regulation by hearsay law — thus eliminating the overbreadth referred to above. Second, that we impose an absolute bar to statements that are testimonial, absent a prior opportunity to cross-examine — thus eliminating the excessive narrowness referred to above.

Where testimonial statements are involved [as they are in this case since Sylvia Crawford's statement is testimonial under any definition], we do not think the Framers meant to leave the Sixth Amendment's protection to the vagaries of the rules of evidence, much less to amorphous notions of "reliability." Certainly none of the authorities discussed above acknowledges any general reliability exception to the common-law rule. Admitting statements deemed reliable by a judge is fundamentally at odds with the right of confrontation. To be sure, the Clause's ultimate goal is to ensure reliability of evidence, but it is a procedural rather than a substantive guarantee. It commands, not that evidence be reliable, but that reliability be assessed in a particular manner: by testing in the crucible of cross-examination. . . .

The *Roberts* test allows a jury to hear evidence, untested by the adversary process, based on a mere judicial determination of reliability. It thus replaces the constitutionally prescribed method of assessing reliability with a wholly foreign one. In this respect, it is very different from exceptions to the Confrontation Clause that make no claim to be a surrogate means of assessing reliability. For example, the rule of forfeiture by wrongdoing (which we accept) extinguishes confrontation claims on essentially equitable grounds; it does not purport to be an alternative means of determining reliability.

. . . Dispensing with confrontation because testimony is obviously reliable is akin to dispensing with jury trial because a defendant is obviously guilty. This is not what the Sixth Amendment prescribes.

The legacy of *Roberts* in other courts vindicates the Framers' wisdom in rejecting a general reliability exception. The framework is so unpredictable that it fails to provide meaningful protection from even core confrontation violations.

Reliability is an amorphous, if not entirely subjective, concept. There are countless factors bearing on whether a statement is reliable . . . .

The unpardonable vice of the *Roberts* test, however, is not its unpredictability, but its demonstrated capacity to admit core testimonial statements that the Confrontation Clause plainly meant to exclude. . . . To add insult to injury, some of the courts that admit untested testimonial statements find reliability in the very factors that make the statements testimonial. As noted earlier, one court relied on the fact that the witness's statement was made to police while in custody on pending charges — the theory being that this made the statement more clearly against penal interest and thus more reliable. Other courts routinely rely on the fact that a prior statement is given under oath in judicial proceedings. That inculpating statements are given in a testimonial setting is not an antidote to the confrontation problem, but rather the trigger that makes the Clause's demands most urgent. It is not enough to point out that most of the usual safeguards of the adversary process attend the statement, when the single safeguard missing is the one the Confrontation Clause demands.

. . . Where nontestimonial hearsay is at issue, it is wholly consistent with the Framers' design to afford the States flexibility in their development of hearsay law — as does *Roberts*, and as would an approach that exempted such statements from Confrontation Clause scrutiny altogether. Where testimonial evidence is at issue, however, the Sixth Amendment demands what the common law required: unavailability and a prior opportunity for cross-examination. We leave for another day any effort to spell out a comprehensive definition of "testimonial." Whatever else the term covers, it applies at a minimum to prior testimony at a preliminary hearing, before a grand jury, or at a former trial; and to police interrogations. These are the modern practices with closest kinship to the abuses at which the Confrontation Clause was directed.

In this case, the State admitted Sylvia's testimonial statement against petitioner, despite the fact that he had no opportunity to cross-examine her. That alone is sufficient to make out a violation of the Sixth Amendment. *Roberts* notwithstanding, we decline to mine the record in search of indicia of reliability. Where testimonial statements are at issue, the only indicium of reliability sufficient to satisfy constitutional demands is the one the Constitution actually prescribes: confrontation. [Reversed]

CHIEF JUSTICE REHNQUIST, with whom JUSTICE O'CONNOR joins, concurring in the judgment.

I dissent from the Court's decision to overrule *Ohio v. Roberts*, 448 U.S. 56 (1980). I believe that the Court's adoption of a new interpretation of the Confrontation Clause is not backed by sufficiently persuasive reasoning to overrule long-established precedent. Its decision casts a mantle of uncertainty over future criminal trials in both federal and state courts, and is by no means necessary to decide the present case.

The Court's distinction between testimonial and nontestimonial statements, contrary to its claim, is no better rooted in history than our current doctrine. Under the common law, although the courts were far from consistent, out-of-court statements made by someone other than the accused and not taken under oath, unlike *ex parte* depositions or affidavits, were generally not considered substantive evidence upon which a conviction could be based. Testimonial statements such as accusatory statements to police officers likely would have been disapproved of in the 18th century, not necessarily because they resembled ex parte affidavits or depositions as the Court reasons, but more likely than not because they were not made under oath. . . .

Thus, while I agree that the Framers were mainly concerned about sworn affidavits and depositions, it does not follow that they were similarly concerned about the Court's broader category of testimonial statements. As far as I can tell, unsworn testimonial statements were treated no differently at common law than were nontestimonial statements, and it seems to me any classification of statements as testimonial beyond that of sworn affidavits and depositions will be somewhat arbitrary, merely a proxy for what the Framers might have intended had such evidence been liberally admitted as substantive evidence like it is today.

I therefore see no reason why the distinction the Court draws is preferable to our precedent. . . . [W]e have never drawn a distinction between testimonial and nontestimonial statements. And for that matter, neither has any other court of which I am aware. I see little value in trading our precedent for an imprecise approximation at this late date.

I am also not convinced that the Confrontation Clause categorically requires the exclusion of testimonial statements. Although many States had their own Confrontation Clauses, they were of recent vintage and were not interpreted with any regularity before 1791. . . . Nor was the English law at the time of the framing entirely consistent in its treatment of testimonial evidence. Generally *ex parte* affidavits and depositions were excluded as the Court notes, but even that proposition was not universal. . . .

. . . Exceptions to confrontation have always been derived from the experience that some out-of-court statements are just as reliable as cross-examined in-court testimony due to the circumstances under which they were made [citing cases involving co-conspirator statements, spontaneous declarations, statements for purposes of procuring medical services, and dying declarations, was well as "countless other hearsay exceptions."]. . . . That a statement might be testimonial does nothing to undermine the wisdom of one of these exceptions.

Indeed, cross-examination is a tool used to flesh out the truth, not an empty procedure. . . . By creating an immutable category of excluded evidence, the Court adds little to a trial's truth-finding function and ignores this longstanding guidance.

In choosing the path it does, the Court of course overrules *Ohio v. Roberts*, 448 U.S. 56 (1980), a case decided nearly a quarter of a century ago. *Stare decisis* is not an inexorable command in the area of constitutional law, but by and large, it "is the preferred course because it promotes the evenhanded, predictable, and consistent development of legal principles, fosters reliance on judicial decisions, and contributes to the actual and perceived integrity of the judicial process." And in making this appraisal, doubt that the new rule is indeed the "right" one should surely be weighed in the balance. Though there are no vested interests involved, unresolved questions for the future of everyday criminal trials throughout the country surely counsel the same sort of caution. The Court grandly declares that "[w]e leave for another day any effort to spell out a comprehensive definition of 'testimonial.'" But the thousands of federal prosecutors and the tens of thousands of state prosecutors need answers as to what beyond the specific kinds of "testimony" the Court lists is covered by the new rule. They need them now, not months or years from now. Rules of criminal evidence are applied every day in courts throughout the country, and parties should not be left in the dark in this manner.

To its credit, the Court's analysis of "testimony" excludes at least some hearsay exceptions, such as business records and official records. To hold otherwise would require numerous additional witnesses without any apparent gain in the truth-seeking process. Likewise to the Court's credit is its implicit recognition that the mistaken application of its new rule by courts which guess wrong as to the scope of the rule is subject to harmless-error analysis. . . .

NOTES

1. *Crawford's rejection of fairly recent precedent. Crawford* is unusual because it overturns a rather recent Supreme Court precedent and substitutes what the Court sees as the common law approach.

2. *Predictability. Crawford* rejects *Ohio v. Roberts* as being too unpredictable. Do you think *Crawford* is likely to be more predictable?

3. *Hearsay only. Crawford* indicated that the confrontation clause applies only to hearsay evidence — *i.e.* an out of court statement used to prove its truth. If a statement is introduced for a non-hearsay use, it is simply not covered by the confrontation clause. Noting that this rule may open the door for prosecutors to avoid the confrontation clause by arguing that evidence is not been offered for a hearsay use ("We want to introduce it to show why the police focused on the defendant rather than to identify the defendant as the robber"). Professor Jeffrey Fisher raises a number of practical concerns. Jeffrey Fisher, *The Truth About the "Not for Truth" Exception to Crawford*, 32 CHAMPION 18 (Jan/Feb 2008); Stephen Ashlett, Comment, *Crawford's Curious Dictum*, 82 TUL. L. REV. 297 (2007).

4. *Unavailability.* Note that under *Crawford*, a testimonial statement ordinarily can only be introduced if the declarant is unavailable and has been subject to cross examination. The Court does not define "unavailability." Does it mean the same as that needed to admit hearsay under Federal Rule of Evidence 804? *See generally* Andrew Petty, *The Unavailability Requirement*, 102 N.W. U. L. REV. COLLOQUY 239 (2008)(meaning of unavailability and impact of unavailability on forfeiture).

5. *Testimonial.* The term "testimonial" is absolutely critical to any analysis under *Crawford*. How important is it that the key term, "testimonial," is not precisely defined in *Crawford*? Do the Court's illustrations of what is "testimonial" suffice to give you an understanding of what statements are testimonial?

Assume a stepfather is charged with sexually abusing his young stepdaughter. The child talks to a number of people but refuses to testify at trial. Which of the following statement(s) is/are "testimonial" and covered by *Crawford* (so the state cannot use them at trial because doing so would violate the defendant's confrontation rights)?

a. The child made a statement to a police officer investigating the crime.

b. The child also spoke with a social worker interviewing the child for purposes of deciding whether she should be removed from the home.

Would it matter whether the social worker worked for a government unit or a private agency?

c. The child also told her mother about the incident.

d. She also described it to her best friend, a fourth grade classmate.

6. *Testimonial II: Seeking assistance v. providing information about past facts. Davis v. Washington: 911 call.* The Court further elucidated the meaning of "testimonial" in *Davis v. Washington*, 547 U.S. 813 (2006), involving a 911 call and statements made to police at the scene of a crime. The 911 caller in *Davis* reported that "he's here jumpin' me again" and he's "usin' his fists." After naming the assailant, the caller reported "He's runnin' now" and he was leaving in a car with another person. The caller did not testify at trial, but the 911 tapes were admitted into evidence. The *Davis* court added to the definition of "testimonial":

> Statements are nontestimonial when made in the course of police interrogation under circumstances objectively indicating that the primary purpose of the interrogation is to enable police assistance to meet an ongoing emergency. They are testimonial when the circumstances objectively indicate that there is no such ongoing emergency, and that the primary purpose of the interrogation is to establish or prove past events potentially relevant to later criminal prosecution.

Applying this test, the Court concluded that the domestic violence victim's 911 call at issue in the case was not testimonial because it was made to obtain assistance to meet an ongoing emergency. According to the Court, the caller was not "acting as a *witness*; she was not *testifying*" (emphasis in original).

On the other hand, in *Hammon v. Indiana*, a case joined with *Davis*, the Court held that an on-the-scene statement made by a domestic violence victim to police was testimonial because it was elicited as part of an investigation of past domestic violence activity by the defendant. The crisis in *Hammon* had ended when the police arrived and began to question the victim.

The distinction between responding to an emergency and relating past facts is often tenuous. What happens if the police respond to a 911 call and find a person dying from a gunshot wound. The police call 911 for an ambulance, then ask, "What happened?" What if they are told the name and address of the shooter. Is this testimonial? In *People v. Nieves-Andino*, 872 N.E.2d 1188 (N.Y. 2007), the New York Court of Appeals held that statement was nontestimonial for purposes of an emergency. Do you agree? For an thoughtful analysis of the case and the need for standards to determine what is an emergency response, see Recent Case, 121 HARV. L. REV. 906 (2008).

7. *Testimonial III: slippery slope. Davis* makes it clear that a statement that is non-testimonial may turn into one that is. This could occur if a statement deigned to cope with an emergency changes character once the emergency is over and the person describes past facts for later criminal investigation. This evolution may require the trial court to admit only those portions that are not testimonial.

8. *Testimonial IV: Primary purpose doctrine.* Sometimes a statement may be difficult to characterize because it contains both testimonial and nontestimonial elements. *Davis* looks at its *primary purpose* in assessing whether it is testimonial. *See generally* Thomas M. Forsyth III, *Just Don't Say You Heard It From Me*, 35 HAST. CONST'L L. QUARTERLY 263 (2008).

9. *Dying declaration: Unique?* Is a testimonial dying declaration admissible after *Crawford* even though the declarant who made the statement is unavailable and cannot be cross-examined? This could occur, for example, if a police officer is called to the scene of a shooting and interrogates the victim about the incident. If the victim later dies and the defendant is tried for the homicide, the defendant may argue that admission of the dying declaration violates the confrontation clause. A footnote in *Crawford* indicated that dying declarations have a significant historical foundation and may be *sui generis* under the confrontation clause. *See State v. Meeks*, 88 P.3d 789 (Kan. 2004) (allowing a dying declaration), and *United States v. Jordan*, 2005 U.S. Dist. LEXIS 3289; *but see*, 66 Fed. R. Evid. Serv. (Callaghan) 790 (D. Colo. 2005) (holding a dying declaration inadmissible because "admission of a testimonial dying declaration after *Crawford* goes against the sweeping prohibition set forth in that case").

10. *Waiver.* Since the right of confrontation protects the criminal accused, he or she may waive it. The waiver should be knowing, intelligent, and voluntary. A waiver of the right of confrontation is routine when the accused pleads guilty and waives many constitutional rights, a process that occurs in over ninety percent of felony prosecutions.

11. *Forfeiture.* What happens when a witness makes a testimonial statement, then the defendant somehow procures the absence of that witness at trial? Can the defendant use the confrontation clause to bar admission of the absent witness's testimonial statement? In both *Crawford* and *Davis* the Supreme Court recognized the doctrine of *forfeiture by wrongdoing,* which "extinguishes confrontation claims on equitable grounds." *Crawford,* 541 U.S. at 62.

Davis explained the concept more directly: a person "who obtains the absence of a witness by wrongdoing forfeits the constitutional right to confrontation." 547 U.S. at 833. In *Giles v. California,* 128 S.Ct. 2678 (2008), the Supreme Court held that a forfeiture of confrontation occurs only when the defendant engaged in conduct *designed* to prevent the witness from testifying. Simply causing the witness' death is not sufficient absent proof of a purpose to keep the victim from being a witness.

12. *Increased use of depositions.* If you were a prosecutor, would *Crawford* change your thoughts on when you should seek to have a deposition taken in a criminal case? When you should insist on a preliminary hearing? If you were defense counsel, would *Crawford* push you toward waiving a preliminary hearing and objecting to a deposition in some cases? What if there were a deposition or preliminary hearing with full cross-examination of a witness who is unavailable for trial, but then new evidence is discovered that would have been helpful in cross-examining that witness had the witness appeared at trial but the evidence was unavailable when the deposition or preliminary hearing was held? Is the deposition or preliminary hearing still admissible at trial because there was cross-examination at the earlier proceeding? *See People v. Jurado,* 38 Cal. 4th 72, 41 Cal. Rptr. 319 (Cal. 2006)(yes).

13. *Helpful articles.* There are many helpful articles in which *Crawford* is discussed and analyzed carefully. *See generally* Richard D. Friedman, *Adjusting to Crawford: High Court Decision Restores Confrontation Clause Protection,* 19 CRIM. JUST. 4 (2004); Robert P. Mosteller, Crawford v. Washington: *Encouraging and Ensuring the Confrontation of Witnesses,* 39 U. RICH. L. REV. 511 (2005); Andrew Dylan, Note, *Working Through the Confrontation Clause after Davis v. Washington,* 76 FORDHAM L. REV. 1905 (2007).

J. JURY TRIAL

[1] Overview

One of the features that distinguishes the American criminal justice process is the role of the *petit jury,* a body of (usually) twelve people who resolve most fact issues in a criminal trial. As described more fully in *Duncan v. Louisiana,* reproduced below, the jury serves a number of important functions. It gives the populace an opportunity to be involved in criminal justice decisions while adding a measure of legitimacy to the process by allowing citizens, not politicians, to make those decisions.

Since the United States Supreme Court "constitutionalized" the jury process by holding that the states and the federal government must accord the criminal accused a jury trial in all but the least serious cases, the details of the jury trial have become an important focus of American criminal procedure. To some extent, rules of criminal procedure provide the working framework for analysis. This chapter discusses these important issues, and provides answers to the following questions.

The first issue, and one often ignored, is what decisions must the jury make? This requires an analysis of the roles of both the jury and the judge. Another key issue is when does the criminal defendant have a right to a jury trial. Is there this right in every case, even the most minor? A related issue is waiver. If the accused has a right to a jury trial, can this right be waived even if the government wants a jury trial?

There are also numerous procedural issues. While a criminal jury is ordinarily comprised of twelve people, can there be a jury of fifteen or seven or three? Another set of issues concerns the procedures used to select a particular jury. Who is eligible for jury service and how is each juror chosen? What are the limits on counsel's ability to exclude an individual juror from hearing a case?

Once a jury is chosen, how does it operate? May individual jurors take notes or ask questions of a witness? When may a judge require jurors to be *sequestered*, or kept separate from their families during the trial?

After the judge has given jury instructions and the jury retires to make its decisions, what are the rules it must follow? Must the verdict be unanimous? What may the judge do if it appears the jury is deadlocked? What if the jury makes decisions, but the decisions are inconsistent with one another? What discretion does the jury have to do "jury justice" — to ignore the law and resolve the case in a way the jury thinks is fair? Finally, when and how can a jury's decision be attacked because of errors in the jury's processing of the case?

[2] Issues Tried by Jury

[a] Questions of Fact and Law

The short-hand, though not completely accurate, rule is that the jury decides questions of fact and the judge decides questions of law. *E.g.*, Ill. Rev. Stat. ch. 38, para. 115-4 ("Questions of law shall be decided by the court and questions of fact by the jury"). Although the exact details of the division of responsibilities between judges and jury are beyond the scope of this book, the true picture is quite complex.

The jury actually performs two interrelated functions. First, it decides what the facts are that relate to the question of guilt or innocence. Second, it decides whether those facts satisfy the legal standards at issue in the case (sometimes this is called applying the law to the facts). For example, assume that the defendant is charged with store burglary in violation of a state statute that defined the crime as "the unlawful entry of a business at night with the intent to commit a felony therein." The jury would listen to the evidence and decide such issues as: (1) did any part of the defendant enter the store, (2) did the defendant have permission to enter, (3) was the building used as a business, (4) what time did the event occur, and (5) what was the defendant's intent at the time of the event.

After resolving these factual issues, the jury would then turn to its second task: deciding whether the facts it found satisfied the elements of the crime. For example, assume that the jury believed witnesses who testified that the entry occurred at 8:45 P.M. Since the burglary statute covered only entries that occur "at night," the jury would have to decide whether 8:45 P.M. was "at night."

How would the jury know whether 8:45 P.M. is "night"? One of the judge's responsibilities is to decide which law is applicable and to instruct the jury on that law, including relevant definitions. Returning to the burglary case, the jury instructions would tell the jury about this statute and may define some of the key terms, including "at night." The jury would then use the statute and the judge's definitions to decide whether an 8:45 P.M. entry occurred "at night" under the burglary law.

Although this pattern is typical, the situation is frequently much more complex. Often the judge also decides questions of fact because some factual questions are not within the jury's bailiwick. In virtually all jurisdictions, the judge imposes the sentence. This means that ordinarily the judge decides both questions of law and fact relevant solely to the sentence. For example, if the jury finds the defendant guilty of the business burglary, the determination of the appropriate sentence may require the judge to ascertain such facts as the defendant's background, likely success if released on probation, employment possibilities, and acceptance of responsibility. The judge may hear witnesses and examine various documents in making these factual determinations.

[b] Capital Cases

Some jurisdictions depart from these rules and give the jury greater responsibility. The best example is the death penalty, where American jurisdictions routinely give the jury the responsibility of deciding whether the guilty defendant should be given the death penalty or a life sentence. *See generally Spaziano v. Florida*, 468 U.S. 447 (1984). Obviously, this requires the jury to make many factual determinations about the offender and the crime in order to apply the standards for imposing the sentence of death. *See, e.g., Ring. v. Arizona*, 536 U.S. 584 (2002).

[c] Fact Questions Jury May Not Address

In some unusual circumstances, a jury is not permitted to resolve factual questions. In *Jackson v. Denno*, 378 U.S. 368 (1964), the Supreme Court struck down a New York procedure that essentially let the jury decide whether a confession was voluntary (and therefore admissible) at the same time it decided guilt or innocence. The Court was critical of the fact that it was impossible to know whether the jury actually dealt with the issue of voluntariness and whether it ignored the confession if the confession was deemed involuntary. To eliminate the possibility that the jury will misuse an involuntary confession, the Court indicated that voluntariness can be decided by the trial judge, another judge, or another jury; it cannot be resolved by the "convicting" jury. *Id.* at 391 n.19. *See also, Commonwealth v. Miller*, 865 N.E.2d 825 (Mass. App. 2007)(judge must determine voluntariness of confession before submitting it to jury).

[d] Mixed Fact-Law Questions

Complex issues may arise in determining mixed questions of law and fact. For example, in *United States v. Gaudin*, 515 U.S. 506 (1995), the Supreme Court held that the question of the "materiality" of a defendant's allegedly false statement, an element of the offense in issue, must be submitted to a jury for determination. Characterizing the issue of materiality as a mixed question of law and fact, the Court explained that the jury's constitutional responsibility "is not merely to determine facts, but to apply the law to those facts and draw the ultimate conclusion of guilt or innocence." Chief Justice Rehnquist noted in his concurring opinion, however, as follows:

> As with many aspects of statutory construction, determination of what elements constitute a crime often is subject to dispute . . . . Federal and State legislatures may reallocate burdens of proof by labeling elements as affirmative defenses or they may convert elements into "sentencing factors" for consideration by the sentencing court. [*Id.* at 525]

[e] Sentencing

As noted by Chief Justice Rehnquist in *Gaudin*, it may be crucial to determine whether a fact specified in a statute is an element of an offense or a sentencing consideration. If the former, it must be charged in the indictment, submitted to the jury for its consideration, and proven beyond a reasonable doubt by the government.

In the past few years the Supreme Court has decided a series of cases beginning with *Apprendi v. New Jersey*, 530 U.S. 466 (2000), that markedly change the judge-jury responsibilities in the sentencing arena. These developments are discussed in greater detail in Chapter 17, which covers sentencing, but *Apprendi* and its progeny merit some discussion here as well.

The Apprendi revolution. In *Apprendi v. New Jersey*, 530 U.S. 466 (2000), the Supreme Court created a seismic revolution by holding in a case involving a New Jersey sentencing enhancement for a crime committed "with a biased purpose." Under the "hate crime" enhancement statute, the sentence for a crime committed with this "biased" purpose could be punished more severely than the maximum allowed for the original crime alone. The trial judge found the presence of bias by a preponderance of the evidence. The Supreme Court reversed by a vote of 5-4, holding that the due process and jury trial rights, mean that:

> Other than the fact of a prior conviction, any fact that increases the penalty for a crime beyond the prescribed statutory maximum must be submitted to a jury, and proved beyond a reasonable doubt.

> [I]t is unconstitutional for a legislature to remove from the jury the assessment of facts that increase the prescribed range of penalties to which a criminal defendant is exposed. It is equally clear that such facts must be established by proof beyond a reasonable doubt. . . . [Noting the traditional "distinction between "elements" and "sentencing factors" the Court indicated that] . . . the relevant inquiry is one not of form, but of effect — does the required finding expose the defendant to a greater punishment than that authorized by the jury's guilty verdict? . . . .

> This is not to suggest that the term "sentencing factor" is devoid of meaning. The term appropriately describes a circumstance, which may be either aggravating or mitigating in character, that supports a specific sentence within the range authorized by the jury's finding that the defendant is guilty of a particular offense. On the other hand, when the term "sentence enhancement" is used to describe an increase beyond the maximum authorized statutory sentence, it is the functional equivalent of an element of a greater offense than the one covered by the jury's guilty verdict. Indeed, it fits squarely within the usual definition of an "element" of the offense.

> . . . The New Jersey procedure challenged in this case is an unacceptable departure from the jury tradition that is an indispensable part of our criminal justice system.

NOTES

1. *Importance of Apprendi.* The *Apprendi* decision has had a significant impact on both federal and state criminal cases. Literally hundreds of cases have addressed explicitly *Apprendi*'s impact upon various sentencing schemes. One commentator describes *Apprendi*'s significance in the following way:[*]

> *Apprendi* is the most recent installment in a series of Supreme Court cases over the past thirty years addressing a core issue in criminal law: what are the constitutional limits on the legislature's discretion in defining crimes and their elements? Over the decades, the Court has famously zigzagged between tantalizing suggestions of broad constitutional limitations and powerful endorsements of legislative primacy, with the latter position obtaining the upper hand at the end of each stage of development. These cases have closely divided the Court over the years, yielding unusual alliances and murky jurisprudence. *Apprendi* is no exception.

Alan C. Michaels, *Truth in Convicting: Understanding and Evaluating Apprendi*, 12 FEDERAL SENTENCING REPORTER 320 (2000) (author concludes by stating that "*Apprendi* . . . may eventually be seen as a cautious step by the Court in creating some modest limitations on legislature's ability to define crimes that, in the long run, may be considered both appropriate and unexceptional.").

2. According to one commentator, in the first year after the Court's *Apprendi* decision, more than four hundred state and federal cases addressed a range of *Apprendi* issues. This, along with the fact that numerous federal statutes have been challenged under *Apprendi*, led him to conclude that "it seems safe to bet that *Apprendi* and its progeny will dominate the field of determinate sentencing law into the foreseeable

---

future." Joseph L. Hoffman, *Apprendi v. New Jersey: Back to the Future?*, 38 AM. CRIM. L. REV. 255 (2001). Likewise, another commentator predicts that *Apprendi* will focus "new attention to the procedures that should be required if due process in sentencing is to be a reality." Stephen H. Saltzburg, *Due Process, History, and Apprendi v. New Jersey*, 38 AM. CRIM. L. REV. 243, 253 (2001). Other articles addressing various *Apprendi* issues include Benjamin J. Priester, *Constitutional Formalism and the Meaning of Apprendi v. New Jersey*, 38 AM. CRIM. L. REV. 281 (2001) (concluding that *Apprendi* is an important addition to the Court's constitutional criminal procedure doctrines), and John Kenneth Zwerling, *Comprendez Apprendi?*, 38 AM. CRIM. L. REV. 309 (2001) (identifying *Apprendi*'s many lessons for defense counsel).

3. *Death penalty cases.* The United States Supreme Court, in *Ring v. Arizona*, 536 U.S. 584 (2002), evaluated the Arizona procedure which allowed the jury to decide whether the accused was guilty of first-degree murder, but then, for the purpose of deciding whether the death penalty should be imposed, allowed the trial judge, alone, to determine the presence of aggravating factors. Finding this incompatible with *Apprendi*, the Court held that this scheme violated the Sixth Amendment jury trial right: "Capital defendants . . . are entitled to a jury determination of any fact on which the legislature conditions an increase in the maximum punishment." By contrast, the Court held that it is consistent with *Apprendi* to permit a judge to determine the existence of a fact which increases the mandatory minimum sentence so long as that determination does not exceed the statutorily authorized maximum sentence. *Harris v. United States*, 536 U.S. 545 (2002) (noting that "whether chosen by the judge or by the legislature- , . . . the judge may impose the minimum, the maximum, or any other sentence within the range . . . without contradicting *Apprendi*).

4. *Blakely.* In *Blakely v. Washington*, 542 U.S. 296 (2004), the Court extended *Apprendi* and continued the process of greater jury involvement in sentencing. *Blakely* involved a state defendant who entered a plea for a kidnaping crime carrying a 53-month maximum sentence. State law allowed the judge to increase that sentence after making a judicial determination that the defendant acted with "deliberate cruelty." Justice Scalia's opinion for the Court held that under *Apprendi* this finding of "deliberate cruelty" had to be made by a jury rather than by the judge, unless the defendant either waived a jury finding on the issue or stipulated the facts necessary for the judge to draw that conclusion. The Court found that the term "statutory maximum" in *Apprendi* applied to "the maximum sentence a judge may impose solely on the basis of the facts reflected in the jury verdict or admitted by the defendant." Accordingly, the statutory maximum is the maximum sentence a judge "may impose without any additional findings." If a greater sentence is given because of other facts, those facts must be found by a jury unless a jury finding is waived or the defendant stipulates to those facts.

The impact of *Blakely* will differ markedly among the jurisdictions, though its practical effect may be less than anticipated. Since virtually all criminal defendants plead guilty, it is likely that the prosecution will insist on a waiver of jury involvement in sentencing as a condition for the plea. This waiver will alleviate *Blakely* concerns. On the other hand, *Blakely* may give the defense a few more chips to use in plea bargaining, perhaps inducing the prosecution to agree to a sentence that does not exceed the "maximum" in order to avoid a convening a jury when the defendant does not contest guilt.

5. *Booker: Federal Sentencing Guidelines.* In *United States v. Booker*, 543 U.S. 738 (2004), discussed more fully in Chapter 17, the Supreme Court applied *Apprendi* to the federal sentencing guidelines and held that the Sixth Amendment required that the guidelines be advisory rather than mandatory. If advisory, the Sixth Amendment does not require jury involvement in the sentencing decision.

[3] Right to a Jury Trial

There are two possible sources of a right to a jury trial. The most obvious is the United States Constitution's Sixth Amendment, as discussed below in the leading case, *Duncan v. Louisiana*. The second source is statutory.

[a] Sixth Amendment

Until 1968 it was not known whether the Sixth Amendment's right to a jury trial was applicable to the states. In *Duncan v. Louisiana*, the United States Supreme Court resolved this issue but left open a number of important questions about the scope of the criminal accused's right to a jury trial.

DUNCAN v. LOUISIANA
391 U.S. 145 (1968)

Mr. Justice White delivered the opinion of the Court.

Appellant, Gary Duncan, was convicted of simple battery in the Twenty-fifth Judicial District Court of Louisiana. Under Louisiana law simple battery is a misdemeanor, punishable by a maximum of two years' imprisonment and a $300 fine. Appellant sought trial by jury, but because the Louisiana Constitution grants jury trials only in cases in which capital punishment or imprisonment at hard labor may be imposed, the trial judge denied the request. Appellant was convicted and sentenced to serve 60 days in the parish prison and pay a fine of $150. Appellant [unsuccessfully] sought review in the Supreme Court of Louisiana, asserting that the denial of jury trial violated rights guaranteed to him by the United States Constitution . . . . [A]ppellant sought review in this Court, alleging that the Sixth and Fourteenth Amendments to the United States Constitution secure the right to jury trial in state criminal prosecutions where a sentence as long as two years may be imposed.

. . . Appellant was 19 years of age when tried. While driving on Highway 23 in Plaquemines Parish on October 18, 1966, he saw two younger cousins engaged in a conversation by the side of the road with four white boys. Knowing his cousins, Negroes who had recently transferred to a formerly all-white high school, had reported the occurrence of racial incidents at the school, Duncan stopped the car, got out, and approached the six boys. At trial the white boys and a white onlooker testified, as did appellant and his cousins. The testimony was in dispute on many points, but the witnesses agreed that appellant and the white boys spoke to each other, that appellant encouraged his cousins to break off the encounter and enter his car, and that appellant was about to enter the car himself for the purpose of driving away with his cousins. The whites testified that just before getting in the car appellant slapped Herman Landry, one of the white boys, on the elbow. The Negroes testified that appellant had not slapped Landry, but had merely touched him. The trial judge concluded that the State had proved beyond a reasonable doubt that Duncan had committed simple battery, and found him guilty.

The Fourteenth Amendment denies the States the power to "deprive any person of life, liberty, or property, without due process of law." In resolving conflicting claims concerning the meaning of this spacious language, the Court has looked increasingly to the Bill of Rights for guidance; many of the rights guaranteed by the first eight Amendments to the Constitution have been held to be protected against state action by the Due Process Clause of the Fourteenth Amendment.

. . . The test for determining whether a right extended by the Fifth and Sixth Amendments with respect to federal criminal proceedings is also protected against state action by the Fourteenth Amendment has been phrased in a variety of ways in the opinions of this Court. The question has been asked whether a right is among those "fundamental principles of liberty and justice which lie at the base of all our civil and political institutions," *Powell v. State of Alabama*, 287 U.S. 45, (1932); whether it is "basic in our system of jurisprudence," *In re Oliver*, 333 U.S. 257, 273 (1948); and whether it is "a fundamental right, essential to a fair trial," *Gideon v. Wainwright*, 372 U.S. 335, 343–344 (1963). The claim before us is that the right to trial by jury guaranteed by the Sixth Amendment meets these tests. The position of Louisiana, on the other hand, is that the Constitution imposes upon the States no duty to give a jury trial in any criminal case, regardless of the seriousness of the crime or the size of the punishment which may be imposed. Because we believe that trial by jury in criminal cases is fundamental to the American scheme of justice, we hold that the Fourteenth Amendment guarantees a right of jury trial in all criminal cases which — were they to be tried in a federal court — would come within the Sixth Amendment's guarantee. Since we consider the appeal before us to be such a case, we hold that the Constitution was violated when appellant's demand for jury trial was refused.

The history of trial by jury in criminal cases has been frequently told. It is sufficient for present purposes to say that by the time our Constitution was written, jury trial in criminal cases had been in existence in England for several centuries and carried impressive credentials traced by many to Magna Carta. Its preservation and proper operation as a protection against arbitrary rule were among the major objectives of the revolutionary settlement which was expressed in the Declaration and Bill of Rights of 1689.

. . . The Constitution itself, in Art. III, § 2, commanded:

> The Trial of all Crimes, except in Cases of Impeachment, shall be by Jury; and such Trial shall be held in the State where the said Crimes shall have been committed.

Objections to the Constitution because of the absence of a bill of rights were met by the immediate submission and adoption of the Bill of Rights. Included was the Sixth Amendment which, among other things, provided:

> In all criminal prosecutions, the accused shall enjoy the right to a speedy and public trial, by an impartial jury of the State and district wherein the crime shall have been committed.

The constitutions adopted by the original States guaranteed jury trial. Also, the constitution of every State entering the Union thereafter in one form or another protected the right to jury trial in criminal cases.

Even such skeletal history is impressive support for considering the right to jury trial in criminal cases to be fundamental to our system of justice, an importance frequently recognized in the opinions of this Court.

. . . Jury trial continues to receive strong support. The laws of every State guarantee a right to jury trial in serious criminal cases; no State has dispensed with it; nor are there significant movements underway to do so.

. . . The guarantees of jury trial in the Federal and State Constitutions reflect a profound judgment about the way in which law should be enforced and justice administered. A right to jury trial is granted to criminal defendants in order to prevent oppression by the Government. Those who wrote our constitutions knew from history and experience that it was necessary to protect against unfounded criminal charges brought to eliminate enemies and against judges too responsive to the voice of higher authority. The framers of the constitutions strove to create an independent judiciary but insisted upon further protection against arbitrary action. Providing an accused with the right to be tried by a jury of his peers gave him an inestimable safeguard against the corrupt or overzealous prosecutor and against the compliant, biased, or eccentric judge. If the defendant preferred the common-sense judgment of a jury to the more tutored but perhaps less sympathetic reaction of the single judge, he was to have it. Beyond this, the jury trial provisions in the Federal and State Constitutions reflect a fundamental decision about the exercise of official power — a reluctance to entrust plenary powers over the life and liberty of the citizen to one judge or to a group of judges. Fear of unchecked power, so typical of our State and Federal Governments in other respects, found expression in the criminal law in this insistence upon community participation in the determination of guilt or innocence. The deep commitment of the Nation to the right of jury trial in serious criminal cases as a defense against arbitrary law enforcement qualifies for protection under the Due Process Clause of the Fourteenth Amendment, and must therefore be respected by the States.

Of course jury trial has its weaknesses and the potential for misuse. We are aware of the long debate, especially in this century, among those who write about the administration of justice, as to the wisdom of permitting untrained laymen to determine the facts in civil and criminal proceedings. . . . Yet, the most recent and exhaustive study of the jury in criminal cases concluded that juries do understand the evidence and come to sound conclusions in most of the cases presented to them and that when juries differ with the result at which the judge would have arrived, it is usually because they are serving some of the very purposes for which they were created and for which they are now employed.

The State of Louisiana urges that holding that the Fourteenth Amendment assures a right to jury trial will cast doubt on the integrity of every trial conducted without a jury. Plainly, this is not the import of our holding. Our conclusion is that in the American States, as in the federal judicial system, a general grant of jury trial for serious offenses is a fundamental right, essential for preventing miscarriages of justice and for assuring that fair trials are provided for all defendants. We would not assert, however, that every criminal trial — or any particular trial — held before a judge alone is unfair or that a defendant may never be as fairly treated by a judge as he would be by a jury. Thus we hold no constitutional doubts about the practices, common in both federal and state courts, of accepting waivers of jury trial and prosecuting petty crimes without extending a right to jury trial. . . .

Louisiana's final contention is that even if it must grant jury trials in serious criminal cases, the conviction before us is valid and constitutional because here the petitioner was tried for simple battery and was sentenced to only 60 days in the parish prison. We are not persuaded. It is doubtless true that there is a category of petty crimes or offenses which is not subject to the Sixth Amendment jury trial provision and should not be subject to the Fourteenth Amendment jury trial requirement here applied to the States. Crimes carrying possible penalties up to six months do not require a jury trial if they otherwise qualify as petty offenses. But the penalty authorized for a particular crime is of major relevance in determining whether it is serious or not and may in itself, if severe enough, subject the trial to the mandates of the Sixth Amendment . . . . In the case before us the Legislature of Louisiana has made simple battery a criminal offense punishable by imprisonment for up to two years and a fine. The question, then, is whether a crime carrying such a penalty is an offense which Louisiana may insist on trying without a jury.

. . . In determining whether the length of the authorized prison term or the seriousness of other punishment is enough in itself to require a jury trial, we . . . refer to objective criteria, chiefly the existing laws and practices in the Nation. In the federal system, petty offenses are defined as those punishable by no more than six months in prison and a $500 fine. In 49 of the 50 States crimes subject to trial without a jury, which occasionally include simple battery, are punishable by no more than one year in jail . . . . We need not, however, settle in this case the exact location of the line between petty offenses and serious crimes. It is sufficient for our purposes to hold that a crime punishable by two years in prison is, based on past and contemporary standards in this country, a serious crime and not a petty offense. Consequently, appellant was entitled to a jury trial and it was error to deny it. [Reversed]

[The concurring opinions of Justices Black and Fortas are omitted.]

Mr. Justice Harlan, whom Mr. Justice Stewart joins, dissenting.

Every American jurisdiction provides for trial by jury in criminal cases. The question before us is not whether jury trial is an ancient institution, which it is; nor whether it plays a significant role in the administration of criminal justice, which it does; nor whether it will endure, which it shall. The question in this case is whether the State of Louisiana, which provides trial by jury for all felonies, is prohibited by the Constitution from trying charges of simple battery to the court alone. In my view, the answer to that question, mandated alike by our constitutional history and by the longer history of trial by jury, is clearly "no."

. . . The argument that jury trial is not a requisite of due process is quite simple. The central proposition . . . is that "due process of law" requires only that criminal trials be fundamentally fair . . . . If due process of law requires only fundamental fairness, then the inquiry in each case must be whether a state trial process was a fair one. The Court has held, properly I think, that in an adversary process it is a requisite of fairness, for which there is no adequate substitute, that a criminal defendant be afforded a right to counsel and to cross-examine opposing witnesses. But it simply has not been demonstrated, nor, I think, can it be demonstrated, that trial by jury is the only fair means of resolving issues of fact.

The jury is of course not without virtues. It affords ordinary citizens a valuable opportunity to participate in a process of government, an experience fostering, one hopes, a respect for law. It eases the burden on judges by enabling them to share a part of their sometimes awesome responsibility. A jury may, at times, afford a higher justice by refusing to enforce harsh laws (although it necessarily does so haphazardly, raising the questions whether arbitrary enforcement of harsh laws is better than total enforcement, and whether the jury system is to be defended on the ground that jurors sometimes disobey their oaths). And the jury may, or may not, contribute desirably to the willingness of the general public to accept criminal judgments as just.

It can hardly be gainsaid, however, that the principal original virtue of the jury trial — the limitations a jury imposes on a tyrannous judiciary — has largely disappeared. We no longer live in a medieval or colonial society. Judges enforce laws enacted by democratic decision, not by regal fiat. They are elected by the people or appointed by the people's elected officials, and are responsible not to a distant monarch alone but to reviewing courts, including this one.

The jury system can also be said to have some inherent defects, which are multiplied by the emergence of the criminal law from the relative simplicity that existed when the jury system was devised. It is a cumbersome process, not only imposing great cost in time and money on both the State and the jurors themselves, but also contributing to delay in the machinery of justice. Untrained jurors are presumably less adept at reaching accurate conclusions of fact than judges, particularly if the issues are many or complex. And it is argued by some that trial by jury, far from increasing public respect for law, impairs it: the average man, it is said, reacts favorably neither to the notion that matters he knows to be complex are being decided by other average men, nor to the way the jury system distorts the process of adjudication.

That trial by jury is not the only fair way of adjudicating criminal guilt is well attested by the fact that it is not the prevailing way, either in England or in this country . . . . This Court, other courts, and the political process are available to correct any experiments in criminal procedure that prove fundamentally unfair to defendants. That is not what is being done today: instead, and quite without reason, the Court has chosen to impose upon every State one means of trying criminal cases; it is a good means, but it is not the only fair means, and it is not demonstrably better than the alternatives States might devise.

NOTES

1. *Unfair trial in Duncan?* Did the majority opinion in *Duncan* hold that *this* defendant had an unfair trial? If not, how could his trial have violated the due process clause?

2. *No longer need to protect against government oppression?* Justice Harlan's dissent argues that the primary justification for the jury trial — to guard against government oppression — is no longer necessary. Do you agree?

3. *Jury trial in absence of Constitutional right?* Does a United States District Court have the authority to grant a defendant's request for a jury trial even where it is not constitutionally mandated? The court found that the defendant was not entitled to a jury trial under the constitution because the offense was a petty offense carrying a maximum jail term of six months or less, as discussed below. Nevertheless, noting that there is "some authority" to support such a request, in *United States v. Greenpeace*, 314 F. Supp. 2d 1252 (S.D. Fla. 2004), despite the lack of a constitutional right to a jury trial, the trial judge granted the request over the government's objection "as a matter of judicial discretion," but commented that this was done because the case was "unusual" and "would benefit from a jury's collective decision-making."

[i]   Petty Offenses: Six Month Rule

The Supreme Court in *Duncan* acknowledged that the constitutional right to a jury trial does not apply to "petty offenses," but did not indicate precisely where the line would be drawn. The key concept is how "serious" the offense is. This is determined by the sanction authorized for the crime. Although it would seem easy to assess whether the crime was serious or petty, the issue is more complex than it would appear. Criminal statutes do not always characterize sanctions in a way consistent with the Supreme Court's categories, as discussed below.

In *Dyke v. Taylor Implement Co.*, 391 U.S. 216, 220 (1968), decided the same day as *Duncan*, the Court held that "a six-month jail sentence is short enough to be "petty." On the other hand, the plurality opinion in *Baldwin v. New York*, 399 U.S. 66, 69 (1969), held that no offense is petty "where imprisonment for more than six months is authorized." Note that the key is the sentence that is *authorized;* not the one actually imposed. Similarly, as *Blanton, infra,* makes clear, a mandatory period of incarceration short of six months does not change a petty offense into a serious one.

State variations. Some state constitutions extend the right to a jury trial explicitly to misdemeanors. *See, e.g.,* W. Va. Const. art. 3, 14; Wyo. Const. art. 1, § 9. *See also* STANDARDS FOR CRIMINAL JUSTICE § 15-1.1 (3d ed. 1996) (jury trial should be available to either the defendant or the state if confinement in jail or prison may be imposed); American Bar Association, PRINCIPLES FOR JURIES AND JURY TRIALS, Prin. 1(B)(same).

Right to jury v. right to counsel. It should be noted that the standards for determining the right to a jury trial differ from those triggering the right to counsel. The Supreme Court held that an indigent defendant is entitled to court-appointed *counsel* under the Sixth Amendment even in petty offense" cases — at least where actual imprisonment (even for one day) is involved. *Argersinger v. Hamlin*, 407 U.S. 25 (1972).

[ii]   Aggregate Sentence Exceeding Six Months

Should a defendant be accorded a constitutional right to a jury trial when he or she is prosecuted in a single proceeding for multiple petty offenses where the aggregate sentence authorized for the offenses exceeds six months' imprisonment? Justice O'Connor, speaking for the majority in *Lewis v. United States*, 518 U.S. 322 (1996), answered the question "no," reasoning as follows:

> The Sixth Amendment reserves the jury trial right to defendants accused of serious crimes. [W]e determine whether an offense is serious by looking to the judgment of the legislature, primarily as expressed in the maximum authorized term of imprisonment. Here, by setting the maximum authorized prison term at six months, the legislature categorized the offense of obstructing the mail as petty. The fact that the petitioner was charged with two counts of a petty

offense does not revise the legislative judgment as to the gravity of that particular offense, nor does it transform the petty offense into a serious one, to which the jury trial right would apply.

. . . Petitioner directs our attention to *Codispoti v. Pennsylvania*, 418 U.S. 506 (1974), for support for the assertion that the "aggregation of multiple petty offenses renders a prosecution serious for jury trial purposes." *Codispoti* is inapposite. There, defendants were each convicted at a single, nonjury trial for several charges of criminal contempt. The Court was unable to determine the legislature's judgment of the character of that offense, however, because the legislature had not set a specific penalty for criminal contempt. In such a situation, where the legislature has not specified a maximum penalty, courts use the severity of the penalty actually imposed as the measure of the character of the particular offense. Here, in contrast, we need not look to the punishment actually imposed, because we are able to discern Congress' judgment of the character of the offense.

Justices Kennedy and Breyer concurred in the judgment because the magistrate judge in the instant case had ruled at the outset that no more than six months' imprisonment would be imposed. They strongly disagreed with the majority's analysis of *Codispoti*, however, noting that this decision will make it easier "for a government to evade the constraints of the Sixth Amendment when it seeks to lock up a defendant for a long time."

Justices Stevens and Ginsburg dissented, arguing that a legislature's determination of the severity of charges should be "measured by the maximum sentence authorized for the prosecution as a whole." Since Lewis was charged with offenses carrying a statutory maximum prison sentence of more than six months, he was entitled to a trial by jury.

[iii]   Probation

What happens if the defendant is sentenced to a jail term of more than six months, but the sentence is suspended and the defendant is placed on probation? Is he or she entitled to a jury trial since no incarceration is actually imposed?

In *Alabama v. Shelton*, 535 U.S. 654 (2002), the Court held that the possibility of incarceration of more than six months if probation is revoked entitles the defendant to a *jury trial* even though he or she is not initially incarcerated. The right to appointed *counsel* is limited to cases of actual incarceration; authorized incarceration alone is insufficient. *Scott v. Illinois*, 440 U.S. 367 (1979). Does the difference in the counsel and the jury trial standards make sense?

[iv]   Other Sanctions

While the six-month incarceration rule provides a fairly clear dividing line in cases where imprisonment is authorized, the line becomes fuzzy when other sanctions are present. Is the right to a jury trial triggered by sanctions other than incarceration? The issue is difficult because often more than one of these sanctions are imposed in lieu of, or in addition to, a short period of imprisonment.

In *Blanton v. City of North Las Vegas*, 489 U.S. 538 (1989), the defendant was convicted of driving under the influence and received a number of "punishments." The Court reaffirmed that it would assess whether a case was "petty" by looking at how serious society regarded the offense. Society's value of it would be determined after examining all the penalties accompanying the conviction, especially the maximum possible period of incarceration. Fines and probation were characterized as involving a significant loss of freedom, though not nearly as severe as incarceration.

Like *Duncan*, the Court in *Blanton* refused to hold that a prison term of six months or less automatically meant that the crime was "petty," but:

. . . we do find it appropriate to presume for purposes of the Sixth Amendment that society views such an offense as "petty." A defendant is entitled to a jury trial in such circumstances only if he can demonstrate that any additional statutory penalties, viewed in conjunction with the maximum authorized period of incarceration, are so severe that they clearly reflect a legislative determination that the offense in question is a "serious" one. This standard, albeit somewhat imprecise, should ensure the availability of a jury trial in the rare situation where a legislature packs an offense it deems "serious" with onerous penalties that nonetheless "do not puncture the 6-month incarceration line." [*Id.* at 543]

Applying these principles, the *Blanton* Court held that the defendants were not entitled to a jury trial despite having to endure several inconveniences, discussed below. Since the maximum possible incarceration for them was less than six months, the Court found a "presumption" that the offense was petty. The Court dismissed as "not constitutionally determinative" the fact that the defendant may have to serve a minimum of two days' incarceration; the proper focus was on the maximum, not the minimum incarceration period.

Loss of driver's license. The *Blanton* defendant argued that his DUI offense was not petty because one of his sanctions was the loss of a driver's license for 45–90 days. Measuring the severity of this sanction against that of six months in prison, the Court held that the license suspension was irrelevant if it ran concurrently with the prison term. Even if it did not, however, the Court held that the license loss was not "that significant as a Sixth Amendment matter, particularly when a restricted license may be obtained after only 45 days." 489 U.S. at 544 n.9.

Attend counseling. The *Blanton* defendant also complained that he would have to attend an alcohol abuse education course as part of his sentence. The Supreme Court dismissed this complaint as "*de minimis.*"

Community service. Another penalty in *Blanton* was that the accused could have been ordered to perform 48 hours of community service dressed in clothing identifying him as a DUI offender. The Court also found this unpersuasive since it was less embarrassing and onerous than six months in jail.

Additional charges as repeat offender. The accused in *Blanton* also argued that he was entitled to a jury trial because he would face additional sanctions if convicted in the future as a recidivist DUI offender under state law. The Supreme Court noted that DUI recidivist penalties are commonplace, but essentially held that the issue was moot since the accused did not face such penalties. A footnote made it clear that the Court in *Blanton* did not consider whether a repeat offender facing enhanced penalties had a valid constitutional objection based on the absence of a jury trial in a previous DUI conviction. 489 U.S. at 545 n.12.

Fine. The defendant in *Blanton* faced a maximum fine of $1000. He argued that this was sufficient to make the crime a "serious" offense, even though the maximum prison term was six months. The *Blanton* Court rejected the claim, noting only that the $1000 figure "was well below the $5000 level set by Congress in its most recent definition of a "petty" offense." 489 U.S at 544, *citing* 18 U.S.C. § 1 (1982).

This amorphous language in *Blanton* leaves open the question of what amount of fine is sufficient to entitled the accused to a jury trial. In *Muniz v. Hoffman,* 422 U.S. 454 (1975), a local labor union was fined $10,000 for criminal contempt under the Labor Management and Relations Act. This was the maximum authorized by the applicable statute; a prison term was not permissible. Noting that fines and imprisonment should be analyzed differently because of their differences in risk and deprivation, the Court held that the union was not entitled to a jury trial. The Court analyzed the extent of risk to the union and found that the deprivation was not of "such magnitude" that a jury was required. Since the union has 13,000 dues-paying members, the $10,000 fine did not work such a hardship as to merit Sixth Amendment protection. On the other hand, a

$52,000,000 criminal contempt fine against a union is clearly a "serious contempt" entitling the union to a jury trial. *United Mine Workers v. Bagwell*, 512 U.S. 821 (1994) (court noted it had not specified the precise difference between a "serious" and "petty" criminal contempt sanction).

Muniz did not indicate whether a $10,000 fine would be sufficient to trigger the right to a jury trial for an individual. Would it matter whether the defendant were wealthy or poor? Does this make sense considering the purposes for the jury trial articulated in *Duncan v. Louisiana*?

Court and related costs. Sometimes the actual out-of-pocket costs far exceed the formal fine in a criminal case. Courts distinguish between court and related costs, and fines. The costs are not computed in assessing the right to a jury. *See, e.g., State v. Washington*, 498 So. 2d 136 (La. Ct. App. 1986) (special DWI costs and reinstatement fees were costs, not fines).

[v]   Juvenile Cases

Although *Duncan v. Louisiana, supra*, held that the Sixth Amendment guaranteed a jury trial in serious criminal cases, the Supreme Court subsequently held that the Sixth Amendment does not apply to juveniles convicted in juvenile court. Justice Blackmun's plurality opinion in *McKeiver v. Pennsylvania*, 403 U.S. 528 (1971), reasoned that a juvenile delinquency proceeding is neither civil nor criminal. In addition, fundamental fairness as guaranteed by the due process clause does not require a jury trial in such proceedings, for accurate fact finding is possible without a jury trial. Moreover, the plurality opinion raised the danger of turning the proceeding into an adversary trial rather than an intimate, informal protective proceeding if the formalities of a Sixth Amendment trial were mandated.

[vi]   De Novo Cases

Just as the Sixth Amendment does not guarantee a jury trial in juvenile cases, it also does not bar a jurisdiction from using a two-tiered trial system in which no jury is provided for the first trial, but the accused has an absolute right to a second trial before a jury. In *Ludwig v. Massachusetts*, 427 U.S. 618 (1976), the Supreme Court considered the constitutionality of the Massachusetts "two-tiered" system. In this state, a person charged with a misdemeanor or certain felonies has the option of first being tried in a bench trial. If convicted, the offender may appeal to a higher court and has the right to receive a jury trial *de novo*.

The Supreme Court in *Ludwig* held that this procedure did not violate the Sixth Amendment by unduly burdening the accused's right to be tried by a jury. The Court found that the possibility of a second trial before a jury satisfied the need to protect an individual from government oppression. Moreover, the Court found that the two-tiered system did not place an unreasonable financial burden on the accused who could essentially waive the first trial and proceed directly to the jury trial. The Court also rejected arguments that the two-tiered system was unconstitutional because it permitted a greater sentence at the second trial than given at the first trial, and because it inflicted too many adverse psychological and physical hardships on the accused.

[b]   Court Rules

The rules of criminal procedure are surprisingly silent on the question of when a jury trial is authorized. In the federal system, the matter is resolved by the constitution rather than by the rules of criminal procedure, which are not helpful on the issue.

FEDERAL RULES OF CRIMINAL PROCEDURE

Rule 23. *Jury or Nonjury Trial*

(a) Jury Trial. If the defendant is entitled to a jury trial, the trial must be by jury unless:

(1)   the defendant waives a jury trial in writing;

(2)   the government consents; and

(3)   the court approves. . . .

[4]   Waiver of Jury Trial

Although the Sixth Amendment gives the criminal accused in "serious" cases a right to a jury trial, a jury trial actually occurs in surprisingly few cases. A national survey of felonies resolved in state courts found that a jury trial was held in only two percent of the cases (ninety-five percent of all defendants pled guilty; of the five percent who went to trial, more than sixty percent opted for a bench trial). United States Dept. of Justice, Sourcebook   of   Criminal   Justice   Statistics   Online, www.albany.edu/sourcebook/pdf/t5462004.pdf (read May 19, 2008).

In recognizing a constitutional right to a jury trial, the Supreme Court in *Duncan v. Louisiana* also upheld "the practices, common in both state and federal courts, of accepting waivers of jury trial." *See also Adams v. United States ex rel. McCann*, 317 U.S. 269, 275 (1942)(" . . . an accused, in the exercise of a free and intelligent choice, and with the considered approval of the court, may waive trial by jury . . . ."). The waiver of this important constitutional right must be knowing, intelligent, and voluntary. *See, e.g., Schneckloth v. Bustamonte*, 412 U.S. 218 (1973).

[a]   Knowing, Intelligent, and Voluntary

It is clear that the "knowing, intelligent, and voluntary" standard is applicable to waivers of a jury trial. *See, e.g., Schneckloth v. Bustamonte*, 412 U.S. 218, 237 (1973) ("knowing and intelligent" standard applies to waiver of jury trial). The trial judge has the responsibility for gathering the information necessary to determine whether this standard is satisfied. The Supreme Court has suggested that the trial court should not accept a waiver of jury trial "as a matter of rote, but with sound and advised discretion, with an eye to avoid unreasonable or undue departures from that mode [the jury] of trial." *Patton v. United States*, 281 U.S. 276, 312–313 (1930). Some courts suggest that the court should personally advise the defendant of the right to a jury trial before accepting a waiver of it. *See, e.g., United States v. Straite*, 425 F.2d 594 (D.C. Cir. 1970). This advice is required by Rule 11 before the court accepts a guilty plea, which involves a waiver of jury trial.

Where circumstances indicate some question about whether the waiver is knowing, intelligent, and voluntary, the court should make special efforts to scrutinize the waiver. In one case, for example, there was considerable evidence that the accused was incompetent at the time he waived jury trial. The appellate court held that the trial judge should have delved into such issues as whether the defendant understood he had a right to a jury trial, the difference between a jury and a non-jury trial, and whether the accused mechanically followed his lawyer's advice to waive the jury. *United States v. David*, 511 F.2d 355 (D.C. Cir. 1975).

[b]   Consent of Government and Court

Note that Rule 23(a) and similar rules in many other jurisdictions permit the accused to waive a jury trial. Frequently, these rules also permit both the court and the government (or just the government), without stating reasons, to block the waiver and require the case to be tried by a jury. This is somewhat anomalous since the right to a jury trial is designed to protect the *accused* from government oppression. Nevertheless, in *Singer v. United States*, 380 U.S. 24, 36 (1965), the Supreme Court upheld this rule in a mail fraud case in which the accused wanted to waive a jury trial but the government objected and the case was tried before a jury:

> In light of the Constitution's emphasis on jury trial, we find it difficult to understand how the petitioner can submit the bald proposition that to compel a defendant in a criminal case to undergo a jury trial against his will is contrary to his right to a fair trial or to due process. A defendant's only constitutional right concerning the method of trial is to an impartial trial by jury. We find no constitutional impediment to conditioning a waiver of this right on the consent of the prosecuting attorney and the trial judge when, if either refuses to consent, the result is simply that the defendant is subject to an impartial trial by jury — the very thing that the Constitution guarantees him.

The *Singer* Court did recognize that there may be unusual situations where the accused's interests in a fair trial could require that the accused's waiver of a jury trial be implemented despite the government's desire to impanel a jury. The Court noted:

> In upholding the validity of Rule 23(a), we reiterate [that] . . . the government attorney in a criminal prosecution is not an ordinary party to a controversy, but a "servant of the law" with a "twofold aim . . . that guilt shall not escape or innocence suffer." It was in light of this concept of the role of prosecutor that Rule 23(a) was framed, and we are confident that it is in this light that it will continue to be invoked by government attorneys. Because of this confidence in the integrity of the federal prosecutor, Rule 23(a) does not require that the Government articulate its reasons for demanding a jury trial at the time it refuses to consent to a defendant's proffered waiver. Nor should we assume that federal prosecutors would demand a jury trial for an ignoble purpose. We need not determine in this case whether there might be some circumstances where a defendant's reasons for wanting to be tried by a judge alone are so compelling that the Government's insistence on trial by jury would result in the denial to a defendant of an impartial trial. Petitioner argues that there might arise situations where "passion, prejudice . . . public feeling" or some other factor may render impossible or unlikely an impartial trial by jury. [380 U.S. at 37]

Contrast with waiver of counsel. By contrast, it should be noted that the Supreme Court has held that a defendant has the right to waive *counsel* even if the government objects. The Sixth Amendment guarantees the right to self-representation. *Faretta v. California*, 422 U.S. 806 (1975). Does the difference in approaches between waiver of jury trial and waiver of counsel make sense?

State variations. Approximately half of the states allow prosecutors to either directly request jury trials or to override the defendant's waiver as was done in *Singer*. By contrast, some states provide the defendant with a unilateral and absolute right to a bench trial. *See* Adam H. Kurland, *Providing a Federal Criminal Defendant with a Unilateral Right to a Bench Trial: A Renewed Call to Amend Federal Rule of Criminal Procedure 23(a)*, 26 U.C. Davis L. Rev. 309 (1993).

[c] Form of Waiver

Rule 23 provides specifically that a waiver of a jury trial must be in writing. Many state provisions are identical. *See, e.g.*, Ariz. R. Crim. P. 18.1(b)(waiver of jury trial must be in writing or in open court). This requirement is designed to assure that the accused is aware of the right to a jury and that the decision to waive it is unequivocal and documented. But what happens when counsel (usually) or the accused orally waives a jury trial without also doing so in writing? If the accused knew of the right to a jury trial and consented to the waiver, the waiver will be upheld despite the lack of written documentation. *United States v. Garrett*, 727 F.2d 1003 (11th Cir. 1984). Any other resolution would let the accused agree orally to be tried by the court and then, if convicted, successfully appeal the lack of a written jury waiver.

To alleviate the issue and the risk of appellate reversal, the prosecuting lawyer and the judge should ensure that an oral waiver of a jury trial is not accepted. The prosecutor should be especially careful since some courts place on the government the burden of proving that the defendant's oral waiver was knowing, intelligent, and voluntary.

[d]   Withdrawal of Waiver

On rare occasions a defendant may waive a jury then have a change of mind. In the unusual case where a criminal rule addresses the issue, it usually permits the withdrawal with the court's permission. Sometimes the withdrawal is possible only before a certain point in the proceedings. *See, e.g.*, Ariz. R. Crim. P. 18.1 (withdrawal of jury waiver permitted with judge's permission but not after court begins taking evidence).

[e]   Recommendations

The American Bar Association recommends that any case where confinement is possible be tried by a jury unless waived by the accused with the prosecutor's consent. The court should accept a waiver only after the defendant is advised in open court of the right to a jury, including the consequences of a waiver, and the accused personally waives jury trial in writing or in open court. American Bar Association, Principles for Juries and Jury Trials, Prin. 1 (2005).

[5]   Jury Size

Generally, a jury in a criminal case is comprised of twelve people, perhaps with a few alternates available for emergencies.

FEDERAL RULES OF CRIMINAL PROCEDURE

Rule 23. *Jury or Nonjury Trial*

. . . .

(b) Jury Size.

(1) In General. A jury consists of 12 persons unless this rule provides otherwise.

(2) Stipulation for a Smaller Jury. At any time before the verdict, the parties may, with the court's approval, stipulate in writing that:

(A) the jury may consist of fewer than 12 persons; or

(B) a jury of fewer than 12 persons may return a verdict if the court finds it necessary to excuse a juror for good cause after the trial begins.

(3) Court Order for a Jury of 11. After the jury has retired to deliberate, the court may permit a jury of 11 persons to return a verdict, even without a stipulation by the parties, if the court finds good cause to excuse a juror.

NOTES

1. *States approve smaller juries.* A significant minority of jurisdictions, however, authorize juries of less than twelve for some or all criminal cases. *E.g.*, Fla. R. Crim. P. 3.270 (jury of 12 in capital cases, 6 in all other criminal cases). Often a 12-person jury is used in serious cases (usually felonies) and a 6-person jury is convened for less serious ones (usually misdemeanors).

2. *Limits on reduction in number of jurors.* Does the Sixth Amendment permit a jury of less than twelve? If so, how small can a criminal jury be? Could a state permit a jury of three, as happens in some European countries where three people (including a judge and two lay people) decide guilt or innocence?

In *Williams v. Florida*, discussed in *Ballew v. Georgia*, below, the United States Supreme Court upheld a Florida statute providing a six person jury in all but capital cases (where a twelve person jury was authorized). *Ballew* addressed the question whether a jury of less than six was permissible under the Sixth Amendment.

BALLEW v. GEORGIA
435 U.S. 223 (1977)

MR. JUSTICE BLACKMUN announced the judgment of the Court and delivered an opinion in which MR. JUSTICE STEVENS joined.

This case presents the issue whether a state criminal trial to a jury of only five persons deprives the accused of the right to trial by jury guaranteed to him by the Sixth and Fourteenth Amendments. Our resolution of the issue requires an application of principles enunciated in *Williams v. Florida*, 399 U.S. 78 (1970), where the use of a six-person jury in a state criminal trial was upheld against similar constitutional attack.

[Petitioner, manager of an adult theater in Atlanta, was convicted of two misdemeanor counts of distributing obscene materials after his theater exhibited a film. He was convicted by a jury of five persons, consistent with Georgia law providing a five person jury in misdemeanor cases, that deliberated only thirty-eight minutes. Petitioner's motion for a twelve person jury was denied. He was sentenced to two concurrent one year sentences, both suspended upon payment of a $2000 fine. The petitioner lost appeals in Georgia state courts and applied for certiorari in the United States Supreme Court.]

The Fourteenth Amendment guarantees the right of trial by jury in all state nonpetty criminal cases. *Duncan v. Louisiana*, 391 U.S. 145 (1968). The Court in *Duncan* applied this Sixth Amendment right to the States because "trial by jury in criminal cases is fundamental to the American scheme of justice." The right attaches in the present case because the maximum penalty for violating § 26-2101, as it existed at the time of the alleged offenses, exceeded six months' imprisonment.

In *Williams v. Florida*, the Court reaffirmed that the "purpose of the jury trial . . . is to prevent oppression by the Government." . . . This purpose is attained by the participation of the community in determinations of guilt and by the application of the common sense of laymen who, as jurors, consider the case.

Williams held that these functions and this purpose could be fulfilled by a jury of six members . . . . Rather than requiring 12 members, then, the Sixth Amendment mandated a jury only of sufficient size to promote group deliberation, to insulate members from outside intimidation, and to provide a representative cross-section of the community. Although recognizing that by 1970 little empirical research had evaluated jury performance, the [*Williams*] Court found no evidence that the reliability of jury verdicts diminished with six-member panels. Nor did the Court anticipate significant differences in result, including the frequency of "hung" juries. Because the reduction in size did not threaten exclusion of any particular class from jury roles, concern that the representative or cross-section character of the jury would suffer with a decrease to six members seemed "an unrealistic one." As a consequence, the six-person jury was held not to violate the Sixth and Fourteenth Amendments.

When the Court in *Williams* permitted the reduction in jury size — or, to put it another way, when it held that a jury of six was not unconstitutional — it expressly reserved ruling on the issue whether a number smaller than six passed constitutional scrutiny. The Court refused to speculate when this so-called "slippery slope" would become too steep. We face now, however, the two-fold question whether a further reduction in the size of the state criminal trial jury does make the grade too dangerous, that is, whether it inhibits the functioning of the jury as an institution to a significant degree, and, if so, whether any state interest counterbalances and justifies the disruption so as to preserve its constitutionality.

[*Williams* and later cases] generated a quantity of scholarly work on jury size. These writings do not draw or identify a bright line below which the number of jurors would not be able to function as required by the standards enunciated in *Williams*. On the other hand, they raise significant questions about the wisdom and constitutionality of a reduction below six. We examine these concerns:

First, recent empirical data suggest that progressively smaller juries are less likely to foster effective group deliberation. At some point, this decline leads to inaccurate fact-finding and incorrect application of the common sense of the community to the facts . . . . As juries decrease in size, then, they are less likely to have members who remember each of the important pieces of evidence or argument. Furthermore, the smaller the group, the less likely it is to overcome the biases of its members to obtain an accurate result . . . . Groups also exhibited increased motivation and self-criticism. All these advantages, except, perhaps, self-motivation, tend to diminish as the size of the group diminishes.

. . . Second, the data now raise doubts about the accuracy of the results achieved by smaller and smaller panels. Statistical studies suggest that the risk of convicting an innocent person (Type I error) rises as the size of the jury diminishes. Because the risk of not convicting a guilty person (Type II error) increases with the size of the panel, an optimal jury size can be selected as a function of the interaction between the two risks. [Two researchers] concluded that the optimal size, for the purpose of minimizing errors, should vary with the importance attached to the two types of mistakes. After weighing Type I error as 10 times more significant than Type II, perhaps not an unreasonable assumption, they concluded that the optimal jury size was between six and eight. As the size diminished to five and below, the weighted sum of errors increased because of the enlarging risk of the conviction of innocent defendants.

Another doubt about progressively smaller juries arises from the increasing inconsistency that results from the decreases. Saks [M. Saks, Jury Verdicts (1977)] argued that the "more a jury type fosters consistency, the greater will be the proportion of juries which select the correct (i.e., the same) verdict and the fewer 'errors' will be made."

. . . Third, the data suggest that the verdicts of jury deliberation in criminal cases will vary as juries become smaller, and that the variance amounts to an imbalance to the detriment of one side, the defense. [Several researchers found that the number of hung juries would decrease as the number of jurors decreased.] . . . [S]tudies emphasized that juries in criminal cases generally hang with only one, or more likely two jurors remaining unconvinced of guilt. Also, group theory suggests that a person in the minority will adhere to his position more frequently when he has at least one other person supporting his argument . . . .

While we adhere to, and reaffirm our holding in *Williams v. Florida*, these studies, most of which have been made since *Williams* was decided in 1970, lead us to conclude that the purpose and functioning of the jury in a criminal trial is seriously impaired, and to a constitutional degree, by a reduction in size to below six members. We readily admit that we do not pretend to discern a clear line between six members and five. But the assembled data raise substantial doubt about the reliability and appropriate representation of panels smaller than six.

. . . Georgia argues that its use of five-member juries does not violate the Sixth and Fourteenth Amendments because they are used only in misdemeanor cases. If six persons may constitutionally assess the felony charge in *Williams*, the State reasons, five persons should be a constitutionally adequate number for a misdemeanor trial. The problem with this argument is that the purpose and functions of the jury do not vary significantly with the importance of the crime . . . . In the present case the possible deprivation of liberty is substantial. The State charged petitioner with misdemeanors . . . and he has been given concurrent sentences of imprisonment, each for one year, and fines totaling $2,000 have been imposed. We cannot conclude that there is less need for the imposition and the direction of the sense of the community in this case than when the State has chosen to label an offense a felony. The need for an effective jury here must be judged by the same standards announced and applied in *Williams v. Florida*.

[T]he retention by Georgia of the unanimity requirement does not solve the Sixth and Fourteenth Amendment problem. Our concern has to do with the ability of the smaller group to perform the functions mandated by the Amendments. That a five-person jury may return a unanimous decision does not speak to the questions whether the group engaged in meaningful deliberation, could remember all the important facts and arguments, and truly represented the sense of the entire community.

. . . Georgia [also] submits that the five-person jury adequately represents the community because there is no arbitrary exclusion of any particular class. We agree that it has not been demonstrated that the Georgia system violates the Equal Protection Clause by discriminating on the basis of race or some other improper classification. But the data outlined above raise substantial doubt about the ability of juries truly to represent the community as membership decreases below six. If the smaller and smaller juries will lack consistency, as the cited studies suggest, then the sense of the community will not be applied equally in like cases. Not only is the representation of racial minorities threatened in such circumstances, but also majority attitude or various minority positions may be misconstrued or misapplied by the smaller groups.

. . . With the reduction in the number of jurors below six creating a substantial threat to Sixth and Fourteenth Amendment guarantees, we must consider whether any interest of the State justifies the reduction. We find no significant state advantage in reducing the number of jurors from six to five.

. . . The point that is to be made, of course, is that a reduction in size from six to five or four or even three would save the States little. They could reduce slightly the daily allowances, but with a reduction from six to five the savings would be minimal. If little time is gained by the reduction from 12 to 6, less will be gained with a reduction from 6 to 5 . . . .

Petitioner, therefore, has established that his trial on criminal charges before a five-member jury deprived him of the right to trial by jury guaranteed by the Sixth and Fourteenth Amendments. [Reversed]

[The concurring opinions of JUSTICES STEVENS, WHITE, and BRENNAN are omitted.]

MR. JUSTICE POWELL, with whom THE CHIEF JUSTICE and MR. JUSTICE REHNQUIST join, concurring in the judgment.

. . . I do not agree . . . that every feature of jury trial practice must be the same in both federal and state courts . . . .

NOTES

1. *Why not five? Ballew* holds that a jury of six is permissible but a jury of five is not. Do the Court's reasons convince you that this is the correct place to draw the line? Can you think of a situation in which a jury of less than six persons may be permissible? *See* Colo. Rev. Stat. Ann. § 13-10-114, providing that juries in municipal courts shall consist of a minimum of three and a maximum of six, persons. Is this constitutional? Is additional information needed to address this question?

2. *What happened between Ballew and Williams? Williams*, decided in 1970, held that a six-person jury was constitutionally permissible. But *Ballew*, in 1977, held that a five-person jury was not. What happened between 1970 and 1977 to convince the Court that six was the bottom limit on jury size? If the Court in *Williams* had the same empirical data as it had in *Ballew*, do you think it would have accepted a six person jury? If not, where would it have drawn the line?

3. *Questioning Williams.* The soundness of Williams has been questioned on both empirical and historical grounds. *See,* Michael J. Saks, *The Smaller the Jury, the Greater the Unpredictability,* 79 JUDICATURE 263, 265 (1996) (arguing that juries smaller than twelve are both unwise and unconstitutional); Alisa Smith, *The Case for Overturning Williams v. Florida and the Six Person Jury: History, Law, and Empirical Evidence,* 60 FLA. L. REV. 441 (2008)(arguing that the clear understanding and contemplation of the Framers of the Sixth Amendment was that juries would be comprised of twelve citizens (albeit, at the time, twelve white male property owners; discussing recent empirical data on impact of jury size).

Query: In view of changes in the personnel of the Supreme Court from the Burger Court of the 1970's to the present Roberts Court, do you think that the present Court would have decided *Williams* differently? Justices Scalia and Thomas, in particular, are strong "originalist" voices on the current Court whose views have led them on several occasions to cast decisive votes in favor of expanded interpretations of defendants' constitutional rights in cases where they have been persuaded that the Court has strayed from the meaning of the Constitution as originally understood by the Framers. *See, e.g., United States v. Hubbell,* 530 U.S. 27 (2000)(Fifth Amendment privilege against self-incrimination, discussed in Ch. 7); *Apprendi v. New Jersey,* 530 U.S. 466 (2000)(Fifth and Sixth Amendment right to have jury decide sentence-enhancing facts, discussed in Ch. 17); *Crawford v. Washington,* 541 U.S. 36 (Sixth Amendment right of confrontation, discussed in this chapter); *Kyllo v. United States,* 533 U.S. 27 (2001)(Fourth Amendment prohibition against unreasonable search and seizure). Might the present Court be hospitable to reconsidering *Williams* if given the opportunity?

4. *Size v. unanimity.* The size of a jury is related to the issue of whether the jury verdict must be unanimous. This issue is discussed later in this chapter.

5. *ABA recommendations.* The American Bar Association recommends the traditional twelve-person rule for serious offenses. STANDARDS FOR CRIMINAL JUSTICE § 15-1.1(a) and (b) (3d ed. 1996) (jury should consist of 12 persons, except a jury of 6 to 11 persons may be provided if the maximum possible penalty is confinement for 6 months or less); American Bar Association, PRINCIPLES FOR JURIES AND JURY TRIALS, Prin. 3 (2005).

6. *Further information.* For more information on this subject, *see* J. Myron Jacobstein & Roy M. Mersky, eds., JURY SIZE: ARTICLES AND BIBLIOGRAPHY FROM THE LITERATURE OF LAW AND THE SOCIAL AND BEHAVIORAL SCIENCES (1998).

[a] Waiver of Full Jury

In most jurisdictions, including the federal system pursuant to Rule 23(b), the accused has a right to a jury of a certain size but is permitted to waive that right and submit to a trial by a smaller jury. *See, e.g.,* Ark. Stat. Ann. § 16-32-202 (jury composed of 12 people, but parties may agree to lesser number in non-felonies). Before accepting a waiver, the court must ensure that both defense counsel and the accused agree to the smaller jury. If the smaller jury is necessitated by the removal of a sitting juror, the accused is not entitled to know the identity of the juror to be removed. *United States v. Yonn,* 702 F.2d 1341 (11th Cir. 1983).

Although a jury of five or fewer members would violate *Ballew,* could the defendant waive a jury of six and agree to be tried by a jury of five or less? This could happen if a jury of six started a case, then one or more jurors had to quit for a legitimate reason, such as illness or a family death. Recall that a defendant may waive a jury trial, so why should the accused be barred from waiving a jury comprised of six members and submit to trial by a jury of five or fewer jurors?

[b] Alternate Jurors

Irrespective of the size of the trial jury, every jurisdiction also provides a mechanism for selecting and using *alternate jurors*. Ordinarily from one to four alternate jurors may be selected, depending on the likely length of the trial. The trial court is usually given the discretion whether to select alternate jurors and how many should be taken. The usual rule is that the alternate jurors are selected in the same manner as the trial jury and hear the same evidence as the trial jury, sometimes even sitting in the jury box during the trial. Ordinarily the alternate jurors are identified as such throughout the trial.

Not identifying alternates and regular jurors until just before deliberation. In some jurisdictions, however, the alternates and regular jurors are not identified as one or the other, and are selected as one jury of, say, fifteen people. Shortly before the jury retires, the judge randomly "deselects" the alternates and sends the remaining jurors to the jury room to deliberate. This novel approach is designed to keep alternate jurors interested in the trial since no juror knows whether he or she is a regular or alternate juror until after final jury instructions. *See* STANDARDS FOR CRIMINAL JUSTICE, § 15-2.9(a) (3d ed. 1993); American Bar Association, PRINCIPLES FOR JURIES AND JURY TRIALS, Prin. 11(G)(2)(status of jurors as regular or alternate jurors should be determined by random selection at the time for jury deliberation). Ordinarily, the alternate jurors are dismissed when the trial jury retires to consider its verdict, though in many locales the court may keep them until verdict in case a regular juror must be replaced during deliberations.

FEDERAL RULES OF CRIMINAL PROCEDURE

Rule 24. *Trial Jurors*

. . . .

[c] Alternate Jurors

(1) *In General.* The court may impanel up to six alternate jurors to replace any jurors who are unable to perform or who are disqualified from performing their duties.

(2) *Procedure.*

(A) Alternate jurors must have the same qualifications and be selected and sworn in the same manner as any other juror.

(B) Alternate jurors replace jurors in the same sequence in which the alternates were selected. An alternate juror who replaces a juror has the same authority as the other jurors.

(3) *Retaining Alternate Jurors.* The court may retain alternate jurors after the jury retires to deliberate. The court must ensure that a retained alternate does not discuss the case with anyone until that alternate replaces a juror or is discharged. If an alternate replaces a juror after deliberations have begun, the court must instruct the jury to begin its deliberations anew.

NOTES

1. *Great judicial discretion.* The trial court is given great discretion in deciding whether and when to replace a regular juror with an alternate juror. Usually the decision will be reversed on appeal only if the defendant can show prejudice. *See, e.g., United States v. Fajardo*, 787 F.2d 1523 (11th Cir. 1986); *see also, United States v. Leahy*, 82 F.3d 624 (5th Cir. 1996) (court would only find prejudice if the replaced juror was discharged without factual support or for a legally irrelevant reason; juror was correctly removed because of a hearing impairment, discovered once deliberations

began, impeded juror's capacity to participate in deliberations). Ordinarily the trial judge will hold a hearing to decide whether a regular juror should be replaced with an alternate.

2. *Illustrations of reasons to replace juror.* To illustrate the variety of reasons for impanelling an alternate juror, the following reasons were held to be acceptable in federal appellate decisions: the regular juror lied while answering questions during voir dire; the juror slept through some of the testimony; the juror's employer submitted a letter indicating that the juror was desperately needed to inspect an Air Force Base; the juror received anonymous telephone calls concerning the trial; the juror tried to contact a defendant; the juror was ten minutes late to trial; in mid-trial the juror indicated that she had already formed an opinion as to guilt; a juror surreptitiously used a cell phone during trial; and a juror's parents-in-law had worked for the defendant, a local politician, in elections.

3. *Role of alternates who replace regular jurors.* If an alternate juror is substituted for a regular juror, the alternate essentially becomes a regular juror and is subject to exactly the same rules and rights as the other trial jurors. The alternate will vote and discuss the case as any other juror.

4. *Role of alternate jurors who do not replace regular jurors.* In most jurisdictions, alternates who do not replace a regular juror are dismissed, completing their involvement in the case. Alternate jurors ordinarily do not accompany the regular jury to the jury room during deliberations or participate in jurors' discussions about the case. *See, e.g., United States v. Beasley*, 464 F.2d 468 (10th Cir. 1972) (reversal because alternate juror went with trial jury to jury room and participated in vote to select foreperson). If an alternate juror does attend the deliberations without participating in them, the conviction will be reversed only if the defendant can show prejudice. *United States v. Olano*, 507 U.S. 725 (1993).

[6] Selection of Jurors

Some lawyers believe that the most important procedural facet of a criminal trial is the selection of the jurors. For many reasons, this process has come under increased scrutiny in recent years, resulting in tighter controls over a process that used to be subject to little meaningful appellate review.

Jury pool. The process starts with the *jury pool*, a large group of people who could be part of a jury. This theoretically includes all eligible jurors in the jurisdiction. Federal law provides that jurors should be randomly selected from a fair cross section of the community. 28 U.S.C. § 1861. Each federal district must have a written plan that implements this policy and ensures that there is no discrimination against people because of various ethnic and economic reasons. 28 U.S.C. § 1863. Failure to adhere to proper selection procedures can result in the dismissal of an indictment. 28 U.S.C. § 1867(d).

Sources of jury pool. People are selected for the jury pool from various lists, including voting lists, lists of driver's license holders, tax rolls, telephone directories, or city directories. Sometimes special efforts are made to obtain the names of persons in groups not adequately represented in the usual sources.

Venire. Often, a computer selects a number, perhaps 100–500 people who constitute the *venire*. The members of the venire then receive a letter or summons that directs them to appear at the courthouse at a specified date and hour.

Process for selecting petit jury. Members of the venire are subjected to a process that will produce the *petit jury*, a jury of from six to twelve persons, plus alternates, who will decide most factual questions in criminal cases. First, venire members, perhaps in groups of from 25 to 50 persons, will be asked general questions to ascertain whether they qualify for jury service. This interrogation process, often referred to as the *voir dire*, is conducted by the judge and, in most jurisdictions, counsel for both sides. Some members of the jury pool are eliminated at that time by the judge *for cause* — a reason why the person cannot (*e.g.*, physical or mental problems, childcare or equivalent responsibilities, job responsibilities) or should not (*e.g.*, related to a party or lawyer in the case, such strong feelings about the case or the legal system that he or she cannot render a fair decision) serve as a juror. For example, if a potential juror is pregnant and likely to have a baby in a few weeks, she may be excluded from the panel for physical reasons. Similarly, if a potential juror is the husband of the prosecutor in the case, he will be excluded.

Those jurors who have remained because they were not excluded for cause may still be excluded by the lawyers through a *peremptory* challenge, discussed in detail later in this chapter. This challenge permits the lawyer for each party to exclude a fixed number of potential jurors. For example, in some jurisdictions each party's lawyer in a felony case may exclude up to eight potential jurors for virtually any reason.

Compensation. Jurors are paid a daily fee for their service, plus mileage costs for travel. *See, e.g.*, 28 U.S.C. § 1871 (federal jurors paid forty dollars per day, travel allowance, and subsistence allowance in some circumstances). Many states provide paltry fees, sometimes as little as two dollars per day. *See, e.g.*, S.C. Code Ann. § 14-7-1370 (jury pay varies by county, with jurors in certain counties paid two dollars per day).

[a]   Eligibility for Jury Service

Virtually any adult is eligible to serve as a juror. Federal law is typical, providing that a person is eligible for jury service unless the person is not: a citizen, 18 years old, a resident of the district for one year, sufficiently capable in English to speak and fill out a questionnaire, mentally or physically capable of serving, or if the person has a felony criminal record or pending felony charges and civil rights have not been restored. 28 U.S.C. § 1865. See also American Bar Association, PRINCIPLES FOR JURIES AND JURY TRIALS, Prin. 2 (2005)(for juror eligibility, persons must be at least age 18, U.S. citizens, a resident of the proper geographical district, and able to communicate in English and no satisfactory interpreter is available, and has not been convicted of a felony and is in actual confinement or under parole or probation or court supervision).

States may require the juror to be a citizen of the state and the county with jurisdiction in the case. Some also bar people who are related to a party or attorney within a specified degree, will be a witness in the case, served on the grand jury that indicted the defendant, served on a prior jury in the same case, or have a material interest in the outcome of the case. *See, e.g.*, Ark. Stat. Ann. § 16-31-102; S.C. Code Ann. § 14-7-830.

As discussed more fully in Chapter 14 (Jurisdiction and Venue), the accused has a right to be tried by a jury from the district or county where the crime was committed. This affects juror eligibility by limiting the geographical area from which jurors may be selected.

If an ineligible juror serves and participates in the rendering of the verdict, the defendant may challenge the validity of the verdict. However, some jurisdictions have enacted statutes that uphold the verdict unless the juror lied during questioning on voir dire. *E.g.*, Ark. Stat. Ann. § 16-31-107.

According to federal law, no citizen shall be excluded from federal jury service because of the person's race, color, religion, sex, national origin, or economic status. 28 U.S.C. § 1862. The next case addresses discrimination in juror eligibility.

TAYLOR v. LOUISIANA
419 U.S. 522 (1975)

Mr. Justice White delivered the opinion of the Court.

[Appellant was sentenced to death for aggravated kidnaping. He argued that the jury venire deprived him of his Sixth Amendment right to a trial by a jury that was representative of the community. Louisiana law provided that a woman should not be selected for jury service unless she had previously filed a written declaration of her desire to be subject to jury service. The Supreme Court accepted the case to consider whether the Louisiana system deprived the appellant of his Sixth Amendment right to an impartial jury trial.]

. . . The Louisiana jury-selection system does not disqualify women from jury service, but in operation its conceded systematic impact is that only a very few women, grossly disproportionate to the number of eligible women in the community, are called for jury service. In this case, no women were on the venire from which the petit jury was drawn. The issue we have, therefore, is whether a jury-selection system which operates to exclude from jury service an identifiable class of citizens constituting 53% of eligible jurors in the community comports with the Sixth and Fourteenth Amendments.

[The Court held that Taylor, a male, had standing to challenge the exclusion of women on the criminal jury that convicted him, as he was entitled to a jury drawn from a fair cross section of the community.]

. . . The background against which this case must be decided includes our holding in *Duncan v. Louisiana*, 391 U.S. 145 (1968), that the Sixth Amendment's provision for jury trial is made binding on the States by virtue of the Fourteenth Amendment. Our inquiry is whether the presence of a fair cross section of the community on venires, panels, or lists from which petit juries are drawn is essential to the fulfillment of the Sixth Amendment's guarantee of an impartial jury trial in criminal prosecutions.

. . . The unmistakable import of this Court's opinions, at least since 1940, and not repudiated by intervening decisions, is that the selection of a petit jury from a representative cross section of the community is an essential component of the Sixth Amendment right to a jury trial.

. . . We accept the fair-cross-section requirement as fundamental to the jury trial guaranteed by the Sixth Amendment and are convinced that the requirement has solid foundation. The purpose of a jury is to guard against the exercise of arbitrary power — to make available the commonsense judgment of the community as a hedge against the overzealous or mistaken prosecutor and in preference to the professional or perhaps overconditioned or biased response of a judge. *Duncan v. Louisiana*. This prophylactic vehicle is not provided if the jury pool is made up of only special segments of the populace or if large, distinctive groups are excluded from the pool. Community participation in the administration of the criminal law, moreover, is not only consistent with our democratic heritage but is also critical to public confidence in the fairness of the criminal justice system.

. . . We are also persuaded that the fair-cross-section requirement is violated by the systematic exclusion of women, who in the judicial district involved here, amounted to 53% of the citizens eligible for jury service. This conclusion necessarily entails the judgment that women are sufficiently numerous and distinct from men and that if they are systematically eliminated from jury panels, the Sixth Amendment's fair-cross-section requirement cannot be satisfied.

. . . There remains the argument that women as a class serve a distinctive role in society and that jury service would so substantially interfere with that function that the State has ample justification for excluding women from service unless they volunteer, even though the result is that almost all jurors are men.

. . . The States are free to grant exemptions from jury service to individuals in case of special hardship or incapacity and to those engaged in particular occupations the uninterrupted performance of which is critical to the community's welfare. It would not appear that such exemptions would pose substantial threats that the remaining pool of jurors would not be representative of the community. A system excluding all women, however, is a wholly different matter. It is untenable to suggest these days that it would be a special hardship for each and every woman to perform jury service or that society cannot spare any women from their present duties. This may be the case with many, and it may be burdensome to sort out those who should be exempted from those who should serve. But that task is performed in the case of men, and the administrative convenience in dealing with women as a class is insufficient justification for diluting the quality of community judgment represented by the jury in criminal trials.

. . . Our holding does not augur or authorize the fashioning of detailed jury selection codes by federal courts. The fair-cross-section principle must have much leeway in application. The States remain free to prescribe relevant qualifications for their jurors and to provide reasonable exemptions so long as it may be fairly said that the jury lists or panels are representative of the community.

. . . It should also be emphasized that in holding that petit juries must be drawn from a source fairly representative of the community we impose no requirement that petit juries actually chosen must mirror the community and reflect the various distinctive groups in the population. Defendants are not entitled to a jury of any particular composition, but the jury wheels, pools of names, panels, or venires from which juries are drawn must not systematically exclude distinctive groups in the community and thereby fail to be reasonably representative thereof. [Reversed]

MR. CHIEF JUSTICE BURGER concurs in the result.

MR. JUSTICE REHNQUIST, dissenting.

. . . The majority opinion canvasses various of our jury trial cases . . . . Relying on carefully chosen quotations, it concludes that the "unmistakable import" of our cases is that the fair-cross-section requirement "is an essential component of the Sixth Amendment right to a jury trial." I disagree. Fairly read, the only "unmistakable import" of those cases is that due process and equal protection prohibit jury-selection systems which are likely to result in biased or partial juries.

. . . Absent any suggestion that appellant's trial was unfairly conducted, or that its result was unreliable, I would not require Louisiana to retry him (assuming the State can once again produce its evidence and witnesses) in order to impose on him the sanctions which its laws provide.

NOTES

1. *Challenge to array.* In barring discrimination against a group, *Taylor* and other cases permit what has been called a challenge to the *array*. Sometimes this is referred to as a challenge to the *panel* (this term may also refer to a challenge to the venire or to the individual body of twelve or so jurors sitting in an individual case). This alleges that the jury pool is somehow defective because it does not include certain groups. Proof of this defect requires considerable demographic data to show that the jury pool is statistically unrepresentative. In order to enable the judge to cure any defects, some jurisdictions require that such challenges be made before the jury is sworn. *E.g.,* N.Y. Crim. Pro. Law § 270.10 (challenge to panel must be made before jury selection begins; otherwise issue is waived).

2. *Taylor not retroactive.* In *Daniel v. Louisiana,* 420 U.S. 31 (1975), decided a week after *Taylor,* the Court held that *Taylor* was not retroactive. It applied only to convictions obtained by juries empaneled prior to the *Taylor* decision. Was *Taylor* based on the fact that the defendant received an unfair trial? If so, shouldn't the case be retroactive? What practical problems would arise if *Taylor* had been made retroactive?

3. *Impact of representation of petit jurors.* Would there be a Sixth Amendment violation if the particular jury that tried the defendant contained no minorities, but the

original venire contained a fair representation of all groups in the community? What if the venire contained a definite underrepresentation of a minority, but the jury that tried the accused was representative of the community?

4. *Exemptions from jury service.* Note that *Taylor* specifically authorizes a jurisdiction to exempt from jury service people who have a special hardship or incapacity or who work in "particular occupations the uninterrupted performance of which is critical to the community's welfare." This permits jurisdictions to excuse physicians, veterinarians, teachers, judges, and other groups. A federal statute excludes from federal jury service active duty armed forces personnel; police and fire officers; and various officials of the executive, legislative, and judicial departments. 28 U.S.C. § 1863.

State statutes contain similar provisions, plus other categories. *E.g.*, Iowa Code §§ 607A.5 and 607A.6 (automatically excludes person solely responsible for daily care of permanently disabled person in their home; discretionary excuses for hardship, inconvenience, or public necessity); N.J. Stat. Ann. § 2B:20-10 (exemptions include those with obligations to care for a sick, aged or infirm dependent or a minor child, those providing highly specialized health care service, teachers during school terms, volunteer firefighters and members of volunteer first aid or rescue squads).

The American Bar Association and a growing number of states reject these occupational (and other) exemptions to jury service in order to provide maximum inclusiveness and representativeness. *See* American Bar Association, Principles for Juries and Jury Trials, Prin. 2 (jury service should not be denied or limited because of occupation).

5. *Burden of proof.* In *Duren v. Missouri*, 439 U.S. 357 (1979), the Court struck down a Missouri rule that automatically exempted from jury service any woman who requested an exemption. The decision clarified the burden of proof needed to establish a fair cross-section violation. The Court in *Duren* held that:

> In order to establish a prima facie violation of the fair-cross-section requirement, the defendant must show (1) that the group alleged to be excluded is a "distinctive" group in the community; (2) that the representation of this group in venires from which juries are selected is not fair and reasonable in relation to the number of such persons in the community; and (3) that this underrepresentation is due to systematic exclusion of the group in the jury-selection process . . . . [O]nce the defendant has made a prima facie showing of an infringement of his constitutional right to a jury drawn from a fair cross section of the community, it is the State that bears the burden of justifying this infringement by showing attainment of a fair cross section to be incompatible with a significant state interest. [439 U.S. at 364, 368]

a. *Distinctive group. Duren* requires proof that a distinctive group was underrepresented. Why is this a requirement? If the underlying problem is the denial of an impartial jury, what difference does it make whether the views that were underrepresented stemmed from a distinctive group? Would there still be a problem if there were no liberals on the jury, irrespective of whether liberals are a distinctive group? What about homosexuals?

What would make a group a "distinctive group"? Must it be distinct in an objective way? Must its members have internal cohesion or be identified as a separate group by society? In *Lockhart v. McCree*, 476 U.S. 162 (1986), the Supreme Court made a minimal effort to define "distinctive group." In holding that persons with strong anti-death penalty views are *not* part of a distinctive group, the Court stated:

> The essence of a "fair-cross-section" claim is the systematic exclusion of "a distinctive group in the community." [citation to *Duren*] In our view, groups defined solely in terms of shared attitudes that would prevent or substantially impair members of the group from performing one of their duties as juror-

s. . .are not "distinctive groups" for fair-cross-section purposes. . . . In sum, . . . any . . . group defined solely in terms of shared attitudes that render members of the group unable to serve as jurors in a particular case, may be excluded from jury service without contravening any of the basic objectives of the fair-cross-section requirement. [*Id.* at 174, 176–77]

Clearly, certain groups qualify as "distinctive groups." *See, e.g., United States v. Kleifgen*, 557 F.2d 1293 (9th Cir. 1977) (blacks and males are cognizable groups; young people, less educated people, and unemployed people are not cognizable groups); *State v. Couture*, 194 Conn. 530, 482 A.2d 300 (1984), *cert. denied*, 469 U.S. 1192 (1985) (hispanics are distinctive group); *United States v. Gelb*, 881 F.2d 1155 (2d Cir. 1989) (Jews are cognizable group).

But what about less identifiable groups? In *Lockhart*, the Court held that those strongly opposed to the death penalty did not comprise a distinctive group. *See also United States v. Salamone*, 800 F.2d 1216 (3d Cir. 1986) (members of National Rifle Association not distinctive group).

b. *Fair and reasonable representation.* In order to make the venire a fair and reasonable representation of the community, is it necessary that the percentage of people in each "distinctive group" be exactly the same in both the venire and the community? If not, how great a difference is permissible? *See United States v. Test*, 550 F.2d 577 (10th Cir. 1976) (fact that disparity is statistically significant does not mean it is legally significant). *See also Anderson v. Casscles*, 531 F.2d 682 (2d Cir. 1976) (although county had 4% black population and jury venire had only 2%, difference insufficient to constitute unreasonable representation). *See generally* Sara Sun Beale, *Integrating Statistical Evidence and Legal Theory to Challenge the Selection of Grand and Petit Jurors*, 46 Law & Contemp. Probs. 269 (Autumn 1983).

c. *Systematic exclusion.* What is the relationship between a "systematic exclusion" and an intentional exclusion? Can a systematic exclusion, barred by *Duren*, be unintentional? What if an accidental computer error excluded a particular group of people? Why is systematic exclusion even an issue? If the concern is the composition of the jury (or even the venire), should it matter whether a group was systematically excluded if it was, in fact, absent from the jury or venire?

d. *Significant state interest. Duren* holds that a state can justify the fair cross section violation by proving that the attainment of a fair cross section is incompatible with a significant state interest. What type of significant state interest would justify this constitutional violation? Why should a significant *state* interest be permitted to justify the violation of the *defendant's* right to a jury comprised of a fair cross section of the community?

[b]   Selecting the Petit Jury: In General

As described above, the selection of the actual panel of 6-12 jurors (plus alternates) proceeds according to a fairly predictable process. In general terms, the entire venire or a smaller group of it is interrogated to see which potential jurors should be disqualified for cause or peremptorily. The Supreme Court has stressed the importance of the voir dire process:

> *Voir dire* plays a critical function in assuring the criminal defendant that his Sixth Amendment right to an impartial jury will be honored. Without an adequate *voir dire* the trial judge's responsibility to remove prospective jurors who will not be able impartially to follow the court's instructions and evaluate the evidence cannot be fulfilled. Similarly, lack of adequate *voir dire* impairs the defendant's right to exercise peremptory challenges . . . . [*Rosales-Lopez v. United States*, 451 U.S. 182, 188 (1981)]

MU'MIN v. VIRGINIA
500 U.S. 415 (1991)

Chief Justice Rehnquist delivered the opinion of the Court.

Petitioner Dawud Majid Mu'Min was convicted of murdering a woman in Prince William County, Virginia, while out of prison on work detail, and was sentenced to death. The case engendered substantial publicity, and 8 of the 12 venirepersons eventually sworn as jurors answered on voir dire that they had read or heard something about the case. None of those who had read or heard something indicated that they had formed an opinion based on the outside information, or that it would affect their ability to determine petitioner's guilt or innocence based solely on the evidence presented at trial. Petitioner contends, however, that his Sixth Amendment right to an impartial jury and his right to due process under the Fourteenth Amendment were violated because the trial judge refused to question further prospective jurors about the specific contents of the news reports to which they had been exposed. We reject petitioner's submission.

. . . Shortly before the date set for trial, petitioner submitted to the trial judge 64 proposed voir dire questions and filed a motion for individual voir dire. The trial court denied the motion for individual voir dire; it ruled that voir dire would begin with collective questioning of the venire, but the venire would be broken down into panels of four, if necessary, to deal with issues of publicity. The trial court also refused to ask any of petitioner's proposed questions relating to the content of news items that potential jurors might have read or seen.

Twenty-six prospective jurors were summoned into the courtroom and questioned as a group. When asked by the judge whether anyone had acquired any information about the alleged offense or the accused from the news media or from any other source, 16 of the potential jurors replied that they had. The prospective jurors were not asked about the source or content of prior knowledge, but the court then [asked whether despite that information they had, the jurors could be impartial].

. . . The trial court then conducted further voir dire of the prospective jurors in panels of four. Whenever a potential juror indicated that he had read or heard something about the case, the juror was then asked whether he had formed an opinion, and whether he could nonetheless be impartial. None of those eventually seated stated that he had formed an opinion, or gave any indication that he was biased or prejudiced against the defendant. All swore that they could enter the jury box with an open mind and wait until the entire case was presented before reaching a conclusion as to guilt or innocence.

[The jury found petitioner guilty of capital murder and recommended a death sentence, which the judge imposed. Petitioner unsuccessfully appealed to the Virginia Supreme Court and certiorari was granted by the United States Supreme Court on the issue whether he was entitled to a new trial because of the judge's failure to permit the proposed voir dire questions.]

. . . Our cases dealing with the requirements of voir dire are of two kinds: those that were tried in federal courts, and are therefore subject to this Court's supervisory power and those that were tried in state courts, with respect to which our authority is limited to enforcing the commands of the United States Constitution.

A brief review of these cases is instructive. In *Connors v. United States*, 158 U.S. 408 (1895), we said:

> [A] suitable inquiry is permissible in order to ascertain whether the juror has any bias, opinion, or prejudice that would affect or control the fair determination by him of the issues to be tried. That inquiry is conducted under the supervision of the court, and a great deal must, of necessity, be left to its sound discretion. This is the rule in civil cases, and the same rule must be applied in criminal cases. [158 U.S. at 413]

In *Aldridge v. United States*, 283 U.S. 308 (1931), counsel for a black defendant sought to have the Court put a question to the jury as to whether any of them might be prejudiced against the defendant because of his race. We held that it was reversible error for the Court not to have put such a question, saying "[t]he Court failed to ask any question which could be deemed to cover the subject." More recently, in *Rosales-Lopez v. United States*, 451 U.S. 182 (1981), we held that such an inquiry as to racial or ethnic prejudice need not be made in every case, but only where the defendant was accused of a violent crime and the defendant and the victim were members of different racial or ethnic groups.

. . . Three of our cases dealing with the extent of voir dire examination have dealt with trials in state courts. The first of these was *Ham v. South Carolina*, 409 U.S. 524 (1973). In that case, the defendant was black and had been active in the civil rights movement in South Carolina; his defense at trial was that enforcement officers were "out to get him" because of his civil rights activities, and that he had been framed on the charge of marijuana possession of which he was accused. He requested that two questions be asked regarding racial prejudice and one question be asked regarding prejudice against persons, such as himself, who wore beards. We held that the Due Process Clause of the Fourteenth Amendment required the court to ask "either of the brief, general questions urged by the petitioner" with respect to race, but rejected his claim that an inquiry as to prejudice against persons with beards be made, "[g]iven the traditionally broad discretion accorded to the trial judge in conducting voir dire . . . ."

In *Ristaino v. Ross*, 424 U.S. 589 (1976), we held that the Constitution does not require a state court trial judge to question prospective jurors as to racial prejudice in every case where the races of the defendant and the victim differ, but in *Turner v. Murray*, 476 U.S. 28 (1986), we held that in a capital case involving a charge of murder of a white person by a black defendant such questions must be asked.

We enjoy more latitude in setting standards for voir dire in federal courts under our supervisory power than we have in interpreting the provisions of the Fourteenth Amendment with respect to voir dire in state courts. But, two parallel themes emerge from both sets of cases: first, the possibility of racial prejudice against a black defendant charged with a violent crime against a white person is sufficiently real that the Fourteenth Amendment requires that inquiry be made into racial prejudice; second, the trial court retains great latitude in deciding what questions should be asked on voir dire.

. . . Petitioner asserts that the Fourteenth Amendment requires more in the way of voir dire with respect to pretrial publicity than our cases have held that it does with respect to racial or ethnic prejudice. Not only must the Court "cover the subject," but it must make precise inquiries about the contents of any news reports that potential jurors have read. Petitioner argues that these "content" questions would materially assist in obtaining a jury less likely to be tainted by pretrial publicity than one selected without such questions. There is a certain common sense appeal to this argument.

Undoubtedly, if counsel were allowed to see individual jurors answer questions about exactly what they had read, a better sense of the juror's general outlook on life might be revealed, and such a revelation would be of some use in exercising peremptory challenges. But, since peremptory challenges are not required by the Constitution, this benefit cannot be a basis for making "content" questions about pretrial publicity a constitutional requirement. Such questions might also have some effect in causing jurors to re-evaluate their own answers as to whether they had formed any opinion about the case, but this is necessarily speculative.

Acceptance of petitioner's claim would require that each potential juror be interrogated individually; even were the interrogation conducted in panels of four jurors, as the trial court did here, descriptions of one juror about pretrial publicity would obviously be communicated to the three other members of the panel being interrogated, with the prospect that more harm than good would be done by the interrogation. Petitioner says that the questioning can be accomplished by juror questionnaires submitted in advance at trial, but such written answers would not give counsel or the court any exposure to the demeanor of the juror in the course of answering the content questions. The trial court in this case expressed reservations about interrogating jurors individually because it might make the jurors feel that they themselves were on trial. While concern for the feelings and sensibilities of potential jurors cannot be allowed to defeat inquiry necessary to protect a constitutional right, we do not believe that "content" questions are constitutionally required.

Whether a trial court decides to put questions about the content of publicity to a potential juror or not, it must make the same decision at the end of the questioning: is this juror to be believed when he says he has not formed an opinion about the case? Questions about the content of the publicity to which jurors have been exposed might be helpful in assessing whether a juror is impartial. To be constitutionally compelled, however, it is not enough that such questions might be helpful. Rather, the trial court's failure to ask these questions must render the defendant's trial fundamentally unfair.

[The Court then addressed defendant's argument that *Irvin v. Dowd*, 366 U.S. 717 (1961), applied to the case. In *Irvin*, the Court held that pretrial publicity had so tainted the jury pool that the defendant was entitled to a change of venue under federal constitutional law. In this case, however, the Court found *Irvin* distinguishable because the publicity was not nearly as prejudicial as in *Irvin*.]

. . . In *Patton v. Yount*, 467 U.S. 1025 (1984), we acknowledged that "adverse pretrial publicity can create such a presumption of prejudice in a community that the jurors' claims that they can be impartial should not be believed," but this is not such a case. Had the trial court in this case been confronted with the "wave of public passion" engendered by pretrial publicity that occurred in connection with Irvin's trial, the Due Process Clause of the Fourteenth Amendment might well have required more extensive examination of potential jurors than it undertook here. But the showings are not comparable; the cases differ both in the kind of community in which the coverage took place and in extent of media coverage. Unlike the community involved in *Irvin*, the county in which petitioner was tried, Prince William, had a population in 1988 of 182,537, and this was one of nine murders committed in the county that year. It is a part of the metropolitan Washington statistical area, which has a population of over 3 million, and in which, unfortunately, hundreds of murders are committed each year. In *Irvin*, news accounts included details of the defendant's confessions to 24 burglaries and six murders, including the one for which he was tried, as well as his unaccepted offer to plead guilty in order to avoid the death sentence. They contained numerous opinions as to his guilt, as well as opinions about the appropriate punishment. While news reports about Mu'Min were not favorable, they did not contain the same sort of damaging information. Much of the pretrial publicity was aimed at the Department of Corrections and the criminal justice system in general, criticizing the furlough and work release programs that made this and other crimes possible. Any killing that ultimately results in a charge of capital murder will engender considerable media coverage, and this one may have engendered more than most because of its occurrence during the 1988 Presidential campaign, when a similar crime committed by a Massachusetts inmate became a subject of national debate. But, while the pretrial publicity in this case appears to have been substantial, it was not of the same kind or extent as that found to exist in *Irvin*.

Petitioner also relies on the Standards for Criminal Justice 8-3.5 (2d ed. 1980), promulgated by the American Bar Association. These standards require interrogation of each juror individually with respect to "what the prospective juror has read and heard about the case," "[i]f there is a substantial possibility that individual jurors will be ineligible to serve because of exposure to potentially prejudicial material." These standards, of course, leave to the trial court the initial determination of whether there is such a substantial possibility. But, more importantly, the standards relating to voir dire are based on a substantive rule that renders a potential juror subject to challenge for cause, without regard to his state of mind, if he has been exposed to and remembers "highly significant information" or "other incriminating matters that may be inadmissible in evidence." That is a stricter standard of juror eligibility than that which we have held the Constitution to require. Under the ABA standard, answers to questions about content, without more, could disqualify the juror from sitting. Under the constitutional standard, on the other hand, "[t]he relevant question is not whether the community remembered the case, but whether the jurors . . . had such fixed opinions that they could not judge impartially the guilt of the defendant." Under this constitutional standard, answers to questions about content alone, which reveal that a juror remembered facts about the case, would not be sufficient to disqualify a juror. "It is not required . . . that the jurors be totally ignorant of the facts and issues involved."

. . . Petitioner in this case insists, as a matter of constitutional right, not only that the subject of possible bias from pretrial publicity be covered — which it was — but that questions specifically dealing with the content of what each juror has read be asked. For the reasons previously stated, we hold that the Due Process Clause of the Fourteenth Amendment does not reach this far, and that the voir dire examination conducted by the trial court in this case was consistent with that provision. Affirmed.

[The concurring opinion of JUSTICE O'CONNOR is omitted]

JUSTICE MARSHALL, with whom JUSTICE BLACKMUN and JUSTICE STEVENS join, dissenting.

. . . In my view, the circumstances of this case presented a clear need for content questioning. Exactly two-thirds of the persons on Mu'Min's jury admitted having been exposed to information about the case before trial . . . . [T]he stories printed prior to trial were extraordinarily prejudicial, and were made no less so by the inflammatory headlines typically used to introduce them. Much of the pretrial publicity was of the type long thought to be uniquely destructive of a juror's ability to maintain an open mind about a case — in particular, reports of Mu'Min's confession, statements by prominent public officials attesting to Mu'Min's guilt, and reports of Mu'Min's unsavory past. Because of the profoundly prejudicial nature of what was published in the newspapers prior to trial, any juror exposed to the bulk of it certainly would have been disqualified as a matter of law under the standards set out in *Irvin* and *Rideau* . . . . At minimum, without inquiry into what stories had been read by the eight members of the jury who acknowledged exposure to pretrial publicity, the trial court was in no position to credit their individual professions of impartiality.

. . . Finally, I reject the majority's claim that content questioning should be rejected because it would unduly burden trial courts . . . . [T]he majority's solicitude for administrative convenience is wholly gratuitous. Numerous Federal Circuits and States have adopted the sorts of procedures for screening juror bias that the majority disparages as being excessively intrusive. In short, the majority's anxiety is difficult to credit in light of the number of jurisdictions that have concluded that meaningful steps can be taken to insulate the proceedings from juror bias without compromising judicial efficiency . . . .

JUSTICE KENNEDY, dissenting.

. . . I fail to see how the trial court could evaluate the credibility of the individuals seated on this jury. The questions were asked of groups, and individual jurors attested to their own impartiality by saying nothing. I would hold, as a consequence, that when a juror admits exposure to pretrial publicity about a case, the court must conduct a sufficient colloquy with the individual juror to make an assessment of the juror's ability to be impartial. The trial judge should have substantial discretion in conducting the voir dire, but, in my judgment, findings of impartiality must be based on something more than the mere silence of the individual in response to questions asked en masse.

NOTES

1. *Questions to ask Mu'Min jurors.* As *Mu'Min* makes clear, the trial court is given much discretion in deciding whether to permit detailed or general questioning of potential jurors. If you were the judge in *Mu'Min*, what questions would you ask to ascertain whether a potential juror were biased because of the publicity?

2. *Individual v. group voir dire.* The trial judge is also given discretion in deciding whether to question (or permit the lawyers to question) jurors individually or in groups, perhaps even small groups. What are the advantages and disadvantages of individual voir dire?

[c]   Voir Dire Procedures: In General

Trial courts are generally given significant discretion in fashioning procedures for selecting the panel of jurors who will sit on a particular case.

[i]   Names and Addresses of Potential Jurors; Anonymous Juries

Lawyers preparing for the jury selection process often prefer to examine a list of the names and addresses of the venire prior to the voir dire process. This enables them to prepare questions appropriate for individual jurors and by providing some minimal demographic data. For example, a person's address may tell something about the person's financial status and ethnicity. Sometimes a statute or court rule will authorize the exchange of this information. *See, e.g.,* 18 U.S.C. § 3432 (capital defendant usually entitled to names and addresses of potential jurors no later than 3 days before trial); 28 U.S.C. § 1867 (f) (setting forth circumstances under which access to jury records should be granted); Ariz. R. Crim. P. 18.3 (parties furnished with names and biographical information about each potential juror; comment states this includes names, addresses, occupation, and age of both juror and spouse, employer's names and addresses, number of years employed, marital status and number and age of children, length of residence in state and county, ownership of real estate, education, experience as law enforcement officer, previous juror service, and courses in law that were taken); Standards for Criminal Justice § 15-2.2(a)(1) (3d ed. 1996) (before voir dire, court and counsel should receive data pertinent to the jurors' qualifications, including name, sex, age, residence, marital status, education level, occupation and occupational history, employment address, previous service as a juror, and present or past involvement as a party to civil or criminal litigation).

Anonymous Jury. In general, however, the trial court ordinarily is given the discretion whether to release this information. *See, e.g., United States v. Barnes,* 604 F.2d 121 (2d Cir. 1979) (trial judge, fearing for jurors' safety, has discretion to withhold their names and addresses). *See also Press-Enterprise Co. v. Superior Ct.,* 464 U.S. 501 (1984) (to protect privacy of jurors, trial court may close voir dire to public, but court order must be narrowly drawn and alternatives to closure, such as withholding juror's name, must be considered; presumption of openness of voir dire can be overcome only by overriding interest); *Jury Serv. Res. Ctr. v. De Muniz,* 134 P.3d 948 (Ore 2006)(First Amendment does not require public access to jury pool information).

Several state and federal courts have expressly approved the use of the anonymous jury under limited circumstances. *See State v. Bowles,* 530 N.W.2d 521 (Minn. 1995) (approving anonymous jury where the trial court finds strong reason to believe that the jury needs protection from external threats to safety or impartiality, so long as the court also takes steps to minimize the resulting prejudice to the defendant); *United States v. Edmond,* 52 F.3d 1080 (D.C. Cir. 1995) (in accord with *Bowles,* further noting that the district court could decide *sua sponte* that an anonymous jury was necessary;

court should look to five factors to determine necessity of jury anonymity: (1) defendant's involvement in organized crime, (2) defendant's participation in a group with the capacity to harm jurors, (3) defendant's past attempts to interfere with the judicial process, (4) the potential that, if convicted, the defendant will suffer a lengthy incarceration and substantial monetary penalties, and (5) extensive publicity that could enhance the possibility that jurors' names would become public and expose them to intimidation or harassment); *United States v. Darden*, 70 F.3d 1507 (8th Cir. 1995) (adopting the guidelines followed by the *Edmond* court, specifically finding that a thorough voir dire and the trial court's explanation to the jury that anonymity served to protect jurors from media harassment adequately protected against prejudice).

Even though apparently every federal circuit court addressing this question has expressly approved the use of the anonymous jury in appropriate cases, it has been noted that empaneling such a jury "is a drastic measure, which should be undertaken only in limited and carefully delineated circumstances." *See, e.g., United States v. Sanchez*, 74 F.3d 562 (5th Cir. 1996) (holding that the district court abused its discretion in empaneling an anonymous jury because there was no factual showing to support the conclusion that anonymity was warranted).

Note that the trial judge in *Darden* informed the jury that anonymity was necessitated because of the need to protect jurors from "media harassment" (most likely untrue!). Other creative justifications include (1) protecting jurors from curiosity seekers and (2) explaining to jurors that an anonymous jury is a "common" practice in federal courts. *See United States v. Shryock*, 342 F.3d 948 (9th Cir. 2003).

Professor Nancy King has noted that some judges and legislatures have taken the position that juror anonymity should occur in almost all criminal cases. Favoring a more "routine use" of anonymous juries, she asserts that "[b]y alleviating juror fear, anonymity can enhance the participation of citizens in jury service, the reliability of the voir dire process, the quality of jury deliberations, and the fairness of criminal verdicts." Nancy J. King, *Nameless Justice: The Case for the Routine Use of Anonymous Juries in Criminal Trials*, 49 VAND. L. REV. 123, 125 (1996).

[ii] Juror Questionnaire

Content. In some courts, potential jurors are required to fill out a questionnaire ranging from a page or two to as many as seventy pages. The questions ask about various demographic data (age, gender, home address, job, marital status, education), exposure to information about the crime, and perhaps attitudes about events or people. The completed questionnaires then are used by the judge and lawyers as background information in selecting jurors.

Significant judicial discretion. Trial courts ordinarily are given the discretion whether to employ questionnaires (although they are mandatory in some jurisdictions) and what questions may be included in the questionnaire. *See, e.g., United States v. McDade*, 929 F. Supp. 815 (E.D. Pa. 1996) (refusing to permit several questions to be asked of prospective jurors because of privacy concerns); *United States v. Serafini*, 57 F. Supp. 2d 108 (M.D. Pa. 1999) (district court excluded questions from defendant questionnaire relating to prospective jurors' place of birth, race, marital status, health, political party affiliation, ownership of stock, income, religious affiliation, government employment or security clearance, television programs watched, membership in social or business organizations, and other personal questions, holding them to be intrusive and not linked to the issues of the case or juror ability to be fair).

Contempt of court. Failure to complete the form may constitute contempt of court. *But see Brandborg v. Lucas*, 891 F. Supp. 352 (E.D. Tex. 1995) (contempt order overturned due to trial court's failure to determine whether questions were relevant and to conduct a balancing test of the jurors' privacy interests versus the defendant's interest in an impartial jury).

[iii]   Expert Consultation

Since the 1970's, some lawyers have used "jury selection experts" or "trial consultants" to assist in jury selection. While some of these experts may be characterized as fortune tellers, others have more traditional credentials, such as a doctorate in psychology and extensive experience. Some lawyers believe that such experts can be of material assistance in selecting jurors most likely to be amenable to their arguments.

These experts perform a range of services. Sometimes they help draft and interpret written juror questionnaires and assess community attitudes toward the defendant or certain issues. They may conduct telephone surveys which will help them prepare a *juror profile*, a study that correlates juror characteristics, attitudes, and verdict preferences. They may also be present at the voir dire proceeding and offer suggestions to counsel about questions to ask or jurors to select.

Sometimes these experts base their recommendations on non-verbal cues, such as facial language, posture, and formation of cliques. For example, a psychologist may suggest that a juror who makes irrelevant hand motions to the head area may be lying while answering questions during voir dire. Jury consultants may also assist in arranging mock trials in which a specific part of the case is presented to mock jurors, such as expert testimony or opening and closing statements. Similarly, "shadow juries" sometimes are used as the actual litigation ensues; these jurors give daily feedback to the attorney, assessing how the evidence is likely being evaluated by the actual jurors. Finally, consultants are available to manage documents and coordinate courtroom technology, *See* Shari Seidman Diamond, *Scientific Jury Selection: What Social Scientists Know and Do Not Know*, 73 JUDICATURE 178 (1990); James W. McElhaney, *The Jury Consultant Bazaar: Know What You're Buying in the Litigation Support Market*, 84 A.B.A. J. 78 (Nov. 1998).

[d]   Interrogation of Potential Jurors: The Voir Dire Process

Judge and/or lawyers. While potential jurors are interrogated in every jurisdiction, the process varies considerably. Judges routinely ask questions of the venire, usually assembled in a group of 25–100 people. Often judges ask counsel for both sides to suggest questions to ask. These questions generally focus on obvious reasons why a particular juror should not serve in this case. Thus, potential jurors are asked whether their health or job would prevent service. They are also asked about their relationship with the parties, witnesses, lawyers, or to the case. Other topics may also be explored.

Many judges also permit the defense lawyer and the prosecutor to question jurors. In order to expedite the process, judges may limit the number of questions or the time each lawyer has. *See* STANDARDS FOR CRIMINAL JUSTICE § 15-2.4 (3d ed. 1996) (voir dire should be conducted initially by judge, but counsel should be permitted a reasonable opportunity to question jurors directly, both as a panel and individually; individual voir dire [discussed after Rule 24] should be permitted when the juror is to be asked about sensitive matters or prior exposure to potentially prejudicial material).

Sometimes rules of court indicate whether lawyers are permitted to question potential jurors. Some specifically permit both the prosecutor and defense counsel to question potential jurors. *E.g.*, Fla. R. Crim. P. 3.300(b). The federal approach is to leave the matter to the judge's discretion.

FEDERAL RULES OF CRIMINAL PROCEDURE

Rule 24. *Trial Jurors*

  (a) Examination.

    (1) In General. The court may examine prospective jurors or may permit the attorneys for the parties to do so.

(2) Court Examination. If the court examines the jurors, it must permit the attorneys for the parties to:

(A) ask further questions that the court considers proper; or

(B) submit further questions that the court may ask if it considers them proper. . . .

NOTE

Individual or group. Besides the question of who should interrogate the prospective jurors, the judge also must decide whether the questions are more appropriately posed to groups of jurors or to the individual jurors. In the latter situation, each potential juror is brought into the courtroom to be questioned by the judge and perhaps the defense lawyer and the prosecutor. The other jurors are not present. Because *individual voir dire* (sometimes called *sequestered voir dire*) is more time consuming than *group voir dire*, most judges prefer the latter. One fairly obvious situation in which sequestered voir dire is preferred, however, is when questions are to be asked of prospective jurors about their exposure to publicity about the case, as discussed above.

[e]   Types of Challenges: Cause and Peremptory

Potential jurors are subject to two kinds of challenges or grounds for exclusion. A *challenge for cause* is a claim that a potential juror is disqualified from service because of an inability to serve or a bias that would prevent the juror from being fair. Although the judge decides whether a potential juror is to be excluded for cause, often a defense attorney or prosecutor asks the judge to exclude the juror on this basis. Either side may challenge a juror for cause. The reasons for this challenge must be given so that the judge can determine whether the juror should be excused.

A *peremptory challenge*, discussed later in this chapter, is a decision by a party's lawyer that a particular juror should not serve on the jury. Ordinarily, each side is given a limited number of peremptory challenges which can be exercised for virtually any reason. Often, lawyers will try to preserve their few peremptory challenges by asking the judge to disqualify a juror for cause. If the juror is removed for cause, the lawyer is able to have the juror excused without spending a peremptory challenge.

[f]   Challenges for Cause

Although frequently the rules of criminal procedure do not mention challenges for cause, this challenge is an important facet of the jury selection process in every jurisdiction. There are few limits on the grounds that can be used for a challenge for cause and no limit on the number of jurors who can be struck for cause. Sometimes the grounds for a challenge for cause are stated in general terms. *E.g.*, Ariz. R. Crim. P. 18.4 (challenge for cause when there is "reasonable ground to believe that a juror cannot render a fair and impartial verdict").

A small number of states have adopted statutes pertaining to challenges for cause and have set forth precise reasons or grounds that permit excusing jurors from service. *See, e.g.*, Fla. Stat. § 913.03 (identifying twelve grounds upon which such challenges may be based).

There are actually two general bases for challenge for cause: an inability to perform the necessary functions and a bias that could compromise the juror's ability to decide the case impartially.

[i]   Inability to Serve

Jury service requires both physical and mental activities, and a potential juror may be disqualified because he or she is not able to perform the necessary functions.

Physical or mental capacity. A person who does not have the physical or mental capacity to perform the services required of a juror can be excluded (or excused) for cause. This includes a potential juror whose mental incompetence means the juror cannot understand or deliberate the issues. *United States v. Vargas*, 606 F.2d 341 (1st Cir. 1979).

Understanding of law. A juror may also be disqualified for cause if he or she is unable to grasp the legal principles at issue. However, it is difficult to assess this ground for exclusion since ordinarily jurors are not instructed in depth about the law until the end of the trial. *See United States v. Vera*, 701 F.2d 1349 (11th Cir. 1983) (although potential juror indicated confusion about burden of proof in criminal case, trial court did not err in barring voir dire of this juror on this issue when court asked general questions about the law and gave clear jury instructions about the burden of proof).

[ii] Possible Bias

A juror must be fair. The Sixth Amendment guarantees a jury trial by an impartial jury. According to the Supreme Court:

> . . . [T]he right to jury trial guarantees the criminally accused a fair trial by a panel of impartial, "indifferent" jurors. The failure to accord an accused a fair hearing violates even the minimal standards of due process. [*Irvin v. Dowd*, 366 U.S. 717, 722 (1961)]

Implicit and actual bias. The process of questioning and excluding potential jurors is the primary vehicle for ensuring that a jury panel is comprised of unbiased people. There are actually two types of challenges for cause based on bias: implied bias and actual bias. *Implied bias* permits an assumption that a potential juror is so likely to be biased that disqualification is appropriate. *Actual bias* involves proof that a particular juror would be biased in a particular case. Actual bias is often difficult to prove since the juror may state during voir dire that he or she will put aside all biases and decide the case on its merits. Sometimes actual bias is detected through circumstantial evidence. If actual bias is discovered during the voir dire process, the court must excuse the juror. *United States v. Allsup*, 566 F.2d 68 (9th Cir. 1977).

According to most courts, the key determination is actual rather than implied bias. The trial court should ask whether *this* potential juror is biased. Questions during the voir dire process should address this issue. Ordinarily, a person should not be excluded for cause simply because of the possibility of bias. In exceptional cases, however, some judges are willing to exclude a potential juror for implied bias. *See Smith v. Phillips*, 455 U.S. 209, 222 (1982) (Justice O'Connor notes that in some situations it may be appropriate to use implied bias to dismiss a juror for cause; examples include a juror who is an employee of the prosecuting agency, is a close relative of a trial participant, or was a witness or otherwise involved in the criminal transaction).

In implied bias cases, some courts use an "average person" test, asking whether an average person in a similar situation would feel prejudice. *See, e.g., United States v. Haynes*, 398 F.2d 980 (2d Cir. 1968) (examples of implied bias include a juror who has served on jury which convicted another defendant in prior case involving same transaction; kinship to the defendant; interest in the proceeding; or being a master, servant, counselor, steward, or attorney of the defendant); *see also United States v. Garcia*, 936 F.2d 648 (2d Cir. 1991) (13 potential jurors had just completed jury service in another narcotics trial, in which the government's witness who was scheduled to testify in the instant case, had also testified; no showing that the jurors were actually biased; court found them unbiased based on their unwavering affirmations of impartiality and the court's favorable evaluation of their demeanor).

Government employment. Since the government is a party in every criminal prosecution, it has been alleged that a government employee should be barred from jury service because of likely bias. In *Dennis v. United States*, 339 U.S. 162 (1950), the United States Supreme Court rejected this argument in a case involving an avowed communist who was charged with failure to obey a subpoena from the House Un-American Activities Committee. The Court refused to presume that all government employees were too biased to serve as criminal jurors:

> [We cannot] without injustice take judicial notice of a miasma of fear to which Government employees are claimed to be peculiarly vulnerable — and from which other citizens are by implication immune. Vague conjecture does not convince [us] that Government employees are so intimidated that they cringe before their Government in fear of investigation and loss of employment if they do their duty as jurors, which duty this same Government has imposed upon them. There is no disclosure in this record that these jurors did not bring to bear, as is particularly the custom when personal liberty hinges on the determination, the sense of responsibility and the individual integrity by which men judge men. [339 U.S. at 172]

Of course, the *Dennis* Court also recognized that a juror could be excluded for cause upon proof that the particular juror would not be fair in this case. *See, e.g., United States v. Apodaca*, 666 F.2d 89 (5th Cir. 1982) (potential juror and her husband had worked for F.B.I.; she knew how much investigation went into grand jury case; she might give more credence to prosecution; it would have been prudent and reasonable to exclude this juror for cause, but no error because juror said she could be impartial).

Exposure to pretrial publicity. A frequent allegation is that a particular juror or an entire panel of jurors should be excluded for cause because of their exposure to pretrial publicity. The argument is that the potential jurors cannot be bias-free because their minds were polluted by publicity.

In the leading case, *Irvin v. Dowd*, 366 U.S. 717 (1961), discussed earlier in *Mu'Min v. Virginia*, the defendant was sentenced to death for six murders in a small community. The local news media extensively publicized the crimes and the defendant's confessions. The trial court denied the defendant's motions for a continuance and a change of venue. The Supreme Court reversed, holding that the accused was denied a fair trial by the massive pretrial publicity and the impact it had on the jurors. However, the Court was careful to note that knowledge of a crime alone is insufficient to render a potential juror unqualified to serve. The key is whether the juror can be fair:

> In these days of swift, widespread and diverse methods of communication, an important case can be expected to arouse the interests of the public in the vicinity, and scarcely any of those best qualified to serve as jurors will not have formed some impression or opinion as to the merits of the case. This is particularly true in criminal cases. To hold that the mere existence of any preconceived notion as to the guilt or innocence of an accused, without more, is sufficient to rebut the presumption of a prospective juror's impartiality would be to establish an impossible standard. It is sufficient if the juror can lay aside his impression or opinion and render a verdict based on the evidence presented in court. [*Id.* at 722–23]

Another court expressed the rule concisely: "Mere awareness of some of the allegations in a case does not disqualify a potential juror." *United States v. Wilson*, 732 F.2d 404, 410 (5th Cir. 1984).

Feelings about this case. A juror may be excluded for cause if he or she has such strong feelings about the case that impartiality is unlikely. For example, if a juror felt strongly that no one was insane, he or she should be disqualified for cause in a case in which the insanity defense is asserted. *See, e.g., United States v. Allsup*, 566 F.2d 68 (9th Cir. 1977). *See also United States v. Gonzalez*, 483 F.2d 223 (2d Cir. 1973) (can exclude juror for cause who said she did not know if she could honestly send a man to jail); *United States v. Devery*, 935 F. Supp. 393 (S.D.N.Y. 1996) (court excluded two jurors because they had engaged in conduct so proximate to the unlawful conduct defendants were accused of that their experience necessarily impacted their ability to weigh the evidence impartially; also the court excluded two other jurors who made clear their predisposition to disregard the testimony of an admitted drug dealer solely on account of the witness's prior unlawful acts).

Even with an opinion about the case, a juror may be accepted on the jury if the juror states he or she can be fair. *See, e.g., State v. Hopkins*, 908 So.2d 1265 (La. App. 2005)(juror formed an opinion about the case because of previous grand jury service that taught her there was an evidentiary basis for the charges, but was acceptable because she said she would hold the state to its burden of proof).

Sometimes it is difficult to assess whether the juror's views of the case are sufficiently strong to merit exclusion for cause. The subtle nature of this determination is reflected in *United States v. Barber*, 668 F.2d 778 (4th Cir. 1982). One juror was not excluded for cause when he stated that he could render a decision based on the evidence even though he "maybe" had an impression the defendant "might be guilty." Another juror was excluded for cause who also said he could render a verdict in accordance with the evidence, but he admitted that he had formed an opinion that the defendant was innocent and his feeling about the case would be difficult to overcome.

Relationship to Party, Lawyer, Witness, Victim, or Crime. Another ground for exclusion for cause is the juror's relationship to a person, entity, or some other facet of the case that could cause the juror to be biased. Examples of reasons for excluding jurors for cause under this premise include: the potential juror in a bank robbery case was an employee of the bank that was robbed; a cab driver was excluded in a case where a cab driver was robbed and killed; jurors were related to defense counsel or had used his professional services; jurors were acquainted with the defendant; juror was "close friends" with each defendant; juror had a pastoral and professional relationship with several members of defendant's family; a juror's parents-in-law had worked for the defendant's election (the defendant was a public official charged with voter bribery); a juror's involvement in prior similar litigation; and a juror in a drug case had sons serving prison terms for drug-related crimes.

Exclusion is not necessarily automatic. Often courts will look closely at the relationship and the juror's response to questions to determine whether it will impair the juror's impartiality. *See, e.g., United States v. Brown*, 540 F.2d 364 (8th Cir. 1976) (citizens of St. Louis not automatically barred for cause in case of fraud against City of St. Louis and its citizens; must be proof of actual bias); *Daut v. United States*, 405 F.2d 312 (9th Cir. 1968) (juror not excluded for cause simply because juror is acquainted with a lawyer in the case; actual bias must be shown); *United States v. Tramunti*, 513 F.2d 1087 (2d Cir. 1975) (in narcotics case, juror's wife's stepson had become addict, but juror indicated he could be fair; juror not excluded); *Tinsley v. Borg*, 895 F.2d 520 (9th Cir. 1990) (juror was not excluded from rape case where she had experience counseling a rape victim but did not exhibit any bias); *United States v. Tab*, 259 Fed. Appx. 684 (6th Cir. 2007)(juror had met shooting victim's father many years ago and was certain it would not affect his judgment); *Johnson v. State*, 642 S.E.2d 170 (Ga. App. 2007)(juror knew wife of police officer victim but said she could be fair).

Membership in Organization. Sometimes a potential juror is a member of an organization that represents views somehow related to the case. Ordinarily, such membership alone is insufficient to prove actual bias and justify exclusion for cause. *See, e.g., United States v. Salamone*, 800 F.2d 1216 (3d Cir. 1986) (juror's membership in National Rifle Association insufficient to exclude juror for cause in case involving illegal firearms).

Prior jury service. If a potential juror has already served on a jury in the same or a similar case, the juror can be excluded for cause if the earlier experience somehow creates actual bias. In general, prior service on unrelated matters, coupled with a juror's statement that he or she could be fair, does not merit excusal for cause. *See, e.g., United*

States v. Gordon, 2007 WL2726874 (5th Cir. 2007)(prior grand jury service; said could be impartial).

Some courts are willing to infer bias if the prior service occurred quite near in time to the present case. *See, e.g., United States v. Franklin,* 700 F.2d 1241 (10th Cir. 1983) (jurors who, between the time of their selection as a juror and actual trial, have served on another jury involving similar legal or factual issues or the same government witnesses can be dismissed for cause).

Courts are more likely to grant a challenge for cause if the potential jurors sat on a previous case involving the same transaction or witnesses at issue in the current case. Similarly, a challenge for cause is routinely granted if the potential jurors participated in a previous case in which the current defendant was convicted. *See, e.g., Graham v. State,* 2008 WL553249 (Tex. App. 2008)(juror was member of grand jury that indicted defendant; excusal for cause proper).

The Supreme Court has also stated that removal for cause is necessary if, during the jury selection process, prospective jurors hear about a prior conviction of the same defendant in a similar case. *Leonard v. United States,* 378 U.S. 544 (1964).

[iii] Unique Procedures in Death Penalty Cases

In a typical criminal case, each lawyer may seek to have the most questionable jurors excused for cause, thus preserving the lawyer's peremptory challenges for use on other jurors. The same procedure applies in death penalty cases, with a slightly different twist.

Jury selection procedures in death penalty cases are unique. During the voir dire process, potential jurors are asked the same questions as jurors in any other criminal case, plus others about their views of the death penalty. The latter questions are important since the capital case jury typically decides whether the accused is guilty and, if so, imposes the sentence.

Sometimes the voir dire process reveals that a potential juror has strong feelings about the death penalty. This may mean that the person has reservations about the ultimate punishment. When a juror indicates anti-death penalty sentiments, often the prosecutor will ask that the juror be excused for cause. The defense lawyer, on the other hand, will fight exclusion for two reasons. First, the defense lawyer would like to fill the jury box with people who oppose the death penalty. During jury deliberations these people may vote and argue against the death penalty and may also be more amenable to defense arguments on guilt or innocence. Second, if the juror is to be excused, defense counsel would like to force the prosecution to exercise one of its precious peremptories rather than having the juror excused for cause.

In the 1960's, when a prosecutor challenged a juror who claimed to have "reservations" about the death penalty, some judges would exclude that juror for cause. Defense lawyers objected, arguing that this left a "conviction-prone" jury and deprived the accused of a jury truly representative of American society, which contains people of varying views of the death penalty. In light of these objections, the Court was called upon to decide a series of cases discussing challenges for cause in capital cases. Note how these cases place limits on a trial court's power to exclude certain jurors for cause. These cases deal only with challenges for cause; they do not address the issue of peremptory challenges.

"Witherspoon excludables." In the early leading case, *Witherspoon v. Illinois,* 391 U.S. 510 (1968), an Illinois statute authorized exclusion for cause of any juror in a death penalty case who had "conscientious scruples against capital punishment." During the jury selection process in *Witherspoon,* the trial judge said, "Let's get these conscientious objectors out of the way, without wasting any time on them." He then excluded 47 potential jurors because of their views of the death penalty. Thirty-nine of these acknowledged having "conscientious or religious scruples against the infliction of

the death penalty" or against its infliction "in a proper case." The defendant objected to the exclusions, arguing that a jury selected in this manner was not a random cross-section of the community and was biased in favor of conviction. The Supreme Court agreed, holding that:

> . . . a State may not entrust the determination of whether a man should live or die to a tribunal organized to return a verdict of death. Specifically, we hold that a sentence of death cannot be carried out if the jury that imposed or recommended it was chosen by excluding veniremen for cause simply because they voiced general objections to the death penalty or expressed conscientious or religious scruples against its infliction. No defendant can constitutionally be put to death at the hands of a tribunal so selected.
>
> Whatever else might be said of capital punishment, it is at least clear that its imposition by a hanging jury cannot be squared with the Constitution. The State of Illinois has stacked the deck against the petitioner. To execute this death sentence would deprive him of his life without due process of law. [*Id.* at 521–523]

While *Witherspoon* made it more difficult for the state to exclude potential jurors who had reservations about the death penalty, it did not say that the juror's views of the death penalty were irrelevant. What if a potential juror said that under no circumstances could he or she vote to impose the death penalty? Would *Witherspoon* be violated if the juror were excluded for cause? A footnote in *Witherspoon* answered this question.

> [N]othing we say today bears upon the power of a State to execute a defendant sentenced to death by a jury from which the only veniremen who were in fact excluded for cause were those who made unmistakably clear (1) that they would *automatically* vote against the imposition of capital punishment without regard to any evidence that might be developed at the trial of the case before them, or (2) that their attitude toward the death penalty would prevent them from making an impartial decision as to the defendant's *guilt*. Nor does the decision in this case affect the validity of any sentence *other* than death. [*Id.* at 522–523 n.21]

Adams' Modifications of Witherspoon. In *Adams v. Texas*, 448 U.S. 38 (1980), the Supreme Court cited the *Witherspoon* footnote but established a slightly different test that indicated that jurors in capital cases can be excluded if they are unwilling to apply the law:

> [Case law] establishes the general proposition that a juror may not be challenged for cause based on his views about capital punishment unless those views would prevent or substantially impair the performance of his duties as a juror in accordance with his instructions and his oath. The State may insist, however, that jurors will consider and decide the facts impartially and conscientiously apply the law as charged by the court. [*Id.* at 45]

Note how the *Adams* court shifted from *Witherspoon*'s concern with people who would automatically vote against the death penalty to persons whose views are so strong as to substantially impair their service as a juror charged with following the law.

Subsequent cases dealt with whether a particular juror's responses on voir dire were sufficient to excuse that juror for cause. In those cases, often both the questions asked and answers given were poorly focused. In *Wainwright v. Witt*, 469 U.S. 412 (1985), a potential juror was excused for cause after the following colloquy occurred between the juror and the prosecutor:

> Prosecutor: Do you have any religious beliefs or personal beliefs against the death penalty?
>
> Juror: . . . I am afraid of being a little personal, but definitely not religious.
>
> Prosecutor: Now, would that interfere with you sitting as a juror in this case?

Juror: I am afraid it would.

Prosecutor: . . . Would it interfere with judging the guilt or innocence of the Defendant in this case?

Juror: I think so.

Prosecutor: . . . Your Honor, I would move for cause at this point.

The defendant appealed, partially on the theory that this juror should not have been excluded for cause because the juror did not indicate that she would *automatically* vote against the death penalty.

The Supreme Court reaffirmed *Adams* in an opinion that stressed the need to give the trial court discretion in deciding whether to exclude a juror for cause:

> [A capital case juror may be excluded for cause because of views on capital punishment when] the juror's views would "prevent or substantially impair the performance of his duties as a juror in accordance with his instructions and his oath." We note that in addition to dispensing with Witherspoon's reference to "automatic" decisionmaking, this standard likewise does not require that a juror's bias be proved with "unmistakable clarity." This is because determinations of juror bias cannot be reduced to question-and-answer sessions which obtain results in the manner of a catechism. What common sense should have realized experience has proved: many veniremen simply cannot be asked enough questions to reach the point where their bias has been made "unmistakably clear"; these veniremen may not know how they will react when faced with imposing the death sentence, or may be unable to articulate, or may wish to hide their true feelings. Despite this lack of clarity in the printed record, however, there will be situations where the trial judge is left with the definite impression that a prospective juror would be unable to faithfully and impartially apply the law . . . . [T]his is why deference must be paid to the trial judge who sees and hears the juror. [*Id.* at 424–25]

See also Uttecht v. Brown, 127 S. Ct. 2218 (2007) (upholding excusal of juror whose answers could have led the trial court to believe juror would have been substantially impaired in his ability to impose the death penalty except when there was no possibility the offender would be released and reoffend; trial court given great discretion because of opportunity to observe juror's demeanor).

Although the trial judge has great discretion in deciding whether a particular juror should be excused for cause and what questions may be asked on voir dire, the Supreme Court held that the judge, if requested by counsel, must ask whether a potential juror would automatically vote for the death penalty if the defendant were found guilty of capital murder. *Morgan v. Illinois*, 504 U.S. 719 (1992). The Court indicated that this question will serve the defendant's

> ability to exercise intelligently his complementary challenge for cause against those biased persons on the venire who as jurors would unwaveringly impose death after a finding of guilt. Were *voir dire* not available to lay bare the foundation of petitioner's challenge for cause against those prospective jurors who would *always* impose death following conviction, his right not to be tried by such jurors would be rendered as nugatory and meaningless as the State's right, in the absence of questioning, to strike those who would *never* do so. [504 U.S. at 733–34]

Justice Scalia dissented from the *Morgan* majority's opinion, noting that the Court has held that the Sixth Amendment does not guarantee a jury for the capital punishment penalty phase. Therefore, there was also no "subsidiary requirement" that a sentencing jury, if provided, be impartial. He stated that seating pro-death penalty jurors does not violate due process any more than does electing pro-death penalty judges. Due process, according to Scalia, mandates that jurors not be precluded from considering mitigating evidence; it does not require that jurors be swayed by it.

Supreme Court's summary of death penalty juror rules. In *Uttecht v. Brown*, 127 S. Ct. 2218, 2224 (2007), the Court summarized its *Witherspoon-Adams* decisions:

> These precedents establish at least four principles of relevance here. First, a criminal defendant has the right to an impartial jury drawn from a venire that has not been tilted in favor of capital punishment by selective prosecutorial challenges for cause. Second, the State has a strong interest in having jurors who are able to apply capital punishment within the framework state law prescribes. Third, to balance these interests, a juror who is substantially impaired in his or her ability to impose the death penalty under the state-law framework can be excused for cause; but if the juror is not substantially impaired, removal for cause is impermissible. Fourth, in determining whether the removal of a potential juror would vindicate the State's interest without violating the defendant's right, the trial court makes a judgment based in part on the demeanor of the juror, a judgment owed deference by reviewing courts.
>
> . . . Deference to the trial court is appropriate because it is in a position to assess the demeanor of the venire, and of the individuals who compose it, a factor of critical importance in assessing the attitude and qualifications of potential jurors.

Conviction-prone jury. In *Lockhart v. McCree*, 476 U.S. 162 (1986), the Supreme Court squarely faced a related question: whether *Witherspoon* and *Adams*, by excluding potential jurors with strong anti-death penalty sentiments, produced an unconstitutional conviction-prone jury. Assuming for purposes of argument that the voir dire process in capital cases does produce a "somewhat more" conviction-prone jury, the Court in *Lockhart* rejected the defendant's allegation that the "death-qualification" process violated the Sixth Amendment's cross-section requirement. The Court held that groups, such as "*Witherspoon* excludables," who are defined solely in terms of shared attitudes that would prevent or substantially impair their members from performing their duties as jurors, are not a "distinctive group" for purposes of the Sixth Amendment's fair cross-section requirement. The fair cross-section requirement, according to *Lockhart*, applies only to the venire; it does not apply to petit juries and it does not guarantee that a particular petit jury will reflect the composition of the community at large. In addition, the Court in *Lockhart* also held that the defendant was not deprived of an impartial jury as guaranteed by the Sixth Amendment because removing *Witherspoon* excludables serves the government's interest in having a jury that can "impartially decide all of the issues" in the case. *Id.* at 180. Do you agree?

The Court followed *Lockhart* in *Buchanan v. Kentucky*, 483 U.S. 402 (1987), and held that a "death-qualified" jury, selected in accordance with *Witherspoon* and *Adams*, does not violate the Sixth Amendment's cross-section requirement when the jury decides guilt or innocence in a joint trial where one of the two defendants is not charged with a capital crime. The non-capital defendant unsuccessfully argued that he was harmed when the conviction-prone, death-qualified jury found him guilty. In rejecting this claim, the Court repeated its often-stated maxim that the Constitution "presupposes" that a jury selected from a fair cross-section of the community is impartial, irrespective of the actual composition of the petit jury and the actual mix of views held by those jurors.

Remedy for erroneous exclusion of capital juror. In *Gray v. Mississippi*, 481 U.S. 648 (1987), the Court held that the erroneous exclusion for cause of a capital juror because of that juror's anti-death penalty views is not subject to "harmless error" analysis. In other words, there should be an automatic reversal of any death sentence imposed by a jury from which a potential juror was excused in violation of *Witherspoon* and *Adams*.

In *Gray*, a juror was erroneously removed for cause, thus saving the prosecution from having to use one of its peremptory challenges to remove the juror who viewed the death penalty with disfavor. In *Ross v. Oklahoma*, 487 U.S. 81 (1988), the facts were the reverse of those in *Gray* and quite unusual. The defendant was sentenced to death for killing a police officer during a robbery. During the voir dire process, a potential juror indicated that if the defendant were found guilty, the juror would vote automatically to impose the death penalty. When the trial judge refused to exclude this juror for cause, defense counsel used one of its peremptory challenges to remove the juror. By the end of voir dire, the defense had used all of its nine peremptory challenges; the prosecution used only five.

The Supreme Court upheld the death sentence, holding that the defendant's Sixth Amendment rights were not violated because the jury that convicted him was impartial, for the pro-death penalty juror was removed by a defense peremptory challenge. The defendant argued that the composition of the jury as a whole could have been affected by the trial court's error because the defense had to use its precious peremptory challenge against the pro-death penalty juror instead of another objectionable juror. In rejecting this argument, the Court in *Ross* held that *Gray* was limited to the erroneous exclusion of a juror; it did not apply to the erroneous seating of a pro-death juror who was later removed by peremptory challenge. The *Ross* Court noted, however, that the case would have been reversed had the pro-death juror been seated as a juror and had the defendant preserved the issue for appeal.

[g] Peremptory Challenges

As noted above, a potential juror may be excluded by two types of challenges: cause and peremptory. While a challenge for cause is based on something that makes the juror incapable of serving, a peremptory challenge is one that traditionally requires no articulated reason whatsoever. Whether based upon an objective reason falling short of excusal for cause or some intuitive judgment, the peremptory challenge is used when the lawyer believes that the juror might favor the opposing side or not favor his or her own side.

In general terms, a peremptory challenge is a way for the parties to achieve an impartial jury. Since the peremptory challenge is not guaranteed by the Constitution, jurisdictions have much leeway in fashioning the peremptory challenge process.

[i] Number of Peremptory Challenges

Number varies with severity of crime. Today, court rules or statutes often prescribe both the number of peremptory challenges and the procedures used to exercise them. In general terms, more peremptory challenges are permitted for more serious crimes. Often the two sides are given the same number of peremptory challenges. *E.g.*, Ariz. R. Crim. P. 18.4(c) (both sides get same number: 10 in capital cases, 6 in cases in Superior Court, 2 in non-record courts); Ill. Rev. Stat. ch. 38, para. 5/115-4 (defendant has 20 in capital case, 10 in other cases where imprisonment in penitentiary is possible, and 5 in all other cases; where there are multiple defendants, each has 12, 6 and 3, respectively; prosecution is allowed same number as all defendants combined).

More for defense. Sometimes the defense is given more than those allotted the prosecution. *E.g.*, Mich. Code Crim. P. 768.13 (in capital case, defendant has 20 peremptories, prosecutor has 15).

Trial judge's discretion to increase. In many jurisdictions the trial judge is given the discretion to increase the number of peremptory challenges in unusual cases, such as those that have engendered significant pretrial publicity. Additional peremptory challenges are usually provided in multi-defendant trials. *See, e.g.*, Ill. statute, above. The American Bar Association recommends that peremptory challenges should be allowed in all cases and in equal number to both sides. The court should have the authority to increase the number of peremptories when necessary. STANDARDS FOR CRIMINAL JUSTICE § 15-2.6 (3d ed. 1996); American Bar Association, PRINCIPLES FOR JURIES AND JURY TRIALS, Prin. 11(D)(2005)(same).

Some jurisdictions require the party seeking additional peremptories (virtually always the defense) to establish that his or her cases would suffer prejudice without the additional challenges. *See, e.g., State v. Cruz*, 181 P.3d 196 (Ariz. 2008)(extensive media coverage merits additional peremptory challenges if defendant can show prejudice).

The federal approach is typical:

FEDERAL RULES OF CRIMINAL PROCEDURE

Rule 24. *Trial Jurors*

. . . .

(b) Peremptory Challenges. Each side is entitled to the number of peremptory challenges to prospective jurors specified below. The court may allow additional peremptory challenges to multiple defendants, and may allow the defendants to exercise those challenges separately or jointly.

> **(1) Capital Case.** Each side has 20 peremptory challenges when the government seeks the death penalty.

> **(2) Other Felony Case.** The government has 6 peremptory challenges and the defendant or defendants jointly have 10 peremptory challenges when the defendant is charged with a crime punishable by imprisonment of more than one year.

> **(3) Misdemeanor Case.** Each side has 3 peremptory challenges when the defendant is charged with a crime punishable by fine, imprisonment of one year or less, or both.

(c) Alternate Jurors.

> . . . .

> **(2) Procedure.**

>> **(A)** Alternate jurors must have the same qualifications and be selected and sworn in the same manner as any other juror.

>> **(B)** Alternate jurors replace jurors in the same sequence in which the alternates were selected. An alternate juror who replaces a juror has the same authority as the other jurors.

> **(3) Retaining Alternate Jurors.** The court may retain alternate jurors after the jury retires to deliberate. The court must ensure that a retained alternate does not discuss the case with anyone until that alternate replaces a juror or is discharged. If an alternate replaces a juror after deliberations have begun, the court must instruct the jury to begin its deliberations anew.

> **(4) Peremptory Challenges.** Each side is entitled to the number of additional peremptory challenges to prospective alternate jurors specified below. These additional challenges may be used only to remove alternate jurors.

>> **(A) One or Two Alternates.** One additional peremptory challenge is permitted when one or two alternates are impaneled.

>> **(B) Three or Four Alternates.** Two additional peremptory challenges are permitted when three or four alternates are impaneled.

>> **(C) Five or Six Alternates.** Three additional peremptory challenges are permitted when five or six alternates are impaneled.

[ii]   Procedures for Peremptory Challenges

Jurisdictions differ markedly in the procedures used for the exercise of peremptory challenges. Ordinarily, peremptory challenges are made after challenges for cause have been made. Two of the most prevalent models are the "strike" and "challenge" approaches.

"Strike" system. One model, called the "strike" system, involves the selection of twelve jurors from the larger venire. Sometimes the entire venire or a portion of it is first questioned to determine if the members should be challenged for cause. Twelve (sometimes the number of alternate jurors and the number of peremptory challenges are added to the twelve) potential jurors are then randomly selected from the venire and provisionally seated as jurors in the case. The judge (and sometimes counsel for both sides) interrogates these provisional jurors. Each side may then attempt to have one or more of the twelve potential jurors excused for cause. At this point, counsel for both sides are permitted to exercise peremptory challenges to remove any objectionable jurors remaining from the original panel of twelve provisional jurors. Jurors remaining after all challenges have been made are selected to try the case. In some jurisdictions a new provisional juror is seated immediately after a provisional juror has been "struck." This means that there are always twelve "provisional" jurors. The process continues until the jury panel has the requisite number of jurors. The American Bar Association recommends the strike system. American Bar Association, PRINCIPLES FOR JURIES AND JURY TRIALS, Prin. 11(D)(4)(2005).

"Challenge" system. Under the "challenge" system, the prosecutor randomly selects twelve potential jurors from the venire, exercises challenges for cause and peremptory challenges, and arrives at a panel of twelve. The defense then takes this potential panel, exercises its challenges for cause and peremptory challenges, adds more jurors (subject, of course, to challenges) until the defense has a panel of twelve. This panel is then examined by the prosecutor, who may challenge for cause or use peremptory challenges to pare the number lower than twelve. The process continues until a panel of twelve jurors, acceptable to both the government and the defendant, is selected.

Anonymous exercise of peremptory challenges. A growing number of jurisdictions have adopted procedures to ensure that potential jurors do not know which side exercised a peremptory challenge. This approach is designed to avoid any adverse reactions to a side's decision to excuse a particular juror. *See* American Bar Association, PRINCIPLES FOR JURIES AND JURY TRIALS, Prin. 11(E)(2005) (all challenges to potential jurors should be addressed to the court outside the presence of the jury, so jury panel is not aware of nature or basis of challenge or party making challenge).

[iii]   Grounds for Peremptory Challenges

Traditionally, there were no legal limits on the grounds for exercising peremptory challenges. Lawyers often used hunches based on experience to decide whether to accept or exclude a particular juror. The details of a case may suggest whether a particular potential juror should be excluded by peremptory challenge. Sometimes the reasons for exercising a peremptory challenge reflect the lawyer's hunches about a juror's predisposition. For example, some prosecutors would not accept a juror who wore a bow tie (too independent), or who belonged to a certain ethnic group (too liberal) or the same racial or religious group as the defendant (too likely to identify with the defendant). Similarly, some criminal defense lawyers would use peremptory challenges to exclude potential jurors with a law enforcement background (too likely to believe police officer witnesses) or a government job (too likely to believe in "the system" and feel threatened by criminals). For a more detailed discussion of this process, see James J. Gobert & Walter E. Jordan, JURY SELECTION (2d ed. 1990); V. Hale Starr & Mark McCormick, JURY SELECTION (2d ed. 1993).

In recent years, however, courts have placed some limits on the use of peremptory challenges.

BATSON v. KENTUCKY

476 U.S. 79 (1986)

JUSTICE POWELL delivered the opinion of the Court.

This case requires us to reexamine that portion of *Swain v. Alabama*, 380 U.S. 202 (1965), concerning the evidentiary burden placed on a criminal defendant who claims that he has been denied equal protection through the State's use of peremptory challenges to exclude members of his race from the petit jury.

Petitioner, a black man, was indicted in Kentucky on charges of second-degree burglary and receipt of stolen goods. On the first day of trial in Jefferson Circuit Court, the judge conducted voir dire examination of the venire, excused certain jurors for cause, and permitted the parties to exercise peremptory challenges. The prosecutor used his peremptory challenges to strike all four black persons on the venire, and a jury composed only of white persons was selected. Defense counsel moved to discharge the jury before it was sworn on the ground that the prosecutor's removal of the black veniremen violated petitioner's rights under the Sixth and Fourteenth Amendments to a jury drawn from a cross section of the community, and under the Fourteenth Amendment to equal protection of the laws. Counsel requested a hearing on his motion. Without expressly ruling on the request for a hearing, the trial judge observed that the parties were entitled to use their peremptory challenges to "strike anybody they want to." The judge then denied petitioner's motion, reasoning that the cross-section requirement applies only to selection of the venire and not to selection of the petit jury itself.

[After being convicted on both counts, petitioner appealed to the Kentucky Supreme Court, alleging that the prosecutor's use of peremptory challenges violated the Sixth Amendment cross-section requirement, the Kentucky Constitution, and the equal protection clause's prohibition of a pattern of racially discriminatory peremptory challenges. The Kentucky Supreme Court affirmed, holding that a fair cross section argument must establish systematic exclusion of a group of jurors from the venire rather than from a single jury.] We granted certiorari and now reverse.

In *Swain v. Alabama*, this Court recognized that a "State's purposeful or deliberate denial to Negroes on account of race of participation as jurors in the administration of justice violates the Equal Protection Clause." We reaffirm the principle today.

. . . In holding that racial discrimination in jury selection offends the Equal Protection Clause, the Court in *Strauder v. West Virginia*, 100 U.S. 303 (1880), recognized, however, that a defendant has no right to a "petit jury composed in whole or in part of persons of his own race." But the defendant does have the right to be tried by a jury whose members are selected pursuant to nondiscriminatory criteria. The Equal Protection Clause guarantees the defendant that the State will not exclude members of his race from the jury venire on account of race, or on the false assumption that members of his race as a group are not qualified to serve as jurors.

Purposeful racial discrimination in selection of the venire violates a defendant's right to equal protection because it denies him the protection that a trial by jury is intended to secure. "The very idea of a jury is a body . . . composed of the peers or equals of the person whose rights it is selected or summoned to determine; that is, of his neighbors, fellows, associates, persons having the same legal status in society as that which he holds." (citing *Strauder*) The petit jury has occupied a central position in our system of justice by safeguarding a person accused of crime against the arbitrary exercise of power by prosecutor or judge. Those on the venire must be "indifferently chosen," to secure the defendant's right under the Fourteenth Amendment to "protection of life and liberty against race or color prejudice."

Racial discrimination in selection of jurors harms not only the accused whose life or liberty they are summoned to try. Competence to serve as a juror ultimately depends on an assessment of individual qualifications and ability impartially to consider evidence presented at a trial. A person's race simply is unrelated to his fitness as a juror. As long ago as *Strauder*, therefore, the Court recognized that by denying a person participation in jury service on account of his race, the State unconstitutionally discriminated against the excluded juror.

The harm from discriminatory jury selection extends beyond that inflicted on the defendant and the excluded juror to touch the entire community. Selection procedures that purposefully exclude black persons from juries undermine public confidence in the fairness of our system of justice. Discrimination within the judicial system is most pernicious because it is "a stimulant to that race prejudice which is an impediment to securing to [black citizens] that equal justice which the law aims to secure to all others."

In *Strauder*, the Court invalidated a state statute that provided that only white men could serve as jurors. We can be confident that no State now has such a law. The Constitution requires, however, that we look beyond the face of the statute defining juror qualifications and also consider challenged selection practices to afford "protection against action of the State through its administrative officers in effecting the prohibited discrimination." *Norris v. Alabama*, 294 U.S. 587, 589 (1935). Thus, the Court has found a denial of equal protection where the procedures implementing a neutral statute operated to exclude persons from the venire on racial grounds, and has made clear that the Constitution prohibits all forms of purposeful racial discrimination in selection of jurors.

. . . Accordingly, the component of the jury selection process at issue here, the State's privilege to strike individual jurors through peremptory challenges, is subject to the commands of the Equal Protection Clause. Although a prosecutor ordinarily is entitled to exercise permitted peremptory challenges "for any reason at all, as long as that reason is related to his view concerning the outcome" of the case to be tried, the Equal Protection Clause forbids the prosecutor to challenge potential jurors solely on account of their race or on the assumption that black jurors as a group will be unable impartially to consider the State's case against a black defendant.

. . . Since the decision in *Swain*, we have explained that our cases concerning selection of the venire reflect the general equal protection principle that the "invidious quality" of governmental action claimed to be racially discriminatory "must ultimately be traced to a racially discriminatory purpose." *Washington v. Davis*, 426 U.S. 229, 240 (1976). As in any equal protection case, the "burden is, of course," on the defendant who alleges discriminatory selection of the venire "to prove the existence of purposeful discrimination." *Whitus v. Georgia*, 385 U.S. 545, 550, (1967), *citing Tarrance v. Florida*, 188 U.S. 519 (1903). In deciding if the defendant has carried his burden of persuasion, a court must undertake "a sensitive inquiry into such circumstantial and direct evidence of intent as may be available." *Arlington Heights v. Metropolitan Housing Development Corp.*, 429 U.S. 252, 266 (1977). Circumstantial evidence of invidious intent may include proof of disproportionate impact.

. . . [The] principles [in the post-*Swain* cases] support our conclusion that a defendant may establish a prima facie case of purposeful discrimination in selection of the petit jury solely on evidence concerning the prosecutor's exercise of peremptory challenges at the defendant's trial. To establish such a case, the defendant first must show that he is a member of a cognizable racial group, and that the prosecutor has exercised peremptory challenges to remove from the venire members of the defendant's race. Second, the defendant is entitled to rely on the fact, as to which there can be no dispute, that peremptory challenges constitute a jury selection practice that permits "those to discriminate who are of a mind to discriminate." *Avery v. Georgia*, 345 U.S. at 562. Finally, the defendant must show that these facts and any other relevant circumstances raise an inference that the prosecutor used that practice to exclude the veniremen from the petit jury on account of their race. This combination of factors in the empaneling of the petit jury, as in the selection of the venire, raises the necessary inference of purposeful discrimination.

In deciding whether the defendant has made the requisite showing, the trial court should consider all relevant circumstances. For example, a "pattern" of strikes against black jurors included in the particular venire might give rise to an inference of discrimination. Similarly, the prosecutor's questions and statements during voir dire examination and in exercising his challenges may support or refute an inference of discriminatory purpose. These examples are merely illustrative. We have confidence that trial judges, experienced in supervising voir dire, will be able to decide if the circumstances concerning the prosecutor's use of peremptory challenges creates a prima facie case of discrimination against black jurors.

Once the defendant makes a prima facie showing, the burden shifts to the State to come forward with a neutral explanation for challenging black jurors. Though this requirement imposes a limitation in some cases on the full peremptory character of the historic challenge, we emphasize that the prosecutor's explanation need not rise to the level justifying exercise of a challenge for cause. But the prosecutor may not rebut the defendant's prima facie case of discrimination by stating merely that he challenged jurors of the defendant's race on the assumption — or his intuitive judgment — that they would be partial to the defendant because of their shared race . . . . The prosecutor therefore must articulate a neutral explanation related to the particular case to be tried. The trial court then will have the duty to determine if the defendant has established purposeful discrimination.

The State contends that our holding will eviscerate the fair trial values served by the peremptory challenge. Conceding that the Constitution does not guarantee a right to peremptory challenges and that *Swain* did state that their use ultimately is subject to the strictures of equal protection, the State argues that the privilege of unfettered exercise of the challenge is of vital importance to the criminal justice system.

While we recognize, of course, that the peremptory challenge occupies an important position in our trial procedures, we do not agree that our decision today will undermine the contribution the challenge generally makes to the administration of justice. The reality of practice, amply reflected in many state-and federal-court opinions, shows that the challenge may be, and unfortunately at times has been, used to discriminate against black jurors. By requiring trial courts to be sensitive to the racially discriminatory use of peremptory challenges, our decision enforces the mandate of equal protection and furthers the ends of justice. In view of the heterogeneous population of our Nation, public respect for our criminal justice system and the rule of law will be strengthened if we ensure that no citizen is disqualified from jury service because of his race.

Nor are we persuaded by the State's suggestion that our holding will create serious administrative difficulties. In those States applying a version of the evidentiary standard we recognize today, courts have not experienced serious administrative burdens, and the peremptory challenge system has survived. We decline, however, to formulate particular procedures to be followed upon a defendant's timely objection to a prosecutor's challenges.[24]

In this case, petitioner made a timely objection to the prosecutor's removal of all black persons on the venire. Because the trial court flatly rejected the objection without requiring the prosecutor to give an explanation for his action, we remand this case for further proceedings. If the trial court decides that the facts establish, prima facie, purposeful discrimination and the prosecutor does not come forward with a neutral

---

[24] In light of the variety of jury selection practices followed in our state and federal trial courts, we make no attempt to instruct these courts how best to implement our holding today. For the same reason, we express no view on whether it is more appropriate in a particular case, upon a finding of discrimination against black jurors, for the trial court to discharge the venire and select a new jury from a panel not previously associated with the case, or to disallow the discriminatory challenges and resume selection with the improperly challenged jurors reinstated on the venire.

explanation for his action, our precedents require that petitioner's conviction be reversed.

JUSTICE MARSHALL, concurring.

. . . The decision today will not end the racial discrimination that peremptories inject into the jury-selection process. That goal can be accomplished only by eliminating peremptory challenges entirely.

. . . I wholeheartedly concur in the Court's conclusion that use of the peremptory challenge to remove blacks from juries, on the basis of their race, violates the Equal Protection Clause. I would go further, however, in fashioning a remedy adequate to eliminate that discrimination. Merely allowing defendants the opportunity to challenge the racially discriminatory use of peremptory challenges in individual cases will not end the illegitimate use of the peremptory challenge.

Evidentiary analysis similar to that set out by the Court has been adopted as a matter of state law in States including Massachusetts and California. Cases from those jurisdictions illustrate the limitations of the approach. First, defendants cannot attack the discriminatory use of peremptory challenges at all unless the challenges are so flagrant as to establish a prima facie case. This means, in those States, that where only one or two black jurors survive the challenges for cause, the prosecutor need have no compunction about striking them from the jury because of their race. Prosecutors are left free to discriminate against blacks in jury selection provided that they hold that discrimination to an "acceptable" level.

Second, when a defendant can establish a prima facie case, trial courts face the difficult burden of assessing prosecutors' motives. Any prosecutor can easily assert facially neutral reasons for striking a juror, and trial courts are ill equipped to second-guess those reasons. How is the court to treat a prosecutor's statement that he struck a juror because the juror had a son about the same age as defendant, or seemed "uncommunicative," or "never cracked a smile" and, therefore "did not possess the sensitivities necessary to realistically look at the issues and decide the facts in this case"? If such easily generated explanations are sufficient to discharge the prosecutor's obligation to justify his strikes on nonracial grounds, then the protection erected by the Court today may be illusory.

Nor is outright prevarication by prosecutors the only danger here. "[I]t is even possible that an attorney may lie to himself in an effort to convince himself that his motives are legal." A prosecutor's own conscious or unconscious racism may lead him easily to the conclusion that a prospective black juror is "sullen," or "distant," a characterization that would not have come to his mind if a white juror had acted identically. A judge's own conscious or unconscious racism may lead him to accept such an explanation as well supported.

. . . The inherent potential of peremptory challenges to distort the jury process by permitting the exclusion of jurors on racial grounds should ideally lead the Court to ban them entirely from the criminal justice system . . . .

CHIEF JUSTICE BURGER, joined by JUSTICE REHNQUIST, dissenting.

We granted certiorari to decide whether petitioner was tried "in violation of constitutional provisions guaranteeing the defendant an impartial jury and a jury composed of persons representing a fair cross section of the community."

. . . Long ago it was recognized that "[t]he right of challenge is almost essential for the purpose of securing perfect fairness and impartiality in a trial." W. Forsyth, HISTORY OF TRIAL BY JURY 175 (1852).

. . . Instead of even considering the history or function of the peremptory challenge, the bulk of the Court's opinion is spent recounting the well-established principle that intentional exclusion of racial groups from jury venires is a violation of the Equal Protection Clause. I too reaffirm that principle, which has been a part of our constitutional tradition since at least *Strauder v. West Virginia*, 100 U.S. 303 (1880).

. . . Unwilling to rest solely on jury venire cases such as *Strauder*, the Court also invokes general equal protection principles in support of its holding. But peremptory challenges are often lodged, of necessity, for reasons "normally thought irrelevant to legal proceedings or official action, namely, the race, religion, nationality, occupation or affiliations of people summoned for jury duty." Moreover, in making peremptory challenges, both the prosecutor and defense attorney necessarily act on only limited information or hunch. The process cannot be indicted on the sole basis that such decisions are made on the basis of "assumption" or "intuitive judgment." As a result, unadulterated equal protection analysis is simply inapplicable to peremptory challenges exercised in any particular case. A clause that requires a minimum "rationality" in government actions has no application to "an arbitrary and capricious right." (citing *Swain*)

. . . That the Court is not applying conventional equal protection analysis is shown by its limitation of its new rule to allegations of impermissible challenge on the basis of race . . . . But if conventional equal protection principles apply, then presumably defendants could object to exclusions on the basis of not only race but also sex, age, religious or political affiliation, mental capacity, number of children, living arrangements, and employment in a particular industry or profession.

In short, it is quite probable that every peremptory challenge could be objected to on the basis that, because it excluded a venireman who had some characteristic not shared by the remaining members of the venire, it constituted a "classification" subject to equal protection scrutiny. Compounding the difficulties, under conventional equal protection principles some uses of peremptories would be reviewed under "strict scrutiny and . . . sustained only if . . . suitably tailored to serve a compelling state interest;" others would be reviewed to determined if they were "substantially related to a sufficiently important government interest;" and still others would be reviewed to determine whether they were "a rational means to serve a legitimate end."

. . . Rather than applying straightforward equal protection analysis, the Court substitutes for the holding in *Swain* a curious hybrid. The defendant must first establish a "prima facie case" of invidious discrimination, then the "burden shifts to the State to come forward with a neutral explanation for challenging black jurors." The Court explains that "the operation of prima facie burden of proof rules" is established in "[o]ur decisions concerning 'disparate treatment'; . . . ." The Court then adds, borrowing again from a Title VII case, that "the prosecutor must give a 'clear and reasonably specific' explanation of his 'legitimate reasons' for exercising the challenges."

While undoubtedly these rules are well suited to other contexts, particularly where (as with Title VII) they are required by an Act of Congress, they seem curiously out of place when applied to peremptory challenges in criminal cases. Our system permits two types of challenges: challenges for cause and peremptory challenges. Challenges for cause obviously have to be explained; by definition, peremptory challenges do not . . . . Analytically, there is no middle ground: A challenge either has to be explained or it does not. It is readily apparent, then, that to permit inquiry into the basis for a peremptory challenge would force "the peremptory challenge [to] collapse into the challenge for cause." *United States v. Clark*, 737 F.2d 679, 682 (7th Cir. 1984).

. . . Confronted with the dilemma it created, the Court today attempts to decree a middle ground. To rebut a prima facie case, the Court requires a "neutral explanation" for the challenge, but is at pains to "emphasize" that the "explanation need not rise to the level justifying exercise of a challenge for cause." I am at a loss to discern the governing principles here. A "clear and reasonably specific" explanation of "legitimate reasons" for exercising the challenge will be difficult to distinguish from a challenge for cause. Anything short of a challenge for cause may well be seen as an "arbitrary and capricious" challenge, to use Blackstone's characterization of the peremptory. Apparently the Court envisions permissible challenges short of a challenge for cause that are just a little bit arbitrary — but not too much. While our trial judges are "experienced in supervising voir dire," they have no experience in administering rules like this.

. . . Today we mark the return of racial differentiation as the Court accepts a positive evil for a perceived one. Prosecutors and defense attorneys alike will build records in support of their claims that peremptory challenges have been exercised in a racially discriminatory fashion by asking jurors to state their racial background and national origin for the record, despite the fact that "such questions may be offensive to some jurors and thus are not ordinarily asked on voir dire."

. . . The Court does not tarry long over any of these difficult, sensitive problems, preferring instead to gloss over them as swiftly as it slides over centuries of history: "[W]e make no attempt to instruct [trial] courts how best to implement our holding today." That leaves roughly 7,000 general jurisdiction state trial judges and approximately 500 federal trial judges at large to find their way through the morass the Court creates today . . . .

JUSTICE REHNQUIST, with whom THE CHIEF JUSTICE joins, dissenting.

The Court states, in the opening line of its opinion, that this case involves only a reexamination of that portion of *Swain v. Alabama*, 380 U.S. 202 (1965), concerning "the evidentiary burden placed on a criminal defendant who claims that he has been denied equal protection through the State's use of peremptory challenges to exclude members of his race from the petit jury." But in reality the majority opinion deals with much more than "evidentiary burden[s]."

. . . In my view, there is simply nothing "unequal" about the State's using its peremptory challenges to strike blacks from the jury in cases involving black defendants, so long as such challenges are also used to exclude whites in cases involving white defendants, Hispanics in cases involving Hispanic defendants, Asians in cases involving Asian defendants, and so on. This case-specific use of peremptory challenges by the State does not single out blacks, or members of any other race for that matter, for discriminatory treatment. Such use of peremptories is at best based upon seat-of-the-pants instincts, which are undoubtedly crudely stereotypical and may in many cases be hopelessly mistaken. But as long as they are applied across-the-board to jurors of all races and nationalities, I do not see — and the Court most certainly has not explained — how their use violates the Equal Protection Clause.

Nor does such use of peremptory challenges by the State infringe upon any other constitutional interests. The Court does not suggest that exclusion of blacks from the jury through the State's use of peremptory challenges results in a violation of either the fair-cross-section or impartiality component of the Sixth Amendment. And because the case-specific use of peremptory challenges by the State does not deny blacks the right to serve as jurors in cases involving nonblack defendants, it harms neither the excluded jurors nor the remainder of the community.

The use of group affiliations, such as age, race, or occupation, as a "proxy" for potential juror partiality, based on the assumption or belief that members of one group are more likely to favor defendants who belong to the same group, has long been accepted as a legitimate basis for the State's exercise of peremptory challenges.

Indeed, given the need for reasonable limitations on the time devoted to voir dire, the use of such "proxies" by both the State and the defendant may be extremely useful in eliminating from the jury persons who might be biased in one way or another. The Court today holds that the State may not use its peremptory challenges to strike black prospective jurors on this basis without violating the Constitution. But I do not believe there is anything in the Equal Protection Clause, or any other constitutional provision, that justifies such a departure from the substantive holding contained in Part II of *Swain*. Petitioner in the instant case failed to make a sufficient showing to overcome the presumption announced in *Swain* that the State's use of peremptory challenges was related to the context of the case. I would therefore affirm the judgment of the court below.

[The concurring opinions of JUSTICES WHITE, STEVENS, and O'CONNOR are omitted.]

NOTES

1. *Role of Sixth Amendment.* Although the defendants in *Batson* argued that the defendant's Sixth Amendment fair cross section and impartial jury rights were violated, the Supreme Court resolved the case on equal protection grounds. This left open questions about the role of the Sixth Amendment in limiting peremptory challenges.

In *Holland v. Illinois*, 493 U.S. 474 (1990), a white defendant argued that the Sixth Amendment barred a prosecutor from using peremptory challenges to exclude all black potential jurors from his criminal trial. The Supreme Court held that the white defendant had standing to raise the Sixth Amendment issues because that amendment

> entitles every defendant to object to a venire that is not designed to represent a fair cross section of the community, whether or not the systematically excluded groups are groups to which he himself belongs. [*Id.* at 477]

The Court then rejected the argument that the Sixth Amendment was violated, holding that the Sixth Amendment protects only against the exclusion of cognizable groups from the venire; it has no bearing on the use of peremptory challenges. In language approving the traditional toleration of peremptory challenges, the Court stated:

> The Sixth Amendment requirement of a fair cross section on the venire is a means of assuring, not a *representative* jury (which the Constitution does not demand), but an *impartial* one (which it does). . . . The fair-cross-section venire requirement assures . . . that in the process of selecting the petit jury the prosecution and defense will compete on an equal basis.

> But to say that the Sixth Amendment deprives the State of the ability to "stack the deck" in its favor is not to say that each side may not, once a fair hand is dealt, use peremptory challenges to eliminate prospective jurors belonging to groups it believes would unduly favor the other side. [*Id.* at 480–481]

Why do you suppose the defendant in *Holland* bothered to raise the Sixth Amendment when *Batson* clearly held that he had a viable equal protection claim? The reason is that *Batson* was not available to the defendant in *Holland* because *Batson* is not applied retroactively. *Allen v. Hardy*, 478 U.S. 255 (1986). *But see Griffith v. Kentucky*, 479 U.S. 314 (1987) (holding that *Batson* applied to all cases pending on direct review or not yet final when *Batson* was decided).

2. *Standing expanded to non-members of excluded group.* Recall that *Batson* was an equal protection case involving a black defendant who objected to a prosecutor's use of peremptory challenges to exclude potential black jurors. Subsequent decisions have dealt with other racial and ethnic combinations. In *Powers v. Ohio*, 499 U.S. 400 (1991), the Supreme Court held that *Batson* applied to a white defendant in a case in which the prosecutor exercised peremptory challenges to exclude six black potential jurors. The Court noted that *Batson* was based in part on the equal protection clause's role in recognizing the potential juror's opportunity to participate in the administration of the criminal justice system. Thus, the defendant has standing to enforce the juror's equal protection right to serve even if he or she is not the same race as those excluded. *See Shaw v. Hunt*, 517 U.S. 899 (1996).

3. *Extended to defense challenges. Batson* dealt with a *prosecutor's* use of race-based peremptory challenges. Although several of the *Batson* Justices opined that the equal protection analysis applied as well to race-based peremptory challenges by *defense counsel*, the matter was not finally resolved until *Georgia v. McCollum*, 505 U.S. 42 (1992). The Court held that the equal protection clause bars defense counsel from using race-based peremptory challenges, reasoning along lines suggested in *Powers* that the equal protection clause protects potential jurors from discrimination on the basis of race.

4. *Civil cases.* Although the focus in this section is *Batson*'s impact upon the conduct of jury selection in criminal cases, it is noteworthy that the Court also held that *Batson* applies equally to civil cases. *Edmonson v. Leesville Concrete Co.*, 500 U.S. 614 (1991).

5. *Gender. Batson* held that the equal protection clause barred race-based peremptory challenges. But what about the validity of peremptory challenges based on classifications other than race?

In *J.E.B. v. Alabama ex rel. T.B.*, 511 U.S. 127 (1994), the Supreme Court held that *Batson*'s equal protection analysis forbids intentional discrimination on the basis of gender. *J.E.B.* involved a civil paternity case where the state used its peremptory challenges to remove male potential jurors, leaving an all-female jury. The Supreme Court specifically rejected arguments that gender-based peremptory challenges are permissible because members of one sex may be more sympathetic to a particular party or argument. According to the Supreme Court, such gender-based stereotypes are barred as a justification for the exercise of peremptory challenges.

The *J.E.B.* decision was careful to note, however, that it was not eliminating all peremptory challenges. Such challenges are permissible to secure a fair trial. Moreover,

> [p]arties may also exercise their peremptory challenges to remove from the venire any group or class of individuals normally subject to "rational basis" review. Even strikes based on characteristics that are disproportionately associated with one gender could be appropriate, absent a showing of pretext. [511 U.S. at 143]

6. *Standard to assess whether a "group" is covered by Batson.* Standards utilized in deciding whether a particular group is subject to equal protection under *Batson* are unclear. One court held that a *Batson* challenge could succeed if the proponent proves that the group is definable and limited by a clearly definable factor; a common thread of attitudes, ideas or experiences runs through the group; and there exists a community of interests among the members such that the group's interest cannot be adequately represented if the group is excluded from the jury selection process. *United States v. Sgro*, 816 F.2d 30 (1st Cir. 1987), *cert. denied*, 484 U.S. 1063 (1988).

7. *Groups covered by Batson. Batson* has been held to apply to the other groups. *See, e.g., Hernandez v. New York*, 500 U.S. 352 (1991) (Latinos or Hispanics); *United States v. Chalan*, 812 F.2d 1302 (10th Cir. 1987) (Native Americans); *Fields v. People*, 732 P.2d 1145 (Colo. 1987) (Spanish surnamed people).

8. *Groups not covered by Batson.* In contrast, other courts have held certain groups outside *Batson*'s limitations. *See, e.g. J.E.B. v. Alabama, ex rel. T.B.*, 511 U.S. 127 (1994) (persons with military experience [disproportionately men] and nurses [disproportionately women]); *United States v. Biaggi*, 853 F.2d 89 (2d Cir. 1988) (Italian-Americans); *United States v. Dennis*, 804 F.2d 1208 (11th Cir. 1986) (black males); *United States v. Nichols*, 937 F.2d 1257 (7th Cir. 1991)(black females); *Webber v. Strippit*, 186 F.3d 907 (8th Cir. 1999)(age).

Religion. In *State v. Davis*, 504 N.W.2d 767 (Minn. 1993), the Minnesota Supreme Court held that *Batson* does not apply to religion-based challenges. The United States Supreme Court denied a writ of certiorari, but a dissenting opinion authored by Justice Thomas maintained that "no principled reason immediately appears for declining to apply *Batson* to any strike based on a classification that is accorded heightened scrutiny under the Equal Protection Clause." *Davis v. Minnesota*, 511 U.S. 1115, 1117 (1994).

In *United States v. Somerstein*, 959 F. Supp. 592 (E.D.N.Y. 1997), the United States District Court adopted Justice Thomas' reasoning, and held that *Batson* applies to religious classifications (in that particular case, persons of the Jewish faith). But the *Somerstein* court noted:

> [B]efore a Court applies *Batson* to a challenge on religious grounds, there must be a determination as to whether the religion of the juror is relevant to the issues of the case. Generally, the religion of a juror is not relevant to the jury

selection process, in the legal sense. Accordingly, the preference of attorneys for one religious group over another should not be the basis for a *Batson* challenge. In a criminal case, only if the religion of the jurors is directly relevant to the crimes at issue, can such a challenge be proper. In this case, the defendants are kosher caterers specializing in making kosher affairs, and they are accused of criminal conduct in connection with an alleged scheme to defraud their employees' benefit funds. Based on the particular and unique facts of this case, in which, arguably, the religious element is intertwined in the criminal charges, the Court rules that the religion of the jurors would be relevant as a foundation for a *Batson* challenge. [*Id.* at 595–596]

[iv] *Batson* Step One: Prima Facie Case

Recall that *Batson* held that the person claiming an equal protection violation must first establish a prima facie case of purposeful discrimination. A successful showing raises an inference of purposeful discrimination.

There are many ways of establishing a prima facie case. Courts look at all the facts to assess whether there is an inference of purposeful discrimination. These include such facts as the questions and statements made during voir dire of all potential jurors, the pattern of peremptory challenges (including how potential jurors who answered questions the same way were treated), the nature and facts of the crime, statements and actions inferring motivation, the race (or other minority status) of the defendant and the victim and the witnesses, and the composition of the venire and the jury that was actually seated. Generally, no single factor is dispositive.

An obvious example of a prima facie case is a prosecutor who uses peremptory challenges to exclude only black jurors. But a challenge to the only Hispanic on the venire also may be sufficient. *See United States v. De Gross*, 913 F.2d 1417 (9th Cir. 1990) (prima facie case established where Hispanic defendant was charged with illegal importation of Mexicans and prosecutor used peremptory challenge to remove only Hispanic on the jury).

Another illustration of a prima facie case is provided by *United States v. Hughes*, 880 F.2d 101 (8th Cir. 1989), which involved six potential black jurors. One was dismissed for cause at the defendant's motion. Three were excluded by government peremptory challenges. Two were seated as jurors. In finding that a prima facie case under *Batson* was established, the Court of Appeals noted that there were no non-discriminatory reasons for using peremptory challenges to bar the three black jurors. One of the three did not answer any questions during the voir dire process; a second had been a victim of a burglary years before but so had half the other potential jurors; and the third had a family member who had been convicted of a crime fifteen years ago but indicated she could be unbiased and both she and her husband had "respectable occupations." Even though two blacks remained on the panel, that was insufficient to overcome other factors.

Courts do not automatically find that a prima facie showing is made under facts similar to *Hughes*. Indeed, many decisions indicate just the opposite. *See, e.g., United States v. Dawn*, 897 F.2d 1444 (8th Cir. 1990) (prosecutor used 6 of 7 peremptory challenges to exclude blacks; no prima facie case); *United States v. Dennis*, 804 F.2d 1208 (11th Cir. 1986) (prosecutor used 4 peremptory challenges, 3 of which excluded blacks; no prima facie case because 2 black jurors were not excluded although government had remaining peremptory challenges; no inference of purposeful discrimination).

Standard of prima facie. Is it permissible for a state to require at step one [prima facie case] that the objecting party must show that it is "more likely than not" that the other party's peremptory challenges, if unexplained, were based on impermissible group bias? In *Johnson v. California*, 545 U.S. 162 (2005), the U.S. Supreme Court held that such a standard was "at odds with the prima facie inquiry mandated by *Batson*."

Turning to the facts of this case, the Court found that a prima facie case had been established where the prosecutor removed all three prospective black jurors peremptorily.

[v] *Batson* Step Two: Neutral Explanation or Pretext

Once the defendant has offered a *prima facie* case, under *Batson* the burden shifts to the government to offer a race neutral explanation. The government need not present its reasons until after a *prima facie* case has been made and many prosecutors delay giving such reasons because they do not want to give the defense information that the defense could use to bolster the *prima facie* proof. However, to facilitate appellate review, some appellate courts strongly recommend that the prosecutor offer an explanation even if the defense does not make out a *prima facie* case. *See, e.g., People v. Zambrano*, 163 P. 3d 4 (Cal. 2007).

One of the main practical problems is assessing the constitutional validity of an explanation given for excluding members of identifiable groups from a jury. The concern is whether the lawyer's "neutral" explanation is actually pretextual — *i.e.*, a race-neutral reason given to cover the true race-based justification for exclusion of certain potential jurors.

In *Hernandez v. New York*, 500 U.S. 352 (1991), the government used four peremptory challenges to exclude potential Latino jurors. The prosecutor said that he excluded two of them because he was uncertain whether they would be able to accept a Spanish interpreter's official translation since both possible jurors spoke Spanish themselves. Following *Batson*'s three-step analysis (defendant's prima facie showing of race-based peremptory challenge, prosecutor's burden of establishing a race-neutral explanation, and defendant's burden of proving purposeful discrimination), the Court, without a majority opinion, upheld the use of the peremptory challenges. Noting that *Batson* held that the trial court's decision on discriminatory intent is to be accorded great deference by appellate courts, Justice Kennedy's plurality opinion in *Hernandez* found that the trial court was not clearly erroneous when it decided that the prosecutor's reason for excluding the two Latino jurors was not pretextual.

Hernandez is important for two reasons. First, it demonstrates how much deference is given to the trial court's decision on whether the prosecutor used a race-based motive. Second, it illustrates the importance of establishing discriminatory intent under *Batson*. There is no doubt that the two jurors were excused because their Latin heritage made them fluent in Spanish. But since they were excused because of their language skills rather than their ethnicity, the Supreme Court upheld the jury selection process.

Hernandez focused upon the question whether the prosecutor's proffered reason for excluding jurors was pretextual. The next case elaborates upon this issue, both substantively and procedurally.

PURKETT v. ELEM
514 U.S. 765 (1995)

OPINION: PER CURIAM.

Respondent was convicted of second-degree robbery in a Missouri court. During jury selection, he objected to the prosecutor's use of peremptory challenges to strike two black men from the jury panel, an objection arguably based on *Batson v. Kentucky*, 476 U.S. 79 (1986). The prosecutor explained his strikes:

> I struck [juror] number twenty-two because of his long hair. He had long curly hair. He had the longest hair of anybody on the panel by far. He appeared to me to not be a good juror for that fact, the fact that he had long hair hanging down shoulder length, curly, unkempt hair. Also, he had a mustache and a goatee type beard. And juror number twenty-four also has a mustache and

goatee type beard. Those are the only two people on the jury . . . with the facial hair . . . . And I don't like the way they looked, with the way the hair is cut, both of them. And the mustaches and the beards look suspicious to me.

The prosecutor further explained that he feared that juror number 24, who had had a sawed-off shotgun pointed at him during a supermarket robbery, would believe that "to have a robbery you have to have a gun, and there is no gun in this case."

The state trial court, without explanation, overruled respondent's objection and empaneled the jury. On direct appeal, respondent renewed his *Batson* claim. The Missouri Court of Appeals affirmed, finding that the "state's explanation constituted a legitimate 'hunch';" and that "[t]he circumstances fail[ed] to raise the necessary inference of racial discrimination."

[The district court found no purposeful discrimination.] . . . The Court of Appeals for the Eighth Circuit reversed and remanded with instructions to grant the writ of habeas corpus. It said:

> [W]here the prosecution strikes a prospective juror who is a member of the defendant's racial group, solely on the basis of factors which are facially irrelevant to the question of whether that person is qualified to serve as a juror in the particular case, the prosecution must at least articulate some plausible race-neutral reason for believing those factors will somehow affect the person's ability to perform his or her duties as a juror. In the present case, the prosecutor's comments, "I don't like the way [he] look[s], with the way the hair is cut. . . . And the mustach[e] and the bear[d] look suspicious to me, do not constitute such legitimate race-neutral reasons for striking juror 22."

It concluded that the "prosecution's explanation for striking juror 22 . . . was pretextual," and that the state trial court had "clearly erred" in finding that striking juror number 22 had not been intentional discrimination.

Under our *Batson* jurisprudence, once the opponent of a peremptory challenge has made out a prima facie case of racial discrimination (step 1), the burden of production shifts to the proponent of the strike to come forward with a race-neutral explanation (step 2). If a race-neutral explanation is tendered, the trial court must then decide (step 3) whether the opponent of the strike has proved purposeful racial discrimination. The second step of this process does not demand an explanation that is persuasive, or even plausible. "At this [second] step of the inquiry, the issue is the facial validity of the prosecutor's explanation. Unless a discriminatory intent is inherent in the prosecutor's explanation, the reason offered will be deemed race neutral."

The Court of Appeals erred by combining *Batson's* second and third steps into one, requiring that the justification tendered at the second step be not just neutral but also at least minimally persuasive, i.e., a "plausible" basis for believing that "the person's ability to perform his or her duties as a juror" will be affected. It is not until the third step that the persuasiveness of the justification becomes relevant — the step in which the trial court determines whether the opponent of the strike has carried his burden of proving purposeful discrimination. At that stage, implausible or fantastic justifications may (and probably will) be found to be pretexts for purposeful discrimination. But to say that a trial judge may choose to disbelieve a silly or superstitious reason at step three is quite different from saying that a trial judge must terminate the inquiry at step two when the race-neutral reason is silly or superstitious. The latter violates the principle that the ultimate burden of persuasion regarding racial motivation rests with, and never shifts from, the opponent of the strike.

. . . The prosecutor's proffered explanation in this case — that he struck juror number 22 because he had long, unkempt hair, a mustache, and a beard — is race neutral and satisfies the prosecution's step two burden of articulating a nondiscriminatory reason for the strike. "The wearing of beards is not a characteristic that is peculiar to any race." And neither is the growing of long, unkempt hair. Thus, the inquiry properly proceeded to step three, where the state court found that the prosecutor was not motivated by discriminatory intent. [Reversed.]

JUSTICE STEVENS, with whom JUSTICE BREYER joins, dissenting.

. . . In *Batson*, the Court held that the Equal Protection Clause of the Fourteenth Amendment forbids a prosecutor to use peremptory challenges to exclude African-Americans from jury service because of their race. The Court articulated a three-step process for proving such violations. First, a pattern of peremptory challenges of black jurors may establish a prima facie case of discriminatory purpose. Second, the prosecutor may rebut that prima facie case by tendering a race-neutral explanation for the strikes. Third, the court must decide whether that explanation is pretextual. At the second step of this inquiry, neither a mere denial of improper motive nor an incredible explanation will suffice to rebut the prima facie showing of discriminatory purpose. At a minimum, as the Court held in *Batson*, the prosecutor "must articulate a neutral explanation related to the particular case to be tried."

. . . Today, without argument, the Court replaces the *Batson* standard with the surprising announcement that any neutral explanation, no matter how "implausible or fantastic," even if it is "silly or superstitious," is sufficient to rebut a prima facie case of discrimination. A trial court must accept that neutral explanation unless a separate "step three" inquiry leads to the conclusion that the peremptory challenge was racially motivated. The Court does not attempt to explain why a statement that "the juror had a beard," or "the juror's last name began with the letter "S," should satisfy step two, though a statement that "I had a hunch" should not. It is not too much to ask that a prosecutor's explanation for his strikes be race neutral, reasonably specific, and trial related. Nothing less will serve to rebut the inference of race-based discrimination that arises when the defendant has made out a prima facie case. That, in any event, is what we decided in *Batson*.

. . . [If a prima facie case is made (step one) and the government offers a race neutral explanation,] I think even this Court would acknowledge that some implausible, fantastic, and silly explanations could be found to be pretextual without any further evidence. Indeed, in *Hernandez* the Court explained that a trial judge could find pretext based on nothing more than a consistent policy of excluding all Spanish-speaking jurors if that characteristic was entirely unrelated to the case to be tried. Parallel reasoning would justify a finding of pretext based on a policy of excusing jurors with beards if beards have nothing to do with the pending case.

In some cases, conceivably the length and unkempt character of a juror's hair and goatee type beard might give rise to a concern that he is a nonconformist who might not be a good juror. In this case, however, the prosecutor did not identify any such concern. He merely said he did not "like the way [the juror] looked," that the facial hair "looked suspicious." I think this explanation may well be pretextual as a matter of law; it has nothing to do with the case at hand, and it is just as evasive as "I had a hunch." Unless a reviewing court may evaluate such explanations when a trial judge fails to find that a prima facie case has been established, appellate or collateral review of *Batson* claims will amount to nothing more than the meaningless charade that the Missouri Supreme Court correctly understood *Batson* to disfavor.

In my opinion, preoccupation with the niceties of a three-step analysis should not foreclose meaningful judicial review of prosecutorial explanations that are entirely unrelated to the case to be tried. I would adhere to the *Batson* rule that such an explanation does not satisfy step two. Alternatively, I would hold that, in the absence of an explicit trial court finding on the issue, a reviewing court may hold that such an explanation is pretextual as a matter of law. The Court's unnecessary tolerance of silly, fantastic, and implausible explanations, together with its assumption that there is a difference of constitutional magnitude between a statement that "I had a hunch about this juror based on his appearance," and "I challenged this juror because he had a moustache," demeans the importance of the values vindicated by our decision in *Batson*.

NOTES

1. *I can't remember.* What if the defendant makes out a *prima facie* case (step one) and the burden then shifts to the prosecutor (step two) who cannot recall why the peremptory challenge at issue was made? In *Yee v. Duncan*, 463 P.3d 893 (9th Cir. 2006), the court held that the lack of explanation is evidence of purposeful discrimination, but the defendant must still meet the step three burden of establishing the motive for the challenge. Looking at the entire record, the *Yee* court found that there was a neutral explanation for the use of the peremptory challenge (the juror had served previously on a jury that considered an issue somewhat similar to one in the instant case).

2. *State rejection of Puckett.* A small number of jurisdictions have refused to follow *Purkett* on state law grounds. *See Bruner v. Cawthon*, 681 So. 2d 173, 182 (Ala. 1996) (noting that state's standard differs from *Purkett* because it discounts "whimsical, ad hoc excuses").

[vi] *Batson* Step Three: Purposeful Discrimination

Step three of *Batson* involves an assessment of whether, considering the government's "neutral explanation" (step two), there was purposeful discrimination. The burden is on the party (the defendant ordinarily) objecting to the use of the peremptory challenge. If the prosecutor's "neutral explanation" is considered to be pretextual, there is an "inference of discriminatory content." *Snyder v. Louisiana*, 128 S. Ct. 1203, 1212 (2008).

Miller-El. The U.S. Supreme Court recently addressed the question whether a defendant had carried his "step three" burden of proving a *Batson* purposeful discrimination violation. *Miller-El v. Cockrell*, 537 U.S. 322 (2003). The precise standard applied to Miller-El's case (because it involved a "certificate of appealability" under the Anti-Terrorism and Effective Death Penalty Act of 1996 [see Chapter 18]) was whether he had made "a substantial showing of the denial of a constitutional right."

Justice Kennedy's majority opinion in *Miller-El* recited extensive evidence in support of Court's conclusion that this case should be heard by the Court of Appeals, making clear that his decision was not a ruling on the merit of petitioner's claim.

Among other things, the Court identified several matters that supported its ruling. First, African-Americans were peremptorily excused in a ratio significantly higher than Caucasians were (91% of eligible black jurors were removed by prosecutors). Second, the manner of questioning venire members as to their views concerning the death penalty "varied by race." Third, the prosecution used "jury shuffling" (a Texas procedure that increases the likelihood that preferable jurors will be moved forward and empaneled) in ways that suggested that black jurors would be less likely to be questioned or to serve. Fourth, the Dallas District Attorney's office had adopted policies encouraging the use of peremptory strikes against minorities. And fifth, "three of the State's proffered race-neutral rationales for striking African-America jurors pertained just as well to some white jurors who were not challenged and who did serve on the jury."

Justice Thomas, the lone dissenter, concluded that Miller-El failed to show "that any peremptory strikes of black veniremen were exercised because of race," and therefore he was not entitled to a certificate of appealability.

NOTES

1. *Subsequent history of Miller-El.* Following the grant of a certificate of appealability, the Fifth Circuit rejected Miller-El's *Batson* claim on the merits. In June, 2005, two years after the earlier *Miller-El* decision, the U.S. Supreme Court held that

Miller-El was entitled to prevail on his *Batson* claim. *Miller-El v. Dretke*, 545 U.S. 231 (2005). Reciting essentially the same evidence as it had done in 2003, the Court, in the words of Justice Breyer (concurring) found "extensive evidence of racial bias." Interestingly, Justice Breyer returned to Justice Marshall's opinion in *Batson* and remarked that "I believe it necessary to reconsider *Batson*'s test and the peremptory challenge system as a whole." Justice Thomas, for the three dissenters, argued that "on the basis of facts and law, rather than sentiments, Miller-El does not merit [relief]."

2. *Prosecutor's challenges generally upheld.* As one would expect, trial and appellate courts rarely find that a prosecutor's decision to remove a juror through the exercise of a peremptory challenge was motivated by discriminatory intent. Courts tend to accept prosecutors' "neutral explanations" to justify striking jurors. Some courts even presume that the prosecution used the challenges in a constitutional manner. *See, e.g., People v. Zambrano*, 163 P.3d 4 (Cal. 2007).

One study found that acceptable explanations included the following: age, occupation, employment, religious beliefs, demeanor, relationship to trial participants, intelligence, socioeconomic status, residence, marital status, previous involvement with criminal justice system and prior jury experience. Michael J. Raphael & Edward J. Ungvarsky, *Excuses, Excuses: Neutral Explanations Under Batson v. Kentucky*, 27 U. MICH. J.L. REF. 229 (1993).

Perhaps the best example of the variety of acceptable excuses is presented by two cases. In one, both the trial and appellate courts approved a peremptory exercised because a potential juror avoided eye contact with the prosecution. *United States v. Cartlidge*, 808 F.2d 1064 (5th Cir. 1987). In the other, the trial and appellate courts upheld a peremptory challenge that was based on a potential juror's too frequent eye contact ("he spent a great deal of time examining me in a way which I felt was in the end becoming rather hostile"). *United States v. Mathews*, 803 F.2d 325 (7th Cir. 1986). Other reasonable explanations may include a juror's work with substance abusers, lack of education, or difficulty answering questions. *Rodriguez v. Senkowski*, 2004 U.S. Dist. LEXIS 3975 (S.D.N.Y. 2004)

Reasoned basis. Given the fact that a prosecutor will not readily admit an outright violation of *Batson*, upon what bases may courts conclude that a prosecutor acted with a discriminatory purpose? First, the explanation offered must present a reasoned basis for the juror's removal. *See, e.g., United States v. Horsley*, 864 F.2d 1543 (11th Cir. 1989) (prosecutor struck only black juror; only explanation was that he "just got a feeling about him"; *Batson* held to be violated); *See also People v. Jackson*, 623 N.Y.S. 2d 881 (App. Div. 1995). (held *Batson* violation where prosecutor's reasons for challenging juror was that he did not "feel comfortable" with her and because juror worked as a counselor who assisted the unemployed in finding jobs she might be unduly sympathetic towards the unemployed defendant. The court determined these arguments to be vague and unrelated to the case since the defendant's employment status would not be introduced into the case and such status did not relate to the specific circumstances of the case.)

Comparison of jurors. Another approach is to compare the excluded juror's characteristics with that of a not-excused juror. For example, if juror #4 (a black female) is excused peremptorily because of her "closeness in age to the robbery victim," yet juror #9 (a white female of the same age) is not excused, a *Batson* violation is likely. Conversely, if all jurors, irrespective of race or gender, were treated the same (perhaps all with a reservation about the death penalty were peremptorily excused), the prosecutor's decisions will be upheld as not based on purposeful race, etc. discrimination.

Such a comparative analysis [of jurors struck and those remaining] "is a well-established tool for exploring the possibility that facially race-neutral reasons are a pretext for discrimination." *Turner v. Marshall*, 121 F.3d 1248, 1251–52 (9th Cir. 1997). In *Turner*, the prosecutor challenged a prospective black male juror because he had "a hesitancy toward looking at gruesome photographs that would be shown." While the prosecutor gave a facially non-discriminatory explanation, she could not explain the acceptance of a white female juror who also expressed a hesitance to view the photographs. Consequently, the Ninth Circuit Court of Appeals found through comparative analysis that racial reasons motivated the prosecutor's dismissal of the black male prospective juror. The court found no basis in the jurors' responses during voir dire upon which to distinguish the challenged and unchallenged juror.

Illustration of comparative analysis. In *Snyder v. Louisiana,* 128 S. Ct. 1203 (2008), the prosecutor used peremptory challenges to remove all five black jurors. Noting that *Batson* would be violated if even one juror were struck for racial reasons, the Supreme Court reversed a murder conviction because one black juror was removed, according to the prosecutor, because he seemed "nervous" and was a student teacher concerned about missing some mandatory training. The Supreme Court discounted the "nervous" explanation for lack of a lower court finding, then reversed because of the student-teaching explanation. Noting that the record simply did not support the conclusion that the standard teaching duties were of significant concern to the juror, the Supreme Court held sufficient evidence of discriminatory intent, based on the prosecutor's implausible explanations, to merit overturning the conviction.

[vii] Procedural Issues in Implementing *Batson*

Timing of Batson objection. Another issue is when a *Batson*-based issue must be raised. Some jurisdictions require counsel to make *Batson* objections after the jury is selected and before the jurors are sworn in order to allow the trial judge to cure the problem and ensure that the jury is properly selected. The United States Supreme Court has characterized this as a "sensible rule." *Ford v. Georgia,* 498 U.S. 411 (1991).

Record of violation. In order to launch a successful *Batson* challenge, there must be a record sufficient to establish a prima facie case. Counsel should ensure that the record accurately reflects the races of both the jurors who were seated and excluded as well as documenting other characteristics given as grounds for exclusion, questions that were asked of the jurors on voir dire, information about the jurors available to the party who excluded them, and any other information about the reasons for the use of peremptory challenges.

Deprivation of peremptory challenge. What if the court erroneously denies a challenge for cause for Juror X and therefore forces the defendant to exercise a peremptory challenge to exclude that juror? If the defendant uses all available peremptory challenges, the court's erroneous decision on Juror X essentially deprives the defendant of the opportunity to use a peremptory challenge against Juror Y. Although this judicial error may force the defendant to be tried by a juror who would otherwise have been excluded, the Supreme Court has held that the error is not of constitutional dimension. In *Ross v. Oklahoma,* 481 U.S. 81 (1988), the Court held that the focus must be on whether the twelve jurors who heard the case were impartial. The key is whether the fair cross-section rule was satisfied. The peremptory challenge is a means to achieve an impartial jury.

The use of a peremptory challenge to remove an objectionable juror does not create a constitutional violation because of an inability to use that same peremptory to remove another juror. *See also United States v. Martinez-Salazar,* 528 U. S. 304 (2000) (same as *Ross* under Federal Rule 24(b)). *Martinez-Salazar* held that reversal may be appropriate if the trial court deliberately misapplied the law to force the defendants to use a peremptory challenge or if the final jury included a juror who should have been excluded for cause.

Need to use all peremptory challenges. In some jurisdictions, an accused, arguing that the conviction was rendered by a jury that was not impartial, may appeal the presence of an objectionable juror only if the accused had used all available peremptory challenges and was therefore unable to exclude the objectionable juror. This process is viewed as fair because it requires the accused to take positive steps to ensure the jury was impartial. The Supreme Court has approved state law following this process, *Ross v. Oklahoma*, 487 U.S. 81, 90 (1988), but has refused to require it as a prerequisite to a claim that the accused was denied a fair trial because forced to use a peremptory challenge to remove a juror who should have been removed for cause. *United States v. Martinez-Salazar*, 528 U. S. 304 (2000).

[viii]   Reaction to *Batson*

Critical scholarship. Batson has generated a substantial amount of critical scholarship. *See, e.g.*, Eric L. Muller, *Solving the Batson Paradox: Harmless Error, Jury Representation, and the Sixth Amendment*, 106 YALE L. J. 93 (1996) (asserting that the discriminatory use of peremptory challenges should trigger a rule of automatic reversal, not because of an equal protection violation; rather, because it violates the Sixth Amendment's guarantee of a jury that represents the community); S. Alexandria Jo, *Reconstruction of the Peremptory Challenge System: A Look at Gender-Based Peremptory Challenges*, 22 PAC. L. J. 1305 (1991); Brian Serr & Mark Maney, *Racism, Peremptory Challenges, and the Democratic Jury: The Jurisprudence of a Delicate Balance*, 79 J. CRIM. L. & CRIMINOLOGY 1 (1988); William T. Pizzi, *Batson v. Kentucky: Curing the Disease But Killing the Patient*, 1987 Sup. Ct. Rev. 97 (1987).

Professor Charles Ogletree has proposed that the government's peremptory challenges in criminal cases, as well as the peremptory challenge available to both sides in civil litigation, be abolished and replaced with an expanded for-cause system. Charles J. Ogletree, *Just Say No!: A Proposal to Eliminate Racially Discriminatory Uses of Peremptory Challenges*, 31 AM. CRIM. L. REV. 1099 (1994). He argues as follows:

> Legislatures or courts should institute punitive sanctions against misuse of peremptories; mandate attorney-conducted voir dire; expand the for-cause challenge; and, where possible, abolish or drastically reduce peremptories for all but criminal defendants. Though the risk to criminal defendants posed by abolishing peremptories would be too great to eliminate them altogether, the value of the challenge to other kinds of litigants does not outweigh the problems created by its use as a veil for racism. [Id. at 1151.]

See also Minetos v. City University of New York, 925 F. Supp. 177 (S.D. N.Y. 1996) (holding that peremptory challenges are a "cloak for discrimination" and should now be banned as an unnecessary waste of time and an obvious corruption of the judicial process).

PROBLEM 15-1: THE LAWYER'S CRAFT OR THE CRAFTY LAWYER

In the last fourteen years, Assistant District Attorney Vickie Miles has conducted approximately one hundred jury trials. She was assigned the prosecution of Frank Benton, a 39 year old white, unemployed construction worker, charged with robbing a K Mart of $2700. The robber wore a paper bag on his head with large eye holes cut out. Defendant Benton claims that he was not the robber. He maintains that the afternoon of the crime he was asleep at his girlfriend's apartment. The girlfriend will probably corroborate the alibi. The K Mart clerk, the victim of the robbery, has identified Benton, who briefly removed the bag from his head when he jumped into his car and drove away. Benton was found with $1700 cash in his pocket. Benton and the clerk are white.

During jury selection, prosecutor Miles used only six of her eight peremptory challenges. Five of the six excused black jurors. The sixth excused a white lawyer. The jury that was selected included ten white jurors and two black jurors. The county was 38% black. The venire was 35% black.

Defense counsel cited *Batson* in challenging the prosecutor's use of the peremptory challenges.

1. Based solely on the above information, has the defense established a prima facie case under *Batson*? If not, what additional information would make this a prima facie case?

Would your answers change if the defendant Benton was black instead of white? If the K Mart witness was black? Why should the race of the defendant or the witnesses matter under *Batson*? Is the race of the *prosecutor* relevant?

2. Assuming that a prima facie case were established, assess the acceptability of the following explanations given by Assistant District Attorney Miles for dismissing the five black jurors:

    a. "Juror A was a 32-year-old construction worker. I felt that he would identify too closely with the defendant because of the similarities in their age and occupation."

    b. "Juror B had this Afro hairstyle. My experience is that I have a hard time convincing this type of person, irrespective of the race of the people in the case."

    c. "Juror C dropped out of school in the fourth grade, was working as a dishwasher, and I felt that he could not understand the issues in the case."

    d. "Juror D, a 50-year-old mechanical engineer, had a traffic ticket last year. Although he stated that it would not affect his view of law enforcement, I felt that he would be hostile to our police witnesses who worked for the same police department that gave Juror D a ticket last year. My experience is that engineers don't like it when a cop pulls them over, blue lights flashing, and gives them a hard time about speeding."

    e. "I have been trying cases for a long time. I have interviewed literally thousands of jurors, have spent thousands of hours discussing jury selection with other prosecutors, have attended many seminars on the issue, and have watched many juries perform. In my professional opinion, based on my intuition that has proven to be right on many occasions, I felt that Juror E would be prone to accept this phony alibi defense. He just seemed to me to be a bit gullible. I don't know what it was. There was something about the way he answered the question and looked around the room."

Would your answer change if the prosecutor said that she excluded Juror E because the research she read showed that black jurors are more likely to favor the defense (irrespective of the defendant's race) and disbelieve white police officers (the officers in this case are all white) than are white jurors? Assume *arguendo* that the prosecutor has correctly summarized the available research.

[h] Ethical Issues

The opportunity to learn the names and addresses of jurors, combined with the perceived need to investigate jurors for possible bias, creates the possibility that the defense lawyer (or defendant) or prosecutor could attempt to influence the juror's performance or unwittingly harass the juror or the juror's family. For example, someone could attempt to sway a potential juror's view of the case so that, if selected, the person would favor one side. A number of ethical rules specifically prohibit lawyers from engaging in such conduct.

The American Bar Association's various professional guidelines specifically limit lawyers in their dealings with both potential and actual jurors. Contact with potential jurors is severely restricted. The Standards of Criminal Justice state that when pretrial investigation of possible jurors is conducted, defense counsel should ensure that the jurors are not harassed or unduly embarrassed, and their privacy is respected. Whenever possible, the investigation should be restricted to existing records and sources of information. Standards of Criminal Justice § 4-7.2 (3d ed. 1993). The Model

Code of Professional Responsibility, DR 7-108(A) (1980), also addresses the issue of contact with *potential* jurors.

> Before the trial of a case a lawyer connected therewith shall not communicate with or cause another to communicate with anyone he knows to be a member of the venire from which the jury will be selected for the trial of the case.

A similar rule bars contact with jurors *during trial*.

During the trial of a case:

> (1) A lawyer connected therewith shall not communicate with or cause another to communicate with any member of the jury.

> (2) A lawyer who is not connected therewith shall not communicate with or cause another to communicate with a juror concerning the case.

Id. DR 7-108(B). *See also* STANDARDS FOR CRIMINAL JUSTICE § 4-7.3 (3d ed. 1993) (defense counsel should not intentionally communicate privately with potential or impaneled jurors; the reality or appearance of such communications should be avoided). *Id.* § 3-5.4 (same for prosecutor); American Bar Association, PRINCIPLES FOR JURIES AND JURY TRIALS, Prin. 13(E)(2005)(during trial, jurors should be instructed that parties are permitted to communicate with jurors only in open court with opposing parties present).

The Model Code of Professional Responsibility also prohibits conduct that directly or indirectly causes a vexatious or harassing investigation of a venireperson, juror, or a member of either's family. Model Code of Professional Responsibility DR 7-108(E). A lawyer must also report to the court any improper conduct towards or by a juror or venireperson. *Id.* DR 7-108(G).

The Model Rules of Professional Conduct are far less specific than either the Model Code or the Standards for Criminal Justice. The Model Rules simply provide that a lawyer shall not influence or communicate with a prospective or sitting juror by illegal means. Model Rules of Professional Conduct Rule 3.5 (1983).

[7] Jurors' Oath

Once a jury panel and alternates are selected, the entire group takes an oath. The purpose of the oath is to increase the likelihood that jurors will be unbiased and truthful. Jurisdictions vary in the exact language of the juror's oath. Some invoke God's name, others give the juror the alternative of affirming or swearing in God's name, while others require the juror to swear or affirm but do not mention the deity. Arizona's is typical:

> Do you swear (or affirm) that you will give careful attention to the proceedings, abide by the court's instructions, and render a verdict in accordance with the law and evidence presented to you (so help you God)?

Ariz. R. Crim. P. 18.6. *See generally* Note, Jonathan Belcher, *Religion-Plus-Speech: The Constitutionality of Juror Oaths and Affirmations Under the First Amendment*, 34 WM. & MARY L. REV. 287 (1992).

[8] Removal of Juror

Sometimes unexpected developments occur after the jury is sworn, and a juror must be removed and perhaps replaced by an alternate juror. Rules of criminal procedure often provide for this possibility, but they rarely describe the grounds for removal of a juror. Instead, they focus on procedural matters such as the minimum number of jurors that can hear the case or the process of replacing original jurors with alternate jurors.

FEDERAL RULES OF CRIMINAL PROCEDURE

Rule 23. *Jury or Nonjury Trial*

. . . .

(b) Jury Size.

(1) **In General.** A jury consists of 12 persons unless this rule provides otherwise.

(2) **Stipulation for a Smaller Jury.** At any time before the verdict, the parties may, with the court's approval, stipulate in writing that:

(A) the jury may consist of fewer than 12 persons; or

(B) a jury of fewer than 12 persons may return a verdict if the court finds it necessary to excuse a juror for good cause after the trial begins.

(3) **Court Order for a Jury of 11.** After the jury has retired to deliberate, the court may permit a jury of 11 persons to return a verdict, even without a stipulation by the parties, if the court finds good cause to excuse a juror.

Rule 24. *Trial Jurors.*

. . . .

(c) Alternate Jurors.

(1) **In General.** The court may impanel up to 6 alternate jurors to replace any jurors who are unable to perform or who are disqualified from performing their duties.

(2) **Procedure.**

(A) Alternate jurors must have the same qualifications and be selected and sworn in the same manner as any other juror.

(B) Alternate jurors replace jurors in the same sequence in which the alternates were selected. An alternate juror who replaces a juror has the same authority as the other jurors.

(3) **Retaining Alternate Jurors.** The court may retain alternate jurors after the jury retires to deliberate. The court must ensure that a retained alternate does not discuss the case with anyone until that alternate replaces a juror or is discharged. If an alternate replaces a juror after deliberations have begun, the court must instruct the jury to begin its deliberations anew.

[a]   Grounds for Removal

Although there are no limits on the grounds for removal of a sworn juror, in general terms jurors are removed because they may not be impartial or they cannot physically or mentally complete the work on the case. Trial courts are given great discretion in these decisions.

A common example of removal because of impartiality concerns is when a juror is exposed to prejudicial publicity about aspects of the case not introduced as evidence. *See, e.g., United States v. Williams*, 568 F.2d 464 (5th Cir. 1978) (jurors saw news program). Other illustrations where jurors have been removed because of partiality include: the only Hispanic juror expressed concerns that he would be blamed for a verdict against an Hispanic defendant; a juror disclosed that his parents-in-law had worked for the defendant's election; shortly before retiring for deliberations a juror put a hand on defendant's shoulder and smiled; in the middle of a trial, a juror indicated she had a strong prejudice against wiretapping and could not render a fair verdict if wiretapping evidence was used; and a juror's daughter received a threatening telephone call.

Sometimes statutes provide grounds for removing a juror. *E.g.*, Ind. Code Ann. § 35-37-2-3 (juror shall be removed if juror has personal knowledge of fact material to the case).

Jurors are also removed if they cannot perform their duties. The broad category encompasses difficulties caused by physical and mental problems as well as schedule conflicts. Illustrative federal cases have approved the removal of jurors on grounds of the illness of a juror or a close relative; the juror's need to attend a close relative's funeral in a distant city; a job-related emergency; absence because of a religious holiday; an inability to remain awake during the testimony; an inability to concentrate because of concerns about missing a scheduled airplane flight; tardy arrival in court after testimony had commenced; arriving for jury service in a state of intoxication; and an inability to hear testimony or to read and write.

Another ground for removal is the discovery that the juror gave false answers during voir dire. *See, e.g., State v. Tatum*, 506 So. 2d 584 (La. Ct. App. 1987) (juror's failure to disclose mental illness; can dismiss juror during trial). *Cf. McDonough Power Equipment, Inc. v. Greenwood*, 464 U.S. 548 (1984) (to obtain new trial on basis of juror's false answers during voir dire, party must demonstrate that a correct response would have provided a challenge for cause).

[b]   Procedural Issues

In the ordinary case a judge will conduct a hearing, outside the presence of the jury, before removing a juror and seating an alternate juror. Lawyers for both sides usually are permitted to speak. In some cases, witnesses or affidavits will be considered. For example, if a juror's partiality is at issue, the juror may appear as a witness at the removal hearing.

At this hearing the key concern is whether the juror can render an impartial decision. The trial court will inquire whether *this* juror's fairness has been compromised. *See Smith v. Phillips*, 455 U.S. 209, 217 (1982) (during trial, juror applied for job as investigator with prosecutor's office; trial court should not have dismissed without inquiring into this juror's actual bias).

If a juror is removed, the issue is whether the juror will be replaced by an alternate, assuming an alternate juror is available. If the removal occurs before deliberations, an alternate juror is virtually always used. Once deliberations have begun, courts are hesitant to substitute with an alternate juror, who will have missed the early deliberations and may have been dismissed when the jury retired. In some jurisdictions, the usual remedy is for the deliberations to continue with one less juror.

Under Rule 23(b) of the Federal Rules of Criminal Procedure, the court can permit an eleven-person jury to decide the case if a juror is removed after deliberations have begun. In other jurisdictions, a jury of twelve (or some other number) is required unless the defendant consents (or both parties consent) to a trial by a smaller jury. Absent such consent, if a juror is removed during the deliberations, the trial judge must order a mistrial.

[9]   Pre-Deliberation Processes

The rules of criminal procedure deal with only a small number of the details of the jury process. In the absence of concrete guidance in court rules or statutes, trial courts are given great discretion in structuring the jury's activities. This section deals with three issues: notetaking by jurors during the trial, questions by jurors during trial, and sequestration of jurors.

[a]   Notetaking by Jurors

While it is likely that a juror's memory may be incapable of recalling accurately the testimony of witnesses at trial, relatively few jurors ask whether they may take notes during the proceedings, and courts are divided on whether notetaking by jurors is permissible. Accordingly, jurors do not take notes during trial in most jurisdictions. This is in sharp contrast to a law student who would justifiably feel outraged if not permitted to take notes during law school classes, or a judge or lawyer who would insist on being permitted to take notes during trial.

Notetaking by jurors can be justified on numerous grounds:

(1) Since memory is fallible, notes would be a valuable aid in remembering evidence.

(2) Jurors would record only names of witnesses and summaries of testimony, so there is little danger of erroneous notes.

(3) A conflict in the notes of jurors could easily be resolved by a request for reading of the record.

(4) Since the law-trained judge routinely takes notes during a trial, jurors should also be permitted to take them.

(5) The danger of undue influence on the part of a superior note taker is alleviated by the fact that other jurors are also literate and will take their own notes.

(6) The process of notetaking forces the juror to pay close attention to the testimony.

(7) Time may be saved as jurors have less need to request that the trial transcript of certain witnesses be read out loud to the jury during deliberations.

See W. Steckler, *Management of the Jury*, 28 F.R.D. 190, 195 n.19 (1960)(discussing the first 5 of these reasons).

An empirical study supports some of these arguments. Comparing a criminal jury that was permitted to take notes with one that was not, a researcher found that notetaking did not increase deliberation time, but jurors allowed to take notes rated the quality of their deliberations higher than those who could not take notes. The notetaking jurors also indicated that their cases were less difficult to decide, they placed less reliance on other jurors, half took more notes at the beginning of trial than at the end, and most reported that they participated more actively in deliberations because of the availability of their notes. Victor E. Flango,*Would Jurors Do a Better Job if They Could Take Notes?* 63 Judicature 436 (1980). *See also* Steven Penrod & Larry Hever, *Tweaking Commonsense: Assessing Aids to Jury Decision Making*, 3 Psychol. Pub. Pol'y & Law 259, 271 (1997) (reviewing literature pertaining to notetaking studies and concluding there are some advantages and no disadvantages).

Because of these advantages, jurors' notetaking has been endorsed by a number of scholars and reports. *See, e.g,* Report of the Judicial Conference Committee on the Operation of the Jury System, The Jury System in the Federal Courts, 26 F.R.D. 411, 424 (1960) (trial judges should have discretion to permit jurors to take notes during trial and use them during deliberations; notes confidential); Michael A. McLaughlin, Note, *Questions to Witnesses and Notetaking by the Jury as Aids in Understanding Complex Litigation*, 18 New Eng. L. Rev. 687 (1983). The American Bar Association recommends that jurors be permitted to take notes during trial and be allowed to use them during trial and deliberations. The notes should then be collected by the court daily and destroyed after the trial. American Bar Association, Principles for Juries and Jury Trials, Prin. 13(A)(2005).

There are some disadvantages to notetaking by jurors:

(1) Notetaking could divert the attention of the jurors from the testimony so that they do not hear critical testimony or do not focus enough on the witness's demeanor.

(2) The notes may emphasize one feature of the case over other equally or more important ones.

(3) The notes of some jurors may be inaccurate. This would provide erroneous information to all the jurors. In addition, the author of the notes may, through stubbornness, insist on the accuracy of the notes despite the strong contrary memory or notes of other jurors.

(4) There may be a conflict in the notes of various jurors.

(5) Counsel, in picking a jury, would become concerned with a potential juror's notetaking ability.

(6) The best notetaker could become the most influential juror.

(7) A juror might purposely falsify notes.

(8) Notes may contain information about evidence that has been ruled inadmissible.

(9) After the verdict, a juror's notes may be read by counsel or the news media and destroy jury secrecy and public confidence in the process.

(10) When a juror's notes conflict with another juror's memory of testimony, the written version may carry more weight with the other jurors.

(11) If, as is likely, a juror takes more and better notes early in the trial and tapers off as the trial progresses, the party who presents testimony early in the trial may have an advantage since there will be a better record of that party's evidence.

(12) Notetaking is unnecessary because of the availability of the trial record.

See W. Steckler, *Management of the Jury*, 28 F.R.D. 190, 195-96 n.20 (1960) (listing the first 7 of these reasons).

Although notetaking by jurors is rare, in most jurisdictions courts have the discretion to permit it in both simple and complex cases. *See, e.g., United States v. Rhodes*, 631 F.2d 43 (5th Cir. 1980). Of course, jurors are free to refuse to take notes during the trial. *See United States v. Standard Oil Co.*, 316 F.2d 884, 896 (7th Cir. 1963) (courts may permit, but should not require, notetaking by jurors). A conviction will only be reversed if somehow notetaking was an abuse of discretion. Often the courts ask whether the accused was prejudiced by the notetaking, a standard that is virtually impossible to establish.

In some jurisdictions, notetaking by jurors is specifically authorized by state law. *E.g.*, Ariz. R. Crim. P. 18.6 (court must instruct jurors that they may take notes; court provides notetaking materials; bailiff destroys notes after verdict); Iowa Code § 813.2, Rule 18(e) (jurors may take notes during testimony; jurors must destroy notes at end of deliberations). Other jurisdictions bar notetaking. *E.g.*, Pa. R. Crim. P. 1113 (jurors not permitted to take notes during course of trial).

Notetaking may occur in several ways. A juror may simply start taking notes during a witness's testimony. In some jurisdictions, notetaking is suggested by one or both lawyers or the judge. Sometimes the court will even furnish paper and pens, as noted above (Arizona).

Some decisions hold that a judge may or should instruct the jury on the proper use of notes. The Fifth Circuit suggested the following instruction:

> The court will permit jurors to take notes during the course of the trial. You of course are not obliged to take any notes, and some feel that the taking of notes is not helpful because it may distract you so that you do not hear and evaluate all of the evidence. If you do take notes, do not allow notetaking to distract you from the ongoing proceedings.

> Your notes should be used only as memory aids. You should not give your notes precedence over your independent recollection of the evidence. If you do not take notes, you should rely on your own independent recollection of the proceedings and you should not be influenced by the notes of other jurors. I emphasize that notes are not entitled to any greater weight than the recollection or impression of each juror as to what the testimony may have been. [*United States v. Rhodes*, 631 F.2d 43, 46 n.3 (5th Cir. 1980)]

If jurors are to be permitted to take notes during the deliberations, it has been suggested that counsel should be permitted during voir dire to ask about a potential juror's written skills. *United States v. Standard Oil Co.*, 316 F.2d 884 (7th Cir. 1963).

[b]   Juror Notebooks

Another "jury reform" is to authorize courts to provide jurors with notebooks to use in organizing their materials, such as their own notes, exhibits, and written jury instructions. Although courts have long had the discretion to permit this practice, only recently has it been included in recommendations for improving jury performance. American Bar Association, PRINCIPLES FOR JURIES AND JURY TRIALS, Prin. 13 (2005).

[c]   Juror's Interrogation of Witnesses, Lawyers, or Judge

The usual role of a juror during the trial is as a passive observer. He or she watches and listens and is often cautioned against discussing the case with anyone, including other jurors, until the jury is sent to deliberate. But what if the juror has a question to ask of a witness, the judge, or a lawyer? Taking the easiest possibility, what if a juror does not hear an important statement by a soft-spoken witness? Can the juror interrupt the witness and ask the witness to repeat the testimony? Or what if the witness was vague or ambivalent in responding to a question by counsel? Can the juror ask a pointed question? What if no one asks about an issue the juror thinks is important? Can the juror ask a witness, lawyer, or judge about the matter? Similarly, what if a juror simply does not understand a jury instruction? Can the juror ask the judge for clarification?

Because of the obvious advantages in permitting jurors to avoid misunderstandings or partial understandings, virtually all jurisdictions hold that the judge has the discretion to permit questions by jurors. *See generally* Jeffrey Reynolds Sylvester, Note, *Your Honor, May I Ask A Question? The Inherent Dangers of Allowing Jurors to Question Witnesses*, 7 COOLEY L. REV. 213 (1990); Michael J. Wulser, Note, *Should Jurors Be Allowed to Ask Witnesses Questions in Criminal Trials?*, 58 U. MO. K. C. L. REV. 445 (1990); *United States v. Rawlings*, 522 F.3d 403 (D.C. Cir. 2008)(noting advantages and disadvantages of juror questions; suggesting procedures for courts to use if they allow juror questions; and noting that all federal circuits that had decided the issue recognize that trial judges have the discretion to permit such questions).

There are a number of advantages in permitting jurors to ask questions:

(1) It increases the likelihood that the jurors will have the information they need to reach a fair decision.

(2) It keeps jurors actively involved in the proof process and may increase their attention to testimony.

(3) It may prevent unintentional omissions as jurors ask questions that lawyers forgot to ask.

(4) It alerts lawyers to the issues that jurors think are important and that may need further proof or clarification.

Of course, there are risks as well:

(1) A juror could ask questions about matters that should not be considered, such as why the defendant did not testify.

(2) A juror could interfere with the logical flow of proof by inquiring about matters to be dealt with later or not at all.

(3) A juror could waste time by focusing on unimportant or irrelevant issues.

(4) A lawyer may make a juror angry by objecting to the juror's question or answering it in a way deemed unacceptable by the juror. This possibility puts the lawyer in an especially awkward position, for the lawyer may waive

appellate review of the alleged error by failing to make a timely objection. Some jurisdictions alleviate this concern by not requiring a timely objection to a juror's question.

(5) A juror who engages in active interrogation of witnesses and others during the trial may find it difficult to remain neutral and may become an advocate for a side. This distorts the juror's role as a neutral decisionmaker.

(6) A juror's questions may indicate the juror favors a particular side. When this is perceived by the other jurors, it may informally start the process of deliberation before that process should begin.

These potential difficulties have led a minority of jurisdictions to ban juror questions. *See, e.g., Morrison v. State*, 845 S.W.2d 882 (Tex. Ct. App. 1992). *See generally* Kara Lundy, Note, *Juror Questions of Witnesses: Questioning the United States Criminal Justice System*, 85 MINN. L. REV. 2007 (2001)(arguing that juror questioning of witnesses should not be permitted because it destroys the jurors' impartiality).

An empirical study of actual trials where jurors were or were not permitted to ask questions substantiated a number of the possible advantages of juror questions. It found that in trials where jurors could ask questions of witnesses, the jurors were more satisfied that they had ample evidence to reach a responsible verdict. The jurors also reported that questions were moderately helpful in clarifying the evidence and the law and in helping the jurors to get to the truth. Trial lawyers felt that the jurors' questions were of little consequence, although they did provide useful feedback on the trial. The lawyers did not report that jurors' questions substantially slowed down the trial or upset trial strategy. Interestingly, the study also found that there were fewer than three questions asked by all jurors combined in an average trial. Lawyers objected to only 17% of the jurors' questions, and jurors reported that the objections did not anger them. Larry Heuer & Steven Penrod, *Increasing Jurors' Participation in Trials*, 12 LAW AND HUM. BEHAV. 231 (1988).

To the extent that the disadvantages of allowing jurors to ask questions are valid, measures should be taken to alleviate these concerns. One commentator makes several recommendations. Jurors' questions about evidence should be framed in a neutral way and limited to clarifications of the evidence that was presented. At the beginning of trial, the court should establish specific time and manner requirements for jurors' questions. Jurors' questions may be communicated in writing or orally, but written questions are preferred. Written questions should be addressed to the judge, who will propound them to the witness if appropriate. A juror's questions to a witness should be asked after the witness has testified but before the witness has left the stand. The judge should conduct a jury-out hearing to discuss the propriety of jurors' questions. Michael A. McLaughlin, Note, *Questions to Witnesses and Notetaking by the Jury as Aids in Understanding Complex Litigation*, 18 NEW ENG. L. REV. 687 (1983).

The American Bar Association has taken no stand one way or the other on the issue. ABA's PRINCIPLES FOR JURIES AND JURY TRIAL, Prin. 13(B)(2005) simply says that in deciding whether to permit jurors to ask questions, courts should consider the historic reasons for disapproving the practice as well as the experience of those jurisdictions that have allowed it.

NOTES

1. Do you think that jurors should be permitted to ask questions during the trial? If so, do you agree with the above recommendations for procedures to minimize the risks of this practice?

2. What about a system that permitted jurors to ask questions, but only in written form addressed to the judge, who would (1) disclose it to the parties, (2) confer with the parties or hold a hearing outside the presence of the jury, (3) decide whether the question in its current or a revised form is permissible, (4) personally ask the question or permit a party to do so, and (5) permit parties to ask follow up questions of the witness? Would this cure most of the problems associated with jurors' questions? *See* American Bar Association, Principles for Juries and Jury Trial, Prin. 13(B)(2005)(recommending this procedure if a judge decides to permit juror questions of witnesses).

[d] Sequestration of Jurors

Just as a trial judge ordinarily is given great discretion in deciding whether jurors may take notes or ask questions during a trial, the court is also given significant leeway in deciding whether a jury should be *sequestered* — housed and fed away from home during the trial and deliberations. While both the prosecutor and defense counsel may argue for or against sequestration, in most jurisdictions the decision is that of the judge alone and can be made despite protests from one or both parties. *See, e.g.,* Ind. Code Ann. § 35-37-2-4 (jurors may separate at end of court day unless judge finds sequestration necessary to assure a fair trial).

In some locales, however, judicial decision or court rules mandate sequestration in some circumstances. *See, e.g.,* La. Code Crim. P. Art. 791 (in capital case, jury must be sequestered after being sworn unless both sides waive sequestration; in non-capital case, jury must be sequestered during deliberations unless waived).

The purpose of sequestration is to prevent the jurors' opinions from being contaminated by contact with outside people or information. It is used most frequently in cases engendering significant media coverage. For example, during sequestration a juror's access to newspapers, and radio and television news broadcasts is controlled to prevent the communication of information about the trial or other matters that might affect the jurors' impartiality.

During sequestration, jurors as a group ordinarily eat in restaurants, attend movies and other recreational activities, and sleep in a motel, all at government expense and under government supervision. One or more bailiffs usually stay in the same motel as the jurors and chaperone the jurors throughout the day. Because of the expense and inconvenience involved, sequestration is ordered rarely. In order to alleviate inconvenience and to improve juror morale, some judges allow sequestered jurors to return home for a short period of time, perhaps a day or a weekend, or to visit with family (and sometimes friends) in a specific location. Often the jurors will receive a special jury instruction before their break. This directs them to avoid any outside influences or communications about the case.

If a jury is to be sequestered, the usual practice is for the court to decide this before voir dire and to include the possibility of sequestration in its screening questions. A juror who could not be away from home at night would be eliminated for cause. Ordinarily, a jury is sequestered for the entire trial, including deliberations, although a court may order sequestration for only part of the process, such as during deliberations only.

Since the accused can rarely prove prejudice caused by the judge's exercise of judgment on whether to sequester a jury, there are virtually no appellate reversals on this issue unless sequestration is made mandatory by statute or court rule. If the jury is not sequestered, the court's jury instructions against outside influence are usually viewed as adequate to prevent prejudice. *See, e.g., State v. Cruz,* 181 P.3d 196 (Ariz. 2008)(no reversal for court's refusal to sequester jury in case involving intense media coverage; jurors instructed to avoid exposure to media and no indication jurors did not follow instructions; defendant did not establish prejudice or abuse of discretion in denial of sequestration).

For a critical look at sequestration, *see* James P. Levine, *The Impact of Sequestration on Juries*, 79 JUDICATURE 266, 272 (1996):[*]

> The negative impacts of sequestration normally appear to outweigh its virtues. Its potential for unnerving and even infuriating jurors is apparent, offsetting whatever advantages it may have in shielding jurors from prejudicial publicity and the distractions of personal life. Its effect on the quality of deliberations is also problematic: while it may bond some juries it may fracture others. It may foster a too-cozy relationship between jurors and court officers; and it is surely a deterrent to jury service.
>
> On balance, sequestration seems to undermine the pursuit of justice. Both the personal well-being of jurors and the public interest in quality decision making seem best served by keeping the jury free unless there is substantial reason to do otherwise. Sequestration should be used quite selectively, reserved for cases that promise to receive frenzied, inescapable media saturation.

The American Bar Association recommends that courts have the discretion to order sequestration, but notes that the costs and adverse impact on jurors' lives "weigh against its use in almost all cases." American Bar Association, PRINCIPLES FOR JURIES AND JURY TRIALS, Prin. 15(E)(2005)(Comment). When sequestration is ordered, it should be as juror-friendly as possible, perhaps limited to only particular parts of the trial, such as deliberations. Jurors should be involved in forming the sequestration rules and the jurors' experience should be monitored so that jury concerns are brought to the court's attention. Post-trial counseling may be needed. *Id.*

[10] Jury Instructions

The general rule, subject to some exceptions, is that the judge resolves questions of law and the jury decides questions of fact. Since jurors are not necessarily trained in law, they must be told of their duties and the applicable law. In some jurisdictions, jurors are given a handbook that explains their functions and the administrative details of jury service. In every jurisdiction, judges will inform jurors of their duties several times during a trial. Often the judge instructs the jury at the beginning of trial, perhaps one or more times during the trial, and at the end of closing arguments by counsel.

[a] Content

Jury instructions in criminal cases address two issues: routine administrative matters and the laws the jurors are to apply. The first category tells jurors such information as when the trial will resume, where the jurors are to dine or sleep, and that they are not to discuss the case with anyone until deliberations begin.

The second category — the law jurors are to apply — includes both general and specific legal principles. The general ones, expressed in identical language in many trials, inform the jury of the burden of proof, the presumption of innocence, and the like. Specific jury instructions relate to the crime being tried. For example, if the offense is a homicide where the accused has raised self-defense, the jury instructions may deal with the elements of homicide, various lesser included offenses, and self-defense.

[i] Comment on the Facts

As a neutral "referee" in the criminal justice system, the judge should remain nonpartisan during the trial. But what about jury instructions? Must they be neutral as well? What if the judge believed witness X and had doubts about the credibility of

---

[*] Reprinted with permission. All rights reserved.

witness Y? Should the judge be permitted to include in the jury charge the judge's personal evaluation of the evidence?

Judge may comment on the evidence. In the federal system, the trial judge is permitted to comment on the evidence. In the leading Supreme Court case, the defendant testified and denied involvement with the illegal drug transactions at issue in the case. The jury instructions included the judge's observations:

> You may have noticed, Mr. Foreman and gentlemen, that he [the defendant] wiped his hands during his testimony. It is rather a curious thing, but that is almost always an indication of lying. Why it should be so we don't know, but that is the fact. I think that every single word that man [the defendant] said, except when he agreed with the Government's testimony, was a lie.

Quercia v. United States, 289 U.S. 466, 468 (1933). On appeal, the Supreme Court reversed the conviction because the judge's remarks were not based on the evidence. The Court observed:

> In charging the jury, the trial judge is not limited to instructions of an abstract sort. It is within his province, whenever he thinks it necessary, to assist the jury in arriving at a just conclusion by explaining and commenting upon the evidence, by drawing their attention to the parts of it which he thinks important, and he may express his opinion upon the facts, provided he makes it clear to the jury that all matters of fact are submitted to their determination.
>
> . . . This privilege of the judge to comment on the facts has its inherent limitations. His discretion is not arbitrary and uncontrolled, but judicial . . . . In commenting upon testimony he may not assume the role of a witness. He may analyze and dissect the evidence, but he may not either distort it or add to it . . . . This court has . . . emphasized the duty of the trial judge to use great care that an expression of opinion upon the evidence [should not mislead or be one-sided or contain deductions or theories not warranted by the evidence.] [*Id.* at 469-70]

Judge may not comment on evidence. Many jurisdictions disagree with the federal approach and bar the judge from commenting on the evidence. *See, e.g.*, Ga. Code Ann. § 17-8-57 (error for trial judge to express or intimate opinion as to what has or has not been proved or as to guilt; violation "shall" cause a reversal of conviction and granting of new trial). The American Bar Association recommends that the trial judge should not tell the jury his or her personal opinion as to either the defendant's guilt or a witness's credibility. Standards for Criminal Justice § 15-4.2 (3d ed. 1996). A small number of states permit the court to summarize or comment on the evidence if both the defense attorney and prosecutor so request. *E.g.*, Mo. Rev. Stat. § 546.380.

NOTES

1. *Fair trial.* Which approach do you favor? Can the defendant get a fair trial if the *judge* tells the jury that the defendant (perhaps the main defense witness) is lying?

2. *Jury instructions on judge's comments.* Note that *Quercia* states that the judge must inform the jury that it, not the judge, decides questions of fact. Is this statement adequate to overcome the impact of the judge's comment on the case?

PROBLEM 15-2: THE JUDICIOUS JUDGE JONES

Fred was charged with bank robbery in New York City on December 6th. He testified that he was in Los Angeles the day of the robbery. Defense witnesses were Allison and Abraham who testified that Fred was in Los Angeles with them that day. Barbara and Benjamin, the tellers who were actually robbed, made an in-court identification of Fred as the robber. They had previously described the robber to police and had picked Fred from a lineup at the police station.

In pertinent part, Judge Jones gave the following jury instructions:

. . . You have heard lots of conflicting testimony today and you are to rely on all you know about the witnesses to determine whom to believe. You are to consider the witness's interests in the case as well as everything else you observed and heard in court. You are not bound by any of my comments; you are the sole judges of the credibility of witnesses.

Assess the following additional instructions in a jurisdiction that follows the federal approach and permits the judge to comment on the evidence.

1. "You have probably heard more than one person commit perjury during this trial."

2. "The testimony of eyewitnesses is significant evidence that should be given much weight."

3. "Recall that during the cross-examination of Allison, she admitted that she was just released from a three-year prison term for embezzlement. I think this casts a huge shadow over her credibility."

4. "I think these two bank tellers are very brave to go through the ordeal of the robbery and then to come in here and relive it."

5. "I admire public-spirited citizens like Barbara and Benjamin who are helping us today."

[ii]   Lesser-Included Offenses

The jury instructions in criminal cases will detail the elements of the offense(s) with which the defendant is charged. They may also include those of *lesser-included* crimes. Federal law is typical:

FEDERAL RULES OF CRIMINAL PROCEDURE

Rule 31. *Verdict*

. . . .

(c) Lesser Offense or Attempt. A defendant may be found guilty of any of the following:

(1) an offense necessarily included in the offense charged;

(2) an attempt to commit the offense charged; or

(3) an attempt to commit an offense necessarily included in the offense charged, if the attempt is an offense in its own right.

NOTES

1. *Importance of definition: jury instructions.* The definition of a lesser-included offense is important to both prosecution and defense since it defines the scope of possible criminal liability and indicates what jury instructions should be given. Assume that the defendant is charged with first degree murder. If the jury is only instructed on this crime, it will have only two choices: guilty or innocent of first degree murder. If there is insufficient proof of first degree murder, the defendant must be acquitted. On the other hand, if other crimes (such as second degree murder, voluntary manslaughter, and involuntary manslaughter) are lesser-included offenses of first degree murder, the jury will have a choice of four offenses. Perhaps the jury will acquit the defendant of first degree murder but convict him or her of voluntary manslaughter.

2. *Tactical issues.* The possibility of a lesser-included crime instruction raises a number of tactical considerations. The prosecution may prefer a jury instruction on lesser-included offenses because it may prefer a conviction for some offense rather than an acquittal of all charges. Similarly, the defense may prefer to give the jury an alternative to the serious offense of first degree murder, perhaps hoping that the jury will show mercy when there is sufficient proof of first degree murder to convict. On the other hand, it is also possible that neither side will want the jury instructed on lesser-included crimes. Perhaps the prosecution believes it has a strong case for first degree murder and does not want the defendant to be convicted of a lesser offense. The defense may also prefer to roll the dice in a case in which it believes it has a defense to first degree murder but not to a lesser-included offense.

3. *Trial judge's options.* The general rule is that the court has the inherent authority to charge the jury on lesser-included offenses. *See, e.g., Bostic v. State*, 656 S.E.2d 546 (Ga. App. 2008). In many locales the court *must* do so if the lesser- included crime is established by the evidence. *See, e.g., United States v. Finley*, 477 F.3d 250 (5th Cir. 2007). The so-called "party autonomy" rule gives either the defendant or prosecution the right to have a lesser-included instruction if the evidence supports guilt of the lesser offense. *See, e.g., Wiggins v. State*, 902 A.2d 1110 (Del. 2006).

California law, however, holds that a court is barred from instructing the jury on a lesser-included crime that was not charged in the pleadings unless the prosecution agrees. *See, e.g., People v. Valentine*, 49 Cal. Rptr.3d 948 (Cal. App. 2006). Do you agree with this unusual approach to jury instructions on less-included crimes?

After years of uncertainty about the proper test for determining what is a lesser-included offense, the Supreme Court resolved the matter.

SCHMUCK v. UNITED STATES
489 U.S. 705 (1989)

JUSTICE BLACKMUN delivered the opinion of the Court.

[Defendant, a used car distributor, was charged with twelve counts of mail fraud. He bought used cars, rolled back the odometers, and then sold the cars to dealers for artificially high prices. The dealers, after reselling the cars to consumers, would mail a title registration form to the Wisconsin Department of Transportation. During trial, the defendant, pursuant to Rule 31(c), asked for a jury instruction on the misdemeanor crime of tampering with an odometer. The trial court rejected the request and instructed the jury only on the more serious crime of mail fraud. The defendant was convicted as charged. On appeal, the Court of Appeals reversed, holding that the trial court should have instructed the jury on the lesser-included crime of odometer tampering.]

[The Court first held that the federal mail fraud statute embraced the mailing of the title registration forms. It then turned to the issue of whether tampering with an odometer is a lesser-included offense to mail fraud.]

. . . Federal Rule of Criminal Procedure 31(c) provides in relevant part: "The defendant may be found guilty of an offense necessarily included in the offense charged." As noted above, the Courts of Appeals have adopted different tests to determine when, under this Rule, a defendant is entitled to a lesser included offense instruction. The Seventh Circuit's original panel opinion applied the "inherent relationship" approach formulated in *United States v. Whitaker*, 447 F.2d 314, 319 (1971):

> [D]efendant is entitled to invoke Rule 31(c) when a lesser offense is established by the evidence adduced at trial in proof of the greater offense, with the caveat that there must also be an "inherent" relationship between the greater and lesser offenses, i.e., they must relate to the protection of the same interests, and must be so related that in the general nature of these crimes, though not necessarily invariably, proof of the lesser offense is necessarily presented as part of the showing of the commission of the greater offense.

The *en banc* Seventh Circuit rejected this approach in favor of the "traditional," or "elements" test. Under this test, one offense is not "necessarily included" in another unless the elements of the lesser offense are a subset of the elements of the charged offense. Where the lesser offense requires an element not required for the greater offense, no instruction is to be given under Rule 31(c).

We now adopt the elements approach to Rule 31(c). As the Court of Appeals noted, this approach is grounded in the language and history of the Rule and provides for greater certainty in its application. It, moreover, is consistent with past decisions of this Court which, though not specifically endorsing a particular test, employed the elements approach in cases involving lesser included offense instructions.[8]

First, the wording of Rule 31(c), although not conclusive, supports the application of the elements approach. The Rule speaks in terms of an offense that is "necessarily included in the offense charged." This language suggests that the comparison to be drawn is between offenses. Since offenses are statutorily defined, that comparison is appropriately conducted by reference to the statutory elements of the offenses in question, and not, as the inherent relationship approach would mandate, by reference to conduct proved at trial regardless of the statutory definitions. Furthermore, the language of Rule 31(c) speaks of the necessary inclusion of the lesser offense in the greater. While the elements test is true to this requirement, the inherent relationship approach dispenses with the required relationship of necessary inclusion: the inherent relationship approach permits a lesser included offense instruction even if the proof of one offense does not invariably require proof of the other as long as the two offenses serve the same legislative goals.

In addition, the inherent relationship approach, in practice, would require that Rule 31(c) be applied in a manner inconsistent with its language. The Rule provides that a defendant "may be found guilty" of a lesser included offense, without distinguishing between a request for jury instructions made by the Government and one made by the defendant. In other words, the language of the Rule suggests that a lesser included offense instruction is available in equal measure to the defense and to the prosecution. Yet, under the inherent relationship approach, such mutuality is impossible.

It is ancient doctrine of both the common law and of our Constitution that a defendant cannot be held to answer a charge not contained in the indictment brought against him. This stricture is based at least in part on the right of the defendant to notice of the charge brought against him. Were the prosecutor able to request an instruction on an offense whose elements were not charged in the indictment, this right to notice would be placed in jeopardy. Specifically, if, as mandated under the inherent relationship approach, the determination whether the offenses are sufficiently related to permit an instruction is delayed until all the evidence is developed at trial, the defendant may not have constitutionally sufficient notice to support a lesser included offense instruction requested by the prosecutor if the elements of that lesser offense are not part of the indictment. Accordingly, under the inherent relationship approach, the defendant, by in effect waiving his right to notice, may obtain a lesser offense instruction in circumstances where the constitutional restraint of notice to the defendant would prevent the prosecutor from seeking an identical instruction. The elements test, in contrast, permits lesser offense instructions only in those cases where the indictment contains the elements of both offenses and thereby gives notice to the defendant that he may be convicted on either charge. This approach preserves the mutuality implicit in the language of Rule 31(c).

Second, the history of Rule 31(c) supports the adoption of the elements approach.

. . . Third, the elements test is far more certain and predictable in its application than the inherent relationship approach. Because the elements approach involves a textual comparison of criminal statutes and does not depend on inferences that may be drawn from evidence introduced at trial, the elements approach permits both sides to know in advance what jury instructions will be available and to plan their trial strategies

---

[8] Our decision in no way alters the independent prerequisite for a lesser included offense instruction that the evidence at trial must be such that a jury could rationally find the defendant guilty of the lesser offense, yet acquit him of the greater. *Keeble v. United States*, 412 U.S. 205, 208 (1973).

accordingly. The objective elements approach, moreover, promotes judicial economy by providing a clearer rule of decision and by permitting appellate courts to decide whether jury instructions were wrongly refused without reviewing the entire evidentiary record for nuances of inference.

The inherent relationship approach, in contrast, is rife with the potential for confusion. Finding an inherent relationship between offenses requires a determination that the offenses protect the same interests and that "in general" proof of the lesser "necessarily" involves proof of the greater . . . In the context of rules of criminal procedure, where certainty and predictability are desired, we prefer the clearer standard for applying Rule 31(c).

Turning to the facts of this case, we agree with the Court of Appeals that the elements of the offense of odometer tampering are not a subset of the elements of the crime of mail fraud. There are two elements in mail fraud: (1) having devised or intending to devise a scheme to defraud (or to perform specified fraudulent acts), and (2) use of the mail for the purpose of executing, or attempting to execute, the scheme (or specified fraudulent acts). The offense of odometer tampering includes the element of knowingly and willfully causing an odometer to be altered. This element is not a subset of any element of mail fraud. Knowingly and willfully tampering with an odometer is not identical to devising or intending to devise a fraudulent scheme.

We conclude that . . . [Schmuck] was not entitled to a lesser included offense instruction on odometer tampering. [Affirmed.]

[The dissent of JUSTICE SCALIA, joined by JUSTICES BRENNAN, MARSHALL, and O'CONNOR is omitted.]

NOTES

1. *Mechanical act or policy analysis?* Is it accurate to say that *Schmuck* has made the determination of whether Crime A is lesser-included in Crime B a mechanical act, devoid of policy analysis?

2. *Permutations. Schmuck* says that the lesser offense may not require an element not required for the greater offense. What if the greater offense requires an element not required of the lesser offense? Can the less serious offense be a lesser-included offense under *Schmuck*?

3. *Footnote 8. Schmuck* follows the traditional "element" approach to assessing what is a lesser-included offense. An offense is lesser included if the

> elements of the lesser offense are a subset of the elements of the charged offense. Where the lesser offense requires an element not required for the greater offense, no instruction is to be given under Rule 31(c). [489 U.S. at 716]

While this language is helpful on the definition of a lesser-included offense, it should not be read as indicating that a lesser-included offense jury instruction should be given every time there is a lesser-included offense in the jurisdiction's criminal law. Footnote 8 of *Schmuck* provides guidance on this issue. Is the paragraph quoted above consistent with Footnote 8? If the elements of Crime A are a subset of those for the more serious Crime B, could a jury ever find the accused guilty of Crime A but not Crime B?

Does Footnote 8 add anything to *Schmuck*? Can you imagine a situation where Crime 2 would be a lesser-included offense to Crime 1, but the accused would not be entitled to a lesser-included offense jury instruction?

4. *Identical crimes.* Sometimes a legislature will enact virtually identical crimes with different punishments. What if the prosecutor chooses to prosecute the defendant under the more serious one? If the two offenses require identical proof, can the defendant successfully request a lesser-included crime instruction for the less serious one under Rule 31(c)? *See Berra v. United States*, 351 U.S. 131 (1956). This issue is discussed in

Chapter 2 in connection with *United States v. Batchelder*, 442 U.S. 114 (1979), where the Court upheld a prosecutor's discretion to charge a defendant under either of two overlapping criminal statutes.

5. *All or nothing.* What should be the result if the defense counsel objects to the giving of an instruction for a lesser-included offense and elects an "all-or-nothing" strategy? In the much publicized case of *au pair* worker Louise Woodward, the defense requested that no instruction be given the jury to the lesser-included offense of manslaughter. The request was granted, and the jury was instructed only on (1) first and (2) second-degree murder over the state's objection. She was convicted of second degree murder, but the trial court thereafter reduced the verdict to manslaughter. The Massachusetts Supreme Judicial Court held that the trial court committed error by refusing the prosecution's request to instruct the jury on manslaughter. The appellate court noted that it is well established that, when supported by evidence, a trial judge must grant a request to instruct the jury on all offenses that may be lesser-included offenses of a charged crime. The court added that "this rule has never been limited to requests by the defendant." *Commonwealth v. Woodward*, 694 N.E.2d 1277 (Mass. 1998).

6. *State variations.* Some states deviate from the *Schmuck* elements test. For example, in *State v. Yates*, 571 A.2d 575 (R.I. 1990), the Rhode Island Supreme Court rejected *Schmuck* and ruled that the "inherent relationship" test was to be utilized in determining what was a lesser-included offense.

7. *State law impacting giving of less-included instructions.* In *Beck v. Alabama*, 447 U.S. 625 (1980), the Supreme Court held unconstitutional a state statute barring lesser-included instructions in capital cases when such instructions were available in non-capital cases. The Court found this to be an "artificial barrier" restricting capital juries to a choice between conviction and acquittal. In *Hopkins v. Reeves*, 524 U.S. 88 (1998), the Court held that *Beck* does not require lesser-included instructions on offenses that are not deemed lesser-included by state law. Nebraska law provided that second degree murder and manslaughter are not lesser-included offenses to felony murder.

8. *Illustration of Schmuck approach.* Assume that the defendant is charged with violating 18 U.S.C. § 2113(a), which makes it a federal offense to "by force and violence, or by intimidation, [take] . . . any . . . thing of value [from a] bank." Assume that § 2113(b) provides for lesser penalties in the case of an individual who "takes and carries away, with intent to steal or purloin, [anything] of value exceeding $1,000 [from a] . . . bank." Is the defendant entitled to a jury instruction on the lesser offense if the defendant's contention at trial is that he or she did not take any of the bank's money "by force and violence, or by intimidation?"

In *Carter v. United States*, 530 U.S. 255 (2000), the Supreme Court applied the "elements test" from *Schmuck* and held that § 2113(b) was not a lesser included offense of § 2113(a) because it required three elements not required for conviction under Subsection (a). As the Court explained,

> First, whereas Subsection (b) requires that the defendant act "with intent to steal or purloin," Subsection (a) contains no similar requirement. Second, whereas Subsection (b) requires that the defendant "tak[e] and carr[y] away" the property, Subsection (a) only requires that the defendant "tak[e]" the property. Third, whereas the first paragraph of Subsection (b) requires that the property have a "value exceeding $1,000" Subsection (a) contains no valuation requirement. [Id. at 262]

In dissent, Justice Ginsburg, joined by Justices Stevens, Souter, and Breyer, observed that at common law, larceny was considered a lesser-included offense of robbery. Therefore, she concluded that "Congress did not depart from that traditional understanding when it [adopted the relevant federal statutes]." She also noted, by a footnote, that " under today's holding the Double Jeopardy Clause would not bar the

Government from bringing a bank larceny prosecution against a defendant who has already been acquitted — or, indeed, convicted — by a jury of bank robbery on the same facts." *Id.* at 275–76.

PROBLEM 15-3: I'M INNOCENT, BUT OF WHAT?

1. Keith is charged with two crimes. Crime 1 contains elements X, Y and Z. Crime 2 contains only elements X and Y. Assume that elements X and Y are the same for both offenses.

> **a.** Is Crime 2 lesser-included in Crime 1 according to *Schmuck*?

> **b.** Could Crime 1 be lesser-included in Crime 2?

> **c.** Would your answer to the above questions change if:

> Crimes 1 and 2 were punished exactly the same? What if Crime 1 were punished more severely than Crime 2? What if the reverse: Crime 2 were punished more severely than Crime 1?

2. Heather was arrested after an undercover agent reported that she had marijuana in her house. After a search revealed a container of marijuana, she was charged with the crime of possession of marijuana with an intent to distribute, as follows:

State Statute § 44-101 — Possession with Intent

Except as otherwise authorized by law, it is unlawful for any person knowingly or intentionally to manufacture, distribute, or dispense, or possess with intent to manufacture, distribute, or dispense, marijuana.

The punishment is 3-5 years in prison.

During trial, two police detectives testified that they searched Heather's apartment and found two tons of baled marijuana in her basement. They also found two small packets of rolling papers, containing a total of 100 sheets. An undercover agent testified that Heather offered to sell him 500 pounds of marijuana.

The judge indicated that she would charge the jury under State Statute § 44-101, possession with intent. Heather has filed a motion requesting that the jury also be instructed on State Statute § 44-201, simple possession.

State Statute § 44-201 — Simple Possession

Except as otherwise authorized by law, it is unlawful for any person knowingly or intentionally to possess marijuana.

The punishment is not more than 1 year in prison.

> **a.** Is simple possession (§ 44-201) a lesser-included offense of the crime of possession with intent (§ 44-101)?

> **b.** Should the judge grant Heather's motion and instruct the jury on simple possession as well as possession with intent?

> **i.** Assume that Heather testified at trial, admitted purchasing the marijuana from someone named Juan whose address and whereabouts are unknown, and stated that her intent was to burn the marijuana so that the youth of the area would not be harmed by it. Should this affect the decision whether to give the instruction on simple possession?

> **ii.** Changing the facts, assume that the detectives had found two pounds of marijuana instead of two tons and that Heather did not testify at trial. Should the judge give the requested jury instruction on simple possession? *See generally United States v. Levy*, 703 F.2d 791 (4th Cir. 1983); *United States v. Seni*, 662 F.2d 277 (4th Cir. 1981), *cert. denied.*, 455 U.S. 950 (1982).

[b] Jury Instruction Procedures

[i] Overview

In general terms, it is the judge's responsibility to prepare and give jury instructions, but lawyers for prosecution and defense are also involved. Before the instructions are given, the attorneys are usually permitted — sometimes encouraged — to request that specific instructions be given and to screen the judge's proposed instructions for possible error.

The rules of criminal procedure routinely describe at least part of the process. The federal provision is typical.

FEDERAL RULES OF CRIMINAL PROCEDURE

Rule 30. *Jury Instructions*

(a) In General. Any party may request in writing that the court instruct the jury on the law as specified in the request. The request must be made at the close of the evidence or at any earlier time during the trial that the court reasonably sets. When the request is made, the requesting party must furnish a copy to every other party.

(b) Ruling on a Request. The court must inform the parties before closing arguments how it intends to rule on the requested instructions.

(c) Time for Giving Instructions. The court may instruct the jury before or after the arguments are completed, or at both times.

(d) Objections to Instructions. A party who objects to any portion of the instructions or to a failure to give a requested instruction must inform the court of the specific objection and the grounds for the objection before the jury retires to deliberate. An opportunity must be given to object out of the jury's hearing and, on request, out of the jury's presence. Failure to object in accordance with this rule precludes appellate review, except as permitted under Rule 52(b).

NOTES

1. *Many unanswered questions.* Note that Rule 30 is quite general, leaving many questions about jury instructions unanswered. For example, jury instructions are given orally. Are they also to be "reduced to writing" and given the jurors for use during deliberations? Must the court conduct a hearing on proposed jury instructions or can the court simply rule on the proposals without according either side an opportunity to argue its case? If a lawyer wants the judge to instruct the jury on a certain topic, must that lawyer provide the court with the precise language to use or can the lawyer simply request a jury instruction on a particular topic? Are oral requests for a particular instruction valid?

2. *Role of common law and local practice.* Courts fill in the gaps in Rule 30 by reference to the common law, common sense, and past practices. Obviously the court is obligated to give certain instructions, whether or not requested by counsel. The judge must instruct on such critical legal issues as the burden of proof, the elements of crimes and defenses, and the role of the jury.

3. *Advance copy of instructions for counsel.* Many states require the judge to provide counsel with a written copy of the jury instructions before they are read to the jury. *See, e.g.,* Wash. Crim. R. Lim. Juris. 6.15(b). This ensures that counsel has the opportunity to carefully review the instructions and facilitates informed objections. Note that Rule 30 does not require the judge to provide counsel with a written copy or to inform counsel of the exact instructions to be given. This makes it more difficult for counsel to carefully scrutinize the judge's work and suggest any changes before the instructions are read.

[ii] Timing of Jury Instructions

Instruction at beginning of trial. The first instruction will ordinarily occur at the beginning of the trial when the court provides basic information about the proceedings and some administrative matters. These preliminary instructions may also provide some information about the law to be applied in the case.

Instructions during trial. The court may also instruct the jury on many occasions during the trial. For example, the court may tell the jury that certain evidence is to be used for one purpose but not another, that certain erroneously admitted testimony should be ignored, and that argument of counsel is not evidence.

Before or after closing argument. Rule 30 specifically requires the court to instruct the jury before or after closing arguments, or at both times. Some recent jury reform proposals suggest that judges depart from the traditional rule (jury instructions are given *after* closing arguments) and give jury instructions regarding the applicable law prior to closing arguments. This practice is designed to help jurors better understand the closing arguments and to provide the attorneys a context from which to argue how the law in the case relates to the facts. Of course, the court is free and likely to instruct the jury at other times.

After closing arguments for both sides, the court usually gives the final instructions. These instructions tell the jury about the applicable laws and jury procedures. To ensure a fair opportunity to object and to participate fully in the trial, all jury instructions should be given in the presence of counsel for all parties and the defendant personally. Ordinarily, this is no problem because the necessary people are already in the jury room during the trial. Sometimes an instruction is given in the defendant's absence, however, but this error is usually deemed "harmless error" and of little consequence to the outcome of the case.

[iii] Written or Oral

At common law, jurors were only given oral instructions. The submission of any written materials to the jury was prohibited due to the concern that literate jurors would have unfair influence over nonliterate jurors. *See* Robert G. Nieland, PATTERN JURY INSTRUCTIONS: A CRITICAL LOOK AT A MODERN MOVEMENT TO IMPROVE THE JURY SYSTEM (1979). It now appears that very few states prohibit the use of written jury instructions. The rationale for the distinct minority view barring written instructions is that a jury may "assess undue weight to the points of law in written instructions and possibly misinterpret or misapply the law" and that this "undue emphasis on portions of the charge has the potential of undermining the integrity of the deliberative process." *Commonwealth v. Karaffa,* 709 A.2d 887 (Pa. 1998).

As noted in a dissenting opinion in *Karaffa,* the federal courts and approximately thirty states favor the submission of written charges to the jury because "written instructions . . . help keep the jury focused on the law applicable to the case, thereby benefitting all parties." Noting that written instructions help jurors process and comprehend the instructions as well as recall and apply them, the American Bar Association recommends that each juror be given a written copy of the jury instructions to use while the court instructs the jury and during deliberations. American Bar Association, PRINCIPLES FOR JURIES AND JURY TRIALS, Prin. 14(B) and comment.

Empirical data. Research has shown that there are considerable advantages in providing the jury with a written copy of the oral instructions. In one study, nearly one quarter of 405 mock juries requested written clarification of instructions. Laurence J. Severance and Elizabeth F. Loftus, *Improving the Ability of Jurors to Comprehend and Apply Criminal Jury Instructions,* 17 LAW & SOCIETY REVIEW 153 (1982). Another study reported that juries with written instructions, when compared with those that had to rely on oral instructions, were more efficient, conducted better deliberations, appeared to be less confused about the law, spent less time trying to understand the instructions, concentrated more on relevant facts and accurate application of the law, and felt better about the quality of their decisions. Robert F. Forston, *Sense and Non-Sense: Jury Trial Communication*, 1975 B.Y.U. L. REV. 601.

[iv]   Counsel's Opportunity to Suggest and Object; Hearing

Parties' opportunity to request jury instruction. Rule 30 and similar rules in every jurisdiction specifically provide that counsel for all parties have an opportunity to suggest language to be used in jury instructions. One reason for this rule is to permit counsel to correct possible errors and therefore minimize appellate reversals.

Timing of request for jury instructions. Rule 30, like many state rules of criminal procedure, also deals with the timing of requests for jury instructions, providing that requests should be made no later than at the close of evidence, and earlier if the court directs. Some judges will also accept jury instructions requests later, even after the regular instructions have been given.

Oral jury instruction requests. While Rule 30 outlines a procedure for written jury instruction requests, oral requests are also routinely permitted by some judges. On the other hand, in some jurisdictions all jury instruction requests must be in writing.

Copy of requested instruction to adversary counsel. Counsel making a written request for a certain jury instructions is obligated by Rule 30 to provide adversary counsel with a copy of the request. Often the request takes the form of a motion styled "Request for Jury Instruction."

Duty to object and timing of objection. Under Rule 30 and many others, the opportunity to suggest jury instructions is also turned into a duty to object to faulty ones. Before a party can appeal an erroneous jury instruction, Rule 30 states that the party must object before the jury begins deliberations. Failure to object in a timely manner is generally viewed as a waiver of any objection to a perceived defect in the instructions. To protect appellate options, counsel must ensure that all appropriate objections are on the record to assist appellate review.

These objections should state clearly the grounds for the objection. To guard against the possibility that somehow that jury will be prejudiced against the party objecting to the instructions and will hear proposed instructions that are not accepted by the court, Rule 30 provides that the court should give counsel an opportunity outside the hearing of the jury and, on request of counsel, outside the presence of the jury.

Charge conference. As a matter of practice, some time during the trial, judges often convene a jury-out hearing on possible jury instructions. In some jurisdictions, this is referred to as a "charge conference." At this time the court may distribute written copies of the court's proposed instructions, invite comment on them, and consider proposed instructions drafted by the parties.

[v]   Judicial Discretion

The court is not obligated to accept counsel's proposed jury instructions. The court may reject the proposed instructions altogether or accept counsel's suggestion that a jury instruction on a certain topic be given, then write and use its own version of the instruction on that issue. In order to permit counsel to discuss jury instructions during the closing argument, Rule 30 requires the judge to inform counsel of its ruling on jury instruction requests before the closing argument.

[11]   Closing Arguments

The closing argument is an attorney's last chance to speak to the jury before deliberation. The purpose of closing arguments, or summation, is for each attorney to tie together the evidence it has presented into a coherent story, and to help the jury to apply the law to that evidence. Although the jury has already heard all the evidence before closing arguments begin, prosecution and defense attorneys know that their arguments, both in content and style of delivery, can have a tremendous psychological impact upon the jurors, and therefore influence the verdict. It is because of the great power of closing arguments that restrictions are necessary to govern the types of arguments that are permissible from both the defense and the prosecution.

There is relatively little law on closing arguments. Trial judges are given immense discretion in controlling the form and content. Appellate reversal for abuse of discretion is rare.

Time limits. Trial courts often set time limits on closing arguments. *See, e.g., United States v. Jamal,* 246 Fed. Appx. 351 (6th Cir. 2007)(upholding 45-minute per side for closing argument); *Dorsey v. State,* 646 S.E.2d 713 (Ga. App. 2007)(upholding trial court giving additional time to conclude closing argument). A few statutes even establish time limits. *E.g.,* Ga. Code Ann. § 17-8-73 (closing argument limited to one hour for each side in non-capital case and two hours in capital case).

Reversal for prejudice. A prosecutor's error in closing argument, such as intentionally referring to facts not in evidence, will cause a reversal only if the court finds it impeded the defendant's right to a fair trial. *See, e.g., Garcia v. State,* 246 S.W.3d 121 (Tex. App. 2007)(error in prosecutor's closing argument reversed only if "extremely or manifestly improper"). If the trial judge gave a curative jury instruction, often the error is deemed non-prejudicial on the theory that the jury follows the jury instructions.

The American Bar Association standards for closing arguments are generally the same for prosecution and defense attorneys. The ABA Standards for Criminal Justice Chapter 3, Section 5.8 contains the standards for prosecutors:[*]

Standard 3-5.8: Argument to the Jury

(a) In closing argument to the jury, the prosecutor may argue all reasonable inferences from evidence in the record. The prosecutor should not intentionally misstate the evidence or mislead the jury as to the inferences it may draw.

(b) The prosecutor should not express his or her personal belief or opinion as to the truth or falsity of any testimony or evidence or the guilt of the defendant.

(c) The prosecutor should not make arguments calculated to appeal to the prejudices of the jury.

(d) The prosecutor should refrain from argument which would divert the jury from its duty to decide the case on the evidence.

The standards for defense attorneys in Chapter 4, Section 7.7 are nearly identical, substituting the words "defense counsel" for "prosecutor." For other related standards, *see* Model Code of Prof'l Responsibility DR 7-102(A)(5); DR 7-106(C)(3), (4) (1969); Model Rules of Prof'l Conduct 3.3(a)(1); 3.4(e); 4.1 (1983); NDAA Nat'l Prosecution Standard 85.1 (2d ed. 1991).

Defense "opening the door" in its closing argument. Since the doctrine of double jeopardy prevents most government appeals, arguments by defense counsel rarely come under direct review by the courts; thus, the majority of applicable cases deal with impropriety by the prosecution. However, some courts have indirectly addressed impermissible closing arguments by the defense. If the defense counsel "opens the door" by using impermissible questioning or arguments, many courts will allow the prosecution to respond in like kind during rebuttal.

The subsections below will describe each of the four types of impermissible arguments as outlined by the ABA standards, and give examples of how they may apply

---

to both defense and prosecution arguments. Although all of the arguments below are considered improper, courts vary in their decisions of which improper arguments constitute reversible error.

[a] Inferences and Misrepresentation

While attorneys are given wide latitude in drawing inferences from the evidence presented, both the defense and the prosecution are forbidden to suggest inferences to the jury that are not reasonably supported by the record. If certain evidence is excluded by the court or inadmissible, it is misrepresentation for counsel to draw attention to that evidence in the closing argument. *See, e.g., People v. Ellison*, 350 N.W.2d 812, 815 (Mich. App. 1984) (holding that counsel's reference to inadmissible fingerprint evidence constituted reversible error).

Another common tactic involves the attorney pointing out absent testimony. Prosecutors may try to infer guilt by drawing attention to the fact of the defendant's silence at trial. In *Griffin v. California*, the Court held that such remarks infringe upon the defendant's Fifth Amendment right against self-incrimination. 380 U.S. 609, 614 (1965). Inferences are not limited to the words used by an attorney, but can also extend to actions and body language. *See United States v. Johnston*, 127 F.3d 380, 397 (5th Cir. 1997).

A similar problem occurs when a prosecutor points to information not in the record but personally known to the prosecutor. In one illustrative case, the prosecutor told the jury, "I'd love to tell you what I know, but I can't." *United States v. Stuckey*, 253 Fed. Appx. 468 (6th Cir. 2007).

[b] Personal Belief

Attorneys should be careful not to give their personal beliefs about the defendant's guilt or the credibility of a witness. One way to avoid this is not to preface comments in a closing argument with "I think" or "I believe." These phrases can serve as red flags, alerting the court and opposing counsel that improper expression of the attorney's personal opinions may follow. Personal endorsement of witness testimony by counsel is effectively testimony itself; to allow counsel to testify as a witness without being sworn and subjected to cross-examination would deprive the parties of due process. Courts are especially sensitive to expressions of personal opinion by the prosecution because they appear to exploit the prestige and influence that accompany the office of prosecutor. Although cases involving prosecutorial expression of personal opinion are more common, the standard for defense counsel is the same.

Whether a personal opinion was offered is often a close question that depends on nuance. For example, in one case the prosecutor's closing argument told the jury that witness Bryant "told you the truth." The Georgia Supreme Court held this did not involve the prosecutor's personal view, but rather simply told the jury the conclusion the prosecutor wished the jury to draw from the evidence. *Adams v. State*, 658 S.E.2d 627 (Ga. 2008). *See also People v. Cepeda*, 851 N.Y.S.2d 505, 2008 N.Y. App. Div. LEXIS 1385 (App. Div. 2008)(not improper for prosecutor to argue, "I believe the People have proven the defendant is the person" who committed the charged offenses); *State v. Jackson*, 157 P.3d 660 (Kan. App. 2007)(improper personal opinion for prosecutor to refer to "doozies" defendant told and to defendant's version as "a crock").

Some jurisdictions are more accepting of opinion argument. *See, e.g., Garcia v. State*, 246 S.W.3d 121 (Tex. App. 2007)(prosecutor may argue her personal opinions if based on evidence in the record and are not unsworn testimony; prosecutor properly argued, "He did it, he knows it").

[c]   Appeals to Prejudice

Inflammatory remarks and comments about a witness's race, religion, or ethnic background are almost always improper in closing argument. These kinds of remarks, designed to appeal to the prejudices of the jurors, introduce anger and fear into the deliberation process, clouding the jurors' abilities to reach a rational decision. Charles L. Cantrell, *Prosecutorial Misconduct: Recognizing Errors in Closing Argument*, 26 AM. J. TRIAL ADVOC. 535, 554 (2003). An extreme example of this type of argument occurs when counsel attempts to dehumanize a particular witness (typically the defendant) through name-calling. *See, e.g., People v. Hernandez*, 829 P.2d 394, 396 (Colo. App. 1991) (stating that "courts have uniformly condemned as improper a prosecutor using such terms as 'rat,' 'dog,' or 'animal,' to describe a defendant"); *United States v. Heron*, 525 F. Supp.2d 729 (E.D. Pa. 2007)(referring to defendant as "common thief" and his expert as "a hack").

While such characterizations are sometimes allowed if the evidence supports the inference, courts more often find reversible error because "this type of shorthand characterization of an accused, not based on evidence, is especially likely to stick in the minds of the jury and influence its deliberations." *Hall v. United States*, 419 F.2d 582, 587 (5th Cir. 1969). It is also inappropriate for counsel to incite the jury's sympathy for a witness; such arguments reinforce juror biases, and cut against the jurors' oaths. Charles L. Cantrell, *Prosecutorial Misconduct: Recognizing Errors in Closing Argument*, 26 AM. J. TRIAL ADVOC. 535, 559 (2003).

[d]   Digression from the Evidence

The fourth category of impermissible arguments is broad, encompassing a variety of arguments that do not fit neatly into the other three categories. One of the most recurring arguments in this category is the "appeal to community interest." These arguments ask the jury to take personal responsibility for the consequence of their chosen verdict on society. *See Bates v. Bell*, 402 F.3d 635, (6th Cir. 2005) (reversing the defendant's death sentence based in part on the prosecution's statements to the jury that they would "become accomplices" to the defendant's crime if they allowed him to live); *People v. Moore*, 824 N.E.2d 1162, 1165 (Ill. App. 2005) (holding that reversible error occurred when the prosecution argued in closing that the jury should convict in order prevent car insurance rates from rising). Other types of arguments in this category include personal attacks on opposing counsel, and suggestions that the jury should punish the defendant for some bad act other than the crime at issue. Encouragement of jury nullification can also fall into this category in some jurisdictions.

[12]   Jury Deliberations

Retire to jury room. After the closing arguments and the jury instructions, the jury leaves the courtroom and goes to the jury room to begin deliberations. Only the jurors are permitted in this room, although a court officer may be nearby to assist the jury and to prevent others from disturbing the jurors. Alternate jurors should not be present.

Alternate jurors. In many jurisdictions, alternate jurors are discharged once deliberations begin. Under the federal approach, however, alternate jurors may be detained during deliberations. Fed. R. Crim. P. 24(e)(3). If alternate jurors do attend and observe the deliberations, the case will be reversed only if prejudice is shown. *See United States v. Olano*, 507 U.S. 725 (1993).

Under supervision of court officer. Sometimes jurors eat meals in the jury room or go to a nearby restaurant. In the latter case, they are under the direct supervision of a court officer to ensure that they are not subjected to outside influences and information.

Select foreperson. Often the jury's first task is to select a "foreperson" or leader. This person will organize the jury's work and serve as a liaison with court officers and the judge. The latter function includes communicating with the judge on matters such as the need to have certain jury instructions repeated or explained, to have the transcript of certain testimony read to the jury, and to report the jury's decisions.

Exhibits in jury room. Often a statute or court rule will permit jurors to take into the jury room all or part of the papers and exhibits, such as maps or physical objects, admitted in evidence in the case. These items may be studied by jurors and used in their deliberations. Exceptions are frequently made for depositions that were read into evidence and for some other documents. These are not permitted in the jury room because of a fear the jury will give them too much weight when compared with oral testimony that is not available for scrutiny in the jury room. Sometimes exhibits in the form of books are not permitted because of concern the jurors will use pages not introduced into evidence. In some locales, jurors are also given copies of the indictment and the jury instructions. Sometimes the parties may agree to add or remove items available to the jury.

Reviewing proof presented during trial. During deliberations, jurors may find they cannot remember or they disagree about the content of evidence admitted during the trial. They are routinely permitted to ask the judge if they may review the questionable proof. For example, they may seek to rehear a 911 recording played during trial or have a witness's testimony read from the transcript.

The judge should receive such requests in open court on the record. Both sides are allowed to comment on whether and how the request should be granted. Although the judge is ordinarily given the discretion to grant or deny the request, a minority of jurisdictions require the judge to approve the request if possible. The court may instruct the jury not to give undue weight to the repeated evidence.

If the jury's request for a review of evidence is approved, the court may order the clerk or someone else to read the pertinent portions of the transcript to the jury. On rare occasions the witness may be recalled for live testimony or the judge may give his or her recollection of the evidence in question.

Juror's own knowledge. Though jurors are required to base their decision on the evidence presented at trial, they need not forget their personal experiences or common knowledge in assessing the proof.

Juror's experiments. Jurors may attempt experiments with evidence presented at trial. In general, such efforts are impermissible since the experiment is not subject to adversarial testing and may be misleading. *See, e.g., State v. Ballew,* 63 S.E. 688 (Ga. 1909)(jury improperly threw a hatchet against a wall to re-enact prosecutor's version of a crime).

Some experiments are upheld, though the reasoning is sometimes strained. *See, e.g., State v. Pease,* 163 P.3d 985 (Alas. App. 2007)(upholding jury experiment to look out jury room window to see if could recognize a person at 200 feet, but improper to leave court house to perform same experiment; not reversible error because did not deny defendant a fair trial).

Continued plea negotiations during deliberations. Sometimes the accused and the prosecutor continue plea negotiations during the trial. Since neither side may want to risk a jury's decision, they may work out a deal while the jury is in the jury room deliberating. The American Bar Association recommends in such cases that the jury be dismissed, without rendering a verdict, as soon as the plea is accepted. If a verdict has been decided, the court should not accept it. STANDARDS FOR CRIMINAL JUSTICE § 15-5.5 (3d ed. 1996).

[13] Verdict

[a] In General

The essential purpose of a trial is the resolution of the issues. The *verdict*, the decision of the jury or judge as to guilt, accomplishes this. The verdict states whether the defendant is guilty or innocent of each charge (or lesser-included offense). Rule 31 of the Federal Rules of Criminal Procedure sketches some of the procedural facets of the verdict:

FEDERAL RULES OF CRIMINAL PROCEDURE

Rule 31. *Jury Verdict*

(a) Return. The jury must return its verdict to a judge in open court. The verdict must be unanimous.

(b) Partial Verdicts, Mistrial, and Retrial.

(1) Multiple Defendants. If there are multiple defendants, the jury may return a verdict at any time during its deliberations as to any defendant about whom it has agreed.

(2) Multiple Counts. If the jury cannot agree on all counts as to any defendant, the jury may return a verdict on those counts on which it has agreed.

(3) Mistrial and Retrial. If the jury cannot agree on a verdict on one or more counts, the court may declare a mistrial on those counts. The government may retry any defendant on any count on which the jury could not agree.

(c) Lesser Offense or Attempt. A defendant may be found guilty of any of the following:

(1) an offense necessarily included in the offense charged;

(2) an attempt to commit the offense charged; or

(3) an attempt to commit an offense necessarily included in the offense charged, if the attempt is an offense in its own right.

(d) Jury Poll. After a verdict is returned but before the jury is discharged, the court must on a party's request, or may on its own, poll the jurors individually. If the poll reveals a lack of unanimity, the court may direct the jury to deliberate further or may declare a mistrial and discharge the jury.

NOTES

1. *Announcement of verdict.* Rule 31 answers some, but not all, questions about the return of the verdict. Ordinarily in open court, the judge asks whether the jury has agreed on a verdict. Then, the foreperson orally, in writing, or both, informs the court or the court clerk of the jury's decision. The defendant has a right to be present at this time.

2. *Jury poll.* Usually, the defendant has a right to have the jury *polled* — questioned individually in open court whether the juror agreed with the verdict announced by the foreperson.

3. *Multiple defendants.* When the jury is resolving criminal charges against more than one defendant, Rule 31 makes it clear that the jury has much leeway in considering the defendants at the same time or seriatim. Thus, the jury in a criminal case involving two defendants could resolve the charges against Defendant A, announce the verdict, then retire to consider the charges against Defendant B.

4. *General and special verdicts.* The usual practice is that the jury issues a *general verdict*, which is a simple "guilty" or "not guilty" decision on each count. The jury does not articulate any reasons for its conclusions.

On occasion, a *special verdict* is used in criminal cases. This verdict requires the jury to answer specific factual questions in addition to resolving the allegations in each count. Usually, the special verdict requires the jury to state whether particular elements were present or absent, then to state its conclusion on guilt or innocence. For example, in a burglary case the court could ask for a special verdict that answered the following questions:

1. Did the defendant, John Smith, break a window to enter the trailer of Sarah Bunker at 123 South Street? (yes or no)

2. Did defendant Smith enter Bunker's trailer? (yes or no)

3. Was Bunker's trailer a dwelling house? (yes or no)

4. If there was a breaking and entry, were they at night? (yes or no)

5. Did defendant Smith break and enter with the intent to commit a felony inside? (yes or no)

The Federal Rules of Criminal Procedure do not discuss a special verdict in a criminal case tried by a jury, but Rule 23(c) authorizes it in non-jury cases. Some state provisions authorize a special verdict in jury cases. *E.g.*, Cal. Penal Code §§ 1150 & 1152 (special verdict permissible when jury is in doubt as to legal consequences of proven facts; jury specifically states proven facts and then court draws conclusions of law).

Although a special verdict is quite helpful to jurors in organizing their discussions and decisions, criminal courts rarely use them and some appellate decisions are critical of them. The primary argument seems to be that the special verdict provides the jury with so much specific guidance that it somehow impinges on the jury's independence and, by focusing on logic, could tilt the scales in favor of conviction. *See generally United States v. Spock*, 416 F.2d 165 (1st Cir. 1969);

An illustration is *State v. Surette*, 544 A.2d 823 (N.H. 1988), a burglary case where the court instructed the jury on the applicable elements, then submitted a special verdict form requiring the jurors to answer four questions relating to the elements. One illustrative question asked, "Did John Surette, on or about March 7, 1986, purposely enter the dwelling occupied by [names] in Bedford in the nighttime?" The New Hampshire Supreme Court reversed the conviction because the special verdict form directed "the jury down a path towards a guilty verdict" by omitting the jury's power to acquit even if it finds the defendant committed all elements of the crime. Do you agree with this logic? If the defendant satisfied the crime elements, shouldn't he or she be found guilty?

In some situations, however, a special verdict is essential. For example, sometimes a defendant is charged with conspiracy or attempt to commit several felonies. In order to assure proper sentencing if the defendant is convicted, the jury must indicate which felony the defendant conspired or attempted to commit. Similarly, in some jurisdictions the quantity of drugs or the amount of money stolen must be included in the verdict in order to impose sentences and assess the amount of restitution. This is especially important because of recent Supreme Court decisions, discussed in Chapter 17, requiring the jury, not judge, to make certain factual determinations affecting sentences. *See United States v. Booker*, 543 U.S. 220 (2005).

A special verdict could also be significant in establishing a collateral estoppel claim, since it is crucial to know precisely what facts were found in an earlier criminal case. *See Ashe v. Swenson*, 397 U.S. 436 (1970), discussed in Chapter 16. Finally, a special verdict is often required in capital cases where the sentencing jury must list such facts as the specific aggravating and mitigating factors it found.

Counsel desiring a special verdict should make a timely request, perhaps even suggesting the exact questions the jury should be asked. Failure to request a special verdict may be deemed a waiver of the issue and make appellate reversal unlikely on this claim.

5. *Qualified verdict.* Sometimes, contrary to the court's instructions, a jury will issue a *qualified verdict*, which is a verdict accompanied by a recommendation. The most typical is a guilty verdict with a recommendation of leniency. Usually these recommendations do not have any binding effect and do not affect the validity of the verdict. *Rogers v. United States,* 422 U.S. 35 (1975) (guilty verdict with recommendation of extreme mercy; conviction reversed because when jury so reported, trial judge failed to provide defense attorney opportunity to be heard before judge instructed jury a second time).

If the verdict contains a condition that suggests that the verdict itself is qualified, the trial court should poll the jury to determine whether the verdict is unqualified and the condition is merely a recommendation. For example, assume that a jury returns the following verdict: "We find the defendant guilty of burglary if the sentence is probation." Since it is unclear whether the jury intends for the defendant to be guilty if the sentence is not probation, the court should poll the jurors to determine whether there would have been a verdict of guilty absent the condition that the offender be placed on probation. If the court is uncertain about the jury's actions, it can declare a mistrial or send the jury for additional deliberations, perhaps after additional jury instructions.

6. *Correction or amendment.* Sometimes a jury verdict in a criminal case is ambiguous, not responsive to the judge's instructions, or incorrect in not accurately representing the jury's decision. Examples include a failure to resolve all charges, a guilty verdict to a crime with which the defendant had not been charged, a failure to specify which degree of murder the defendant committed, and a failure to sign the correct verdict form. In such cases, ordinarily the court can simply send the jury back to the jury room to correct the error. If the jury has been discharged, however, usually the trial court cannot reconvene the panel and a mistrial is declared.

After a verdict of acquittal is accepted, the double jeopardy clause bars further proceedings even if the verdict was in error. *See, e.g., State v. Taylor,* 544 So. 2d 1387 (Miss. 1989) (jury verdict of acquittal was ordered filed; jury was polled and one juror disagreed with the acquittal; court ordered jury to retire for additional deliberations and jury found defendant guilty as charged; conviction reversed).

[b] Unanimity

The traditional American view is that a jury in a criminal case consists of twelve people who must vote unanimously in order to convict or acquit a defendant. If the jury is not unanimous, under this view there is a *hung jury* or a *deadlocked jury,* resulting in a mistrial. As early as 1824, the Supreme Court held that the double jeopardy clause does not bar a retrial following a hung jury. *United States v. Perez,* 22 U.S. 579 (1824).

[i] Due Process and Equal Protection

Although the rule requiring a unanimous jury has a long history, it is not mandated by the constitution. In *Johnson v. Louisiana,* 406 U.S. 356 (1972), the defendant was convicted after a 9-3 vote by a 12 person jury, consistent with Louisiana criminal procedure that provided for a guilty verdict if 9 of the 12 jurors voted for conviction. The Supreme Court upheld the conviction against both due process and equal protection challenges. The due process clause was not offended because there was nothing in the record to suggest that the nine jurors who voted guilty did not listen to the dissenting jurors and did not apply the court's instruction on the meaning of guilty beyond a reasonable doubt. Moreover, the fact that three jurors voted against conviction does not mean that there was not proof beyond a reasonable doubt.

The equal protection clause was not violated by this less-than-unanimous procedure, even though Louisiana law mandated a unanimous verdict in capital cases and certain lesser felonies where a five-person jury was authorized. The Supreme Court held that the Louisiana procedures served a rational purpose in that the Louisiana legislature chose to save money by using smaller juries in less serious cases. The Supreme Court found no constitutional violation in the defendant's argument that Louisiana had made it easier to convict in a non-unanimous twelve-person jury than in a unanimous five-person jury. Do you agree that this difference is not of constitutional dimension? Recall that the twelve-person jury is used in more serious cases than the five-person jury.

[ii] Sixth Amendment

Although *Johnson* resolved the issue whether the due process and equal protection clauses would permit a less than unanimous verdict, the companion case dealt with the more difficult question of whether the Sixth Amendment permitted this practice.

APODACA v. OREGON
406 U.S. 404 (1972)

MR. JUSTICE WHITE announced the judgment of the Court in an opinion in which THE CHIEF JUSTICE, MR. JUSTICE BLACKMUN, and MR. JUSTICE REHNQUIST joined.

[The three defendants were convicted of various offenses in separate Oregon state trials. Two of them were convicted by a 10-2 jury vote and one by an 11-1 vote, consistent with Oregon law authorizing a conviction by no less than 10-2. Each defendant claimed that the Sixth Amendment barred a conviction by a non-unanimous jury verdict.]

In *Williams v. Florida*, 399 U.S. 786 (1970), we had occasion to consider a related issue: whether the Sixth Amendment's right to trial by jury requires that all juries consist of 12 men. After considering the history of the 12-man requirement and the functions it performs in contemporary society, we concluded that it was not of constitutional stature. We reach the same conclusion today with regard to the requirement of unanimity.

Like the requirement that juries consist of 12 men, the requirement of unanimity arose during the Middle Ages and had become an accepted feature of the common law jury by the 18th century. But, as we observed in *Williams*, "the relevant constitutional history casts considerable doubt on the easy assumption . . . that if a given feature existed in a jury at common law in 1789, then it was necessarily preserved in the Constitution."

. . . As we observed in *Williams*, one can draw conflicting inferences from this legislative history. . . . And, as in *Williams*, our inability to divine "the intent of the Framers" when they eliminated references to the "accustomed requisites" requires that in determining what is meant by a jury we must turn to other than purely historical considerations.

Our inquiry must focus upon the function served by the jury in contemporary society. As we said in *Duncan*, the purpose of trial by jury is to prevent oppression by the Government by providing a "safeguard against the corrupt or overzealous prosecutor and against the compliant, biased, or eccentric judge." "Given this purpose, the essential feature of a jury obviously lies in the interposition between the accused and his accuser of the commonsense judgment of a group of laymen. . . . " A requirement of unanimity, however, does not materially contribute to the exercise of this commonsense judgment. . . . In terms of this function we perceive no difference between juries required to act unanimously and those permitted to convict or acquit by votes of 10 to two or 11 to one. Requiring unanimity would obviously produce hung juries in some situations where non-unanimous juries will convict or acquit. But in either case, the interest of the defendant in having the judgment of his peers interposed between himself and the officers of the State who prosecute and judge him is equally well served.

[The opinion rejected the claim that a unanimous verdict is essential to protect the Sixth Amendment's guarantee of proof of guilt beyond a reasonable doubt. The Sixth

Amendment does not embrace the beyond-reasonable-doubt guarantee, which is part of due process.]

Petitioners also cite quite accurately a long line of decisions of this Court upholding the principle that the Fourteenth Amendment requires jury panels to reflect a cross section of the community. They then contend that unanimity is a necessary precondition for effective application of the cross-section requirement, because a rule permitting less than unanimous verdicts will make it possible for convictions to occur without the acquiescence of minority elements within the community.

There are two flaws in this argument. One is petitioners' assumption that every distinct voice in the community has a right to be represented on every jury and a right to prevent conviction of a defendant in any case. All that the Constitution forbids, however, is systematic exclusion of identifiable segments of the community from jury panels and from the juries ultimately drawn from those panels; a defendant may not, for example, challenge the makeup of a jury merely because no members of his race are on the jury, but must prove that his race has been systematically excluded. No group, in short, has the right to block convictions; it has only the right to participate in the overall legal processes by which criminal guilt and innocence are determined.

We also cannot accept petitioners' second assumption — that minority groups, even when they are represented on a jury, will not adequately represent the viewpoint of those groups simply because they may be outvoted in the final result. They will be present during all deliberations, and their views will be heard. We cannot assume that the majority of the jury will refuse to weigh the evidence and reach a decision upon rational grounds, just as it must now do in order to obtain unanimous verdicts, or that a majority will deprive a man of his liberty on the basis of prejudice when a minority is presenting a reasonable argument in favor of acquittal. We simply find no proof for the notion that a majority will disregard its instructions and cast its votes for guilt or innocence based on prejudice rather than the evidence. [Affirmed.]

MR. JUSTICE DOUGLAS, with whom MR. JUSTICE BRENNAN and MR. JUSTICE MARSHALL concur, dissenting.

. . . I dissent from this radical departure from American traditions.

The Constitution does not mention unanimous juries. Neither does it mention the presumption of innocence, nor does it say that guilt must be proved beyond a reasonable doubt in all criminal cases. Yet it is almost inconceivable that anyone would have questioned whether proof beyond a reasonable doubt was in fact the constitutional standard.

. . . I had similarly assumed that there was no dispute that the Federal Constitution required a unanimous jury in all criminal cases. . . . Today the bases of those cases are discarded and two centuries of American history are shunted aside.

The result of today's decisions is anomalous: though unanimous jury decisions are not required in state trials, they are constitutionally required in federal prosecutions [by *Andres v. United States*, 333 U.S. 740 (1948)]. How can that be possible when both decisions stem from the Sixth Amendment?

. . . I would construe the Sixth Amendment, when applicable to the States, precisely as I would when applied to the Federal Government.

The plurality approves a procedure which diminishes the reliability of a jury. First, it eliminates the circumstances in which a minority of jurors (a) could have rationally persuaded the entire jury to acquit, or (b) while unable to persuade the majority to acquit, nonetheless could have convinced them to convict only on a lesser-included offense. Second, it permits prosecutors in Oregon and Louisiana to enjoy a conviction-acquittal ratio substantially greater than that ordinarily returned by unanimous juries.

The diminution of verdict reliability flows from the fact that non-unanimous juries need not debate and deliberate as fully as must unanimous juries. As soon as the requisite majority is attained, further consideration is not required either by Oregon or by Louisiana even though the dissident jurors might, if given the chance, be able to convince the majority. . . . Indeed, if a necessary majority is immediately obtained, then no deliberation at all is required in these States.

. . . I fail to understand why the Court should lift from the States the burden of justifying so radical a departure from an accepted and applauded tradition and instead demand that these defendants document with empirical evidence what has always been thought to be too obvious for further study.

To be sure, in *Williams v. Florida* we held that a State could provide a jury less than 12 in number in a criminal trial. [*Williams* noted that empirical studies and common sense show that a 12-person jury is not necessarily more advantageous to the defendant than a smaller jury.]

. . . That rationale of *Williams* can have no application here. *Williams* requires that the change be neither more nor less advantageous to either the State or the defendant. It is said that such a showing is satisfied here since a 3:9 (Louisiana) or 2:10 (Oregon) verdict will result in acquittal. Yet experience shows that the less-than-unanimous jury overwhelmingly favors the States.

Moreover, even where an initial majority wins the dissent over to its side, the ultimate result in unanimous-jury States may nonetheless reflect the reservations of uncertain jurors. I refer to many compromise verdicts on lesser-included offenses and lesser sentences. Thus, even though a minority may not be forceful enough to carry the day, their doubts may nonetheless cause a majority to exercise caution. Obviously, however, in Oregon and Louisiana, dissident jurors will not have the opportunity through full deliberation to temper the opposing faction's degree of certainty of guilt.

The new rule also has an impact on cases in which a unanimous jury would have neither voted to acquit nor to convict, but would have deadlocked. In unanimous-jury States, this occurs about 5.6% of the time. Of these deadlocked juries, Kalven and Zeisel [in The American Jury (1966)] say that 56% contain either one, two, or three dissenters. In these latter cases, the majorities favor the prosecution 44% (of the 56%) but the defendant only 12% (of the 56%). Thus, by eliminating these deadlocks, Louisiana wins 44 cases for every 12 that it loses, obtaining in this band of outcomes a substantially more favorable conviction ratio (3.67 to 1) than the unanimous-jury ratio of slightly less than two guilty verdicts for every acquittal. By eliminating the one-and-two- dissenting-juror cases, Oregon does even better, gaining 4.25 convictions for every acquittal. While the statutes on their face deceptively appear to be neutral, the use of the non-unanimous jury stacks the truth-determining process against the accused. Thus, we take one step more away from the accusatorial system that has been our proud boast.

It is my belief that a unanimous jury is necessary if the great barricade known as proof beyond a reasonable doubt is to be maintained.

. . . Suppose a jury begins with a substantial minority but then in the process of deliberation a sufficient number changes to reach the required 9:3 or 10:2 for a verdict. Is not there still a lingering doubt about that verdict? Is it not clear that the safeguard of unanimity operates in this context to make it far more likely that guilt is established beyond a reasonable doubt?

. . . Today the Court approves a nine-to-three verdict. Would the Court relax the standard of reasonable doubt still further by resorting to eight-to-four verdicts, or even a majority rule? Moreover, in light of today's holdings and that of *Williams v. Florida*, in the future would it invalidate three-to-two or even two-to-one convictions?

Is the next step the elimination of the presumption of innocence?

. . . Proof beyond a reasonable doubt and unanimity of criminal verdicts and the presumption of innocence are basic features of the accusatorial system. What we do today is not in that tradition but more in the tradition of the inquisition. Until amendments are adopted setting new standards, I would let no man be fined or imprisoned in derogation of what up to today was indisputably the law of the land.

[JUSTICE BLACKMUN'S concurring opinion stated that a less than unanimous verdict system is constitutional even though it is unwise.]

JUSTICE POWELL concurred in the judgment. He argued that a less than unanimous verdict does not offend the due process clause because it is not fundamental to the essentials of a jury trial. The jury's function of guarding against arbitrary law enforcement is preserved with or without a unanimous jury verdict requirement. Minority perspectives are not unconstitutionally compromised under the Oregon system because there is no evidence that jurors in Oregon will not listen to all views before rendering a decision.

JUSTICES BRENNAN'S dissent argued that a unanimous jury requirement means that minority views will have to be taken seriously, which is not necessary in a non-unanimous jurisdiction.

JUSTICES MARSHALL and STEWART also wrote dissenting opinions.]

NOTES

1. *Protection against government oppression.* The plurality opinion in *Apodaca* suggested that a non-unanimous jury could protect against government oppression, but had little empirical support for this assertion. Do you think this protection is as likely in a non-unanimous jurisdiction, such as one that permitted guilt to be determined by a 9-3 vote?

2. *Effect on deliberations.* What effect do you think a non-unanimous model will have on jury deliberations? Will they be shorter or longer than under a unanimous approach? More or less heated? Will minority views be given more or less respect? Will more innocent people be convicted? More guilty people acquitted?

3. *Effect on compromises.* Will there be more, less, or the same number of compromises in a non-unanimous and a unanimous jury system? Is this good? Do you agree that compromises on guilt or innocence (which usually means guilt for a lesser included crime) are appropriate in the criminal justice system?

4. *Size v. unanimity.* Recall that in *Williams v. Florida* and *Ballew v. Georgia*, both discussed earlier in this chapter, the Supreme Court held that juries in state courts do not have to consist of twelve people, but they cannot have less than six. Combining these cases with *Apodaca*, what is the relationship between jury size and jury unanimity? Could a state have a jury of six people and require only a two-thirds vote for conviction (thus a person could be convicted by a vote of 4-2)?

In *Burch v. Louisiana*, 441 U.S. 130 (1979), the Supreme Court invalidated obscenity convictions obtained by a 5-1 vote of jurors, as authorized by Louisiana law. Finding the issue to be "a close one," the Supreme Court held that conviction by a non-unanimous six-member jury violated the accused's Sixth Amendment right to a jury trial. The Court stated:

> . . . [M]uch the same reasons that led us in *Ballew* to decide that use of a five-member jury threatened the fairness of the proceeding and the proper role of the jury, lead us to conclude now that conviction for a nonpetty offense by only five members of a six-person jury presents a similar threat to preservation of the substance of the jury trial guarantee and justifies our requiring verdicts rendered by six-person juries to be unanimous. *[Id. at 138]*

Do you agree with the Supreme Court in *Burch*? If a verdict of 9 of 12 jurors (75%) is valid, what is wrong with a verdict of 5 of 6 jurors (83%)? Will it be less reflective? Less accurate? Recall that the Supreme Court upheld a unanimous verdict by a six-person jury. Is an almost-unanimous verdict by 5 of 6 jurors less likely to protect against government oppression? Less likely to involve the community in the decision and the process?

5. The American Bar Association recommends a unanimous verdict in all jury cases. Recall the ABA also recommends a jury of twelve for serious offenses (more than six months' confinement) unless the parties, with court approval, stipulate that the jury shall consist of a smaller number, though not smaller than six. However, the ABA also states that, at any time before verdict, the parties, with court approval, may stipulate to a non-unanimous jury verdict so long as it is made clear the number of concurring jurors required for the verdict to be valid. American Bar Association, PRINCIPLES FOR JURIES AND JURY TRIALS, Prin. 4 (2005).

6. *What must be unanimous?* Does the right to a unanimous jury verdict mean, literally, that the jurors must agree unanimously about each and every fact in dispute? In *Richardson v. United States*, 526 U.S. 813 (1999), the United States Supreme Court held that in a federal criminal prosecution under the "Continuing Criminal Enterprise" statute, the jurors must agree unanimously on the specific drug violations constituting the "continuing series of [drug law] violations." Basing its decision largely upon statutory interpretation, the six-person majority rejected the government's claim that the jurors were not obligated to agree on which particular offenses the defendant committed. In so holding, however, the Court noted that in some instances factual disagreements are permissible. It explained:

> [A] federal jury need not always decide unanimously which of several possible sets of underlying brute facts make up a particular element, say, which of several possible means the defendant used to commit an element of the crime. Where, for example, an element of robbery is force or the threat of force, some jurors might conclude that the defendant used a knife to create the threat; others might conclude he used a gun. But that disagreement — a disagreement about means — would not matter as long as all 12 jurors unanimously concluded that the Government had proved the necessary related element, namely that the defendant had threatened force. [526 U.S. at 817]

[c] Deadlock

Hung jury and mistrial. Recall that a jury in a criminal case can acquit or convict a defendant of a crime only if the jury returns a verdict that meets a specific vote standard. Usually this means that the jury must be unanimous, although a less-than-unanimous verdict is permissible in some jurisdictions. Assuming that a jurisdiction requires a unanimous vote, what happens if the jury is deadlocked 11-1 in favor of conviction? The jury is a *hung jury* and the court must order a mistrial. The prosecution is free to retry the defendant since the double jeopardy clause does not bar a retrial after a hung jury, as discussed in Chapter 16. Since the defendant was neither convicted nor acquitted, he or she is in a state of limbo, where further prosecution is possible but frequently not conducted.

"Dynamite" or Allen charge. What should the judge do when the foreperson reports that the jury is deadlocked? Often the court inquires whether further deliberations would be fruitful or a waste of time. Sometimes the court also gives an additional jury instruction, often referred to as an *Allen charge* or *dynamite charge.* This instruction was approved in substance by the United States Supreme Court in *Allen v. United States*, 164 U.S. 492, 501 (1896), as follows:

> [I]n a large proportion of cases absolute certainty could not be expected; that, although the verdict must be the verdict of each individual juror, and not a mere acquiescence in the conclusion of his fellows, yet they should examine the question submitted with candor, and with a proper regard and deference to the opinions of each other; that it was their duty to decide the case if they could conscientiously do so; that they should listen, with a disposition to be convinced, to each other's arguments; that, if much the larger number were for conviction, a dissenting juror should consider whether his doubt was a reasonable one which made no impression upon the minds of so many men, equally honest,

equally intelligent with himself. If, upon the other hand, the majority were for acquittal, the minority ought to ask themselves whether they might not reasonably doubt the correctness of a judgment which was not concurred in by the majority.

Opponents of the *Allen* charge contend that it is too coercive, essentially telling those jurors in the minority to reconsider their vote. Some opponents characterize this as judicial intimidation of the hold-outs. This coercion deprives the accused (and the state) of the opportunity for a hung jury, sometimes characterized as an important safeguard against conviction of innocent persons. It also may deflect the jurors from focusing on the evidence to considering the need to reach a decision on something. *See generally* Karen Pelletier O'Sullivan, *Deadlocked Juries and the Allen Charge*, 37 Me. L. Rev. 167 (1985); Note, *On Instructing Deadlocked Juries*, 78 Yale L.J. 100 (1968).

Because of these concerns, a number of jurisdictions have limited the *Allen* charge in various ways. Some simply do not use it. Other jurisdictions limit the timing or frequency of an *Allen*-type charge. In the latter group are those that permit the *Allen* charge to be given only one time, not repeatedly to the same jury, or only during the regular jury instructions and not during deliberations. *E.g.*, Wash. Crim. R. Lim. Juris. 6.15(e) (after jury begins deliberations, court shall not instruct jury on need for agreement, consequences of no agreement, or the length of time the jury will be required to deliberate).

ABA alternate instruction. Finally, a growing number of jurisdictions have replaced the *Allen* instruction with one recommended by the American Bar Association and included in the Standards for Criminal Justice § 15-5.4 (3d ed. 1996). *See, e.g., Commonwealth v. Mitchell*, 943 S.W.2d 625 (Ky. 1997). *See also State v. Howard*, 537 N.E.2d 188 (Ohio 1989) (approving an instruction that incorporates aspects of both *Allen* and the A.B.A. model, but specifically requesting that jurors on *both sides* of the issue reconsider their views).

In *Lowenfield v. Phelps*, 484 U.S. 231, 235 (1988), the Supreme Court, noting that a criminal defendant "is entitled to the uncoerced verdict" of a jury, approved use of the following instruction that paraphrased the American Bar Association's recommendation:

> When you enter the jury room it is your duty to consult with one another to consider each other's views and to discuss the evidence with the objective of reaching a just verdict if you can do so without violence to that individual judgment.

> Each of you must decide the case for yourself but only after discussion and impartial consideration of the case with your fellow jurors. You are not advocates for one side or the other. Do not hesitate to reexamine your own views and to change your opinion if you are convinced you are wrong but do not surrender your honest belief as to the weight and effect of evidence solely because of the opinion of your fellow jurors or for the mere purpose of returning a verdict.

NOTES

1. *Allen or ABA.* Compare the *Allen* and the ABA instructions. Is the ABA approach less coercive? Is it coercive at all? Should either be given? Does either put too much pressure on an individual juror to yield the juror's individual view to that of the majority?

2. *When to give.* How is a trial court to know whether to give an *Allen*-type instruction? One method is for the court to poll the jurors to determine whether additional deliberations would be fruitless or worthwhile. *Lowenfield v. Phelps*, 484 U.S. 231 (1988). Is this process coercive? In *Brasfield v. United States*, 272 U.S. 448 (1926), the Supreme Court held that polling a deadlocked jury to ascertain the numerical division of the jurors is an automatic ground for reversal.

Most state courts, however, have determined that *Brasfield* does not apply to the states either because it is an interpretation of a federal procedural rule (see *State v. Fowler*, 322 S.E.2d 389 (N.C. 1984)) or was a ruling based upon the Supreme Court's supervisory authority over federal courts (*See Scoggins v. State*, 726 So. 2d 762 (Fla. 1999).

Generally, the states take a "totality of the circumstances" approach to jury coercion, and the polling of the jury is but one factor to be considered in determining whether coercion existed. In *Fowler*, for example, the court held that the trial judge who polled the jury on its numerical division but who requested not to be told whether the majority was for acquittal or conviction was not unduly coercive. On the other hand, in *State v. McCrimmon*, 927 P.2d 1298 (Ariz. 1996), coercion was established where the trial judge polled a jury and then repeatedly asked the lone dissenter in private whether she could reach a verdict.

3. *Determining coercion.* In assessing whether a jury was unduly coerced to arrive at a verdict rather than be deadlocked, appellate courts usually look at the entire situation, including the content of jury instructions and other communications between the jury and the judge. *See Lowenfield v. Phelps*, 484 U.S. 231 (1988).

Another key factor is whether the jurors were told that they should not surrender their individual preferences simply to reach a unanimous verdict. *See, e.g., United States v. Bonam*, 772 F.2d 1449 (9th Cir. 1985).

4. *Partial verdict.* Recall that Rule 31(b) permits the jury in a multi-defendant trial to return a verdict on the defendants separately. If the jury cannot agree on the verdict for all the defendants, it may report a verdict on some of the defendants and be a hung jury on the others. In some cases the jury may deliberate for some time, then report to the court that it has reached a verdict on some defendants and is deadlocked on others. Defense counsel may then request a Rule 31(b) instruction, telling the jurors that they may return a partial verdict. Most appellate courts hold that the trial judge need not give this instruction, but must not indicate that a partial verdict is unacceptable. *See, e.g., United States v. Burke*, 700 F.2d 70 (2d Cir.), *cert. denied*, 464 U.S. 816 (1983).

PROBLEM 15-4: WHEN IS ENOUGH, ENOUGH?

Dorothy was tried for two bank robberies that occurred on the same day. The only issue was identity. Tellers at both banks identified Dorothy as the lone robber. Dorothy and her alibi witnesses claimed that she was in another town the day of the robberies. Three hours after the jury began deliberations, it returned to the courtroom and the foreperson gave the judge a note which read, "We are unable to agree on a verdict on both counts because of insufficient evidence."

1. The judge then asked the foreperson how the vote was split. You are Dorothy's attorney. Would you object to the judge's question? If so, on what basis? Would you object if the judge asked, "Are you closer to a unanimous verdict on one count than on the other?"

2. The judge then gave additional jury instructions. Assess the validity of each.

   a. "Ladies and gentlemen. You have got to reach a decision in this case." *See Jenkins v. United States*, 380 U.S. 445 (1965).

   b. "Ladies and gentlemen. This is an important case, a very important one. The taxpayers of our state have paid a lot to have it tried. They pay me, the prosecutor, all the court personnel you see, the costs of maintaining this beautiful courthouse, your expenses, everything. In addition, there is a tremendous backlog of cases in our jurisdiction. If you fail to reach a verdict, we may have to retry this case at considerable expense and delay. Now I have done my job. I have tried to be as fair as I could. Now you must do your job so we can get on with the business of our criminal justice system." *See United States v. Rey*, 811 F.2d 1453 (11th Cir.), *cert. denied*, 482 U.S. 830 (1987).

[d] Jury Justice or Nullification

American juries generally operate in secrecy. Their deliberations are conducted in private and individual jurors ordinarily cannot be questioned about the jury's processes or the juror's personal views or vote. Moreover, during the trial, lawyers for both sides may try to appeal to the jurors' emotions and common sense. It should not be surprising that on occasion a jury does what has been called *jury justice* — renders a verdict that is not justified by the evidence but was influenced by reasons of fairness or prejudice, or some arbitrary factor. Of course jury justice can be used to favor either the defendant or the government. Jury justice favoring the accused is often referred to as *jury nullification*.

Jury justice can take several forms. The obvious one is a conviction or acquittal on all charges, but jury justice may also produce a conviction for a lesser crime or on some but not all charges. Assume, for example, the defendant is a woman charged with intentional murder of her husband, for which there is clearly proof of guilt beyond a reasonable doubt. She killed with repeated doses of a slow-acting poison that she discovered while reading an article entitled, "How to Kill Without Being Caught." Manslaughter is a lesser-included crime. It is possible that despite the evidence, a jury will acquit the defendant of murder and convict her of manslaughter because of sympathy for her and an antipathy for the deceased victim, who had beaten the defendant many times during a long marriage but had not beaten her for several months before his death.

Juries may exercise their nullification powers for many reasons. They may disagree with the crime, the punishment, or the application of the law in the particular case. A more politically interesting rationale is to send a message, such as by acquitting the environmentalists who trespass on lawn to protest a new strip mine that is opposed by the local populace.

The actual impact of jury justice is difficult to assess because of the double jeopardy clause. If jury justice results in a conviction contrary to the evidence of innocence, the accused can appeal. If the jury relies on jury justice to acquit the accused, however, the double jeopardy clause, discussed in Chapter 16, bars the government from appealing.

In eighteenth century America, "it was commonly accepted that a defendant had the right to a jury which found both facts and determined whether the law should apply." Arie Rubenstein, Note, *Verdicts of Conscience, Nullification, and the Modern Jury Trial*, 106 COL. L. REV. 959, 960 (2006). Today, most jurisdictions reject the traditional view and conclude that jury justice is inconsistent with many important legal principles. Jurors are instructed to follow the law, to be fair to all sides, and to base their decision on the evidence presented at trial. If a jury acquits a defendant because he or she was poor or uneducated, because the victim deserved the beating, or because the jury disliked the prosecutor, many people argue that the rule of law is compromised and the jury is not performing its proper functions. Reflecting the trend against jury nullification, the Supreme Court itself noted,

> Public and private safety alike would be in peril if the principle be established that juries in criminal cases may, of right, disregard the law as expounded to them by the court, and become a law unto themselves.

Sparf v. United States, 156 U.S. 51, 101 (1895). *See also United States v. Krzyske*, 836 F.2d 1013 (6th Cir. 1988) (jury instructed there was no such thing as jury nullification and that jury would violate its oath if it returned a verdict contrary to the law).

Despite these concerns, American courts have consistently held that jury justice is permissible if it results in leniency. In the leading case, the Supreme Court observed:

> The main reason ordinarily assigned for a recognition of the right of the jury, in a criminal case, to take the law into their own hands, and to disregard the

directions of the court in matters of law, is that the safety and liberty of the citizen [defendant] will be thereby more certainly secured. [*Sparf v. United States*, 156 U.S. 51, 106 (1895)]

Perhaps one reason jury nullification is tolerated is that there is no way to stop it, since acquittals and jury processes are not reviewable.

The California Supreme Court has recognized that "nullification jurors" may be discharged at the deliberation stage of a criminal case. While acknowledging that juries have the power to return verdicts of acquittal contrary to law, when a juror expresses unwillingness to follow the trial judge's instructions, that juror may be removed for the "[inability] to perform his duty." Moreover, a clear refusal to deliberate also may result in the juror's discharge. The court cautioned, however, that trial judges must find that there is a "demonstrable reality" that the juror is unable or unwilling to deliberate before removing that juror. Finally, this inquiry should focus on the juror's conduct and not on the content of deliberations. *People v. Williams*, 21 P.3d 1209 (Cal. 2001), *People v. Cleveland*, 21 P.3d 1225 (Cal. 2001).

[i] Jury Instructions on Nullification

If jury nullification is part of the American criminal justice system (perhaps because there is nothing that can be done when it happens), should jurors be instructed on it as part of the routine package of jury instructions outlining the jury's duties? Obviously defense counsel would prefer that such instructions be given. One requested the following:

> If you feel strongly about the values involved in this case [alleging failure to file tax returns], so strongly that your conscience is aroused, then you may, as the conscience for the community, disregard the strict requirements of the law. You should disregard the law only if the requirements of the law cannot justly be applied in this case. By disregarding the law, you may use your common sense judgment and find a verdict according to your conscience.

Following the traditional view, the court refused defense counsel's request. *United States v. Powell*, 955 F.2d 1206, 1213 (9th Cir. 1992).

Majority view: reject nullification instruction. The usual reason for rejecting such jury instructions is a fear that "anarchy would result from instructing the jury that it may ignore the requirements of the law." *Id.* Another court noted that a jury instruction on nullification would "have undermined the impartial determination of justice based on law." *United States v. Krzyske*, 836 F.2d 1013 (6th Cir. 1988).

Minority view: permit nullification instruction. A distinct minority of jurisdictions permit jury instructions on nullification. *See, e.g., State v. Mayo*, 480 A.2d 85 (N.H. 1984) (nullification instructions discretionary).

Impact of nullification instruction. The presence or absence of jury nullification instructions appears to affect both the content and the outcome of jury deliberations. One study shows that when a jury is instructed that it has the discretion whether to apply the law to the facts, the jury is more prone to acquit sympathetic defendants and more likely to convict unsympathetic ones. If the nullification suggestion occurs in counsel's argument and is countered by adversary counsel's objection, the jury generally is not swayed toward nullification. I. Horowitz, *Jury Nullification: The Impact of Judicial Instructions, Arguments, and Challenges on Jury Decision Making*, 12 L. & HUM. BEHAV. 439 (1988).

Policy dilemma. The refusal to instruct on jury nullification creates an anomaly that reflects the criminal justice system's conflicted approach to the issue. While American law permits jury nullification in order to protect the citizen from the state, in most jurisdictions it simultaneously bars a jury instruction on the issue. Does this conflicting approach make sense?

The issue is magnified by empirical data showing the general public is unaware of a jury's nullification power. *See* David C. Brody & Craig Rivera, *Examining the Dougherty "All-Knowing" Assumption": Do Jurors Know About Their Jury Nullification Power*, 33 CRIM. L. BULL. 151 (1997)(less than 5% of potential New York jurors aware of nullification power).

[ii] Argument by Counsel on Nullification

Even if jury instructions do not include guidance on jury nullification, can defense counsel use closing argument to ask the jury to disregard the law and acquit the accused? Most courts do not permit this form of argument, reasoning that it would violate the rule that the jury is to apply the law contained in the jury instructions. *See, e.g., United States v. Trujillo*, 714 F.2d 102 (11th Cir. 1983).

A minority of courts do permit defense counsel to discuss jury nullification in closing argument. *See, e.g., United States v. Krzyske*, 836 F.2d 1013 (6th Cir. 1988); *State v. Mayo*, 480 A.2d 85 (N.H. 1984). When defense counsel makes an emotional appeal on behalf of the defendant, however, is there any way to prevent an indirect appeal for jury nullification? *See generally* Christopher C. Schwan, Comment, *Right Up to the Line: The Ethics of Advancing Nullification Arguments to the Jury*, 29 J. LEGAL. PROF. 293 (2005)(techniques lawyers may use).

[iii] Other Procedural Aspects of Jury Justice

The possibility of jury nullification may influence many procedural facets of the criminal trial. Since jury nullification is technically a violation of the jurors' oaths, many judges will attempt to limit the information that could influence jurors to ignore the judge's instruction and render a jury justice verdict. Lawyers for both sides, on the other hand, may attempt to provide the jury with information that would promote jury justice for one side or against the other side.

Jury selection. The possibility of jury justice may influence the jury selection process. For example, the defense lawyer may seek jurors who will be empathetic toward the defendant and sufficiently independent to ignore the judge's jury instructions and may reject jurors who will rigidly apply the law and have little sympathy for the defendant.

For an excellent article arguing that jury selection procedures designed to counter jury nullification interfere with the defendant's right to a heterogeneous jury, *see* Chaya Weinbert-Brodt, Note, *Jury Nullification and Jury-Control Procedures*, 65 N.Y.U. L. REV. 825 (1990) (proposing a defendant-centered system which openly faces and sometimes endorses jury nullification). It should be noted, however, that courts have excluded "nullifiers" from the jury box throughout the years because of their refusal to abide by the law. Indeed, recent cases intimate that judges are quick to excuse for cause those potential jurors who have been exposed to pro-nullification advocacy. *See* Nancy J. King, *Silencing Nullification Advocacy Inside the Jury Room and Outside the Courtroom*, 65 U. CHI. L. REV. 433 (1998).

Evidence. Jury nullification may also affect the evidence that is offered and the court's ruling on objections. For example, in order to elicit sympathy for the accused, the defense lawyer may attempt to introduce evidence about the victim's bad character and the defendant's good character. The prosecution may file a motion *in limine* to exclude it, arguing that this evidence should be excluded if its only relevance is jury nullification. In order to reduce the likelihood of jury justice, the judge may throw out marginal evidence that could affect jurors' sympathy toward a party.

[iv] Recent Jury Nullification Proposals

African-American considerations. Professor Paul Butler urges African-American jurors to "approach their work cognizant of its political nature and their prerogative to exercise their power in the best interests of the black community." Paul Butler, *Racially Based Jury Nullification: Black Power in the Criminal Justice System*, 105 YALE L.J. 677, 715 (1995). Specifically, he proposes as follows:[*]

> In cases involving violent *malum in se* crimes like murder, rape, and assault, jurors should consider the case strictly on the evidence presented, and, if they have no reasonable doubt that the defendant is guilty, they should convict. For non-violent *malum in se* crimes such as theft or perjury, nullification is an option that the juror should consider, although there should be no presumption in favor of it. A juror might vote for acquittal, for example, when a poor woman steals from Tiffany's, but not when the same woman steals from her next-door neighbor. Finally, in cases involving non-violent, *malum prohibitum* offenses, including "victimless" crimes like narcotics offenses, there should be a presumption in favor of nullification.

Professor Butler acknowledges the need to convey this information to jurors and that, because of *Sparf*, jury instructions would likely not be the appropriate vehicle for doing so. Accordingly, he proposes that this information be disseminated through a variety of intraracial communication techniques such as black newspapers and magazines, rap songs, ministers' sermons and convention gatherings.

Bifurcated deliberations. Professors David Dorfman and Chris Iijima propose that jury nullification be accommodated through a bifurcated deliberation process. David Dorfman and Chris Iijima, *Fictions, Fault and Forgiveness: Jury Nullification in a New Context*, 28 U. MICH. J. L. REF. 861 (1995). Under their recommendation, the first stage would be similar to the usual jury deliberation in which the jury applies the law received from the judge to the facts. If, as a result of this deliberation, the jury finds the defendant not guilty, the deliberations are over and the case is concluded. On the other hand, if the jury finds the defendant guilty, it would be instructed by the court to return to the jury room "for a second deliberation to determine whether, as a matter of conscience, [the individual] circumstances present the extraordinary situation where a verdict of guilty will result in an injustice of such magnitude that the defendant should be acquitted notwithstanding [the jury's] provisional finding of guilt." Interestingly, the authors propose that if not more than five jurors vote not guilty during the "nullification" stage, the jury should return a verdict of guilty based upon its findings during the first stage of deliberations. However, if six or more (but not all) vote not guilty at the second stage, it should report to the judge that there is "an impasse." And if the impasse remains, a mistrial should be declared. Thus, a unanimous vote of not guilty notwithstanding factual guilt is the only vote sufficient to permit a verdict of not guilty once the second stage has been reached.

The authors recommend this procedure because of their sense that it will encourage "true deliberation rather than confusion, caprice, or bad faith." They also acknowledge that such a system may not be efficient:

> Implementation of such procedures will not necessarily make trial procedure more efficient. It probably will not diminish the length of most trials and may even lengthen others. It will do very little for clogged court calendars and overcrowded jails. But it will enhance integrity in the jury's work. Instead of nullifying the judge's instructions by focusing on surrogate issues . . . the jury will be given the opportunity to consider directly the issue of justice. [*Id.* at 925]

Legislation. It is interesting to note that in 1995, ten legislatures introduced measures to require that trial judges instruct juries on their nullification right. *See*

David C. Brody, *Sparf and Dougherty Revisited: Why the Court Should Instruct the Jury of its Nullification Right*, 33 Am. Crim. L. Rev. 89 (1995) (evaluating the opposing arguments and articulating both a model instruction and procedures a trial court can take when nullification may be an issue).

[e] Inconsistent Verdicts

Sometimes a jury returns *inconsistent verdicts* — multiple verdicts that are inconsistent with one another. The inconsistency may be one of two kinds: *multiple-count inconsistency* or *multiple-defendant inconsistency*. A multiple-count inconsistency may arise when a defendant is charged with a compound crime, a crime based upon the commission of another crime. For example, a defendant could be charged with possessing cocaine with the intent to distribute and also with the offense of using a telephone to commit that offense. The telephone count is a compound crime in that it has as an element the commission of a separate crime, the possession of cocaine. A jury could acquit the defendant of the possession charge but convict him or her of using a telephone to commit the possession offense. The jury, then, has effectively said that the defendant is both guilty and not guilty of the crime of possession; it has produced an inconsistent verdict.

An example of a multiple-defendant inconsistency is the case of a defendant and his or her co-defendant charged with committing the crime of conspiracy (requiring an agreement between at least two people to commit an illegal act). The jury could acquit one defendant of conspiracy while convicting the other, thereby producing an inconsistent verdict. *See*, Eric L. Muller, *The Hobgoblin of Little Minds? Our Foolish Law of Inconsistent Verdicts*, 111 Harv. L. Rev. 771 (1998) (discussing these hypotheticals in detail).

Inconsistent verdicts were rarely an issue in America until the twentieth century, when multiple-count indictments became permissible. In *Dunn v. United States*, 284 U.S. 390 (1931), the defendant was indicted for three crimes: maintaining a nuisance by keeping for sale intoxicating liquor; unlawful possession of intoxicating liquor; and unlawful sale of intoxicating liquor. The evidence showed that a revenue agent bought whiskey from a bar located in a room at the back of defendant's fishing tackle store. The jury convicted the defendant of the first count and acquitted him of the other two. On appeal, the defendant argued that the acquittal for the last two counts was inconsistent with his conviction on the first count, which should be dismissed. Rather than discuss whether the counts really were inconsistent, the Supreme Court held that consistency is not necessary. Each count in an indictment is treated as if it were a separate indictment. According to the Supreme Court, an inconsistent verdict may mean that the jury did not vote in accordance with its true beliefs as to guilt or innocence but rather showed lenity, compromise, or even mistake.

Dunn established the general rule that inconsistent verdicts are permissible. Subsequent decisions cast doubt on this rule, however, when the doctrine of collateral estoppel was applied in criminal cases. *See Ashe v. Swenson*, 397 U.S. 436 (1970), discussed in Chapter 16. If the defendant is acquitted of one charge, collateral estoppel doctrine holds that the facts resolved in the acquittal cannot be relitigated in another criminal case. For example, *Ashe* involved the robbery of a number of people at the same time. If the defendant were acquitted of one of the robberies, he or she could not be convicted of the others, assuming all the crimes happened at the same time and were committed by the same person.

In *United States v. Powell*, 469 U.S. 57 (1984), the Supreme Court reaffirmed *Dunn*. The defendant in *Powell* was indicted on 10 counts of violating federal drug laws. The jury acquitted the defendant of (count 1) conspiracy to possess cocaine with intent to distribute, (count 9) possession of cocaine with intent to distribute, and one count (count 6) of using a telephone to facilitate a drug conspiracy. The jury convicted the defendant of three counts (counts 3, 4, 5) of using a telephone to facilitate a conspiracy. Because of the facts of the case, both the defense and the government agreed that the verdicts were inconsistent. If the defendant were guilty of the three telephone facilitation counts (counts 3-5), she would also be guilty of the conspiracy (count 1) and the possession offenses (count 9), since the latter crimes were elements of the telephone facilitation crimes.

The *Powell* defendant argued that acquittal of counts 1 and 6 mandated acquittal on counts 3–5. The Supreme Court disagreed and affirmed the convictions. The Court reaffirmed the *Dunn* Court's holding that inconsistent verdicts do not offend the Constitution. The Court reasoned:

> We believe that the *Dunn* rule rests on a sound rationale that is independent of its theories of res judicata, and that it therefore survives an attack based upon its presently erroneous reliance on such theories . . . . The rule that the defendant may not upset such a verdict embodies a prudent acknowledgment of a number of factors. First, . . . inconsistent verdicts — even verdicts that acquit on a predicate offense while convicting on the compound offense — should not necessarily be interpreted as a windfall to the Government at the defendant's expense. It is equally possible that the jury, convinced of guilt, properly reached its conclusion on the compound offense, and then through mistake, compromise, or lenity, arrived at an inconsistent conclusion on the lesser offense. But in such situations the Government has no recourse if it wishes to correct the jury's error; the Government is precluded from appealing or otherwise upsetting such an acquittal by the Constitution's Double Jeopardy Clause.

> Inconsistent verdicts therefore present a situation where "error," in the sense that the jury has not followed the court's instructions, most certainly has occurred, but it is unclear whose ox has been gored. Given this uncertainty, and the fact that the Government is precluded from challenging the acquittal, it is hardly satisfactory to allow the defendant to receive a new trial on the conviction as a matter of course.

> . . . We also reject, as imprudent and unworkable, a rule that would allow criminal defendants to challenge inconsistent verdicts on the ground that in their case the verdict was not the product of lenity, but of some error that worked against them. Such an individualized assessment of the reason for the inconsistency would be based either on pure speculation, or would require inquiries into the jury's deliberations that courts generally will not undertake.

> . . . Finally, we note that a criminal defendant already is afforded protection against jury irrationality or error by the independent review of the sufficiency of the evidence undertaken by the trial and appellate courts. This review should not be confused with the problems caused by inconsistent verdicts. Sufficiency-of-the-evidence review involves assessment by the courts of whether the evidence adduced at trial could support any rational determination of guilty beyond a reasonable doubt. This review should be independent of the jury's determination that evidence on another count was insufficient. [*Id.* at 64–67]

NOTES

1. *Inconsistent verdict and jury nullification.* Does *Powell* reaffirm the propriety of jury nullification?

2. *Fairness.* Both *Dunn* and *Powell* focus on the likelihood that inconsistent verdicts result from jury leniency. But both opinions also recognize that the inconsistent results could also stem from prejudice or error. Do you think *Powell* provides adequate assurances that criminal defendants will not be convicted of crimes because a jury was prejudiced or simply mistaken?

3. *Jury instructions.* If inconsistent verdicts are not reversible error, should the jury be instructed that it may return inconsistent verdicts?

4. *Special verdicts.* If special verdicts were used in multiple-count and multiple-defendant cases, would their use effectively negate the underpinnings of *Dunn* and *Powell* by eliminating uncertainty about the jury's rationale?

5. *Collateral estoppel.* When *Powell* held that inconsistent verdicts do not invalidate either verdict, it created a significant block to the use of collateral estoppel in certain circumstances. As discussed more fully in Chapter 16, collateral estoppel would prevent a subsequent trial of the same issue that resulted in an acquittal in an earlier trial. But if there is an inconsistent verdict when a jury convicted the defendant of one count and acquitted on the other count, *Powell* indicates that the doctrine of collateral estoppel is inapplicable to invalidate the conviction. *See generally* Anne Bowen Poulin, *Collateral Estoppel in Criminal Cases: Reuse of Evidence After Acquittal*, 58 U. Cin. L. Rev. 1, 39–48 (1989).

6. *State variations.* Some state courts apply state law to reverse inconsistent verdicts. In *DeSacia v. State*, 469 P.2d 369 (Alas. 1970), the Alaska Supreme Court reversed a conviction involving inconsistent verdicts because under Alaska law there must be at least a minimal degree of reasonableness in a jury's decision. Similarly, at least two states recognize that trial judges act appropriately in refusing to accept inconsistent verdicts. *See People v. Klingenberg*, 665 N.E.2d 1370 (Ill. 1996); *State v. Peters*, 855 S.W.2d 345 (Mo. 1993).

[f] Impeachment of Jury Verdict

If a jury convicts the defendant of a crime, he or she may decide to challenge the verdict. Several possible grounds relate to the jury processes. The range of possible misconduct is vast. Examples include allegations that a juror was biased (perhaps also lied during voir dire), drunk, insane, bribed, or slept through the trial or deliberations; that jurors used outside information, such as a newspaper or book, in their deliberations; that during deliberations someone, other than a juror, spoke with a juror about the case; and that jurors misunderstood the jury instructions.

The defendant may allege that one or more such problems caused the jury to perform in a way that violated due process or the Sixth Amendment's jury trial guarantee of a competent jury. The Supreme Court has held that the criminal defendant has a right to a tribunal that is both impartial and mentally competent to afford a hearing. *Tanner v. United States*, 483 U.S. 107, 126 (1987).

Another theory is that the jury processes violated the accused's Sixth Amendment right to confront the accusers. *See, e.g., Rushen v. Spain*, 464 U.S. 114 (1983) (*ex parte* communications between the judge and a juror, never reported to either counsel, may violate confrontation right); *Parker v. Gladden*, 385 U.S. 363 (1966) (bailiff told several jurors during deliberations that defendant was guilty and Supreme Court would correct any error if defendant were found guilty; violated confrontation rights).

In order to succeed, however, the convicted defendant has what may be a difficult burden of proving prejudice. *See, e.g., United States v. Taliaferro*, 558 F.2d 724 (4th Cir. 1977) (defendant unable to prove prejudice when jurors consumed liquor during meal eaten while jury deliberating).

[i] Bias and Lies During Voir Dire

One ground for attacking a verdict is that a juror was biased against the accused, thereby violating the Sixth Amendment's guarantee of an impartial jury. Usually this ground alleges that the juror lied or somehow withheld information during the voir dire process.

McDonough Power Equipment, Inc. v. Greenwood, 464 U.S. 548 (1984), was a civil case involving injuries caused by a lawnmower. During voir dire, a juror did not disclose that a member of his family had suffered a severe accidental injury, despite being questioned on that point. Assuming that the juror did not intend to mislead counsel during voir dire, the Supreme Court established a standard of review:

> We hold that to obtain a new trial in such a situation, a party must first demonstrate that a juror failed to answer honestly a material question on *voir dire*, and then further show that a correct response would have provided a valid basis for a challenge for cause. The motives for concealing information may vary, but only those reasons that affect a juror's impartiality can truly be said to affect the fairness of a trial. *[Id.* at 556]

The *Greenwood* court remanded the case to apply the new test. This standard was applied to reverse a conviction where the juror lied about knowing the defendant and prior involvement in litigation. *United States v. Perkins*, 748 F.2d 1519 (11th Cir. 1984) (with emphasis on the fact that the juror gave false answers during voir dire). *Cf. State v. Thomas*, 830 P.2d 243 (Utah 1992) (applying *Greenwood* but disagreeing with the *Perkins* emphasis on the juror's purposeful act; juror's partiality, not her intent, is key consideration).

[ii]   The Problem of Proof

Even if a juror misbehaved and the error would cause the verdict to be overturned, there may be no way of proving it. In order to protect jurors from harassment and to encourage finality in judicial proceedings, American courts have traditionally barred jurors from testifying about most facets of the deliberations. The usual rule is that jurors may not testify about "internal" jury processes. This is read as barring their testimony about the deliberative process. A juror can be questioned about "external" influences, such as contact with outsiders or the use of evidence not introduced during the trial. Federal Rule of Evidence 606(b) is typical:

FEDERAL RULES OF EVIDENCE

Rule 606. Competency of Juror as Witness

> . . . .

> (b) *Inquiry into validity of verdict or indictment.* Upon an inquiry into the validity of a verdict or indictment, a juror may not testify as to any matter or statement occurring during the course of the jury's deliberations or to the effect of anything upon that or any other juror's mind or emotions as influencing the juror to assent to or dissent from the verdict or indictment or concerning the juror's mental processes in connection therewith, except that a juror may testify on the question whether extraneous prejudicial information was improperly brought to the jury's attention or whether any outside influence was improperly brought to bear upon any juror. Nor may a juror's affidavit or evidence of any statement by the juror concerning a matter about which the juror would be precluded from testifying be received for these purposes.

NOTES

1. *Illustrations of impermissible topics.* Courts interpreting Rule 606(b) have held that after a verdict, jurors are not competent to testify about the following misconduct that occurred during deliberations or the trial: a juror was intoxicated or asleep; the judge's jury instructions were coercive or not followed; the jurors hurried their deliberations in order to finish quickly; and a juror feared government recriminations if the juror voted to acquit. *See Tanner v. United States*, 483 U.S.107 (1987) (cannot inquire into drug and alcohol use during trial).

2. *Illustrations of permissible topics.* On the other hand, federal courts have permitted jurors to testify about "extraneous" influences such as the fact that individual jurors had received threats; a juror conducted an experiment designed to test plaintiff's theory; or a juror had been present at the trial of three other persons charged in the crime and heard testimony not presented at this trial.

3. *Other methods of proof.* Although it may be impossible to prove malfeasance by the testimony or affidavits of jurors, other methods of proof are possible. In *United States v. Taliaferro,* 558 F.2d 724 (4th Cir. 1977), for example, the defendant alleged that the conviction should be overturned because the jurors drank liquor during deliberations. As proof, he introduced the records of the restaurant where the jurors dined and the testimony of the marshall who accompanied the jurors.

Can *Tanner* and *Taliaferro* be reconciled? Consider the following case: The defendant was on trial for having been involved in a fatal accident while allegedly under the influence of intoxicants at the time of the collision. During cross-examination of a defense witness, the prosecutor referred to a prior incident in which the defendant had been ticketed for speeding. The trial judge sustained a defense objection, and the jury was instructed to disregard the speeding ticket. After a verdict of guilt, the jury foreperson stated under oath that, despite the court's instruction, members of the jury had discussed the speeding ticket during deliberations. Specifically, he stated that he had been holding out for an acquittal until three members of the jury used the prior ticket to persuade him to vote guilty. Based upon this statement, which was contradicted by other jurors, the trial judge granted the defendant a new trial. The Florida Supreme Court held that the trial judge acted improperly by inquiring into matters occurring in the jury room and by permitting a juror to testify to such matters. The matters involved in this case were ones that "inhere in the verdict itself" and cannot be explored. Such matters, according to the court, are "subjective in nature whereas matters that are extrinsic to the verdict, and may therefore be the subject of post-verdict inquiry, are objective. To permit the verdict to be impugned on the basis of the foreperson's allegations "would sow the seeds for the destruction of" the jury system. *Devoney v. State,* 717 So. 2d 501 (Fla. 1998).

[iii]   Attorney's Post-Trial Contact with Jurors

After a jury verdict, counsel for the losing (and sometimes winning) party may be interested in learning about what happened during the jury's deliberations. One reason is simply to improve counsel's performance in the next trial by getting feedback on various facets of the trial. For example, a lawyer may be interested in learning whether a particular witness or closing argument was effective. A second reason for inquiring into the jury's processes is to determine whether there is any ground to reverse the judgment. Recall that reversal is possible for some malfeasance in the jury room.

To achieve these goals, counsel has to communicate with the jurors. This may pose few practical problems since the trial lawyers likely have the jurors' names and addresses. The problem, of course, is that during this communication the jurors may feel harassed or intimidated, and jurors may be less than candid during jury deliberations because of the concern that their comments will be the subject of aggressive post-trial inquiries by trial counsel.

Because of these fears, many jurisdictions have adopted rules limiting counsel's post-trial contact with the trial jurors. A common example is a court rule barring lawyers from having post-trial contact with jurors without court permission, which is given after a showing of "good cause." Other rules permit such contacts only in open court under the judge's supervision and/or only after notice to adversary counsel or the court. Another approach is to encourage the court to permit lawyer-juror contact after the trial is over. *See, e.g.,* American Bar Association, PRINCIPLES FOR JURIES AND JURY TRIALS, Prin. 18 (after trial, court should instruct jurors they have a right to discuss or not discuss the case with anyone; court should ordinarily permit the parties to contact jurors after the end of the juror's term of jury service).

Surprisingly, the various ethical and professional standards contain relatively few restrictions on counsel's post-trial contact with jurors. The most comprehensive discussion is provided by the American Bar Association's Defense Function, which states:

> After discharge of the jury from further consideration of a case, defense counsel should not intentionally make comments to or ask questions of a juror for the purpose of harassing or embarrassing the juror in any way which will tend to influence judgment in future jury service. If defense counsel believes that the verdict may be subject to legal challenge, he or she may properly, if no statute or rule prohibits such course, communicate with jurors to determine whether such challenge may be available.

STANDARDS FOR CRIMINAL JUSTICE § 4–7.3(c) (3d ed. 1993). There is a similar standard for prosecutors. *Id.* § 3–5.4(c).

The Model Code of Professional Responsibility simply bars a lawyer, after discharge of the jury, from communicating with former jurors in a way calculated to harass or embarrass the juror or influence the juror's actions in future deliberations. MODEL CODE OF PROFESSIONAL RESPONSIBILITY DR 7-108(D) (1980). Another section extends this to the former juror's family. *Id.* DR 7-108(F). The Model Rules of Professional Conduct bar an attorney from using means designed to embarrass, delay or burden a former juror, or that violate the person's legal rights. MODEL RULES OF PROFESSIONAL CONDUCT Rule 4.4 (1983). For a critical discussion of restrictions on post-trial contact by attorneys with jurors, see Benjamin M. Lawsky, Note, *Limitations on Attorney Postverdict Contact with Jurors: Protecting the Criminal Jury and its Verdict at the Expense of the Defendant*, 94 COLUM. L. REV. 1950 (1994) (concluding that such limitations tread on a criminal defendant's Sixth Amendment rights by impeding discovery of jury misconduct).

[g] Non-Jury Verdicts

If a criminal defendant waives a jury or is not entitled to one because the case is considered to be a "petty crime," the trial will be conducted by the judge. In such cases, it is often said that the judge's responsibility is to weigh the evidence, determine the credibility of witnesses, and find the facts. Although the judge may render a decision any time after final argument, usually the decision on guilt or innocence comes quite quickly after the closing arguments. The judge may delay imposing sentence until a later date to permit both sides and the probation department to gather information about the offense and the defendant and to explore sentencing alternatives.

In most jurisdictions the court simply pronounces whether the defendant is guilty or innocent on each count. Federal law also gives either side a right to have the judge make a *specific finding* in some circumstances. A special finding is a decision as to the specific facts that formed the basis for the general verdict.

FEDERAL RULES OF CRIMINAL PROCEDURE

Rule 23. *Jury or Nonjury Trial*

. . . .

(c) Nonjury Trial. In a case tried without a jury, the court must find the defendant guilty or not guilty. If a party requests before the finding of guilty or not guilty, the court must state its specific findings of fact in open court or in a written decision or opinion.

NOTES

Note that the right to a specific finding on the facts is triggered by request of counsel. The rule specifically provides that the request must be made before the judge returns a general verdict in the trial (it does not apply to decisions on motions). A request made after the general verdict is issued is viewed as being untimely and constitutes a waiver of the right to a verdict. Of course, the judge is free to provide specific findings even without a request by either side. Since Rule 23 states that the specific findings may be made orally, they are usually made at the same time the general verdict is announced in open court.

This request should be made in especially complex cases where it is possible the judge may misunderstand the issues or base the conviction on an erroneous finding of fact. It will greatly facilitate appellate review since it will provide the appellate court with data about the logic used by the trial court.

K. MOTIONS AFTER GUILTY VERDICT

Just as numerous motions may be filed with the court before and during a criminal trial, the defendant may submit motions after a verdict of guilty has been returned either by the jury or the trial judge. In some jurisdictions, the failure to file an appropriate motion after a guilty verdict may preclude an assertion of certain arguments on appeal. Counsel should carefully assess all possible motions, with particular emphasis on the subject matter germane to each motion and specified time limitations.

[1] Motion for Judgment of Acquittal

A motion for judgment of acquittal must be granted "if the evidence is insufficient to sustain a conviction." In most jurisdictions, this motion is made routinely by the defense after the prosecution has presented its proof but may also be made at the close of the defendant's proof and even after the jury has been discharged following its return of a guilty verdict. Even if the motion is made at or before the close of all the evidence, the court may reserve ruling on the motion, submit the case to the jury, and then make the appropriate ruling after the jury returns a guilty verdict or is discharged without returning a verdict. Usually, a post-verdict motion for judgment of acquittal may be made even if an earlier motion was not submitted by counsel. The federal rule is typical.

FEDERAL RULES OF CRIMINAL PROCEDURE

Rule 29. *Motion for a Judgment of Acquittal*

. . . .

(b) **Reserving Decision.** The court may reserve decision on the motion, proceed with the trial (where the motion is made before the close of all the evidence), submit the case to the jury, and decide the motion either before the jury returns a verdict or after it returns a verdict of guilty or is discharged without having returned a verdict. If the court reserves decision, it must decide the motion on the basis of the evidence at the time the ruling was reserved.

(c) **After Jury Verdict or Discharge.**

(1) **Time for a Motion**. A defendant may move for a judgment of acquittal, or renew such a motion, within 7 days after a guilty verdict or after the court discharges the jury, whichever is later, or within any other time the court sets during the 7-day period.

(2) Ruling on the Motion. If the jury has returned a guilty verdict, the court may set aside the verdict and enter an acquittal. If the jury has failed to return a verdict, the court may enter a judgment of acquittal.

(3) No Prior Motion Required. A defendant is not required to move for a judgment of acquittal before the court submits the case to the jury as a prerequisite for making such a motion after jury discharge.

(d) Conditional Ruling on a Motion for a New Trial.

(1) Motion for a New Trial. If the court enters a judgment of acquittal after a guilty verdict, the court must also conditionally determine whether any motion for a new trial should be granted if the judgment of acquittal is later vacated or reversed. The court must specify the reasons for that determination.

(2) Finality. The court's order conditionally granting a motion for a new trial does not affect the finality of the judgment of acquittal.

(3) Appeal.

(A) Grant of a Motion for a New Trial. If the court conditionally grants a motion for a new trial and an appellate court later reverses the judgment of acquittal, the trial court must proceed with the new trial unless the appellate court orders otherwise.

(B) Denial of a Motion for a New Trial. If the court conditionally denies a motion for a new trial, an appellee may assert that the denial was erroneous. If the appellate court later reverses the judgment of acquittal, the trial court must proceed as the appellate court directs.

NOTES

1. *Double jeopardy.* If the court grants an acquittal motion, the double jeopardy guarantee usually bars a government appeal of the motion. When an acquittal motion is granted after a jury verdict of guilt, however, the government is permitted an appeal in order to demonstrate error by the trial court in granting the acquittal motion. If the government prevails, its requested relief is reinstatement of the guilty verdict. *See United States v. Martin Linen Supply Co.*, 430 U.S. 564 (1977).

2. *Timeliness.* Note that a Rule 29 motion must be made or renewed within 7 days after the jury is discharged. Does a federal district court have authority to grant such a motion if it is filed one day late? No, answered the United States Supreme Court in *Carlisle v. United States*, 517 U.S. 416 (1996). Finding the rule plain and unambiguous, Justice Scalia also concluded that a district court's "inherent power" does not include the power "to develop rules that circumvent or conflict with the Federal Rules of Criminal Procedure." Therefore the Court affirmed the circuit court's reversal of the judgment of acquittal and remanded for reinstatement of the jury's verdict.

[2]   Motion for New Trial

This motion may encompass a wider range of issues than the motion for judgment of acquittal. In federal criminal cases, this motion is governed by Rule 33:

FEDERAL RULES OF CRIMINAL PROCEDURE

Rule 33. *New Trial*

(a) Defendant's Motion. Upon the defendant's motion, the court may vacate any judgment and grant a new trial if the interest of justice so requires. If the case was tried without a jury, the court may take additional testimony and enter a new judgment.

(b) Time to File.

(1) **Newly Discovered Evidence.** Any motion for a new trial grounded on newly discovered evidence must be filed within 3 years after the verdict or finding of guilty. If an appeal is pending, the court may not grant a motion for a new trial until the appellate court remands the case.

(2) **Other Grounds.** Any motion for a new trial grounded on any reason other than newly discovered evidence must be filed within 7 days after the verdict or finding of guilty, or within such further time as the court sets during the 7-day period.

NOTES

1. *Types of errors.* Due to the vague standard enunciated in Rule 33 ("interests of justice"), a wide range of errors may be specifically alleged. According to one commentator, bases for a new trial include prosecutorial misconduct, prejudicial exposure of jurors to news accounts, incorrect jury instructions, improper introduction of evidence, and misconduct of the jury. *See* James C. Cissell, FEDERAL CRIMINAL TRIALS § 13-1(b) (5th ed. 1999). Some states permit the granting of a new trial based upon an assessment of the evidence itself. *See* Tenn. R. Crim. P. 33(f): "The trial court may grant a new trial following a verdict of guilty if it disagrees with the jury about the weight of the evidence."

2. *Newly discovered evidence.* Note that Rule 33 also authorizes a court to order a new trial because of "newly discovered evidence." In federal cases, an exacting test must be satisfied before a judge will grant a new trial on this ground: the evidence must not have been known to the defendant at the time of the trial, the newly discovered evidence must be material to the issues involved, and the evidence must be so significant that it probably would produce an acquittal. *See* James C. Cissell, FEDERAL CRIMINAL TRIALS § 13-1(a) (5th ed. 1999). It also should be noted that the period of time in which such a motion can be made is three years, as opposed to seven days.

[3]   Motion in Arrest of Judgment

This post-verdict judgment, which can even be granted after a plea of guilty, is usually limited to very precise matters. The granting of such a motion renders the judgment void. In federal criminal cases, this is governed by Rule 34:

FEDERAL RULES OF CRIMINAL PROCEDURE

Rule 34. *Arresting Judgment*

(a) **In General.** Upon the defendant's motion or on its own, the court must arrest judgment if:

(1) the indictment or information does not charge an offense; or

(2) the court does not have jurisdiction of the charged offense.

(b) **Time to File.** The defendant must move to arrest judgment within 7 days after the court accepts a verdict or finding of guilty, or after a plea of guilty or nolo contendere, or within such further time as the court sets during the 7-day period.

NOTES

1. *State variations.* Some states list additional grounds for the granting of such a motion. Also, some jurisdictions provide for a longer time period in which such a motion may be filed. *See* Tenn. R. Crim. P. 34 (providing that such a motion may be made orally in open court, but requiring that it be reduced to writing and filed within 30 days of pronouncement of sentence).

2. *Decided on record only.* Since the issues addressed in this motion are quite technical, in many jurisdictions the motion can be resolved by reviewing the record

without regard to the evidence. For example, if the motion alleges that the indictment charges no offense, this defect can be assessed by reviewing the indictment and does not depend on the proof in the case.

Chapter 16
DOUBLE JEOPARDY

A. GENERAL OVERVIEW

The Fifth Amendment to the United States Constitution provides that "no person shall . . . be subject for the same offence to be twice put in jeopardy of life or limb . . . ." In *Benton v. Maryland*, 395 U.S. 784, 794 (1969), this guarantee was held applicable to the states through the Fourteenth Amendment because it "represents a fundamental idea in our constitutional heritage." Noting that virtually every state has some form of double jeopardy prohibition (either by state constitution or by common law), the *Benton* Court explained:

> [T]he underlying idea . . . is that the State with all its resources and power should not be allowed to make repeated attempts to convict an individual for an alleged offense, thereby subjecting him to embarrassment, expense, and ordeal and compelling him to live in a continuing state of anxiety and insecurity, as well as enhancing the possibility that even though innocent he may be found guilty. This underlying notion has from the very beginning been part of our constitutional tradition. Like the right to trial by jury, it is clearly fundamental to the American scheme of justice. [*Id.* at 796, *quoting*, in part, *Green v. United States*, 355 U.S. 184 (1957)]

Another Supreme Court decision characterized the double jeopardy rule "principally as a restraint on courts and prosecutors." *Brown v. Ohio*, 432 U.S. 161, 165 (1977).

The Supreme Court has observed repeatedly that the double jeopardy guarantee consists of three separate constitutional protections:

> It protects against a second prosecution for the same offense after acquittal.
> It protects against a second prosecution for the same offense after conviction.
> And it protects against multiple punishments for the same offense.

North Carolina v. Pearce, 395 U.S. 711, 717 (1969).

Despite what appears to be clear language in the double jeopardy clause and the Supreme Court's summary of its coverage, there continue to be many situations in which the defendant can be tried and sentenced twice for the same criminal act. As discussed more fully in this chapter, some of the key issues related to this phenomenon include: (1) determining the precise statutory definitions of the relevant crimes; (2) exploring the reasons why the initial trial did not resolve the guilt-innocence question; and (3) identifying the governmental entities prosecuting the cases.

Burden of proof. The general rule is that a defendant asserting a double jeopardy claim must establish a *prima facie* case. The burden then shifts to the government to establish that the offenses are separate. *See, e.g., United States v. Delgado*, 256 F.3d 264 (5th Cir. 2001)(defendant failed to establish a *prima facie* case that a prior conspiracy conviction was for the same conspiracy now on trial).

B. "SAME OFFENSE"

[1] *Blockburger* Test

Note that the Fifth Amendment provides a double jeopardy guarantee as to "the same offense." Given the fact that one criminal episode may subject an offender to charges under various criminal statutes, what determines whether or not a defendant is being charged twice with the "same offense?" For example, assume that the prosecutor believes that Carol robbed the ABC Liquor Store and killed the clerk who reached beneath the counter to get a shotgun. Does the double jeopardy clause permit Carol to be convicted of both robbery and murder, or only one of the two? Does it matter whether the theory of murder is felony-murder, using the robbery as the felony? What about convicting her of both attempted murder (for pointing her pistol at the clerk) and murder (for pulling the trigger)? The answer depends on the meaning of "same offense" in the Fifth Amendment.

Whether double jeopardy applies requires an examination of both the elements of the crimes and the alleged conduct sought to be proven to satisfy those elements. As a starting point for analysis, the courts routinely note that "separate statutory crimes need not be identical — either in constituent elements or in actual proof — in order to be the same [offense] within the meaning of the [double jeopardy] . . . prohibition." *Brown v. Ohio*, 432 U.S. 161, 164 (1977).

The current rule is the so-called *Blockburger* test from *Blockburger v. United States*, 284 U.S. 299 (1932):

> [W]here the same act or transaction constitutes a violation of two distinct statutory provisions, the test to be applied to determine whether there are two offenses or only one, is whether each provision requires proof of a fact which the other does not. [284 U.S. at 304]

Under *Blockburger*, a court examines the elements of the two crimes. If *each* requires proof of a fact that the other does not, the two crimes are not the "same offense," even if there is considerable overlap in their elements. On the other hand, if one crime requires the *same* evidence as another, the two are the "same offense."

Under this so-called "same elements" or "same evidence" (some commentators reject the term "same evidence" as misleading and argue "same elements" is more accurate) standard, for example, the Supreme Court has held that the crime of joyriding (taking or operating a vehicle without the owner's consent) and auto-theft (joyriding plus the intention to permanently deprive the owner of possession) are the "same offense" for double jeopardy purposes and therefore the defendant may not be convicted of both crimes. *Brown v. Ohio*, 432 U.S. 161 (1977). Auto-theft requires proof of a fact (intent to permanently deprive the owner of the vehicle) that joyriding does not; but joyriding does not require proof of a fact beyond those required for auto-theft. Therefore, since the greater offense (auto-theft) is the "same offense" for double jeopardy purposes as the lesser offense (joyriding), double jeopardy bars conviction or punishment for both. *See also United States v. Mena*, 933 F.2d 19 (1st Cir. 1991) (air piracy and boarding aircraft with explosives are not the "same offense"; each requires proof of distinctive fact; the latter requires proof of bringing an explosive device aboard a plane; former requires proof of exercising control over plane); *McIntyre v. Caspari*, 35 F.3d 338 (8th Cir. 1994) (tampering with a vehicle and auto theft are not separate offenses under *Blockburger* because the former is a lesser included offense of the latter; since the defendant had already been prosecuted for tampering, subsequent prosecution for auto theft was barred by double jeopardy).

The federal offenses of "conducting a continuing criminal enterprise" and conspiracy both require proof that the accused acted "in concert" with another. Could an individual be convicted of both crimes? *No*, answered the Supreme Court in *Rutledge v. United States*, 517 U.S. 292 (1996), holding that "a straightforward application of the *Blockburger* test leads to the conclusion that conspiracy . . . does not define a different offense from the [continuing criminal enterprise] offense." *Id.* at 300.

PROBLEM 16-1. DRUGS . . . MORE DRUGS

Hubert Putt harvested a small amount of marijuana from his back-yard garden. He then distributed the contraband to Betty Dyal, an undercover police officer, in exchange for $25. He was immediately arrested. Subsequently, he was charged with (1) unlawful cultivation of marijuana, (2) possession of marijuana, (3) possession with intent to sell marijuana, and (4) unlawful sale of marijuana.

1. Would the double jeopardy guarantee permit Putt to be convicted on all 4 counts? Could Putt be convicted of more than one offense? If so, which ones?

2. How significant would the precise wording of the relevant state statutes be to the *Blockburger* analysis?

3. What if each of the 4 counts was alleged to have been committed on a different date?

NOTES

1. *Multiple convictions v. multiple sentences.* While *Blockburger* may provide a fairly workable standard with regard to successive *prosecutions* of the same defendant, does it apply equally to the cumulative *punishment* issue? In other words, if Putt could be *prosecuted* for all four crimes in a single trial, could he also be *sentenced* for all four, perhaps even receiving a total of four consecutive prison terms? The Court answered "yes" in *Missouri v. Hunter*, 459 U.S. 359 (1983), when it held that even if prosecution under two statutes might fall within the "same offense" standard of *Blockburger*, cumulative punishments under such statutes in a single trial are permitted as long as the legislature has specifically authorized that punishment scheme. Multiple punishments and *Hunter* are discussed later in this chapter.

For a critical evaluation of the *Blockburger* test, see Akhil Reed Amar, *Double Jeopardy Law Made Simple*, 106 Yale L.J. 1807 (1997) (characterizing *Blockburger* as "a mess, legally and logically" and arguing that "we [can] do better"; suggesting that the due process guarantee should play a greater role in what are now only double jeopardy issues); *See also* Anne Bowen Poulin, *Double Jeopardy Protection from Successive Prosecution: A Proposed Approach*, 92 Geo. L. J. 1183 (2004)(proposing rejection of *Blockburger* in favor of a test that balances interests of the government against the defendant's double jeopardy interests).

2. *Unit of production.* What if a defendant robs both A and B. Can he or she be prosecuted for two robberies or would this violate the double jeopardy clause? Or what if a defendant secretly opened a cash register and took two $20 bills. Would the crime be one or two larcenies? Courts resolve this common dilemma by applying what is sometimes called a *unit of production* test. It involves an assessment of legislative intent. How did the legislature define the minimum scope of conduct for the particular criminal statute?

In the robbery illustration above, courts routinely find that the legislature intended for each robbery to be a separate offense. The unit of prosecution is a single victim. On the other hand, the theft case would be one larceny on the theory that the legislature meant to aggregate the thefts that occur from one victim in one transaction. *See, e.g.,* *State v. Green*, 172 P.3d 1213 (Kan. App. 2007)(defendant engaged in identity theft by using another person's name to open, or charge items to, credit accounts in several stores; each account was a separate crime under Kansas identity theft law).

[2]   Same Transaction/Lesser-Included Offense Analysis in Successive Prosecutions

[a]   More Serious First

Blockburger readily answers the "same offense" question for most criminal prosecutions, but there are instances in which additional considerations come into play in the context of defining the scope of the double jeopardy guarantee. As illustrated by the following cases, these particular problems usually occur in cases of *successive prosecutions*. For example, in *Harris v. Oklahoma*, 433 U.S. 682 (1977), the defendant, charged in connection with the killing of a grocery store clerk in the course of a robbery by his companion, was convicted of felony-murder in an Oklahoma state court. The robbery was the predicate felony. At a later date, he was brought to trial and convicted on a separate information of robbery with firearms for the same grocery store robbery. Proof of the robbery had been used to establish the intent necessary for the felony-murder conviction in his first trial. In a *per curiam* opinion, the United States Supreme Court held that the second trial was barred by the double jeopardy clause: "When . . . conviction of a greater crime, murder, cannot be had without conviction of the lesser crime, robbery with firearms, the Double Jeopardy Clause bars prosecution for the lesser crime after conviction of the greater one."

[b] Less Serious First

[i] General Rule: More Serious Barred

In *Harris*, the more serious crime, murder, was tried first. What if the less serious is first? In *Illinois v. Vitale*, 447 U.S. 410 (1980), a juvenile was convicted of failing to reduce speed to avoid an accident in violation of state law. The day after this traffic conviction, a petition was filed in juvenile court charging him with two counts of involuntary manslaughter (two children were killed as a result of the incident giving rise to the earlier charges). The state supreme court affirmed the dismissal of the second petition, concluding that the manslaughter cases were barred by the double jeopardy guarantee because of the earlier traffic conviction. The United States Supreme Court observed that "if, as a matter of Illinois law, a careless failure to slow is always a necessary element of manslaughter by automobile, then the two offenses are the 'same' under *Blockburger*." The Court explained:

> It may be that to sustain its manslaughter case the State may find it necessary to prove a failure to slow or to rely on conduct necessarily involving such failure; it may concede as much prior to trial. In that case, because Vitale has already been convicted for conduct that is a necessary element of the more serious crime for which he has been charged, his claim of double jeopardy would be substantial under . . . [*Harris v. Oklahoma*] [447 U.S. at 420]

The *Vitale* Court characterized its earlier holding in *Harris* as one in which the second robbery trial involved prosecution of a "species of lesser-included offense."

[ii] Short-Lived *Grady* "Same Conduct" Approach

In a significant, but relatively short-lived, case, the United States Supreme Court reaffirmed *Harris* and *Vitale* and (at least some would say) enlarged the scope of the double jeopardy guarantee. In *Grady v. Corbin*, 495 U.S. 508 (1990), the defendant, Corbin, was involved in an automobile accident that killed one person and injured another. He was issued two traffic tickets, one for the misdemeanor of driving while intoxicated and the other for failing to keep to the right of the median. He appeared in a town justice court and pled guilty to the two traffic tickets. The presiding judge was not informed of the fatality or an impending homicide investigation. Later, Corbin was charged by a grand jury with reckless manslaughter, criminally negligent homicide, and third-degree reckless assault. A bill of particulars specified the acts upon which the prosecution would rely to prove these charges: (1) operating a motor vehicle in an intoxicated condition, (2) failing to keep to the right of the median, and (3) driving too fast for the weather and road conditions. Following denial of a motion to dismiss on double jeopardy grounds, an appellate court held that the second prosecution would be barred if the prosecution sought to establish an essential element of the second crime by proving the conduct for which the defendant was convicted in the first prosecution, relying upon *Illinois v. Vitale*.

The United States Supreme Court affirmed:

> We have long held [citing *Blockburger*] that the Double Jeopardy Clause of the Fifth Amendment prohibits successive prosecutions for the same criminal

act or transaction under two criminal statutes whenever each statute does not "requir[e] proof of a fact which the other does not." In *Illinois v. Vitale*, 447 U.S. 410 (1980), we suggested that even if two successive prosecutions were not barred by the *Blockburger* test, the second prosecution would be barred if the prosecution sought to establish an essential element of the second crime by proving the conduct for which the defendant was convicted in the first prosecution. Today we adopt the suggestion set forth in *Vitale*. We hold that the Double Jeopardy Clause bars a subsequent prosecution if, to establish an essential element of an offense charged in that prosecution, the government will prove *conduct* that constitutes an offense for which the defendant has already been prosecuted. [*Id.* at 510 (emphasis added)]

The *Grady* majority recognized that a comparison of the elements of two offenses, under *Blockburger*, did not sufficiently protect defendants from the burdens of multiple trials:

If *Blockburger* constituted the entire double jeopardy inquiry in the context of successive prosecutions, the State could try Corbin in four consecutive trials for failure to keep right of the median, for driving while intoxicated, for assault, and for homicide. The State could improve its presentation of proof with each trial, assessing which witnesses gave the most persuasive testimony, which documents had the greatest impact, and which opening and closing arguments most persuaded the jurors. Corbin would be forced either to contest each of these trials or to plead guilty to avoid the harassment and expense.

Thus, a subsequent prosecution must do more than merely survive the *Blockburger* test. As we suggested in *Vitale*, the Double Jeopardy Clause bars any subsequent prosecution in which the government, to establish an essential element of offense charged in that prosecution, will prove conduct that constitutes an offense for which the defendant has already been prosecuted. The critical inquiry is what conduct the State will prove, not the evidence the State will use to prove that conduct. [495 U.S. at 520–521]

With regard to the facts of *Corbin*, the Supreme Court expressed sympathy for an overworked prosecutorial staff that failed to monitor the proceedings brought against Corbin. Thus, "with adequate preparation and foresight, the State could have prosecuted Corbin for the offenses charged in the traffic tickets and the subsequent indictment in a single proceeding, thereby avoiding this double jeopardy question." 495 U.S. at 524.

Grady's "same conduct" test could have had a profound impact on the American criminal justice system. If the prosecution did not prosecute all crimes at the same time, there was the possibility that the defense could find a cooperative court (or one ignorant of all the facts) and enter a quick guilty plea to one of the lesser charges. Under *Grady*, this could preclude prosecution for the greater charges. Additionally, the *Grady* principle could have been read to essentially mandate the practice of "mandatory joinder," as discussed in Chapter 8. *Grady* quickly engendered significant concern by law enforcement officials who feared that minor administrative errors could cause serious felony cases to be dismissed

[iii]   Demise of *Grady*: *Dixon*

In *United States v. Dixon*, 509 U.S. 688 (1993), *Grady* was overturned and *Blockburger* restored as the primary double jeopardy test. The procedural posture of the two cases consolidated for a review in *Dixon* was nearly identical to that of *Harris*, *Vitale*, and *Grady*. In the first, defendant Dixon was released on bail. One condition of release was that he not commit any criminal offense. He also was warned that any violation of the condition of release would subject him to prosecution for contempt of court. While awaiting trial, Dixon was arrested and indicted for possession of cocaine with intent to distribute. At a hearing to determine whether he should be held in contempt, the government proved beyond a reasonable doubt that Dixon was in possession of drugs and that the drugs were possessed with the intent to distribute. He was found guilty of criminal contempt and sentenced to 180 days in jail. He then moved to dismiss the cocaine indictment on double jeopardy grounds.

On review, the United States Supreme Court noted that *Dixon* "resembles the situation that produced our judgment of double jeopardy in *Harris v. Oklahoma*." The *Dixon* trial court's order, according to the Supreme Court, "incorporated the entire governing criminal code in the same manner as the *Harris* felony-murder statute incorporated the several enumerated felonies. Here, as in *Harris*, the underlying substantive criminal offense, is a species of lesser-included offense." Therefore, since Dixon's drug offense did not include any element that was not already contained in his previous contempt offense, the subsequent drug prosecution was barred by the double jeopardy guarantee because of *Blockburger*.

The Court also reconsidered and then overturned *Grady*:

> Unlike *Blockburger* analysis, whose definition of what prevents two crimes from being the "same offence," has deep historical roots and has been accepted in numerous precedents of this court, *Grady* lacks constitutional roots. The "same-conduct" rule it announced is wholly inconsistent with earlier Supreme Court precedent and with the clear common-law understanding of double jeopardy. [509 U.S. at 704]

Justice Scalia also declared that *Grady*, though only decided three years earlier, was a "mistake" because the decision contradicted an unbroken line of Supreme Court decisions, contained inaccurate historical analysis, and had produced confusion.

[iv] Exception: New Events and Defendant's Fault

While the general rule is that a defendant convicted of a lesser-included offense may not later be prosecuted for the greater offenses, there are several exceptions.

Subsequent events. One exception is when all the events needed for the greater crime have not occurred when the prosecution for the lesser-included crime began. This could occur if the defendant were a defendant who is convicted of assault, then the victim dies. Prosecution for the homicide is permissible despite the previous assault conviction. *See Diaz v. United States*, 223 U.S. 442 (1912).

Late discovery of facts necessary for the greater crime. The later discovery of facts necessary for the greater crime, despite due diligence, may also be an exception permitting prosecution for the greater offense. *Jeffers v. United States*, 432 U.S. 137, 151 (1977).

Subsequent proceedings as defendant's fault. Another exception is when the defendant asks for separate trials on the lesser and greater crimes or does not raise the issue that the first trial concerns a lesser-included offense of a later one. *Id.* The second proceeding is caused by the defendant's fault and is permitted.

NOTES

1. *State variations.* The double jeopardy protection guaranteed under a state constitution may, of course, be more extensive than that afforded by the federal constitution. This has occurred in the context of the *Grady-Dixon* dichotomy. For example, in *State v. Lessary*, 865 P. 2d 150 (Hawaii 1994), the Hawaii Supreme Court adopted a minority position and ruled that *Grady* "is necessary to afford adequate double jeopardy protection," and rejected the *Dixon* holding as one that "does not adequately protect individuals from [double jeopardy]."

2. *Summary contempt proceedings. Dixon* does not establish that the double jeopardy protection applies to "summary" criminal contempt proceedings — prosecutions of persons for contumacious conduct committed in the presence of a judge.

Professor Rudstein has noted that "nearly every lower court . . . has concluded that the protection against double jeopardy does not extend" to such prosecutions. David S. Rudstein, *Double Jeopardy and Summary Contempt Prosecutions*, 69 NOTRE DAME L. REV. 691, 714 (1994) (citing, as an example, *United States v. Rollerson*, 449 F.2d 1000 (D.C. Cir. 1971), where the court "held that the summary criminal contempt conviction of a defendant for hitting a federal prosecutor with an ice-filled water pitcher during the trial did not bar the defendant's subsequent prosecution for either assault with a dangerous weapon or assault on a federal officer"). While Professor Rudstein asserts that the double jeopardy guarantee should apply to summary criminal contempt prosecutions, he predicts that the current Supreme Court would rule otherwise.

[3] Collateral Estoppel

Recall that Justice Scalia, dissenting in *Grady*, conceded that the double jeopardy guarantee would bar a second prosecution that would require relitigation of issues resolved in the defendant's favor in a prior prosecution. This principle, sometimes referred to as *collateral estoppel*, was recognized by the Supreme Court in *Ashe v. Swenson*, 397 U.S. 436 (1970). In that case, Ashe was charged with the armed robbery of several individuals, each of whom was engaged in a poker game at the time of the robbery. Ashe was tried on the charge of robbing only one of the victims (Knight), but was found not guilty "due to insufficient evidence" (the evidence that Ashe was one of the three or four alleged robbers was described as "weak"). Six weeks later, Ashe was tried again — this time for the robbery of another named victim (Roberts) — and was found guilty. The United States Supreme Court reversed:

> The federal decisions have made clear that the rule of collateral estoppel in criminal cases is not to be applied with the hypertechnical and archaic approach of a 19th century pleading book, but with realism and rationality. Where a previous judgment of acquittal was based upon a general verdict, as is usually the case, this approach requires a court to "examine the record of a prior proceeding, taking into account the pleadings, evidence, charge, and other relevant matter, and conclude whether a rational jury could have grounded its verdict upon an issue other than that which the defendant seeks to foreclose from consideration."

> . . . Straightforward application of the federal rule to the present case can lead to but one conclusion. For the record is utterly devoid of any indication that the first jury could rationally have found that an armed robbery had not occurred, or that Knight had not been a victim of that robbery. The single rationally conceivable issue in dispute before the jury was whether the petitioner had been one of the robbers. And the jury by its verdict found that he had not. The federal rule of law, therefore, would make a second prosecution for the robbery of Roberts wholly impermissible.

> The ultimate question to be determined . . . is whether this established rule of federal law is embodied in the Fifth Amendment guarantee against double jeopardy. We do not hesitate to hold that it is. For whatever else that constitutional guarantee may embrace, it surely protects a man who has been acquitted from having to "run the gantlet" a second time.

> The question is not whether Missouri could validly charge the petitioner with six separate offenses for the robbery of the six poker players. It is not whether he could have received a total of six punishments if he had been convicted in a single trial of robbing the six victims. It is simply whether, after a jury determined by its verdict that the petitioner was not one of the robbers, the State could constitutionally hale him before a new jury to litigate that issue again.

> After the first jury had acquitted the petitioner of robbing Knight, Missouri could certainly not have brought him to trial again upon that charge. Once a jury

had determined upon conflicting testimony that there was at least a reasonable doubt that the petitioner was one of the robbers, the State could not present the same or different identification evidence in a second prosecution for the robbery of Knight in the hope that a different jury might find that evidence more convincing. The situation is constitutionally no different here, even though the second trial related to another victim of the same robbery. For the name of the victim, in the circumstances of this case, had no bearing whatever upon the issue of whether the petitioner was one of the robbers.

In this case the State in its brief has frankly conceded that following the petitioner's acquittal, it treated the first trial as no more than a dry run for the second prosecution: "No doubt the prosecutor felt the state had a provable case on the first charge and, when he lost, he did what every good attorney would do — he refined his presentation in light of the turn of events at the first trial." But this is precisely what the constitutional guarantee forbids. [397 U.S. at 444–447]

NOTES

1. *Collateral estoppel as additional limit to Blockburger.* Note the relationship between the *Blockburger* same-elements test and collateral estoppel. As in *Ashe*, collateral estoppel bars a second prosecution that is permissible under *Blockburger*. This means that *Blockburger* is not the only standard for determining whether successive prosecutions are permissible under the double jeopardy clause.

2. *One way street.* Note that the collateral estoppel bars the government from relitigating a fact that was the basis of an acquittal. It does not stop the *defendant* from relitigating a fact that was the basis of an earlier conviction.

3. *Burden of establishing collateral estoppel.* The party arguing that collateral estoppel bars a second proceeding has the burden of demonstrating that the issue in the second trial was actually decided in that party's favor in the first proceeding. See, e.g., *United States v. McGowan*, 58 F.3d 8 (2d Cir. 1995). Does this allocation of the burdens of production and persuasion make sense? Should it be the government's job to ensure that a citizen is not put "twice in jeopardy" since the government made the decision to proceed in both the first and second cases?

4. *Issues actually resolved in first trial.* The application of collateral estoppel requires a close analysis of the issues actually resolved in the first trial. To make it clear what facts were found by a jury that acquitted the defendant, Professor Amar recommends that the defendant be permitted to request a specific verdict after an acquittal. Akhil Reed Amar, *Double Jeopardy Law Made Simple*, 106 Yale L.J. 1807, 1829 (1997).

Assume that a person enters the United States without declaring to customs officials that he or she is in possession of valuable jewelry. Thereafter, this person is acquitted of charges of violating a federal statute that requires a determination that the defendant "willfully and knowingly, with intent to defraud the United States," smuggled those items into the country. The federal government then institutes a civil forfeiture action under a statute that requires that the government need only prove that the property was brought into the country without the required declaration; that is, there is no requirement of proving mens rea. Under those circumstances, should the civil forfeiture action be barred under the *Ashe* collateral estoppel principle?

In *One Lot Emerald Cut Stones and One Ring v. United States*, 409 U.S. 232 (1972), the United States Supreme Court held that the forfeiture action was allowed. First, the Court noted that the doctrine of collateral estoppel itself would not bar the forfeiture proceeding because the earlier criminal acquittal did not resolve the key issues in the forfeiture action. The acquittal on the criminal charge may have been based upon a finding that the defendant's act was done without the requisite intent. Because the civil forfeiture action does not require a finding of intent, "the criminal acquittal may not be regarded as a determination that the property was not unlawfully brought into the United States, and the forfeiture proceeding will not involve an issue previously litigated and finally determined between these parties."

Additionally, the Court in *One Lot* declared that the difference in the burden of proof in criminal and civil cases precludes application of the double jeopardy doctrine of collateral estoppel to bar a civil proceeding because of a previous finding in a criminal case. The criminal acquittal means only that the trier of fact did not find guilt beyond a reasonable doubt. It is not a finding on whether a fact was proven by the civil preponderance-of-the-evidence standard. Finally, the Court held that the double jeopardy clause was inapplicable because it reached successive *criminal* prosecutions, not a criminal prosecution followed by a civil action.

5. *Evidentiary use of prior act for which was acquitted.* The Supreme Court extended this logic in *Dowling v. United States*, 493 U.S. 342 (1990), and held that collateral estoppel does not bar the later use of evidence of a prior act for which the witness had been acquitted. The defendant was first acquitted of attempted robbery during which the robber wore a ski mask. At a later trial for another bank robbery, where the robber also wore a ski mask, a government witness testified that the defendant had worn a ski mask at the earlier attempted robbery (for which the defendant had been acquitted). The Supreme Court in *Dowling* held that the prior acquittal did not bar the later evidentiary use of the prior attempted robbery because the acquittal meant only that the beyond-a-reasonable-doubt standard was not satisfied. It did not mean that the lower standard for admitting evidence was not met.

6. *Two parties.* Assume that Alvin Taylor and James Daniels plan a liquor store robbery. Taylor is to remain in the getaway car and Daniels is to enter the liquor store and obtain cash from the clerk at gunpoint. In the course of the robbery, an individual is killed. Daniels is tried first and is convicted of the robbery but acquitted of the murder charge. Thereafter, Taylor is also charged with both robbery and murder. Under these circumstances, should the collateral estoppel doctrine preclude the state from obtaining a murder conviction against Taylor? In *People v. Taylor*, 527 P.2d 622 (Cal. 1974), the Supreme Court of California answered that question "yes." Emphasizing that the defendant's subsequent conviction for murder could result only upon a finding that his confederate, Daniels, was guilty of the homicide, collateral estoppel applied notwithstanding the lack of identity of the parties involved. The Court was careful to point out, however, that this decision was limited to the unique facts of this case "where an accused's guilt must be predicated on his vicarious liability for the acts of a previously acquitted confederate." *Id.* at 631. Do you agree with the *Taylor* analysis? Is it not possible that Daniels' acquittal was based upon "jury mercy" (or nullification)? Does this question suggest the need for a special verdict (*i.e.*, one in which the first jury is required to explain the basis upon which it decided to acquit)?

7. *Inconsistent verdicts.* If it is difficult to utilize collateral estoppel in a general verdict case because of an inability to ascertain the precise issues resolved, it is virtually impossible to do so when the jury has reached inconsistent verdicts. *See, e.g., United States v. Powell*, 469 U.S. 57, 68 (1984) (once it is established a jury reached inconsistent verdicts, "established principles of collateral estoppel — which are predicated on the assumption that the jury acted rationally and found certain facts in reaching its verdict — are no longer useful").

PROBLEM 16-2. BIRTH PAINS

William Blaine was tried for two crimes: Count I — wilful possession of an unlawfully issued birth certificate with intent to defraud. Count II— wilfully making false statements on a passport application for purposes of obtaining a passport.

Blaine is an attorney who, according to government proof, made false representations to obtain a certified copy of a birth certificate in the name of Harold Linden. He also obtained a fake social security number in Linden's name. Blaine then used these two items to obtain a United States passport for his client, a Canadian citizen named Timothy Wiggins. The passport bore the name Harold Linden but the photo of Timothy Wiggins, permitting Wiggins to use it.

At trial, defendant Blaine argued lack of intent because he actually believed his client Timothy Wiggins was really Harold Linden. The jury acquitted him of Count I (birth certificate) and could not reach a verdict on Count II (passport).

The government then obtained another indictment for conspiracy (with Wiggins) to make false statements in a passport application.

Should the second prosecution barred by collateral estoppel? *See, United States v. White*, 936 F.2d 1326 (D.C. Cir.), *cert. denied*, 502 U.S. 942 (1991).

C. MULTIPLE PUNISHMENTS

Just as the double jeopardy clause prohibits the government from convicting a person more than once for the same offense, the guarantee also proscribes multiple punishments for the same offense. For example, a defendant may not be convicted of robbery and sentenced to ten years in prison, then convicted again (at the same or a subsequent trial) for exactly the same crime and given another ten-year sentence. This would involve double punishment for the same offense. Of course, the judge could achieve the same result by imposing a twenty-year sentence for the first robbery conviction if authorized by statute. If that occurred, the primary constitutional issue is whether that penalty is disproportionate to the crime and therefore in violation of the Eighth Amendment's ban on cruel and unusual punishment. See Chapter 17.

[1] Multiple Punishment in Single Trial

Sometimes a person is charged with several related crimes in one trial. What are the limits on multiple punishments? As the following case concludes, the answer is different from *Blockburger's* same element test.

MISSOURI v. HUNTER
459 U.S. 359 (1983)

CHIEF JUSTICE BURGER delivered the opinion of the Court.

[The defendant and two accomplices robbed a supermarket. During the robbery, the defendant struck the store manager with the butt of a revolver and shot at a police officer at the scene. Defendant was convicted under Missouri law of (1) first degree robbery and (2) armed criminal action. (A third charge is not relevant). First degree robbery is defined under Missouri law as feloniously taking property from another's person or presence by violence to the person or by putting the person in fear of immediate injury. The second crime, armed criminal action, is defined as the use of a dangerous weapon to commit a felony. The Missouri legislature specified that the penalty for armed criminal action is a prison term of not less than three years, to be served in addition to the punishment imposed for the felony (here, robbery) for which the weapon was used. Defendant was sentenced to 10 years' imprisonment for robbery and 15 years for armed criminal action.]

On appeal the defendant claimed that a sentence for both robbery and armed criminal action violated double jeopardy. The Missouri Court of Appeals agreed.

. . . The Double Jeopardy Clause is cast explicitly in terms of being "twice put in jeopardy." We have consistently interpreted it "to protect an individual from being subjected to the hazards of trial and possible conviction more than once for an alleged offense." *Burks v. United States*, 437 U.S. 1, 11 (1978), *quoting Green v. United States*, 355 U.S. 184, 187 (1957). Because respondent has been subjected to only one trial, it is not contended that his right to be free from multiple trials for the same offense has been violated . . . . With respect to cumulative sentences imposed in a single trial, the

Double Jeopardy Clause does no more than prevent the sentencing court from prescribing greater punishment than the legislature intended.

. . . Here, the Missouri Supreme Court has construed the two statutes at issue as defining the same crime. In addition, the Missouri Supreme Court has recognized that the legislature intended that punishment for violations of the statutes be cumulative. We are bound to accept the Missouri court's construction of that State's statutes.

. . . Our analysis and reasoning in *Whalen v. United States*, 445 U.S. 684 (1980)[legislature did not intend for multiple punishments for crime of rape and crime of murder during course of rape] . . . [leads] inescapably to the conclusion that simply because two criminal statutes may be construed to proscribe the same conduct under the *Blockburger* test does not mean that the Double Jeopardy Clause precludes the imposition, in a single trial, of cumulative punishments pursuant to those statutes. The rule of statutory construction noted in *Whalen* is not a constitutional rule requiring courts to negate clearly expressed legislative intent. Thus far, we have utilized that rule only to limit a federal court's power to impose convictions and punishments when the will of Congress is not clear. Here, the Missouri Legislature has made its intent crystal clear. Legislatures, not courts, prescribe the scope of punishments.

Where, as here, a legislature specifically authorizes cumulative punishment under two statutes, regardless of whether those two statutes proscribe the "same" conduct under *Blockburger*, a court's task of statutory construction is at an end and the prosecutor may seek and the trial court or jury may impose cumulative punishment under such statutes in a single trial. [Reversed]

JUSTICE MARSHALL, with whom JUSTICE STEVENS joins, dissenting.

The Double Jeopardy Clause forbids either multiple prosecutions or multiple punishment for "the same offence." Respondent was convicted of both armed criminal action and the lesser included offense of first-degree robbery, and he was sentenced for both crimes. Had respondent been tried for these two crimes in separate trials, he would plainly have been subjected to multiple prosecutions for "the same offence" in violation of the Double Jeopardy Clause.[1] For the reasons stated below, I do not believe that the phrase "the same offence" should be interpreted to mean one thing for purposes of the prohibition against multiple prosecutions and something else for purposes of the prohibition against multiple punishment.

. . . A State has wide latitude to define crimes and to prescribe the punishment for a given crime. For example, a State is free to prescribe two different punishments (*e.g.*, a fine and a prison term) for a single offense. But the Constitution does not permit a State to punish as two crimes conduct that constitutes only one "offence" within the meaning of the Double Jeopardy Clause. For whenever a person is subjected to the risk that he will be convicted of a crime under state law, he is "put in jeopardy of life or limb." If the prohibition against being "twice put in jeopardy" for "the same offense" is to have any real meaning, a State cannot be allowed to convict a defendant two, three, or more times simply by enacting separate statutory provisions defining nominally distinct crimes. If the Double Jeopardy Clause imposed no restrictions on a legislature's power to authorize multiple punishment, there would be no limit to the number of convictions that a State could obtain on the basis of the same act, state of mind, and result. A State would be free to create substantively identical crimes differing only in name, or to create a series of greater and lesser included offenses, with the first crime a lesser included offense of the second, the second a lesser included offense of the third, and so on.

. . . [T]he entry of two convictions and the imposition of two sentences cannot be justified on the ground that the legislature could have simply created one crime but

---

[1] The Double Jeopardy Clause would have forbidden multiple prosecutions regardless of which charge was brought first, and regardless of whether the first trial ended in a conviction or an acquittal.

prescribed harsher punishment for that crime. This argument incorrectly assumes that the total sentence imposed is all that matters, and that the number of convictions that can be obtained is of no relevance to the concerns underlying the Double Jeopardy Clause.

When multiple charges are brought, the defendant is "put in jeopardy" as to each charge. To retain his freedom, the defendant must obtain an acquittal on all charges; to put the defendant in prison, the prosecution need only obtain a single guilty verdict. The prosecution's ability to bring multiple charges increases the risk that the defendant will be convicted on one or more of those charges. The very fact that a defendant has been arrested, charged, and brought to trial on several charges may suggest to the jury that he must be guilty of at least one of those crimes. Moreover, where the prosecution's evidence is weak, its ability to bring multiple charges may substantially enhance the possibility that, even though innocent, the defendant may be found guilty on one or more charges as a result of a compromise verdict. The submission of two charges rather than one gives the prosecution "the advantage of offering the jury a choice — a situation which is apt to induce a doubtful jury to find the defendant guilty of the less serious offense rather than to continue the debate as to his innocence." *Cichos v. Indiana*, 385 U.S. 76, 81 (1966) (Fortas, J., dissenting from dismissal of certiorari).

The Government's argument also overlooks the fact that, quite apart from any sentence that is imposed, each separate criminal conviction typically has collateral consequences, in both the jurisdiction in which the conviction is obtained and in other jurisdictions. The number of convictions is often critical to the collateral consequences that an individual faces. For example, a defendant who has only one prior conviction will generally not be subject to sentencing under a habitual offender statute.

Furthermore, each criminal conviction itself represents a pronouncement by the State that the defendant has engaged in conduct warranting the moral condemnation of the community. Because a criminal conviction constitutes a formal judgment of condemnation by the community, each additional conviction imposes an additional stigma and causes additional damage to the defendant's reputation.

. . . In light of these considerations, the Double Jeopardy Clause cannot reasonably be interpreted to leave legislatures completely free to subject a defendant to the risk of multiple punishment on the basis of a single criminal transaction . . . . The Court has long assumed that the *Blockburger* test is also a rule of constitutional stature in multiple-punishment cases, and I would not hesitate to hold that it is. If the prohibition against being "twice put in jeopardy" for "the same offence" is to provide meaningful protection, the phrase "the same offence" must have content independent of state law in both contexts. Since the Double Jeopardy Clause limits the power of all branches of government, including the legislature, there is no more reason to treat the test as simply a rule of statutory construction in multiple-punishment cases than there would be in multiple-prosecution cases.

NOTES

1. *What is Hunter saying?* Recall that double jeopardy is read as barring "multiple punishments for the same offense." In *Hunter* is the Supreme Court saying the two sentences (1) are not "multiple punishment," (2) are not the "same offense," or (3) something else?

2. *Hunter as legislative intent exception.* Justice Marshall's dissent in *Hunter* says that the term "same offense" should be interpreted the same way for both multiple prosecutions and multiple punishments. Does Chief Justice Burger's majority opinion disagree with this proposition? Could the *Hunter* majority opinion be read as authorizing a "legislative intent" exception to *Blockburger* on both issues (multiple prosecutions and multiple punishments) as long as both occurred in the same trial?

In *Daniels v. Bronson*, 932 F.2d 102 (2d Cir. 1991), the defendant was convicted in one trial of capital murder (for killing a mother and daughter in one event) and of murder of the mother. He was sentenced to serve consecutive prison terms. He claimed the two punishments were barred by double jeopardy. The Court of Appeals found they were the "same offense" under *Blockburger*, but noted that multiple punishment may still be permissible under *Hunter* if there was a clear indication that the Connecticut legislature intended to permit multiple punishments. Finding no such evidence of legislative intent, the Court of Appeals held that multiple convictions and sentences were barred by double jeopardy.

3. *Changing Hunter facts.* In *Hunter* the defendant was convicted of first degree robbery and armed criminal action in a single trial. What if he were first convicted of the robbery, then at a later trial convicted of armed criminal action, and given a sentence to be served on completion of the robbery sentence. Would this offend *Blockburger*? Would this offend *Missouri v. Hunter*? Would your answer change if it were clearly established that the legislature intended for there to be successive prosecutions?

Revisit the policies behind the double jeopardy clause. Are they served if consecutive trials are barred, but multiple charges for the "same offense" in the same trial are permitted?

4. *State legislature defines double jeopardy?* After *Hunter*, the resolution of some double jeopardy issues will depend largely on state legislative intent. Is it fair to say that *Hunter* lets a state legislature define the meaning of "same offense" in the federal double jeopardy guarantee?

5. *Legislative intent.* How clear must legislative intent be to resolve a multiple punishment issue under *Hunter*? The rule of lenity is sometimes used in criminal cases when legislative intent is unclear. This rule resolves ambiguities in favor of the accused. Should this rule ever be used to resolve double jeopardy issues?

If *Blockburger* is a rule of statutory construction, when does it apply in multiple punishment cases? If legislative intent is clear? Unclear? When there is a slight indication that multiple punishments are permissible? Impermissible?

Some legislatures have enacted statutes to express their intent in this area. *See, e.g.,* Kan. Stat. Ann. § 21-3107 (if same conduct constitutes more than one crime, defendant may be persecuted for each crime, but may not be convicted of both the crime charged and a lesser-included crime).

6. *Multiple punishment intended.* Many cases after *Hunter* have found a legislative intent allowing multiple punishments. *See, e.g., United States v. Patel*, 370 F.3d 108 (1st Cir. 2004)(double jeopardy did not bar imposition of multiple punishments for arson and causing fire to commit mail fraud); *Birr v. Shillinger*, 894 F.2d 1160 (10th Cir.) *cert. denied*, 496 U.S. 940 (1990) (consecutive sentences for felony murder and underlying felony); *Banner v. Davis*, 886 F.2d 777 (6th Cir. 1989) (aggravated assault and firing into occupied dwelling).

7. For critical assessments of *Hunter*, see ; Anne Bowen Poulin, *Double Jeopardy and Multiple Punishment: Cutting the Gordian Knot*, 77 U. Colo. L. Rev. 595 (2006); George C. Thomas III, *Multiple Punishments for the Same Offense: The Analysis after Missouri v. Hunter*, 62 Wash. U.L.Q. 79 (1984).

[2] What is Punishment?

[a] Criminal and Civil Penalties

Difficult double jeopardy questions arise when two sanctions are not similar. What if the robber is sentenced to a ten-year prison term and a $10,000 fine? More problematic, what if the robber receives the ten-year prison sentence, a $10,000 fine, and then, in the same or a separate proceeding, is assessed a $50,000 civil penalty or tax? Does the $50,000 assessment violate double jeopardy? Would it matter if it were $500 rather than $50,000?

Justice O'Connor, dissenting in *Department of Revenue of Montana v. Kurth Ranch*, 511 U.S. 767 (1994), summarized several principles applicable to the multiple punishment concept:

> Congress may impose both a criminal and a civil sanction in respect to the same act or omission; for the double jeopardy clause prohibits merely *punishing* twice, or attempting a second time to punish criminally, for the same offense. . . . [A] civil proceeding following a criminal prosecution . . . is not a second "jeopardy." But . . . the Constitution constrains the States' ability to denominate proceedings as "civil" and so dispense with the criminal procedure protections embodied in the Bill of Rights. Some governmental exactions are so punitive that they may only be imposed in a criminal proceeding. And because the Double Jeopardy Clause prohibits successive criminal proceedings for the same offense, the government may not sanction a defendant for conduct for which he has already been punished *insofar as the subsequent sanction is punitive*, because to do so would necessitate a criminal proceeding prohibited by the Constitution. [*Id.* at 793]

[i] Civil Penalties

In *United States v. Halper*, 490 U.S. 435 (1989), the defendant was convicted of numerous separate violations of a federal criminal false claims statute. He received a two-year prison sentence and a fine of $5,000. After imposition of the sentence, the federal government filed a separate action to recover a $2,000 civil penalty for each of the criminal violations. The district judge found that the total amount sought ($130,000) in civil penalties was more than 220 times greater than the federal government's identifiable loss, and therefore was a second "punishment" that was barred by the double jeopardy prohibition. On direct appeal, the United States Supreme Court acknowledged that the "criminal" vs. "civil" labels were not necessarily binding in assessing such double jeopardy issues. That is, "a defendant who already has been punished in a criminal prosecution may not be subjected to an additional civil sanction to the extent that the second sanction may not fairly be characterized as remedial, but only as a deterrent or retribution." 490 U.S. at 448–449. And a civil penalty would be treated as "remedial" if it simply reimbursed the government for actual costs arising from the defendant's criminal conduct. Accordingly, the case was remanded for a calculation of the portion of the civil penalty that legitimately could be awarded as compensation for the government's actual damages.

The *Halper* analysis, however, was reconsidered in *Hudson v. United States*, 522 U.S. 93 (1997). In *Hudson*, the defendants used their bank positions to arrange a series of loans to a third individual in violation of banking statutes and regulations. Thereafter, the Office of the Comptroller of Currency (OCC) imposed monetary penalties and occupational debarment on the defendants. Later, these defendants were indicted for numerous federal crimes, all of which rested on the lending transactions that had formed the basis for the prior administrative actions brought by OCC. The district court dismissed the indictment on double jeopardy grounds, but the Court of Appeals reversed, relying upon *Halper*, because the fines imposed were not so disproportional to the damage to the government as to render these sanctions "punishment" for double jeopardy purposes. The Supreme Court affirmed the judgment of the Court of Appeals but disavowed the method of analysis used in *Halper*.

The Court reasoned that because the double jeopardy protection extends only to imposition of criminal punishments for the same offense, the first step of analysis should be to determine whether a particular punishment is criminal or civil as a matter of statutory construction. The Court found the *Halper* analysis to have been "ill considered" because it deviated from traditional double jeopardy doctrine in two key respects:

> First, the *Halper* Court bypassed the threshold question: whether the successive punishment at issue is a "criminal" punishment . . . . The second significant departure in *Halper* was the Court's decision to "assess the character of the actual sanctions imposed," rather than . . . evaluating the "statute on its face" to determine whether it provided for what amounted to a criminal sanction. [*Id.* at 101]

Applying the more "traditional" double jeopardy analysis to the facts of this case, the Court found that Congress had intended the OCC penalties and debarment sanctions to be "civil" in nature and therefore the double jeopardy clause posed no obstacle to trial on the pending indictments.

[ii] Taxes

While *Hudson* appears to clarify the double jeopardy analysis in civil fine cases, does the same analysis apply to taxing schemes? In 1994 — after *Halper* but prior to *Hudson* — the Supreme Court addressed this question in *Department of Revenue of Montana v. Kurth Ranch*, 511 U.S. 767 (1994). There, the defendants pled guilty to drug charges related to marijuana plants found during a raid of their farm by Montana law enforcement officers. Thereafter, the State Revenue Department brought a second action to collect a state tax imposed on the possession and storage of dangerous drugs. The tax was imposed upon "the possession and storage of dangerous drugs," and collected only after "any state or federal fines or forfeitures have been satisfied." The amount of the tax was either 10% of the assessed market value of the drugs or a specified amount depending upon the particular drug in question. Additionally, taxpayers were obligated to file a return within 72 hours of their arrest; indeed, taxpayers had no obligation to file a return or to pay any tax until they were arrested.

The defendants challenged the tax in bankruptcy proceedings. The bankruptcy court, noting that the assessment on the marijuana harvest resulted in a tax eight times the product's market value, held that it was a form of double jeopardy. Later, the Ninth Circuit Court of Appeals, applying *Halper*, affirmed the lower court's decision because the state had refused to offer any evidence to show that the tax sanction was rationally related to the damages suffered by the state.

In the Supreme Court, Justice Stevens' majority opinion concluded that the state drug tax was "a concoction of anomalies too far-removed in crucial respects from a standard tax assessment to escape characterization as punishment for the purpose of Double Jeopardy analysis." He pointed out, for example, that the state tax is conditioned on the commission of a crime, is exacted only after the taxpayer has been arrested, and is levied on goods that the taxpayer neither owns nor possesses when the tax is imposed. Contrary to the Ninth Circuit, however, he reasoned that it would be "inappropriate" to subject the state drug tax to *Halper's* test for civil penalties: "[T]ax statutes serve a purpose quite different from civil penalties, and *Halper's* method of determining whether the exaction was remedial or punitive simply does not work in the case of a tax statute." He concluded:

> This drug tax is not the kind of remedial sanction that may follow the first punishment of a criminal offense. Instead, it is a second punishment . . . and therefore must be imposed during the first prosecution or not at all.[*]

---

[*] Justice Stevens noted in an earlier portion of his opinion that whether activity is unlawful or not does not prevent its taxation. He explained that the state "could collect its tax on the possession of marijuana . . . if it had not previously punished the taxpayer for the same offense, or, indeed, if it had assessed the tax in the same proceeding that resulted in his conviction." [*Id.* at 778.]

The proceeding Montana initiated to collect a tax on the possession of drugs was the functional equivalent of a successive criminal prosecution that placed the Kurths in jeopardy a second time "for the same offense." [*Id.* at 784]

Chief Justice Rehnquist's dissent agreed with Justice Stevens that the *Halper* mode of analysis should not be applied in the case of a tax statute. He also agreed that an assessment which is labeled a "tax" could, "under some conceivable circumstances, constitute punishment for purposes of the Double Jeopardy Clause." He concluded, however, that this particular tax provision did not constitute a "punishment": "[T]he Montana tax has a nonpenal purpose of raising revenue, as well as the legitimate purpose of deterring conduct, such that it should be regarded as a genuine tax for double jeopardy purposes." [*Id.* at 791.

Justice O'Connor's dissent argued that the tax provision should be analyzed under *Halper*, as follows:

> [T]he defendant must first show the absence of a rational relationship between the amount of the sanction and the government's nonpunitive objectives; the burden then shifts to the government to justify the sanction with reference to the particular case. This bifurcated approach to the double jeopardy question makes good sense. The presumption of constitutionality to which every state statute is entitled means in this context that a sanction denominated as civil must be presumed to be nonpunitive. This presumption would be rendered nugatory if the government were required to prove that the sanction is in fact nonpunitive before imposing it in a particular case. Rather, the defendant must show that the sanction may be punitive as applied to him before the government can be required to justify its imposition. [*Id.* at 796]

Justice Scalia, with whom Justice Thomas joined, asserted that "there is not . . . a multiple-punishments component of the Double Jeopardy Clause." Rather, the question was whether the Montana tax proceeding constituted a second criminal "prosecution." Since it did not, and since the Montana legislature authorized these specific taxes in addition to the criminal penalties for possession of marijuana, Justice Scalia concluded that "these taxes did not violate the principle of due process, sometimes called the multiple-punishments component of the Double Jeopardy Clause."

[iii] In Rem Proceedings

In *United States v. Ursery*, 518 U.S. 267 (1996), the United States Supreme Court noted that neither *Halper* nor *Kurth Ranch* dealt with *in rem* civil forfeitures. In consolidated cases involving civil forfeiture proceedings against an individual's house (alleging that it had been used to facilitate illegal drug transactions) as well as another civil in rem action against various properties seized from individuals (alleging that each item was subject to forfeiture because it had been involved in illegal activities) the United States Supreme Court held that those specific civil forfeitures as well as "civil forfeitures generally" do not constitute "punishment" for purposes of the double jeopardy clause. Justice Stevens concurred in part and dissented in part. He agreed with the majority that the forfeiture of proceeds of unlawful activity, "like the confiscation of money stolen from a bank, does not punish [the defendant] because it exacts no price in liberty or lawfully derived property." As to the seizure of a home where there is no evidence that the house had been purchased with the proceeds of unlawful activity and no evidence that the house, itself, was contraband, however, he asserted that "none of the reasons supporting the forfeiture of proceeds or contraband provides a sufficient basis for concluding that the confiscation of [a] home was not punitive."

[iv] Civil Commitment

In yet another ruling, the United States Supreme Court held that a "civil" commitment of a person scheduled for release from prison was not punishment for either double jeopardy or *ex post facto* purposes. *Kansas v. Hendricks*, 521 U.S. 346 (1997). The Court upheld a Kansas statute under which persons, due to either mental abnormality or personality disorder, and likely to engage in acts of sexual violence, can be civilly committed involuntarily. The finding of non-punitiveness was based upon a determination that (1) the statute did not implicate the primary objectives of criminal punishment, (2) the statute's purpose was not retributive, and (3) the term of confinement under the statute, while potentially indefinite, was tied to a finding that the person's mental abnormality no longer caused a threat to others.

Justice Breyer, writing for the four dissenters, asserted that the effort to commit Hendricks was "to inflict further punishment upon him" and therefore prohibited under the *ex post facto* clause because his crimes were committed before enactment of the statute.

[v] Deportation

Deportation is widely considered to be a civil penalty and not affected by a criminal prosecution for the same conduct that caused the deportation. *But see* Won Kidane, *Committing a Crime While a Refugee: Rethinking the Issue of Deportation in Light of the Principle Against Double Jeopardy*, 34 HAST. CONST. L. Q. 383 (2007)(arguing double jeopardy should bar deportation of refugees who have been convicted of a deportable crime, have served the sentence, and will be deported to a country where they will be criminally prosecuted).

[b] Sentencing Enhancement

Does the defendant suffer a double jeopardy violation when convicted and sentenced for a crime involving conduct that was considered in determining the defendant's sentence for a prior conviction? The United States Supreme Court answered that question in the following case.

WITTE v. UNITED STATES
515 U.S. 389 (1995)

JUSTICE O'CONNOR delivered the opinion of the Court.

The Double Jeopardy Clause of the Fifth Amendment to the United States Constitution prohibits successive prosecution or multiple punishment for "the same offence." This case, which involves application of the United States Sentencing Guidelines, asks us to consider whether a court violates that proscription by convicting and sentencing a defendant for a crime when the conduct underlying that offense has been considered in determining the defendant's sentence for a previous conviction.

[In 1991, Witte was charged with conspiring and attempting to possess marijuana with intent to distribute. Thereafter, he pled guilty to the attempted possession count and the government agreed to dismiss the conspiracy count . . . . In calculating Witte's offense level under the Guidelines, the district court concluded that the defendant's "relevant conduct" included earlier activities concerning importation of cocaine and marijuana which were not a part of the same course of conduct as the 1991 marijuana offense. In 1992, another grand jury returned an indictment against Witte for conspiracy and attempting to import cocaine. Witte moved to dismiss, arguing that he had already been punished for the cocaine offenses because the cocaine involved had been considered as "relevant conduct" at sentencing for the 1991 marijuana offense. The district court dismissed the indictment on grounds that punishment for the indicted offenses would violate double jeopardy, but the Fifth Circuit Court of Appeals reversed.]

Petitioner clearly was neither prosecuted for nor convicted of the [earlier] cocaine offenses during the first criminal proceeding. The offense to which petitioner pleaded guilty and for which he was sentenced in 1992 was attempted possession of marijuana with intent to distribute it, whereas the crimes charged in the instant indictment are conspiracy to import cocaine and attempted importation of the same.

Petitioner nevertheless argues that, because the conduct giving rise to the cocaine charges was taken into account during sentencing for the marijuana conviction, he effectively was "punished" for that conduct during the first proceeding. As a result, he contends, the Double Jeopardy Clause bars the instant prosecution. Thus, if petitioner is correct that the present case constitutes a second attempt to punish him criminally for the same cocaine offenses, then the prosecution may not proceed. We agree with the Court of Appeals, however, that petitioner's double jeopardy theory — that consideration of uncharged conduct in arriving at a sentence within the statutorily authorized punishment range constitutes "punishment" for that conduct — is not supported by our precedents, which make clear that a defendant in that situation is punished, for double jeopardy purposes, only for the offense of which the defendant is convicted.

. . . [W]e specifically have rejected the claim that double jeopardy principles bar a later prosecution or punishment for criminal activity where that activity has been considered at sentencing for a separate crime. *Williams v. Oklahoma*, 358 U.S. 576 (1959), arose out of a kidnapping and murder committed by the petitioner while attempting to escape from police after a robbery. Following his arrest, Williams pleaded guilty to murder and was given a life sentence. He was later convicted of kidnapping, which was then a capital offense in Oklahoma, and the sentencing court took into account, in assessing the death penalty, the fact that the kidnapping victim had been murdered. We rejected Williams' contention that this use of the conduct that had given rise to the prior conviction [for murder] violated double jeopardy. Emphasizing that "the exercise of a sound discretion in such a case required consideration of all the circumstances of the crime," we made clear that "one of the aggravating circumstances involved in this kidnapping crime was the fact that petitioner shot and killed the victim in the course of its commission," and rejected the claim "that the sentencing judge was not entitled to consider that circumstance, along with all the other circumstances involved, in determining the proper sentence to be imposed for the kidnapping crime." We then disposed of the petitioner's double jeopardy claim as follows: "In view of the obvious fact that, under the law of Oklahoma, kidnapping is a separate crime, entirely distinct from the crime of murder, the court's consideration of the murder as a circumstance involved in the kidnapping crime cannot be said to have resulted in punishing petitioner a second time for the same offense . . . ." We thus made clear that use of evidence of related criminal conduct to enhance a defendant's sentence for a separate crime within the authorized statutory limits does not constitute punishment for that conduct within the meaning of the Double Jeopardy Clause.

We find this case to be governed by *Williams;* it makes no difference in this context whether the enhancement occurred in the first or second sentencing proceeding.

Williams, like this case, concerned the double jeopardy implications of taking the circumstances surrounding a particular course of criminal activity into account in sentencing for a conviction arising therefrom. Similarly, we have made clear in other cases, which involved a defendant's background more generally and not conduct arising out of the same criminal transaction as the offense of which the defendant was convicted, that "enhancement statutes, whether in the nature of criminal history provisions such as those contained in the Sentencing Guidelines, or recidivist statutes which are common place in state criminal laws, do not change the penalty imposed for the earlier conviction." In repeatedly upholding such recidivism statutes, we have rejected double jeopardy challenges because the enhanced punishment imposed for the later offense "is not to be viewed as either a new jeopardy or additional penalty for the earlier crimes," but instead as "a stiffened penalty for the latest crime, which is considered to be an aggravated offense because a repetitive one."

. . . Because consideration of relevant conduct in determining a defendant's sentence within the legislatively authorized punishment range does not constitute punishment for that conduct, the instant prosecution does not violate the Double Jeopardy Clause's prohibition against the imposition of multiple punishments for the same offense. Affirmed.

JUSTICE SCALIA, with whom JUSTICE THOMAS joins, concurring in the judgment.

. . . It is not true that (as the Court claims) "the language of the Double Jeopardy Clause protects against . . . the actual imposition of two punishments for the same offense." What the Clause says is that no person "shall . . . be subject for the same offence to be twice put in jeopardy of life or limb," which means twice prosecuted for the same offense. Today's decision shows that departing from the text of the Clause, and from the constant tradition regarding its meaning, as we did six years ago in *United States v. Halper*, requires us either to upset well-established penal practices, or else to perceive lines that do not really exist. Having created a right against multiple punishments *ex nihilo*, we now allow that right to be destroyed by the technique used on the petitioner here: "We do not punish you twice for the same offense," says the Government, "but we punish you twice as much for one offense solely because you also committed another offense, for which other offense we will also punish you (only once) later on." I see no real difference in that distinction, and decline to acquiesce in the erroneous holding that drives us to it.

In sum, I adhere to my view that "the Double Jeopardy Clause prohibits successive prosecution, not successive punishment." Since petitioner was not twice prosecuted for the same offense, I concur in the judgment.

JUSTICE STEVENS, concurring in part and dissenting in part.

Petitioner pleaded guilty to attempting to possess with intent to distribute more than 100 kilograms of marijuana. At petitioner's sentencing hearing, the District Court heard evidence concerning petitioner's participation in a conspiracy to import cocaine. Pursuant to its understanding of the Guidelines, the District Court considered the cocaine offenses as "relevant conduct" and increased petitioner's sentence accordingly. Petitioner received exactly the same sentence that he would have received had he been convicted of both the marijuana offenses and the cocaine offenses. The Government then sought to prosecute petitioner for the cocaine offenses.

The question presented is whether the Double Jeopardy Clause bars that subsequent prosecution. The Court today holds that it does not. In my view, the Court's holding is incorrect and unprecedented. More importantly, it weakens the fundamental protections the Double Jeopardy Clause was intended to provide.

. . . Traditional sentencing practices recognize that a just sentence is determined in part by the character of the offense and in part by the character of the offender. Within this framework, the admission of evidence of an offender's past convictions reflects the longstanding notion that one's prior record is strong evidence of one's character. A recidivist should be punished more severely than a first offender because he has failed to mend his ways after a first conviction. Thus, when a sentencing judge reviews an offender's prior convictions at sentencing, the judge is not punishing that offender a second time for his past misconduct, but rather is evaluating the nature of his individual responsibility for past acts and the likelihood that he will engage in future misconduct. Recidivist statutes are consistent with the Double Jeopardy Clause not because of the formalistic premise that one can only be punished or placed in jeopardy for the "offense of conviction," but rather because of the important functional understanding that the purpose of the prior conviction is to provide valuable evidence is to the offender's character. The majority's reliance on recidivist statutes is thus unavailing.

When the offenses considered at sentencing are somehow linked to the offense of conviction, the analysis is different. . . . [I]nsofar as the sentencer relies on the offense as aggravation of the underlying offense, the Double Jeopardy Clause is necessarily implicated. At that point, the defendant is being punished for having committed the offense at issue, and not for what the commission of that offense reveals about his character. In such cases, the defendant has been "put in jeopardy" of punishment for the offense because he has in fact been punished for that offense.

Under many sentencing regimes, of course, it is difficult if not impossible to determine whether a given offense has affected the judge's assessment of the character of the offender, the character of the offense, or both. However, under the federal Sentencing Guidelines, the role played by each item in the sentencing calculus is perfectly clear. The Guidelines provide for specific sentencing adjustments for "criminal history" (*i.e.*, character of the offender) and for "relevant conduct" (*i.e.*, character of the offense). Under the Guidelines, therefore, an offense that is included as "relevant conduct" does not relate to the character of the offender (which is reflected instead by criminal history), but rather measures only the character of the offense. Even if all other mitigating and aggravating circumstances that shed light on an offender's character have been taken into account, the judge must sentence the offender for conduct that affects the seriousness of the offense.

The effect of this regime with respect to drug crimes provides a particularly striking illustration of why this mandatory consideration of relevant conduct implicates the Double Jeopardy Clause under anything but a formalistic reading of the Clause. Under the Guidelines, the severity of a drug offense is measured by the total quantity of drugs under all offenses that constitute "relevant conduct," regardless of whether those offenses were charged and proved at the guilt phase of the trial or instead proved at the sentencing hearing. For example, as I have noted above, petitioner's guidelines range was determined by adding the quantity of marijuana to the quantity of cocaine (using the conversion formula set forth in the Guidelines). Petitioner has thus already been sentenced for an actual offense that includes the cocaine transactions that are the subject of the second indictment. Those transactions played precisely the same role in fixing his punishment as they would have if they had been the subject of a formal charge and conviction. The actual imposition of that punishment must surely demonstrate that petitioner was just as much in jeopardy for the offense as if he had been previously charged with it. . . .

D.   WHEN DOES JEOPARDY ATTACH?

Just as it is critically important to determine whether a defendant has been twice charged with the "same offence," it is equally important to determine, for double jeopardy purposes, if jeopardy has "attached" to the defendant's case. The double jeopardy guarantee is inapplicable until jeopardy attaches. For example, assume that a defendant is indicted and the case is set for trial. Two days before the trial is to begin, the trial judge orders that the case be dismissed. Thereafter, the defendant is indicted a second time for the exact same offense. The defendant now files a motion to dismiss on the ground that a trial on the second charge is barred by the double jeopardy guarantee. Should the judge grant the motion to dismiss?

Simply stated, in a case that is to be tried by a jury, "jeopardy" does not attach until the jury is selected and sworn (sometimes expressed as "empaneled and sworn"); termination of the case prior to that time does not afford the defendant any double jeopardy protection. *See, e.g., Crist v. Bretz*, 437 U.S. 28 (1978). In non-jury cases, jeopardy does not attach until the first witness for the prosecution is sworn. When the criminal charge is resolved through the plea negotiation process, jeopardy attaches when the defendant's plea of guilty is accepted and a judgment of guilt is subsequently entered.

Some state statutes define the attachment of jeopardy. *See, e.g.,* 720 Ill. Con. Stat. 5/3-4(a)(3)(jeopardy attaches after jury is impaneled and sworn, or in a bench trial after the first witness was sworn but before findings were rendered by the trier of fact, or after a guilty plea was accepted by the court).

Rules concerning when jeopardy attaches appear to be somewhat arbitrary. As noted in *Crist*, however, they serve as stern reminders that once a case has begun, the task of arriving at a final verdict should not be abandoned.

E.   REPROSECUTION FOLLOWING DISMISSAL OR ACQUITTAL

[1]   Acquittal by Jury

[a]   Bar to Retrial

A jury verdict of not guilty (*i.e.,* an acquittal) is given absolute finality for double jeopardy purposes and therefore bars a retrial on the same issue in the same jurisdiction. The United States Supreme Court's strong adherence to this principle is reflected in *United States v. DiFrancesco*, 449 U.S. 117, 129–130 (1980):

> The Constitutional protection against double jeopardy unequivocally prohibits a second trial following an acquittal, for the "public interest in the finality of criminal judgments is so strong that an acquitted defendant may not be retried even though the acquittal was based upon an egregiously erroneous foundation." See *Fong Foo v. United States*, 369 U.S. 141, 143 (1962). If the innocence of the accused has been confirmed by a final judgment, the Constitution conclusively presumes that a second trial would be unfair.
>
> . . . This is justified on the ground that, however mistaken the acquittal may have been, there would be an unacceptably high risk that the Government, with its superior resources, would wear down a defendant, thereby "enhancing the possibility that even though innocent he may be found guilty." *Green v. United States*, 355 U.S. 184, 187 (1957).

As suggested by the *DiFrancesco* analysis, sometimes it may appear that an acquittal is flatly contrary to the government's proof. One commentator has expressed the view that the double jeopardy guarantee in this regard is a recognition of the jury's "nullification" power. *See* Peter Westen, *The Three Faces of Double Jeopardy: Reflections on Government Appeals of Criminal Sentences*, 78 MICH. L. REV. 1001, 1012 (1980) (asserting that "the most coherent . . . justification for the absolute finality of jury acquittals . . . is that the rule is a consequence of the jury's prerogative to acquit against the evidence").

[b]   Exception in Interests of Justice

[i]   Fraud or Intimidation

Should an acquittal obtained through fraud bar a subsequent prosecution for the same offense? The general rule is that the acquittal still bars the retrial. Based upon an analysis of the policies underlying the double jeopardy guarantee, Professor Rudstein agrees with this conclusion, "even though that acquittal may have been the result of bribery, blackmail, intimidation, or other improper conduct on the part of the accused or with her knowledge and acquiescence." David S. Rudstein, *Double Jeopardy and the Fraudulently-Obtained Acquittal*, 60 MO. L. REV. 607 (1995) (discussing an Illinois case in which an indictment was returned against a person who had previously been acquitted of the offense; prosecutor quoted as saying that double jeopardy did not protect the accused "because his acquittal resulted from a $10,000 bribe paid to the trial judge"). Do you agree with this conclusion? Could the doctrine of waiver be used to permit retrial?

[ii] Newly Discovered Evidence

What if the defendant is acquitted, then newly discovered evidence (perhaps DNA) becomes available clearly establishing guilt. Should double jeopardy prevent a retrial? The general rule is that retrial is barred, though perhaps a prosecution for perjury is possible if the defendant testified falsely and the statute of limitations has not run.

English law now grants an exception to its double jeopardy guarantee in this situation. *See generally* Justin W. Curtis, *The Meaning of Life (or Limb): an Originalist Proposal for Double Jeopardy Reform*, 41 U. Rich. L. Rev. 991 (1997)(citing case where man acquitted of murdering a baby later confessed to the crime; arguing retrial should be permissible based on historical notions of double jeopardy); Note, 44 Am. Crim. L. Rev. 1179 (2007)(citing data showing in 6.79% of acquittals the judge could not understand how the jury acquitted the defendant; arguing for constitutional amendment permitting retrial for newly discovered evidence).

If retrial for new evidence is permitted, what limits would you put on it? Would the evidence have to be decisive or could it just be "strong" or "better than was offered at trial?" Would you require that the evidence not have been available at trial had the government made good faith efforts to find it?

[2] Acquittal by Judge

Noting that the double jeopardy clause does not distinguish between jury and non-jury trials, the Supreme Court treats directed acquittals entered by the judge the same as a jury verdict of not guilty. *Sanabria v. United States*, 437 U.S. 54 (1978). This situation is to be contrasted, however, with the rare case in which a judge enters a judgment of acquittal *after* the jury has returned a verdict of guilty. In that instance, the government is permitted to appeal the judge's acquittal. If the government prevails on appeal, the appellate court is permitted to reinstate the verdict of guilty. *United States v. Jenkins*, 420 U.S. 358 (1975). As explained in *United States v. Scott*, 437 U.S. 82 (1978), a judgment of acquittal bars the government from an appeal only when, if the government wins its appeal, a second trial would be necessitated. Since this is not the case where a jury first returns a verdict of guilty and then the judge orders an acquittal, the government's appeal is allowed. The appeal simply restores the jury's original guilty verdict.

[3] Dismissal by Judge

A *dismissal* of the criminal charges (as opposed to an *acquittal*) by the judge normally presents no double jeopardy constraint on reprosecution because dismissals normally occur prior to the attachment of jeopardy. But what should be the result if a trial judge dismisses criminal charges *after* empaneling and swearing in the jury?

In *United States v. Scott*, 437 U.S. 82 (1978), the trial judge granted the defendant's motion to dismiss two (of three) counts on the ground of prejudicial pretrial delay; this came during trial and at the close of all the evidence. The Supreme Court refused to treat this dismissal as an acquittal; accordingly, the government was permitted to appeal the dismissal and, if successful on appeal, to reprosecute the defendant. Distinguishing between a judge's acquittal versus dismissal during trial, the Supreme Court noted:

[A] defendant is acquitted only when the ruling of a judge, whatever its label, actually represents a resolution [in the defendant's favor], correct or not, of some or all of the factual elements of the offense charged.

. . . [T]he defendant, by deliberately choosing to seek termination of the proceedings against him on a basis unrelated to factual guilt or innocence-. . . suffers no injury cognizable under the Double Jeopardy Clause . . . .
[437 U.S. at 97–99]

Justice Brennan, writing for the three dissenters, argued that a retrial should be barred even if the judgment favorable to the accused was based upon a ground other than factual innocence. He asserted that double jeopardy concerns apply equally in either "acquittal" or "dismissal" cases: heavy personal strain upon the accused, increased risk of a guilty verdict at the second trial, and the government's ability to benefit by shoring up weaknesses exposed in the first proceeding. Finally, he expressed uneasiness with the way in which the Court's acquittal standard would be applied, maintaining that there would be "few instances" in which defense claims could be found unrelated to factual innocence.

NOTE

The principle applies irrespective of the proceure that led to termination of the trial. *See, e.g., In re State*, 932 A.2d 848 (N.H. 2007)(court granted directed verdict for defendant because of improper venue; retrial permitted because was not adjudication on merits).

F.   RETRIAL FOLLOWING MISTRIAL: "MANIFEST NECESSITY" AND THE ISSUE OF DEFENDANT'S CONSENT

[1]   Manifest Necessity: Hung Jury and Other Circumstances

It occasionally happens that, after jeopardy has attached, a criminal case fails to end in a final judgment. Yet even then, the double jeopardy guarantee may not protect the defendant from being compelled to face a second trial. This occurs when the trial judge orders a *mistrial* either with or without the defendant's consent. In a mistrial, unlike a dismissal, the court simply ends the trial without dismissing the criminal charges.

The United States Supreme Court has long held that trial judges may declare a mistrial over the objection of the defendant whenever there is *manifest necessity* for the mistrial. In *United States v. Perez*, 22 U.S. 579 (1824), the Supreme Court recognized that when a trial ends in the declaration of a mistrial because of a "hung jury" (hopelessly deadlocked and unable to reach a verdict), such manifest necessity exists and double jeopardy does not preclude retrial. This is so because there has been no final verdict and the circumstances are such that the judge truly has no alternative to granting a mistrial. As explained in *Illinois v. Somerville*, 410 U.S. 458 (1973), the *Perez* doctrine of manifest necessity also reflects the notion that trial judges should not be pressed into permitting a trial to proceed to conviction when an obvious procedural error makes appellate reversal a certainty. The "ends of justice" are not served by wasting governmental services on a trial that will be automatically reversed if the government succeeds in obtaining a conviction.

To determine whether or not the "manifest necessity" standard is met, the trial judge must determine whether or not effective alternatives to a mistrial are present. Many courts say that mistrial should be a last resort. *See, e.g., United States v. Lara-Ramirez*, 519 F.3d 76 (1st Cir. 2008); *Tritt v. State*, 173 P.3d 1017 (Alas. App. 2008)(court should order mistrial without defendant's consent only in "very extraordinary and striking circumstances").

For example, in *United States v. Jorn*, 400 U.S. 470 (1971), the defendant was charged with assisting in the preparation of fraudulent income tax returns. At trial the prosecutor called as a witness the taxpayer whose return the defendant allegedly had aided in preparing. The trial judge refused to permit the witness to testify until he had consulted an attorney. The judge then discharged the jury, thereby aborting the trial, to give the witness time to talk with counsel. When later the case was set for retrial before another jury, the defendant moved for dismissal on the ground of double jeopardy. Dismissal was granted and the United States Supreme Court affirmed. The Court explained:

> It is apparent from the record that no consideration was given to the possibility of a trial continuance; indeed, the trial court acted so abruptly in discharging the jury that, had the prosecutor been disposed to suggest a continuance, or the defendant to object to the discharge of the jury, there would have been no opportunity to do so. When one examines the circumstances surrounding the discharge of this jury, it seems abundantly apparent that the trial judge made no effort to exercise a sound discretion to assure that, taking all the circumstances into account, there was a manifest necessity for the *sua sponte* declaration of this mistrial. Therefore, we must conclude that in the circumstances of this case, [defendant's] reprosecution would violate the double jeopardy provision of the Fifth Amendment. [400 U.S. at 487]

NOTE

1. *Case illustrations of manifest necessity.* A survey of cases found the following illustrations of manifest necessity: deadlocked jury; death, illness or absence of a judge, jurors, lawyer or the defendant; the judge disqualified himself mid-trial because surprising testimony made it appear the judge cold not be impartial; ineffective assistance of defense counsel; and defense counsel, mid-trial, discovered serious conflict of interest).

2. *Case illustrations finding no manifest necessity.* Illustrations of where manifest necessity was not present to support a mistrial include: *Tritt v. State*, 173 P.3d 1017 (Alas. App. 2008)(error to declare mistral because of improper opening statement; could have been cured by clarifying jury instruction); *State v. Voigt*, 734 N.W.2d 787 (N.D. 2007)(confusion about whether defense counsel represented defendant did not merit discharge of jury since court could have released and then reconvened same jury after issue resolved); *Paul v. People*, 105 P.3d 628 (Colo. 2005)(docket overcrowding and unexpectedly long trial not manifest necessity).

3. *Enough is enough.* Though double jeopardy does not bar retrials after a hung jury, some courts have the inherent authority to dismiss subsequent prosecution in the interests of "fair play" or "substantial justice" or the like. *See, e.g., State v. Kyles*, 706 So.2d 611 (La. App. 1998)(refusing to use its inherent authority to dismiss fifth murder prosecution following several mistrials); *State v. Abbati*, 493 A.2d 513 (N.J. 1985)(recognizing inherent authority; extensive case and policy analysis, including factors to be considered before exercising inherent authority).

Do you agree this is an appropriate judicial decision? Or could the separation of powers doctrine suggest this is a prosecutorial, not judicial, decision? In exercising its inherent authority, should a court consider the strength of the persecution's case? Or focus on the harm to the defendant?

[2] Defendant Requests or Consents to Mistrial: No Provocation

Where the *defendant* moves for a mistrial, reprosecution usually is allowed. As explained in *United States v. Dinitz*, 424 U.S. 600, 606–607 (1976):

> [w]hether . . . there can be a new trial after a mistrial has been declared without the defendant's request or consent depends on whether "there is a manifest necessity for the [mistrial], or the ends of public justice would otherwise be defeated." Different considerations obtain, however, when the mistrial has been declared at the defendant's request.

The Court in *Dinitz* noted that it is basically the defendant's decision whether (1) to continue the trial, notwithstanding the alleged judicial or prosecutorial error, or (2) to ask for a mistrial and therefore surrender the right to have the matter determined by the first jury.

NOTE

1. *What constitutes consent?* Whether a retrial is permissible may depend on whether the the the accused requested the mistrial. The easy case is when the defendant — alone or joined by the prosecution — formally requests the mistrial. But what if the defense lawyer is silent or fails to object to the mistrial? Many courts hold that neither constitutes consent. *See, e.g., Dawson v. State*, 2008 WL941784 (Fla. App. 2008)(defense counsel stated "the defense has no position" when court considered whether to declare a mistrial; defense did not consent to mistrial).

Other courts are more flexible, finding consent when the defendant "sits silently by and does not object" to the mistrial when there is a fair opportunity to do so. *See United States v. Lara-Ramirez*, 519 F.3d 76 (1st Cir. 2008)(no consent; defense counsel urged alternatives to mistrial, giving "unmistakable notice of objection to mistrial" even though never used words, "I object"); *United States v. Gantley*, 172 F.3d 422 (6th Cir. 1999)(failure to object to mistrial implies consent only if sum of surrounding circumstances positively indicates silence was tantamount to consent; implied consent found when defense counsel suggested court's reaction caused prejudice, court suggested mistrial was needed, and defense counsel twice refused to comment when asked if there was "anything else"); *Pelligrine v. Commonwealth*, 844 N.E.2d 608 (Mass. 2006)(consent to mistrial inferred from silence when defense counsel had opportunity to object and remained silent in situation when judge's conduct was not intimidating).

A statute may also define consent. *See* Colo. Rev. Stat. Ann. § 18-1-301(2)(a)(consent is a waiver of objection to mistrial; defendant is deemed to consent unless objections to mistrial are on the record at time of court order of mistrial).

2. *Must defendant personally consent?* If consent to a mistrial constitutes a waiver of double jeopardy (which is the usual rule), can defense counsel waive it or must the defendant personally do so? Most courts conclude the decision is for defense counsel as part of professional judgment, but a minority view is that the waiver must be knowing, intelligent, and voluntary and can only be done by the accused personally. *See generally, Nero v. District of Columbia*, 936 A.2d 310 (D.C. 2007)(reviewing authorities and concluding that the decision to move for mistrial is within defense counsel's discretion and may be made over the defendant's objection). Which view do you think is best?

3. *Withdrawal of consent.* What if a defendant requests, or consents to, a mistrial, then withdraws the request or consent after the mistrial is granted.? Courts routinely reject the withdrawal. *See, e.g., Tinsley v. Million*, 399 F.3d 796 (6th Cir. 2005)(defense counsel moved and argued for mistrial, then objected when mistrial granted).

However, if the withdrawal of consent is made before the mistrial is ordered, the defendant is not deemed to have consented. *See, e.g., Weston v. Kernan*, 50 F.3d 633 (9th Cir. 1995)(prior to court's ruling on mistrial, defense clarified that his motion was for mistrial with prejudice; no consent to mistrial without prejudice, as was the case).

[3]   Defendant Provoked to Request or Consent to Mistrial

What should be the result if the defendant is provoked into requesting a mistrial because of some intentional misbehavior on the part of the prosecuting attorney? *Dinitz* held that a different rule applies in that instance:

> The Double Jeopardy Clause does protect a defendant against governmental actions intended to provoke mistrial requests and thereby to subject defendants to the substantial burdens imposed by multiple prosecutions. It bars retrials where "bad-faith conduct by judge or prosecutor" threatens the "harassment of an accused by successive prosecutions or declarations of a mistrial so as to afford the prosecution a more favorable opportunity to convict" the defendant. [424 U.S. at 611]

Whether the prosecutor intended to provoke a mistrial is a question decided by the judge, not jury, and the decision is given great deference on appeal.

How workable is the standard requiring intentional provocation? Assume that a witness for the prosecution is asked by defense counsel on cross examination whether the witness had ever filed a criminal complaint against the accused (so as to establish the witness' bias against the defendant). After the witness has admitted filing a complaint, the prosecutor on redirect examination now seeks to rehabilitate the witness by eliciting reasons why such a complaint may have been filed against the defendant. The following colloquy occurs:

Prosecutor: Have you ever done business with [the defendant]?

Witness: No, I have not.

Prosecutor: Is that because he is a crook?

At that point, the defendant's motion for a mistrial is granted by a trial judge. Would retrial of the defendant be barred by the double jeopardy guarantee?

These facts were at issue in *Oregon v. Kennedy*, 456 U.S. 667 (1982), where a state trial court found that "it was not the intention of the prosecutor in this case to cause a mistrial," and therefore permitted retrial of the defendant. A state appellate court disagreed, however, concluding that retrial was barred because the prosecutor's conduct was "overreaching" — notwithstanding the fact that the appellate court accepted the finding that the prosecutor did not actually intend to cause a mistrial. The United States Supreme Court rejected the appellate court's analysis and adopted a standard that focuses on the intent of the prosecutor:

> Only where the governmental conduct in question is intended to "goad" the defendant into moving for a mistrial may a defendant raise the bar of double jeopardy to a second trial after having succeeded in aborting the first on his own motion. [456 U.S. at 676]

The Court in *Kennedy* explained why the "prosecutorial intent" standard was preferable to a more generalized standard of "bad faith conduct" or "harassment":

> The difficulty with the more general standards which would permit a broader exception than one based merely on intent is that they offer virtually no standards for their application. Every act on the part of a rational prosecutor during a trial is designed to "prejudice" the defendant by placing before the judge or jury evidence leading to a finding of his guilt. Given the complexity of the rules of evidence, it will be a rare trial of any complexity in which some proffered evidence by the prosecutor or by the defendant's attorney will not be found objectionable by the trial court. Most such objections are undoubtedly curable by simply refusing to allow the proffered evidence to be admitted, or in the case of a particular line of inquiry taken by counsel with a witness, by an admonition to desist from a particular line of inquiry.
>
> More serious infractions on the part of the prosecutors may provoke a motion for mistrial on the part of the defendant, and may in the view of the trial court

warrant the granting of such a motion. The "overreaching" [or harassment] standard . . . would add another classification of prosecutorial error, one requiring dismissal of the indictment, but without supplying any standard by which to assess that error.

By contrast, a standard that examines the intent of the prosecutor, though certainly not entirely free from practical difficulties, is a manageable standard to apply. It merely calls for the court to make a finding of fact. Inferring the existence or nonexistence of intent from objective facts and circumstances is a familiar process in our criminal justice system. [456 U.S. at 674–675]

Because the Oregon trial court found that the prosecutor's conduct culminating in the termination of the trial was not intended to provoke the defendant into moving for a mistrial, no double jeopardy violation occurred.

NOTES

1. *Proof of intent to provoke.* The defendant has a difficult task of meeting the burden of proving that the judge or prosecutor intended to provoke a motion for a mistral. Factors courts look at include the tone and manner of the judge's or prosecutor's improper actions, the response to the defendant's mistrial motion (did the state strongly oppose it?), the strength of the state's cases (no intent for mistrial if case strong), and any motive for the judge's or state's action.

The difficulty of proving intent explains why few cases hold the government actually did goad the defense into requesting a mistrial. The cases finding the improper intent involve egregious government misconduct. *See, e.g., Anderson v. State,* 645 S.E.2d 647 (Ga. App. 2007)(prosecutor knowingly elicited testimony that defendant refused to answer police questions and requested a lawyer).

Motives are often found to be legitimate. *See, e.g., Lee-Thomas v. United States,* 921 A.2d 773 (D.C. 2007)(court strongly suggested defense counsel's trial representations were deficient and defendant requested mistrial; court's motives were not improper since intent was to benefit defendant's right to a fair trial).

2. *State rejection of "intentional goading" test.* Interestingly, the Supreme Court of Oregon later considered the issue under the Oregon Constitution and rejected the United States Supreme Court's test of "intentional provocation of mistrials." *Oregon v. Kennedy,* 666 P.2d 1316 (Ore. 1983). The Oregon Supreme Court observed that the "intentional provocation" test has two significant shortcomings. First, in focusing only upon the behavior of prosecutors, the focus is too limited because other officials (judges, bailiffs, or other courthouse officials) could also cause a mistrial or a reversal. Second, a finding of "intentional provocation" would likely constitute contempt of court and could also lead to disbarment or other discipline as a violation of professional standards. Given the possible invocation of additional penalties against the offending prosecutor, "that places too heavy a burden on the inference that a defendant must ask a judge to draw from the objective conduct and circumstances." [*Id.* at 1326]

In its place, the following standard was adopted:

[R]etrial is barred by [the Oregon Constitution] when improper official conduct is so prejudicial to the defendant that it cannot be cured by means short of a mistrial, and if the official knows that the conduct is improper and prejudicial and either intends or is indifferent to the resulting mistrial or reversal. When this occurs, it is clear that the burden of a second trial is not attributable to the defendant's preference for a new trial over completing the trial infected by an error. Rather, it results from the state's readiness, though perhaps not calculated intent, to force the defendant to such a choice.

Id. See also *State v. Rogan,* 984 P.2d 1231 (Hawaii 1999) (holding under state constitutional law that reprosecution of a defendant after a mistrial as a result of prosecutorial misconduct is barred if the misconduct was so egregious, from an objective standpoint, to deny the defendant a fair trial); *Ex parte Wheeler*, 203 S.W.3d 317 (Tex. Crim. App. 2006)(intentional goading *or* reckless misconduct); *People v. Batts*, 68 P. 3d 357 (Cal. 2003) (retrial barred if "prosecutorial misconduct deprived the defendant of a reasonable prospect of an acquittal").

PROBLEM 16-3. PIZZO'S DECAPITATED RODENT

Sam Stevens was charged with theft of valuable construction equipment. Paul Pizzo, a crucial government witness, was to testify that Stevens had made incriminating comments to him about the crime. The prosecutor referred to this expected testimony in his opening statement, though he knew that Pizzo might be hesitant to testify.

On the third day of the trial, Pizzo's attorney, Rachel Rich, informed the prosecutor that Pizzo would refuse to testify "whether or not he was granted immunity." Specifically, Pizzo was concerned about the well-being of his family, had received telephone threats, and had found a decapitated rodent left at his door.

When Pizzo was called to the stand, he refused to testify. The prosecutor offered immunity and explained to Pizzo that he was now obligated to answer all questions truthfully. Still, he refused to answer. After being held in contempt and jailed, Pizzo again was called to testify. Again, he refused to testify.

Conceding that without Pizzo's testimony there was insufficient evidence to convict, the prosecutor moved for a mistrial. The trial judge granted the motion and denied the defendant's motion for a judgment of acquittal.

Stevens was re-indicted, and his attorney moved to dismiss the indictment on double jeopardy grounds.

1. What arguments should defense counsel make in support of the motion?

2. How should those arguments be countered by the prosecutor?

3. If you were judge, how would you rule on the motion? *See United States v. Stevens*, 177 F.3d 579 (6th Cir. 1999).

G. REPROSECUTION FOLLOWING CONVICTION AND REVERSAL

[1] Conviction Reversed on Appeal; General Approach

If the defendant's trial ends in conviction, the defendant may pursue an appeal (or some other post-conviction remedy) to set aside the guilty verdict on the basis of an alleged error at trial. If the defendant's appeal succeeds and the conviction is overturned, the double jeopardy guarantee does not prevent the government from prosecuting the defendant a second time. As explained in *United States v. DiFrancesco*, 449 U.S. 117, 131 (1980):

> It would be a high price indeed for society to pay were every accused granted immunity from punishment because of any defect sufficient to constitute reversible error in the proceedings leading to conviction. To require a criminal defendant to stand trial again after he has successfully invoked a statutory right of appeal to upset his first conviction is not an act of governmental oppression of the sort against which the Double Jeopardy Clause was intended to protect.

[2] Exception: Reversal for Insufficiency of Evidence

In *Burks v. United States*, 437 U.S. 1 (1978), the United States Supreme Court recognized, however, that retrial of the convicted defendant is *not* allowed when the basis for appellate reversal is insufficiency of the evidence. The contrast was explained as follows:

[R]eversal for trial error, as distinguished from evidentiary insufficiency, does not constitute a decision to the effect that the government has failed to prove its case. As such, it implies nothing with respect to the guilt or innocence of the defendant. Rather, it is a determination that a defendant has been convicted through a judicial process which is defective in some fundamental respect, *e.g.*, incorrect receipt or rejection of evidence, incorrect instructions, or prosecutorial misconduct. When this occurs, the accused has a strong interest in obtaining a fair readjudication of his guilt, free from error, just as society maintains a valid concern for insuring that the guilty are punished.

The same cannot be said when a defendant's conviction has been overturned due to a failure of proof at trial, in which case the prosecution cannot complain of prejudice, for it has been given one fair opportunity to offer whatever proof it could assemble. Moreover, such an appellate reversal means that the government's case was so lacking that it should not have been *submitted* to the jury. Since we necessarily afford absolute finality to a jury's *verdict* of acquittal — no matter how erroneous its decision — it is difficult to conceive how society has any greater interest in retrying a defendant when, on review, it is decided as a matter of law that the jury could not properly have returned a verdict of guilty. [437 U.S. at 15–16]

Reversal for weight of evidence. Sometimes the basis for appellate court reversal is expressed in terms of *weight* of the evidence rather than *legal sufficiency* of the evidence. In *Tibbs v. Florida*, 475 U.S. 31 (1981), the state supreme court had overturned the defendant's conviction on this basis (in the court's words, "the evidence, although sufficient to support the jury's verdict, did not fully persuade the court of Tibbs' guilt"). In this instance, the United States Supreme Court concluded that double jeopardy would *not* bar a retrial. As the Court explained:

While [reversal of a conviction] based on the weight of the evidence . . . fails to implicate the policies supporting *Burks*, it does involve the usual principles permitting retrial after a defendant's successful appeal. Just as the Double Jeopardy Clause does not require society to pay the high price of freeing every defendant whose first trial was tainted by prosecutorial error, it should not exact the price of immunity for every defendant who persuades an appellate panel to overturn an error-free conviction and give him a second chance at acquittal. Giving the defendant this second opportunity, when the evidence is sufficient to support the first verdict, hardly amounts to governmental oppression of the sort against which the Double Jeopardy Clause was intended to protect. [457 U.S. at 44]

NOTES

1. *Conviction on lesser-included offense.* Assume that a defendant is charged with aggravated robbery, a class A felony, but is convicted of the lesser-included offense of robbery, a class B felony. If the defendant successfully appeals the robbery conviction on a ground other than evidence sufficiency, is the government allowed to charge him or her once again with aggravated robbery? Normally, the jury's verdict of guilt on the lesser-included offense is treated as an implicit acquittal as to the greater offense of aggravated robbery. Accordingly, double jeopardy bars the reinstatement of the greater charge on retrial. *See Green v. United States*, 355 U.S. 184 (1957).

2. *Greater sentence on retrial.* With regard to sentencing, it is usually permissible to impose a more severe sentence following conviction on retrial. This is not permissible, however, when the harsher sentence is based on judicial or prosecutorial vindictiveness. *North Carolina v. Pearce*, 395 U.S. 711 (1969). *See* Chapters 2 and 18.

3. *Government appeal of sentence.* Double jeopardy also does not bar the government from seeking appellate review of a sentence. In *United States v. DiFrancesco*, 449 U.S. 117 (1980), the Supreme Court held that increasing a sentence on appeal does not violate double jeopardy because imposition of the lesser sentence is not tantamount to an "implied acquittal" of the greater sentence. *See* James C. Cissell, FEDERAL CRIMINAL TRIALS § 10-5 (5th ed. 1999).

Whether the government is permitted to appeal the sentence imposed requires an analysis of both statutes and rules of procedure. Some states allow either the government or the defendant to seek appellate review of the sentence. The appellate court may affirm, reduce or increase the sentence, and its review may be *de novo* or may entail some deference to the trial judge's assessment of the appropriate sentence. Other jurisdictions prohibit appellate review of sentencing upon the government's request. With the current trend toward presumptive or "guideline" sentencing (see Chapter 17), however, it appears that an increasing number of jurisdictions permit both the prosecution and the defense to initiate appellate review for the purpose of seeking an increased or reduced sentence.

4. *Retrial after completion of sentence.* What if the defendant is convicted and appeals, and has completed service of the sentence when the original conviction was overturned. Is retrial permissible? *See State v. Jordan*, 716 A.2d 1004 (Me. 1998)(no double jeopardy bar).

[3]   Exception: Serious Prosecutorial Misconduct

What if the prosecution's trial behavior is egregious, the jury convicts, the defendant appeals and wins because of the prosecutor's misconduct. The general rule is that the defendant may be retried because he or she appealed the case.

A minority of states, however, analogize the situation to a mistrial intentionally provoked by the government. They bar a retrial if a conviction is reversed because of intentional government misconduct or other similar standard. *See, e.g., State v. Rogan*, 984 P.2d 1231 (Haw. 1999)(under Hawaii double jeopardy clause, reprosecution after mistrial or conviction reversed on appeal, will be barred if prosecutor made highly prejudicial error that was so egregious, from an objective standpoint, it clearly denied a defendant the right to a fair trial; prosecutor made racist comments in closing argument); *State v. Jorgenson*, 10 P.3d 1177 (Ariz. 2000)(retrial barred when conviction reversed because of the state's "egregiously, intentional, improper conduct"); *State v. Breit*, 930 P.3d 792 (N.M. 1996)(under state constitution, retrial barred if official misconduct is so unfairly prejudicial it cannot be cured without mistrial or motion for new trial, and official knew the conduct was improper and prejudicial, and the official intended to provoke a mistrial or acted in willful disregard of the resulting mistrial, new trial, or reversal).

H.   REPROSECUTION BY A SEPARATE SOVEREIGN

[1]   General Rule: Prosecution Permitted by Different Sovereigns

It is not uncommon that a single criminal episode violates both a state and a federal criminal statute. The double jeopardy clause does not prohibit prosecution by a state simply because the accused has been convicted or acquitted of the same offense by a federal court or vice versa. *Abbate v. United States*, 359 U.S. 187 (1959); *Bartkus v. Illinois*, 359 U.S. 121 (1959). This principle of double jeopardy law is known as "the dual sovereignty" or "separate sovereign" doctrine. Its underlying rationale was explicated by the United States Supreme Court in *Heath v. Alabama*, 474 U.S. 82, 88 (1985):

> The dual sovereignty doctrine is founded on the common-law conception of crime as an offense against the sovereignty of the government. When a defendant in a single act violates the "peace and dignity" of two sovereigns by breaking the laws of each, he has committed two distinct "offences." *United States v. Lanza*, 260 U.S. 377, 382 (1922) . . . . Consequently, when the same

act transgresses the laws of two sovereigns, "it cannot be truly averred that the offender has been twice punished for the same offence; but only that by one act he has committed two offences, for each of which he is justly punishable."

Another rationale for the dual sovereignty rule is the fear that without it a person could escape fair punishment by obtaining a lenient sentence in one jurisdiction and thereby barring other jurisdictions from imposing more appropriate sanctions. The scenario becomes more compelling if it is hypothesized that the lenient jurisdiction is where the defendant, a politically influential person, lives and receives "home cooking" by a politically sensitive judge who is facing reelection.

NOTES

1. *Doctrine criticized.* The separate sovereign doctrine has been strongly criticized. Justice Black, dissenting in *Abbate* and *Bartkus*, protested that "double prosecutions for the same offense are . . . contrary to the spirit of our free country." He continued:

> The Court [in *Bartkus*] takes the position that a second trial for the same act is somehow less offensive if one of the trials is conducted by the Federal Government and the other by a State. [F]rom the standpoint of the [defendant], this notion is too subtle for me to grasp. If double punishment is what is feared, it hurts no less for two "sovereigns" to inflict it than one. [359 U.S. at 150, 155]

For scholarly criticism of the dual sovereignty doctrine, see Harlan R. Harrison, *Federalism and Double Jeopardy: A Study in the Frustration of Human Rights*, 17 U. MIAMI L. REV. 306 (1963), and Raymond C. Hurley, Note, *The Continued Validity of Successive Prosecutions by State and Federal Governments for the Same Conduct*, 14 WAKE FOREST L. REV. 823 (1978).

2. *Federal government's policy.* Under the *Petite* policy (so named because the policy was mentioned by the United States Supreme Court in *Petite v. United States*, 361 U.S. 529 (1960)), generally United States attorneys will not initiate or continue a federal prosecution following a state prosecution based upon substantially the same act unless there is substantial federal interest, prior state prosecution left that interest unvindicated, and there is sufficient evidence for a federal conviction and a compelling reason for doing so. This internal policy constraint, which now appears as § 9-2.031 in the United States Attorneys' Manual, is not constitutionally mandated and is not enforceable against the government by the accused.

One prominent federal interest which has sometimes persuaded the United States government to prosecute, even after a defendant has been acquitted or not charged at all in state court, has been the vindication of civil rights. On occasion, the Department of Justice has investigated and prosecuted certain acts which constitute criminal federal civil rights violations, as well as crimes under state law. Examples include the prosecution of Los Angeles police officers in the 1990's for the beating of Rodney King after he was in handcuffs and not resisting arrest, the investigation of the murderers of civil rights workers in Mississippi in the 1960's, and prosecution of the fatal bombing of an African American church in Birmingham, Alabama in the same era. These cases suggest that the dual sovereignty doctrine can be used by one jurisdiction to correct the errors of another.

[2] Different Units of Same Government

Where separate prosecutions are pursued by different units of the *same government*, however, the double jeopardy prohibition applies. For example, a court-martial trial bars a successive trial for the same crime in a federal district court. *Grafton v. United States*, 206 U.S. 333 (1907). Similarly, successive municipal (or county) and state prosecutions are barred. See *Waller v. Florida*, 397 U.S. 387 (1970) (observing that cities are not separate sovereigns, but rather are "subordinate governmental instrumentalities" of the state).

In *United States v. Lara*, 541 U.S. 193 (2004), the Court held that a tribal court's prosecution of a non-member Native American was "in its capacity of a separate sovereign." Thus the Double Jeopardy guarantee did not bar the Federal Government from prosecuting the defendant for essentially the same offense (assaulting a federal officer). (Note, however, that Indian tribes generally do not have criminal jurisdiction to prosecute non-Indians. *See Oliphant v. Suquamish Indian Tribe*, 435 U.S. 191 (1978)). *See generally* Symposium, 40 TULSA L. REV. 1-153 (2004)(*Lara* decision).

[3] Two States

Does the dual sovereignty doctrine permit successive prosecutions by two states? In *Heath v. Alabama*, 474 U.S. 82 (1985), the Supreme Court answered "yes." There, a resident of Alabama arranged for the kidnapping and murder of his wife. The kidnapping occurred in Alabama. The homicide victim's body was found in an automobile in Georgia, where it was later established the murder actually took place. Both Georgia and Alabama law enforcement officials pursued investigations, and ultimately the defendant was arrested by Georgia authorities. He pled guilty in Georgia to a murder charge in exchange for a sentence of life imprisonment. Approximately three months later, an Alabama grand jury investigated the same crime and returned an indictment against the defendant for the capital offense of murder during a kidnapping. The defendant's double jeopardy objection to the Alabama indictment was rejected on the basis of the dual sovereignty doctrine. Thereafter, he was convicted in Alabama of "murder during a kidnapping" in the first degree and received a death sentence.

The United States Supreme Court affirmed the Alabama death sentence. Justice O'Connor, writing for the seven-person majority, explained that the dual sovereignty doctrine applies fully to successive prosecutions by two states. Next, she turned to the defendant's argument that the dual sovereignty principle should be restricted to cases where both jurisdictions can demonstrate that allowing only one entity to exercise jurisdiction over the defendant will interfere with the unvindicated interests of the second entity.

> This balancing of interests approach . . . cannot be reconciled with the dual sovereignty principle . . . . If the States are separate sovereigns, as they must be under the definition of sovereignty which the Court consistently has employed, the circumstances of the case are irrelevant.
>
> . . . Foremost among the prerogatives of sovereignty is the power to create and enforce a criminal code. To deny a State its power to enforce its criminal laws because another State has won the race to the courthouse "would be a shocking and untoward deprivation of the historic right and obligation of the States to maintain peace and order within their confines." *Bartkus v. Illinois*, 359 U.S. 121, 137 (1959).
>
> Such a deprivation of a State's sovereign powers cannot be justified by the assertion that under "interest analysis" the State's legitimate penal interests will be satisfied through a prosecution conducted by another State. A State's interest in vindicating its sovereign authority through enforcement of its laws by definition can never be satisfied by another State's enforcement of *its* own laws. [*Id.* at 92–93]

Justice Marshall, with whom Justice Brennan joined, dissented. He maintained:

> Where two States seek to prosecute the same defendant for the same crime in two separate proceedings, the justifications found in the federal-state context for an exemption from double jeopardy constraints simply do not hold. Although the two States may have opted for different policies within their assigned territorial jurisdictions, the sovereign concerns with whose vindication each

State has been charged are identical. Thus, in contrast to the federal-state context, barring the second prosecution would still permit one government to act upon the broad range of sovereign concerns that have been reserved to the States by the Constitution. The compelling need in the federal-state context to subordinate double jeopardy concerns is thus considerably diminished in cases involving successive prosecutions by different States. Moreover, from the defendant's perspective, the burden of successive prosecutions cannot be justified as a *quid pro quo* of dual citizenship. [*Id.* at 100–101]

NOTES

1. *Subsequent history of Heath.* Heath was executed by Alabama authorities in 1992. For a critical assessment of *Heath*, see Ronald J. Allen & John P. Ratnaswamy, *Heath v. Alabama: A Case Study of Doctrine and Rationality in the Supreme Court*, 76 J. CRIM. L. & CRIMINOLOGY 801, 804 (1985) (characterizing the analysis as "simplistic," "unresponsive to the reasons that gave rise to the rules the Court purports to apply," and "an example of poor judicial craftsmanship").

2. *State rejection of doctrine.* A significant number of states have rejected the dual sovereignty doctrine either under a state statute or state constitutional provisions. See, for example, *People v. Morgan*, 785 P.2d 1294 (Colo. 1990), characterizing the dual sovereignty doctrine as "harsh." The Colorado statute, applied in that case, provides:

> If conduct constitutes an offense within the concurrent jurisdiction of this state and of the United States, or another state, or of a municipality, a prosecution in any other of these jurisdictions is a bar to a subsequent prosecution in this state [if] the first prosecution resulted in a conviction or an acquittal . . . and the subsequent prosecution is based on the same conduct . . . . [Colo. Rev. Stat. § 18-1-303 (1999)]

Chapter 17
SENTENCING

A. INTRODUCTION

This chapter provides an introduction to some of the main issues within the complex topic of sentencing in criminal cases. Students interested in more information on this difficult topic should consult the materials cited throughout the chapter. *See generally* Lynn S. Branham & Michael S. Hamden, The Law and Policy of Sentencing And Corrections (7th Ed. 2005); Arthur W. Campbell, Law Of Sentencing (3d ed. 2004); Norval Morris & Michael Tonry, Between Prison and Probation (1990); Michael Tonry, Sentencing Matters (1996).

[1] Importance of Sentencing

In many ways, sentencing is the most important part of the criminal justice system. To those charged with a crime, the chances are great that critical aspects of their future life will be determined by the sentencing process. Approximately ninety percent of them will plead guilty and their sentences will usually be the product of negotiations between the prosecutor and the defense counsel. Those proceeding to trial will face a similar result. Most will be found guilty and receive some kind of sentence. Therefore, it is no exaggeration to say that in the vast majority of criminal cases, the key issue to defendants, prosecutors, and victims alike is not guilt or innocence but rather, what is the most appropriate sentence.

To the extent that sentencing practices affect both the volume and types of crimes committed, sentencing may also affect the quality of life of average citizens. For example, if a particular sentencing approach creates a deterrent to crime, it may reduce the incidence of that offense. This will spare members of the public the human and financial costs of being crime victims and becoming criminals. It will also contribute to society's sense of safety. Conversely, a sentencing scheme could actually encourage crime, thereby increasing the risk of victimization. An example would be a system that imposed such heavy fines on the poor that many turn to crime in order to pay their penalties.

Just as sentencing affects citizens' safety, it also affects their perceptions of the criminal justice system and government (or at least the legal system) in general. If sentences are viewed as inappropriate (perhaps because they are too harsh or too lenient, or because they are unfairly arrived at), people may lose faith in the justice system. A 2007 national poll found that only 19% of those surveyed reported that they had "a great deal" or "quite a lot" of confidence in the criminal justice system. U.S. Dep't of Justice Sourcebook of Criminal Justice Statistics [online] ("Sourcebook")(Ann L. Pastore and Kathleen Maguire, eds., 2006), available at http://www.albany.edu/sourcebook/pdf/t2112007.pdf. Thirty-three percent of respondents reported "very little" confidence in the criminal justice system. It is likely that dissatisfaction with sentencing contributed to those dismal results.

To some extent the public's interest in the criminal justice system is reflected in the political world. Crime and the criminal justice system have been and continue to be political issues. Politicians routinely decry lenient sentences, "country club-like" prisons, and the early release of prisoners. These themes are consistent with public opinion polls. In 2002, for example, a national survey asked whether the courts in a respondent's area dealt "too harshly," "not harshly enough," or "about right" with criminals. The results showed that 67% answered "not harshly enough"; 9% "too harshly"; and 18% "about right." Sourcebook, at http://www.albany.edu/sourcebook/pdf/t247.pdf.

As a political issue, sentencing generates both rhetoric and proposals for change. In addition to sentencing guidelines, two of the most current proposals are "Truth in Sentencing" (the sentence a criminal actually serves should be about the same as that announced by the judge) and "Three Strikes You're Out" (third time felony offenders should receive a sentence of life or life without possibility of parole).

[2] General Features

Although sentencing structure is discussed in more detail below, a few general parameters are important to understand at this point.

[a] Discretion

One of the key features of the American sentencing system is *discretion*. Judges (and formerly juries) historically have been given much leeway in deciding the appropriate sentence for a given offender. Typically the statutory scheme provided the judge with a range of options and furnished little guidance in selecting among the choices. For example, a state criminal law may have authorized a prison term of from one to five years, and also may have permitted the judge to impose a probation term in lieu of prison. As discussed below, appellate review of sentences is relatively rare (other than in jurisdictions with recently enacted *sentencing guidelines*) and reinforces the trial judge's broad discretion in selecting sentences.

Sometimes, however, the judge's sentencing discretion is limited. For example, the legislature may establish a mandatory minimum sentence (*e.g.*, no less than five years in prison with no possibility of probation or parole until the minimum required time has been served) or even a set sentence (*e.g.*, a $500 fine) that must be imposed. As described later in this chapter, some recent sentencing guideline systems have considerably structured and confined the exercise of judicial sentencing discretion.

[b] Role of Plea Bargaining

Although it is true that sentencing laws assign the sentencing function almost exclusively to judges, this theoretical truism masks the fact that most sentencing decisions are driven, as a practical matter, by the plea bargaining process rather than made by judges. As discussed more fully in Chapter 11, over ninety percent of persons charged with a crime plead guilty. Virtually all of these pleas are the result of plea agreements between the defense and the prosecution. Routinely, the "deal" sets the sentence the defendant will receive and/or the exact crimes of which the defendant will be convicted. The court ordinarily rubber stamps the deal, but typically has the final word as to whether or not to accept the plea agreement. If the sentence imposed by the court embraces the terms of the plea bargain, the defendant will be considered to have waived the right to appeal the sentence in most situations. *See, e.g.*, 18 U.S.C. § 3742(c). Many commentators have suggested that by shaping the terms of negotiated guilty pleas, the prosecutor, not the judge, has the predominant role in determining the actual sentence that will be imposed, especially with regard to sentencing in federal courts under the United States Sentencing Guidelines, discussed later in this chapter.

[c] Role of System Capacity and Resource Limitations

The many theoretical facets of sentencing are sometimes pushed aside by a critically important fact: sentencing decisions are severely limited by the capacity of the criminal justice system. Well over half of the states' correctional systems have been declared unconstitutional at some time, in significant part because of overcrowding. When a jurisdiction's jails and prisons are full, sentencing decisions must reflect this reality. For example, if all beds in a local jail are occupied, or if an overcrowded correctional system or facility is under a court order not to exceed a maximum population, a sentencing judge in that jurisdiction may have to sentence a person charged with a minor crime to probation rather than a short jail term. In some jurisdictions, a formula or other mechanism is used to provide an early release from prison for some offenders in order to free bed space for new arrivals when overcrowding reaches a certain level.

The American Bar Association recommends that legislatures "not promulgate sentencing provisions that will result in prison populations beyond the capacity of existing facilities unless [the respective legislature] appropriates funds for timely construction of additional facilities sufficient to accommodate the projected populations." Standards for Criminal Justice § 18-4.4(c)(i) (3d ed. 1994). Similarly, the ABA recommends that legislatures amend sentencing provisions to reduce the length of sentences so as to relieve prison overcrowding. *Id.* § 18-4.4(c)(ii).

Just as prison and jail space limitations affect sentencing decisions, some sentencing options are legally permissible but practically impossible because of other limited resources. For example, a judge may believe that a sex offender would profit from an intensive therapy regime, but the jurisdiction's resources cannot fund this expensive option.

[d] Race and Gender

Race. Although an in-depth treatment is beyond the scope of this brief survey of sentencing, it must be noted that the role of race and gender in the sentencing process has become the focus of much political and scholarly attention. As noted in Chapter 1 and later in this chapter, race is not irrelevant in several aspects of sentencing. Research has demonstrated that the incarceration rate for African-Americans, who constitute about 12% of the population, is seven times that of white Americans. Moreover, African-Americans comprise about half of the prison population, and serve comparatively longer prison sentences, have higher arrest and conviction rates and higher bail requirements. Nearly 100 black men are arrested for each one who is graduated from college. David Cole, No EQUAL JUSTICE 4–5 (1999). These data have led many commentators to decry the devastating impact that the criminal justice system inflicts disproportionally on the African-American community in general and on the African-Americans (and their families) enmeshed in a race-based system. See generally Elliott Currie, CRIME AND PUNISHMENT IN AMERICA (1998); Randall Kennedy, RACE, CRIME, AND THE LAW (1999); Marc Mauer, RACE TO INCARCERATE (revised ed. 2006); James F. Short, Jr., POVERTY, ETHNICITY AND VIOLENT CRIME (1997).

Gender. Gender, like race, has also been scrutinized in the sentencing process. Noting that various sentencing reforms, such as guidelines, designed to minimize judicial discretion, have resulted in an increase in the number and percentage of women in prison, some commentators have argued that the changes have been especially harmful to women.

As primary caregivers in many families, women who are incarcerated often lose their children either to foster care or even permanently. Moreover, their children may suffer the loss of their only caregiving parent. Observing that the recidivism rate of women is lower than that of men, these analysts suggest that gender-neutral sentencing practices should be replaced by ones that recognize the social and behavioral differences between men and women. *See generally* Christopher M. Alexander, *Crushing Equality: Gender Equal Sentencing in America*, 6 AM. UNIV. J. OF GENDER & LAW 199 (1997).

Both race and gender. Some commentators have taken the additional step of looking at the combination of race and gender in sentencing. They point out that for some crimes African-American women are incarcerated at about the same rate as white men, that African-American women are over three times as likely to serve a prison sentence as white women, and that African-American women constitute over forty percent of women in state prisons. *Id.* at 215. They conclude that sentencing reforms have not eliminated disparity, especially for African-American women, and that, on the contrary, some purported reforms have actually aggravated previously race-based sentencing disparities. *See, e.g.*, Nekima Levy-Pounds, *From the Frying Pan into the Fire: How*

Poor Women of Color and Children are Affected by Sentencing Guidelines and Mandatory Minimums, 47 Santa Clara L. Rev. 287 (2007).

[e] Determinate vs. Indeterminate

Sentences can be *determinate* or *indeterminate*. A determinate sentence is one for a set amount of time. For example, a sentence of two years in prison is a determinate sentence. An indeterminate sentence is one where the actual release date is not established at the time of sentencing. Ordinarily, the parole board or some other executive branch agency will determine the exact date of release. For example, a sentence of 5–10 years in prison is indeterminate. The offender may serve as long as ten years or be released in five years (or even earlier), depending on conduct while in prison and other factors. He or she will not know the exact duration of incarceration until at least some part of the sentence has been served.

Although sentences are sometimes spoken of as being *either* indeterminate *or* determinate, determinacy versus indeterminacy is actually a relative matter. A sentence of 10 years without any possibility of parole or deduction for good behavior (in other words, 10 years imposed equals exactly 10 years served) would be fully determinate, but sentences that are fully, day-for-day determinate are exceedingly rare. At the other extreme, a sentence of from one day (minimum) to life (maximum) is as indeterminate as one can posit, and equally rare. (Note, however, that certain commitments under state "sexual predator" or "sexually dangerous person" laws, although denominated as civil rather than criminal in nature, do in fact carry one-day-to-life total indeterminacy.) Although this topic is generally beyond the scope of this book, see *Kansas v. Hendricks*, 521 U.S. 346 (1997)(upholding Kansas' one-day-to-life sexual predator commitment statute against due process, double jeopardy, and *ex post facto* challenges). All sentences falling between the two polar extremes given above are, relatively, either more or less determinate or indeterminate.

[f] Concurrent vs. Consecutive Sentences

If an offender is convicted of more than one crime, the sentencing judge will determine whether the sentence for the separate crimes will be served concurrently or consecutively. A *concurrent sentence* is one that is served at the same time as another sentence. A *consecutive sentence* is one that is served after completion of another sentence. For example, assume that an offender is convicted of two burglaries and sentenced to five years in prison on each. If the sentences are concurrent, the offender will be released after serving a maximum of five years. On the other hand, if the sentences are consecutive, the offender will serve the sentence for one burglary after completing the sentence for the other (a total of ten years maximum). The sentencing judge ordinarily determines whether sentences are to be consecutive or concurrent. Some sentencing statutes or case law provide factors for the court to use in making this determination, while other legislation may mandate that consecutive sentences be imposed for certain offenses. By and large, concurrent sentences tend to be the "rule" in practice, and consecutive sentences the exception.

[g] Mandatory Sentence

Minimum sentences. Sentencing statutes sometimes severely limit a judge's discretion to impose a criminal sentence. Most criminal laws impose a maximum sentence that can be imposed. For example, a particular crime may be punishable by a sentence of no more than twenty years in prison. Since this scheme does not establish a minimum sentence, a judge could impose either a very short sentence, or no sentence of incarceration at all, on the offender convicted of this offense. Many legislatures have been critical of these short sentences, especially for serious felonies, and have altered the sentencing laws to assure that such overly lenient sentences do not occur.

Mandatory minimum sentences. One common model is for a statute to establish a *mandatory minimum* sentence that must be imposed. For example, a state may provide that the court must impose a sentence of at least four years in prison for someone convicted of possession of more than a certain amount of cocaine. In theory, the court cannot impose a sentence of, say, three years for this offense, but defense lawyers (and sometimes even prosecutors) often find ways to avoid the harshness of mandatory minimum sentences. In many jurisdictions, for example, the defendant could plead guilty to possession of less than the amount necessary to trigger the mandatory minimum sentence.

Fixed or mandatory specific sentences. A related limit on a judge's authority is a statutorily *fixed*, or *mandatory specific sentence.* This reflects the legislature's decision to ensure that each person convicted of a certain crime, say illegal possession of a weapon, receives a set sentence, such as five years. The trial court may lack the authority to impose a greater or lesser sentence for this offense.

Policy considerations. A mandatory minimum or specific sentence sometimes leads to harsh results because courts are not allowed to consider mitigating or extenuating circumstances with respect to the sentence imposed upon an individual offender. Also, mandatory minimum sentencing schemes may exacerbate prison overcrowding. The American Bar Association recommends that legislatures "should not prescribe a minimum term of total confinement for any offense." STANDARDS FOR CRIMINAL JUSTICE § 18-3.21(b) (3d ed. 1993). *See* Nekima Levy-Pounds, *From the Frying Pan into the Fire: How Poor Women of Color and Children are Affected by Sentencing Guidelines and Mandatory Minimums,* 47 SANTA CLARA L. REV. 287 (2007).

"Three strikes" laws. A number of jurisdictions have passed "three strikes" measures. In California, for example, any person with two prior violent felonies who is convicted of a third felony, even if that felony is a non-violent felony, may receive a mandatory sentence of from twenty-five years to life. In 1998, the California Attorney General's Office reported that this legislation was largely responsible for a decrease in violent crime. *But see* Linda S. Beres and Thomas D. Griffith, *Did "Three Strikes" Cause the Recent Drop in California Crime? An Analysis of the California Attorney General's Report,* 32 LOY. L.A. L. REV. 101 (1998) (concluding that "there is no evidence that Three Strikes played an important role in the drop in the crime rate").

B. THEORIES OF PUNISHMENT

[1] Why Punish?

What is punishment? There is little debate about the general notion that ordinarily persons convicted of a crime should be punished. It is assumed that punishment is appropriate for a violation of a criminal law. We rarely even discuss what punishment is, although some theoreticians have tried. For example, one scholar has found that punishment consists of seven features: the infliction of something unwelcome; the infliction is both intentional and purposeful; the punishment is regarded as authorized; the punishment is for violation of a law; the person punished has somehow voluntarily violated a law; the punisher offers a justification for the punishment; and whether it is punishment is determined from the perspective of the punisher rather than the person punished. Nigel Walker, Why Punish 1–3 (1991).

Should a particular person or act be punished? Although we rarely question whether, in general, we should punish the violation of a criminal law, the question does arise in the context of particular individuals. For example, although a seriously ill person may have committed a crime, a judge may impose no sentence of incarceration because of the defendant's grave physical condition. The question of whether to punish also arises when we ask whether certain conduct should be proscribed by the criminal law. For example, should there be a crime of smoking in a non-smoking area? For some actions, we may conclude that punishment by imprisonment is not an appropriate way to regulate human conduct. Perhaps it would be too costly to inflict punishment because there are too many violators or perhaps punishment would not affect the criminals' conduct. The American experience in the 1920's with prohibition of alcohol is often cited as an example of an instance in which criminal penalties were unsuccessful in eliminating the consumption of alcoholic beverages.

[2] The Principal Theories

Although punishment is an accepted consequence of a violation of criminal law, the precise reason for imposing a sanction has generated a massive amount of discussion and literature. American scholars generally list four primary rationales for punishment: rehabilitation, deterrence, incapacitation, and retribution (or just desserts). These rationales are important for two practical reasons. First, they may determine the general sentencing scheme. If retribution is the goal of punishment for a particular crime or penal code, the sentencing structure will differ markedly from one in which rehabilitation is the goal. Second, the selection of a sentence for a particular offender may vary according to the reason for the sanction. Accordingly, the sentence that a particular drunk driver receives based on the goal of rehabilitation will probably differ from the sentence that another person, convicted of the same crime, will receive through sentencing based on deterrence.

[a] Deterrence

A well-accepted rationale for punishment is deterrence. Deterrence is designed to reduce future criminal activity by causing potential criminals to fear the consequences of violating the criminal law.

General and special deterrence. There are two varieties of deterrence: general and special (or specific). *General deterrence* is deterrence aimed at potential lawbreakers other than the offender being punished. *Special (or specific) deterrence* is designed to deter the offender being punished. For example, consider a drug-addicted burglar who commits the offense to obtain money to buy drugs. If the court imposes a sentence for general deterrence purposes, it will punish this burglar in order to deter other potential burglars (or, more generally, lawbreakers). If a special deterrent sentence is imposed, it will sanction this burglar in order to deter this burglar from repeating the crime.

Evaluation. Critics of general deterrence often question the morality of general deterrence. Is it appropriate for a society to impose a sentence on one citizen in order to affect the behavior of others? Other critics also note the lack of empirical support to prove that deterrence actually works. Unfortunately, it is true that most empirical studies do not support the general proposition that increasing criminal sanctions causes a decrease in crime. *See generally* Roger G. Hood, THE DEATH PENALTY: A WORLDWIDE PERSPECTIVE (3d ed. 2002) (analysis of studies of deterrent effect of death penalty from admittedly abolitionist perspective, concluding the studies do not prove any deterrent effect). Increasing the likelihood of swift apprehension and adjudication may be a better deterrent than increasing the sanction for those offenders who are caught.

[b] Incapacitation

A second rationale for punishment is *incapacitation*. An incapacitative sentence will somehow disable the offender so that he or she cannot reoffend for the duration of the punishment. The most obvious incapacitative punishment is the death penalty. The recent focus on "three strikes you're out" and life without parole also reflects a desire to incapacitate. Prison also is generally an incapacitation since most offenders will not be able to continue their criminal ways (at least against non-prisoners) during their incarceration.

Selective incapacitation. In recent years there has been much discussion of *selective incapacitation*. This theory is based on research showing that some offenders commit many crimes, while other criminals commit relatively few offenses. By informed sentencing decisions, those offenders who are likely to commit many crimes should receive lengthy sentences, thus greatly reducing the incidence of crime by removing the source of much criminality.

Evaluation. Critics of incapacitation note that, like rehabilitation and deterrence, empirical studies raise serious questions about the wisdom of this theory. The problem is that it is difficult or impossible to make accurate predictions of dangerousness. By definition, an incapacitative sentence keeps an offender from committing offenses against non-prisoners during the period of incapacitation. But no one knows with much certainty which offenders need to be incapacitated and for how long. Predictions of future dangerousness tend to engender a number of "false positives" — predictions that a particular offender will recidivate when in fact that person will not do so.

[c] Retribution (or Just Desserts)

Perhaps the most controversial and complex theory of punishment is *retribution*. Sometimes called *dessert* or *just dessert*, this theory posits that a criminal should be punished because he or she deserves it for violating a criminal law. Some theorists argue that punishing offenders is a government's moral imperative. They note that by punishing an offender, one also treats the offender as an intelligent human being capable of making rational decisions.

Actually, retribution has two facets. It not only justifies punishment, it also limits punishment. It has been noted that the concept of "an eye for an eye" means that it is appropriate to punish someone who violates the law. But it also means that the punishment should be proportionate to the offense. In other words, in theory one can remove the eye of the criminal who destroyed the victim's eye, but one cannot do more than the equivalent of removing the offender's eye. Under this view, retribution places significant restraints on the degree of punishment that the state may select.

[d] Rehabilitation

Although rehabilitation has been a leading goal of punishment in the United States, whether it remains one today is open to serious question. In general terms, it means that a criminal offender is given a sentence that will somehow reform the defendant so that he or she will not recidivate. To a large extent, this concept is based on what has been termed a "medical model of crime." It assumes that the accused is "sick" and can be "cured" by the proper dose of punishment and/or treatment. Perhaps the best example is the drug-addicted burglar who commits the offense to obtain money to buy drugs. A rehabilitative sentence may require the offender to participate in a therapy program that deals with the underlying problem: drug addiction. In theory, if the offender is cured of this addiction, he or she will live crime-free.

Despite the inherent appeal of this approach, since the 1970's it has been heavily criticized by both liberals and conservatives. *See generally* American Friends Service Committee, STRUGGLE FOR JUSTICE (1971); Andrew Von Hirsch, DOING JUSTICE: THE CHOICE OF PUNISHMENTS (1976); Francis A. Allen, THE DECLINE OF THE REHABILITATIVE IDEAL: PENAL POLICY AND SOCIAL PURPOSE (1981); Alan M. Dershowitz, FAIR AND CERTAIN PUNISHMENT (1976); Robert R. Martinson, *New Findings, New Views: A Note of Caution Regarding Sentencing Reform*, 7 HOFSTRA L. REV. 243 (1979).

Conservatives object because a rehabilitative sentence is often viewed as too lenient and too expensive. Liberals, on the other hand, complain that a rehabilitative sentence may be too harsh or so discretionary that it thwarts sentencing uniformity and opens the door to discrimination on the basis of such inappropriate factors as wealth, gender, or race. Moreover, some liberal critics complain that the state has no business trying to change the mind-set of its people. It is appropriate to punish those who violate the laws, but the state should not try to alter the thinking processes of its citizens. Both liberals and conservatives also note that some scholars have found little evidence that various treatment modalities actually rehabilitate offenders. If this is true and most rehabilitation efforts are not effective in bringing about positive behavioral changes, they argue, why should sentences be based on a theory that does not work and is subject to abuse?

[e]   Other Theories

While the four theories listed above dominate discussions of punishment in America, other theories have also been advanced. The most common of these "minor" approaches is *public education*. According to this approach, punishing a criminal teaches the public about the boundaries of acceptable behavior. In a sense, it is a lesson in what is acceptable and what is not. It also teaches relative values when certain behavior, such as robbery, is punished more severely than other conduct, like shoplifting. It may also teach that certain acts, such as homicide, are especially grave crimes because the punishment is so severe. These lessons are then translated into values which guide individual decisions. For example, if prostitutes are punished, it teaches us that prostitution is wrong and may lead some people to refrain from being either prostitutes or their customers.

The American Bar Association has identified two additional societal purposes in designing a sentencing scheme. The first, which is considered to be related to the deterrence rationale, is "to foster respect for the law." Second, the sentencing system also should "provide *restitution* or reparation to victims of crimes." Standards for Criminal Justice § 18-2.1(a) (3d ed. 1994).

For an interesting argument that sentencing decisions should be evidence-based — *i.e.* based on sound scientific studies of what sanctions actually reduce the risk of recidivism, see Roger K. Warren, *Evidence-Based Practices and State Sentencing Policy: Ten Policy Initiatives to Reduce Recidivism*, 82 Ind. L. J. 1307 (2007).

PROBLEM 17-1. THEORIES IN PRACTICE

1.   Compare the four main theories of punishment.

   a.   Which are designed to change future behavior?

   b.   Assume that X and Y rob a bank. Under each of the four theories, would the sentence for each criminal be the same (*i.e.* under rehabilitation, would X and Y receive identical sentences; under general deterrence, would each receive an identical sentence)?

   c.   In calculating an appropriate sentence under each of the four theories, what role is played by the individual characteristics of the offender? The particular features of this offense?

   d.   General deterrence, education, and retribution focus on the needs of the public. What are these needs?

2.   Assume that you are a judge in a jurisdiction that gives you all reasonable sentencing alternatives. You have just concluded a drunk driving trial and are considering the appropriate sentence. Your jurisdiction authorizes up to a year in jail or, alternatively, up to a year on probation subject to reasonable conditions of release.

   a.   What information will you need to select the best sentence? Where will you get that information?

   b.   Assume that you learn that the defendant, Barry, worked as an assistant department manager at a small supermarket. The day before the drunk driving incident he was fired because his supervisor thought he had stolen some cigarettes. He has denied the theft and the store will not prosecute for it. He is 25 years old and married. Three years ago he was arrested for possession of marijuana. The marijuana charge was dismissed when he successfully completed a diversion program for first offenders. He is a high school graduate.

    i.   What other information do you need?

    ii.   Assume that your sole goal is rehabilitation. What sentence would you impose? What if your only goal were general deterrence? Special deterrence? Retribution? Incapacitation?

  c. Changing the facts slightly, assume that the crime was armed robbery of a convenience food market. The robber used a pistol and threatened to kill the clerk if the police were notified. The other facts remain the same. The jurisdiction authorizes a prison term up to fifteen years or probation up to five years. If sent to prison, the offender would be eligible for parole after serving 50% of the prison term. What sentence would you impose under each theory?

C. LEGAL LIMITATIONS ON SENTENCING

[1] Statutory

Criminal sentences are governed by statute. Accordingly, the statute authorizing a particular sanction and the procedures used during the sentencing process must be closely examined for each case. This is especially true in jurisdictions adopting complex sentencing guidelines.

[2] Constitutional

A complete discussion of constitutional limits on sentences is beyond the scope of this book, but a few general observations are possible.

[a] Equal Protection

Equal protection has infrequently been successful in challenging sentences or sentencing procedures. The key is finding an impermissible discrimination. *See, e.g., People v. Bolton*, 589 P.2d 396 (1979) (overturning sentence that discriminated against the defendant because he was on welfare and had illegitimate children).

For constitutional and other reasons, the American Bar Association recommends that the following personal characteristics not be considered with regard to sentencing: (1) race, (2) gender or sexual orientation, (3) national origin, (4) religion or creed, (5) marital status and (6) political affiliation or belief. STANDARDS FOR CRIMINAL JUSTICE, § 18-3.4(d) (3d ed. 1994).

[b] Eighth Amendment

[i] United States Constitution

The Eighth Amendment's cruel and unusual punishment clause has been used as a limit on sentencing in both state and federal courts. Most of the United States Supreme Court's cruel and unusual punishment decisions relate to capital punishment, discussed below.

In non-capital cases, the cruel and unusual punishment clause has been used to challenge the severity of a sentence. The offender claims that a particular sentence is so harsh that it is unconstitutional. These claims are rarely successful. One reason is that it is not clear to what extent the Eighth Amendment embraces a requirement that sentences in non-capital cases be proportionate to the offense.

In *Harmelin v. Michigan*, 501 U.S. 957 (1991), the defendant was convicted of possession of 672 grams of cocaine and was given the mandatory sentence of life without possibility of parole. He argued that the sentence violated the Eighth Amendment's prohibition against cruel and unusual punishment because it was significantly disproportionate to the crime. His argument was supported by *Solem v. Helm*, 463 U.S. 277 (1983), in which the Supreme Court held that the Eighth Amendment was violated by a South Dakota sentence of life without parole for a recidivist who had been convicted of many non-violent crimes: three burglaries, one false pretenses, one grand larceny, one drunk driving, and one for writing a bad check.

The Court in *Harmelin* refused to apply *Solem*, although there was no majority opinion. The *Harmelin* Court divided over whether the Eighth Amendment even contains a proportionality requirement. Justices Scalia and Rehnquist looked at the history of the Eighth Amendment and concluded that there is no such principle in non-capital cases. To them, *Solem v. Helm* was wrongly decided. Justices Kennedy, O'Connor and Souter disagreed, recognizing a narrow proportionality principle inherent in the Eighth Amendment. There need not be strict proportionality between crime and sentence. To them, the limit is that there cannot be extreme sentences that are grossly disproportionate to the crime. Dissenting Justices White, Blackmun and Stevens found a somewhat broader proportionality guarantee in the Eighth Amendment. Following *Solem*, these Justices argued that the Eighth Amendment includes a proportionality principle that involves assessing the gravity of the offense and the harshness of the penalty, the sentences imposed on other criminals in the same jurisdiction, and those in other jurisdictions for persons committing the same offense. Another way to count the votes in this case is that seven of the nine Justices on the *Harmelin* court (except only Scalia and Thomas) were of the view that there *is* a proportionality principle in non-capital cases, but they differ as to the principle's extent. *Harmelin* is discussed in Peter Mathis Spett, Note, 24 COLUM. HUM. RTS. L. REV. 203 (1992-93); Chris Baniszewski, Note, 25 ARIZ. ST. L. J. 929 (1993); Stephen E. Meltzer, Note, 27 NEW ENG. L. REV. 749 (1993).

Two more recent U.S. Supreme Court cases underscore the notion that a "narrow proportionality principle" applies to non-capital sentences. In *Ewing v. California*, 538 U.S. 11 (2003), the Court held that a sentence under California's "three strike" law of 25 years to life for grand theft (three golf clubs, worth $399 a piece) committed by Ewing (who had previously been convicted of four felony convictions arising out of three burglaries) was not grossly disproportionate to the crime committed. Therefore, this sentence did not violate the cruel and unusual punishment clause of the Eighth Amendment.

Similarly, in *Lockyer v. Andrade*, 538 U.S. 63 (2003), a federal habeas case, the Court held that it was not an unreasonable application of the Eighth Amendment's proportionality standards for a California appellate court to affirm Andrade's sentence of two consecutive sentences of 25 years to life for thefts (five videotapes worth $84.70) committed by a person with three prior convictions for serious or violent felonies. For a sobering account of the *Andrade* case, written by Andrade's advocate both in the U.S. Circuit Court of Appeals and in the Supreme Court, see Erwin Chemerinsky, *Cruel and Unusual: The Story of Leandro Andrade*, 52 DRAKE L. REV. 1 (2003). For an interesting discussion of waiving Eighth Amendment protections, see Lystra Batchoo, *Voluntary Surgical Castration of Sex Offenders: Waiving the Eighth Amendment Protection from Cruel and Unusual Punishment*, 72 BROOK. L. REV. 689 (2007).

[ii] State Constitutions

Although the federal cruel and unusual punishment clause is not likely to lead to appellate reversal of lengthy sentences, occasionally a state constitution's own cruel and unusual punishment clause (or an equivalent provision) will result in a successful challenge to a harsh sentence. *See, e.g., People v. Bullock*, 485 N.W.2d 866 (Mich. 1992) (mandatory life-without-parole sentence for possessing 650 grams of cocaine mixture violated state constitution's cruel or unusual punishment guarantee); *State v. Barker*, 410 S.E.2d 712 (W. Va. 1991) (life sentence for repeat offender, with no history of crimes involving personal violence, violated state cruel and unusual punishment clause).

For a discussion of the *Harmelin* and *Bullock* decisions and the ways in which a state court may interpret its state's cognate constitutional provision differently from the way the Supreme Court has interpreted the analogous provision of the federal constitution, see Stanley E. Adelman, *Towards an Independent State Constitutional Jurisprudence, or, How to Disagree with the Supreme Court and How Not To*, 2002 ARKANSAS LAW NOTES 1 (available on Lexis and WestLaw).

[iii] *Ex Post Facto*

The Constitution bars both Congress and the states from passing an *ex post facto* law. U.S. Const. art I, §§ 9, 10. This provision is designed to prevent legislatures from passing vindictive legislation and to provide potential lawbreakers with fair warnings about what conduct is criminal and about penalties. A law violates the *ex post facto* provision if it is (1) retrospective, applying to events occurring before the new law took effect, and (2) disadvantageous to the offender. *Weaver v. Graham*, 450 U.S. 24, 29 (1981).

Not every law that causes a criminal defendant to suffer a disadvantage, however, offends this provision. The Supreme Court has distinguished between disadvantageous changes affecting *procedure* and those altering *substantial personal rights*. The *ex post facto* provision was not designed to limit the legislature's prerogative of altering both remedies and procedures which do not involve matters of substance. *Dobbert v. Florida*, 432 U.S. 282, 293 (1977).

Megan's laws. All states have adopted versions of "Megan's Law" designed to protect communities from sex offenders. In *Smith v. Doe*, 538 U.S. 84 (2003), the U.S. Supreme Court held that Alaska's Sex Offender Registration Act was a civil, nonpunitive scheme. Because the legislature's purpose was to not impose punishment, it was not an unconstitutional *ex post facto* law as applied to persons convicted of sex offenses prior to its enactment.

Sentencing procedures. The *ex post facto* provision can be involved any time a change in sentencing rules is applied to an offender who committed a crime before the new provisions were enacted. In *Miller v. Florida*, 482 U.S. 423 (1987), the defendant committed a sexual battery at a time when Florida law authorized a presumptive sentence of three to four years in prison. By the time he was sentenced, Florida law had increased the presumptive sentence to somewhere between five to seven years in prison. Using the new guidelines, the sentencing judge gave the defendant a seven year sentence. The Supreme Court held that the *ex post facto* clause was violated because the sentence substantially increased the offender's punishment for conduct occurring before the new law was effective. The Court refused to find the change, which only increased the penalty for sexual battery, merely "procedural" and hence outside the *ex post facto* guarantee.

Conversely, in *Dobbert v. Florida*, 432 U.S. 282 (1977), the defendant committed a murder at a time when Florida law provided that the penalty for murder was death unless the jury recommended mercy. At the time of the trial, however, the law was changed so that the jury merely advised the judge about the penalty; it could no longer veto the death penalty by a recommendation of mercy. The *Dobbert* Court held that the change was merely procedural, and therefore not barred by the *ex post facto* guarantee because it only altered the methods used to determine whether the death penalty was imposed; it did not change the "quantum of punishment attached to the crime." *Id.* at 294. According to the *Dobbert* Court, the new Florida procedures did not change the definition of the crime or the amount of proof necessary for guilt. *See also Hopt v. Utah*, 110 U.S. 574 (1884) (change in witness competency rules, so that prosecution witness became competent to testify at trial, merely procedural); *Thompson v. Missouri*, 171 U.S. 380 (1898) (change in evidence law held procedural even though it permitted certain prosecution evidence, formerly barred, to be admissible at trial).

D. SENTENCING OPTIONS

American jurisdictions have adopted a significant array of sentencing options. The following sections provide a brief sketch of many of these options and the legal limits on them.

[1] Death Penalty

Because of the unique nature of the death penalty itself and the procedures used in imposing and carrying out a sentence of death, the subject of capital punishment is treated separately later in this chapter.

[2] Incarceration

Increased use. Incarceration in a prison or jail is a typical punishment for more serious offenses. It is also one that is being used with increased frequency in America. One study noted that between 1972 and 1998, America's prison population rose 500% while the national population increased only 28%. Between 1985 and 1995, federal and state governments opened a new prison each week. Marc Mauer, RACE TO INCARCERATE 1 (1999).

One study of federal convictions found that 76% percent of the defendants were incarcerated. Sourcebook, at http://www.albany.edu/sourcebook/pdf/t5202003.pdf. For federal drug offenders, 92% were incarcerated. Violent federal offenders were incarcerated 93% of the time, but only about 60% of property offenders were imprisoned. The average federal prison sentence was 63 months. *Id.* at http://www.albany.edu/sourcebook/pdf/t5252006.pdf.

The state statistics are similar. About 70% of convicted state felons are sentenced to jail or prison. *Sourcebook* at http://www.albany.edu/sourcebook/pdf/t5472004.pdf. The average maximum state prison sentence was 57 months. Most countries use imprisonment less frequently than America, which may have the highest incarceration rate (prisoners per 100,000 people) in the world. Harry R. Dammer & Erika S. Fairchild, Comparative Criminal Justice Systems 197 (3d ed. 2006).

Disproportionate impact. The heavy reliance on incarceration falls especially heavily on African-Americans and Hispanics. According to one study, while African-Americans constitute about 13% of the population, they comprise about half of all prison inmates. About one in fourteen black males is in an American prison on an average day. In 1995, about one in three black males between 20–29 years of age was in prison, jail, or on probation or parole. A black male infant born in 1991 stood a 29% chance of being imprisoned sometime in his life, while a Hispanic boy had a 16% chance and a white boy a 4% chance. In sum, according to this study an African-American has a seven times greater chance of being incarcerated than does a white person. Marc Mauer, RACE TO INCARCERATE 118–126 (1999).

Recommendations. Many jurisdictions and the American Bar Association recommend that incarceration in a prison or jail be utilized only when it is absolutely necessary. *See* STANDARDS FOR CRIMINAL JUSTICE §§ 18-3.11(c) (3d ed. 1994) (total confinement should not be the mandated sanction "unless the legislature can contemplate no mitigating circumstances that would justify a less restrictive sanction"); 18-6.4(a & b) (the sentencing court should "prefer sanctions not involving total confinement in the absence of affirmative reasons to the contrary"; total confinement may be the appropriate sanction if the offender threatened or caused serious bodily injury, other types of sanctions have been proven ineffective for prior offenses involving the defendant, incarceration "is necessary so as not to depreciate unduly the seriousness of the offense and thereby foster disrespect for the law," or confinement for a brief period is necessary to impress upon the defendant that the offense could have resulted in a longer incarceration; this Standard also admonishes a sentencing court to "not select a sanction of total confinement because of community hostility to the offender or because of the offender's apparent need for rehabilitation or treatment").

Determination of exact duration of incarceration. Ordinarily the trial judge imposes the prison sentence (*e.g.*, five years) and an administrative agency, usually the state correctional department, decides in which institution the sentence will be served. The precise time to be served is the product of a number of laws permitting reductions in sentence for good behavior and other achievements (*e.g.*, obtaining of a G.E.D.) in prison. Often a *parole board*, a group of three or more executive branch officials, will decide the actual release date. If the offender is deemed trustworthy and/or has exhibited exemplary behavior during confinement, he or she may be released on parole before the expiration of the full prison term. While on parole the offender must abide by a list of conditions, such as holding a job, and must be in contact with a parole officer on a regular basis. A serious violation of these conditions may result in revocation of parole and return of the offender to imprisonment.

American prisons are often classified by security needs. A maximum security prison differs markedly from a minimum security one. The latter are ordinarily for minor offenders and prisoners near the end of their sentences.

[3] Semi-Incarceration

Incarceration in America is expensive and often prisons and jails are filled to capacity. Moreover, incarceration can separate an offender from his or her family and job, reducing the likelihood of rehabilitation. Because of these concerns, there are now a number of semi-incarceration punishments that involve the deprivation of liberty, but not to the same extent as incarceration.

[a] House Arrest

A recent trend is toward *house arrest* or *home confinement*, although it is more often used for pretrial detainees than convicted criminals. *See generally* Paul J. Hofer & Barbara S. Meierhoefer, HOME CONFINEMENT: AN EVOLVING SANCTION IN THE FEDERAL CRIMINAL JUSTICE SYSTEM (1987); Richard A. Ball, HOUSE ARREST AND CORRECTIONAL POLICY (Inciardi ed. 1987). The offender, usually a non-violent person with a minimal criminal history, is required to remain at home during a certain period, such as six months, or during certain hours each day. For example, an offender could be required to be at home during all hours he or she is not at work.

Electronic monitoring. To ensure that the offender does not leave home during the restricted periods, an electronic monitoring system may be used. A device is placed in the offender's home that picks up a signal from a plastic anklet, wristlet, or necklace that the offender is required to wear. When the offender leaves the home, the device automatically places a telephone call to a probation office or computer service.

The American Bar Association applauds the use of home detention as an authorized sentence with the proviso, however, that "use of electronic monitoring devices as part of a sentence to home detention is appropriate, but the availability of such devices should not be a prerequisite for such sentences." STANDARDS FOR CRIMINAL JUSTICE § 18-3.20(d) (3d ed. 1994).

Evaluation. The concept of house arrest has many appealing features. It saves the state or local government money since offenders pay their own expenses. Moreover, it relieves overcrowded jails and prisons. The downside, of course, is that it may expose the community to the risk of recidivism as the offender can usually ignore the limit on travel or commit a new crime while on a permissible journey, such as going to work. It may also be perceived as too lenient punishment, making it inappropriate for retributive or deterrent purposes. Another problem is that "house arrest" may be inappropriate for homeless defendants, those without telephones, or offenders who cannot afford to pay the fees for renting the system. With respect to the financial inequality concern, the American Bar Association recommends that ability of an offender to pay the cost of an electronic monitoring device "should not be considered . . . in determining whether to use the sanction of . . . home detention." STANDARDS FOR CRIMINAL JUSTICE § 18-3.20(d) (3d ed. 1994).

[b]   Halfway House

Another common punishment is an order that the offender reside in a *halfway house,* ordinarily a relatively small residential facility where offenders live when not at work or in a therapeutic or educational program. The American Bar Association recommends what it characterizes as "intermittent confinement in a facility" — one that allows the defendant to leave for "employment, education, vocational training, or other approved purpose, but requires the offender to return to the facility for specified hours or period, such as nights or weekends." STANDARDS FOR CRIMINAL JUSTICE § 18-3.19(a) (3d ed. 1994). While in the halfway house, the offenders' behavior is monitored by staff and the offenders may be required to participate in group or individual therapy sessions. A halfway house may be an attractive option for offenders in need of some structure and supervision but who have a job or other responsibilities that they should not have to forego. Many jurisdictions use a halfway house as a way station between prison and outright release.

[4]   Probation

Probation may be the most common punishment assessed by American judges in criminal cases. While the American Bar Association endorses the concept of probation, it has chosen the characterization of "compliance program" in place of probation — arguing that such programs "should promote offenders' future compliance with the law." STANDARDS FOR CRIMINAL JUSTICE § 18-3.13(c)(i) (3d ed. 1994). Probation is routinely used in misdemeanor cases. A 2004 study also found it used in about 28% of state felony cases. Sourcebook, at http://www.albany.edu/sourcebook/pdf/t5472004.pdf. The average length of a state probation sentence was 38 months.

[a]   Suspended Execution or Imposition of Sentence

Traditionally, a person is placed on probation in one of two ways. The sentencing judge may *suspend execution* of a sentence or *suspend imposition* of the sentence and put the offender on probation. If the court suspends execution of the sentence, it imposes a prison sentence (of, for example, three years), then suspends the actual service of the prison term and releases the offender on probation. If the offender successfully completes probation, the prison term is never served. If the court suspends imposition of a sentence, it places the offender on probation without actually imposing a prison sentence (sometimes called a sentence to *straight probation*). If the offender violates probation, the court then imposes a prison term as if the offender had never been on probation. The primary difference between the two approaches is that, in case of a probation violation, the court may be bound by the original prison sentence it imposed in the suspended execution model, but there are no such limits in the suspended imposition model. The American Bar Association recommends that judges should not utilize the suspended execution procedure. STANDARDS FOR CRIMINAL JUSTICE

§ 18-7.3(e) (3d ed. 1994) (providing that the "initial sentence should not specify the terms of a resentence in the event that the offender violates [a compliance] program").

[b] Limits on Probation Eligibility

Many jurisdictions impose limits on probation. For example, this sanction may be unavailable for more serious offenses. Another common limit is that an offender cannot be on probation for more than a fixed number of years, such as eight or ten years. The reason for this limit is that at some stage the offender should be ready to live crime-free without government supervision. If a probationer has not violated the conditions of release for this period of time, the scarce probation resources could better be devoted to recent offenders.

[c] Limits on Probation Conditions

A probationer is ordinarily obligated to adhere to a list of *probation conditions*. The number of conditions may exceed fifteen; fairly common conditions include: (1) violate no criminal law, (2) hold a job, (3) support dependents, and (4) report for regular counseling visits with a probation officer. The American Bar Association recommends that any such restrictions "have a reasonable relationship to the individual's current offense and criminal history," and may include such matters as making restitution to the victim, maintaining residence in a prescribed area, submitting to random drug or alcohol testing, or performing specified public or community service. STANDARDS FOR CRIMINAL JUSTICE § 18-3.13(d) (3d ed. 1994).

A recent trend, sometimes referred to as *split confinement*, combines incarceration and probation. The offender first serves a short prison or jail term, then is released on probation for the remainder of the sentence. This innovation gives the offender an unpleasant experience without long-term removal from family and job. A variation of this has the offender spend some time, perhaps weekends, in jail and the rest of the time at home and work. Recently, conditions of probation that utilize modern technology, such as electronic monitoring bracelets and global positioning devices, have been gaining wider use and acceptance by the courts.

Courts have wide discretion to impose probation conditions which are reasonably related to legitimate penological goals. *See, e.g., United States v. Rearden*, 349 F.3d 608 (9th Cir. 2003) (defendant convicted of sending child pornography over the Internet; condition prohibiting him from accessing the Internet without prior approval of probation officer upheld as reasonably related to penological goals of deterrence, rehabilitation, and public protection); *State v. Oakley*, 629 N.W.2d 200 (Wis. 2001) ("deadbeat dad" sentenced to probation for nonsupport of nine children he had fathered by four different women; condition prohibiting him from fathering another child unless he could first demonstrate ability to support all his children upheld as reasonably related to rehabilitative purposes of probation and to societal goal of assuring financial support to children, despite partial infringement on constitutional right to procreate).

However, some conditions of probation (or parole as well) have been struck down as not reasonably related to the proper goals of supervision, as unauthorized by the probation statute, or as violating a constitutional guarantee. *See e.g., United States v. Evans*, 155 F.3d 245 (3d Cir. 1998) (cannot order reimbursement of defense counsel's fees as condition of probation); *Commonwealth v. Pike*, 701 N.E.2d 951 (Mass. 1998) (condition banishing probationer from state held violative of right to interstate travel and not reasonably related to correctional purposes); *Inouye v. Kemna*, 504 F. 3d 705 (9th Cir. 2007) (parole officer violated Establishment Clause of the First Amendment by ordering Buddhist parolee, as a condition of parole, to attend a 12-step drug treatment program that required participation in meetings that had a "substantial religious component," and then recommending revocation of parolee's parole because he refused to participate).

Query: what if an AA program is the "only game in town" and there are no secular alcohol or drug treatment programs available?

Shame sentences. So-called "shame sentences," requiring probationers to wear self-condemning signboards in public, write public letters of apology, or wear clothing or post signs warning the public that they are criminal offenders have been particularly controversial, and judicial opinion has been mixed. *Compare, United States v. Gementera,* 379 F.3d 596 (9th Cir. 2004)(upholding condition requiring convicted mail thief to wear a signboard outside post office saying, "I stole mail. This is my punishment."), with *People v. Letterlough,* 655 N.E.2d 146 (N.Y. 1995)(striking down probation condition requiring convicted drunk driver to affix a fluorescent sign stating "convicted dwi" to any vehicle he drives).

[d]   Modification of Conditions

A trial court has other options when a probationer violates the terms of release. It may modify and tighten the supervision conditions rather than incarcerate the offender. For example, if the offender acquires a drinking problem, the court may add a probation condition that the offender attend Alcoholics Anonymous sessions. Ordinarily this is done after a court hearing where the defendant has an opportunity to oppose or otherwise comment on the modification.

[e]   Revocation

If the offender violates a condition of release, the court may *revoke probation,* sending the offender to prison. But there are limits on this process. In *Bearden v. Georgia,* 461 U.S. 660 (1983), the Supreme Court held that the due process clause's fundamental fairness guarantee bars a sentencing court from automatically revoking probation for the failure to comply with a condition of release requiring the payment of money. If the probationer willfully refused to pay or make sufficient efforts to get the necessary funds, incarceration may be ordered at the probation revocation hearing. But if the offender could not pay despite reasonable efforts to do so, the court must consider alternate measures of punishment other than incarceration for the failure to adhere to the probation terms. Incarceration is permissible in such cases only when the state's interest in punishing the offender cannot be served by means other than a prison term. Similarly, the American Bar Association recommends that resentencing of such an offender to imprisonment should occur only after a finding that the defendant "has committed a substantial violation of a material requirement or condition of [a compliance program]." STANDARDS FOR CRIMINAL JUSTICE § 18-7.3(a) (3d ed. 1994).

According to *Gagnon v. Scarpelli,* 411 U.S. 778 (1973), probationers enjoy a conditional liberty which cannot be taken away without certain due process procedures. Before probation can be revoked, the offender is usually entitled to a preliminary and final hearing. The preliminary revocation hearing is to determine whether there is probable cause to believe that the probationer violated release conditions. The final revocation proceeding is to determine whether probation should be revoked. The defendant has a qualified right to counsel and to present evidence at both proceedings. *See generally* Neil P. Cohen, THE LAW OF PROBATION AND PAROLE (2d ed. 1999).

[5]   Fines

Fines have long been a sanction for violation of criminal law and are used routinely in Western Europe. As pressures on government finances and overcrowded correctional facilities increase, the fine becomes an even more attractive sentencing alternative in America. Since a fine is paid to a state agency, it differs markedly from restitution, paid to the crime victim as compensation. A fine serves several penal purposes. If sufficiently severe, it may satisfy retribution and could be both a general and special deterrent. The obvious problem with fines is that they may discriminate against the poor. The other side of the coin is that they may favor the wealthy who can afford to pay. The American Bar Association recommends that legislatures not set minimum fines for any offense; fine amounts should be set by utilizing one or more of the following factors: (1) the defendant's income and assets, (2) the amount of the victim's loss or the offenders' gain, and (3) the "difficulty of detection of the offense." STANDARDS FOR CRIMINAL JUSTICE § 18-3.16(b) and (c) (3d ed. 1994).

Monetary fines are frequently imposed in state and federal white collar crimes cases. For example, federal offenders are now subject to substantially increased fines since the adoption of sentencing guidelines. *See, e.g.*, 18 U.S.C. § 3571 (authorizing fine up to $250,000 for individuals convicted of felonies and up to $500,000 for organizations convicted of felonies). Among the factors that a federal court must consider in determining whether to impose a fine, and, if so, in determining the amount, are (1) the defendant's ability to pay, (2) the burden that payment of the fine will impose on both the defendant and his or her dependents, and (3) whether restitution has been or will be made by the defendant to the victim. 18 U.S.C. § 3572(a).

Day fines. Many countries have adopted the Scandinavian *day-fine*, a fine based on the amount of money a person makes in a day. Thus, a particular offender may be required to pay a day fine equivalent to the earnings of one hundred days of work. It can be argued that the day fine system is fair to both rich and poor since it punishes them equally, despite differences in the amount of their particular fine. *See generally* Sally T. Hillsman, Joyce L. Sichel, Barry Mahoney, FINES IN SENTENCING: A STUDY OF THE USE OF THE FINE AS A CRIMINAL SANCTION (1984); Sally T. Hillsman, *Fines and Day-Fines*, 12 CRIME AND JUSTICE: A REVIEW OF RESEARCH 49 (Tonry & Morris, eds. 1990).

[6]   Community Service

In recent years many American jurisdictions have added a new sentencing option: community service. The offender is ordered to spend a set number of hours, say one hundred, working at no pay for a public or charitable purpose. Examples include picking up trash in a park, working in a hospital emergency room, painting the houses of elderly citizens, repairing roads or playgrounds, and speaking to school groups about the dangers of drugs.

This option, used extensively in Britain, has many advantages. It not only provides a valuable service to the people or agency receiving the free work, it, in theory at least, aids rehabilitation by teaching the offender about the needs of the community and making the offender feel a part of the collective enterprise of citizenship. If sufficiently rigorous, it also could deter future criminality and satisfy the need for retribution.

Community service is not without costs. It requires human and financial resources for supervision, equipment, supplies, and insurance. Community service workers could also perform jobs that would otherwise be done by paid public or private employers, thus increasing employment problems of some law-abiding citizens. It also raises serious questions about liability for injuries caused by the offender (*e.g.*, negligent use of a shovel causing injury to a co-worker) or to the offender (*e.g.*, back injury incurred performing community service). Because of a concern about increasing the risk of harm to the public as some offenders on community release may recidivate while doing their community service, many jurisdictions limit this option to offenders convicted of nonviolent crimes or with little or no prior criminal record.

[7]   Forfeiture

Property used to commit offense. Another sentencing option is a *forfeiture* of property. The typical pattern is a statute that permits a court to order forfeiture of property in two contexts. First, a court may be authorized to order the forfeiture of property used in the commission of a particular offense, such as a drug violation. In some locales, a car, boat, or house used in illegal drug activities can be ordered to be forfeited to the government.

Proceeds of crime. The second approach reaches the proceeds of illegal activity. A statute may authorize the forfeiture of property obtained by money earned in certain crimes. A good example is the so-called RICO (Racketeer Influenced and Corrupt Organizations Act) law which, in general terms, bars a person receiving income from a pattern of racketeering activity or unlawful debt collection to use or invest such income in an enterprise affecting interstate commerce. 18 U.S.C. § 1962. Among the authorized penalties is the forfeiture of "any interest in; security of; claim against; or property or contractual right of any kind affording a source of influence over; any enterprise which the person has established, operated, controlled, conducted, or participated in the conduct of" in violation of the RICO statute. 18 U.S.C. § 1963(a)(3). It also reaches "any property constituting, or derived from, any proceeds which the person obtained, directly or indirectly, from racketeering activity or unlawful debt collection" in violation of RICO. *Id.* The Supreme Court has upheld the forfeiture of drug proceeds that were to have been used to pay for criminal defense counsel. *Caplin & Drysdale, Chartered v. United States*, 491 U.S. 617 (1989).

Proceeds of media publications: "Son of Sam" laws. A related variety of forfeiture mandates that a criminal offender forfeit financial benefits from some income derived from the media. Called *Son of Sam* laws (referring to the New York serial killer, David Berkowitz), these statutes usually take away money an offender earns from books, interviews, movies, and the like that relate to the crime for which the offender was convicted. The funds are placed in an escrow account and are paid to the offender's victim and creditors. While acknowledging that the state has a compelling interest in stripping criminals of the fruits of their crimes and in compensating victims, the United States Supreme Court struck down the New York *Son of Sam* statute as violating the First Amendment. In *Simon and Schuster v. New York Crime Victims Bd.*, 502 U.S. 105 (1991), the Court held that the New York provision singled out a particular kind of speech and placed on it a financial burden that was not placed on speech involving other content.

Some states have adopted revised *Son of Sam* statutes to meet the *Simon and Schuster* objections, but their constitutionality is uncertain.

Constitutional limits. Forfeitures can present significant constitutional issues. In *United States v. Bajakajian*, 524 U.S. 321 (1998), the Supreme Court, for the first time, applied the Eighth Amendment's excessive fines clause to strike down a forfeiture. The case involved a man who was apprehended leaving the United States with $357,144 in his luggage, in violation of a federal statute requiring reporting of currency in excess of $100,000 taken out of the country. A lower court authorized forfeiture of the $357,144 in accordance with federal law. The Supreme Court held that the forfeiture violated the excessive fines clause since the forfeiture was punitive rather than remedial and bore no relationship to the injury suffered by the government. Had the government suffered some injury and the forfeiture been designed to reimburse the government for that loss or had the defendant been involved in a separate offense such as money laundering or tax evasion, the majority opinion, authored by Justice Thomas, indicated that the forfeiture may have been sustained. In 1996, the Supreme Court had held that civil forfeitures in general do not constitute punishment and therefore do not offend the double jeopardy clause. Such forfeitures are viewed as actions against the property rather than actions against the owner. *United States v. Ursery*, 518 U.S. 267 (1996).

Procedural issues. Forfeitures create a number of unique procedural difficulties. Many stem from the fact that property subject to forfeiture can be transferred to others or may be owned at least in part by several people. Statutes routinely permit a court to order that property subject to forfeiture not be transferred to other persons. There are also provisions to protect the interests of non-criminals who own an interest in property subject to forfeiture. *See, e.g.*, 18 U.S.C. § 1963. Finally, the due process clause requires that, absent exigent circumstances, the government in a civil forfeiture case cannot seize real property without first providing the owner notice and an opportunity to be heard. *See United States v. James Daniel Good Real Property*, 510 U.S. 43 (1993) (due process violated when 4 1/2 years after marijuana seized from defendant's home, government obtained *ex parte* forfeiture warrant for this home and surrounding 4 acres); *cf. Bennis v. Michigan*, 516 U.S. 442 (1996) (due process not offended when car, jointly owned by husband and wife, was forfeited because of husband's use of it with prostitute; wife accorded opportunity to contest forfeiture).

[8] Restitution

In an era when the plight of criminal victims is an important national issue, jurisdictions routinely permit restitution to be a sentencing alternative, often in combination with other sanctions. Some require it for nonviolent crimes. For example, the federal Crime Victim's Rights Act states specifically that a crime victim has the right "to full and timely restitution" as provided by law. 18 U.S.C. § 3771(a)(6).

Restitution is compensation by the offender for the harm he or she caused. For example, a burglar may be sentenced to repay the value of the items taken (*e.g.*, $750) plus the cost of replacing a door damaged in the entry (*e.g.*, $200). Restitution may also be authorized for such amounts as lost wages, medical costs, and even pain and suffering. The American Bar Association recommends that restitution should be limited "to the greater of the benefit to [the defendant] or actual loss to [the victim]." Victims seeking exemplary, punitive damages, or consequential damages, such as pain and suffering or loss of profits, should be limited to civil remedies. The ABA also recommends that "appropriate provisions [be enacted] to integrate the criminal sanction of restitution or reparation with a victim's right of civil action against an offender." STANDARDS FOR CRIMINAL JUSTICE § 18-3.15(c) and (d) (3d ed. 1994).

Procedural issues. The amount of restitution should be set only after a hearing in which the accused has an opportunity to offer proof on the value of the losses for which restitution is authorized. The procedure becomes more complicated if there are multiple offenders, particularly if some have not been apprehended or have no resources to pay a restitution order. The issue is what share each offender must pay.

Theoretical basis. Although restitution is now an accepted part of sentencing, its theoretical basis is often ignored. One approach is the notion that restitution is actually not punishment at all. If X steals Y's lawn mower, is it punishment if X is ordered to return the lawn mower? After all, the lawn mower never belonged to X, the thief. Another explanation, following both more traditional themes and more recent notions of *restorative justice*, is that restitution is rehabilitative in that it forces the offender to come to grips with and repair the harm he or she caused. This acceptance of responsibility is often viewed as an important step toward rehabilitation. It can also be argued that restitution contributes to deterrence since it conveys the message that the criminal will not profit from the offense, thereby reducing the likelihood that the crime will benefit the potential criminal.

[9] Diversion

Another sentencing option is *diversion*, ordinarily involving an early removal of the offender from the "criminogenic" environment of the criminal justice system. Diversion can occur at various stages of the criminal justice system and can be quite informal or very structured. An example of the former is a police officer or prosecutor who agrees to "sit on" or drop charges or never initiate charges if the offender does not get arrested for another crime in the next six months. A *structured diversion* may be done by a judge who enters a formal order that charges will be dropped (or never filed) if the offender is not convicted of another crime in a year. Sometimes, a diversion is ordered only if the offender satisfies certain conditions, such as paying court costs or restitution or performing a specified number of hours of community service.

The primary purpose of diversion is rehabilitation, especially for first-time and non-violent offenders. Some offenders could become more crime-prone by getting involved in the criminal justice system, where they are likely to meet and learn from other offenders and they may begin to think of themselves as criminals.

Diversion, like the other options, has a downside. Ordinarily it is lenient treatment and may involve little retribution, deterrence, or incapacitation. On the other hand, certain diversion programs such as drug courts and boot camps can be very rigorous and demanding on their participants.

E. PROCEDURES

Sentencing involves procedures ranging from informal to very formal. Recent innovations, such as guidelines, markedly change many facets of sentencing procedures.

[1] Procedures in General

Irrespective of the precise procedural details that may vary from one jurisdiction to another, most sentencing decisions are based on a common model. In general terms, sentencing in America is done by the judge. The American Bar Association explicitly recommends that jury sentencing be abolished. STANDARDS FOR CRIMINAL JUSTICE § 18-1.4(a) (3d ed. 1994) (noting that sentencing the offender is a "judicial function" and that the "jury's role in a criminal trial should not extend to determination of the appropriate sentence"). The main exception is capital cases, where the jury, not the judge, after finding the defendant guilty of a capital offense, finds the facts on which the decision whether or not to impose the death penalty will be made. *See, Ring v. Arizona*, 536 U.S. 584 (2002), discussed later in this chapter. In a few states such as Arkansas and Oklahoma, however, in all cases tried to a jury, the jury recommends the sentence, which the trial judge, by practice and tradition, most often follows.

Hearing. Ordinarily the sentence is decided after a *sentencing hearing*, described below. If the conviction is the product of a guilty plea, the sentence may be imposed shortly after the plea is accepted. If the conviction resulted from a bench or jury trial, the sentence will usually be decided after a hearing held weeks or even months after the conviction.

At the sentencing hearing, the government will be represented by a prosecutor and the defendant by defense counsel, unless a defense lawyer has been waived. Usually the prosecution will speak first, perhaps even offering witnesses and sometimes advocating a certain sentence. Defense counsel may cross-examine government witnesses and present its own proof, including both witnesses and documents. Often the rules of evidence do not apply at sentencing hearings, making hearsay evidence both admissible and frequently used. Normally, the standard of proof on all issues of fact is by a preponderance of the evidence. *See* STANDARDS FOR CRIMINAL JUSTICE § 18-5.18(a)(i) (3d ed. 1994). But query, does this standard of proof need to be reexamined in light of the *Apprendi* line of cases (facts that increase a sentence beyond the maximum otherwise allowable must be found by a jury, absent waiver, beyond a reasonable doubt), discussed later in this chapter?

If there has been a plea bargain, the sentencing hearing may last only a few minutes as the court rubber stamps the deal worked out by counsel and satisfies the procedural requirements mandated for guilty pleas. *See* Chapter 11. In the absence of a plea agreement, a sentencing hearing, in exceptional cases, could last several days or longer, although the usual one lasts an hour or less.

[2] Data Used in Sentencing: Reports and Other Information

Although frequently the sentence is actually determined as the result of a plea bargain between the prosecution and the defense lawyer, sometimes the court makes an independent determination of the appropriate sentence. In order to arrive at a sentence that best serves the judge's sentencing goal(s) in a particular case, the court will need additional information about the defendant and perhaps the offense itself. For example, if the judge would like to impose a sentence designed to rehabilitate the offender, the court must have information about the defendant's social history in order to determine an appropriate sentence. A defendant with a fourth grade education and a poor work record may be handled quite differently than one with a college degree and a lengthy employment history.

Courts obtain information about the defendant and the offense from three sources, as explained below and in the next subsection.

Written presentence report. First, often the court will have a *presentence report* prepared by a probation officer or the equivalent. In essence, the presentence report is a social history of the accused. This report may also include information about the crime, the effect on the victim, and even a suggested sentence. This report will routinely detail such information as the defendant's family situation, educational and work history, physical and mental condition, and financial status. *See* Fed. R. Crim. P. 32(c) and (d). It may also include information about the impact of the crime on the victim and others, such as the victim's family. The American Bar Association recommends that a statement "prepared by a victim" should be "included as an attachment to the presentence report." STANDARDS FOR CRIMINAL JUSTICE § 18-5.4(c) (3d ed. 1994).

According to the Federal Rules of Criminal Procedure, the presentence report may not include information that, if disclosed, might result in harm to the defendant or other persons, or that was obtained upon a promise of confidentiality. Fed. R. Crim. P. 32(d)(3). The American Bar Association recommends that presentence reports be confidential (not a part of a public record) but that they should be available to the parties; it also recommends that rules of procedure should provide that parties are "entitled . . . to copies of the written presentence report and any similar reports." STANDARDS FOR CRIMINAL JUSTICE §§ 18-5.6(a) and 18-5.7(a) (3d ed. 1994).

Ensuring accurate information. Rules of criminal procedure routinely provide protections against inaccurate information used in sentencing decisions. The Federal Rules of Criminal Procedure are especially protective. The federal rules give defense counsel the right to attend any interview of the defendant by the probation officer conducting a presentence investigation. They also require the probation officer to disclose the presentence report to the defendant, defense lawyer, and the government more than a month before the sentencing hearing. Since some states do nor mandate disclosure, the American Bar Association recommends that states adopt rules of procedure entitling parties to "copies of the written presentence report and any similar reports." STANDARDS FOR CRIMINAL JUSTICE § 18-5.7(a) (3d ed. 1994). If the parties object to any facts in the report, the rules provide procedures and deadlines for resolving the problems. Fed. R. Crim. P. 32(f) and (g).

Information from lawyers and victim. The second source of information is the lawyers for both sides. Ordinarily, each may submit its own presentence memorandum to the court, stressing information that may or may not be available from other sources. Sometimes the victim also is permitted to provide the court with information about his or her feelings about the crime and the possible sentence. The victim's information may be included in the presentence report or a separate document, or through live testimony at the sentencing hearing (sometimes referred to as *victim allocution*). For example, the federal Crime Victims' Rights Act gives victims "the right to be reasonably heard at any public proceeding . . . involving . . . sentencing." 18 U.S.C. § 3771(a)(4). Additional data may be presented during the trial or earlier proceedings.

The defendant's prior criminal record (or "rap sheet") is also typically considered by the judge prior to sentencing the defendant.

The American Bar Association recommends that states adopt rules of procedure establishing mechanisms for providing notice to victims of "all important steps in the sentencing process." In addition to the victims' statements submitted in writing and attached to presentence reports, the ABA states that victims also should be permitted to make oral statements at sentencing hearings "concerning the physical, psychological, economic, or social effects of the offense on the victim or the victim's family." The ABA does not explicitly endorse the notion of permitting the crime victim to comment on the appropriate or recommended sentence. STANDARDS FOR CRIMINAL JUSTICE §§ 18-5.9(a), 5.10(a) and 5.11(a) (3d ed. 1994).

[3]   Sentencing Hearing

The third source of information is the *sentencing hearing*, an adversary proceeding in which both the prosecution and defense are permitted to provide the court with information relevant to the sentencing decision. In all except capital cases, the sentencing hearing is virtually always conducted by the judge without the use of a jury. A small number of states, however, empower the jury to recommend a sentence to the judge, who then has the final word. In these states, especially where judges are elected, judges may be reluctant to overrule jury sentencing recommendations with any degree of frequency.

Since, in general terms, a judge conducts fact finding on sentencing issues and a jury (unless waived) finds the facts with regard to the elements of the crime, on occasion there must be a determination whether a particular fact in a criminal statute is an element of the crime (hence to be found by the jury using the beyond-a-reasonable-doubt standard) or a sentencing consideration (resolved by the judge, perhaps on some lesser standard of proof). When the statute is ambiguous on this issue, courts look at the structure of the statute, including paragraphing and internal consistency, the history of the statute, practice in other jurisdictions, and the historical role of the jury. For example, in *Jones v. State*, 526 U.S. 227 (1999), the Court was presented with a carjacking statute that increased the penalty if "serious bodily injury" occurred. Conceding that the question was close, Justice Souter's opinion for the Court looked at the above factors and held that "serious bodily injury" was an element rather than merely a sentencing consideration. Two concurring opinions concluded that it would violate due process to remove from the jury the assessment of facts that increase the prescribed range of penalties to which a criminal defendant is exposed. This issue is also discussed in Chapter 15.

The sentencing hearing may be held immediately after the trial or guilty plea, or several weeks or even months later. The defendant is entitled to be represented by counsel at the sentencing hearing if he or she is entitled to one at trial. In some jurisdictions the victim is permitted to testify or provide written information about the crime and the sentence. *See, e.g.*, 18 U.S.C. § 3771(a)(4).

Although procedures differ markedly among the jurisdictions, ordinarily the sentencing hearing is less formal than the trial. The rules of evidence may be inapplicable or only applied to some kinds of information. For example, some written reports may be admissible at a sentencing hearing though they would be inadmissible under the hearsay rule at a trial. Both sides may present witnesses. In a typical case, the defense will offer testimony from the defendant, members of the defendant's family, and character witnesses to talk about the defendant and the impact of a particular sentence. The defendant is accorded the right of *allocution* which permits him or her personally to address the judge in open court. If the defense counsel offers a plan for a probation sentence, a useful witness would be the person who has promised to employ the defendant if the court orders probation instead of prison. The prosecution's witness may be the victim who will describe the crime, the extent of the loss, and perhaps even comment on the appropriate sentence.

[4] Sentencing Factfinding and the *Apprendi* Line of Cases

[a] *Apprendi v. New Jersey*

An important sentencing issue is whether a fact that affects a sentence must be found by a judge or jury and whether the standard of proof is beyond a reasonable doubt or some lesser standard. Although in some earlier cases the Court had resolved this question by determining whether a particular fact was an *element of the crime* (to be decided by a jury using the standard of beyond a reasonable doubt) or a *sentencing factor* (to be decided by a judge, often using the preponderance of evidence standard), the Court rejected the significance of this distinction in *Apprendi v. New Jersey*, 536 U.S. 584 (2000), and expanded on the ruling in subsequent decisions.

APPRENDI v. NEW JERSEY
530 U.S. 466 (2000)

JUSTICE STEVENS delivered the opinion of the Court.

[Following his arrest, Charles Apprendi admitted that he fired shots into the home of an African-American family. Although later retracted by Apprendi, he also stated that he did not want the victims in the neighborhood "because they are black in color." He later agreed to plead guilty to two firearms counts (punishable by a penalty range of 5 to 10 years) and another offense punishable by 3 to 5 years' imprisonment. The plea agreement allowed the State to request an "enhanced" sentence on the ground that the offense "was committed with a biased purpose," while Apprendi reserved the right to "challenge the hate crime sentence enhancement on the ground that it violates the United States Constitution." After a hearing, at which time several witnesses, including Apprendi, testified on the issue of Apprendi's "purpose" for shooting, the judge found by a preponderance of the evidence that Apprendi's actions were taken "with a purpose to intimidate" (*i.e.*, the crime "was motivated by racial bias") and sentenced him to a 12-year term of imprisonment, to run concurrently with the other sentences.]

At stake in this case are constitutional protections of surpassing importance: the proscription of any deprivation of liberty without "due process of law," and the guarantee that "[i]n all criminal prosecutions, the accused shall enjoy the right to a speedy and public trial, by an impartial jury." Taken together, these rights indisputably entitle a criminal defendant to "a jury determination that [he] is guilty of every element of the crime with which he is charged, beyond a reasonable doubt."

. . . [O]ur reexamination of our cases in this area, and of the history upon which they rely, confirms the opinion that we expressed in *Jones*. Other than the fact of a prior conviction, any fact that increases the penalty for a crime beyond the prescribed statutory maximum must be submitted to a jury, and proved beyond a reasonable doubt. With that exception, we endorse the statement of the rule set forth in the concurring opinions in that case: "[I]t is unconstitutional for a legislature to remove from the jury the assessment of facts that increase the prescribed range of penalties to which a criminal defendant is exposed. It is equally clear that such facts must be established by proof beyond a reasonable doubt."

The New Jersey statutory scheme that Apprendi asks us to invalidate allows a jury to convict a defendant of a second-degree offense based on its finding beyond a reasonable doubt that he unlawfully possessed a prohibited weapon; after a subsequent and separate proceeding, it then allows a judge to impose punishment identical to that New Jersey provides for crimes of the first degree based upon the judge's finding, by a preponderance of the evidence, that the defendant's "purpose" for unlawfully possessing the weapon was "to intimidate" his victim on the basis of a particular characteristic the victim possessed. In light of the constitutional rule explained above, and all of the cases supporting it, this practice cannot stand.

. . . [T]he New Jersey Supreme Court correctly recognized that it does not matter whether the required finding is characterized as one of intent or of motive, because "[l]abels do not afford an acceptable answer." That point applies as well to the constitutionally novel and elusive distinction between "elements" and "sentencing factors." Despite what appears to us the clear "elemental" nature of the factor here, the relevant inquiry is one not of form, but of effect — does the required finding expose the defendant to a greater punishment than that authorized by the jury's guilty verdict?[1]

. . . The New Jersey procedure challenged in this case is an unacceptable departure from the jury tradition that is an indispensable part of our criminal justice system.

[JUSTICE THOMAS, joined by JUSTICE SCALIA, concurred and argued for a broader rule than the majority:]

A long line of essentially uniform authority addressing accusations, and stretching from the earliest reported cases after the founding and well into the 20th century, establishes that the original understanding of which facts are elements was even broader than the rule that the Court adopts today.

This authority establishes that a "crime" includes every fact that is by law a basis for imposing or increasing punishment (in contrast with a fact that mitigates punishment). Thus, if the legislature defines some core crime and then provides for increasing the punishment of that crime upon a finding of some aggravating fact — of whatever sort, including the fact of a prior conviction — the core crime and the aggravating fact together constitute an aggravated crime, just as much as grand larceny is an aggravated form of petit larceny. The aggravating fact is an element of the aggravated crime. Similarly, if the legislature, rather than creating grades of crimes, has provided for setting the punishment of a crime based on some fact — such as a fine that is proportional to the value of stolen goods — that fact is also an element. No multi-factor parsing of statutes . . . is necessary. One need only look to the kind, degree, or range of punishment to which the prosecution is by law entitled for a given set of facts. Each fact necessary for that entitlement is an element. . . .

[T]his traditional understanding — that a "crime" includes every fact that is by law a basis for imposing or increasing punishment . . . reflect[s] the original meaning of the Fifth and Sixth Amendments.

JUSTICE O'CONNOR, with whom THE CHIEF JUSTICE, JUSTICE KENNEDY, and JUSTICE BREYER join, dissenting.

Last Term, in *Jones v. United States*, this Court found that our prior cases suggested the following principle: "[U]nder the Due Process Clause of the Fifth Amendment and the notice and jury trial guarantees of the Sixth Amendment, any fact (other than prior conviction) that increases the maximum penalty for a crime must be charged in an indictment, submitted to a jury, and proven beyond a reasonable doubt." At the time, JUSTICE KENNEDY rightly criticized the Court for its failure to explain the origins, contours, or consequences of its purported constitutional principle; for the inconsistency of that principle with our prior cases; and for the serious doubt that the holding cast on sentencing systems employed by the Federal Government and States

---

[1] This is not to suggest that the term "sentencing factor" is devoid of meaning. The term appropriately describes a circumstance, which may be either aggravating or mitigating in character, that supports a specific sentence within the range authorized by the jury's finding that the defendant is guilty of a particular offense. On the other hand, when the term "sentence enhancement" is used to describe an increase beyond the maximum authorized statutory sentence, it is the functional equivalent of an element of a greater offense than the one covered by the jury's guilty verdict. Indeed, it fits squarely within the usual definition of an "element" of the offense.

alike. Today, in what will surely be remembered as a watershed change in constitutional law, the Court imposes as a constitutional rule the principle it first identified in *Jones*.

[JUSTICE O'CONNOR asserted that the majority failed to offer any "meaningful justification" for its "increase in the maximum penalty" rule. She also noted that the impact of this ruling could be far reaching:]

The decision will likely have an even more damaging effect on sentencing conducted in the immediate future under current determinate-sentencing schemes. Because the Court fails to clarify the precise contours of the constitutional principle underlying its decision, federal and state judges are left in a state of limbo. Should they continue to assume the constitutionality of the determinate-sentencing schemes under which they have operated for so long, and proceed to sentence convicted defendants in accord with those governing statutes and guidelines? The Court provides no answer, yet its reasoning suggests that each new sentence will rest on shaky ground. The most unfortunate aspect of today's decision is that our precedents did not foreordain this disruption in the world of sentencing. Rather, our cases traditionally took a cautious approach to questions like the one presented in this case. The Court throws that caution to the wind and, in the process, threatens to cast sentencing in the United States into what will likely prove to be a lengthy period of considerable confusion. . . .

JUSTICE BREYER, with whom CHIEF JUSTICE REHNQUIST joins, dissenting.

The majority holds that the Constitution contains the following requirement: "any fact [other than recidivism] that increases the penalty for a crime beyond the prescribed statutory maximum must be submitted to a jury, and proved beyond a reasonable doubt." This rule would seem to promote a procedural ideal — that of juries, not judges, determining the existence of those facts upon which increased punishment turns. But the real world of criminal justice cannot hope to meet any such ideal. It can function only with the help of procedural compromises, particularly in respect to sentencing. And those compromises, which are themselves necessary for the fair functioning of the criminal justice system, preclude implementation of the procedural model that today's decision reflects. At the very least, the impractical nature of the requirement that the majority now recognizes supports the proposition that the Constitution was not intended to embody it. . . .

NOTES

1. *What's the big deal?* Why is *Apprendi* regarded as a minor revolution in American sentencing law? Does it help or hurt the criminal accused? The state? Do you think it will result in longer, shorter, or the same sentences as imposed before *Apprendi*?

2. Does *Apprendi* mean that juries will have to be involved in every sentencing decision in every state? Don't forget that criminal defendants plead guilty in over ninety percent of all felony cases. Part of the plea process involves a formal waiver of a jury trial. If the defendant waives a jury *trial*, does this also mean that there is a waiver of a jury's involvement in *sentencing*?

3. *Apprendi* is based on the concept of the "statutory maximum" sentence. Was the sentence enhancement in *Apprendi* actually beyond the statutory maximum since it was authorized by statute to be added to the sentence for the base crime?

4. How does the Thomas concurrence differ from the Stevens opinion for the Court? Can you come up with a crime that illustrates the differences?

5. *See generally*, Mohammed Saif-Alden, *The Meaning of Guilt: Rethinking Apprendi*, 33 NEW ENG. J. ON CRIM. & CIV. CONFINEMENT 501 (2007).

The following cases will help you understand the impact of *Apprendi*, especially in death penalty cases and in jurisdictions using sentencing guidelines, including the federal system.

[b] Post-*Apprendi*

[i] *Ring v. Arizona*: Capital Cases

Post-*Apprendi* decisions have further elevated the importance of the role of juries in the process of finding facts that may enhance sentence severity. In *Ring v. Arizona*, 536 U.S. 584 (2002), the Supreme Court applied *Apprendi* to capital cases. Arizona law authorized the death penalty only when, after a jury finds guilt of first degree murder, the judge (without a jury) finds the presence of one or more aggravating circumstances. The judge imposed the death penalty, finding that the testimony at the sentencing hearing established two aggravating factors: that Ring was a major participant in the armed robbery that led to the killing and that he exhibited a reckless disregard or indifference for human life.

The Supreme Court overturned the death penalty, reasoning that under *Apprendi*'s reading of the Sixth Amendment, the determination regarding aggravating factors, and therefore the facts on which the life-or-death sentencing decision will depend, must be made by juries rather than judges. The Court reasoned from *Apprendi* that since *life* was the maximum penalty allowable on the basis of the jury's verdict of guilt *standing alone*, the ultimate penalty of *death* could only be imposed if the facts that lead to the imposition if the death penalty are found by the jury, not the judge. *Ring*, in effect, invalidated death penalty procedures in several other states which had assigned the finding of aggravating versus mitigating circumstances in capital cases to the trial judge.

[ii] *Blakely v. Washington*: Maximum Sentence Definition

Blakely v. Washington, 542 U.S. 296 (2004), continued the *Apprendi* approach. Blakely pleaded guilty to kidnapping his estranged wife. Under Washington law, the maximum sentence he could receive at that time was 53 months in prison. But Washington law authorized an increase if "substantial and compelling reasons" justified "an exceptional sentence." This could increase Blakely's sentence to 90 months if the court found that he acted with "deliberate cruelty," one of several aggravating factors permitting the judge to increase the sentence upon finding the aggravating factor to be present. After hearing evidence, including the victim's testimony about the incident, the trial judge issued 32 findings of fact and imposed the 90-month sentence.

The *Blakely* Court invalidated the increase because "the statutory maximum" for *Apprendi* purposes is the maximum sentence a judge may impose "*solely on the basis of the facts reflected in the jury verdict or admitted by the defendant.*" *Apprendi* barred increasing a sentence beyond the maximum the judge "may impose based solely on the facts admitted in the guilty plea." 542 U.S. at 303 (emphasis in original).

Blakely made it clear, however, that the prosecution and defense may avoid jury factfinding in the sentencing process if the defendant executes a valid waiver of a jury trial and agrees to be sentenced by the court, or if both sides stipulate to the relevant enhancing facts. *See generally* Joanna Shepherd, *Blakely's Silver Lining: Sentencing Guidelines, Judicial Discretion, and Crime*, 58 Hast. L. J. 533 (2007).

[iii] *United States v. Booker*: Federal Sentencing Guidelines

Although *Blakely* reviewed a provision of state law, the decision placed the constitutionality of the United States Sentencing Guidelines in doubt, inasmuch as the U.S. Guidelines, by design, frequently allow sentences to be enhanced on the basis of judge-made factual determinations under a preponderance-of-the-evidence standard. Shortly after *Blakely*, in *United States v. Booker*, 543 U.S. 220 (2005), the Court found that the Federal Sentencing Guidelines violated *Apprendi* and *Blakely* in certain instances, *i.e.*, where the judge after sentencing factfinding imposes a greater sentence than could have been given on the basis of the jury's verdict of guilty (or the defendant's plea of guilty) alone.

In *Booker*, the defendant was convicted of possessing at least 50 grams of crack cocaine. The maximum guideline sentence for the offense itself was 262 months, but the trial court used the Guidelines' departure rules to impose a longer sentence (360 months) based on the judge's finding by a preponderance of evidence that Booker actually possessed 566 grams of cocaine. No jury was involved in establishing the additional quantity of drugs and the initial jury verdict did not authorize a sentence for anything more than possession of 50 grams of cocaine.

Advisory rather than mandatory. Booker first found the sentence to be unconstitutional under *Apprendi* and held that the U.S. Sentencing Guidelines scheme was partially unconstitutional (to the extent that they allow defendants to be sentenced, on the basis of *judge-found* facts, to more time than would be otherwise be allowable on the basis of the *jury-found* verdict of guilt alone). The Court noted, however, that the guidelines would be upheld if they were merely advisory rather than mandatory. *Booker* recognized the longstanding rule that a trial judge may make factual determinations needed to impose sentence within the range authorized by the jury verdict. Thus, if a sentencing scheme authorized a sentence of 5–15 years for Crime X and provided a set of factors for the court to use in determining the exact sentence within that range, the court alone (without the jury) could assess whether the sentencing factors are present. This would occur after the jury found the defendant guilty of Crime X, which then authorized the court to decide the sentence within the 5–15 year range for Crime X.

Having found that the federal guidelines were unconstitutional in part, the *Booker* Court had to confront the issue of *severability* in framing its remedy. The Court determined that the Federal Guidelines would not violate the Sixth Amendment if their application were to be construed as *advisory*, rather than mandatory. But the question of severability required the Court to assess Congress's intent in light of the Court's determination that the Guidelines were partially unconstitutional. Would Congress prefer that the Guidelines be struck down in their entirety if it regarded the mandatory operation of the Guidelines as central to the whole statutory scheme? Or would Congress prefer to retain the Guidelines as glossed by the Court to be merely advisory in operation (in order to comply with the Sixth Amendment right to have a jury decide sentence-enhancing facts)?

A closely and sharply divided Court chose the latter view and rather than striking down the federal guidelines in their entirety, adopted the saving construction of treating them as advisory rather than mandatory. Although the guidelines are advisory, they still have enormous importance because federal sentencing judges must still "take into account" the Guidelines and other sentencing goals. More particularly, federal judges must in each particular case consider the Guidelines' sentencing range for the offense and defendant, the Sentencing Commission's policy statements, the need to avoid unwarranted disparities, and the need for restitution.

Standard of review on appeal of sentence. Booker further clarified *Apprendi*, ruling that sentences under the Guidelines should be upheld on appeal so long as they are "reasonable" (supplanting the *de novo* standard of review applicable to sentences that depart from the Guidelines, which Congress had enacted in 2003). In *Booker* and again in *United States v. Rita*, 127 S. Ct. 2456 (2007), the Court likened the review of sentences for "reasonableness" to appellate review under an abuse-of-discretion standard. In both decisions, the Court emphasized the need to preserve a significant degree of latitude and discretion for federal judges to sentence either within or outside of the Guidelines, in order for the Federal Guidelines to be truly "advisory" rather than "mandatory" in their operation.

References. See generally, Frank C. Damrell, Jr., *Observations: Sentencing Guideline Law and Practice in a Post-Booker World,* 39 McGeorge L. Rev. 823 (2008); Robert L. Boone, *Booker Defined: Examining the Application of United States v. Booker in the Nation's Most Divergent Circuit Courts,* 95 Cal. L. Rev. 1079 (2007); Paul Hofer, *Empirical Questions and Evidence in Rita v. United States,* 85 Denv. U. L. Rev. 27 (2007).

[iv] *Cunningham v. California*: Presumptive Sentences

In *Cunningham v. California,* 127 S. Ct. 856 (2007), the Supreme Court applied the *Apprendi* line of reasoning to invalidate California's enhanced sentencing provisions enacted under its 1977 Determinate Sentencing Law, which created a presumptive sentencing system to limit judges' sentencing discretion. That statutory scheme, as implemented by court rules, provided for judges to sentence convicted felons to one of three terms (designated respectively as the "lower," the "middle," and the "upper" terms) for a given crime. The middle term, also designated as the "presumptive" term, is to be imposed under the statutory scheme unless the judge finds either that certain "mitigating factors" justify sentencing to the lower term, or that "aggravating factors" justify sentencing to the upper term. Assessing the presence or absence of these factors required the judge to engage in factfinding about the defendant and the offense.

Following *Apprendi* and its progeny, the Court held that the Cunningham had been sentenced to the upper term on the basis of constitutionally impermissible factfinding by the sentencing judge: "Because the [California Determinate Sentencing Law] authorizes the judge, not the jury, to find facts permitting an upper term sentence, the system cannot withstand measurement under our Sixth Amendment precedent." *Id.* at 871. The "relevant statutory maximum" for *Apprendi* purposes, the Court reiterated, is "not the maximum sentence a judge may impose after finding additional facts, but the maximum he may impose *without* any additional findings." 127 S. Ct. at 865, quoting from *Blakely,* 542 U.S. at 303 (emphasis in original). *See* Laurie Jaeckel, *Cunningham v. California: The Shifting Balance of Judge and Jury,* 85 Denv. U. L. Rev. 153 (2007).

[v] State Responses to *Apprendi*

States with guideline and enhanced sentencing systems have responded to the *Apprendi* line of decisions in two ways in order to conform their systems to the Sixth Amendment. Some have added a second jury factfinding process after the jury has found guilt. The jury reconvenes and decides whether statutory aggravating or enhancing factors are present. For example, if the jurisdiction authorized an enhanced sentence for the presence of a loaded weapon at a crime, the jury would first find guilt, then reconvene to determine whether the defendant had a loaded weapon at the crime scene.

The second approach is to adopt the Supreme Court's *Booker* remedy, making state guidelines advisory rather than mandatory and thus eliminating the need to involve a jury in the sentencing process.

[5] Sentence Reduction by Trial Court

Sentence reduction. After a trial court imposes a sentence, most jurisdictions permit that same judge to reduce the sentence within a certain period after imposition. This practice is usually justified as permitting the court to receive new information or to reprocess old information. Many jurisdictions follow the former federal rule and permit the court to lower the sentence within 120 days of its imposition, although other time limits are also used. *See, e.g.,* Fla. R. Crim. P. 3.800(c) (within 60 days); Me. R. Crim. P. 35(c) (within 1 year, on grounds that original sentence was influenced by a mistake of fact which existed at time of sentencing).

In the federal courts, the judge may reduce a sentence for a defendant's substantial assistance in investigating or prosecuting another person. Ordinarily, the government must move for this reduction within one year after the sentence is imposed. Fed. R. Crim. P. 35(b).

Usually the sentence reduction process is triggered when the defendant files a Motion to Reduce Sentence. Courts differ on whether a hearing must be held on the motion and whether the court must provide findings of fact and law in ruling on the motion.

Vacating improper sentence. Sometimes a court erroneously imposes a sentence that is not authorized by law. For example, the court could mistakenly impose a seven year sentence on an offender when a five year sentence was the maximum permitted by statute. Most jurisdictions permit this improper sentence to be corrected, even beyond the term permitted by rule or statute for a sentence reduction.

[6] Appellate Review

[a] Review in Traditional (Non-Guideline) Sentencing Systems

Despite the obvious importance of the judge's sentencing decision, appellate courts in many American jurisdictions have been reluctant to second guess the trial judge's (or jury's) selection of a sentence. Prior to the adoption of the federal sentencing guidelines, federal courts simply refused to review most sentencing issues. Sometimes this refusal led to sweepingly broad statements. *See, e.g., Dorszynski v. United States,* 418 U.S. 424, 431 (1974) ("once it is determined that a sentence is within the limitations set forth in the statute under which it is imposed, appellate review is at an end"). Nonetheless, even federal courts reviewed some issues in sentencing.

Many state courts continue to follow this tradition and refuse to overturn a trial court's sentence unless there has been an "abuse of discretion" or even a "gross abuse of discretion," standards that give great deference to the trial court's decision and rarely lead to an appellate reversal. The decisions tend to be fact specific.

The American Bar Association recommends that state legislatures authorize appellate courts to review sentences, at the initiative of either the defendant or the prosecution. The appropriate reviewing court should be authorized to (1) affirm the sentence, (2) reverse the sentence and remand to the original sentencing court for resentencing, or (3) "substitute for the sentence under review any other disposition that was available to the sentencing court." STANDARDS FOR CRIMINAL JUSTICE §§ 18-8.1(a), 8.3 and 8.4(a) (3d ed. 1994).

[b] Review in Guideline Systems

Appeal by either side. With the advent of sentencing guideline systems (discussed later in this chapter) that seek to structure and set bounds on the exercise of traditional, almost completely unlimited sentencing discretion, there has also come a recent trend toward greater appellate review of sentences. A sentence under the federal sentencing guidelines, for example, can be appealed by either the prosecution or defense. 18 U.S.C. § 3742. Appeal by the government was upheld in *United States v. DiFrancesco,* 449 U.S. 117 (1980) (double jeopardy clause not violated if government appeals lenient sentence and offender given longer sentence). *DiFrancesco* is also discussed in Chapter 16.

Some, but not all, sentencing guideline systems (discussed later in this chapter) provide for appellate review of sentences that fall outside of the guideline sentencing range in a given case. One ground for appeal of a federal sentence is that it was "imposed as a result of an incorrect application of the sentencing guidelines." 18 U.S.C. § 3742(a)(2). But neither side can appeal a sentence that is consistent with a plea agreement between the two sides.

Deference to trial court's decision. As noted earlier in this chapter, the Supreme Court determined in *Booker v. United States*, 543 U.S. 220 (2005), that sentences imposed under the U.S. Sentencing Guidelines are to be upheld on appeal so long as they are "reasonable." In *United States. v. Rita*, 127 S. Ct. 2456 (2007), the Court held that when reviewing federal sentences for reasonableness, appellate courts *may* (but are not required to) apply a rebuttable presumption that a properly calculated sentence which falls within the applicable guideline range is a reasonable one. However, the converse does not apply — appellate courts are *not* to presume that a sentence that falls *outside* of the Guidelines is *unreasonable. See generally, Rita v. United States Leaves More Open Than it Answers*, 20 FED. SENT. R. 28 (2007).

The Supreme Court emphasized in *Booker* and *Rita*, and again in two later cases decided on the same day, *Gall v. United States*, 128 S.Ct. 586 (2007), and *Kimbrough v. United States*, 128 S.Ct. 558 (2007), that the circuit courts of appeal are to review sentencing decisions under the Guidelines with considerable deference. In *Gall*, the Court upheld as reasonable (in other words, not an abuse of discretion) the sentencing judge's downward departure from the Guideline range (which would have called for a sentence of 30 to 37 months imprisonment) in sentencing the defendant to 36 months on probation in light of the fact that the defendant had withdrawn from an ecstasy distribution conspiracy and had lived productively and crime-free for years prior to being charged. In *Kimbrough*, the Court upheld as reasonable a trial judge's downward departure from the Guidelines, sentencing a defendant for crack cocaine and weapons offenses to 15 years (the minimum allowable by statute), rather than within the Guideline range of 19 to 22 years. The sentencing judge's stated reason for this departure was that the Guidelines' highly controversial 100:1 crack-to-powder cocaine ratio (treating one gram of crack as the equivalent, for sentencing purposes, of 100 grams of powder, widely criticized as racially invidious), prevented the judge from imposing a sentence that is just and sufficient, but no greater than necessary. (As discussed later in this chapter, the United States Sentencing Commission, with the tacit approval of Congress, acted retroactively in 2007 to lessen the sentencing disparity between crack and powder cocaine.)

The *Gall* decision is a virtual primer both for sentencing courts in applying and departing from the federal sentencing guidelines, and for federal appellate courts in reviewing federal sentences:

> [A] district judge must give serious consideration to the extent of any departure from the Guidelines and must explain his conclusion that an unusually lenient or an unusually harsh sentence is appropriate in a particular case with sufficient justifications. . . .

> In reviewing the reasonableness of a sentence outside the Guidelines range, appellate courts may therefore take the degree of variance into account and consider the extent of a deviation from the Guidelines. We reject, however, an appellate rule that requires "extraordinary" circumstances to justify a sentence outside the Guidelines range. We also reject the use of a rigid mathematical formula that uses the percentage of a departure as the standard for determining the strength of the justifications required for a specific sentence. . . .

> [A] district court should begin all sentencing proceedings by correctly calculating the applicable Guidelines range. As a matter of administration and to secure nationwide consistency, the Guidelines should be the starting point and the initial benchmark. The Guidelines are not the only consideration, however. Accordingly, after giving both parties an opportunity to argue for whatever sentence they deem appropriate, the district judge should then consider all of the [statutory sentencing] factors to determine whether they

support the sentence requested by a party. In so doing, he may not presume that the Guidelines range is reasonable. He must make an individualized assessment based on the facts presented. If he decides that an outside-Guidelines sentence is warranted, he must consider the extent of the deviation and ensure that the justification is sufficiently compelling to support the degree of the variance. We find it uncontroversial that a major departure should be supported by a more significant justification than a minor one. After settling on the appropriate sentence, he must adequately explain the chosen sentence to allow for meaningful appellate review and to promote the perception of fair sentencing. . . .

Regardless of whether the sentence imposed is inside or outside the Guidelines range, the appellate court must review the sentence under an abuse-of-discretion standard. It must first ensure that the district court committed no significant procedural error, such as failing to calculate (or improperly calculating) the Guidelines range, treating the Guidelines as mandatory, failing to consider the [statutory sentencing] factors, selecting a sentence based on clearly erroneous facts, or failing to adequately explain the chosen sentence – including an explanation for any deviation from the Guidelines range. Assuming that the district court's sentencing decision is procedurally sound, the appellate court should then consider the substantive reasonableness of the sentence imposed under an abuse-of-discretion standard. When conducting this review, the court will, of course, take into account the totality of the circumstances, including the extent of any variance from the Guidelines range. If the sentence is within the Guidelines range, the appellate court may, but is not required to, apply a presumption of reasonableness. But if the sentence is outside the Guidelines range, the court may not apply a presumption of unreasonableness. It may consider the extent of the deviation, but must give due deference to the district court's decision that the [statutory] factors, on a whole, justify the extent of the variance. The fact that the appellate court might reasonably have concluded that a different sentence was appropriate is insufficient to justify reversal of the district court. [128 S. Ct. at 594-597]

Prior to *Booker* and *Rita*, guideline-departure sentences under circumstances such as presented in *Gall* and *Kimbrough* might have invited appellate reversal (indeed, in both cases, the Supreme Court reinstated the district court's sentences after the circuit courts had reversed them). However, the Court has made it "pellucidly clear" in this line of decisions that the circuit courts of appeal are not to scrutinize sentencing decisions too closely. Appellate courts are not to presume departure sentences to be unreasonable, or to second guess the sentencing court's calculus of how much, if any, departure, either upward or downward, is justified under the circumstances of a given case. To do so would be too close to exercising *de novo* appellate review, which is flatly contrary to "reasonableness" or "abuse of discretion" review.

This rather remarkable line of cases, from *Booker* to *Kimbrough* — treating the Guidelines as advisory rather than mandatory and giving considerable latitude for departure — has restored to federal judges a substantial amount of the sentencing discretion that they had been widely believed to have lost under the United States Sentencing Guidelines.

[7]   Good Time, Parole, and Supervised Release

The sentencing judge determines the sentence that the offender could serve, but in many jurisdictions, the judge only controls the outer limits of the sentence the defendant actually will serve. The actual sentence is usually determined by a mix of three factors. First, the judge sets the maximum (and sometimes minimum) sentence.

[a] Prison Credits

Second, the correctional authorities are usually authorized by statute to reduce that sentence by giving various forms of credit. For example, many jurisdictions give prisoners "good time" credits, which reduce the maximum (and sometimes minimum) sentence for good behavior while in prison. Other credits may be given for educational achievement (perhaps a sentence reduction for earning a high school, college, or vocational degree) and participation in certain prison programs (giving blood, fighting forest fires). Sometimes prison overcrowding problems also result in sentence reductions through an emergency release provision in state law.

[b] Parole

The third factor in determining the length of time that will actually be served is the parole process. *Parole* is an executive branch process that determines when an offender will be released from prison. An executive agency, usually called a *parole board* or commission and comprised of three or more people, is authorized by statute to make an individual determination of how much time each offender (at least the more serious offenders) will spend in prison and how much on parole after release. Counsel is usually permitted but is not constitutionally required.

Hearing. Ordinarily, the decision is made after a *parole hearing* in which the offender is present and provided an opportunity to argue in favor of release. The parole board will review the offense (perhaps including the views of the victim, the prosecuting lawyer, and even the sentencing judge), the offender's prison record, the recommendations of prison officials, and other relevant data. If the offender is paroled, he or she usually will serve the remainder of the sentence under the supervision of a *parole officer*, a state-paid counselor who in many jurisdictions also has police powers.

Conditions. The offender will be subject to various *parole conditions*. The conditions are similar to probation conditions and may include such items as committing no crimes, refraining from getting intoxicated, submitting to drug testing, holding a job, supporting dependents, meeting with a parole officer at regular intervals, remaining in a certain geographical area unless given permission to leave, and staying away from certain people (perhaps the victim of the original crime).

Revocation. Violation of a parole condition can cause the offender to be subjected to revocation proceedings before the parole board (or sometimes the courts) and to be reincarcerated for all or part of the unexpired prison term. Due Process requires that parolees, like probationers, be afforded a hearing prior to the revocation of their parole, (actually, two hearings — a preliminary probable cause type hearing and a final revocation hearing — are often required, *see, Morrissey v. Brewer*, 408 U.S. 471 (1972)). At the revocation hearing, the offender's rights are much less comprehensive than at a criminal trial. *See, e.g., Pennsylvania Bd. of Probation v. Scott*, 524 U.S 357 (1998) (parole boards need not exclude evidence obtained in violation of the Fourth Amendment).

Abolition or severe limits on parole. A minority of American jurisdictions, including the federal government, rejected the concept of discretionary parole in the 1980's and 1990's. As of 1999, thirteen states had either abolished or severely limited parole. However, the movement to abolish or restrict parole appears to have crested in the 1990's, and three states (Connecticut, Colorado and Florida) have reinstated some form of parole after efforts to remove it caused massive prison overcrowding. *See 85* A.B.A.J. 14 (May 1999); 2005 Paroling Authorities Survey, Association of Paroling Authorities, International, *available* at http://www.apaintl.org/content/en/pdf/2005_ParolingAuthorities_Survey.pdf.

There appears to be a correlation between the elimination of parole and the adoption of sentencing guidelines. Jurisdictions abolishing the parole process believe that parole destroys predictability and uniformity in sentencing since at the time of sentencing the offender and others cannot tell exactly how long the offender will serve in prison. Moreover, they are often dissatisfied with the amount of discretion given the parole authority. The American Bar Association urges states to adopt truth-in-sentencing as a part of the guidelines process, recommending that "the sentences imposed will determine the length of sentences served, apart from credit for good time." STANDARDS FOR CRIMINAL JUSTICE § 18-4.4(c) (3d ed. 1994). If there is inadequate "determinacy in sentencing," however, the Bar Association suggests that the jurisdiction should establish a board of parole. *Id.* § 18-3.21(g).

Supervised release. When parole is eliminated, the usual practice, as exemplified by the federal system, is to add a system of *supervised release.* Under this approach, at the time of the initial sentencing the offender is given both a prison term and a specific period of supervised release to be served after completing the prison term. *See* 18 U.S.C. § 3583. A person on supervised release, like a parolee, is subject to a number of release conditions. Violation of these terms of release can subject the supervised releasee to another term of prison. The primary difference between supervised release and parole is that the judge, at the time of sentencing, determines the duration of supervised release while the parole board, a branch of the executive department, decides when the offender is to be paroled after considering the offender's behavior in prison. *See generally* Neil P. Cohen, THE LAW OF PROBATION AND PAROLE (2d ed. 1999).

[8]   Executive Sentencing Review: Clemency and Pardons

Although sentencing is virtually always the bailiwick of the judicial branch of government, the executive branch plays a role as well. For example, the executive branch ordinarily handles the parole granting process. Another area is executive clemency. Both federal and state constitutions authorize the executive to grant some form of *executive clemency. See generally* Kathleen Dean Moore, PARDONS: JUSTICE, MERCY AND THE PUBLIC INTEREST (1989).

The nomenclature for this process and procedural details vary considerably among the jurisdictions and may include the terms *pardon, commutation, reprieve, and remission.* In general, federal or state constitutional provisions authorize the President or Governor to reduce all or part of a sentence, to delay implementation of a sentence, or to absolve the offender from all consequences of conviction. Sometimes the chief executive's decision must be based on the recommendation of a panel or board.

The precise procedures that must be accorded an applicant for executive clemency have not been fully articulated by the Supreme Court, which has expressed a hesitancy to set standards. *See Ohio Adult Parole Authority v. Woodard,* 523 U.S. 272 (1998) (pardon and commutation decisions traditionally have not been the business of courts and are rarely, if ever, appropriate subjects for judicial review). A gubernatorial or presidential grant or denial of clemency is typically not subject to any form of judicial review.

Although the various forms of executive clemency are seldom used in most jurisdictions, they have occasionally been relied on in several contexts. One use is to correct injustice, such as when new evidence shows that a long-time prisoner, perhaps now deceased, was actually innocent of the charges. Another is to spare judicial resources. For example, the sentences of many capital offenders were commuted to life imprisonment after the jurisdiction's death penalty was declared unconstitutional; this spared the judiciary the need to resentence many offenders. A third use is to recognize unique circumstances that make a change in sentence appropriate. Thus, a life prisoner with terminal cancer may be given executive clemency to spend the last weeks of life at home, or an elderly prisoner with a lengthy exemplary prison record is given executive clemency to shorten a very long sentence imposed fifty years earlier. *See* Carol Jacobsen, *et al.,* Battered *Women, Homicide Convictions, and Sentencing: The Case for Clemency,* 18 HAST. WOMEN'S L.J. 321 (2007).

Conditions of release. Sometimes a grant of executive clemency is given subject to the prisoner's adherence to a list of conditions of release, similar to parole and probation. For example, a governor may grant a pardon or commute a sentence on the condition that the released offender commit no more felonies, support dependents, and refrain from involvement in a certain business. A violation of such a condition can lead to a revocation of executive clemency and a return to prison.

Clemency decisions of governors and presidents are often politically charged and controversial. Examples include President Ford's pardon of former President Nixon even in the absence of any criminal prosecution of the former president, President Clinton's end-of-term pardons of several allegedly "well connected" individuals, and President George W. Bush's commutation of the sentence of former vice-presidential aide, Lewis I. "Scooter" Libby, sparing him from serving any period of imprisonment. *See generally* Margaret Love, *Reinventing the President's Pardon Power*, 20 Fed. Sent. Rep. 5 (2007); Molly Gill, *Into the Bottomless Black Box: the Prisoner's Perspective on the Commutation Process*, 20 Fed. Sent. Rep. 16 (2007).

F. STRUCTURE OF THE SENTENCING DECISION

[1] Traditional Model

Under the traditional sentencing model, still used by many jurisdictions, the judge is given much discretion in selecting the sentence. The legislature sets some general limits. For example, a crime may be punishable by a maximum sentence ("no more than twenty years in prison"), a minimum sentence ("not less than five years in prison"), both a stated minimum and maximum ("not less than five years more nor than twenty years in prison"), or, on rare occasions, a fixed penalty ("one year in jail").

Often the court has an array of options. For example, the statute defining the crime or the sentencing laws may authorize a prison term as well as a fine. In lieu of the prison term for less serious offenses, the court may be authorized to impose probation. A short jail term may be imposed as a probation condition. Many modern statutes also require restitution unless there is some good reason why restitution should not be ordered.

[2] Guidelines Model

In recent years there has been a great deal of dissatisfaction with the traditional approach to sentencing. The key objections are that the sentencing judge has too much unbridled discretion, there is unfair sentencing disparity, and sentences are too lenient (rarely is there a complaint that they are too harsh). *See* ABA Standards for Criminal Justice § 18-2.5(b) (3d ed. 1994) (recommending that legislatures create a sentencing structure "that sufficiently guides the exercise of sentencing courts' discretion to the end that unwarranted and inequitable disparities in sentences are avoided"). A related concern is that prisons are overcrowded and can be better controlled by a structured sentencing system that makes prison population easier to predict. These complaints have led an increasing number of jurisdictions, including the federal government, to adopt *sentencing guidelines*, a structured set of rules to be used in sentencing in criminal cases. As will be discussed later, some sentencing guideline systems, especially the U.S. Sentencing Guidelines, have themselves been the source of sharp criticism and controversy. *See, e.g.*, Nekima Levy-Pounds, *From the Frying Pan into the Fire: How Poor Women of Color and Children are Affected by Sentencing Guidelines and Mandatory Minimums*, 47 Santa Clara L. Rev. 287 (2007).

[a] Sentencing Commission

In virtually all guideline jurisdictions, the guidelines are the product of a study by a group called a *sentencing commission*, usually comprised of representatives of various constituencies involved in the criminal justice system in that jurisdiction. Commission members may include judges, prosecutors, law enforcement and correctional officials, public defenders, academics, legislators, and members of the general public. The commission may have as few as seven members or as many as twenty or so. Usually it will have a professional staff to aid in drafting and researching. Indeed, according to the American Bar Association, a sentencing commission's "empirical research capacity should be given highest priority and should be adequately funded by the legislature." STANDARDS FOR CRIMINAL JUSTICE § 18-4.2(d) (3d ed. 1994). A primary advantage is that it can provide far more detailed sentencing guidelines than would be possible using the traditional legislative processes. Ordinarily the guidelines apply only to felonies.

[b] Voluntary or Mandatory

In general terms, sentencing guidelines greatly restrict the sentencing judge's discretion. Guidelines may be either *voluntary* or *mandatory*. Voluntary guidelines are simply recommendations that judges may or may not follow. Although a number of American states adopted voluntary guidelines in the 1970's, empirical research showed that they did not meet their expectations in reducing sentencing disparity. *See, e.g.,* Michael H. Tonry, SENTENCING REFORM IMPACTS 37-43 (1987). Mandatory guidelines, by far the predominant model today, are obligatory. Note, however, that in light of *United States v. Booker*, 543 U.S. 220 (2004), discussed earlier in this chapter, mandatory guideline systems may now be constitutionally suspect if they rely on sentence-enhancing facts found by the judge rather than the jury.

[c] Presumptive Sentence

Most sentencing guidelines involve a *presumptive sentence*, a sentence or range from which sentence should be imposed in the typical case. Courts usually are given some discretion to depart from the presumptive sentence or range in unusual cases. Such departures ordinarily must be explained in writing and can be appealed by either side. To determine the presumptive sentence, often one must consult a grid or matrix that combines two or more variables. The usual model has two dimensions: offense severity and offender characteristics. Each crime is placed in one of perhaps ten classes of offenses. For example, robbery may be a Class Five offense. Each offender is also placed in a category, usually based on prior convictions. For example, an offender with two prior felony convictions could be in Category Two.

Guidelines often indicate a preference for non-custodial sentences for less serious offenses. Some states, like Minnesota, establish standards for imposing sentences to probation and other non-incarceration dispositions, as well as sentences to imprisonment. Many continue to use parole. *See generally* Bureau of Justice Assistance, National Assessment of Structured Sentencing (1996).

The following two sections of this chapter describe two very contrasting sentencing guideline systems: The Minnesota and the United States Sentencing Guidelines. They both aim to reduce unwarranted sentencing disparity and both operate to confine judges' sentencing discretion. But beyond these similarities they are designed to serve very different sentencing goals. As you read these sections, make note of the ways you find these systems to be both similar and different from each other.

[d] Minnesota

Minnesota, the first jurisdiction to appoint a sentencing commission (1978), is an example of the guideline process. It had nine part-time members. The Minnesota Sentencing Commission's work was characterized by several features:

The Minnesota Commission made a number of bold policy decisions. First, it decided to be "prescriptive" and explicitly to establish its own sentencing priorities . . . . Second, the Commission decided to de-emphasize imprisonment as a punishment for property offenders and to emphasize imprisonment for violent offenders . . . . Third, in order to attack sentencing disparities, the Commission established very narrow sentencing ranges (for example 30–34 months, or 50–58 months) and to authorize departures from guideline ranges only when "substantial and compelling" reasons were present. Fourth, the Commission elected to adopt "just desserts" as the governing premise of its policies concerning who receives prison sentences. Fifth, the Commission chose to interpret an ambiguous statutory injunction that it take correctional resources into "substantial consideration" as a mandate that its guidelines not increase prison population beyond existing capacity constraints. This meant that the Commission had to make deliberate trade-offs in imprisonment policies. If the Commission decided to increase the length of prison terms for one group of offenders, it either had to decrease prison terms for another group or to shift the "in/out" line and divert some group of prisoners from prison altogether. Sixth, the Commission forbade consideration at sentencing of many personal factors — such as education, employment, marital status, living arrangements — that many judges believed to be legitimate. This decision resulted from a policy that sentencing decisions not be based on factors that might directly or indirectly discriminate against minorities, women, or low income groups.

Michael H. Tonry, SENTENCING REFORM IMPACTS 48 (1987). *See generally* Andrew Von Hirsch, Kay A. Knapp, Michael Tonry, THE SENTENCING COMMISSION AND ITS GUIDELINES (1987); Richard S. Frase, *The Role of the Legislature, the Sentencing Commission, and Other Officials under the Minnesota Sentencing Guidelines*, 28 WAKE FOREST L. REV. 345 (1993).

The Minnesota sentencing matrix follows.

The Minnesota Sentencing Guidelines

Presumptive Sentence Lengths in Months

Italicized numbers within the grid denote the range within which a judge may sentence without the sentence being deemed a departure. Offenders with nonimprisonment felony sentences are subject to jail time according to law.

SEVERITY LEVEL OF CONVICTION OFFENSE (Common offenses listed in italics)		CRIMINAL HISTORY SCORE						
		0	**1**	**2**	**3**	**4**	**5**	**6 or more**
Sale of Simulated Controlled Substance	I	12[1]	12[1]	12[1]	13	15	17	19 *18-20*
Theft Related Crimes ($2500 or less) Check Forgery ($200-$2500)	II	12[1]	12[1]	13	15	17	19	21 *20-22*
Theft Crimes ($2500 or less)	III	12[1]	13	15	17	19 *18-20*	22 *21-23*	25 *24-26*
Nonresidential Burglary Theft Crimes (Over $2500)	IV	12[1]	15	18	21	25 *24-26*	32 *30-34*	41 *37-45*
Residential Burglary Simple Robbery	V	18	23	27	30 *29-31*	38 *36-40*	46 *43-49*	54 *50-58*
Criminal Sexual Conduct, 2nd Degree (a) & (b)	VI	21	26	30	34 *33-35*	44 *42-46*	54 *50-58*	65 *60-70*
Aggravated Robbery	VII	48 *44-52*	58 *54-62*	68 *64-72*	78 *74-82*	88 *84-92*	98 *94-102*	108 *104-112*
Criminal Sexual Conduct, 1st Degree Assault, 1st Degree	VIII	86 *81-91*	98 *93-103*	110 *105-115*	122 *117-127*	134 *129-139*	146 *141-151*	158 *153-163*
Murder, 3rd Degree Murder, 2nd Degree (felony Murder)	IX	150 *144-156*	165 *159-171*	180 *174-186*	195 *189-201*	210 *204-216*	225 *219-231*	240 *234-246*
Murder, 2nd Degree (with intent)	X	306 *299-313*	326 *319-333*	346 *339-353*	366 *359-373*	386 *379-393*	406 *399-413*	426 *419-433*

☐ Presumptive stayed sentence; at the discretion of the judge, up to a year in jail and/or other non-jail sanctions can be imposed as conditions of probation. However, certain offenses in this section of the grid always carry a presumptive commitment to a state prison. These offenses include Third Degree Controlled Substance Crimes when the offender has a prior felony drug conviction, Burglary of an Occupied Dwelling when the offender has a prior felony burglary conviction, second and subsequent Criminal Sexual Conduct offenses and offenses carrying a mandatory minimum prison term due to the use of a dangerous weapon (e.g., Second Degree Assault). See sections II.C. Presumptive Sentence and II.E. Mandatory Sentences.

☐ Presumptive commitment to state imprisonment. First Degree Murder is excluded from the guidelines by law and continues to have a mandatory life sentence. See section II.E. Mandatory Sentences for policy regarding those sentences controlled by law, including minimum periods of supervision for sex offenders released from prison.

[1] One year and one day

[e] Federal Guidelines

The federal sentencing guidelines are quite different from those of Minnesota and other American jurisdictions. In general terms, they are far more complex, rely much more on incarceration as the sentencing sanction of choice, involve more factors, and require a somewhat more complicated mathematical calculation to determine the appropriate sentence. *See generally* Daniel J. Freed & Marc Miller, Federal Sentencing Reporter (published quarterly); Thomas W. Hutchison, Peter Hoffman, Deborah

Young, and Sigmund Popko, FEDERAL SENTENCING LAW AND PRACTICE (2007 ed.); Michael Tonry, SENTENCING MATTERS 72-99 (1996); Symposium, *The Federal Sentencing Guidelines: Ten Years Later*, 91 NW. U. L. REV. 1231-1598 (1997) (10 excellent articles).

Development of federal guidelines. Prior to the federal sentencing guidelines, federal sentences used an indeterminate sentence model. Federal judges had great discretion in assigning a sentence and the United States Parole Board determined the prisoner's actual release date. The indeterminate structure was strongly criticized on the bases that it (1) was based on a rehabilitative model that had proved to be unsuccessful, (2) facilitated sentencing disparity among federal judges, and (3) produced a lack of certainty (and "honesty") about when a federal offender would be released from prison. The federal sentencing guidelines were the product of several earlier developments. In 1958 Congress authorized judicial sentencing institutes and joint sentencing councils to help establish criteria for sentencing. In 1973 the United States Parole Commission had adopted guidelines to assist in determining parole release dates.

Congress rejected the traditional sentencing system in 1984 when it passed legislation (the Sentencing Reform Act) that created the seven-member United States Sentencing Commission and charged it with drafting mandatory guidelines to be used in all federal sentencing. The law also abolished the Parole Commission and established a determinate system in which the offender is to serve virtually all the sentence imposed by the judge. The United States Supreme Court upheld the federal guidelines against a constitutional challenge based on unlawful delegation of sentencing authority to an administrative agency and an alleged unconstitutional violation of the separation of powers doctrine. *Mistretta v. United States*, 488 U.S. 361 (1989).

Now advisory only. As discussed earlier in this chapter, a series of United States Supreme Court decisions, beginning with *Apprendi v. New Jersey*, has made the federal sentencing guidelines advisory rather than mandatory. This means that federal judges must consider the guidelines but need not adhere to them.

[i]   Procedure Under Federal Guidelines: In General

In order to determine a sentence under the Federal Sentencing Guidelines, one must consult a thick manual of several hundred pages that lists many guidelines and other tables. In general terms, the sentence can only be ascertained after calculating two numbers: the *offense level* and the *criminal history* category. Both of these numbers are determined only after a sometimes lengthy process of adding and subtracting points for various factors. When the two items are computed, the sentence can be determined by consulting a Sentencing Table contained in the Guidelines. The offense level is the vertical category and the criminal history category is the horizontal category. To assist in applying these complex rules, the Guidelines include "Application Notes" that provide detailed explanations of various sections.

[ii] Guidelines Table

The table for most offenses follows:

Federal Sentencing Guidelines Table

Criminal History

Offense Level	I (0 or 1)	II (2 or 3)	III (4, 5, 6)	IV (7, 8, 9)	V (10, 11, 12)	VI (13 or more)
6						12-18
7					12-18	15-21
8					15-21	18-24
9				12-18	18-24	21-27
10				15-21	21-27	24-30
11			12-18	18-24	24-30	27-33
12		12-18	15-21	21-27	27-33	30-37
13	12-18	15-21	18-24	24-30	30-37	33-41
14	15-21	18-24	21-27	27-33	33-41	37-46
15	18-24	21-27	24-30	30-37	37-46	41-51
16	21-27	24-30	27-33	33-41	41-51	46-57
17	24-30	27-33	30-37	37-46	46-57	51-63
18	27-33	30-37	33-41	41-51	51-63	57-71
19	30-37	33-41	37-46	46-57	57-71	63-78
20	33-41	37-46	41-51	51-63	63-78	70-87
21	37-46	41-51	46-57	57-71	70-87	77-96
22	41-51	46-57	51-63	63-78	77-96	84-105
23	46-57	51-63	57-71	70-87	84-105	92-115
24	51-63	57-71	63-78	77-96	92-115	100-125
25	57-71	63-78	70-87	84-105	100-125	110-137
26	63-78	70-87	78-97	92-115	110-137	120-150
27	70-87	78-97	87-108	100-125	120-150	130-162
28	78-97	87-108	97-121	110-137	130-162	140-175
29	87-108	97-121	108-135	121-151	140-175	151-188
30	97-121	108-135	121-151	135-168	151-188	168-210
31	108-135	121-151	135-168	151-188	168-210	188-265
32	121-151	135-168	151-188	168-210	188-235	210-262
33	135-168	151-188	168-210	188-235	210-262	235-293
34	151-188	168-210	188-235	210-262	235-293	262-327
35	168-210	188-235	210-262	235-293	262-327	292-365
36	188-235	210-262	235-293	262-327	292-365	324-405
37	210-262	235-293	262-327	292-365	324-405	360-life
38	235-293	262-327	292-365	324-405	360-life	360-life
39	262-327	292-365	324-405	360-life	360-life	360-life
40	292-365	324-405	360-life	360-life	360-life	360-life
41	324-405	360-life	360-life	360-life	360-life	360-life
42	360-life	360-life	360-life	360-life	360-life	360-life
43	life	life	life	life	life	life

[iii]   Offense Level

The first calculation is to find the offense level. The first step in this process is to ascertain the federal crime(s) involved. Then consult an Appendix to the Guidelines which will locate the specific Guideline for the offense(s) charged. After locating the correct Guideline, one finds the "base offense level" for that crime.

For example, assume that an offender is convicted of burglary of a post office, in violation of 18 U.S.C. § 2115. The Appendix to the Sentencing Guidelines indicates that the proper Guideline is § 2B2.1:

§ 2B2.1 Burglary of a Residence or structure other that a Residence

(a) Base Offense Level:

    (1) 17, if a residence; or

    (2) 12, if a structure other than a residence.

(b) Specific Offense Characteristics

    (1) If the offense involved more than minimal planning, increase by 2 levels.

    (2) If the loss exceeded $2,500, increase the offense level as follows:

<u>Loss</u> (Apply the Greatest)	<u>Increase in Level</u>
(A) $2,500 or less	No Increase
(B) More than $2,500	add 1
(C) More than $10,000	add 2
(D) More than $50,000	add 3
(E) More than $250,000	add 4
(F) More than $800,000	add 5
(G) More than $1,500,000	add 6
(H) More than $2,500,000	add 7
(I) more than $5,000,000	add 8

    (3) If a firearm, destructive or controlled substance was taken, or if the taking of such item was an object of the offense, increase by 1 level.

    (4) If a dangerous weapon (including a firearm) was possessed, increase by 2 levels.

This Guideline indicates that the base offense level is 12 for this offense.

Specific offense characteristics. The next step is to add the "Specific Offense Characteristics" to the base offense level. This involves fine-tuning of the base offense level to permit increases or decreases based on differences that the Sentencing Commission thought sufficiently important to affect the sentence. Returning to our post office burglary hypothetical, assume that the offender used a firearm. Under (b)(4) in the above Guideline, the base offense level would be increased 2 levels, making a total base offense level of 14.

Adjustments. The next step is to make "adjustments" to the base offense level. Chapter Three of the Guidelines contains many topics that permit the court to add points to or subtract them from the base offense level. For example, there is a victim-related adjustment. If the victim is unusually vulnerable because of age, physical or mental condition or otherwise particularly susceptible to the criminal conduct, the base offense level is increased by two points. Guidelines § 3A1.1. Similar adjustments are also authorized if the victim was a public official or was physically restrained.

Other categories of adjustments relate to the offender's role in the offense (levels added if the defendant played an organizing or leading role in a crime involving numerous people and levels deducted if the offender's role was minor); the abuse of a position of public or private trust; the offender used special skills in the crime; the obstruction of justice during the case's processing; and the creation of a substantial risk of death or serious bodily injury while fleeing.

There are special rules for calculating the offense level for multiple offenses. The offense level is also reduced if the defendant accepts responsibility for the offense and has timely provided information on his or her involvement in the crime or timely notified authorities of the intent to plead guilty.

Real offense sentencing: relevant conduct. A controversial aspect of the guidelines is called "real offense" sentencing. The drafters of the federal guidelines opted to focus as much as possible on the defendant's actual conduct in committing the crime. Accordingly, the guidelines permit the court to use "relevant conduct" in determining the defendant's base offense level, specific offender characteristics, and other Chapter 3 adjustments. "Relevant conduct" refers generally to conduct that a court determines is relevant to establishing the base offense level. It includes the defendant's acts and reasonably foreseeable acts of others involved in the crime, whether or not these other acts were charged as crimes.

For example, in *United States v. Crawford*, 991 F.2d 1328 (7th Cir. 1993), the defendant entered a plea of guilty to the crime of possession with intent to distribute marijuana. In determining the base offense level, the judge considered both the 875 pounds of marijuana that the defendant admitted he "off-loaded" plus an additional 736 pounds of marijuana which was never actually delivered (it was described as having been "under negotiation" between an accomplice and a police informant). The base level calculation was affirmed because the record established that the defendant participated in the negotiations for the purchase of the 736 pounds. In other words, the "relevant conduct" approach permitted the sentencing court to rely upon facts (*i.e.*, the additional marijuana) as to which the defendant was not convicted.

Interestingly, the American Bar Association recommends that sentences should not be based upon "real offense"; rather, the sentence should reflect the "offense of conviction," which should be "fixed by the charges proven at trial or established as the factual basis for a plea of guilty or nolo contendere." STANDARDS FOR CRIMINAL JUSTICE § 18-3.6 (3d ed. 1994). Similarly, the Minnesota guidelines specifically reject the "real offense" sentencing approach, and their accompanying Commentary suggests that sentencing on the basis of an offense other than the offense "of record" for which the defendant was actually convicted, is ethically questionable. No state has emulated this aspect of the federal sentencing guidelines.

Acquittal. The United States Supreme Court held that a sentencing court may consider conduct of which a jury acquitted a defendant if the government proves that conduct by a preponderance of the evidence. *United States v. Watts*, 519 U.S. 148 (1997). The Court reasoned that the guidelines do not alter the sentencing judge's discretion to consider relevant conduct and that the use of relevant conduct, even if the subject of a prior acquittal, does not impose punishment in violation of the double jeopardy clause. Consequently, in *Watts*, the Court upheld the district court's finding that the defendant possessed a gun in connection with his drug offense (despite a jury's acquittal of using a firearm in relation to a drug offense) and permitted the adding of two points to the base offense level under the guidelines. Although *Watts* has been heavily criticized, *see, e.g.*, J. Nicodemus, *Watts v. United States*, 25 AM. J. CRIM. L. 437 (1998), the Supreme Court in *Booker v. U.S.*, 543 U.S. 220 (2005), in essence reaffirmed *Watts*'s approval of "real offense" sentencing under the federal guidelines.

For analyses of "real offense" sentencing, *see* William W. Wilkins & John R. Steer, *Relevant Conduct: the Cornerstone of the Federal Sentencing Guidelines*, 41 S.C. L. REV. 495 (1990)(pro); David Yellen, *Illusion, Illogic, and Injustice; Real Offense Sentencing and the Federal Sentencing Guidelines*, 78 MINN. L. REV. 403 (1993)(contra);

W. Crews Lott, Note, 45 BAYLOR L. REV. 877 (1993)(concluding that determining relevant conduct by only a preponderance of the evidence is constitutionally insufficient).

The "crack/powder cocaine" disparity. Until recently, the Federal Sentencing Guidelines treated possession of one gram of cocaine in "crack" form as the equivalent, for sentencing purposes, of 100 grams of cocaine in its "powder" form. According to the United States Sentencing Commission, this disparity often resulted in sentences for crack possession that were from three to six times greater than for possession of cocaine powder. The basis of this differential treatment was the perception that crack is more quickly addictive than powder, and that the crack trade is more closely associated with violence, such as drive–by shootings, than trade in powder. This disparity has been widely criticized as being racially invidious — its impact falling much more severely on African Americans than on white or Hispanic drug defendants. *See, Kimbrough v. United States*, 128 S.Ct. 558 (2007)(discussed earlier in this chapter), and the dissent of Justice Stevens (appearing in Chapter 2) in *United States v. Armstrong*, 517 U.S. 456 (1996).

In 2007, the United States Sentencing Commission amended its policy, effective May 1, 2008, with the approval of Congress, to significantly ameliorate the crack/powder disparity and to make this amendment retroactive. As a result of this change, many federal prisoners serving sentences which were enhanced on the basis of the previous disparity between possession of crack and powder, may now move for sentence reductions from the original sentencing court. The Department of Justice opposed making this change retroactive based on its stated concern that retroactivity would result in a flood of immediate releases of dangerous drug offenders from federal prisons.

[iv]   Criminal History

After determining the score for the offense conduct, the next step is to consult Chapter Four of the federal guidelines to calculate the defendant's criminal history. For example, an offender receives three points for each prior sentence of imprisonment exceeding thirteen months, two points for each other one at least sixty days long, and one point for each other prior sentence. Two points are also added if the current offense was committed while the offender was on release on probation, parole, and the like, and another one or two if the defendant committed the instant offense less than two years after release from imprisonment, while in prison, or while in escape status. Guidelines § 4A1.1.

There are specific rules for calculating the point scores for juvenile offenses, expunged convictions, and other variations. The court is also authorized to depart from the formula for calculating the criminal history category if the ordinary formula would inadequately reflect the seriousness of the defendant's criminal history or risk of recidivism. Guidelines § 4A1.3. There are especially harsh provisions if the offender is a "career offender," someone with two prior convictions for violence or drug crimes and the current one is a violent felony or a drug crime. Guidelines § 4B1.1.

[v]   Departures

Despite the mathematical precision used to calculate most sentences under the federal guidelines, there is still a considerable degree of flexibility for judges to depart from the calculated guideline sentencing range, especially after the *Booker* line of decisions. Departures may be downward or upward, and judges must state in writing their reasons, subject to appellate review, for departing either upward or downward. In 2006, the year after *Booker* was decided, downward departures were given in about 36% of all federal sentences; upward departures in less than 2%. Sourcebook, at http://www.albany.edu/sourcebook/pdf/t5362006.pdf.

Substantial assistance. The most frequent downward departure, used in about 14.5% of all federal cases, is given if the defendant has provided *substantial assistance* to the authorities in the investigation or prosecution of another offender. *Id.* Since the guidelines provide that this departure can only be given if the government requests it, this rule provides a major incentive for the defendant to satisfy the government's interest in prosecuting other people suspected of being involved in this or any other crime. Guidelines § 5K1.1. According to one report, the term "substantial assistance" has not been given a consistent meaning; therefore, improper factors such as gender, race and ethnicity continue to influence the size of departures awarded under the substantial assistance rubric. *See* Linda Drazga Maxfield and John H. Kramer, *Substantial Assistance: An Empirical Yardstick Gauging Equity in Current Federal Policy and Practice*, cited and discussed in 62 CRIMINAL LAW REPORTER 1430 (February 18, 1998).

Generic departure provision. The guidelines also include a generic departure rule. If the court finds there is "an aggravating or mitigating circumstance of a kind, or to a degree, not adequately taken into consideration by the Sentencing Commission in formulating the guidelines that should result in a sentence different from that described," the court may impose an appropriate sentence irrespective of the guidelines sentence. 18 U.S.C. § 3553(b)(1). The court must give its reasons for any such departure.

Departures prior to Booker. A 1996 pre-*Booker* study explored when and how federal sentencing judges depart from the Guidelines. The study concluded that (1) downward departures were used to resist incarcerating white collar criminals, (2) upward departures were quite rare, (3) criminal history categories were sufficiently malleable to permit downward departures, (4) there was no difference in departures by judges appointed by different Presidents, (5) federal circuits differed in their receptivity to departures, and (6) some departures occur in ordinary cases rather than the atypical cases envisioned by the Sentencing Commission. *See* Michael S. Gelacak, Ilene H. Nagel and Barry L. Johnson, *Departures Under the Federal Sentencing Guidelines: An Empirical and Jurisprudential Analysis*, 81 MINN. L. REV. 299 (1996). Among the study's results is the conclusion that departures are not always consistent with congressional intent. The authors concluded that the following "lesson" can be drawn from their analysis of departure practices:

> [T]he apparent incursion of judges' preferences into departure decisions and the tendency of departure patterns to mirror pre-Guidelines severity levels highlight the inherent limitations of legislative control over judicial decision-making. As long as some discretion is left in the system, some disparity in the application of general rules to specific cases will occur. [*Id.* at 365]

Appellate review of departures: Koon. The standard for reviewing such departures under 18 U.S.C. § 3553(b) was initially established in *Koon v. United States*, 518 U.S. 81 (1996), involving a federal criminal trial for four Los Angeles Police Department officers charged with violating Rodney King's civil rights. The officers previously had been acquitted by a Los Angeles state jury. After the federal conviction, the district judge found that the federal sentencing guidelines made the offense a level 27 which carried a 70–87 months' prison term. But the judge then granted an eight level downward departure to a level 19 with a sentencing range of 30–37 months. A five-level downward departure was because the victim's wrongful conduct contributed significantly to provoke the defendant's behavior. The three-level departure was based on a combination of four factors (likely abuse in prison, job loss, burden of successive state and federal prosecutions, and no need to protect the public from future criminality). In reviewing this sentence, the Supreme Court announced that it would apply an *abuse of discretion* standard. The case was remanded when the Court held that the trial court should not have considered either the job loss or low likely recidivism since both were considered in the formulation of the applicable sentencing guidelines.

The short-lived "Feeney Amendment." In 2003, Congress passed legislation (known by acronym as the "PROTECT Act") which created a national "Amber Alert" notification system for child abductions. An amendment to the Amber Alert legislation, adopted without the usual committee study and hearing process or floor debate (referred to as the "Feeney Amendment") further restricted judicial discretion to grant downward departures under the Guidelines. The amendment established the much less deferential *de novo* standard for appellate review of guideline-departure sentences (effectively abrogating the *Koon* abuse of discretion standard), and required the Justice Department to inform Congress of individual judges' decisions granting such departures. This amendment was in response at least in part to a perception that too many "soft" federal judges were granting too many downward departures, in contravention of Congress's intention to provide greater uniformity in sentencing and to limit departures to cases that are truly atypical.

The Feeney Amendment engendered considerable scholarly and judicial criticism. One commentator predicted the following undesirable consequences:

> The likely result is many fewer Guideline departures, less judicial discretion, and more prosecutorial control. . . . Prosecutorial leverage to plea bargain will be at an all-time high, resulting in fewer trials, more bargains, and higher sentences. Judges used to check prosecutorial harshness, but now they are increasingly powerless unless prosecutors deign to grant leniency.

Stephanos Bibas, *The Feeney Amendment and the Continuing Rise of Prosecutorial Power to Plea Bargain*, 94 J. CRIM. L. & CRIMINOLOGY 295 (2004).

Regarding the requirement of reports on individual judges who depart, two United States District Court decisions held the provision unconstitutional as violative of separation-of-powers principles. *See, United States v. Mendoza*, 2004 U.S. Dist. LEXIS 1449 (C.D. Cal.) (Feeney Amendment unconstitutional because it "chills and stifles judicial independence"); *accord, United States v. Detwiler*, 338 F.Supp.2d 1166 (D.Or. 2004). The late Chief Justice William H. Rehnquist also criticized the reporting requirement as "an unwarranted and ill-considered effort to intimidate individual judges in the performance of their official duties" (2005 address to the Federal Judges Association Board of Directors, *available at* www.supremecourtus.gov/publicinfo/speeches/sp_05-05-03.html).

As discussed earlier in this chapter, however, the *Booker* line of decisions (especially including *Rita* and *Gall*) has effectively supplanted the Feeney Amendment's *de novo* standard of review of "departure" sentences with an appellate standard of "reasonableness" that is similar to, if not indistinguishable from, the pre-Feeney abuse of discretion standard articulated in *Koon*.

Upward departures. Examples of upward departures (sentence greater than that authorized by the applicable guideline range) include: *United States v. Melvin*, 187 F.3d 1316 (11th Cir. 1999) (upward departure in credit card fraud prosecution permissible because of number and vulnerability of hospitalized children whose names were used for the credit cards); and *United States v. Merritt*, 988 F.2d 1298 (2d Cir. 1993) (upward departure from 37–60 months permissible for conspiracy to defraud U.S. when defendant made significant efforts to conceal assets and avoid payment of restitution; departure necessary for punishment and deterrence).

Downward departures. Examples of downward departures include *United States v. Mignott*, 184 F.3d 1288 (11th Cir. 1999) (downward departure for consent to deportation despite nonfrivolous defense to deportation); and *United States v. Martinez-Ramos*, 184 F.3d 1055 (9th Cir. 1999) (downward departure for disparity in plea bargaining practices among California federal districts). *See generally* Kirk D. Houser, Note, 31 DUQ. L. REV. 361 (1993); J. Gordon Seymour, Note, 59 U. CHI. L. REV. 837 (1992) (post-offense drug rehabilitation efforts as grounds for downward departure).

Review of departure sentences, for "reasonableness" or "abuse of discretion" since Rita and Gall. Since the Supreme Court's most recent decisions in *Rita, Gall,* and *Kimbrough,* the circuit courts of appeal are now reviewing departure sentences under the more lenient reasonableness standard. It appears that departure sentences are being upheld on appeal more frequently than they were prior to *Rita* and *Gall*, but there have also been instances of reversal even under this more deferential standard.

Examples of downward departures affirmed since *Gall* include *United States v. Munoz-Nava*, 2008 WL 1947011 (10th Cir.) (significant downward departure for defendant convicted of possession of heroin with intent to distribute upheld on basis of defendant's long and consistent work history and sole support of young child and ailing elderly parents, absence of a prior felony record; sentence which ordered stringent post-release supervision conditions held to appropriately reflect the seriousness of the offence and to provide "just punishment"); and *United States v. Pauley*, 511 F. 3d 468 (4th Cir. 2008) (downward departure for possessor of images of child pornography upheld as furthering rehabilitation and diminishing likelihood of reoffending under court-imposed counseling requirements, and on basis of defendant's remorse and possession of a relatively small number of photographs, which did not show child's face). *But see* cases reversing downward departures even under more deferential appellate review, including *United States v. Livesay*, 2008 WL 1810195 (11th Cir.) (downward departure for defendant in high profile health care fraud conspiracy, from guideline range of 78 to 97 months imprisonment to 60 months of probation with the first 6 months served as home detention, held *not* justified by the fact that the defendant had repudiated the conspiracy early on and cooperated with prosecutors; sentencing judge held to have inadequately stated reasons for departure); and *United States v. Williams*, 2008 WL 1836371 (2d Cir.) (downward departure from guideline range held *not* justified by sentencing judge's view that prosecution for sale of crack cocaine should have been in state, not federal, court, and that the federal sentence should be adjusted downward to approximate sentence that could have been expected from state court).

For examples of upward departures affirmed since *Gall, see United States v. Austad*, 519 F. 3d 431 (8th Cir. 2008) (significant upward departure for defendant convicted of mailing threatening communications, held to be explained with "sufficient justifications" and therefore not an abuse of discretion); and *United States v. Briggs*, 511 F. 3d 808 (8th Cir. 2008) (upward departure for defendant convicted of fraudulent use of unauthorized access device held not to be abuse of discretion, upholding district court's enhancement based on defendant's persistent criminal behavior).

Whether reviewing either upward or downward departures, appellate courts in the most recent cases appear to be taking seriously *Gall*'s prescriptions — that sentencing judges must still properly calculate the applicable guideline range and must adequately state their reasons for guideline departures, and that appellate judges review all sentences, whether within or outside the applicable guideline ranges, under the deferential abuse-of-discretion standard. In effect, all federal sentencing decisions (except in cases where the sentence reflects an negotiated agreement between prosecution and defense) must now be adequately explained — a far cry from the days when no explanations were required and appellate review of sentences was virtually nonexistent.

[vi]   Continuing Controversy and Future Uncertainty

In the final analysis, there is a certain inevitable degree of tension between the guideline goals of sentencing uniformity (and reducing unwarranted sentencing disparity) and the goal of preserving the ability of judges to "do justice" in individual cases. Whether Congress will choose to respond further to *Booker* and its progeny remains to be seen. Despite the greater degree of freedom to depart from the Guidelines under the *Booker/Rita* "reasonableness" standard, federal district judges do not appear to have markedly increased their guideline departure rate in the wake of these decisions. Some federal circuits have continued to reverse departure sentences, even under the more lenient standard, in instances where they have found the sentencing judge's reasons for departure to be inadequately or erroneously explained. This subject continues to receive detailed coverage and discussion, with links to newly decided federal district and circuit court decisions, in the comprehensive "blog" of Professor Douglas A. Berman, Sentencing Law and Policy, available at http://sentencing.typepad.com.

As one would expect from such a complex, significant change from prior sentencing procedures, the federal sentencing guidelines have engendered a tremendous amount of analysis and criticism. Many critics argued that the Guidelines, at least as they existed and were implemented prior to *Booker*, *Rita*, and *Gall*, were a system of virtual mandatory minimum penalties that deprived judges of necessary discretion and resulted in unduly harsh sentences in some circumstances. *See generally* Orrin G. Hatch, *The Role of Congress in Sentencing: The United States Sentencing Commission, Mandatory Minimum Sentences, and the Search for a Certain and Effective Sentencing System*, 28 WAKE FOREST L. REV. 185 (1993); Gary T. Lowenthal, *Mandatory Sentencing Laws: Undermining the Effectiveness of Determinate Sentencing Reform*, 81 CAL. L. REV. 61 (1993); Stephen J. Schulhofer, *Rethinking Mandatory Minimums*, 28 WAKE FOREST L. REV. 199 (1993).

Moreover, the Guidelines' relatively narrow sentencing ranges have been criticized as contributing to prison overcrowding while doing little to rehabilitate offenders, and even as exacerbating the kinds of unwarranted disparities based on race and ethnicity that the Guidelines were intended to cure. Another source of controversy (discussed above) has been the Guidelines' "real offense" feature, which permits sentences to be enhanced based on the court's perception of the offense that the defendant actually committed (even if the perceived real offense was dismissed during plea bargaining or the defendant was acquitted of it), as opposed to the offense of record for which the defendant was actually convicted. A related concern is the relatively low preponderance–of– the–evidence standard of proof used in factfinding under the guidelines. at least prior to *Booker. See, e.g.*, Edward Becker, *Insuring Reliable Fact Finding in Guidelines Sentencing: Must the Guarantees of the Confrontation Clause and Due Process Clauses be Applied?*. 151 F.R.D. 153 (1993); Kevin R. Reitz, *Sentencing Facts: Travesties of Real-Offense Sentencing*, 45 STAN. L. REV. 523 (1993); Deborah Young, *Fact-finding at Federal Sentencing: Why the Guidelines Should Meet the Rules*, 79 CORNELL L. REV. 299 (1994).

For a response to the many criticisms of the Guidelines, *see* Frank O. Bowman III, *The Quality of Mercy Must Be Restrained, and Other Lessons in Learning to Love the Federal Sentencing Guidelines*, 1996 WIS. L. REV. 679; *see also* Michael Goldsmith, *Sentencing Reform that Works*, Wash. Post, Nov. 14, 1996, at A21 ("Churchill's adage about democracy may also be true of the guidelines: They are the worst form of sentencing except for all the rest"). Justice Stephen Breyer, who was a member of the original Sentencing Commission prior to his appointment to the Supreme Court, also defends the federal Guidelines:

> Despite the criticism of the guidelines, and even recognizing the bias that may arise from my own participation in the creation of the guidelines, I remain cautiously optimistic about their future. They have opened up the "black box" of sentencing. They have begun to lead broader segments of the legal community to focus upon the question of punishment. They have helped to diminish disparity in sentencing. And most importantly, they have begun to put in place a system for sentencing research that, in principle, can transmit to sentencing policymakers the results of judicial sentencing experience in the field. For all these reasons, I would not recommend a return to preguidelines practice. I do believe it important, however, to focus upon areas where change is desirable and possible. [14 Criminal Justice 28, 35 (Spring 1999)]

Among the many excellent discussions of the federal guidelines prior to the *Booker* line of cases, *see* Albert W. Alschuler, *The Failure of Sentencing Guidelines: a Plea for Less Aggregation*, 58 U. CHI. L. REV. 901 (1991); Gerald W. Heaney, *The Reality of Guidelines Sentencing: No End to Disparity*, 28 AM. CRIM. L. REV. 161 (1991); Ralph J.

Henham, *Evaluating the United States Federal Sentencing Guidelines*, 21 ANGLO-AM. L. REV. 399 (1992); Eric P. Berlin, Note, 1993 WIS. L. REV. 187 (1993) (failure to eliminate disparity).

A number of articles deal with guideline sentencing in particular kinds of cases:

Sentencing of corporations and white collar crimes: Jennifer Moore, *Corporate Culpability under the Federal Sentencing Guidelines*, 34 ARIZ. L. REV. 743 (1992); Ellen Podgor, *The Challenge of White Collar Sentencing*, 97 J. CRIM. L. & CRIMINOLOGY 731 (2007).

Environmental crimes: Jane Barrett, *Sentencing Environmental Crimes Under the United States Sentencing Guidelines — A Sentencing Lottery*, 22 ENVTL. L. 1421 (1992).

[3] Sentencing Panels

Efforts to change sentencing practices have addressed structural changes other than guidelines. One suggested reform is to have sentencing done by a group or panel of judges rather than a single judge. This proposed reform is designed to eliminate or at least minimize disparity by requiring the sentencing decision to be the product of a group process that, in theory at least, will reduce the likelihood of extremely long or short sentences. *See generally* Marvin E. Frankel, CRIMINAL SENTENCES: LAW WITHOUT ORDER 69–74 (1973) (sentencing councils).

G. DEATH PENALTY

The death penalty has long been a part of the American sentencing system, although it has been virtually abandoned in most other developed countries. Because of a series of legal developments that are beyond the scope of this book, the area has become quite complex. In general terms, roughly three-quarters of the American jurisdictions authorize the death penalty. The American public overwhelmingly believes in the death penalty. Since 1976, between 60 and 70% of all Americans consistently report that they believe in capital punishment. Sourcebook, at http://www.albany.edu/sourcebook/pdf/ t2512006.pdf. Only about 40% of African-Americans do so, however. *Id.* at http:// www.albany.edu/sourcebook/pdf/t2522006.pdf. *See generally* Frank E. Zimring & Gordon Hawkins, Capital Punishment and the American Agenda (1986); Roger G. Hood, THE DEATH PENALTY: A WORLDWIDE PERSPECTIVE (3d ed. 2002); Hugo Adam Bedau, ed., THE DEATH PENALTY IN AMERICA (4th ed. 1997).

[1] Constitutionality: In General

[a] Temporary Unconstitutionality: *Furman* (1972)

The death penalty survived most constitutional attacks until 1972 when the United States Supreme Court decided *Furman v. Georgia*, 408 U.S. 238 (1972). In a 5-4 decision, the *Furman* majority was able to agree only on a one paragraph *per curiam* decision that held simply that "the imposition and carrying out of the death penalty in these cases constitute cruel and unusual punishment in violation of the Eighth and Fourteenth Amendments." At stake were the death sentences of approximately 600 prisoners in various states. Five Justices wrote concurring opinions (Douglas, Brennan, Stewart, White, and Marshall) and four wrote dissents (Burger, Blackmun, Powell, and Rehnquist). The nine opinions totaled about 250 pages and constituted the longest set of opinions in the history of the Court.

Proponents of the death penalty read the opinions carefully and noted that the majority was comprised of at least three justices whose votes could change in certain circumstances. Since the vote was 5-4, a change in even one vote could reverse the *Furman* decision and restore the death penalty as a constitutionally permissible punishment. Among the *Furman* majority, it was clear that Justices Brennan and

Marshall were unlikely to change their votes because they believed that the death penalty itself was cruel and unusual punishment in violation of the Eighth Amendment.

Three other justices in the majority, however, were not as adamant. Justices Douglas, Stewart, and White focused on the *process* of determining who lives and who dies rather than on the death penalty itself. All three were concerned that juries had so much untrammeled discretion that this crucial decision could be made in an arbitrary manner. They felt that this element of arbitrariness violated the Eighth Amendment's ban on cruel and unusual punishment. Justice Stewart summarized these views when he noted in an often-quoted phrase that the death penalty is cruel and unusual "in the same way that being struck by lightning is cruel and unusual." He continued, "I simply conclude that the Eighth and Fourteenth Amendments cannot tolerate the infliction of a sentence of death under legal systems that permit this unique penalty to be so wantonly and freakishly imposed."

After *Furman*, a number of state legislatures enacted new death penalty provisions designed to appeal to at least one of the three majority Justices who were concerned with the arbitrary manner in which death sentences were imposed. One approach was to enact a mandatory death penalty so that everyone convicted of certain offenses would receive a death sentence. Under this approach, it was argued, neither the jury nor judge could be "arbitrary" since neither had the discretion to depart from the mandatory sentence. The other approach also attempted to minimize arbitrariness by establishing criteria for the sentencing authority (usually a jury) to use in determining which offenders were sentenced to death. These standards somewhat confined the sentencer's discretion. *See generally*, Corinna Barrett Lain, *Furman Fundamentals*, 82 WASH. L. REV. 1 (2007).

[b] Constitutional Again: *Gregg* (1976)

Four years later, in 1976, the pro-death penalty advocates won when the Supreme Court decided several cases that paved the way for the end of *Furman*'s *de facto* moratorium on the death penalty. Both Justices White and Stewart, who had joined the majority in *Furman*, voted to uphold the death penalty in certain circumstances. In *Gregg v. Georgia*, 428 U.S. 153 (1976), the Court upheld Georgia's death penalty statute and decided that the Eighth Amendment does not bar the death penalty for the crime of murder. Irrespective of its value as a deterrent, the death penalty was upheld as a permissible method of serving the goal of retribution. Georgia's death penalty statute provided the sentencing authority with sufficient guidance to overcome *Furman*'s concern with the possibility of an arbitrary and capricious death sentence.

The Georgia provision, later adopted in some form by many other states, included a bifurcated procedure. During the first trial (the "guilt phase"), the trier of fact determines the issue of guilt or innocence. If the defendant is found guilty of a capital offense, a second hearing (the "penalty phase") is held to determine whether the sentence should be life imprisonment or death. The death penalty is permissible only if one of ten listed aggravating circumstances specified by statute is found to be present beyond a reasonable doubt. The trier of fact also considers whether there are any mitigating circumstances, and whether the aggravating factors militating in favor of the death penalty outweigh the mitigating factors that militate against it. After a death sentence is imposed, the Georgia statute authorized a direct review by the Georgia Supreme Court. Part of the review is to determine whether the death sentence was excessive or disproportionate to the penalty imposed in similar cases. Justices Brennan and Marshall, in contrast to White and Stewart, rejected the Georgia provision and repeated their *Furman* view that the death penalty categorically violates the Eighth Amendment's cruel and unusual punishment ban.

The same day as *Gregg*, the Supreme Court decided four other capital cases that answered a number of questions raised by *Furman*. The Court was particularly concerned with whether the statutory scheme at issue imposed sufficient restraints to protect against the arbitrary use of the death penalty. In *Jurek v. Texas*, 428 U.S. 262 (1976), the Court upheld the Texas death penalty statute which authorized the death penalty only if the trier of fact found beyond a reasonable doubt that the homicide was deliberate with the reasonable expectation that death would result, that there was a probability that the defendant would commit criminal acts of violence in the future, and that the killing, if provoked, was an unreasonable response. The Court found that these questions sufficiently narrowed the decisionmaker's discretion to avoid arbitrariness. In what could be considered a departure from its concern with restricted discretion, the *Jurek* Court also held that the Eighth Amendment mandates that the death sentencing decision be individualized so that the jury could consider any evidence in mitigation of death.

Proffitt v. Florida, 428 U.S. 242 (1976), decided with *Gregg*, upheld the Florida death penalty statute, which required the judge to consider specific aggravating and mitigating factors before imposing a death sentence. The judge was required to give written findings about these factors when imposing a death sentence. A jury issued an advisory opinion on the issue and the Florida Supreme Court automatically reviewed each death sentence. The continued vitality of *Proffitt* is doubtful, however, since *Ring v. Arizona*, 536 U.S. 584 (2002), discussed above, where the Supreme Court held that juries, not judges, must decide the facts relevant to the decision whether or not to impose the death penalty unless the defendant has waived the right to a jury.

The United States Supreme Court in *Proffitt* rejected the argument that some of the statutory aggravating circumstances were so vague that they did not provide adequate restrictions on sentencing discretion. Thus, the *Proffitt* Court upheld aggravating circumstances that the killing was "especially heinous, atrocious, or cruel" as defined by the Florida courts.

Mandatory death penalty. Woodson v. North Carolina, 428 U.S. 280 (1976), and *Roberts v. Louisiana*, 428 U.S. 325 (1976), were different than the other three cases decided that day. Both involved mandatory death penalty statutes enacted in an effort to satisfy *Furman's* concern with arbitrary sentencing decisions. These two cases involved statutes that imposed the death penalty for *all* first degree murders. Justice Stewart's plurality opinion in both cases (he was joined by Justices Powell and Stevens) found the provisions unconstitutional because they failed to help guide the jury's decision whether to convict the defendant of first or second degree murder and to permit the jury to consider the particular relevant aspects of the character and record of each convicted defendant. Justices Brennan and Marshall wrote separate concurring decisions reiterating their views that the death penalty itself was unconstitutional. The dissenters argued that the mandatory death penalty was constitutional because it did not make the sentencing decision arbitrary.

Since 1976. After 1976, it was clear that the United States Supreme Court would uphold the death penalty in homicide cases. Subsequent death penalty decisions refined the 1976 cases and, because of personnel changes on the Court, gradually produced a solid majority. Many of the decisions focused on a particular jurisdiction's procedures. A common theme in the cases is that "death is different." Because of a death sentence's impact on both the defendant and the community, the procedures used to impose it must be more reliable than those required for ordinary criminal cases.

Critique of Furman. For an insightful critique of Furman "consistency" goal and an argument for a different Eighth Amendment approach, see Scott W. Howe, *Furman's Mythical Mandate*, 40 U. Mich. J. L. Reform 435 (2007); *see also* William W. Berry III, *Following the Yellow Brick Road of Evolving Standards of Decency: The Ironic Consequences of Death-is-Different Jurisprudence*, 28 Pace L. Rev. 15 (2007).

[2] Culpability Needed for Death Penalty

Non-homicide crimes. Historically in Anglo-American common law, the death penalty was authorized for a large number of offenses, including blasphemy, adultery, and a youth's sassing his or her parents. Over time it became clear that the Eighth Amendment's cruel and unusual punishment clause contained a proportionality limitation that restricted the use of the gravest penalty to crimes that merited society's ultimate condemnation. The plurality opinion in *Coker v. Georgia*, 433 U.S. 584 (1977), held that the death penalty for rape of an adult woman was grossly disproportionate to the gravity of the offense and therefore violated the cruel and unusual punishment clause. *Coker* was reaffirmed by a majority of the Court in *Enmund v. Florida*, 458 U.S. 782 (1982).

More recently, the Supreme Court, by a 5–4 majority, also prohibited, on Eighth Amendment proportionality grounds, the imposition of the death penalty for the crime of rape of a child. *Kennedy v. Louisiana* 128 S.Ct. 2641 (2008). The decision in *Kennedy* effectively ruled out the death penalty for all crimes against the person which do not result in the death of the victim. However, the majority opinion of Justice Kennedy specifically noted that the case did not present the question of the death penalty for non-homicide offenses against the State such as "treason, espionage, terrorism, and drug kingpin activity."

Varieties of homicide. It remained unclear exactly what participation in a homicide was necessary before a death penalty was permissible. What about the situation when the defendant did not kill intentionally? Perhaps the defendant was an accomplice, such as the lookout or getaway car driver, or was the killer but did not intend for death to result, yet was legally responsible for the murder because of the felony murder or joint enterprise rule. Can the death penalty be applied constitutionally in these cases?

Limit: kill, attempt to kill, or intend to kill. In *Enmund v. Florida*, 458 U.S. 782 (1982), the defendant Enmund was in the car near the scene of a double robbery-murder. Apparently the jury found that he was waiting to help in the robbers' escape and therefore was an aider and abetter in the robbery. There was no evidence that he was present at the killing, or knew or intended that a death would occur. Nevertheless, under Florida law he was considered a principal and received the death penalty. The death sentence was challenged as violating the Eighth Amendment.

In a 5-4 decision, Justice White's majority opinion reversed the sentence, holding that it violated the Eighth Amendment's cruel and unusual punishment clause. He first reviewed state capital statutes and found virtually none that authorized the death penalty simply because a person participated in a robbery where a death resulted. The Eighth Amendment, the majority reasoned, bars penalties that are disproportionate to the crime. In assessing proportionality, the focus must be on the individual defendant's own conduct, "not on that of those who committed the robbery and shot the victims." "Putting Enmund to death to avenge two killings that he did not commit and had no intention of committing or causing does not measurably contribute to the retributive end of ensuring that the criminal gets his just desserts." *See also Cabana v. Bullock*, 474 U.S. 376 (1986) (determination under *Enmund* of defendant's personal culpability can be made at any stage in the criminal process, including on appeal; *Enmund* read as barring death penalty for killers who did not personally kill, attempt to kill, or intend to kill).

Limit: Major participation and deliberate indifference. Enmund was refined in *Tison v. Arizona*, 481 U.S. 137 (1987), a case in which the defendants assisted their father's escape from prison, then helped him detain and rob a family of four. They were also present when their father shot all four family members, but claimed surprise at their father's violence. After the homicides, they escaped with their father and others involved in the killings. Although the *Tison* Court refused to "precisely delineate the particular types of conduct and states of mind warranting imposition of the death penalty," it held that "major participation in the felony committed, combined with reckless indifference to human life," satisfied *Enmund*'s proportionality concerns. *Id.* at 158. *See generally*, Melanie A. Renken, *Revisiting Tison v. Arizona: the Constitutionality of Imposing the Death Penalty on Defendants Who Did Not Kill or Intend to Kill*, 51 St. Louis U. L. J. 895 (2007).

[3]   Persons Who May Not Be Executed: Juveniles, The Mentally Retarded, The Insane

Echoing the concern expressed in *Coker v. Georgia* that the death penalty, unique in its severity and finality, only be imposed proportionally in the "worst of the worst" cases, the Supreme Court has prohibited its imposition under the Eighth Amendment for several categories of defendants whom the Court has determined do not have sufficient culpability to merit the imposition of a sentence of death.

[a]   Under Eighteen Years Old

In *Thompson v. Oklahoma*, 487 U.S. 815 (1988), a four-justice plurality of the Supreme Court concluded that the Eighth Amendment bars the death penalty for a defendant who was under sixteen when he committed murder. Then, after initially holding in *Stanford v. Kentucky*, 492 U.S. 361 (1989) (upholding the death penalty where the killer was sixteen or seventeen years old at the time of the homicide), that lack of maturity does not bar the imposition of the death penalty, the Court reversed itself in *Roper v. Simmons*, 543 U.S. 1 (2005), prohibiting the execution of offenders who were under the age of eighteen when their crimes were committed.

[b]   Insane and Mentally Retarded

It is also unconstitutional to execute an offender who is insane. The Supreme Court explained this rule as based on either (1) protecting the offender from fear and pain without the comfort of understanding, or (2) protecting the dignity of society from the barbarity of exacting mindless vengeance. *Ford v. Wainwright*, 477 U.S. 399 (1986). Similarly, the Eighth Amendment bars execution of a mentally retarded offender. *Atkins v. Virginia*, 536 U.S. 304 (2002) (overruling the Court's contrary determination 13 years earlier in *Penry v. Lynaugh*, 492 U.S. 302 (1989)). The Court noted that such executions raise serious questions whether either retribution or deterrence would be served, and therefore the death penalty is excessive under the circumstances.

In both *Roper v. Simmons* and *Atkins v. Virginia*, the Supreme Court majority, over vigorous dissents, applied the principle, as stated in *Trop v. Dulles*, 356 U.S. 86 (1958), that Eighth Amendment standards may change over time, guided by the "evolving standards of decency that mark the progress of a maturing society." In *Atkins* and again in *Roper*, the Court concluded, on the basis of recent trends in state legislatures and appellate courts and in actual sentencing practice, that the "national consensus" had swung away from approval of executing both mentally retarded persons and minors. The dissenters in *Roper* and *Atkins* express the "originalist" view that the meaning of the Eighth Amendment should be determined on the basis of the intent of its Framers in 1791, not on the later "subjective" views of a majority of the members of the Supreme Court. *See generally*, Richard J. Bonnie, *The Challenge of Implementing Atkins v. Virginia: How Legislatures and Courts Can Promote Accurate Assessments and Adjudications of Mental Retardation in Death Penalty Cases*, 41 U. Rich. L. Rev. 811 (2007). For an interesting argument against automatic exclusions of juveniles and mentally regarded offenders, see Dora W. Klein, *Categorical Exclusions from Capital Punishment: How Many Wrongs Make a Right?*, 72 Brook. L. Rev. 1211 (2007).

[4] Aggravating Circumstances

Since the 1976 decisions, death penalty statutes routinely include a list of as many as ten aggravating or limiting factors or questions. Typically, a defendant is eligible for the death penalty only if at least one of the circumstances is present. Aggravating circumstances focus on the nature of the offense (was it especially cruel or did it involve torture); the nature of the victim (was the victim very young, old, disabled, a police officer, a public official); the status of the defendant (on bail, parole, probation; a repeat violent offender), and future dangerousness. Ordinarily, the jury considers the aggravating circumstances at the sentencing hearing. In some jurisdictions these limiting factors are used at the guilt phase when the jury is asked whether certain facts are present. If so, the defendant is then eligible for the state's death penalty. The penalty phase will then determine whether the death penalty should be imposed in this case.

Functions. According to the Supreme Court, aggravating circumstances serve two functions. First, they limit the application of the death penalty to the most serious crimes. An aggravating circumstance would be unconstitutional if it were present in virtually every homicide because it would not assist in restricting the death penalty to the most egregious killings. Second, they channel the jury's discretion and therefore minimize the discretion and arbitrariness found lacking in *Furman. See, e.g., Lowenfield v. Phelps*, 484 U.S. 231 (1988) (upholding death statute permitting death penalty if jury found that the defendant knowingly created a risk of death or great bodily harm to more than one person).

Some aggravating factors have been invalidated because they do not serve these purposes. For example, an aggravating factor that is too vague is invalid because it does not channel the jury's discretion by providing principled guidance for the choice between death and a lesser penalty. In assessing vagueness, the United States Supreme Court will look at a state court's interpretation of its state statute. *See, e.g., Arave v. Creech*, 507 U.S. 463 (1993) (aggravating factor that defendant acted with "utter disregard for human life" not unconstitutionally vague because of limiting interpretation by Idaho Supreme Court); *Walton v. Arizona*, 497 U.S. 639 (1990) (aggravating factor "especially heinous, cruel or depraved" killing upheld because of narrowing interpretation of Arizona court); *Maynard v. Cartwright*, 486 U.S. 356 (1988) (aggravating factor "especially heinous, atrocious, or cruel" is unconstitutionally vague because not sufficiently narrowed by Oklahoma court); *Godfrey v. Georgia*, 446 U.S. 420 (1980) (aggravating factor "outrageously or wantonly vile, horrible, or inhuman" is unconstitutionally vague). *See* Brian Sites, *The Danger of Future Dangerousness in Death Penalty Use*, 34 Fla. St. U. L. Rev. 959 (2007).

Impact of invalid condition. A number of cases have considered the impact of an aggravating circumstance that was used at a capital sentencing proceeding and later found to be invalid. If the jury was instructed to consider an aggravating circumstance that was invalid because it was constitutionally impermissible or irrelevant (*e.g.*, defendant's race, religion, or political persuasion), due process mandates that the death sentence be overturned. *Zant v. Stephens*, 462 U.S. 862 (1983). Other errors in instructing a jury on invalid aggravating circumstances have not always caused a reversal. The result depends on the aggravating circumstance and its procedural weight in the case. A state appellate court or federal court can "reweigh" the various factors to determine whether the use of the invalid factor was harmless error. *See, e.g., Richmond v. Lewis*, 506 U.S. 40 (1992) (in a state where the jury must "weigh" or balance aggravating and mitigating factors to determine which prevail, it is constitutional error to give weight to unconstitutionally vague aggravating factor, even if other valid factors are present); *Sochor v. Florida*, 504 U.S. 527 (1992) (if invalid aggravating factor used in weighing aggravating versus mitigating factors, federal court can reweigh without the invalid aggravating factor or determine that invalid factor was harmless error); *Zant v. Stephens*, 462 U.S. 862 (1983) (one aggravating circumstance held vague but no reversal because jury found two other valid aggravating circumstances).

Proof. The existence of an aggravating circumstance has an effect on the evidence presented by both parties. The prosecution must prove the aggravating circumstance and the defense must be permitted to rebut it. In *Simmons v. South Carolina*, 512 U.S. 154 (1994), the prosecution's closing argument suggested that the jury should impose a death sentence because of the defendant's future dangerousness. The Supreme Court, in a plurality opinion, held that this argument gave the defense the right to tell the jury that a life sentence actually meant life without parole under state law. Due process does not permit a person to be executed on the basis of information the person had no chance to explain or deny. Without knowing the actual effect of a life sentence, the jury might vote for a death sentence because of a misperception about the consequences of the life term.

Victim impact evidence. Closely related to aggravating circumstances is "victim impact" evidence. Some states permit the prosecution at the capital sentencing hearing to present evidence and jury arguments about the victim's uniqueness and the effect of the victims loss on the family and community. This evidence may be offered by the prosecution as a victim impact statement, or in the form of testimony from the victim or the victim's survivors, or *victim allocution*. To some extent, victim impact testimony and evidence are offered to counter mitigating evidence offered by the defendant in the hope of arousing the jury's sympathy. In *Payne v. Tennessee*, 501 U.S. 808, 825 (1991), the Supreme Court held that the constitution does not bar such victim impact evidence:

> We are now of the view that a State may properly conclude that for the jury to assess meaningfully the defendant's moral culpability and blameworthiness, it should have before it at the sentencing phase evidence of the specific harm caused by the defendant.

This "evidence about the victim and about the impact of the murder on the victim's family is relevant to the jury's decision as to whether or not the death penalty should be imposed." *Id.* at 827. Note that *Payne* is somewhat limited. It did not authorize victim impact testimony about the "family members' characterizations and opinions about the crime, the defendant, and the appropriate sentence." *Id.* at 830 n.2.

Critics of *Payne* point out that it departs from the post-*Furman* cases confining the death penalty jury's discretion by requiring structured decision procedures. Accordingly, some states have opted to keep such evidence out of capital cases. *See generally* Michael Vitiello, *Payne v. Tennessee: A "Stunning Ipse Dixit,"* 8 Notre Dame J. of L., Ethics, & Pub. Pol'y 165 (1994); Randall Coyne, *Inflicting Payne on Oklahoma: The Use of Victim Impact Evidence During the Sentencing Phase of Capital Cases*, 45 Okla. L. Rev. 589 (1992); Michael Ira Oberlander, Note, 45 Vand. L. Rev. 1621 (1992).

[5] Mitigating Circumstances

Although it may appear that *Furman*'s concern with too much discretion would lead the Supreme Court to severely limit the issues a capital jury may consider, the Court has actually increased jury discretion as to evidence used to suggest that the death penalty *not* be imposed. In *Lockett v. Ohio*, 438 U.S. 586 (1978), a four-justice plurality struck Ohio's death penalty statute because it did not permit the trier of fact to consider relevant mitigating factors, such as the defendant's character, prior criminal record, age, lack of specific intent to cause death, and minor role in the crime. A number of cases after *Lockett* have held that the cruel and unusual punishment clause of the Eighth Amendment mandates that the jury in a capital case must be permitted to consider any aspect of a defendant's character and background and any of the circumstances of the offense that the defendant offers to convince the jury to impose a sentence other than death. This "individualized" approach is necessary, according to the Court, in order to treat offenders as unique people and to provide respect for humanity's value of compassion. *See, e.g., Johnson v. Texas*, 509 U.S. 350 (1993) (defendant's youth is mitigating factor that capital jury must be permitted to consider); *McKoy v. North Carolina*, 494 U.S. 433 (1990) (striking North Carolina requirement that mitigating factor can only be considered if all jurors find it present; procedure unduly limits role of mitigating factor because one juror can prevent others from considering specific mitigating factor); *Skipper v. South Carolina*, 476 U.S. 1 (1986) (at capital sentencing hearing, defendant entitled to present evidence that defendant had made good jail adjustment); *Eddings v. Oklahoma*, 455 U.S. 104 (1982) (trial court erred in not considering capital defendant's family history and mental problems).

The necessary individualized approach is not unlimited. Jurors can be instructed to base their decision on factors presented at the trial and to avoid extraneous emotional factors, even if these instructions would cause them to be less favorable toward the accused. *See, e.g., California v. Brown*, 479 U.S. 538 (1987) (upholding jury instruction that jurors must not be swayed by mere sentiment, conjecture, sympathy, passion, prejudice, public opinion, or public feeling).

Jurors' assessment of aggravating and mitigation factors. Although most states require a jury before deciding on a sentence of death to find that the aggravating factors urged by the prosecution outweigh the mitigating factors urged by the defense, Kansas's unusual statute *requiring* the jury to impose the death penalty if it finds the aggravating and mitigating factors to be "in equipoise" (*i.e.*, evenly balanced) was upheld by a majority of the Supreme Court in *Kansas v. Marsh*, 548 U.S. 163 (2006).

To some extent, what is mitigating evidence may depend on what the prosecution presents. If the prosecution argues that the defendant merits the death penalty because he or she presents a future danger, the defendant is entitled to inform the jury that he or she is not parole eligible if state law bars parole in the case. *Cf. O'Dell v. Netherland*, 521 U.S. 151 (1997).

[6] Lesser-Included Offenses

Subsequent cases have amplified many of the procedural issues raised in the 1976 cases. In *Beck v. Alabama*, 447 U.S. 625 (1980), the Court held that the jury in a capital case must be permitted to consider lesser-included offenses if the evidence warrants the instruction. But such instructions are not necessary if the alleged lesser-included crime is not provable or viable under state law. *See Spaziano v. Florida*, 468 U.S. 447 (1984) (jury need not be instructed on lesser-included offenses for which the defendant could not be convicted because of the statute of limitations); *Hopper v. Evans*, 456 U.S. 605 (1982) (jury instructions on lesser-included offenses necessary only if evidence supports the lesser-included crimes); *Hopkins v. Reeves*, 524 U.S. 88 (1998) (since under Nebraska law neither second-degree murder nor manslaughter is a lesser-included offense of felony murder, the court need not give a jury instruction on either one).

[7] Roles of Judge and Jury

As discussed earlier in this chapter, facts that will determine whether or not the defendant will receive the death penalty are for the jury (unless waived), not the judge, to decide. *Ring v. Arizona*, 536 U.S. 584 (2002). The *Ring* decision was based upon the jury trial guarantee, as analyzed in *Apprendi v. New Jersey*, 530 U.S. 466 (2000). *See generally*, Donald M. Houser, *Reconciling Ring v. Arizona with the Current Structure of the Federal Capital Murder Trial: The Case for Trifurcation*, 64 WASH. & LEE L. REV. 349 (2007).

In making its crucial life-or-death decision, the jury must not be led to believe that the ultimate responsibility for the decision is held by some other body, such as a higher appellate court that will review the case. *Caldwell v. Mississippi*, 472 U.S. 320 (1985).

The Court in *Caldwell* was concerned that the jury would be prone to select the death penalty rather than a life sentence because any mistake would later be corrected on appeal.

[8] Discriminatory Application of Death Penalty

It is obvious that the death penalty should not be applied in a way that discriminates on the basis of race, ethnicity, and the like. Proof of such discrimination is difficult. In *McCleskey v. Kemp*, 481 U.S. 279 (1987), the defendant, a black man, was given the death penalty for killing a white police officer during the course of a furniture store robbery. The defendant presented empirical studies showing that (1) persons who kill whites are more likely to receive the death penalty than persons who murder blacks, and (2) blacks who kill are more likely to be given the death penalty than whites who kill.

Despite this evidence, the Supreme Court held that neither the equal protection guarantee nor the cruel and unusual punishment clause was offended. Equal protection was not violated because the defendant was unable to prove that there was purposeful discrimination that had a discriminatory effect on him. The empirical studies did not — and could not — establish that any decisionmaker (judge, jurors, prosecutor, legislator) in *his* case acted with a discriminatory purpose. The Eighth Amendment challenge was unsuccessful because the defendant could not prove that his sentence was disproportionate to either the gravity of the crime or the sentences received by others who killed during the course of a robbery. Moreover, the Court found that the empirical studies did not demonstrate a constitutionally significant risk that the jury acted in a racially biased way. The Court acknowledged the existence of statistical correlations showing possible biases, but found that some disparity is inherent in a criminal justice system that confers discretion on decisionmakers.

McCleskey engendered several spirited dissents. Justice Brennan argued that the Eighth Amendment's cruel and unusual punishment clause was violated simply because the empirical studies showed that there was a risk that race might have affected the jury's decision; the precedents do not require proof that this particular jury was so motivated. Justice Blackmun's dissent in *McCleskey* maintained that equal protection was violated because the conviction was based on race discrimination. McCleskey was a member of a recognized group who produced sufficient empirical proof that his sentence was affected by racial factors. Justice Stevens' dissent argued that there was a strong probability that racial issues entered the jury's processes. This violated the rule that the death sentence must be imposed consistently and fairly or not at all.

The *McCleskey* data were influential in convincing Justice Blackmun to conclude that the death penalty, as currently administered, is unconstitutional because it does not eliminate arbitrariness and discrimination. *Callins v. Collins*, 510 U.S. 1141 (1994) (Blackmun, J., dissenting to denial of certiorari). *See generally* David Cole, No Equal Justice 132-141 (1999) (*McCleskey's* failure to deal with racial disparity legitimated the view that such disparities are inevitable, and need not be explained or justified, and allowed the white majority to assume "tough on crime" attitudes while imposing most of the cost of these tough criminal penalties on minorities); Ray Sebastian Pantle, *Blacker than Death Row: How Current Equal Protection Analysis Fails Minorities Facing Capital Punishment*, 35 Cap. U. L. Rev. 811 (2007); Brooke Butler, *Death Qualification and Prejudice: The Effect of Implicit Racism, Sexism, and Homophobia on Capital Defendants' Right to Due Process*, 25 Beh. Sci. & L. 857 (2007); *Symposium on Pursuing Racial Fairness in Criminal Justice: Twenty Years after McCleskey v. Kemp*, 39 Colum. Hum. Rts. L. Rev. 1–285 (2007)(excellent series of articles on post-*McCleskey* developments); David C. Baldus & George Woodworth, *Race Discrimination and the Legitimacy of Capital Punishment: Reflections on the Interaction of Fact and Perception*, 53 DePaul L. Rev. 1411, 1423–26 (2004) (impact of race of victim and defendant); Glenn L. Pierce & Michael L. Radelet, *The Impact of*

Legally Inappropriate Factors on Death Sentencing for California Homicides, 1990–1999, 46 Santa Clara L. Rev. 1, 19–25 (2005) (likelihood of death penalty based on race and ethnicity of victim); Nancy J. King, *How Different is Death? Jury Sentencing in Capital and Non-Capital Cases Compared*, 2 Ohio St. J. Crim. L. 195, 204 (2004) (impact on death sentence of race of homicide victim).

[9] Access to Information

Because the death penalty is unique and irreversible, the Court has mandated special procedures to ensure reliable verdicts. One is that the accused is entitled to access to information used by the sentencing authority to decide whether the sentence should be death or some lesser sentence. *Gardner v. Florida*, 430 U.S. 349 (1977) (reversal because confidential information in presentence report was used as partial basis for imposition of death sentence but was not disclosed to defendant or defense counsel).

[10] Appeal

Because of the importance of the decision and the history of criminal procedure, in capital cases every jurisdiction permits an appeal of both the conviction and death sentence. Often there are expedited procedures that bypass intermediate appellate courts and send the case directly from the trial court to the state's highest court.

Proportionality review. As part of the appellate process in capital cases, some states undertake a "comparative proportionality review" in which the sentence of someone receiving the death penalty is compared with the sentences of those who were convicted of the same type of crime but did not receive the death penalty. This form of review is designed to protect against improper sentencing disparity. In *Pulley v. Harris*, 465 U.S. 37 (1984), the Supreme Court held that this proportionality review is not constitutionally required as long as the jurisdiction has ample procedures to guard against the arbitrary application of the death penalty. For a criticism of the *Pulley* decision and a call for state appellate courts to engage in comparative proportionality review, see Penny J. White, *Can Lightning Strike Twice? Obligations of State Courts After Pulley v. Harris*, 70 U. Colo. L. Rev. 813 (1999).

[11] Method of Execution

Early in our nation's history, hanging was the predominant method of carrying out a sentence of death. Over time, states came to prefer a succession of other methods (including firing squads, poison gas, and electrocution) intended to make executions more humane and less painful. With the advent in recent years of execution by lethal injection almost all states have come to abandon other means of execution, or to give the condemned prisoner a choice between death by injection or by some other means.

In *Baze v. Rees*, 128 S.Ct. 1520 (2008), the Supreme Court rejected an Eighth Amendment challenge to the procedures used in Kentucky (and in most other death penalty states) to administer lethal injections. Lethal injection typically involves three drugs: first, a massive sedative to render the condemned unconscious and insensitive to pain, second, a paralytic agent to eliminate grotesque muscular twitching, and third, a drug to stop the heart and cause death.

The defendant and the State in *Rees* agreed on some facts. First, that the sequence of drugs, if properly administered would produce a virtually pain-free death. Second, a botched execution in which the condemned is subjected unnecessarily to substantial pain would be cruel and unusual punishment in violation of the Eighth Amendment.

The Court, via a three-justice plurality opinion by Chief Justice Roberts and five concurring opinions (by Justices Alito, Stevens, Scalia, Thomas, and Breyer), rejected the defendant's argument that use of the paralytic agent, pancuronium bromide, could mask outward signs of massive pain that could result if the condemned had not first been adequately sedated. The Roberts plurality opinion held that the defendant had simply not proved this contention. Notably, the Thomas concurrence (joined by Justice Scalia) argued that only those executions *designed* to inflict a torturous or lingering death violate the Eighth Amendment.

Justice Stevens, in sharp contrast, acknowledged that the death penalty is not *per se* unconstitutional in light of *Gregg* and other precedents, but argued that the death penalty itself violates the Eighth Amendment and urged that the Court reconsider its holding in *Gregg* in the future.

Justice Ginsburg, joined by Justice Souter, dissented only to the extent that between the administration of the sedative and the paralytic agent, the Eighth Amendment, in her view, requires that the executioner check for signs of consciousness (by flicking the defendant's eyelashes, shaking him, pinching the skin, placing an ammonia tablet under the nose, or calling out his name, as is done in some states), in order to minimize the possibility of an unnecessarily painful death. Justice Stevens thus appears to be the only Justice on the present Court who believes that the death penalty, *per se*, is unconstitutionally cruel and unusual punishment.

More than a hundred years prior to *Baze*, the Supreme Court held in *Wilkerson v. Utah*, 99 U.S. 130 (1870), and in *In re Kemmler*, 136 U.S. 436 (1890), respectively, that execution by firing squad and by electrocution do not violate the Eighth Amendment. With the passage of time and the common use of lethal injection, Nebraska became the only state to use electrocution as the sole method of execution. However, in *State v. Mata*, 745 N.W. 2d 229 (decided February 8, 2008, two months before *Baze*), the Nebraska Supreme Court held that electrocution, by causing a needlessly painful death, violates that state's constitutional prohibition against cruel and unusual punishment. Thus it now appears that no state requires any method of execution other than lethal injection, although some still permit the condemned prisoner to choose between lethal injection and some other method.

H. ETHICAL ISSUES IN SENTENCING

Sentencing, like every other issue in criminal practice, presents ethical issues for both the prosecutor and defense lawyer. The different responsibilities for the two create slightly different obligations.

[1] Defense Counsel

For the defense lawyer, recall that *Strickland v. Washington*, 466 U.S. 668 (1984), establishes the standard for the Sixth Amendment's guarantee of the effective assistance of counsel in sentencing matters. In *Strickland* the defendant was sentenced to death for three homicides. He sought to have the sentence overturned because of defense counsel's inadequate representation during the sentencing hearing. The Supreme Court held that the key consideration is "whether counsel's conduct so undermined the proper functioning of the adversarial process that the trial cannot be relied on as having produced a just result." The *Strickland* Court adopted a two-pronged test.

Deficient performance. First, the defendant must show that counsel's performance was "deficient." This means that defense counsel acted unreasonably under prevailing professional norms. Professional standards are guides but not dispositive. Counsel's conduct must be judged in the context of the particular case. There is a presumption that counsel was adequate.

Prejudice. The second *Strickland* prong is that counsel's deficient performance must have been prejudicial to the defense. Prejudice is presumed if counsel has an actual conflict of interest that adversely affected his or her performance. In other situations, the defendant can prove prejudice by showing a reasonable probability (*i.e.*, a probability sufficient to undermine confidence in the outcome) that, but for the lawyer's unprofessional errors, the result of the proceeding would have been different. Counsel's defective representation that results in an increase in a prison term is prejudicial under *Strickland*. *Glover v. United States*, 531 U.S. 198 (2001).

Applying this test in *Strickland*, the Supreme Court found no Sixth Amendment violation. The defendant, against the advice of defense counsel, had pled guilty. During the plea proceedings, the defendant accepted responsibility for the homicides, and stated he had no significant prior criminal record and was under extreme emotional disturbance at the time of the offense. The trial judge seemed sympathetic. At the subsequent sentencing hearing, defense counsel devoted little effort to finding character witnesses and did not request a psychiatric examination. The defense lawyer explained this as a strategic decision. Since helpful information was relayed to the seemingly sympathetic judge during the guilty plea procedure, counsel thought that it would be better to present no more information on those points at sentencing. He did not request a presentence report because he feared it would be harmful in its inclusion of the defendant's criminal history. By relying heavily on the earlier plea proceedings, defense counsel also prevented the prosecution from cross-examining the defendant and from bringing in pro-prosecution psychiatric expert testimony.

The Supreme Court found that counsel's performance was not ineffective under *Strickland*'s two-pronged test. The decision to rely on the guilty plea procedure was professionally reasonable under the particular circumstances and the defendant could not prove that counsel's performance, even if deficient, was prejudicial.

The opposite result was reached in another extraordinary capital case involving a homicide during the course of a burglary. In *Horton v. Zant*, 941 F.2d 1449 (11th Cir. 1991), at the closing argument during the sentencing hearing the defense counsel actually told the jury:

> [T]he one you judge is not a very good person . . . . I ask you for the life of a worthless man." And, the prosecutor's closing "made me hate my client. But then I . . . try to be reasonable about the whole situation; and I don't hate him as much . . . Mr. Briley [the prosecutor] has admirably told you just exactly why it is that Jimmy Lee [the defendant] has got to die. And it becomes my turn to try and explain to you why you don't have to say he's got to die . . . . I find my task virtually impossible . . . . Maybe Mr. Briley is right, maybe he is not. Maybe he ought to die, but I don't know."

Id. at 1462. Defense counsel also introduced no mitigating evidence and called no witnesses at the sentencing proceeding on the mistaken theory that such evidence was only helpful in torture cases. The appellate court found defense counsel's performance at the sentencing hearing to be below the *Strickland* standard. *See also Hardwick v. Crosby*, 320 F.3d 1127 (11th Cir. 2003)(defense counsel's failure to investigate and present any of considerable mitigating evidence at sentencing demonstrated misunderstanding of law, caused prejudice to the defendant, and established ineffective assistance of counsel); *Lewis v. Lane*, 832 F.2d 1446 (7th Cir. 1987) (reversal for stipulating existence of four nonexistent prior felony convictions that affected sentence); *United States v. Phillips*, 210 F.3d 345 (5th Cir. 2000) (reversal because defense counsel did not correct erroneous application of sentencing guidelines that resulted in enhanced sentence).

Additional effectiveness of counsel claims in death penalty cases have been addressed by the United States Supreme Court in recent years with mixed results.

In *Bell v. Cone*, 535 U.S. 685 (2002), defendant Cone was charged with two counts of first degree murder in the perpetration of a burglary. At his trial, defense counsel sought to establish that the defendant was not guilty by reason of insanity. The jury found him guilty on all charges. At the sentencing stage, Cone's attorney called the jury's attention to mitigating evidence, which had been considered at the guilt stage. While he made various attempts to convince the jury to show mercy and not impose the death penalty, he elected to waive his final argument, thereby preventing the lead prosecutor from arguing in rebuttal. The jury found four aggravating factors and no mitigating circumstances substantial enough to outweigh them. Therefore, the death penalty was imposed.

The United States Supreme Court held that the defendant had failed to establish a Sixth Amendment counsel violation. The Court's analysis focused principally upon *United States v. Cronic*, 466 U.S. 648 (1984), where the Court opined that a trial would be presumptively unfair (that is, there is no separate requirement of proving prejudice) where the accused is denied the presence of counsel at a critical stage or if "counsel entirely fails to subject the prosecution's case to meaningful adversarial testing." As to that latter point, the Court emphasized that the attorney's failure to test the prosecutor's case "must be complete." Because Cone's attorney failed to oppose prosecution at "specific points" only, the Court rejected the notion that prejudice must be presumed. Finally, as to the defense attorney's decision to waive closing argument, the Court echoed a theme developed in *Strickland* that the defendant must overcome the presumption that the challenged action constituted "sound trial strategy."

Justice Stevens, dissenting, argued that the *Cronic* rule applied because the defense attorney did not interview witnesses aside from those relative to guilt, he did not present testimony relevant to mitigation from witnesses who were available, and he made no plea for Cone's life or closing remarks after the state's case.

Conflict of interest. Two months prior to *Bell*, the Court in *Mickens v. Taylor*, 535 U.S. 162 (2002), addressed the question, as articulated by Justice Breyer, whether the defendant may receive the death penalty "after [the state of Virginia] appointed to represent him as his counsel a lawyer, who at the time of the murder, was representing the very person Mickens was accused of killing." The majority expressed the issue somewhat differently. To them the question was "what a defendant must show in order to demonstrate a Sixth Amendment violation where the trial court fails to inquire into a potential conflict of interest about which it knew or reasonably should have known." Relying upon *Cuyler v. Sullivan*, 446 U.S. 335 (1980), the Court ruled that a defendant must demonstrate that a conflict of interest actually affected the adequacy of his representation. That is, prejudice under *Strickland* will be presumed only if the conflict sufficiently affected the attorney's performance. Here, because that finding had not been made and because the defendant did not establish prejudice, no relief was granted. Justice Breyer asserted in dissent that automatic reversal was required because, by appointing this attorney to represent *Mickens*, the state created a "structural defect" in the process.

Failure to present mitigating evidence. Contrary to *Bell* and *Mickens, Williams v. Taylor*, 529 U.S. 362 (2000), holds that a denial of effective assistance of counsel is established when attorneys fail to investigate and present substantial mitigating evidence during the sentencing phase of a capital murder trial. Simply stated, at the defendant's sentencing hearing, his lawyer failed to discover and present any significant mitigating evidence. Indeed, the defense attorney's closing argument was devoted to explaining that it was difficult to find a reason why the jury should spare Mr. Williams's life.

In a six to three decision, the United States Supreme Court found a Sixth Amendment counsel violation under *Strickland*. First, the Court pointed out in considerable detail evidence that could have been discovered by the defense attorney that would have been relevant for mitigation purposes. Justice Stevens, writing for the majority, also examined whether or not this might have been justified as a reasonable tactical decision: "the failure to introduce the comparatively voluminous amount of evidence that did speak in Williams' favor was not justified by a tactical decision to focus on Williams' voluntary confession." Continuing, he stated that "those omissions. . .clearly demonstrate that trial counsel did not fulfill their obligation to conduct a thorough investigation of the defendant's background." The Court finally concluded that the lawyer's unprofessional service prejudiced the defendant within the meaning of *Strickland*:

> Mitigating evidence unrelated to dangerousness may alter the jury's selection of penalty, even if it does not undermine or rebut the prosecution's death-eligibility case. The Virginia Supreme Court did not entertain that possibility. It thus failed to accord appropriate weight to the body of mitigation evidence available to trial counsel. . . . The entire postconviction record, viewed as a whole and accumulative of mitigation evidence presented originally, raised a "reasonable probability that the result of the sentencing proceeding would have been different" if competent counsel had presented and explained the significance of all the available evidence. [*Id.* at 398–399]

Most recently, the *Williams* principle was applied by the United States Supreme Court to a death penalty case in which trial counsel failed to perform a reasonable investigation into the defendant's family history and background. As a result, mitigation arguments were not made at the sentencing hearing. Justice O'Connor, writing for the seven-person majority (Justices Scalia and Thomas dissenting), concluded that the evidence not discovered was "powerful" and that the attorneys chose to "abandon their investigation at an unreasonable juncture, making a fully informed decision with respect to sentencing strategy impossible." *Wiggins v. Smith*, 539 U.S. 510 (2003).

Regarding the question whether this ineffectiveness prejudiced the defendant (*i.e.*, the jury's decision to impose the death penalty), the Court in *Wiggins* found the mitigating evidence in this case was stronger than that present in *Williams* and also that the state's evidence in support of the death penalty was weaker in this case than in *Williams*. Therefore, the Court concluded that "had the jury been confronted with this considerable mitigating evidence, there is a reasonable probability that it would have returned with a different sentence."

Reiterating the importance of referring to ABA Standards as a benchmark for determining reasonable competence, the U.S. Supreme Court, applying *Strickland* and *Wiggins*, held that "even when a capital defendant's family members and the defendant himself have suggested that no mitigating evidence is available, his lawyer is bound to make reasonable efforts to obtain and review material that counsel knows the prosecution will probably rely on as evidence of aggravation at the sentencing of trial." *Rompilla v. Beard*, 545 U.S. 374 (2005).

In sum. In general, the cases interpreting the Sixth Amendment provide little specific guidance for the criminal defense lawyer. The American Bar Association's Standards for Criminal Justice are only slightly more helpful. They obligate the defense attorney to become familiar with the available sentencing alternatives and the judge's sentencing practices, and to ensure that the court and prosecution have information helpful to the accused. Defense counsel at the sentencing hearing is acting as an advocate for the defendant. Accordingly, counsel "should present to the court any ground which will assist in reaching a proper disposition favorable to the accused." STANDARDS FOR CRIMINAL JUSTICE § 4–8.1(b) (3d ed. 1993). The Commentary notes that at a sentencing hearing, defense counsel "is an advocate in a representative capacity participating in an adversary proceeding." Of course, the adversarial nature of the sentencing process does not authorize defense counsel to mislead the court or prosecution.

> Counsel may not present facts that are known to be false in a manner that creates an inference that they are true. Counsel may not, for example, present facts concerning the defendant's character that would suggest to the judge that the defendant does not have a prior record of crime if it is known that the defendant has such a record and that fact has not been disclosed to the court. [*Id.* § 4–8.1 commentary (3d ed. 1993)]

[2] Prosecution

Given society's "get tough" attitude with respect to crime and punishment, a prosecutor may feel obligated to seek the most severe sentence possible in every case. This, it can be argued, is the prosecutor's function — to convey the sentiments of society through the criminal justice process. A prosecutor, especially one seeking re-election to office, could see and present this as evidence of prosecutorial effectiveness.

The American Bar Association's Standards for Criminal Justice squarely address this issue:

> The prosecutor should not make the severity of sentences the index of his or her effectiveness. To the extent that the prosecutor becomes involved in the sentencing process, he or she should seek to assure that a fair and informed judgment is made on the sentence and to avoid unfair sentence disparities.

STANDARDS FOR CRIMINAL JUSTICE § 3–6.1(a) (3d ed. 1993). The commentary to this section stresses the prosecutor's role as a "minister of justice" whose "overriding obligation is to see that justice is fairly done." This is "achieved by seeking to make the sentencing process operate in a fair and equitable manner with the best available information." *Id.*, commentary.

The ABA Standards also address how a prosecutor should function with respect to sentencing information:

> The prosecutor should assist the court in basing its sentence on complete and accurate information for use in the presentence report. The prosecutor should disclose to the court any information in the prosecutor's files relevant to the sentence. If incompleteness or inaccurateness in the presentence report comes to the prosecutor's attention, the prosecutor should take steps to present the complete and correct information to the court and to defense counsel. The prosecutor should disclose to the defense and to the court at or prior to the sentencing proceeding all unprivileged mitigating information known to the prosecutor, except when the prosecutor is relieved of this responsibility by a protective order of the tribunal.

STANDARDS FOR CRIMINAL JUSTICE § 3–6.2(a) and (b) (3d ed. 1993).

NOTE

Note that the ABA Standards impose an affirmative duty on the prosecutor to disclose information helpful to the defense relative to sentencing. Do they impose a similar duty on the defense lawyer (*i.e.*, must he or she disclose evidence to the prosecution that would suggest a harsh sentence)? If not, what are the limits on the defense counsel's ability to keep harmful information secret?

Chapter 18
POST-CONVICTION REMEDIES

A. INTRODUCTION

After a criminal conviction (and occasionally even before the conviction), both the defendant and the government may seek to have another court alter the conviction, sentence, or, less frequently, a judicial decision occurring before the conviction. Virtually every criminal conviction and sentence is subject to challenge by a complicated, often technical array of *post-conviction remedies.* For state offenders, sometimes both state and federal remedies are available.

This chapter provides a brief introduction to the primary post-conviction remedies and issues, but it is not designed as a complete treatment. *See generally* David G. Knibb, FEDERAL COURT OF APPEALS MANUAL (5th ed. 2007); Herbert Monte Levy, HOW TO HANDLE AN APPEAL (4th ed. 1999); Michael E. Tigar & Jane B. Tigar, FEDERAL APPEALS (1999); James S. Liebman & Randy Hertz, FEDERAL HABEAS CORPUS PRACTICE AND PROCEDURE (5th ed. 2005).

[1] Categories of Post-Conviction Remedies

[a] Direct Appeals and Collateral Challenges

In general terms, there are two types of post-conviction remedies: *direct appeals* and *collateral challenges.* A direct appeal is a request to a higher court to alter a judge's ruling. Ordinarily, it is made shortly after the ruling or conviction and may be "as a matter of right" — *i.e.,* the higher court must entertain the appeal. Collateral challenges ordinarily are made after direct appeals have been exhausted and are often limited to certain issues, such as constitutional violations. Thus, collateral remedies may be available for a much narrower group of errors than direct appeal. Collateral remedies, unlike direct appeals, are usually first sought from a trial court. Sometimes the various collateral remedies are referred to as "post-conviction" (as opposed to "appellate") remedies.

Procedural rules often dictate whether an offender will take a direct appeal or pursue collateral remedies. There may be a number of both statutory and common law collateral remedies theoretically available in a jurisdiction. Sometimes it is not clear whether the statutes have supplanted all or part of the common law remedies.

[b] Civil Rights Actions

Although clearly beyond the scope of this book, there is still another remedy used frequently by prisoners. *Civil rights actions,* based on 42 U.S.C. § 1983, provide a civil remedy for state violations of a person's "rights, privileges, or immunities secured by the Constitution and laws." Relief can be in the form of monetary damages or injunctive relief, both unavailable in direct criminal appeals or habeas corpus actions. If the civil rights suit is successful, the government defendant may be required to pay the plaintiff's legal fees.

In 2006, state prisoners filed 15,531 civil rights actions and 19,195 federal habeas corpus petitions. U.S. Dep't of Justice Sourcebook of Criminal Justice Statistics [online] (Ann L. Pastore and Kathleen Maguire, eds., 2006), *available at* http://www.albany.edu/sourcebook/pdf/t5652006.pdf. Most civil rights actions filed by prisoners deal with the conditions of their confinement, including the quality of food and medical care, alleged assaults by guards and other prisoners, searches, and interference with mail, visitors, freedom of speech, and the like.

Occasionally, however, a civil rights action is brought on grounds that could also be argued on appeal or in a habeas corpus petition. Because of differences in the various remedies, federal courts have had to distinguish them. In *Preiser v. Rodriguez*, 411 U.S. 475 (1973), state prisoners filed a civil rights action to challenge the deprivation of good-time credits earned in prison. By filing a civil rights action rather than a habeas corpus petition, the prisoners sought to avoid the exhaustion-of-state-remedies rule required for habeas corpus actions, discussed below. Thus, they filed directly in federal court without first giving a state court the opportunity to address the federal constitutional issues. The Supreme Court resolved the issue by holding:

> What is involved here is the extent to which § 1983 is a permissible alternative to the traditional remedy of habeas corpus. Upon that question, we hold today that when a state prisoner is challenging the very fact or duration of his physical imprisonment, and the relief he seeks is a determination that he is entitled to immediate release or a speedier release from that imprisonment, his sole federal remedy is a writ of habeas corpus. [*Id.* at 500]

Since the *Preiser* plaintiffs would have been released earlier if their civil rights action had prevailed, the Court held that habeas corpus was the only remedy available to them. *See also Hutcherson v. Riley*, 468 F.3d 750 (11th Cir. 2006)(§ 1983 available for challenge to circumstances of confinement but not validity of conviction or validity or duration of sentence, which are cognizable in habeas corpus).

Damages. Preiser essentially removed civil rights actions as a viable remedy for criminal procedural issues when the aggrieved person seeks to overturn a conviction or reduce a sentence. But what about a case where the aggrieved person seeks *damages* under § 1983 rather than a decree that a conviction or sentence is invalid? In *Heck v. Humphrey*, 512 U.S. 477 (1994), the Supreme Court held that a § 1983 action is inappropriate to challenge actions that would require the court to find that a conviction or sentence is invalid. Before bringing an action under § 1983, the prisoner must first prove that the conviction or sentence was reversed on direct appeal, expunged, invalidated by a state court, or called into question by a federal court's issuance of a writ of habeas corpus.

Immunity. The doctrines of absolute immunity or qualified immunity can limit recovery in a civil rights action. *See, e.g., Kalina v. Fletcher*, 522 U.S. 118 (1997) (prosecutor has absolute immunity for preparation and filing of charging documents, but may be liable under § 1983 for service as a complaining witness). But sometimes these lawsuits are successful when constitutional criminal procedures are not followed. *See, e.g., Monroe v. Pape*, 365 U.S. 167 (1961) (civil rights action for unreasonable search and seizure); *Robinson v. Solano County*, 278 F. 3d 1007 (9th Cir. 2002)(officer pointing gun at head of unarmed, unresisting misdemeanor suspect constituted excessive force, actionable under § 1983); *Morgan v. Woessner*, 975 F.2d 629 (9th Cir. 1992) (unlawful airport arrest); *Goodwin v. Metts*, 885 F.2d 157 (4th Cir. 1989) (law enforcement officers' failure to disclose exculpatory evidence to prosecutor; compensatory damages awarded but punitive damages denied). *See generally* Joseph G. Cook & John L. Sobieski, Jr., CIVIL RIGHTS ACTIONS (1999).

[2] Federal and State Remedies

Both federal and state courts offer direct appeals and various remedies. The applicable procedure depends on whether the offender was convicted in a federal or state court.

Federal defendant. A criminal defendant convicted in a federal court will ordinarily pursue a federal direct appeal in the applicable United States Circuit Court of Appeals and seek certiorari in the United States Supreme Court. If unsuccessful, the federal offender can file a § 2255 Motion to Vacate Sentence. 28 U.S.C. § 2255. A federal prisoner must use a § 2255 Motion rather than a habeas corpus petition if the former is available and adequate. *Id.* Both remedies are discussed below.

State defendant. A criminal defendant convicted in a state court will ordinarily take a direct appeal to the state's intermediate appellate court and then, if unsuccessful, to the state's highest court. The defendant can then ask the United States Supreme Court to review the state court's alleged violation of the federal laws applicable to the case.

After state direct appeal has been exhausted, the defendant may try both state and federal collateral procedures. Ordinarily, the state defendant will use the state collateral procedures first, although a state is not constitutionally required to offer state collateral remedies and the offender is not necessarily required to use them. After direct state appeals have been used unsuccessfully (i.e., *exhausted*), the defendant may try federal collateral remedies, especially federal habeas corpus, discussed below.

B. DIRECT APPEAL

Both the criminal defendant and, to some extent, the government may appeal certain judicial decisions in a criminal proceeding. The procedural requirements vary according to who is taking the appeal and at what point in the proceeding the appeal is requested.

In a criminal proceeding, the defendant usually appeals only after a final judgment has been ordered by the court. This occurs after the court imposes sentence. In many jurisdictions, the government may also appeal certain issues, though far fewer than the defendant. Usually the government is authorized to appeal the sentence imposed on the defendant and decisions on some pretrial and post-trial motions. This limited appeal by the government does not conflict with the double jeopardy clause of the Fifth Amendment to the United States Constitution. The double jeopardy clause is discussed in Chapter 16.

Appellate review appears to be quite common in most countries. In England, although the right to appeal is well established, "appeals are rarely admitted by the courts, and convictions are rarely overturned." Harry R. Dammer & Erika S. Fairchild, COMPARATIVE CRIMINAL JUSTICE SYSTEMS 205 (3d ed. 2006). In France, by contrast, criminal cases are appealed to the "Court of Cassation"; this court of last resort, contrary to United States Supreme Court, "does not have the authority to turn down cases." *Id.* at 205.

While double jeopardy principles prohibit American prosecutors from appealing acquittals, such appeals are allowed in both Germany and Saudi Arabia. In the latter country, however, the appellate court is not permitted to overturn the judgment, but can only "return [it] for reconsideration to the lower court." *Id.* at 220.

[1] Limits on Appellate Review

[a] Mootness

As discussed further below with regard to habeas corpus, appellate courts will routinely dismiss a criminal appeal that has become *moot*. Although some decisions hold that this occurs when the defendant has completed service of the sentence, other decisions take a broader view of mootness and permit an appeal even after the sentence is served. In *Sibron v. New York*, 392 U.S. 40 (1968), the Supreme Court recognized that, for federal appellate purposes, a case is not moot in several post-sentence situations. First, it is not moot if it could not be appealed before expiration of the sentence. This rule is especially important for minor offenses where the sanctions are minimal. Second, and more importantly, a case is not moot in federal court if, under either state or federal law, additional penalties or disabilities could still be imposed because of the offense. In *Sibron*, the Court noted that the conviction being appealed could cause the offender to be impeached in a later case or have a sentence increased if he were to recidivate. It is obvious that *Sibron* virtually eliminated the doctrine of mootness in federal criminal appeals since some kind of disability is a possible consequence of virtually every criminal conviction. For example, a criminal conviction always raises the possibility that the accused will be denied a professional license, life or health insurance, a loan, the opportunity to run for certain elective offices, the right to serve on a jury, or the right to vote. *See, e.g., Minnesota v. Dickerson*, 508 U.S. 366 (1993) (case not moot even though charges were dismissed under diversion program; dismissed charges could be used in future to increase sanction for future crime).

Many states have followed the *Sibron* approach, although some require proof that the appellant will suffer a particular disability from the conviction. The matter is more complicated if the offender has a previous conviction that could also cause some disability. Some states require the appellant to prove that the second conviction will have adverse consequences apart from those already caused by the first offense.

[b]   Failure to Raise Issue at Trial and Plain Error

A maxim of appellate practice is that an appellate court will consider an issue only if the issue was first raised at trial. Sometimes this precept is referred to as the *contemporaneous exception rule* and is often justified on the basis of either (1) a waiver or (2) forfeiture of the right to raise the issue on appeal. This widely recognized rule serves the policy of judicial efficiency. If the trial court corrects its own error or properly decides the issue in question, the time-consuming and expensive process of appellate reversal and retrial may be unnecessary. This serves society's interest in the prompt, efficient resolution of legal issues.

As with any rule barring appellate review, this rule has a number of exceptions that vary among the jurisdictions. One common exception is that at least some jurisdictional issues can be raised at any time, including on appeal. The theory is that the proceedings are void if the trial court had no jurisdiction over the case. Another exception is recognized where a procedural hurdle prevents raising an issue at trial. If a person is effectively barred from raising an issue at trial, appellate courts generally will overlook the failure and will hear the appeal.

The plain error rule. Many jurisdictions have a catch-all exception, permitting appellate courts to consider issues that were not raised at trial. Sometimes, the standard is expressed in terms of judicial economy (*i.e.*, would it be more efficient for the appellate court to consider the issue despite the failure to bring it before the trial judge?).

Federal appellate courts and most state courts are allowed to consider *plain errors or defects* affecting substantial rights that were not brought to the trial court's attention. Fed. R. Crim. P. 52(b). Often this is used to allow appeal of an issue that defense counsel negligently failed to raise properly at trial

Some state plain error provisions limit the types of issues that are deemed "plain error," and some states do not recognize the plain error doctrine as a matter of their own law. *See, Wicks v. State*, 606 S.W. 2d 366 (Ark. 1980). While the federal rule is typical in not limiting the issues that can constitute plain error, the Supreme Court has noted that the federal plain error rule should be used sparingly to allow a defendant to pursue an issue on appeal that he or she did not properly raise at or before trial.

FEDERAL RULES OF CRIMINAL PROCEDURE

Rule 52. *Harmless and Plain Error*

. . . .

(b) Plain Error. A plain error that affects substantial rights may be considered even though it was not brought to the court's attention.

NOTES

1. *Error.* Rule 52(b) actually involves three issues. First, there must be an "error." This means that there must have been a deviation from a legal rule, and the right to complain about it was not waived by the failure to object at trial. A "waiver" occurs if the decision to not object was the product of an "intentional relinquishment or abandonment of a known right." *United States v. Olano*, 507 U.S. 725, 733 (1993), *quoting Johnson v. Zerbst*, 304 U.S. 458, 464 (1938). If there was no objection and no waiver, the matter is considered to be a "forfeiture" (rather than a waiver) under Rule 52(b). As explained by the Supreme Court, "[i]f a legal rule was violated . . . and if the defendant did not waive the rule, then there has been an 'error'; . . . despite the absence of a timely objection." *United States v. Olano*, 507 U.S. 725, 734 (1993).

2. *Plain.* The second issue under Rule 52(b) is whether the error was "plain," a word synonymous with the words "clear" or "obvious." *United States v. Olano*, 507 U.S. 725, 734 (1993). This means that the mistake was clear under existing law. Rule 52(b) does not authorize reversal for errors that were based on law that did not exist at the time of the trial but were later applied retroactively.

3. *Affecting substantial rights.* The third issue under Rule 52(b) is the most difficult for the defendant to establish. Rule 52(b) applies only to errors "affecting substantial rights." The Supreme Court has stated that "[n]ormally, although perhaps not in every case, the defendant must make a specific showing of prejudice to satisfy [this prong] of Rule 52(b)." *United States v. Olano*, 507 U.S. 725, 734 (1993). Additionally, the Court noted that in "most" cases the error must have been prejudicial; this means it "must have affected the outcome of the District Court proceedings." *Id.* Even if this prejudice test is satisfied, however, Rule 52(b) still does not require reversal. The express terms of the rule indicate that it is *discretionary* with the appellate court. According to the Supreme Court,

> The Court of Appeals should correct a plain forfeited error affecting substantial rights if the error "seriously affect[s] the fairness, integrity or public reputation of judicial proceedings."

United States v. Olano, 507 U.S. 725, 736 (1993), *quoting United States v. Atkinson*, 297 U.S. 157, 160 (1936). Some appellate decisions have held that the plain error should have been so important that it probably affected the outcome of the trial and a failure to correct it would result in a miscarriage of justice.

4. *Considered in context.* A plain error claim usually is considered in the context of the entire trial in order to assess the importance of the error. Accordingly, plain error cases are resolved on a case-by-case basis. Because of the difficulty of showing prejudice to the defendant, most plain error claims are rejected. *See, e.g., United States v. Cotton*, 535 U.S. 625 (2002)(failure to allege quantity of cocaine in indictment for possession with intent to distribute; held erroneous but non-prejudicial); *United States v. Olano*, 507 U.S. 725 (1993) (alternate jurors attended jury deliberations but did not participate); *United States v. Rena*, 981 F.2d 765 (5th Cir. 1993) (improper cumulative evidence).

5. *Plain error occasionally found.* In unusual cases, appellate courts do find plain error. *See, e.g., United States v. Watson*, 476 F. 3d 1020 (D.C. Cir. 2007) (court's miscalculation of applicable federal sentencing guideline range held plain error which affected defendant's substantial rights); *United States v. Carter*, 481 F.3d 601 (8th Cir. 2007)(plain error found where district court failed to impose a mandatory minimum sentence; error found to seriously affect substantial rights and the fairness, integrity, and public reputation of judicial proceedings, noting that "fairness concerns run both ways" and that prosecution, as well as defense, may invoke plain error rule on sentence appeal), *but see Green v. United States* 2008 WL 2484861 (U.S. Sup. Ct.) (absent government appeal or cross-appeal of sentence, appellate court may not, on its own initiative, order increase in sentence based on plain error rule);*United States v. Hernandez*, 125 F.3d 859 (9th Cir. 1997) (prosecutor's comment on defendant's post-*Miranda* silence held plain error, but conviction still affirmed because evidence was sufficient to convict); *United States v. Mann*, 557 F.2d 1211 (5th Cir. 1977) (unduly suggestive pretrial identification).

The decision of the Ninth Circuit in *Hernandez* is an apt illustration of the principle that reversal for plain error is not automatic, but rather is a matter committed to the court's discretion. The court there found all three required elements of the doctrine to be present, but denied relief in reliance on *Olano* because in its view, the error was not one that "seriously affected the fairness, integrity, or public reputation" of the proceedings in that case. Stated differently, "[only] if all three conditions are met, an appellate court may then exercise its discretion to notice a forfeited error." *Johnson v. United States*, 520 U.S. 461, 467 (1997)(internal quotations and citations omitted).

[c]   Harmless Error and Automatic Reversal

If trials were required to be legally "perfect" in all respects, virtually every conviction would be reversed on appeal, resulting in the possibility of never-ending litigation and a paralyzed legal system. To prevent this absurd situation, every jurisdiction has adopted a *harmless error rule*, which means that trial errors will ordinarily not merit appellate reversal unless the error was somehow significant. As one would expect, the distinction between harmless errors and those sufficiently harmful to cause a reversal has produced varying standards and a vast amount of judicial and academic verbiage. Some errors are deemed so egregious that they will cause an *automatic reversal* without consideration of the actual impact on the proceedings, as discussed below.

The general rule followed in every jurisdiction is that a trial error that is "harmless" will not lead to appellate reversal. In the federal system, this is expressed in the Federal Rules of Criminal Procedure:

FEDERAL RULES OF CRIMINAL PROCEDURE

Rule 52. *Harmless Error and Plain Error.*

(a) Any error, defect, irregularity, or variance that does not affect substantial rights must be disregarded.

NOTES

The obvious issue is ascertaining whether a particular error satisfies this standard. The answer may depend upon whether the error was constitutional or not. Additionally, appellate courts typically will closely evaluate the entire case to assess the impact of the error. The harmless error rule applies to federal appeals and federal habeas corpus actions. *See Brecht v. Abrahamson*, 507 U.S. 619 (1993).

Nonconstitutional error. If the trial error at issue is one that does not involve a constitutional violation, the general standard of harmless error is expressed in many ways. One formulation is whether the error had a significant tendency to promote a guilty verdict. Another version is whether the error likely produced a guilty verdict.

There are thousands of decisions where nonconstitutional errors have been deemed harmless. *See, e.g., United States v. Pridgen*, 518 F.3d 87 (1st Cir. 2008)(for non-constitutional error, test is whether it is highly probable the error did not affect the verdict; harmless error found when trial court may have erroneously excluded extrinsic evidence of a government witness's prior inconsistent statement).

Constitutional error: In general. The rules change when the error is of constitutional dimension. In the leading case, *Chapman v. California*, 386 U.S. 18 (1967), the prosecutor violated the defendants' Fifth Amendment rights by commenting on their failure to testify at their joint trial for homicide. The petitioners argued that since the prosecutor deprived them of a constitutional right, the Supreme Court should reverse automatically and not apply harmless error analysis. The Court in *Chapman* agreed that there are some constitutional errors that merit automatic reversal, but also held that:

> there may be some constitutional errors which in the setting of a particular case are so unimportant and insignificant that they can, consistent with the Federal Constitution, be deemed harmless, not requiring the automatic reversal of the conviction. [*Id.* at 22]

Trial v. structural errors. The question is, which constitutional violations are analyzed by harmless error standards and which result in automatic reversal without consideration of their impact? In *Arizona v. Fulminante*, 499 U.S. 279 (1991), the Court distinguished the two categories of errors by using a trial process-structure dichotomy. Constitutional violations merit harmless error analysis if they are "trial errors." This refers to an:

> error which occurred during the presentation of the case to the jury, and which may therefore be quantitatively assessed in the context of other evidence presented in order to determine whether its admission was harmless beyond a reasonable doubt. In applying harmless-error analysis to these many different constitutional violations, the Court has been faithful to the belief that the harmless-error doctrine is essential to preserve the "principle that the central purpose of the criminal trial is to decide the factual question of the defendant's guilt or innocence, and promotes public respect for the criminal process by focusing on the underlying fairness of the trial rather than on the virtually inevitable presence of immaterial error." [*Id.* at 307–308, *quoting Delaware v. Van Arsdall*, 475 U.S. 673, 681 (1986)]

Grave doubt of effect. In *O'Neal v. McAnich*, 513 U.S. 432 (1995), the United States Supreme Court further refined the harmless error standard in federal habeas corpus cases. In such cases, if the federal judge at the habeas proceeding is in "grave doubt" about whether a trial error of federal constitutional law had substantial and injurious effect or influence in determining the jury's verdict, the error is not harmless. This means that the risk of doubt is on the state, not the defendant. The Court rejected imposing a burden of proof on either party or using a presumption to resolve the issue.

Automatic reversal rule. The automatic reversal rule, on the other hand, is applied to errors that involve "structural defects in the constitution of the trial mechanism." *Arizona v. Fulminante*, 499 U.S. at 309. Such structural defects affect the framework within which the trial proceeds as opposed to an error in the trial process itself. These structural errors violate a basic protection and defy measurement of their affect on a particular trial process. The Supreme Court has held that there is a strong presumption that constitutional errors are subject to the harmless error analysis. Which violations are in which category?

Constitutional error: harmless error analysis applied. Decisions after *Chapman v. California* have found that most constitutional violations are subject to harmless error analysis. *Arizona v. Fulminante*, 499 U.S. 279, 306–307 (1991), lists seventeen examples of constitutional errors analyzed under the harmless error approach. Many involve errors in jury instructions, including overbroad jury instructions at a capital sentencing proceeding, an erroneous charge regarding a conclusive or rebuttable presumption, a misstatement of an element of the crime, and the failure to instruct on the presumption of innocence.

Other decisions cited in *Fulminante* deal with the erroneous admission or exclusion of evidence. Examples include the admission of evidence secured in violation of the Sixth Amendment right to counsel or the Fourth Amendment right to be free from an unreasonable search and seizure, and the exclusion of the defendant's testimony concerning the circumstances of a confession.

Harmless error analysis has also been applied to errors in unduly restricting cross-examination on the issue of bias, improperly commenting on the defendant's silence, and the denial of counsel at a preliminary hearing.

Harmless beyond a reasonable doubt. If the harmless error rule applies, what degree of harm must be shown before a conviction will be reversed? *Chapman v. California*, 386 U.S. 18 (1967), held that "before a federal constitutional error can be held harmless, the court must be able to declare a belief that it was harmless beyond a reasonable doubt." *Id.* at 24. Since the government benefitted from the alleged error, according to

Chapman the government has the burden of proving "beyond a reasonable doubt that the error complained of did not contribute to the verdict obtained." *Id.*

In assessing whether this test is satisfied, the reviewing court will look at the entire record *de novo*. If the appellate court cannot assess whether the error affected the trial, it is possible the error may be analyzed under the automatic-reversal standard rather than the harmless error rule. *See Sullivan v. Louisiana*, 508 U.S. 275 (1993). When the *Chapman* Court applied the harmless error test, it held that the prosecutor's improper comments about the defendant's silence at trial were not harmless beyond a reasonable doubt and reversed the conviction.

Constitutional error: no harmless error analysis — automatic reversal. Chapman v. California and later decisions have recognized that some constitutional violations are so egregious that they will always invalidate a criminal conviction, irrespective of proof of harm. As noted above, this category involves constitutional errors that relate to the structural integrity of the trial mechanism.

Arizona v. Fulminante, 499 U.S. 299 (1991), listed a number of decisions holding that the constitutional errors were so fundamental that they were not subject to the harmless error approach. These include: the total deprivation of the right to trial counsel, the right to self-representation, and the right to a public trial, a biased judge, and the exclusion of members of the defendant's race from the grand jury. *See also Sullivan v. Louisiana*, 508 U.S. 275 (1993) (error in instructing jury on reasonable doubt causes automatic reversal without proof of harm).

Interestingly, *Fulminante* itself involved a 5-4 split, with the majority holding that harmless error analysis applies to the use of a coerced confession because it is a "trial process" rather than a "structural" error. Do you agree? If the use of a coerced confession is a "trial process" error subject to harmless error analysis, why is the exclusion of members of a person's race from the grand jury a structural error? Can't the grand jury error be "cured" by a subsequent fair trial using a properly selected trial jury where the accused is convicted by proof beyond a reasonable doubt?

[2] Appellate Structure

Article III of the Constitution allows for the creation of inferior courts, "as Congress may from time to time ordain and establish." U.S. Const. art. III. Congress, as we know, created in the federal system numerous trial courts as well as intermediate appellate courts to harmonize with the already-established Supreme Court. Most state systems have copied the federal model and provide intermediate courts between the lowest court and the Supreme Court. Generally, an intermediate court hears the first appeal in a criminal case.

In the relatively few states that do not have an intermediate appellate court, the first appeal goes directly to the state's highest court. In other states, some cases, such as death penalty cases, are appealed directly to the highest court, bypassing the intermediate appellate court. *E.g.*, N.Y. Crim. Proc. Law § 450.70; Idaho Code § 19-2827; Nev. Stat. 177.055. Finally, some states' intermediate appellate courts have limited subject matter jurisdiction (*e.g.*, civil cases are assigned to one appellate court and criminal cases to another). In most instances, decisions of each specialized appellate court may be appealed to the state's highest court.

[3] Types of Appeals by Criminal Defendant

[a] Appeals "As of Right"

Most appeals in criminal cases occur when a defendant appeals a conviction or sentence. Although the United States Supreme Court has long held that the constitution does not require a state to grant a criminal defendant an appeal, *Evitts v. Lucey*, 469 U.S. 387, 393 (1985), American jurisdictions routinely accord the defendant at least one "appeal as of right." Typically, the defendant must be informed of the right to appeal. *See, e.g.*, Fed. R. Crim. P. 32(j)(1). *See also* Fed. R. Crim. P. 58(c)(4) (appeals from misdemeanor convictions).

To some extent the concept of an "appeal as of right" is misleading, for not all convicted defendants who appeal actually receive full appellate consideration. In many jurisdictions an appellate court has the right to give a particular case less than full scrutiny via procedures such as summary affirmance with either only a brief opinion or no opinion at all, or deciding an appeal on the briefs only, without hearing oral argument. The decision whether to grant full or truncated appellate review is generally based on whether the defendant has raised a substantial legal issue or, in some limited cases, a substantial factual issue that must be resolved by the appellate court. For example, an appellate court may give limited scrutiny to issues related to the sufficiency of evidence.

This right of appeal ordinarily does not extend in the same way to defendants who plead guilty or *nolo contendere* unless the jurisdiction has a conditional plea procedure. See Chapter 11 for a detailed discussion of conditional pleas. Also, the defendant who pleads guilty may, in some situations, be permitted to appeal the sentence imposed following the plea.

[i]   The Decision Whether to Appeal

Although all convicted defendants have the right to file the notice of appeal once the conviction is final, many do not exercise that right because of the many factors that must be considered. The judge should inform the defendant of the right to appeal. Fed. R. Crim. P. 32(j)(1)(A),(B) (appeal conviction and sentence). Failure to provide this information is reversible error only if the defendant suffered prejudice. *Deguero v. United States*, 526 U.S. 23 (1999).

The defendant's attorney has an ethical obligation to explain all of these factors to the defendant to facilitate an informed decision of whether to appeal. The ultimate decision whether to appeal is made by the client. *See generally* American Bar Association, Standards for Criminal Justice § 4-8.2 (3d ed. 1993).

One reason for foregoing an appeal, of course, is that the defendant is not dissatisfied with the result or has no real grounds to appeal. As discussed below, the defense attorney may consider the appeal "frivolous" and refuse to file it. Further, the defendant's appeal may be unsuccessful if it is based on an error that is "harmless," *i.e.*, the error had no substantial affect on the outcome of the trial. Finally, the error alleged must have been preserved in the trial record or the error must be a "plain error."

Other factors that the defendant considering an appeal should explore are the wisdom of engaging a new attorney to handle the appeal, the costs of the appeal, and, most importantly, the possible adverse consequences of a *successful* appeal.

[ii]   *North Carolina v. Pearce:* Harsher Sentence After Successful Appeal

An important factor in assessing whether to appeal is the possible result if the appeal is successful. Could the accused actually be in *a worse* condition after winning the appeal? In *North Carolina v. Pearce*, 395 U.S. 711 (1969), the United States Supreme Court held that in some circumstances the defendant could actually receive a harsher sentence on retrial following a successful appeal or habeas corpus petition. *Pearce* involved several state defendants who were convicted of a crime and sentenced to prison. After their convictions were overturned on appeal, each was retried, convicted, and given a sentence that was harsher than that imposed in the first trial. Each defendant in *Pearce* filed a federal habeas corpus action alleging that the double jeopardy, equal protection, and due process guarantees bar the imposition of a more severe punishment after the retrial of a conviction that has been reversed.

The Supreme Court started its analysis by rejecting both the double jeopardy and equal protection claims. The Court noted that the double jeopardy clause places no limit on the length of sentence following a retrial. After the first conviction is reversed by a higher court, the slate is "wiped clean" for purposes of double jeopardy and any lawful sentence may be imposed on retrial. The Court in *Pearce* also stated that equal protection is not violated if the accused receives a harsher sentence on retrial. At the second trial, the offender could receive no sentence, a shorter sentence, the same sentence, or a longer sentence than imposed at the first trial. Because of these possibilities, the state has not established an invalid classification scheme for those who seek new trials.

Although the *Pearce* Court rejected the double jeopardy and equal protection arguments, it found part of the due process claim compelling. The Court held that the due process clause prohibits the state from imposing a heavier sentence on retrial for the purpose of punishing those who use the courts to overturn a conviction. The harsher sanction creates a presumption of vindictiveness that the sentencing judge must overcome. According to *Pearce*:

> Due process of law, then, requires that vindictiveness against a defendant for having successfully attacked his first conviction must play no part in the sentence he receives after a new trial. And since the fear of such vindictiveness may unconstitutionally deter a defendant's exercise of the right to appeal or collaterally attack his first conviction, due process also requires that a defendant be freed of apprehension of such a retaliatory motivation on the part of the sentencing judge.

> In order to assure the absence of such a motivation, we have concluded that whenever a judge imposes a more severe sentence upon a defendant after a new trial, the reasons for his doing so must affirmatively appear. Those reasons must be based upon objective information concerning identifiable conduct on the part of the defendant occurring after the time of the original sentencing proceeding. And the factual data upon which the increased sentence is based must be made part of the record, so that the constitutional legitimacy of the increased sentence may be fully reviewed on appeal. [*Id.* at 725–26]

NOTES

1. *Retroactivity. North Carolina v. Pearce* announced both substantive and procedure rules. The substantive rule is that due process bars actual judicial vindictiveness that results in a harsher sentence on retrial. The procedural rule establishes a rebuttable presumption that a harsher sentence is due to vindictiveness and must be justified on the basis of post-trial conduct. A subsequent Supreme Court decision held that the procedural rule is not retroactive. *Michigan v. Payne*, 412 U.S. 47 (1973). This rule was characterized as "prophylactic," designed to protect against possible vindictiveness. But *Pearce's* substantive rule banning retaliatory motivation in sentencing was considered a part of basic due process, not just a prophylactic rule, and was made retroactive. *Id.* at 55.

2. *Exceptions to Pearce: Proof of vindictiveness.* The *Pearce* decision's concern with the possibility of vindictiveness has led subsequent Supreme Court decisions to create several exceptions where this possibility is either eliminated or minimized. According to the Supreme Court, *Pearce* applies only when there is a reasonable likelihood "that the increase in sentence is the product of actual vindictiveness on the part of the sentencing authority. Where there is no such reasonable likelihood, the burden remains upon the defendant to prove actual vindictiveness." *Alabama v. Smith*, 490 U.S. 794, 799 (1989). This means that the defendant can still bar the harsher sentence by proving this particular sentencing authority was actually motivated by vindictiveness in imposing the harsher sentence.

3. *Harsher sentence imposed by jury.* Another exception to *Pearce* is when the sentence in the second trial is imposed by a jury rather than a judge. The issue appears infrequently today because the jury imposes sentences in very few American jurisdictions. In *Chaffin v. Stynchcombe*, 412 U.S. 17 (1973), a jury convicted the defendant of robbery and sentenced him to fifteen years in prison. After his conviction was overturned because of an erroneous jury instruction, a second jury convicted him again and imposed a life sentence. The Supreme Court rejected the argument that the greater sentence was barred by *North Carolina v. Pearce*. The Court reasoned that *Pearce* did not apply because there is only a *de minimis* potential that the second jury's sentence was motivated by the vindictiveness barred by *Pearce*. The second jury was not informed about the first jury's sentence, although it may have known about the prior trial. Moreover, according to *Stynchcombe*, the second sentence was imposed by a different jury that had no motive to be vindictive. Unlike a judge, a jury will probably have no interest in discouraging appeals.

4. *First sentence imposed by jury, second by judge.* A third exception to *Pearce* was noted in a factually unique case when the first sentence was imposed by a jury and the harsher second sanction was exacted by a judge. In *Texas v. McCullough*, 475 U.S. 134 (1986), the defendant was convicted by a jury that sentenced him to twenty years in prison. After the trial judge granted the defendant's motion for a new trial, the defendant was convicted again by a jury but asked that the judge conduct the resentencing. The trial judge then sentenced the defendant to fifty years in prison. Based on these highly unusual facts, the Supreme Court held that *Pearce* did not bar a harsher sentence following the retrial.

First, the Court in *McCullough* found nothing in the record to suggest that this particular judge had a vindictive motive. The trial judge herself reversed the first conviction because of prosecutorial misconduct rather than judicial error. The Court refused to hold that this alone created the possibility that the trial judge would punish the defendant for bothering her with a second proceeding. Moreover, the defendant had asked the judge rather than the jury to impose the second sentence. This indicated that even the defense thought the judge capable of a fair decision. The mere fact that the defendant's desire to move for a new trial could be chilled by the possibility of a harsher sentence was rejected as an inadequate ground under *Pearce* to bar a greater sentence on retrial. Finally, even if *Pearce* applied, the Supreme Court in *McCullough* held that the trial court complied with *Pearce* in justifying the harsher sentence on new evidence about the crime that was not presented at the first trial. It should be noted that the new evidence was known to the authorities (though not the judge) at the first trial; it was not based on the defendant's conduct occurring after the trial. This is a subtle change from the *Pearce* Court's focus on the defendant's conduct *since* the first sentencing hearing.

5. *Harsher sentence after vacated guilty plea.* A related exception involves a harsher sentence imposed after a defendant pleads guilty, has the plea vacated, and is sentenced again after a trial. In *Alabama v. Smith*, 490 U.S. 794 (1989), the Supreme Court held that there is no presumption of vindictiveness when the first sentence followed a guilty plea but the second sentence occurred after a trial. The increased sanction is not likely to be the product of vindictiveness. Rather, the new sentence probably will be based on far more information (including the defendant's conduct during trial) than that available in the guilty plea proceeding. Also, the plea-based sentence may have been more lenient because of the defendant's willingness to accept responsibility for the crime.

6. *Different judges.* Some other courts have combined the Supreme Court decisions after *Pearce* to arrive at another exception: *Pearce* does not apply when separate sentences are imposed by different bodies or judges because the chance of vindictiveness is minimal. *See, e.g., United States v. Lippert*, 740 F.2d 457 (6th Cir. 1984). Do you agree with the assumption that the chance of vindictiveness is remote when different judges impose the two sentences?

7. *Is second sentence harsher?* One obvious difficulty with implementing *Pearce* is determining whether the second sentence is actually harsher than the first. The problem occurs when the two sentences are not expressed in the same "currency." For example, a three-year prison sentence is obviously harsher than a two-year prison sentence. But what about a three-year prison sentence versus a two-year jail term followed by five years on probation. The former sentence expires in three years while the latter will take seven years to complete. On the other hand, the former includes three years of incarceration while the latter demands only two. Which is harsher?

The problem is illustrated by *Gauntlett v. Kelley*, 658 F.Supp. 1483 (W.D. Mich. 1987), *aff'd*, 849 F.2d 213 (6th Cir. 1988), in which the defendant was convicted of several counts of child sex abuse. His first sentence was to five years probation with the conditions that the defendant must spend the first year in jail and submit to "chemical castration" for five years. After this sentence was overturned on appeal, the defendant was sentenced to a 5–15 year prison term. Assessing whether *Pearce* was violated because the second sentence was harsher than the first, the district judge candidly admitted that he did not know how to determine whether chemical castration was harsher than a substantial prison term. Since he could not conclude that it was harsher, he refused to find *Pearce v. North Carolina* applicable. Do you agree?

Comparing concurrent and consecutive sentences can also present difficulties in determining degrees of harshness. The Illinois Court of Appeals addressed this issue in *Illinois v. Walker*, 663 N.E.2d 148 (Ill. App. 1995). The defendant had initially been *consecutively* sentenced to 100 to 150 years for rape, 100 to 150 years for armed robbery and 19 to 20 years for attempted murder. After an appeal, the defendant received *concurrent* sentences of 100 to 300 years for each conviction. Illinois prohibited judges from imposing greater sentences on resentencing. The defendant argued and the court agreed that the increase in the defendant's sentences for his individual convictions was a violation of Illinois law, notwithstanding the fact that the total number of years he must actually serve did not increase.

8. *Prosecution's increase in charges at second trial. North Carolina v. Pearce* applies when a judge imposes a harsher sentence on retrial. Does it also apply to a *prosecutor* who, following a successful appeal, increases the charges that the appellant must face at the second trial? In *Blackledge v. Perry*, 417 U.S. 21 (1974), the defendant was charged with a misdemeanor assault stemming from a prison fight. After being convicted and receiving a six month sentence, he appealed the decision by requesting a trial *de novo* in accordance with state law. Prior to the new trial, the prosecutor obtained an indictment charging felony assault for the same fight that was the basis for the earlier misdemeanor conviction. He pled guilty to the new charge and was sentenced to five to seven years in prison. Citing *North Carolina v. Pearce*, the Supreme Court in *Blackledge* held that due process entitles an accused to pursue a statutorily-guaranteed right to a trial *de novo* without fear that the prosecution will retaliate by increasing the seriousness of the defendant's exposure at the second proceeding. This means that the *Pearce* presumption applies and the prosecution must explain a decision to increase the charges for defendants pursuing an appeal. *See also United States v. Goodwin*, 457 U.S. 368 (1982). Prosecutorial vindictiveness, including discussion of both *Blackledge* and *Goodwin*, is covered in Chapter 2.

PROBLEM 18-1. WHEN IT RAINS, IT POURS

Fran is convicted of unarmed robbery. At the sentencing hearing, the government informed Judge Phillips that Fran had a charge of marijuana possession pending in another state. Since the marijuana charge had not been tried, Judge Phillips did not consider it and imposed a three-year sentence, with all but six months suspended. This means that Fran would serve six months in jail and then two-and-a-half years on probation.

Fran appealed the robbery case on a procedural issue and the conviction was overturned. She was convicted again on retrial in Judge Phillips'court. Between the first and second trials, Fran pleaded *nolo contendere* to the marijuana charge and was given a three-month jail term. After the second unarmed robbery conviction, Judge Phillips sentenced her to a five-year prison term. He noted for the record that the sentence was, in part, based on the recent marijuana conviction.

1. Does the five-year sentence violate *North Carolina v. Pearce? See Wasman v. United States*, 468 U.S. 559 (1984).

2. Changing the facts, what if Fran had been convicted of the marijuana charge before the first trial, but the prosecution did not discover the conviction until shortly before the second trial? Can it be used to justify a harsher sentence on retrial?

3. Changing the facts again, assume that the marijuana charges were still pending when the second sentence was imposed. Assume further that Judge Phillips ignored the pending charges in the first trial, but Judge Stein (who conducted the second trial) took them in consideration in imposing the five year sentence. While Judge Phillips had an informal policy of ignoring pending charges, Judge Stein considered them as some evidence of the defendant's rehabilitative potential. (Assume also that state law permitted both approaches.) Is *Pearce* violated?

[iii] Appellate Procedure

Trial motions. The defendant may file several post-trial motions before filing a notice of appeal. These include a Motion for a New Trial based on such grounds as new evidence or faulty jury instructions, a Motion for a Judgment of Acquittal, and a Motion for Arrest of Judgment. *See, e.g.*, Fed. R. Crim. P. 33 (motion for new trial), 34 (motion for arrest of judgment). These motions are discussed more fully in Chapters 9 and 15.

Notice of appeal. The usual formality for appealing a criminal case is to file a notice of appeal with the trial court. *See, e.g.*, Fed. R. App. P. 3(a). In the federal system, the defendant must file the notice of appeal with the clerk of the district court, who then transmits a copy to the appropriate Court of Appeals. Fed. R. App. P. 3(d). The court clerk also serves a copy of the notice of appeal on the defendant (defense counsel may have prepared it) and on the lawyer for each party other than the appellant.

In order to facilitate both finality and orderly procedures, court rules routinely establish a time-limit for filing a notice of appeal. In general, a notice of appeal in a federal case must be filed by a criminal defendant within ten days after the entry of the judgment or order being appealed. Fed. R. App. P. 4(b). A federal defendant who exceeds the timely notice requirement may file a motion stating why the filing is late. The late defendant must show "excusable neglect" to justify the tardy filing, but the federal court will not allow an extension to reach beyond 30 days.

Some states allow the notice of appeal to be filed up to 20 and 30 days after judgment has been rendered. *E.g.*, N.Y. Crim. Proc. Law § 460.10 (McKinney 1994); Ariz. R. Crim. P. 31.3 (20 days).

Some states do not require the defendant to file a notice of appeal in certain cases. In some jurisdictions, for example, if the defendant is sentenced to death, the clerk will automatically file the necessary notice with the court of appeals. *E.g.*, Ariz. R. Crim. P. 31.2(b).

The exact information required to be included in the notice of appeal varies in every jurisdiction. Under federal procedure, the notice must designate the parties taking the appeal, the judgment appealed from, and the court to which the appeal is taken. Fed. R. App. P. 3(c).

Briefs. After the notice of appeal is served, the appellant must file a brief. *See, e.g.*, Fed. R. App. P. 28–32. The appellee may then file a reply brief. After the briefs are filed with the court, often both the appellant and the appellee are permitted to give oral arguments supporting their propositions. In an increasing number of cases, however, oral arguments are waived by the parties or not permitted by the court. *See* Fed. R. App. P. 34.

Once the court hears oral argument, it will enter an order disposing of the appeal. In some cases, there is a significant lapse of time between argument and final decision. See Chapter 13 for discussion of the right to speedy trial as applied to the appellate process. A federal defendant who loses the appeal may ask the United States Supreme Court to review the case or may file a petition for rehearing in the same appellate court not more than 14 days after final disposition. Fed. R. App. P. 40. If the petition for rehearing is denied, or if it is successful but relief is still not granted, the defendant may seek permission for review from the highest court.

Indigent defendants. Trial and appellate courts are required to make special arrangements to ensure that indigent defendants are not denied access to appellate processes because of their indigency. The right to appointed counsel is discussed below. *See, e.g., Griffin v. Illinois*, 351 U.S. 12 (1956) (state must provide free transcript to indigent defendant if free transcript is only way to assure defendant has adequate and effective appeal); *Burns v. Ohio*, 360 U.S. 252 (1959) (overturning rule that indigent defendants had to pay filing fee as prerequisite to filing notice of appeal); *Draper v. Washington*, 372 U.S. 487 (1963) (invalidating state rule that free transcript is available to indigent defendant only if trial judge stated that appeal was not frivolous).

[iv] Misdemeanor Appeals

Defendants convicted of a misdemeanor may also appeal, although few actually do. The procedure is generally the same as with felony convictions. *See, e.g.*, Fed. R. Crim. P. 58(g)(2)(b). However, some jurisdictions require that the misdemeanor appeal first go to a higher level trial court where the case may be tried *de novo* or, rarely, considered as an appeal. If relief is denied at this level, the defendant may appeal through the normal state appellate processes.

[v] Conditional Pleas

A conditional plea, discussed in Chapter 11, occurs when a criminal defendant pleads guilty while preserving for appeal issues raised at pretrial proceedings. Fed. R. Crim. P. 11(a)(2). Since the guilty plea serves as a final judgment, the defendant may then proceed with an appeal. The conditional plea is used frequently when a defendant desires to pursue appellate review of a denial of a motion to suppress important prosecution evidence.

[vi] Right to Counsel and Ethical Issues

Right to counsel. Since 1963, the Supreme Court has held that an indigent criminal accused has an equal protection right to appointed counsel at a first direct appeal as of right. However, the accused does not have a constitutional right to represent himself or herself at this appeal. *Martinez v. Court of Appeal of California*, 528 U.S. 152 (2000).

An appeal as of right, like every other facet of criminal practice, raises important ethical issues for lawyers. *Douglas v. California*, 372 U.S. 353 (1963).

Standard of counsel's performance. In *Evitts v. Lucey*, 469 U.S. 387 (1985), the Court embellished the right to counsel guarantee by holding that the due process clause mandates that counsel on direct appeal satisfy the Sixth Amendment's standard of rendering *effective* assistance of counsel. In *Evitts*, the defendant was convicted of a drug offense and authorized his retained counsel to appeal. The appeal was dismissed when the retained lawyer failed to file certain required documents with the Kentucky Court of Appeals. After state courts refused to permit the appeal, the defendant filed a federal habeas corpus petition alleging that he had been denied the effective assistance of counsel guaranteed by the Fourteenth Amendment.

The United States Supreme Court in *Evitts* granted relief and agreed that the due process guarantee provides that a criminal accused is entitled to the "effective assistance of counsel" on the first direct appeal in a criminal case. The Court noted that a defendant who has ineffective representation on appeal is no better than one with no counsel at all. Chief Justice Burger filed a spirited dissent, arguing that the *Evitts* majority simply added another barrier to finality without offering a real contribution to fairer justice. Similarly, Justice Rehnquist's dissent raised the fear that *Evitts* would simply provide convicted criminals with another possible ground for habeas corpus relief: that counsel on appeal was inadequate. He also criticized the majority for making it virtually impossible for states to enforce their own appellate procedural rules. He observed that when defense counsel fails to follow state rules pertaining to appellate procedure, federal courts will excuse the error and authorize the appeal.

NOTES

1. *Standard of effectiveness of appellate counsel. Evitts* held that the accused on the first direct appeal is entitled to the effective assistance of counsel but did not specify how to assess whether this standard is satisfied. It is clear, however, that the total failure to appoint counsel for this appeal is reversible error. *Cf. Penson v. Ohio*, 488 U.S. 75, 88 (1988). Similarly, "nominal" counsel is inadequate.

According to *Evitts*, appellate counsel is necessary to ensure meaningful appellate review. This means that appellate counsel must assist in preparing and submitting a brief to the appellate court. 469 U.S. at 394. But it does not mean that appellate counsel must advance every argument suggested by the defendant or even every arguable issue. *See also Jones v. Barnes*, 463 U.S. 745 (1983) (appellate counsel for indigent appellee need not raise every nonfrivolous issue that client wants raised; attorney must make professional evaluation of issues to raise; sometimes it is better to raise only solid issues and not include weaker ones).

In general terms, as discussed in Chapters 9 and 11, the Sixth Amendment's test for ineffective assistance of counsel was announced in *Strickland v. Washington*, 466 U.S. 668 (1984): the accused has a right to reasonably effective legal assistance. The defendant alleging ineffective assistance of counsel must show that counsel's representation fell below an objective standard of reasonableness, and the deficient representation prejudiced the defendant.

Cases after *Evitts* have been quite inconsistent in establishing the minimal standard for appellate counsel. Counsel is not usually expected to anticipate the course of future Supreme Court or other appellate caselaw, and the failure to raise issues on appeal which became palpable only after a later change in caselaw has been held not to constitute ineffective assistance. *See, e.g., Horne v. Trickey*, 895 F.2d 497 (8th Cir. 1990); *United States v. Barth*, 488 F.Supp.2d 874 (D.N.D. 2007)(not ineffective assistance where counsel failed to anticipate and raise an objection to sentence enhancement based on *Blakely v. Washington* [see Chapter 17] prior to that decision — sometimes referred to as the "clairvoyance" principle); *Spence v. Nix*, 945 F.2d 1030 (8th Cir. 1991), *cert. denied*, 502 U.S. 1105 (1992) (appellate counsel failed to file required motion, causing dismissal of state appeal on issue of voluntariness of guilty plea; no reversal because though counsel was deficient, there was no prejudice since even absent counsel's error, appeal challenging guilty plea would not have succeeded on the merits); *Lombard v. Lynaugh*, 868 F.2d 1475 (5th Cir. 1989) (appellate counsel's brief, which asserted that no arguable grounds for appeal exist but which failed to raise nonfrivolous appellate issues, held ineffective assistance of counsel on appeal)(see discussion, below, of *Anders* briefs).

2. *Prejudice.* A key issue after *Evitts* is whether appellate counsel's poor performance can cause an order for a new appeal without proof that somehow the inadequate legal work caused prejudice. The problem is best exemplified if appellate counsel somehow failed to perfect the appeal, perhaps by missing a deadline or failing to file necessary forms. If the accused must prove prejudice by the lack of an appeal, relief may turn on whether the appeal, if properly perfected, would have been successful.

Denial of counsel. The United States Supreme Court has held that the total denial of counsel on the first direct appeal is legally presumed to be prejudicial. This "casts such doubt on the fairness of the trial process, that it can never be considered harmless error." *Penson v. Ohio*, 488 U.S. 75, 88 (1988) (appellate counsel filed a timely notice of appeal but then filed a Certification of Meritless Appeal and participated no further in the appeal).

Failure to file notice of appeal. What happens if trial counsel does not file a notice of appeal, thereby foreclosing at least some appellate remedies? In *Roe v. Flores-Ortega*, 528 U.S. 470 (2000), trial counsel did not file a notice of appeal. In a subsequent habeas corpus action alleging ineffective assistance of counsel for this error, the Supreme Court held that there were three separate situations to assess under *Strickland* whether counsel was ineffective when there was a failure to file a notice of appeal. First, if the defendant specifically instructed defense counsel to file a notice of appeal, counsel's failure to do so is professionally unreasonable, satisfying the first prong of *Strickland*. The "prejudice" or second prong of *Strickland* is satisfied in such cases because the defendant was harmed since he or she would have taken an appeal had defense counsel performed as instructed.

Second, where the defendant explicitly tells defense counsel not to file an appeal, the defendant cannot later allege that counsel's performance was deficient. Third, where the defendant does not instruct defense counsel to file or not to file an appeal, the issue turns of whether counsel discussed the issue with the defendant. *Roe* held that defense counsel has a constitutional and reasonable professional duty to consult with the defendant about an appeal when there is reason to think either that a rational defendant would want to appeal or that this particular defendant reasonably demonstrated to counsel that he or she was interested in appealing. If counsel violates this standard of reasonable professional performance, *Roe* permits a finding of ineffective assistance of counsel if there is a reasonable probability that, but for counsel's deficient performance, the defendant would have timely appealed. The *Roe* Court specifically held that the likely success of the appeal was not a factor in assessing prejudice.

Other deficiencies. Courts are divided on whether lesser inadequacies by defense counsel require proof of prejudice before a habeas petition will be granted. *Compare, Lombard v. Lynaugh*, 868 F.2d 1475 (5th Cir. 1989) (appellate counsel filed a two-page appellate brief which said that the defendant's conviction was valid and the appeal was without merit; no grounds to appeal were alleged; prejudice must be shown if appellate counsel simply failed to raise, brief, or argue specific issues on appeal, but no prejudice need be proven if there was actual or constructive (counsel was worthless) complete denial of appellate counsel's assistance) with *Kimball v. State*, 490 A.2d 653 (Me. 1985) (must show that result of appeal would have been different but for counsel's lack of diligence).

If prejudice must be shown, how would a new lawyer convince a court that the result would have changed had a prior lawyer acted differently? If new counsel can convince a habeas court that appellate counsel's work was inadequate and prejudicial, what is the remedy? Should it be reversal of the conviction and a new trial, or simply a new appeal?

[vii] Appealing Meritless Issues: The *Anders* Brief

Criminal appeals raise considerable ethical problems for even the most conscientious lawyer. A major problem area is the conflict in views between the lawyer and the now-convicted client. The client may want to appeal every possible issue or particular issues. Appellate counsel, on the other hand, may study the trial record and conclude that only some issues have merit or that no issue has merit. Recall that a lawyer cannot file a "frivolous" appeal. According to the United States Supreme Court:

> Neither paid nor appointed counsel may deliberately mislead the court with respect to either the facts or the law, or consume the time and the energies of the court or the opposing party by advancing frivolous arguments. An attorney, whether appointed or paid, is therefore under an ethical obligation to refuse to prosecute a frivolous appeal.

McCoy v. Court of Appeals, 486 U.S. 429, 436 (1988). *See also Ellis v. United States*, 356 U.S. 674 (1958) (appointed counsel convinced that appeal is frivolous may ask to withdraw; appellate court can then dismiss appeal if it believes counsel was diligent and appeal is meritless).

What if appellate counsel believes that there is no issue to appeal? Perhaps counsel believes that the trial or plea was conducted properly and all legal issues were correctly resolved. If counsel is retained, the answer is simple. Counsel has a duty to inform the client of this assessment and withdraw from the case. The client can then hire other counsel who may provide a fresh evaluation of the record and find an issue of merit to appeal. On the other hand, if appellate counsel has been appointed for an indigent defendant, the lawyer may find it impossible to withdraw without compromising the client's position. If the lawyer in requesting to withdraw is candid with the appellate court, the likelihood of meaningful appellate review could be reduced. After all, if appellate counsel believes the appeal has no merit, will the appellate court take the appeal seriously? Moreover, if the court permits the appellate attorney to withdraw, the client may have to pursue the appeal *pro se* without benefit of legal expertise.

In *Anders v. California*, 386 U.S. 738 (1967), counsel was appointed to file an appeal for an indigent person convicted of a drug offense. After reviewing the case, the appointed attorney filed a letter informing the state appellate court that he would file no appellate brief because the appeal had no merit. The appellate court refused to appoint a second lawyer, and the defendant filed a *pro se* brief that was inadequate to raise all the issues. After the conviction was affirmed by state courts, the prisoner filed a habeas corpus petition. The United States Supreme Court reversed, holding that due process and equal protection were violated by a procedure that discriminated against indigent defendants.

The *Anders* Court was careful to note that appellate counsel was not obligated to present frivolous arguments on appeal. But before appointed appellate counsel could opt out of a case, he had to file what has become known as an *Anders* brief. According to the Supreme Court:

> [Appointed counsel for an indigent must] support his client's appeal to the best of his ability. Of course, if counsel finds his case to be wholly frivolous, after a conscientious examination of it, he should so advise the court and request permission to withdraw. That request must, however, be accompanied by a brief referring to anything in the record that might arguably support the appeal. A copy of counsel's brief should be furnished the indigent and time allowed him to raise any points that he chooses; the court — not counsel — then proceeds, after a full examination of all the proceedings, to decide whether the case is wholly frivolous. If it so finds it may grant counsel's request to withdraw and dismiss the appeal insofar as federal requirements are concerned, or proceed to a decision on the merits, if state law so requires. On the other hand, if it finds any of the legal points arguable on their merits (and therefore not frivolous) it must, prior to decision, afford the indigent the assistance of counsel to argue the appeal.
>
> This requirement would not force appointed counsel to brief his case against his client but would merely afford the latter that advocacy which a nonindigent defendant is able to obtain. It would also induce the court to pursue all the more vigorously its own review because of the ready references not only to the record,

but also to the legal authorities as furnished it by counsel. . . . Moreover, such handling would tend to protect counsel from the constantly increasing charge that he was ineffective and had not handled the case with that diligence to which an indigent defendant is entitled. This procedure will assure penniless defendants the same rights and opportunities on appeal — as nearly as is practicable — as are enjoyed by those persons who are in a similar situation but who are able to afford the retention of private counsel. [*Id.* at 744–745]

NOTES

1. *Conflicting roles. Anders* represents an attempt to deal with appellate counsel's two, sometimes conflicting, roles. As an advocate for a convicted criminal, counsel must represent the client's interests. On the other hand, as an officer of the court a lawyer has important duties to the system of justice. Does *Anders* adequately resolve these conflicting obligations?

Is it fair to say that *Anders* forces appellate defense lawyers to become advocates *against* their indigent clients? If so, doesn't it create a significant gap between the representation of the rich and the poor? Remember that *Anders* will have little impact on retained counsel. On the other hand, perhaps it doesn't matter. If defense counsel, whether retained or appointed, believes that there is no merit to an appeal, isn't it likely that the appeal would fail even if vigorously pressed by competent appellate counsel?

2. *Alternatives to Anders.* While *Anders* provides a detailed description of what counsel should do when he or she believes the appeal would be frivolous, in *Smith v. Robbins*, 528 U.S. 259 (2000), the Court held that the *Anders* procedure is not the only permissible one. States are free to adopt different procedures so long as those procedures adequately safeguard a defendant's right to appellate counsel. The *Smith* Court upheld a California procedure that differed from *Anders*. It requires that defense counsel, believing an appeal would be frivolous, must file a brief summarizing the factual and procedural history of the case, attesting that he or she has examined the record, explained the evaluation of the case to the client, given the client a copy of the brief, informed the client of the right to file a *pro se* supplemental brief, and requesting the court to examine independently the record for arguable issues. Unlike the *Anders* procedures, defense counsel need not explicitly indicate that the appeal is frivolous nor ask permission to withdraw; he or she may remain available to brief any issues the court directs to be briefed. Do you agree with the *Smith* Court that the California procedure adequately protects the defendant's right to appellate counsel?

3. *Content of Anders brief.* Note that the "*Anders* brief" described in *Anders* must include a statement of "anything in the record that might arguably support the appeal." It does not appear to require counsel to indicate *why* each of these issues lacks merit. Thus, *Anders* may not mandate inclusion of citations to cases or statutes suggesting the issues are not even arguably meritorious. Was this an important omission? Recall that the *Anders* brief is filed with a request to withdraw because the appeal is frivolous. Do you think that citations and arguments on the meritless nature of the issues are unnecessary? Or is more involved?

In *McCoy v. Court of Appeals*, 486 U.S. 429 (1988), the Supreme Court upheld a Wisconsin rule requiring that *Anders* briefs contain a discussion of why each issue lacks merit. This requirement, though not mandated by *Anders*, is permissible because it (1) may assist appellate counsel in finding support for an argument originally thought to be baseless, (2) will assist the appellate court in assessing whether counsel was diligent in investigating the case, and (3) will assist the appellate court in determining whether the appeal is actually frivolous. Do you agree with *McCoy*? Does it go too far in forcing lawyers to become advocates against their clients? Does it create a different standard for appellate consideration of rich and poor clients?

4. *Efforts to prepare Anders brief. Anders* did not specify what efforts counsel must expend before filing an *Anders* brief. In *McCoy v. Court of Appeals*, 486 U.S. 429, 438–439 (1988), the Supreme Court held lawyers to a high standard:

> The appellate lawyer must master the trial record, thoroughly research the law, and exercise judgment in identifying the arguments that may be advanced on appeal. In preparing and evaluating the case, and in advising the client as to the prospects for success, counsel must consistently serve the client's interest to the best of his or her ability. Only after such an evaluation has led counsel to the conclusion that the appeal is "wholly frivolous" is counsel justified in making a motion to withdraw. This is the central teaching of *Anders*.

Since counsel must "thoroughly research" as well as file an *Anders* brief, would it make more sense to require counsel to file a formal appellate brief rather than withdraw? Would this approach save time or waste time for both counsel and the court? *See Commonwealth v. Moffett*, 418 N.E.2d 585 (Mass. 1981)(suggesting that counsel's briefing even of "well nigh hopeless" issues would be more efficient for the court and less inimical to client's interests than filing an *Anders* brief; hopeless points should be stated as briefly and succinctly as possible; notice to court and client required if counsel is utterly unable to come up with even thinly arguable appellate issues).

5. The American Bar Association's Standards for Criminal Justice make the distinction between an appeal or a ground for appeal that is frivolous and one that lacks merit. STANDARDS FOR CRIMINAL JUSTICE § 4-8.3. (3d ed. 1993). The Standards provide that appellate counsel is not permitted to withdraw because counsel believes the appeal lacks merit, but may do so if it is frivolous. Do you agree with this distinction? Could a court actually implement it? How would the court determine whether an appeal or issue is frivolous or simply without merit?

If appellate counsel believes that some issues are not frivolous but the client insists on including an issue that appellate counsel believes is frivolous, the ABA Standards counsel that:

> In this situation, it is proper for the lawyer to brief and argue the points he or she believes are supportable and tactically or strategically advisable to make and to omit the others. *Id.* Commentary.

[b] Discretionary Appeals

[i] Appeal After a Direct Appeal as of Right: Supreme Court

Appeals after the initial appeal "as of right" are discretionary in most jurisdictions. The appellate court does not have to accept the case. If an intermediate appellate court upholds the conviction, interlocutory order, or denial of collateral relief, the defendant desiring another appeal often must file a petition, sometimes called a writ of *certiorari*, with the next higher court, usually the state supreme court, requesting the appeal be accepted.

This pattern is used in the federal system. The United States Supreme Court has discretion to decide what criminal cases it will hear. The Supreme Court's Rules state that a writ of *certiorari* will be granted only "for compelling reasons." These reasons generally involve a conflict among lower federal or sometimes state courts as to the interpretation of a federal law, or a lower court decision that conflicts with a Supreme Court decision or presents an issue that should be settled by the Supreme Court. Sup. Ct. R. 10.

Under federal procedure, the person seeking a writ of *certiorari* to overturn a Court of Appeals decision must file a petition for writ of *certiorari* in the United States Supreme Court within 90 days of the date the judgment is rendered or the date a petition for rehearing is denied. A Justice may extend the date the petition is due, but such an extension period cannot exceed 60 days. Sup. Ct. R. 13.

The content of the petition for *certiorari* is specified in detail in the Supreme Court's Rules. Sup. Ct. R. 14. A petition can be denied for failure to comply with these rules. In general terms, the petition for *certiorari* resembles an appellate brief that states the relevant issues and legal authorities in a way designed to convince the Court to grant the petition.

After a petition for *certiorari* is filed, the other side files a brief in opposition to the petition for a writ of *certiorari*. The petitioner can then file a reply brief to the brief in opposition. Sup. Ct. R. 15.

After consideration of the petition for a writ of *certiorari*, the United States Supreme Court enters an appropriate order. If the petition is granted, the Court will notify the interested parties and the case will be scheduled for briefing and oral argument. If the order is denied, the Supreme Court notifies the interested parties of the decision. Sup. Ct. R. 16.

[ii]   Prior to Final Judgment: Interlocutory Appeals

In a criminal proceeding, the criminal defendant ordinarily appeals only after conviction and sentencing. In this post-sentence appeal the defendant raises every available issue, including those raised unsuccessfully in pretrial motions. For example, many criminal defendants appeal their convictions on the ground that either an illegal confession or physical evidence was admitted into evidence following an unsuccessful pretrial motion to suppress.

On occasion, however, the defendant wants an immediate appeal of a judge's decision on a pretrial motion (or even a decision made during trial). If the appeal is successful, it could alter the course of the trial or prevent it entirely. For example, in a drug case if a suppression motion is initially denied but then granted on appeal before the trial has begun, the prosecution may have to drastically alter the charges or even dismiss the case for lack of evidence.

As one would expect, courts do not welcome interlocutory appeals, for they can cause significant delay in processing a case and can play havoc with a judge's efforts to schedule cases. The Supreme Court has used strong language to express its negative feelings about interlocutory appeals:

> All our jurisprudence is strongly colored by the notion that appellate review should be postponed, except in certain narrowly defined circumstances, until after final judgment has been rendered by the trial court. This general policy against piecemeal appeals takes on added weight in criminal cases, where the defendant is entitled to a speedy resolution of the charges against him. [*Will v. United States*, 389 U.S. 90, 96 (1967)]

This preference has led to the so-called *final judgment* or *final order* rule, generally permitting appeals only after a final judgment. In the federal system, the courts of appeals have jurisdiction in appeals "from all final decisions" of district courts. 28 U.S.C. § 1291. According to the Supreme Court, a final judgment or decision in a criminal case occurs only after conviction and sentence. *Flanagan v. United States*, 465 U.S. 259, 263 (1984). Does the final judgment rule make sense? Whose interest does it serve? Does it have any relationship to the likelihood of a fair trial? Does it save judicial resources? Does it save prosecution or defense costs? Does it serve society's interest in the speedy resolution of criminal charges?

In unusual cases, virtually all jurisdictions have a procedure that authorizes *interlocutory appeals*. An interlocutory procedure occurs between the commencement of the case and the final judgment. Interlocutory appeals are actually authorized in two ways: by the collateral order doctrine and by statute. A third category, independent proceedings, is different in that it may not actually involve an interlocutory appeal. Each is discussed below.

Collateral order doctrine. The *collateral order doctrine*, derived from federal case law originally dealing with civil cases, permits, in federal criminal cases, the appeal of certain pretrial orders that are viewed as if they were final judgments. *See generally Cohen v. Beneficial Industrial Loan Corp.*, 337 U.S. 541 (1949) (civil case establishing collateral order doctrine).

The collateral order doctrine:

> . . . considers as "final judgments," even though they do not "end the litigation on the merits," decisions "which finally determine claims of right separate from, and collateral to, rights asserted in the action, too important to be denied review and too independent of the cause itself to require that appellate jurisdiction be deferred until the whole case is adjudicated." To fall within the limited class of final collateral orders, an order must (1) "conclusively determine the disputed question," (2) "resolve an important issue completely separate from the merits of the action," and (3) "be effectively unreviewable on appeal from a final judgment."

Midland Asphalt Corp. v. United States, 489 U.S. 794, 798–799 (1989), *quoting Cohen v. Beneficial Industrial Loan Corp., supra*, and *Coopers & Lybrand v. Livesay*, 437 U.S. 463 (1978). The third prong is the most difficult to prove in criminal cases. It requires the appellant to convince the appellate court that the trial court's order involves "an asserted right the legal and practical value of which would be destroyed if it were not vindicated before trial." *United States v. MacDonald*, 435 U.S. 850 (1978).

Consistent with the general judicial hesitancy to permit interlocutory appeals, the collateral order doctrine is interpreted "with the utmost strictness" in criminal cases. Nevertheless, a few Supreme Court decisions do permit collateral order interlocutory appeals in such cases. *See, e.g., Helstoski v. Meanor*, 442 U.S. 500 (1979) (motion to dismiss under speech or debate clause is collateral order); *Abney v. United States*, 431 U.S. 651 (1977) (denial of motion to dismiss for double jeopardy is collateral order); *Stack v. Boyle*, 342 U.S. 1 (1951) (denial of bail is collateral order).

Most cases refuse to apply the collateral order exception. *See, e.g., Midland Asphalt Corp. v. United States*, 489 U.S. 794 (1989) (denial of motion to dismiss because of improper disclosure of grand jury information not collateral order; is not completely separate from merits of action); *United States v. Hollywood Motor Car Co.*, 458 U.S. 263 (1982) (denial of motion to dismiss because of prosecutorial vindictiveness is not collateral order; is reviewable on appeal; court suggests collateral order rule extends to situations where there is a right not to be tried as opposed to a right to have charges dismissed); *United States v. MacDonald*, 456 U.S. 1 (1982) (denial of motion to dismiss because of speedy trial violation not collateral order; is reviewable on appeal).

Statutes. Statutes in most jurisdictions authorize an interlocutory appeal in limited circumstances. Typically, the accused must obtain the permission of a trial court or, occasionally, appellate judge before taking an interlocutory appeal. Some of these statutes present the court with a list of factors to consider in determining whether to permit an interlocutory appeal. In some circumstances, the government is granted more opportunities than the defendant to take an interlocutory appeal. Government appeals are discussed below.

Independent proceedings. On rare occasions a criminal case involves issues or people separate from the criminal case being tried. For example, the police may conduct a search and obtain property belonging to the defendant and third parties. The third parties file a motion to have their property returned to them. If the motion is denied, it may be immediately appealed if it is considered "independent of, and unaffected by, another litigation with which it happens to be entangled." *Radio Station WOW v. Johnson*, 326 U.S. 120, 126 (1945).

The leading case involved an attempt to appeal the denial of a motion to suppress in a drug case. In *DiBella v. United States*, 369 U.S. 121, 131–132 (1962), Justice Frankfurter observed, "[o]nly if the motion is solely for return of property and is in no way tied to a criminal prosecution *in esse* against the movant can the proceedings be regarded as independent." To illustrate, this test was satisfied where IRS agents seized bank records but the persons filing the suppression motion had not been arrested or indicted. Their action was deemed independent of any pending criminal case and the denial of the suppression motion could be appealed. *First National Bank of Tulsa v. Department of Justice*, 865 F.2d 217 (10th Cir. 1989).

[4] Appeals by the Government

With respect to appeals, the government in a criminal case is in an unusual situation. Because of the double jeopardy clause, discussed in Chapter 16, it may not appeal acquittals in criminal cases. Moreover, concerns about government abuse and the citizen's right to face prosecution only once have led to the rule that "in the federal jurisprudence . . . appeals by the Government in criminal cases are something unusual, exceptional, not favored." *Carroll v. United States*, 354 U.S. 394, 400 (1957).

Although appeals by the government are not welcomed, they are permitted by statutes to a limited extent. Under federal law and in most states, statutes authorize the government to appeal a court order "dismissing an indictment or information or granting a new trial after verdict or judgment." 18 U.S.C. § 3731. *See also*, Ill. Sup. Ct. Rule 604; N.Y. Crim. Proc. Law § 450.20. However, the government may not appeal this type of order if the "double jeopardy clause of the United States Constitution prohibits further prosecution." 18 U.S.C. § 3731. For example, this would occur if, after jeopardy attached, the case was dismissed because of the defendant's innocence.

The government in many jurisdictions is also permitted to appeal the sentence imposed on the defendant, *e.g.*, 18 U.S.C. § 3742(b); N.Y. Crim. Proc. Law § 450.30 (government may appeal only on ground that sentence is invalid as a matter of law), as well as many bail issues. 18 U.S.C. § 3731. The federal government is also often authorized to appeal an order suppressing or excluding evidence if the order is made before the defendant has been put in jeopardy, the appeal is not taken for purpose of delay, and the suppressed evidence is substantial proof of a fact material in the proceeding. 18 U.S.C. § 3731. The rationale behind allowing an interlocutory appeal in the pretrial motion context is that the government may have insufficient proof to continue the prosecution if it is unable to admit certain evidence at trial. *See also* Fla. Stat. Ann. § 924.071. Recall that the defendant, unlike the government, is often *not* permitted to appeal interlocutory orders. Does it make sense to permit the government, but not the defendant, to appeal interlocutory orders?

In general terms, the procedure that the government follows when appealing is much like that of the criminal defendant. *See generally* David G. Knibb, Federal Court of Appeals Manual § 15.3 (5th ed. 2007). There may be small differences that vary among the jurisdictions. In the federal system, for example, the government, unlike the criminal defendant, has thirty days to file its notice of appeal from a district court judgment. 18 U.S.C. § 3731.

C. COLLATERAL REMEDIES

The best known, and most frequently invoked, collateral remedy is the writ of *habeas corpus*, discussed in detail below. For *state* prisoners, federal habeas entails seeking review in *federal* court of the constitutionality of the underlying conviction or sentence, after direct state appeals have been exhausted. The other significant collateral remedy, the writ of error *coram nobis*, in contrast, seeks relief (either before or after direct appeals are exhausted) from the court that originally imposed the conviction and sentence.

[1] *Coram Nobis*

The common law writ of error *coram nobis* (or its cousin *coram vobis*) still exists in the federal courts and many state jurisdictions, although it is used infrequently. *Coram nobis* is designed to permit a criminal conviction to be challenged because of a factual error detrimental to the defense. In *United States v. Morgan*, 346 U.S. 502 (1954), the United States Supreme Court held that federal *coram nobis* was a valid remedy for a state prisoner to use in challenging the validity of a prior federal conviction that was obtained in violation of the defendant's right to counsel. The Court stated:

> The writ of error *coram nobis* was available at common law to correct errors of fact. It was allowed without limitation of time for facts that affect the "validity and regularity" of the judgment and was used in both civil and criminal cases. While the occasions for its use were infrequent, no one doubts its availability at common law . . . . It has been used, in the United States, with and without statutory authority but always with references to its common law scope — for example, to inquire as to the imprisonment of a slave not subject to imprisonment, insanity of a defendant, a conviction on a guilty plea through the coercion of fear of mob violence, [and the] failure to advise of right to counsel.

See, e.g., People v. Chaklader, 29 Cal. Rptr. 2d 344 (Cal. App. 1994) (*coram nobis* relief available if guilty plea induced by mistake, fraud, or coercion); *Dugart v. State*, 578 So.2d 789 (Fla. Dist. Ct. App. 1991) (*coram nobis* appropriate for ineffective assistance of trial counsel in providing misinformation about effect of plea); *State v. Cottingham*, 410 N.W.2d 498 (Neb. 1987) (*coram nobis* petition based on new evidence should be denied when new evidence was cumulative and probably would not have affected result).

The defendant and defense counsel must not have been negligent in failing to bring this fact to the judge's attention at trial. The writ will succeed if the factual error was so serious that, if known at trial, it would have prevented the conviction. For reasons that will make sense later in this chapter, *coram nobis* can be an important remedy for a prisoner who attacks a conviction for which he or she is not currently in custody and therefore cannot use remedies such as federal habeas corpus. Some courts have characterized *coram nobis* as a remedy of last resort, meaning that it cannot be used if habeas corpus or some other collateral remedy is available. In some jurisdictions a *coram nobis* action will be dismissed if the petitioner had not previously used all available remedies to challenge the alleged error. *See, e.g., State v. Davis*, 515 N.W.2d 205 (S.D. 1994) (voluntary dismissal of direct appeal bars subsequent *coram nobis* action on issue raised in dismissed appeal). The procedures for using *coram nobis* vary considerably among the jurisdictions. In general, the writ first must be filed in the court where the conviction being challenged occurred.

[2] Habeas Corpus

[a] Nature and History of the Writ

The writ of habeas corpus, sometimes referred to as The Great Writ of Liberty or simply The Great Writ, exists under federal law and in many states, and is the primary vehicle (other than direct appellate review of a conviction or sentence) by which persons under confinement can challenge the constitutionality of their incarceration. As discussed later in this chapter, federal court habeas petitions are usually "collateral" attacks by state prisoners on their underlying convictions and/or sentences. However, the writ is also available for persons in federal custody. With origins extending to at least the twelfth century in England, habeas corpus has been an important judicial check on the government's actions in depriving its citizens of their liberty. *See Hamdi v. Rumsfeld*, 542 U.S. 507, 525 (2004)(habeas is a "critical check on the Executive ensuring that it does not detain individuals except in accordance with law," and citing, to the same effect, *I.N.S. v. St. Cyr*, 533 U.S. 289 (2001)); *see also*, James S. Liebman and Randy Hertz, FEDERAL HABEAS CORPUS PRACTICE AND PROCEDURE (5th ed. 2005); Daniel J. Meador, HABEAS CORPUS AND MAGNA CARTA; DUALISM OF POWER AND LIBERTY (1966).

Civil case to produce petitioner. The phrase "habeas corpus" means "have or produce the body." Historically, and under the governing statutes and rules, a habeas petition is treated as a civil action, even though it is usually a collateral attack on a criminal conviction and/or sentence. The person bringing the petition is called the *petitioner*, or *applicant*, and the official who has custody over the petitioner, and to whom the writ is addressed, is called the *respondent*. In general terms habeas corpus is a court order, addressed to the respondent (usually the prison warden), to bring the petitioner before the court to determine the validity of the petitioner's confinement.

Habeas as a constitutionally protected procedure to obtain immediate release from unlawful confinement. In *Fay v. Noia*, 372 U.S. 391, 401–402 (1963), one of the leading Supreme Court habeas corpus precedents, the Court addressed the fundamental purpose of the Great Writ:

> Although in form the Great Writ [of habeas corpus] is simply a mode of procedure, its history is inextricably intertwined with the growth of fundamental rights of personal liberty. For its function has been to provide a prompt and efficacious remedy for whatever society deems to be intolerable restraint. Its root principle is that in a civilized society, government must always be accountable to the judiciary for a man's imprisonment: if the imprisonment cannot be shown to conform with the fundamental requirements of law, the individual is entitled to his immediate release.

The Constitution recognizes this important role and provides that "[t]he privilege of the Writ of Habeas Corpus shall not be suspended, unless when in Cases of Rebellion or Invasion the public safety may require it." U.S. Const. art. 1, § 9. Recently, in *Hamdi v. Rumsfeld*, 542 U.S. 507 (2005), the Supreme Court held as a matter of due process that a United States citizen detained as an accused "enemy combatant" must be able to challenge that designation via habeas corpus. The Court in *Hamdi* reaffirmed the importance and the availability of habeas as a procedural mechanism for citizens to challenge the legality of their confinement:

> [A]bsent suspension, the writ of habeas corpus remains available to every citizen detained in the United States. [*Id., at 525*]

In *Boumediene v. Bush*, 128 S.Ct. 229 (2008), the court extended the constitutional "privilege" of habeas corpus to "enemy combatants" being detained at the United States military detention facility in Guantanamo Bay, Cuba.

Availability of the writ to federal and state prisoners. Originally federal habeas corpus was limited to federal prisoners, but in 1867 the writ became available on a limited basis to state prisoners held in violation of selected federal constitutional provisions. Gradually, many of these limitations were removed, making the writ of habeas corpus a viable remedy for state prisoners claiming their state custody was in violation of the United States Constitution. By 1942, the Supreme Court was able to state that federal habeas corpus " . . . extends . . . to those exceptional cases where the conviction has been in disregard of the constitutional rights of the accused, and where the writ is the only effective means of preserving his rights." *Waley v. Johnston*, 316 U.S. 101, 105 (1942) (state prisoner can use federal habeas corpus to challenge custody resulting from coerced guilty plea).

Stone v. Powell preclusion rule. Despite the wording of the federal habeas corpus statute, not all federal constitutional violations are cognizable in federal habeas corpus.

For policy reasons, the Supreme Court has held that habeas corpus relief is unavailable for certain constitutional claims. In *Stone v. Powell*, 428 U.S. 465 (1976), the Supreme Court held that a state prisoner is not constitutionally entitled to habeas corpus relief on the ground that evidence, obtained in an unconstitutional search or seizure, was introduced at trial. The key is whether the defendant was afforded "an opportunity for full and fair litigation" of the Fourth Amendment claim in state court. According to *Stone*, if this opportunity exists, the purpose of the "exclusionary rule" in deterring unlawful police conduct has been adequately served and the possibility of federal habeas corpus relief is unnecessary as an added deterrent.

The so-called "*Stone v. Powell* preclusion rule" has not been extended to other constitutional areas. Therefore *Stone* did not lead to the complete destruction of access to habeas corpus, as some commentators had predicted. *See Kimmelman v. Morrison*, 477 U.S. 365 (1986) (*Stone* not extended to claims of Sixth Amendment violation of right to effective assistance of counsel); *Withrow v. Williams*, 507 U.S. 680 (1993) (not extended to *Miranda* violation); *Cardwell v. Taylor*, 461 U.S. 571 (1983) (suggesting *Stone* not extended to involuntary statements); *Rose v. Mitchell*, 443 U.S. 545 (1979) (not extended to discriminatory grand jury selection). The *sui generis* nature of the ruling in *Stone* is probably best explained by the Court's continuing discomfort with the exclusionary rule (a topic which is beyond the scope of this book).

Federal and state habeas corpus. Although states have habeas corpus and related procedures, federal habeas corpus is the most important such remedy and is considered in this chapter. Habeas corpus is a critical aspect of American procedures designed to protect the individual from government oppression. *See generally* Dallin H. Oaks, *Habeas Corpus in the States — 1776–1865*, 32 U. CHI. L. REV. 243 (1965).

Present statutory basis. The statutory authority for federal habeas corpus is now contained in 28 U.S.C. §§ 2241–2254 (for persons on state custody) and § 2255 (for persons in federal custody). Some procedural details are contained in Rules Governing Section 2254 Cases in the United States District Courts, originally adopted in 1977. In general terms, federal habeas corpus is available to a state (and sometimes federal) prisoner held in custody in violation of federal law. In 2006, state prisoners filed over 19,000 federal habeas corpus petitions and federal prisoners filed almost 4,000. Sourcebook, at http://www.albany.edu/sourcebook/pdf/t5652006.pdf.

AEDPA. In 1996 Congress passed the Antiterrorism and Effective Death Penalty Act ("AEDPA"), Pub.L. 104-132. This legislation significantly restricted prisoners' access to federal habeas corpus or relief under Section 2255, discussed below. AEDPA's major stated purpose was to make the death penalty more "effective" by cutting down on the time, often measured in decades, between the pronouncement and the actual execution of death sentences. However, despite the suggestion in the Act's title that it is targeted primarily at death penalty and terrorism cases, AEDPA's restrictions on habeas corpus relief apply to *all* federal habeas petitions filed after the Act's date, in both capital and non-capital cases and in both terrorism and non-terrorism cases alike. *Lindh v. Murphy*, 521 U.S. 320 (1997).

AEDPA initially drew much scholarly criticism on both constitutional and policy grounds. *See e.g.*, Mark Tushnet and Larry W. Yackle, *Symbolic Statutes and Real Laws: The Pathologies of the Antiterrorism and Effective Death Penalty Act and the Prison Litigation Reform Act*, 47 DUKE L. J. 1 (1997); Marshall J. Hartman & Jeanette Nyden, *Habeas Corpus and the New Federalism after the Anti-Terrorism and Effective Death Penalty Act of 1996*, 30 J. MARSHALL L. REV. 337 (1997); A.A. Kochan, Note, *The Antiterrorism and Effective Death Penalty Act of 1996: Habeas Corpus Reform?*, 52 WASH. U. J. URB. & CONTEMP. L 399 (1997). However, in *Felker v. Turpin*, 518 U.S. 651 (1996), the United States Supreme Court upheld the constitutionality of AEDPA, noting that although the Act imposes new conditions on the Court's authority to grant relief, it does not deprive the Supreme Court of "jurisdiction to entertain original habeas petitions."

[b] The Custody and Mootness Requirements

[i] Custody

The federal habeas corpus statute extends to a prisoner who is "in custody," a term that is not defined. 28 U.S.C. § 2241(c). The Supreme Court explained this limitation in *Hensley v. Municipal Court*, 411 U.S. 345, 351 (1973):

> The custody requirement of the habeas corpus statute is designed to preserve the writ of habeas corpus as a remedy for severe restraints on individual liberty. Since habeas corpus is an extraordinary remedy whose operation is to a large extent uninhibited by traditional rules of finality and federalism, its use has been limited to cases of special urgency, leaving more conventional remedies for cases in which the restraints on liberty are neither severe nor immediate.

In *Hensley*, a state offender, released on his own recognizance pending execution of sentence, challenged his conviction on various federal constitutional grounds. The Supreme Court found that he was in sufficient "custody" to satisfy federal habeas corpus even though he was not confined in an institution and was free to live at home and conduct a normal life. The Court noted that he was subject to restraints not shared by the general public and that he could be incarcerated as soon as a stay was removed.

Other decisions have further broadened the concept of "custody" beyond penal confinement to include a person who is on parole or probation, but not to a person sentenced to pay a fine or whose driver's license has been suspended. Custody also includes a prisoner incarcerated on one sentence who wishes to attack a consecutive sentence to be served at the completion of the first term. And it includes a prisoner, incarcerated for parole revocation, who files a habeas corpus petition attacking the revocation, then is released on parole. A person whose later sentence is enhanced by an allegedly constitutionally invalid prior sentence is also considered to be in sufficient custody from the prior sentence to use federal habeas corpus to attack that prior sentence. *Lackawanna County District Attorney v. Coss*, 532 U.S. 394 (2001). The petitioner's custody status is determined at the time of filing the petition. *Spencer v. Kemna*, 523 U.S. 1 (1998).

Query: Does *Hensley*'s rationale, limiting the concept of custody to "severe and immediate" restraints on liberty, make sense? If the defendant was convicted in violation of the constitution, why should it matter whether he or she is still in custody? Isn't it true that the government is responsible for the illegality which led to harm to the defendant's reputation and job prospects as well as other facets of his or her daily life?

[ii] Mootness

A federal habeas corpus petition will be dismissed if the issue is moot. The mootness rule is based on a lack of a "case or controversy" under Article III, § 2 of the Constitution. This provision requires the offender to have a stake in the outcome. Mootness is related to the concept of custody. A case often becomes moot once the offender is no longer in custody. It can become moot if the petitioner escapes from custody, is pardoned, or dies. But in *Carafas v. LaVallee*, 391 U.S. 234 (1968), the Court held that collateral consequences, such as an inability to hold a license because of a criminal conviction, were sufficient to keep a habeas petition from being deemed moot. Although the petitioner in *Carafas* had been unconditionally released from prison, the Supreme Court held that he could still challenge his conviction because it continued to cause consequences such as an inability to conduct certain businesses, vote, or serve as a juror. *But see Spencer v. Kemna*, 523 U.S. 1 (1998) (habeas corpus moot when parole violator released from prison and attacks parole revocation procedures; inadequate proof of collateral consequences); *Lane v. Williams*, 455 U.S. 624 (1982) (habeas corpus moot when parole violator released from custody; insufficient civil disabilities result from fact of earlier parole violation).

[c]   In Violation of Federal Law

[i]   Federal Constitution, Statutes, or Treaties

Federal habeas corpus is available to a prisoner "in custody in violation of the Constitution or laws or treaties of the United States." 28 U.S.C. § 2241. This means that a state prisoner cannot use federal habeas corpus to challenge state custody without alleging a violation of federal law. Although technically the federal provision can be a treaty or statute, virtually always it is a federal constitutional provision.

Sometimes habeas corpus petitioners strain to turn a state court's error into a federal constitutional violation. *See, e.g., Estelle v. McGuire*, 502 U.S. 62 (1991) (even though state court erroneously admitted evidence in violation of state evidence law, due process clause not necessarily violated); *Hill v. United States*, 368 U.S. 424 (1962) (failure to offer defendant opportunity to make statement before sentencing does not constitute due process violation authorizing collateral relief).

Harmless error. The harmless error doctrine, discussed earlier in this chapter, applies to habeas corpus cases. *See Calderon v. Coleman*, 525 U.S. 141 (1998); *Brecht v. Abrahamson*, 507 U.S. 619 (1993).

[ii]   Actual Innocence: *Herrera*

An obvious habeas corpus claim is that the prisoner is actually innocent of the charges and therefore is being held unconstitutionally. The argument is that surely due process is violated if an innocent person is incarcerated for a crime he or she did not commit. Although in a just system the prisoner would eventually be freed if this were true, in *Herrera v. Collins*, 506 U.S. 390 (1993), the United States Supreme Court made it extremely difficult for such claims to prevail. The petitioner in *Herrera* was convicted of capital murder and, after unsuccessful state court appeals and habeas corpus proceedings, filed a federal habeas corpus petition alleging that recently acquired affidavits supported his claim of innocence. The Supreme Court denied relief, holding that an assertion of actual innocence does not raise a separate constitutional ground. The Court was concerned that any other holding would destroy finality and interfere with the comity-based principle that federal courts should not unduly interfere with the proceedings of state courts. It should be noted that Herrera did not argue that his trial was constitutionally deficient; he argued that he was innocent. As discussed below, a strong showing of actual innocence may still permit a prisoner to seek habeas relief on an issue that should have been raised in an earlier proceeding.

Herrera did not go so far as to make a claim of actual innocence totally irrelevant (and insufficient as grounds for relief) to a habeas corpus petition in the absence of a separate claim of constitutional error. The Court assumed *arguendo* that in extraordinary cases a federal habeas corpus proceeding could be brought at any time if the prisoner could meet a very high standard of establishing actual innocence. The Court refused to specify the exact standard to be satisfied, but did indicate that it "would necessarily be extraordinarily high." *Id.* at 869. Justice Blackmun's dissent argued that a habeas corpus petition should be granted if the petitioner can prove that he or she is "probably innocent." *See generally,* Arleen Anderson, *Responding to the Challenge of Actual Innocence Claims After Herrera v. Collins*, 71 Temp. L. Rev. 489 (1998); Kevin M. Zielke, Note, *The Governor, God, and the Great Writ of Habeas Corpus*, 1993 Det. C. L. Rev. 1393.

In *House v. Bell*, 547 U.S. 518 (2006), the Supreme Court determined that the federal habeas petitioner there, who had been convicted of murder and sentenced to death, had proffererd sufficient evidence of his likely innocence (especially including

DNA evidence that semen found on the victim's clothing had come from her husband, rather than from the defendant as argued by the prosecution at trial, but also including other forensic and testimonial evidence that undermined the prosecution's circumstantial case) to warrant his habeas petition proceeding despite the fact that he had not raised this issue in a timely manner. The Court reiterated, however, that such a determination regarding likely actual innocence will only be made in those "rare" cases where the habeas petitioner meets the "extraordinarily high" requirement under *Herrera* of showing that reasonable trial jurors would likely have had a reasonable doubt of the petitioner's guilt had they heard the evidence presented later to the habeas court.

The Innocence Project and attempting to reopen old convictions on claims of innocence. First begun at Yeshiva University School of Law in 1992 and dedicated to seeking the exoneration of convicted persons who could be proved factually innocent by DNA testing, the Innocence Project is now a network of similar projects in law schools and universities in some 40 states. According to the Innocence Project's website, 217 persons (as of May 30, 2008) have been exonerated in the United States in recent years on the basis of modern DNA testing technology, including 15 who had been sentenced to death. *See,* Innocence Project, Mission Statement, *available at* http://www.innocenceproject.org. Many of these exonerated persons had been convicted at a time when DNA testing was either not available or when the available DNA testing technology had not yet attained its present enormous power either to convict or to exonerate. Also, see discussion in Chapter 10 of *Arizona v. Youngblood*, 488 U.S. 51 (1988)(government's duty to preserve evidence). Typically, persons represented by the Innocence Project, like Larry Youngblood, had been convicted and sentenced many years ago and exhausted all their available direct and collateral post-conviction remedies.

Many states now have enacted statutes or have judicial decisions requiring DNA testing in certain situations as part of their postconviction relief process. If the jurisdiction has a time limitation for filing such claims, some states authorize their executive clemency process to obtain DNA testing.

Some prosecutors, invoking the need for finality, have vigorously opposed reopening convictions years after the fact to permit state-of-the-art DNA testing, while others, and some courts, have agreed to allow testing years after conviction, especially where life or death of the defendant may hang in the balance. The very effort to obtain later DNA testing can sometimes face insurmountable barriers. If the prosecution is unwilling to agree to a DNA test, the defendant may bring a habeas petition and seek a court order for DNA testing pursuant to the discovery procedures that apply to habeas corpus proceedings. Under a strict reading of *Herrera*, however, a *claim* of innocence is an insufficient ground on which to seek habeas relief absent a *showing* of probable innocence. Query, how does the habeas petitioner, who asserts innocence but does not have DNA testing or other strong evidence required to show probable innocence, avoid dismissal under *Herrera* at the outset and reach the discovery stage at which potentially exonerating DNA testing may be ordered and obtained?

In many cases DNA testing done at the defendant's behest actually establishes guilt rather than innocence. Some commentators argue that the defendant should be penalized for obtaining the tests which wasted both time and money. *See, e.g.,* Gwendolyn Carroll, *Proven Guilty: An Examination of the Penalty-Free World of Post-Conviction DNA Testing*, 97 Crim. Law & Crimin. 665 (2007)(recommending prisoner loses good time prison credits for requesting DNA testing that confirms guilt). Do you think this is a good idea?

Also, as discussed later in this chapter, the severe limitations in AEDPA on bringing successive habeas petitions and on seeking federal habeas corpus relief on claims that have not been exhausted in the state courts may preclude a defendant from bringing a post-appellate habeas petition as a means to obtain potentially exculpatory DNA testing. In light of some very high profile DNA-based exonerations in recent years (see Innocence Project's website, above), judicial and prosecutorial resistance to allowing DNA testing to show possible actual innocence years after conviction appear to be softening somewhat. For an interesting and troubling empirical study of cases involving innocent people who were erroneously convicted, see Brandon L. Garrett, *Judging Innocence*, 108 COLUM. L. REV. 55 (2008).

[d]   Exhaustion of State Remedies

A long-standing principle in habeas corpus jurisprudence, called the *exhaustion requirement*, is that before being allowed to seek habeas corpus relief in *federal* court, *state* prisoners should first attempt to have the question of the legality of their confinement resolved in state court.

[i]   Federal Statutes Mandating Exhaustion

Accordingly, even if a state prisoner petitioning for federal habeas corpus relief adequately meets the requirements, discussed above, of showing "custody" that is "in violation of federal law," relief will be denied (subject to some narrow exceptions) unless the petitioner has satisfied the exhaustion requirement, now codified in 28 U.S.C. § 2254(b) and (c):

(b)(1)   [Habeas relief will be denied unless the petitioner has]

    (A)   . . . exhausted the remedies available in the courts of the State; or

    (B)

        (i)   there is an absence of available State corrective process; or

        (ii)   circumstances exist that render such process ineffective to protect the rights of the applicant.

(2)   An application for a writ of habeas corpus may be denied on the merits notwithstanding the failure of the applicant to exhaust the remedies available in the courts of the State.

(3)   A State shall not be deemed to have waived the exhaustion requirement or be estopped from reliance upon the requirement unless the State, through counsel, expressly waives the requirement.

(c)   An applicant shall not be deemed to have exhausted the remedies available in the courts of the State, within the meaning of this section, if he has the right under the law of the State to raise, by any available procedure, the question presented.

NOTES

1. *Deny petition even without exhaustion.* Note that subsection 2254(b)(2) is an exception to the exhaustion rule, though not one that benefits the petitioner. The federal court is authorized to dismiss the habeas corpus petition even if the petitioner has not exhausted state remedies on all claims. This permits the federal court to dismiss patently frivolous petitions without burdening state courts with the need to act on the issues and without requiring the federal court to take the time to consider the case again at a future date after state remedies have been exhausted.

2. *State may waive exhaustion.* Subsection (b)(3) authorizes states to waive the exhaustion requirement, but the waiver must be express rather than implied.

[ii] Rationale for Exhaustion Requirement

The exhaustion requirement, based on the principles of federalism and federal-state comity, is designed to permit state courts to play a role in enforcing federal law. It has been said that this will assist in minimizing friction between state and federal systems of justice. Do you agree that the exhaustion rule helps reduce this friction? Could it actually aggravate it?

Another rationale for the exhaustion rule is to save federal court resources by providing federal courts with a complete record of the issue developed in a state court proceeding. Think about these rationales. Does the exhaustion rule actually save federal judicial resources, since the issue of exhaustion itself must be litigated by federal court? Could the exhaustion doctrine actually waste *state* judicial resources?

The importance of the exhaustion requirement is demonstrated by *Duckworth v. Serrano*, 454 U.S. 1 (1981), in which an Indiana state prisoner filed a federal habeas corpus petition alleging the ineffective assistance of counsel at his state murder trial. Before the state trial, defense counsel had been retained by a prosecution witness to represent her at a later proceeding. This representation created an obvious conflict of interest for the defense counsel. The defendant did not raise the ineffective counsel issue on direct appeal to the Indiana Supreme Court or in a habeas corpus petition to a federal district court. It was first presented in a habeas corpus petition to the United States Court of Appeals. The Court of Appeals acknowledged that the issue had not been raised in a state forum or in the federal district court, but nevertheless reversed in order to conserve judicial resources since the matter was a "clear violation" of the defendant's Sixth Amendment rights. The Supreme Court reversed the Court of Appeals and dismissed the habeas petition for failure to exhaust state remedies, even if the habeas corpus petition raised a "clear violation" of defendant's constitutional rights. The Court feared that a "clear violation" exception would invite habeas corpus petitioners to bypass state procedures and file initially in federal court. The *Duckworth* Court observed that "it would be unseemly in our dual system of government for the federal courts to upset a state-court conviction without affording to the state courts the opportunity to correct a constitutional violation." [454 U.S. at 4]

[iii] Meaning of Exhaustion

In general terms, the exhaustion rule means that a state prisoner's habeas corpus action will not be allowed to proceed in federal court unless the state court system has first been given the chance to rule on the federal constitutional claim presented in the federal habeas corpus petition. For example, if a state prisoner allegedly held in custody in violation of the federal constitution has available a direct appeal in state court to raise this issue, the state remedy ordinarily must be pursued before federal habeas corpus is available. The prisoner should ensure that the state courts are presented with the substance of the federal claim. But if the prisoner is unsuccessful in having state court grant relief on the federal issue, he or she does not have to seek a writ of *certiorari* from the United States Supreme Court in order to have exhausted state remedies.

The exhaustion requirement is not always applied literally. The Supreme Court has specifically held that in special circumstances federal courts can dispense with or modify the exhaustion rule. For example, state collateral remedies, such as state habeas corpus, need not ordinarily be pursued before a state prisoner can seek federal habeas relief if an issue was already raised on direct appeal in state courts. It is usually not necessary to give state courts more than one opportunity to address the federal issue. Similarly, when a state appellate court has been presented with a federal constitutional issue but has ignored it, state remedies may be considered to have been exhausted even if other state procedures are still available. *See Castille v. Peoples*, 489 U.S. 346 (1989).

Fairly presented to state courts. Before a federal constitutional issue is exhausted, it must have been fairly presented to the state court for a determination. This means that the defendant ordinarily must have meaningfully raised the federal issue in the state proceedings. *See Anderson v. Harless*, 459 U.S. 4 (1982) (defense counsel in state proceeding did not directly raise federal constitutional issue).

Futility. The exhaustion requirement does not demand the impossible. If a federal issue was not raised in a state court because doing so would have been futile, the rule will be deemed satisfied. For example, no exhaustion is necessary if the identical issue was raised unsuccessfully by another person before the state's highest court or by this petitioner, and the state court has failed to issue a ruling despite the passage of considerable time. *See, e.g., House v. Mayo*, 324 U.S. 42 (1945). On the other hand, a recent change in state law may require submission of the issue once again to state courts.

The exhaustion rule has generated countless decisions dealing with particular procedures and facts. Each is resolved in a case-by-case basis and is beyond the scope of this book. *See, e.g., Rose v. Lundy*, 455 U.S. 509 (1982) (if habeas corpus petition contains some exhausted and some unexhausted claims, petition should be dismissed until all claims exhausted).

[e] Related Doctrines Dealing with Failure to Exhaust State Remedies

Several related doctrines, some grounded in statute and some based on the Supreme Court's habeas corpus jurisprudence, have provided further specificity to the traditional exhaustion requirement. All of the following doctrines and rules, sometimes with only slight shades of difference between them, are variations on the same basic exhaustion theme — that federal habeas courts will not consider an unexhausted claim unless there is compelling reason to do so and a good reason why the claim was not presented and exhausted in state court

[i] Deliberate Bypass

A now-rejected doctrine, called the "deliberate bypass" rule, gave a federal judge the discretion to deny a habeas corpus petition to a state prisoner who intentionally failed to raise the federal issue in a state court, and was then precluded from doing so under state rules. To cause the denial of a federal habeas corpus petition, the bypass of state remedies must have been intentional and knowing — "an intentional relinquishment or abandonment of a right or privilege." This rule was designed to force reliance on state procedures. *See Fay v. Noia*, 372 U.S. 391 (1963).

To ensure that the prisoner was not prejudiced by a decision of defense counsel, the deliberate bypass rule ordinarily required that the prisoner personally have made the decision to forego raising the issue in state court. But sometimes defense counsel's strategic decision not to raise a federal issue in a state proceeding would constitute a deliberate bypass even if the defendant did not personally participate in the decision. *Cf. Henry v. Mississippi*, 379 U.S. 443 (1965).

Often a decision to plead guilty, which involves a waiver of appeal on many issues, was deemed a deliberate bypass and prevented subsequent habeas corpus relief. *See, e.g., McMann v. Richardson*, 397 U.S. 759 (1970) (guilty plea was deliberate bypass of issue whether plea was product of coerced confession); *Francis v. Henderson*, 425 U.S. 536 (1976) (deliberate bypass for failure to abide by state procedure rule mandating raising certain issues within specified time limit; since the issue could no longer be raised in state court, there was deliberate bypass because of the defense's procedural error).

[ii] Procedural Default: Cause and Prejudice

The deliberate bypass rule has undergone significant change in recent years, resulting in the dismissal of habeas actions even where the bypass of state remedies has not been "deliberate." The Supreme Court has increasingly refused to allow habeas petitions where state remedies have not first been fully utilized. When a federal habeas petitioner has failed to take a direct appeal in state court or has not adequately presented and developed a constitutional issue before a state court, the United States Supreme Court has rejected the *Fay v. Noia* approach (generally permitting federal habeas corpus consideration unless there was a knowing and deliberate waiver of the issue in state court) and held that the deliberate bypass rule should not be applied.

In its place, the Supreme Court has adopted a more restrictive approach called the *procedural default* rule, which has had a devastating affect on the likelihood of a successful habeas corpus petition on an unexhausted issue. Under this approach, failure to raise an issue at a state trial or to exhaust direct state appellate remedies is considered to be a procedural *waiver* of that issue, which will be excused by a federal habeas court only on a showing of *cause and prejudice* or a *fundamental miscarriage of justice.*

Definition. The cause-and-prejudice rule means the habeas corpus petitioner must show (1) some excusable cause for the procedural default, and (2) that it produced actual prejudice. *See generally Wainwright v. Sykes*, 433 U.S. 72 (1977). Both factors, as defined, are difficult for the petitioner to establish.

Rationale. The purpose of the cause-and-prejudice rule, like the prior deliberate bypass rule and the exhaustion rule itself, is to force state defendants to utilize fully state procedures. It permits fewer habeas corpus petitions than the deliberate bypass rule since there is no need to prove an intentional decision to bypass a state remedy. Cases applying the cause and prejudice rule to deny access to habeas relief include: *Bousley v. United States*, 523 U.S. 614 (1998) (cause and prejudice rule applicable to failure to use direct appeal to challenge voluntariness of guilty plea); *Keeney v. Tamayo-Reyes*, 504 U.S 1 (1992) (cause and prejudice standard applicable to excuse failure to develop material fact in state court proceedings); *Wainwright v. Sykes*, 433 U.S. 72 (1977) (defendant's failure to object to admission of confession at trial court, under Florida law, constituted a waiver of a later challenge in Florida courts; federal habeas corpus permissible only if defendant can prove cause and prejudice of the failure to object); *Francis v. Henderson*, 425 U.S. 536 (1976) (failure to make timely objection to racial composition of grand jury, therefore barring state court consideration of issue, cognizable in federal habeas corpus only on showing of cause and prejudice of failure to make timely objection).

Cause. "Cause" for a procedural default ordinarily means that "some objective factor external to the defense impeded counsel's efforts to comply with the State's procedural rule." *Murray v. Carrier*, 477 U.S. 478, 488 (1986). Examples include an inability to comply because the factual or legal basis for invoking the procedural rule was not reasonably available to counsel, perhaps because of its novelty, or because officials somehow interfered with compliance with the state procedure. On the other hand, a defense attorney's ignorance or inadvertence is not deemed "cause" unless counsel's legal work is so poor that it violates the Sixth Amendment's guarantee of the effective assistance of counsel. Criminal defendants are generally considered to be responsible for their lawyers' actions. But when a defense lawyer's conduct is so deficient that it violates the Sixth Amendment, the Supreme Court has held that the harm is "external" to the accused and is somehow attributed to the state. *Coleman v. Thompson*, 501 U.S. 722 (1991) (lawyer filed late notice of appeal in state court, thereby barring consideration of issues raised in the appeal). But the claim of ineffective assistance of counsel, if used to establish cause for the procedural default of some other constitutional claim (such as insufficiency of the evidence), must also, itself, satisfy the cause and prejudice standard. *Edwards v. Carpenter*, 529 U.S. 446 (2000).

Exception for ineffective assistance allegations. In *Massaro v. United States*, 538 U.S. 500 (2003), the Supreme Court retreated from requiring cause and prejudice in cases involving claims of ineffective assistance of trial counsel. While recognizing the general rule that claims not raised on direct appeal may not be raised on collateral review unless the petitioner shows cause and prejudice, the Court created an exception for ineffective assistance claims. The unanimous Court reasoned that the dual policies of finality and conservation of judicial resources would not be served by requiring early resolution of this issue since the facts may not be fully developed in time to present them on direct appeal. Accordingly, an ineffective assistance claim by a federal prisoner may be brought in a collateral proceeding under 28 U.S.C. § 2255 (and, presumably, also by a state prisoner under § 2254) whether or not the issue could have been raised on direct appeal.

The AEDPA "cause and innocence" rule. AEDPA altered the "cause and prejudice" standard even more restrictively. It now provides in 28 U.S.C § 2254:

> (e)(2) If the applicant has failed to develop the factual basis of a claim in State court proceedings, the court shall not hold an evidentiary hearing on the claim unless the applicant shows that —
>
> (A) The claim relies on —
>
> (i) a new rule of constitutional law, made retroactive to cases on collateral review by the Supreme Court, that was previously unavailable; or
>
> (ii) a factual predicate that could not have been previously discovered through the exercise of due diligence; and
>
> (B) the facts underlying the claim would be sufficient to establish by clear and convincing evidence that but for constitutional error, no reasonable factfinder would have found the applicant guilty of the underlying offense.

NOTE

When federal basis not developed in state court. Note the even heavier burden placed on the federal habeas petitioner who has not developed the factual and legal basis for the claim in state court. An evidentiary hearing may only be held if the claim involves a new rule of constitutional law that is retroactive or newly discovered evidence that was missed despite due diligence. *See, Williams v. Taylor*, 529 U.S. 420 (2000) (a failure to develop a factual claim is not established unless there is a lack of diligence or some greater degree of fault attributable to the prisoner or prisoner's counsel). In addition, the petitioner must show more than just "prejudice" (a significant possibility that the outcome would have been different but for the alleged constitutional error). The habeas petitioner must convince the federal court by clear and convincing evidence that no reasonable factfinder would have found the offender guilty but for the error. This standard has become known as the "cause and innocence" rule.

[iii] Procedural Default: Fundamental Miscarriage of Justice

If cause and prejudice cannot be shown to excuse a failure to exhaust, a federal court still has the discretion to entertain a habeas corpus petition to prevent a fundamental miscarriage of justice. The Supreme Court characterized this as occurring "in an extraordinary case, where a constitutional violation has probably resulted in the conviction of one who is actually innocent." *Murray v. Carrier*, 477 U.S. 478, 496 (1986). This means that the petitioner must demonstrate that it is more likely than not that no reasonable juror would have convicted him. *Bousley v. United* States, 523 U.S. 614 (1998). The Supreme Court has explained that this means the accused is factually innocent, not that the evidence at trial was legally insufficient. To counter the defendant's efforts to establish innocence, the prosecution at the habeas proceeding may introduce any admissible evidence, even if not presented at the trial. *Id. See also, Schlup v. Delo,* 513 U.S. 298 (1995). Examples of actual innocence include the conviction of the wrong person or, in capital cases, a death sentence for a defendant who did not meet the statutory eligibility requirements for the death penalty. Note the focus on actual as opposed to legal innocence. The burden of proof is on the petitioner to establish that there is a fair probability that had the constitutional errors not occurred, the trier of fact would have had a reasonable doubt as to guilt. *Cf. Sawyer v. Whitley,* 505 U.S. 333 (1992).

[iv] Independent and Adequate State Grounds

The United States Supreme Court has long held that it will not review a question of federal law decided by a state court if the state court's decision is based on state law that is independent of the federal issue and adequate to support the decision. In such cases the federal question would become merely advisory since federal courts do not have jurisdiction to resolve questions of purely state law. For example, assume that a state criminal defendant did not follow a state procedure and therefore was barred from having state courts resolve a certain question. The failure to follow the state procedure is considered an independent and adequate *state law* ground and would therefore also bar a federal court from considering the same issue. *See generally Lambrix v. Singletary,* 520 U.S. 518 (1997); *Harris v. Reed,* 489 U.S. 255 (1989).

Determining whether decision based on state ground. It is often difficult to ascertain whether a state court decision was based on an adequate and independent state ground. The Supreme Court has adopted several rules to assist in this determination. The Court has held that a state procedural default does not bar federal habeas relief unless the last state court rendering judgment "clearly and expressly" indicates that its ruling rests on a state procedural bar. *Harris v. Reed,* 489 U.S. 255 (1989). Sometimes this rule is called the "plain statement" rule. But if the state decision appears to rest primarily on federal law or at least is "interwoven" with federal law and when the adequacy and independence of a state legal ground is not clear, there is a presumption that there is no independent and adequate state ground. *Coleman v. Thompson,* 501 U.S. 722 (1991).

Relationship of independent state ground and cause-and-prejudice. The doctrines of independent-and-adequate-state-grounds and cause-and-prejudice are, in actuality, part of the same formula. According to the Supreme Court, an adequate and independent finding of procedural default will bar federal habeas review of the federal claim unless the habeas petitioner can establish either "cause and prejudice" or a "fundamental miscarriage of justice." *Harris v. Reed,* 489 U.S. 255, 262 (1989). In other words, a state procedural default that bars state review of a federal claim may also bar a federal review of it unless cause and prejudice or a fundamental miscarriage of justice can be shown. All of the successive elaborations on the exhaustion requirement discussed above, culminating in the AEDPA cause and innocence and miscarriage of justice rules, have increasingly made habeas relief virtually impossible to obtain for petitioners who have not fully presented and developed their claims (with the notable exception of claims of ineffective assistance claims of counsel) in state court.

[f] Effect of Previous Proceedings and Adjudications

A pervasive problem with federal habeas corpus is that prisoners frequently file repeated federal habeas corpus petitions raising the same issue or new issues that could have been presented in the first petition. A related problem is the effect of prior state adjudications of the same issues raised in a federal habeas corpus petition. To some extent these problems result from the historical principle that the doctrine of *res judicata* does not apply to a federal court's denial of habeas corpus relief. Both of these problems raise important questions about the conservation of limited judicial resources and the respect that should be accorded decisions on the same issue by other judges (sometimes from other jurisdictions).

Courts have often denied relief on successive habeas petitions that either allege the same old grounds as a previous petition or conjure up new, often fanciful grounds, as being an *abuse of the writ*. As discussed below, ADEPA has created procedures for weeding out repetitious and abusive petitions.

[i] Successive Petitions from the Same Prisoner

Successive petitions on the same issue. The changes in the federal habeas corpus statute enacted by AEDPA make it extremely difficult for a prisoner to obtain relief in a second habeas corpus petition on grounds already raised in a previous petition. *See* 28 U.S.C. § 2244:

> (a) No circuit or district judge shall be required to entertain an application for a writ of habeas corpus to inquire into the detention of a person pursuant to a judgment of a court of the United States if it appears that the legality of such a detention has been determined by a judge or court of the United States on a prior application for a writ of habeas corpus, except as provided in section 2255.

> (b)(1) A claim presented in a second or successive habeas corpus application under section 2254 that was presented in a prior application shall be dismissed.

NOTE

This provision requires the federal court to decide whether a petition is a second or successive one. *See generally, Stewart v. Martinez-Villareal*, 523 U.S. 637 (1998) (habeas corpus claim dismissed as premature does not bar later petition on same issue; later petition is essentially a resolution of the first petition).

Successive petitions on different issues. AEDPA also makes it difficult to raise an issue in a second federal habeas corpus petition that was *not* raised in the first one. Following some earlier precedent, AEDPA makes it imperative that a person in custody bring all available claims in the first habeas petition; otherwise they will be deemed to be procedurally defaulted.

This rule is stated in 28 U.S.C. § 2244(b):

(2) A claim presented in a second or successive habeas corpus application under section 2254 that was not presented in a prior application shall be dismissed unless —

> (A) the applicant shows that the claim relies on a new rule of constitutional law, made retroactive to cases on collateral review by the Supreme Court, that was previously unavailable; or

> (B)(i) the factual predicate for the claim could not have been discovered previously through the exercise of due diligence; and

> (ii) the facts underlying the claim, if proven and viewed in light of the evidence as a whole, would be sufficient to establish by clear and convincing evidence that, but for constitutional error, no reasonable fact finder would have found the applicant guilty of the underlying offense.

NOTE

A habeas corpus petition filed after an earlier such petition was dismissed without adjudication on the merits because of a failure to exhaust state remedies is not a "second or successive" petition. *Slack v. McDaniel*, 529 U.S. 473 (2000).

Procedural hurdles to second petition: permission by court of appeals. As an added hurdle to the successful filing of a second habeas corpus petition, AEDPA now requires the applicant to receive permission to file the successive petition from a three-judge panel of the Court of Appeals.

This is contained in 28 U.S.C. § 2244:

(3) . . .

(A) Before a second or successive application permitted by the section is filed in the district court, the applicant shall move in the appropriate court of appeals for an order authorizing the district court to consider the application.

(B) A motion in the court of appeals for an order authorizing the district court to consider a second or successive application shall be determined by a three-judge panel of the court of appeals.

(C) The court of appeals may authorize the filing of a second or successive application only if it determines that the application makes a prima facie showing that the application satisfies the requirements of this subsection.

(D) The court of appeals shall grant or deny the authorization to file a second or successive application not later than 30 days after the filing of the motion.

(E) The grant or denial of an authorization by a court of appeals to file a second or successive application shall not be appealable and shall not be the subject of a petition for rehearing or for a writ of *certiorari*.

(4) A district court shall dismiss any claim presented in a second or successive application that the court of appeals has authorized to be filed unless the applicant shows that the claim satisfies the requirements of this section.

NOTES

1. *Severe limits.* Note the high standard designed to severely limit second filings in a district court. A three judge appellate court, acting as a "gatekeeper," must be convened and is under a strict thirty-day time limit for rendering a decision on whether to authorize the filing of the second petition. The panel's decision is final; there will be no review for either side in the United States Supreme Court by an appeal or writ of *certiorari*.

2. *Constitutionality.* This procedural hurdle imposed by AEDPA has withstood constitutional attack. *See Felker v. Turpin*, 518 U.S. 651 (1996), discussed in Joseph T. Thai, Recent Development, 20 HARV. J. L. & PUB. POL'Y 605 (1997). *See also Calderon v. Thompson*, 523 U.S. 538 (1998) (appellate court *sua sponte* changing its mind and opting to revisit its own earlier decision denying habeas corpus relief to a state prisoner may do so only to avoid a miscarriage of justice).

3. *Habeas corpus by Supreme Court.* Persons unable to surmount this hurdle may still apply directly to the Supreme Court for a writ of habeas corpus, though such writs are granted only in exceptional circumstances (*i.e.*, virtually never). Sup. Ct. R. 20(4)(a); *Felker*, 518 U.S. at 665.

[ii]   Prior Adjudications of the Same Issue in Other Cases

Prior Supreme Court adjudication of an issue. Habeas corpus law has long stated that a prior decision by the United States Supreme Court in the case is generally dispositive in a subsequent habeas corpus petition on the same point. The federal habeas corpus statute as amended by AEDPA now provides in 28 U.S.C. § 2244:

(c) In a habeas corpus proceeding brought in behalf of a person in custody pursuant to the judgment of a State court, a prior judgment of the Supreme Court of the United States on an appeal or review by a writ of *certiorari* at the instance of a prisoner of the decision of such State court, shall be conclusive as to all issues of fact or law with respect to an asserted denial of a Federal right which constitutes ground for discharge in a habeas corpus proceeding, actually adjudicated by the Supreme Court therein, unless the applicant for the writ of habeas corpus shall plead and the court shall find the existence of a material and controlling fact which did not appear in the record of the proceeding in the Supreme Court and the court shall further find that the applicant for the writ of habeas corpus could not have caused such fact to appear in such record by the existence of reasonable diligence.

Prior state court adjudication of an issue. The AEDPA amendments to habeas corpus law reflect a strong deference to state court adjudications. If a state court has resolved an issue against a person (perhaps in a direct appeal or a state post-conviction petition) who then files a federal habeas corpus petition addressing that same issue, the federal court must give the state court's decision great deference. Indeed, there is a presumption under AEDPA that the state court correctly resolved a factual issue, and the petitioner has a heavy burden of establishing that the state court decision was incorrect.

The prior-adjudication limits are in 28 U.S.C. § 2254:

(d) An application for a writ of habeas corpus on behalf of a person in custody pursuant to the judgment of a State court shall not be granted with respect to any claim that was adjudicated on the merits in State court proceedings unless the adjudication of the claim —

> (1) resulted in a decision that was contrary to, or involved an unreasonable application of, clearly established Federal law, as determined by the Supreme Court of the United States; or

> (2) resulted in a decision that was based on an unreasonable determination of the facts in light of the evidence presented in the State court proceeding.

(e)(1) In a proceeding instituted by an application for a writ of habeas corpus by a person in custody pursuant to the judgment of a State court, a determination of a factual issue made by a state court shall be presumed to be correct. The applicant shall have the burden of rebutting the presumption of correctness by clear and convincing evidence.

NOTE

1. *Decision on federal law.* Note that this great degree of deference even embraces a state court's decision on *federal* law. A state court's reasonable, though arguably erroneous, application of a clearly established federal law appears to be able to withstand reversal in a habeas corpus action. However, federal habeas corpus may be granted if the state court arrived at a conclusion of law opposite to that reached by the United States Supreme Court, or if the state court decided a case differently than the Supreme Court did on a set of materially indistinguishable facts. *Williams v. Taylor,* 529 U.S. 420 (2000).

Overturned if unreasonable. Moreover, a state court's determination of the facts will not be overturned unless it rises to the level of being "unreasonable" in light of the evidence before the state court. This means that the state court correctly identified the governing legal principle but unreasonably applied that principle to the facts of the prisoner's case. *Williams v. Taylor,* 529 U.S. 362, 412 (2000).

[iii]　Retroactivity: *Teague*

Federal habeas corpus relief ordinarily is sought after a state court judgment has become final. Since the state trial and direct appellate decisions may have occurred years ago, the habeas petition may be based on legal developments occurring since the state decision or a new theory that has not yet been accepted. For example, if the United States Supreme Court expands the scope of a constitutional provision, state prisoners convicted years before the new decision may argue that the new Supreme Court rule should cause their earlier state court decision to be reversed. For habeas petitioners to be successful, however, the new decision will have to be applied retroactively — to convictions that were final before the new decision was announced. Recent Supreme Court decisions have greatly reduced the chances that a habeas corpus petitioner will be able to get relief based on a recent decision or a novel theory.

In a complicated set of sometimes inconsistent decisions, often marked by no majority opinion, the United States Supreme Court has severely limited the retroactive application of new decisions in habeas corpus cases. In the leading case, *Teague v. Lane*, 490 U.S. 1031 (1989), the habeas corpus petitioner's state conviction became final in 1983, several years before the Supreme Court decided in *Batson v. Kentucky*, 476 U.S. 79 (1986), that the equal protection clause barred the use of peremptory challenges based on a potential juror's race. The habeas petitioner in *Teague* had been convicted by an all-white jury selected after the prosecutor had used his ten peremptory challenges to exclude blacks.

There was no majority opinion in *Teague*, although Justice White's partial concurrence found the plurality's approach "acceptable." Justice O'Connor's plurality opinion noted that the retroactive application of new decisions severely interferes with the important value of finality in criminal cases. The plurality held that new rules of constitutional criminal procedure will ordinarily not be applied to cases that became final before the date the new rules were announced. There were two exceptions. First, a new rule would be retroactive if it placed certain conduct beyond the authority of the substantive criminal law. This could include a new decision holding that it was a violation of due process to convict a drug addict of the crime of using narcotics. It should be obvious that this exception will rarely arise. The second *Teague* exception is also extremely unlikely to occur. New procedures are applied retroactively if, without them, the likelihood of an accurate conviction is seriously diminished. The concern is whether the new procedure is a "watershed" rule of criminal procedure that alters our understanding of the "bedrock procedural elements" essential to the fairness of a trial. Under this standard, the Court in *Teague* held that *Batson* should be applied retroactively.

Application of Teague. Teague has been followed in subsequent Supreme Court decisions as if the plurality decision were a majority. In *Graham v. Collins*, 506 U.S. 461 (1993), for example, the Court held that under *Teague* new rules will neither be applied nor announced in collateral review cases unless one of the two *Teague* exceptions applies. A "new rule" was defined in *Graham* as one that breaks new ground, imposes a new obligation on either the "states or the federal government, or was not dictated by precedent existing at the time the petitioner's [state] conviction became final." *Id.* at 897. *See, e.g., Bousley v. United States*, 523 U.S. 614 (1998) (*Teague* does not bar habeas corpus review of meaning of federal statute); *O'Dell v. Netherland*, 521 U.S. 151 (1997) (*Teague* bars habeas corpus review of death sentence imposed in violation of "new rule" permitting accused to inform sentencing jury of parole ineligibility); *Lambrix v. Singletary*, 520 U.S. 518 (1997) (*Teague* bars habeas corpus petition alleging death sentence to be in violation of "new rule" concerning validity of aggravating circumstances).

The "extremely narrow" exceptions to the general rule of non-retroactivity have made *Teague* a virtually insurmountable obstacle to both direct appellants and habeas petitioners seeking retroactive application of new rules of criminal procedure.

Apprendi v. New Jersey, 536 U.S. 584 (2000), discussed at length in Chapters 15 and 17, (facts that lead to certain sentencing enhancements must be found beyond a reasonable doubt by jury, not judge) and its progeny have not been applied retroactively. In a significant application of *Teague*, a 5-4 majority of the Supreme Court in *Schriro v. Summerlin*, 542 U.S. 348 (2004), held *Ring v. Arizona*, 536 U.S. 584 (2002), to be non-retroactive. Recall that *Ring* (also discussed in Chapters 15 and 17) held that facts which will determine whether the defendant in capital case will be sentenced to life or death must be found by the jury, not the judge. The *Summerlin* Court reasoned that in allocating the finding and weighing of aggravating vs. mitigating facts in capital cases to the jury, *Ring* was not a "watershed" decision but merely one dealing with procedure rather than substance. Also, the 5-4 majority opinion of Justice Breyer in *U.S. v. Booker*, 543 U.S. 220 (2004) (holding enhanced sentences under the U.S. Sentencing Guidelines subject to *Apprendi* analysis) hints strongly in dicta (by stating that ordinary "prudential principles" such as the plain error rule apply) that *Booker* should not be applied retroactively by the lower federal courts.

Similarly, the Supreme Court in *Whorton v. Bockting*, 127 S. Ct. 1173 (2007), refused retroactive application to *Crawford v. Washington*, 541 U.S. 36 (2004), discussed in Chapter 15 (Sixth Amendment's confrontation guarantee requires that testimonial statement of a witness absent from trial may only be admitted where the declarant is unavailable and where the defendant has had a prior opportunity to cross-examine the witness). The Court noted in *Whorton* that it has almost never granted retroactive application to decisions in the area of criminal procedure; no other attempt to persuade the Court to grant retroactivity has been successful since *Teague* held *Batson* to be retroactive in 1989, and aside from *Teague*, only the Supreme Court's landmark right-to-counsel decision in *Gideon v. Wainwright*, 372 U.S. 335 (1963), has been accorded such exalted "watershed" status. The Court observed in *Whorton* that the *Crawford* rule, "while certainly important, is not in the same category with *Gideon*." 127 S.Ct. at 1183–84.

In *Danforth v. Minnesota*, 128 S. Ct. 1029 (2008), however, the Supreme Court determined that the *Teague* rule of very limited retroactivity is not binding on state courts, which are free to retroactively apply new Supreme Court precedents more liberally. Therefore, the Court determined that *Whorton v. Bockting* did not preclude the Minnesota Supreme Court from applying *Crawford* retroactively as a matter of *state* law. *Teague*, the Court explained, was only intended to limit *federal* habeas courts' review of state court criminal convictions.

When a habeas corpus petition is filed, the federal court will treat the issue of retroactivity as a threshold issue to be resolved before considering the merits of the petition. If granting the relief requested in the petition would create or apply a new rule of constitutional law, the petition will be dismissed unless one of the above two *Teague* exceptions applies.

Teague and its progeny have greatly reduced the likelihood that a habeas corpus petition will achieve positive results except in cases where the state courts have flatly misapplied Supreme Court precedents. It is now extremely difficult for the petitioner either to take advantage of recent constitutional decisions or to convince a habeas court to announce a new rule of constitutional criminal law. As a result, now a criminal defense lawyer must try to raise every possible new ground for relief (whether recently recognized or still merely theoretical) at or before trial, or on direct appeal within the state system, and even on petition for *certiorari* to the United States Supreme Court. Otherwise, it may be too late to raise the issue in a habeas corpus petition. In other words, it is possible to seek to break new doctrinal ground on direct appeal and *certiorari*, but nearly impossible to do so on habeas.

[g] Procedures

[i] Statute of Limitations

The AEDPA changes in federal habeas corpus law drastically modify previous practice by establishing a one year statute of limitations on filing most habeas corpus petitions. The purpose of this change is to expedite the final resolution of habeas corpus petitions. 28 U.S.C. § 2244 now provides:

(d) . . .

(1) A 1-year period of limitation shall apply to an application for a writ of habeas corpus by a person in custody pursuant to the judgment of a State court. The limitation period shall run from the latest of —

(A) the date on which the judgment became final by the conclusion of direct review or the expiration of the time seeking such review;

(B) the date on which the impediment to filing an application created by State action in violation of the Constitution or laws of the United States is removed, if the applicant was prevented from filing by such State action;

(C) the date on which the constitutional right asserted was initially recognized by the Supreme Court and made retroactively applicable to cases on collateral review; or

(D) the date on which the factual predicate of the claim or claims presented could have been discovered through the exercise of due diligence.

(2) The time during which a properly filed application for State post-conviction or other collateral review with respect to the pertinent judgment or claim is pending shall not be counted toward any period of limitation under this subsection.

NOTE

This rule means that in most cases the offender will have one year from the date the conviction and sentence become final after the direct review process in state appellate courts. The precise meaning of this standard is unclear. For example, when does the clock begin running if the defendant applies for *certiorari* in the United States Supreme Court after the state supreme court has refused to hear the case on direct appeal or has ruled against the offender?

If the prisoner seeks state post-conviction relief after an unsuccessful direct appeal, the one year limitation period is tolled while the state post-conviction matter is pending. However, if the petition for state post-conviction relief is itself untimely, then the one year statute of limitations under AEDPA is not tolled. *See, Pace v. DeGuglielmo*, 544 U.S. 408 (2005)(statute not equitably tolled for time period during which untimely petition for state post-conviction relief was pending prior to filing of federal habeas petition); *Allen v. Siebert*, 128 S. Ct. 2 (2007)(same result as *Pace*; federal habeas petitioner may not rely on "untimely filed" state post-conviction petition to toll AEDPA's one-year statute of limitations).

An even shorter statute of limitations applies, theoretically, to habeas corpus petitions for review of death penalty convictions sentences in states that have agreed to certain minimum standards for defense services in capital cases. *See* 28 U.S.C. § 2263 (in qualifying states, a federal habeas corpus petition involving a state capital case must be filed within 180 days of conclusion of direct review in state court). However, one author notes that as of 2005, no state had yet qualified for this reduced limitations period. *See*, John H. Blume, *AEDPA: the "Hype" and the "Bite,"* 91 CORNELL L. REV. 259 (2006).

[ii] Written Procedures

In addition to the habeas corpus statute, 28 U.S.C. §§ 2241–2254, Congress has adopted a set of rules for federal habeas corpus proceedings. These Rules Governing Section 2254 Cases in the United States District Courts provide detailed information about habeas corpus petitions and other procedures.

[iii]   Who May Bring

Ordinarily the person in custody brings the habeas corpus petition, but it can also be brought by someone else if the person in custody is unable to do so, perhaps because of age, physical condition, or circumstances of custody. *See* 28 U.S.C. § 2242(a)(petition may be signed and verified by the person seeking relief, "or by someone acting in his behalf"); *Hamdi v. Rumsfeld*, 542 U.S. 507 (2004)(habeas petition filed by father of petitioner, alleging son was being held incommunicado as alleged enemy combatant and therefore unable to file on his own behalf). If the petitioner is currently in custody, the respondent is the state official having custody over the petitioner. Usually this is the prison warden.

[iv]   Petition

Form of petition. Because of the historical importance of the writ, courts have been very tolerant of habeas corpus petitions that lack technical perfection. This is especially true if, as is often the case, the petition is written and filed by an indigent prisoner. To assist in obtaining the proper information, some courts use a mandatory or permissive form that is designed to be completed with ease. A prisoner seeking to file a habeas corpus petition will be sent a blank form to fill out and return. This form often contains a laundry list of possible constitutional violations. It requires the petitioner to indicate whether he or she is complaining about each listed violation. Failure to raise an issue in this petition can be grounds to reject a later petition raising it.

The Rules Governing Section 2254 Cases provide a sample form used in many federal districts. Inadequate habeas corpus petitions can be amended. The petition must be in writing (it can be handwritten), signed, and verified by the petitioner. 28 U.S.C. § 2242. A petitioner unable to pay the usual filing fee in federal district court may seek permission to proceed in forma pauperis.

Content of petition. The habeas corpus petition must:

> allege the facts concerning the applicant's commitment or detention, the name of the person who has custody over him and by virtue of what claim or authority, if known. [28 U.S.C. § 2242]

[v]   Issuance of Writ

Once a habeas corpus petition is filed, the court receiving it has two choices. First, it can dismiss the petition if "it appears from the application that the applicant or person detained is not entitled" to it. 28 U.S.C. § 2243. Second, it can "award the writ or issue an order directing the respondent to show cause why the writ should not be granted." *Id.* Contrary to popular belief, if the writ is issued, the prisoner is not immediately freed. All that happens is that the custodian, usually the warden or sheriff, must produce the prisoner in federal court for a hearing to assess the validity of the imprisonment. Habeas corpus petitions are given special priority on the court docket.

[vi]   Answer and Reply

Unlike the usual civil procedure, a respondent named in a habeas corpus petition is not obligated to make any response unless ordered to do so by the court. If a writ or show cause order is issued, the custodian must file an "answer" which essentially explains the legal basis of the custody and why the writ should be denied. It must also deal with such procedural issues as whether the petitioner exhausted state remedies. It must describe what transcripts of other relevant proceedings are available and include relevant portions of available records. Rules Governing Section 2254 Proceedings, Rule 5.

[vii] Stay of State Court Proceedings

If a habeas corpus petitioner is currently engaged in state litigation, the federal judge before whom the habeas petition is pending has the authority to issue an order that stays the state court proceedings. 28 U.S.C. § 2251. This provision is designed to prevent state authorities from issuing an order that may be declared unconstitutional by a federal court.

[viii] Right to Counsel

As a general rule, there is no constitutional right to appointed counsel in either state or federal habeas corpus proceedings. *See, e.g., Pennsylvania v. Finley*, 481 U.S. 551 (1987) (no due process or equal protection right of counsel for indigent prisoners pursuing state habeas corpus relief). Virtually all jurisdictions, however, have a mechanism that gives a judge the discretion to appoint counsel in such cases. Federal law authorizes the appointment of counsel for indigent habeas corpus petitioners in some circumstances. *See, e.g.*, Rules Governing Section 2254 Cases, Rule 6 (appointment of counsel to assist in discovery); Rule 8(c) (appointment of counsel for evidentiary hearing).

[ix] Discovery

Although a federal habeas corpus action is technically a civil case, the Federal Rules of Civil Procedure are not applied as in normal civil cases. The rules of discovery do not apply, but federal courts can mandate some discovery in appropriate cases. Rules Governing Section 2254 Cases, Rule 6. According to the Supreme Court, in federal habeas corpus cases the federal courts are free to "fashion appropriate modes of procedure, by analogy to existing rules or otherwise in conformity with judicial usage." *Harris v. Nelson*, 394 U.S. 286, 299 (1969).

[x] Hearing

The usual rule is that unless the petition contains only issues of law or is dismissed on the basis of the petition and return, the federal district court or magistrate will convene an evidentiary hearing. As noted above, however, the 1996 AEDPA amendments severely limit evidentiary hearings when the applicant failed to develop the factual basis for the claim in state court. 28 U.S.C. § 2254(e)(2). If an evidentiary hearing is held, the prisoner is entitled to be present. 28 U.S.C. § 2243. The rules of evidence are somewhat relaxed at the hearing. The judge who conducted the original state trial may present a "certificate" that describes what happened at the trial. 28 U.S.C. § 2245. Evidence may include oral testimony, depositions, and if the judge permits, affidavits. Written interrogatories are permissible if affidavits are used. 28 U.S.C. § 2246. Judges are given great discretion in deciding whether to issue a subpoena for a witness.

[xi] Appeal

In a habeas corpus or § 2255 proceeding, the district judge's final order is subject to review by the appropriate court of appeals, but there is no appeal as of right. 28 U.S.C. § 2253(a). An appeal may be taken only if a circuit or district judge issues a *certificate of appealability* upon finding that the applicant has made a "substantial showing of the denial of a constitutional right." 28 U.S.C. § 2253(c)(2); Fed. R. App. P. 22(b). If the district court rejected the constitutional claim on its merits, this showing is satisfied if the applicant has established that "reasonable jurists would find the district court's assessment of the constitutional claims debatable or wrong." *Slack v. McDaniel*, 529 U. S. 473, 484 (2000). But if the district court denied the habeas petition on procedural grounds without reaching the underlying constitutional claim, a certificate of appealability should issue if the petitioner shows "that jurists of reason would find it debatable whether the petition states a valid claim of a denial of a constitutional right and that jurists of reason would find it debatable whether the district court was correct in its procedural ruling." *Id.* Ordinarily the district judge will decide whether to issue the certificate. If that judge refuses to approve the certificate, the offender can ask the court of appeals to issue it.

Since this certificate must state precisely which specific issue or issues satisfy this standard, 28 U.S.C. § 2253(c)(3), the court of appeals may permit an appeal on only some of the habeas corpus petition's issues. This unusual process is designed to limit severely the appeals in such cases by removing marginal cases from the appellate calendar. The habeas corpus petitioner has no right to be physically present at the appeal, but the United States Courts of Appeals have the discretion to order the defendant to be brought to the court for the hearing.

If the circuit court denies a certificate of appealability, the prisoner may ask the Supreme Court to review the denial. *Hohn v. United States*, 524 U.S. 236 (1998).

[3]   Federal Prisoners: Motion to Vacate Sentence (§ 2255 Motion)

While federal habeas corpus is used primarily by state prisoners, a *Motion to Vacate Sentence* is used by federal prisoners to challenge the constitutionality of their incarceration. This motion is provided in 28 U.S.C. § 2255 and is ordinarily referred to as a § 2255 Motion. *See also* Rules Governing Section 2255 Proceedings for the United States District Courts. In 2006, federal prisoners filed 6,515 Motions to Vacate Sentence and 3,789 federal habeas corpus petitions. Sourcebook, at http://www.albany.edu/sourcebook/pdf/t5652006.pdf.

A § 2255 Motion involves virtually the same issues and procedures as federal habeas corpus. For example, the Motion is appropriate to challenge a federal prisoner's custody that is in violation of a federal constitutional or statutory provision. Section 2255 specifically provides that it, rather than federal habeas corpus, must be used unless a § 2255 Motion would be inadequate.

The § 2255 Motion is filed in the federal district court which imposed the sentence. The federal judge has the authority under this statute to vacate, set aside, or correct the federal sentence. This can result in an order discharging or resentencing the offender, or requiring a new trial. As with habeas corpus, the court can deny the Motion if the same issue was resolved in an earlier § 2255 Motion.

While a habeas corpus petition is filed in the federal district where the state offender is in *custody*, a § 2255 Motion is filed in the district where the *sentence was imposed*. This jurisdictional feature for § 2255 Motions was designed to alleviate caseload overcrowding in federal districts in which large federal prisons are located. It also recognized that the sentencing court, rather than the court where the prison is located, is more likely to have the records, witnesses, and knowledge necessary to process the motion efficiently. Since the prisoner filing the § 2255 Motion may be incarcerated in a federal prison far from the district where the sentence occurred, the statute states that the prisoner need not be present in person at any hearing on a § 2255 Motion.

NOTES

1. *What's left of federal habeas corpus after AEDPA and Teague?* Under the 1996 AEDPA amendments to the federal habeas corpus laws, federal habeas relief is still possible, despite an adverse state court judgment on point, when the state judgment is contrary to clearly established federal law or involves an unreasonable application of clearly established federal law. 28 U.S.C. § 2254(d)(1). Also, under AEDPA, if a habeas petitioner has failed to develop the factual basis for a claim in *state* court, the federal court should not hold an evidentiary hearing on the issue unless the claim relies on a

new rule of constitutional law that is retroactive. 28 U.S.C. § 2254(e)(2). Both of these sections suggest that some habeas petitioners, at least in theory, might still be able to benefit retroactively from rare new Supreme Court "watershed" decisions. Otherwise, the utility of habeas corpus relief appears now to be limited to curing plainly erroneous state court applications of Supreme Court precedent.

For an ironic view, that ADEPA did not live up to predictions that it would gut federal habeas corpus as an effective remedy because the Supreme Court's recent habeas corpus jurisprudence had already substantially eviscerated it, *see* John H. Blume, *AEDPA: the "Hype" and the "Bite,"* 91 Cornell L. Rev. 259 (2006)(noting that post-AEDPA habeas petitions have had the same rate of success in the Supreme Court as pre-AEDPA petitions, but that success rates post-AEDPA have declined in the lower federal courts).

2. *Claims of innocence in "closed" cases and DNA testing.* If you are representing a prisoner serving a long sentence or perhaps even facing the death penalty in a case dating back to a time when current state-of-the-art DNA testing procedures were not generally available, what strategies might you consider to try to get the prosecutor, the sentencing judge, or even a habeas court (despite all the obstacles previously discussed) to order or agree to a DNA test that might establish your client's actual innocence?

3. In your view, are the previously discussed constrictions in recent years on the availability of habeas relief, both pre– and post– AEDPA, excessively harsh and inappropriate diminutions on the utility and the stature of the Great Writ, or are they reasonable limitations that appropriately serve the interests of federalism, finality, efficiency, and prevention of abuse of the Great Writ? Do you think Congress could have struck a better balance — between the interest in preserving habeas corpus as an expeditious remedy for unlawful confinement and those countervailing interests — than the one it struck when it enacted AEDPA in 1996?

4. For various points of view on the preceding question, *see: Symposium: Pro Se Litigation Ten Years After AEDPA,* 41 Harv. C.R. — C.L. L. Rev. 289-412 (2006); Kent S. Scheiddeger, *Habeas Corpus, Relitigation, and the Legislative Power,* 98 Colum. L. Rev. 888 (1998); Tung Yin, *A Better Mousetrap: Procedural Default as a Retroactivity Alternative to Teague v. Lane and the Antiterrorism and Effective Death Penalty Act of 1996,* 25 Am. J. Crim.. L. 203 (1998); Mark Tushnet and Larry W. Yackle, *Symbolic Statutes and Real Laws: The Pathologies of the Antiterrorism and Effective Death Penalty Act and the Prison Litigation Reform Act,* 47 Duke L. J. 1 (1997); Ronald J. Tabak & J. Mark Lane, *Judicial Activism and Legislative "Reform" of Federal Habeas Corpus: A Critical Analysis of Recent Developments and Current Proposals,* 55 Alb.. L. Rev. 1 (1991); Robert Weisberg, *A Great Writ While It Lasted,* 81 J. Crim. L. & Criminology 9 (1990).

TABLE OF CASES

[References are to pages]

[References are to pages]

C

[References are to pages]

[References are to pages]

[References are to pages]

[References are to pages]

[References are to pages]

[References are to pages]

[References are to pages]

[References are to pages]

[References are to pages]

INDEX

[References are to pages.]

[References are to pages.]

[References are to pages.]

[References are to pages.]

[References are to pages.]

[References are to pages.]

[References are to pages.]

[References are to pages.]

[References are to pages.]

V

W

[References are to pages.]